SCHOOL LAW

By

KERN ALEXANDER

Professor
University of Florida

ST. PAUL, MINN.
WEST PUBLISHING CO.
1980

Library of Congress Cataloging in Publication Data

Alexander, Kern.
    School law.

    Includes index.
    1. Educational law and legislation—United States—Cases. I. Title.
KF4118.A44   344.'73'07   79–24471

ISBN 0–8299–2078–1

Alexander School Law MTB

1st Reprint—1980

To my
Mother and Father

without whose unfailing support and encouragement
this book could not have been completed

*

PREFACE

This book is intended to provide the educational administrator and teacher with a broad based and comprehensive view of the law governing the state school systems of America. *School Law* seems to be a fitting title since the book conveys rules of law under which the elementary and secondary schools of this nation were formed and continue to operate today. The term "school" is used because the book is delimited to exclude legal considerations bearing on higher education, and although the book is primarily about the law governing the public, common schools, some of the material holds important implications for private and parochial schools as well.

Education in America is large and diverse and, unlike European systems of education, is truly a federalistic governmental function with each of the fifty states having a certain uniqueness of educational origin and purpose which adds strength and viability to the whole. Because of the decentralized nature of our educational structure, it is many times difficult to identify any one, single rule of law which prevails in all states. Even with the great sweep of constitutional precedents which the U.S. Supreme Court, from time to time, delivers, the law governing our schools can often be difficult to accurately assess and summarize. Beyond constitutional law, which is sometimes tighter knit because the Supreme Court can give the final word, we have a great mass of law pertaining to contracts, property, torts, general administrative law, et cetera which all bear on the administration of the schools. Too, substantial variation may be found from state to state, not merely because of the differing statutory bases, but also because of widely varying perspectives and philosophies of education which the judges, themselves, may have in viewing particular school litigation.

The reader of this book should, therefore, keep fully in mind that the author, of necessity, had to select from the great mass of case law among the hundreds of jurisdictions in this country the cases which appear to best exemplify the prevailing view of the courts in the various areas of law and among the many courts. Certainly, the precedents identified by the author may not neatly fit the multitude of situations and conditions which can exist in all the local school districts across the nation. For this reason, the reader will be well advised to carefully compare the precedents of the book with the rule of law in his or her own locality before drawing hard and fast conclusions. Also, as explained in the first chapter of the text, the reader should, at all times, realize that the facts of the case are of utmost importance and small variations in facts may result in very large differences in rules of law.

This book employs the casebook approach to convey the law. Over the years, this method of instruction has been tried and tested and has, generally, been given high marks as one of the best approaches to relating the abstractions of law to the everyday dilemmas which confront both administrator and teacher in the schools. The technique allows each person to relate the law to a concrete, factual situation which may be similar to experiences already encountered by the seasoned educator. For the fledgling educator it provides a firm foothold in a mock educational dispute which may effectively provide an ounce of prevention.

An effort is made, herein, to present an encompassing book, ranging across civil, criminal, and constitutional law as they touch the student, teacher, administrator and school district. Several chapters in the book may be of primary interest to teachers who are concerned with such matters as control over the curriculum, teacher tenure, contracts, constitutional restraints, and collective bargaining. While these may, of course, be essential information for the administrator, additional administrative legal problems are addressed in chapters on financing, property law, desegregation and intergovernmental relations. In totality, the book represents an attempt to convey to the educator a fully comprehensive treatment of the law, whether emanating from common law, statute or constitutional law.

I have obligations to several wonderful and dedicated individuals who helped me in different ways in completion of this book. Of course, I owe much to my graduate students who, with their quest for knowledge, have kept me constantly aware of the perpetual motion with which the law evolves. Certain of my graduate students deserve special recognition for their timely assistance and insightful commentary. Jill S. Louv, graduate assistant, University of Florida; Nelda Cambron, now of Miami University, Oxford, Ohio and Thomas Melcher, now of the Minnesota State Department of Education all gave unselfishly of their time to help with this project. I am also indebted to Cindy Scott for her typing of the manuscript. I am particularly grateful to Deborah Inman, University of Florida, for the many hours she spent in helping me coordinate and edit the materials and manuscript and for bringing to my attention the passages which needed to be revised or strengthened. Further, every man's productivity is greatly dependent on his wife and family, and I am no exception. My four boys, Kern III, King, Klint and Kane, have been of great personal satisfaction to me and their presence has constantly

PREFACE

reinforced in me a desire to be more academically responsible and productive. As I have indicated on the dedicatory page, I am thankful to my Mother and Father, both educators, for the inspiration and encouragement they gave me throughout this entire endeavor.

KERN ALEXANDER

Gainesville, Florida
November, 1979

*

SUMMARY OF CONTENTS

---

*

TABLE OF CONTENTS

TABLE OF CONTENTS

CHAPTER 3. ROLE OF THE FEDERAL GOVERNMENT

CHAPTER 4. EDUCATION, A STATE FUNCTION

TABLE OF CONTENTS

TABLE OF CONTENTS

TABLE OF CONTENTS

TABLE OF CONTENTS

TABLE OF CONTENTS

CHAPTER 8. STUDENT RIGHTS

TABLE OF CONTENTS

TABLE OF CONTENTS

TABLE OF CONTENTS

CHAPTER 10. TEACHERS AND THE LAW

TABLE OF CONTENTS

TABLE OF CONTENTS

TABLE OF CONTENTS

CHAPTER 12. TORTS

TABLE OF CONTENTS

TABLE OF CONTENTS

CHAPTER 13. FINANCE

TABLE OF CONTENTS

TABLE OF CONTENTS

*

TABLE OF CASES

Principal cases are in italic type. Nonprincipal cases are in roman type.
References are to pages.

TABLE OF CASES

TABLE OF CASES

TABLE OF CASES

TABLE OF CASES

TABLE OF CASES

TABLE OF CASES

TABLE OF CASES

TABLE OF CASES

TABLE OF CASES

TABLE OF CASES

TABLE OF CASES

*

SCHOOL LAW

Chapter 1

THE LEGAL SYSTEM

INTRODUCTION

The law of the school includes all those areas of jurisprudence which bear on the operation of public elementary and secondary schools in the United States. School law as a field of study is a generic term covering a wide range of legal subject matter including the basic fields of contracts, property, torts, constitutional law, and other areas of law which directly affect the educational and administrative processes of the educational system. Because of the breadth of the subject matter involved it is necessary for the school law student to be versed in certain fundamental concepts of the American legal system and be able to apply this knowledge to situations which daily affect school operation.

Since public schools are, in fact, governmental agencies their conduct is circumscribed by legal concepts of general administrative law supplemented by those necessary legal doctrines which have uniquely evolved from the historical traditions surrounding an educational organization which is state established, yet locally administered. In this setting legal and educational structural issues must be considered, the most important of which is the basis for the power to operate, control and manage the schools. In analyzing the American educational system and comparing it to state systems of education in foreign countries one is struck by the diversity of power and authority under which the American public schools are governed. The American federalism is nowhere more pronounced or obvious than in the public school system where there are not only fifty separate state systems but several thousand local school districts. Through all of this organizational multiformity and, indeed complexity, runs the legal basis on which the entire system is founded. The fundamental principles of legal control are quite simply those prescribed by our constitutional system, generally, from which the basic organic law of the land emanates, the written constitutions of the fifty states and the federal government. Constitutions at both levels of government are basic since the positive power to create public education systems is assumed by state constitutions and provisions of both the state and federal constitutions serve as restraints to protect the people from unwarranted denial of basic constitutional rights and freedoms.

The power for operation of the public educational system, therefore, originates with a constitutional delegation to the legislature to provide for a system of education. With legislative enactments providing the basis for public school law, it then becomes the role of the courts, through litigation, to interpret the will of the legislature. The combination of constitutions, statutes, and court or case law form the primary legal foundation on which the public schools are based.

Constitutions

A constitution is a body of precepts which provides a framework of law within which orderly governmental processes may operate. The constitutions of this country are characterized by their provisions for securing fundamental personal, property and political rights. One of the primary precepts embodied in a constitution is the provision for authorized modification of the document. Experience in human and governmental relations teaches that to be effective a constitution must be flexible and provide for systematic change processes. The Constitution of the United States expressly provides in Article V a process for proposing amendments by a two-thirds vote of each house of Congress or by a convention which shall be called by Congress upon application by two-thirds of the state legislatures. Amendments must be ratified by the legislatures of three-fourths of the states or by conventions in three-fourths of the states.

Another precept reflected in the state and federal constitutions of this country is the importance of a government of separated powers. While all state constitutions do not expressly provide for a separation of the legislative, executive and judicial departments, in actual practice all states have governments of separated powers. There is no requirement in the federal constitution that the states have constitutions which require a separation of powers. Theoretically, if a state so desired, it could clothe an officer or an agency with not only executive but plenary judicial and legislative powers. However, as indicated previously this is not the case and all states have governments with separate branches each of which exercises checks and balances on the powers of other branches.

State constitutions of every state make provision for a system of free public schools. Such provisions range from very specific educational provisions to a simple mandate that the legislature of the state shall provide funds for the support of a public school system.

Statutes

A statute, is an act of the legislative department of government expressing its will and constituting a law of the state. Statute is a word derived from the Latin term *statutum,* which means, "it is decided." Statutes, in our American form of government, are the most viable and effective means of making new law or changing old law. Statutes enacted at the state or federal level may either react to custom or forge ahead and establish law which shapes the future of the citizenry.

Statutes in this country are subject to review by the judiciary to determine constitutionality. This procedure is different from England where the legislature has ultimate authority and there is no means by which the courts can hold legislation unconstitutional. This is true primarily because in England the constitution for the most part is unwritten and the legislature, Parliament, may amend the constitution when it so desires.

The public schools of the United States are governed by statutes enacted by state legislatures. The schools have no inherent powers and the authority to operate them must be found in either express or implied terms of statute. The specificity of statutes in governing the operation of public schools varies from state to state and from subject to subject. For example, one state may only generally require for appropriate measures to be followed in budgeting and accounting for public funds, while in another state the legislature may actually specify each line item of the budget for school systems and lay down intricate details for accounting for these funds.

Rules and regulations of both state and local boards of education fall within the category of statutory sources of school law. As a general rule, the legislature cannot delegate its legislative powers to govern the schools to a subordinate agency or official. Boards of education must, in devising rules and regulations for the administration of the schools, do so within the limits defined by the legislature and cannot exercise legislative authority. However, the legislature may through statute expressly or impliedly confer administrative duties upon an agency or official. These administrative powers must be well defined and "canalized" within definitely circumscribed channels.

Court or Case Law

The third source of school law is judge-made or case law, sometimes called common law. The terms case law or common law are used to distinguish rules of law which are enunciated by the courts from those which have originated in legislative bodies. The term common law in its broadest sense may sometimes be used to contrast the entire system of Anglo-American law with the law of non-English speaking countries sometimes referred to as having systems of civil law. Civil law is a system of statutes where there is no reliance on precedent. Common law originated in England where the word "common" was derived as customs of the various parts of the country became common to the entire country. The customs of various parts of the country became crystalized into legal principles which were applied and used as precedent throughout England.

Powers and Functions of the Courts

The question of what powers may be exercised by the judiciary in reviewing decisions or enactments by the other two branches of government is essential to our system of government. The courts have traditionally maintained and enforced the concept of "separation of powers" when confronted with cases involving education. They will not usually question the judgment of either the administrative agencies of the executive branch or the legislative branch. This is true at the federal level as well as the state.

One court, in describing the hesitancy of the courts to interfere with the other two branches of government, said:

> This reluctance is due, in part, to an awareness of the sometimes awesome responsibility of having to circumscribe the limits of their authority. Even more persuasive is an appreciation of the importance in our system of the concept of separation of powers so that each division of government may function freely within the area of its responsibility. This safeguarding of the separate powers is essential to preserve the balance which has always been regarded as one of the advantages of our system.[1]

In accordance with this reasoning, the courts presume that legislation or administrative actions were enacted conscientiously with due deliberation and are not arbitrary nor capricious.[2] When the courts do intervene they perform three types of judicial functions, (a) settle controversies by applying principles of law to a specific set of facts, (b) construe or interpret enactments of the legislature, and (c) determine the constitutionality of legislative or administrative actions.

In applying principles of law to factual situations, the court may find the disputants to be either school districts, individuals or both. Although school law cases will generally involve the school district itself, they may in some instances concern litigation between individuals, a teacher and a student. In many cases the principles of law governing the situation are vague and statutory and constitutional guidance are difficult to find or virtually nonexistent. In such instances the judges must look to judicial law precedent for guidance. Cardoza related the process in this manner:

> Where does the judge find the law he embodies in his judgment? There are times when the source is obvious. The

---

1. Ricker v. Board of Ed. of Millard County School Dist., 16 Utah 2d 106, 396 P.2d 416 (1964).

2. Latham v. Board of Ed. of City of Chicago, 31 Ill.2d 178, 201 N.E.2d 111 (1965).

rule that fits the case may be supplied by the constitution or by statute. If that is so, the judge looks no further. The correspondence ascertained, his duty is to obey. The constitution overrides a statute, but a statute, if consistent with the constitution, overrides the law of judges. In this sense, judge-made law is secondary and subordinate to the law that is made by legislators *   *   *. We reach the land of mystery when constitution and statute are silent, and the judge must look to the common law for the rule that fits the case. He is the "living oracle of the law" in Blackstone's vivid phrase.[3]

The second function of the courts, the task of construing and interpreting statutes, is the most common litigation involving public school operation. Since statutes are merely words to which many definitions and interpretations may be applied courts may actually affect the meaning of the legislation. Pound conceives of four ways with which legislation may be dealt by the courts once litigation arises.[4]

"(1) They might receive it fully into the body of the law as affording not only a rule to be applied but a principle from which to reason, and hold it, as a later and more direct expression of the general will, of superior authority to judge-made rules on the same general subject; and so reason from it by analogy in preference to them.

(2) They might receive it fully into the body of the law to be reasoned from by analogy the same as any other rule of law, regarding it, however, as of equal or coordinate authority in this respect with judge-made rules upon the same general subject.

(3) They might refuse to receive it fully into the body of the law and give effect to it directly only; refusing to reason from it by analogy but giving it, nevertheless, a liberal interpretation to cover the whole field it was intended to cover.

(4) They might not only refuse to reason from it by analogy and apply it directly only, but also give to it a strict and narrow interpretation, holding it down rigidly to those cases which it covers expressly."

The fourth hypothesis is probably the orthodox, traditional approach; however, the courts today, in interpreting statutes, tend to adhere more and more to the second and third hypotheses.

---

3. Cardoza, Benjamin N., *The Nature of the Judicial Process*, Yale University Press, New Haven and London, 1962, pp. 18–19.

4. Pound, Roscoe, "Common Law and Legislation," 21 *Harvard Law Review*, pp. 383, 385 (1908). Copyright © 1908 by The Harvard Law Review Association.

The philosophy of the courts toward statutory interpretation varies not only among judges and courts but also in the content of the legislation being interpreted. The courts are generally more willing to grant implied authority to perform educational programs where large sums of public monies are not involved. In cases where taxing authority is in question or where large capital outlay programs are at issue, the courts tend to require very specific and express statutory authority in order for a school board to perform.[5]

The functions and responsibility of the judiciary in determining the constitutionality of legislation were set out early in Marbury v. Madison,[6] in prescribing the power of the United States Supreme Court. This case shaped the American view of the role of the judiciary. Chief Justice Marshall's landmark opinion stated:

> It is emphatically, the province and duty of the judicial department, to say what the law is. Those who apply the rule to particular cases, must of necessity expound and interpret that rule. If two laws conflict with each other, the courts must decide on the operation of each. So, if a law be in opposition to the constitution; if both the law and the constitution apply to a particular case, so that the court must either decide that case, conformable to the law, disregarding the constitution; or conformable to the constitution, disregarding the law; the court must determine which of these conflicting rules governs the case; this is of the very essence of judicial duty. If then, the courts are to regard the constitution, and the constitution is superior to any ordinary act of the legislature, the constitution, and not such ordinary act, must govern the case to which they both apply.

In determining the constitutionality of statutes the courts first presume the act to be constitutional and anyone maintaining the contrary must bear the burden of proof. The Florida Supreme Court has related the principle in this manner: " * * * We have held that acts of the legislature carry such a strong presumption of validity that they should be held constitutional if there is any reasonable theory to that end * * *. Moreover, unconstitutionality must appear beyond all reasonable doubt before an Act is condemned * * * ."[7] If a statute can be interpreted in two different ways, one by which it will be constitutional, the courts will adopt the constitutional interpretation.[8]

With specific regard to the U. S. Supreme Court's review of legislation, either state or federal, the judicial duty in the eyes of Justice

5. Marion & M. Ry. Co. v. Alexander, 63 Kan. 72, 64 P. 978 (1901).

6. 5 U.S. (1 Cranch) 137 (1803).

7. Bonvento v. Board of Public Instruction of Palm Beach County, 194 So.2d 605 (Fla.1967).

8. Hobbs v. County of Moore, 267 N.C. 665, 149 S.E.2d 1 (1966).

Brandeis was that: "It must be evident that the power to declare legislative enactment void is one which the judge, conscious of the fallibility of human judgment, will shrink from exercising in any case where he can conscientiously and with due regard to duty and official oath decline the responsibility." [9] Using this basic philosophy Justice Brandeis in 1936 set out certain criteria for judicial review which are still generally referred to today in considering the standing of litigants before the Supreme Court.

1. The Court will not pass upon the constitutionality of legislation in a friendly, non-adversary, proceeding, declining because to decide such questions is legitimate only in the last resort, and as a necessity in the determination of real, earnest and vital controversy between individuals.

2. The Court will not anticipate a question of constitutional law in advance of the necessity of deciding it. It is not the habit of the court to decide questions of a constitutional nature unless absolutely necessary to a decision of the case.

3. The Court will not formulate a rule of constitutional law broader than is required by the precise facts to which it is to be applied.

4. The Court will not pass upon a constitutional question although properly presented by the record, if there is also present some other ground upon which the case may be disposed of. This rule has found most varied application. Thus, if a case can be decided on either of two grounds, one involving a constitutional question, the other a question of statutory construction or general law, the Court will decide only the latter.

5. The Court will not pass upon the validity of a statute upon complaint of one who fails to show that he is injured by its operation. Among the many applications of this rule, none is more striking than the denial of the right of challenge to one who lacks a personal or property right. Thus, the challenge by a public official interested only in the performance of his official duty will not be entertained.

6. The Court will not pass upon the constitutionality of a statute at the instance of one who has availed himself of its benefits.

7. When the validity of an act of Congress is drawn in question, and even if a serious doubt of constitutionality is raised, it is a cardinal principle that this Court will first ascertain whether the construction of the statute is fairly possible by which the question may be avoided.[10]

9. Ashwander v. Tennessee Valley Authority, 297 U.S. 288, 56 S.Ct. 466 (1936).

10. Supra.

Stare Decisis

Implicit in the concept of common or case law is the reliance on past court decisions which reflect the historical development of legal controversies. Precedents established in the past cases form the groundwork for decisions in the future. In the United States the doctrine of precedent or the rule of *stare decisis*, "let the decision stand," prevails and past decisions are generally considered to be binding on subsequent cases which have the same or substantially the same factual situations. The rule of *stare decisis* is rigidly adhered to by lower courts when following decisions by higher courts in the same jurisdiction. Courts can limit the impact of the doctrine of precedent by carefully distinguishing the facts of the case from those of the previous case which established the rule of law. Aside from distinguishing factual situations, courts of last resort can reverse their own previous decisions and change a rule of law which they themselves established.

Stare decisis in American law does not constitute the strict adherence to older decisions as is found in English courts. The American rule of today is probably best stated by Justice Brandeis when he said that: "stare decisis is usually the wise policy * * * "[11] and Justice Cardoza observed that: "I think adherence to precedent should be the rule and not the exception."[12]

The Historical Development of the Doctrine of Precedent

(Reprinted with permission, Harold J. Berman and William R. Greiner,
The Nature and Functions of Law, The Foundation Press, 1966,
pp. 491–494.)

If we go back to the early history of modern English law, we find that by the end of the 12th century, virtually as soon as records of court proceedings were kept, there developed an interest in judicial decisions as guides to what the law is. Bracton in his treatise on English law, written in the middle of the 13th century, referred to about 500 decided cases; he also wrote a Notebook containing digests of 2000 cases. The word "precedent," however, is entirely absent from Bracton's vocabulary; cases for him and for his contemporaries were not binding authorities but merely illustrations of legal principles.

In the 14th, 15th and early 16th centuries law students kept notes of oral arguments in court cases. These notes, preserved in the so-called Yearbooks, show that not only the students but also the courts were concerned with analogizing and distinguishing cases. Again, however, the decisions were not treated as authorities in any sense, and if a judge did not approve of a decision he would just say it was wrong.

11. Burnet v. Coronado Oil & Gas Co.,   12. Supra, p. 149.
285 U.S. 393, 52 S.Ct. 443 (1932).

In the 16th and 17th centuries we get the first systematic reports of cases and the first mention of precedent. Judges then began to say that they are bound by precedents in matters of procedure, and especially in matters of pleading, and the practice of citing previous cases became firmly established. It is interesting to note, however, that in the first known use of the word precedent, in 1557, it is stated that a decision was given "notwithstanding two presidents." Indeed, the doctrine of precedent which developed in those centuries did not provide that a single decision was binding but rather that a line of decisions would not be overturned. Lord Mansfield could still say, in the latter part of the 18th century, "The reason and spirit of cases make law; not the letter of particular precedents."

Nevertheless, with the development in the 17th century of the distinction between dictum and holding, the way was paved for the modern doctrine. It should be noted that the 17th century in England was a time when analogical reasoning also became prevalent in fields other than law.

In the later 19th century for the first time there developed the rule that a holding by a court in a previous case is binding on the same court (or on an inferior court) in a similar case. The doctrine was called *stare decisis*—"to stand by the decisions." It was never absolute. The court is only bound "in the absence of weighty reasons." There is always the possibility of over-ruling the previous holding—except in the case of the House of Lords sitting as the supreme court in England, which adopted the rule that it cannot overrule one of its own precedents. (It should be added that the House of Lords has developed to a fine art the practice of distinguishing earlier cases of which it disapproves.)

Not only is *stare decisis* not absolute but it also has no clear meaning. As is seen from the cases on manufacturer's liability, the ratio decidendi of a case is never certain. Moreover, the doctrine of precedent has different values in different fields of law. In dealing with questions of property law or commercial law a court is reluctant to overturn the holdings of previous cases since the community relies upon the stability of court decisions in making property or business transactions; indeed the expression "rule of property" is sometimes used with reference to a doctrine laid down in previous decisions which the court will not overturn because business people rely upon it (whether or not the doctrine relates to property law as such). In dealing with questions of tort law, on the other hand, courts have less reason to be reluctant to overrule precedent or to "distinguish away" past cases; presumably if a driver of a car proceeds carelessly through an intersection when another careless driver is approaching from the opposite direction, he does not do so in reliance upon the rule that the contributory negligence of the other driver will bar the latter's recovery. Nevertheless, predictability of judicial decision is a factor to be considered in tort cases as in any other, if only for the reason that the lawyers for the parties rely on past decisions in bringing suit or in defending.

In matters of constitutional law—to take a third example—the doctrine of precedent has still less value than in matters of tort law, since it is a function of the courts under our system of law to adapt the provisions of the Constitution to the changing needs of society. This does not mean that the Constitution has no fixed meaning and that the courts will overturn previous constitutional decisions whenever they disapprove of them; on the contrary, the Constitution has an extraordinary stability as a framework of our social, economic and political life over the centuries, and the Supreme Court of the United States, in interpreting it, is strongly influenced by its own past decisions. But the interpretation of the Constitution is bound to be more flexible than the interpretation, say, of a contract.

Finally, *stare decisis* is often given a rather different value in matters of statutory interpretation because of a theory that a prior judicial decision interpreting a statute is presumed to have the approval of the legislature unless the legislature has overruled the decision by amending the statute. Thus a kind of legislative "rule of property", so to speak, is sometimes introduced into the field of statutory interpretation.

In the heyday of the doctrine of *stare decisis,* that is, in the last quarter of the 19th and the first quarter of the 20th century, belief was prevalent that certainty in law could be obtained by a scientific use of precedent. The legislature alone was thought to have the function of changing the law; the court's function was "merely" to apply the law, and to apply it in accordance with the holdings of previous decisions. The common law as an organically growing body of experience and doctrine was supposed, in effect, to have been superseded by a body of fixed rules which could be mechanically applied.

The idea that the common law is a body of fixed rules vanished in the second quarter of the 20th century, and perhaps earlier, in the face of overwhelming changes in social, economic and political life. The mathematical or mechanical jurisprudence of the late 19th century which denied that there is an ethical element in the analogizing and distinguishing of cases can seldom be found today among leaders of legal thought, at least in the United States. This does not mean, however, that the doctrine of precedent has been repudiated. It means, rather, that there has been a return to an older concept of precedent. Precedent is seen as a means of marshalling past experience, of providing a historical context, for making the choice at hand. While condemning the hocus-pocus aspects of the strict 19th century doctrine, many American thinkers about law would agree with Lord Mansfield that "the common law works itself pure."

Understanding Judicial Decisions

In order to determine the rule of a case, it is necessary to find the *ratio decidendi* or the point of which the judgment balances. This is done primarily by carefully analyzing the facts of the case which are treated by the judge as being material. Only the material facts are relevant to the identification of the *ratio decidendi* of a case. Conclusions of a judge departing from the *ratio* are not binding as precedent and are considered to be *obiter dicta*. Essentially there are two types. First, a statement of law is *obiter* if it is based on facts which were not found to exist, or if the facts are present they are immaterial. Second, it may also be a statement of law which, although based on established facts of the case, does not form the rationale for the decision. A statement of law supporting a dissenting opinion is one example. Another instance of *obiter* may be where a court makes a statement of law leading to one conclusion but then reaches a contrary decision on the facts for a different reason.[13]

Karl N. Llewellyn [14], late Professor of Law, University of Chicago, in his work *The Bramble Bush* probably offers the best and most concise explanation of what to look for when reading case law. Since the case method is employed in presenting most of the materials in this book it seems appropriate to quote a portion of Llewellyn's comments or reading and analyzing judicial opinions.

" * * * The first thing to do with an opinion, then, is read it. The next thing is to get clear the actual decision, the judgment rendered. Who won, the plaintiff or defendant? And watch your step here. You are after in first instance the plaintiff and defendant below, in the trial court. In order to follow through what happened you must therefore first know the outcome below; else you do not see what was appealed from, nor by whom. You now follow through in order to see exactly what further judgment has been rendered on appeal. The stage is then cleared of form—although of course you do not yet know all that these forms mean, that they imply. You can turn now to what you peculiarly do know. Given the actual judgments below and above as your indispensable framework—what has the case decided, and what can you derive from it as to what will be decided later?

"You will be looking, in the opinion, or in the preliminary matter plus the opinion, for the following: a statement of the facts the court assumes; a statement of the precise way the question has come before the court—which includes what

13. R. J. Walker & M. G. Walker, *The English Legal System*, Butterworths London, (1972) p. 124.

14. K. N. Llewellyn, *The Bramble Bush, On Our Law and Its Study*, Oceana Publications, New York, 1960, pp. 41–43.

the plaintiff wanted below, and what the defendant did about it, the judgment below, and what the trial court did that is complained of; then the outcome on appeal, the judgment; and finally the reasons this court gives for doing what it did. This does not look so bad. But it is much worse than it looks. For all our cases are decided, all our opinions are written, all our predictions, all our arguments are made, on certain four assumptions. * * * (1) *The court must decide the dispute that is before it*. It cannot refuse because the job is hard, or dubious, or dangerous. (2) *The court can decide only the particular dispute which is before it*. When it speaks to that question it speaks *ex cathedra, with authority*, with finality, with an almost magic power. When it speaks to the question before it, it announces law, and if what it announces is new, it legislates, it makes the law. But when it speaks to any other question at all, it says mere words, which no man needs to follow. Are such words worthless? They are not. We know them as judicial *dicta*; when they are wholly off the point at issue we call them *obiter dicta*—words dropped along the road, wayside remarks. Yet even wayside remarks shed light on the remarker. They may be very useful in the future to him, or to us. But he will not feel bound to them, as to his *ex cathedra* utterance. They came not hallowed by a Delphic frenzy. He may be slow to change them; but not so slow as in the other case. (3) *The court can decide the particular dispute only according to a general rule which covers a whole class of like disputes.* Our legal theory does not admit of single decision standing on their own. If judges are free, are indeed forced, to decide new cases for which there is no rule, they must at least make a new rule as they decide. So far, good. But how wide or how narrow, is the general rule in this particular case? That is a troublesome matter. The practice of our case-law, however, is I think, fairly stated thus: It pays to be suspicious of general rules which look too wide; it pays to go slow in feeling certain that a wide rule has been laid down at all, or that, if seemingly laid down, it will be followed. For there is a fourth accepted canon: (4) *Everything, everything, everything, big or small, a judge may say in an opinion, is to be read with primary reference to the particular dispute, the particular question before him*. You are not to think that the words mean what they might if they stood alone. You are to have your eye on the case in hand, and to learn how to interpret all that has been said merely as a reason for deciding that case that way. * * * "

Judicial Procedure

Judicial procedure is substantially different for criminal and civil law. In contradistinction to a "civil" action a typical "criminal" case is one initiated by the state for the purpose of attaining obedience to the law by punishment or correction of a lawbreaker. Although criminal law may potentially involve school personnel or students it does not usually directly involve the school district as a public entity and is therefore beyond the scope of this book. Most school law cases are "civil" in nature; a typical one being carried forward by an individual against another person or the school district. The redress sought for the alleged wrong is commonly the payment of money, or the specific performance of a contract, though in many school law cases the plaintiff seeks to compel the officials of a school district to either perform or refrain from doing something which the plaintiff feels is detrimental to his interests.

Any person may initiate a civil action in the appropriate courts of a state to obtain civil redress. The tasks of these courts is to decide specific disputes brought by persons who are unable to settle their own controversies. The basic outlines of a typical civil action, how it gets to court, what transpires before the court and how the court resolves the problems is discussed below.

An Outline of the Proceedings in a Civil Action

(Reprinted with permission, Austin W. Scott and Robert B. Kent, *Cases and Other Materials on Civil Procedure*, Little, Brown and Company, Boston, 1967, pp. 13–24.)

1. *Selection of a Court*. The decision to litigate having been made, plaintiff's counsel must select a tribunal, a court which, by the law of its creation, has the power to determine the class of controversies to which his particular case belongs. This power is called jurisdiction of the subject matter. The plaintiff may have a choice among different courts of the same state or courts of different states. He may sue in a federal court if the case is one falling within the jurisdiction of such a court. The court selected must be one capable of acquiring jurisdiction over the defendent (personal jurisdiction) or at least over his property. The method of acquiring such jurisdiction is discussed below. * * * The law (usually statutory) governing the place where actions may be brought is referred to as "venue." Venue is frequently dependent upon the residence of the parties, sometimes upon the place where the operative facts took place.

2. *Commencement of the Action; Service of Process*. In some states the civil action is started by the issuance and service of process upon the defendant; in others and in the federal courts the action is commenced by filing a complaint with the court. If the complaint is filed first the process is then issued and served. * * *

Ordinarily it is necessary to serve the defendant personally with process within the boundaries of the state in which the action is brought. If the defendent is personally present within the state and process is there served upon him, the court acquires jurisdiction over him, though he is not a resident of the state, and even though he merely happens to be passing through the state. * * *

3. *The Pleadings.* In order that the defendant may know what the plaintiff's claim against him is, the plaintiff is required to make a written statement of the circumstances on which he relies as the basis of his claim against the defendant. Similarly, in order that the plaintiff may know what the defendant's defense is, the defendant is required to make a written statement of his defense. Where the defendent does not merely deny the plaintiff's allegations but sets up additional facts by way of affirmative defense, further pleading may be required, although in modern practice this is usually not necessary. The defendent may include claims against the plaintiff on which the defendant seeks affirmative relief. All these written statements made by the parties are called the pleadings. * * *

The pleadings may disclose that there is an issue of law which may be determinative of the case; a hearing may be held, the outcome of which may render a trial of facts unnecessary. The pleadings will also indicate whether the case is one in which a trial of the facts warrants the impaneling of a jury or whether trial to the court alone is indicated. The pleadings will also assist the judge in determining what evidence is material to the claims and defenses of the parties. * * *

A fundamental rule of pleading at common law is that all material facts alleged by one party and not denied by the other party are to be taken as admitted. * * * Under the common law principles of pleading, the plaintiff in his statement of his cause of action, which is called a *declaration,* alleges the facts constituting his cause of action. * * *

If the defendant believes that the plaintiff's declaration, although it states facts which are true, nevertheless fails to state facts sufficient to constitute a cause of action, he will file a *demurrer.* In this demurrer he does not deny the plaintiff's allegations nor does he set up new facts by way of defense. He simply alleges that the declaration is insufficient in law. By filing such a demurrer an issue is reached —an issue of law, not an issue of fact. This issue will be determined by the court and not by a jury, since it involves a question of law. Under the procedure in many states today, the functions of a demurrer are served by a substitute introduced by statute or by rule, usually called a *motion to dismiss.* * * *

4. *The Hearing on Demurrer.* Where the pleadings terminate in a demurrer, the issue of law thus raised will be set down for hearing before the court sitting without a jury. * * * In the United

States the hearing is ordinarily before a single judge. The court either sustains or overrules the demurrer. If the demurrer is sustained, judgment will be given for the demurrant, unless the other party asks for and obtains leave to amend his pleading, which leave is now ordinarily granted as a matter of course. If the demurrer is overruled, judgment will be given against the demurrant, unless he asks for and obtains leave to plead over, which leave is also now ordinarily granted as a matter of course.

5. *Pretrial Discovery*. The conclusion of the pleadings frequently leaves the case in a position in which a trial is necessary; that is, factual allegations of one party have been denied by the other. In the great majority of states the parties may elicit additional information prior to trial by what are commonly called discovery devices. * * * Discovery includes the taking of oral depositions of parties and witnesses, the submission of written interrogatories to be answered under oath, the production of documents and things for copying or inspection, the conduct of physical and mental examinations under court order when physical or mental conditions are an issue, and the request for admission of facts by one's adversary, wherein the refusal to admit must be supported by a sworn statement.

These devices are designed to augment the pleadings, to reduce the element of surprise in litigation, and to emphasize the trial as a search for truth rather than a sporting contest between lawyers.

6. *Summary Judgment*. In many states and in the federal courts either party may move for summary judgment in his favor. Such a motion is usually accompanied by affidavits setting forth circumstances which, if true, demonstrate that there is no genuine issue of fact to be tried. The nonmoving party then has an opportunity to submit counter-affidavits which may well disclose that there are issues which require trial. If the uncontradicted affidavits of the moving party disclose circumstances in which he is entitled to judgment as matter of law, such summary judgment will be immediately entered. However, on a motion for summary judgment the court will not judge as between conflicting affidavits, and if a conflict appears it will deny the motion, leaving the issues to be determined at the trial. Even if the affidavits disclose no genuine issue of fact, the moving party may not be entitled to judgment as matter of law, and in such circumstances the motion will be denied.

7. *Pretrial Conference*. In many states and in the federal courts the court may order, prior to trial, a conference among counsel and the court to explore the possibility of settlement or at least the feasibility of reaching agreements as to what matters are and what matters are not actually in dispute, and any other agreements which will simplify and shorten the trial itself. * * *

8. *The Trial*. Where the pleadings terminate in a denial, the issue of fact thus raised will be set down for trial. * * * Cases may

be assigned for trial on specific days. In the meantime a jury panel has been selected and the prospective jurors summoned to attend court. When the case is reached, twelve jurors are selected from the panel by drawing their names from a wheel or box, and the first twelve so drawn, if not challenged or excused, will constitute the *jury* for the trial of the case. By consent of the parties, an action at law may be tried by a judge without a jury, and many cases are so tried. * * * After all the evidence is in, the defendent may make a motion for *directed verdict*, or, indeed, the plaintiff may make such a motion. If the motion is denied, the defendent's counsel then addresses the jury, after which the plaintiff's counsel does the same. The trial judge then gives his *charge* or instructions to the jury, stating the law and usually summarizing the evidence. In a few states the charge of the court precedes the arguments of counsel. The jury then retires to consider its *verdict*. When a verdict has been agreed upon by the jurors it is reported by the foreman to the court. Ordinarily the verdict is a simple statement that the jury finds for the defendant or that it finds for the plaintiff in a certain amount. * * *

9. *Motions in the Trial Court after Verdict*. The party who is dissatisfied with a verdict may make a *motion for a new trial*. The grounds for such a motion are various. It may be based upon a mistake of the judge at the trial, either in admitting or excluding the evidence, or in giving an erroneous instruction to the jury. It may be based upon misconduct of the jurors or misconduct of opposing counsel at the trial. It may be based upon the insufficiency of the evidence to support the verdict. It may be based upon the ground that the damages awarded are excessive or inadequate. * * *

10. *The Judgment*. The judgment is the final determination of the controversy by the court. * * * After reciting the proceedings which have taken place it states

> that it is ordered, adjudged, and decreed that, the plaintiff recover a certain sum, or, if the defendant is successful, that the plaintiff take nothing. * * *

Costs. At common law the successful party to an action is ordinarily entitled to costs against the other as a matter of right. If the plaintiff succeeds, he recovers a judgment for the amount of the jury's verdict plus costs; if the defendant succeeds, he recovers a judgment against the plaintiff for costs. * * *

11. *Execution of the Judgment*. If the plaintiff has obtained a judgment against the defendant and the defendant does not pay or otherwise satisfy the judgment, the plaintiff is entitled to execution. In the case of a judgment for money, the plaintiff obtains a writ from the court directing the sheriff to seize property of the defendant, sell it, and with the proceeds pay to the plaintiff the amount of his judgment. * * *

12. *Appellate Review.* After a final judgment is rendered, the losing party can ordinarily carry the case to a higher court. * * *

The official record of what happened in the lower court is called the *record.* It contains those matters which the upper court is to consider in deciding whether to affirm or reverse the judgment below. At common law it contained only the pleadings, verdict, and judgment, unless matters happening at the trial were included by means of a bill of exceptions. Under modern procedure the record on appeal is likely to contain not only the pleadings, verdict, and judgment but also the proceedings at the trial, or such much thereof as the parties' counsel may regard as important.

The American Court System

In our federal form of government it is necessary to have a dual judicial system, state and federal. Cases involving public schools may be litigated at either level and while most actions involve non-federal questions and are decided by state courts, recent years have brought on a substantial increase in the number of school cases handed down by federal courts.

State Courts

State constitutions will generally prescribe the powers and the jurisdiction of the primary or main state courts. The legislature, through power granted in the constitution, provides for the specific operation of the constitutional courts and it may create new and additional courts if so authorized by the constitution.

The types of state courts may be classified into four categories; [15] those of general jurisdiction, special jurisdiction, small claims and appeals.

Courts of General Jurisdiction are usually called district or circuit courts. The jurisdiction of these courts cover all cases except those reserved for special courts. The subject matter of cases of general jurisdiction sometimes overlap with courts of special jurisdiction.

Courts of Special Jurisdiction are set up to handle cases involving litigation in special subject matter areas which generally involve large numbers of cases. Probate courts, domestic relation courts and juvenile courts are common types of courts of special jurisdiction.

Small Claims Courts are established to handle lawsuits involving small amounts of money. Justice of the peace courts are usually classified as small claims courts, however, some states may classify small claims courts and justice of the peace courts as having separate jurisdictions; for example, in Florida small claims courts have civil jurisdiction in cases at law in which the demand or value of the prop-

---

15. Auerbach, Carl A., Garrison, Lloyd K., Hurst, Willard, Mermin, Samuel, *The Legal Process,* Chandler Publishing Company, San Francisco, 1961, pp. 3–4.

erty does not exceed two hundred and fifty dollars [16] while the justice of the peace courts have jurisdiction over disputes involving actions for not more than one hundred dollars.[17]

Appellate Courts are found in all states and in most are the only courts to which appeals may be made involving decisions of trial courts of general jurisdiction. These courts are usually called Supreme Courts or Courts of Appeals. Some states, because of the sheer volume of cases, have established intermediate appellate courts. For example, New York and California have intermediate appellate courts, and Indiana has both a Court of Appeals and a Supreme Court. In states with intermediate courts of appeals, certain cases on appeal may terminate at the intermediate appellate court while other cases can be appealed to the state's highest court.

Federal Courts

Article III of the Constitution of the United States provides in part: "The judicial power of the United States, shall be vested in one supreme court, and in such inferior courts as the Congress may from time to time ordain and establish." [18] Pursuant to this provision Congress has created a network of courts.

Today the federal court system in the United States includes District Courts, Courts of Appeals, Special Federal Courts and the Supreme Court.

There is at least one District Court in each state and usually more than two. Cases litigated before federal district courts may largely be classified into two types: (1) cases between citizens of different states and (2) cases involving litigation of federal statutes or the federal Constitution. Cases before district courts are usually presided over by one judge, however, in cases of injunction against the enforcement of a state or federal statute a three-judge court is required. A three-judge court is made up of the district judge, to whom the injunction is presented, and two other federal judges, one of which must be a circuit judge. Decisions of district courts may be appealed to the federal Courts of Appeals, and in some instances directly to the Supreme Court of the United States. There are eleven Courts of Appeals each in one of the eleven federal judicial circuits. For example, the United States Court of Appeals for the Eighth Circuit includes the states of North Dakota, South Dakota, Nebraska, Minnesota, Iowa, Missouri, and Arkansas.

In addition, federal courts have been established by the Congress to handle special problems or to cover special jurisdictions. These courts are the courts of the District of Columbia, the Court of Claims, the Tax Court, the Customs Courts, the Courts of Customs

---

16. F.S.A. (Fla.) 42.03.

17. F.S.A. (Fla.) 37.01(1).

18. U.S.C.A. Const. Art. III, 1.

and Patent Appeals, the Emergency Court of Appeals, and the territorial courts.

The Supreme Court of the United States is the highest court in the land beyond which there is no redress. Cases may be brought before the Supreme Court by appeal, *writ of certiorari* or through the original jurisdiction of the Court.

Most school cases which go to the Supreme Court are taken on *writs of certiorari,* certiorari being an original action whereby a case is removed from an inferior to a superior court for trial. Cases may be taken to the Supreme Court from state courts by *writ of certiorari* where a state statute or federal statute is questioned as to its validity under the federal Constitution or where any title, right, privilege or immunity is claimed under the Constitution. Since most school law cases fall within this category, the *writ of certiorari* is the most common means of getting a case before the Supreme Court.

Chapter 2

HISTORICAL PERSPECTIVE

The law of public education is shaped by the philosophical, political, and social traditions of the United States. Early, the colonies quite naturally assumed the pattern of the class oriented English educational system in which free and universal education was far beyond the eye of the most progressive leaders. Children of the poor and lower class families received no education at all or were attached as apprentices to learn a trade and develop manual skills.

Even though there was some governmental recognition of the benefits of education, as evidenced by a 1642 statute in Massachusetts in which all parents were charged with seeing to the education of their children and later in 1647 when the legislature required certain towns to appoint a teacher and permitted taxes for education, by in large early colonial legislatures tended to ignore education. What efforts were made to educate were through pauper school laws which provided that if indigent parents would declare themselves paupers their children could be sent to specified private or pay schools for a free education.[1] A vestige of the English system which was utilized in some colonies was the "rate bill", which required the parent to pay an amount for each child to supplement inadequate school revenues. The amount assessed was collected from the parents through ordinary tax bills. Such rate bills were still in effect in New York state as late as 1867.[2]

It was not until the 18th Century that a new political philosophy developed which conceived of education as essential to the welfare of the state. Until then the benefits of education were viewed as largely personal; the external value of education to society had not yet been realized. As the colonies began to struggle for independence from England, the concept of free public education gained momentum. Americans became obsessed with freedom and schools were viewed as the primary means by which freedom could be obtained and maintained. As Butts has observed, " *   *   * the really important reason for believing in the value of education is that it can be the foundation of freedom. In the first place, a truly democratic society must rest upon the knowledge, intelligence, and wisdom of all the people."[3] Americans generally embraced the words of Jefferson, that "a people who mean to be their own Governors must arm themselves with the power which knowledge gives." More than any other, Jefferson's

---

1. Ellwood P. Cubberley, *A Brief History of Education*, Houghton Mifflin Company, Boston, 1922, p. 374.

2. Ibid, p. 376.

3. R. Freeman Butts, "Search for Freedom: The Story of American Education", *NEA Journal*, March 1960, pp. 33–48.

words redounded the public or common school philosophy which in generations to come was to sweep the young nation. Typical of Jefferson's position was his letter from Paris in 1786 to his old professor George Wythe written in support of a bill for general education, he said:

> I think by far the most important bill in our whole code is that for the diffusion of knowledge among the people. No other sure foundation can be devised for the preservation of freedom and happiness. * * * Preach, my dear sir, a crusade against ignorance; establish and improve the law for educating the common people. Let our countrymen know * * * that the tax which will be paid for this purpose is not more than the thousandth part of what will be paid to kings, priests, and nobles who will rise up among us if we leave the people in ignorance.[4]

In this new era not only was universal education in greater demand but a discernible shift toward more practical studies was in evidence and the old Latin grammar school began to deteriorate as the major source of learning. After 1750 the enthusiasm for schools based on religious motivations began to die down and the European traditions for both types and methods of education no longer satisfied the American appetite for knowledge.[5] A concept of public education evolved which was uniquely American. During this period general school laws in older states, which marked the progression of public education, required maintenance of schools by towns for a definite term each year, imposed taxation, and generally statutorily sanctioned the public school movement which had evolved over a century and one-half.[6]

A clearly defined role of the state in education, however, had not emerged by 1796 when George Washington in his Farewell Address called for the American people to:

> Promote, then, as an object of primary importance, institutions for the general diffusion of knowledge. In proportion as the structure of a government gives force to public opinion, it is essential that public opinion be enlightened.[7]

To progress from the sporadic and inadequate early general school laws to uniform state systems of free public education was a

4. Letter from Thomas Jefferson to George Wythe, Paris, August 14, 1786, Bernard Mayo, *Jefferson Himself*, University Press of Virginia, Charlottesville 1942, p. 89.

5. Cubberley, Ibid, p. 286.

6. Ibid, General school laws were enacted in: Connecticut in 1700, 1712, and 1714, Vermont in 1782, in addition to earlier statutes in Massachusetts (1647), and New Hampshire (1680). Georgia created a state system of academies in 1783. In 1795 New York provided for a state system of elementary education. Delaware established a state school fund in 1796 and Virginia enacted an optional school law in 1796.

7. Ibid, p. 288.

laborious journey with battles over the tax support and sectarianism marking the way. By 1825 it had become commonly recognized that a state system of education would require general and direct taxation of a major source of revenue such as real property. A broad base of taxation became the watchword; "The wealth of the State must educate the children of the State," aptly described the principle of taxation for education which was to eventually emerge.[8]

Established traditions were not easily overcome and it was difficult to convince many of the citizens that pauper schools were not the appropriate educational concept since it was believed to be merely the poor and poverty stricken who would benefit from free public schools.

Major impetus for education had come from the churches which sought to advance Christianity through knowledge of the Bible. Early states generally recognized and supported these efforts and several states set aside lands to help church schools. As the new philosophy of public education became entrenched and people started to grasp its benefits, new advocates for state education emerged and conflict with church leaders developed. The inherent discord between sectarian education and free state education were soon manifested in bitter struggles in several states, the story of which is more fully developed in a later chapter of this book.

Into the vortex of these conflicts stepped public education advocates, such as Horace Mann of Massachusetts,[9] who preached an educational awakening which was ultimately to form the basis for state systems of public education as we know them today—free secular public schools supported by both local and state general taxation.

The early 19th Century saw an extraordinary group of dedicated and effective leaders who were "public school men" to emerge in several states. They argued against tuition in any shape or form and most importantly they maintained that the term "free school" should no longer mean merely a place where the poor were given a free education and all others paid tuition. Class distinctions, they argued, would be reduced if all children could be given a free education financed with revenues from taxes levied on everyone.[10]

This view was reflected in an 1822 report to the Kentucky legislature which advocated free common schools and specifically rejected the pauper school approach saying:

> To be separated from the rest of the community as a distinct and inferior caste, and held out to the world as the objects of public charity, is a degradation too humiliating for the pride of freemen.[11]

8.   *Cubberley*, p. 371.

9.   Horace Mann.

10.   *Butts*, supra.

11.   *House Journal 1822*, Commonwealth of Kentucky, p. 236.

Legislatures gradually accepted the idea of free or common schools for all and by statute began to require local school districts to tax themselves to support the public schools. In this early period it became clear that the states must require rather than permit localities to establish free schools. Local control of education gradually became limited by state constitutions, and actions by state legislatures. Uniformity of education across states, it was decided, would be better brought to fruition by a degree of central state planning rather than through completely decentralized local school control.[12]

By 1852 when Massachusetts enacted the first compulsory attendance law the responsibility for public education was firmly lodged at the state level. The idea of free common schools was well established but the implementation of the concept developed slowly. It remained for succeeding generations to deal with the pervasive issues of "uniformity" and "equality" which have grown to be as vital to the public school movement as the word "freedom" was originally.

As a major governmental enterprise the development of the public school system was accompanied by a continuous string of legal controversies in every state in the nation. As a result, court decisions have to a great extent given form and substance to the philosophical base on which the public schools are founded. The courts have made it quite clear that "Public education is not merely a function of government; it is of government."[13] In legal theory, the function of the public schools is not only to confer benefits on the individual but just as importantly the school exists because the very existence of a civil society demands it.[14] Of such importance is the public education function that the state can, under certain conditions, limit parental control in order to advance the common weal.[15] The role of the public school in society is probably best defined by the Supreme Court of New Hampshire:

> The primary purpose of the maintenance of the common school system is the promotion of the general intelligence of the people constituting the body politic and thereby to increase the usefulness and efficiency of the citizens, upon which the government of society depends. Free schooling furnished by the state is not so much a right granted to pupils as a duty imposed upon them for the public good. If they do not voluntarily attend the schools provided for them, they may be compelled to do so. While most people regard the public schools as the means of great personal advantage to the pupils, the fact is too often overlooked that they are governmental means of protecting the state from

12. *Butts*, supra.

13. Newton Edwards, *The Courts and The Public Schools*, The University of Chicago Press, 1955, p. 23.

14. Ibid, p. 24.

15. Meyer v. State of Nebraska, 262 U. S. 390, 43 S.Ct. 625 (1923).

the consequences of an ignorant and incompetent citizenship.[16]

This judicial philosophy is stated in various ways by the decisions in other state supreme courts. The high court for Tennessee, for example, saw a need for a uniform system of public schools to promote the general welfare " * * * by educating the people, and thus, by providing and securing a higher state of intelligence and morals, conserve the peace, good order, and well-being of society."[17]

Development of the public schools was accompanied by an expansion of public school services beyond merely the elementary school level. Earlier, education above elementary school had to be acquired at private academies and colleges for which a tuition fee was charged and few if any poor children attended. In fact, the precise definition of common schools included only elementary schools, while the term public schools as later developed included high schools. Free public high schools soon became a democratic necessity. Cubberley observed that " * * * the rising democracy of the second quarter of the nineteenth century now demanded and obtained the democratic high school."[18] Gradually the high school became an integral part of the state school system but not before some classic litigation tested the expansion of state legislation. One of the best known and clearest historical examples of the judicial acceptance and promotion of the vital role of the public schools in society was the Kalamazoo Case [19] in which the Michigan Supreme Court gave such a positive response that it strongly influenced the expansion of the common schools through high school education in many states.

MASSACHUSETTS SCHOOL LAW OF 1647

Sec. 1. It being one chief project of the old deluder, Satan, to keep men from the knowledge of the Scriptures, as in former times by keeping them in an unknown tongue, so in these latter times by persuading them from the use of tongues that so at least the true sense and meaning of the original might be clouded by false glosses of saint-seeming deceivers, that learning may not be buried in the grave of our fathers in the church and commonwealth, the Lord assisting our endeavors,

It is therefore ordered by this court and authority thereof, that every township in this jurisdiction, after the Lord hath increased them to the number of fifty householders, shall then forthwith appoint one within their town to teach all such children as shall resort to him to write and read, whose wages shall be paid either by the parents or masters of such children, or by the inhabitants in general, by way of

16. Fogg v. Board of Educ., 76 N.H. 296, 82 A. 173 (1912).

17. Leeper v. State, 103 Tenn. 500, 53 S.W. 962 (1899).

18. *Cubberley*, supra, p. 386.

19. Stuart v. School Dist. No. 1 of the Village of Kalamazoo, 30 Mich. 69 (1814).

supply, as the major part of those that order the prudentials of the town shall appoint; provided, those that send their children be not oppressed by paying much more then they can have them taught for in other towns.

Sec. 2. It is further ordered, that where any town shall increase to the number of one hundred families or householders they shall set up a grammar school, the master thereof being able to instruct youth so far as they may be fitted for the university; and if any town neglect the performance hereof above one year, every such town shall pay five pounds per annum to the such school till they shall perform this order.
* * *

PREAMBLE TO A BILL FOR THE MORE GENERAL DIFFUSION OF KNOWLEDGE (1779) *

Whereas it appeareth that however certain forms of government are better calculated than others to protect individuals in the free exercise of their natural rights, and are at the same time themselves better guarded against degeneracy, yet experience hath shown, that even under the best forms, those entrusted with power have, in time, and by slow operations, perverted it into tyranny; and it is believed that the most effectual means of preventing this would be, to illuminate, as far as practicable, the minds of the people at large, and more especially to give them knowledge of those facts, which history exhibiteth, that, possessed thereby of the experience of other ages and countries, they may be enabled to know ambition under all its shapes, and prompt to exert their natural powers to defeat its purposes. And whereas it is generally true that people will be happiest whose laws are best, and are best administered, and that laws will be wisely formed, and honestly administered, in proportion as those who form and administer them are wise and honest; whence it becomes expedient for promoting the publick happiness that those persons, whom nature hath endowed with genius and virtue, should be rendered by liberal education worthy to receive, and able to guard the sacred deposit of the rights and liberties of their fellow citizens, and that they should be called to that charge without regard to wealth, birth or other accidental condition or circumstance; but the indigence of the greater number disabling them from so educating, at their own expense, those of their children whom nature hath fitly formed and disposed to become useful instruments for the public, it is better that such should be sought for and educated at the common expence of all, than that the happiness of all should be confided to the weak or wicked: * * *

* From *The Works of Thomas Jefferson*, collected and edited by Paul Leicester Ford, Volume II, Federal Edition (New York: G. P. Putnam's Sons, 1904), pp. 414–426, abridged.

A BILL FOR THE MORE GENERAL DIFFUSION OF
KNOWLEDGE BY THOMAS JEFFERSON,
VIRGINIA, (1779)

Be it therefore enacted by the General Assembly, that in every county within this commonwealth, there shall be chosen annually, by the electors qualified to vote for Delegates, three of the most honest and able men of their county, to be called the Aldermen of the county; and that the election of the said Aldermen shall be held at the same time and place, before the same persons, and notified and conducted in the same manner as by law is directed for the annual election of Delegates for the county. * * * The said Aldermen shall forthwith proceed to have a school-house built at the said place, and shall see that the same be kept in repair, and, when necessary that it be rebuilt; but whenever they shall think necessary that it be rebuilt, they shall give notice as before directed, to the electors of the hundred to meet at the said school-house, on such day as they shall appoint, to determine by vote, in the manner before directed, whether it shall be rebuilt at the same, or what other place in the hundred.

At every of these schools shall be taught reading, writing, and common arithmetick, and the books which shall be used therein for instructing the children to read shall be such as will at the same time make them acquainted with Graecian, Roman, English, and American history. At these schools all the free children, male and female, resident within the respective hundred, shall be intitled to receive tuition gratis, for the term of three years, and as much longer, at their private expence, as their parents, guardians or friends, shall think proper.

Over every ten of these schools (or such other number nearest thereto, as the number of hundreds in the county will admit, without fractional divisions) an overseer shall be appointed annually by the Aldermen at their first meeting, eminent for his learning, integrity, and fidelity to the commonwealth whose business and duty it shall be, from time to time, to appoint a teacher to each school, who shall give assurance of fidelity to the commonwealth, and to remove him as he shall see cause; to visit every school once in every half year at the least; to examine the scholars; see that any general plan of reading and instruction recommended by the visiters of William and Mary College shall be observed; and to superintend the conduct of the teacher in every thing relative to his school.

Every teacher shall receive a salary * * * which, with the expences of building and repairing the school-houses, shall be provided in such manner as other county expences are by law directed to be provided and shall also have his diet, lodging, and washing found him, to be levied in like manner, save only that such levy shall be on the inhabitants of each hundred for the board of their own teacher only.

And in order that grammar schools may be rendered convenient to the youth in every part of the commonwealth, Be it farther enacted, that on the first Monday in November, after the first appointment of overseers for the hundred schools, *   *   * the said overseers appointed for the schools *   *   * shall fix on such place in some one of the counties in their district as shall be most proper for situating a grammar school-house, endeavouring that the situation be as central as may be to the inhabitants of the said counties, that it be furnished with good water, convenient to plentiful supplies of provision and fuel, and more than all things that it be healthy. *   *   *

The said overseers shall forthwith proceed to have a house of brick or stone, for the said grammar school, with necessary offices, built on the said lands, which grammar school-house shall contain a room for the school, a hall to dine in, four rooms for a master and usher, and ten or twelve lodging rooms for the scholars.

To each of the said grammar schools shall be allowed out of the public treasury, the sum of pounds,* out of which shall be paid by the Treasurer, on warrant from the Auditors, to the proprietors or tenants of the lands located, the value of there several interests as fixed by the jury, and the balance thereof shall be delivered to the said overseers to defray the expence of the said buildings.

In these grammar schools shall be taught the Latin and Greek languages, English grammar, geography, and the higher part of numerical arithmetick, to wit, vulgar and decimal fractions, and the extraction of the square and cube roots.

A visiter from each county constituting the district shall be appointed, by the overseers, for the county, in the month of October annually, either from their own body or from their county at large, which visiters or the greater part of them, *   *   * shall have power to choose their own Rector, who shall call and preside at future meetings, to employ from time to time a master, and if necessary, an usher, for the said school, to remove them at their will, and to settle the price of tuition to be paid by the scholars. They shall also visit the school twice in every year at the least, either together or separately at their discretion, examine the scholars, and see that any general plan of instruction recommended by the visiters of William and Mary College shall be observed. The said masters and ushers, before they enter on the execution of their office, shall give assurance of fidelity to the commonwealth.

A steward shall be employed, and removed at will by the master, on such wages as the visiters shall direct; which steward shall see to the procuring provisions, fuel, servants for cooking, waiting, house cleaning, washing, mending, and gardening on the most reasonable terms; the expence of which, together with the steward's wages,

---

* Editor's note: number missing in original.

shall be divided equally among all the scholars boarding either on the public or private expence. And the part of those who are on private expence, and also the price of their tuitions due to the master or usher, shall be paid quarterly by the respective scholars, their parents, or guardians, and shall be recoverable if withheld, together with costs on motion in any Court of Record, * * *.

Every overseer of the hundred schools shall, in the month of September annually, after the most diligent and impartial examination and enquiry, appoint from among the boys who shall have been two years at the least at some one of the schools under his superintendence, and whose parents are too poor to give them farther education, some one of the best and most promising genius and disposition, to proceed to the grammar school of his district; which appointment shall be made * * * in the presence of the Aldermen, * * *.

Every boy so appointed shall be authorised to proceed to the grammar school of his district, there to be educated and boarded during such time as is hereafter limited; and his quota of the expences of the house together with a compensation to the master or usher for his tuition, at the rate of twenty dollars by the year, shall be paid by the Treasurer quarterly on warrant from the Auditors.

A visitation shall be held, for the purpose of probation, annually at the said grammar school * * * at which one third of the boys sent thither by appointment of the said overseers, and who shall have been there one year only, shall be discontinued as public foundationers, being those who, on the most diligent examination and enquiry, shall be thought to be of the least promising genius and disposition; and of those who shall have been there two years, all shall be discontinued, save one only the best in genius and disposition, who shall be at liberty to continue there four years longer on the public foundation, and shall thence forward be deemed a senior.

The visiters * * * after diligent examination and enquiry as before directed, shall chuse one among the said seniors, of the best learning and most hopeful genius and disposition, who shall be authorised by them to proceed to William and Mary College, there to be educated, boarded, and clothed three years; the expence of which annually shall be paid by the Treasurer on warrant from the Auditors.

JEFFERSON'S EXPLANATION OF HIS "BILL FOR THE MORE GENERAL DIFFUSION OF KNOWLEDGE" *

Another object of the revision is, to diffuse knowledge more generally through the mass of the people. This bill proposes to lay off every country into small districts of five or six miles square, called hundreds and in each of them to establish a school for teaching, read-

* From Thomas Jefferson, *Notes on the State of Virginia*, J. W. Randolph, Richmond, Va., 1853, pp. 157–160.

ing, writing, and arithmetic. The tutor to be supported by the hundred, and every person in it entitled to send their children three years gratis, and as much longer as they please, paying for it. These schools to be under a visitor who is annually to chuse the boy of best genius in the school, of those whose parents are too poor to give them further education, and to send him forward to one of the grammar schools, of which twenty are proposed to be erected in different parts of the country, for teaching Greek, Latin, geography, and the higher branches of numerical arithmetic. Of the boys thus sent in any one year, trial is to be made at the grammar schools one or two years, and the best genius of the whole selected, and continued six years, and the residue dismissed. By this means twenty of the best geniuses will be raked from the rubbish annually, and be instructed, at the public expence, so far as the grammar schools go. At the end of six years instruction, one half are to be discontinued (from among whom the grammar schools will probably be supplied with future masters); and the other half, who are to be chosen for the superiority of their parts and disposition, are to be sent and continued three years in the study of such sciences as they shall chuse, at William and Mary college, the plan of which is proposed to be enlarged, as will be hereafter explained, and extended to all the useful sciences. The ultimate result of the whole scheme of education would be the teaching all the children of the State reading, writing, and common arithmetic; turning out ten annually, of superior genius, well taught in Greek, Latin, geography, and the higher branches of arithmetic; turning out ten others annually, of still superior parts, who, to those branches of learning, shall have added such of the sciences as their genius shall have them them led to; the furnishing to the wealthier part of the people convenient schools at which their children may be educated at their own expence.—The general objects of this law are to provide an education adapted to the years, to the capacity, and the condition of every one, and directed to their freedom and happiness. Specific details were not proper for the law. These must be the business of the visitors entrusted with its execution. The first stage of this education being the schools of the hundreds, wherein the great mass of the people will receive their instruction, the principal foundations of future order will be laid here. Instead, therefore, of putting the Bible and Testament into the hands of the children at an age when their judgments are not sufficiently matured for religious inquiries, their memories may here be stored with the most useful facts from Grecian, Roman, European, and American history. The first elements of morality too may be instilled into their minds; such as, when further developed as their judgments advance in strength, may teach them how to work out their own greatest happiness, by shewing them that it does not depend on the condition of life in which chance has placed them, but is always the result of a good conscience, good health, occupation, and freedom in all just pursuits.—Those whom either the wealth of their parents or the adoption of the state shall destine to higher degrees of learning, will go on to the grammar schools, which constitute the next stage, there to be instructed in the languages. The learning Greek and Latin, I am told, is going into disuse in Europe. I know not what their manners and occupations may call for: but it would be very ill-judged in us to follow their example in this instance. There is a certain period of life, say from eight to fifteen or sixteen years of age, when the mind like the body is not yet firm enough for laborious and close operations. If applied to such, it falls an early victim to premature exertion; exhibiting, indeed, at first, in these young and tender subjects, the flattering appearance of their being men while they are yet children, but ending in reducing them to be children when they should be men. The memory is then most susceptible and tenacious of impressions; and the learning of languages being chiefly a work of memory, it seems precisely fitted to the powers of this period, which is long enough too for acquiring the most useful languages, ancient and modern. I do not pretend that language is science. It is only an instrument for the attainment of science. But that time is not lost which is employed in providing tools for future operation: more especially as in this case the books put into the hands of the youth for this purpose may be such as will at the same time impress their minds with useful facts and good principles. If this period be suffered to pass in idleness, the mind becomes lethargic and impotent, as would the body it inhabits if unexercised during the same time. The sympathy between body and mind during their rise, progress and decline, is too strict and obvious to endanger our being misled while we reason from the one to the other. —As soon as they are of sufficient age, it is supposed they will be sent on from the grammar schools to the university, which constitutes our third and last stage, there to study those sciences which may be adapted to their views.—By that part of our plan which prescribes the selection of the youths of genius from among the classes of the poor, we hope to avail the state of those talents which nature has shown as liberally among the poor as the rich, but which perish without use, if not sought for and cultivated.—But of all the views of this law none is more important, none more legitimate, than that of rendering the people the safe, as they are the ultimate, guardians of their own liberty. For this purpose the reading in the first stage, where *they* will receive their whole education, is proposed, as has been said, to be chiefly historical. History, by apprising them of the past, will enable them to judge of the future; it will avail them of the experience of other times and other nations; it will qualify them as judges of the actions and designs of men; it will enable them to know ambition under every disguise it may assume; and knowing it, to defeat its views. In every government on earth is some trace of human weakness, some germ of corruption and degeneracy, which cunning will discover, and wickedness insensibly open, cultivate and improve. Every government degenerates when trusted to the rulers of the people alone. The people themselves therefore are its only safe depositories. And to render even them safe, their minds must be improved to a certain degree. This indeed is not all that is necessary, though it be essentially necessary. An amendment of our constitution must here come in aid of the public education. The influence over government must be shared among all the people. If every individual which composes their mass participates of the ultimate authority, the government will be safe; because the corrupting the whole mass will exceed any private resources of wealth; and public ones cannot be provided but by levies on the people. In this case every man would have to pay his own price. The government of Great Britain has been corrupted, because but one man in ten has a right to vote for members of parliament. The sellers of the government, therefore, get nine-tenths of their price clear. It has been thought that corruption is restrained by confining the right of suffrage to a few of the wealthier of the people; but it would be more effectually restrained by an extension of that right to such members as would bid defiance to the means of corruption.

HORACE MANN'S 10TH AND 12TH ANNUAL REPORTS TO THE MASSACHUSETTS BOARD OF EDUCATION

From the 10th Report (1846): *

I believe in the existence of a great, immutable principle of natural law, or natural ethics, a principle antecedent to all human institutions and incapable of being abrogated by any ordinances of man, a principle of divine origin, clearly legible in the ways of Providence as those ways are manifested in the order of nature and in the history of the race, which proves the *absolute right* of every human being that comes into the world to an education; and which, of course, proves the correlative duty of every government to see that the means of that education are provided for all.

In regard to the application of this principle of natural law, that is, in regard to the extent of the education to be provided for all, at the public expense, some differences of opinion may fairly exist, under different political organizations; but under a republican government, it seems clear that the minimum of this education can never be less than such as is sufficient to qualify each citizen for the civil and social duties he will be called to discharge; such an education as teaches the individual the great laws of bodily health; as qualifies for the fulfilment of parental duties; as is indispensable for the civil functions of a witness or a juror; as is necessary for the voter in municipal affairs; and finally, for the faithful and conscientious discharge of all those duties which devolve upon the inheritor of a portion of the sovereignty of this great republic.

* From the 10th Annual Report, published in *The Common School Journal*, Vol. IX, No. 9, edited by Horace Mann (Boston: William B. Fowle, 1847); the 12th Annual Report, published separately from the *Journal* by Fowle in 1849.

From the 12th Report (1848):

> The Capacities of Our Present School System to Improve the Pecuniary Condition, and to Elevate the Intellectual and Moral Character of the Commonwealth

Under the Providence of God, our means of education are the grand machinery by which the "raw material" of human nature can be worked up into inventors and discoverers, into skilled artisans and scientific farmers, into scholars and jurists, into the founders of benevolent institutions, and the great expounders of ethical and theological science. By means of early education, those embryos of talent may be quickened, which will solve the difficult problems of political and economical law; and by them, too, the genius may be kindled which will blaze forth in the Poets of Humanity. Our schools, far more than they have done, may supply the Presidents and Professors of Colleges, and Superintendents of Public Instruction, all over the land; and send, not only into our sister states, but across the Atlantic, the man of practical science, to superintend the construction of the great works of art. Here, too, may those judicial powers be developed and invigorated, which will make legal principles so clear and convincing as to prevent appeals to force; and, should the clouds of war ever lower over our country, some hero may be found, the nursling of our schools, and ready to become the leader of our armies, the best of all heroes, who will secure the glories of a peace, unstained by the magnificent murders of the battlefield.   *   *   *

Without undervaluing any other human agency, it may be safely affirmed that the Common School, improved and energized, as it can easily be, may become the most effective and benignant of all the forces of civilization. Two reasons sustain this position. In the first place, there is a universality in its operation, which can be affirmed of no other institution whatever. If administered in the spirit of justice and conciliation, all the rising generation may be brought within the circle of its reformatory and elevating influences. And, in the second place, the materials upon which it operates are so pliant and ductile as to be susceptible of assuming a greater variety of forms than any other earthly work of the Creator.   *   *   *

I proceed, then, in endeavoring to show how the true business of the schoolroom connects itself, and becomes identical, with the great interests of society. The former is the infant, immature state of those interests; the latter, their developed, adult state. As "the child is father to the man," so may the training of the schoolroom expand into the institutions and fortunes of the State.

According to the European theory, men are divided into classes —some to toil and earn, others to seize and enjoy. According to the Massachusetts theory, all are to have an equal chance for earning, and equal security in the enjoyment of what they earn. The latter tends to equality of condition; the former to the grossest inequalities.

Tried by any Christian standard of morals, or even by any of the better sort of heathen standards, can any one hesitate, for a moment, in declaring which of the two will produce the greater amount of human welfare; and which, therefore, is the more conformable to the Divine will? * * *

I suppose it to be the universal sentiment of all those who mingle any ingredient of benevolence with their notions on Political Economy, that vast and overshadowing private fortunes are among the greatest dangers to which the happiness of the people in a republic can be subjected. Such fortunes would create a feudalism of a new kind; but one more oppressive and unrelenting than that of the Middle Ages. The feudal lords in England, and on the continent, never held their retainers in a more abject condition of servitude, than the great majority of foreign manufacturers and capitalists hold their operatives and laborers at the present day. The means employed are different, but the similarity in results is striking. What force did then, money does now. * * * The baron prescribed his own terms to his retainers; those terms were peremptory, and the serf must submit or perish. The British manufacturer or farmer prescribes the rate of wages he will give to his work-people; he reduces these wages under whatever pretext he pleases; and they too have no alternative but submission or starvation. In some respects, indeed, the condition of the modern dependent is more forlorn than that of the corresponding serf class in former times. Some attributes of the patriarchal relation did spring up between the lord and his lieges, to soften the harsh relations subsisting between them. Hence came some oversight of the condition of children, some relief in sickness, some protection and support in the decrepitude of age. But only in instances comparatively few, have kindly offices smoothed the rugged relation between British Capital and British Labor. The children of the work-people are abandoned to their fate; and, notwithstanding the privations they suffer, and the dangers they threaten, no power in the realm has yet been able to secure them an education; and when the adult laborer is prostrated by sickness, or eventually worn out by toil and age, the poorhouse, which has all along been his destination, becomes his destiny.

Now, surely, nothing but Universal Education can counter-work this tendency to the domination of capital and the servility of labor. If one class possesses all the wealth and the education, while the residue of society is ignorant and poor, it matters not by what name the relation between them may be called; the latter, in fact and in truth, will be the servile dependents and subjects of the former. But if education be equably diffused, it will draw property after it, by the strongest of all attractions; for such a thing never did happen, and never can happen, as that an intelligent and practical body of men should be permanently poor. * * *

<u>Education, then, beyond all other devices of human origin, is the great equalizer of the conditions of men—the balance-wheel of the social machinery.</u> I do not here mean that it so elevates the moral nature as to make men disdain and abhor the oppression of their fellow-men. This idea pertains to another of its attributes. But I mean that it gives each man the independence and the means, by which he can resist the selfishness of other men.   *   *   *

    *   *   *

For the creation of wealth, then—for the existence of a wealthy people and a wealthy nation—intelligence is the grand condition. The number of improvers will increase, as the intellectual constituency, if I may so call it, increases. In former times, and in most parts of the world even at the present day, not one man in a million has ever had such a development of mind, as made it possible for him to become a contributor to art or science. Let this development precede, and contributions, numberless, and of inestimable value, will be sure to follow. That Political Economy, therefore, which busies itself about capital and labor, supply and demand, interest and rents, favorable and unfavorable balances of trade; but leaves out of account the element of a wide-spread mental development, is nought but stupendous folly. The greatest of all the arts in political economy is to change a consumer into a producer; and the next greatest is to increase the producing power—an end to be directly attained, by increasing his intelligence.   *   *   *

Political Education

    *   *   * Such being the rule established by common consent, and such the practice, observed with fidelity under it, it will come to be universally understood, that political proselytism is no function of the school; but that all indoctrination into matters of controversy between hostile political parties is to be elsewhere sought for, and elsewhere imparted. Thus, may all the children of the Commonwealth receive instruction in the great essentials of political knowledge, in those elementary ideas without which they will never be able to investigate more recondite and debatable questions; thus, will the only practicable method be adopted for discovering new truths, and for discarding, instead of perpetuating, old errors; and thus, too, will that pernicious race of intolerant zealots, whose whole faith may be summed up in two articles, that they, themselves, are always infallibly right, and that all dissenters are certainly wrong, be extinguished, not by violence, nor by proscription, but by the more copious inflowing of the light of truth.

Moral Education

Moral education is a primal necessity of social existence. The unrestrained passions of men are not only homicidal, but suicidal; and a community without a conscience would soon extinguish itself. *   *   *

* * *

But to all doubters, disbelievers, or despairers, in human progress, it may still be said, there is one experiment which has never yet been tried.　It is an experiment which, even before its inception, offers the highest authority for its ultimate success.　Its formula is intelligible to all; and it is as legible as though written in starry letters on an azure sky.　It is expressed in these few and simple words: *"Train up a child in the way he should go, and when he is old he will not depart from it."*　This declaration is positive.　If the conditions are complied with, it makes no provision for a failure.　Though pertaining to morals, yet, if the terms of the direction are observed, there is no more reason to doubt the result, than there would be in an optical or a chemical experiment.

But this experiment has never yet been tried.　Education has never yet been brought to bear with one hundredth part of its potential force, upon the natures of children, and, through them, upon the character of men, and of the race.　In all the attempts to reform mankind which have hitherto been made, whether by changing the frame of government, by aggravating or softening the severity of the penal code, or by substitution a government-created, for a God-created religion; in all these attempts, the infantile and youthful mind, its amenability to influences, and the enduring and self-operating character of the influences it receives, have been almost wholly unrecognized.　Here, is a new agency, whose powers are but just beginning to be understood, and whose mighty energies, hitherto, have been but feebly invoked; and yet, from our experience, limited and imperfect as it is, we do know that, far beyond any other earthly instrumentality, it is comprehensive and decisive.　* * *

Religious Education

　　* * * If, then a government would recognize and protect the rights of religious freedom, it must abstain from subjugating the capacities of its children to any legal standard of religious faith, with as great fidelity as it abstains from controlling the opinions of men.　It must meet the unquestionable fact, that the old spirit of religious domination is adopting new measures to accomplish its work—measures, which, if successful, will be as fatal to the liberties of mankind, as those which were practiced in by-gone days of violence and terror.　These new measures are aimed at children instead of men.　They propose to supersede the necessity of subduing free thought, *in the mind of the adult,* by forestalling the development of any capacity of free thought, *in the mind of the child.*　They expect to find it easier to subdue the free agency of children, by binding them in fetters of bigotry, than to subdue the free agency of men, by binding them in fetters of iron.　For this purpose, some are attempting to deprive children of their right to labor, and, of course, of their daily bread, unless they will attend a government school, and receive its sectarian instruction. Some are attempting to withhold all means, even of secular education, from the poor, and thus punish them with ignorance, unless, with the secular knowledge which they desire, they will accept theological knowledge which they condemn. Others, still, are striving to break down all free Public School systems, where they exist, and to prevent their establishment, where they do not exist, in the hope, that on the downfall of these, their system will succeed. The sovereign antidote against these machinations is Free Schools for all, and the right of every parent to determine the religious education of his children.

Taxes May be Levied on the General Public to Expand
Common School Program Through High School

STUART v. SCHOOL DIST. NO. 1 OF THE VILLAGE OF KALAMAZOO

Supreme Court of Michigan, 1874.
30 Mich. 69.

COOLEY, J.: The bill in this case is filed to restrain the collection of such portion of the school taxes assessed against complainants for the year 1872, as have been voted for the support of the high school in that village, and for the payment of the salary of the superintendent. While, nominally, this is the end sought to be attained by the bill, the real purpose of the suit is wider and vastly more comprehensive than this brief statement would indicate, inasmuch as it seeks a judicial determination of the right of school authorities, in what are called union school districts of the state, to levy taxes upon the general public for the support of what in this state are known as high schools, and to make free by such taxation the instruction of children in other languages than the English. The bill is, consequently, of no small interest to all the people of the state; and to a large number of very flourishing schools, it is of the very highest interest, as their prosperity and usefulness, in a large degree, depend upon the method in which they are supported, so that a blow at this method seems a blow at the schools themselves. * * *

The complainants rely upon two objections to the taxes in question, one of which is general, and the other applies only to the authority or action of this particular district. The general objection has already been indicated; the particular objection is that, even conceding that other districts in the state may have authority under special charters or laws, or by the adoption of general statutes, to levy taxes for the support of high schools in which foreign and dead languages shall be taught, yet this district has no such power, because the special legislation for its benefit, which was had in 1859, was invalid for want of compliance with the constitution in the forms of enactment, and it has never adopted the general law * * * by taking a vote of the district to establish a union school in accordance with its provisions, * * *.

Whether this particular objection would have been worthy of serious consideration had it been made sooner, we must, after this lapse of time, wholly decline to consider. This district existed *de facto*, and we suppose *de jure*, also, for we are not informed to the contrary, when the legislation of 1859 was had, and from that time to the present it has assumed to possess and exercise all the franchises which are now brought in question, and there has since been a steady concurrence of action on the part of its people in the election of officers, in the levy of large taxes, and in the employment of teachers for the support of a high school. The state has acquiesced in this assumption of authority, and it has never, so far as we are advised, been questioned by any one until, after thirteen years user, three individual tax payers, out of some thousands, in a suit instituted on their own behalf, and to which the public authorities give no countenance, come forward in this collateral manner and ask us to annul the franchies. * * * If every municipality must be subject to be called into court at any time to defend its original organization and its franchises at the will of any dissatisfied citizen who may feel disposed to question them, and subject to dissolution, perhaps, or to be crippled in authority and powers if defects appear, however complete and formal may have been the recognition of its rights and privileges, on the part alike of the state and of its citizens, it may very justly be said that few of our municipalities can be entirely certain of the ground they stand upon, and that any single person, however honestly inclined, if disposed to be litigious, or over technical and precise, may have it in his power in many cases to cause infinite trouble, embarrassment and mischief.

　　　* * *

The more general question which the record presents we shall endeavor to state in our own language, but so as to make it stand out distinctly as a naked question of law, disconnected from all considerations of policy or expediency; in which light alone are we at liberty to consider it. It is, as we understand it, that there is no authority in this state to make the high schools free by taxation levied on the people at large. The argument is that while there may be no constitutional provision expressly prohibiting such taxation, the general course of legislation in the state and the general understanding of the people have been such as to require us to regard the instruction in the classics and in living modern languages in these schools as in the nature not of practical and therefore necessary instruction for the benefit of the people at large, but rather as accomplishments for the few, to be sought after in the main by those best able to pay for them, and to be paid for by those who seek them, and not by general tax. And not only has this been the general state policy, but this higher learning of itself, when supplied by the state, is so far a matter of private concern to those who receive it that the courts ought to declare it incompetent to supply it wholly at the public expense. This is in sub·stance, as we understand it, the position of the complainants in this suit.

* * *

It is not disputed that the dissemination of knowledge by means of schools has been a prominent object from the first, and we allude to the provision of the ordinance of 1787 on that subject, and to the donation of lands by congress for the purpose. * * *

* * *

Thus stood the law when the constitution of 1835 was adopted. The article on education in that instrument contained the following provisions:

"2. The legislature shall encourage by all suitable means the promotion of intellectual, scientific and agricultural improvement. * * *

"3. The legislature shall provide for a system of common schools, * * *."

* * * Two things are specially noticeable in these provisions: *first*, that they contemplated provision by the state for a complete system of instruction, beginning with that of the primary school and ending with that of the university; *second*, that while the legislature was required to make provision for district schools for at least three months in each year, no restriction was imposed upon its power to establish schools intermediate the common district school and the university, and we find nothing to indicate an intent to limit their discretion as to the class or grade of schools to which the proceeds of school lands might be devoted, or as to the range of studies or grade of instruction which might be provided for in the district schools.

* * *

The system adopted by the legislature, and which embraced a university and branches, and a common or primary school in every school district of the state, was put into successful operation, and so continued, with one important exception, until the adoption of the constitution of 1850. The exception relates to the branches of the university, which the funds of the university did not warrant keeping up, and which were consequently abandoned. Private schools to some extent took their place; but when the convention met to frame a constitution in 1850, there were already in existence, in a number of the leading towns, schools belonging to the general public system, which were furnishing instruction which fitted young men for the university. These schools for the most part had been organized under special laws, which, while leaving the primary school laws in general applicable, gave the districts a larger board of officers and larger powers of taxation for buildings and the payment of teachers. As the establishment and support of such schools were optional with the people, they encountered in some localities considerable opposition, which, however, is believed to have been always overcome, and the authority of the districts to provide instruction in the languages in these union schools was not, so far as we are aware, seriously contested. * * *

It now becomes important to see whether the constitutional convention and the people, in 1850, did any thing to undo what previously had been accomplished towards furnishing high schools as a part of the primary school system. The convention certainly did nothing to that end. On the contrary, they demonstrated in the most unmistakable manner that they cherished no such desire or purpose. * * *

The instrument submitted by the convention to the people and adopted by them provided for the establishment of free schools in every school district for at least three months in each year, and for the university. By the aid of these we have every reason to believe the people expected a complete collegiate education might be obtained. The branches of the university had ceased to exist; the university had no preparatory department, and it must either have been understood that young men were to be prepared for the university in the common schools, or else that they should go abroad for the purpose, or be prepared in private schools. Private schools adapted to the purpose were almost unknown in the state, and comparatively a very few persons were at that time of sufficient pecuniary ability to educate their children abroad. The inference seems irresistible that the people expected the tendency towards the establishment of high schools in the primary school districts would continue until every locality capable of supporting one was supplied. * * *

If these facts do not demonstrate clearly and conclusively a general state policy, beginning in 1817 and continuing until after the adoption of the present constitution, in the direction of free schools in which education, and at their option the elements of classical education, might be brought within the reach of all the children of the state, then, as it seems to us, nothing can demonstrate it. We might follow the subject further, and show that the subsequent legislation has all concurred with this policy, but it would be a waste of time and labor. We content ourselves with the statement that neither in our state policy, in our constitution, or in our laws, do we find the primary school districts restricted in the branches of knowledge which their officers may cause to be taught, or the grade of instruction that may be given, if their voters consent in regular form to bear the expense and raise the taxes for the purpose.

Having reached this conclusion, we shall spend no time upon the objection that the district in question had no authority to appoint a superintendent of schools, and that the duties of superintendency should be performed by the district board. We think the power to make the appointment was incident to the full control which by law the board had over the schools of the district, and that the board and the people of the district have been wisely left by the legislature to follow their own judgment in the premises.

It follows that the decree dismissing the bill was right, and should be affirmed.

The other justices concurred.

Chapter 3

ROLE OF THE FEDERAL GOVERNMENT

Historically, the federal government has exhibited an active interest in education. Even before the adoption of the Constitution, The Ordinance of 1785 included the provision that "there shall be reserved the lot number 16 of every township for the maintenance of public schools in each township". Two years later the policies set forth in 1785 were put into effect in The Ordinance of 1787 with the sale of lands to the Ohio Company. The Ordinance of 1787 enunciated the federal government's policy toward education in the often quoted statement: "Religion, morality and knowledge being necessary to good government and the happiness of mankind, schools and the means of education shall be forever encouraged." These federal land grants served to stimulate interest in public schools and as the funds derived from the land grants became insufficient the states began to supplement the funding. In this way the federal policy toward education established a precedent which the states followed and have so fully developed in our present state systems of public education. This early method of federal land grants for education was notable in two particular aspects. First, the grants were made for the purpose of creating and aiding public schools directly, thus espousing a federal interest in mass general common school education for everyone, and second, the federal government exercised no control over education as a condition for receiving the grants.[1] From these beginnings it was established that the federal government was to play an indirect role in the development of public education, to serve a stimulus function without direct control of educational policy and operation.

Over the years the federal government's role has remained one of indirect support of education; never directly controlling education, but generally in a positive and affirmative manner, the Congress has from time to time fashioned educational policy to address certain perceived national interests. The first Morrill Act passed by Congress in 1862, like the early land grants, shaped American education policy by providing a grant of land to each state to be sold with the proceeds to be used for the "endowment, maintenance and support of at least one college where the leading object shall be, without excluding other scientific and classical studies and including military tactics, to teach such branches of learning as are related to agriculture and mechanic arts in such manner as the legislatures of the states may respectively prescribe."[2] In reliance on this Act the great land grant colleges

---

1. Roe L. Johns and Edgar L. Morphet, *The Economics and Financing of Education* (3rd ed.), Prentice-Hall, Inc., Englewood Cliffs, New Jersey, 1975, p. 370.

2. U.S.C.A., Title 20, Education 81 to 1686.

were established and supported.   Herein, Congress advanced a role of higher education which transcended the traditional, narrow European model by expanding and giving credibility to the study of agriculture and engineering, disciplines which a new and developing nation so badly needed.   Subsequent legislation, the second Morrill Act of 1890 and the Hatch Act of 1887, the Adams Act of 1906 and other provisions expanded the activities of the land-grant colleges and introduced grants-in-aid as another type of federal support.

Following these initial steps the federal government has continued to provide assistance to various phases of education.   Categorical grants which were geared toward bringing about a particular educational emphasis became the method of allocation most relied upon. Federal grants of particular importance have been: The Smith-Lever Act of 1914 which was quite specific in purpose prescribing the expenditure of grant funds for, among other things, extension services by county agents for agriculture and homemaking and for training of teachers in these areas; the Smith-Hughes Act of 1917 which provided for funds for vocational education below college level; the National Defense Education Act of 1958, the response to Sputnik I which instituted several types of programs at the elementary, secondary and higher education levels to give impetus to scientific training and research; the Higher Education Facilities Act of 1963 creating financial assistance for construction at all levels of higher education; the Vocational Education Act of 1963 substantially increasing federal appropriations for vocational education, and the Elementary and Secondary Education Act of 1965, the most important elementary and secondary program ever enacted by Congress which provided funding primarily for the educations of culturally disadvantaged children.[3]

In each of these acts the role of the federal government is conveyed by Congress to be one of supplementary assistance to the state systems of education.   The Congress has sought to shape educational policy through the indirect means of categorical grants giving direction to certain educational programs once states accept the funds.   In each instance the states have the option of accepting or rejecting the funds, but once they are accepted the states must abide by the federal guidelines for use of the resources.   As states have accepted the conditions of these categorical grants over the years the role of the federal government in guiding educational choices has become more predominant and some commentators have maintained that too much control is today vested in the federal government.   As a result, even though the federal government's role in education is said to be indirect and secondary, the impact of myriad regulations and conditions bear down quite heavily on the public schools and has led some to question the legal scope of federal powers.   Unfortunately legal definition of the role of the federal government in education is as hazy

3.   Ibid.

and uncertain as the legal parameters of our federal system of government itself. Courts continue today to ponder the nature of the states' relationship to the central government not only in education, but in all areas of domestic activity.

Reserved State Powers

The powers of the federal government are circumscribed by delegation within the Constitution and are specifically limited by the Tenth Amendment of the Constitution which provides that "The powers not delegated to the United States by the Constitution, nor prohibited by it to the States, are reserved to the States respectively or to the people." Education is not mentioned in the Constitution and is therefore presumably reserved "to the states or to the people." The Tenth Amendment was intended to reconfirm the implicit understanding at the time of the Constitution's adoption that powers not granted to the central government were reserved.[4] James Madison at the urging of Jefferson sponsored the Tenth Amendment and in the course of debate which took place while the Amendment was still pending over Hamilton's proposal to establish a national bank, Madison declared that: "Interference with the power of the States was no constitutional criterion of the power of Congress. If the power was not given, Congress could not exercise it; if given, they might exercise it, although it should interfere with the laws, or even the Constitutions of the States." [5]

A discrete boundary line between federal and state power was not to evolve, however, in spite of Madison's apparently clear conception of the doctrine. Chief Justice Marshall in the famous case of McCulloch v. Maryland [6] added ambiguity by noting that the word "expressly" was not included in the Tenth Amendment as it had been in the Articles of Confederation effectively leaving the issue "whether the particular power which may become the subject of contest has been delegated to the one government, or prohibited to the other", to depend upon a fair construction of the whole instrument.[7] Justice Marshall's view of the Tenth Amendment was merely a restatement of the already presumed and established relationship which is delineated in other parts of the Constitution. In *Darby* the Court said:

> The Amendment states but a truism that all is retained which has not been surrendered. There is nothing in the history of its adoption to suggest that it was more than declaratory of the relationship between the national and state

4. United States v. Sprague, 282 U.S. 716, 51 S.Ct. 220 (1931).

5. Annals of Congress, 1897 (1791). (See: Edward S. Corwin (ed.), *The Constitution of the United States of America*, U. S. Government Printing Office, Wash. D.C., 1964, pp. 1035–1036.)

6. Wheat 316 (1819).

7. Ibid. p. 406.

governments as it had been established by the Constitution before the amendment or that its purpose was other than to allay fears that the new national government might seek to exercise powers not granted, and that the states might not be able to exercise fully their reserved powers.[8]

Standing alone the Tenth Amendment does little more than bear witness to the fact that our system of government assumes some separation of powers and prevents federal activity without express or implied constitutional authority. As such, there is a presumption of state power which effectively places the burden on the federal government to justify in court its involvement in affairs which may have been presumed to be left to the states. As Justice Cardoza declared, the Tenth Amendment voices an assumption of "quasi-sovereignty * * * which the state is privileged to redress as a suitor in the courts."[9] This presumption on behalf of the states provides a Constitutional basis through which a state can seek legal redress in challenging a federal statute. Without the Tenth Amendment no such action would be possible. In the face of such challenges the federal government has been forced on many occasions to identify other Constitutional provisions which justify its activity in regulation of functions which states have assumed to be within their prerogative. In this light the federal government does not possess general police powers, as such, and in justifying its many activities has invoked implied powers of the general welfare and commerce clauses of the Constitution.

Federal Control of Education

By virtue of the Tenth Amendment federal control over education is secondary to the power exercised by the states. While a state can create, organize, and reorganize school districts, employ and dismiss personnel, prescribe curriculum, establish and enforce accredation standards and govern all management and operation functions of the public schools directly, the federal government can only intervene in a peripheral and oblique way. Federal controls emanate from three sources: (1) acquiescence by states in accepting federal grants which are provided under the authority given the Congress by the general welfare clause; (2) public schools may come under certain standards or regulations which the Congress has authorized within the commerce clause; and (3) courts may constrain public school actions where they come in conflict with federal constitutional provisions protecting individual rights and freedoms.

Education and General Welfare

Two major questions concern education and general welfare—first, does education come under the definition of general welfare and

---

8. United States v. Darby, 312 U.S. at 124, 61 S.Ct. 451 (1941).

9. Hopkins Federal Sav. and Loan Ass'n v. Cleary, 296 U.S. 315, 56 S.Ct. 235 (1935).

secondly, how can Congress provide for education if it does come within the definition? Section 8 of Article I gives Congress the power to tax and spend: "The Congress shall have Power to lay and collect Taxes, Duties, Imports and Excises, to pay the Debts and provide for the common Defense and General Welfare of the United States * * *." [10]

The interpretation of the meaning of the general welfare clause has been the subject of much debate and controversy. James Madison contended that the clause "amounted to no more than a reference to other powers enumerated in subsequent clauses of the same section; that, as the United States is a government of limited and enumerated powers, the grant of power to tax and spend for the general welfare must be confined to the enumerated legislative fields committed to the Congress." [11] Madison pointed out that the framers of the Constitution borrowed the phrase from the Articles of Confederation, and it was not looked upon as a phrase to extend the parameters of federal authority. In taking an opposing point of view, Hamilton maintained that this Article conferred upon the Congress a substantive power to tax and spend for purposes which would provide for the general welfare of the United States.

The Supreme Court adopted the Hamiltonian philosophy in a 1936 case which tested the constitutionality of the Agriculture Adjustment Act. [12] The Court stated that Congress was not limited in the expenditure of public monies to the direct or express grants of legislative power found in the Constitution.

In a later case, Helvering v. Davis, [13] the Supreme Court upheld the Social Security Act and in so doing ruled conclusively that Congress can tax and spend under the general welfare clause. In this case, the Court said that the general welfare concept is not static but is flexible, and Congress may tax and expend public money for general welfare purposes so long as it does not demonstrate a display of arbitrary power. With this elastic definition of general welfare, the Congress is free to define education as general welfare and to tax and appropriate funds for educational purposes.

With the prerogative to broadly define general welfare as inclusive of education, Congress then looks to the taxing power of the clause for the instrumentality to "provide" for education. Jefferson explained the power and purpose of the clause in this manner: "* * * the laying of taxes is the *power,* and the general welfare the *purpose* for which the power is to be exercised. They [Congress] are not to lay taxes *ad libitum for any purpose they please,* but only *to pay the debts or provide for the welfare of the Union.* In like

10.   Article I, Sec. 8, cl. 1.

11.   United States v. Butler, 297 U.S. 1, 56 S.Ct. 312 (1936).

12.   297 U.S. 1, 56 S.Ct. 312 (1936).

13.   301 U.S. 619, 57 S.Ct. 904 (1937).

manner, they are not *to do anything they please* to provide for the general welfare, but only to *lay taxes* for that purpose." [italics added] [14] This clause therefore expresses not an unlimited power but only a qualified one. Congress has never acted to assert an unlimited power to tax and the Court has therefore never been compelled to decide the point.[15]

The last sentence in Jefferson's statement raises the point quite clearly that Congress cannot provide for the general welfare in any manner other than through its taxing and appropriation power. With regard to education, this means that Congress can only involve itself in educational matters through the indirect means of appropriation of funds and does not have the power to directly legislate changes in education. It is for this reason that Congress has so consistently used the categorical aid approach to bring about change in education. Constitutionally, regulation of educational functions can only be acquired through conditional grants.

The federal government cannot, therefore, affirmatively and directly require that states alter educational policy, such would be an affront to state autonomy. Constitutionally, the issue is really one of inducement versus compulsion, as one commentator has observed:

> The Constitution counts upon the necessary participation of the states * * * not by direct command but by incentive of not losing the opportunity of participation.[16]

In matters of education then the Congress can only effect change through persuasion or of giving the states an option which allows a state to act of its own volition. Welch says:

> The volitional nature of the state's acquiescence to conditional spending programs touches the very core of political autonomy. * * * Undoubtedly, economic necessity often forces states to alter governmental operations to qualify for federal funds; yet, the conditioning of needed funds does not preempt the state's decision-making process. Although the distinction may often be one of form rather than substance, the Court treats it as a critically important question of form. Such observance of form is more than a ritualistic bow to the founders' respect for the states. Apparently, the Court considers the sanctity of a state's decision making process a necessary component of the Constitution's structure which endows the states with at least a degree of autonomous, volitional control.[17]

14. 3 Writings of Thomas Jefferson, pp. 147–149 (Library Edition, 1904).

15. Corwin, *op.cit.* p. 145.

16. Henry Hart, "The Relations Between State and Federal Law", 54 *Columbia Law Review* 489 (1954).

17. Richard E. Welch III, "At Federalism's Crossroads: National League of Cities v. Usery", *Boston University Law Review* 178 (1977).

A choice of accepting the grant and the conditions attached thereto must be provided the state. Under the General Welfare Clause, then, a state may elect not to participate in a federal program if the conditions are educationally, financially, or legally offensive.[18]

Education and Commerce

Increasingly, Congress has relied on the <u>Commerce Clause</u> to require affirmative action by states. Quite beyond the limitations governing general welfare <u>the Congress has power under this Clause to</u> "<u>* * * regulate Commerce with foreign Nations, and among the several States, and with the Indian Tribes.</u>" [19] Education can be affected by congressional action pursuant to this clause in many different ways, but most notably, safety, transportation and labor regulations have touched education. While one would naturally assume that the term commerce included commercial activity, to buy, sell and trade goods to and fro among states, the definition as applied by the Supreme Court has been given broader meaning. In Gibbons v. Ogden [20] Chief Justice Marshall rejected the narrow "trading" definition and maintained that it was "something more—intercourse". Commerce as intercourse was defined in *Gibbons* as not merely an exchange of goods but as a means for "advancement of society, labor, transportation, *intelligence,* care, and various mediums of exchange, become commodities, and enter into commerce * * *." [italics added]

As a mere limitation on states to prevent interference with interstate commerce such a definition has little practical effect on education, but when read in its larger context in relation to the "necessary and proper clause" [21] then Congress may act to improve commerce in an affirmative way rather than merely acting to prevent state impediments. <u>This coupled with the fact that commerce regulation is not limited to interstate but may also, under certain conditions, include intrastate activities brings public education within the purview of the clause.</u>[22] <u>In this broad context, education could conceivably be brought within the scope of commerce in that the movement of an intelligent citizenry among the states is vital to the growth and prosperity of the nation.</u>

With this definition the courts are presented with a difficult dilemma of weighing the state powers under the Tenth Amend-

18. Wheeler v. Barrera, 417 U.S. 402, 94 S.Ct. 2274 (1974).

19. Article 1, Sec. 8, cl. 3.

20. 22 U.S. (9 Wheat) 1 (1924).

21. The power of Congress "To make all Laws which shall be necessary and proper for carrying into Execution the foregoing Powers, * * *" Article I, Sec. 8, cl. 18.

22. Justice Marshall in Gibbons stated: "* * * the power of Congress does not stop at the jurisdictional lines of the several States", but "must be exercised whenever [wherever?] the subject exists. * * * Commerce among the States must, of necessity, be commerce [within?] the States." Gibbons v. Ogden, 22 U.S. (9 Wheat) 1 (1924).

ment against the apparent boundless scope of "commerce." Until recently, few decisions were rendered in favor of state prerogative; in expounding the philosophy that the "political process", in which each state has representation in the Congress and this representation will protect state interests, the Supreme Court largely exhibited a hands-off attitude toward the expansion of the federal role through the Commerce Clause.[23]

This prevailing view, though, was apparently changed, if not reversed, in the National League of Cities v. Usery [24] handed down by the Supreme Court in 1976. Under litigation was the 1974 Amendments to the Fair Labor Standards Act which extended wage and hour standards to almost all public employment, including local school districts.[25] In this case the Court, while admitting that the amendments were within the scope of the Commerce Clause, nevertheless, held that the Tenth Amendment was violated. The decision enunciated a more restricted view of the Commerce Clause and interpreted the Tenth Amendment as an affirmative limitation upon the power of Congress to regulate activities of state and local governments.[26] Justice Rehnquist writing for the majority maintained that the state's power to determine wages of its own employees is an "undoubted attribute of state sovereignty" and that the functions performed by the affected state employees were "essential to the separate and independent existence" of the state.[27]

The net effect of the Amendments had been to greatly increase the minimum wage of local school employees, thus placing a substantial burden on the local school districts. States had no recourse but to follow the mandate, no element of inducement or volition was present. The overall effect of this decision was to revitalize the importance of the Tenth Amendment as a restraint on federal action but more specifically where education is concerned it provided better definition of the role of the federal government in education.

This case suggested that the role of the federal government in education may be more carefully circumscribed by the courts in the future. Certainly any definition by the Court in the future would probably be interpreted as a limitation on federal power since up until this point, pre-*Usery,* judicial specification of the boundary be-

23. "[T]he power over commerce * * * is vested in Congress as absolutely as it would be in a single government, having in its constitution the same restrictions on the exercise of the power as are found in the constitution of the United States. The wisdom and the discretion of Congress, their identity with the people, and the influence which their constituents possess at elections, are * * * the sole restraints on which they have relied, to secure them from its abuse. They are the restraints on which the people must often rely solely, in all representative governments." Gibbons v. Ogden, 22 U.S. (9 Wheat) 1 (1924).

24. 426 U.S. 833, 96 S.Ct. 2465 (1976).

25. 29 U.S.C.A. § 203(s)(5).

26. Welch, *op. cit.* pp. 178–179.

27. National League of Cities v. Usery, *op. cit.*

tween federal interest and the states' sovereign powers has been virtually nonexistent.

Constitutional Rights and Freedoms of Individuals

Under our system of government state laws which violate or deny individual rights or freedoms may be invalidated by the courts through application of the U. S. Constitution. Many of the restraints which educators refer to as "federal control" emanates from the application of federal constitutional provisions to state statutes, regulations or actions by agents of the public school system. Virtually all of the cases which have held state actions unconstitutional have been based on either the First or the Fourteenth Amendments to the Constitution, with a scattering involving the Fourth, Fifth, Sixth, and even the Eighth Amendments. Outside the Amendments proper some early litigation was directed toward the impairment of contracts provision of the Constitution, Article I, Section 10, which prohibits unilateral abrogation of contracts by government. *

Judicial action through injunctive relief on behalf of a student, teacher, or parent may well serve to limit state options in educational policy issues. Most notable, among these has been the pervasive impact of the federal courts in shaping educational policy to effect racial integration in the public schools. Each of these actions are taken by the courts, though, on a case by case basis and judicial control is only imposed where past state action has denied individual constitutional rights.

Suppression of individual freedoms which are given constitutional status in the First Amendment also serve as the basis for frequent litigation and many times subsequent judicial control of educational activity. Personal freedoms and civil rights found in the First Amendment pertain to religion, speech, association, press, and assembly. Each of these have been brought into play as restraints on objectionable activities by state school systems.

Each of these constitutional issues will be fully discussed in subsequent chapters of this book, but it is important here to note that it is these legitimate constitutional concerns involving personal freedoms and rights which are primarily responsible for the "federal involvement in education." Such activity by the federal courts in no way violates the sovereign power of the states to operate the public schools.

Beyond these direct judicial controls whereby the court normally enjoins or mandates, the Congress has evolved certain power from the Fourteenth Amendment to bring about enforce constitutional purposes. Federal regulation of state employment practices as justified under the Fourteenth Amendment has been upheld by the Supreme

---

* These cases will be discussed in a later chapter of this text.

Court. In Fitzpatrick v. Bitzer [28] Justice Rehnquist appeared to distinguish between Congress' Fourteenth Amendment and Commerce Clause powers by maintaining that the Fourteenth Amendment "clearly contemplates limitations on [the states'] authority". From such precedents then it appears that the federal role in education extends to both judicial action to prevent unconstitutional state action and to affirmative Congressional action to effectuate equality through the Fourteenth Amendment.

*General Welfare is Expansive Giving Congress Powers
Beyond those Specifically Enumerated
in the Constitution*

UNITED STATES v. BUTLER

Supreme Court of the United States, 1936.
297 U.S. 1, 56 S.Ct. 312.

Mr. Justice ROBERTS delivered the opinion of the Court.

In this case we must determine whether certain provisions of the Agricultural Adjustment Act, 1933,[1] conflict with the Federal Constitution.

* * *

* * * The government asserts that even if the respondents may question the propriety of the appropriation embodied in the statute, their attack must fail because article 1, § 8 of the Constitution, authorizes the contemplated expenditure of the funds raised by the tax. This contention presents the great and the controlling question in the case. We approach its decision with a sense of our grave responsibility to render judgment in accordance with the principles established for the governance of all three branches of the government.

* * *

The question is not what power the federal government ought to have, but what powers in fact have been given by the people. It hardly seems necessary to reiterate that ours is a dual form of government; that in every state there are two governments; the state and the United States. Each state has all governmental powers save such as the people, by their Constitution, have conferred upon the United States, denied to the states, or reserved to themselves. The federal union is a government of delegated powers. It has only such as are expressly conferred upon it and such as are reasonably to be implied from those granted. In this respect we differ radically from nations where all legislative power, without restriction or limitation, is vested in a parliament or other legislative body subject to no restrictions except the discretion of its members.

28.   427 U.S. 445, 96 S.Ct. 2666 (1976).   1.   May 12, 1933, c. 25, 48 Stat. 31.

Article 1, § 8, of the Constitution, vests sundry powers in the Congress. * * *

The clause thought to authorize the legislation, the first, confers upon the Congress power "to lay and collect Taxes, Duties, Imposts and Excises, to pay the Debts and provide for the common Defence and general Welfare of the United States. * * * " It is not contended that this provision grants power to regulate agricultural production upon the theory that such legislation would promote the general welfare. The government concedes that the phrase "to provide for the general welfare" qualifies the power "to lay and collect taxes." The view that the clause grants power to provide for the general welfare, independently of the taxing power, has never been authoritatively accepted. Mr. Justice Story points out that, if it were adopted, "it is obvious that under color of the generality of the words, to 'provide for the common defence and general welfare', the government of the United States is, in reality, a government of general and unlimited powers, notwithstanding the subsequent enumeration of specific powers." [11] The true construction undoubtedly is that the only thing granted is the power to tax for the purpose of providing funds for payment of the nation's debts and making provision for the general welfare.

Nevertheless, the government asserts that warrant is found in this clause for the adoption of the Agricultural Adjustment Act. The argument is that Congress may appropriate and authorize the spending of moneys for the "general welfare"; that the phrase should be liberally construed to cover anything conducive to national welfare; that decision as to what will promote such welfare rests with Congress alone, and the courts may not review its determination; and, finally, that the appropriation under attack was in fact for the general welfare of the United States.

The Congress is expressly empowered to lay taxes to provide for the general welfare. Funds in the Treasury as a result of taxation may be expended only through appropriation. Article 1, § 9, cl. 7. They can never accomplish the objects for which they were collected, unless the power to appropriate is as broad as the power to tax. The necessary implication from the terms of the grant is that the public funds may be appropriated "to provide for the general welfare of the United States." These words cannot be meaningless, else they would not have been used. The conclusion must be that they were intended to limit and define the granted power to raise and to expend money. How shall they be construed to effectuate the intent of the instrument?

Since the foundation of the nation, sharp differences of opinion have persisted as to the true interpretation of the phrase. Madison

11. Story, Commentaries on the Constitution of the United States (5th Ed.) vol. I, § 907.

asserted it amounted to no more than a reference to the other powers enumerated in the subsequent clauses of the same section; that, as the United States is a government of limited and enumerated powers, the grant of power to tax and spend for the general national welfare must be confined to the enumerated legislative fields committed to the Congress. In this view the phrase is mere tautology, for taxation and appropriation are or may be necessary incidents of the exercise of any of the enumerated legislative powers. Hamilton, on the other hand, maintained the clause confers a power separate and distinct from those later enumerated, is not restricted in meaning by the grant of them, and Congress consequently has a substantive power to tax and to appropriate, limited only by the requirement that it shall be exercised to provide for the general welfare of the United States. Each contention has had the support of those whose views are entitled to weight. This court has noticed the question, but has never found it necessary to decide which is the true construction. Mr. Justice Story, in his Commentaries, espouses the Hamiltonian position. We shall not review the writings of public men and commentators or discuss the legislative practice. Study of all these leads us to conclude that the reading advocated by Mr. Justice Story is the correct one. While, therefore, the power to tax is not unlimited, its confines are set in the clause which confers it, and not in those of section 8 which bestow and define the legislative powers of the Congress. It results that the power of Congress to authorize expenditure of public moneys for public purposes is not limited by the direct grants of legislative power found in the Constitution.

But the adoption of the broader construction leaves the power to spend subject to limitations.

As Story says: "The Constitution was, from its very origin, contemplated to be the frame of a national government, of special and enumerated powers, and not of general and unlimited powers."

Again he says: "A power to lay taxes for the common defence and general welfare of the United States is not in common sense a general power. It is limited to those objects. It cannot constitutionally transcend them."

That the qualifying phrase must be given effect all advocates of broad construction admit. Hamilton, in his well known Report on Manufacturers, states that the purpose must be "general, and not local." Monroe, an advocate of Hamilton's doctrine, wrote: "Have Congress a right to raise and appropriate the money to any and to every purpose according to their will and pleasure? They certainly have not." [16] Story says that if the tax be not proposed for the common defense or general welfare, but for other objects wholly extraneous, it would be wholly indefensible upon constitutional principles.

16. Richardson, Messages and Papers
of the Presidents, vol. II, p. 167.

And he makes it clear that the powers of taxation and appropriation extend only to matters of national, as distinguished from local, welfare.

* * *

We are not now required to ascertain the scope of the phrase "general welfare of the United States" or to determine whether an appropriation in aid of agriculture falls within it. Wholly apart from that question, <u>another principle embedded in our Constitution prohibits the enforcement of the Agricultural Adjustment Act. The act invades the reserved rights of the states</u>. It is a statutory plan to regulate and control agricultural production, a matter beyond the powers delegated to the federal government. The tax, the appropriation of the funds raised, and the direction for their disbursement, are but parts of the plan. They are but means to an unconstitutional end.

From the accepted doctrine that the United States is a government of delegated powers, it follows that those not expressly granted, or reasonably to be implied from such as are conferred, are reserved to the states or to the people. To forestall any suggestion to the contrary, the Tenth Amendment was adopted.[18] The same proposition, otherwise stated, is that <u>powers not granted are prohibited. None to regulate agricultural production is given, and therefore legislation by Congress for that purpose is forbidden</u>.

It is an established principle that the attainment of a prohibited end may not be accomplished under the pretext of the exertion of powers which are granted. * * *

"Congress cannot, under the pretext of executing delegated power, pass laws for the accomplishment of objects not intrusted to the federal government. And we accept as established doctrine that any provision of an act of Congress ostensibly enacted under power granted by the Constitution, not naturally and reasonably adapted to the effective exercise of such power, but solely to the achievement of something plainly within power reserved to the states, is invalid and cannot be enforced." Linder v. United States, 268 U.S. 5, 17, 45 S.Ct. 446, 449.

* * *

The power of taxation, which is expressly granted, may, of course, be adopted as a means to carry into operation another power also expressly granted. But resort to the taxing power to effectuate an end which is not legitimate, not within the scope of the Constitution, is obviously inadmissible.

"<u>Congress is not empowered to tax for those purposes which are within the exclusive province of the states</u>." Gibbons v. Ogden, 9 Wheat. 1, 199. * * *

18. The Tenth Amendment declares:
    "The powers not delegated to the United States by the Constitution, nor prohibited by it to the States, are reserved to the States respectively, or to the people."

* * *   If the taxing power may not be used as the instrument to enforce a regulation of matters of state concern with respect to which the Congress has no authority to interfere, may it, as in the present case, be employed to raise the money necessary to purchase a compliance which the Congress is powerless to command? The government asserts that whatever might be said against the validity of the plan, if compulsory, it is constitutionally sound because the end is accomplished by voluntary co-operation. There are two sufficient answers to the contention. The regulation is not in fact voluntary. The farmer, of course, may refuse to comply, but the price of such refusal is the loss of benefits. The amount offered is intended to be sufficient to exert pressure on him to agree to the proposed regulation. The power to confer or withhold unlimited benefits is the power to coerce or destroy. If the cotton grower elects not to accept the benefits, he will receive less for his crops; those who receive payments will be able to undersell him. The result may well be financial ruin. The coercive purpose and intent of the statute is not obscured by the fact that it has not been perfectly successful. It is pointed out that, because there still remained a minority whom the rental and benefit payments were insufficient to induce to surrender their independence of action, the Congress has gone further, and, in the Bankhead Cotton Act, used the taxing power in a more directly minatory fashion to compel submission. This progression only serves more fully to expose the coercive purpose of the so-called tax imposed by the present act. It is clear that the Department of Agriculture has properly described the plan as one to keep a nonco-operating minority in line. This is coercion by economic pressure. The asserted power of choice is illusory.

* * *

But if the plan were one for purely voluntary co-operation it would stand no better so far as federal power is concerned. At best, it is a scheme for purchasing with federal funds submission to federal regulation of a subject reserved to the states.

* * *   Is a statute less objectionable which authorizes expenditure of federal moneys to induce action in a field in which the United States has no power to intermeddle? The Congress cannot invade state jurisdiction to compel individual action; no more can it purchase such action.

* * *

We are not here concerned with a conditional appropriation of money, nor with a provision that if certain conditions are not complied with the appropriation shall no longer be available. By the Agricultural Adjustment Act the amount of the tax is appropriated to be expended only in payment under contracts whereby the parties bind themselves to regulation by the federal government. There is an obvious difference between a statute stating the conditions upon which moneys shall be expended and one effective only upon assumption of a contractual obligation to submit to a regulation which otherwise could not be enforced. Many examples pointing to the distinction might be cited. We are referred to appropriations in aid of education, and it is said that no one has doubted the power of Congress to stipulate the sort of education for which money shall be expended. But an appropriation to an educational institution which by its terms is to become available only if the beneficiary enters into a contract to teach doctrines subversive of the Constitution is clearly bad. An affirmance of the authority of Congress so to condition the expenditure of an appropriation would tend to nullify all constitutional limitations upon legislative power.

* * *

Congress has no power to enforce its commands on the farmer to the ends sought by the Agricultural Adjustment Act. It must follow that it may not indirectly accomplish those ends by taxing and spending to purchase compliance. The Constitution and the entire plan of our government negative any such use of the power to tax and to spend as the act undertakes to authorize. It does not help to declare that local conditions throughout the nation have created a situation of national concern; for this is but to say that whenever there is a widespread similarity of local conditions, Congress may ignore constitutional limitations upon its own powers and usurp those reserved to the states. If, in lieu of compulsory regulation of subjects within the states' reserved jurisdiction, which is prohibited, the Congress could invoke the taxing and spending power as a means to accomplish the same end, clause 1 of section 8 of article 1 would become the instrument for total subversion of the governmental powers reserved to the individual states.

* * *

Until recently no suggestion of the existence of any such power in the federal government has been advanced. The expressions of the framers of the Constitution, the decisions of this court interpreting that instrument and the writings of great commentators will be searched in vain for any suggestion that there exists in the clause under discussion or elsewhere in the Constitution, the authority whereby every provision and every fair implication from that instrument may be subverted, the independence of the individual states obliterated, and the United States converted into a central government exercising uncontrolled police power in every state of the Union, superseding all local control or regulation of the affairs or concerns of the states.

Hamilton himself, the leading advocate of broad interpretation of the power to tax and to appropriate for the general welfare, never suggested that any power granted by the Constitution could be used for the destruction of local self-government in the states. Story countenances no such doctrine. It seems never to have occurred to them, or to those who have agreed with them, that the general welfare of the United States (which has aptly been termed "an indestructible Union, composed of indestructible States,") might be served by obliterating the constituent members of the Union. But to this fatal conclusion the doctrine contended for would inevitably lead. And its sole premise is that, though the makers of the Constitution, in erecting the federal government, intended sedulously to limit and define its powers, so as to reserve to the states and the people sovereign power, to be wielded by the states and their citizens and not to be invaded by the United States, they nevertheless by a single clause gave power to the Congress to tear down the barriers, to invade the states' jurisdiction, and to become a parliament of the whole people, subject to no restrictions save such as are self-imposed. The argument, when seen in its true character and in the light of its inevitable results, must be rejected.

Since, as we have pointed out, there was no power in the Congress to impose the contested exaction, it could not lawfully ratify or confirm what an executive officer had done in that regard. Consequently the Act of 1935, * * * does not affect the rights of the parties.

The judgment is affirmed.

NOTES

1.   In an early case, the Kentucky Court of Appeals described the relationship of the federal government to the states: "The power of the states to establish and maintain systems of common schools, to raise money for that purpose by taxation, and to govern, control, and regulate such schools when established, is one of 'the powers not delegated to the United States by the Constitution, nor prohibited by it to the states,' and consequently it is reserved to the states respectively or to their people." Marshall v. Donovan, 10 Bush 681 (1874).

2.   In the case of Helvering v. Davis, 301 U.S. 619, 57 S.Ct. 904 (1937), the Supreme Court of the United States was called upon to determine the constitutionality of the Social Security Act of 1935. Although this case does not directly involve education, it provides precedent for interpreting the meaning of the "general welfare clause." In this case, the Court makes two especially important determinations. (a) In drawing the line between what is "general" welfare, and what is "particular," the determination of Congress must be respected by the courts, unless it be plainly arbitrary. (b) The concept of "general welfare" is not static but adapts itself to the crises and necessities of the times. The Court said:

Congress may spend money in aid of the "general welfare." Constitution, Art. I, section 8; United States v. Butler, 297 U.S. 1, 65, 56 S.Ct. 312 (1936), Steward Machine Co. v. Davis, supra. There have been great statesmen in our history who have stood for other views. We will not resurrect the contest. It is now settled by decision. United States v. Butler, supra. The conception of the spending power advocated by Hamilton and strongly reinforced by Story has prevailed over that of Madison, which has not been lacking in adherents. Yet difficulties are left when the power is conceded. The line must still be drawn between one welfare and another, between particular and general. Where this shall be placed cannot be shown through a formula in advance of the event. There is a middle ground or certainly a penumbra in which discretion is at large. The discretion, however, is not confined to the courts. The discretion belongs to Congress, unless the choice is clearly wrong, a display of arbitrary power, not an exercise of judgment. This is now familiar law. * * *

When such a contention comes here we naturally require a showing that by no reasonable possibility can the challenged legislation fall within the wide range of discretion permitted to the Congress. United States v. Butler, supra, p. 67. Cf. Cincinnati Soap Co. v. United States, ante, p. 308; United States v. Realty Co., 163 U.S. 427, 440, 16 S.Ct. 1120 (1896); Head Money Cases, 112 U.S. 580, 595, 5 S.Ct. 247 (1884). Nor is the concept of the general welfare static. Needs that were narrow or parochial a century ago may be interwoven in our day with the well-being of the Nation. What is critical or urgent changes with the times.

3. Powers not expressly or impliedly conferred by the Constitution to the federal government are reserved to the "States respectively or to the people." (Amendment X, Constitution of the United States of America). James Madison in debate concerning the pending Tenth Amendment declared that: "Interference with the power of the States was no constitutional criterion of the power of Congress. If the power was not given, Congress could not exercise it; if given, they might exercise it, although it should interfere with the laws, or even the constitutions of the States." (Annals of Congress, 1897, 1791).

4. It is interesting to note that in 1788, before the Tenth Amendment was enacted, Madison described the federal government relationship to the states in the new Constitution thusly:

The powers delegated by the proposed Constitution to the Federal Government, are few and defined. Those which are to remain in the State Governments are numerous and indefinite. The former will be exercised principally on external objects, as war, peace, negotiation, and foreign commerce; with which the power of taxation will for the most part be connected. The powers reserved to the several States will extend to all the objects, which, in the ordinary course of affairs, concern the lives, liberties and properties of the people; and the internal order, improvement, and prosperity of the State. (The Federalist, No. 45, January 26, 1788)

5. The United States Supreme Court has summarily rejected doctrines of nullification and interposition. The doctrine of interposition being a

concept based on the proposition that the United States is a compact of States, any one of which may interpose its sovereignty against the enforcement within its borders of any decision of the

Supreme Court or act of Congress, irrespective of the fact that the constitutionality of the act has been established by decision of the Supreme Court * * *.

* * * interposition is not a constitutional doctrine * * * [and] if taken seriously, it is illegal defiance of constitutional authority. (Bush v. Orlean School Bd., 364 U.S. 500, 81 S.Ct. 260 (1960); 188 F.Supp. 916 (E.D.La.1960).)

The Supreme Court had this to say about interposition as it concerns education. Although "the responsibility of public education is primarily the concern of the States * * *, such responsibilities * * * must be exercised consistently with federal constitutional requirements as they apply to state action." Cooper v. Aaron, 358 U.S. 1, 78 S.Ct. 1401 (1958).

Congress May Not Use the Commerce Clause to Intrude into Integral State Governmental Function

NATIONAL LEAGUE OF CITIES v. USERY

Supreme Court of the United States, 1976.
426 U.S. 833, 96 S.Ct. 2465.

Mr. Justice REHNQUIST delivered the opinion of the Court.

Nearly 40 years ago Congress enacted the Fair Labor Standards Act,[1] and required employers covered by the Act to pay their employees a minimum hourly wage and to pay them at one and one-half times their regular rate of pay for hours worked in excess of 40 during a workweek. * * *

I

In a series of amendments beginning in 1961 Congress began to extend the provisions of the Fair Labor Standards Act to some types of public employees. * * *

In 1974, Congress again broadened the coverage of the Act, 88 Stat. 55. The definition of "employer" in the Act now specifically "includes a public agency," 29 U.S.C.A. § 203(d). In addition, the critical definition of "[e]nterprise[s] engaged in commerce or in the production of goods for commerce" was expanded to encompass "an activity of a public agency," * * *. By its 1974 amendments, then, Congress has now entirely removed the exemption previously afforded States and their political subdivisions, * * *. of several specific capacities. 29 U.S.C.A. § 203(e)(2)(C). The Act thus imposes upon almost all public employment the minimum wage and maximum hour requirements previously restricted to employees engaged in interstate commerce. These requirements are essentially identical to those imposed upon private employers, although the Act

1. The Fair Labor Standards Act of 1938, 52 Stat. 1060, 29 U.S.C.A. § 201 et seq.

does attempt to make some provision for public employment relationships which are without counterpart in the private sector, such as those presented by fire protection and law enforcement personnel.
* * *

II

It is established beyond peradventure that the Commerce Clause of Art. I of the Constitution is a grant of plenary authority to Congress. That authority is, in the words of Mr. Chief Justice Marshall in Gibbons v. Ogden, 9 Wheat. 1, 6 L.Ed. 23 (1824), "the power to regulate; that is, to prescribe the rule by which commerce is to be governed." Id., at 196. * * * Congressional power over areas of private endeavor, even when its exercise may preempt express state-law determinations contrary to the result which has commended itself to the collective wisdom of Congress, has been held to be limited only by the requirement that "the means chosen by [Congress] must be reasonably adapted to the end permitted by the Constitution." Heart of Atlanta Motel v. United States, 379 U.S. 241, 262, 85 S.Ct. 348, 360, 13 L.Ed.2d 258 (1964).

Appellants in no way challenge these decisions establishing the breadth of authority granted Congress under the commerce power. Their contention, on the contrary, is that when Congress seeks to regulate directly the activities of States as public employers, it transgresses an affirmative limitation on the exercise of its power akin to other commerce power affirmative limitations contained in the Constitution. * * * Appellants' essential contention is that the 1974 amendments to the Act, while undoubtedly within the scope of the Commerce Clause, encounter a similar constitutional barrier because they are to be applied directly to the States and subdivisions of States as employers. This Court has never doubted that there are limits upon the power of Congress to override state sovereignty, even when exercising its otherwise plenary powers to tax or to regulate commerce which are conferred by Art. I of the Constitution. In *Wirtz,* for example, the Court took care to assure the appellants that it had "ample power to prevent * * * 'the utter destruction of the State as a sovereign political entity,'" which they feared. 392 U.S., at 196, 88 S.Ct., at 2024. * * * In *Fry,* supra, the Court recognized that an express declaration of this limitation is found in the Tenth Amendment:

"While the Tenth Amendment has been characterized as a 'truism,' stating merely that 'all is retained which has not been surrendered,' United States v. Darby, 312 U.S. 100, 124, 61 S.Ct. 451, 462, 85 L.Ed. 609 (1941), it is not without significance. The Amendment expressly declares the constitutional policy that Congress may not exercise power in a fashion that impairs the States' integrity or their ability to function effectively in a federal system." 421 U.S., at 547, 95 S.Ct., at 1795 n. 7.

*   *   *

The expressions in these more recent cases trace back to earlier decisions of this Court recognizing the essential role of the States in our federal system of government. Mr. Chief Justice Chase, perhaps because of the particular time at which he occupied that office, had occasion more than once to speak for the Court on this point. In Texas v. White, 7 Wall. 700, 725, 19 L.Ed. 227 (1869), he declared that "[t]he Constitution, in all its provisions, looks to an indestructible Union, composed of indestructible States." *   *   *

One undoubted attribute of state sovereignty is the States' power to determine the wages which shall be paid to those whom they employ in order to carry out their governmental functions, what hours those persons will work, and what compensation will be provided where these employees may be called upon to work overtime. The question we must resolve here, then, is whether these determinations are " 'functions essential to separate and independent existence,' " id., at 580, 31 S.Ct., at 695, quoting from Lane County v. Oregon, supra, 7 Wall. at 76, so that Congress may not abrogate the States' otherwise plenary authority to make them.

In their complaint appellants advanced estimates of substantial costs which will be imposed upon them by the 1974 amendments. *   *   *

Judged solely in terms of increased costs in dollars, these allegations show a significant impact on the functioning of the governmental bodies involved. *   *   *

Quite apart from the substantial costs imposed upon the States and their political subdivisions, the Act displaces state policies regarding the manner in which they will structure delivery of those governmental services which their citizens require. The Act, speaking directly to the States *qua* States, requires that they shall pay all but an extremely limited minority of their employees the minimum wage rates currently chosen by Congress. It may well be that as a matter of economic policy it would be desirable that States, just as private employers, comply with these minimum wage requirements. But it cannot be gainsaid that the federal requirement directly supplants the considered policy choices of the States' elected officials and administrators as to how they wish to structure pay scales in state employment. The State might wish to employ persons with little or no training, or those who wish to work on a casual basis, or those who for some other reason do not possess minimum employment requirements, and pay them less than the federally prescribed minimum wage. It may wish to offer part-time or summer employment to teenagers at a figure less than the minimum wage, and if unable to do so may decline to offer such employment at all. But the Act would forbid such choices by the States. The only "discretion" left to them under the Act is either to attempt to increase their revenue to meet the additional financial burden imposed upon them by paying congressionally prescribed wages to their existing complement of employees, or to reduce that complement to a number which can be paid the federal minimum wage without increasing revenue.

This dilemma presented by the minimum wage restrictions may seem not immediately different from that faced by private employers, who have long been covered by the Act and who must find ways to increase their gross income if they are to pay higher wages while maintaining current earnings. The difference, however, is that a State is not merely a factor in the "shifting economic arrangements" of the private sector of the economy, * * * but is itself a coordinate element in the system established by the Framers for governing our Federal Union.

*   *   *

Our examination of the effect of the 1974 amendments, as sought to be extended to the States and their political subdivisions, satisfies us that both the minimum wage and the maximum hour provisions will impermissibly interfere with the integral governmental functions of these bodies. We earlier noted some disagreement between the parties regarding the precise effect the amendments will have in application. We do not believe particularized assessments of actual impact are crucial to resolution of the issue presented, however. For even if we accept appellee's assessments concerning the impact of the amendments, their application will nonetheless significantly alter or displace the States' abilities to structure employer-employee relationship in such areas as fire prevention, police protection, sanitation, public health, and parks and recreation. These activities are typical of those performed by state and local governments in discharging their dual functions of administering the public law and furnishing public services. Indeed, it is functions such as these which governments are created to provide, services such as these which the States have traditionally afforded their citizens. If Congress may withdraw from the States the authority to make those fundamental employment decisions upon which their systems for performance of these functions must rest, we think there would be little left of the States' " 'separate and independent existence.' " Coyle, 221 U.S., at 580, 31 S.Ct., at 695. Thus, even if appellants may have overestimated the effect which the Act will have upon their current levels and patterns of governmental activity, the dispositive factor is that Congress has attempted to exercise its Commerce Clause authority to prescribe minimum wages and maximum hours to be paid by the States in their capacities as sovereign governments. In so doing, Congress has sought to wield its power in a fashion that would impair the States' "ability to function effectively in a federal system," Fry, 421 U.S., at 547, 95 S.Ct., at 1796 n. 7. This exercise of congressional authority does not comport with the federal system of government embodied in the Constitution.   We hold that insofar as the challenged amendments operate to directly displace the States' freedom to structure integral operations in areas of traditional governmental functions, they are not within the authority granted Congress by Art. I, § 8, cl. 3.

    *   *   *

But we have reaffirmed today that the States as States stand on a quite different footing from an individual or a corporation when challenging the exercise of Congress' power to regulate commerce. * * * Congress may not exercise that power so as to force directly upon the States its choices as to how essential decisions regarding the conduct of integral governmental functions are to be made.   We agree that such assertions of power if unchecked, would indeed, as Mr. Justice Douglas cautioned in his dissent in *Wirtz,* allow "the National Government [to] devour the essentials of state sovereignty," 392 U.S., at 205, 88 S.Ct., at 2028, and would therefore transgress the bounds of the authority granted Congress under the Commerce Clause. * * *

The judgment of the District Court is accordingly reversed, and the cases are remanded for further proceedings consistent with this opinion.

So ordered.

*State Statute Impeding Intent of Federal
Statute Violates Supremacy Clause*

SHEPHEARD v. GODWIN

U.S.Dist.Ct. of Eastern Virginia, 1968.
280 F.Supp. 869.

OPINION

ALBERT V. BRYAN, Circuit Judge:

"Impacted" school areas are those whose school populations have been substantially enlarged by the attendance of Federal employees' children, but at the same time are losing school tax revenues because of the United States government's immunity from land taxes, both factors arising from increased Federal activities in the area.   These conditions prompted Congress to provide financial aid for operation of the local educational facilities, P.L. 874.

In applying a State formula for State assistance to local school districts, Virginia has deducted from the share otherwise allocable to the district a sum equal to a substantial percentage of any Federal "impact" funds receivable by the district.

Residents, real estate owners and taxpayers of the City of Norfolk, later joined by those of the County of Fairfax, Virginia, in behalf of themselves and others similarly situated, here attack this deduction *   *   * as violative of the purpose and intent of the act of Congress and as transgressing the Fourteenth Amendment. We uphold their contention.

*   *   *

The theory of the deduction in toto was that the Federal moneys were substituting for the taxes lost to the district by reason of the immunity of the Government property, and hence should be charged to the locality, just as the taxes would have been, in fixing the State supplementary aid. *   *   *

The grievance of the plaintiffs is obvious: any deduction whatsoever of the Federal supplement in apportioning State aid, pro tanto burdens them as taxpayers, for they and the other property owners in Norfolk and Fairfax have to make up the unindemnified portion of the impact costs. They contend that any deduction is prohibited by the purpose and plan of the Federal act.

The rejoinder of the defendant officials is, first, that the impact pupils are counted by the State in computing the minimum program cost in the district, and in accounting with the district for the State's supplementary aid it is not inequitable to insist upon a deduction of a commensurate amount of the impact moneys. At first appealing, this argument ignores the fact that the Federal children are to a large extent paying their own way so far as the *State* is concerned. Quite soundly, the Congressional Committee on Education and Labor in recommending passage of P.L. 874, observed that the influx of Federal employees, and the withdrawal of real estate from taxes, did not diminish the tax sources of the State or otherwise burden the State.
*   *   *

Our conclusion is that the State formula wrenches from the impacted localities the very benefaction the act was intended to bestow. The State plan must fall as violative of the supremacy clause of the Constitution. Our decision rests entirely on the terms, pattern and policy of the act.

The act makes these propositions clear: (1) the Federal funds are exclusively for supplementation of the local sources of revenues for school purposes; and (2) the act was not intended to lessen the efforts of the State. Those postulates are manifested in the statute by these provisions, especially: that the Federal contribution be paid directly to the local school agency on reports of the local agency, and that the contribution be computed by reference to the expenditures "made from revenues derived from local sources" in comparable school districts.

But the State formula at once sets these precepts at naught. It uses the impact funds to account in part for fulfillment of the State's pledge of supplementary aid to the community; and the State moneys thus saved are available for State retention or such use as Virginia determines. Without the inclusion of the Federal sums the State's annual payments towards supplementary aid would be increased, it is estimated, by more than $10,000,000.

This commandeering of credit for the Federal moneys severely injures both the community and the pupil. First and foremost, it does not relieve the local taxpayers to the extent Congress contemplated. Next, without the exclusive application of the funds to the areas where the need arose and remains, the result may be to lower the standard of education provided in an impacted district. Instead of maintaining the previous standards for the additional pupils, the impact money when thinned by the State would obviously be inadequate to continue that level for the increased school attendance, a result certainly thwarting the aim of the Federal law.

The construction and the implications we put upon the act find confirmation in its legislative history. * * * The exposition underscores the Congressional mandate that the impact payments are for local use and are not to be applied to compensate the State in any respect. Thus, at p. 13, it is stated:

> "The effect of the payments provided for in this section is to compensate the local educational agency for loss in its *local* revenues. *There is no compensation for any loss in States revenues.* * * * " (Accent added.)
>
> * * *

Since its explanation in 1950 when P.L. 874 was passed that no compensation was intended for the State, Congress has reiterated this intention. In this repetition it definitely disapproves the accounting use Virginia's formula makes of the impact moneys. The House of Representatives Committee Report No. 1814, dated August 5, 1966, in proposing an amendment to P.L. 874 stated:

> "Fifteen States offset the amount of Public Law 874 funds received by their school districts by reducing part of their State aid to those districts. *This is in direct contravention to congressional intent.* Impact aid funds are intended to compensate districts for loss of tax revenues due to Federal connection, not to substitute for State funds the districts would otherwise receive.
>
> * * *

The committee report and the amendment are cited merely as evidence of Congressional intendment. The amendment provides only an administrative remedy of the Government and does not deprive the plaintiffs of standing to prevent future State infringement of their Constitutional right to the benefits of the aid proposed by Congress. Necessarily, then, the upshot is that the defendants must be enjoined from hereafter in any way denying to the impacted area the exclusive use and enjoyment of the impact funds.

*   *   *

An order implementing this opinion is filed herewith.

*   *   *

State is Not Obligated to Expend Federal Funds for Purposes which Violate the State Constitution

WHEELER v. BARRERA

Supreme Court of the United States, 1974.
417 U.S. 402, 94 S.Ct. 2274.

Mr. Justice BLACKMUN delivered the opinion of the Court.

Title I of the Elementary and Secondary Education Act of 1965, as amended, 20 U.S.C.A. § 241a et seq., provides for federal funding of special programs for educationally deprived children in both public and private schools.

This suit was instituted on behalf of parochial school students who were eligible for Title I benefits and who claimed that the public school authorities in their area, in violation of the Act, failed to provide adequate Title I programs for private school children as compared with those programs provided for public school children. The defendants answered that the extensive aid sought by the plaintiffs exceeded the requirements of Title I and contravened the State's Constitution and state law and public policy. First Amendment rights were also raised by the parties. The District Court, concluding that the State had fulfilled its Title I obligations, denied relief. The United States Court of Appeals for the Eighth Circuit, by a divided vote, reversed. We granted certiorari to examine serious questions that appeared to be present as to the scope and constitutionality of Title I.
*   *   *

I

The questions that arise in this case concern the scope of the State's duty to insure that a program submitted by a local agency under Title I provides "comparable" services for eligible private school children.

Plaintiff-respondents are parents of minor children attending elementary and secondary nonpublic schools in the inner city area of Kansas City, Missouri. They instituted this class action in the United States District Court for the Western District of Missouri on behalf of themselves and their children, and others similarly situated, alleging that the defendant-petitioners, the then State Commissioner of Education and the members of the Missouri Board of Education, arbitrarily and illegally were approving Title I programs that deprived eligible nonpublic school children of services comparable to those offered eligible public school children. The complaint sought an injunction restraining continued violations of the Act and an accounting and restoration of some $13,000,000 in Title I funds allegedly misapplied from 1966 to 1969.

* * *

In what perhaps may be described as something less than full cooperation by both sides, the possibility of providing "comparable" services was apparently frustrated by the fact that many parochial schools would accept only services in the form of assignment of federally funded Title I teachers to teach in those schools during regular school hours. At the same time, the petitioners refused to approve any program providing for on-the-premises instruction on the grounds that it was forbidden under both Missouri law and the First Amendment and, furthermore, that Title I did not require it. Since the larger portion (over 65%) of Title I funds allocated to Missouri has been used to provide personnel for remedial instruction, the effect of this stalemate is that substantially less money per pupil has been expended for eligible students in private schools, and that the services provided in those schools in no sense can be considered "comparable."

* * *

In response to petitioners' argument that Missouri law forbids sending public school teachers into private schools, the court held that the state constitutional provision barring use of "public" school finds in private schools had no application to Title I funds. The court reasoned that although the Act was generally to be accommodated to state law, the question whether Title I funds were "public," within the meaning of the Missouri Constitution,[9] must necessarily be decided by federal law. * * *

In this Court the parties are at odds over two issues: First, whether on this record Title I requires the assignment of publicly employed teachers to provide remedial instruction during regular school hours on the premises of private schools attended by Title I eligible students, and, second, whether that requirement, if it exists, contravenes the First Amendment. We conclude that we cannot reach and decide either issue at this stage of the proceedings.

A. *Title I requirements.* As the case was presented to the District Court, petitioners clearly had failed to meet their statutory commitment to provide comparable services to children in nonpublic schools. The services provided to the class of children represented by

9. In Special District v. Wheeler, 408 S.W.2d 60, 63 (1966), the Supreme Court of Missouri held that "the use of public school moneys to send speech teachers * * * into the parochial schools for speech therapy" was not a use "for the purpose of maintaining free public schools," within the meaning of Art. 9, § 5, of the State's Constitution, and therefore was a practice "unlawful and invalid." That case did not involve federal funds. * * *

respondents were plainly inferior, both qualitatively and quantitatively, and the Court of Appeals was correct in ruling that the District Court erred in refusing to order relief. But the opinion of the Court of Appeals is not to be read to the effect that petitioners *must* submit and approve plans that employ the use of Title I teachers on private school premises during regular school hours.

The legislative history, the language of the Act, and the regulations clearly reveal the intent of Congress to place plenary responsibility in local and state agencies for the formulation of suitable programs under the Act. There was a pronounced aversion in Congress to "federalization" of local educational decisions. * * * Although this concern was directed primarily at the possibility of HEW's assuming the role of a national school board, it has equal application to the possibility of a federal court's playing an overly active role in supervising the manner of Title I expenditures.

At the outset, we believe that the Court of Appeals erred in holding that federal law governed the question whether on-the-premises private school instruction is permissible under Missouri law. Whatever the case might be if there were no expression of specific congressional intent, Title I evinces a clear intention that state constitutional spending proscriptions not be pre-empted as a condition of accepting federal funds. The key issue, namely, whether federal aid is money "donated to any state fund for public school purposes," within the meaning of the Missouri Constitution, Art. 9, § 5, is purely a question of state and not federal law. By characterizing the problem as one involving "federal" and not "state" funds, and then concluding that federal law governs, the Court of Appeals, we feel, in effect nullified the Act's policy of accommodating state law. The correct rule is that the "federal law" under Title I is to the effect that state law should not be disturbed. If it is determined, ultimately, that the petitioners' position is a correct exposition of Missouri law, Title I requires, not that that law be preempted, but, rather, that it be accommodated by the use of services not proscribed under state law. The question whether Missouri law prohibits the use of Title I funds for on-the-premises private school instruction is still unresolved.

Furthermore, in the present posture of this case, it was unnecessary for the federal court even to reach the issue whether on-the-premises parochial school instruction is permissible under state law. The state-law question appeared in the case by way of petitioners' defense that it could not provide on-the-premises services because it was prohibited by the State's Constitution. But, as is discussed more fully below, the State is not obligated by Title I to provide on-the-premises instruction. The mandate is to provide "comparable" services. Assuming, *arguendo*, that state law does prohibit on-the-premises instruction, this would not provide a defense to repondents' complaint that comparable services are not being provided. The choice of programs is left to the State with the proviso that comparable (not identical) programs are also made available to eligible private school children. If one form of services to parachial school children is rendered unavailable because of state constitutional proscriptions, the solution is to employ an acceptable alternative form. In short, since the illegality under state law of on-the-premises instruction would not provide a defense to respondents' charge of noncompliance with Title I, there was no reason for the Court of Appeals to reach this issue. By deciding that on-the-premises instruction was not barred by state law, the court in effect issued an advisory opinion. Even apart from traditional policies of abstention and comity, it was unnecessary to decide this question in the current posture of the case.

The Court of Appeals properly recognized, as we have noted that petitioners failed to meet their broad obligation and commitment under the Act to provide comparable programs. "Comparable," however, does not mean "identical," and, contrary to the assertions of both sides, we do not read the Court of Appeals' opinion or, for that matter, the Act itself, as ever requiring that identical services be provided in nonpublic schools. Congress recognized that the needs of educationally deprived children attending nonpublic schools might be different from those of similar children in public schools; it was also recognized that in some States certain programs for private and parochial schools would be legally impossible because of state constitutional restrictions, most notably in the church-state area. Title I was not intended to override these individualized state restrictions. Rather, there was a clear intention that the assistance programs be designed on local levels so as to accommodate the restrictions.

Inasmuch as comparable, and not identical, services are required, the mere fact that public school children are provided on-the-premises Title I instruction does not necessarily create an obligation to make identical provision for private school children. Congress expressly recognized that different and unique problems and needs might make it appropriate to utilize different programs in the private schools. A requirement of identity would run directly counter to this recognition. It was anticipated, to be sure, that one of the options open to the local agency in designing a suitable program for private school children was the provision of on-the-premises instruction,[18] and on remand this is an option open to these petitioners and the local agency. If, however, petitioners choose not to pursue this meth-

---

18. The Senate Report outlined the circumstances in which this type of service would be appropriate:

  "It is anticipated however, that public school teachers will be made available to other than public school facilities only to provide specialized services which contribute particularly to meeting the special educational needs of educationally deprived children (such as therapeutic, remedial or welfare services) and only where such specialized services are not normally provided by the nonpublic school." S.Rep. No. 146, 89th Cong., 1st Sess., 12 (1965). See 45 CFR § 116.9(e); 111 Cong.Rec. 5747 (1965) (remarks of Congs. Perkins and Carey).

od, or if it turns out that state law prevents its use, three broad options still remain:

First, the State may approve plans that do not utilize on-the-premises private school Title I instruction but, nonetheless, still measure up to the requirement of comparability.   *   *   *   In essence, respondents are asking this Court to hold, as a matter of federal law, that one mode of delivering remedial Title I services is superior to others.   To place on this Court, or on any federal court, the responsibility of ruling on the relative merits of various possible Title I programs seriously misreads the clear intent of Congress to leave decisions of that kind to the local and state agencies.   It is unthinkable, both in terms of the legislative history and the basic structure of the federal judiciary, that the courts be given the function of measuring the comparative desirability of various pedagogical methods contemplated by the Act.

In light of the uncontested statutory proscription in Missouri against dual enrollment, it may well be a significant challenge to these petitioners and the local agencies in their State to devise plans that utilize on-the-premises public school instruction and, at the same time, forgo on-the-premises private school instruction.   *   *   *

Of course, the cooperation and assistance of the officials of the private school are obviously expected and required in order to design a program that is suitable for the private school.   It is clear, however, that the Act places ultimate responsibility and control with the public agency, and the overall program is not to be defeated simply because the private school refuses to participate unless the aid is offered in the particular form it requests.   The private school may refuse to participate if the local program does not meet with its approval.   But the result of this would then be that the private school's eligible children, the direct and intended beneficiaries of the Act, would lose.   The Act, however, does not give the private school a veto power over the program selected by the local agency.

In sum, although it may be difficult, it is not impossible under the Act to devise and implement a legal local Title I program with comparable services despite the use of on-the-premises instruction in the public schools but not in the private schools.   On the facts of this case, petitioners have been approving plans that do not meet this requirement, and certainly, if public school children continue to receive on-the-premises Title I instruction, petitioners should not approve plans that fail to make a genuine effort to employ comparable alternative programs that make up for the lack of on-the-premises instruction for the nonpublic school children.   A program which provides instruction and equipment to the public school children and the same equipment but no instruction to the private school children cannot, on its face, be comparable.   In order to equalize the level and quality of services offered, something must be substituted for the private school children. The alternatives are numerous. Providing nothing to fill the gap, however, is not among the acceptable alternatives.

Second, if the State is unwilling or unable to develop a plan which is comparable, while using Title I teachers in public but not in private schools, it may develop and submit an acceptable plan which eliminates the use of on-the-premises instruction in the public schools and, instead, resorts to other means, such as neutral sites or summer programs that are less likely to give rise to the gross disparity present in this case.

Third, and undoubtedly least attractive for the educationally deprived children, is nonparticipation in the program. Indeed, under the Act, the Commissioner, subject to judicial review, 20 U.S.C.A. § 241k, may refuse to provide funds if the State does not make a bona fide effort to formulate programs with comparable services. 20 U.S. C.A. § 241j.

B. *First Amendment.* The second major issue is whether the Establishment Clause of the First Amendment prohibits Missouri from sending public school teachers paid with Title I funds into parochial schools to teach remedial courses. The Court of Appeals declined to pass on this significant issue, noting that since no order had been entered requiring on-the-premises parochial school instruction, the matter was not ripe for review. We agree. As has been pointed out above, it is possible for the petitioners to comply with Title I without utilizing on-the-premises parochial school instruction. Moreover, even if, on remand, the state and local agencies do exercise their discretion in favor of such instruction, the range of possibilities is a broad one and the First Amendment implications may vary according to the precise contours of the plant that is formulated.

* * *

* * * It would be wholly inappropriate for us to attempt to render an opinion on the First Amendment issue when no specific plan is before us. A federal court does not sit to render a decision on hypothetical facts, and the Court of Appeals was correct in so concluding.

* * * The comparability mandate is a broad one, and in order to implement the overriding concern with localized control of Title I programs, the District Court should make every effort to defer to the judgment of the petitioners and of the local agency. Under the Act, <u>respondents are entitled to comparable services, and they are, therefore, entitled to relief.</u> As we have stated repeatedly herein, they are not entitled to any particular form of service, and it is the role of the state and local agencies, and not of the federal courts, at least at this stage, to formulate a suitable plan.

On this basis, the judgment of the Court of Appeals is affirmed.

Chapter 4

EDUCATION, A STATE FUNCTION

State government through statute regulates and controls education subject only to limitations placed on it by the state and federal constitutions. The courts have consistently held that the power over education is an essential attribute of state sovereignty of the same order as the power to tax, exercise of police power, and to provide for the welfare of the citizenry. In the exercise of this pervasive function states have established systems of public schools which are operated as administrative arms of the state government.

The broad power of the state extends to provision for education generally within its boundaries and not merely to the public schools alone. Education in this broader context encompasses educational purposes and pursuits of the populace and the schools, both public and private. The interest in an educated citizenry is such an important part of state sovereignty that a certain minimal quality of education for all children is guaranteed whether their education is acquired in public or private schools.

Court decisions abundantly support the preeminence of the state in control of education. Interestingly, most precedents indicate that the legislature has the prerogative to govern education, when what they actually mean is that education is governed by the democratic legislative process, which requires action by both the legislative and executive branches of government. The legal principals controlling education have been stated many times in different ways by state courts; for example; the legislature has plenary power to set up public schools,[1] the maintenance of common schools is a concern of the state and legislature,[2] or a uniform system of public schools is exclusively within the province of the legislature.[3] The pervasiveness of this power is adequately illustrated by a Michigan decision which states that, "The legislature has entire control over the schools of the state, * * *. The division of the territory of the state into districts, the conduct of the schools, the qualifications of teachers, the subjects to be taught therein, are all within its (the state's) control." [4]

An Ohio court has briefly encapsulated this power as follows:

* * * that the control of schools, be they public or private, providing elementary and secondary education for the

---

1. State Tax Comm. v. Board of Educ. of Jefferson County, 235 Ala. 388, 179 So. 197 (1938).

2. Board of Educ. v. Stoddard, 294 N.Y. 667, 60 N.E.2d 757 (1945).

3. Moore v. Board of Educ., 212 N.C. 499, 193 S.E. 732 (1937).

4. Child Welfare Society of Flint v. Kennedy School Dist., 220 Mich. 290, 189 N.W. 1002 (1922).

youth of Ohio, reposes in the Legislature of our state. When the General Assembly speaks on matters concerning education it is exercising *plenary* power and its action is subject only to the limitations contained in the Constitution. * * * We can, therefore, indulge in generalities and make a broad statement to the effect that the Legislature of Ohio, in passing laws concerning elementary and secondary schools, is restrained only by its own conscience, [and] fear of the electorate, * * *.[5]

The power of the state to control education has sometimes been characterized as emanating from the state's police power.[6] Although police power has not been fully defined by the courts, it is clear that the term encompasses all the elements vested in state sovereignty including those powers necessary to preserve the peace, morals, good order, and well-being of society.[7] It embraces the broad prerogatives of general welfare. The U. S. Supreme Court has said: "The police power of a state extends to the protection of the lives, limbs, health, comfort, and quiet of all persons, and to the protection of all property, within the state, and hence to the making of all regulations promotive of domestic order, morals, health, and safety." [8] Within this framework is the power of the state to protect the individual and society through provision for a system of education.

In holding that education is a state function, the courts maintain that the state's authority over education is not a distributive one to be exercised by local government but is a central power residing in the state. The legislature has the unrestricted prerogative to prescribe the methods of education, and the courts will not intervene unless the legislation is contrary to constitutional provisions.

The state legislature holds plenary power for purposes of education and civil government. In matters of education as in all other functions of state government, the state constitution is fundamental and is determinative of the broad scope within which the legislature can operate. The fact that the legislature is created by the constitution and given law making authority, in conjunction with the executive branch, is in and of itself a pervasive and general delegation which is not limited to special conditions or situations. In way of explanation of this prerogative, the Court of Appeals of New York has said: "The people, in framing the constitution, committed to the legislature the whole law making power of the state, which they did not expressly or impliedly withhold. Plenary power in the legislature of

5. Board of Educ. of Aberdeen-Huntington Local School Dist. v. State Bd. of Educ., 116 Ohio App. 515, 189 N.E.2d 81 (1962).

6. Campbell v. Aldrich, 159 Or. 208, 79 P.2d 257, appeal dismissed, 305 U.S. 559, 59 S.Ct. 87 (1938).

7. Leeper v. State, 103 Tenn. 500, 53 S. W. 962 (1899).

8. Railroad Co. v. Husen, 95 U.S. 465 (1877).

all purposes of civil government is the rule." [9]   Unlike the Congress of the United States which has only those powers delegated to it by the Constitution, state legislatures have plenary power and may pass any act which is not expressly or impliedly forbidden by the state constitution.[10] A constitutional mandate that the legislature provide education for a certain class of the population is not, as a rule, considered to be a limitation on the educational opportunities which may be made available to other classes. According to Edwards, "The legislature must do so much; it may do more." [11]

Regulation of Common Schools is Within the Power of the Legislature

STATE EX REL. CLARK v. HAWORTH

Supreme Court of Indiana, 1890.
122 Ind. 462, 23 N.E. 946.

ELLIOTT, J. * * *   It is sufficient, to bring the question clearly enough before the mind for investigation and consideration, to say that the relator petitioned for a writ of mandate to compel the appellee, as school trustee of Monroe township, in the county of Howard, to certify to the county superintendent of schools the number of text-books required by the children of the township for use in the public schools, and to procure and furnish such books as the law requires * * * Elliott's Supp. § 1289 (Acts 1889, p. 74.)

<u>The act assailed does not impinge in the slightest degree upon the right of local self-government</u>. The right of local self-government is an inherent, and not a derivative, one. Individualized, it is the right which a man possesses in virtue of his character as a free man. It is not bestowed by legislatures, nor derived from statutes. But the courts which have carried to its utmost extent the doctrine of local self-government have never so much as intimated that it exists as to a matter over which the constitution has given the law-making power supreme control; nor have they gone beyond the line which separates matters of purely local concern from those of state control. Essentially and intrinsically, the schools in which are educated and trained the children who are to become the rulers of the commonwealth are matters of state, and not of local, jurisdiction. <u>In such matters the state is a unit, and the legislature the source of power</u>. The authority over schools and school affairs is not necessarily a distributive one,

---

9. People v. Draper, 15 N.Y. 532 (1857).

10. See Edwards, *op. cit.* p. 27; Also, Commonwealth v. Hartman, 17 Pa. 118 (1851); Moseley v. Welch, 209 S. C. 19, 39 S.E.2d 133 (1946); Board of Educ. of Chicago v. Upham, 357 Ill. 263, 191 N.E. 876 (1934); Board of

Educ. v. State Bd. of Educ., 116 Ohio App. 515, 189 N.E.2d 81 (1962); Associated Schools of Independent Dist. No. 63 v. School Dist. No. 83 of Renville County, 122 Minn. 254, 142 N.W. 325 (1913).

11. Edwards, p. 28.

to be exercised by local instrumentalities; but, on the contrary, it is a central power, residing in the legislature of the state. It is for the law-making power to determine whether the authority shall be exercised by a state board of education, or distributed to county, township, or city organizations throughout the state. With that determination the judiciary can no more rightfully interfere than can the legislature with a decree or judgment pronounced by a judicial tribunal. The decision is as conclusive and inviolable in the one case as in the other; and an interference with the legislative judgment would be a breach of the constitution which no principle would justify, nor any precedent excuse.

* * * Judge Cooley has examined the question with care, and discussed it with ability; and he declares that the legislature has plenary power over the subject of the public schools. He says, in the course of his discussion, that "to what degree the legislature shall provide for the education of the people at the cost of the state, or of its municipalities, is a question which, except as regulated by the constitution, addresses itself to the legislative judgment exclusively." Again, he says, "The governing school boards derive all their authority from the statute, and can exercise no powers except those expressly granted, and those which result by necessary implication from the grant." Const.Lim. (5th Ed.) p. 225, note 1. No case has been cited by counsel, and none has been discovered by us,—although we have searched the reports with care,—which denies the doctrine that the regulation of the public schools is a state matter, exclusively within the dominion of the legislature.

* * *

As the power over schools is a legislative one, it is not exhausted by exercise. The legislature, having tried one plan, is not precluded from trying another. It has a choice of methods, and may change its plans as often as it deems necessary or expedient; and for mistakes or abuses it is answerable to the people, but not to the courts. It is clear, therefore, that, even if it were true that the legislature had uniformly intrusted the management of school affairs to local organizations, it would not authorize the conclusion that it might not change the system. To deny the power to change, is to affirm that progress is impossible, and that we must move forever "in the dim footsteps of antiquity." But the legislative power moves in a constant stream, and is not exhausted by its exercise in any number of instances, however great. It is not true, however, that the authority over schools was originally regarded as a local one. On the contrary, the earlier cases asserted that the legislature could not delegate the power to levy taxes for school purposes to local organizations, but must itself directly exercise the power; thus denying, in the strongest possible form, the theory of local control. * * * All the public schools have been established under legislative enactments, and all rules and regulations have been made pursuant to statutory authority. <u>Every school that has been established owes its existence to leg-islation, and every school officer owes his authority to the statute.</u>

It is impossible to conceive of the existence of a uniform system of common schools without power lodged somewhere to make it uniform; and, even in the absence of express constitutional provisions, that <u>power must necessarily reside in the legislature</u>. If it does reside there, then that body must have, as an incident of the principal power, the authority to prescribe the course of study, and the system of instruction, that shall be pursued and adopted, as well as the books which shall be used. This general doctrine is well entrenched by authority. Hovey v. State, 119 Ind. 395, 21 N.E.Rep. 21; Hovey v. Riley, 119 Ind. 386, 21 N.E.Rep. 890; State v. Hawkins, 44 Ohio St. 98, 5 N.E.Rep. 228; State v. Harmon, 31 Ohio St. 250. Having this authority, the legislature may not only prescribe regulations for using such books, but it may also declare how the books shall be obtained and distributed. If it may do this, then it may provide that they shall be obtained through the medium of a contract awarded to the best or lowest bidder, since, if it be true, as it unquestionably is, that the power is legislative, it must also be true that the legislature has an unrestricted discretion, and an unfettered choice of methods. It cannot be possible that the courts can interfere with this legislative power, and adjudge that the legislature shall not adopt this method or that method; for, if the question is at all legislative, it is so in its whole length and breadth. * * *

Either the state has power to regulate and control the schools it owns, or it has not. That it does not have the power, we venture to say, no one will affirm. If it does have the power, it must reside in the law-making department, for it is impossible for it to exist elsewhere. If the power does reside in the law-making department, then that department must exercise its discretion, and adopt such measures as it deems best; and, if the measures adopted lead to the exclusion of some book-owners, it is an incident that no ingenuity can escape, nor any system avoid. The denial of the right to select the books is the denial of the right of regulation and control, and we cannot conceive it possible to deny this right. If the right of regulation and control exists, then the fact that the exercise of the right does not exclude some publisher is an inseparable and unavoidable condition of the exercise of the right. Without it, the right is annihilated. If a clear and manifest legislative right cannot be exercised without conferring privileges in the nature of a monopoly, then, as the authorities all agree, a monopoly may be created; for a denial of the right will not be suffered. This doctrine is discussed by Judge Cooley in his work on Torts, and by Mr. Tiedeman in his work on the Police Power, to which we refer without comment. Cooley, Torts, 277; Tied. Lim. 315 et seq. But we need not enter the field traveled by those authors, for here there is no denial of a right to sell books to a community. All that is here done is to provide that the person who receives, after fair and open competition, the contract for supplying books to the school children, shall enjoy an exclusive privilege for the period prescribed by the statute. Judge Cooley says that "it is held competent for the state to contract with a publisher to supply all the schools of the state with text-books of a uniform character and price." Const. Lim. (5th Ed.) p. 225, note 1. * * *

* * * Judgment reversed, with instructions to proceed in accordance with this opinion.

* * *

Legislature has Plenary Power to Govern
the Educational System

COHEN v. STATE

Supreme Court of New York, 1966.
52 Misc.2d 324, 275 N.Y.S.2d 719.

IRVING L. LEVEY, Justice.

Plaintiff, a resident of the Bronx and the father of two children attending a public school maintained by the Board of Education, sues the defendants State of New York, the City of New York, and others, on his own behalf and on behalf of those similarly situated, for a declaratory judgment declaring Section 2553, subdivision 2 of the Education Law unconstitutional.

The plaintiff alleges that under this law the members of the Board of Education are nominated by the Selection Board composed of heads of various private organizations and the nominations are submitted to the Mayor of the City of New York, who must select therefrom the names of persons for appointment to vacancies on the Board of Education.

The plaintiff further alleges that outside the City of New York in the various school districts such as Common School Districts, Union Free School Districts, Central School Districts and City School Districts of cities less than 125,000 inhabitants, and in the cities of Rochester and Syracuse, the Education Law provides that boards of education are to be elected by the vote of the people and the population of those school districts and cities which so elect their boards of education was, in 1960, 8,147,201, compared to 7,781,984 in the City of New York.

It is plaintiff's contention that by providing for the election of boards of education in districts and cities having such population but failing to provide for such elections in the City of New York, there has been created by the State an unreasonable and unconstitutional classification of persons and citizens and that the State has denied to the plaintiff and all other residents of the City of New York the right to equal protection of the laws, in violation of Section 1 of the Fourteenth Amendment to the Constitution of the United States and Section 11 of Article I of the Constitution of the State of New York and by such law the State of New York has disenfranchised the plaintiff and other residents of the City of New York and deprives them of rights and privileges received by other citizens, in violation of Section 1 of Article 1 of the New York State Constitution.

* * *

Plaintiff has shown no constitutional or statutory authority indicating that the officers of the boards of education are to be elected. Moreover, Article XI, Section 1, of the New York State Constitution sets forth:

> "The legislature shall provide for the maintenance and support of a system of free common schools, wherein all the children of this state may be educated."

The Appellate Division has held that "[t]he power of the Legislature over the educational system of the state is plenary. It may allocate functions among units of the educational system in accordance with its judgment as to what will best serve the educational interests of the state * * * ." (Union Free School District No. 22, etc. v. Wilson, 281 App.Div. 419, 424, 120 N.Y.S.2d 483.)

This power granted to the Legislature is unrestricted within, of course, the confines of the State and Federal Constitutions (Adler v. Deegan, 251 N.Y. 467, 167 N.E. 705; Matter of McAneny v. Board of Estimate and Apportionment of City of New York, 232 N.Y. 377, 134 N.E. 187).

Although there is no case in this jurisdiction directly in point on the question of the right of the Legislature to determine the selection of the Board of Education in any particular manner, it has been held that there is no constitutional right to vote on the question of consolidation of school districts by the Legislature (Johnson v. Parsons, 207 Misc. 107, 135 N.Y.S.2d 672, aff'd Janowsky v. Parsons, 285 App.Div. 601, 139 N.Y.S.2d 676).

I find that the Legislature under the plenary power granted by Article 11, Section 1 of the New York State Constitution has the right to provide for the selection of the New York City Board of Education in the manner set forth in Section 2553, subdivision 2 of the Education Law (78 C.J.S. Schools and School Districts § 107; 47 Am.Jur., § 30). I further find that the plaintiff has failed to show any legal authority that the officers of the Board of Education must be elected.

* * *

The second attack on Section 2553, subdivision 2 of the Education Law is based upon the plaintiff's claim that by permitting Boards of Education to be elected by the vote of the people in school districts and cities having a population of 8,147,201 and directing the Board of Education in the City of New York with a population of 7,781,984 to be appointed in the manner prescribed by such section violates the equal protection clause of both the Federal and State Constitutions.

* * *

There are ample, reasonable bases for the establishment by the Legislature of both elected and appointed Boards of Education in different areas of the State, and the factors warranting such distinction are numerous.

Except for the "Big 6" city school districts of New York, Buffalo, Albany, Yonkers, Rochester and Syracuse which are coterminous with the city boundaries, the remaining 991 school districts cross town, village, and county boundaries. More than one-half of the central and union free school districts are located in more than one county. It would therefore be almost impossible to provide for appointment of Boards in such districts not wholly within any political subdivision. Moreover, the "Big 6" city school districts are not financially independent, but rely on their own city legislative bodies for financing. The other school districts are permitted to levy taxes and to incur indebtedness so that they are not dependent on their political subdivision in connection with their fiscal affairs. It follows from these facts that the legislature was reasonable and not arbitrary in enacting legislation permitting the residents of these financially independent school districts to elect their Boards of Education. Plaintiff's claim of geographical discrimination regarding the cities of Syracuse and Rochester which elect their boards is without merit. State legislation concerning education affecting only certain political subdivisions has been held immune from attack based upon geographical classification, Young, J., in holding that a Section of the Education Law which established town boards of education in all counties except Nassau was not an unreasonable classification stated in Brown v. Bunselmeyer, 101 Misc. 625, at 629–630, 167 N.Y.S. 993, at 996.

"It is not for the Courts to determine whether the legislative reason for the exclusion of one county from the provisions of the act and the inclusion of another, apparently similarly situated, is good or bad. To attempt such review opens a wide field of pure speculation. To the Legislature has been entrusted power to provide 'for the maintenance and support of a system of free common schools wherein all the children of the State may be educated' * * * and it is clearly within its province to provide the necessary legislation to accomplish that purpose. Clearly this constitutional provision does not require it to provide the same system and organization for each locality in the state." * * *

Accordingly, I find that Section 2553, subdivision 2 of the Education Law is not violative of the equal protection clauses of the State or Federal Constitution.

For the foregoing reasons, the defendants' motions to dismiss the complaint are granted and plaintiff's motion for summary judgment is denied.

NOTES

Police Power of the State. The Supreme Court of Tennessee early explained the role of the state in exercising police power over public education:

"We are of the opinion that the legislature, under the constitutional provision, may as well establish a uniform system of schools and a uniform administration of them, as it may establish a uniform system of criminal laws and of courts to execute them. The object of the criminal laws is, by punishment, to deter others from the commission of crimes, and thus preserve the peace, morals, good order and well-being of society; and the object of the public-school system is to prevent crime, by educating the people, and thus, by providing and securing a higher state of intelligence and morals, conserve the peace, good order, and well-being of society. The prevention of crime, and preservation of good order and peace, is the highest exercise of the police power of the state, whether done by punishing offenders or educating the children. What is the scope and meaning of the term 'police power' has never been defined. The supreme court of the United States has expressly declined to define its limits. Stone v. Mississippi, 101 U.S. 814 (1879). In Mayor, etc., v. Miln, 36 U.S. 102, 11 Pet. 102 (1835), it is said: 'It embraces every law which concerns the welfare of the whole people, of the state or any individual within it, whether it relates to their rights or duties, whether it respects them as men or citizens of the state, whether in their public or private relations, whether it relates to the rights of persons or property of the whole people of the state or of any individual within it.' In Railroad Co. v. Husen, 95 U.S. 465 (1877), it is said: 'The police power of a state extends to the protection of the lives, limbs, health, comfort, and quiet of all persons, and to the protection of all property, within the state, and hence to the making of all regulations promotive of domestic order, morals, health, and safety.' In Smith v. State, 100 Tenn. 494, 46 S.W. 566, it is said, in substance, that it extends to all questions of health, morals, safety, order, comfort, and well-being of the public, and that this enumeration does not make the list complete. Similar language has but recently been used in the case of Harbison v. Iron Co., [103 Tenn. 421] 53 S.W. 955, and this is no new doctrine, either in this state or in the United States." Leeper v. State, 103 Tenn. 500, 53 S.W. 962 (1899).

*Public Schools as State Institutions are Not
Subject to Local Municipal Control*

CITY OF LOUISVILLE v. COMMONWEALTH

Court of Appeals of Kentucky, 1909.
134 Ky. 488, 121 S.W. 411.

J. O'REAR, An act of the Legislature of 1908, approved March 24, 1908 (Acts 1908, p. 156, c. 61), the minimum levy of taxes for school purposes in cities of the first class was fixed at 36 cents on the $100. This appeal involves the constitutionality of that act.

*   *   *

The main feature of the question presented is: Is it competent for the Legislature to fix a minimum sum to be raised by a city for school purposes, and to require that sum to be raised without discretion? It is claimed by appellant that section 181 of the Constitution prohibits the legislative action. That section reads: "The General Assembly shall not impose taxes for the purpose of any county, city, town or other municipal corporation, but may by general laws confer upon the proper authorities thereof respectively power to assess and collect such taxes." If the maintenance of a public school is a purely municipal purpose, then the section would seem to be conclusive of the matter. But education is not a subject pertaining alone, or pertaining essentially, to a municipal corporation. Whilst public education in this country is now deemed a public duty in every state, and since before the first federation was regarded as a proper public enterprise, it has never been looked upon as being at all a matter of local concern only. On the contrary, it is regarded as an essential to the preservation of liberty—as forming one of the first duties of a democratic government. The place assigned it in the deliberate judgment of the American people is scarcely second to any. If it is essentially a prerogative of sovereignty to raise troops in time of war, it is equally so to prepare each generation of youth to discharge the duties of citizenship in time of peace and war. Upon preparation of the younger generations for civic duties depends the perpetuity of this government. The power to levy taxes is an essential attribute of the sovereignty. That is so because the necessity of conducting the government requires that money be raised for the purpose by some sort of taxation. So is the power to educate the youth of a state, to fit them so that the state may prosper; else the taxes raised could scarcely meet the demands made upon a government in these times. Whilst the power named is older in point of adoption as a legal maxim, the other is modernly found to be of no less importance. It may be doubted if the state could strip itself of either quality of its sovereignty. Certainly it will not be deemed to have attempted it upon language open to debate.

In this state the subject of public education has always been regarded and treated as a matter of state concern. In the last Constitution, as well as in the one preceding it, the most explicit care was evinced to promote public education as a duty of the state. Besides setting apart a very considerable capital sum as an inviolable asset of the school fund, the Constitution provides: "The General Assembly shall, by appropriate legislation, provide for an efficient system of common schools throughout the state." Const. Sec. 183. In obedience to that requirement the General Assembly has provided a system of common schools, in connection with other branches of public education. The subject requires different provisions for localities differing in density of population. For rural settlements there is the district school. For villages and towns a more extended term may be had, including high schools, because the population makes it practical to do so. In cities a still more elaborate, and consequently more expensive system is set up. All have the one main essential—that they are free schools, open to all the children of proper school age residing in the locality, and affording, so long as the term lasts, equal opportunity for all to acquire the learning taught in the various common school branches. The school funds raised directly by the state for common school purposes are apportioned ratably among them all. In the cities the government of the public schools is committed to boards of education. Each city of certain classes, including the class to which Louisville belongs, is made a separate school district. Local taxation is provided for in every instance to supplement the fund paid to the district out of the state money. In some it is left to the option of the voters of the district; in others, to the discretion of the trustees; while in others it is left to the city council and board of education. But in none is the question left entirely to the locality whether a public school shall be maintained for it. Nor does the state take its hands off the control of the school system, by allowing, or by requiring, the different localities to take steps toward supplementing the general appropriation by local taxation. The school is none the less a state institution for that matter. If the public schools of Louisville were local affairs, over which that municipality had the sole control, it may be doubted if it would be competent for the state to levy a tax on its other citizens to help support them. But they are not municipal institutions at all. * * * The city schools, including high schools, are part of the state's common school system. Their trustees are officers of the state. * * *

Our conclusion is that the statute is a valid exercise of legislative power and discretion. The council should have levied at least the minimum rate fixed by the statute. Their refusal was a failure to obey an express requirement of law. The writ of mandamus was the proper remedy, and was correctly applied * * *, including for the year of 1909, which was manifestly intended to be embraced by the terms of the act.

Judgment affirmed.

NOTES

1. Constitutional provisions requiring an "efficient" system of schools is a command to the legislature to provide a fair and efficient system open to all children. People ex rel. Tuohy v. Barrington Consol. High School Dist. No. 224, 396 Ill. 129, 71 N.E.2d 86 (1947); Fiedler v. Eckfeldt, 335 Ill. 11, 166 N.E. 504 (1929).

2. The efficiency and fairness of a state school system is for the determination of the legislature. McLain v. Phelps, 409 Ill. 393, 100 N.E.2d 753 (1951).

3. Constitutional requirements of a "uniform" system of free public schools are distinguished from other state educational institutions in determination of the uniformity of the system. State ex rel. Clark v. Henderson, 137 Fla. 666, 188 So. 351 (1939).

4. The requirement of uniformity does not mean that all schools have a uniform school government nor that all children be provided the same means of instruction, it simply means that all areas of the state may enjoy the same sort of school based on a particular class or grade, Landis v. Ashworth, 57 N.J. Law 509, 31 A. 1017 (1895); Smith v. Simmons, 129 Ky. 93, 110 S.W. 336 (1908).

5. Because of the public concern for education, the legislature can require compulsory attendance, provided such requirement does not violate constitutional limitations. See Everson v. Board of Educ. of Ewing Twp., 330 U.S. 1, 67 S.Ct. 504 (1947), and Pierce v. Society of the Sisters of the Holy Names of Jesus and Mary, 268 U.S. 510, 45 S.Ct. 571 (1925) in later chapters.

6. In an early Virginia decision the court explained the power of the state to enact legislation governing the public schools. The court said:

> While the Constitution of the state provides in mandatory terms that the Legislature shall establish and maintain public free schools, there is neither mandate nor inhibition in the provisions as to the regulation thereof. The Legislature, therefore, has the power to enact any legislation in regard to the conduct, control, and regulation of the public free schools, which does not deny to the citizen the Constitutional right to enjoy life and liberty, to pursue happiness and to acquire property. Flory v. Smith, 145 Va. 164, 134 S.E. 360 (1926).

Sovereign Power of Legislature is Restricted
by Direct Constitutional Limitation

IN RE KINDERGARTEN SCHOOLS

Supreme Court of Colorado, 1893.
18 Colo. 234, 32 P. 422.

The opinion of the court is in response to the following question by the house of representatives: "Does the general assembly possess power, under the constitution of the state of Colorado, to provide for the establishment and maintenance of a kindergarten department in the public school system of the state, and for the education therein of children of an age less than six (6) years?"

PER CURIAM.   As we are advised, the particular provision of the constitution that gave rise to the doubt your honorable body entertains in regard to the validity of the proposed legislation, is section 2, art. 9, which is as follows: "The general assembly shall, as soon as practicable, provide for the establishment and maintenance of a thorough and uniform system of free public schools throughout the state, wherein all residents of the state, between the ages of six and twenty-one years, may be educated gratuitously.   One or more public schools shall be maintained in each school district within the state, at least three months in each year; any school district failing to have such school shall not be entitled to receive any portion of the school fund for that year."   And we understand that such doubt is as to whether the language of this section limits the power of the legislature to establish any free schools other than therein specifically mentioned.   The rule of construction to be applied to our constitution is announced in Alexander v. People, 7 Colo. 155, 2 Pac.Rep. 894, as follows: "The legislature being invested with complete power for all the purposes of civil government, and the state constitution being merely a limitation upon that power, the court will look into it, not to see if the enactment in question is authorized, but only to see if it is prohibited."   Unless, therefore, the constitution, in express terms or by necessary implication, limits it, the legislature may exercise its sovereign power in any way that, in its judgment, will best subserve the general welfare.   Read in the light of this rule of interpretation, and the wise and liberal policy of the state in educational matters, the section is clearly mandatory, and requires affirmative action on the part of the legislature to the extent and in the manner specified, and is in no measure prohibitory or a limitation of its power to provide free schools for children under six years of age, whenever it deems it wise and beneficial to do so.   *   *   *   We are of opinion that the legislature has the power, under the constitution, to provide for the establishment and maintenance of a kindergarten department in the public school system for the education of children of an age less than six years.

NOTES

1.   Constitutional or statutory provisions using the term "common schools" have caused the courts to interpret and delineate precisely what is meant by the term.   In interpreting that community junior colleges are not "common schools" the Supreme Court of Kansas referred to the following definitions:

A common school is one which is open to all within the school boundaries and is supported at public expense through taxation, free of any charge to the attending students. C.J.S. Schools and School Districts § 1, p. 606; 47 Am.Jur., Schools § 3, p. 298.

"Common schools," as that term is used in the Kansas Constitution, means free schools common or accessible to all. Board of Education of City of Lawrence v. Dick, 70 Kan. 434, 78 P. 812 (1904).

The Kansas Court held that community junior colleges were not "common schools" primarily because they were not free, and part of the operating expenses of such schools came from student tuition. State ex rel. Londerholm v. Hayden, 197 Kan. 199, 416 P.2d 61 (1966).

2. A California court has held that kindergarten is not a part of the system of common schools required by the constitution to be established by the legislature in that state. Los Angeles County v. Kirk, 148 Cal. 385, 83 P. 250 (1905).

3. Courts have generally held that schools for adults do not fall within the system of public schools as described by constitutional provision.

4. Neither legislative assertions nor court pronouncements can make an institution part of the state common school system contrary to constitutional mandate. Hodgkin v. Board for Louisville & Jefferson County Children's Home, Ky., 242 S.W.2d 1008 (1951).

5. A school for the blind is not a part of the public nor common school system. Walls v. State Bd. of Educ., 195 Ark. 955, 116 S.W.2d 354 (1938).

6. Such pronouncements by the courts concerning the make-up of the common or public school system do not generally prohibit establishment of special schools but do prohibit common school funds from being expended for such additional educational programs. Associated Schools of Ind. Dist. No. 63 of Hector v. Renville County Dist. No. 83, 122 Minn. 254, 142 N.W. 325 (1913).

7. The authority of the legislature is not limited to certain common branches of education but extends to higher branches of education. State Bank of Commerce of Brockport v. Stone, 261 N.Y. 175, 184 N.E. 750 (1933).

8. A high school is within the definition of public, free common schools as described by state constitution. Young v. Board of Trustees of Broadwater County High School, 90 Mont. 576, 4 P.2d 725 (1931). See also People ex rel. Bd. of Ed. of Deerfield-Shields Tp. High School Dist. No. 113, Lake County v. Read, 344 Ill. 397, 176 N.E. 284 (1931).

9. In the absence of constitutional restrictions, the state legislature may establish normal schools or other higher education. Briggs v. Johnson County, C.C.Mo., F.Cas.No.1,872, 4 Dill. 148 (1930).

State Education Agencies

All states and the federal government have networks of administrative agencies usually called boards, commissions, bureaus, or offices which have been created to implement and administer statutes. State legislatures and the U.S. Congress have not seen fit historically to actually administer legislative enactments themselves even though the legislative branch of government could conceivably assume the role of program administration. Traditionally, the view has been that the legislature should not perform the multi-duties of enacting legislation, appropriating funds and then administering the funds, thereby invading the gray area of executive responsibility. In education, for example, it would be tedious and legislatively cumbersome for a state legislature to attempt to establish by statute rules and regulations governing specific certification requirements for teachers. Jaffe has suggested the reasoning for such delegation of regulatory power by saying:

> Power should be delegated where there is agreement that a task must be performed and it cannot be effectively performed by the legislature without the assistance of a delegate or without an expenditure of time so great as to lead to the neglect of equally important business.[12]

The result has been for the state legislature to create agencies which handle the administrative functions necessary to properly implement legislation. This delegation by the legislature in most states manifests itself in a state board of education which may be either elected or appointed and has authority to perform administrative and supervisory functions. An alternative to this approach is to vest officials of the executive branch with regulatory and attendant authority to administer the school system of the state; such officers are generically referred to as chief state school officers.

Functions of State Agencies

Functions of public agencies can generally be classified as (1) legislative, (2) administrative or executive, and (3) judicial (or quasi-judicial). As agencies of government, both state and local education authorities have these basic powers.

Administration encompasses the rule making and adjudication processes and incidental powers such as coordinating, supervising, investigating, prosecuting, advising, and declaring.[13] The exercise of administrative functions may be reviewed by the courts to determine if duties have been carried forth within the scope of law and whether proper procedures are followed.

Delegation of Legislative Powers

Legislative functions of the state agency include the promulgation of rules and regulations made pursuant to and within the scope of statute. The legislative function performed by state agencies has been justified on the grounds that the agency was merely "filling in

12. Jaffe, Louis L., *Essay on Delegation of Legislative Power*, 47 Col.L. Rev. 359, 361 (1947).

13. Kenneth Culp Davis, *Administrative Law Treatise*, West Publishing Company, St. Paul, Minn. (Vol. 1), 1958, p. 5.

the details" within the meaning of general statute.[14]   In the public interest, it is said the state agency should not have legislative powers since agency officials are not direct representatives of the people with constitutionally sanctioned law making prerogative.   This is a basic tenet of representative government recognized early by John Locke. In his treatises on civil government, he said:

> The legislature cannot transfer the power of making laws to any other hands, for it being but a delegated power from the people, they who have it cannot pass it over to others. * * *   nobody else can say other men shall make laws for them; nor can they be bound by any laws but such as are enacted by those whom they have chosen and authorized to make laws for them.[15]

Exclusive powers of the legislature should not therefore be delegated away to subordinate agencies.   In way of clarification of this theory of government, a Michigan court has said:

> This is not to say, however, that a subordinate body or official may not be clothed with authority to say when the law shall operate, or to whom, or upon what occasion, provided, however, that the standards prescribed for guidance are as reasonably precise as the subject matter requires or permits.[16]

Davis maintains, though, that formulations by state courts which attempt to circumscribe the legislative function of subordinate agencies are largely without substance.[17]   While generally it appears that most courts seek to restrain too broad a delegation in order to prevent arbitrary use of uncontrolled power by subordinate officials, the actual legal theory and its implementation by the courts is sometimes difficult to follow.   Basically the theory of delegation appears to have been justified on the grounds of "adequacy of standards".   Does the statute provide sufficient delineation of the particular requirement or prohibition so that in light of the surrounding facts and circumstances the agency can ascertain, interpret, and implement the true purpose of the act?   The legislature must prescribe a "reasonably adequate standard".[18]   Some courts maintain that "definite standards are indispensable, not only to avoid a delegation of the essential legislative power, but to guard against an arbitrary use of the delegated administrative authority".[19]   Limitations on legislative delegation to

---

14.   Ibid, p. 102.

15.   John Locke, *Two Treatises of Civil Government*, Book II, Ch. XI, Sec. 141.

16.   Osius v. City of St. Clair Shores, 344 Mich. 693, 75 N.W.2d 25 (1956).

17.   Davis, *op. cit.* p. 103.

18.   Ward v. Scott, 11 N.J. 117, 93 A.2d 385 (1952).

19.   *Ibid.*

<u>subordinate agencies may have been best described by a Washington</u>
<u>court which said</u>:

> The legislature may delegate these legislative controls to an
> administrative agency of the state, provided, in so doing, it
> defines what is to be done; the instrumentality's authority
> in so doing, by prescribing reasonable administrative
> standards.[20]

This statement probably represents the prevailing view of the courts
but the doctrine of delegation is one which must be treated as highly
flexible.   Courts, for example, will tend to restrict agency prerogatives in the area of taxation, property rights or individual civil rights.
On the other hand, state education agencies may have broad latitude
in dealing with regulation of purely educational matters such as
school district organization.   For example, a Wisconsin statute was
contested as being unconstitutional because it authorized the state superintendent to merge certain school districts of low assessed valuation with contiguous school districts.   The Wisconsin Supreme Court
said that "the power to exercise discretion in determining whether
such districts shall be altered * * * may be delegated without any
standard whatsoever to guide in the exercise of the power
delegated".[21]

   <u>The tendency has been in recent years for the courts to follow a</u>
<u>much more lenient policy toward delegation of legislative power</u>.[22]
Changes in the nature of modern government and the increasing
complexity of society necessitates that public agencies have more
general authority to assume broader prerogatives.   As it now stands
the delegation principle is still applicable to the state educational process and it remains in use to prevent unconstitutional usurpation of
unauthorized powers, but it is much less pervasive than before.   The
rule today as expounded by state courts is best exemplified by a New
York court[23] which quoted with approval the standard established by
the U.S. Supreme Court, which said: That a legislative body,

> * * * does not abdicate its functions when it de-
> scribes what job must be done, who must do it, and what is
> the scope of his authority.   In our complex economy that in-
> deed is frequently the only way in which the legislative pro-
> cess can go forward.[24]

20. State v. Kinnear, 70 Wash.2d 482, 423 P.2d 937 (1967).

21. School Dist. No. 3 of Town of Adams v. Callahan, 237 Wis. 560, 297 N.
W. 407 (1941).

22. Schinck v. Board of Educ. of West-
wood Consolidated School Dist., 60 N.
J.Super. 448, 159 A.2d 396 (1960).

23. Jokinen v. Allen, 15 Misc.2d 124, 182 N.Y.S.2d 166 (1958).

24. Bowles v. Willingham, 321 U.S. 503, 64 S.Ct. 641 (1944).

Although, the rationale of the courts continues to follow the delegation doctrine it should be observed that proper delegation and guarantee against arbitrary action by agencies cannot be assured through the specification of standards in legislative declarations. Protection against inappropriate action and injustice in education are to be found more in procedural safeguards and various checks and balances; the most effective of which is, of course, justification of the action to the voters and taxpayers.

Limitations Prescribed by the Legislature in Delegation of Power Must be Strictly Followed

SCHOOL DISTRICT NO. 8 OF SHERMAN COUNTY v. STATE BD. OF EDUC.

Supreme Court of Nebraska, 1964.
176 Neb. 722, 127 N.W.2d 458.

CARTER, Justice. This is a suit to enjoin the State Board of Education and the Commissioner of Education from enforcing an order disapproving the high school of School District No. 8 of Sherman County for the collection of free high school tuition money as provided in section 79–328, R.S.Supp., 1961. The trial court held the statute to be unconstitutional and entered judgment in favor of School District No. 8. The State Board of Education and the Commissioner of Education have appealed.

For convenience we shall hereafter refer to the State Board of Education as the state board, the Commissioner of Education as commissioner, and School District No. 8 of Sherman County as school district.

Pursuant to the authority granted by section 79–328, R.S.Supp., 1961, rules and regulations were adopted and issued by the commissioner on January 5, 1960, prior to the happening of the events herein detailed. On February 2, 1962, the school district was informed that the state board would, on February 13, 1962, consider the recommended disapproval of Rockville High School, the high school here involved, for free high school tuition money, and invited the attendance of the members of the board of the school district at the hearing. The hearing was held with the representatives of the school district in attendance. On February 14, 1962, the school district was informed that Rockville High School had been disapproved by the state board for the 1962–1963 school year for the collection of free high school tuition money for failure to maintain the high school in accordance with the rules and regulations issued by the commissioner. On April 16, 1962, this suit was commenced.

The school district contends that section 79–328(5) (c), R.S.Supp., 1961, is unconstitutional in that it is an invalid delegation of legislative authority and power to an administrative agency. This section provides that the state board shall have the power and it shall be its duty to "(c) establish rules and regulations based upon the program of studies, guidance services, the number and preparation of teachers in relation to the curriculum and enrollment, instructional materials and equipment, science facilities and equipment, library facilities and materials, health and safety factors in buildings and grounds, and procedures for classifying, approving, and accrediting schools, for approving the opening of new schools, for the continued legal operation of all schools, and for the approval of high schools for the collection of free high school tuition money in accordance with the rules and regulations provided for in this subdivision; Provided, that the State Board of Education shall approve a school for the collection of free high school tuition money where a hardship would result to the students and a substantial effort is being made to comply with the rules and regulations established, * * *."

The law appears to be well settled that the Legislature may properly delegate authority to an executive or administrative agency to formulate rules and regulations to carry out the expressed legislative purpose, or to implement such expressed purpose in order to provide for the complete operation and enforcement of the statute. The purpose of the delegation of authority ordinarily must be limited by express standards which have the effect of restricting the actions of the agency to the expressed legislative intent. In State ex rel. Martin v. Howard, 96 Neb. 278, 147 N.W. 689, this court approved the following: "In order to justify the courts in declaring invalid as a delegation of legislative power a statute conferring particular duties or authority upon administrative officers, it must clearly appear beyond a reasonable doubt that the duty or authority so conferred is a power that appertains exclusively to the legislative department, and the conferring of it is not warranted by the provisions of the Constitution. * * * Authority to make rules and regulations to carry out an expressed legislative purpose, or for the complete operation and enforcement of a law within designated limitations, is not an exclusively legislative power. Such authority is administrative in its nature and its use by administrative officers is essential to the complete exercise of the powers of all the departments." * * *

The difference between a delegation of legislative power and the delegation of authority to an administrative agency to carry out the expressed intent of the Legislature and the details involved has long been a difficult and important question. Increased complexity of our social order, and the multitude of details that necessarily follow, has led to a relaxation of the specific standards in the delegating statute in favor of more general ones where a specialized state agency is concerned. It is almost impossible for a legislature to prescribe all the rules and regulations necessary for a specialized agency to accomplish the legislative purpose. The delegation of authority to a specialized department under more generalized standards has been the natural trend as the need for regulation has become more evident and complex.   *   *   *

The Constitution provides: "There is hereby established a State Department of Education which shall be comprised of a State Board of Education and a Commissioner of Education. The State Department of Education shall have general supervision and administration of the school system of the state and of such other activities as the Legislature may direct." Art. VII, § 14, Constitution of Nebraska. It is provided by Article VII, section 15, Constitution of Nebraska, however, that the powers and duties of the state board shall be prescribed by the Legislature. The Legislature has done this and fixed the area in which the state board shall operate by section 79–328, R.S.Supp., 1961. The general supervision and administration of the school system of the state by the State Department of Education is thereby a constitutional grant of power dependent only upon implementing legislative action. In dealing with the powers of the state superintendent of public instruction under a similar constitutional provision in the Kansas Constitution, the Kansas court said: "Realizing that many questions pertaining to educational matters naturally would arise, and which would need the attention of a competent official who could investigate and determine what is best to be done, our Constitution gave to the superintendent of public instruction 'the general supervision of the * ` * * educational interests of the state,' and specifically authorized him to 'perform such other duties as may be prescribed by law,' without limiting those duties to such as might be classified as executive or administrative only. He is authorized to perform any duties pertaining to the educational interests of the state which the Legislature deems wise and prudent to impose upon him. <u>Under these provisions, it cannot be said that the Legislature is without authority to authorize the state superintendent of public instruction to perform duties, or determine questions, with respect to the educational interests of the state which, in the general classification of powers of government, would be regarded as legislative in character.</u>   *   *   *

     *   *   *

In dealing with the same subject the Missouri court said: "Art. II of the present Constitution divides the power of government into the legislative, executive and judicial departments and provides that no person or collection of persons charged with the exercise of power properly belonging to one of those departments shall exercise any power properly belonging to either of the others, '*except in the instances in this Constitution expressly directed or permitted.*' (Italics ours.) The legislative powers vested in a senate and house of representatives by Art. III, Sec. 1. Since the State Board of Education is a constitutional board with duties defined by the Constitution and 'shall have such other powers and duties as may be prescribed by law', it follows that <u>the state legislature can confer on that board duties that are legislative in character as distinguished from those clas-</u>

sified as executive or administrative only. Such duties would come within the exception of Art. II of the Constitution." State ex rel. Reorganized School Dist., etc. v. Holmes, 360 Mo. 904, 231 S.W.2d 185. We are in accord with the reasoning of the foregoing opinions and, in our judgment, whether or not the power granted is legislative or administrative is of no importance if it is within the scope of the Legislature's implementing legislation. The intent of Article VII, section 14, of the Constitution, was to confer powers upon the state board, which it did not and could not previously have. If this is not so there would have been no purpose in adopting it as an amendment to the Constitution in 1952. The Legislature was already authorized to delegate administrative authority to the state board and the constitutional grant of the general supervision and administration of the school system of the state, and such other activities as the Legislature may direct, necessarily included authority by the Legislature to grant purely legislative power if it was to have any added meaning at all.

*   *   *

Contrary to the contentions of the school district, we think the delegation of authority by the Legislature contains adequate descriptive terms. Complaint is made that there are no restricting words such as "all in accordance with sound educational practices." But we point out that subdivision (5)(c) of section 79–328, R.S.Supp., 1961, specifies the matters to be considered in promulgating rules and regulations which are limiting in effect and confine them within the grant of power contained in Article VII, section 14, of the Constitution. Standards are not required in the constitutional grant of legislative power.

We conclude that subdivision (5)(c) of section 79–328, R.S.Supp., 1961, is not violative of Article II, Section 1, Constitution of Nebraska. We hold also that the delegation of power by the Legislature to the State Department of Education pursuant to Article VII, section 14, of the Constitution, is adequately described, and that said section 79–328, R.S.Supp., 1961 is not so vague, ambiguous, and indefinite as to be unconstitutional.

*   *   *

*   *   * It is the province of the Legislature to determine the manner in which delegated powers shall be exercised and a failure to comply with the conditions and limitations imposed is an unlawful exercise of the powers purportedly granted.

Section 84–913, R.S.Supp., 1961, is an independent act providing for notice and hearing by administrative agencies in specified instances. The same section of the statute provides: "Each agency shall adopt appropriate rules of procedure for notice and hearing in contested cases." The State Department of Education failed to provide rules for the procedure for notice and hearing. The provision for requiring such rules is mandatory and within the competence of the Legislature to require. Until the State Department of Education adopts appropriate rules of procedure for notice and hearing, and thereby initiates its authority to provide notice and hearing, its authority to give notice and hearing is dormant and its attempt to provide it is without validity. If the State Department of Education could with impunity disregard a mandatory provision of the statute in the delegation of authority to it, it could disregard others on the authority of the first, with the result that the control of the Legislature would be lost. Compliance with the mandate of the Legislature in the delegation of power and authority to an agency of government is in effect a condition precedent to the exercise of such power and authority.

The delegation of authority and power does not ordinarily imply a parting with the powers of the Legislature, but points rather to the conferring of authority or power to do the things which otherwise the Legislature would have to do itself. <u>The Legislature may therefore provide the conditions and limitations with which the agency must comply before the authority or power may be exercised.</u>

      *   *   *

      *   *   * It is the failure of the state board and the commissioner to comply with the statute, and not any deficiency in the statute itself, that results in the invalidation of the state board's finding that the school district was not entitled to its free high school tuition money.

For the reasons stated, the order of the state board and the commissioner, under date of February 14, 1962, is void and of no force and effect. The judgment of the district court, therefore, is correct in permanently enjoining the enforcement of the order of the state board denying free high school tuition money to the school district.

      Affirmed.

Mere Doubt of Constitutionality of Legislative Delegation of Power Will Not Invalidate Statute

DICKEN v. KENTUCKY STATE BD. OF EDUC.

Court of Appeals of Kentucky, 1947.
304 Ky. 343, 199 S.W.2d 977.

THOMAS, Justice. At its regular session in 1934 the Legislature of this Commonwealth enacted Chapter 65 of the published acts for that year. It superseded all preceding statutes for the creating, management and enforcement of our free public school system; imposing certain duties on the State Superintendent of Public Instruction; creating the State Board of Education with the State Superintendent of Public Instruction, by virtue of his office, made chairman thereof, and describing the qualifications for the other members of that Board, who were required to be professional educators. * * *

Parts of that enactment are now sections 156.160 and 158.100 of KRS. The first one (156.160) authorizes the Superintendent of Public Instruction, with the approval of the State Board of Education, to prescribe:

> "Rules and regulations for grading, classifying and accrediting all common schools, and for determining the scope of instruction that may be offered in the different classes of schools, and the minimum requirements for graduation from the courses offered;"

> * * *

Pursuant to its rule making power so authorized, the State Superintendent with the approval of the State Board of Education promulgated this rule with reference to high schools:

> "Four-year high schools (grades 9–12) shall employ at least three full-time teachers and have a bona fide enrollment of not fewer than sixty pupils."

The rules which the State Board of Education promulgates and adopts are uniform throughout the state and to be observed and followed by all county boards of education.

The attendance of high grade pupils in the area of the A. J. Jolly School was * * * considerably less than 60 pupils in the school year of 1945–46, and the State Board of Education so notified the county board of education of Campbell County. * * * that thereafter the high school at that location should be abandoned and that the high school pupils theretofore attending that school should be transferred to the class "A" high school at Alexandria, located in the same county and 12 miles distant from the A. J. Jolly School and where the faculty consisted of eleven members. * * *

Plaintiffs prayed for a declaration of rights, to be followed by a mandatory injunction against the County Board of Education (which had theretofore entered an order abandoning the A. J. Jolly High School) and its members requiring them to continue to provide for and maintain the A. J. Jolly High School * * *.

Plaintiffs appear to admit in their brief, filed in this court that pursuant to authority conferred by KRS 156.160 the State Board of Education may make rules for the governing, classifications, etc., of the public schools of the Commonwealth which do not infringe upon pure legislative authority, but they insist that the rule herein attacked fixing a minimum of pupil attendance to maintain a high school is the exercise of a legislative function by the State Board of Education which section 28 of our Constitution expressly forbids. Section 27 of that instrument divides the powers of government into three departments, the Legislative, the Executive and the Judicial, and section 28 prescribes that "no person or collection of persons, being of one of those departments, shall exercise any power properly belonging to either of the others, except in the instances hereinafter expressly directed or permitted." Since we regard this contention as the only one deserving consideration, all of the other grounds and arguments made by learned counsel for appellants will be dismissed as immaterial and valueless for the obtention of the relief sought.

A late case cited by appellants, and largely relied on to sustain their contention, is that of Bloemer v. Turner, 281 Ky. 832, 137 S.W. 2d 387, 390, involving the right under statutory authority to make rules and regulations governing the administration of the statute there involved of the Director of the Kentucky Agricultural Experiment Station, to add to what the label on a package of dog food should contain by annexing an additional requirement. The statute enumerated the specific facts that should be put upon the label of the package containing the dog food, but the administrators of the act attempted to add an additional requirement to be so stated, which it was insisted could be done under conferred authority or regulation. The trial court sustained that contention, but we reversed the judgment and held that the added requirement was a legislative act and not a regulatory one. In doing so we said that if the delegated authority to the administrative agency were authorized to add to the specific requirements contained in the statute, then the same agency could likewise take from the specific requirements of the statute, or, we may add, such administrative authority might dispense entirely with such specific statutory requirements, which would logically and essentially be legislative action. There is here presented for our determination no such question as was involved and determined in that case. * * *

Further along in the same opinion we approvingly inserted this excerpt from the Pennsylvania Supreme Court in Locke's Appeal, 72 Pa. 491, 13 Am.Rep. 716:

> " 'The legislature cannot delegate its power to make a law; but it can make a law to delegate a power to determine some fact or state of things upon which the law makes, or intends to make, its own action depend. To deny this would be to stop the wheels of government. There are many things upon which wise and useful legislation must depend, which cannot be known to the law-making power, and must, therefore, be a subject of inquiry and determination outside of the halls of legislation.' "

* * *

The 1934 school code is a comprehensive statute, in the enforcement of which a number of administrative agencies are provided, each of which necessarily requires the performance of a multiplicity of duties so as to accomplish the purpose of the Legislature in enacting it, which was to construct, and administer the most efficient formula for the education of the school children of the Commonwealth. The Legislature fixed therein the classes of the schools provided for, and enacted that the four grades following the eighth should be considered as what are commonly understood as High Schools, and required that each county board should maintain or make provision for at least one high school in its county district, but did not restrict the number of them that might be established therein. The very fact that the statute expressly required only one of such schools to be established is an indication that the members of the Legislature realized the fact that such high schools could not be established in every community where there was a small number of high school pupils located in the particular area. It, therefore, left it to the State Board of Education, under its authorized power to make rules, classifications, etc. to fix the minimum number of pupils necessary for the maintenance of a high school, and which we conclude was permitted regulation instead of a delegation of legislative authority.

* * *

The Supreme Court of the United States in the case of Louisville Bridge Company v. United States, 242 U.S. 409, 37 S.Ct. 158, 162, 61 L.Ed. 395, was presented with the same question relating to the construction of a bridge across the Ohio River, a navigable stream. The Congressional Act authorizing such construction required, in substance, that the bridge so authorized should not *unreasonably* obstruct navigation, but it provided no specific plans or standards as to what was or was not "unreasonable obstruction" to navigation, and delegated the authority to the Secretary of War to make such standard. In the course of the opinion the court, speaking by Mr. Justice Pitney, said:

> "Congress thereby declared that whenever the Secretary of War should find any bridge theretofore or thereafter constructed over any of the navigable waterways of the United States to be an unreasonable obstruction to the free navigation of such waters on account of insufficient height, width of span, or otherwise, it should be the duty of the Secretary, after hearing the parties concerned, to take action looking to the removal or alteration of the bridge, so as to render navigation through or under it reasonably free, easy, and unobstructed. As this court repeatedly has held, this is not an unconstitutional delegation of legislative or judicial power to the Secretary." (Citing authorities.)

The line separating that which is purely regulation, and that which is purely legislation, is necessarily indistinct, and becomes more so as the line separating such authority is approached. Therefore, courts, when no more than a doubt exists as to which side of the separating line the act in question falls, will resolve the doubt in favor of the validity of the act rather than holding it invalid, which is analogous to the well established rule that a mere doubt as to the constitutionality of a statute will be resolved in favor of its validity rather than its invalidity, and which is especially true when the act is essential and necessary for the carrying out the broad purpose and intent of the Legislature. We therefore conclude that the petition was insufficient to the relief sought therein, and that the court properly sustained a demurrer to it and dismissed it after plaintiff declined to plead further.

Wherefore, the judgment is affirmed.

*Proper Delegation of Legislative Authority Does Not Invest
Education Officials With Power to Determine
Whether Law Shall or Shall Not be Enforced*

SCHOOL DIST. NO. 39 OF WASHINGTON COUNTY v. DECKER

Supreme Court of Nebraska, 1955.
159 Neb. 693, 68 N.W.2d 354.

CHAPPELL, Justice. Plaintiff, School District No. 39 of Washington County, generally known as Rose Hill School District, is a rural Class II school district conducting both elementary and ninth and tenth high school grades in Washington County. It brought this action in equity to enjoin the enforcement of Rule III–3 of Section B, "Criteria for Approved Schools" promulgated as of July 1, 1952, by defendant Freeman Decker, then Superintendent of Public Instruction, under purported authority granted him by the last sentence of section 79–307, R.R.S.1943. Such section provides: "The Superintendent of Public Instruction shall prescribe forms for making all reports and regulations for all proceedings under the general school laws of the state. *He shall also formulate rules and regulations for the approval of all high schools for the collection of free high school tuition money.*" (Italics supplied.)

Rule III–3 also provides: "The teacher-pupil ratio for high school (grades 9–12) shall not be less than 1–5."

On May 12, 1953, defendant had removed plaintiff's high school from the list of approved schools for the school year 1953–1954 because its teacher-pupil ratio was "1–4 which is less than the minimum standards" required by Rule III–3. Concededly, such removal made plaintiff ineligible for collection of free high school tuition for nonresident pupils, deprived it of exemption from the free high school tax levy together with the right to be considered for accreditation status, and, as stated by defendant, "so far as our records are concerned, there is no high school in Rose Hill."

Insofar as important here, plaintiff sought injunctive relief primarily upon the ground that the last sentence of section 79–307, R. R.S.1943, was an unconstitutional and invalid delegation of legislative authority and power to an executive or administrative officer of the state. In other words, plaintiff contended that Rule III–3 was invalid and unenforceable because such statute granted defendant authority to "formulate rules and regulations for the approval of all high schools for the collection of free high school tuition money" without therein or otherwise in any statute in pari materia therewith providing any legislative numerical limitations, standards, rules, or criteria for the guidance of defendant in so doing.

Upon issues duly joined there was a hearing in the district court whereat evidence was adduced and a judgment was rendered finding and adjudging the issues generally for defendant and against plaintiff. In doing so, it was found and adjudged that section 79–307, R.R.S. 1943, was a valid, legal statute, and not unconstitutional as a delegation of legislative powers, and that Rule III–3 promulgated thereunder was valid and enforceable.

* * *

As disclosed by the record, defendant admitted that there is no magic in the ratio of 1–5 required by Rule III–3, and that it could as well have been higher or lower, but should be higher. As a matter of fact, defendant also admitted that there are only eight ninth and tenth grade high schools left in Nebraska, but that in the recent past he had waived the ratio of 1–5 for two or three other like high schools in Washington County because they had prospects for more students in the future, or had suggested the possibility of reorganization.

Thus the Superintendent of Public Instruction has been delegated a free hand without legislative limitations or standards to make or change at will any numerical ratio or standard required for approval of high schools for the collection of free high school tuition money when it would have been a simple matter for the Legislature, which had the power and authority, to have incorporated limits and standards in the statute. As a consequence, without questioning the motives or ability of the Superintendent of Public Instruction, there might well be approval of some high schools upon one standard and a withholding of approval from others by a qualification of such standard or by virtue of another. Thus, defendant had arbitrary power over the life or death of all high schools in this state and the preservation or destruction of their property and the grant or denial of free high school revenue, dependent upon the granting or refusal of approval.

Article II, section 1, Constitution of Nebraska provides: "The powers of the government of this state are divided into three distinct departments, the legislative, executive and judicial, and no person or collection of persons being one of these departments, shall exercise any power properly belonging to either of the others, except as hereinafter expressly directed or permitted."

* * *

As said in 42 Am.Jur., Public Administrative Law, § 45, p. 342, citing authorities from many states: "It is a fundamental principle of our system of government that the rights of men are to be determined by the law itself, and not by the let or leave of administrative officers or bureaus. This principle ought not to be surrendered for convenience, or in effect nullified for the sake of expediency. However, it is impossible for the legislature to deal directly with the host of details in the complex conditions on which it legislates, and when the legislature states the purpose of the law and sets up standards to guide the agency which is to administer it, there is no constitutional objection to vesting discretion as to its execution in the administrators. * * * A statute which in effect reposes an absolute, unregulated, and undefined discretion in an administrative body bestows arbitrary powers and is an unlawful delegation of legislative powers. The presumption that an officer will not act arbitrarily but will exercise sound judgment and good faith cannot sustain a delegation of unregulated discretion." Also, as said in 42 Am.Jur., Public Administrative Law, § 49, p. 353, citing authorities from many states: "The legislature, having declared its policy and purpose and provided standards for the exercise of the power, may confer upon administrative authorities the power to enact rules and regulations to promote the purpose and spirit of the legislation and carry it into effect, and, even though such rules and regulations are given the force and effect of law, there is no violation of the constitutional inhibition against delegation of the legislative function."

* * *

For reasons heretofore set forth, the judgment of the trial court should be and hereby is reversed and the cause is remanded with directions to render judgment for plaintiff in conformity with this opinion. All costs are taxed to defendant.

Reversed and remanded with directions.

NOTES

1. The courts have held that discretionary administrative powers may be delegated while legislative powers cannot. In this regard the Supreme Court of Nebraska has said:

"The legislature cannot delegate legislative authority to an individual. It can prescribe the terms and conditions which may bring into operation a dissolution or consolidation of school districts. This is the legislative act. It then can authorize the county superintendent to determine if the facts exist which call the law into operation."

Bierman v. Campbell, 175 Neb. 877, 124 N.W.2d 918 (1963).

An Illinois court has said that the legislature may not delegate legislative authority but it may "give an administrative body discretionary powers to decide an issue if it establishes standards under which that discretion may be exercised." People ex rel. Community Unit School Dist. No. 1 v. Decatur School Dist. No. 61, 45 Ill.App.2d 33, 194 N.E.2d 659 (1963).

2. The courts have held that the Superintendent of Public Instruction of Illinois is the head of the public school system of that state and has been vested by the General Assembly with the duty of establishing standards in education, along the lines delineated by statute. Games v. County Bd. of School Trustees of McDonough County, 13 Ill.2d 78, 147 N.E.2d 306 (1958).

3. A Massachusetts court has held that the state Commissioner of Education has the power to compel local school officials to produce information by racial census. The court said that the Commissioner had the implied authority to do in an ordinary and reasonable manner those things required for efficient exercise of powers and satisfactory performance of duties. School Committee of New Bedford v. Commissioner of Educ., 349 Mass. 410, 208 N.E.2d 814 (1965).

4. In a Kentucky case concerning the constitutionality of delegation of legislative power to agencies in general and county boards of education in particular, the court said:

> "It has been suggested that the statute in this respect * * * is unconstitutional as being a delegation of legislative power to the several county boards of education. Such bodies may and do have conferred upon them legislative authority in a degree, for rules and regulations partake of that function. But delegation of legislative power in relation to constitutional limitations means delegation of discretion as to what the law shall be, and does not mean that the legislature may not confer discretion in the administration of the law itself. * * * Many are the instances where powers more nearly approaching the legislative prerogative than this have been vested in executive or administrative agencies and sustained as valid. This authority given the school boards is administrative and not legislative, and the act does not offend the Constitution in this regard."

Board of Education of Bath County v. Goodpaster, 260 Ky. 198, 84 S.W.2d 55 (1935).

5. A decision by the Commissioner of Education of New York requiring school boards to furnish transportation of non-public school children was held not to be arbitrary even though the decision was rendered under two "somewhat inconsistent rules". Board of Education of Cornwall v. Nyquist, 61 A.D.2d 132, 401 N.Y.S.2d 589 (1978).

Executive Functions

Although activities of state education agencies are difficult to compartmentalize it is possible to identify certain ones which may be more readily described as executive rather than legislative or judicial. In fact, the organizational structures of state education agencies tend to adhere to such definition in that the legislative functions are usually vested in a state board of education, the executive functions in a chief state school officer and his staff, the state department of education, while the quasi-judicial functions may be found within the prerogatives of either or both.

The distinction between legislative and executive acts can be expressed as the difference between the general and the particular. "A legislative act is the creation and promulgation of a general rule of conduct without reference to particular cases; an administrative act cannot be exactly defined, but it includes the adoption of policy, the making and issue of specific direction, and the application of a general rule to a particular case in accordance with the requirements of policy or expediency or administrative practice." [25]

Activities of the state education agency which may be classified as purely executive are declaring and enforcing policy as well as advising and supervising implementation of policy. One can easily identify such activities as they are performed daily in state agencies; for example, when a policy is established it must be properly interpreted and conveyed to the local school district administrators, then advice may be given and certain supervisory activities may be followed to assist in implementation. Should problems arise steps must be taken to assure enforcement of the particular policy.

Executive actions can also be viewed in the more commonly used legislative categories of ministerial and discretionary functions. Ministerial refers to those required duties performed by the administrator and no exercise of judgment is permitted. Discretionary functions, on the other hand, are judgmental and represent exercise of substantial administrative prerogative. An administrator can pass on to a subordinate ministerial functions, but cannot delegate duties discretionary in nature. Discretionary functions, of course, represent an area of major overlap with the broader quasi-judicial functions of agencies. The maxim *delegatus non protest delegare* has, on the whole, been more strictly enforced when applied to sub-delegation than at the primary or legislative level of delegation. In other words, courts tend to examine more critically the internal delegation of a discretionary function from the state superintendent down to an assistant than from the legislature to the agency itself. For example, where statute vests a specific discretionary power in a state board, the board cannot sub-delegate to one board member or to some other officer such as the state superintendent. Similarly, statutory discretion vested in the state superintendent cannot be re-delegated to a deputy or assistant. Ministerial functions, on the other hand, can be sub-delegated.

25. S. A. de Smith, *Judicial Review of Administrative Action*, Stevens & Sons, London, 1973, p. 60.

Will [26] has pointed out that there is a discernible trend toward the separation of the legislative function and the executive powers in state educational administration. He describes the pattern in this way:

> Students of state educational administration commonly hold that the central education agency should consist of a state board of education, a chief state school officer, and the necessary staff. The state board of education is looked upon as the agency's legislative policy-making body, the chief state school officer as the agency's executive officer, and the organized staff as the agency's work force. A virtually complete separation of legislative and executive powers at the administrative level is intended under this pattern.[27]

The powers and duties of the state board of education, the chief state school officer and the state department of education varies from state to state; however, general rules governing the delegation of legislative powers, the exercises of discretionary authority, and the quasi-judicial role of central state agencies are carefully circumscribed by court decisions.

Courts Will Not Substitute Their Discretion for
That of Authorized Officers or Boards

STATE EX REL. SCHOOL DIST. NO. 29, FLATHEAD COUNTY v. COONEY

Supreme Court of Montana, 1936.
102 Mont. 521, 59 P.2d 48.

MORRIS, Justice. The petition in this action was filed in the district court for Lewis and Clark county July 23, 1935, and alleges, in substance, that school district No. 29, Flathead county, Mont., has maintained an accredited 2-year high school for a period of 16 years; that "during the school year 1934–1935," the board of trustees determined it was for the best interests of the school to provide for a third year of high school work; that the prescribed course of study as required by the state board of education was provided for, duly installed, and given by competent instructors, and by reason of the school's compliance with the standards fixed by the state board it has become the duty of the state board to accredit the plaintiff school as a 3-year high school; that demand was made upon the state board for such

26. Will, Robert F., *State Education, Structure and Organization*, U.S. Department of Health Education and Welfare, U.S. Office of Education, 1964, pp. 8–10.

27. Will, *State Education, Structure and Organization*.

accrediting, and by the state board arbitrarily and capriciously denied. This action followed.

* * *

It is obvious that the controversy arises out of a misconception of the relative functions of the state board of education and the superintendent of public instruction, on the one hand, and the local board of school trustees, on the other. Certain duties and powers are vested in the former, and others in the local board, and each, acting within the law, is supreme in its respective sphere so long as no act is done arbitrarily or capriciously. Among the duties imposed upon the state educational officials, generally speaking, is that of establishing and maintaining a general uniform and thorough system of public instruction. A specific duty is that they shall establish uniform standards of study and maintain certain standards to which all local schools must conform before such local schools are entitled to be placed upon the accredited list. Certain powers of local control and management are vested in the local school board, such as the employment of teachers, the admission of students from other districts, the selection of school sites, etc. Both the state board and superintendent and the local board are quasijudicial bodies or officials, and both exercise discretionary powers * * *, and when such powers are exercised in the manner prescribed by law, no right of review exists. This phase of the controversy will be adverted to later.

We think a review of the powers and duties, respectively, of the state board of education, the superintendent of public instruction, the board of trustees of the school district, and consideration of the facts as shown by the record, will readily suggest the correct determination of the controversy.

The state board of education is a constitutional board (article 11, § 11); that section of the Constitution provides in part: "The general control and supervision of the state university and the various other state educational institutions shall be vested in a state board of education, whose powers and duties shall be prescribed and regulated by law. The said board shall consist of eleven members." The following mandate is imposed upon the Legislature by the Constitution: "It shall be the duty of the legislative assembly of Montana to establish and maintain a general, uniform and thorough system of public, free, common schools." Article 11, § 1. The state board of education is a part of the executive department of the state government. * * * The provision of the Constitution first above mentioned vests in the state board general control over and supervision of all state educational matters, including district and high schools. * * * The state board may prescribe and accredit such high schools as maintain the standards prescribed. Subsection 4, § 836, Rev.Codes 1921. It shall have power, and it shall be its duty, to adopt rules and regulations for the execution of the duties and powers conferred. Subsection 2, § 836, Id.; see, also, section 70, ch. 148, Laws of 1931.

The superintendent of public instruction is one of the seven exec-utive officers of the state provided for by the Constitution (article 7, § 1); a constitutional member of the state board of land commission-ers having control of the school lands (article 11, § 4); a constitu-tional member of the state board of education (article 11, § 11). By statute the superintendent has supervision of all public schools of the state, subject to general supervision of the state board (section 932, Rev.Codes 1921), and must report annually to the Governor (section 939, Id.); "shall prepare, or cause to be prepared, with the co-opera-tion and approval of such educators as may be named by the state board of education, a course of study for all the public elementary and high schools of the state, and shall prescribe to what extent the same is to be used" (section 941, Id.); shall decide all appeals from decisions of county superintendents (section 943, Id.); shall be the secretary of the state board of education (section 833, Id.); shall have general supervision over the budgets of elementary schools and the enforcement thereof (section 25, ch. 146, Laws of 1931); on ap-proval of the state board of education, shall appoint a supervisor of high schools who shall inspect all such schools of the state and report from time to time (section 69, ch. 148, Laws of 1931.)

"When the Board of Trustees of any school district desires to es-tablish a high school, it shall petition the Superintendent of Public Instruction, prior to June first of the current year for the permission to do so. * * * An investigation shall be made thereafter by a designated representative of the Superintendent of Public Instruction and his report on the petition filed with it before the petition is acted upon. The Superintendent of Public Instruction must have passed fa-vorably on any such petition before the high school proposed may be established by the district." Chapter 9, Laws of 1933, amending sec-tion 38 of chapter 148, Laws of 1931.

* * *

The structure outlined in the mandatory provisions of the Con-stitution heretofore quoted looking to the establishment of a system of free public schools, and perfected by legislative act, is built around the state board of education and the superintendent of public instruc-tion. Both of these state agencies are executive in character. The Constitution provides, and this court has said in the cases cited, that the state board has general supervision of all institutions of learning that are public in nature; that is, schools maintained in whole or in part at public expense. They are the state agencies upon which the state has imposed, by the Constitution and legislative acts, the duties to build and maintain the state's system of public instruction, and the Legislature has vested in the board power to make and enforce rules and regulations consonant with law to accomplish the purposes for which the state board was created. The members of the board by legislative act must serve without compensation, and it is obvious that the Legislature intended to have other state officers and employees assemble the necessary facts and information essential to the exercise of the board's supervising power. It will not be presumed that a state board serving without compensation shall be required to assemble the necessary data upon which it bases its decision. The superintendent of public instruction is the secretary of the board, and the department of the superintendent is the chief source of the detailed information upon which the board must depend. Any attack upon the system should be made upon the Constitution and through the Legislature; not here.

The facts established by the evidence or admitted are: (1) That the Somers school attempted to provide for the third year high school work before obtaining the approval of the superintendent of public instruction; such act being contrary to the provisions of chapter 9, Laws of 1933, and also contrary to a rule adopted and published by the state board to the same effect. (2) It is alleged in the petition that a third year of high school work was provided for and that such third year was authorized by the board of trustees of the Somers school, but no evidence was produced, either in the form of a minute entry or by the testimony of any member of the board of trustees, to support the affidavit that any such action was taken or authorized by the board of trustees. Neither is there any evidence in the record to show that legal demand was made upon the board to accredit the school. It cannot be said that the state board is in default until legal demand is shown and refused. * * *

It is suggested by counsel for the defendants that there never has been any hearing on plaintiffs' alleged application in any sense by the state board. Obviously the state board cannot be forced to act when a provision of the statute and one of its rules have been ignored in an essential preliminary matter. The Somers school failed to come before the board with the approval of the superintendent of public instruction. True, the state board might have waived these requirements, but we think it would have been derelict in its duty as the supervising power of the schools if it had done so. No great amount of activity was shown by any party on behalf of the Somers school, except by the principal, who, for reasons stated, was not properly accredited with authority to show any right to act for the board. He was accompanied to the informal hearing before the state board of education by two members of the local school board, but neither of the members of the school board took any part in the proceedings, and there was nothing before the board to show any "clear legal right" that would justify the state board in overriding the opposition of the superintendent of public instruction. Even if the records of the minutes of the board authorizing the additional work and demand on the state board for accrediting were in evidence, there is still ample in the record to justify the superintendent's refusal to approve the application, and until such approval was obtained the applicant was not legally before the state board nor entitled to be heard.

The physical facilities of the school and the question as to whether the additional third year of high school might adversely affect the financial interest of the grade schools are questions that are in dispute, but are matters to be determined at the discretion of the superintendent of public instruction and the state board.

We think that all that has been said so far is consonant with the intention of our lawmakers as expressed in the Constitution and in legislative acts, but the final barrier to the plaintiffs' demands is the discretionary power in the state board. That the state board acted arbitrarily or capriciously in denying the application of the plaintiffs is to say that the Legislature acted arbitrarily or capriciously in vesting the powers in the state board and the superintendent of public instruction that they are required to exercise in supervising our public schools, and we think that any such contention is shown to be without merit by even a casual investigation of the laws referred to heretofore, and if the state board did not act arbitrarily or capriciously, then no legal ground remains to justify the issuance of the writ. "Repeatedly, and consistently, this court has adhered to the rule that courts will not substitute their discretion for the discretion reposed in officers or boards by legislative enactment." * * * The state board acts in a quasijudicial capacity in determining all such matters as that involved here, and "it would greatly impair the government and efficiency of the common schools if the honest judgment and the discretion of the board, exercised in good faith, could be reviewed and reversed by a jury" (or a court). In the Peterson Case, it was sought to compel the school board of district No. 1 of Cascade county to admit a pupil not a resident of the district without tuition. To determine whether the pupil was entitled to attend such school without paying the tuition fixed by the board or not, was held to be within the discretion of the school board and with which the courts would not interfere.

If the plaintiff school has been given no legal hearing by the state board, a fact which we believe the record shows, the state board may be compelled to meet and act in the premises, but only after the local board establishes by satisfactory evidence that all preliminary steps have been taken, and approval to install the third year's work must first be obtained from the superintendent of public instruction. Even if the state board be compelled to grant a hearing, it cannot be compelled to accredit the Somers school unless it be clearly shown that the denial of the application of the Somers school by the state board would be an arbitrary or capricious act. The writ will lie to compel the board to act, and exercise its discretion, but not to direct its conclusions nor the judgment it shall reach; this, of course, means legal discretion. * * *

There is no evidence here that any power vested in the state board has been exercised arbitrarily or capriciously. We think the issuance of the writ in this case clearly an invasion of the discretionary power vested in the state board of education, and the judgment is therefore reversed, and the cause remanded to the district court, with instructions to quash the writ and dismiss the action.

NOTES

The Commissioner of Education of New York acted within his authority when he approved the closing of several schools by a local school board. DeVito v. Nyquist, 43 N.Y.2d 681, 401 N.Y.S.2d 25, 371 N.E.2d 788 (1977).

Judicial Functions

In their tripartite capacity administrative agencies hand down many more decisions affecting individuals than do the formal courts of this country. Decisions by educational tribunals form an important source of law under which education operates. Authority for decisions by educational tribunals may be found at federal, state, and local levels. At the federal level statute often vests the U.S. Commissioner of Education with quasi-judicial authority to render decisions in disputes over federal grant processes and procedures which may have direct impact on individuals or states. At the state level quasi-judicial authority may be given to state boards of education, to state superintendents, or in some cases to other legislatively authorized bodies. New Jersey and New York are good examples of such powers being vested in the chief state school officer.

The state commissioner of education of New Jersey has the authority to decide cases involving internal administrative operations of the public schools of that state. A New Jersey court has said that a statute providing that the state commissioner shall decide all controversies under the school laws of the state is evidence of legislative purpose to set up a comprehensive system of internal appeals with broad powers. Such an authority invested in administrative tribunals assures that controversies are justly disposed of in accordance with the law.[28]

In another New Jersey case illustrating the judicial function of the state commissioner of education, the court said that the commissioner must enforce all rules and regulations prescribed by the state board and decide all questions arising under rules and regulations of the state board.[29]

Determinations by these tribunals are binding on the parties involved and serve additionally to establish a type of quasi-judicial *stare decisis* within the agencies' jurisdiction. Agencies in exercise of their judicial powers are required generally to merely provide fair treatment to the parties involved. Some states through administrative procedure acts may provide specific definition of the require-

28. Laba v. Board of Educ. of Newark, 23 N.J. 364, 129 A.2d 273 (1966).

29. In re Masiello, 25 N.J. 590, 138 A. 2d 393 (1966).

ments of fairness, and when administrative tribunals are dealing with disputes involving constitutional interests more elaborate procedures are necessary. In the absence, though, of statutory or constitutional restraints the courts have been very liberal in allowing educational tribunals to establish their own procedures. In so doing courts more or less adhere to a requirement similar to the English doctrine of *audi alteram partem* of natural justice which requires that tribunals must adjudicate fairly. <u>Fairness is not always easily defined but may be roughly equated to reasonableness and good faith</u>. These two standards are not the same but may be viewed as complimentary. It has been said that "some of the most honest people are the most unreasonable; and some excesses may be sincerely believed in but yet quite beyond the limits of reasonableness." [30] It is true, however, that the actions of one conducting a hearing could be so unreasonable as to be arbitrary and capricious and as such appear to be taken in bad faith.

To ensure fairness, members of tribunals should not have special interests in the outcome of a particular issue. A personal conflict of interest on the part of the adjudicator will invalidate a decision. However, the mere fact that the public agency is, as a body, a party to the dispute is not alone an indication of bias.[31]

ROBERT H. JACKSON,* THE ADMINISTRATIVE PROCESS

5 Journal of Social Philosophy 143, 146–49 (1940).

"* * * From the very beginning the administrative tribunal has faced the hostility of the legal profession. The lawyer is inclined by habit and training to prefer the court over the administrative tribunal. Its personnel, procedure, and atmosphere are more congenial to him. I frankly share that preference for a court as a forum in which to practice.

The court belongs to the lawyers; lawyers only preside, and lawyers alone address it. The administrative tribunal generally includes lawyers, but some of its members are apt to be laymen, sometimes with special training, such as accountancy, or engineering.

Most lawyers like court procedure, which is somewhat ceremonial and moves according to a prescribed ritual. Administrative bodies, on the other hand, generally sit informally. Their procedure is not rigid, and many of them admit laymen to practice. The court re-

30. R. v. Roberts, 2 K.B. 695 (1924). See also: Kern Alexander, "Administrative Prerogative: Restraints of Natural Justice on Student Discipline", 7 *Journal of Law and Education* 3, 331–358, July 1978.

31. Hortonville Joint School Dist. No. 1 v. Hortonville Educ. Ass'n, 426 U.S. 482, 96 S.Ct. 2308 (1976).

* Former Associate Justice, Supreme Court of the United States; former Attorney General of the United States, etc.

ceives evidence only according to technical rules of presentation, competence and relevance. None but the lawyers understand these rules, and they are generally in disagreement about their application which makes a trial something of a drama of objections and exceptions, with lawyers playing all speaking roles. The administrative tribunal is non-technical about the receipt of evidence, its procedure is flexible, and even mistakes are easily amended. A layman may actually understand what one of these administrative tribunals is doing. Such a tribunal may have a better knowledge of the problems at issue than the lawyer who presents the case. It may have its own corps of experts to advise and assist it. Such a tribunal is not as dependent as the ordinary court upon the arguments of partisan counsel to get at the truth.

When the cause reaches the stage of decision, the court follows the lawyer's doctrine of stare decisis. It will generally yield its present opinion to follow precedents laid down in more or less like cases by other courts of superior jurisdiction and by earlier judges of the same court. The administrative tribunal is relatively free from the restraints of this rule. It is often penetrating into new fields where precedents do not exist. Its concern is with the future more than with the past, and it counts the probable progeny of its decisions as of more importance than their ancestry. The courts and their methods are therefore naturally favored by lawyers.

This lawyerly hostility has lately taken on political aspects because the New Deal has had occasion to create new agencies in greater numbers than any previous administration. Those who dislike such activities of the government as regulation of the utility holding companies, of labor relations, or of the marketing of securities, rightly conceive that if they can destroy the administrative tribunal which enforces regulation, they would destroy the whole plan of regulation itself. It may be said that the administrative tribunal is the heart of nearly every reform which attempts to give a new validity to the rights of large numbers of people on the one hand against powerful interests on the other. * * *

[No friend of the administrative process believes] that its administrators are always at their best or that the process is not capable of abuses. * * * The record of the administrative tribunal in review of actual cases, however, gives no support for intemperate attacks upon administrative agencies as generally, or often, usurping, partisan, arbitrary, ignorant, or of doubtful integrity. * * * Each of these vices, when at times they do appear, may be matched by examples of the same vices in the judiciary. * * *

The problem of adapting the administrative process to the magnitude of its task is still a formidable one, but it is not hopeless. The necessity for administrative tribunals is too apparent to permit the enemies of effective government to destroy them. On the other hand, the need for the process to be committed to hands that are dispassionate and disciplined is too obvious to allow any widespread or long-continued abuses of their position. The leisurely process of political evolution may try the patience of impetuous men, but it is the source of hope for the far-sighted ones.   *   *   * "

Judicial Review of Administrative Actions

Whether the administrative actions be legislative, or executive or judicial, the courts agree that school boards or officials may exercise those powers expressly granted by statute, and those fairly and necessarily implied.

> The rule respecting such powers is that, in addition to the powers expressly given by statute to an officer or board of officers, he or it has by implication such additional powers as are necessary for the due and efficient exercise of the powers expressly granted or which may be fairly implied from the statute granting the express powers.[32]

While some flexibility in discretion is necessary, indeed indispensable for the schools to operate efficiently, the courts cannot usurp the legislative function by too broad an interpretation of administrative powers.[33]

In challenging the exercise of administrative powers by an educational agency, be they express or implied, the aggrieved parties are required by the courts to exhaust their administrative remedies before they are allowed to bring an action before the courts. Such a rule assures the courts that issues have been properly treated at lower levels, within the realm of administrative authority, thus preventing continuous involvement of the courts in educational disputes where legitimate legal controversy is not present. Examples of the hesitancy of courts to intervene until administrative remedies are exhausted may be found in many instances.[34]

In New York, the state administrative decisions are considered to have substantial weight owing largely to a statute which provides that decisions of the commissioner of education "shall be final and conclusive, and not subject to question or review in any place or court whatsoever". While this provision on its face would appear to preclude any judicial intervention, the true "intent" has been inter-

---

32. A. H. Andrews Co. v. Delight Special School Dist., 95 Ark. 26, 128 S.W. 361 (1910).

33. Edwards, op. cit. p. 147.

34. Knox County Bd. of Educ. v. Fultz, 241 Ky. 265, 43 S.W.2d 707 (1931); Lyerley v. Manila School Dist., 214 Ark. 245, 215 S.W.2d 733 (1948);

Board of Educ. v. County Bd. of School Trustees, 25 Ill.App.2d 390, 166 N.E.2d 472 (1960); Detroit Edison Co. v. East China Township School Dist., 366 Mich. 638, 115 N.W.2d 298 (1962); School Dist. No. 12, Phillips County v. Hughes, 170 Mont. 267, 552 P.2d 328 (1976).

preted to mean that <u>the decisions of the commissioner would stand so long as they were not arbitrary.</u>[35]

Quasi-judicial authority of the state board of education in Kentucky has, likewise, been held to be final unless it clearly appears that the board's actions are "unreasonable, arbitrary or capricious". The general rule of law is probably best expounded by an Illinois court which stated:

> * * * A court of review cannot substitute its judgment for the judgment of the administrative tribunal. The question is not simply whether the court of review agrees or disagrees with the finding below. It has been said that courts should not disturb administrative findings unless such findings are arbitrary, or constitute an abuse of discretion, or are without substantial foundation in evidence, or are obviously and clearly wrong, or unless an opposite conclusion is clearly evident.[36]

While this rule governing judicial review of administrative actions is generally followed by courts across the country, the individual interpretations of the rule are widely variant ranging from rather strict adherence to what some would consider to be relative disregard. As a matter of fact, courts may exercise their prerogatives to intervene and alter administrative action with several different legal bases. <u>Ministerial actions of government agencies have been successfully challenged under the ancient legal doctrines of nonfeasance, misfeasance or malfeasance.</u> Under each of these the public official or board has a particular function to perform but does not do so in a manner which is anticipated by legislation. Failure to respond properly may be remedied by the courts by use of the common law remedy, writ of *mandamus*. <u>If the aggrieved party is seeking to prevent an inappropriate action, then an *injunction* may be the appropriate legal remedy.</u>

On the other hand, if discretionary actions are in question, then the person challenging the action may proceed from a broader legal basis. As mentioned above, fairness and reasonableness of action are requisite to appropriate use of quasi-judicial authority of an agency. More directly, discretionary powers may be viewed quite broadly and if an agency acts beyond the scope of its powers it may well be *ultra vires*. A discretionary power may be abused in either good faith or in bad faith, but in both instances the action may be voided by the courts.[37] Beyond inquiry into *vires*, judicial intervention may be jus-

---

35. Board of Educ. of City of New York v. Allen, 6 N.Y.2d 127, 188 N.Y. S.2d 515, 160 N.E.2d 60 (1959).

36. Board of Educ. v. County Bd. of School Trustees, 32 Ill.App.2d 1, 176 N.E.2d 633 (Ill.1961).

37. de Smith, *op. cit.* p. 283.

tifiable if: (1) A power granted to an agency is not properly applied. Here the courts will seek to determine whether the agency had either express or implied statutory power to perform as it did and if the statute was broad enough with possibly a plurality of purposes sufficient to support the action. The court here will generally apply certain tests including seeking to ascertain (a) the true purpose for the action, (b) the dominant purpose, and (c) if there was an unauthorized or illicit purpose,[38] whether the action is taken in bad faith may come into play. (2) Exercise of discretionary power may also be challenged if the agency, official or tribunal was influenced by considerations which could not have been lawfully taken into account or if it ignored obviously relevant considerations. Plaintiff, though, must show that irrelevant considerations were actually relied upon in the decision. Certainly if extraneous or irrelevant matters are set out as reasons in support of the decision then courts may consider the result to be invalid. (3) Prescription of law is not followed in effecting administrative actions. While most instances which come to mind here involve ministerial functions e. g., following election procedures or budgetary submission processes, the educational agency's action may also be challenged if it fails to recognize or appreciate the amplitude of its discretion.[39] For example, a state authority may have the statutory power to grant salary increases or increase fringe benefits but misconstrues and through misunderstanding fails to recognize the discretion. Here it is not the reasonableness of the decision made by the agency but the failure of the agency to recognize its power which is judicially questionable. (4) A public education board binds itself through its own regulation in such a way as to constrict or disable itself from fulfilling the primary purposes for which it was created. Where a public body is entrusted by the legislature with certain powers and duties either express or implied for public purposes, the body cannot divest itself of such powers and duties. Regulations or bylaws which effectively thwart statutory intent, for example, by contracting away a power or requiring the exercise of a broad power in a restrictive way, may be unreasonable and incompatible with public purpose.

Courts will not penalize a state agency for possible error in the exercise of discretion where judgment or opinion of the public officials are in contest. If there are reasonable grounds the judge has no further duty to inquire. The criterion of reasonableness is not subjective, but objective in the sense that it must be weighed in light of surrounding facts and circumstances.

38. Ibid, pp. 288, 289.   39. Ibid, p. 279.

*Action by State Board of Education Relating to Internal
Education Affairs is Final Unless Found to be
Arbitrary, Capricious, or Fraudulent*

BLAIR v. BOARD OF TRUSTEES, TRINITY IND. SCHOOL DIST.

Court of Civil Appeals of Texas, Galveston, 1942.
161 S.W.2d 1030.

MONTEITH, Chief Justice. This suit was brought by appellant, E. L. Blair, to set aside an order of the Board of Trustees of the Trinity Independent School District and the Board of Education of the State of Texas finding him guilty of certain charges brought against him by the Board of Trustees and discharging him as Superintendent of Schools of the Trinity Independent School District.

The Board of Trustees charged appellant with withholding, mishandling, and misapplying funds belonging to the school district and with failure to divulge information in reference to the handling of said funds, and notified him that he would be given a hearing on said charges before the Board. Upon a hearing thereon, an order was entered by the Board finding him guilty of said charges and discharging him from his position as Superintendent of its schools. He appealed from this order to the State Superintendent of Public Instruction, who, after a hearing, reversed the order of the Board of Trustees and reinstated appellant as Superintendent of Schools of said district. The Board of Trustees then appealed to the State Board of Education, which Board, after a hearing, reversed the order of the Superintendent of Public Instruction and affirmed the order of the Board of Trustees.

This suit is an appeal to the district court of Trinity County, Texas, from the order of the State Board of Education.

*   *   *

The controlling questions to be determined in the appeal are, (1) whether or not the charges brought against appellant by said Board of Trustees and its order based thereon discharging him as superintendent of its schools involved matters relating to the internal affairs of the school and the efficient management thereof, and (2) whether or not the action of the State Board of Education in its hearing of the appeal from the order of the State Superintendent of Instruction was arbitrary, capricious, or fraudulent.

The parts of Article 2656, R.S.1925, material to this appeal provide: "The State Superintendent shall be charged with the administration of the school laws and a general superintendency of the business relating to the public schools of the State * * *. He shall hear and determine all appeals from the rulings and decisions of subordinate school officers, and all of the officers and teachers shall conform to his decisions. Appeal shall always be from his rulings to the State Board. * * *

In discussing the confusion that has heretofore existed concerning the effect to be given the findings of fact by an administrative agency, upon a contest of an order of such agency in court, the Supreme Court, speaking through Chief Justice Alexander, in the case of Railroad Commission of Texas et al. v. Shell Oil Co., Inc., et al., 161 S. W.2d 1022, in an opinion handed down on March 11, 1942, has laid down the following rule: "* * * our statutes do not provide for the making of any findings of fact by an administrative agency. Nevertheless, when the validity of an order of such an agency is contested in court, certain presumptions are indulged in favor of the validity of such order in some instances. If the matter covered by the order is one committed to the agency by the Legislature, and involves the exercise of its sound judgment and discretion in the administration of the matter so committed to it, the court will not undertake to put itself in the position of the agency, and determine the wisdom or advisability of the particular ruling or order in question, but will sustain the action of the agency so long as its conclusions are reasonably supported by substantial evidence. This is so because, since the Legislature has seen fit to vest the authority to exercise sound judgment and discretion in the particular matter in the administrative agency, courts will not undertake to usurp the powers committed to the agency, and to exercise the agency's judgment and discretion for it. For example, in contesting an order of a commissioners' court fixing a tax rate, or an order of a school board concerning the management of schools, the court will not put itself in the position of the administrative agency for the purpose of determining whether or not the action was wise. Wright v. Allen, Tex.Civ.App., 257 S.W. 980, par. 4, writ refused; Young County Board of School Trustees v. Bailey, Tex.Civ.App., 61 S.W.2d 130, par. 2, writ refused. In such a case the issue is not whether or not the agency came to the proper fact conclusion on the basis of conflicting evidence, but whether or not it acted arbitrarily and without regard to the facts. * * * In Texas, in all trials contesting the validity of an order, rule, or regulation of an administrative agency, the trial is not for the purpose of determining whether the agency actually heard sufficient evidence to support its orders, but whether at the time such order was entered by the agency there then existed sufficient facts to justify the same. Whether the agency heard sufficient evidence is not material. * * * "

* * *

"By the provisions of the above statute [Art. 2656, R.S.1925] the Legislature has committed to the state superintendent, as one specially trained and experienced in school matters, the responsibility of deciding all questions relating to the internal affairs and management of the public schools of Texas. His decisions in such matters are final unless reversed by the state board of education. When an appeal is taken from his decision to the state board of education, the decision of that board becomes final and cannot and will not be interfered with by the courts unless such board acts arbitrarily or is actuated by fraud or abuses its discretion. The findings of such board on matters committed to its jurisdiction, when not arbitrary or capricious, are prima facie true and are as binding on the courts as is the verdict of a jury, and the court will not put itself in the position of the board and try the question anew for the purpose of testing the expediency or wisdom of the decision of the board, nor for the purpose of determining whether or not under similar testimony it would have made a similar or a different ruling."

The question before the school board and the State Board of Education in the instant case was one of fact relating to the manner in which appellant was performing his duties as superintendent of schools in connection with the handling and application of the finances of the school district which had been entrusted to his care. There was no implication in the findings made by the school board that appellant had been guilty of an intentional misapplication of the funds belonging to the school district, or of an intention on his part to appropriate the funds of the school to his own use and benefit. The board simply found as a fact that appellant had, "withheld, mishandled and misapplied funds belonging to the Trinity Independent School District" which had been entrusted to his custody as superintendent of its schools, and that he had "failed to divulge material information relative to the handling of said funds to the trustees of the school district." The question as to whether appellant should have been discharged for one or more of the reasons set out in the charges preferred against him were, we think, matters of fact relating to the internal affairs of the school and the efficient management thereof and "came within the purview of the matters committed by the Legislature to such board for its determination" and the decision of the State Board that appellant had been properly discharged was final on that issue.

Appellant's contention that the State Board of Education acted arbitrarily, capriciously, or fraudulently in affirming the judgment of the Board of Trustees of the Trinity Independent School District cannot be sustained. As stated by the Supreme Court in the case of Railroad Commission of Texas v. Shell Oil Co., Inc., et al., supra, it is generally recognized that where the order of the agency under attack involves the exercise of the sound judgment and discretion of the agency in a matter committed to it by the Legislature, the court will sustain the order if the action of the agency in reaching such conclusion is reasonably supported by substantial evidence, and, at the time such order was entered by the agency, there then existed sufficient facts to justify the entry of the order.

* * * A transcript of all evidence heard by the State Superintendent was before the State Board of Education on the appeal from the ruling of the State Superintendent. The record shows that appellant was present and was represented by counsel at all hearings before the school authorities, and that no objection was made to the introduction in evidence of the audit made by the accountant employed by the school board, or the report thereon. As above stated, the fact to be determined in the hearing before the State Board was whether it was shown by substantial evidence that sufficient facts existed to justify the entry of the order. Under the above facts we think that there was ample evidence in the record to support the decision of the State Board of Education and appellant's contention that such decision was arbitrary, capricious or unreasonable, for that reason cannot be sustained.

* * *

It follows from above conclusions that the judgment of the trial court must be, in all things, affirmed. It is so ordered.

Affirmed.

NOTES

1. Concerning the judicial nature of the actions of the New York Commissioner of Education a New York court said:

"In appraising the judicial nature of the act of the Commissioner of Education it must be remembered that he combines both judicial and administrative functions, when he decides appeals where he has occasion to construe statutes, he undoubtedly acts in a judicial capacity. But in passing upon the propriety of educational policy by a particular school board or school district he acts in a broader capacity than the courts, by reviewing at times administrative acts of discretion of which a court would refuse to take cognizance."

Craig v. Board of Educ. of City of New York, 173 Misc. 969, 19 N.Y.S.2d 293 (1940); affirmed on appeal, 262 App.Div. 706, 27 N.Y.S. 993.

"There is some suggestion also that under Section 310 of the Education Law the remedy of the plaintiffs is by appeal to the Commissioner of Education. It is true that under that section, the courts have held that in matters involving policy, administration or intradepartmental disputes or the like, the remedy provided by that section is exclusive but that is not so in matters involving a tax levy or third parties not connected with the Education Department; that in such cases the Supreme Court has jurisdiction. * * * Also it has been held that where the right of a party depends upon the interpretation of a statute and it is claimed that a school board or official has proceeded to act in violation of an express statute, and thereby the party complaining is being deprived of valuable rights, the courts will not be ousted of jurisdiction to determine the matter, notwithstanding another method of settling the controversy has been provided."

Finley v. Spaulding, 192 Misc. 860, 81 N.Y.S.2d 890 (1948).

2. The decision of the Commissioner of Education of New York in interpreting statute is to be given great weight by the courts and unless irrational or unreasonable it will be upheld. Board of Educ. of Roslyn Union Free School Dist. v. Nyquist, 90 Misc.2d 955, 396 N.Y.S.2d 567 (1977).

3. Administrative agencies in quasi-judicial hearings have traditionally not been held to the intricate procedural requirement of the courts, however, there are fundamental requirements of a fairness which must be observed. A West Virginia court had this to say concerning the conduct of hearings by administrative agencies.

> "An administrative body, clothed by law with quasi-judicial powers, must never depart from those elemental principles of discreetness and circumspection which our system of law requires in all tribunals which purport to conduct trials. * * * There was a time in the history of English jurisprudence when a felon was not entitled to have the assistance of an attorney at law, but in America, the very word 'hearing', both in common and legal parlance, implies some kind of trial, formal or informal, and presupposes permission to have legal aid if desired."

State ex rel. Rogers v. Board of Educ. of Lewis County, 125 W.Va. 579, 25 S.E.2d 537 (1943).

4. Legislation in Texas has been interpreted to mean that all administrative steps should be taken to resolve a dispute before appeal can be taken to the courts. Exception to this rule is only found where an action involves a question of taxation (City of Dallas v. Mosely, 286 S.W. 497 (Texas 1926), if the facts are undisputed and the issue is one purely of law and not of education; in such instances direct access to the courts is available. (Alvin Independent School Dist. v. Cooper, 404 S.W.2d 76 (Texas 1966).

5. A Maryland court has held that the State Board of Education has the last word on any matter concerning educational policy or administration of the system of public instruction; however, it cannot finally decide pure questions of law nor exercise its visitatorial power fraudulently, in bad faith or in breach of trust. Where the State Board of Education of Maryland set a rule of a county board of education requiring fingerprint cards of all employees to be submitted to local police, the court upheld the action of the State Board as being a valid exercise of its authority. Wilson v. Board of Ed. of Montgomery County, 234 Md. 561, 200 A.2d 67 (1964).

6. A Missouri court has held that, where four local school districts were unable to reorganize because of refusal of one to discuss the matter, the state board of education was vested with exclusive jurisdiction to make the decision for the board and once this decision by the state board was approved by the voters, the school district became officially and legally organized. Eagleton ex rel. Reorganized School Dist. R—I of Miller County v. Van Landuyt, Mo., 359 S.W.2d 773 (1962).

7. Examples of grants of legislative and judicial power to the United States Commissioner of Education are demonstrated in the Elementary and Secondary Education Act of 1965:

> "Whenever the Commissioner, after reasonable notice and opportunity for hearing to any state educational agency, finds that there has been a failure to comply substantially with any assurance set

forth in the application of that state approved under Section 205(c) or 260(b), the Commissioner shall notify the agency that further payments will not be made to the State under this title * * * until he is satisfied that there is no longer any failure to comply."

In this instance there is, of course, no federal board of education which coincides with a state board of education. The complete regulatory and quasi-judicial authority is vested in one man, the Commissioner of Education. With the action taken by the Congress in 1979, creating a new Department of Education, the locus of authority will change to the Secretary of Education, but the governmental model will remain the same.

Chapter 5

LOCAL GOVERNANCE OF SCHOOLS

Local governance of the public schools is vested in the school board which promulgates regulations and exercises discretion in the public interest. The local school district is a state agency, created by either statute or constitution, to which the legislature by law delegates the power to govern the schools. A Michigan court described the legal relationship between the state and local school districts in this way:

> Fundamentally, provision for and control of our public school system is a state matter, delegated and lodged in the state legislature by the Constitution in a separate article entirely distinct from that relating to local government. The general policy of the state has been to retain control of its school system, to be administered throughout the state under state laws by local state agencies organized with plenary powers independent of the local government with which, by location and geographical boundaries, they are necessarily closely associated and to a greater or lesser extent authorized to co-operate. "Education belongs to the state." [1]

Since local school districts are state agencies, it follows that school board members are state, not local officials. [2] Local school boards are vested with a portion of the sovereignty of the state through delegation by which they acquire certain administrative functions having attributes of all three branches of government, executive, quasi-judicial and regulatory or quasi-legislative. As creatures of the legislature or constitution, local school districts abide within their legal prerogatives and cannot give away or re-delegate their judgmental powers to other agencies or individuals.

The courts commonly divide the administrative functions of the local school board into two categories, discretionary and ministerial. The meaning of discretionary powers here is those acts which require judgment on the part of the board. Examples of such responsibilities could be the location of a school building site, the employment of a particular teacher or the purchase of a certain type of school bus. The greatest portion of a board's powers may be classified as discretionary. In exercising these discretionary powers a board of education is only limited by the requirements and restrictions of the law. As has been pointed out in the case of state education agencies, the

---

1. MacQueen v. City Comm. of City of Port Huron, 194 Mich. 328, 160 N.W. 627 (1916).

2. Board of Educ. Louisville v. Society of Alumni of Louisville Male High School, 239 S.W.2d 931 (Ky.1951).

118

courts will not interfere with a board's exercise of discretion even though the judgment is unwise except where the board's action violates the law, abuses authority, or is an ultra vires act.

Ministerial acts neither require nor permit the exercise of subjective judgment. Specifically ministerial duties may be requirements that a board publish an annual financial report, obtain a signature on a contract, or prepare a budget for approval by the board of education. *Courts have generally held that a board can delegate ministerial powers to subordinate employees of the school district, but cannot delegate discretionary powers.

The operation of school districts is based upon the express or implied authority of statute. The courts in circumscribing the authority of school boards from statutory implication have held that in the absence of statute, travel expenses can be paid for the recruitment of teachers outside the state,[3] a school district can establish a cafeteria,[4] and a school board can establish a school health inspection department made up of doctors, dentists and nurses.[5] On the other hand, authority has been denied for a school district to pay for surgical and dental operations for pupils,[6] for medical care for pupils injured in athletic contests,[7] and for purchase of basketball uniforms to be used on land not under school control.[8]

School Districts Can Exercise Only Those Powers Fairly Implied or Expressly Granted by Statute

McGILVRA v. SEATTLE SCHOOL DIST., NO. 1

Supreme Court of Washington, 1921.
113 Wash. 619, 194 P.2d 817.

PARKER, J. The plaintiffs, McGilvra and others, residents and taxpayers of Seattle school district No. 1, of King county, suing for themselves and in behalf of all others similarly situated, commenced this action in the superior court for that county seeking an injunction to restrain the school district and its officers from maintaining in one of its school buildings and expending funds of the school district for the maintenance therein of a so-called "clinic," which, as we proceed we think it will appear would be more properly designated as a "hospital," for the medical, surgical, and dental treatment of the physical ailments of pupils of the schools of the district, whose parents or

3. School District No. 1, Multnomah County v. Bruck, 225 Or. 496, 358 P.2d 283 (1960).

4. Goodman v. School Dist., 32 F.2d 586 (C.C.A.Colo.1929).

5. Hallett v. Post Printing & Pub. Co., 68 Colo. 573, 192 p. 658 (1920).

6. McGilvra v. Seattle School Dist. No. 1, 113 Wash. 619, 194 p. 817 (1921).

7. Jarrett v. Goodall, 113 W.Va. 478, 168 S.E. 763 (1933).

8. Brine v. City of Cambridge, 265 Mass. 452, 164 N.E. 619 (1929).

guardians are financially unable to furnish such treatment. Trial in the superior court upon the merits resulted in findings and judgment denying the relief prayed for, from which the plaintiffs have appealed to this court.

* * *

The question to be here answered is: Have the school district and its officers legal authority for so furnishing the use of, and equipping rooms in its buildings and the maintenance therein of such clinic, by the expenditure of the taxpayers' funds collected and placed at their disposal, for the sole purpose of maintaining the public schools of the district? At the outset let us be reminded in the language of Judge Dillon, in his work on Municipal Corporations, quoted with approval by this court in State ex rel. Winsor v. Mayor and Council, 10 Wash. 4, 37 Pac. 761, that—

"It is a general and undisputed proposition of law that a municipal corporation possesses and can exercise the following powers, and no others: First, those granted in express words; second, those necessarily or fairly implied in or incident to the powers expressly granted; third, those essential to the declared objects and purposes of the corporation—not simply convenient but indispensable. Any fair or reasonable doubt concerning the existence of power is resolved by the courts against the corporation, and the power is denied."

This view of the law is of added weight when applied to school districts, because they are municipal corporations with powers of a much more limited character than are cities, or towns, or even than counties. * * *

* * *

We are quite unable to find in * * * statutory provisions any power given to the school district officers, other than the power to cause inspection of the buildings and premises of the district to be made with a view to making them sanitary and healthful, and to cause inspection of persons with a view to the exclusion from the school premises of all persons afficted with contagious diseases, to the end that such diseases shall not obtain a foothold among the pupils and other persons whose duties require them to be upon the school premises.

Counsel for the school district officers call our attention to, and rely upon, our decision in State ex rel. School District No. 56 v. Superior Court, 69 Wash. 189, 124 Pac. 484, and Sorenson v. Perkins & Co., 72 Wash. 16, 129 Pac. 577, commonly known as the "playground" and "gymnasium" cases, wherein it was held that a school district has the power to acquire, by expenditure of the funds of the district, additional land for playgrounds for the pupils, and also at the expense of the district to construct and equip gymnasiums. We do not think these cases are of any controlling force touching the present inquiry. Playgrounds in connection with public schools have for generations been so common that it must be presumed that the Legislature by giving the general power to maintain public schools incidentally intended to also give the authority to provide such playgrounds in connection therewith; and, while gymnasiums in connection with public schools have not been so common, the work and exercise of the students carried on therein is manifestly so intimately connected with the education of the pupil as to warrant the assumption that the Legislature intended the school districts and their officers to possess the power of providing the same as a proper public school equipment. The rendering of medical, surgical, and dental services to the pupils, however, is, and always has been, we think, so foreign to the powers to be exercised by a school district or its officers, that such power cannot be held to exist in the absence of express legislative language so providing.

*   *   *

The specific legislative enumeration of these powers which it seems could with much sounder reason be considered as implied powers in the absence of express language in the statute than the claimed powers here in question, argues, in the light of well-settled rules of statutory construction, that the Legislature has not intended that there should be an exercise of such claimed powers. We see no argument lending any substantial support, in a legal way, to the view that a school district and its officers possess the powers they are seeking to exercise and threatening to continue to exercise. There is much in the argument of counsel for the school officers which might be considered as lending support to the view that such powers ought to be possessed by the school district and its officers, and it is probable that counsel has many well meaning people upon his side of that question. The Legislature may give heed to such arguments, but the courts cannot do so.

The judgment of the trial court is reversed, and the case remanded to that court, with directions to render a judgment enjoining the school district and its officers from furnishing or equipping upon the school premises, or elsewhere, appliances for the medical, surgical, or dental treatment of the physical ailments of the pupils of the schools at the expense of the district, and from employing physicians, dentists, or nurses for the rendering of such medical, surgical, or dental treatment; it being understood, however, that such injunction shall not restrain the school district or its officers from the doing of these things at the expense of the district in connection with, and as may be necessary in, the maintenance of the parental schools of the district and the proper care of the pupils committed to such schools.

NOTES

The school district is a state agency. Moreover, it is of legislative creation. It is true that it was provided for in obedience to a constitutional requirement; and whatever we may think of the right of the district to administer in a local way the affairs of the district, under the Constitution, we cannot doubt that such management must be in conformity to the provisions of such laws of a general character as may from time to time be passed, and that the property of the district is in no sense private property, but is public property devoted to the purposes of the state, for the general good, just as almshouses and courthouses are, although confided to local management, and applied to uses which are in a sense local, though in another sense general. Attorney General v. Lowrey, 131 Mich. 639, 92 N.W. 289 (1902).

School Board Cannot Re-delegate Its
Rule-making Power

BUNGER v. IOWA HIGH SCHOOL ATHLETIC ASS'N

Supreme Court of Iowa, 1972.
197 N.W.2d 555.

UHLENHOPP, Justice. This case involves the validity of a rule of the Iowa High School Athletic Association (which we will refer to as IHSAA or the association).

IHSAA is an unincorporated association in charge of boys' interscholastic athletic events in Iowa, including tournaments. Waverly-Shell Rock Community School District is a member of IHSAA, as are all other high schools in Iowa except the school at Kalona. Member schools agree to abide by the constitution and bylaws of IHSAA, which may be amended by referendum of the members. * * *

Under the constitution and bylaws, a member school cannot allow an athlete who is known to be ineligible to engage in interscholastic athletic events. Nor can a member school engage in such events with a nonmember school. A member school violating the constitution or bylaws is subject to probation, suspension, or expulsion. One portion of the constitution and bylaws deals with eligibility of athletes to participate in interscholastic events.

The member schools strongly oppose the use of alcoholic beverages by athletes. In recent years, the drinking problem has increased, particularly the drinking of beer. Attempts by individual school boards to deal with the problem proved unsatisfactory. School boards and administrators were sometimes under local pressure to play outstanding athletes notwithstanding infractions, and different boards had varying rules relating to similar violations.

Largely at the behest of the schools themselves, a committee of IHSAA studied the problem and proposed rules which were adopted by a substantial majority vote of the membership.   *   *   *

     *   *   *

Item 2: In the event a boy pleads guilty or is found guilty of using alcoholic beverages or pleads guilty or is found guilty of the use of dangerous drugs, or the transportation of either such beverages or drugs, he shall be declared ineligible for participation in interscholastic athletic competition for a minimum of six weeks for the first offense. (Individual member schools may exclude a boy for more than six weeks.)   *   *   *

This section is known as the Good Conduct Rule and Item 2 of it is known as the "beer rule."

Purporting to interpret the beer rule, the board of control adopted the following ruling (which we will refer to as "the interpretation" or "the rule"):

A boy shall lose at least 6 weeks of interscholastic competition if he is found guilty of possession, consumption or transportation of alcoholic beverages or dangerous drugs, or if he admits to a school administrator, the coach or an officer of the law that he has possessed or consumed such beverages or drugs. A boy is also subject to the same loss of eligibility if he is in a vehicle stopped by a law officer and alcoholic beverages and/or dangerous drugs are found in the vehicle.   *   *   *

The State Department of Public Instruction approved the Good Conduct Rule and the interpretation of it and IHSAA disseminated that Rule and the interpretation among its members. The members made the Rule and interpretation known to athletes, including plaintiff William Hal Bunger. William is a 16-year-old football player of ability on the outstanding Waverly-Shell Rock team.

On the evening of June 7, 1971, William and three other minors were riding in a car containing a case of beer. William knew the beer was in the car. An Iowa highway patrolman stopped the four minors, discovered the beer, and issued summonses to all four for possession of beer as minors. Three pleaded guilty. William pleaded not guilty, and the charges against him were subsequently dismissed by the county attorney.

On June 10, 1971, William reported the beer incident to his school athletic director and stated he knew at the time that the beer was in the car. Thereupon, the school officials declared William ineligible for six weeks commencing with the opening of the fall football season.

William brought the present suit to enjoin enforcement of the rule. The trial court upheld the rule, and William appealed.

William levels a number of charges against the rule. We think, however, that we need not consider all of his claims, for two basic questions control the case. First, does IHSAA have authority to promulgate the rule in question? Second, is the rule valid on its merits? We confine ourselves to the rule before us rendering ineligible an athlete who occupies a car with knowledge of the presence of beer which is found by a law officer.

I. *Authority to Promulgate the Rule.* In our scheme of things, authority to provide for the educational interests of the state is confided in the General Assembly. * * * Pursuant to that authority, the legislature has provided for school districts, to be under the control of elected district directors. * * *

Can a school board re-delegate its rule-making power regarding pupils to some other organization? Several courts have considered this question to more or less extent, although under statutes or facts distinguishable from the present ones * * *.

Rule-making by school boards involves the exercise of judgment and discretion. The legislature has delegated rule-making to those boards, and the general principle is that while a public board or body may authorize performance of ministerial or administrative functions by others, it cannot re-delegate matters of judgment or discretion. * * * The general principle is stated thus in 2 Am.Jur.2d Administrative Law § 222 at 52:

> It is a general principle of law, expressed in the maxim "delegatus non potest delegare," that a delegated power may not be further delegated by the person to whom such power is delegated, and that in all cases of delegated authority, where personal trust or confidence is reposed in the agent and especially where the exercise and application of the power is made subject to his judgment or discretion, the authority is purely personal and cannot be delegated to another unless there is a special power of substitution either express or necessarily implied.

As to school authorities in particular, this is stated in C.J.S. Schools and School Districts § 122 at 910:

> In accordance with the rule applicable to public boards and officers generally * * * a board of education, or of directors, trustees, or the like, of a school district or other local school organization cannot lawfully delegate to others, whether to one or more of its members, or to any school officer, or to any other board, the exercise of any discretionary power conferred on it by law. * * *

Cases are legion involving application of the principle to various agencies and governmental units, including schools. * * *

But IHSAA contends the rule in question is actually a rule of each individual school board, in that each board agrees to abide by the rules of IHSAA when it joins the association. By joining the association, IHSAA says, each board promulgates IHSAA's rules as its own.

We think this contention is inconsonant with the realities of the situation. The rules are actually association rules. A rule is initially adopted by majority vote of the association members. Bearing in mind that a school board cannot re-delegate its rule-making power, how can we say that a school which votes against a proposed rule has itself promulgated that rule? Again, a school which joins IHSAA after a number of rules have been adopted has no choice as to the rules it will accept. It must take them all and abdicate its nondelegable responsibility to select the rules it wishes to have. Then what about a member school which becomes dissatisfied with a rule? It has no power to repeal the rule. To say the school can withdraw from IHSAA is no answer. If it leaves IHSAA voluntarily, or involuntarily for violating the rule, its boys' interscholastic athletic program is at an end—except for playing Kalona. Its hands are tied. The power is actually in the association, not in each school board where the statute places it.

What we have here, in fact, is an association which started out arranging inter-school games and tournaments and grew into an organization above individual schools, regulating all manner of affairs relating to athletes. The association did not usurp the regulatory functions of individual schools; the schools turned over those functions to the association.

IHSAA also contends that a statute has been enacted which makes the rule valid in two separate ways—by authorizing schools to delegate their rule-making power to an association, and by authorizing the association itself to make rules subject to the approval of the State Board of Public Instruction. The statute is § 257.25(10), Code, 1971. * * *

> * * * For the purposes of this subsection "organization" means any corporation, association, or organization which has as one of its primary purposes the sponsoring or administration of extracurricular interscholastic contests or competitions; but shall not include any agency of this state, any public or private school or school board, or any athletic conference or other association whose interscholastic contests or competitions do not include more than twenty schools.

Enactment of § 257.25(10) probably resulted in part from a desire on the part of schools to obtain interscholastic activity rules of statewide uniformity.

Our statutes also provide that if a state agency promulgates a rule of general application, as distinguished from a rule relating solely to the internal operation of the agency, the agency must submit the rule to the Attorney General and the Legislative Departmental Rules Committee for a prescribed procedure. Code, 1971, ch. 17A.

In accordance with § 257.25(10), the State Board of Public Instruction in 1966 promulgated several rules regarding athletic associations and interscholastic athletic events, and complied with the procedure prescribed by chapter 17A. See 1971 Iowa Dept'l Rules 656–657. But none of the rules related to the subject matter of the rule before us.

In 1968 IHSAA adopted the Good Conduct Rule and the interpretation of it and reported them to the State Department of Public Instruction, which approved them. But the State Board did not promulgate them as its own rules or put them through chapter 17A procedure.

IHSAA's first contention, that § 257.25(10) authorizes school boards to redelegate to it their rule-making authority, overextends the statute. The language of § 257.25(10) is that public schools shall not allow students to participate in an interscholastic contest or competition "which is sponsored or administered by an organization as defined in this subsection" unless the organization registers and files financial statements with the State Department of Public Instruction and complies with the Board's rules. An "organization" is defined to include an association such as IHSAA.

This language of § 257.25(10) clearly means that schools may participate in interscholastic events sponsored by qualifying organizations, and we think it also means, inferentially, that schools may belong to such organizations. But the language cannot be stretched to mean that schools may turn over their statutory rule-making authority to such organizations.

IHSAA's second contention, that § 257.25(10) authorizes IHSAA itself to promulgate rules if approved by the State Department of Public Instruction is contrary to the language of the statute. Subsection 10 permits schools to allow students to participate in interscholastic events sponsored by organizations that are, among other things, "in compliance with rules and regulations which the *state board of public instruction shall adopt* for the proper administration, supervision, operation, *eligibility requirements*, and scheduling of such extracurricular interscholastic contests and competitions. * * *" (Italics added.) Thus the eligibility rule-making authority, so far as § 257.25(10) is concerned, is in the State Board, not in IHSAA. Moreover, since promulgation of eligibility rules involves judgment and discretion, we think the State Board cannot re-delegate its rule-making authority under § 257.25(10) any more than a school board can re-delegate its rule-making authority under § 279.8. * * *

The rule before us is, in fact, a rule of IHSAA and not of the Waverly-Shell Rock Board of Education or of the State Board. Neither of the latter public bodies could re-delegate its rule-making authority. We hold that the rule is invalid for want of authority in IHSAA to promulgate it.

* * *

NOTES

Validity of athletic association rules have been challenged on both the "delegation" grounds of *Bunger* and on the grounds of "reasonableness" as in Robinson v. Illinois High School Ass'n, 45 Ill.App.2d 277, 195 N.E.2nd 38 (1963), certiorari denied 379 U.S. 960, 85 S.Ct. 647 (1965). The South Carolina Supreme Court upheld a rule of the state high school athletic association that excluded a transfer student from high school athletic competition for a period of one year. The court said the rule was reasonable because it prevented interschool recruitment of high school athletes. The issue of illegal delegation was apparently not tested in this case. Bruce v. South Carolina High School League, 258 S.C. 546, 189 S.E.2d 817 (1972).

In line with *Bunger*, a California court held that educational institutions can delegate to athletic associations only as much power as they themselves are given to delegate by the legislature. Cabrillo Community College Dist. of Santa Cruz County v. California Junior College Ass'n, 44 Cal.App. 3d 367, 118 Cal.Rptr. 708 (1975).

School Board Cannot Re-delegate Its Discretionary Powers

JOHNSON v. SABINE PARISH SCHOOL BD.

Court of Appeal of Louisiana, Second
Circuit, Second Division, 1932.
19 La.App. 243, 140 So. 87.

STEPHENS, J. The plaintiff brought this suit against the defendant to enforce the specific performance of an alleged contract; or, in the alternative, for damages in the sum of $866 for its breach.

* * *

The plaintiff stated the case in his petition as follows:

"That on the 6th day of August, 1930, the Sabine Parish School Board passed the following resolutions, to-wit:

" 'On motion duly seconded and carried Mr. Cates was authorized to secure a driver for the transfer route driven by Mr. Kegley to the Noble School for session 1930–31;' and the said resolution was published in the minutes of the Sabine Parish School Board, in the Sabine Index, August 15, 1930.

"That acting under and by virtue of the authority conferred upon him, by the said resolution, the said A. B. Cates for, and in the name of the Sabine Parish School Board, offered to contract and did contract with your petitioner, on the 23rd day of August, 1930, to drive the school transfer on the Kegley Transfer Route to the Noble School for the session of 1930 and 1931, at a salary of Eighty-five and No/100 ($85.00) Dollars per month for nine months.

"That G. C. Reeves, Superintendent of the Public Schools of Sabine Parish, and Secretary of the Sabine Parish School Board, assured your petitioner on the 25th day of August, 1930, that A. B. Cates had the authority as published in the resolution contained in the Minutes of the Sabine Parish School Board in the Sabine Index, on August 15th, 1930, to employ a driver to transfer the children for the Kegley Transfer Route to the Noble School for the session of 1930 and 1931; and that the said contract with and through the said A. B. Cates was valid and binding on the Sabine Parish School Board.

*   *   *

"That notwithstanding the said contract made with your petitioner, and accepted by petitioner in good faith, and the expense incurred by petitioner, as hereinabove set forth, preparatory to complying with, and carrying out his part of said contract, the Sabine Parish School Board, on the 3rd day of September, 1930, met in special session, and with full knowledge of all the facts herein set forth willfully disregarded and violated said contract with petitioner, by employing another man to transfer the school children on the Kegley transfer route to the Noble School.   *   *   * "

The statute which empowers the school boards of the several parishes to provide transportation for school children reads as follows: "That the Parish school boards shall have the authority to provide transportation for children attending any school approved by the State Board of Education for children living more than two miles from a school of suitable grade." Section 29, Act No. 100 of 1922, as amended by Act No. 202 of 1928.

A public board is constituted to act in the interest of the public welfare as a deliberative body with each of its members assisting the board to arrive at a conclusion which reflects the result of their united wisdom and experience. The board alone, therefore, must finally determine every subject committed to its discretion and judgment.

The general rule, succinctly stated, is that legislative and discretionary powers devolved by law on a public board or governing body politic cannot be delegated or referred to the discretion and judgment of its subordinates or any other authority. A contrary rule prevails, however, as to ministerial duties or administrative functions of such board or body.

*   *   *

The act of the Legislature above quoted which confers the power and authority, and imposes the duty on the school board to provide for the transportation of school children, is general in its terms. The method by which the purpose of the act is to be accomplished is not specified, and is therefore impliedly committed to the discretion of the board.

Mr. A. B. Cates, acting under the authority of the resolution, as set forth in the petition, contracted with the plaintiff in the name of the defendant board, thereby exercising its power to contract, and substituting his judgment and discretion for that of the board in determining the person to be employed as driver of the transfer route, and the compensation to be paid for that service.

Clearly, the action of the defendant board in delegating its power to contract with reference to a matter in which it was necessary to exercise a discretion, and in referring the exercise of that discretion to an individual, is without statutory authority or other legal sanction.

"The common council cannot, however, in the absence of legislative authority, delegate its power to contract to a board, committee or officer where the exercise of discretion in making the contract is necessary." Excerpt from McQuillin, Municipal Corporations, § 1279.

It is not contended that the contract entered into by Mr. Cates was subsequently ratified by the school board, but, on the contrary, it is alleged in the petition that the board entered into a contract with another person to drive the route in question; which action by the board, of course, repudiated the alleged contract with plaintiff.

As Mr. Cates was without legal authority to bind the defendant school board, the contract which he made with the plaintiff was without legal effect, and the plaintiff is not entitled to the relief sought in the premises.

We are of the opinion that the exception of no cause or right of action was correctly sustained, and the judgment appealed from is therefore affirmed.

School Board Regulations Must be Reasonable

HENNESSEY v. INDEPENDENT SCHOOL DIST. NO. 4, LINCOLN COUNTY, 1976.

Supreme Court of Oklahoma, 1976.
552 P.2d 1141.

DOOLIN, Justice. This is an action filed in the district court by the Wellston Parent Teacher Association (PTA) seeking a writ of mandamus to require Independent School District No. 4, Lincoln County School Board (Board) to allow PTA use of school facilities for its meetings. * * *

Board has uniformly permitted outside organizations such as Lions Club, Young Homemakers' Organization, Booster Club, 4H Club, Boy Scouts, Bible Lovers' League and Vocational Agriculture Teachers to use the building as authorized by 70 O.S.1971 § 5–130. * * *

* * *

At some time after PTA's first request was denied, Board adopted rules for use of school property by outside organizations. These rules, in addition to general platitudes, contained the following provisions:

"* * *

The Wellston School Board will not tolerate nor continue affiliation with any organization that it determines to be disruptive to or *unsupportive* of the school board or any part of the school system. * * *

* * *

Board's refusal to allow PTA to use its building fails for the following reasons:

First, there is no evidence any of Board's stated rules, constitutional or otherwise, have been violated. The record is absolutely void of any testimony as to any legitimate reason why PTA should be forbidden use of the building, or that PTA is not supportive of the school system. The Superintendent of Schools testified he had no personal knowledge of any past action of PTA that would be considered a violation of Board's regulations.

The general statement in the minutes of the Board that use by PTA of school facilities would not be in best interests of community is unsupported by *any* evidence. To the contrary, it was shown that in the past PTA has sponsored many admittedly worthwhile activities for the community children. The superintendent admitted the guidelines and objectives of PTA are all worthwhile. He indicated PTA's request was refused because a vote of the teachers showed a majority of them were not interested in becoming members of PTA. PTA is chartered and supported by both the state and national Parent-Teacher Association. There is nothing in either organization's rules or guidelines requiring teachers to be members in order to be recognized.

Board's reasoning is *circulus in probanda;* PTA is not comparable to other organizations, because the Board does not officially recognize it, since it is not comparable to other organizations. 70 O.S. 1971 § 5–130 was certainly not intended to omit PTA objectives from its list of permitted purposes and it cannot be successfully argued PTA is not comparable to the acceptable organizations.

The other grounds for reversal are constitutional. Board's rules and regulations as set forth above and their implementation violate the first and fourteenth amendments to the Constitution of the United States as an abridgment of freedom of speech, and a denial of equal protection and further are a violation of the Constitution of Oklahoma Art. 2, § 22. A regulation by a governmental body such as a school board which permits a public official or body to determine what expressions or views will be permitted or allows the board to engage in invidious discrimination among groups by use of a statute granting discretionary powers and by a system of selective enforcement cannot stand. * * *

* * *

There is no doubt 70 O.S.1971 § 5–130 gives Board absolute discretionary authority as to whether or not to open a school building to activities and meetings of outside organizations. The only absolute discretion exercised however is whether to open the building to outside organizations or not to open it. Once this discretion has been exercised and the decision has been made to permit use of property for any of the enumerated purposes, then it must not adopt a discriminatory and unconstitutional policy as to who will be allowed access to its facilities. Its classifications must be reasonable. Discretion of an administrative body must not be used in a discriminatory matter. Administrative action must have a reasonable or rational basis if it is to avoid the stigma of arbitrariness. All governmental bodies must remain within bounds of the Constitution.

A school board may withhold school facilities altogether from use by non-scholastic groups or may make *reasonable* classifications in determining availability. The state may control the use made of its premises but not without regard to the Constitution. The equal protection clause precludes a school from censoring expressions because it does not like its content or message, and it requires a state authority to deal with similarly situated organizations in an even handed manner. The privilege of using a school should be available on a reasonable basis.

A state is under no duty to make school buildings available for public gatherings and a school board is not prevented from barring its use for unlawful purposes. But where a school district allows a number of organizations to use its facilities for non-academic purposes, a board must not unconstitutionally discriminate against any comparable applicant in deciding who will and who will not be permitted its use.

Reversed.

School Officers

A school officer as opposed to a school employee is one who holds public office by virtue of which he possesses a delegation of sovereign power. An Indiana court[9] has defined a public office as " * * * a position to which a portion of the sovereignty of the state attaches for the time being, and which is exercised for the benefit of the public." The most important characteristic which may be said to distinguish an office from an employment is, that the duties of an office must involve an exercise of some portion of the sovereignty; there are powers and duties conferred by the legislature or the constitution. The duties must be performed independently without the control of a superior power unless statute provides for a subordinate office. Other characteristics which typically identify the office are a permanency or continuity of office, a required oath of office, and a procedure for removal which is usually fixed by statute. In addition, employees may exercise only ministerial powers and have no authority to exercise discretionary powers.

A superintendent of a local school district is, in most states, considered an employee. A case in point is where a local superintendent in California was discharged by the board of education and claimed he could only be discharged by the grand jury since he was a school officer. The school code provided that the school board shall "elect" a superintendent for a four-year term. Other provisions of the code said the school board may "employ" a superintendent. The superintendent in this case asserted that the term "elect" was indicative of public office. The court, however, held that the terms "elect" and "employ" in this case meant the same thing. The court further pointed out that the position of superintendent did not exercise a sovereign power, was not created by the constitution or statute, and statutes did not impose independent police power duties upon the individual.[10]

Public officers are not allowed to hold two offices which are in conflict. Offices may be incompatible when one exercises control over the other, one office is subordinate to another or the offices are held in more than one branch of the government at the same time. For example a judge cannot also be a prosecuting attorney, a legislator cannot also be school board member and a governor cannot also be a legislator. Extending this principle further, it has been held that teachers, even though they are only employees, cannot also serve as board members in the same school district.[11]

Some state constitutions may say that a person cannot hold two lucrative offices regardless of whether one is subordinate to the other.

9. Shelmadine v. City of Elkhart, 75 Ind.App. 493, 129 N.E. 878 (1921).

10. Main v. Claremont Unified School Dist., 161 Cal.App.2d 189, 326 P.2d 573 (1958).

11. Maddox v. State, 220 Ark. 762, 249 S.W.2d 972 (1952).

The Indiana Constitution provides, "No person holding a lucrative office or appointment under the United States or under this State, shall be eligible to a seat in the General Assembly; nor shall any person hold more than one lucrative office at the same time, except as in this Constitution expressly prohibited * * * ".[12] Such "lucrative offices" have been held to prevent a person from serving both as a justice of the peace and a school board member, or to be sheriff while serving as a school board member.

Nearly all states have statutes which prevent public officers from having an interest in contracts made with the agencies they administer. A case illustrating conflict of interest occurred where a board member with an interest in an insurance company wrote a policy for his own school district. The court held that this board member could be removed because he had wrongfully gained advantage through his public position.[13]

A public office, theoretically, is a public duty and an officer must have the consent of the governing power before he can resign. In other words, a public office is held at the will of both parties, and the public has a right to the services of its citizens, therefore, a resignation must be accepted. Without acceptance the resignation is of no effect and the officer remains in office.[14] Although this is one theory of vacation of a public office some states provide for an "absolute" right to resign.[15] In states where the officer has an "absolute" right to resign, if he tenders a resignation he cannot withdraw it. There is immediate unconditional acceptance. In states which follow the "public duty" theory, a resignation probably can be withdrawn prior to acceptance or prior to an effective date if resignation specifies such a date. An Illinois court has held that resignations in advance are not legal. In a case where a mayor required board members to put resignations in writing at the time of appointment, and the mayor later accepted, the court said that such resignations were invalid as they were not contemplated by the law.[16]

Statutes provide the procedure to be used for the removal of public officers. In the absence of statute, removal is an incidental power of the appointing agency. For removal for cause only a notice and a hearing are generally required. Cause may be malfeasance, improper or illegal performance of duties or breach of good faith, inefficiency, and incapacity. A public officer cannot be removed during a term of office, when the term is fixed by statute, unless for cause. In a case where school board members took "kickbacks" from a contractor for violation of competitive bid law, the court removed the board. The

---

12. Constitution of Indiana, Art. 2, § 9.

13. People v. Becker, 112 Cal.App.2d 324, 246 P.2d 103 (1952).

14. Green v. Jones, 144 W.Va. 276, 108 S.E.2d 1 (1959).

15. Leech v. State, 78 Ind. 570 (1881).

16. People v. Reinberg, 263 Ill. 536, 105 N.E. 715 (1914).

court held that even in the absence of statute, the board members could be punished under common law for wilful misconduct in office.[17]

Common Law Incompatibility May Exist Where a Person Holds Two Public Offices

STATE v. WHITE

Supreme Court of Iowa, 1965.
275 Iowa 606, 133 N.W.2d 903.

STUART, Justice. Two related questions are involved on this appeal. May a person serve as a member of a local school board and the county board of education at the same time? If not, in which office does the vacancy occur?

Plaintiff proceeded under R.C.P. 300, 58 I.C.A. to obtain leave of court to file this quo warranto action. The petition alleged defendant was elected to the Board of Directors of the Davenport Community School District in Scott County. He qualified for the three year term on September 18, 1961. On September 9, 1963 he was elected as the member at large of the Board of Education for Scott County and qualified for that position on October 7, 1963. He assumed the duties of both offices. Plaintiff further alleged the duties of the two offices as prescribed by statute are incompatible and that it is contrary to public policy for one person to hold them both concurrently.

* * *

III. There is no constitutional or statutory provision which prohibits defendant from holding the two offices in question at the same time. The case therefore turns on the well settled common law rule: "[I]f a person, while occupying one office, accepts another incompatible with the first, he *ipso facto* vacates the first office, 'and his title thereto is thereby terminated without any other act or proceeding.' "

* * *

"The principal difficulty that has confronted the courts in cases of this kind has been to determine what constitutes incompatibility of offices, and the consensus of judicial opinion seems to be that the question must be determined largely from a consideration of the duties of each, having, in so doing, a due regard for the public interest. It is generally said that incompatibility does not depend upon the incidents of the office, as upon physical inability to be engaged in the duties of both at the same time. Bryan v. Cattell, supra. But that the test of incompatibility is whether there is an inconsistency in the functions of the two, as where one is subordinate to the other 'and subject in some degree to its revisory power," or where the duties of the two offices 'are inherently inconsistent and repugnant.' * * * A still different

17. Commonwealth v. Fahey, 156 Pa.
Super. 254, 40 A.2d 167 (1944).

definition has been adopted by several courts. It is held that incompatibility in office exists 'where the nature and duties of the two offices are such as to render it improper, from considerations of public policy, for an incumbent to retain both.' " State, ex rel. Crawford v. Anderson, 155 Iowa 271, 273, 136 N.W. 128, 129.

Similar language is contained in 42 Am.Jur., Public Officers, § 70, pages 935, 936.

The trial court examined the pertinent statutes and analyzed them as follows:

"It is obvious that the curriculum of a school, the instruction in the schools, the transportation of pupils to school where required by law, the union or merger of school districts, the changing or adjusting of boundary lines of contiguous school corporations are important matters which are the concern of the board of directors of a community school district. The action of the board of such school district, however, in said matters is subject to review by the county board. Section 273.13, Par. 3, makes it a specific duty of the county board to approve the curriculum of the county school system in conformity with the course of study prescribed by the State Department of Public Instruction; Section 274.15, [273.18] Par. 7, makes it the duty of and grants the power to the county superintendent, under the direction of the county board, to supervise or arrange for supervision of instruction in the schools of the county school system; Section 273.13, Par. 7, and Section 289.9 [285.9] make it the specific duty of the county board to enforce all laws, rules and regulations of the Department of Public Instruction for the transportation of pupils to and from public schools in all school districts of the county, and if the community district board fails to arrange for such transportation, the county board may do so and the service provided must be paid for by the community board. Section 285.12 makes the county board an appellate body over disagreements between a school patron and the community board as to matters of transportation; and Section 290.1 makes the county superintendent, a person appointed by the county board for a three year term (and subject to not being reappointed at the end of that period), the appeal body for persons aggrieved by any decision or order of the community board.

"Section 274.37 makes any action of the board of directors of contiguous school corporations changing boundary lines subject to the approval of the county board; and Sections 274.42, 274.43 and 274.44 give the county board power to adjust boundary lines between districts under certain circumstances, and its decision is final. Section 274.46 gives the county board the power to determine matters of reimbursement for loss of taxes caused by adjustment of boundary lines provided for in Section 274.42.

"It thus appears that in many important matters the community school board is subordinate to the county board and subject to its revisory power in some degree."

We hold these statutes show that a definite and clear incompatibility exists between the duties and powers of a local school board and a county board of education and it is contrary to public policy for one person to hold the offices concurrently.

Appellant cites Thie v. Cordell, 199 Iowa 709, 202 N.W. 532, to support his contention there is no common law rule against concurrent holding of offices, one of which has revisory or appellate power over the other. There it was held a county superintendent sitting ex officio as a member of the county board of education was entitled to vote on an appeal to the board from his decision as county superintendent. We do not think the cases are analogous. The statutes involved there made the county superintendent by virtue of that office a member of the county board and gave the board authority to review the decision of the superintendent. Members of the board directly interested were disqualified by statute but there was no bar to a vote by the superintendent. We said:

"In this perfectly obvious situation, the Legislature has seen fit to provide, not for his disqualification by reason of his having rendered the decision appealed from, but only for the disqualification of a member of the board who lives or owns property in the district, and must be deemed to have intended that the county superintendent should participate, as a member of the board in the review of his own decisions on appeal, and to have contemplated the possibility that his might be the deciding vote."

The court there determined the legislature intended the superintendent to have a vote as he was made a member of the board and not disqualified. The legislature could provide that one person could serve on both boards here if it so desires, but in the absence of a statute expressing such intention the common law rule of incompatibility must be applied. *   *   *

*   *   *

Appellee on his cross appeal concedes Iowa has thus far followed the general rule that when a person accepts appointment to a second office he vacates or by implication resigns the first. *   *   *   However, he vigorously urges that we recognize an exception in this case because section 277.24 of the code provides for members of local school boards to serve "for the term for which elected and until their successors are elected or appointed and qualified" and that even though one resigns an office he continues in office until his successor qualifies. * * *

We have, however, held a member of a school board can resign his office and create a vacancy in spite of such statutory provision. Board of Directors of Menlo Consolidated School Dist. of Menlo v. Blakesley, 240 Iowa 910, 36 N.W.2d 751. As the acceptance of the second office by implication is a resignation of the first, it appears that we should not apply the exception in Iowa.

This is an area of the law in which it is more important for the rule to be settled and the public to know the effect of the acceptance of a second office than for exceptions to be engrafted onto the general rule. No such injustices or inequities result from the application of the general rule to require a court of equity to search its conscience before applying it.

Affirmed.

School Elections

Legal issues relating to school elections are nearly as diverse as the general election laws of a state. No attempt is made here to fully encompass this wide body of law, but it is necessary to observe election law with regard to reapportionment precedents and to those legal requirements pertaining to compliance with election statutes, generally.

Until 1962, the view of the courts prevailed that legislative representation and how it was apportioned throughout a state was a matter for only the legislature to determine. Malapportionment and rottenboroughs were of grave concern to many and the problems became more acute as population mobility left some voters with very little legislative power, while others reaped disproportionately great political muscle. Judicial precedent, which permitted this to transpire, was found in Colegrove v. Green,[18] in which case Justice Frankfurter writing for the Supreme Court had opted to keep the courts out of the "political thicket." Frankfurter said:

> To maintain this action would cut very deep into the very being of Congress. Courts ought not to enter this political thicket. The remedy for unfairness in distributing is to secure state legislatures that will apportion properly, or to invoke the ample powers of Congress. * * * The Constitution has left the performance of many duties in our governmental scheme to depend on the fidelity of the executive and legislative action and, ultimately, in the vigilance of the people in exercising their political rights.[19]

After this decision it soon became clear that the problems of apportionment would not be corrected by the legislators, themselves,

18.   328 U.S. 549, 66 S.Ct. 1198 (1946).   19.   Ibid.

and the people were powerless to fully exercise the political rights. In reevaluation of its position the Supreme Court handed down new precedent in Baker v. Carr [20] in 1962. In so doing, the court found that the Equal Protection Clause was violated by the resulting discrimination against some votes which was not reasonable or rational but instead was arbitrary and capricious.

This case has had bearing on school district elections in the same manner as it has influenced state-wide elections; if officials are elected by popular vote, then the Constitution assures "that each person's vote counts as much, insofar as it is practicable, as any other person's." [21]

Statute Limiting Franchise Cannot Sustain Compelling Interest Test

KRAMER v. UNION FREE SCHOOL DISTRICT

Supreme Court of the United States, 1969.
395 U.S. 621, 89 S.Ct. 1886.

Mr. Chief Justice WARREN delivered the opinion of the Court.

In this case we are called on to determine whether § 2012 of the New York Education Law, McKinney's Consol.Laws, c. 16, is constitutional. The legislation provides that in certain New York school districts residents who are otherwise eligible to vote in state and federal elections may vote in the school district election only if they (1) own (or lease) taxable real property within the district, or (2) are parents (or have custody of) children enrolled in the local public schools. * * *

* * *

Appellant is a 31-year-old college-educated stockbroker who lives in his parents' home in the Union Free School District No. 15, a district to which § 2012 applies. He is a citizen of the United States and has voted in federal and state elections since 1959. However, since he has no children and neither owns nor leases taxable real property, appellant's attempts to register for and vote in the local school district elections have been unsuccessful. After the school district rejected his 1965 application, appellant instituted the present class action challenging the constitutionality of the voter eligibility requirements.

* * *

At the outset, it is important to note what is *not* at issue in this case. The requirements of § 2012 that school district voters must (1) be citizens of the United States, (2) be bona fide residents of the

20. 369 U.S. 186, 82 S.Ct. 691 (1962).

21. Hadley v. Junior College Dist. of Metropolitan Kansas City, Mo., 397 U.S. 50, 90 S.Ct. 791 (1970).

school district, and (3) be at least 21 years of age are not challenged. Appellant agrees that the States have the power to impose reasonable citizenship, age, and residency requirements on the availability of the ballot. * * * The sole issue in this case is whether the *additional* requirements of § 2012—requirements which prohibit some district residents who are otherwise qualified by age and citizenship from participating in district meetings and school board elections—violate the Fourteenth Amendment's command that no State shall deny persons equal protection of the laws.

* * * "[S]ince the right to exercise the franchise in a free and unimpaired manner is preservative of other basic civil and political rights, any alleged infringement of the right of citizens to vote must be carefully and meticulously scrutinized." Reynolds v. Sims, 377 U.S. 533, 562, 84 S.Ct. 1362, 1381, 12 L.Ed.2d 506 (1964). * * *

* * * Therefore, if a challenged state statute grants the right to vote to some bona fide residents of requisite age and citizenship and denies the franchise to others, the Court must determine whether the exclusions are necessary to promote a compelling state interest. * * *.

* * * The presumption of constitutionality and the approval given "rational" classifications in other types of enactments are based on as assumption that the institutions of state government are structured so as to represent fairly all the people. However, when the challenge to the statute is in effect a challenge of this basic assumption, the assumption can no longer serve as the basis for presuming constitutionality. * * *

The need for exacting judicial scrutiny of statutes distributing the franchise is undiminished simply because, under a different statutory scheme, the offices subject to election might have been filled through appointment. States do have latitude in determining whether certain public officials shall be selected by election or chosen by appointment and whether various questions shall be submitted to the voters. In fact, we have held that where a county school board is an administrative, not legislative, body, its members need not be elected. Sailors v. Kent County Bd. of Education, 387 U.S. 105, 108, 87 S.Ct. 1549, 1552, 18 L.Ed.2d 650 (1967). However, "once the franchise is granted to the electorate, lines may not be drawn which are inconsistent with the Equal Protection Clause of the Fourteenth Amendment." Harper v. Virginia Bd. of Elections, supra, 383 U.S., at 665, 86 S.Ct., at 1080.

Nor is the need for close judicial examination affected because the district meetings and the school board do not have "general" legislative powers. Our exacting examination is not necessitated by the subject of the election; rather, it is required because some resident citizens are permitted to participate and some are not. * * *

* * *

We turn therefore to question whether the exclusion is necessary to promote a compelling state interest. First appellees argue that the State has a legitimate interest in limiting the franchise in school district elections to "members of the community of interest"—those "primarily interested in such elections." Second, appellees urge that the State may reasonably and permissibly conclude that "property taxpayers" (including lessees of taxable property who share the tax burden through rent payments) and parents of the children enrolled in the district's schools are those "primarily interested" in school affairs.

We do not understand appellees to argue that the State is attempting to limit the franchise to those "subjectively concerned" about school matters. Rather, they appear to argue that the State's legitimate interest is in restricting a voice in school matters to those "directly affected" by such decisions. The State apparently reasons that since the schools are financed in part by local property taxes, persons whose out-of-pocket expenses are "directly" affected by property tax changes should be allowed to vote. Similarly, parents of children in school are thought to have a "direct" stake in school affairs and are given a vote.

* * *

We need express no opinion as to whether the State in some circumstances might limit the exercise of the franchise to those "primarily interested" or "primarily affected." Of course, we therefore do not reach the issue of whether these particular elections are of the type in which the franchise may be so limited. For, assuming, *arguendo*, that New York legitimately might limit the franchise in these school district elections to those "primarily interested in school affairs," close scrutiny of the § 2012 classifications demonstrates that they do not accomplish this purpose with sufficient precision to justify denying appellant the franchise.

Whether classifications allegedly limiting the franchise to those resident citizens "primarily interested" deny those excluded equal protection of the laws depends, *inter alia*, on whether all those excluded are in fact substantially less interested or affected than those the statute includes. In other words, the classifications must be tailored so that the exclusion of appellant and members of his class is necessary to achieve the articulated state goal. Section 2012 does not meet the exacting standard of precision we require of statutes which selectively distribute the franchise. * * *

Nor do appellees offer any justification for the exclusion of seemingly interested and informed residents—other than to argue that the § 2012 classifications include those "whom the State could understandably deem to be the most intimately interested in actions taken by the school board," and urge that "the task of * * * balancing the interest of the community in the maintenance of orderly school district elections against the interest of any individual in voting in such elections should clearly remain with the Legislature." But the issue is not whether the legislative judgments are rational. A more exacting standard obtains. The issue is whether the § 2012 requirements do in fact sufficiently further a compelling state interest to justify denying the franchise to appellant and members of his class. The requirements of § 2012 are not sufficiently tailored to limiting the franchise to those "primarily interested" in school affairs to justify the denial of the franchise to appellant and members of his class.

The judgment of the United States District Court for the Eastern District of New York is therefore reversed. The case is remanded for further proceedings consistent with this opinion.

It is so ordered.

Constitutionality of One-Man One-Vote Is Not Applicable to Appointive Boards

SAILORS v. BOARD OF EDUC. OF COUNTY OF KENT

Supreme Court of the United States, 1967.
387 U.S. 105, 87 S.Ct. 1549.

Mr. Justice DOUGLAS delivered the opinion of the Court.

Appellants, qualified and registered electors of Kent County, Michigan, brought this suit in the Federal District Court to enjoin the Board of Education of Kent County from detaching certain schools from the city of Grand Rapids and attaching them to Kent County, to declare the county board to be unconstitutionally constituted, and to enjoin further elections until the electoral system is redesigned. Attack is also made on the adequacy of the statutory standards governing decisions of the county board in light of the requirements of due process. We need not bother with the intricate problems of state law involved in the dispute. For the federal posture of the case is a very limited one. The people of Michigan (qualified school electors) elect the local school boards. No constitutional question is presented as respects those elections. The alleged constitutional questions arise when it comes to the county school board. It is chosen, not by the electors of the county, but by delegates from the local boards. Each board sends a delegate to a biennial meeting and those delegates elect a county board of five members, who need not be members of the local boards, from candidates nominated by school electors. It is argued that this system of choosing county board members * * * violates the principle of "one man, one vote" which we held * * * in Reynolds v. Sims, 377 U.S. 533, 84 S.Ct. 1362, 12 L.Ed.2d 506, was constitutionally required in state elections. A vast array of facts is assembled showing alleged inequities in a system which gives one vote to every local school board (irrespective of population, wealth, etc.) in the selection of the county board. * * *

* * *

We start with what we said in Reynolds v. Sims, supra, at 575, 84 S.Ct. at 1388:

> "Political subdivisions of States—counties, cities or whatever—never were and never have been considered as sovereign entities. Rather, they have been traditionally regarded as subordinate governmental instrumentalities created by the State to assist in the carrying out of state governmental functions. As stated by the Court in Hunter v. City of Pittsburgh, 207 U.S. 161, 168 [28 S.Ct. 40, 52 L.Ed. 151,] these governmental units are 'created as convenient agencies for exercising such of the governmental powers of the state, as may be entrusted to them,' and the 'number, nature and duration of the powers conferred upon [them] * * * and the territory over which they shall be exercised rests in the absolute discretion of the state.'"

We find no constitutional reason why state or local officers of the nonlegislative character involved here may not be chosen by the governor, by the legislature, or by some other appointive means rather than by an election. * * *

* * *

A State cannot of course manipulate its political subdivisions so as to defeat a federally protected right, as for example, by realigning political subdivisions so as to deny a person his vote because of race. * * *

* * *

The Michigan system for selecting members of the county school board is basically appointive rather than elective. We need not decide at the present time whether a State may constitute a local legislative body through the appointive rather than the elective process. * * * We do not have that question here, as the County Board of Education performs essentially administrative functions; and while they are important, they are not legislative in the classical sense.

Viable local governments may need many innovations, numerous combinations of old and new devices, great flexibility in municipal arrangements to meet changing urban conditions. We see nothing in the Constitution to prevent experimentation. At least as respects nonlegislative officers, a State can appoint local officials or elect them or combine the elective and appointive systems as was done here. If we assume *arguendo* that where a State provides for an election of a local official or agency—whether administrative, legislative, or judicial—the requirements of * * * Reynolds v. Sims must be met, no question of that character is presented. For while there was an election here for the local school board, no constitutional complaint is raised respecting that election. Since the choice of members of the county school board did not involve an election and since none was required for these nonlegislative offices, the principle of "one man, one vote" has no relevancy.

Affirmed.

NOTES

A statute limiting franchise to school elections to parents of children enrolled in the public schools and owners and leasees of taxable real property denies equal protection. Kramer v. Union Free School Dist., No. 15, 395 U.S. 621, 89 S.Ct. 1886 (1969).

Similarly, the Supreme Court has held unconstitutional a statute which limited electors in a public utility bond election to only "property taxpayers.' Cipriano v. City of Houma, 395 U.S. 701, 89 S.Ct. 1897 (1969).

Equality of Voting Power Is Required
in Local District Elections

HADLEY v. JUNIOR COLLEGE DIST. OF METROPOLITAN KANSAS CITY, MO.

Supreme Court of the United States, 1970.
397 U.S. 50, 90 S.Ct. 791.

Mr. Justice BLACK delivered the opinion of the Court.

This case involves the extent to which the Fourteenth Amendment and the "one man, one vote" principle apply in the election of local governmental officials. Appellants are residents and taxpayers of the Kansas City School District, one of eight separate school districts that have combined to form the Junior College District of Metropolitan Kansas City. Under Missouri law separate school districts may vote by referendum to establish a consolidated junior college district and elect six trustees to conduct and manage the necessary affairs of that district. The state law also provides that these trustees shall be apportioned among the separate school districts on the basis of "school enumeration," defined as the number of persons between the ages of six and 20 years, who reside in each district. In the case of the Kansas City School District this apportionment plan results in the election of three trustees, or 50% of the total number from that district. Since that district contains approximately 60% of the total school enumeration in the junior college district, appellants brought suit claiming that their right to vote for trustees was being unconstitutionally diluted in violation of the Equal Protection Clause of the Fourteenth Amendment. The Missouri Supreme Court upheld the trial court's dismissal of the suit, stating that the "one man, one vote" principle was not applicable in this case. * * * [F]or the reasons set forth below we reverse and hold that the Fourteenth Amendment requires that the trustees of this junior college district be apportioned in a manner that does not deprive any voter of his right to have his own vote given as much weight, as far as is practicable, as that of any other voter in the junior college district.

* * *

This Court has consistently held in a long series of cases that in situations involving elections, the States are required to insure that each person's vote counts as much, insofar as it is practicable, as any other person's. We have applied this principle in congressional elections, state legislative elections, and local elections. The consistent theme of those decisions is that the right to vote in an election is protected by the United States Constitution against dilution or debasement. While the particular offices involved in these cases have varied, in each case a constant factor is the decision of the government to have citizens participate individually by ballot in the selection of certain people who carry out governmental functions. Thus in the case now before us, while the office of junior college trustee differs in certain respects from those offices considered in prior cases, it is exactly the same in the one crucial factor—these officials are elected by popular vote.

* * * While there are differences in the powers of different officials, the crucial consideration is the right of each qualified voter to participate on an equal footing in the election process. It should be remembered that in cases like this one we are asked by voters to insure that they are given equal treatment, and from their perspective the harm from unequal treatment is the same in any election, regardless of the officials selected.

* * *

It has also been urged that we distinguish for apportionment purposes between elections for "legislative" officials and those for "administrative" officers. Such a suggestion would leave courts with an * * * unmanageable principle since governmental activities "cannot easily be classified in the neat categories favored by civics texts," * * * and it must also be rejected. We therefore hold today that as a general rule, whenever a state or local government decides to select persons by popular election to perform governmental functions, the Equal Protection Clause of the Fourteenth Amendment requires that each qualified voter must be given an equal opportunity to participate in that election, and when members of an elected body are chosen from separate districts, each district must be established on a basis that will insure, as far as is practicable, that equal numbers of voters can vote for proportionally equal numbers of officials.

* * *

* * *

Although the statutory scheme reflects to some extent a principle of equal voting power, it does so in a way that does not comport with constitutional requirements. This is so because the Act necessarily results in a systematic discrimination against voters in the more populous school districts. This discrimination occurs because whenever a large district's percentage of the total enumeration falls within a certain percentage range it is always allocated the number of trustees corresponding to the bottom of that range. Unless a particularly large district has exactly 33⅓%, 50% or 66⅔% of the total enumeration it will always have proportionally fewer trustees than the small districts. As has been pointed out, in the case of the Kansas City School District approximately 60% of the total enumeration entitles that district to only 50% of the trustees. Thus while voters in large school districts may frequently have less effective voting power than residents of small districts, they can never have more. Such built-in discrimination against voters in large districts cannot be sustained as a sufficient compliance with the constitutional mandate that each person's vote count as much as another's, as far as practicable. * * * We have said before that mathematical exactitude is not required * * * but a plan that does not automatically discriminate in favor of certain districts is.

In holding that the guarantee of equal voting strength for each voter applies in all elections of governmental officials, we do not feel that the States will be inhibited in finding ways to insure that legitimate political goals of representation are achieved. We have previously upheld against constitutional challenge an election scheme that required that candidates be residents of certain districts that did not contain equal numbers of people. * * * Since all the officials in that case were elected at large, the right of each voter was given equal treatment. We have also held that where a State chooses to select members of an official body by appointment rather than election, and that choice does not itself offend the Constitution, the fact that each official does not "represent" the same number of people does not deny those people equal protection of the laws. * * * And a State may, in certain cases, limit the right to vote to a particular group or class of people. * * * But once a State has decided to use the process of popular election and "once the class of voters is chosen and their qualifications specified, we see no constitutional way by which equality of voting power may be evaded." * * *

    * * *

Election May Not be Voided if Directory

GANN v. HARRISBURG COMMUNITY UNIT SCHOOL DIST.

Appellate Court of Illinois, Fifth Circuit, 1966.
73 Ill.App.2d 103, 218 N.E.2d 833.

GEORGE J. MORAN, Justice. * * *

The appellants alleged in their complaint that, pursuant to the filing of a petition and a hearing on the petition in accordance with Ill.Rev.Stat., Ch. 122, Section 11–6, an election was held on May 27, 1965, for the purpose of determining whether or not a community unit school district should be established in certain contiguous areas in Saline County; that each of the appellants had been a resident of the territory included within the proposed district at the time of the election; that, in accordance with the statute, the Saline County Superintendent of Schools designated five precincts for the election; that the precinct designated number 3 did not lie within the territory comprising the proposed school district; and that, therefore, the election, which resulted in favor of the formation of the proposed district, was void and of no effect and that it should be set aside. The appellee made a motion to strike the complaint for failure to state a cause of action. The trial court sustained the motion and dismissed the complaint. The appellants seek to reverse the dismissal in order that the complaint may be heard and be determined on the merits. There are no allegations that any fraud occurred or that any voters were deterred from voting. Nor is there any allegation that persons voted who were not residents of the territory sought to be organized.

The statute governing the formation of community unit school districts expressly provides that the polling place for a particular precinct must lie within the boundaries of the precinct. Ill.Rev.Stat., Ch. 122, Sec. 11–6, provides that after a petition has been presented concerning the formation of a school district and after the petition has been approved, the county superintendent "shall call an election to be held in the manner provided in Article 9 of this Act * * *." Chapter 122, Sec. 9–7, provides in part that:

> In elections in all other school districts, including non-high school districts, the board of education shall establish a suitable number of voting precincts and fix the boundaries thereof for the accommodation of the voters of the district. If more than one voting precinct is established the voting precincts shall be designated by number. In each voting precinct there shall be one polling place designated by the board. * * *
>
> At an election called by the superintendent of schools, unless otherwise provided, voting precincts shall be estab-

lished and polling places designated by the county superintendent of schools in accordance with the provisions of this section * * *.

The appellants contend that this statutory provision is mandatory and, therefore, that the failure to designate polling places within the territory sought to be organized should render the election void.

A similar contention was made and overruled in People ex rel. v. Graham, 267 Ill. 426, 108 N.E. 699, a case in which the court held that the designation of a polling place for three city wards across the street from the boundary lines of two of the wards would not void a municipal election. In its decision, the court reviewed cases in other jurisdictions and stated, at 440, 108 N.E. at 705:

> The courts of last resort in a majority of these cases have held that where it was shown that no legal voter was thereby deprived of his vote and the location was not selected from any improper motive, no fraud or other harm being shown or charged, such location of a polling place would not avoid the election. (Cases cited.)

Even though there was no express statutory provision governing the location of a polling place in the Graham case, the decision is nonetheless applicable; for the court held that such a provision was implied by the spirit of the election law.

This position has also been taken in C.J.S. Elections § 199, where it is stated that:

> (T)he rule is that, where the polling place selected by the proper officers is outside the election district, the electors of the district who vote thereat are not disenfranchised on that account if the election is otherwise lawfully conducted.

Generally, an election should be held at the time and in the place provided by law in order that it have validity. * * * However, a distinction has been drawn between directory and mandatory provisions. * * * The failure to follow a mandatory provision will invalidate an otherwise valid election, while the failure to follow a directory provision will not. * * * This is not to say, however, that a directory provision may or should be disregarded, but only that an entire election will not be invalidated for the failure to follow such a provision. * * * This analysis has been used not only for general elections, but also for special school elections. * * *

The determination whether a statutory provision is mandatory or directory has depended upon the following criteria: (1) Whether the statutory scheme expressly or impliedly provides that the failure to follow the provision shall render an election void; (2) whether the failure interfered in any way with the result of the election; (3) whether any person legally entitled to vote was not permitted to do so; (4) whether any person voted who was not a resident of the territory sought to be organized; (5) whether the polling place was chosen for any improper motive; and (6) whether any fraud occurred in or as a result of the selection of the polling place. * * * Generally, "statutory provisions regulating the conduct of an election are deemed directory after an election in which no improper voting has occurred." * * *

In this case, the statutory scheme does not expressly or impliedly provide that a failure to follow the provision shall render an election void. In addition, none of the adverse effects mentioned above were alleged to have occurred as a result of the failure. Nor was there any fraud alleged. Hence, the provision is directory, not mandatory, and the election need not be voided.

For the foregoing reasons, the judgment of the lower court is affirmed.

Judgment affirmed.

NOTES

1. Where there is no fraud, bad faith, nor misleading of the voters, it is a well settled rule that statutory provisions which are treated as mandatory before an election will be construed as directory after the election. Lindahl v. Independent School Dist. No. 306, 270 Minn. 164, 133 N.W.2d 23 (1965).

2. A Minnesota court in Bakken v. Schroeder, 269 Minn. 381, 130 N. W.2d 579 (1964), challenges to consolidation proceedings will not serve to invalidate the election unless there is proof of prejudice and that statutory requirements are treated as directory rather than mandatory when election proceedings are contested following the election. In a case involving challenge the court quoted an earlier decision entitled, Erickson v. Sammons, 242 Minn. 345, 65 N.W.2d 198, and said:

> It is the general rule that, before an election is held, statutory provisions regulating the conduct of the election will usually be treated as mandatory and their observance may be insisted upon and enforced. After an election has been held, the statutory regulations are generally construed as directory and such rule of construction is in accord with the policy of this state, which from its beginning has been that, in the absence of fraud or bad faith or constitutional violation, an election which has resulted in a fair and free expression of the will of the legal voters upon the merits will not be invalidated because of a departure from the statutory regulations governing the conduct of the election except in those cases where the legislature has clearly and unequivocally expressed an intent that a specific statutory provision is an essential jurisdictional prerequisite and that a departure therefrom shall have the drastic consequence of invalidity. * * *

3. Where a statute requires a resolution by the board of education for the initiation of a bond election the courts have held that the resolution

need not be formal, "Be it resolved," nor need it even be in writing. The statute is fulfilled by any official action by the board. Lindahl v. Independent School Dist. No. 306, 270 Minn. 164, 133 N.W.2d 23 (1965).

4. The Supreme Court of Texas in McKinney v. O'Conner, 26 Tex. 5 (1861), has stated the rule for elections as:

> * * * rules prescribing the manner in which the qualified electors shall hold the election, at the time and place designated, and those prescribing the manner in which their act, when done, shall be authenticated, so as to import verity on its face, are directory. Irregularities in their observance will not vitiate an election, unless they be such that the true result of the ballot cannot be arrived at with reasonable certainty. The ultimate test of the validity of an election is involved in the questions: *Did the qualified electors, at the time and place designated, acting in concert, either actively or by acquiescence, hold an election and cast their votes in the ballot box; and has it been done in a matter sufficiently conformable to the directions of the law, as that the true* result can be arrived at with reasonable certainty? (Emphasis supplied.)

5. Judicial reluctance to overthrow an election was illustrated in Stafford v. Stegle, Tex.Civ.App., 271 S.W.2d 833 (1954), wherein the court said:

> While those charged with conducting elections would use every precaution possible to see that elections are conducted strictly in accordance with the provisions of the Election Code, nevertheless, after an election has been held and it appears that it has been fairly conducted and the result correctly declared and there [are] no charges of fraud, misconduct or illegality, the entire election will not be set aside for irregularities in the manner of conducting the election, unless the statutes governing such matters state that the election must be vitiated.

6. In a case contending a lack of sufficiency of notice for a special election, a Missouri court said that: "Generally, statutory provisions as to notice of special elections are mandatory, must be strictly followed, the failure to properly call a special election will invalidate it. * * * A special election, however, will not be vitiated by failure to comply strictly with the statutory requirements with respect to the giving of notice where the electors were in fact informed of the time, place and purpose of the election and generally voted on the question submitted; where it is not shown that the electors did not participate in the election because of lack of notice or knowledge or that a different result would have obtained if the full statutory notice had been given. State v. Whittle, Mo., 401 S.W.2d 401 (1966).

*Election May be Voided if Irregularities
Are too Great*

WOOLSEY v. CARNEY

Supreme Court of Montana, 1963.
141 Mont. 476, 378 P.2d 658.

JOHN C. HARRISON, Justice. * * * These facts are fairly well agreed upon. The voters of two adjoining rural school districts, 23 and 29, located in the southern part of Sweet Grass County held an election on August 7, 1961, to determine whether or not they should consolidate their school districts. This was the second election held, there having been a previous election on the same issue, on July 1, 1961, at which time the consolidation had failed to carry. All of the necessary statutory procedures were followed up to the day of election. The notice of the election was published and posted showing the date and the hours of the election, and judges were properly appointed. All went well until the day of the election when a series of events occurred, which could serve as the basis for a Gilbert-Sullivan operetta. Due to an oversight the ballots failed to arrive at the two school election houses where the elections were held, so the election judges made up their own ballots placing on each a box marked "FOR" and "AGAINST". There was, however, no explanation of FOR what or AGAINST what, even though the statute requires the ballots be marked FOR consolidation and AGAINST consolidation. It was in the election judges' opinion unnecessary to put the word consolidation due to the fact they thought everybody knew what they were voting for. It is undenied that over five ballots were cast by people who were never present at the election. This was explained by the election judges by saying that they let some persons vote before the polls opened at the legal hour of 2:00 o'clock on the 7th due to the inconvenience to these persons having to come to the voting place during the hours of the said election. The hours of election were from 2:00 p. m. to 6:00 p. m. Too, one judge cast a vote of her husband who she said was busy on the ranch, though when examined she could only explain that she was certain, as only a wife can be, that her husband was FOR consolidation. In school district 29, after the judges had closed the polls and due to an objection to the system of voting absentee, the election judges withdrew five FOR votes, leaving a total of fifty votes, there having been prior to the withdrawal fifty-five votes cast. This left a total vote of fifty with twenty-six FOR and twenty-four AGAINST. It would appear that in this district there were more than five absentee voters, probably eight, and it is unknown how the other three would have voted, but had three more FOR vote ballots been withdrawn the election there would have failed. To further complicate the voting in district 29 it is alleged that two voters who said that they were against consolidation appeared at the polls and were refused the right to vote even though they said they had arrived before 6:00 p. m. by their watches. The judges explained this by saying they opened and closed the polls "by their time."

To further complicate the picture in the adjoining district 23, the voting was sixteen FOR and fifteen AGAINST, but at the time of the hearing on the order to show cause one lady testified she thought she was voting "For keeping the school, not FOR CONSOLIDATION." So had her vote been cast as she thought it was, her vote would have changed the election, making sixteen AGAINST consolidation and fifteen FOR consolidation.

Several Montana Statutes are involved here and we must determine whether having failed to follow the statutes on consolidated school districts the defendants may still prevail due to the failure on the part of the plaintiff to pursue thereafter an appeal through administrative proceedings rather than going to the court.

Section 75–1813, R.C.M.1947, covers consolidated districts, procedure in the event of consolidation, and amount of debt. Subsection 2 states as follows:

> "(2) The votes at such election shall be by ballot, which shall read 'For consolidation' or 'Against consolidation.' The presiding officer at such election shall, within ten (10) days thereafter, certify the result of the vote to the county superintendent of the county in which the district lies."

There can be no question, based on the facts above set forth, that the ballots prepared by the judges at the time of the election failed to comply with the statute, and that therefore any election held was on its face null and void. The testimony presented at the time of the order to show cause clearly showed that in at least one instance a lady who voted thought she was voting for keeping her schoolhouse rather than for consolidation, and that this vote in district 23 changed the outcome of the election in that district.

Concerning the withdrawal by the judges of the five votes in question section 75–1612, R.C.M.1947, is controlling. It is in part:

> *Poll and tally list, certificate of judges and canvass of the votes.* At every election held under this act, a poll list shall be kept by the judges and the clerk at each polling place, and immediately after the close of the polls the judges shall count the ballots, and if there be more ballots than votes cast the judges must draw by lot from the ballots, without seeing them, sufficient number of ballots to make the ballots remaining correspond with the number of votes cast."

All of the testimony was to the effect that there was never a drawing by lot of the five ballots in question to make the number of ballots cast tally with the number of votes contained in the poll list as required by the above statute.

This court in its most recent pronouncement on school election matters in a case of Hehn v. Olson, 138 Mont. 576, 358 P.2d 431, said this in quoting from Thompson v. Chapin, 64 Mont. 376, 209 P. 1060:

> " * * * [w]hile it is true that irregularities invite a concealed fraud, yet, where the fault lies with the election officials rather than the elector, they should be disregarded, unless the statute expressly declares that the same is fatal to the election, or *unless they are such as to themselves change or render doubtful the result of the election.*"

> It should be noted here that failure on the part of the election officials to follow the provisions of section 75–1612, would not be fatal to the election *unless the failure to follow the statute* would *"change or render doubtful the result of the election."*

Here, clearly, the testimony is that in district 23 one woman would have voted AGAINST rather than FOR had the word "consolidation" been on the ballot. Too, the improper procedure on the part of the officials in withdrawing five votes in district 29 has created such a situation in that district that it is doubtful that the result of the election would have been as it is recorded had they properly withdrawn the ballots according to statute.

The respondents contend that however illegal the election may have been that the appellants cannot prevail due to their failure to follow the provisions of section 75–1518, which fixes the duties of the county superintendent of schools with regard to school controversies. This section provides as follows:

> "He shall decide all matters in controversy arising in his county in the administration of the school law or appealed to him from the decision of school officers or boards. An appeal may be taken from his decision, in which case a full written statement of the facts, together with the testimony and his decision in the case, shall be certified to the state superintendent for his decision in the matter, which decision shall be final, subject to adjudication or the proper legal remedies in the state courts."

> * * *

> * * * The holding of elections on school matters whether voting for the school trustees, school levy, a school bond or school consolidation, is not an administrative function within the provisions of section 75–1518, where for some reason, the election is contested.

This court recently said in Hehn v. Olson, 138 Mont. 576, 358 P.2d 431: "However, even though § 75–1605 provides that the conduct of elections in second and third class school districts is 'by ballot without reference to the general election laws in regard to nominations, form of ballot, or manner of voting' election officials must be governed by some rules in determining the validity of votes. We hold that the rule stated in § 23–1704, with reference to determining the validity of ballots in *general* elections should also apply to school elections."

In this case, as in the above-quoted Hehn v. Olson, case, in an election controversy in a school district the county officials should have been guided by the election laws governing election controversies rather than by the school law upon which they relied.

Had this case been a case under section 75–1522, wherein the county superintendent had the power to consolidate a school district administratively, the case most certainly would have been a case wherein the protesting parties would have had to have followed the administrative procedure set forth in section 75–1518. This court in a series of cases * * * has held that the superintendent, acting under the statute giving her the administrative power to abandon the school district, which is section 75–1522, R.C.M.1947, will be sustained in her decision if the parties contesting the abandonment or consolidation do not follow the proper administrative appeal procedures set forth in section 75–1518. There is, however, a difference in her exercising an administrative function given to her by the legislature and the function of determining the legality of the procedure followed settling a vote dispute which is not contemplated in an election within the statute, upon which she relied.

The judgment of the district court is reversed.

School Board Meetings

A fundamental rule of school board meetings is that the meeting must be held within the geographic boundaries of the school district. A Missouri court has explained the reasons for this requirement in this manner " * * * it is obvious that considerations of public policy demand that the official meetings of public bodies be held within the limits of their territorial jurisdictions; otherwise, public servants might do in secret that which they would not attempt to do under public scrutiny, and thereby much injury might be done the public welfare * * *. It would be just as proper for the state legislature to hold its sessions outside the state or for a county court to transact business in another county * * *."

The courts have traditionally been rather lenient concerning the procedure used by boards of education in meetings. Unless the rules of procedure are prescribed by statute, a board of education may establish its own rules of procedure. Where neither statutes nor adopted board procedures are used the generally accepted rules of parliamentary procedure will control. As indicated the courts are indulgent concerning procedure and will not insist on a specific set of rules. The court is primarily concerned that every board member has been given a right to be heard and to vote.

The actual board meeting is an important prerequisite to an action by a board of education. Action taken separately or individually by board members outside a board meeting has no validity. Likewise, promises made by individual board members outside official meetings have no legal validity. However, a board of education, if it chooses, may ratify a previous individual commitment made a board member. Official action at a later meeting is necessary for ratification.

School Records are Open to Public and May be Photographed

PEOPLE EX REL. GIBSON v. PELLER

Appellate Court of Illinois, 1962.
34 Ill.App.2d 372, 181 N.E.2d 376.

BURKE, Justice. Plaintiffs are residents and taxpayers of the area comprising School District 89 and have children who attend a school of the district. Defendants are members of the Board of Education of the district and govern and administer the schools within the district. On April 4, 1960, at a designated time and place previously consented to by the defendants for the inspection of the financial records of the Board of Education of the district for the years 1955 through 1960, the plaintiffs were refused the right to make photographic reproduction thereof. They had brought a professional photographer with them to enable them to photographically reproduce the records. In their pleadings plaintiffs allege the right to photograph the records under the common law as well as pursuant to the State Records Act, Sec. 43.7, Ch. 116, Ill.Rev.Stat.1959. The pleadings present the issue whether relators have the right to photograph the records. From the judgment that a writ of mandamus issue commanding the defendants to permit relators to examine and reproduce by photographic means the financial records of expenditures and receipts of the Board for the years 1955 to 1960, inclusive, the defendants appeal.

Defendants insist that the State Records Act does not apply to them. They concede the right of relators to inspect the records and take copies thereof when necessary to the attainment of justice. They deny the right of relators to photograph the records for the period mentioned. We are of the opinion that the State Records Act applies to members of a Board of Education and to the public records in custody of the members and the Board. A Board of Education is an agency of the state government. * * * The Board of Education is an executive administrative agency of the state. Inasmuch as it is an agency of the state government and its members public officers of the state government, Sec. 43.7 of the State Records Act applies to permit the relators to photograph the records of the Board of Education.

The right of relators to reproduce the public records is not solely dependent upon statutory authority. There exists at common law the right to reproduce, copy and photograph public records as an incident to the common law right to inspect and use public records. Good public policy requires liberality in the right to examine public records. In C.J.S. Records § 35, p. 133, the author states: "The right of access to, and inspection of, public records is not entirely a matter of statute. The right exists at common law. * * * all authorities are agreed that at common law a person may inspect public records * * * or make copies or memoranda thereof." In Clay v. Ballard, 87 Va. 787, 790, 13 S.E. 262, 263, the court said that at common law the right to inspect includes the right to copy. * * *

Defendants say that relators have the right to look, examine and inspect with the naked eye the public records and copy by hand these public records, but that they have no right to photograph the records. This argument cannot be sustained by logic or common knowledge. Modern photography is accurate, harmless, noiseless and time saving. It does nothing more than capture that which is seen with the naked eye. Neither defendants nor the public can be harmed by the reproduction of the records exactly as they exist. The fact that more modern methods of copying are devised should not lessen the basic right given under the common law. The State Records Act declares the public policy relating to public records in the State of Illinois. It does not abrogate the common law.

The trial judge was right in entering judgment for the relators, and the judgment is affirmed.

Judgment affirmed.

NOTES

1. Open Meetings: Some states require open school board meetings by statute (Sunshine Laws), but even in the absence of statute board meetings are required to be open by the courts. The primary difference lies in that by common law boards can adjourn to executive session to consider any issue, but can only act in public. Most sunshine statutes require both deliberations and actions to be taken in public; the exception being only for sensitive matters which would, if aired in public, be personally detrimental to some party or would harm the public interest.

In New Jersey a statute requires open meetings. A board meeting was called for 8:00 P.M. to consider the appointment of a superintendent of schools. Three members (of the 5) met at 7:00 P.M. and without notifying the other two members privately agreed to appoint a certain individual as superintendent. At 8:00 P.M. the "resolution" was announced; the remainder of the board objected. The court held the appointment was void and said that for a public meeting to be valid there must be a fair opportunity for discussion. This did not prevent "advance" meetings of the board for "tentative" discussion, but it did preclude final action as was taken in this case. Cullum v. Board of Educ., 27 N.J.Super. 243, 99 A.2d 323 (1953).

In a Utah case the court held that "unless matters [are] * * * of such a delicate nature or of the type where public policy dictates non-dissemination, the meeting itself should be open to the public and press * * *. The truth about official acts of public servants always should be displayed in the public market place, subject to public appraisal." Conover v. Board of Educ., 1 Utah 2d 375, 267 P.2d 768 (1954).

A New York court has held that "All official action (of a school board) must be taken at a public meeting, and not at a closed one which only certain members of the public are permitted to attend." Application of Flinn, 154 N.Y.S.2d 124 (1956).

2. *Executive Sessions.* Executive sessions, where the board retires to privacy, may be utilized for discussion, but not for action. Where a board met in open session, adjourned for an hour or so, reconvened in executive session, and then met again in open session, teachers' contracts were terminated in the open session after discussion in the executive session and the teachers sued questioning the validity of the action. The court said the meeting was a legal one, despite the fact that the contracts were discussed in the executive session. The requirements of the law were met when the official action of the board was taken in open session. Alva v. Sequoia Union High School Dist., 98 Cal.App.2d 656, 220 P.2d 788 (1950); Dryden v. Marcelluse Community Schools, 401 Mich. 76, 257 N.W.2d 79 (1977).

In a later case, in Illinois, the board of education voted in an executive session to condemn land. Action was later ratified in an open meeting. The action was challenged and the court held that the action in the executive session was "not an effective exercise of the power of the board to commence condemnation. The original petition was, thus, insufficient." However, since the board had later ratified the action in an official meeting, the condemnation proceedings were legal. Goldman v. Zimmer, 64 Ill. App.2d 277, 212 N.E.2d 132 (1965).

3. *Procedure.* As pointed out earlier courts are rather flexible as to the procedure used by local school boards.

In 1960, a New Hampshire court upheld action by a school board where there was considerable irregularity in parliamentary procedure. The court said that a board's action could not be voided so long as no statutes were violated. If the machinery of government were not allowed a little play in its joints it would not work. Lamb v. Danville School Bd., 102 N.H. 569, 162 A.2d 614 (1960).

However, the courts will not go too far in upholding flimsy procedure. In a Missouri case, two board members, without notifying a third, got together informally at home and decided to call a special school election. No minutes were kept. The court said in this case that school elections called as a result of the meeting were invalid. The board meeting was not a legal one: "While there is no question but that the motives of the (board members) * * * were of the highest, we think their manner of getting together had no more dignity than any ordinary fence-row conference." State ex rel. Stewart v. Consolidated School Dist., Mo., 281 S.W.2d 511 (1955).

Boards of education should adopt rules of procedure, however, when they do they are bound by their own rules. In an early Kentucky case, illustrating the binding force of a board rule, a board made a rule that purchases of supplies and materials of $500 or less could be made without bid. Pianos were purchased in an amount of $2,500 without bids. The membership of the board changed and the new board refused to pay for the pianos. The vendor sued. The action of the vendor was unsuccessful. The court held that the school board rules had the force of law upon the board itself, which the board could not disregard. Montenegro-Riehm Music Co. v. Bd. of Ed. of Louisville, 147 Ky. 720, 145 S.W. 740 (1912).

An Ohio school board passed a rule which provided that bus drivers, involved in five accidents causing police investigation, shall be dismissed. A bus driver arrived home from a vacation trip at three in the morning, arose four hours later to drive a school bus. The bus left the road and struck an embankment 17 feet from the highway. No one was injured. The board dismissed the driver and the driver sued. The court held for the driver saying that the rule of five accidents of the board was "unfortunate." Since there was evidence of only one accident and even though the discharge of the driver was desirable, the board could not discharge him because of its own regulation. State ex rel. Edmundson v. Board of Educ., 2 Ohio Misc. 137, 201 N.E.2d 729 (1964).

4. *Quorum.* A quorum under common law is a simple majority of the total membership. In the absence of statute the common law rule will be applied. Gunnip v. Lautenklos, 33 Del. 415, 94 A.2d 712 (1953).

A Kentucky court has held that where there was one vacancy on a five member board the four remaining members represented a quorum. Trustees v. Brooks, 163 Ky. 200, 173 S.W. 305 (1915). The number required for a quorum is not reduced by a reduction in the membership due to vacancies. This means that in the case of a five member board, which has three vacancies, the two remaining board members cannot take action.

5. *Voting.* Boards, in the absence of statute, may establish voting procedures (voice vote, show of hands, secret ballot). There is no authority for a board member to allow someone else to vote for him.

Where a board member refuses to vote, the general rule is, that this vote is considered as assent to the will of the majority. Mullins v. Eveland, 234 S.W.2d 639 (Mo.1950). In a Tennessee case where a board of seven members considered a motion to execute a contract, three voted in favor, two opposed, and two did not vote. The court said the motion carried by a vote of five to two, those not voting were considered as assenting to majority. Collins v. Janey, 147 Tenn. 477, 249 S.W. 801 (1923).

Common law does not require that individual votes be recorded in the board minutes so long as the totals are made a part of the record. Diefenderfer v. Budd, 563 P.2d 1355 (Wyo.1977).

6. *Minutes and Records.* Courts hold that the school boards can act only through their minutes. The minutes of a board member are the only legal evidence of what has transpired during the meeting. An Illinois court has said that: "Proper minutes and records should be kept by a board of education to the end that the persons who are carring the tax load may make reference thereto and the future boards may be advised of the manner

of disposition of questions that have arisen." Hankenson v. Board of Educ., 10 Ill.App.2d 79, 134 N.E.2d 356 (1956).

A board secretary may record minutes after the meeting has adjourned. Kent v. School District, 166 Okl. 30, 233 P. 431 (1925).

Memoranda kept by the board secretary cannot be examined by the public prior to transcribing to minutes. In a 1954 case, on the day after a board meeting, citizens requested permission to examine minutes. The school board secretary had not as yet transcribed his notes and refused permission to the group. The court upheld the board and said " * * * the clerk's untranscribed notes reasonably are not classifiable as a public writing * * * whereas the transcribed minutes, in final form, but awaiting only approval and placement in the journal, are a public writing * * *." Conover v. Board of Educ., 1 Utah 2d 375, 267 P.2d 768 (1954).

The form and wordage used in school board minutes are looked upon with indulgence by the court. "Although they may be unskillfully drawn, if by fair and reasonable interpretation their meaning can be ascertained, they will be sufficient to answer the requirements of law." Noxubee Co. v. Long, 141 Miss. 72, 106 So. 83 (1925).

A public records law may require that names of applicants screened for superintendent's position be released to press. Attorney General v. School Committee of Northampton, 375 N.E.2d 1188 (Mass.1978).

7. *Notice of Meetings.* In order for a board meeting to be legal, proper notice must be given, all members notified in time to be given an opportunity to participate. A reasonable time in advance of a meeting for notice to be given is "sufficient time to the party notified for preparation and attendance at the time and place of such meeting." Green v. Jones, 144 W. Va. 276, 108 S.E.2d 1 (1959).

Where a board meeting was called with a few minutes notice, the chairman was unable to attend, and the board employed a teacher, the court held the employment invalid. "* * * (The chairman) was hardly bound to quit the work he had started to do and rush over to attend a suddenly called meeting of the board. The notice should have given him reasonable opportunity to attend. It did not." Wood v. School Dist., 137 Minn. 138, 162 N.W. 1081 (1917).

Notice should include the time and the place of the meeting. Members should be notified of any changes.

Where a meeting is held, without notice, and all members are present and consent to act, the requirement of notice is waived.

Notice is not required at regular board meetings because members have constructive notice. For example, boards usually establish a regular meeting date each month for which special notice is not required. Notice is only required for special board meetings.

8. *Special Board Meetings.* Notice of a special board meeting must include the purpose for the meeting. If a purpose is specified actions taken by the board on other subjects are null and void. Where a special board meeting was called to consider the budget, "and all other matters to come before the board," and during the meeting a tenure teacher submitted her resignation and later attempted to rescind it; the court held that the board had acted within the law since it had included the "catchall" phrase "and

other matters" in the notice. Evens v. Board of Educ., 65 N.J.Super. 68, 167 A.2d 39 (1961).

School District Organization

Power and responsibility for creation and control of school districts lies with the state. The legislature, as the governing body of the state, concerns itself with creation, alteration and abolition of school districts. The power over school districts may be exercised through direct legislative action or through the delegation of quasi-legislative power to administrative agents such as school boards. An Ohio court [22] described this relationship.

"Education is a matter of state concern. The public school system in Ohio is a creature of both the Constitution and the laws of the State * * * The State has a duty to establish and maintain public schools and to provide for the organization, administration, and control of them. The state performs this duty and obligation through the local school boards in the designated areas within its geographical boundary."

The case of People v. Decatur School Dist. No. 61,[23] illustrates the process of creation and alteration of school district boundaries. The legislature itself established the boundaries of the Decatur school district, and provided by statute that alteration of the district's boundaries may be had by three-fourths of the legal residents of an area petitioning the school board to be annexed. In this case, the area owned by a private company was inhabited by three people, two of voting age, both of whom petitioned the board to be included in the Decatur school district. The court upheld the annexation as in conformance with a valid statute.

The courts have held that if the legislature demands, school districts may be created and altered by school boards and by the authority of a public election. Individuals who merely have a property interest in the school district may not control the creation and alteration of school districts' boundaries. The Illinois legislature provides for administrative examination and determination of the propriety of annexation of special charter school districts within sixty days of annexation. Either of the concerned boards can set aside annexation if it finds that "the public interest and welfare of the districts and persons involved indicated [a] desirability of or need therefore." Individuals do not have a property interest in school district boundaries and there is no validity to the argument that they are deprived of property in violation of the due process clause of the constitution.

The right of citizens to challenge the creation and consolidation of school districts is limited. In most cases only the State may chal-

22. Board of Education of Miami v. Marting Trace Local Sch., 185 N.E.2d 597 (Ohio 1962).

23. 45 Ill.App.2d 33, 194 N.E.2d 659 (1963).

lenge the existence of school districts in a *quo warranto* proceeding. As a general rule, the citizen can only challenge the legality of a school district if he has personal interest in its being ruled illegal. For example, a citizen may have an interest more pervasive than the general public if an illegally constituted district is attempting to condemn his property through eminent domain.

The creation, alteration, and abolition of school districts is, in the main, controlled by the legislature and protected by the courts. The cases that follow further illustrate the extent, as well as the limitations on school district organization.

*State Has Absolute Power to Create
and Change School Districts*

KIES v. LOWREY

Supreme Court of the United States, 1905.
199 U.S. 233, 26 S.Ct. 27.

Mr. Justice McKENNA delivered the opinion of the court.

The constitution of the State of Michigan requires the legislature to establish and provide a system of public schools, whereby a school shall be kept open at least three months in each year in every school district in the State. In fulfillment of this requirement legislation was enacted from time to time providing for the formation of school districts. Under this legislation (1881) four school districts were organized in the townships of Somerset and Moscow, county of Hillsdale. In 1901 the legislature passed an act known as "Act Number 315 of the Local Acts of the State of Michigan for the Year 1901," entitled "An act to incorporate the public schools of the village of Jerome, Hillsdale County, Michigan; define the boundaries thereof, provide for the election of trustees and fix their powers and duties, and provide for the distribution of the territory of the disorganized districts." By this act one of the districts formed in the townships of Somerset and Moscow, in which the village of Jerome is situated, and portions of other districts, was set off and incorporated in one school district, to be known as "the public schools of the village of Jerome." The act appointed defendants in error trustees of the new district, to continue in office until their successors should be elected, as provided in the act. The act gave to the new district the property within its limits which had belonged to the districts from which it was created, and required the new district to assume and pay the debts and obligations of the old districts. The new district did not include all the lands of the old districts.

On the seventh of October, 1901, an information was filed in the nature of a *quo warranto* by the attorney general of the State upon the relation of L. E. Kies, W. E. Alley, J. B. Strong and Stephen Mc-

Cleary, charging defendants in error with usurping, intruding into and unlawfully claiming to exercise "a false, fictitious and pretended public office, to wit, trustees and officers of the pretended school district known as 'The public schools of the village of Jerome,' and *ex officio* 'The board of school inspectors of the public schools of the village of Jerome,' to wit, at the county of Hillsdale aforesaid, in contempt of the people of the State of Michigan, and to their great damage and prejudice."

The Circuit Court rendered a judgment of ouster against defendants in error. The Supreme Court entered the following judgment: "The judgment of ouster should be affirmed as to such officers as now hold under the legislative appointment, if there be any thus holding. As to others, if any, it will be reversed."

The grounds of attack upon the validity of the act creating the new district in the Supreme Court of the State were as follows:

First. It deprives this school district or municipality of the right of local self-government, guaranteed to all municipalities by the constitution.

Second. The title to the act indicates and the act itself embraces more than one object.

Third. The act is broader than the title; the body of the act embraces many objects not covered by the title.

Fourth. The act as passed impairs the obligation of contracts, within the meaning of the Constitution of the United States and the constitution of the State of Michigan.

With the first three grounds we have no concern. They present strictly local questions. We are concerned with the fourth ground only in so far as it invokes the Constitution of the United States. The Supreme Court disposed of this ground as follows: "We have already shown that the obligation of contracts is not impaired. The districts did not hold this property under any contract with the State, but as a public agency." In other words, the non-existence of a contract was rested on the construction of the constitution and laws of the State, and hence defendant in error contends that the decision of the court did not involve a Federal question. This, however, overlooks the power and duty of this court to determine for itself the existence or non-existence of a contract. Other grounds in support of the motion to dismiss are urged which, we think are also untenable. The motion is therefore denied.

Plaintiff in error broadened in this court his objections to the act, based on the Constitution of the United States. He urges, besides, the contract clause of the Constitution, that provision of the Fourteenth Amendment which protects private property from deprivation without due process of law, and section 4, Article IV, which provides "The United States shall guarantee to every State in the Union a republican form of government." But the grounds all depend ultimately upon the same arguments. If the legislature of the State has the power to create and alter school districts and divide and apportion the property of such districts no contract can arise, no property of a district can be said to be taken, and the action of the legislature is compatible with a republican form of government even if it be admitted that section 4, Article IV, of the Constitution applies to the creation of, or the powers or rights of property of, the subordinate municipalities of a State. We may omit, therefore, that section and Article from further consideration. The decision of the other grounds urged we may rest upon the opinion of the Supreme Court of the State and the case of Laramie County v. Albany County et al., 92 U.S. 307. It is there said in many ways, with citation of many supporting cases, that the legislature of a State has absolute power to make and change subordinate municipalities. The following quotation meets exactly the contentions of plaintiff in error:

"Institutions of the kind, whether called counties or towns, are the auxiliaries of the State in the important business of municipal rule, and cannot have the least pretension to sustain their privileges or their existence upon anything like a contract between them and the legislature of the State, because there is not and cannot be any reciprocity of stipulation, and their objects and duties are utterly incompatible with everything of the nature of compact. Instead of that, the constant practice is to divide large counties and towns, and to consolidate small ones, to meet the wishes of the residents, or to promote the public interests as understood by those who control the action of the legislature. Opposition is sometimes manifested but it is everywhere acknowledged that the legislature possesses the power to divide counties and towns at their pleasure and to apportion the common property and the common burdens in such manner as to them may seem reasonable and equitable." Many cases are cited. See also Worcester v. Worcester Street Railway Co., 196 U.S. 539, 25 S.Ct. 327.

Judgment affirmed.

NOTES

1. The term "school reorganization," as generally used, means the changing of boundary lines of a school district and may also mean changes in the organizational structure within a school district. School reorganization is also known by other terms such as "consolidation," "unification," "centralization," "annexation" and "merger."

2. Some states have reorganized school districts by direct legislative enactment. This procedure is relatively rare; usually reorganization statutes are permissive and leave reorganization to local districts. Examples of abolition of existing districts and creation of new ones by the legislature are: County units were adopted in Maryland in 1868; in Louisiana, 1912; in West Virginia, 1933; in Florida, 1947; and in Nevada, 1956. Modified

county units were adopted in Alabama, 1903; in Tennessee, 1907; Kentucky, 1908; Utah, 1915; in Virginia, 1923; in Georgia, 1945.

3. Litigation involving school district reorganization involve either state or federal constitutional issues. A reorganization statute in Oregon required county committees to prepare a plan for reorganization. If the boundaries were to be changed a vote of citizens was provided for, if no change in boundaries then there was no provision for a vote. This provision was challenged as violation of equal protection. The court held that the statute was constitutional. "The inhabitants of a district have no vested right in the status of a school district and none of their rights, constitutional or otherwise, are violated by legislation requiring district reorganization." Padberg v. Martin, 225 Or. 135, 357 P.2d 255 (1960).

In an Indiana case, plaintiff contended a school district reorganization act was unconstitutional because it was enacted by a legislature that had failed to reapportion itself, contrary to the state constitution. The court in ruling against the plaintiff said that legislators who hold office under color of election and discharge their duties in full view of the public without being usurpers or intruders are at least de facto officers. The authority of a de facto officer cannot be collaterally attacked. For protection of the public, acts of a de facto officer are as valid as acts of a de jure officer. Fruit v. Metropolitan School Dist. of Winchester-White Township, 241 Ind. 621, 172 N.E.2d 864 (1961).

A Washington court held constitutional provisions prohibiting taking of property without due process of law are not violated by a statute providing for school district reorganization without a vote of the electorate. Electors have no absolute right to vote on matters of school district reorganization. Goodnoe Hills School Dist. v. Forry, 52 Wash.2d 868, 329 P.2d 1083 (1959).

Impairment of Obligation of Contract

In an Indiana case the plaintiff contended that school debts of other townships in a reorganization plan was not his debt—he had no voice in formation of the contract for the debts and therefore contracts could not be enforced after reorganization of school districts because he was not a party to the original contract. The court held against the plaintiff and said that the contract was between bondholders and school officials as representatives of the taxpayers. The plaintiff had no contractual interest in this contract and therefore his contractual rights were not impaired. Cottongim v. Congleton, 245 Ind. 387, 199 N.E.2d 96 (1964).

4. Petitions submitted requesting school reorganization are sometimes a source of litigation.

Under common law a petitioner may withdraw his name prior to filing with the proper agency. A Kentucky court has stated that the "right * * * to withdraw an inherent and natural right * * *. Would it not be logical to say that if, after requesting the withdrawal of his name from the petition he changes his mind and concludes to stand by his original act in signing it, should he not be permitted to revoke such withdrawal, provided the revocation is made before the court takes action on the petition?" Horton v. Botts, 158 Ky. 11, 164 S.W. 352 (1914).

In Nebraska a county superintendent had the authority to divide or establish new school districts upon petition of 55 percent of the legal voters. A petition was filed, but prior to action by the county superintendent, two people withdrew their names, making less than the required 55 percent. The superintendent ignored the request to withdraw and proceeded to separate the district as was requested in the petition. The court said the action of the superintendent was illegal, "We do not discover anything improper in a citizen, who thinks he is now better advised, changing his mind a second time * * *. It seems better to us to say (that the citizen) has absolute control of the matter as to whether or not his name shall remain upon the petition up to the moment that the board acts upon it." State v. Morrison, 155 Neb. 309, 51 N.W.2d 626 (1952).

Although the above cases seem to state the general rule of law regarding withdrawal of names from petitions, a South Carolina court has ruled to the contrary denying the right of 17 petitioners to withdraw on the last day fixed by statute for filing a petition for election. The court reasoned that such late changes, "when it was too late to add other names to the original petition or for the filing of a new one by those favoring an election," would prejudice, "the other signers of the original petition in the enjoyment of their political rights." Hawkins v. Carroll, 190 S.C. 11, 1 S.E.2d 898 (1939).

5. The right of a board of education to change plans after reorganization is consummated has been contested.

In Arkansas the Perryville board made a "deal" with the voters of the Cherry Hill district to maintain a school in that district if the people voted to reorganize. After 12 years, the school was discontinued. Patrons sued to mandate the continuation of the school or to deconsolidate. The court held against the plaintiffs and said that there was no statutory authority for a school board to contract to maintain a school at a certain place indefinitely. Powers of a board are conferred by statute and a board cannot restrict its powers by such an agreement. Brown v. Gardner, 232 Ark. 197, 334 S.W.2d 889 (1960).

In an Idaho case involving a change of plans by a board of education, after reorganization, the court once again upheld the board. Here a reorganization plan as approved by the State and ratified by the voters provided for the transfer of certain pupils out of the district. The board found the costs too high and decided to educate the pupils themselves. Plaintiffs brought suit to prevent this. The court said that proposals contained in a plan do not constitute a rigid, fixed permanent pattern for operation of schools of the district. Found against the plaintiff. Hay v. Class B. School Dist., 84 Idaho 501, 373 P.2d 922 (1962).

6. Generally, when school districts are consolidated, the new school district must pay prior indebtedness of consolidated districts. This is not true, however, in states where the constitution requires a vote of the electors to incur indebtedness. Walker v. Bennett, 125 S.C. 389, 118 S.E. 779 (1923).

7. The actions of a school district may be challenged because of some irregularity in its formation. In order to prevent impedance of public business, courts have created the legal fiction of a de facto school district. In the matter of business corporations de facto corporation is defined: "A de

facto corporation exists so that the legality of its subsistence cannot be attacked collaterally, where (1) there is a special act or general law under which such a corporation may lawfully live, (2) a bona fide attempt to organize under the law in colorable compliance with the statutory requirements, and (3) actual user or exercise of corporate powers in pursuance of such law and attempted organization." DeBerg v. County Bd. of Educ., 248 Iowa 1039, 82 N.W.2d 710 (1957).

The definition of a de facto business corporation above embodies the elements necessary for a de facto school district. Applied to school districts these are: (1) there must be some law under which the district could have organized legally, (2) there must have been an attempt to organize the school district under that law, and (3) it must be claimed that rights conferred by that law were used.

A case in point is a Minnesota case where a district was reorganized but there was a defect in the reorganization petition. Plaintiff sought to enjoin operation on the grounds that the district was illegal. The court held that this was a de facto district. A law had been passed, there was an attempt to follow the law, and the district was operated for a period of time. Although the district had not been operated for a longer period of time, the essential thing was that the district was a *user* for an appreciable length of time. This court went on to point out that the legality of a school district can only be attacked in a quo warranto proceeding. It cannot be attacked directly or collaterally by an ordinary citizen. The reason is that public rights must be vindicated by public authority, and since a school district is a creature of the state its legality can only be challenged by the state. Evens v. Anderson, 132 Minn. 59, 155 N.W. 1040 (1916).

The de facto doctrine protects the school district against challenges to its authority. In summary the doctrine provides:

(1) To all but the state, a *de facto* district has all the qualities of a *de jure* district.

(2) Acts of a *de facto* district are as valid as acts of a *de jure* district.

(3) The legality of a *de facto* district is not subject to direct or collateral attack by a private citizen, unless the citizen can show a special interest apart from the public's as a whole is at stake. *De facto* district can only be attacked by the state itself in a *quo warranto* proceeding.

Chapter 6

CHURCH AND STATE

Centuries of religious strife in Europe left an indelible mark on the minds of the fathers of the American Constitution. Diversity of religious background among the American colonies was so great and religious sentiments so deep that representatives at the Convention in Philadelphia in 1787 were loath to address the issue lest the Convention founder on the shoals of religious dissension. Avoidance was implicitly agreed upon by all and everyone, more or less, adopted the position of John Adams who assumed that if the issue was not mentioned both the state and religion would be best served. Adams expressed the hope that "Congress will never meddle with religion further than to say their own prayers, and to fast and to give thanks once a year." [1] Some believed that simple omission was not the appropriate solution to the religious dilemma and although it was not acted upon by the Convention, Pinckney of South Carolina sought to make the absence of Congressional power in religion explicit by proposing that the new Constitution provide that " * * * the Legislature of the United States shall pass no law on the subject of religion." [2] Even though no general religious provision was acted upon, there is little doubt that the failure resulted from the delegates' firm belief that such a provision was not necessary to preserve religious liberty. While no general religious separation provision was thought to be needed, the Convention did decide to specifically prohibit states from imposing religious tests for federal office. Madison explained that it might be implied that "without [an] exception, a power would have been given to impose an oath involving religious test as a qualification for office." [3] Obviously, it was in the interest of the central government to prevent states with different religious ties to require religious tests for federal office. With cognizance of this the Convention adopted Pinckney's motion that " * * * no religious test shall ever be required as a qualification to any office or public trust under the United States; " this became the last clause of Article VI in the Constitution.

Thus, when the Constitution was ratified by the states only the "religious test" of office provision was included and no other reference was made regarding religious toleration. This omission was not taken lightly when the states were called upon to ratify the document.

1. Evarts B. Green, *Religion and The State in America*, New York University Press, New York, 1941, p. 83.

2. Jonathan Elliot, *The Debates in the Several State Conventions on the Adoption of the Federal Constitution,* 2d ed., J. B. Lippincott & Co., Philadelphia, 1888, v. p. 131.

3. Leo Pfeffer, *Church, State and Freedom*, Beacon Press, Boston, 1967, p. 123.

Six states ratified but proposed amendments guaranteeing religious liberty and two other states, North Carolina and Rhode Island, refused to ratify until a bill of rights including religious freedom was promulgated.[4] Although Madison defended the omission saying, "the government has no jurisdiction over it [religion]",[5] it was argued by others that there was no security for the rights of conscience. Jefferson ultimately convinced Madison that a religious provision in a bill of rights was necessary. In a letter to Madison from Paris, commenting on the proposed constitution, where Jefferson was serving as ambassador, he said:

> I will now add what I do not like. First, the omission of a bill of rights providing clearly and without the aid of sophisms for freedom of religion, freedom of the press, protection against monopolies, the eternal and unremitting force of the habeas corpus laws, and trials by juries. * * * [A] bill of rights is what the people are entitled to against every government on earth, general or particular, and what no just government should refuse or rest on inference.[6]

The very uncertainty itself of whether such rights were implied in the Constitution was evidence enough that a bill of rights protecting religious freedom and assuring disestablishment was necessary. Madison, with Jefferson's urging and his own experience in persuading the states to ratify only after promising amendments as specific affirmation of individual rights and freedoms stated that he now favored amendment to provide for "all essential rights, particularly the rights of Conscience in the fullest latitude, the freedom of the press, trial by jury, etc." [7] In accordance with this position, Madison introduced to the House of Representatives in 1789 a compilation of proposals for amendments which he maintained would prevent encroachments by the sovereign power into individual rights and liberties. Madison's proposals before the House were to finally become the Bill of Rights which were approved by the requisite number of states in 1791. Prominent among these rights was the separation of church and state provision which guaranteed religious freedom and prohibited establishment of religion by government. The First Amendment states:

> Congress shall make no law respecting an establishment of religion, or prohibiting the free exercise thereof; or abridging the freedom of speech, or of the press; or the right of the people peaceably to assembly and to petition the Government for a redress of grievances.

4. R. Freeman Butts, *The American Tradition in Religion and Education,* Beacon Press, Boston, 1950, p. 72.

5. Pfeffer, *op. cit.* p. 125.

6. Ibid.

7. Ibid. p. 126.

Antecedents of The First Amendment

Much of the history of Western civilization has had its basis in religious controversy. Disputes between tribal chiefs and priests were fertile ground for discord that materially affected both church and state. In more primitive eras the state did not attempt to delineate religious from secular activities, with some polytheistic societies merely cataloguing and assigning gods to a particular divine hierarchy, as in the Code of Hammurabi.[8] In most instances the state and religion were entwined in the interests and affairs of the day, but it was very clear that of the two forces, the state was supreme. In ancient Greece, the head of state was also chief priest and served as the supreme guardian of religion. As the Athenian republic became well established the unity of religion with state continued.[9]

Rome, too, was originally a state of many gods with the innovation that great heads of state, upon death, were placed among the ranks of the gods.[10] So long as there were many gods to worship and everyone recognized the state was supreme, little conflict developed; however, with the advent of Christianity, full-fledged discord became apparent. Christians ascribed to a dogmatic exclusiveness which was not tolerated by the Romans. Religious persecution of Christians began with Nero with the justification that they were "enemies of mankind" and "arsonists", conveniently serving as scapegoats for the burning of Rome.[11] Persecution continued until Constantine when he and his two co-rulers of the empire issued the Edict of Milan in 312 or 313 A.D., a document of great importance in religious history, providing "that liberty of worship shall not be denied to any, but that the mind and will of every individual shall be free to manage divine affairs according to his own choice."[12] From this point on the Christian religion became dominant as Constantine adopted it as a primary means of consolidating his empire.[13]

In the centuries which followed the Christian Church gained power and authority, to the point that it became quite clear that the church was supreme over any head of state. Strength of the Church was demonstrated by Pope Gelasius I in 496 when he proclaimed to the emperor:

> There are two things, most august emperor, by which this world is chiefly ruled: the sacred authority of the priesthood and the royal power. Of these two the priests carry

8. Leo Pefeffer, *op. cit.* p. 4.

9. Ibid.

10. Pfeffer.

11. Williston Walker, *A History of the Christian Church*, Charles Scribner's Sons, New York 1929, p. 464.

12. *History of Christianity in the Light of Modern Knowledge*, Blackie and Son, London, 1929, p. 464.

13. Pfeffer, *op. cit.* p. 14.

the greater weight, because they will have to render account in the divine judgment even for the kings of men.[14]

Although Christianity had, under the Romans, been the oppressed, when it gained dominion it became the oppressor and little tolerance was exhibited. St. Augustine strongly advanced the conviction that the civil power of the state should be used to suppress dissidents of the church. Compulsion was the watchword and St. Augustine espoused the belief that "freedom to err" was the worst killer of the soul. In keeping with that philosophy; "the Medieval Church was intolerant, was the source and author of persecution, justified and defended the most violent measures which could be taken against those who differed from it."[15]

From this basis, the development of medieval Europe was almost solely that of continual struggle between church and state, with kings rebelling against the Church, and the sword of the state being alternatively put to use to stamp out heretics and nonconformists.

While most people are aware of the centuries of intolerance on the European continent, the most extreme example of which is probably the Spanish Inquisition, our more direct church-state antecedents derive from English origin. With the Reformation, problems of church and state were compounded as new religious doctrines were advanced and various ideologies began to emerge as separate and viable religions. Intolerance prevailed, whether Catholics or Protestants were in power. Henry VIII's conflict with Rome blossomed into bloody internal strife as Edward VI, Mary and Elizabeth took the throne and in succession persecuted religious opponents. For her deeds, Mary was remembered in history as "Bloody Mary". During Elizabeth's long reign the Church of England was firmly established as the state religion and the supremacy of the state over the church was complete. Ecclesiastical offices were regulated by her proclamations and opposing religious viewpoints were not tolerated. From this point in England there existed a church which was Protestant in nature and entirely subject to state authority and control. Intra-Protestant struggles developed, and internal Protestant religious peace was not actually achieved in England until 1689 with the act of Toleration.

Even though the great religious wars of Europe were not of the same era with the lifespan of the Constitutional forefathers of the United States, the strife of the Old World was still much in their minds. The Supreme Court of the United States has best expressed the situation:

The centuries immediately before and contemporaneous with the colonization of America had been filled with tur-

14. M. Searle Bates, *Religious Liberty: An Inquiry*, International Missionary Council, New York and London, 1945, p. 134.

15. Alexander J. Carlyle, *The Christian Church and Liberty*, J. Clark, London, 1924, p. 96.

moil, civil strife, and persecution, generated in large part by
established sects determined to maintain their absolute political and religious supremacy. With the power of government to support them, at various times and places, Catholics
had persecuted Protestants, Protestants had persecuted
Catholics, Protestant sects had persecuted other Protestant
sects, Catholics of one shade of belief had persecuted Catholics of another shade of belief, and all of these had from
time to time persecuted Jews.[16]

When the matter of religion was to be considered in 1787, there
were essentially three rationalizations for church-state relationships
which had arisen out of the Reformation: the Erastian (named after
the German philosopher Erastus), the theocratic, and the separatist.
Dominate among these was the Erastian view which assumed state
superiority over ecclesiastical affairs and religion was used to further
the interests of the state. It was during the Elizabethan era in England that the Erastian philosophy was fully implemented. The second, the theocratic, was founded in the idea that the church is supreme and the state should be used to further ecclesiastical policy.
Third, complete separation, was advanced as the proper course by minority dissident groups in Europe but did not find full expression until 1791 in America.[17] It was, however, John Locke on whom both
Madison and Jefferson relied for their basic philosophical ideas concerning separation. In his _Letter Concerning Toleration,_ Locke
maintained that, "The care of souls cannot belong to the civil magistrate because his power consists only in outward force, but true and
saving religion consists in the inward persuasion of the mind
* * *."[18]

Locke's ideas were developed and expanded under fire in the great
dispute in Virginia over established religion which had been carefully
protected by statutes promulgated by the Anglican Church until the
Revolution. These laws provided for religious services according to
the laws and orders of the Church of England: compulsory attendance at religious services, regulation of nonconformists, glebe lands
for support of the clergy, and a system of governmentally sanctioned
vestries empowered to levy tithes for upkeep of the Church and ministers' salaries.

Jefferson, more than any other individual led in enunciating and
implementing the separation principle. In 1776 while he was in Philadelphia writing the _Declaration of Independence_ he drafted a proposed constitution for Virginia which stated that "All persons shall
have full and free liberty of religious opinion; nor shall any be com-

---

16. Everson v. Board of Educ., 330 U.S.
1, 67 S.Ct. 504 (1947).

17. Pfeffer, _op. cit._ p. 26.

18. John Locke, _A Letter Concerning
Toleration,_ Liberal Arts Press, 1955,
pp. 17–18.

pelled to frequent or maintain any religious institution."[19]　Although this particular measure was not passed, it nevertheless set the tone for religious freedom for Virginia in the era to come.　In spite of Jefferson's position, however, in 1779, a bill was introduced in the Virginia legislature which declared that "the Christian Religion shall in all times coming be deemed and held to be the established Religion of the Commonwealth."[20]　It required every person to enroll his name with the county clerk and designate the society which he intended to support, whereupon, the clerk would present the role and the appropriate religious group to determine assessment rates;　these were then collected by the sheriff and the proceeds were turned over to the church.　Taxes obtained from persons failing to enroll in a religious society had their payments spread across all religious groups.[21]

In 1784 the bill was called up for a vote;　entitled a "Bill Establishing a Provision for Teachers of the Christian Religion," it was sponsored by Patrick Henry.　Although the bill was defeated, from the preceding and ensuing debate two of the most important documents in religious freedom were written, Jefferson's *Bill for Establishing Religious Freedom* and Madison's *Memorial and Remonstrance against Religious Assessments*.　When Jefferson's bill was finally enacted into law in 1786 it set forth among other provisions

> * * * that no man shall be compelled to frequent or support any religious worship, place or ministry whatsoever, nor shall be enforced, restrained, molested or burdened in his body or goods, nor shall otherwise suffer on account of his religious opinions or beliefs, but that all men shall be free to profess, and by argument to maintain, their opinions in matters of religion, and that the same shall in no wise diminish, enlarge or affect their civil capacities.

Madison's *Memorial*, in opposition to Henry's bill for religious assessments, was of great historical significance.　The philosophy stated therein has often been referred to by the U.S. Supreme Court in support of its opinions.　The *Memorial* presents several arguments against the religious assessment bill but more importantly it conveys a philosophy of separation which, along with Jefferson's, provided the logic and rationale for the "wall of separation" provisions of the First Amendment in 1791.

AN ACT FOR ESTABLISHING RELIGIOUS FREEDOM

by Thomas Jefferson (1786)

Well aware that Almighty God hath created the mind free;　that all attempts to influence it by temporal punishments or burdens, or

19. Saul K. Pandover, *The Complete Jefferson*, Duell, Sloan & Pearce, New York, 1943.

20. Ibid.

21. Pfeffer, *op. cit.* p. 109.

by civil incapacitations, tend only to beget habits of hypocrisy and meanness, and are a departure from the plan of the Holy Author of our religion, who being Lord both of body and mind, yet chose not to propagate it by coercions on either, as was in his Almighty power to do;

That the impious presumption of legislators and rulers, civil as well as ecclesiastical, who, being themselves but fallible and uninspired men, have assumed dominion over the faith of others, setting up their own opinions and modes of thinking as the only true and infallible, and as such endeavoring to impose them on others, hath established and maintained false religions over the greatest part of the world, and through all time;

That to compel a man to furnish contributions of money for the propagation of opinions which he disbelieves, is sinful and tyrannical; that even the forcing him to support this or that teacher of his own religious persuasion, is depriving him of the comfortable liberty of giving his contributions to the particular pastor whose morals he would make his pattern, and whose power he feels most persuasive to righteousness, and is withdrawing from the ministry those temporal rewards, which proceeding from an approbation of their personal conduct, are an additional incitement to earnest and unremitting labors for the instruction of mankind;

That our civil rights have no dependence on our religious opinions, more than our opinions in physics or geometry; that, therefore, the proscribing any citizen as unworthy the public confidence by laying upon him an incapacity of being called to the offices of trust and emolument, unless he profess or renounce this or that religious opinion, is depriving him injuriously of those privileges and advantages to which in common with his fellow citizens he has a natural right;

That it tends also to corrupt the principles of that very religion it is meant to encourage, by bribing, with a monopoly of worldly honors and emoluments, those who will externally profess and conform to it; that though indeed these are criminal who do not withstand such temptation, yet neither are those innocent who lay the bait in their way;

That to suffer the civil magistrate to intrude his powers into the field of opinion and to restrain the profession or propagation of principles, on the supposition of their ill tendency, is a dangerous fallacy, which at once destroys all religious liberty, because he being of course judge of that tendency, will make his opinions the rule of judgment, and approve or condemn the sentiments of others only as they shall square with or differ from his own;

That it is time enough for the rightful purposes of civil government, for its officers to interfere when principles break out into overt acts against peace and good order;

And finally, that truth is great and will prevail if left to herself, that she is the proper and sufficient antagonist to error, and has nothing to fear from the conflict, unless by human interposition disarmed of her natural weapons, free argument and debate, errors ceasing to be dangerous when it is permitted freely to contradict them.

Be it therefore enacted by the General Assembly, That no man shall be compelled to frequent or support any religious worship, place or ministry whatsoever, nor shall be enforced, restrained, molested, or burthened in his body or goods, nor shall otherwise suffer on account of his religious opinions or belief; but that all men shall be free to profess, and by argument to maintain, their opinions in matters of religion, and that the same shall in nowise diminish, enlarge, or affect their civil capacities.

And though we well know this Assembly, elected by the people for the ordinary purposes of legislation only, have no power to restrain the acts of succeeding assemblies, constituted with the powers equal to our own, and that therefore to declare this act irrevocable, would be of no effect in law, yet we are free to declare, and do declare, that the rights hereby asserted are of the natural rights of mankind, and that if any act shall be hereafter passed to repeal the present or to narrow its operation, such act will be an infringement of natural right.

MEMORIAL AND REMONSTRANCE AGAINST RELIGIOUS ASSESSMENTS

by James Madison

To the Honorable the General Assembly of the Commonwealth of Virginia. A Memorial and Remonstrance.

We, the subscribers, citizens of the said Commonwealth, having taken into serious consideration, a Bill printed by order of the last Session of General Assembly, entitled "A Bill establishing a provision for teachers of the Christian Religion," and conceiving that the same, if finally armed with the sanctions of a law, will be a dangerous abuse of power, are bound as faithful members of a free State, to remonstrate against it, and to declare the reasons by which we are determined. We remonstrate against the said Bill,

Because we hold it for a fundamental and undeniable truth, "that religion, or the duty which we owe to our Creator, and the manner of discharging it, can be directed only by reason and conviction, not by force or violence." [22] The Religion then of every man must be left to the conviction and conscience of every man; and it is the right of every man to exercise it as these may dictate. This right is in its nature an unalienable right. * * *

---

22. Decl. Rights, Art. 16. [Note in the original.]

Because, it is proper to take alarm at the first experiment on our liberties. We hold this prudent jealousy to be the first duty of citizens, and one of [the] noblest characteristics of the late Revolution. The freemen of America did not wait till usurped power had strengthened itself by exercise, and entangled the question in precedents. They saw all the consequences in the principle, and they avoided the consequences by denying the principle. We reverse this lesson too much, soon to forget it. Who does not see that the same authority which can establish Christianity, in exclusion of all other Religions, may establish with the same ease any particular sect of Christians, in exclusion of all other Sects? That the same authority which can force a citizen to contribute three pence only of his property for the support of any one establishment, may force him to conform to any other establishment in all cases whatsoever?

Because, the bill violates that equality which ought to be the basis of every law, and which is more indispensable, in proportion as the validity or expediency of any law is more liable to be impeached. If "all men are by nature equally free and independent," [23] all men are to be considered as entering into Society on equal conditions; as relinquishing no more, and therefore retaining no less, one than another, of their natural rights. Above all are they to be considered as retaining an "equal title to the free exercise of Religion according to the dictates of conscience." [24] Whilst we assert for ourselves a freedom to embrace, to profess and to observe the Religion which we believe to be of divine origin, we cannot deny an equal freedom to those whose minds have not yet yielded to the evidence which has convinced us. If this freedom be abused, it is an offense against God, not against man: To God, therefore, not to men, must an account of it be rendered. As the Bill violates equality by subjecting some to peculiar burdens; so it violates the same principle, by granting to others peculiar exemptions. Are the Quakers and Menonists the only sects who think a compulsive support of their religions unnecessary and unwarrantable? Can their piety alone be entrusted with the care of public worship? Ought their Religions to be endowed above all others, with extraordinary privileges, by which proselytes may be enticed from all others? We think too favorably of the justice and good sense of these denominations, to believe that they either covet preeminencies over their fellow citizens, or that they will be seduced by them, from the common opposition to the measure.
* * *

What influence in fact have ecclesiastical establishments had on Civil Society? In some instances they have been seen to erect a spiritual tyranny on the ruins of Civil authority; in many instances they have been seen upholding the thrones of political tyranny; in no in-

23. Decl. Rights, Art. 1. [Note in the original.]   24. Art. 16 [Note in the original.]

stance have they been seen the guardians of the liberties of the people. Rulers who wished to subvert the public liberties, may have found an established clergy convenient auxiliaries. A just government, instituted to secure and perpetuate it, needs them not. Such a government will be best supported by protecting every citizen in the enjoyment of his Religion with the same equal hand which protects his person and his property; by neither invading the equal rights by any Sect, nor suffering any Sect to invade those of another.

Because the proposed establishment is a departure from that generous policy, which offering an asylum to the persecuted and oppressed of every Nation and Religion, promised a lustre to our country, an accession to the number of its citizens. What a melancholy mark is the Bill of sudden degeneracy? Instead of holding forth an asylum to the persecuted, it is itself a signal of persecution. It degrades from the equal rank of citizens all those whose opinions in Religion do not bend to those of the Legislative authority. Distant as it may be, in its present form, from the Inquisition it differs from it only in degree. The one is the first step, the other the last in the career of intolerance. * * *

Because, it will destroy that moderation and harmony which the forbearance of our laws to intermeddle with Religion, has produced amongst its several sects. Torrents of blood have been spilt in the old world, by vain attempts of the secular arum to extinguish Religious discord, by proscribing all difference in Religious opinions. Time has at length revealed the true remedy. Every relaxation of narrow and rigorous policy, wherever it has been tried, has been found to assuage the disease. The American Theatre has exhibited proofs, that equal and complete liberty, if it does not wholly eradicate it, sufficiently destroys its malignant influence on the health and prosperity of the State. If with the salutary effects of this system under our own eyes, we begin to contract the bonds of Religious freedom, we know no name that will too severely reproach our folly. At least let warning be taken at the first fruit of the threatened innovation. The very appearance of the Bill has transformed that "Christian forbearance,"[25] love and charity," which of late mutually prevailed, into animosities and jealousies, which may not soon be appeased. What mischiefs may not be dreaded should this enemy to the public quiet be armed with the force of a law? * * *

Because, finally, "the equal right of every citizen to the free exercise of his Religion according to the dictates of conscience" is held by the same tenure with all our other rights. If we recur to its origin, it is equally the gift of nature; if we weigh its importance, it cannot be less dear to us; if we consult the Declaration of those rights which pertain to the good people of Virginia, as the "basis and foundation of Government," [26] it is enumerated with equal solemnity,

25. Art. 16. [Note in the original.]　　　26. Dec. Rights-title [Note in the original.]

or rather studied emphasis. Either then, we must say, that the will of the Legislature is the only measure of their authority; and that in the plentitude of this authority, they may sweep away all our fundamental rights; or, that they are bound to leave this particular right untouched and sacred: Either we must say, that they may control the freedom of the press, may abolish the trial by jury, may swallow up the Executive and Judiciary powers of the State; nay that they may despoil us of our very right of suffrage, and erect themselves into an independent and hereditary assembly: or we must say, that they have no authority to enact into law the Bill under consideration. We, the subscribers, say, that the General Assembly of this Commonwealth have no such authority: And that no effort may be omitted on our part against so dangerous an usurpation, we oppose to it, this remonstrance; earnestly praying, as we are in duty bound, that the Supreme Lawgiver of the Universe, by illuminating those to whom it is addressed, may on the one hand turn their councils from every act which would affront his holy prerogative, or violate the trust committed to them: and on the other, guide them into every measure which may be worthy of his [blessing, may re] dound to their own praise, and may establish more firmly the liberties, the prosperity, and the Happiness of the Commonwealth. II Madison, 183–191.

The Public School and Religion

Public education is founded on three fundamental assumptions which relate either directly or indirectly to the issue of church and state. First, that education is a benefit to the entire society and that the legislature has power to tax all for support. Essential to this concept is that general taxation is used for support and that taxation is not levied merely on those who use the public schools—the childless and those who sent their children to private schools must all pay their fair share. Thaddeus Stevens in 1835, in dramatically defeating a legislative proposal to repeal general taxation for education, enunciated the principle of universal responsibility for universal education in Pennsylvania. It was claimed that it was unjust to tax people to educate children of others; Stevens responded thusly:

> It is for their own benefit, inasmuch as it perpetrates the government and ensures the due administration of the laws under which they live, and by which their lives and property are protected. Why do they not urge the same objection against all other taxes? The industrious, thrifty, rich farmer pays a heavy county tax to support criminal courts, build jails, and pay sheriffs and jail keepers, and yet probably he never has had and probably never will have any direct personal use for them. * * * He cheerfully pays burdensome taxes which are necessarily levied to support and punish convicts, but loudly complains of that which goes to pre-

vent his fellowbeing from becoming a criminal and to obviate the necessity of those humiliating institutions.[27]

To Stevens, education was a public obligation which must be nurtured to develop the entire civic intelligence to better govern through an elective republic. Those who do not directly benefit from public education certainly gain indirectly through association with an enlightened citizenry.

Second, that education provided by the state must be secular and individual religious beliefs should not be inhibited. An important element of the secular state envisioned by Jefferson was a system of public schools which could convey all necessary temporal knowledge and yet not impede religious freedom. The power of the state could not be utilized to inculcate religious beliefs nor could the authority of the state to tax be used to assist religious training.

The First Amendment has two religious clauses which protect the individual's religious liberty, "the establishment" clause and the "free exercise" clause. These two combined prevent the use of public schools to proselytize and correspondingly forbid the expenditure of public tax funds to support religion. An extract from an opinion by the Supreme Court of Iowa forcefully illuminates this:

> If there is any one thing which is well settled in the policies and purposes of the American people as a whole, it is the fixed and unalterable determination that there shall be an absolute and unequivocal separation of church and state, and that our public school system, supported by the taxation of the property of all alike—Catholic, Protestant, Jew, Gentile, believer and infidel—shall not be used directly or indirectly for religious instruction, and above all that it shall not be made an instrumentality of proselyting influence, in favor of any, religious organization, sect, creed, or belief.[28]

The third assumption, that the state can compel all parents to provide their children with a minimum secular education, is essential to the concept of general mass education. Every government has as a goal its own continuation and preservation, and in a republic an educated electorate is fundamental. As such, the state must be conceived as *parens patriae* in enforcing minimum educational and welfare requirements. The validity of the state's interest was established several years ago in Prince v. Massachusetts.[29]

The primary issue emanates from placing the force and power of the state, whether it be through taxation or other public policy decision, in a position to either enhance or inhibit religion. This was one of the most obstinate problems which Horace Mann was forced to over-

27. V. T. Thayer, *The Attack Upon the American Secular School*, Beacon Press, Boston, 1951, pp. 26–27.

28. Knowlton v. Baumhover, 182 Iowa 691, 166 N.W. 202 (1918).

29. 321 U.S. 158, 64 S.Ct. 438 (1944).

come in his great crusade to found free common schools in Massachusetts. Mann vigorously maintained that the only purpose of religious education in the schools was to convey to each child the idea and respect of religious liberty. According to him the child should be able:

> * * * to judge for himself according to the dictates of his own reason and conscience, what his religious obligations are and whither they lead. But if a man is taxed to support a school where religious doctrines are inculcated which he believes to be false, and which he believes that God condemns, then he is excluded from the school by the divine law, at the same time that he is compelled to support it by the human law. This is a double wrong.[30]

Today the public schools of America are secular and not merely nonsectarian, such is necessary if separation of church and state is to be complete. The important position of education in the governmental process is the key to maintaining religious liberty. Pfeffer observes that to be secular does not mean to be "Godless"; it is merely a guarantee that the state will not dictate or encroach on religious beliefs of the individual. He says:

> A secular state requires a secular state school; but the secularization of the state does not mean the secularization of society. Only by accepting a totalitarian philosophy, either in religion or politics or both, can the state be equated with society. We are a religious people even though our government is secular. Our democratic state must be secular, for it does not purport or seek to pre-empt all of societal life. Similarly the public school need not and should not be the totality of the education process.[31]

In this regard our Constitution precludes religious indoctrination in the public schools and prohibits use of public funds in supporting religion in parochial schools and it also proscribes the state from pre-empting all the child's time, thereby allowing substantial opportunity for religious training outside the school by parents and churches.[32]

Textbooks and Transportation for Parochial School Pupils

The United States Supreme Court, in the case of Cochran v. Louisiana, ruled that a state plan to provide textbooks to parochial school students does not violate the Fourteenth Amendment.[33] The Court in this decision was not asked to determine whether the First Amendment was violated.

30. Joseph L. Blow, *Cornerstones of Religious Freedom in America*, Beacon Press, Boston, 1949, pp. 179–182.

31. Pfeffer, *op. cit.* p. 338.

32. Wisconsin v. Yoder, 406 U.S. 205, 92 S.Ct. 1526 (1972).

33. Cochran v. Louisiana State Board of Education, 281 U.S. 370, 50 S.Ct. 335 (1930).

The decision in the Cochran case was rendered in 1930, ten years before the Court decided in the Cantwell case that the religious liberties of the First Amendment not only provided protection against actions by the Congress but when applied through the Fourteenth Amendment protected the individual from arbitrary acts of the States.[34] However, the Court in this case did identify and adopt the "child benefit" concept which has subsequently been used in many instances to defend the appropriation of public funds for private and parochial school use.

The Supreme Court in the Everson case, a 1947 decision, held that the funds for transportation of parochial school children does not violate the First Amendment. However, many state constitutions impose stricter regulations concerning separation of church and state than does the United States Constitution and, as a result, the highest courts in several states have ruled that their state constitutions would be violated if public funds were used to provide transportation for parochial school pupils.

In the Everson case the legislature of New Jersey enacted a law which allowed boards of education to provide transportation for parochial school children at public expense. A school board, acting under this statute, authorized reimbursement of parents for bus fares spent in sending their children to parochial schools. The plaintiff attacked the statute on the grounds that it violated the First and Fourteenth Amendments of the federal Constitution. The Court in a 5–4 decision ruled that that statute did not violate the Constitution. The Court adopted the "child benefit" doctrine and reasoned that the funds were expended for the benefit of the individual child and not for religious purposes. The transportation law was a general program which provided assistance in getting children safely to and from school regardless of their religion.

In 1968, the Supreme Court applied the reasoning of the Cochran and Everson cases in upholding as constitutional a New York statute which provided textbooks distributed free of charge to students attending parochial schools. The court stated that there was no indication that the books were being used to teach religion and that since private schools serve a public purpose and perform a secular as well as a sectarian function, such an expenditure of public funds is not unconstitutional.[35]

34. Cantwell v. Connecticut, 310 U.S. 296, 60 S.Ct. 900 (1940).

35. Board of Ed. of Central School Dist. v. Allen, 392 U.S. 236, 88 S.Ct. 1923 (1968).

State Law Providing Free Books to Parochial School
Students Does Not Constitute Taking Property
for a Private Purpose

COCHRAN v. LOUISIANA STATE BD. OF EDUC.

Supreme Court of the United States, 1930.
281 U.S. 370, 50 S.Ct. 335.

Mr. Chief Justice HUGHES delivered the opinion of the Court.

The appellants, as citizens and taxpayers of the state of Louisiana, brought this suit to restrain the State Board of Education and other state officials from expending any part of the severance tax fund in purchasing school books and in supplying them free of cost to the school children of the state, under Acts No. 100 and No. 143 of 1928, upon the ground that the legislation violated specified provisions of the Constitution of the state and also section 4 of article 4 and the Fourteenth Amendment of the Federal Constitution. The Supreme Court of the state affirmed the judgment of the trial court which refused to issue an injunction. 168 La. 1030, 123 So. 664.

Act No. 100 of 1928 provided that the severance tax fund of the state, after allowing funds and appropriations as required by the state Constitution, should be devoted "first, to supplying school books to the school children of the State." The Board of Education was directed to provide "school books for school children free of cost to such children." Act No. 143 of 1928 made appropriations in accordance with the above provisions.

* * *

The contention of the appellant under the Fourteenth Amendment is that taxation for the purchase of school books constituted a taking of private property for a private purpose. Citizens' Sav. & Loan Association v. Topeka, 20 Wall. 655, 22 L.Ed. 455. The purpose is said to be to aid private, religious, sectarian, and other schools not embraced in the public educational system of the state by furnishing text-books free to the children attending such private schools. The operation and effect of the legislation in question were described by the Supreme Court of the state as follows (168 La. page 1020, 123 So. 655, 660): "One may scan the acts in vain to ascertain where any money is appropriated for the purchase of school books for the use of any church, private, sectarian, or even public school. The appropriations were made for the specific purpose of purchasing school books for the use of the school children of the state free of cost to them. It was for their benefit and the resulting benefit to the state that the appropriations were made. True, these children attend some school, public or private, the latter, sectarian or nonsectarian, and that the books are to be furnished them for their use, free of cost, whichever they attend. The schools, however, are not the beneficiaries of these appropriations. They obtain nothing from them, nor are they relieved of a single obligation, because of them. The school children and the state alone are the beneficiaries. It is also true that the sectarian schools, which some of the children attend, instruct their pupils in religion, and books are used for that purpose, but one may search diligently the acts, though without result, in an effort to find anything to the effect that it is the purpose of the state to furnish religious books for the use of such children.   *   *   *   What the statutes contemplate is that the same books that are furnished children attending public schools shall be furnished children attending private schools. This is the only practical way of interpreting and executing the statutes, and this is what the state board of education is doing. Among these books, naturally, none is to be expected, adapted to religious instruction." The court also stated, although the point is not of importance in relation to the Federal question, that it was "only the use of the books that is granted to the children, or, in other words, the books are lent to them."

Viewing the statute as having the effect thus attributed to it, we cannot doubt that the taxing power of the state is exerted for a public purpose. The legislation does not segregate private schools, or their pupils, as its beneficiaries or attempt to interfere with any matters of exclusively private concern. Its interest is education, broadly; its method, comprehensive. Individual interests are aided only as the common interest is safeguarded.

Judgment affirmed.

NOTES

1. Until the Cantwell case in 1940 the Supreme Court had not applied the protection of the Fourteenth Amendment to the "establishment" and "free exercise" clauses of the First Amendment. This was the reason that the Louisiana statute was attacked under the Fourteenth Amendment directly instead of under the religious issue of the First Amendment. The Court in the Cantwell case stated:

> The First Amendment declares that Congress shall make no law respecting an establishment of religion or prohibiting the free exercise thereof. The Fourteenth Amendment has rendered the legislatures of the states as incompetent as Congrss to enact such laws. The constitutional inhibition of legislation on the subject of religion has a double aspect. On the one hand, it forestalls compulsion by law of the acceptance of any creed or the practice of any form of worship. Freedom of conscience and freedom to adhere to such religious organization or form of worship as the individual may choose cannot be restricted by law. On the other hand, it safeguards the free exercise of the chosen form of religion. Thus, the amendment embraces two concepts,—freedom to believe and freedom to act. The first is absolute but, in the nature of things, the second cannot be. Cantwell v. Connecticut, 310 U.S. 296, 60 S.Ct. 900(1940).

2. What is the logic given in the Cochran case which supports the "public purpose" and "child benefit" theories?

3. Is it significant that the books were merely loaned to the children and not granted to them?

Establishment Clause Does Not Prohibit
Spending Tax Funds to Pay Bus Fares
for Parochial School Students

EVERSON v. BOARD OF EDUC.

Supreme Court of the United States, 1947.
330 U.S. 1, 67 S.Ct. 504.

Mr. Justice BLACK delivered the opinion of the Court.

A New Jersey statute authorizes its local school districts to make rules and contracts for the transportation of children to and from schools. The appellee, a township board of education, acting pursuant to this statute authorized reimbursement to parents of money expended by them for the bus transportation of their children on regular busses operated by the public transportation system. Part of this money was for the payment of transportation of some children in the community to Catholic parochial schools. These church schools give their students, in addition to secular education, regular religious instruction conforming to the religious tenets and modes of worship of the Catholic Faith. The superintendent of these schools is a Catholic priest.

The appellant, in his capacity as a district taxpayer, filed suit in a State court challenging the right of the Board to reimburse parents of parochial school students. He contended that the statute and the resolution passed pursuant to it violated both the State and the Federal Constitutions. That court held that the legislature was without power to authorize such payment under the State constitution. 132 N.J.L. 98, 39 A.2d 75. The New Jersey Court of Errors and Appeals reversed, holding that neither the statute nor the resolution passed pursuant to it was in conflict with the State constitution or the provisions of the Federal Constitution in issue. 133 N.J.L. 350, 44 A.2d 333. The case is here on appeal under 28 U.S.C. § 344(a), 28 U.S.C. A. § 344(a).

* * *

The only contention here is that the State statute and the resolution, in so far as they authorized reimbursement to parents of children attending parochial schools, violate the Federal Constitution in these two respects, which to some extent, overlap. First. They authorize the State to take by taxation the private property of some and bestow it upon others, to be used for their own private purposes. This, it is alleged violates the due process clause of the Fourteenth Amendment. Second. The statute and the resolution forced inhabitants to pay taxes to help support and maintain schools which are dedicated to, and which regularly teach, the Catholic Faith. This is alleged to be a use of State power to support church schools contrary to the prohibition of the First Amendment which the Fourteenth Amendment made applicable to the states.

First. The due process argument that the State law taxes some people to help others carry out their private purposes is framed in two phases. The first phase is that a state cannot tax A to reimburse B for the cost of transporting his children to church schools. This is said to violate the due process clause because the children are sent to these church schools to satisfy the personal desires of their parents, rather than the public's interest in the general education of all children. This argument, if valid, would apply equally to prohibit state payment for the transportation of children to any non-public school, whether operated by a church, or any other non-government individual or group. But, the New Jersey legislature has decided that a public purpose will be served by using tax-raised funds to pay the bus fares of all school children, including those who attend parochial schools. The New Jersey Court of Errors and Appeals has reached the same conclusion. The fact that a state law, passed to satisfy a public need, coincides with the personal desires of the individuals most directly affected is certainly an inadequate reason for us to say that a legislature has erroneously appraised the public need.

* * *

It is much too late to argue that legislation intended to facilitate the opportunity of children to get a secular education serves no public purpose. Cochran v. Louisiana State Board of Education, 281 U.S. 370, 50 S.Ct. 335, 74 L.Ed. 913; * * *. The same thing is no less true of legislation to reimburse needy parents, or all parents, for payment of the fares of their children so that they can ride in public busses to and from schools rather than run the risk of traffic and other hazards incident to walking or "hitchhiking." See Barbier v. Connolly, supra, 113 U.S. at page 31, 5 S.Ct. at page 359. * * * Nor does it follow that a law has a private rather than a public purpose because it provides that tax-raised funds will be paid to reimburse individuals on account of money spent by them in a way which furthers a public program. See Carmichael v. Southern Coal & Coke Co., 301 U.S. 495, 518, 57 S.Ct. 868, 876, * * *. Subsidies and loans to individuals such as farmers and home owners, and to privately owned transportation systems, as well as many other kinds of businesses, have been commonplace practices in our state and national history.

Insofar as the second phase of the due process argument may differ from the first, it is by suggesting that taxation for transportation of children to church schools constitutes support of a religion by the State. But if the law is invalid for this reason, it is because it violates the First Amendment's prohibition against the establishment of religion by law. This is the exact question raised by appellant's second contention, to consideration of which we now turn.

Second. The New Jersey statute is challenged as a "law respecting an establishment of religion." The First Amendment, as made applicable to the states by the Fourteenth, Murdock v. Commonwealth of Pennsylvania, 319 U.S. 105, 63 S.Ct. 870, 872, * * * commands that a state "shall make no law respecting an establishment of religion, or prohibiting the free exercise thereof." These words of the First Amendment reflected in the minds of early Americans a vivid mental picture of conditions and practices which they fervently wished to stamp out in order to preserve liberty for themselves and for their posterity. Doubtless their goal has not been entirely reached; but so far has the Nation moved toward it that the expression "law respecting an establishment of religion," probably does not so vividly remind present-day Americans of the evils, fears, and political problems that caused that expression to be written into our Bill of Rights. * * *

* * *

The "establishment of religion" clause of the First Amendment means at least this: Neither a state nor the Federal Government can set up a church. Neither can pass laws which aid one religion, aid all religions, or prefer one religion over another. Neither can force nor influence a person to go to or to remain away from church against his will or force him to profess a belief or disbelief in any religion. No person can be punished for entertaining or professing religious beliefs or disbeliefs, for church attendance or non-attendance. No tax in any amount, large or small, can be levied to support any religious activities or institutions, whatever they may be called, or whatever form they may adopt to teach or practice religion. Neither a state nor the Federal Government can, openly or secretly, participate in the affairs of any religious organizations or groups and vice versa. In the words of Jefferson, the clause against establishment of religion by law was intended to erect "a wall of separation between Church and State." Reynolds v. United States, supra, 98 U.S. at page 164, 25 L.Ed. 244.

We must consider the New Jersey statute in accordance with the foregoing limitations imposed by the First Amendment. But we must not strike that state statute down if it is within the state's constitutional power even though it approaches the verge of that power. * * * New Jersey cannot consistently with the "establishment of religion" clause of the First Amendment contribute tax-raised funds to the support of an institution which teaches the tenets and faith of any church. On the other hand, other language of the amendment commands that New Jersey cannot hamper its citizens in the free exercise of their own religion. Consequently, it cannot exclude individual Catholics, Lutherans, Mohammedans, Baptists, Jews, Methodists,

Non-believers, Presbyterians, or the members of any other faith, *because of their faith, or lack of it,* from receiving the benefits of public welfare legislation. While we do not mean to intimate that a state could not provide transportation only to children attending public schools, we must be careful, in protecting the citizens of New Jersey against state-established churches, to be sure that we do not inadvertently prohibit New Jersey from extending its general State law benefits to all its citizens without regard to their religious belief.

Measured by these standards, we cannot say that the First Amendment prohibits New Jersey from spending tax-raised funds to pay the bus fares of parochial school pupils as a part of a general program under which it pays the fares of pupils attending public and other schools. It is undoubtedly true that children are helped to get to church schools. There is even a possibility that some of the children might not be sent to the church schools if the parents were compelled to pay their children's bus fares out of their own pockets when transportation to a public school would have been paid for by the State. The same possibility exists where the state requires a local transit company to provide reduced fares to school children including those attending parochial schools, or where a municipally owned transportation system undertakes to carry all school children free of charge. Moreover, state-paid policemen, detailed to protect children going to and from church schools from the very real hazards of traffic, would serve much the same purpose and accomplish much the same result as state provisions intended to guarantee free transportation of a kind which the state deems to be best for the school children's welfare. And parents might refuse to risk their children to the serious danger of traffic accidents going to and from parochial schools, the approaches to which were not protected by policemen. Similarly, parents might be reluctant to permit their children to attend schools which the state had cut off from such general government services as ordinary police and fire protection, connections for sewage disposal, public highways and sidewalks. Of course, cutting off church schools from these services, so separate and so indisputably marked off from the religious function, would make it far more difficult for the schools to operate. But such is obviously not the purpose of the First Amendment. That Amendment requires the state to be a neutral in its relations with groups of religious believers and non-believers; it does not require the state to be their adversary. State power is no more to be used so as to handicap religions, than it is to favor them.

      *   *   *

The First Amendment has erected a wall between church and state. That wall must be kept high and impregnable. We could not approve the slightest breach. New Jersey has not breached it here.

Affirmed.

NOTES

1. <u>At least two states have constitutions which authorize public transportation of parochial school pupils, New York and New Jersey.</u> The state constitution of New York was amended to authorize such transportation after a 1938 court decision (Judd v. Board of Educ., 278 N.Y. 200, 15 N.E. 2d 576 [1938]) which invalidated a parochial school transportation statute as being repugnant to a constitutional restriction against direct or indirect aid to sectarian education. Several other states have statutes providing public funds for parochial pupil transportation, including California, Connecticut, Illinois, Indiana, Kansas, Kentucky, Louisiana, Maine, Maryland, Massachusetts, Michigan, New Hampshire, New Mexico, North Dakota, Ohio, Oregon, Pennsylvania, and Rhode Island.

In three of these states, Kentucky, Louisiana and New Mexico, transportation of parochial pupils is left to the discretion of local officials. In Maryland the statutory authorization is by special act for certain counties and does not apply to the state as a whole.

2. <u>In some twenty states other decisions or statutes specifically prohibit transportation of parochial or nonpublic school pupils.</u> Mississippi statute provides for transportation of only those pupils in attendance in the public schools. Courts in six of these twenty states, Alaska, Delaware, Missouri, Oklahoma, Washington and Wisconsin, have held that transportation of parochial school children at public expense violates these states' constitutions. The decisions in these six were as follows:

(a) In Alaska it was held that free transportation to nonpublic schools furnished a direct benefit to such schools; therefore, it was unconstitutional. Matthews v. Quinton, 362 P.2d 932, 939 (Alaska, 1961).

(b) The court in Delaware held that a statute appropriating funds for transportation of pupils in religiously affiliated schools violated Article X, Section 3 of the Delaware Constitution even though the funds were not given directly to the school. State ex rel. Traub v. Brown, 36 Del. 181, 172 A. 835 (1934), writ of error dismissed 39 Del. 187, 197 A. 478 (1938).

(c) The Missouri constitution provides for the use of state school funds solely for the purpose of free public schools (Article IX, Section 5). Referring to this provision the high court of that state held that a statute providing free transportation for private school pupils was unconstitutional. McVey v. Hawkins, 364 Mo. 44, 258 S.W.2d 927 (1953).

(d) In Oklahoma public funds for transportation of parochial school pupils violates constitutional provisions which prohibit expenditure of public monies for sectarian purposes. Board of Educ. for Ind. School Dist. No. 52 v. Antone, 384 P.2d 911 (Okl.1963); Gurney v. Ferguson, 190 Okl. 254, 122 P.2d 1002 (1942).

3. How is the *Everson* case related to the *Cochran* case? Is the "child benefit" theory employed here? Are any limitations placed on the "child benefit" theory?

4. What is the reasoning of the court in the majority opinion in ruling that the New Jersey statute does not violate the "establishment of religion" clause?

5. Relate the historical background and rationale of Jefferson's *Bill for Establishing Religious Freedom* and *Madison's Memorial and Remonstrance Against Religious Assessments* to *Everson*.

6. Is the state's contribution under the New Jersey law in defraying the cost of conveying pupils to a place where they will receive primarily religious instruction in fact a substitution of resources for parents and an encouragement to aid religion?

7. Do you believe that the "child benefit" or "public purpose" theory contradicts the effect of the First Amendment?

8. Statutes which authorize public transportation for parochial school children to travel to and from the private schools do not constitute mandatory authority for the public schools to also transport such children for educational field trips. Cook v. Griffin, 47 A.D.2d 23, 364 N.Y.S.2d 632 (1975).

Loan of Textbooks to Parochial School Students
Does Not Violate Establishment Clause

BOARD OF EDUC. OF CENTRAL SCHOOL DIST. NO. 1 v. ALLEN

Supreme Court of the United States, 1968.
392 U.S. 236, 88 S.Ct. 1923.

Mr. Justice WHITE delivered the opinion of the Court.

A law of the State of New York requires local public school authorities to lend textbooks free of charge to all students in grades seven through 12; students attending private schools are included. This case presents the question whether this statute is a "law respecting an establishment of religion, or prohibiting the free exercise thereof," and so in conflict with the First and Fourteenth Amendments to the Constitution, because it authorizes the loan of textbooks to students attending parochial schools. We hold that the law is not in violation of the Constitution.

* * *

* * * Beginning with the 1966–1967 school year, local school boards were required to purchase textbooks and lend them without charge "to all children residing in such district who are enrolled in grades seven to twelve of a public or private school which complies with the compulsory education law."[1] The books now loaned are "text-books which are designated for use in any public, elementary or secondary schools of the state or are approved by any boards of education," and which—according to a 1966 amendment—"a pupil is required to use as a text for a semester or more in a particular class in the school he legally attends."

1. New York Education law § 701 (1967 suppl.).

Appellant Board of Education of Central School District No. 1 in Rensselaer and Columbia Counties, brought suit in the New York courts against appellee James Allen.[2] The complaint alleged that § 701 violated both the State and Federal Constitutions; that if appellants, in reliance on their interpretation of the Constitution, failed to lend books to parochial school students within their counties appellee Allen would remove appellants from office; and that to prevent this, appellants were complying with the law and submitting to their constituents a school budget including funds for books to be lent to parochial school pupils. Appellants therefore sought a declaration that § 701 was invalid, an order barring appellee Allen from removing appellants from office for failing to comply with it, and another order restraining him from apportioning state funds to school districts for the purchase of textbooks to be lent to parochial students.   *   *   *

*   *   *

Everson and later cases have shown that the line between state neutrality to religion and state support of religion is not easy to locate. "The constitutional standard is the separation of Church and State. The problem, like many problems in constitutional law, is one of degree." Zorach v. Clauson, 343 U.S. 306, 314, 72 S.Ct. 679, 684, 96 L.Ed. 954 (1952).   *   *   *   Based on Everson, Zorach, McGowan, and other cases, Abington Tp. School District v. Schempp, 374 U.S. 203, 83 S.Ct. 1560, 10 L.Ed.2d 844 (1963), fashioned a test subscribed to by eight Justices for distinguishing between forbidden involvements of the State with religion and those contacts which the Establishment Clause permits:

> "The test may be stated as follows: what are the purpose and the primary effect of the enactment? If either is the advancement or inhibition of religion then the enactment exceeds the scope of legislative power as circumscribed by the Constitution. That is to say that to withstand the strictures of the Establishment Clause there must be a secular legislative purpose and a primary effect that neither advances nor inhibits religion. Everson v. Board of Education   *   *   *."
> 374 U.S. at 222, 83 S.Ct., at 1571.

This test is not easy to apply, but the citation of *Everson* by the *Schempp* Court to support its general standard made clear how the *Schempp* rule would be applied to the facts of *Everson*. The statute upheld in *Everson* would be considered a law having "a secular legislative purpose and a primary effect that neither advances nor inhibits religion." We reach the same result with respect to the New York law requiring school books to be loaned free of charge to all students in specified grades. The express purpose of § 701 was stated by the New York Legislature to be furtherance of the educational opportuni-

2. Commissioner of Education of New
York.

ties available to the young. Appellants have shown us nothing about the necessary effects of the statute that is contrary to its stated purpose. The law merely makes available to all children the benefits of a general program to lend school books free of charge. Books are furnished at the request of the pupil and ownership remains, at least technically, in the State. Thus no funds or books are furnished to parochial schools, and the financial benefit is to parents and children, not to schools. Perhaps free books make it more likely that some children choose to attend a sectarian school, but that was true of the state-paid bus fares in *Everson* and does not alone demonstrate an unconstitutional degree of support for a religious institution.

* * *

The major reason offered by appellants for distinguishing free textbooks from free bus fares is that books, but not buses, are critical to the teaching process, and in a sectarian school that process is employed to teach religion. However this Court has long recognized that religious schools pursue two goals, religious instruction and secular education. In the leading case of Pierce v. Society of Sisters, 268 U.S. 510, 45 S.Ct. 571, 69 L.Ed. 1070 (1925), the Court held that although it would not question Oregon's power to compel school attendance or require that the attendance be at an institution meeting State-imposed requirements as to quality and nature of curriculum, Oregon had not shown that its interest in secular education required that all children attend publicly operated schools. A premise of this holding was the view that the State's interest in education would be served sufficiently by reliance on the secular teaching that accompanied religious training in the schools maintained by the Society of Sisters. Since *Pierce*, a substantial body of case law has confirmed the power of the States to insist that attendance at private schools, if it is to satisfy state compulsory-attendance laws, be at institutions which provide minimum hours of instruction, employ teachers of specified training, and cover prescribed subjects of instruction. Indeed, the State's interest in assuring that these standards are being met has been considered a sufficient reason for refusing to accept instruction at home as compliance with compulsory education statutes. These cases were a sensible corollary of Pierce v. Society of Sisters: if the State must satisfy its interest in secular education through the instrument of private schools, it has a proper interest in the manner in which those schools perform their secular educational function. Another corollary was Cochran v. Louisiana State Board of Education, 281 U.S. 370, 50 S.Ct. 335, 74 L.Ed. 913 (1930), where appellants said that a statute requiring school books to be furnished without charge to all students, whether they attended public or private schools, did not serve a "public purpose," and so offended the Fourteenth Amendment. Speaking through Chief Justice Hughes, the Court summarized as follows its conclusion that Louisiana's interest in the secular education being provided by private schools made provision of textbooks to students in those schools a properly public concern: "[The State's] interest is education, broadly; its method, comprehensive. Individual interests are aided only as the common interest is safeguarded." 281 U.S., at 375, 50 S.Ct., at 336.

Underlying these cases, and underlying also the legislative judgments that have preceded the court decisions, has been a recognition that private education has played and is playing a significant and valuable role in raising national levels of knowledge, competence, and experience. Americans care about the quality of the secular education available to their children. They have considered high quality education to be an indispensable ingredient for achieving the kind of nation, and the kind of citizenry, that they have desired to create. Considering this attitude, the continued willingness to rely on private school systems, including parochial systems, strongly suggests that a wide segment of informed opinion, legislative and otherwise, has found that those schools do an acceptable job of providing secular education to their students. This judgment is further evidence that parochial schools are performing, in addition to their sectarian function, the task of secular education.

Against this background of judgment and experience, unchallenged in the meager record before us in this case, we cannot agree with appellants either that all teaching in a sectarian school is religious or that the processes of secular and religious training are so intertwined that secular textbooks furnished to students by the public are in fact instrumental in the teaching of religion. This case comes to us after summary judgment entered on the pleadings. Nothing in this record supports the proposition that all textbooks, whether they deal with mathematics, physics, foreign languages, history, or literature, are used by the parochial schools to teach religion. No evidence has been offered about particular schools, particular courses, particular teachers, or particular books. We are unable to hold, based solely on judicial notice, that this statute results in unconstitutional involvement of the State with religious instruction or that § 701, for this or the other reasons urged, is a law respecting the establishment of religion within the meaning of the First Amendment.

*   *   *

Mr. Justice BLACK, dissenting.

*   *   *   I believe the New York law held valid is a flat, flagrant, open violation of the First and Fourteenth Amendments which together forbid Congress or state legislatures to enact any law "respecting an establishment of religion." For that reason I would reverse the New York Court of Appeals' judgment. *   *   *

The *Everson* and *McCollum* cases plainly interpret the First and Fourteenth Amendments as protecting the taxpayers of a State from being compelled to pay taxes to their government to support the agencies of private religious organizations the taxpayers oppose. To authorize a State to tax its residents for such church purposes is to put the State squarely in the religious activities of certain religious groups that happen to be strong enough politically to write their own religious preferences and prejudices into the laws. This links state and churches together in controlling the lives and destinies of our citizenship—a citizenship composed of people of myriad religious faiths, some of them bitterly hostile to and completely intolerant of the others. It was to escape laws precisely like this that a large part of the Nation's early immigrants fled to this country. It was also to escape such laws and such consequences that the First Amendment was written in language strong and clear barring passage of any law "respecting an establishment of religion."

It is true, of course, that the New York law does not as yet formally adopt or establish a state religion. But it takes a great stride in that direction and coming events cast their shadows before them. The same powerful sectarian religious propagandists who have succeeded in securing passage of the present law to help religious schools carry on their sectarian religious purposes can and doubtless will continue their propaganda, looking toward complete domination and supremacy of their particular brand of religion.[1] And it nearly always is by insidious approaches that the citadels of liberty are most successfully attacked.[2]

I know of no prior opinion of this Court upon which the majority here can rightfully rely to support its holding this New York law constitutional. In saying this, I am not unmindful of the fact that the New York Court of Appeals purported to follow Everson v. Board of Education, supra, in which this Court, in an opinion written by me, upheld a New Jersey law authorizing reimbursement to parents for the transportation of children attending sectarian schools. That law did not attempt to deny the benefit of its general terms to children of any faith going to any legally authorized school. Thus, it was treated in the same way as a general law paying the streetcar fare *of all school children,* or a law providing midday lunches for all children or all school children, or a law to provide police protection for children going to and from school, or general laws to provide police and fire protection for buildings, including, of course, churches and church school buildings as well as others.

As my Brother DOUGLAS so forcefully shows, in an argument with which I fully agree, upholding a State's power to pay bus or streetcar fares for school children cannot provide support for the validity of a state law using tax-raised funds to buy school books for a religious school. The First Amendment's bar to establishment of religion must preclude a State from using funds levied from all of its citizens to purchase books for use by sectarian schools, which, al-

---

1. See dissenting opinion of Mr. Justice Douglas.

2. See Boyd v. United States, 116 U.S. 616, 6 S.Ct. 524, 29 L.Ed. 746.

though "secular," realistically will in some way inevitably tend to propagate the religious views of the favored sect. Books are the most essential tool of education since they contain the resources of knowledge which the educational process is designed to exploit. In this sense it is not difficult to distinguish books, which are the heart of any school, from bus fares, which provide a convenient and helpful general public transportation service. With respect to the former, state financial support actively and directly assists the teaching and propagation of sectarian religious viewpoints in clear conflict with the First Amendment's establishment bar; with respect to the latter, the State merely provides a general and nondiscriminatory transportation service in no way related to substantive religious views and beliefs.

This New York law, it may be said by some, makes but a small inroad and does not amount to complete state establishment of religion. But that is no excuse for upholding it. It requires no prophet to foresee that on the argument used to support this law others could be upheld providing for state or federal government funds to buy property on which to erect religious school buildings or to erect the buildings themselves, to pay the salaries of the religious school teachers, and finally to have the sectarian religious groups cease to rely on voluntary contributions of members of their sects while waiting for the Government to pick up all the bills for the religious schools. Arguments made in favor of this New York law point squarely in this direction, namely, that the fact that government has not heretofore aided religious schools with tax-raised funds amounts to a discrimination against those schools and against religion. And that there are already efforts to have government supply the money to erect buildings for sectarian religious schools is shown by a recent Act of Congress which apparently allows for precisely that. See Higher Education Facilities Act of 1963, 77 Stat. 363, 20 U.S.C.A. § 701 et seq.

I still subscribe to the belief that tax-raised funds cannot constitutionally be used to support religious schools, buy their school books, erect their buildings, pay their teachers, or pay any other of their maintenance expenses, even to the extent of one penny. The First Amendment's prohibition against governmental establishment of religion was written on the assumption that state aid to religion and religious schools generates discord, disharmony, hatred, and strife among our people, and that any government that supplies such aids is to that extent a tyranny. And I still believe that the only way to protect minority religious groups from majority groups in this country is to keep the wall of separation between church and state high and impregnable as the First and Fourteenth Amendments provide. The Court's affirmance here bodes nothing but evil to religious peace in this country.

*   *   *

NOTES

1. Observe that Justice Black wrote the majority opinion in *Everson* and dissented in *Allen*. This is particularly interesting since the majority opinion by Justice White relied heavily on the interpretation and meaning of the majority in *Everson*.

2. Under Title II of the Elementary and Secondary Education Act of 1965 (P.L. 89–10), the Congress provided funds for the "acquisition of library resources (which for the purposes of this title means books, periodicals, documents, audio-visual materials, and other related library materials), textbooks, and other printed and published instructional materials for the use of children and teachers in public and private elementary and secondary schools." Section 205(a) of this Act makes provision for the technical ownership of these library resources and materials to remain with a public agency.

3. At least six states have laws which permit or provide for textbooks, purchased with public funds, to be distributed to pupils in private schools. These states are: Iowa, Louisiana, Mississippi, New Mexico, New York, and Rhode Island. As previously presented, the *Cochran* case of Louisiana and the case of Board of Education v. Allen upheld laws in Louisiana and New York which provided textbooks for private or sectarian school children. The *Cochran* case in Louisiana was preceded by Borden v. Louisiana State Bd. of Educ., 168 La. 1005, 123 So. 655 (1929) which held that the Acts of 1928, Nos. 100 and 143, the same acts contested in *Cochran*, were not violative of religious constitutional prohibitions, nor did the acts violate constitutional provisions prohibiting public funds for private or benevolent purposes and were not adverse to due process requirements. Laws in Iowa, Mississippi and Rhode Island provide for the loan of textbooks to private school children.

4. A statute, in South Dakota, providing for free textbooks to "pupils" without designation as to whether the pupils were to be in public or private schools, or both, was held to exclude pupils in private, sectarian and parochial schools. Haas v. Independent School Dist. No. 1 of Yankton, 69 S.D. 303, 9 N.W.2d 707 (1943).

In an Oregon case the court held that distribution of free textbooks to parochial schools violated state constitutional prohibitions against public aid to religious institutions. Dickman v. School Dist. No. 62C, Oregon City, 232 Or. 238, 366 P.2d 533 (1961), cert. denied 371 U.S. 823, 83 S.Ct. 41 (1962).

5. Appellants in *Allen* argue that transportation of parochial pupils may be constitutional while providing textbooks is not. How does the court react to this argument? Compare the courts' opinion to the dissenting opinion of Justice Jackson in the *Everson* case.

6. What is the implication of Justice White's statement that "parochial schools are performing, in addition to their sectarian function, the task of secular education?"

7. How does Justice Black in dissent in *Allen* distinguish textbooks from transportation in *Everson* in which he wrote the majority opinion?

8. In an advisory opinion to the state senate the Supreme Court of Michigan held that provision of textbooks and supplies to religious schools

violated the Michigan Constitution. The court reasoned that both textbooks and supplies were primary elements necessary for schools to exist and it therefore constituted aid to religion. In re Advisory Opinion re Constitutionality of 1974, P.A. 242, 394 Mich. 41, 228 N.W.2d 772 (Mich.1975).

State Financial Aid to Parochial Schools

The decision by the Supreme Court in the *Allen* case [36] created many questions on the part of both public and parochial school leaders throughout the country. The language by Justice White speaking for the majority was unclear failing to delineate First Amendment restrictions in providing state aid to parochial schools. White applied the public purpose theory and apparently reasoned that the state could give assistance to religious schools so long as the aid was provided for only secular services in the operation of parochial schools. He said:

> a wide segment of informed opinion, legislative and otherwise, has found that those schools [parochial] do an acceptable job of providing secular education to their students. *This judgment is further evidence that parochial schools are performing, in addition to their sectarian function, the task of secular education.*

This statement was taken by many parochial school educators to mean that a state could permissibly provide funds to parochial schools for such things as teachers' salaries, operation, building, et cetera, so long as the funds were used by the parochial school only for "public secular purposes." State legislatures were suddenly flooded with hundreds of bills to provide state support to parochial schools, some were passed and others for various reasons failed.

It was into this fertile area of conjecture that the Supreme Court of the United States walked in 1971 when it was asked to rule on the constitutionality of two such state acts from Pennsylvania and Rhode Island, both states relying on the vagueness of *Allen* were attempting to aid parochial schools. The Supreme Court struck down the statutes of both states. The court found the "secular purpose" standard alone to be inadequate and added its own standard of "excessive entanglement." This new standard seeks to prevent the state from infringing on the separate rights of religion by becoming too intermingled with the process of religion. The Supreme Court summarized three tests for determining constitutionality of a state statute and applied and discussed each of these in Lemon v. Kurtzman, the tests are: (1) the statute must have a secular legislative purpose, (2) its principal or primary effect must be one that neither advances nor inhibits religion, and (3) it must not foster excessive government en-

36. Board of Educ. of Central School Dist. No. 1 v. Allen, 392 U.S. 236, 88 S.Ct. 1923 (1968).

tanglement with religion. Subsequent Supreme Court cases have further delineated the boundaries prescribed by these tests.[37]

In this series of cases the Supreme Court held that reimbursement to parents for tuition expense,[38] auxiliary services including counseling, testing and psychological services, and therapy for exceptional children,[39] loans spending state money for instructional materials and equipment in parochial schools and permitting parochial school students to take field trips to museums and other points of interest at public expense [40] were all unconstitutional.

On the other hand, the state financed educationally peripheral activities of loaning of textbooks, administering standardized tests to parochial school students, treatment for speech and hearing problems, and taking care of students' dental needs have been held constitutional.[41]

State Aid to Parochial Schools Through Salary Supplements and Purchase of Services Constitutes Impermissible Entanglement Between Church and State

LEMON v. KURTZMAN

Supreme Court of the United States, 1971.
403 U.S. 602, 91 S.Ct. 2105.

Mr. Chief Justice BURGER delivered the opinion of the Court.

These two appeals raise questions as to Pennsylvania and Rhode Island statutes providing state aid to church-related elementary and secondary schools. Both statutes are challenged as violative of the Establishment and Free Exercise Clauses of the First Amendment and the Due Process Clause of the Fourteenth Amendment.

Pennsylvania has adopted a statutory program that provides financial support to nonpublic elementary and secondary schools by way of reimbursement for the cost of teachers' salaries, textbooks, and instructional materials in specified secular subjects. Rhode Island has adopted a statute under which the State pays directly to teachers in nonpublic elementary schools a supplement of 15% of their annual salary. Under each statute state aid has been given to church-related educational institutions. We hold that both statutes are unconstitutional.

37. Sloan v. Lemon, 413 U.S. 825, 93 S. Ct. 2982 (1973), reh. denied 414 U.S. 881, 94 S.Ct. 30; Committee for Public Educ. and Religious Liberty v. Nyquist, 413 U.S. 756, 93 S.Ct. 2955 (1973).

38. Sloan v. Lemon, 413 U.S. 825, 93 S. Ct. 2982 (1973).

39. Meek v. Pittinger, 421 U.S. 349, 95 S.Ct. 1753 (1975).

40. Wolman v. Walter, 433 U.S. 229, 97 S.Ct. 2593 (1977).

41. Ibid.

I

The Rhode Island Statute

The Rhode Island Salary Supplement Act [1] was enacted in 1969. It rests on the legislative finding that the quality of education available in nonpublic elementary schools has been jeopardized by the rapidly rising salaries needed to attract competent and dedicated teachers. The Act authorizes state officials to supplement the salaries of teachers of secular subjects in nonpublic elementary schools by paying directly to a teacher an amount not in excess of 15% of his current annual salary. As supplemented, however, a nonpublic school teacher's salary cannot exceed the maximum paid to teachers in the State's public schools, and the recipient must be certified by the state board of education in substantially the same manner as public school teachers.

In order to be eligible for the Rhode Island salary supplement, the recipient must teach in a nonpublic school at which the average per-pupil expenditure on secular education is less than the average in the State's public schools during a specified period. Appellant State Commissioner of Education also requires eligible schools to submit financial data. If this information indicates a per-pupil expenditure in excess of the statutory limitation, the records of the school in question must be examined in order to assess how much of the expenditure is attributable to secular education and how much to religious activity.

The Act also requires that teachers eligible for salary supplements must teach only those subjects that are offered in the State's public schools. They must use "only teaching materials which are used in the public schools." Finally, any teacher applying for a salary supplement must first agree in writing "not to teach a course in religion for so long as or during such time as he or she receives any salary supplements" under the Act.

Appellees are citizens and taxpayers of Rhode Island. * * * Appellants are state officials charged with administration of the Act, teachers eligible for salary supplements under the Act, and parents of children in church-related elementary schools whose teachers would receive state salary assistance.

A three-judge federal court was convened pursuant to 28 U.S.C. A. §§ 2281, 2284. It found that Rhode Island's non-public elementary schools accommodated approximately 25% of the State's pupils. About 95% of these pupils attended schools affiliated with the Roman Catholic church. To date some 250 teachers have applied for benefits under the Act. All of them are employed by Roman Catholic schools.

1. R.I.Pen.Laws Ann. § 16–51–1 et seq. (Supp.1970).

The court held a hearing at which extensive evidence was introduced concerning the nature of the secular instruction offered in the Roman Catholic schools whose teachers would be eligible for salary assistance under the Act. Although the court found that concern for religious values does not necessarily affect the content of secular subjects, it also found that the parochial school system was "an integral part of the religious mission of the Catholic Church."

The District Court concluded that the Act violated the Establishment Clause, holding that it fostered "excessive entanglement" between government and religion. In addition two judges thought that the Act had the impermissible effect of giving "significant aid to a religious enterprise." 316 F.Supp. 112. We affirm.

The Pennsylvania Statute

Pennsylvania has adopted a program that has some but not all of the features of the Rhode Island program. The Pennsylvania Nonpublic Elementary and Secondary Education Act [3] was passed in 1968 in response to a crisis that the Pennsylvania Legislature found existed in the State's nonpublic schools due to rapidly rising costs. The statute affirmatively reflects the legislative conclusion that the State's educational goals could appropriately be fulfilled by government support of "those purely secular educational objectives achieved through nonpublic education * * * ."

The statute authorizes appellee state Superintendent of Public Instruction to "purchase" specified "secular educational services" from nonpublic schools. Under the "contracts" authorized by the statute, the State directly reimburses nonpublic schools solely for their actual expenditures for teachers' salaries, textbooks, and instructional materials. A school seeking reimbursement must maintain prescribed accounting procedures that identify the "separate" cost of the "secular educational service." These accounts are subject to state audit. The funds for this program were originally derived from a new tax on horse and harness racing, but the Act is now financed by a portion of the state tax on cigarettes.

There are several significant statutory restrictions on state aid. Reimbursement is limited to courses "presented in the curricula of the public schools." It is further limited "solely" to courses in the following "secular" subjects: mathematics, modern foreign languages,[4] physical science, and physical education. Textbooks and instructional materials included in the program must be approved by the state Superintendent of Public Instruction. Finally, the statute prohibits reimbursement for any course that contains "any subject matter expressing religious teaching, or the morals or forms of worship of any sect."

---

3. Pa.Stat.Ann., Tit. 24, §§ 5601–5609 (Supp.1971).

4. Latin, Hebrew, and classical Greek are excluded.

The Act went into effect on July 1, 1968, and the first reimbursement payments to schools were made in September 2, 1969. It appears that some $5 million has been expended annually under the Act. The State has now entered into contracts with some 1,181 nonpublic elementary and secondary schools with a student population of some 535,215 pupils—more than 20% of the total number of students in the State. More than 96% of these pupils attend church-related schools, and most of these schools are affiliated with the Roman Catholic church.

Appellants brought this action in the District Court to challenge the constitutionality of the Pennsylvania statute. The organizational plaintiffs-appellants are associations of persons resident in Pennsylvania declaring belief in the separation of church and state; individual plaintiffs-appellants are citizens and taxpayers of Pennsylvania. Appellant Lemon, in addition to being a citizen and a taxpayer, is a parent of a child attending public school in Pennsylvania. Lemon also alleges that he purchased a ticket at a race track and thus had paid the specific tax that supports the expenditures under the Act.
* * *

* * * The District Court held that the individual plaintiffs-appellants had standing to challenge the Act, 310 F.Supp. 42.
* * *

The court granted appellees' motion to dismiss the complaint for failure to state a claim for relief. 310 F.Supp. 35. It held that the Act violated neither the Establishment nor the Free Exercise Clause, Chief Judge Hastie dissenting. We reverse.

II

In Everson v. Board of Education, 330 U.S. 1, 67 S.Ct. 504, 91 L. Ed. 711 (1947), this Court upheld a state statute that reimbursed the parents of parochial school children for bus transportation expenses. There Mr. Justice Black, writing for the majority, suggested that the decision carried to "the verge" of forbidden territory under the Religion Clauses. Id., at 16, 67 S.Ct., at 511. Candor compels acknowledgment, moreover, that we can only dimly perceive the lines of demarcation in this extraordinarily sensitive area of constitutional law.

The language of the Religion Clauses of the First Amendment is at best opaque, particularly when compared with other portions of the Amendment. Its authors did not simply prohibit the establishment of a state church or a state religion, an area history shows they regarded as very important and fraught with great dangers. Instead they commanded that there should be "no law *respecting* an establishment of religion." A law may be one "respecting" the forbidden objective while falling short of its total realization. A law "respecting" the proscribed result, that is, the establishment of religion, is not always easily identifiable as one violative of the Clause. A given law might not *establish* a state religion but nevertheless be one "respecting" that end in the sense of being a step that could lead to such establishment and hence offend the First Amendment.

In the absence of precisely stated constitutional prohibitions, we must draw lines with reference to the three main evils against which the Establishment Clause was intended to afford protection: "sponsorship, financial support, and active involvement of the sovereign in religious activity." Walz v. Tax Commission, 397 U.S. 664, 668, 90 S.Ct. 1409, 1411, 25 L.Ed.2d 697 (1970).

Every analysis in this area must begin with consideration of the cumulative criteria developed by the Court over many years. Three such tests may be gleaned from our cases. First, the statute must have a secular legislative purpose; second, its principal or primary effect must be one that neither advances nor inhibits religion, Board of Education v. Allen, 392 U.S. 236, 243, 88 S.Ct. 1923, 1926, 20 L. Ed.2d 1060 (1968); finally, the statute must not foster "an excessive government entanglement with religion." Walz, supra, at 674, 90 S. Ct., at 1414.

Inquiry into the legislative purposes of the Pennsylvania and Rhode Island statutes affords no basis for a conclusion that the legislative intent was to advance religion. On the contrary, the statutes themselves clearly state that they are intended to enhance the quality of the secular education in all schools covered by the compulsory attendance laws. There is no reason to believe the legislatures meant anything else. A State always has a legitimate concern for maintaining minimum standards in all schools it allows to operate. As in *Allen*, we find nothing here that undermines the stated legislative intent; it must therefore be accorded appropriate deference.

In *Allen* the Court acknowledged that secular and religious teachings were not necessarily so intertwined that secular textbooks furnished to students by the State were in fact instrumental in the teaching of religion. 392 U.S., at 248, 88 S.Ct., at 1929. The legislatures of Rhode Island and Pennsylvania have concluded that secular and religious education are identifiable and separable. In the abstract we have no quarrel with this conclusion.

The two legislatures, however, have also recognized that church-related elementary and secondary schools have a significant religious mission and that a substantial portion of their activities is religiously oriented. They have therefore sought to create statutory restrictions designed to guarantee the separation between secular and religious educational functions and to ensure that State financial aid supports only the former. All these provisions are precautions taken in candid recognition that these programs approached, even if they did not intrude upon, the forbidden areas under the Religion Clauses. We need not decide whether these legislative precautions restrict the principal or primary effect of the programs to the point where they do not offend the Religion Clauses, for we conclude that the cumulative impact of the entire relationship arising under the statutes in each State involves excessive entanglement between government and religion.

* * *

(a) *Rhode Island program*

The District Court made extensive findings on the grave potential for excessive entanglement that inheres in the religious character and purpose of the Roman Catholic elementary schools of Rhode Island, to date the sole beneficiaries of the Rhode Island Salary Supplement Act.

The church schools involved in the program are located close to parish churches. This understandably permits convenient access for religious exercises since instruction in faith and morals is part of the total educational process. The school buildings contain identifying religious symbols such as crosses on the exterior and crucifixes, and religious paintings and statues either in the classrooms or hallways. Although only approximately 30 minutes a day are devoted to direct religious instruction, there are religiously oriented extracurricular activities. Approximately two-thirds of the teachers in these schools are nuns of various religious orders. Their dedicated efforts provide an atmosphere in which religious instruction and religious vocations are natural and proper parts of life in such schools. Indeed, as the District Court found, the role of teaching nuns in enhancing the religious atmosphere has led the parochial school authorities to attempt to maintain a one-to-one ratio between nuns and lay teachers in all schools rather than to permit some to be staffed almost entirely by lay teachers.

On the basis of these findings the District Court concluded that the parochial schools constituted "an integral part of the religious mission of the Catholic Church." The various characteristics of the schools make them "a powerful vehicle for transmitting the Catholic faith to the next generation." This process of inculcating religious doctrine is, of course, enhanced by the impressionable age of the pupils, in primary schools particularly. In short, parochial schools involve substantial religious activity and purpose.

The substantial religious character of these church-related schools gives rise to entangling church-state relationships of the kind the Religion Clauses sought to avoid. Although the District Court found that concern for religious values did not inevitably or necessarily intrude into the content of secular subjects, the considerable religious activities of these schools led the legislature to provide for careful governmental controls and surveillance by state authorities in order to ensure that state aid supports only secular education.

* * *

* * * The Rhode Island Legislature has not, and could not, provide state aid on the basis of a mere assumption that secular teachers under religious discipline can avoid conflicts. The State must be certain, given the Religion Clauses, that subsidized teachers do not inculcate religion—indeed the State here has undertaken to do so. To ensure that no trespass occurs, the State has therefore carefully conditioned its aid with pervasive restrictions. An eligible recipient must teach only those courses that are offered in the public schools and use only those texts and materials that are found in the public schools. In addition the teacher must not engage in teaching any course in religion.

A comprehensive, discriminating, and continuing state surveillance will inevitably be required to ensure that these restrictions are obeyed and the First Amendment otherwise respected. Unlike a book, a teacher cannot be inspected once so as to determine the extent and intent of his or her personal beliefs and subjective acceptance of the limitations imposed by the First Amendment. These prophylactic contacts will involve excessive and enduring entanglement between state and church.

There is another area of entanglement in the Rhode Island program that gives concern. The statute excludes teachers employed by nonpublic schools whose average per-pupil expenditures on secular education equal or exceed the comparable figures for public schools. In the event that the total expenditures of an otherwise eligible school exceed this norm, the program requires the government to examine the school's records in order to determine how much of the total expenditures is attributable to secular education and how much to religious activity. This kind of state inspection and evaluation of the religious content of a religious organization is fraught with the sort of entanglement that the Constitution forbids. It is a relationship pregnant with dangers of excessive government direction of church schools and hence of churches. The Court noted "the hazards of government supporting churches" in Walz v. Tax Commission, supra, 397 U.S., at 675, 90 S.Ct., at 1414, and we cannot ignore here the danger that pervasive modern governmental power will ultimately intrude on religion and thus conflict with the Religion Clauses.

(b) *Pennsylvania program*

The Pennsylvania statute also provides state aid to church-related schools for teachers' salaries. The complaint describes an educational system that is very similar to the one existing in Rhode Island. According to the allegations, the church-related elementary and secondary schools are controlled by religious organizations, have the purpose of propagating and promoting a particular religious faith, and conduct their operations to fulfill that purpose. Since this complaint was dismissed for failure to state a claim for relief, we must accept these allegations as true for purposes of our review.

As we noted earlier, the very restrictions and surveillance necessary to ensure that teachers play a strictly nonideological role give rise to entanglements between church and state. The Pennsylvania statute, like that of Rhode Island, fosters this kind of relationship. Reimbursement is not only limited to courses offered in the public schools and materials approved by state officials, but the statute excludes "any subject matter expressing religious teaching, or the morals or forms of worship of any sect." In addition, schools seeking reimbursement must maintain accounting procedures that require the State to establish the cost of the secular as distinguished from the religious instruction.

The Pennsylvania statute, moreover, has the further defect of providing state financial aid directly to the church-related schools. This factor distinguishes both *Everson* and *Allen*, for in both those cases the Court was careful to point out that state aid was provided to the student and his parents—not to the church-related school. * * * In Walz v. Tax Commission, supra, 397 U.S., at 675, 90 S. Ct., at 1414, the Court warned of the dangers of direct payments to religious organizations:

> "Obviously a direct money subsidy would be a relationship pregnant with involvement and, as with most governmental grant programs, could encompass sustained and detailed administrative relationships for enforcement of statutory or administrative standards * * * ."

The history of government grants of a continuing cash subsidy indicates that such programs have almost always been accompanied by varying measures of control and surveillance. The government cash grants before us now provide no basis for predicting that comprehensive measures of surveillance and controls will not follow. In particular the government's post-audit power to inspect and evaluate a church-related school's financial records and to determine which expenditures are religious and which are secular creates an intimate and continuing relationship between church and state.

A broader base of entanglement of yet a different character is presented by the divisive political potential of these state programs. In a community where such a large number of pupils are served by church-related schools, it can be assumed that state assistance will entail considerable political activity. Partisans of parochial schools, understandably concerned with rising costs and sincerely dedicated to both the religious and secular educational missions of their schools, will inevitably champion this cause and promote political action to achieve their goals. Those who oppose state aid, whether for constitutional, religious, or fiscal reasons, will inevitably respond and employ all of the usual political campaign techniques to prevail. Candidates will be forced to declare and voters to choose. It would be unrealistic to ignore the fact that many people confronted with issues of this kind will find their votes aligned with their faith.

Ordinarily political debate and division, however vigorous or even partisan, are normal and healthy manifestations of our democratic system of government, but political division along religious lines was one of the principal evils against which the First Amendment was intended to protect.   *   *   *   The potential divisiveness of such conflict is a threat to the normal political process.   *   *   *

     *   *   *

The potential for political divisiveness related to religious belief and practice is aggravated in these two statutory programs by the need for continuing annual appropriations and the likelihood of larger and larger demands as costs and populations grow.   *   *   *

In *Walz* it was argued that a tax exemption for places of religious worship would prove to be the first step in an inevitable progression leading to the establishment of state churches and state religion. That claim could not stand up against more than 200 years of virtually universal practice imbedded in our colonial experience and continuing into the present.

The progression argument, however, is more persuasive here. We have no long history of state aid to church-related educational institutions comparable to 200 years of tax exemption for churches. Indeed, the state programs before us today represent something of an innovation. We have already noted that modern governmental programs have self-perpetuating and self-expanding propensities. These internal pressures are only enhanced when the schemes involve institutions whose legitimate needs are growing and whose interests have substantial political support. Nor can we fail to see that in constitutional adjudication some steps, which when taken were thought to approach "the verge," have become the platform for yet further steps. A certain momentum develps in constitutional theory and it can be a "downhill thrust" easily set in motion but difficult to retard or stop. Development by momentum is not invariably bad; indeed, it is the way the common law has grown, but it is a force to be recognized and reckoned with. The dangers are increased by the difficulty of perceiving in advance exactly where the "verge" of the precipice lies. As well as constituting an independent evil against which the Religion Clauses were intended to protect, involvement or entanglement between government and religion serves as a warning signal.

Finally, nothing we have said can be construed to disparage the role of church-related elementary and secondary schools in our national life. Their contribution has been and is enormous. Nor do we ignore their economic plight in a period of rising costs and expanding need. Taxpayers generally have been spared vast sums by the maintenance of these educational institutions by religious organizations, largely by the gifts of faithful adherents.

The merit and benefits of these schools, however, are not the issue before us in these cases. The sole question is whether state aid to these schools can be squared with the dictates of the Religion Clauses. Under our system the choice has been made that government is to be entirely excluded from the area of religious instruction and churches excluded from the affairs of government. The Constitution decrees that religion must be a private matter for the individual, the family, and the institutions of private choice, and that while some involvement and entanglement are inevitable, lines must be drawn.

The judgment of the Rhode Island District Court in No. 569 and No. 570 is affirmed. The judgment of the Pennsylvania District Court in No. 89 is reversed, and the case is remanded for further proceedings consistent with this opinion.

* * *

NOTES

1. *Lemon* prohibited aid to sectarian schools but did not proscribe state assistance to private nonsectarian schools.

2. Lease of classroom space from a parochial school by the public school system was held to be constitutional where the public schools actually faced a severe classroom shortage and the classrooms were in a separable part of the parochial school where no religious impediments were present. A significant effort had been made by the public schools, it was found, to prevent intermingling of the two school programs. Thomas v. Schmidt, 397 F.Supp. 203 (D.C.R.I.1975).

3. Lease of public school facilities for religious activities is unconstitutional where the rental charge covered only the cost of janitorial services and the lease extended for an indefinite period of time. The court found that such nominal rent is functionally a subsidy to the church. Resnick v. East Brunswick Township Bd. of Educ., 135 N.J. Super. 257, 343 A.2d 127 (1975).

Maintenance and Repair Grants for Parochial Schools as Well as Tuition Reimbursement and Income Tax Benefits to Parents of Parochial School Children are Unconstitutional

COMMITTEE FOR PUBLIC EDUC. AND RELIGIOUS LIBERTY v. NYQUIST

Supreme Court of the United States, 1973.
413 U.S. 756, 93 S.Ct. 2955.

Mr. Justice POWELL delivered the opinion of the Court.

These cases raise a challenge under the Establishment Clause of the First Amendment to the constitutionality of a recently enacted New York law which provides financial assistance, in several ways, to nonpublic elementary and secondary schools in that State. The cases involve an intertwining of societal and constitutional issues of the greatest importance.

James Madison, in his Memorial and Remonstrance Against Religious Assessments, admonished that a "prudent jealousy" for religious freedoms required that they never become "entangled * * * in precedents." His strongly held convictions, coupled with those of Thomas Jefferson and others among the Founders, are reflected in the first Clauses of the First Amendment of the Bill of Rights, which state that "Congress shall make no law respecting an establishment of religion, or prohibiting the free exercise thereof." Yet, despite Madison's admonition and the "sweep of the absolute prohibitions" of the Clauses, this Nation's history has not been one of entirely sanitized separation between Church and State. It has never been thought either possible or desirable to enforce a regime of total separation, and as a consequence cases arising under these Clauses have presented some of the most perplexing questions to come before this Court. Those cases have occasioned thorough and thoughtful scholarship by several of this Court's most respected former Justices, including Justices Black, Frankfurter, Harlan, Jackson, Rutledge, and Chief Justice Warren.

As a result of these decisions and opinions, it may no longer be said that the Religion Clauses are free of "entangling" precedents. Neither, however, may it be said that Jefferson's metaphoric "wall of separation" between Church and State has become "as winding as the famous serpentine wall" he designed for the University of Virginia. * * * Indeed, the controlling constitutional standards have become firmly rooted and the broad contours of our inquiry are now well defined. Our task, therefore, is to assess New York's several forms of aid in the light of principles already delineated.

I

In May 1972, the Governor of New York signed into law several amendments to the State's Education and Tax Laws. The first five sections of these amendments established three distinct financial aid programs for nonpublic elementary and secondary schools. * * *

The first section of the challenged enactment, entitled "Health and Safety Grants for Nonpublic School Children," provides for direct money grants from the State to "qualifying" nonpublic schools to be used for the "maintenance and repair of * * * school facilities and equipment to ensure the health, welfare and safety of enrolled pupils." A "qualifying" school is any nonpublic, nonprofit elementary or secondary school which "has been designated during the [immediately preceding] year as serving a high concentration of pupils from low-income families for purposes of Title IV of the Federal Higher Education Act of nineteen hundred sixty-five (20 U.S.C.A. § 425)." Such schools are entitled to receive a grant of $30 per pupil per year, or $40 per pupil per year if the facilities are more than 25 years old. * * *

"Maintenance and repair" is defined by the statute to include "the provision of heat, light, water, ventilation and sanitary facilities; cleaning, janitorial and custodial services; snow removal; necessary upkeep and renovation of buildings, grounds and equipment; fire and accident protection; and such other items as the commissioner may deem necessary to ensure the health, welfare and safety of enrolled pupils." * * *

The remainder of the challenged legislation—§§ 2 through 5—is a single package captioned the "Elementary and Secondary Education Opportunity Program." It is composed, essentially, of two parts, a tuition grant program and a tax benefit program. Section 2 establishes a limited plan providing tuition reimbursements to parents of children attending elementary or secondary nonpublic schools. * * *

* * *

The remainder of the "Elementary and Secondary Education Opportunity Program," contained in §§ 3, 4, and 5 of the challenged law, is designed to provide a form of tax relief to those who fail to qualify for tuition reimbursement. Under these sections parents may subtract from their adjusted gross income for state income tax purposes a designated amount for each dependent for whom they have paid at least $50 in nonpublic school tuition. * * *

* * *

Plaintiffs argued below that because of the substantially religious character of the intended beneficiaries, each of the State's three enactments offended the Establishment Clause. The District Court, in an opinion carefully canvassing this Court's recent precedents, held unanimously that § 1 (maintenance and repair grants) and § 2 (tuition reimbursement grants) were invalid. As to the income tax provisions of §§ 3, 4, and 5, however, a majority of the District Court, over the dissent of Circuit Judge Hays, held that the Establishment Clause had not been violated. * * * We affirm the District Court insofar as it struck down §§ 1 and 2 and reverse its determination regarding §§ 3, 4, and 5.

II

The history of the Establishment Clause has been recounted frequently and need not be repeated here. * * * It is enough to note that it is now firmly established that a law may be one "respecting an establishment of religion" even though its consequence is not to promote a "state religion," * * * and even though it does not aid one religion more than another but merely benefits all religions alike. * * * It is equally well established, however, that not every law that confers an "indirect," "remote," or "incidental" benefit upon re-

ligious institutions is, for that reason alone, constitutionally invalid.
* * *

Most of the cases coming to this Court raising Establishment
Clause questions have involved the relationship between religion and
education. Among these religion-education precedents, two general
categories of cases may be identified: those dealing with religious activities within the public schools, and those involving public aid in
varying forms to sectarian educational institutions. While the New
York legislation places this case in the latter category, its resolution
requires consideration, not only of the several aid-to-sectarian-educa-
tion cases, but also of our other education precedents and of several
important noneducation cases. For the now well-defined three-part
test that has emerged from our decisions is a product of considerations derived from the full sweep of the Establishment Clause cases.
Taken together, these decisions dictate that to pass muster under the
Establishment Clause the law in question first must reflect a clearly
secular legislative purpose, * * * second, must have a primary
effect that neither advances nor inhibits religion, * * * and,
third, must avoid excessive government entanglement with religion,
* * *

In applying these criteria to the three distinct forms of aid involved in this case, we need touch only briefly on the requirement of
a "secular legislative purpose." As the recitation of legislative purposes appended to New York's law indicates, each measure is adequately supported by legitimate, nonsectarian state interests. We do
not question the propriety, and fully secular content, of New York's
interest in preserving a healthy and safe educational environment for
all of its schoolchildren. And we do not doubt—indeed, we fully recognize—the validity of the State's interest in promoting pluralism
and diversity among its public and nonpublic schools. Nor do we
hesitate to acknowledge the reality of its concern for an already overburdened public school system that might suffer in the event that a
significant percentage of children presently attending nonpublic
schools should abandon those schools in favor of the public schools.

But the propriety of a legislature's purposes may not immunize
from further scrutiny a law which either has a primary effect that
advances religion, or which fosters excessive entanglements between
Church and State. Accordingly, we must weigh each of the three aid
provisions challenged here against these criteria of effect and entanglement.

A

The "maintenance and repair" provisions of § 1 authorize direct
payments to nonpublic schools, virtually all of which are Roman
Catholic schools in low-income areas. The grants, totaling $30 or $40
per pupil depending on the age of the institution, are given largely
without restriction on usage. So long as expenditures do not exceed

50% of comparable expenses in the public school system, it is possible for a sectarian elementary or secondary school to finance its entire "maintenance and repair" budget from state tax-raised funds. No attempt is made to restrict payments to those expenditures related to the upkeep of facilities used exclusively for secular purposes, nor do we think it possible within the context of these religion-oriented institutions to impose such restrictions. Nothing in the statute, for instance, bars a qualifying school from paying out of state funds the salaries of employees who maintain the school chapel, or the cost of renovating classrooms in which religion is taught, or the cost of heating and lighting those same facilities. <u>Absent appropirate restrictions on expenditures for these and similar purposes, it simply cannot be denied that this section has a primary effect that advances religion in that it subsidizes directly the religious activities of sectarian elementary and secondary schools.</u>

* * *

It might be argued, however, that while the New York "maintenance and repair" grants lack specifically articulated secular restrictions, the statute does provide a sort of statistical guarantee of separation by limiting grants to 50% of the amount expended for comparable services in the public schools. * * * Quite apart from the language of the statute, our cases make clear that a mere statistical judgment will not suffice as a guarantee that state funds will not be used to finance religious education. * * *

What we have said demonstrates that New York's maintenance and repair provisions violate the Establishment Clause because their effect, inevitably, is to subsidize and advance the religious mission of sectarian schools. We have no occasion, therefore, to consider the further question whether those provisions as presently written would also fail to survive scrutiny under the administrative entanglement aspect of the three-part test because assuring the secular use of all funds requires too intrusive and continuing a relationship between Church and State, Lemon v. Kurtzman, supra.

B

New York's tuition reimbursement program also fails the "effect" test, for much the same reasons that govern its maintenance and repair grants. The state program is designed to allow direct, unrestricted grants of $50 to $100 per child (but no more than 50% of tuition actually paid) as reimbursement to parents in low-income brackets who send their children to non-public schools, the bulk of which is concededly sectarian in orientation. * * *

* * * The controlling question here, then, is whether the fact that the grants are delivered to parents rather than schools is of such significance as to compel a contrary result. The State and intervenor-appellees rely on *Everson* and *Allen* for their claim that grants to parents, unlike grants to institutions, respect the "wall of separation" required by the Constitution. It is true that in those cases the Court upheld laws that provided benefits to children attending religious schools and to their parents: As noted above, in *Everson* parents were reimbursed for bus fares paid to send children to parochial schools, and in *Allen* textbooks were loaned directly to the children. But those decisions make clear that, far from providing a per se immunity from examination of the substance of the State's program, the fact that aid is disbursed to parents rather than to the schools is only one among many factors to be considered.

In *Everson*, the Court found the bus fare program analogous to the provision of services such as police and fire protection, sewage disposal, highways, and sidewalks for parochial schools. 330 U.S., at 17–18, 67 S.Ct., at 512–513. Such services, provided in common to all citizens, are "so separate and so indisputably marked off from the religious function," id., at 18, 67 S.Ct., at 513 that they may fairly be viewed as reflections of a neutral posture toward religious institutions. *Allen* is founded upon a similar principle. The Court there repeatedly emphasized that upon the record in that case there was no indication that textbooks would be provided for anything other than purely secular courses. "Of course books are different from buses. Most bus rides have no inherent religious significance, while religious books are common. However, the language of [the law under consideration] does not authorize the loan of religious books, and the State claims no right to distribute religious literature. * * * Absent evidence, we cannot assume that school authorities * * * are unable to distinguish between secular and religious books or that they will not honestly discharge their duties under the law." * * *

The tuition grants here are subject to no such restrictions. There has been no endeavor "to guarantee the separation between secular and religious educational functions and to ensure that State financial aid supports only the former." * * * Indeed, it is precisely the function of New York's law to provide assistance to private schools, the great majority of which are sectarian. By reimbursing parents for a portion of their tuition bill, the State seeks to relieve their financial burdens sufficiently to assure that they continue to have the option to send their children to religion-oriented schools. And while the other purposes for that aid—to perpetuate a pluralistic educational environment and to protect the fiscal integrity of overburdened public schools—are certainly unexceptionable, the effect of the aid is unmistakably to provide desired financial support for non-public, sectarian institutions.

* * *

Although we think it clear, for the reasons above stated, that New York's tuition grant program fares no better under the "effect" test than its maintenance and repair program, in view of the novelty of the question we will address briefly the subsidiary arguments made by the state officials and intervenors in its defense.

First, it has been suggested that it is of controlling significance that New York's program calls for *reimbursement* for tuition already paid rather than for direct contributions which are merely routed through the parents to the schools, in advance of or in lieu of payment by the parents. The parent is not a mere conduit, we are told, but is absolutely free to spend the money he receives in any manner he wishes. There is no element of coercion attached to the reimbursement, and no assurance that the money will eventually end up in the hands of religious schools. The absence of any element of coercion, however, is irrelevant to questions arising under the Establishment Clause. * * * [I]f the grants are offered as an incentive to parents to send their children to sectarian schools by making unrestricted cash payments to them, the Establishment Clause is violated whether or not the actual dollars given eventually find their way into the sectarian institutions. Whether the grant is labeled a reimbursement, a reward, or a subsidy, its substantive impact is still the same. In sum, we agree with the conclusion of the District Court that "[w]hether he gets it during the current year, or as reimbursement for the past year, is of no constitutional importance."

* * *

Finally, the State argues that its program of tuition grants should survive scrutiny because it is designed to promote the free exercise of religion. The State notes that only "low-income parents" are aided by this law, and without state assistance their right to have their children educated in a religious environment "is diminished or even denied." It is true, of course, that this Court has long recognized and maintained the right to choose nonpublic over public education. * * * It is also true that a state law interfering with a parent's right to have his child educated in a sectarian school would run afoul of the Free Exercise Clause. But this Court repeatedly has recognized that tension inevitably exists between the Free Exercise and the Establishment Clauses, * * * and that it may often not be possible to promote the former without offending the latter. As a result of this tension, our cases require the State to maintain an attitude of "neutrality," neither "advancing" nor "inhibiting" religion. In its attempt to enhance the opportunities of the poor to choose between public and nonpublic education, the State has taken a step which can only be regarded as one "advancing" religion. However great our sympathy, * * * for the burdens experienced by those who must pay public school taxes at the same time that they support other schools because of the constraints of "conscience and discipline," ibid., and notwithstanding the "high social importance" of the State's purposes, * * * neither may justify an eroding of the limitations of the Establishment Clause now firmly emplanted.

C

Sections 3, 4, and 5 establish a system for providing income tax benefits to parents of children attending New York's nonpublic schools. * * *

These sections allow parents of children attending nonpublic elementary and secondary schools to subtract from adjusted gross income a specified amount if they do not receive a tuition reimbursement under § 2, and if they have an adjusted gross income of less than $25,000. * * *

In practical terms there would appear to be little difference, for purposes of determining whether such aid has the effect of advancing religion, between the tax benefit allowed here and the tuition grant allowed under § 2. The qualifying parent under either program receives the same form of encouragement and reward for sending his children to nonpublic schools. The only difference is that one parent receives an actual cash payment while the other is allowed to reduce by an arbitrary amount the sum he would otherwise be obliged to pay over to the State. * * *

Appellees defend the tax portion of New York's legislative package on two grounds. First, they contend that it is of controlling significance that the grants or credits are directed to the parents rather than to the schools. This is the same argument made in support of the tuition reimbursements and rests on the same reading of the same precedents of this Court, primarily *Everson* and *Allen*. Our treatment of this issue in Part II–B is applicable here and requires rejection of this claim. Second, appellees place their strongest reliance on Walz v. Tax Comm'n, supra, in which New York's property tax exemption for religious organizations was upheld. We think that *Walz* provides no support for appellees' position. Indeed, its rationale plainly compels the conclusion that New York's tax package violates the Establishment Clause.

Tax exemptions for church property enjoyed an apparently universal approval in this country both before and after the adoption of the First Amendment. The Court in *Walz* surveyed the history of tax exemptions and found that each of the 50 States has long provided for tax exemptions for places of worship, that Congress has exempted religious organizations from taxation for over three-quarters of a century, and that congressional enactments in 1802, 1813, and 1870 specifically exempted church property from taxation. In sum, the Court concluded that "[f]ew concepts are more deeply embedded in the fabric of our national life, beginning with pre-Revolutionary colonial times, than for the government to exercise at the very least this kind of benevolent neutrality toward churches and religious exercise generally." * * * We know of no historical precedent for New York's recently promulgated tax relief program. Indeed, it seems clear that tax benefits for parents whose children attend parochial schools are a recent innovation, occasioned by the growing financial plight of such nonpublic institutions and designed, albeit unsuccessfully, to tailor state aid in a manner not incompatible with the recent decisions of this Court. *   *   *

But historical acceptance without more would not alone have sufficed, as "no one acquires a vested or protected right in violation of the Constitution by long use." *   *   * It was the reason underlying that long history of tolerance of tax exemptions for religion that proved controlling. A proper respect for both the Free Exercise and the Establishment Clauses compels the State to pursue a course of "neutrality" toward religion. Yet governments have not always pursued such a course, and oppression has taken many forms, one of which has been taxation of religion. Thus, if taxation was regarded as a form of "hostility" toward religion, "exemption constitute[d] a reasonable and balanced attempt to guard against those dangers." *   *   * Special tax benefits, however, cannot be squared with the principle of neutrality established by the decisions of this Court. To the contrary, insofar as such benefits render assistance to parents who send their children to sectarian schools, their purpose and inevitable effect are to aid and advance those religious institutions.

*   *   *

One further difference between tax exemption for church property and tax benefits for parents should be noted. The exemption challenged in *Walz* was not restricted to a class composed exclusively or even predominantly of religious institutions. Instead, the exemption covered all property devoted to religious, educational, or charitable purposes. As the parties here must concede, tax reductions authorized by this law flow primarily to the parents of children attending sectarian, nonpublic schools. Without intimating whether this factor alone might have controlling significance in another context in some future case, it should be apparent that in terms of the potential divisiveness of any legislative measure the narrowness of the benefited class would be an important factor.

In conclusion, we find the *Walz* analogy unpersuasive, and in light of the practical similarity between New York's tax and tuition reimbursement programs, we hold that neither form of aid is sufficiently restricted to assure that it will not have the impermissible effect of advancing the sectarian activities of religious schools.

III

Because we have found that the challenged sections have the impermissible effect of advancing religion, we need not consider whether such aid would result in entanglement of the State with religion in the sense of "[a] comprehensive, discriminating, and continuing state surveillance." *   *   * But the importance of the competing societal interests implicated here prompts us to make the further observation that, apart from any specific entanglement of the State in particular religious programs, assistance of the sort here involved carries grave potential for entanglement in the broader sense of continuing political strife over aid to religion.

*   *   *

*   *   * All three of these programs start out at modest levels: the maintenance grant is not to exceed $40 per pupil per year in approved schools; the tuition grant provides parents not more than $50 a year for each child in the first eight grades and $100 for each child in the high school grades; and the tax benefit, though more difficult to compute, is equally modest. But we know from long experience with both Federal and State Governments that aid programs of any kind tend to become entrenched, to escalate in cost, and to generate their own aggressive constituencies. And the larger the class of recipients, the greater the pressure for accelerated increases. Moreover, the State itself, concededly anxious to avoid assuming the burden of educating children now in private and parochial schools, has a strong motivation for increasing this aid as public school costs rise and population increases. In this situation, where the underlying issue is the deeply emotional one of Church-State relationships, the potential for seriously divisive political consequences needs no elaboration. And while the prospect of such divisiveness may not alone warrant the invalidation of state laws that otherwise survive the careful scrutiny required by the decisions of this Court, it is certainly a "warning signal" not to be ignored. *   *   *

Our examination of New York's aid provisions, in light of all relevant considerations, compels the judgment that each, as written, has a "primary effect that advances religion" and offends the constitutional prohibition against laws "respecting an establishment of religion." We therefore affirm the three-judge court's holding as to §§ 1 and 2, and reverse as to §§ 3, 4, and 5.

It is so ordered.

Affirmed in part and reversed in part.

NOTES

Following the precedent established by the U.S. Supreme Court in *Nyquist*, the United States Court of Appeals for the Third Circuit struck down a $4.4 million tax deduction plan which would have assisted parents with children in parochial schools. The statute enacted in 1976 provided for a personal income tax deduction of $1000 for each child attending a nonpublic elementary and secondary school on a full-time basis. The federal court found that the statute had a secular purpose, but failed to meet the primary effect test and thus was constitutionally deficient because it advanced religion. Since the act violated the primary effect standard the

Court saw no need to evaluate it under the excessive entanglement criterion. The U.S. Supreme Court on a vote of 6 to 3 upheld without a hearing the lower Court's decision. The denial of a hearing before the Supreme Court indicates that the rationale of *Nyquist* prevails as strong precedent where tax deductions or credits are challenged. Public Funds for Public Schools of New Jersey v. Byrne, 590 F.2d 514 (1979).

Tuition Reimbursement to Parents of Parochial School Children Is Unconstitutional

SLOAN v. LEMON

Supreme Court of the United States, 1973.
413 U.S. 825, 93 S.Ct. 2982.

Mr. Justice POWELL delivered the opinion of the Court.

* * *

Pennsylvania's "Parent Reimbursement Act for Nonpublic Education" provides for reimbursement to parents who pay tuition for their children to attend the State's nonpublic elementary and secondary schools. Qualifying parents are entitled to receive $75 for each dependent enrolled in an elementary school, and $150 for each dependent in a secondary school, unless that amount exceeds the amount of tuition actually paid. The money to fund this program is to be derived from a portion of the revenues from the State's tax on cigarette sales, and is to be administered by a five-member committee appointed by the Governor, known as the "Pennsylvania Parent Assistance Authority." In an effort to avoid the "entanglement" problem that flawed its prior aid statute, Lemon v. Kurtzman, *supra*, the new legislation specifically precludes the administering authority from having any "direction, supervision or control over the policy determinations, personnel, curriculum, program of instruction or any other aspect of the administration or operation of any nonpublic school or schools." Similarly, the statute imposes no restrictions or limitations on the uses to which the reimbursement allotments can be put by the qualifying parents.

Like the New York tuition program, the Pennsylvania law is prefaced by "legislative findings," which emphasize its underlying secular purposes: parents who send their children to nonpublic schools reduce the total cost of public education; "inflation, plus sharply rising costs of education, now combine to place in jeopardy the ability of such parents fully to carry this burden"; if the State's 500,000 nonpublic school children were to transfer to the public schools, the annual operating costs to the State would be $400 million, and the added capital costs would exceed $1 billion; therefore, "parents who maintain students in nonpublic schools provide a vital service" and deserve at least partial reimbursement for alleviating an otherwise "intolerable public burden." We certainly do not question now, any more than we did two Terms ago in Lemon v. Kurtzman, the reality and legitimacy of Pennsylvania's secular purposes. * * *

* * *

For purposes of determining whether the Pennsylvania tuition reimbursement program has the impermissible effect of advancing religion, we find no constitutionally significant distinctions between this law and the one declared invalid today in *Nyquist.* Each authorizes the States to use tax-raised funds for tuition reimbursements payable to parents who send their children to nonpublic schools. Neither tells parents how they must spend the amount received. While the Pennsylvania grants are more generous ($75 to $150 as opposed to $50 to $100), and while Pennsylvania imposes no ceiling on the number of children for whom parents may claim tuition reimbursement or on the percentage of the tuition bill for which parents may be reimbursed, these considerations are irrelevant to the First Amendment question.

* * * Intervenors suggest that New York's law might be differentiated on the ground that because tuition grants there were available only to parents in an extremely low income bracket (less than $5,000 of taxable income), it would be reasonable to predict that the grant would, in fact, be used to pay tuition, rendering the parent a mere "conduit" for public aid to religious schools. Since Pennsylvania authorizes grants to all parents of children in nonpublic schools —regardless of income level—it is argued that no such assumption can be made as to how individual parents will spend their reimbursed amounts.

Our decision, however, is not dependent upon any such speculation. Instead we look to the substance of the program, and no matter how it is characterized its effect remains the same. The State has singled out a class of its citizens for a special economic benefit. Whether that benefit be viewed as a simple tuition subsidy, as an incentive to parents to send their children to sectarian schools, or as a reward for having done so, at bottom its intended consequences is to preserve and support religion-oriented institutions. We think it plain that this is quite unlike the sort of "indirect" and "incidental" benefits that flowed to sectarian schools from programs aiding *all* parents by supplying bus transportation and secular textbooks for their children. Such benefits were carefully restricted to the purely secular side of church-affiliated institutions and provided no special aid for those who had chosen to support religious schools. Yet such aid approached the "verge" of the constitutionally impermissible. Everson v. Board of Education, 330 U.S. 1, 16, 67 S.Ct. 504, 511, 91 L.Ed. 711 (1947). In Lemon v. Kurtzman, we declined to allow *Everson* to be used as the "platform for yet further steps" in granting assistance to "institutions whose legitimate needs are growing and whose interests have substantial political support." Again today we decline to approach or overstep the "precipice" against which the Establishment

Clause protects. <u>We hold that Pennsylvania's tuition grant scheme violates the constitutional mandate against the "sponsorship" or "financial support" of religion or religious institutions</u>. * * *

* * *

In holding today that Pennsylvania's post-Lemon v. Kurtzman attempt to avoid the Establishment Clause's prohibition against government entanglements with religion has failed to satisfy the parallel bar against laws having a primary effect that advances religion, we are not unaware that appellants and those who have endeavored to formulate systems of state aid to nonpublic education may feel that the decisions of this Court have, indeed, presented them with the "insoluble paradox" to which Mr. Justice White referred in his separate opinion in Lemon v. Kurtzman. But if novel forms of aid have not readily been sustained by this Court, the "fault" lies not with the doctrines which are said to create a paradox but rather with the Establishment Clause itself: "Congress" and the States by virtue of the Fourteenth Amendment "shall make no law respecting an establishment of religion." With that judgment we are not free to tamper, and while there is "room for play in the joints," * * * the Amendment's proscription clearly forecloses Pennsylvania's tuition reimbursement program.

Affirmed.

State Financing of Auxiliary Services and Direct Loans for Instructional Materials and Equipment for Parochial Schools are Unconstitutional

MEEK v. PITTENGER

Supreme Court of the United States, 1975.
421 U.S. 350, 95 S.Ct. 1753.

Mr. Justice STEWART announced the judgment of the Court and delivered the opinion of the Court (Parts I, II, IV, and V), together with an opinion (Part III), in which Mr. Justice BLACKMUN and Mr. Justice POWELL, joined.

This case requires us to determine once again whether a state law providing assistance to nonpublic, church-related, elementary and secondary schools is constitutional under the Establishment Clause of the First Amendment, made applicable to the States by the Fourteenth Amendment. * * *

I

With the stated purpose of assuring that every schoolchild in the Commonwealth will equitably share in the benefits of auxiliary services, textbooks, and instructional material provided free of charge to children attending public schools, the Pennsylvania General Assembly in 1972 added Acts 194 and 195, July 12, 1972, Pa.Stat.Ann., Tit. 24, § 9–972, to the Pennsylvania Public School Code of 1949, Pa.Stat.Ann., Tit. 24, §§ 1–101 to 27–2702.

Act 194 authorizes the Commonwealth to provide "auxiliary services" to all children enrolled in nonpublic elementary and secondary schools meeting Pennsylvania's compulsory-attendance requirements. "Auxiliary services" include counseling, testing, and psychological services, speech and hearing therapy, teaching and related services for exceptional children, for remedial students, and for the educationally disadvantaged, "and such other secular, neutral, nonideological services as are of benefit to nonpublic school children and are presently or hereafter provided for public school children of the Commonwealth." Act 194 specifies that the teaching and services are to be provided in the nonpublic schools themselves by personnel drawn from the appropriate "intermediate unit," part of the public school system of the Commonwealth established to provide special services to local school districts.

Act 195 authorizes the State Secretary of Education, either directly or through the intermediate units, to lend textbooks without charge to children attending nonpublic elementary and secondary schools that meet the Commonwealth's compulsory-attendance requirements. The books that may be lent are limited to those "which are acceptable for use in any public, elementary, or secondary school of the Commonwealth."

Act 195 also authorizes the Secretary of Education, pursuant to requests from the appropriate nonpublic school officials, to lend directly to the nonpublic schools "instructional materials and equipment, useful to the education" of nonpublic school children. "Instructional materials" are defined to include periodicals, photographs, maps, charts, sound recordings, films, "or any other printed and published materials of a similar nature." "Instructional equipment," as defined by the Act, includes projection equipment, recording equipment, and laboratory equipment.

* * *

In judging the constitutionality of the various forms of assistance authorized by Acts 194 and 195, the District Court applied the three-part test that has been clearly stated, if not easily applied, by this Court in recent Establishment Clause cases. * * * First, the statute must have a secular legislative purpose. * * * Second, it must have a "primary effect" that neither advances nor inhibits religion. * * * Third, the statute and its administration must avoid excessive government entanglement with religion. * * *

These tests constitute a convenient, accurate distillation of this Court's efforts over the past decades to evaluate a wide range of governmental action challenged as violative of the constitutional prohibition against laws "respecting an establishment of religion," and thus

provide the proper framework of analysis for the issues presented in
the case before us. It is well to emphasize, however, that the tests
must not be viewed as setting the precise limits to the necessary constitutional inquiry, but serve only as guidelines with which to identify
instances in which the objectives of the Establishment Clause have
been impaired. * * *

* * *

The District Court held that the textbook loan provisions of Act
195 are constitutionally indistinguishable from the New York textbook loan program upheld in Board of Education v. Allen, 392 U.S.
236, 88 S.Ct. 1923, 20 L.Ed.2d 1060. We agree.

* * *

Like the New York program, the textbook provisions of Act 195
extend to all schoolchildren the benefits of Pennsylvania's well-established policy of lending textbooks free of charge to elementary and
secondary school students. As in _Allen_, Act 195 provides that the
textbooks are to be lent directly to the student, not to the nonpublic
school itself, although, again as in _Allen_, the administrative practice
is to have student requests for the books filed initially with the nonpublic school and to have the school authorities prepare collective
summaries of these requests which they forward to the appropriate
public officials. Thus, the financial benefit of Pennsylvania's textbook program, like New York's, is to parents and children, not to the
nonpublic schools.

* * * Moreover, the record in the case before us, like the record in _Allen_, * * * contains no suggestion that religious textbooks will be lent or that the books provided will be used for anything other than purely secular purposes.

In sum, the textbook loan provisions of Act 195 are in every material respect identical to the loan program approved in _Allen_. Pennsylvania, like New York, "merely makes available to all children the
benefits of a general program to lend school books free of charge."
As such, those provisions of Act 195 do not offend the constitutional
prohibition against laws "respecting an establishment of religion."

Although textbooks are lent only to students, Act 195 authorizes
the loan of instructional material and equipment directly to qualifying nonpublic elementary and secondary schools in the Commonwealth. The appellants assert that such direct aid to Pennsylvania's
nonpublic schools, including church-related institutions, constitutes an
impermissible establishment of religion.

* * *

The only requirement imposed on nonpublic schools to qualify
for loans of instructional material and equipment is that they satisfy
the Commonwealth's compulsory-attendance law by providing, in the
English language, the subjects and activities prescribed by the stan-

dards of the State Board of Education. Commonwealth officials, as a matter of state policy, do not inquire into the religious characteristics, if any, of the nonpublic schools requesting aid pursuant to Act 195. The Coordinator of Nonpublic School Services, the chief administrator of Acts 194 and 195, testified that a school would not be barred from receiving loans of instructional material and equipment even though its dominant purpose was the inculcation of religious values, even if it imposed religious restrictions on admissions or on faculty appointments, and even if it required attendance at classes in theology or at religious services. In fact, of the 1,320 nonpublic schools in Pennsylvania that comply with the requirements of the compulsory-attendance law and thus qualify for aid under Act 195, more than 75% are church-related or religiously affiliated educational institutions. Thus, the primary beneficiaries of Act 195's instructional material and equipment loan provisions, like the beneficiaries of the "secular educational services" reimbursement program considered in Lemon v. Kurtzman, and the parent tuition-reimbursement plan considered in Sloan v. Lemon, are nonpublic schools with a predominant sectarian character.

*   *   *

The church-related elementary and secondary schools that are the primary beneficiaries of Act 195's instructional material and equipment loans typify such religion-pervasive institutions. The very purpose of many of those schools is to provide an integrated secular and religious education; the teaching process is, to a large extent, devoted to the inculcation of religious values and belief. * * * Substantial aid to the educational function of such schools, accordingly, necessarily results in aid to the sectarian school enterprise as a whole. "[T]he secular education those schools provide goes hand in hand with the religious mission that is the only reason for the schools' existence. Within the institution, the two are inextricably intertwined." * * * For this reason, Act 195's direct aid to Pennsylvania's predominantly church-related, nonpublic elementary and secondary schools, even though ostensibly limited to wholly neutral, secular instructional material and equipment, inescapably results in the direct and substantial advancement of religious activity, * * * and thus constitutes an impermissible establishment of religion.

Unlike Act 195, which provides only for the loan of teaching material and equipment, Act 194 authorizes the Secretary of Education, through the intermediate units, to supply professional staff, as well as supportive materials, equipment, and personnel, to the nonpublic schools of the Commonwealth. The "auxiliary services" authorized by Act 194—remedial and accelerated instruction, guidance counseling and testing, speech and hearing services—are provided directly to nonpublic school children with the appropriate special need. But the services are provided only on the nonpublic school premises, and only when "requested by nonpublic school representatives." * * *

* * * The appellants concede the validity of this secular legislative purpose. Nonetheless, they argue that Act 194 constitutes an impermissible establishment of religion because the auxiliary services are provided on the premises of predominantly church-related schools.

* * *

We need not decide whether substantial state expenditures to enrich the curricula of church-related elementary and secondary schools, like the expenditure of state funds to support the basic educational program of those schools, necessarily result in the direct and substantial advancement of religious activity. For decisions of this Court make clear that the District Court erred in relying entirely on the good faith and professionalism of the secular teachers and counselors functioning in church-related schools to ensure that a strictly nonideological posture is maintained.

In Earley v. DiCenso, a companion case to Lemon v. Kurtzman, supra, the Court invalidated a Rhode Island statute authorizing salary supplements for teachers of secular subjects in nonpublic schools. The Court expressly rejected the proposition, relied upon by the District Court in the case before us, that it was sufficient for the State to assume that teachers in church-related schools would succeed in segregating their religious beliefs from their secular educational duties. * * *

The prophylactic contacts required to ensure that teachers play a strictly nonideological role, the Court held, necessarily give rise to a constitutionally intolerable degree of entanglement between church and state. * * * The same excessive entanglement would be required for Pennsylvania to be "certain," as it must be, that Act 194 personnel do not advance the religious mission of the church-related schools in which they serve. * * *

That Act 194 authorizes state funding of teachers only for remedial and exceptional students, and not for normal students participating in the core curriculum, does not distinguish this case from Earley v. DiCenso and Lemon v. Kurtzman, supra. Whether the subject is "remedial reading," "advanced reading," or simply "reading," a teacher remains a teacher, and the danger that religious doctrine will become intertwined with secular instruction persists. The likelihood of inadvertent fostering of religion may be less in a remedial arithmetic class than in a medieval history seminar, but a diminished probability of impermissible conduct is not sufficient: "The State must be certain, given the Religion Clauses, that subsidized teachers do not inculcate religion." * * * And a state-subsidized guidance counselor is surely as likely as a state-subsidized chemistry teacher to fail on occasion to separate religious instruction and the advancement of religious beliefs from his secular educational responsibilities.

The fact that the teachers and counselors providing auxiliary services are employees of the public intermediate unit, rather than of the church-related schools in which they work, does not substantially eliminate the need for continuing surveillance. To be sure, auxiliary-services personnel, because not employed by the nonpublic schools, are not directly subject to the discipline of a religious authority. * * * But they are performing important educational services in schools in which education is an integral part of the dominant sectarian mission and in which an atmosphere dedicated to the advancement of religious belief is constantly maintained. * * * The potential for impermissible fostering of religion under these circumstances, although somewhat reduced, is nonetheless present. To be certain that auxiliary teachers remain religiously neutral, as the Constitution demands, the State would have to impose limitations on the activities of auxiliary personnel and then engage in some form of continuing surveillance to ensure that those restrictions were being followed.

In addition, Act 194, like the statutes considered in Lemon v. Kurtzman, and Committee for Public Education & Religious Liberty v. Nyquist, creates a serious potential for divisive conflict over the issue of aid to religion—"entanglement in the broader sense of continuing political strife." * * * The recurrent nature of the appropriation process guarantees annual reconsideration of Act 194 and the prospect of repeated confrontation between proponents and opponents of the auxiliary services program. The Act thus provides successive opportunities for political fragmentation and division along religious lines, one of the principal evils against which the Establishment Clause was intended to protect. * * * This potential for political entanglement, together with the administrative entanglement which would be necessary to ensure that auxiliary-services personnel remain strictly neutral and nonideological when functioning in church-related schools, compels the conclusion that Act 194 violates the constitutional prohibition against laws "respecting an establishment of religion."

The judgment of the District Court as to Act 194 is reversed; its judgment as to the textbook provisions of Act 195 is affirmed, but as to that Act's other provisions now before us its judgment is reversed.

It is so ordered.

Judgment reversed in part and affirmed in part.

NOTES

1. A New York law permitting the state to reimburse parochial schools for state-required record keeping and testing services was held unconstitutional by the U.S. Supreme Court. The law was found to constitute both direct aid to religion and to involve excessive entanglement. Levitt v. Cathedral Academy, 409 U.S. 977, 93 S.Ct. 316 (1973).

2. In a Vermont suit by a taxpayer against a town school district the question was presented: does the payment of tuition for attendance of students at a religious school by a public entity create a fusion of secular and sectarian education? The court held the payment of students' tuition to the religious denominational high school violates the Federal Constitution. The court quoted the U.S. Supreme Court in Zorach v. Clauson, 343 U.S. 306, 72 S.Ct. 679 (1952) stating: "Government may not finance religious groups nor undertake religious instruction nor blend secular and sectarian education nor use secular institutions to force one or some religion on any person." Swart v. South Burlington Town School Dist., 122 Vt. 177, 167 A.2d 514 (1961).

3. In Virginia an Appropriation Act providing money for education of orphans of soldiers, sailors, and marines for tuition, institutional fees, etc., at any educational institution whether public or nonpublic was held to violate the First Amendment and Virginia constitutional prohibitions against public appropriations schools not under public control. Almond v. Day, 197 Va. 419, 89 S.E.2d 851 (1955).

Certain Services to Nonpublic School Students Are Constitutional While Provision for Instructional Materials and Equipment and Field Trip Services Is Violative of First Amendment

WOLMAN v. WALTER

Supreme Court of the United States, 1977.
433 U.S. 229, 97 S.Ct. 2593.

Mr. Justice BLACKMUN delivered the opinion of the Court (Parts I, V, VI, VII, and VIII), together with an opinion (Parts II, III, and IV), in which The CHIEF JUSTICE, Mr. Justice STEWART, and Mr. Justice POWELL joined.

This is still another case presenting the recurrent issue of the limitations imposed by the Establishment Clause of the First Amendment, made applicable to the States by the Fourteenth Amendment, Meek v. Pittenger, on state aid to pupils in church-related elementary and secondary schools. * * *

I

Section 3317.06 was enacted after this Court's May 1975 decision in Meek v. Pittenger, supra, and obviously is an attempt to conform to the teachings of that decision. * * * In broad outline, the statute authorizes the State to provide nonpublic school pupils with books, instructional materials and equipment, standardized testing and scoring, diagnostic services, therapeutic services, and field trip transportation.

The initial biennial appropriation by the Ohio Legislature for implementation of the statute was the sum of $88,800,000. Funds so appropriated are paid to the State's public school districts and are then expended by them. All disbursements made with respect to nonpublic schools have their equivalents in disbursements for public schools, and the amount expended per pupil in nonpublic schools may not exceed the amount expended per pupil in the public schools.

The parties stipulated that during the 1974–1975 school year there were 720 chartered nonpublic schools in Ohio. Of these, all but 29 were sectarian. More than 96% of the nonpublic enrollment attended sectarian schools, and more than 92% attended Catholic schools. It was also stipulated that, if they were called, officials of representative Catholic schools would testify that such schools operate under the general supervision of the Bishop of their Diocese; that most principals are members of a religious order within the Catholic Church; that a little less than one-third of the teachers are members of such religious orders; that "in all probability a majority of the teachers are members of the Catholic faith"; and that many of the rooms and hallways in these schools are decorated with a Christian symbol. All such schools teach the secular subjects required to meet the State's minimum standards. The state-mandated five-hour day is expanded to include, usually, one-half hour of religious instruction. Pupils who are not members of the Catholic faith are not required to attend religion classes or to participate in religious exercises or activities, and no teacher is required to teach religious doctrine as a part of the secular courses taught in the schools.

The parties also stipulated that nonpublic school officials, if called, would testify that none of the schools covered by the statute discriminate in the admission of pupils or in the hiring of teachers on the basis of race, creed, color, or national origin.

* * *

II

The mode of analysis for Establishment Clause questions is defined by the three-part test that has emerged from the Court's decisions. In order to pass muster, a statute must have a secular legislative purpose, must have a principal or primary effect that neither advances nor inhibits religion, and must not foster an excessive government entanglement with religion. * * *

In the present case we have no difficulty with the first prong of this three-part test. We are satisfied that the challenged statute reflects Ohio's legitimate interest in protecting the health of its youth and in providing a fertile educational environment for all the school children of the State. As is usual in our cases, the analytical difficulty has to do with the effect and entanglement criteria.

We have acknowledged before, and we do so again here, that the wall of separation that must be maintained between church and state "is a blurred, indistinct, and variable barrier depending on all the circumstances of a particular relationship." * * * Nonetheless, the Court's numerous precedents "have become firmly rooted," * * *

and now provide substantial guidance. We therefore turn to the task of applying the rules derived from our decisions to the respective provisions of the statute at issue.

III

Textbooks

Section 3317.06 authorizes the expenditure of funds:

"(A) To purchase such secular textbooks as have been approved by the superintendent of public instruction for use in public schools in the state and to loan such textbooks to pupils attending nonpublic schools within the district or to their parents. Such loans shall be based upon individual requests submitted by such nonpublic school pupils or parents. Such requests shall be submitted to the local public school district in which the nonpublic school is located. Such individual requests for the loan of textbooks shall, for administrative convenience, be submitted by the nonpublic school pupil or his parent to the nonpublic school which shall prepare and submit collective summaries of the individual requests to the local public school district. As used in this section, 'textbook' means any book or book substitute which a pupil uses as a text or text substitute in a particular class or program in the school he regularly attends."

The parties' stipulations reflect operation of the textbook program in accord with the dictates of the statute. In addition, it was stipulated:

"The secular textbooks used in nonpublic schools will be the same as the textbooks used in the public schools of the state. Common suppliers will be used to supply books to both public and nonpublic school pupils.

"Textbooks, including book substitutes, provided under this Act shall be limited to books, reusable workbooks, or manuals, whether bound or in looseleaf form, intended for use as a principal source of study material for a given class or a group of students, a copy of which is expected to be available for the individual use of each pupil in such class or group."

This system for the loan of textbooks to individual students bears a striking resemblance to the systems approved in Board of Education v. Allen, and in Meek v. Pittenger. Indeed, the only distinction offered by appellants is that the challenged statute defines "textbook" as "any book or book substitute." Appellants argue that a "book substitute" might include auxiliary equipment and materials that, they assert, may not constitutionally be loaned. We find this argument untenable in light of the statute's separate treatment of instructional materials and equipment in its subsections (B) and (C), and in light of the stipulation defining textbooks as "limited to books, reusable workbooks, or manuals." * * * We find no grounds, * * * to doubt the Board of Education's reading of the statute, or to fear that the Board is using the stipulations as a subterfuge. As read, the statute provides the same protections against abuse as were provided in the textbook programs under consideration in Allen and in Meek.

In the alternative, appellants urge that we overrule Allen and Meek. This we decline to do. Accordingly, we conclude that § 3317.-06(A) is constitutional.

IV

Testing and Scoring

Section 3317.06 authorizes expenditure of funds:

"(J) To supply for use by pupils attending nonpublic schools within the district such standardized tests and scoring services as are in use in the public schools of the state."

These tests "are used to measure the progress of students in secular subjects." Nonpublic school personnel are not involved in either the drafting or scoring of the tests. The statute does not authorize any payment to nonpublic school personnel for the costs of administering the tests.

In Levitt v. Committee for Public Education, this Court invalidated a New York statutory scheme for reimbursement of church-sponsored schools for the expenses of teacher-prepared testing. The reasoning behind that decision was straightforward. The system was held unconstitutional because "no means are available, to assure that internally prepared tests are free of religious instruction."

There is no question that the State has a substantial and legitimate interest in insuring that its youth receive an adequate secular education. The State may require that schools that are utilized to fulfill the State's compulsory education requirement meet certain standards of instruction, Allen, and may examine both teachers and pupils to ensure that the State's legitimate interest is being fulfilled. Levitt, * * * Under the section at issue, the State provides both the schools and the school district with the means of ensuring that the minimum standards are met. The nonpublic school does not control the content of the test or its result. This serves to prevent the use of the test as a part of religious teaching, and thus avoids that kind of direct aid to religion found present in Levitt. Similarly, the inability of the school to control the test eliminates the need for the supervision that gives rise to excessive entanglement. We therefore agree with the District Court's conclusion that § 3317.06(J) is constitutional.

V

Diagnostic Services

Section 3317.06 authorizes expenditures of funds:

"(D) To provide speech and hearing diagnostic services to pupils attending nonpublic schools within the district. Such service shall be provided in the nonpublic school attended by the pupil receiving the service.

* * * * * * * * * * * *

"(F) To provide diagnostic psychological services to pupils attending nonpublic schools within the district. Such services shall be provided in the the school attended by the pupil receiving the service."

It will be observed that these speech and hearing and psychological diagnostic services are to be provided within the nonpublic school. It is stipulated, however, that the personnel (with the exception of physicians) who perform the services are employees of the local board of education; that physicians may be hired on a contract basis; that the purpose of these services is to determine the pupil's deficiency or need of assistance; and that treatment of any defect so found would take place off the nonpublic school premises.

Appellants assert that the funding of these services is constitutionally impermissible. They argue that the speech and hearing staff might engage in unrestricted conversation with the pupil and, on occasion, might fail to separate religious instruction from secular responsibilities. They further assert that the communication between the psychological diagnostician and the pupil will provide an impermissible opportunity for the intrusion of religious influence.

The District Court found these dangers so insubstantial as not to render the statute unconstitutional. We agree. This Court's decisions contain a common thread to the effect that the provision of health services to all school children—public and nonpublic—does not have the primary effect of aiding religion. * * *

In *Meek* the Court did hold unconstitutional a portion of a Pennsylvania statute at issue there that authorized certain auxiliary services—"remedial and accelerated instruction, guidance counseling and testing, speech and hearing services"—on nonpublic school premises. The Court noted that the teacher or guidance counselor might "fail on occasion to separate religious instruction and the advancement of religious beliefs from his secular educational responsibilities." The Court was of the view that the publicly employed teacher or guidance counselor might depart from religious neutrality because he was "performing important educational services in schools in which education is an integral part of the dominant sectarian mission and in which an atmosphere dedicated to the advancement of religious belief is constantly maintained." The statute was held unconstitutional on entanglement grounds, namely, that in order to insure that the auxiliary teachers and guidance counselors remained neutral, the State would have to engage in continuing surveillance on the school premises. * * * The Court in Meek explicitly stated, however, that the provision of diagnostic speech and hearing services by Pennsylvania seemed "to fall within that class of general welfare services for children that may be provided by the State regardless of the incidental benefit that accrues to church-related schools." The provision of such services was invalidated only because it was found unseverable from the unconstitutional portions of the statute.

The reason for considering diagnostic services to be different from teaching or counseling is readily apparent. First, diagnostic services, unlike teaching or counseling, have little or no educational content and are not closely associated with the educational mission of the nonpublic school. Accordingly, any pressure on the public diagnostician to allow the intrusion of sectarian views is greatly reduced. Second, the diagnostician has only limited contact with the child, and that contact involves chiefly the use of objective and professional testing methods to detect students in need of treatment. The nature of the relationship between the diagnostician and the pupil does not provide the same opportunity for the transmission of sectarian views as attends the relationsip between teacher and student or that between counselor and student.

We conclude that providing diagnostic services on the nonpublic school premises will not create an impermissible risk of the fostering of idealogical views. It follows that there is no need for excessive surveillance, and there will not be impermissible entanglement. We therefore hold that §§ 3317.06(D) and (F) are constitutional.

VI

Therapeutic Services

Sections 3317.06(G), (H), (I), and (K) authorize expenditures of funds for certain therapeutic, guidance, and remedial services for students who have been identified as having a need for specialized attention. Personnel providing the services must be employees of the local board of education or under contract with the State Department of Health. The services are to be performed only in public schools, in public centers, or in mobile units located off the nonpublic school premises. The parties have stipulated: "The determination as to whether these programs would be offered in the public school, public center, or mobile unit will depend on the distance between the public and nonpublic school, the safety factors involved in travel, and the adequacy of accommodations in public schools and public centers."

Appellants concede that the provision of remedial, therapeutic, and guidance services in public schools, public centers, or mobile units is constitutional if both public and nonpublic school students are served simultaneously. Their challenge is limited to the situation where a facility is used to service only nonpublic school students. They argue that any program that isolates the sectarian pupils is impermissible because the public employee providing the service might tailor his approach to reflect and reinforce the ideological view of the sectarian school attended by the children. Such action by the employee, it is claimed, renders direct aid to the sectarian institution. Appellants express particular concern over mobile units because they perceive a danger that such a unit might operate merely as an annex of the school or schools it services.

At the outset, we note that in its present posture the case does not properly present any issue concerning the use of a public facility as an adjunct of a sectarian educational enterprise. The District Court construed the statute, as do we, to authorize services only on sites that are "neither physically nor educationally identified with the functions of the nonpublic school." Thus, the services are to be offered under circumstances that reflect their religious neutrality.

We recognize that, unlike the diagnostician, the therapist may establish a relationship with the pupil in which there might be opportunities to transmit ideological views. In Meek the Court acknowledged the danger that publicly employed personnel who provide services analogous to those at issue here might transmit religious instruction and advance religious beliefs in their activities. But, as discussed in Part V, supra, the Court emphasized that this danger arose from the fact that the services were performed in the pervasively sectarian atmosphere of the church-related school. * * * The danger existed there not because the public employee was likely deliberately to subvert his task to the service of religion, but rather because the pressures of the environment might alter his behavior from its normal course. So long as these types of services are offered at truly religiously neutral locations, the danger perceived in Meek does not arise.

The fact that a unit on a neutral site on occasion may serve only sectarian pupils does not provoke the same concerns that troubled the Court in Meek. The influence on a therapist's behavior that is exerted by the fact that he serves a sectarian pupil is qualitatively different from the influence of the pervasive atmosphere of a religious institution. The dangers perceived in Meek arose from the nature of the institution, not from the nature of the pupils.

Accordingly, we hold that providing therapeutic and remedial services at a neutral site off the premises of the nonpublic schools will not have the impermissible effect of advancing religion. Neither will there be any excessive entanglement arising from supervision of public employees to insure that they maintain a neutral stance. It can hardly be said that the supervision of public employees performing public functions on public property creates an excessive entanglement between church and state. Sections 3317.06(G), (H), (I), and (K) are constitutional.

VII

Instructional Materials and Equipment

Sections 3317.06(B) and (C) authorize expenditures of funds for the purchase and loan to pupils or their parents upon individual request of instructional materials and instructional equipment of the kind in use in the public schools within the district and which is "incapable of diversion to religious use." Section 3717.06 also provides that the materials and equipment may be stored on the premises of a nonpublic school and that publicly hired personnel who administer the lending program may perform their services upon the nonpublic school premises when necessary "for efficient implementation of the lending program."

Although the exact nature of the material and equipment is not clearly revealed, the parties have stipulated: "It is expected that materials and equipment loaned to pupils or parents under the new law will be similar to such former materials and equipment except that to the extent that the law requires that materials and equipment capable of diversion to religious issues will not be supplied." Equipment provided under the predecessor statute, * * * included projectors, tape recorders, record players, maps and globes, science kits, weather forecasting charts, and the like. * * *

In Meek, * * * the Court considered the constitutional validity of a direct loan to nonpublic schools of instructional material and equipment, and, despite the apparent secular nature of the goods, held the loan impermissible. * * * Thus, even though the loan ostensibly was limited to neutral and secular instructional material and equipment, it inescapably had the primary effect of providing a direct and substantial advancement of the sectarian enterprise.

Appellees seek to avoid Meek by emphasizing that it involved a program of direct loans to nonpublic schools. In contrast, the material and equipment at issue under the Ohio statute are loaned to the pupil or his parent. In our view, however, it would exalt form over substance if this distinction were found to justify a result different from that in Meek. Before Meek was decided by this Court, Ohio authorized the loan of material and equipment directly to the nonpublic schools. Then, in light of Meek, the state legislature decided to channel the goods through the parents and pupils. Despite the technical change in legal bailee, the program in substance is the same as before: the equipment is substantially the same; it will receive the same use by the students; and it may still be stored and distributed on the nonpublic school premises. In view of the impossibility of separating the secular education function from the sectarian, the state aid inevitably flows in part in support of the religious role of the schools.

Indeed, this conclusion is compelled by the Court's prior consideration of an analogous issue in Committee for Public Education v. Nyquist. There the Court considered, among others, a tuition reimbursement program whereby New York gave low income parents who sent their children to nonpublic schools a direct and unrestricted cash grant of $50 to $100 per child (but no more than 50% of tuition actually paid). The State attempted to justify the program, as Ohio does here, on the basis that the aid flowed to the parents rather than to the church-related schools. The Court observed, however, that, unlike the bus program in Everson v. Board of Education, * * * and the book program in Allen, there "has been no endeavor 'to guarantee the separation between secular and religious educational functions and to insure that State financial aid supports only the former.'" * * * The Court thus found that the grant program served to establish religion. If a grant in cash to parents is impermissible, we fail to see how a grant in kind of goods furthering the religious enterprise can fare any better. Accordingly, we hold §§ 3317.06(B) and (C) to be unconstitutional.

VIII

Field Trips

Section 3317.06 also authorizes expenditures of funds:

> "(L) To provide such field trip transportation and services to nonpublic school students as are provided to public school students in the district. School districts may contract with commercial transportation companies for such transportation service if school district busses are unavailable."

There is no restriction on the timing of field trips; the only restriction on number lies in the parallel the statute draws to field trips provided to public school students in the district. The parties have stipulated that the trips "would consist of visits to governmental, industrial, cultural, and scientific centers designed to enrich the secular studies of students." The choice of destination, however, will be made by the nonpublic school teacher from a wide range of locations.

The District Court, held this feature to be constitutionally indistinguishable from that with which the Court was concerned in Everson v. Board of Education. We do not agree. In Everson the Court approved a system under which a New Jersey board of education reimbursed parents for the cost of sending their children to and from school, public or parochial, by public carrier. The Court analogized the reimbursement to situations where a municipal common carrier is ordered to carry all school children at a reduced rate, or where the police force is ordered to protect all children on their way to and from school. The critical factors in these examples, as in the Everson reimbursement system, are that the school has no control over the expenditure of the funds and the effect of the expenditure is unrelated to the content of the education provided. Thus, the bus fare program in Everson passed constitutional muster because the school did not determine how often the pupil traveled between home and school—every child must make one round trip every day—and because the travel was unrelated to any aspect of the curriculum.

The Ohio situation is in sharp contrast. First, the nonpublic school controls the timing of the trips and, within a certain range, their frequency and destinations. Thus, the schools, rather than the children, truly are the recipients of the service and, as this Court has recognized, this fact alone may be sufficient to invalidate the program as impermissible direct aid. * * * Second, although a trip may be to a location that would be of interest to those in public schools, it is the individual teacher who makes a field trip meaningful. The experience begins with the study and discussion of the place to be visited; it continues on location with the teacher pointing out items of interest and stimulating the imagination; and it ends with a discussion of the experience. The field trips are an integral part of the educational experience, and where the teacher works within and for a sectarian institution, an unacceptable risk of fostering of religion is an inevitable byproduct. * * * Funding of field trips, therefore, must be treated as was the funding of maps and charts in Meek v. Pittenger, supra, the funding of buildings and tuition in Committee for Public Education v. Nyquist, supra, and the funding of teacher-prepared tests in Levitt v. Committee for Public Education; it must be declared an impermissible direct aid to sectarian education.

Moreover, the public school authorities will be unable adequately to insure secular use of the field trip funds without close supervision of the nonpublic teachers. This would create excessive entanglement: * * *.

We hold § 3317.06 (L) to be unconstitutional.

IX

In summary, we hold constitutional those portions of the Ohio statute authorizing the State to provide nonpublic school pupils with books, standardized testing and scoring, diagnostic services, and therapeutic and remedial services. We hold unconstitutional those portions relating to instructional materials and equipment and field trip services.

* * *

Released Time for Religious Instruction

The practice of releasing public school children during regular school hours for religious instruction first began in the United States in Gary, Indiana, in 1914. Since then the Supreme Court has had before it two cases involving release time. The first was the *McCollum* case in 1948,[42] in which pupils were released to attend religious instruction in the classrooms of the public school building. Students who did not want to participate were not released, but were required to leave their classrooms and go to another part of the building to pursue their secular studies. The Supreme Court held that this "release time" program violated the First Amendment of the Constitution.

In 1952 the Supreme Court was once again called upon to test the constitutionality of "release time." In this case a New York statute permitted pupils to leave the school building and grounds to attend religious centers for religious instruction.[43] Students who did not wish to participate in such services stayed in their classrooms, and no supervision or approval of their activities was required. The Supreme Court found that this statute did not violate the doctrine of separation of church and state. The Court pointed out that while the Constitution forbids the government financing of religious groups and the promotion of religious instruction, the First Amendment does not require governmental hostility toward religion. From this decision it is clear that the Supreme Court does not prohibit some cooperation between schools and churches, but the nature and degree of the cooperation is important; and, if it exceeds certain reasonable limitations, the relationship will violate the Constitution.

Released Time for Religious Instruction on Public
School Premises Is Unconstitutional

PEOPLE OF STATE OF ILLINOIS EX REL. McCOLLUM v. BOARD OF EDUC. OF SCHOOL DIST. NO. 71, CHAMPAIGN COUNTY, ILL.

Supreme Court of the United States, 1948.
333 U.S. 203, 68 S.Ct. 461.

Mr. Justice BLACK delivered the opinion of the Court.

This case relates to the power of a state to utilize its tax-supported public school system in aid of religious instruction insofar as that power may be restricted by the First and Fourteenth Amendments to the Federal Constitution.

---

42. People of State of Illinois ex rel McCollum v. Board of Educ. of School Dist. No. 71, 333 U.S. 203, 68 S.Ct. 461 (1948).

43. Zorach v. Clauson, 343 U.S. 306, 72 S.Ct. 679 (1952).

* * *

Appellant's petition for mandamus alleged that religious teachers, employed by private religious groups, were permitted to come weekly into the school buildings during the regular hours set apart for secular teaching, and then and there for a period of thirty minutes substitute their religious teaching for the secular education provided under the compulsory education law. The petitioner charged that this joint public-school religious-group program violated the First and Fourteenth Amendments to the United States Constitution. The prayer of her petition was that the Board of Education be ordered to "adopt and enforce rules and regulations prohibiting all instruction in and teaching of all religious education in all public schools in Champaign District Number 71, * * * and in all public school houses and buildings in said district when occupied by public schools."

* * *

Although there are disputes between the parties as to various inferences that may or may not properly be drawn from the evidence concerning the religious program, the following facts are shown by the record without dispute. In 1940 interested members of the Jewish, Roman Catholic, and a few of the Protestant faiths formed a voluntary association called the Champaign Council on Religious Education. They obtained permission from the Board of Education to offer classes in religious instruction to public school pupils in grades four to nine inclusive. Classes were made up of pupils whose parents signed printed cards requesting that their children be permitted to attend; they were held weekly, thirty minutes for the lower grades, forty-five minutes for the higher. The council employed the religious teachers at no expense to the school authorities, but the instructors were subject to the approval and supervision of the superintendent of schools. The classes were taught in three separate religious groups by Protestant teachers, Catholic priests, and a Jewish rabbi, although for the past several years there have apparently been no classes instructed in the Jewish religion. Classes were conducted in the regular classrooms of the school building. Students who did not choose to take the religious instruction were not released from public school duties; they were required to leave their classrooms and go to some other place in the school building for pursuit of their secular studies. On the other hand, students who were released from secular study for the religious instructions were required to be present at the religious classes. Reports of their presence or absence were to be made to their secular teachers.

The foregoing facts, without reference to others that appear in the record, show the use of tax-supported property for religious instruction and the close cooperation between the school authorities and the religious council in promoting religious education. The operation of the state's compulsory education system thus assists and is integrated with the program of religious instruction carried on by separate religious sects. Pupils compelled by law to go to school for secular education are released in part from their legal duty upon the condition that they attend the religious classes. This is beyond all question a utilization of the tax-established and tax-supported public school system to aid religious groups to spread their faith. And it falls squarely under the ban of the First Amendment (made applicable to the States by the Fourteenth) as we interpreted it in Everson v. Board of Education, 330 U.S. 1, 67 S.Ct. 504. * * *

* * *

To hold that a state cannot consistently with the First and Fourteenth Amendments utilize its public school system to aid any or all religious faiths or sects in the dissemination of their doctrines and ideals does not, as counsel urge, manifest a governmental hostility to religion or religious teachings. A manifestation of such hostility would be at war with our national tradition as embodied in the First Amendment's guaranty of the free exercise of religion. For the First Amendment rests upon the premise that both religion and government can best work to achieve their lofty aims if each is left free from the other within its respective sphere. Or, as we said in the Everson case, the First Amendment has erected a wall between Church and State which must be kept high and impregnable.

Here not only are the state's tax-supported public school buildings used for the dissemination of religious doctrines. The State also affords sectarian groups an invaluable aid in that it helps to provide pupils for their religious classes through use of the state's compulsory public school machinery. This is not separation of Church and State.

The cause is reversed and remanded to the State Supreme Court for proceedings not inconsistent with this opinion.

Reversed and remanded.

NOTES

1. *Released Time.* Courts upholding discretionary power of boards of education to provide released time programs: People ex rel. Lewis v. Graves, 245 N.Y. 195, 156 N.E. 663 (1927); People ex rel. Latimer v. Board of Ed. of City of Chicago, 394 Ill. 228, 68 N.E.2d 305 (1946); Dilger v. School Dist., 222 Or. 108, 352 P.2d 564 (1960). Some decisions indicated parents had the right to have children excused or released from school for religious purposes: Lewis v. Spaulding, 193 Misc. 66, 85 N.Y.S.2d 682 (1948), appeal dismissed 299 N.Y. 564, 85 N.E.2d 791 (1949); Gordon v. Board of Ed. of City of Los Angeles, 78 Cal.App.2d 464, 178 P.2d 488 (1947); Perry v. School Dist. No. 61, Spokane, 54 Wash.2d 886, 344 P.2d 1036 (1959).

2. In this case, how do the compulsory attendance laws of the state assist religion?

3. How does the court answer the argument that the First Amendment was intended only to forbid government preference of one religion over another, not an impartial governmental assistance of all religions?

Released Time for Public School Students to Attend Religious Classes Off Public School Grounds Is Constitutional

ZORACH v. CLAUSON

Supreme Court of the United States, 1952.
343 U.S. 306, 72 S.Ct. 679.

Mr. Justice DOUGLAS delivered the opinion of the Court.

New York City has a program which permits its public schools to release students during the school day so that they may leave the school buildings and school grounds and go to religious centers for religious instruction or devotional exercises. A student is released on written request of his parents. Those not released stay in the classrooms. The churches make weekly reports to the schools, sending a list of children who have been released from public school but who have not reported for religious instruction.

This "released time" program involves neither religious instruction in public school classrooms nor the expenditure of public funds. All costs, including the application blanks, are paid by the religious organizations. The case is therefore unlike McCollum v. Board of Education, 333 U.S. 203, 68 S.Ct. 461, 92 L.Ed. 249, which involved a "released time" program from Illinois. In that case the classrooms were turned over to religious instructors. We accordingly held that the program violated the First Amendment which (by reason of the Fourteenth Amendment) [3] prohibits the states from establishing religion or prohibiting its free exercise.

Appellants, who are taxpayers and residents of New York City and whose children attend its public schools,[4] challenge the present law, contending it is in essence not different from the one involved in the McCollum case. Their argument, stated elaborately in various ways, reduces itself to this: the weight and influence of the school is put behind a program for religious instruction; public school teachers police it, keeping tab on students who are released; the classroom activities come to a halt while the students who are released for religious instruction are on leave; the school is a crutch on which the churches are leaning for support in their religious training; without the cooperation of the schools this "released time" program, like the one in the McCollum case, would be futile and ineffective. The New

---

3. See Stromberg v. California, 283 U. S. 359, 51 S.Ct. 532, 75 L.Ed. 1117; Cantwell v. Connecticut, 310 U.S. 296, 60 S.Ct. 900, 84 L.Ed. 1213; Murdock v. Pennsylvania, 319 U.S. 105, 63 S.Ct. 870, 87 L.Ed. 1292.

4. No problem of this Court's jurisdiction is posed in this case since, unlike the appellants in Doremus v. Board of Education, 342 U.S. 429, 72 S.Ct. 394, 96 L.Ed. 475, appellants here are parents of children currently attending schools subject to the released time program.

York Court of Appeals sustained the law against this claim of unconstitutionality.   *   *   *

          *   *   *

It takes obtuse reasoning to inject any issue of the "free exercise" of religion into the present case. No one is forced to go to the
religious classroom and no religious exercise or instruction is brought
to the classrooms of the public schools. A student need not take religious instruction. He is left to his own desires as to the manner or
time of his religious devotions, if any.

There is a suggestion that the system involves the use of coercion to get public school students into religious classrooms. There is
no evidence in the record before us that supports that conclusion.
The present record indeed tells us that the school authorities are neutral in this regard and do no more than release students whose parents so request. If in fact coercion were used, if it were established
that any one or more teachers were using their office to persuade or
force students to take the religious instruction, a wholly different
case would be presented. Hence we put aside that claim of coercion
both as respects the "free exercise" of religion and "an establishment
of religion" within the meaning of the First Amendment.

          *   *   *

We would have to press the concept of separation of Church and
State to these extremes to condemn the present law on constitutional
grounds.   *   *   *

We are a religious people whose institutions presuppose a Supreme Being. We guarantee the freedom to worship as one chooses.
We make room for as wide a variety of beliefs and creeds as the spiritual needs of man deem necessary. We sponsor an attitude on the
part of government that shows no partiality to any one group and
that lets each flourish according to the zeal of its adherents and the
appeal of its dogma. When the state encourages religious instruction
or cooperates with religious authorities by adjusting the schedule of
public events to sectarian needs, it follows the best of our traditions.
For it then respects the religious nature of our people and accommo-
dates the public service to their spiritual needs. To hold that it may
not would be to find in the Constitution a requirement that the government show a callous indifference to religious groups. That would
be preferring those who believe in no religion over those who do believe. Government may not finance religious groups nor undertake
religious instruction nor blend secular and sectarian education nor
use secular institutions to force one or some religion on any person.
But we find no constitutional requirement which makes it necessary
for government to be hostile to religion and to throw its weight
against efforts to widen the effective scope of religious influence.
The government must be neutral when it comes to competition between sects. It may not thrust any sect on any person. It may not

make a religious observance compulsory. It may not coerce anyone to attend church, to observe a religious holiday, or to take religious instruction. But it can close its doors or suspend its operations as to those who want to repair to their religious sanctuary for worship or instruction. No more than that is undertaken here.

* * *

In the McCollum case the classrooms were used for religious instruction and the force of the public school was used to promote that instruction. Here, as we have said, the public schools do no more than accommodate their schedules to a program of outside religious instruction. We follow the McCollum case. But we cannot expand it to cover the present released time program unless separation of Church and State means that public institutions can make no adjustments of their schedules to accommodate the religious needs of the people. We cannot read into the Bill of Rights such a philosophy of hostility to religion.

Affirmed.

NOTES

1. *Shared Time:* "Dual Enrollment" or "shared time" is an arrangement between a public school and a private school by which the shared use of the public school facilities is provided for private school teachers or students. A pupil may be a part-time student in a public school while concurrently attending a nonpublic school part-time.

The Elementary and Secondary Education Act of 1965 included provisions for dual enrollment of shared time programs. P.L. 89–10, 79 Stat. 29. This act was passed by the Congress of the United States for the purpose of strengthening and improving educational opportunities and quality in the nation's elementary and secondary schools.

The Act and federal regulations pursuant to the Act provided that the number of children from private and parochial schools who share in this aid:

> be consistent with the number of educationally deprived children in the school district of the local educational agency who are enrolled in private elementary and secondary schools, the local educational agency just make provision for including special educational services and arrangements (such as dual enrollment, educational radio and television, and mobile educational services and equipment) in which such children can participate. Federal Regulations 116.9 (a), in Federal Reprints, Sept. 15, 1965, p. 11813.

Four (Titles I, II, III, and VI) of the six Titles or P.S. 89–10 provided for dual enrollment arrangements with pupils of private and parochial schools. Elementary and Secondary Education Act Amendments of 1966, 89th Cong. 2d Sess. Report No. 2309 (H.R.).

2. In a case involving "shared time" the Supreme Court of Missouri held that use of public monies to send speech teachers of a school district

into parochial schools for speech therapy was not for the purpose of maintaining free public schools and was therefore unconstitutional (Section 5 of Article IX, Missouri Constitution). Also, where the school district provided speech therapy for parochial school children in buildings maintained by the school district and parochial children who desired such therapy were released from school for part of their regular six-hour day, such practice violated compulsory attendance laws which required each school child to attend school regularly for six hours a school day. Special District for the Educ. and Training of Handicapped Children of St. Louis County v. Wheeler, 408 S.W.2d 60 (Mo.1966).

3. An Illinois court reached a conclusion different from that of the Missouri court concerning shared time. Plaintiffs in this case sought to enjoin the Board of Education from maintaining a dual enrollment program where children were enrolled part-time in a public school and part-time in a nonpublic school, on the grounds that the program violated statutory and constitutional provisions. The court held that the dual enrollment program did not violate either statutory or constitutional provisions.

> The object of compulsory attendance law is that all children be educated and not that they be educated in any particular manner or place, and part-time enrollment in a public school and part-time enrollment in a nonpublic school under a dual enrollment program is permitted so long as the child receives a complete education.

Morton v. Board of Educ. of City of Chicago, 69 Ill.App.2d 38, 216 N.E.2d 305 (1966).

4. How does the released time program of the *Zorach* case differ from the program in the *McCollum* case?

5. What does the court say about the relationship between church and state? What is the role of the state in dealing with religion?

6. Relate the reasoning in the decisions by the Supreme Court in *McCollum* and *Zorach* to the concept of dual enrollment. What legal principles of the cases may be applied in a case involving dual enrollment?

7. A shared time program where the school district leased parochial school facilities and public school teachers taught classes therein, the court held that neither the state nor federal constitutions were violated. This was true even in light of one fact that the parochial school students attended classes in both the public and private school classes which were conducted in the same building. Citizens to Advance Public Educ. v. Porter, 65 Mich.App. 168, 237 N.W.2d 232 (1975).

Prayer and Bible Reading in the Public Schools

Prayer and Bible reading in the public schools have been the source of much judicial controversy. Over half the states have at some point permitted or required prayer and Bible reading in public schools. Prior to 1962 at least twelve states and the District of Columbia required Bible reading. The typical attitude of the courts was that the Bible and general prayer were not sectarian in nature, and their use did not violate constitutional religious guarantees.[44] That the Bible was not sectarian was even reflected in statute; the North Dakota legislature had provided:

> The Bible shall not be deemed a sectarian book. It shall not be excluded from any public school. It may at the option of the teacher be read in school without sectarian comment, not to exceed ten minutes daily. No pupil shall be required to read it nor be present in the schoolroom during the reading thereof contrary to the wishes of his parents or guardian or other person having him in charge.[45]

Voluntariness of the exercise, whether it was Bible reading or prayer was thought to be an important factor as evidenced by this type of legislation. Proponents of religious exercises generally relied upon this, tradition, and nonsectarianism of the Bible as the primary defense of the practice. In 1962, however, the U. S. Supreme Court, in Engel v. Vitale, found a New York Regents prayer unconstitutional, and a year later held both prayer and Bible reading offensive to the First Amendment even though the defendants claimed that the exercises were voluntary and the Bible was nondenominational. This result could probably have been anticipated since the position established by the Court in *McCollum* in 1948 indicated that neither the nature of the religious instruction nor the voluntariness of the exercise were valid defenses. In *McCollum*, Justice Frankfurter stated:

> That a child is offered an alternative may reduce the constraint; it does not eliminate the operation of influence by the school in matters sacred to conscience and outside the school's domain. The law of imitation operates, and nonconformity is not an outstanding characteristic of children. The result is an obvious pressure upon children to attend.
> * * * "[46]

Likewise, the nondenominational nature of a prayer was found to be no defense when the issue was raised in *Engel*. The Court explained that neither the fact that a prayer is denominationally neutral nor that it is voluntary can serve to free it from the limitations of the Establishment Clause of the First Amendment. According to the Court:

> The Establishment Clause, unlike the Free Exercise Clause, does not depend upon any showing of direct governmental

44. Hackett v. Brooksville Graded School Dist., 120 Ky. 608, 87 S.W. 792 (1905).

45. North Dakota Compiled Laws, Sec. 1388 (1913).

46. People ex rel. McCollum v. Board of Educ., 333 U.S. 203, 68 S.Ct. 461 (1948).

compulsion and is violated by the enactment of laws which establish an official religion whether those laws operate directly to coerce non-observing individuals or not. * * * " 47

The result of both the *Engel,* the *Schempp* and its companion case, *Murray,*48 in 1963, was that religious exercises in the public schools are clearly unconstitutional. Neither state, nor school, nor teacher can hold religious services of any type in the public schools. The Court did point out, however, that the study of the Bible and religion, as a part of a secular program of education for their literary and historic values would not be unconstitutional.

Use of Public School Classroom to Encourage
Recitation of State Promulgated Prayer
Is Unconstitutional

ENGEL v. VITALE

Supreme Court of the United States, 1962.
370 U.S. 421, 82 S.Ct. 1261.

Mr. Justice BLACK delivered the opinion of the Court.

The respondent Board of Education of Union Free School District No. 9, New Hyde Park, New York, acting in its official capacity under state law, directed the School District's principal to cause the following prayer to be said aloud by each class in the presence of a teacher at the beginning of each school day:

> "Almighty God, we acknowledge our dependence upon Thee, and we beg Thy blessings upon us, our parents, our teachers and our Country."

This daily procedure was adopted on the recommendation of the State Board of Regents, a governmental agency created by the State Constitution to which the New York Legislature has granted broad supervisory, executive, and legislative powers over the State's public school system.[1] These state officials composed the prayer which they recommended and published as a part of their "Statement on Moral and Spiritual Training in the Schools," saying: "We believe that this Statement will be subscribed to by all men and women of good will, and we call upon all of them to aid in giving life to our program."

     * * *

47. Engel v. Vitale, 370 U.S. 421, 82 S.Ct. 1261 (1962).

48. School Dist. of Abington Township v. Schempp and Murray v. Curlett, 374 U.S. 203, 83 S.Ct. 1560 (1963).

1. See New York Constitution, art. V, § 4; New York Education Law, McKinney's Consol.Laws, c. 16, §§ 101, 120 et seq., 202, 214–219, 224, 245 et seq., 704, and 801 et seq.

We think that by using its public school system to encourage recitation of the Regents' prayer, the State of New York has adopted a practice wholly inconsistent with the Establishment Clause. There can, of course, be no doubt that New York's program of daily classroom invocation of God's blessings as prescribed in the Regents' prayer is a religious activity. It is a solemn avowal of divine faith and supplication for the blessings of the Almighty. The nature of such a prayer has always been religious. * * *

The petitioners contend among other things that the state laws requiring or permitting use of the Regents' prayer must be struck down as a violation of the Establishment Clause because that prayer was composed by governmental officials as a part of a governmental program to further religious beliefs. For this reason, petitioners argue, the State's use of the Regents' prayer in its public school system breaches the constitutional wall of separation between Church and State. We agree with that contention since we think that the constitutional prohibition against laws respecting an establishment of religion must at least mean that in this country it is no part of the business of government to compose official prayers for any group of the American people to recite as a part of a religious program carried on by government.

* * *

There can be no doubt that New York's state prayer program officially establishes the religious beliefs embodied in the Regents' prayer. The respondents' argument to the contrary, which is largely based upon the contention that the Regents' prayer is "nondenominational" and the fact that the program, as modified and approved by state courts, does not require all pupils to recite the prayer but permits those who wish to do so to remain silent or be excused from the room, ignores the essential nature of the program's constitutional defects. Neither the fact that the prayer may be denominationally neutral nor the fact that its observance on the part of the students is voluntary can serve to free it from the limitations of the Establishment Clause, as it might from the Free Exercise Clause, of the First Amendment, both of which are operative against the States by virtue of the Fourteenth Amendment. Although these two clauses may in certain instances overlap, they forbid two quite different kinds of governmental encroachment upon religious freedom. The Establishment Clause, unlike the Free Exercise Clause, does not depend upon any showing of direct governmental compulsion and is violated by the enactment of laws which establish an official religion whether those laws operate directly to coerce nonobserving individuals or not. This is not to say, of course, that laws officially prescribing a particular form of religious worship do not involve coercion of such individuals. When the power, prestige and financial support of government is placed behind a particular religious belief, the indirect coercive pressure upon religious minorities to conform to the prevailing officially approved religion is plain. But the purposes underlying the Establishment Clause go much further than that. Its first and most immediate purpose rested on the belief that a union of government and religion tends to destroy government and to degrade religion. The history of governmentally established religion, both in England and in this country, showed that whenever government had allied itself with one particular form of religion, the inevitable result had been that it had incurred the hatred, disrespect and even contempt of those who held contrary beliefs. That same history showed that many people had lost their respect for any religion that had relied upon the support of government to spread its faith. The Establishment Clause thus stands as an expression of principle on the part of the Founders of our Constitution that religion is too personal, too sacred, too holy, to permit its "unhallowed perversion" by a civil magistrate. * * * The New York laws officially prescribing the Regents' prayer are inconsistent both with the purposes of the Establishment Clause and with the Establishment Clause itself.

It has been argued that to apply the Constitution in such a way as to prohibit state laws respecting an establishment of religious services in public schools is to indicate a hostility toward religion or toward prayer. Nothing, of course, could be more wrong. * * * It is neither sacrilegious nor antireligious to say that each separate government in this country should stay out of the business of writing or sanctioning official prayers and leave that purely religious function to the people themselves and to those the people choose to look to for religious guidance.

It is true that New York's establishment of its Regents' prayer as an officially approved religious doctrine of that State does not amount to a total establishment of one particular religious sect to the exclusion of all others—that, indeed, the governmental endorsement of that prayer seems relatively insignificant when compared to the governmental encroachments upon religion which were commonplace 200 years ago. To those who may subscribe to the view that because the Regents' official prayer is so brief and general there can be no danger to religious freedom in its governmental establishment, however, it may be appropriate to say in the words of James Madison, the author of the First Amendment:

> "[I]t is proper to take alarm at the first experiment on our liberties. * * * Who does not see that the same authority which can establish Christianity, in exclusion of all other Religions, may establish with the same ease any particular sect of Christians, in exclusion of all other Sects? That the same authority which can force a citizen to contribute three pence only of his property for the support of

any one establishment, may force him to conform to any other establishment in all cases whatsoever?" [22]

The judgment of the Court of Appeals of New York is reversed and the cause remanded for further proceedings not inconsistent with this opinion.

Reversed and remanded.

State Enforced Bible Reading and Prayer in the Public Schools Is Unconstitutional

SCHOOL DIST. OF ABINGTON TOWNSHIP v. SCHEMPP AND MURRAY v. CURLETT

Supreme Court of the United States, 1963.
374 U.S. 203, 83 S.Ct. 1560.

Mr. Justice CLARK delivered the opinion of the Court.

Once again we are called upon to consider the scope of the provision of the First Amendment to the United States Constitution which declares that "Congress shall make no law respecting an establishment of religion, or prohibiting the free exercise thereof * * * ." These companion cases present the issues in the context of state action requiring that schools begin each day with readings from the Bible. While raising the basic questions under slightly different factual situations, the cases permit of joint treatment. In light of the history of the First Amendment and of our cases interpreting and applying its requirements, we hold that the practices at issue and the laws requiring them are unconstitutional under the Establishment Clause, as applied to the States through the Fourteenth Amendment.

I.

The Facts in Each Case: No. 142. The Commonwealth of Pennsylvania by law, 24 Pa.Stat. § 15–1516, as amended, Pub.Law 1928 (Supp.1960) Dec. 17, 1959, requires that "At least ten verses from the Holy Bible shall be read, without comment, at the opening of each public school on each school day. Any child shall be excused from such Bible reading, or attending such Bible reading, upon the written request of his parent or guardian." The Schempp family, husband and wife and two of their three children, brought suit to enjoin enforcement of the statute, contending that their rights under the Fourteenth Amendment to the Constitution of the United States are,

22. Memorial and Remonstrance Against Religious Assessments, II Writings of Madison 183, at 185–186.

have been, and will continue to be violated unless this statute be declared unconstitutional as violative of these provisions of the First
Amendment.   They sought to enjoin the appellant school district,
wherein the Schempp children attend school, and its officers and the
Superintendent of Public Instruction of the Commonwealth from continuing to conduct such readings and recitation of the Lord's Prayer
in the public schools of the district pursuant to the statute. * * *

* * *

No. 119.   In 1905 the Board of School Commissioners of Baltimore City adopted a rule pursuant to Art. 77, § 202 of the Annotated
Code of Maryland.   The rule provided for the holding of opening exercises in the schools of the city, consisting primarily of the "reading,
without comment, of a chapter in the Holy Bible and/or the use of
the Lord's Prayer."   The petitioners, Mrs. Madalyn Murray and her
son, William J. Murray III, are both professed atheists.   Following
unsuccessful attempts to have the respondent school board rescind
the rule, this suit was filed for mandamus to compel its rescission and
cancellation.   It was alleged that William was a student in a public
school of the city and Mrs. Murray, his mother, was a taxpayer
therein; that it was the practice under the rule to have a reading on
each school morning from the King James version of the Bible; that
at petitioners' insistence the rule was amended [4] to permit children to
be excused from the exercise on request of the parent and that William had been excused pursuant thereto; that nevertheless the rule
as amended was in violation of the petitioners' rights "to freedom of
religion under the First and Fourteenth Amendments" and in violation of "the principle of separation between church and state, contained therein. * * * "

* * *

Applying the Establishment Clause principles to the cases at
bar we find that the States are requiring the selection and reading
at the opening of the school day of verses from the Holy Bible
and the recitation of the Lord's Prayer by the students in unison.
These exercises are prescribed as part of the curricular activities of
students who are required by law to attend school.   They are held in
the school buildings under the supervision and with the participation
of teachers employed in those schools.   None of these factors, other
than compulsory school attendance, was present in the program up-

---

4.   The rule as amended provides as follows:

"Opening Exercises.   Each school,
either collectively or in classes, shall
be opened by the reading, without
comment, of a chapter in the Holy
Bible and/or the use of the Lord's
Prayer.   The Douay version may be
used by those pupils who prefer it.

Appropriate patriotic exercises should
be held as a part of the general opening exercise of the school or class.
Any child shall be excused from participating in the opening exercises or
from attending the opening exercises
upon the written request of his parent or guardian."

held in Zorach v. Clauson. The trial court in No. 142 has found that such an opening exercise is a religious ceremony and was intended by the State to be so. We agree with the trial court's finding as to the religious character of the exercises. Given that finding, the exercises and the law requiring them are in violation of the Establishment Clause.

There is no such specific finding as to the religious character of the exercises in No. 119, and the State contends (as does the State in No. 142) that the program is an effort to extend its benefits to all public school children without regard to their religious belief. Included within its secular purposes, it says, are the promotion of moral values, the contradiction to the materialistic trends of our times, the perpetuation of our institutions and the teaching of literature. The case came up on demurrer, of course, to a petition which alleged that the uniform practice under the rule had been to read from the King James version of the Bible and that the exercise was sectarian. The short answer, therefore, is that the religious character of the exercise was admitted by the State. But even if its purpose is not strictly religious, it is sought to be accomplished through readings, without comment, from the Bible. Surely the place of the Bible as an instrument of religion cannot be gainsaid, and the State's recognition of the pervading religious character of the ceremony is evident from the rule's specific permission of the alternative use of the Catholic Douay version as well as the recent amendment permitting nonattendance at the exercises. None of these factors is consistent with the contention that the Bible is here used either as an instrument for nonreligious moral inspiration or as a reference for the teaching of secular subjects.

The conclusion follows that in both cases the laws require religious exercises and such exercises are being conducted in direct violation of the rights of the appellees and petitioners. Nor are these required exercises mitigated by the fact that individual students may absent themselves upon parental request, for that fact furnishes no defense to a claim of unconstitutionality under the Establishment Clause. * * * Further, it is no defense to urge that the religious practices here may be relatively minor encroachments on the First Amendment. The breach of neutrality that is today a trickling stream may all too soon become a raging torrent and, in the words of Madison, "it is proper to take alarm at the first experiment on our liberties." Memorial and Remonstrance Against Religious Assessments. * * *

It is insisted that unless these religious exercises are permitted a "religion of secularism" is established in the schools. We agree of course that the State may not establish a "religion of secularism" in the sense of affirmatively opposing or showing hostility to religion, thus "preferring those who believe in no religion over those who do believe." Zorach v. Clauson, supra, 343 U.S., at 314, 72 S.Ct., at 684, 96 L.Ed. 954. We do not agree, however, that this decision in any sense has that effect. In addition, it might well be said that one's education is not complete without a study of comparative religion or the history of religion and its relationship to the advancement of civilization. It certainly may be said that the Bible is worthy of study for its literary and historic qualities. Nothing we have said here indicates that such study of the Bible or of religion, when presented objectively as part of a secular program of education, may not be effected consistently with the First Amendment. But the exercises here do not fall into those categories. They are religious exercises, required by the States in violation of the command of the First Amendment that the Government maintain strict neutrality, neither aiding nor opposing religion.

Finally, we cannot accept that the concept of neutrality, which does not permit a State to require a religious exercise even with the consent of the majority of those affected, collides with the majority's right to free exercise of religion. While the Free Exercise Clause clearly prohibits the use of state action to deny the rights of free exercise to *anyone*, it has never meant that a majority could use the machinery of the State to practice its beliefs. Such a contention was effectively answered by Mr. Justice Jackson for the Court in West Virginia Board of Education v. Barnette, 319 U.S. 624, 638, 63 S.Ct. 1178, 1185, 87 L.Ed. 1628 (1943):

> "The very purpose of a Bill of Rights was to withdraw certain subjects from the vicissitudes of political controversy, to place them beyond the reach of majorities and officials and to establish them as legal principles to be applied by the courts. One's right to * * * freedom of worship * * * and other fundamental rights may not be submitted to vote; they depend on the outcome of no elections."

The place of religion in our society is an exalted one, achieved through a long tradition of reliance on the home, the church and the inviolable citadel of the individual heart and mind. We have come to recognize through bitter experience that it is not within the power of government to invade that citadel, whether its purpose or effect be to aid or oppose, to advance or retard. In the relationship between man and religion, the State is firmly committed to a position of neutrality. Though the application of that rule requires interpretation of a delicate sort, the rule itself is clearly and concisely stated in the words of the First Amendment. Applying that rule to the facts of these cases, we affirm the judgment in No. 142. In No. 119, the judgment is reversed and the cause remanded to the Maryland Court of Appeals for further proceedings consistent with this opinion.

It is so ordered.

Judgment in No. 142 affirmed; judgment in No. 119 reversed and cause remanded with directions.

NOTES

1. Many decisions were rendered by state courts before the *Engel* and *Schempp* cases which found that morning religious activities did not violate constitutional or statutory provisions. Some of these were: Hackett v. Brooksville Graded School Dist., 120 Ky. 608, 87 S.W. 792 (1905); Donahoe v. Richards, 38 Me. 379, 61 Am.Dec. 256 (1854); Moore v. Monroe, 64 Iowa 367, 20 N.W. 475 (1884); Billard v. Board of Educ. of City of Topeka, 69 Kan. 53, 76 P. 422 (1904); Knowlton v. Baumhover, 182 Iowa 691, 166 N.W. 202 (1918); McCormick v. Burt, 95 Ill. 263 (1880).

Other state courts listed below found religious exercises offended their constitutions: State ex rel. Weiss v. District Bd., 76 Wis. 177, 44 N.W. 967 (1890); State ex rel. Freeman v. Scheve, 65 Neb. 853, 91 N.W. 846 (1902); People ex rel. Ring v. Board of Educ. of Dist. 24, 245 Ill. 334, 92 N.E. 251 (1910); Herold v. Parish Bd. of School Directors, 136 La. 1034, 68 So. 116 (1915); State ex rel. Finger v. Weedman, 55 S.D. 343, 226 N.W. 348 (1929).

2. How does the court distinguish the "Establishment" clause from the "Free Exercise" clause?

3. Does prohibition against state laws which require or permit religious services in public schools indicate an hostility to religion? What does the court say?

4. A statute requiring a period of silence for prayer or meditation at the opening of each school day does not violate the Free Exercise Clause. Lack of mandatory direction indicated to the court that the state intended to maintain neutrality. Gaines v. Anderson, 421 F.Supp. 337 (D.Mass. 1976).

5. A school district was held to be acting in aid of religion in violation of the First Amendment where; (1) student council members read the Lord's Prayer and read verses from the Bible over the school's public address system each day, (2) The Gideon society was regularly invited to distribute religious books and give talks, (3) certain teachers required their classes to memorize prayers and conducted Bible-reading sessions during class, and (4) various ministers were invited to address classes during which time students were questioned about their religious beliefs. Plaintiffs, however, failed to meet the burden of proving that another part of the exercises, the conduct of Baccalaureate services on school grounds prior to graduation, was also unconstitutional. The court relied on both *Schempp* and *McCollum* in rendering the decision. Goodwin v. Cross County School Dist., 394 F.Supp. 417 (E.D.Ark.1973).

6. *Religious Garb in Public Schools.* Whether public school teachers can wear religious garb of any particular religious order or society has been litigated on several occasions. While there is no precise definition of what constitutes religious garments, some states have sought prohibition of any apparel which showed that the person belonged to a particular sect, denomination, or order. (See: Donald E. Boles, *The Two Swords,* Iowa State University Press, 1967, p. 222.)

In 1894, the Supreme Court of Pennsylvania held that the wearing by nuns of garb and insignia of the Sisterhood of St. Joseph while teaching in the public schools did not constitute sectarian teaching. Hysong v. Gallitzin Borough School Dist., 164 Pa. 629, 30 A. 482 (1894). The court reasoned that to deny wearing of such apparel would violate the teachers' religious liberty. Later, the Legislature of Pennsylvania prohibited the wearing of garb by public school teachers while in performance of their duties. This statute was subsequently upheld by the Pennsylvania Supreme Court. This time the Court maintained that the Act was a reasonable exercise of state power in regulating the educational system to prevent sectarian control. The court found that the legislation "is directed against acts, not beliefs, and only against acts of the teacher while engaged in the performance of his or her duties as such teacher." Commonwealth v. Herr, 229 Pa. 132, 78 A. 68 (1910).

Litigation over the years in other states has been split on the issue. A New York Court in 1906 held that "the influence of such apparel is distinctly sectarian." O'Connor v. Hendrick, 184 N.Y. 421, 77 N.E. 612 (1906). Similarly, the Nebraska Supreme Court refused to mandate that the State Superintendent distribute state school trust funds to a school because of the school's religious nature. The school rested on church property, was adorned with religious emblems, and the teachers wore distinctive garb, including the rosary, indicative of the Catholic sisterhood. State ex rel. Public School Dist. No. 6 v. Taylor, 122 Neb. 454, 240 N.W. 573 (1932); see also: Zellers v. Huff, 55 N.M. 501, 236 P.2d 949 (1951).

On the other hand, the wearing of religious garb has been upheld by at least three state supreme courts. In a North Dakota case, the court held that there was no evidence that nuns imparted religious instruction even though they were dressed in religious garb of the Sisterhood of St. Benedict. Gerhardt v. Heid, 66 N.D. 444, 267 N.W. 127 (1936); see also: City of New Haven v. Town of Torrington, 132 Conn. 194, 43 A.2d 455 (1945) and Rawlings v. Butler, 290 S.W.2d 801 (Ky.1956.)

Lack of concensus by the courts is due to their legitimate hesitancy to invade either the religious rights of teachers or students. The issue boils down to one of a weighing of interests in view of the particular facts of the case. As the Connecticut Supreme Court has said:

> The decisions in these cases, however, are, as is to be expected, based upon a wide diversity of facts. The only definite conclusion that may be drawn from them is that whether sectarian influence connected with a school is such as to affect its public character is ordinarily a question of fact for the trial court. City of New Haven v. Town of Torrington, 132 Conn. 194, 43 A.2d 455 (1945).

Flag Salute

The flag-salute ceremony in the United States originated in 1892 after a substantial rise in national sentiment to stimulate patriotism in the schools. In 1898, New York passed the first flag-salute statute only one day after the United States declared war on Spain.[49] By

49. Donald E. Bowles, *The Two Swords*, The Iowa State University Press, Ames, Iowa, 1967, p. 139.

1940, eighteen states had statutes making provision for "some sort of teaching regarding the flag." [50]   Even though the statutes did not specifically require individual recitation, the reality of the classroom regimentation tended to make such statutory pronouncement unnecessary.[51]   Opposition sprang up on sporadic bases from certain religious groups, the most persistent of which was from Jehovah's Witnesses.   In early litigation the Georgia Supreme Court held that the Witnesses' religious freedom was not violated since the flag salute was merely an exercise in patriotism and not a religious rite.[52]   Other rulings were unfavorable to the plaintiffs, the most intolerant of which stated that "Those who do not desire to conform with the demands of the statute can seek their school elsewhere." [53]   In California, that state's high court upheld the expulsion of pupils for refusing to salute the flag.[54]   Similarly, a New York court in 1939, held that "The flag has nothing to do with religion"; therefore, religious freedoms could not be offended.[55]

Nationalistic fervor just before World War II brought on more heated controversy, and the Supreme Court, in 1940, rendered a decision.   In this case Justice Frankfurter, speaking for an eight-to-one majority, held that <u>freedom of religion guaranteed by the First Amendment was not violated by a Pennsylvania statute which required a flag salute and pledge of allegiance</u>.   Significantly, the opinion concluded that:

> Conscientious scruples have not, in the course of the long struggle for religious toleration, relieved the individual from obedience to a general law not aimed at the promotion or restriction of religious beliefs.   The mere possession of religious convictions which contradict the relevant concerns of a political society does not relieve the citizen from the discharge of political responsibilities.[56]

This decision engendered substantial controversy, and the legal and academic community generally disapproved of the decision as an infringement on individual constitutional rights.[57]   Some state courts tended to ignore the federal constitutional implications and held that flag-salute requirements violated their own state constitutions.[58]

50.   D. R. Manwaring, *Render Unto Caesar: The Flag-Salute Controversy,* University of Chicago Press, Chicago, 1962.

51.   Ibid.

52.   Leoles v. Landers, 184 Ga. 580, 192 S.E. 218 (1937), appeal dismissed 302 U.S. 656, 58 S.Ct. 364 (1937).

53.   Hering v. State Bd. of Educ., 117 N.J.L. 455, 189 A. 629 (1937).

54.   Gabrielli v. Knickerbocker, 12 Cal. 2d 85, 82 P.2d 391 (1938).

55.   People ex rel. Fish v. Sandstrom, 279 N.Y. 523, 18 N.E.2d 840 (1839).

56.   Minersville School Dist. v. Gobitis, 310 U.S. 586, 60 S.Ct. 1010 (1940).

57.   Boles, *op. cit.* p. 148.

58.   State v. Smith, 155 Kan. 588, 127 P.2d 518 (1942); Bolling v. Superior

Other state courts followed the decision.[59] Disenchantment with the *Gobitis* decision was so great and the constitutional foundation so weak that the case was officially overruled in West Virginia State Bd. of Educ. v. Barnette in 1943.[60] In reconsideration of the issues, Justice Jackson, writing for a six-man majority, held that a state may require pupils to attend educational exercises based on American history and civics to teach patriotism, but, ceremonies involving compulsory rituals, such as flag salute, were unconstitutional. Justices Black, Douglas, and Murphy had changed their minds, and even though Frankfurter remained steadfast, the precedent of *Gobitis* was overturned. The swing vote of the three justices was predictable by the announcement a year earlier, in 1942, in Jones v. Opelika [61] that: "Since we joined in the opinion in the Gobitis Case, we think this is an appropriate occasion to state that we now believe that it was * * * wrongly decided."

Required Participation in Flag Salute Is Unconstitutional

WEST VIRGINIA STATE BD. OF EDUC. v. BARNETTE

Supreme Court of the United States, 1943.
319 U.S. 624, 63 S.Ct. 1178.

Mr. Justice JACKSON delivered the opinion of the Court.

Following the decision by this Court on June 3, 1940, in Minersville School District v. Gobitis, 310 U.S. 586, 60 S.Ct. 1010, 84 L.Ed. 1375, 127 A.L.R. 1493, the West Virginia legislature amended its statutes to require all schools therein to conduct courses of instruction in history, civics, and in the Constitutions of the United States and of the State "for the purpose of teaching, fostering and perpetuating the ideals, principles and spirit of Americanism, and increasing the knowledge of the organization and machinery of the government." Appellant Board of Education was directed, with advice of the State Superintendent of Schools, to "prescribe the courses of study covering these subjects" for public schools. The Act made it the duty of private, parochial and denominational schools to prescribe courses of study "similar to those required for the public schools."

The Board of Education on January 9, 1942, adopted a resolution containing recitals taken largely from the Court's Gobitis opinion and ordering that the salute to the flag become "a regular part of the program of activities in the public schools," that all teachers and pupils "shall be required to participate in the salute honoring the Na-

Court, 16 Wash.2d 373, 133 P.2d 803 (1943).

59. Matter of Latrecchia, 128 N.J.L. 472, 26 A.2d 881 (1942); State v. Davis, 58 Ariz. 444, 120 P.2d 808 (1942).

60. 319 U.S. 624, 63 S.Ct. 1178 (1943).

61. 316 U.S. 584, 62 S.Ct. 1231 (1942); see: Bates, *op. cit.* pp. 151–152.

tion represented by the Flag; provided, however, that refusal to salute the Flag be regarded as an Act of insubordination, and shall be
dealt with accordingly."

* * *

Appellees, citizens of the United States and of West Virginia,
brought suit in the United States District Court for themselves and
others similarly situated asking its injunction to restrain enforcement
of these laws and regulations against Jehovah's Witnesses. The Witnesses are an unincorporated body teaching that the obligation imposed by law of God is superior to that of laws enacted by temporal
government. Their religious beliefs include a literal version of Exodus,
Chapter 20, verses 4 and 5, which says: "Thou shalt not make unto
thee any graven image, or any likeness of anything that is in heaven
above, or that is in the earth beneath, or that is in the water under the
earth; thou shalt not bow down thyself to them nor serve them."
They consider that the flag is an "image" within this command. For
this reason they refuse to salute it.

* * *

This case calls upon us to reconsider a precedent decision, as the
Court throughout its history often has been required to do. Before
turning to the Gobitis case, however, it is desirable to notice certain
characteristics by which this controversy is distinguished.

The freedom asserted by these appellees does not bring them into
collision with rights asserted by any other individual. It is such conflicts which most frequently require intervention of the State to determine where the rights of one end and those of another begin. But
the refusal of these persons to participate in the ceremony does not
interfere with or deny rights of others to do so. Nor is there any
question in this case that their behavior is peaceable and orderly.
The sole conflict is between authority and rights of the individual.
The State asserts power to condition access to public education on
making a prescribed sign and profession and at the same time to
coerce attendance by punishing both parent and child. The latter
stand on a right of self-determination in matters that touch individual opinion and personal attitude.

* * *

Nor does the issue as we see it turn on one's possession of particular religious views or the sincerity with which they are held. While
religion supplies appellees' motive for enduring the discomforts of
making the issue in this case, many citizens who do not share these
religious views hold such a compulsory rite to infringe constitutional
liberty of the individual. It is not necessary to inquire whether non-
conformist beliefs will exempt from the duty to salute unless we first
find power to make the salute a legal duty.

The Gobitis decision, however, *assumed*, as did the argument in
that case and in this, that power exists in the State to impose the

flag salute discipline upon school children in general. The Court only examined and rejected a claim based on religious beliefs of immunity from an unquestioned general rule. The question which underlies the flag salute controversy is whether such a ceremony so touching matters of opinion and political attitude may be imposed upon the individual by official authority under powers committed to any political organization under our Constitution.   *   *   *

*   *   *

The Fourteenth Amendment, as now applied to the States, protects the citizen against the State itself and all of its creatures— Boards of Education not excepted. These have, of course, important, delicate, and highly discretionary functions, but none that they may not perform within the limits of the Bill of Rights. That they are educating the young for citizenship is reason for scrupulous protection of Constitutional freedoms of the individual, if we are not to strangle the free mind at its source and teach youth to discount important principles of our government as mere platitudes.

*   *   *

The very purpose of a Bill of Rights was to withdraw certain subjects from the vicissitudes of political controversy, to place them beyond the reach of majorities and officials and to establish them as legal principles to be applied by the courts. One's right to life, liberty, and property, to free speech, a free press, freedom of worship and assembly, and other fundamental rights may not be submitted to vote; they depend on the outcome of no elections.

*   *   *

National unity as an end which officials may foster by persuasion and example is not in question. The problem is whether under our Constitution compulsion as here employed is a permissible means for its achievement.

*   *   *

If there is any fixed star in our constitutional constellation, it is that no official, high or petty, can prescribe what shall be orthodox in politics, nationalism, religion, or other matters of opinion or force citizens to confess by word or act their faith therein. If there are any circumstances which permit an exception, they do not now occur to us.

We think the action of the local authorities in compelling the flag salute and pledge transcends constitutional limitations on their power and invades the sphere of intellect and spirit which it is the purpose of the First Amendment to our Constitution to reserve from all official control.

The decision of this Court in Minersville School District v. Gobitis and the holdings of those few per curiam decisions which preceded and foreshadowed it are overruled, and the judgment enjoining enforcement of the West Virginia Regulation is affirmed.

*   *   *

NOTES

Where a student was offered the option of either leaving the classroom or standing silently during the Pledge of Allegiance, the court held that to leave the classroom is a benign type of punishment for nonparticipation, while to compel the student to stand in silence was to compel an act of acceptance to the Pledge over the student's deeply held contrary convictions. The requirement of the school was therefore unconstitutional regardless of option. Goetz v. Ansell, 477 F.2d 636 (2nd Cir. 1973).

Chapter 7

COMPULSORY EDUCATION AND CURRICULUM

Introduction

The abiding faith that education is the key to enhancement of the culture, governmental stability and social equality is manifested in the state's interest in public instruction of the masses. Madison's admonition that "a popular government without popular information or means of acquiring it is but a prologue to a farce or a tragedy, or, perhaps, both," has been highly regarded among all the states. Mass, general education in the United States has been brought to fruition by state requirements that; first, children must attend a school, and second, a minimal prescribed educational program can be mandated by the state in conveying the kind of instructional program which the state deems necessary. This chapter deals with the legal ramifications of both these, compulsory education and publicly prescribed instructional programs.

Legal authority for the state to provide for compulsory public instruction is found in the common law doctrine of *parens patriae* which maintains, essentially, that as father to all persons, the state has the inherent prerogative to provide for the common wealth and individual welfare. As such, it can through the exercise of the police power of the legislature establish reasonable laws, not repugnant to the constitution, as it may judge for the good of the state. As guardian over everyone the state has the authority to protect those who are not legally competent to act in their own behalf, *non sui juris.** This protection was quite naturally interpreted to apply to minor children who because of their age were unable to take care of themselves. Unavoidably, the state's interest in the child was to collide with parental interest and this, today, still forms the framework on which most compulsory education and curriculum controversies are litigated. It is though well established, going back into English law, that the state's or the King's prerogative are superior to that of the parent when the parent's natural right is improperly exercised. Authority for the power of the state was clearly stated in English precedent and *parens patriae* was adopted throughout the United States "to the end that the health, patriotism, morality, efficiency, industry, and integrity of its citizenship may be preserved and protected, looking to the preservation and stability of the state." [1] In this country the desirability of the doctrine as a rudiment of governmental responsibility was well expressed in an 1882 Illinois case, wherein the court said:

---

* Means literally "not his own master."   1. Strangway v. Allen, 194 Ky. 681, 240 S.W. 384 (1922).

It is the unquestioned right and imperative duty of every enlightened government, in its character of *parens patriae*, to protect and provide for the comfort and well-being of such of its citizens as by reason of infancy * * * were unable to take care of themselves. The performance of these duties is justly regarded as one of the most important of governmental functions, and all constitutional limitations must be so understood and construed as not to interfere with its proper and legitimate exercise.[2]

A child has a right to be protected not only from patent abuses of his parents but also against the ignorance of his parents. The state has recognized more truth than fiction in the adage, "There are no delinquent children, only delinquent parents." In support of this view, juvenile courts and welfare agencies of the state have traditionally intervened between parent and child in cases of parental abuse. Public education may thus serve as a mechanism to free the child from the shackles of unfit parents.

To protect the child from the parent requires affirmative state action. A child has no constitutional protection from the parent; such protection must come in the form of statutory action by the state to protect the child, examples of which are compulsory attendance laws and requirements that children be exposed to certain kinds of educational curricula. On the other hand, the state's action must be supported by a compelling or, at least, a rational state interest before either the child's or the parent's rights can be restricted or infringed upon.

In the United States today a dual set of precedents have emerged. One tends to limit *parens patriae*, as is evidenced by court-imposed limitations on state handling of juvenile cases.[3] More recently this was illustrated by the exception from state compulsory attendance laws in *Yoder*[4]. The second precedent is a tendency of the courts to allow the state to protect the infant from parental abuse. This was reflected by the United States Supreme Court in Ford v. Ford[5] in 1962:

Unfortunately, experience has shown that the question of custody, so vital to a child's happiness and well-being, frequently cannot be left to the discretion of the parents. This is particularly true where, as here, the estrangement of husband and wife beclouds parental judgment with emotion and prejudices.

2. County of McLean v. Humphrey, 104 Ill. 378 (1882).

3. In re Gault, 387 U.S. 1, 87 S.Ct. 1428 (1967).

4. Wisconsin v. Yoder, 406 U.S. 205, 92 S.Ct. 1526 (1972).

5. Ford v. Ford, 371 U.S. 187, 83 S.Ct. 273 (1962).

The language of the Supreme Court in Pierce v. Society of Sisters [6] indicated that only limited tolerance would be given the state in interfering with the parent's control of the child:

> In this day and under our civilization, the child of man is his parent's child and not the state's. * * * It is not seriously debatable that the parental right to guide one's child intellectually and religiously is a most substantial part of the liberty and freedom of the parent.

This does not mean that parental rights fully preempt those of the state. On the contrary, it would appear that a parent may forfeit his right to control his child by either omission or commission. In such case, the parent has no immunity from state intervention.

Nearly twenty years after *Pierce*, in 1943, the Supreme Court more clearly defined its position toward state intervention in Prince v. Massachusetts. [7] Here, a legal guardian was found guilty of contributing to the delinquence of a minor by permitting her nine-year-old ward to sell Jehovah's Witnesses publications on a public street. The act was found to be in violation of Massachusetts' child labor laws. The Supreme Court addressed the conflicting claims of parent and state saying:

> [T]he family itself is not beyond regulation in the public interest * * * acting to guard the general interest in youth's well being, the state as *parens patriae* may restrict the parent's control by requiring school attendance, regulating or prohibiting the child's labor and in many other ways.

More recently in *Yoder*, the court said that the power of the parent, even when linked to free exercise of religion, may be subject to limitation if it appears that parental decisions will jeopardize the health or safety of the children or have "potential for significant social burdens."

A common thread running through these precedents is a renewed judicial concern for the child himself, with the parental interest and the state interest secondary. However, the general welfare is always a concern of the state and the maxim *salus populi suprema lex esto*, let the welfare of the people be the supreme law, is always sufficient justification for the exercise of the *parens patriae* doctrine.

This chapter is concerned with two aspects of this legal issue, compulsory attendance and the state's authority to govern the educational curriculum.

6. 268 U.S. 510, 45 S.Ct. 571 (1925).

7. Prince v. Massachusetts, 321 U.S. at 166, 64 S.Ct. at 442 (1943).

Compulsory Attendance *

Few would dispute the state's legal competence in requiring children be exposed to a certain amount of education.[8] Although compulsory attendance restrains a child's liberty, these laws have had uniform acceptance by the courts.

State intervention to compel education includes distinguishable premises: the state may provide education for all who cannot appropriately educate themselves, protect infants from those who would deny them education, and compel all citizens to act in ways most beneficial to the child and society.[9] Reflecting state concern in these areas, compulsory attendance laws both require education and provide enforcement to protect the child from undesirable parental conduct.[10]

Cases involving challenges to compulsory attendance laws generally emanate from disputes between parents and officials. This may be due, in part, to the old notion that "the basic right of a juvenile is not to liberty but to custody.[11]" It may also result directly from enforcement provisions in compulsory attendance laws that penalize the parent, rather than the child.

Confrontation between state and parent instead of between state and child is probably the result of two subtle theories suggested by Kleinfeld.[12] One is that parents have a duty to a child to educate him, and the state may compel fulfillment of this duty. The other is that parents have a duty to the state to educate their children, which the state may compel them to perform.

Whether the judgment of the parent should prevail over the collective judgment of the state in educational matters is a much broader question, however, than may be evidenced by simple challenges to compulsory attendance laws. In a dispute between parent and state regarding an educational matter, parents may be pictured as intelligent, well-meaning, and motivated for the betterment of the child. This is not always the case. The invocation of the doctrine of *parens patriae* in matters of education may result from broken homes where parents will not assist or support the child in obtaining an education. Where children have sought financial assistance from parents toward a common school education, the courts have uniformly

* This discussion is taken from Kern Alexander and K. Forbis Jordan, *Legal Aspects of Educational Choice: Compulsory Attendance and Student Assignment*, NOLPE Monograph Series, No. 4, 1973.

8. Jackson v. Hankinson, 51 N.J. 230, 238 A.2d 685 (1968).

9. Andrew Jay Kleinfeld, "The Balance of Power Among Infants, Their Parents and the State", ABA Family Law Quarterly 5 (1971), p. 107.

10. Salem Community School Corp. v. Easterly, 150 Ind.App. 11, 275 N.E.2d 317 (Ind.1971).

11. Id. p. 92.

12. Id. p. 93.

termed such education as "necessary" and granted the support. Common school education is a "necessary," just as food, lodging, clothing, and medicine are.[13]

In the courts' view, education has traditionally been of such importance that even items assisting school attendance have been considered necessary for child support purposes. For example, one early Texas court held that a buggy may be a "necessary" if it is needed to convey a child to and from school.[14] In some states, the courts have given alimony decrees that consider education over and beyond the normal public school education as a "necessary."[15]

Exercise of *parens patriae* by the state may result in more severe action than that of requiring a child to attend school or mandating that a parent furnish resources for attendance in school or college. The child-parent relationship can be partly or totally severed by judicial enforcement of divorce, neglect,[16] or child abuse statutes.[17] Most states have such statutes. The concept of *parens patriae* extends to compulsory medical care over the objection of parents. Some states have explicit statutory language declaring a parent neglectful if he fails to provide medical care for his child. Under a finding of neglect, the court is empowered to provide the necessary medical care.[18] Courts have made children the wards of the state and required medical care, acting in *parens patriae,* in the absence of statute and under common law.[19]

It should be noted that the invocation of *parens patriae* by the states does not restrict parental authority in all cases. In some instances, such action may even strengthen it. In cases where parents are unable to control their own children, the child's action produces not only disharmony within the family but sometimes becomes a nuisance to the public generally. For such situations, some states have enacted "stubborn child laws [20]" that protect the public from children who are "runaways, night walkers, common railers and brawlers."

13. Morris v. Morris, 92 Ind.App. 65, 171 N.E. 386 (1930); Sisson v. Schultz, 251 Mich. 553, 232 N.W. 253 (1930).

14. Heffington v. Jackson and Norton, 43 Tex.Civ.App. 560, 96 S.W. 108 (1906).

15. Luques v. Luques, 127 Me. 356, 143 A. 263 (1928).

16. Hiram D. Gordon, "Terminal Placements of Children and Permanent Termination of Parental Rights: The New York Permanent Neglect Statute," *St. Johns Law Review* 46 (1971): 215.

17. Harvey J. Eger and Anthony J. Popeck, "The Abused Child: Problems and Proposals," *Duquesne Law Review* 8 (1969–70): 136.

18. State v. Perricone, 37 N.J. 463, 181 A.2d 751 (1962); People v. Pierson, 176 N.Y. 201, 68 N.E. 243 (1903).

19. Morrison v. State, 252 S.W.2d 97 (Mo.App.1952).

20. Massachusetts Gen.Laws Ann., ch. 272, § 53 (1958).

In upholding the power of the state to enact and enforce a stubborn child law, the Massachusetts Supreme Judicial Court has said:

> While the state defers to the parents with respect to most decisions on family matters, it has an interest in insuring the existence of harmonious relations between family members, and between the family unit and the rest of public society.   To protect this interest, the State may properly require that unemancipated children obey the reasonable and lawful commands of their parents, and it may impose criminal penalties on the children if they persistently disobey such commands.   The State is not powerless to prevent or control situations which threaten the proper functioning of a family unit as an important segment of the total society.[21]

Exceptions to Compulsory Attendance

When compulsory attendance laws are mentioned, one usually thinks of children being compelled to attend only public schools. However, many alternatives and exceptions exist.   A child may have the prerogative of home instruction or attendance at private, profit, nonprofit, sectarian, or secular schools.   A child may also be exempt from required attendance because of religion, marriage, physical or mental incapacity, distance of travel, and so on.   Courts have established many precedents that even today are in a state of transition.

Instruction in Private Schools

Few cases have defined "private school" as used in compulsory attendance laws.[22]   Precise definition is lacking perhaps partly because in several jurisdictions children are not required to attend either public or private schools but must obtain "equivalent instruction."[23]   Although vaguely defining the term "equivalent" as meaning "equal," the court generally refers to the qualifications of the instructor and the available teaching materials as the primary criteria for determining equivalency of instruction.

To be "recognized" a private school must provide instruction equivalent to the free instruction furnished in public schools.   To have equivalent instruction, it is also necessary for the private school to comply with the statutory period of attendance.[24]

A correspondence school was not within the contemplated definition of private school even where parents served as tutors for their children.   In this particular California case, the court ruled that the parents did not have state teaching credentials.   The parents admit-

---

21. Commonwealth v. Brasher, 359 Mass. 550, 270 N.E.2d 389 (1971).

22. See Alexander v. Bartlett, 14 Mich. App. 177, 165 N.W.2d 445 (1968).

23. 14 A.L.R.2d 1369; Knox v. O'Brien, 7 N.J.Super. 608, 72 A.2d 389 (1950).

24. State v. Garber, 197 Kan. 567, 419 P.2d 896 (1966).

ted that they had not provided the children with instruction in civics and California history, as required by law.[25]

Although the state can require instruction equivalent to that of a public school, it cannot deny the parent the right to send his child to a private school.[26] Instead, the private school itself, as a corporation, claimed denial of due process of law because an Oregon compulsory attendance statute required all children ages eight to sixteen to attend public schools. The appellees in the case were the Society of Sisters and Hill Military Academy, both private, profit-making corporations. The schools claimed that enforcement of the compulsory attendance law would deprive them of students, destroy the profitable features of their businesses, and diminish the value of their property.

No question was raised challenging the power of the state to reasonably regulate, inspect, supervise, and examine all schools, teachers, and pupils and to see that nothing was taught that was inimical to the public welfare. Apparently, the law was originally enacted to combat Bolshevism, syndicalism, and communism. Supporters of the law sought to place all education more directly under the control of the state to prevent the teaching of certain economic doctrines.

In ruling in the plaintiffs' favor, in *Pierce,* the United States Supreme Court decided the case on the grounds that the state cannot, through improper regulation, deprive a business corporation of its patrons or customers. The law deprived the corporations of a liberty protected by the Fourteenth Amendment, according to the Court.

In a statement that must be considered *dictum,* since neither parents or children were appellants, the Court remarked on the rights of both parent and child:

> The fundamental theory of liberty upon which all governments in this union repose excludes any general power of the state to standardize its children by forcing them to accept instruction from public teachers only. The child is not the mere creature of the state; those who nurture him and direct his destiny have the right, coupled with the high duty, to recognize and prepare him for additional obligations.[27]

Instruction at Home

Courts are not in agreement on whether home instruction constitutes instruction in a private school. Key elements in determining the validity of home instruction are the educational level of the parents and the regularity and time of instruction.

25. In re Shinn, 195 Cal.App.2d 683, 16 Cal.Rptr. 165 (1961).

26. Pierce v. Society of Sisters of the Holy Names of Jesus and Mary, 268 U.S. 510, 45 S.Ct. 571 (1925).

27. Supra, note 26.

An early Washington case rejected the home as a private school. In the case, the parent claimed his home instruction was authorized by a statute providing that children must attend "the public school of the district in which the child resides, for the full time such school may be in session, or . . . attend a private school for the same time." The parent further claimed that he was a qualified and competent teacher giving home instruction within the definition to the statute. This claim was rejected by the court.

The court explained:

> We do not think that the giving of instruction by a parent to a child, conceding the competency of the parent to fully instruct the child in all that is taught in the public schools, is within the meaning of the law "to attend a private school." Such a requirement means more than home instruction; it means that the same character of school as the public school, a regular, organized and existing institution making a business of instructing children of school age in the required studies and for the full time required by the laws of this state. * * * There may be a difference in institution and government, but the purpose and end of both public and private schools must be the same—the education of children of school age. The parent who teaches his children at home, whatever be his reason for desiring to do so, does not maintain such a school.[28]

Home instruction has been rejected because of difficulty of supervision. The state bears the responsibility of reasonable supervision to guarantee that students obtain an adequate education. If home instruction imposes an unreasonable burden on the state's performance of its duties, the instruction is not allowed. For example, a situation may exist where parents use education units so small or facilities of such doubtful quality that supervision creates an unusual expense for the state. The state requires that proper educational facilities be provided for the child and supplied in a way that the state can ascertain facts about the instructional program and maintain proper direction without undue cost.[29]

Critics have charged that home instruction does not comply with statutory requirements that a child attend a public, private, denominational, or parochial school and be taught by a competent instructor. In Kansas, the legislature reenacted a compulsory attendance law, leaving out a former provision for home instruction as a valid exemption from compulsory attendance. A court said that exclusion of home instruction, while including private, denominational, and paro-

---

28. State v. Counort, 69 Wash. 361, 124 P. 910 (1912).

29. State v. Hoyt, 84 N.H. 38, 146 A. 170 (1929).

chial instruction as valid, indicated legislative intent to disallow home instruction as an excuse of nonattendance.[30]

Another Kansas case distinguished between a "private school" and "scheduled home instruction." Here parents operated a "school," serving as tutors themselves, with only their own children in attendance. The only grades taught were those in which their own children were enrolled. The court interpreted this as falling short of the definition of a private school, and ruled that the instruction given did not meet statutory requirements. In the view of the court, the program was nothing more than "home instruction." [31]

Where reference to home instruction was excluded from the statute, a California court refused to officially regard home instruction programs as qualified "private schools." [32]

Other cases, however, have established that home instruction may constitute "private school" instruction in contemplation of the law. For example, a parent who employs a competent, noncertified school teacher to instruct his child in the same curriculum and for the same period of time as the public schools is complying with the law, which requires instruction in a public, private, or parochial school.[33] The court said,

> The law was made for the parent who does not educate his child, and not for the parent who employs a teacher and pays him out of his private purse, and so places within the reach of the child the opportunity and means of acquiring an education equal to that obtainable in the public schools of the State.

In a similar case, an Illinois court held that parental instruction in the home was within the meaning of a statute requiring that all children must attend a public, private, or parochial school where children are taught branches of education corresponding to that offered in the public schools. The court ruled that the mother, who had received training in education, was giving her child commensurate instruction including regular hours of study and recitation.[34] This court maintained that the number of children taking instruction was irrelevant. Further, the court said, the burden of proof was on the parent to show that (1) instruction was being provided in good faith, and (2) the prescribed courses of training were being met.

A New York state court approved a home instruction program in which the children were found to be reading above grade level when

30. State v. Well, 99 Kan. 167, 160 P. 1025 (1916).

31. State v. Lowry, 191 Kan. 701, 383 P. 2d 962 (1963).

32. People v. Turner, 121 Cal.App.2d 861, 263 P.2d 685 (1953).

33. State v. Peterman, 32 Ind.App. 665, 70 N.E. 550 (1904).

34. People v. Levisen, 404 Ill. 574, 90 N.E.2d 213 (1950).

tested by the court. Testimony indicated that the children had formal lessons with their mother during the day and then did "homework" at night. In addition, the attendance officer testified, a surprise visit to the home found the children pursuing a discernible course of study.[35]

The parent is obliged to introduce evidence showing that home instruction is, in fact, being conducted. In a situation where a child was being taught regular public grade school subjects by the mother, the court still held that such instruction fell short of private school status. Grounds for this decision were the mother's failure to report the child's attendance in a private school and the fact that she had made no attempt to qualify the home as a private school.[36]

On the other hand, the state's case will not prevail if it merely assumes that the child is receiving no home instruction. Beyond this, the state must produce evidence documenting the parents' failure to furnish adequate home instruction.[37] The parent is, therefore, required to show evidence of home instruction. However, the final burden of proof is on the state to show that the home instruction is not equivalent education as required by law.[38]

Other cases have upheld the right of a parent to educate his child through private instruction,[39] but these cases were not decided directly on the private school issue. In Commonwealth v. Bey a Pennsylvania statute made provision for instruction by properly qualified private tutors. In another case, In Re Richards, the court's decision was based on the extenuating circumstance that the distance from schools and the lonely roads made home instruction necessary.

Aside from the importance of the statute's wording, one can probably conclude that the courts will measure home instruction against the standards of equivalency to public school instruction. In Knox v. O'Brien,[40] the court set out three tests to determine equivalent education. The first test was consideration of the qualifications of the parent or instructor. Although not all compulsory attendance cases are decided on this point, the qualifications of the teacher are generally the foremost consideration. The second standard established by *O'Brien* concerned the teaching material, and the third was whether the children received the full advantages supplied by the public schools.

35. In re Foster, 69 Misc.2d 400, 330 N.Y.S.2d 8 (1972).

36. State ex rel. Shoreline School Dist. v. Superior Court, 55 Wash.2d 177, 346 P.2d 999 (1959).

37. Sheppard v. State, 306 P.2d 346 (Okl.Cr.1957).

38. State v. Massa, 95 N.J.Super. 382, 231 A.2d 252 (1967).

39. Commonwealth v. Bey, 166 Pa.Super. 136, 70 A.2d 693 (1950); Connell v. Board of School Directors of Kennett Township, 356 Pa. 585, 52 A.2d 645 (1947); In re Richards, 255 App. Div. 922, 7 N.Y.S.2d 722 (1938); Wright v. State, 21 Okl.Crim. 430, 209 p. 179 (1922); Bevan v. Shears, 2 K.B. 936, Ann.Cas. 1912 A. 370 (1911).

40. 7 N.J. 608, 7 A.2d 389 (1950).

This last standard is the most difficult to accommodate, because it concerns association with other children. If children are educated alone at home, with no opportunity to interact with other children, one of the primary purposes of the public schools is foiled and equivalency is not provided. This represents a substantial departure from the view of earlier courts,[41] which generally held that the purpose of compulsory attendance was education generally and not education in any particular way.[42]

If the courts adopt this general philosophy with regard to home instruction, the number of children will become important to the question of equivalency. Further, an extension of this doctrine could mean that true education is not accomplished unless a reasonable cross-section of society, or at least a random sample, is present to ensure the "commonness" of the common schools.

The court's view can best be summarized by noting that private school or home instruction must provide the child with an educational experience that is not restricted to the presence of teachers, materials, and facilities but that offers a minimum public school education.[43]

Exemption from Compulsory Attendance

While private schools and home instruction provide alternatives to attendance in public schools, the child nevertheless is compelled to attend some school. Another kind of litigation that has arisen over the years has sought exemption from attending any school at all. The claims for exemption have generally been based on religious grounds, reasons of mental or physical unfitness, and marriage.

Religion

Following Pierce v. Society of Sisters,[44] it was rather uniformly assumed that children could be compelled to attend a public, private, or parochial school, but that no child had a right *not* to attend school at all.

Early cases established that the child's and the parents' rights of religious freedom, as protected by the First Amendment of the United States Constitution, were not sufficient to diminish the state's power to compel compulsory attendance. Justice Cardozo, in a concurring opinion in Hamilton v. Regents [45] (a case dealing with the rights of a conscientious objector), maintained that undesirable re-

---

41. Commonwealth v. Roberts, 159 Mass. 372, 34 N.E. 402 (1893).

42. See also Stephens v. Bongart, 15 N.J.Misc. 80, 189 A. 131 (1937).

43. Sheppard, supra note 37, at 344.

44. Pierce, supra note 26.

45. Hamilton v. Regents, 293 U.S. 245, 55 S.Ct. 197 (1934).

sults may evolve where religious scruples predominate over reasonable state laws. In delivering the opinion Cardozo said:

> Manifestly a different doctrine would carry us to lengths that have never yet been dreamed of. The conscientious objector, if his liberties were to be thus extended, might refuse to contribute taxes in furtherance of any other end condemned by his conscience as irreligious or immoral. The right of private judgment has never yet been so exalted above the powers and the compulsion of the agencies of government. One who is a martyr to a principle—which may turn out in the end to be a delusion or an error—does not prove by his martyrdom that he has kept within the law.

Following this rationale, other courts have concluded that the individual cannot be permitted, on religious grounds, to be the judge of his duty to obey reasonable civil requirements enacted in the interest of public welfare.

In a 1945 Virginia case,[46] the parents of three families sought to prevent enforcement of compulsory attendance laws on religious grounds. These parents interpreted the Bible as commanding parents to teach and train their own children. They believed that sending their children to public schools was incompatible with the primary religious obligation they felt they owed their Maker. Their willful intent to violate the law was solely because of sincere religious convictions.

The court, in deciding against the parents, declared:

> No amount of religious fervor he [parent] may entertain in opposition to adequate instruction should be allowed to work a lifelong injury to his child. Nor should he, for this religious reason, be suffered to inflict another illiterate citizen on his community or his state.

According to the court, religious grounds did not permit the individual to be the judge of his duty to obey reasonable laws. Although the religious issue was the *ratio decidendi* in the case, the court ruled that the parents were not capable of adequately educating the children themselves.

Religious grounds have been ruled insufficient to limit the number of days a child attends school. A Moslem parent claimed that his religion prevented him from sending his children to school on Fridays.[47] Regardless of the validity of his religious motives, the court said the state allowed parental choice among public, private,

---

46. Rice v. Commonwealth, 49 S.E.2d 342, 3 A.L.R.2d 1392 (1948).

47. Commonwealth v. Bey, 57 York Leg.Rec. (Pa.) 200, 92 Pitts.Leg.J. 84 (1944).

and parochial schools. The parent and child did not, however, have the option of nonattendance on Fridays.[48]

Until recently, the prevailing view of the courts was that religious beliefs cannot impair achievement of the state's objective—universal compulsory education. The precedent-setting case that has radically altered this view is Wisconsin v. Yoder.[49] This case contested the power of the state to require the school attendance of Amish children after the eighth grade. Although the issue in this case is limited to the compulsory attendance of Amish children between the time they complete the eighth grade and the time they reach sixteen years of age, it nevertheless has profound implications for all future cases involving compulsory attendance.

The decision of the Court in this case can be summarized in three points. First, although the state has power to impose reasonable regulation, this power must be balanced against fundamental rights and interests of individuals. Second, beliefs that are philosophical rather than personal are not sufficient to invoke free exercise of religion. Third, where parents show that enforcement of compulsory education will endanger their religious beliefs, the *parens patriae* power of the state must give way to the free exercise clause of the First Amendment.

Two dramatic limitations on the general applicability of *Yoder* are the objection of the Amish only to post-eighth-grade compulsory attendance of fourteen-and-fifteen-year-olds and the well-established Amish customs of living near the soil and shunning modern society generally. These features of the case tend to diminish the compelling interest of the state: they eliminate the possibility of illiteracy by providing at least eight years of schooling and negate the chance of these children becoming unproductive members of society.

The ultimate question of who will determine the child's destiny is not answered by the case. The court is content, instead, to speak rather vaguely of balancing the fundamental religious freedom of the parents against the interest of the state.

Marriage

Exemption from compulsory attendance is a dubious benefit of marriage. Courts have uniformly agreed that when a minor of less than sixteen years (otherwise required to attend school) is married, he or she is exempt from further compulsory attendance.

One of the precedents in this area was derived by the Supreme Court of Louisiana. A fifteen-year-old girl and her husband sought to set aside a judgment of a lower court committing her to the State

---

48. See also In re Currence, 42 Misc.2d 418, 248 N.Y.S.2d 251 (1963). Here religious observance was no defense for withdrawing a boy from school weekly on Wednesday afternoons and Thursday mornings.

49. Yoder, supra note 4.

Industrial School for Girls as a result of her truancy and alleged juvenile delinquency.[50] The girl did not deny truancy but claimed that her legal marriage exempted her from attendance. Although the marriage of a female under sixteen years of age was prohibited by law, the court ruled that once a girl is married, she enjoys the status of wife and has a right to live as such, emancipated from both school and parents. The court stated:

> The marriage relationship, regardless of the age of the persons involved, creates conditions and imposes obligations upon the parties that are obviously inconsistent with compulsory school attendance or with either the husband or wife remaining under the legal control of parents or other persons.

In another Louisiana case, a girl was truant and, in the lower court's opinion, a neglected child.[51] The girl, fourteen years of age, was married only a few days after the truant officer had taken her into custody. The lower court judge ignored the previous case (*Priest*) and committed the girl for an indefinite period to a state girls' school. The judge, exercising *parens patriae*, was of the opinion that the girl needed the care and protection of the state. The Supreme Court of Louisiana, while sympathetically viewing the judge's concern for the girl's welfare, held that the lower juvenile court could not commit her to the girls' school or prevent her from assuming the responsibilities of a married woman. The court stated that the power of such public policy determinations rested with the legislature and not the court.

A New York court followed the rationale of these two cases. The girl had not been committed to a state school or been determined to be a delinquent, but she had resisted attempts to force her to attend school because she was married and wanted to be a housewife and homemaker.[52] The court, while recognizing the state's sovereignty concerning compulsory attendance, decided for the girl, observing that times and mores had changed since the compulsory attendance law was passed. The court also expressed doubt that the legislature had anticipated the question of such youthful marriage in passing the law.

In the eyes of the law, then, youthful marriage is another valid exemption from compulsory attendance laws. This determination, in the absence of specific statutory exemption, is predicated on the assumption that the responsibility of the minor, once married, is to be a productive member of society and that this is better achieved by es-

---

50. State v. Priest, 210 La. 389, 27 So. 2d 173 (1946).

51. In re State, 214 La. 1062, 39 So.2d 731 (1949).

52. In re Rogers, 36 Misc.2d 680, 234 N.Y.S.2d 179 (1962).

tablishing and supporting a home. The net effect of this reasoning is to remove both state and parental control over the alternatives available to the minor. Consequently, he has the choice and the right to decide on his own further education.

Vaccination

To protect the health and welfare of citizens, states have required school children to be vaccinated. Children going unvaccinated are not allowed to attend school. Courts have generally held that, if a parent violates a statute requiring vaccination, the parent is subject to arrest or fine, even if he claims religious, conscientious, or scientific objections.

In 1905 the United States Supreme Court held that a board of health requirement that all persons in Cambridge, Massachusetts, be vaccinated did not violate personal liberties secured under the Fourteenth Amendment.[53] In this case, the Court noted that "the liberty secured by the Constitution of the United States to every person within its jurisdiction does not impart an absolute right in each person to be, at all times and in all circumstances, wholly freed from restraint. There are manifold restraints to which every person is necessarily subject for the common good."

Although this particular decision directly challenged the vaccination regulation rather than compulsory attendance, the Supreme Court [54] nevertheless cited several state court decisions approving state statutes and making vaccination of children a condition of the right to attend public schools.[55]

In Viemeister v. White,[56] a turn-of-the-century New York decision, the appellant argued that vaccination not only did not prevent smallpox but tended instead to bring on other harmful diseases. The court, while not ruling that vaccination was a smallpox preventative, nevertheless maintained that laymen and physicians alike commonly believed that it did prevent smallpox. Acknowledging the difference between universal and common belief, the court observed that few beliefs are accepted by everyone. The court then concluded that, even if it could not be conclusively proved that the vaccination was a preventative, in our Republican form of government the legislature has the right to pass laws based on common belief and the will of the people to promote health and welfare.

53. Jacobson v. Commonwealth of Massachusetts, 197 U.S. 11, 25 S.Ct. 358 (1905).

54. Id. p. 364.

55. Blue v. Beach, 155 Ind. 121, 56 N.E. 89 (1900); Morris v. Columbus, 102 Ga. 792, 30 S.E. 850 (1898); State v. Hay, 126 N.C. 999, 35 S.E. 459; Abeel v. Clark, 84 Cal. 226, 24 P. 383 (1890); Bissell v. Davidson, 65 Conn. 183, 32 A. 348 (1894); Hazen v. Strong, 2 Vt. 427 (1830); Duffield v. Williamsport School District, 162 Pa. 476, 29 A. 742 (1894).

56. Viemeister v. White, 179 N.Y. 235, 72 N.E. 97 (1904).

Is a parent guilty of violating the compulsory attendance law, then, if he sends his child to school without vaccination and the child is sent home by school authorities? Answering this question in the affirmative, a New York court said that attendance at a public school imposes certain conditions on a child. These requirements must be met in order for him to attend. However, the 1915 decision went on to say that under the public health law, vaccination was only required for children attending public schools. The parent could offer private equivalent education to the child and avoid vaccination. Here, however, the parent had not provided equivalent education and was, therefore, subject to penalty under the compulsory attendance law.[57]

In an earlier New York case, little tolerance was illustrated for parents who used vaccination as an excuse to prevent their children's attendance in public schools.

> It is obvious that a parent should not be allowed to escape his duty to send his children to school as provided by law on any excuse which is not an ample justification for such course. Our public school system has been developed with great pains and solicitude, and its maintenance and support have been recognized as so important for the welfare of the state that they have been provided for and safeguarded in the Constitution itself. As a part of this system a statute has been passed requiring attendance at school of children within certain limits. If indifferent or selfish parents, for ulterior purposes, such as the desire to place young children at labor, instead of school, or from capricious or recalcitrant motives, may be allowed to manufacture easy excuses for not sending their children to school, a ready method will have been developed for evading the statute compelling such attendance, and, if the statute which requires parents to see to it that their children attend and take advantage of this school system may be lightly and easily evaded, the purposes of the state in providing and insisting on education will be frustrated and impaired. Failure to comply with the statute ought not to be excused, except for some good reason.[58]

The earlier cases concerning school vaccinations were not generally related to First Amendment religious protections. In fact, the Supreme Court did not clarify the application of the "no state" provision of the Fourteenth Amendment until 1940, in Cantwell v. Connecticut.[59] The precedent of religious exemption from compulsory attendance, established in *Yoder*,[60] has bold implications for cases

57. People v. McIlwain, 151 N.Y.S. 366 (1915).

58. People v. Ekerold, 211 N.Y. 386, 105 N.E. 670 (1914).

59. Cantwell v. Connecticut, 310 U.S. 296, 60 S.Ct. 900, 128 ALR 1352 (1940).

60. Yoder, supra note 4.

involving religious freedom from vaccination. In the past and present, however, the courts have ruled that a statute requiring vaccination does not violate the free exercise of religion.

Parents in State v. Drew refused to have their child vaccinated, giving reasons as "partly religious and partly because they did not want that poison injected into their child." The Supreme Court of New Hampshire upheld the parents' conviction for violating the compulsory attendance law and said:

> The defendant's individual ideas, whether "conscientious," "religious," or "scientific" do not appear to be more than opinions. * * * The defendant's views cannot affect the validity of the statute or entitle him to be excepted from its provisions. * * * It is for the Legislature, not for him or for us to determine the question of policy involved in public health regulations.[61]

Another factor that has often emerged in vaccination cases is the extenuating circumstance of an epidemic. Where epidemic is imminent, there is no question concerning the state's power to protect the citizenry by requiring vaccination. However, where there is no evidence of the imminence of an epidemic, how do the courts view the issue? The question revolves around the further question of what is a reasonable state regulation? Can the state's requirement of vaccination be a reasonable and permissible restraint on constitutional rights in the absence of epidemic?

In *Maas* [62] the defendant argued that compulsory vaccination and immunization were not needed in Mountain Lakes because there had been no smallpox or diphtheria for almost a decade. The court disagreed and ruled that the absence of an emergency does not warrant a denial of the exercise of preventive means. The court said, "A local board of education need not await an epidemic, or even a single sickness or death, before it decides to protect the public. To hold otherwise would be to destroy prevention as a means of combating the spread of disease."

Likewise, in Stull v. Reber,[63] the fact there had been no smallpox in the borough for forty years did not prevent enforcement of the compulsory vaccination regulation. Health authorities were not required to wait until an epidemic existed before acting to prevent one, the court said.[64] Neither would the fact that an epidemic had already

61. State v. Drew, 89 N.H. 54, 192 A. 629 (1937).

62. Board of Education of Mountain Lakes v. Maas, 56 N.J.Super. 245, 152 A.2d 394 (1959).

63. Stull v. Reber, 215 Pa. 156, 64 A. 419 (1906).

64. Hill v. Bickers, 171 Ky. 703, 188 S. W. 766 (1916).

started and it was too late to prevent the closing of school have been a reason to prevent compulsory vaccination.[65]

If the state board of health enacts a compulsory vaccination regulation made pursuant to statute, general statutory requirements requiring all pupils to comply with law are sufficient grounds for the board of education to enforce the statute.[66]

All these cases contested duly promulgated board rules that were enacted pursuant to state statutes. However, where no statute exists to empower school or health boards to pass compulsory vaccination regulations, the issues shift quite drastically. First, a board cannot enact regulations unless they are based on existing statutes. Where the board acts regardless of statute, the act is *ultra vires* (in excess of legal authority). Second, a board rule restricting school attendance cannot prevail over a legislative act granting free unlimited admittance to public schools.

Accordingly, two Illinois courts have decided that in the absence of a compulsory vaccination statute, an unvaccinated child cannot be denied a public education.[67] In both of these old cases, however, it appeared the school boards made little effort to draw enabling implications from health or education statutes.

In summary, one can reasonably make several conclusions regaring compulsory attendance and vaccination: (1) The legislature has power to enact a statute providing for vaccination and including a penalty for noncompliance. (2) Neither the parent nor the child has a constitutional right to schooling without complying with the statutory requirement of vaccination. (3) A parent cannot escape conviction for failing to have his child vaccinated by demanding the child be admitted to school unvaccinated. (4) Religious objection has not generally prevented enforcement of compulsory vaccination and attendance requirements.

---

65. Board of Trustees v. McMurtry, 169 Ky. 457, 184 S.W. 390 (1916).

66. Mosier v. Barren County Board of Health, 308 Ky. 829, 215 S.W.2d 967 (1948).

67. Potts v. Breen, 167 Ill. 67, 47 N.E. 81 (1897); People ex rel. LaBaugh v. Board of Education of District No. 2, 52 N.E. 850 (1899).

*Compulsory Education Law Requiring All Children to Attend
Public Schools Violates Due Process Clause*

PIERCE v. SOCIETY OF THE SISTERS OF THE HOLY NAMES OF JESUS AND MARY

Supreme Court of the United States, 1925.
268 U.S. 510, 45 S.Ct. 571.

Mr. Justice McREYNOLDS delivered the opinion of the Court.

These appeals are from decrees, based upon undenied allegations, which granted preliminary orders restraining appellants from threatening or attempting to enforce the Compulsory Education Act adopted November 7, 1922 (Laws Or.1923, p. 9), under the initiative provision of her Constitution by the voters of Oregon. Judicial Code, § 266 (Comp.St. § 1243). * * *

The challenged act, effective September 1, 1926, requires every parent, guardian, or other person having control or charge or custody of a child between 8 and 16 years to send him "to a public school for the period of time a public school shall be held during the current year" in the district where the child resides; and failure so to do is declared a misdemeanor. There are exemptions—not specially important here—for children who are not normal, or who have completed the eighth grade, or whose parents or private teachers reside at considerable distances from any public school, or who hold special permits from the county superintendent. The manifest purpose is to compel general attendance at public schools by normal children, between 8 and 16, who have not completed the eighth grade. And without doubt enforcement of the statute would seriously impair, perhaps destroy, the profitable features of appellees' business and greatly diminish the value of their property.

Appellee the Society of Sisters is an Oregon corporation, organized in 1880, with power to care for orphans, educate and instruct the youth, establish and maintain academies or schools, and acquire necessary real and personal property. It has long devoted its property and effort to the secular and religious education and care of children, and has acquired the valuable good will of many parents and guardians. * * * It owns valuable buildings, especially constructed and equipped for school purposes. The business is remunerative—the annual income from primary schools exceeds $30,000—and the successful conduct of this requires long time contracts with teachers and parents. The Compulsory Education Act of 1922 has already caused the withdrawal from its schools of children who would otherwise continue, and their income has steadily declined. The appellants, public officers, have proclaimed their purpose strictly to enforce the statute.

After setting out the above facts, the Society's bill alleges that the enactment conflicts with the right of parents to choose schools where their children will receive appropriate mental and religious training, the right of the child to influence the parents' choice of a school, the right of schools and teachers therein to engage in a useful business or profession, and is accordingly repugnant to the Constitution and void. And, further, that unless enforcement of the measure is enjoined the corporation's business and property will suffer irreparable injury.

Appellee Hill Military Academy is a private corporation organized in 1908 under the laws of Oregon, engaged in owning, operating, and conducting for profit an elementary, college preparatory, and military training school for boys between the ages of 5 and 21 years. * * * It owns considerable real and personal property, some useful only for school purposes. The business and incident good will are very valuable. * * *

The Academy's bill states the foregoing facts and then alleges that the challenged act contravenes the corporation's rights guaranteed by the Fourteenth Amendment and that unless appellants are restrained from proclaiming its validity and threatening to enforce it irreparable injury will result. The prayer is for an appropriate injunction.

* * * The court ruled that the Fourteenth Amendment guaranteed appellees against the deprivation of their property without due process of law consequent upon the unlawful interference by appellants with the free choice of patrons, present and prospective. It declared the right to conduct schools was property and that parents and guardians, as a part of their liberty, might direct the education of children by selecting reputable teachers and places. * * *

No question is raised concerning the power of the state reasonably to regulate all schools, to inspect, supervise and examine them, their teachers and pupils; to require that all children of proper age attend some school, that teachers shall be of good moral character and patriotic disposition, that certain studies plainly essential to good citizenship must be taught, and that nothing be taught which is manifestly inimical to the public welfare.

The inevitable practical result of enforcing the act under consideration would be destruction of appellees' primary schools, and perhaps all other private primary schools for normal children within the state of Oregon. Appellees are engaged in a kind of undertaking not inherently harmful, but long regarded as useful and meritorious. Certainly there is nothing in the present records to indicate that they have failed to discharge their obligations to patrons, students or the state. And there are no peculiar circumstances or present emergencies which demand extraordinary measures relative to primary education.

Under the doctrine of Meyer v. Nebraska, we think it entirely plain that the Act of 1922 unreasonably interferes with the liberty of parents and guardians to direct the upbringing and education of children under their control. As often heretofore pointed out, rights guaranteed by the Constitution may not be abridged by legislation which has no reasonable relation to some purpose within the competency of the state. The fundamental theory of liberty upon which all governments in this Union repose excludes any general power of the state to standardize its children by forcing them to accept instruction from public teachers only. The child is not the mere creature of the state; those who nurture him and direct his destiny have the right, coupled with the high duty, to recognize and prepare him for additional obligations.

Appellees are corporations, and therefore, it is said, they cannot claim for themselves the liberty which the Fourteenth Amendment guarantees. Accepted in the proper sense, this is true. * * * But they have business and property for which they claim protection. These are threatened with destruction through the unwarranted compulsion which appellants are exercising over present and prospective patrons of their schools. And this court has gone very far to protect against loss threatened by such action. * * *

* * *

Generally, it is entirely true, as urged by counsel, that no person in any business has such an interest in possible customers as to enable him to restrain exercise of proper power of the state upon the ground that he will be deprived of patronage. But the injunctions here sought are not against the exercise of any proper power. Appellees asked protection against arbitrary, unreasonable, and unlawful interference with their patrons and the consequent destruction of their business and property. Their interest is clear and immediate, * * *.

* * *

The decrees below are affirmed.

NOTE

Where it was shown that a handicapped child was receiving an adequate education at home from two certified teachers who made regular visits, the court held that the attendance law was satisfied. Cleary v. Lash, 92 Misc.2d 642, 401 N.Y.S.2d 124 (1977).

Parents Have No Constitutional Right to Deprive
Their Children of an Education

COMMONWEALTH v. BEY

Superior Court of Pennsylvania, 1950.
166 Pa.Super. 136, 70 A.2d 693.

RENO, Judge. Appellants, husband and wife, were convicted in a summary proceeding before an alderman and on appeal in the court below of violating the compulsory attendance provisions of the School Code.

The offense was committed on January 19, 1949, and the applicable statute is the Act of May 18, 1911, P.L. 309, § 1414, as last amended by the Act of June 24, 1939, P.L. 786, § 2, 24 P.S. § 1421. It requires "every parent * * * of any child or children of compulsory school age [between the ages of eight and seventeen years] * * * to send such child or children to a *day school* * * *; and such child or children shall attend such school *continuously* through the entire term * * * Provided, That the certificate of any principal or teacher of a *private school,* or of any *institution for the education of children* * * * setting forth that the work of said school is in compliance with the provisions of this act, shall be sufficient and satisfactory evidence thereof: * * * Regular daily instruction * * * by a properly qualified *private tutor,* shall be considered as complying with the provisions of this section, if such instruction is satisfactory to the proper county or district superintendent of schools." (Emphasis added.) Provision is made for the allowance of other exceptions which are not material to this case.

It will be observed that the requirement of compulsory attendance can be satisfied in a "day school" which may be a public school, "a private school," or an "institution for the education of children". The last two classifications include parochial or denominational schools. Daily instruction by an approved private tutor will also satisfy the statute.

The provision that children shall attend "continuously through the entire term" recognizes the obvious fact that each day's school work is built upon the lessons taught on the preceding day. It is virtually impossible properly to educate a child who is absent one day a week. Friday's instruction is the foundation for understanding Monday's lesson. By such regularly recurring absences the child loses not only one-fifth of the instruction, but the continuity of the course of study is broken and the pupil is not able to keep pace with his classmates. The requirement is reasonable and enforceable.

Appellants are Mohammedans, and they have persistently refused to send their children of compulsory attendance age to school on Fridays, the sacred day of that religion. They have sent them to the public schools on all other days except Friday. They invoke the guarantees of religious freedom contained in the State and Federal constitutions. Appellants were convicted for the same offense in 1943 and 1944.

At common law the most important duty resting upon parents was to give their children "an education suitable to their station in life." Having stated the duty, Blackstone lamented: "Yet the municipal laws of most countries seem to be defective in this point, by not constraining the parent to bestow a proper education upon his children."

Nevertheless, he discerned that the right of the parent to give or withhold an education was not absolute or unlimited. In the apprenticing laws of his day he discovered power in the state to subject at least some children to educative processes. " * * * [T]he poor and laborious part of the community, when past the age of nurture, are taken out of the hands of their parents, by the statutes for apprenticing poor children, and are placed out by the public in such a manner, as may render their abilities, in their several stations, of the greatest advantage to the commonwealth." 1 Commentaries 451. See also 47 Am.Jur., Schools, §§ 6, 156.

In Pennsylvania the power of state to require that children be educated has never been doubted. Even aside from the constitutional provisions establishing the common school system the appellate courts, though recognizing the natural right of control by parents, held that the right may be restricted and regulated by law. In an early case, 1839, the Supreme Court, in a per curiam opinion, said: "It is to be remembered that the public has a paramount interest in the virtue and knowledge of its members, and that of strict right, *the business of education belong to it. * * * The right of parental control is a natural, but not an unalienable one.* It is not excepted by the declaration of rights out of the subjects of ordinary legislation; and it consequently remains subject to the ordinary legislative power which, if wantonly or inconveniently used, would soon be constitutionally restricted, but the competency of which, as the government is constituted, cannot be doubted." (Emphasis added.) Ex parte Crouse, 4 Whart. 9, 11. In short, parents have no constitutional right to deprive their children of the blessings of education or prevent the state from assuring children adequate preparation for the independent and intelligent exercise of their privileges and obligations as citizens in a free democracy.

*   *   *

Speaking for this Court, Judge Orlady said in Com. v. Gillen, 65 Pa.Super. 31, 36: "it must be conceded by all right thinking persons, that the enforcement of the compulsory school code is a matter of paramount importance, to which the views of the individual view must yield, and this must be so, whether such view is based on a prejudice against a legislative requirement, or even a conscientious difference of opinion as to a health regulation." More recently the Supreme Court of the United States has held: "But the family itself is not beyond regulation in the public interest, as against a claim of religious liberty. * * * And neither rights of religion nor rights of parenthood are beyond limitation. Acting to guard the general interest in youth's well being, *the state as parens patriae may restrict the parent's control by requiring school attendance,* regulating or prohibiting the child's labor, and in many other ways. *Its authority is not nullified merely because the parent grounds his claim to control the* *child's course of conduct on religion or conscience."* Prince v. Massachusetts, 321 U.S. 158, 166, 64 S.Ct. 438, 442, 88 L.Ed. 645. (Emphasis added.)

Thus, in this realm the right of the state is superior to that of the parents. It is subject to only one limitation. Parents cannot be compelled to send their children to public schools exclusively and debar them from attending parochial or private schools. While it recognized "the power of the state * * * to require that all children of proper age attend some school", nevertheless the United States Supreme Court held in Pierce v. Society of the Sisters of the Holy Names, 268 U.S. 510, 534, 535, 45 S.Ct. 571, 573, 69 L.Ed. 1070, 39 A.L.R. 468: "The fundamental theory of liberty upon which all governments in this Union repose excludes any general power of the state to standardize its children by forcing them to accept instruction from public teachers only." See also Meyer v. Nebraska, 262 U.S. 390, 43 S.Ct. 625, 67 L.Ed. 1042, 29 A.L.R. 1446. Our statute is completely free of objection upon that score. It permits attendance at private and parochial schools. All that it requires is continuous attendance at a day-school of the kind and character mentioned in the statute, or daily instruction by a private tutor. Since the parent may avail himself of other schools, including parochial or denominational schools, the statute does not interfere with or impinge upon the religious freedom of parents or the guarantees of either the Federal or State constitution. The requirement is within the constitutional power of the state.

Having exercised the option provided by the statute and elected to send their children to the public schools, appellants are bound to perform all the requirements of the compulsory attendance provisions. They cannot send their children to the public schools upon condition that they shall be excused on Fridays. They have no constitutional right to submit to only a part of the statute or to a part of regulations made pursuant to it.

Judgment and sentence affirmed.

State Cannot Compel Amish Children to Attend Public High School

STATE OF WISCONSIN v. YODER

Supreme Court of the United States, 1972.
406 U.S. 205, 92 S.Ct. 1526.

* * *

Respondents Jonas Yoder and Wallace Miller are members of the Old Order Amish religion, and respondent Adin Yutzy is a member of the Conservative Amish Mennonite Church. They and their families are residents of Green County, Wisconsin. Wisconsin's compulsory school-attendance law required them to cause their children to attend public or private school until reaching age 16 but the respondents declined to send their children, ages 14 and 15, to public school after they complete the eighth grade. The children were not enrolled in any private school, or within any recognized exception to the compulsory-attendance law, and they are conceded to be subject to the Wisconsin statute.

On complaint of the school district administrator for the public schools, respondents were charged, tried, and convicted of violating the compulsory-attendance law in Green County Court and were fined the sum of $5 each. Respondents defended on the ground that the application of the compulsory-attendance law violated their rights under the First and Fourteenth Amendments. *   *   *

*   *   * The history of the Amish sect was given in some detail, beginning with the Swiss Anabaptists of the 16th century who rejected institutionalized churches and sought to return to the early, simple, Christian life de-emphasizing material success, rejecting the competitive spirit, and seeking to insulate themselves from the modern world. As a result of their common heritage, Old Order Amish communities today are characterized by a fundamental belief that salvation requires life in a church community separate and apart from the world and worldly influence. This concept of life aloof from the world and its values is central to their faith.

*   *   *

Formal high school education beyond the eighth grade is contrary to Amish beliefs, not only because it places Amish children in an environment hostile to Amish beliefs with increasing emphasis on competition in class work and sports and with pressure to conform to the styles, manners, and ways of the peer group, but also because it takes them away from their community, physically and emotionally, during the crucial and formative adolescent period of life. *   *   *

The Amish do not object to elementary education through the first eight grades as a general proposition because they agree that their children must have basic skills in the "three R's" in order to read the Bible, to be good farmers and citizens, and to be able to deal with non-Amish people when necessary in the course of daily affairs. They view such a basic education as acceptable because it does not significantly expose their children to worldly values or interfere with their development in the Amish community during the crucial adolescent period. While Amish accept compulsory elementary education generally, wherever possible they have established their own elementary schools in many respects like the small local schools of the past. In the Amish belief higher learning tends to develop values they reject as influences that alienate man from God.

*   *   *

I

There is no doubt as to the power of a State, having a high responsibility for education of its citizens, to impose reasonable regulations for the control and duration of basic education. See, e. g., Pierce v. Society of Sisters, 268 U.S. 510, 534, 45 S.Ct. 571, 573, 69 L.Ed. 1070 (1925). Providing public schools ranks at the very apex of the function of a State. Yet even this paramount responsibility was, in *Pierce*, made to yield to the right of parents to provide an equivalent education in a privately operated system. There the Court held that Oregon's statute compelling attendance in a public school from age eight to age 16 unreasonably interfered with the interest of parents in directing the rearing of their offspring, including their education in church-operated schools. As that case suggests, the values of parental direction of the religious upbringing and education of their children in their early and formative years have a high place in our society. * * * Thus, a State's interest in universal education, however highly we rank it, is not totally free from a balancing process when it impinges on fundamental rights and interests, such as those specifically protected by the Free Exercise Clause of the First Amendment, and the traditional interest of parents with respect to the religious upbringing of their children so long as they, in the words of *Pierce*, "prepare [them] for additional obligations." 268 U.S., at 535, 45 S.Ct., at 573.

It follows that in order for Wisconsin to compel school attendance beyond the eighth grade against a claim that such attendance interferes with the practice of a legitimate religious belief, it must appear either that the State does not deny the free exercise of religious belief by its requirement, or that there is a state interest of sufficient magnitude to override the interest claiming protection under the Free Exercise Clause. * * *

The essence of all that has been said and written on the subject is that only those interests of the highest order and those not otherwise served can overbalance legitimate claims to the free exercise of religion. We can accept it as settled, therefore, that, however strong the State's interest in universal compulsory education, it is by no means absolute to the exclusion or subordination of all other interests. * * *

II

We come then to the quality of the claims of the respondents concerning the alleged encroachment of Wisconsin's compulsory school-attendance statute on their rights and the rights of their children to the free exercise of the religious beliefs they and their forbears have adhered to for almost three centuries. In evaluating those claims we must be careful to determine whether the Amish religious faith and their mode of life are, as they claim, inseparable and interdependent. A way of life, however virtuous and admirable, may not be interposed as a barrier to reasonable state regulation of education if it is based on purely secular considerations; to have the protection of the Religion Clauses, the claims must be rooted in religious belief. Although a determination of what is a "religious" belief or practice entitled to constitutional protection may present a most delicate question,[6] the very concept of ordered liberty precludes allowing every person to make his own standards on matters of conduct in which society as a whole has important interests. Thus, if the Amish asserted their claims because of their subjective evaluation and rejection of the contemporary secular values accepted by the majority, much as Thoreau rejected the social values of his time and isolated himself at Walden Pond, their claims would not rest on a religious basis. Thoreau's choice was philosophical and personal rather than religious, and such belief does not rise to the demands of the Religion Clauses.

Giving no weight to such secular considerations, however, we see that the record in this case abundantly supports the claim that the traditional way of life of the Amish is not merely a matter of personal preference, but one of deep religious conviction, shared by an organized group, and intimately related to daily living. * * *

* * *

As the society around the Amish has become more populous, urban, industrialized, and complex, particularly in this century, government regulation of human affairs has correspondingly become more detailed and pervasive. The Amish mode of life has thus come into conflict increasingly with requirements of contemporary society exerting a hydraulic insistence on conformity to majoritarian standards. So long as compulsory education laws were confined to eight grades of elementary basic education imparted in a nearby rural schoolhouse, with a large proportion of students of the Amish faith, the Old Order Amish had little basis to fear that school attendance would expose their children to the worldly influence they reject. But modern compulsory secondary education in rural areas is now largely carried on in a consolidated school, often remote from the student's home and alien to his daily home life. As the record so strongly shows, the values and programs of the modern secondary school are in sharp conflict with the fundamental mode of life mandated by the Amish religion; modern laws requiring compulsory secondary education have accordingly engendered great concern and conflict. The conclusion is inescapable that secondary schooling, by exposing Amish children to worldly influences in terms of attitudes, goals, and values contrary to beliefs, and by substantially interfering with the religious development of the Amish child and his integration into the way of life of the Amish faith community at the crucial adolescent stage of development, contravenes the basic religious tenets and practice of the Amish faith, both as to the parent and the child.

---

6. See Welsh v. United States, 398 U.S. 333, 351–361, 90 S.Ct. 1792, 1802–1807, 26 L.Ed.2d 308 (1970) (Harlan, J., concurring in result); United States v. Ballard, 322 U.S. 78, 64 S.Ct. 882, 88 L.Ed. 1148 (1944).

The impact of the compulsory-attendance law on respondents' practice of the Amish religion is not only severe, but inescapable, for the Wisconsin law affirmatively compels them, under threat of criminal sanction, to perform acts undeniably at odds with fundamental tenets of their religious beliefs.   *   *   *

In sum, the unchallenged testimony of acknowledged experts in education and religious history, almost 300 years of consistent practice, and strong evidence of a sustained faith pervading and regulating respondents' entire mode of life support the claim that enforcement of the State's requirement of compulsory formal education after the eighth grade would gravely endanger if not destroy the free exercise of respondents' religious beliefs.

III

*   *   *

The State advances two primary arguments in support of its system of compulsory education. It notes, as Thomas Jefferson pointed out early in our history, that some degree of education is necessary to prepare citizens to participate effectively and intelligently in our open political system if we are to preserve freedom and independence. Further, education prepares individuals to be self-reliant and self-sufficient participants in society. We accept these propositions.

However, the evidence adduced by the Amish in this case is persuasively to the effect that an additional one or two years of formal high school for Amish children in place of their long-established program of informal vocational education would do little to serve those interests. Respondents' experts testified at trial, without challenge, that the value of all education must be assessed in terms of its capacity to prepare the child for life. It is one thing to say that compulsory education for a year or two beyond the eighth grade may be necessary when its goal is the preparation of the child for life in modern society as the majority live, but it is quite another if the goal of education be viewed as the preparation of the child for life in the separated agrarian community that is the keystone of the Amish faith.

*   *   *

The State attacks respondents' position as one fostering "ignorance" from which the child must be protected by the State. No one can question the State's duty to protect children from ignorance but this argument does not square with the facts disclosed in the record. Whatever their idiosyncrasies as seen by the majority, this record strongly shows that the Amish community has been a highly successful social unit within our society, even if apart from the conventional "mainstream." Its members are productive and very law-abiding members of society; they reject public welfare in any of its usual modern forms. The Congress itself recognized their self-sufficiency by authorizing exemption of such groups as the Amish from the obligation to pay social security taxes.

* * *

Insofar as the State's claim rests on the view that a brief additional period of formal education is imperative to enable the Amish to participate effectively and intelligently in our democratic process it must fall. The Amish alternative to formal secondary school education has enabled them to function effectively in their day-to-day life under self-imposed limitations on relations with the world, and to survive and prosper in contemporary society as a separate, sharply identifiable and highly self-sufficient community for more than 200 years in this country. In itself this is strong evidence that they are capable of fulfilling the social and political responsibilities of citizenship without compelled attendance beyond the eighth grade at the price of jeopardizing their free exercise of religious belief. When Thomas Jefferson emphasized the need for education as a bulwark of a free people against tyranny, there is nothing to indicate he had in mind compulsory education through any fixed age beyond a basic education. Indeed, the Amish communities singularly parallel and reflect many of the virtues of Jefferson's ideal of the "sturdy yeoman" who would form the basis of what he considered as the ideal of a democratic society. Even their idiosyncratic separateness exemplifies the diversity we profess to admire and encourage.

The requirement for compulsory education beyond the eighth grade is a relatively recent development in our history. Less than 60 years ago, the educational requirements of almost all of the States were satisfied by completion of the elementary grades, at least where the child was regularly and lawfully employed. The independence and successful social functioning of the Amish community for a period approaching almost three centuries and more than 200 years in this country are strong evidence that there is at best a speculative gain, in terms of meeting the duties of citizenship, from an additional one or two years of compulsory formal education. Against this background it would require a more particularized showing from the State on this point to justify the severe interference with religious freedom such additional compulsory attendance would entail.

* * *

* * * There is no intimation that the Amish employment of their children on family farms is in any way deleterious to their health or that Amish parents exploit children at tender years. Any such inference would be contrary to the record before us. Moreover, employment of Amish children on the family farm does not present the undesirable economic aspects of eliminating jobs that might otherwise be held by adults.

IV

Finally, the State, on authority of Prince v. Massachusetts, argues that a decision exempting Amish children from the State's requirement fails to recognize the substantive right of the Amish child to a secondary education, and fails to give due regard to the power of the State as *parens patriae* to extend the benefit of secondary education to children regardless of the wishes of their parents.   Taken at its broadest sweep, the Court's language in *Prince,* might be read to give support to the State's position.   However, the Court was not confronted in *Prince* with a situation comparable to that of the Amish as revealed in this record; this is shown by the Court's severe characterization of the evils that it thought the legislature could legitimately associate with child labor, even when performed in the company of an adult.   321 U.S., at 169–170, 64 S.Ct., at 443–444. The Court later took great care to confine *Prince* to a narrow scope in Sherbert v. Verner, when it stated:

> "On the other hand, the Court has rejected challenges under the Free Exercise Clause to governmental regulation of certain overt acts prompted by religious beliefs or principles, for 'even when the action is in accord with one's religious convictions, [it] is not totally free from legislative restrictions.'   Braunfeld v. Brown, 366 U.S. 599, 603, 81 S.Ct. 1144, 1146, 6 L.Ed.2d 563.   The conduct or actions so regulated have invariably posed some substantial threat to public safety, peace or order.   See, e. g., Reynolds v. United States, 98 U.S. 145, 25 L.Ed. 244; Jacobson v. Massachusetts, 197 U.S. 11, 25 S.Ct. 358, 49 L.Ed. 643; Prince v. Massachusetts, 321 U.S. 158, 64 S.Ct. 438, 88 L.Ed. 645.   *   *   *"   374 U.S., at 402–403, 83 S.Ct., at 1793.

This case, of course, is not one in which any harm to the physical or mental health of the child or to the public safety, peace, order, or welfare has been demonstrated or may be properly inferred.   The record is to the contrary, and any reliance on that theory would find no support in the evidence.

*   *   *

Our holding in no way determines the proper resolution of possible competing interests of parents, children, and the State in an appropriate state court proceeding in which the power of the State is asserted on the theory that Amish parents are preventing their minor children from attending high school despite their expressed desires to the contrary.   Recognition of the claim of the State in such a proceeding would, of course, call into question traditional concepts of parental control over the religious upbringing and education of their minor children recognized in this Court's past decisions.   It is clear that such an intrusion by a State into family decisions in the area of religious training would give rise to grave questions of religious freedom comparable to those raised here and those presented in Pierce v. Society of Sisters, 268 U.S. 510, 45 S.Ct. 571, 69 L.Ed. 1070 (1925). On this record we neither reach nor decide those issues.

The State's argument proceeds without reliance on any actual conflict between the wishes of parents and children. It appears to rest on the potential that exemption of Amish parents from the requirements of the compulsory-education law might allow some parents to act contrary to the best interests of their children by foreclosing their opportunity to make an intelligent choice between the Amish way of life and that of the outside world. The same argument could, of course, be made with respect to all church schools short of college. There is nothing in the record or in the ordinary course of human experience to suggest that non-Amish parents generally consult with children of ages 14–16 if they are placed in a church school of the parents' faith.

Indeed it seems clear that if the State is empowered, as *parens patriae*, to "save" a child from himself or his Amish parents by requiring an additional two years of compulsory formal high school education, the State will in large measure influence, if not determine, the religious future of the child. Even more markedly than in *Prince*, therefore, this case involves the fundamental interest of parents, as contrasted with that of the State, to guide the religious future and education of their children. The history and culture of Western civilization reflect a strong tradition of parental concern for the nurture and upbringing of their children. This primary role of the parents in the upbringing of their children is now established beyond debate as an enduring American tradition. * * *

* * *

* * * The record strongly indicates that accommodating the religious objections of the Amish by forgoing one, or at most two, additional years of compulsory education will not impair the physical or mental health of the child, or result in an inability to be self-supporting or to discharge the duties and responsibilities of citizenship, or in any other way materially detract from the welfare of society.

In the fact of our consistent emphasis on the central values underlying the Religion Clauses in our constitutional scheme of government, we cannot accept a *parens patriae* claim of such all-encompassing scope and with such sweeping potential for broad and unforeseeable application as that urged by the State.

V

For the reasons stated we hold, with the Supreme Court of Wisconsin, that the First and Fourteenth Amendments prevent the State from compelling respondents to cause their children to attend formal high school to age 16. Our disposition of this case, however, in no way alters our recognition of the obvious fact that courts are not school boards or legislatures, and are ill-equipped to determine the "necessity" of discrete aspects of a State's program of compulsory education. This should suggest that courts must move with great circumspection in performing the sensitive and delicate task of weighing a State's legitimate social concern when faced with religious claims for exemption from generally applicable educational requirements. It cannot be overemphasized that we are not dealing with a way of life and mode of education by a group claiming to have recently discovered some "progressive" or more enlightened process for rearing children for modern life.

Aided by a history of three centuries as an identifiable religious sect and a long history as a successful and self-sufficient segment of American society, the Amish in this case have convincingly demonstrated the sincerity of their religious beliefs, the interrelationship of belief with their mode of life, the vital role that belief and daily conduct play in the continued survival of Old Order Amish communities and their religious organization, and the hazards presented by the State's enforcement of a statute generally valid as to others. Beyond this, they have carried the even more difficult burden of demonstrating the adequacy of their alternative mode of continuing informal vocational education in terms of precisely those overall interests that the State advances in support of its program of compulsory high school education. In light of this convincing showing, one that probably few other religious groups or sects could make, and weighing the minimal difference between what the State would require and what the Amish already accept, it was incumbent on the State to show with more particularity how its admittedly strong interest in compulsory education would be adversely affected by granting an exemption to the Amish. * * *

Nothing we hold is intended to undermine the general applicability of the State's compulsory school-attendance statutes or to limit the power of the State to promulgate reasonable standards that, while not impairing the free exercise of religion, provide for continuing agricultural vocational education under parental and church guidance by the Old Order Amish or others similarly situated. The States have had a long history of amicable and effective relationships with church-sponsored schools, and there is no basis for assuming that, in this related context, reasonable standards cannot be established concerning the content of the continuing vocational education of Amish children under parental guidance, provided always that state regulations are not inconsistent with what we have said in this opinion.

Affirmed.

Failure of Public School to Teach Indian Culture Does
Not Negate Compulsory Education Statute

MATTER OF McMILLAN

Court of Appeals of North Carolina, 1976.
226 S.E.2d 693.

ARNOLD, Judge. It is unchallenged, and the court found, that Shelby and Abe McMillan were "well fed, clothed, and cared for except for their lack of academic instruction." The court concluded that the children "are neglected within the meaning of G.S. 7A–278(4) on account of the wilful failure and refusal" of their parents "to send said children to school."

The issue presented in this appeal is whether children whose parents wilfully refuse to allow them to attend school may be "neglected" within the meaning of G.S. 7A–278(4). A child is neglected, as defined in that statute, when he or she does not "receive proper care or supervision or discipline * * *, or who has been abandoned, or who is not provided necessary medical care or other remedial care recognized under State law, or who lives in an environment injurious to his welfare * * *."

We reject appellants' argument that the court exceeded its authority in this matter. They contend that the proceeding was brought to compel compliance with the compulsory school attendance law, and that the exclusive means to enforce compulsory school attendance is G.S. 115–166. That statute provides that "No person shall encourage, entice or counsel any such child [between the ages of seven and sixteen] to be unlawfully absent from school." Violation of G.S. 115–166 is a misdemeanor. G.S. 115–169.

The purpose of G.S. 115–166 is to prevent those in charge or control of children from encouraging or enticing said children to be absent from school unlawfully. * * *

In the instant case the disposition of the neglect petition is coincident with the policy of G.S. 115–166 that children between the ages of seven and sixteen attend school. However, the essence of the petition is not to enforce the compulsory school attendance law but to determine and provide for the needs of the children.

It was said in Tucker v. Tucker, 288 N.C. 81, 216 S.E.2d 1 (1975), that the natural and legal right of parents to the custody, companionship, control and bringing up of their children is not absolute. It may be interfered with or denied for substantial and sufficient reason, and it is subject to judicial control when the interest and welfare of the children require it.

We do not accept appellants' position that a deep-rooted conviction for Indian heritage is on an equal constitutional plane with religious beliefs and thus protected by the First Amendment. This case is not like the one cited by appellants, Wisconsin v. Yoder, 406 U.S. 205, 92 S.Ct. 1526, 32 L.Ed.2d 15 (1972), which dealt with religious beliefs of the Amish.   There is no showing that Shelby and Abe McMillan receive any mode of educational programs alternative to those in the public school.   There is also no showing that the Indian heritage or culture of these children will be endangered or threatened in any way by their attending school.

The parents of Shelby and Abe McMillan wilfully refused to permit them to attend the public schools because those schools do not teach the particular heritage and culture the parents deem appropriate.   Moreover, the parents do not provide any sufficient alternative education or training for these children.   In our opinion the court exercised its control to interfere with the natural right of the parents in the best interest and welfare of the children.

It is fundamental that a child who receives proper care and supervision in modern times is provided a basic education.   A child does not receive "proper care" and lives in an "environment injurious to his welfare" when he is deliberately refused this education, and he is "neglected" within the meaning of G.S. 7A–278(4).   The trial court did not err in so finding, and the order is

Affirmed.

NOTES

Mother who strongly identified with the American Indian rights movement could not withdraw child from school as reaction to some perceived lack of sympathy by the school for the Indian movement.

The court said:

We cannot approve or sanction a parent's defiance of our compulsory school attendance law as a means of compelling a school system to change the kind of education made available to its students, provided its procedures comply with law.

In the Matter of Baum, 61 A.D.2d 123, 401 N.Y.S.2d 514 (1978).

Curriculum *

Once entered into the public school, the child becomes subject to administrative regulations at the state and local levels, as well as to state laws governing public education.   The regulations are an exercise of police power that provides each child an appropriate education.   The curriculum content making up that education, however, may be viewed differently by different people—not only educators, but by parents and students as well.

Few will argue that to be appropriate the public educational program should be expansive and nonrestrictive in broadening the

* See Alexander and Jordan, supra.

perspective of knowledge. This role of education has been quite accurately defined as provision of a "marketplace of ideas".

The crucial role of education in a democratic society is self-evident. Over the years, the courts have come to conclude that society is best served by an educational system that teaches "through wide exposure to that robust exchange of ideas which discovers truth 'out of a multitude of tongues [rather] than through any kind of authoritative selection.' " [68] Thus, because of the importance of the schools and because this "robust exchange of ideas" is so vital to the educational process, the perpetuation of that exchange is, at all levels of the educational system, "a special concern of the First Amendment." [69] No school can function as "a marketplace of ideas" unless both students and faculty enjoy an atmosphere conducive to debate and scholarly inquiry. Thus, this first amendment attaches to a teacher's classroom activities not only for the teacher's benefit, but also to create an intellectual "marketplace." ("Academic Freedom in The Public Schools: The Right to Teach", *New York University Law Review*, Vol. 48, Dec. 1973, p. 1183.

Courts have generally given a wide berth to the state in school matters involving the educational program. In one notable case, parents sought a writ of *mandamus* to prevent using the novel *Slaughterhouse-Five* as a part of the instructional program. [70] The parents alleged that the material was obscene, profane, and repugnant to the religious provisions of the First Amendment.

The court, in an exposition on the law, first observed that, although there may have been religious references in the work, the book itself did not violate the students' and parents' religious freedom. To declare otherwise, the court concluded, would censor and prevent the public schools from making use of and reference to many great works of the past.

> If plaintiffs' contention was correct, then public school students could no longer marvel at Sir Galahad's saintly quest for the Holy Grail, nor be introduced to the dangers of Hitler's *Mein Kampf* nor read the mellifluous poetry of John Milton and John Donne. Unhappily, Robin Hood would be forced to forage without Friar Tuck and Shakespeare would have to delete Shylock from *The Merchant of Venice*. Is this to be the state of our law? Our Constitution does not command ignorance; on the contrary, it assures the people

68. Keyishian v. Board of Regents, 385 U.S. 589, 603, 87 S.Ct. 675, 683, 684 (1967), quoting United States v. Associated Press, 52 F.Supp. 362, 372 (S. D.N.Y.1943), aff'd 326 U.S. 1, 65 S.Ct. 1416 (1945); see Weiman v. Updegraff, 344 U.S. 183, 197–198, 73 S.Ct. 215, 221–222 (1952) (Frankfurter, J., concurring).

69. Keyishian v. Board of Regents, 385 U.S. 589, 603, 87 S.Ct. 675, 683, 684 (1967).

70. Todd v. Rochester Community Schools, 41 Mich.App. 320, 200 N.W.2d 90 (1972).

that the state may not relegate them to such a status and guarantees to all the precious and unfettered freedom of pursuing one's own intellectual pleasures in one's own personal way.[71]

Even more to the point, the court observed that the judges are not to be the experts in what subject matter is offered in the schools. Citing Justice Brennan's admonition in *Schempp*,[72] the court contended that curriculum determination should be entrusted to the experienced school officials of the nation's public schools and not to the judges. The appellate court reprimanded the lower trial court for imposing its judgment of "right" and "morality" over that of the school authorities. Such action by a court was forbidden by the state constitution and a matter for the lawfully elected school board to determine. The appellate court concluded that the judicial censor was *persona non grata* in the formation of public education curriculum policies.

Parental intervention does not always promote greater freedom and choice for students. In many instances, such intervention may amount to an attempt to restrict knowledge and limit educational prerogative. Similarly, a court, unless it exercises sufficient restraint, could find itself sanctioning restriction rather than protecting freedom.

The school, in this context, is an arm of the state.[73] It is a creature of the legislature over which the legislature has complete control. The actual control of public schools is vested in the school board, which is required by the legislature to conduct the school in the best interest of the pupils. The determination of subject matter and required teaching force are solely within the discretion of the board.[74]

The educational program of the public school has both academic and disciplinary aspects. Courts have been very hesitant to enter into the academic arena. The position of the courts is stated by the U.S. Supreme Court in a higher education case which has applicability for elementary and secondary school operation. In *Horowitz,* the Court said: [75]

> Academic evaluations of a student, in contrast to disciplinary determinations, bear little resemblance to the judicial and administrative fact-finding proceedings to which we have traditionally attached a full learning requirement.

71. Id.

72. School Dist. of Abington Township v. Schempp, 374 U.S. at 300, 83 S.Ct. at 1612 (1963).

73. Sturgis v. County of Allegan, 343 Mich. 209, 72 N.W.2d 56 (1955).

74. Kelly v. Dickson County School Dist., 64 Lack.Jur. 13 (1962).

75. Board of Curators of Univ. of Missouri v. Horowitz, 435 U.S. 78, 98 S. Ct. 948 (1978).

* * * Like the decision of an individual professor as to the proper grade for a student in his course, the determination whether to dismiss a student for academic reasons requires expert evaluation of cumulative information and is not readily adapted to the procedural tools of judicial or administrative decisionmaking. * * * Courts are particularly ill-equipped to evaluate academic performance.

The courts have generally supported the school boards when they have expanded the school program or introduced innovative curricula. Thus far, the courts have agreed that the school has the power to regulate and develop curriculum for the well-being of the students. These cases also establish that not all parental discontent is aimed at broadening student knowledge and choice. In many instances, parents seek to restrict or "contract the spectrum of knowledge." As a result, the courts will tend to weigh such grievances very carefully, even when a parent feels that a constitutional right is being offended.

This judicial position has been demonstrated where the school board sought to reduce the length of the school day, thereby restricting the educational program. For lack of funds, the school board decided to hold one-half sessions and to teach certain subjects on a compressed schedule.[76] The Supreme Court of Michigan decided that in the absence of state board regulations limiting local school board authority in this area, the reduction in the school program was valid.

Although the content of the school program itself is an area of concern to parents, an even more direct concern is the placement of their children. Aside from the recent statutory emphasis and litigation dealing with handicapped children, much of the controversy between parent and school has arisen during the child's first few years of schooling. It is at this level that the parent and the child are experiencing the removal of the child from the home and placing him or her in the hands of strangers at school.

In one such New York State case, a mother petitioned the court for an order directing the board of education to admit her son to the first grade.[77] Previously, the boy had established quite a reputation as a "disciplinary problem." The school had demoted the boy from the first grade back to kindergarten, an action the parent maintained was arbitrary, capricious, unreasonable, and in violation of the Fourteenth Amendment and the New York Constitution. The board defended itself by maintaining the school principal had made an "educational decision" based on the boy's inability to perform first-grade work, his test results, and his lack of self-control. The petitioner was unable to rebut the test results. The court held that the placement of the child was within the school's authority "to provide rules and reg-

76. Welling v. Board of Educ., 382 Mich. 620, 171 N.W.2d 545 (1969).

77. Pittman v. Board of Education of Glen Cove, 56 Misc.2d 51, 287 N.Y.S.2d 551 (1967).

ulations for promotion from grade to grade, based not on age but on training, knowledge and ability.[78]

In a similar New York State decision, the parents of a five-year-old child sought to compel the school board to accept the child into the first grade.[79]   According to New York law, a five-year-old is entitled to attend public schools, and the boy's parents claimed that kindergarten was not the public schools.   The court disagreed with the parent, arguing that when a kindergarten is established it becomes a part of the public school system.   Since the boy was already in *public school,* the court maintained, the parents had no right to insist that the boy be admitted to a particular *grade or class* in the public school.

Most precedents indicated that the courts, though sympathetic with the intentions of the parent, generally defer to authorized and trained educational experts in matters of school policy establishment. In recent years, however, there has been a greater tendency by the courts to delve deeper into the justification and rationale supporting educational policy.   School authorities, therefore, are well advised to document placement and curriculum decisions with solid educational rationale.

The collective judgment of the school holds substantial influence with the courts.   Courts, therefore, hesitate to substitute their knowledge of children for that of educators.   Although the school has generally prevailed in curriculum and placement disputes with parents, the school's power is by no means absolute.   Where legitimate constitutional concerns are present, the courts stand ready to invalidate the offending regulations, particularly if the action of the school tends to contract rather than expand knowledge.   Such judicial intervention is not uncommon and has been demonstrated in several notable United States Supreme Court cases.

In Meyer v. State of Nebraska,[80] the Court ruled that legislative determination of educational matters was subject to supervision by the courts.   Nebraska had attempted to contract available knowledge by forbidding the teaching of foreign languages in public and private schools before the eighth grade.   The Court rejected the rather elusive notion that the state, in the exercise of its police power, was protecting the child's health by limiting his mental activities.

Curriculum content was also the issue in a more recent Supreme Court case where the old Scopes "monkey law" controversy was resurrected.[81]   As in *Meyer,* this action was brought by a teacher who was subjected to criminal prosecution for teaching Darwin's theory of evolution.   In holding the law unconstitutional, the Court commented that judicial interference in the operation of public schools

---

78. Id.

79. Isquith v. Levitt, 285 App.Div. 833, 137 N.Y.S.2d 497 (1955).

80. Meyer, supra.

81. Epperson v. Arkansas, 393 U.S. 99, 89 S.Ct. 266 (1968).

requires care and restraint. Furthermore, the Supreme Court said the courts should not intervene in conflicts that arise in the daily operation of the schools, so long as the conflicts do not involve basic constitutional values. On the other hand, neither would the Court "tolerate laws which cast a pall of orthodoxy over the classroom."[82]

Technically, the basic constitutional value involved was freedom of religion, but the entire tone of the antievolution statute was to limit or restrict the knowledge available to children. This result, as pointed out, will usually engender judicial suspicion.[83]

The court delivered a similar opinion in Sweezy v. New Hampshire: [84]

> Scholarship cannot flourish in an atmosphere of suspicion and distrust. Teachers and students must always remain free to inquire, to study and to evaluate * * * [The state cannot] chill that free play of the spirit which all teachers ought especially to cultivate and practice.[85]

These cases firmly establish the precedent for judicial intervention in education matters where constitutional rights and freedoms are at issue. Several other Supreme Court decisions have also established that the state cannot compel students to perform rituals that violate their freedom of religion.[86] All these precedents combine to limit somewhat state school power in favor of individual freedom of choice for the teacher and student. However, the state does have a legitimate interest in prescribing a public school curriculum and such will be upheld unless it cast a "pall of orthodoxy" or tends to contract the spectrum of knowledge.

Board Has the Power to Enforce Reasonable Rules Prescribing Specific Curriculum

STATE EX REL. ANDREW v. WEBBER

Supreme Court of Indiana, 1886.
108 Ind. 31, 8 N.E. 708.

HOWK, C. J. * * *

The relator * * * said that he was the father and natural guardian of one Abram Andrew, who was a white male child, between the ages of 6 and 21 years, to-wit, of the age of 12 years * * *.

---

82. Keyishian v. Board of Regents, 385 U.S. 589, 87 S.Ct. 675 (1967).

83. Epperson, *supra* note 81.

84. Sweezy v. New Hampshire, 354 U.S. 234, 77 S.Ct. 1203 (1957).

85. Wieman v. Updegraff, 344 U.S. 183, 73 S.Ct. 215 (1952).

86. McCollum v. Board of Educ., 333 U.S. 203, 68 S.Ct. 461 (1948); Engel v. Vitale, 370 U.S. 421, 82 S.Ct. 1261 (1962); School Dist. of Abington Township v. Schempp, 374 U.S. 203, 83 S.Ct. 1560 (1963); West Virginia State Bd. of Educ. v. Barnette, 319 U.S. 624, 63 S.Ct. 1178 (1943).

* * * The said Abram Andrew being sufficiently advanced in his studies, in accordance with the relator's desire and consent, and in compliance with his legal rights in the premises, was admitted as a pupil in such high school, to receive instruction therein, and thereafter, until his suspension, as hereinafter stated, was regular in his attendence and deportment, and was obedient and respectful to his teachers, and properly subordinate to the rules and regulations of such school; that among the exercises prescribed by such superintendent, with the sanction of such board of trustees, for the pupils of the high school, was a requirement that each of the pupils should, at stated intervals, employ a certain period of time in the study and practice of music, and that they should provide themselves with prescribed books for that purpose; that the relator, believing it was not for the best interest of said Abram Andrew, and not in accordance with the relator's wishes regarding the instruction of his said son, in a respectful manner asked of such superintendent that Abram Andrew might be excused from the study and practice of music at such exercises, and directed Abram Andrew not to participate therein, all in good faith, and in a respectful manner, and with no intention of in any manner interfering with the government, rules, and regulations of such schools, except in so far as he might legally control and direct the education of his said son, which purpose and desire were fully communicated by him to such superintendent.

But the relator said that, notwithstanding his said desire and request so communicated to such superintendent as aforesaid, the superintendent, on or about the fourteenth day of October, 1885, in disregard of the relator's wishes and request, required said Abram Andrew to participate in the practice and study of music, and upon the refusal of said Abram Andrew to participate in such exercises and study, which he did without disrespect to such superintendent, and entirely because of the relator's direction, which was so communicated to such superintendent as aforesaid, the superintendent suspended said Abram Andrew from such school, without assigning any cause therefor, * * *

* * * This action is brought by the father and natural guardian of the suspended pupil, to compel, by mandate, the governing authorities of the school corporation to revoke such suspension, and to readmit such pupil to the high school.

The question for our decision in this case, as it seems to us, may be thus stated: Is the rule or regulation for the government of the pupils of the high school of the school city of La Porte, in relation to the study and practice of music, a valid and reasonable exercise of the discretionary power conferred by law upon the governing authorities of such school corporation? In section 4497, Rev.St.1881, in force since August 16, 1869, it is provided as follows: "The common schools of the state shall be taught in the English language; and the trustee shall provide to have taught in them orthography, reading, writing, arithmetic, geography, English grammar, physiology, history of the United States, and good behavior, and such other branches of learning, and other languages, as the advancement of pupils may require, and the trustees from time to time direct." Under this statutory provision and others of similar purport and effect, to be found in our school laws, it was competent, we think, for the trustees of the school city of La Porte to enact necessary and reasonable rules for the government of the pupils of its high school, directing what branches of learning such pupils should pursue, and regulating the time to be given to any particular study, and prescribing what book or books should be used therein. Such trustees were and are required, by the express provisions of section 4444, Rev.St.1881, in force since March 8, 1873, to "take charge of the educational affairs" of such city of La Porte; "they may also establish graded schools, or such modifications of them as may be practicable, and provide for admitting into the higher departments of the graded school, from the primary schools of their townships, such pupils as are sufficiently advanced for such admission."

The power to establish graded schools carries with it, of course, the power to establish and enforce such reasonable rules as may seem necessary to the trustees, in their discretion, for the government and discipline of such schools, and prescribing the course of instruction therein. Confining our opinion strictly to the case in hand, we will consider and decide these two questions, in the order of their statement, namely: (1) Has the appellant's relator shown, by the averments of his verified complaint, that the rule or regulation for the government of the pupils of the high school, in the school city of La Porte, of which he complains, was or is an unreasonable exercise of the discretionary power conferred by law upon the trustees of such school corporation and the superintendent of its schools? (2) Conceding or assuming such rule or regulation to be reasonable and valid, has the relator shown, in his complaint herein, any sufficient or satisfactory excuse for the non-compliance therewith, and the disobedience thereof, of his son, Abram Andrew, a pupil of such high school, or any sufficient or legal ground for the revocation of the suspension of his son, or for his son's readmission, as a pupil in such high school?

1. As to the first of these questions * * * we think, that the legislature has given the trustees of the public school corporations the discretionary power to direct, from time to time, what branches of learning, in addition to those specified in the statute, shall be taught in the public schools of their respective corporations. Where such trustees may have established a system of graded schools, or such modifications of them as may be practicable, within their respective corporations, they are clothed by law with the discretionary power to prescribe the course of instruction in the different grades of their public schools. We are of opinion that the rule or regulation of

which the relator complains in the case under consideration was within the discretionary power conferred by law upon the governing authorities of the school city of La Porte; that it was not an unreasonable rule; but that it was such a one as each pupil of the high school, in the absence of sufficient excuse, might lawfully be required to obey and comply with. * * *

2. * * * The only cause or reason assigned by the relator for requiring his son to disobey such rule or regulation was that he did not believe it was for the best interest of his son to participate in the musical studies and exercises of the high school, and did not wish him to do so. The relator has assigned no cause or reason, and it may be fairly assumed that he had none, in support either of his belief or his wish. The important question arises, which should govern the public high school of the city of La Porte, as to the branches of learning to be taught and the course of instruction therein,—the school trustees of such city, to whom the law has confided the direction of these matters, or the mere arbitrary will of the relator, without cause or reason in its support? We are of opinion that only one answer can or ought to be given to this question. The arbitrary wishes of the relator in the premises must yield and be subordinated to the governing authorities of the school city of La Porte, and their reasonable rules and regulations for the government of the pupils of its high school. * * *

* * *

For the reasons given, our conclusion is that no error was committed by the court below in sustaining appellees' demurrer to the relator's complaint.

The judgment is affirmed, with costs.

School Alone Has Power to Determine if
Student Is Delinquent in His Studies

BARNARD v. INHABITANTS OF SHELBURNE

Supreme Judicial Court of Massachusetts, 1913.
216 Mass. 19, 102 N.E. 1095.

RUGG, C. J. This is an action of tort to recover damages (as alleged in his declaration) for wrongful exclusion of the plaintiff from the "public high school" of Shelburne. The court ruled that there was no evidence that the plaintiff might not have gone to a school of the ninth grade. This ruling appears to have been right and became the law of the case for the purposes of that trial.

The evidence tended to show that the plaintiff entered the high school in its freshman class in the autumn of 1910, and that from the first he fell below the required standard of excellence in one or more branches of instruction, information as to which was sent to his father once at least, and that in December written notice was given to his father that he could no longer continue in the high school, accompanied with a suggestion that the boy go to a Miss Johnstone, who was teacher of a ninth grade school in the same village, for the rest of the year, and with an expression of hope that he then would be able with this additional preparation do to the high school work. It was testified by the principal of the high school that the conduct of the boy had nothing to do with the letters written about his ability to keep up with his class. There is nothing in the record to control this evidence. It is plain from the reports of teachers as to his standing that he failed to attain a standard of 60 per cent. or was deficient in three branches, and the plaintiff himself testified that he thought this was so.

A rule adopted by the school committee was put in evidence to the effect that "pupils standing below 60 per cent. in two or more subjects shall be demoted one grade, and when such deficiency occurs in the freshman class the delinquent shall be dropped from the roll of the school." Apparently this merely was putting in more permanent form a standard previously adopted by the faculty of the school. It properly might apply to pending cases. The only ground of exclusion which finds any support in the reported evidence is deficiency in studies. * * *

Two questions were submitted to the jury which, with their answers, were as follows:

(1) "Was the plaintiff excluded from the public schools of the town of Shelburne?" The jury answered: "He was."

(2) "If the jury answer that he was excluded from the public schools, what was the grounds of such exclusion?" The jury answered: "His standing in the school not being high enough; such facts, however, in the minds of the jury not sustained by the evidence."

* * * There is nothing in the evidence as reported to give color to a contention that he was excluded for any other reason than that his standing was not high enough.

The right of every child to attend the public schools is subject to such reasonable regulations as to qualifications of pupils to be admitted and retained in the respective schools as the school committee shall prescribe. The school committee have general charge and superintendence over all public schools. * * * For the promotion of the best interests of pupils and of all the people, it necessarily has been construed broadly by the court." The care and management of schools which is vested in the school committee includes the establishment and maintenance of standards for the promotion of pupils from one grade to another and for their continuance as members of any particular class. So long as the school committee act in good faith their conduct in formulating and applying standards and making decisions touching this matter is not subject to review by any other tribunal. It is obvious that efficiency of instruction depends in no small degree upon this feature of our school system. It is an educational question, the final determination of which is vested by law in the public officers charged with the performance of that important duty. Although this precise point never has been determined in this commonwealth, it plainly follows, from the general principles by which public schools are governed, and from numerous decisions in which the powers of the school committee to establish reasonable rules and regulations for the government, discipline and general management of the public schools under their charge have been stated with clearness and precision as applicable to a considerable variety of circumstances. * * *

When the real ground for exclusion from a particular school or grade is failure to maintain a proper standard of scholarship and there is opportunity afforded to the pupil to attend another school adapted to his ability and accomplishments, there is no illegal exclusion from school within the meaning of the statute. It would seem from the latter part of the answer of the jury to the second question that the trial proceeded upon the theory that the jury had power to pass upon the inquiry whether in fact the plaintiff was delinquent in his studies and thus revise the conclusion of the school committee in this respect. But that was a matter plainly outside their province. When it had been ruled that there had been no exclusion of the plaintiff from the next lower grade of school then the only possible issue was whether the exclusion of the plaintiff from the High School was an act of bad faith by the school committee. The burden of proving that as an affirmative proposition rested upon the plaintiff. It required support by evidence and could not be left wholly to surmise, conjecture or speculation. The record is bare of any evidence tending to show the existence of bad faith on the part of the school committee.

It has been argued that, because the school committee did not grant a hearing to the father upon his request, the exclusion was illegal, and reliance is placed upon Bishop v. Rowley, 165 Mass. 460, 43 N.E. 191, Morrison v. Lawrence, 186 Mass. 456, 72 N.E. 91, and Jones v. Fitchburg, 211 Mass. 66, 97 N.E. 612. These cases have no application. When the real ground of exclusion is not misconduct there is no obligation on the part of the school committee to grant a hearing. R.L. c. 44, §§ 7, 8. Failure to attain to a given standard of excellence in studies is not misconduct in itself. The reason for this distinction in the statute is obvious. Misconduct is a very different matter from failure to attain a standard of excellence in studies. A determination as to the fact involves investigation of a quite different kind. A public hearing may be regarded as helpful to the ascertainment of misconduct and useless or harmful in finding out the truth as to scholarship.

Exceptions sustained.

Statute Prohibiting Teaching of Foreign Language
Violates Substantive Due Process

MEYER v. NEBRASKA

Supreme Court of the United States, 1923.
262 U.S. 390, 43 S.Ct. 625.

Mr. Justice McREYNOLDS delivered the opinion of the Court.

Plaintiff in error was tried and convicted in the district court for Hamilton county, Nebraska, under an information which charged that on May 25, 1920, while an instructor in Zion Parochial School he unlawfully taught the subject of reading in the German language to Raymond Parpart, a child of 10 years, who had not attained and successfully passed the eighth grade. The information is based upon "An act relating to the teaching of foreign languages in the state of Nebraska," approved April 9, 1919 (Laws 1919, c. 249), which follows:

"Section 1. No person, individually or as a teacher, shall, in any private, denominational, parochial or public school, teach any subject to any person in any language than the English language.

"Sec. 2. Languages, other than the English language, may be taught as languages only after a pupil shall have attained and successfully passed the eighth grade as evidenced by a certificate of graduation issued by the county superintendent of the county in which the child resides.

*　*　*

The Supreme Court of the state affirmed the judgment of conviction. 107 Neb. 657, 187 N.W. 100. It declared the offense charged and established was "the direct and intentional teaching of the German language as a distinct subject to a child who had not passed the eighth grade," in the parochial school maintained by Zion Evangelical Lutheran Congregation, a collection of Biblical stories being used therefor. And it held that the statute forbidding this did not conflict with the Fourteenth Amendment, but was a valid exercise of the police power. The following excerpts from the opinion sufficiently indicate the reasons advanced to support the conclusion.

"The salutary purpose of the statute is clear. The Legislature had seen the baneful effects of permitting foreigners, who had taken residence in this country, to rear and educate their children in the language of their native land. The result of that condition was found to be inimical to our own safety. To allow the children of foreigners, who had emigrated here, to be taught from early childhood the language of the country of their parents was to rear them with that language as their mother tongue. It was to educate them so that they must always think in that language, and, as a consequence, naturally inculcate in them the ideas and sentiments foreign to the best interests of this country. The statute, therefore, was intended not only to require that the education of all children be conducted in the English language, but that, until they had grown into that language and until it had become a part of them, they should not in the schools be taught any other language. The obvious purpose of this statute was that the English language should be and become the mother tongue of all children reared in this state. The enactment of such a statute comes reasonably within the police power of the state. * * *

* * *

The problem for our determination is whether the statute as construed and applied unreasonably infringes the liberty guaranteed to the plaintiff in error by the Fourteenth Amendment. "No state * * * shall deprive any person of life, liberty or property without due process of law."

While this court has not attempted to define with exactness the liberty thus guaranteed, the term has received much consideration and some of the included things have been definitely stated. Without doubt, it denotes not merely freedom from bodily restraint but also the right of the individual to contract, to engage in any of the common occupations of life, to acquire useful knowledge, to marry, establish a home and bring up children, to worship God according to the dictates of his own conscience, and generally to enjoy those privileges long recognized at common law as essential to the orderly pursuit of happiness by free men. * * * The established doctrine is that this liberty may not be interfered with, under the guise of protecting the public interest, by legislative action which is arbitrary or without reasonable relation to some purpose within the competency of the state to effect. Determination by the Legislature of what constitutes proper exercise of police power is not final or conclusive but is subject to supervision by the courts. * * *

The American people have always regarded education and acquisition of knowledge as matters of supreme importance which should be diligently promoted. The Ordinance of 1787 declares; "Religion, morality and knowledge being necessary to good government and the happiness of mankind, schools and the means of education shall forever be encouraged." Corresponding to the right of control, it is the natural duty of the parent to give his children education suitable to their station in life; and nearly all the states, including Nebraska, enforce this obligation by compulsory laws.

Practically, education of the young is only possible in schools conducted by especially qualified persons who devote themselves thereto. The calling always has been regarded as useful and honorable, essential, indeed, to the public welfare. Mere knowledge of the German language cannot reasonably be regarded as harmful. Heretofore it has been commonly looked upon as helpful and desirable. Plaintiff in error taught this language in school as part of his occupation. His right thus to teach and the right of parents to engage him so to instruct their children, we think, are within the liberty of the amendment.

* * *

That the state may do much, go very far, indeed, in order to improve the quality of its citizens, physically, mentally and morally, is clear; but the individual has certain fundamental rights which must be respected. The protection of the Constitution extends to all, to those who speak other languages as well as to those born with English on the tongue. Perhaps it would be highly advantageous if all had ready understanding of our ordinary speech, but this cannot be coerced by methods which conflict with the Constitution—a desirable end cannot be promoted by prohibited means.

* * *

The power of the State to compel attendance at some school and to make reasonable regulations for all schools, including a requirement that they shall give instructions in English, is not questioned. Nor has challenge been made of the state's power to prescribe a curriculum for institutions which it supports. Those matters are not within the present controversy. Our concern is with the prohibition approved by the Supreme Court. Adams v. Tanner, 244 U.S. 594, 37 S.Ct. 662, pointed out that mere abuse incident to an occupation ordinarily useful is not enough to justify its abolition, although regulation may be entirely proper. No emergency has arisen which renders knowledge by a child of some language other than English so clearly harmful as to justify its inhibition with the consequent infringement of rights long freely enjoyed. We are constrained to conclude that the statute as applied is arbitrary and without reasonable relation to any end within the competency of the State.

As the statute undertakes to interfere only with teaching which involves a modern language, leaving complete freedom as to other matters, there seems no adequate foundation for the suggestion that the purpose was to protect the child's health by limiting his mental activities. It is well known that proficiency in a foreign language seldom comes to one not instructed at an early age, and experience shows that this is not injurious to the health, morals or understanding of the ordinary child.

The judgment of the court below must be reversed and the cause remanded for further proceedings not inconsistent with this opinion.

Reversed.

Statute Forbidding the Teaching of Evolution
Is Unconstitutional

EPPERSON v. STATE OF ARKANSAS

Supreme Court of the United States, 1968.
393 U.S. 97, 89 S.Ct. 266.

Mr. Justice FORTAS delivered the opinion of the Court.

I.

This appeal challenges the constitutionality of the "anti-evolution" statute which the State of Arkansas adopted in 1928 to prohibit the teaching in its public schools and universities of the theory that man evolved from other species of life. * * *

The Arkansas law makes it unlawful for a teacher in any state-supported school or university "to teach the theory or doctrine that mankind ascended or descended from a lower order of animals," or "to adopt or use in any such institution a textbook that teaches" this theory. Violation is a misdemeanor and subjects the violator to dismissal from his position.

The present case concerns the teaching of biology in a high school in Little Rock. According to the testimony, until the events here in litigation, the official textbook furnished for the high school biology course did not have a section on the Darwinian Theory. Then, for the academic year 1965–1966, the school administration, on recommendation of the teachers of biology in the school system, adopted and prescribed a textbook which contained a chapter setting forth "the theory about the origin * * * of man from a lower form of animal."

Susan Epperson, a young woman who graduated from Arkansas' school system and then obtained her master's degree in zoology at the University of Illinois, was employed by the Little Rock school system in the fall of 1964 to teach 10th grade biology at Central High School. At the start of the next academic year, 1965, she was confronted by the new textbook (which one surmises from the record was not unwelcome to her). She faced at least a literal dilemma because she was supposed to use the new textbook for classroom instruction and presumably to teach the statutorily condemned chapter; but to do so would be a criminal offense and subject her to dismissal.

* * *

* * * Only Arkansas and Mississippi have such "anti-evolution" or "monkey" laws on their books. There is no record of any prosecutions in Arkansas under its statute. It is possible that the statute is presently more of a curiosity than a vital fact of life in these States. Nevertheless, the present case was brought, the appeal

as of right is properly here, and it is our duty to decide the issues presented.

II.

At the outset, it is urged upon us that the challenged statute is vague and uncertain and therefore within the condemnation of the Due Process Clause of the Fourteenth Amendment. The contention that the Act is vague and uncertain is supported by language in the brief opinion of Arkansas' Supreme Court. That court, perhaps reflecting the discomfort which the statute's quixotic prohibition necessarily engenders in the modern mind, stated that it "expresses no opinion" as to whether the Act prohibits "explanation" of the theory of evolution or merely forbids "teaching that the theory is true." Regardless of this uncertainty, the court held that the statute is constitutional.

On the other hand, counsel for the State, in oral argument in this Court, candidly stated that, despite the State Supreme Court's equivocation Arkansas would interpret the statute "to mean that to make a student aware of the theory * * * just to teach that there was such a theory" would be grounds for dismissal and for prosecution under the statute; and he said "that the Supreme Court of Arkansas' opinion should be interpreted in that manner." He said: "If Mrs. Epperson would tell her students that 'Here is Darwin's theory, that man ascended or descended from a lower form of being,' then I think she would be under this statute liable for prosecution."

In any event, we do not rest our decision upon the asserted vagueness of the statute. On either interpretation of its language, Arkansas' statute cannot stand. It is of no moment whether the law is deemed to prohibit mention of Darwin's theory, or to forbid any or all of the infinite varieties of communication embraced within the term "teaching." Under either interpretation, the law must be stricken because of its conflict with the constitutional prohibition of state laws respecting an establishment of religion or prohibiting the free exercise thereof. The overriding fact is that Arkansas' law selects from the body of knowledge a particular segment which it proscribes for the sole reason that it is deemed to conflict with a particular religious doctrine; that is, with a particular interpretation of the Book of Genesis by a particular religious group.

* * *

Judicial interposition in the operation of the public school system of the Nation raises problems requiring care and restraint. Our courts, however, have not failed to apply the First Amendment's mandate in our educational system where essential to safeguard the fundamental values of freedom of speech and inquiry and of belief. By and large, public education in our Nation is committed to the control of state and local authorities. Courts do not and cannot intervene in the resolution of conflicts which arise in the daily operation of school systems and which do not directly and sharply implicate basic constitutional values.   On the other hand, "[t]he vigilant protection of constitutional freedoms is nowhere more vital than in the community of American schools," Shelton v. Tucker, 364 U.S. 479, 487, 81 S.Ct. 247, 251, 5 L.Ed.2d 231 (1960).   As this Court said in Keyishian v. Board of Regents, the First Amendment "does not tolerate laws that cast a pall of orthodoxy over the classroom."   385 U.S. 589, 603, 87 S.Ct. 675, 683, 17 L.Ed.2d 629 (1967).

* * *

There is and can be no doubt that the First Amendment does not permit the State to require that teaching and learning must be tailored to the principles or prohibitions of any religious sect or dogma.
* * *

* * *

In the present case, there can be no doubt that Arkansas has sought to prevent its teachers from discussing the theory of evolution because it is contrary to the belief of some that the Book of Genesis must be the exclusive source of doctrine as to the origin of man.   No suggestion has been made that Arkansas' law may be justified by considerations of state policy other than the religious views of some of its citizens.   It is clear that fundamentalist sectarian conviction was and is the law's reason for existence.   Its antecedent, Tennessee's "monkey law," candidly stated its purpose: to make it unlawful "to teach any theory that denies the story of the Divine Creation of man as taught in the Bible, and to teach instead that man has descended from a lower order of animals."   Perhaps the sensational publicity attendant upon the *Scopes* trial induced Arkansas to adopt less explicit language.   It eliminated Tennessee's reference to "the story of the Divine Creation of man" as taught in the Bible, but there is no doubt that the motivation for the law was the same: to suppress the teaching of a theory which it was thought "denied" the divine creation of man.

* * *

The judgment of the Supreme Court of Arkansas is reversed.

NOTES

The Supreme Court of Mississippi struck down the last of the anti-evolution students in Smith v. State, 242 So.2d 692 (Miss.1970).

Tennessee's legislature repealed the anti-evolution statute which had created the Scopes Controversy, Scopes v. State of Tennessee, 154 Tenn. 105, 289 S.W. 363 (1927), and subsequently the use of any textbook which discussed evolution unless the book contained a disclaimer saying that the doctrine was merely a theory and was not based on scientific facts about the origin of man.   Further, the statute mandated that the Genesis version of creation be included if any version was treated by the text and under the statute the Genesis version needed no disclaimer when included alone.   The United States Court of Appeals, Sixth Circuit, held this statute to be unconstitutional because it gave preference to the Biblical version of creation. Daniel v. Waters, 515 F.2d 485 (6th Cir. 1975).

State Can Validly Require a Course in Sex Education for All Students

CORNWELL v. STATE BD. OF EDUC.

United States District Court, Maryland, 1969.
314 F.Supp. 340 (D.Md.1969), affirmed
428 F.2d 471 (4th Cir. 1970),
cert. denied 400 U.S. 942, 91 S.Ct. 240 (1970).

HARVEY, District Judge: In this civil action, Baltimore County taxpayers are suing the Maryland State Board of Education seeking to prevent the implementation in the Baltimore County Schools of a program of sex education. In particular, the plaintiffs, who are school children and their parents, seek to have this Court declare unconstitutional a bylaw duly adopted by the State Board. The provision in question is By-Law 720, Section 3, Subsection 4, which provides as follows:

> "It is the responsibility of the local school system to provide a comprehensive program of family life and sex education in every elementary and secondary school for all students as an integral part of the curriculum including a planned and sequential program of health education."

* * *

In determining whether there is here a substantial question of constitutionality, this Court concludes initially that no question whatsoever arises under the Fourteenth Amendment. There is first no denial of substantive due process to the plaintiffs. Under Section 6 of Article 77 of the Maryland Code (as amended and re-codified by Chapter 405 of the Acts of 1969), the State Board is directed to determine the educational policies of the state and to enact bylaws for the administration of the public school system, which when enacted and published shall have the force of law. Assuredly it cannot be said that the bylaw here is an arbitrary or unreasonable exercise of the authority vested in the State Board to determine a teaching curriculum, nor that there is no basis in fact for the legislative policy expressed in the bylaw. Furthermore, it does not appear that the bylaw denies equal protection of the laws, as on its face it applies to all pupils equally.

Plaintiffs allege that the enactment of this bylaw was based on a study made in reference to pregnant pupils. But whatever the genesis of the bylaw, it is not the study that is being attacked here but the bylaw itself, and it is being attacked on its face. It is the provisions of the bylaw then that must be examined in the light of the

United States Constitution. The plaintiffs' argument that the bylaw is defective because it applies to non-pregnant as well as to pregnant pupils is difficult to follow. There would appear to be just as much reason for the State Board to provide sex education for the non-pregnant (and, incidentally, for the non-impregnating) as for those students who, because of a lack of information on the subject (or for other reasons), have become pregnant or who have caused pregnancy.

The plaintiffs further assert that they have the exclusive constitutional right to teach their children about sexual matters in their own homes, and that such exclusive right would prohibit the teaching of sex in the schools. No authority is cited in support of this novel proposition, and this Court knows of no such constitutional right. This Court, then, is satisfied that the claims asserted in this complaint under the Fourteenth Amendment are so insubstantial that they do not confer jurisdiction here.

In support of their First Amendment claim, the plaintiffs assert that they have been denied the free exercise of their religious concepts and that the teaching of sex in the Baltimore County Schools will in fact establish religious concepts. * * *

    * * *

Applying the principles that have been established by the various cases, it is quite clear to this Court that the purpose and primary effect of the bylaw here is not to establish any particular religious dogma or precept, and that the bylaw does not directly or substantially involve the state in religious exercises or in the favoring of religion or any particular religion. The bylaw may be considered quite simply as a public health measure. As the Supreme Court indicated in Prince v. Massachusetts, 321 U.S. 158, 64 S.Ct. 438 (1944), the State's interest in the health of its children outweighs claims based upon religious freedom and the right of parental control. The Court in that particular case said this (at pages 168–169):

> "A democratic society rests * * * upon the healthy, well-rounded growth of young people into full maturity as citizens * * *. It is too late now to doubt that legislation appropriately designed to reach such evils is within the state's police power, whether against the parent's claim to control of the child or one that religious scruples dictate contrary action."

In summary, then, the Court concludes that the federal question here is plainly insubstantial. Construing the allegations in a light most favorable to the plaintiffs, as the Court must do on these motions to dismiss, this Court finds that the constitutional questions relied upon are obviously without merit. The unsoundness and insubstantiality of the plaintiffs' position is clearly indicated by the various decisions of the Supreme Court to which I have alluded.

For these reasons then, the two motions to dismiss are granted.

NOTES

Sex education does not invade the privacy of school children or parents. Medeiros v. Kiyosaki, 478 P.2d 314 (Hawaii 1970).

Academic Freedom Extends to Protect Teacher in Use of "Dirty" Word if Conveyed for Demonstrated Educational Purpose

KEEFE v. GEANAKOS

United States Court of Appeals, First Circuit, 1969.
418 F.2d 359.

ALDRICH, Chief Judge. * * *

Reduced to fundamentals, the substance of plaintiff's position is that as a matter of law his conduct which forms the basis of the charge did not warrant discipline. Accordingly, he argues, there is no ground for any hearing. He divides this position into two parts. The principal one is that his conduct was within his competence as a teacher, as a matter of academic freedom, whether the defendants approved of it or not. The second is that he had been given inadequate prior warning by such regulations as were in force, particularly in the light of the totality of the circumstances known to him, that his actions would be considered improper, so that an ex post facto ruling would, itself, unsettle academic freedom. The defendants, essentially, deny plaintiff's contentions. They accept the existence of a principle of academic freedom to teach, but state that it is limited to proper classroom materials as reasonably determined by the school committee in the light of pertinent conditions, of which they cite in particular the age of the students. Asked by the court whether a teacher has a right to say to the school committee that it is wrong if, in fact, its decision was arbitrary, counsel candidly and commendably (and correctly) responded in the affirmative. This we consider to be the present issue. * * *

On the opening day of school in September 1969 the plaintiff gave to each member of his senior English class a copy of the September 1969 Atlantic Monthly magazine, a publication of high reputation, and stated that the reading assignment for that night was the first article therein. September was the educational number, so-called, of the Atlantic, and some 75 copies had been supplied by the school department. Plaintiff discussed the article, and a particular word that was used therein, and explained the word's origin and context, and the reasons the author had included it. The word, admittedly highly offensive, is a vulgar term for an incestuous son. Plaintiff stated that any student who felt the assignment personally distasteful could have an alternative one.

The next evening the plaintiff was called to a meeting of the school committee and asked to defend his use of the offending word. Following his explanation, a majority of the members of the committee asked him informally if he would agree not to use it again in the classroom. Plaintiff replied that he could not, in good conscience, agree. His counsel states, however, without contradiction, that in point of fact plaintiff has not used it again. No formal action was taken at this meeting. Thereafter plaintiff was suspended, as a matter of discipline, and it is now proposed that he should be discharged.

The Lifton article, which we have read in its entirety, has been described as a valuable discussion of "dissent, protest, radicalism and revolt." It is in no sense pornographic. We need no supporting affidavits to find it scholarly, thoughtful and thought-provoking. The single offending word, although repeated a number of times, is not artificially introduced, but, on the contrary, is important to the development of the thesis and the conclusions of the author. Indeed, we would find it difficult to disagree with plaintiff's assertion that no proper study of the article could avoid consideration of this word. It is not possible to read the article, either in whole or in part, as an incitement to libidinous conduct, or even thoughts. If it raised the concept of incest, it was not to suggest it, but to condemn it; the word was used, by the persons described, as a superlative of opprobrium. We believe not only that the article negatived any other concept, but that an understanding of it would reject, rather than suggest the word's use.

*   *   *

Hence the question in this case is whether a teacher may, for demonstrated educational purposes, quote a "dirty" word currently used in order to give special offense, or whether the shock is too great for high school seniors to stand. If the answer were that the students must be protected from such exposure, we would fear for their future. We do not question the good faith of the defendants in believing that some parents have been offended. With the greatest of respect to such parents, their sensibilities are not the full measure of what is proper education.

We of course agree with defendants that what is to be said or read to students is not to be determined by obscenity standards for adult consumption. *   *   * At the same time, the issue must be one of degree. A high school senior is not devoid of all discrimination or resistance. Furthermore, as in all other instances, the offensiveness of language and the particular propriety or impropriety is dependent on the circumstances of the utterance.

*   *   *

*   *   * We accept the conclusion of the court below that "some measure of public regulation of classroom speech is inherent in every provision of public education." But when we consider the facts at bar as we have elaborated them, we find it difficult not to think that its application to the present case demeans any proper concept of education. The general chilling effect of permitting such rigorous censorship is even more serious.

We believe it equally probable that the plaintiff will prevail on the issue of lack of any notice that a discussion of this article with the senior class was forbidden conduct. The school regulation upon which defendants rely, although unquestionably worthy, is not apposite. It does not follow that a teacher may not be on notice of impropriety from the circumstances of a case without the necessity of a regulation. In the present case, however, the circumstances would have disclosed that no less than five books, by as many authors, containing the word in question were to be found in the school library. It is hard to think that any student could walk into the library and receive a book, but that his teacher could not subject the content to serious discussion in class.

Such inconsistency on the part of the school has been regarded as fatal. * * * We, too, would probably so regard it. At the same time, we prefer not to place our decision on this ground alone, lest our doing so diminish our principal holding, or lead to a bowdlerization of the school library.

Finally, we are not persuaded by the district court's conclusion that no irreparable injury is involved because the plaintiff, if successful, may recover money damages. Academic freedom is not preserved by compulsory retirement, even at full pay.

The immediate question before us in whether we should grant interlocutory relief pending appeal. This question, as defendants point out, raises the ultimate issue of the appeal itself. The matter has been extensively briefed and argued by both sides. We see no purpose in taking two bites, and believe this a case for action under Local Rule 5. The order of the district court denying an interlocutory injunction pending a decision on the merits is reversed and the case is remanded for further proceedings consistent herewith.

NOTES

In a case where a secondary school teacher wrote on the board and used a four letter word to illustrate changes in standards of morality, the court held that the teacher must be able to show that the methods used are in keeping with the preponderant opinion of the teaching profession.

The court said:

While secondary schools are not rigid disciplinary institutions, neither are they open forums in which mature adults, already habituated to social restraints, exchange ideas on a level of parity. Moreover, it cannot be accepted as a premise that the student is voluntarily in the classroom and willing to be exposed to a teaching method which, though, reasonable, is not approved by the school authorities or by the weight of professional opinion. A secondary school student, unlike most college students, is usually required to attend school classes, and may have no choice as to his teacher.

Bearing in mind these competing considerations, this court rules that when a secondary school teacher uses a teaching method which he does not prove has the support of the preponderant opinion of the teaching profession or of the part of it to which he belongs, but which he merely proves is relevant to his subject and students, is regarded by experts of significant standing as serving a serious educational purpose, and was used by him in good faith the state may suspend or discharge a teacher for using that method but it may not resort to such drastic sanctions unless the state proves he was put on notice either by a regulation or otherwise that he should not use that method. Mailloux v. Kiley, 323 F.Supp. 1387 (D.Mass.1971).

On appeal of this case, the higher court cast some doubt on the feasibility of the rule measuring the validity of a teaching method on the preponderant opinion of other educators and noted that each case must be examined on an independent basis, the court considering that "the propriety of regulations or sanctions must depend on such circumstances as the age and sophistication of the students, the closeness of the relation to the specific [teaching] technique used and some concededly valid educational objective, and the context and manner of presentation." Mailloux v. Kiley, 448 F.2d 1242 (1st Cir. 1971).

Book Selection Is Within the Proper Discretion of School Board

PRESIDENTS COUNCIL, DIST. 25 v. COMMUNITY SCHOOL BD.

United States Court of Appeals, Second Circuit, 1972.
457 F.2d 289.

MULLIGAN, Circuit Judge. * * *

The plaintiffs-appellants in this case are the Presidents Council, District 25, an organization of presidents and past presidents of various parent and parent-teacher associations in the district, three junior high school students enrolled in schools in the district, seven parents and guardians of minors who attend junior high schools in the district, two teachers, a librarian and the principal of a junior high school, all within the district and under the jurisdiction of the Board. This litigation commenced as a result of the decisions of the duly elected Community School Board (hereinafter Board) of Community School District 25 (hereinafter District), which in executive session on March 31, 1971, voted five to three to remove from all junior high school libraries in the District all copies of *Down These Mean Streets*, a novel by Piri Thomas. * * *

* * *

* * *

The book, which has created the controversy and provoked the action of the Board, *Down These Mean Streets*, is an autobiographical account by Piri Thomas, of a Puerto Rican youth growing up in the East Side Barrio (Spanish Harlem) in New York City. Predictably the scene is depressing, ugly and violent. The argot of the vicinage is replete with four letter and twelve letter obscenities unreported by Tom Swift or even Tom Jones. Acts of criminal violence, sex, normal and perverse, as well as episodes of drug shooting are graphically described. * * *

Since the Legislature of the State of New York has by law determined that the responsibility for the selection of materials in the public school libraries in New York City is to be vested in the Community School Board and the Commissioner of Education of that State has defined the purposes of the public school library, and in further view of the procedures for administrative and state court review provided in New York, we do not consider it appropriate for this court to review either the wisdom or the efficacy of the determinations of the Board. Our function is purely one of constitutional adjudication on the facts and the record before us: has the Board transgressed the first amendment rights of the plaintiff teachers, parents, librarian and children. * * *

After a careful review of the record before us and the precedents we find no impingement upon any basic constitutional values. Since we are dealing not with the collection of a public book store but with the library of a public junior high school, evidently some authorized person or body has to make a determination as to what the library collection will be. It is predictable that no matter what choice of books may be made by whatever segment of academe, some other person or group may well dissent. The ensuing shouts of book burning, witch hunting and violation of academic freedom hardly elevate this intramural strife to first amendment constitutional proportions. If it did, there would be a constant intrusion of the judiciary into the internal affairs of the school. Academic freedom is scarcely fostered by the intrusion of three or even nine federal jurists making curriculum or library choices for the community of scholars. When the court has intervened, the circumstances have been rare and extreme and the issues presented totally distinct from those we have here. * * *

* * * Here, patently we have no religious establishment or free exercise question, and neither do we have the banning of the teaching of any theory or doctrine. The problems of the youth in the ghetto, crime, drugs and violence have not been placed off limits by the Board. A book has been removed but the librarian has not been penalized, and the teacher is still free to discuss the Barrio and its problems in the classroom. The action of the Board does not even preclude the teacher from discussing *Down These Mean Streets* in class or from assigning it for outside reading. In those libraries which have the book, the parent can borrow it and, if he sees fit, can loan it to his child if he wishes to read it. The intrusion of the Board here upon any first amendment constitutional right of any category of plaintiffs is not only not "sharp" or "direct", it is miniscule.

* * * The public school library obviously does not have to become the repository, at public expense, for books which are deemed by the proper authorities to be without merit either as works of art or science, simply because they are not obscene within the statute. If someone authored a book advocating that the earth was flat, it could hardly be argued that the work could not be removed from the public school library unless it was also obscene. Appellants concede, or at least do not reject, the proposition that the Board has ultimate authority for the initial selection of the public school library collection. They suggest, however, that we have a different case where, as here, the book was once shelved and is now removed. They analogize the shelving and unshelving of a book to the constitutional right of a person to obtain public employment and his rights to retain such employment when it is sought to be terminated. This concept of a book acquiring tenure by shelving is indeed novel and unsupportable under any theory of constitutional law we can discover. It would seem clear to us that books which become obsolete or irrelevant or where improperly selected initially, for whatever reason, can be removed by the same authority which was empowered to make the selection in the first place.

* * *

* * * The appellant conveniently ignores the factual setting of *Tinker* but would have us apply its test. Since the shelving of *Down These Mean Streets* did not create any disruption or disorder, it is argued, it should remain on the shelf. There is here no problem of freedom of speech or the expression of opinions on the part of parents, teachers, students or librarians. As we have pointed out, the discussion of the book or the problems which it encompasses or the ideas it espouses have not been prohibited by the Board's action in removing the book.

The administration of any library, whether it be a university or particularly a public junior high school, involves a constant process of selection and winnowing based not only on educational needs but financial and architectural realities. To suggest that the shelving or unshelving of books presents a constitutional issue, particularly where there is no showing of a curtailment of freedom of speech or thought, is a proposition we cannot accept.

* * *

In view of the facts in the record before us and the controlling precedents, we find no constitutional infirmity in the resolutions of the Board.

Affirmed.

NOTES

In an Ohio case the court held that the school board had the power to select books for the library but could not censor and pull books from the library shelves without regard to the First Amendment. The court said:

> Clearly, discretion as to the selection of textbooks must be lodged somewhere and we can find no federal constitutional prohibition which prevents its being lodged in school board officials who are elected representatives of the people. To the extent that this suit concerns a question as to whether the school faculty may make its professional choices of textbooks prevail over the considered decision of the Board of Education empowered by the state law to make such decisions, we affirm the decision of the District Judge in dismissing that portion of plaintiff's complaint. In short, we find no federal constitutional violation in this Board's exercise of curriculum and textbook control as empowered by the Ohio statute.

> * * *

> A library is a storehouse of knowledge. When created for a public school it is an important privilege created by the state for the benefit of the students in the school. That privilege is not subject to being withdrawn by succeeding school boards whose members might desire to "winnow" the library for books the content of which occasioned their displeasure or disapproval.

> * * *

> In the absence of any explanation of the Board's action which is neutral in First Amendment terms, we must conclude that the School Board removed the books because it found them objectionable in content and because it felt that it had the power, unfettered by the First Amendment, to censor the school library for subject matter which the Board members found distasteful.

> Neither the State of Ohio nor the Strongsville School Board was under any federal constitutional compulsion to provide a library for the Strongsville High School or to choose any particular books. Once having created such a privilege for the benefit of its students, however, neither body could place conditions on the use of the library which were related solely to the social or political tastes of school board members.

> * * *

> A public school library is also a valuable adjunct to classroom discussion. If one of the English teachers considered Joseph Heller's *Catch 22* to be one of the more important modern American novels (as, indeed, at least one did), we assume that no one would dispute that the First Amendment's protection of academic freedom would protect both his right to say so in class and his student's right to hear him and to find and read the book. Obviously, the students' success in this last endeavor would be greatly hindered by the fact that the book sought had been removed from the school library. The removal of books from a school library

is a much more serious burden upon freedom of classroom discussion than the action found unconstitutional
in *Tinker v. Des Moines Independent Community School
Dist.* (armband case). Minarcini v. Strongsville City
School Dist., 541 F.2d 577 (6th Cir. 1976).

*School System's Failure to Provide English Language
Instruction to Chinese Speaking Children Violates
the Civil Rights Act of 1964*

LAU v. NICHOLS

Supreme Court of the United States, 1974.
414 U.S. 563, 94 S.Ct. 786.

Mr. Justice DOUGLAS delivered the opinion of the Court.

* * *

This class suit brought by non-English-speaking Chinese students
against officials responsible for the operation of the San Francisco
Unified School District seeks relief against the unequal educational
opportunities, which are alleged to violate the Fourteenth Amendment. No specific remedy is urged upon us. Teaching English to the
students of Chinese ancestry who do not speak the language is one
choice. Giving instructions to this group in Chinese is another.
There may be others. Petitioners ask only that the Board of Education be directed to apply its expertise to the problem and rectify the
situation.

* * *

The Court of Appeals reasoned that "every student brings to
the starting line of his educational career different advantages and
disadvantages caused in part by social, economic and cultural background, created and continued completely apart from any contribution by the school system,". Yet in our view the case may not be so
easily decided. This is a public school system of California and § 71
of the California Education Code states that "English shall be the basic language of instruction in all schools." That section permits a
school district to determine "when and under what circumstances instruction may be given bilingually." That section also states as "the
policy of the state" to insure "the mastery of English by all pupils in
the schools." And bilingual instruction is authorized "to the extent
that it does not interfere with the systematic, sequential, and regular
instruction of all pupils in the English language."

Moreover, § 8573 of the Education Code provides that no pupil
shall receive a diploma of graduation from grade 12 who has not met
the standards of proficiency in "English," as well as other prescribed
subjects. Moreover, by § 12101 of the Education Code children between the ages of six and 16 years are (with exceptions not material
here) "subject to compulsory full-time education."

Under these state-imposed standards there is no equality of treatment merely by providing students with the same facilities, text-books, teachers, and curriculum; for students who do not understand English are effectively foreclosed from any meaningful education.

Basic English skills are at the very core of what these public schools teach. Imposition of a requirement that, before a child can effectively participate in the educational program, he must already have acquired those basic skills is to make a mockery of public education. We know that those who do not understand English are certain to find their classroom experiences wholly incomprehensible and in no way meaningful.

We do not reach the Equal Protection Clause argument which has been advanced but rely solely on § 601 of the Civil Rights Act of 1964, 42 U.S.C.A. § 2000d, to reverse the Court of Appeals.

That section bans discrimination based "on the ground of race, color, or national origin," in "any program or activity receiving Federal financial assistance." The school district involved in this litigation receives large amounts of federal financial assistance. HEW which has authority to promulgate regulations prohibiting discrimination in federally assisted school systems, 42 U.S.C.A. § 2000d–1; in 1968 issued one guideline that "school systems are responsible for assuring that students of a particular race, color, or national origin are not denied the opportunity to obtain the education generally obtained by other students in the system." 33 CFR 4955. In 1970 HEW made the guidelines more specific, requiring school districts that were federally funded "to rectify the language deficiency in order to open" the instruction to students who had "linguistic deficiencies," 35 Fed.Reg. 11595.

By § 602 of the Act HEW is authorized to issue rules, regulations, and orders to make sure that recipients of federal aid under its jurisdiction conduct any federally financed projects consistently with § 601. HEW's regulations, 45 CFR § 80.3(b)(1), specify that the recipients may not

> "Provide any service, financial aid, or other benefit to an individual which is different, or is provided in a different manner, from that provided to others under the program;
> * * *
> "Restrict an individual in any way in the enjoyment of any advantage or privilege enjoyed by others receiving any service, financial aid, or other benefit under the program."

Discrimination among students on account of race or national origin that is prohibited includes "discrimination * * * in the availability or use of any academic * * * or other facilities of the grantee or other recipient." Id., § 80.5(b).

Discrimination is barred which has that *effect* even though no purposeful design is present: a recipient "may not   *   *   * utilize criteria or methods of administration which have the effect of subjecting individuals to discrimination" or have "the effect of defeating or substantially impairing accomplishment of the objectives of the program as respect individuals of a particular race, color or national origin." Id., § 80.3(b)(2).

It seems obvious that the Chinese-speaking minority receive fewer benefits than the English-speaking majority from respondents' school system which denies them a meaningful opportunity to participate in the educational program—all earmarks of the discrimination banned by the regulations. In 1970 HEW issued clarifying guidelines (35 Fed.Reg. 11595) which include the following:

> "Where inability to speak and understand the English language excludes national origin-minority group children from effective participation in the educational program offered by a school district, the district must take affirmative steps to rectify the language deficiency in order to open its instructional program to these students" (Pet.Br.App. 1a).

> "Any ability grouping or tracking system employed by the school system to deal with the special language skill needs of national origin-minority group children must be designed to meet such language skill needs as soon as possible and must not operate as an educational deadend or permanent track." (Pet.Br. p. 2 a).

Respondent school district contractually agreed to "comply with title VI of the Civil Rights Act of 1964   *   *   * and all requirements imposed by or pursuant to the Regulation" of HEW (45 CFR pt. 80) which are "issued pursuant to that title   *   *   *" and also immediately to "take any measures necessary to effectuate this agreement." The Federal Government has power to fix the terms on which its money allotments to the States shall be disbursed.   *   *   * Whatever may be the limits of that power,   *   *   * they have not been reached here. Senator Humphrey, during the floor debates on the Civil Rights Act of 1964, said:

> "Simple justice requires that public funds, to which all taxpayers of all races contribute, not be spent in any fashion which encourages, entrenches, subsidizes, or results in racial discrimination."

We accordingly reverse the judgment of the Court of Appeals and remand the case for the fashioning of appropriate relief.

Reversed.   *   *   *

NOTES

1. School district may admit students with achievement in the top 15 percent to a preferred, college-preparatory high school without violating the

Civil Rights Act or the Fourteenth Amendment, even though the percentage of black and Spanish-American is disproportionately low. The court found that the school districts legitimate interest outweighed any harm imagined or suffered by students whose achievement had not qualified them for admission. Berkelman v. San Francisco Unified School District, 501 F.2d 1264 (9th Cir. 1974).

2. A federal district court has within its inherent legal prerogative the equitable power to fashion a bilingual-bicultural program which will assure that Spanish surnamed children receive meaningful education. Serna v. Portales Municipal Schools, 499 F.2d 1147 (10th Cir. 1974).

*Establishment and Operation of Nongraded School
Is Within Discretion of School Board*

SCHWAN v. BOARD OF EDUC. OF LANSING SCHOOL DISTRICT

Court of Appeals of Michigan, Division 2, 1971.
27 Mich.App. 391, 183 N.W.2d 594.

PER CURIAM. The only issue presented by this appeal is whether defendant board of education has authority to establish and operate a nongraded school program in its elementary schools. We reach this conclusion after examining the trial court record, plaintiffs' amended complaint, the pretrial statement, plaintiffs' trial court brief, the opinion and judgment of the trial court, all of which indicate that this was the only issue presented to and decided by the trial court.

The trial court held that except as provided in M.C.L.A. §§ 340.-745 and 340.746 (Stat.Ann.1968 Rev. §§ 15.3745 and 15.3746), the defendant board had no authority to establish ungraded schools. This was error. The statutory sections referred to are part of the chapter of the school code dealing with compulsory education and they have no bearing on the issue before us.

M.C.L.A. § 340.583 (Stat.Ann.1968 Rev. § 15.3583) provides:

"Every board shall establish and carry on such grades, schools and departments as it shall deem necessary or desirable for the maintenance and improvement of the schools; determine the courses of study to be pursued and cause the pupils attending school in such district to be taught in such schools or departments as it may deem expedient:"

This grant of discretionary authority is sufficiently broad to encompass the establishment and operation of nongraded school programs in elementary schools. Courts should not interfere with the exercise of that discretion absent a showing of abuse thereof. * * * The record before us does not establish an abuse of discretion.

General supervision over all public education is vested in the state board of education. Const.1963, art. 8, § 3. * * * We have not been apprised of any action by that board prohibiting the establishment of a nongraded program in elementary schools. We conclude that section 340.583, supra, remains in full force and effect.

Reversed and remanded to the trial court for entry of an order dismissing plaintiffs' complaint with prejudice. Plaintiffs' cross-appeal is dismissed. A public question being involved, no costs are allowed.

Chapter 8

STUDENT RIGHTS

School authorities are vested with broad powers for the establishment and conduct of the educational program. This prerogative, however, is by no means absolute and school officials must act within the scope of reasonable rules and regulations. Reasonable regulations are those which measurably contribute to the maintenance and advancement of the educational process. Traditionally, courts have given wide discretion in promulgation of regulations governing student conduct but they cannot be so broad or vague as to allow arbitrary or capricious application and administration. School regulations may be held to be sufficiently definitive where they provide students with the adequate information as to what is expected of them and are so stated that persons of common intelligence are not required to guess at their meaning. Reasonable certainty of interpretation requires only the use of ordinary and commonly used terminology. Reasonableness, however, is not predicated on formal adoption and publication of rules before they can have effect, and the absence of a preexisting rule on the books does not prohibit official action. Absence of such formality may, though, make it much more difficult to convince a court that the rule was necessary and that its enforcement was not arbitrary or capricious.

This chapter discusses the power of school boards, in promulgation of rules of student conduct and the reasonableness of the application by school administrators and teachers. Much of the chapter is devoted to limitations which the courts will impose to protect the students where governmental actions have been unreasonable, vague, arbitrary, or direct violations of constitutional rights or freedoms.

In Loco Parentis

To act to control pupils in the absence of a formal rule is a necessity which has long been recognized as the *in loco parentis* doctrine. Courts are aware that a teacher in the day to day activities of working with children must be given considerable supervisory leeway. Immediate classroom control of pupil conduct is put in perspective in an old Wisconsin case:

> While the principal or teacher in charge of a public school is subordinate to the school board or board of education of his district or city, and must enforce rules and regulations adopted by the board for the government of the school, and execute all its lawful orders in that behalf, he does not derive all his power and authority in the school and over his

pupils from affirmative action of the board. He stands for the time being *in loco parentis* to his pupils, and because of that relation he must necessarily exercise authority over them in many things concerning which the board may have remained silent. In the school, as in the family, there exists on the part of the pupils the obligations of obedience to lawful commands, subordination, civil deportment, respect for the rights of other pupils and fidelity to duty. These obligations are inherent in any proper school system, and constitute, so to speak, the common law of the school.[1]

Students have a constitutionally protected interest in attending the public schools which cannot be denied or impaired without due process of law. Within the school setting, students are "persons" and their fundamental rights and freedoms are protected by the United States Constitution. Of course, no child is free to exercise a constitutional right in such a way as to infringe on the rights of other students and to cause disruption of the school. To loudly exercise one's freedom of speech, using a quiet school library as a forum, is naturally not defensible. Unlimited individual freedom in many instances must give way to the rights of other students, the interests of the community, parents and teachers in conducting a well-run and efficient school system. The courts, therefore, recognizing the importance of discipline and decorum in the schools, attempt to "balance the interests" of the student against the interests of the school in each particular factual situation.

That school teachers have the legal authority to physically punish school childen in order to maintain discipline in schools is well documented. For centuries courts have sanctioned corporal punishment and continue to do so today. The legality of corporal punishment has been sanctioned by the courts in much the same manner as governmental immunity; that is, in the absence of limiting statutes, the teachers have the power to administer corporal punishment. In the same manner in which governmental immunity is derived from the common law doctrine, "the king can do no wrong," the authority to physically punish children in school is gained from the common law doctrine of "in loco parentis."

While it would not be correct to say that all courts have always upheld corporal punishment, it is certainly true that the vast majority of the courts, and the people for that matter, have generally accepted the idea that the schools must have the authority to physically punish children if classroom decorum and discipline is to be maintained. Consequently, the cases have generally dealt with the degree and reasonableness of the punishment and not whether corporal punishment should be administered at all.

---

1.   State ex rel. Burpee v. Burton, 45 Wis. 150, 30 Am.Rep. 706 (1878).

A teacher's right to discipline students within his charge is subject to the same standard of reasonableness which is applicable to parents in disciplining their own children.[2] Courts have advanced two standards governing a teacher's corporal punishment of a child; (a) the reasonableness standard e. g. "must be exerted within bounds of reason and humanity,"[3] and (b) the good faith standard, "The authority of a teacher over his pupil being regarded as a delegation of at least a portion of the parental authority, the presumption is in favor of the correctness of the teacher's action in inflicting corporal punishment upon the pupil. The teacher must not have been activated by malice, nor have inflicted the punishment wantonly. For an error in judgment, although the punishment is unnecessarily excessive, if it is not of a nature to cause lasting injury and he acts in good faith, the teacher is not liable."[4]

Of late, the legality of corporal punishment in the public schools has been drawn into question from several different perspectives. The primary arguments are encompassed in three broad categories; (1) the social and psychological arguments that society has progressed past the physical punishment stage; (2) the idea that legally corporal punishment is "cruel and unusual" punishment as prohibited by the Eighth Amendment, and (3) that corporal punishment should not be administered without first providing the student with procedural due process of law as prescribed in the Fourteenth Amendment.

The first of these arguments is nonlegal but the other two were of sufficient legal consequence to have the U.S. Supreme Court to render an opinion which apparently finally resolved the issues.[5] Prior to the Supreme Court's decision lower courts had held that corporal punishment was not *ipso facto* cruel and unusual but it could be if it were immoderate and excessive.

Teachers have always been liable in tort for too severely administering punishment and are, of course, subject to state statutes against assault and battery, but to be liable for cruel and unusual punishment introduced a new kind of liability under the Civil Rights Act of 1871. The issue was, therefore, of some magnitude particularly from the teacher's perspective.

In resolving the question the U.S. Supreme Court in Ingraham v. Wright[6] ruled flatly that corporal punishment as administered in the schools could not be construed to fall within the ambit of the Eighth

2. People v. Ball, 58 Ill.2d 36, 317 N.E. 2d 54 (1974).

3. Fletcher v. People, 52 Ill. 395 (1869); People v. Parris, 130 Ill. App.2d 933, 267 N.E.2d 39 (1971).

4. Fox v. People, 84 Ill.App. 270 (1899); People v. Ball, 58 Ill.2d 36, 317 N.E.2d 54 (1974).

5. Ingraham v. Wright, 430 U.S. 651, 97 S.Ct. 1401 (1977).

6. 430 U.S. 651, 97 S.Ct. 1401 (1977).

Amendment. As such, the Court said the prohibition against cruel and unusual punishment did not apply to paddling in schools, but instead was designed to protect those convicted of crimes. The Amendment's intent is threefold; to limit the kinds of punishment that can be imposed on those convicted of crimes, proscribe punishment grossly disproportionate to the severity of the crime, and impose substantive limits on what can be made criminal and punished as such. In this light it is difficult to conceive of corporal punishment as being circumscribed by the Eighth Amendment and was not, according to the court, so intended. Regarding due process, the court held that a notice and hearing are not required prior to imposition of corporal punishment.

Court Will Not Interfere Unless School Board
Abuses Discretion

KINZER v. DIRECTORS OF INDEPENDENT
SCHOOL DIST. OF MARION

Supreme Court of Iowa, 1906.
129 Iowa 441, 105 N.W. 686.

McCLAIN, C. J. It appears from the allegations in plaintiff's petition that plaintiff was by a resolution of the defendant board of directors suspended from the high school of which he was a pupil until he should apologize to the superintendent before the school, and through the superintendent to the board, for the willful violation of a rule adopted by the board, of which violation the board on investigation found plaintiff to be guilty. The rule was as follows: Resolved, that the board of directors disfavor football on account of injuries to life and limb. The board will lend all assistance, morally and financially, in support of baseball, the gymnasium, or track work, but for the above reasons will not permit football or practice under the auspices of the High School or on the school grounds. The violation charged consisted in participating in a game of football, as a member of a team composed largely of the students of the high school, which was played on a Saturday afternoon at the fair grounds.

*   *   *

     *   *   *

We are required, therefore to decide whether the rule of the defendant board, for the alleged violation of which plaintiff was excluded from the high school, was within the power of the board to enact. And here it may be suggested that the court should hesitate to interfere with the regularly constituted school authorities in their management of the scholars which are placed under their charge. The Legislature is expressly authorized to provide for the educational interests of the state, in such manner as shall seem best and proper. See article 9 of section 15 of the state Constitution. And in the exercise of this power school districts have been created, authorized to have exclusive jurisdiction in all school matters over their respective territories. Code, § 2743. It is further provided that the affairs of each school corporation shall be conducted by a board of directors. Code, § 2745. And the directors are, as already indicated, expressly authorized to make and enforce rules. It was plainly intended, therefore, that the management of school affairs should be left to the discretion of the board of directors, and not to the courts, and we ought not to interfere with the exercise of discretion on the part of a school board as to what is a reasonable and necessary rule, except in a plain case of exceeding the power conferred. A rule may be so far unreasonable or beyond the exercise of discretion that the courts will say that the board acted without authority in making and enforcing it. * * * But the presumption is in favor of the reasonableness and propriety of the action of the board.

It is contended that the rule of defendant board already quoted, under which plaintiff was suspended, does not apply to the conduct of pupils of the school on holidays and outside of school hours, and that, if it is to be construed as having application to the action of pupils away from the school grounds and on a day when the school is not in session, it is unreasonable and invalid. But, in view of the general discretion given to boards of directors, as above indicated, we are not disposed to hold that the rule as applied in the present case by the defendant board is unreasonable or in excess of authority. The general character of the school and the conduct of its pupils, as affecting the efficiency of the work to be done in the school room and the discipline of the scholars, are matters to be taken into account by the school board, making rules for the government of the school. They have no concern, it is true, with the individual conduct of the pupils wholly outside of the school room and school grounds and while they are presumed to be under the control of their parents, or after they are beyond the age of parental control, to be governed by the rules which regulate the conduct of all members of the body politic; but the conduct of pupils which directly relates to and affects the management of the school and its efficiency is within the proper regulation of the school authorities. Thus it has been held that rules as to absence and tardiness of pupils and their misconduct on the way to school, or on going home from school, are properly within the scope of the power of school officers. * * * We have no doubt as to the power of the defendant board, in the exercise of its reasonable discretion as to the management of the high school, to determine that it was detrimental to the best interests of the school that pupils should be encouraged by their school associations to engage in games of football with teams of other high schools, and we think that their proper power, with reference to the encouragement or discouragement of the playing of football by pupils of the school, was not limited to the high school grounds, but extended to participation by the pupils in games as members of a team purporting to represent in any way the high school under the control of defendant board; and we therefore reach the conclusion that, giving to the rule the interpretation which the board gave it in holding it to be applicable to the act of plaintiff, such rule was not unreasonable nor in excess of the powers of the board. Whether or not the conduct of the plaintiff was in fact a violation of such reasonable rule as thus interpreted was, as we think, a question, not of the jurisdiction of the board, but of the propriety of its action, which we cannot review in the present proceeding. In short, we hold that the defendants as a board had authority to prohibit and did prohibit, the pupils of the high school from playing football in a game purporting to be played under the auspices of the school or on a team purporting to be a team representing the school.

The other questions presented on this appeal may be briefly disposed of in accordance with principles already announced. If the board had the power to make the rule in question, then the findings as to whether the rule had been violated by the plaintiff and whether the apology tendered by him was sufficient or not are not subject to review in this proceeding and can be tested only by appeal to the county superintendent. Plainly it is not intended that the courts shall interfere with the action of the school authorities in matters of discipline, as to which such authorities are vested with discretionary power. * * *

The action of the trial court in sustaining the demurrer to plaintiff's petition and rendering judgment for defendant was correct, and it is affirmed.

Court Is Not Concerned with Wisdom of Regulation but Whether It Is Reasonable

FLORY v. SMITH

Supreme Court of Appeals of Virginia, 1926.
145 Va. 164, 134 S.E. 360.

CAMPBELL, J. The object of this suit is to test the legality of a rule promulgated by the school board of Gloucester county. This rule is as follows:

"Student Regulation.—Leaving the campus between the hours of 9 a. m. and 3:35 p. m. is strictly prohibited, unless students are accompanied by a teacher."

* * *

It was the desire of the appellees that their children be relieved of the restriction placed upon them by the rule stated, supra, and that the children be permitted to eat their midday meal, either in the home, situated about a mile distant from the school, or to eat same with their father at the hotel in the town.

The special privilege was denied by the principal of the school.
* * *

* * *

The court, on final hearing, overruled the demurrer and entered a decree enjoining and restraining E. D. Flory, principal of the school, from prohibiting and preventing the children of appellees "from eating their midday meals either in the home of their parents or with their father in Botetourt Hotel.

* * *

While the Constitution of the state provides in mandatory terms that the Legislature shall establish and maintain public free schools, there is neither mandate nor inhibition in the provisions as to the regulation thereof. The Legislature, therefore, has the power to enact any legislation in regard to the conduct, control, and regulation of the public free schools, which does not deny to the citizen the constitutional right to enjoy life and liberty, to pursue happiness and to acquire property.

In the conduct of the public schools it is essential that power be vested in some legalized agency in order to maintain discipline and promote efficiency. In considering the exercise of this power, the courts are not concerned with the wisdom or unwisdom of the act done. The only concern of the court is the reasonableness of the regulation promulgated. To hold otherwise would be to substitute judicial opinion for the legislative will.

* * *

While appellees allege in their bill "that it is their right to select and provide the best and most suitable food for the nourishment of their children, and to select the mode and manner by which such food shall be received by their children, to the end that their children may be best nourished and their physical development may be best promoted," it is nowhere alleged that the physical condition of the children is such that results detrimental to their physical well-being will follow if the right alleged is denied.

While it may be argued with force that a warm meal at midday is preferable to a cold lunch, it is not conclusive that the latter is destructive of health. It is a matter of common knowledge that in the towns and rural sections the vast majority of school children partake of a cold lunch at midday. In the larger cities, where paternalism is further advanced, children are encouraged to partake of hot food furnished them for a consideration.

Considering the regulation from the viewpoint afforded us by the bill of complaint, demurrer, and answer, we are unable to say that the regulation is an unreasonable one. However, while a rule may be legally reasonable, it should not be without elasticity. In the enforcement of every law there should be brought into play the element of common sense.

We have no serious trouble in disposing of the contention that appellees have a property right in the public schools of the commonwealth. * * *

* * *

While it may be a restraint upon liberty and an infringement upon happiness for the Legislature to inhibit a parent from sending his child to any school, it is neither restraint nor infringement for the Legislature to enact laws to debar a child from the mere privilege of acquiring an education at the expense of the state until he is willing to submit himself to all reasonable regulations enacted for the purpose of promoting efficiency and maintaining discipline. There is a marked difference between the inherent right to conduct a private school—that is, to select and pursue a given legitimate vocation—and the right to attend a public school.

* * *

The last contention of appellees is that they have been penalized without notice and deprived of their right to seek redress by appeal.

* * *

* * * Immediately upon the suspension of appellees' child, notice of such suspension was given to the father. We are of the opinion that this was sufficient notice; that upon the receipt thereof he had the absolute right to have the matter reviewed by the county school board within a reasonable time from the date of the receipt of such notice.

For the reasons stated, the decree of the circuit court must be reversed, and this court will enter a decree dismissing the bill of complaint.

Reversed.

NOTES

1. For other related cases on this point, see Bozeman v. Morrow, 34 S.W.2d 654 (Tex.Civ.App.1931); Richardson v. Braham, 125 Neb. 142, 249 N.W. 557 (1933); and Haffner v. Braham, 125 Neb. 147, 249 N.W. 560 (1933).

2. A parent arranged for her daughter to receive private music lessons off campus. The school officials refused to permit the child to leave the school premises during school hours to take the private instruction. When the pupil disobeyed this direction of the school officials, she was suspended. Judgment for whom and why? See Christian v. Jones, 211 Ala. 161, 100 So. 99 (1924).

School Master Has the Power to Reasonably Punish Pupil for Acts Detrimental to the Good Order of the School Whether Committed in School Hours or After Pupil Has Returned Home

LANDER v. SEAVER

Supreme Court of Vermont, 1859.
32 Vt. 114, 76 Am.Dec. 156.

Trespass for assault and battery. Defendant pleaded the general issue, and two special pleas in bar. The first special plea alleged that defendant was a school-master; that plaintiff was one of his pupils, and was guilty of misbehavior as such pupil; that for the purpose of punishing him for it, defendant did, in his school, a little beat and bruise the plaintiff, but that no unnecessary injury was done him. This was alleged to be the trespass complained of by plaintiff. The second special plea justified upon the same ground, except that the pupil's offense was stated to have been the use of saucy and disrespectful language towards defendant after the close of the school, but in the presence of other pupils of defendant; that such language tended to degrade the latter in the opinion of such other pupils. The plaintiff replied *de injuria*, etc. The jury rendered a verdict for defendant, and judgment being entered thereon, the plaintiff appealed. The offense of the pupil, a boy eleven years of age, was committed an hour and a half after the close of school, after he had returned home, and while he was driving his father's cow past the teacher's house. Plaintiff, in the presence of some fellow-pupils, and of the master, called the latter "old Jack Seaver." The next morning after school convened, defendant reprimanded the plaintiff for said language, and whipped him with a small rawhide. * * *

George F. Edmunds, for the defendant.

By Court, ALDIS, J. The defendant was a teacher in a public school in Burlington; the plaintiff, his pupil. The first question presented is, Has a school-master the right to punish his pupil for acts of misbehavior committed after the school has been dismissed, and the pupil has returned home and is engaged in his father's service?

I. It is conceded that his right to punish extends to school hours, and there seems to be no reasonable doubt that the supervision and control of the master over the scholar extend from the time he leaves home to go to school till he returns home from school. Most parents would expect and desire that teachers would take care that their children, in going to and returning from school should not loiter, or seek evil company, or frequent vicious places of resort. But in this case, as appears from the bill of exceptions, the offense was committed an hour and a half after the school was dismissed, and after the boy had returned home, and while he was engaged in his father's service. When the child has returned home, or to his parents' control, then the parental authority is resumed and the control of the teacher ceases, and then, for all ordinary acts of misbehavior, the parent alone has the power to punish. It is claimed, however, that in this case "the boy, while in the presence of other pupils of the same school, used toward the master and in his hearing contemptuous language, with a design to insult him, and which had a direct and immediate tendency to bring the authority of the master over his pupils into contempt and lessen his hold upon them and his control over the school." This, under the charge of the court, must have been found by the jury.

This misbehavior, it is especially to be observed, has a direct and immediate tendency to injure the school, to subvert the master's authority, and to beget disorder and insubordination. It is not misbehavior generally, or towards other persons, or even towards the master in matters in no way connected with or affecting the school; for as to such misconduct, committed by the child after his return home from school, we think the parents, and they alone, have the power of punishment.

But where the offense has a direct and immediate tendency to injure the school and bring the master's authority into contempt, as in this case, when done in the presence of other scholars and of the master, and with a design to insult him, we think he has the right to punish the scholar for such acts if he comes again to school.

The misbehavior must not have merely a remote and indirect tendency to injure the school. All improper conduct or language may perhaps have, by influence and example, a remote tendency of that kind. But the tendency of the acts so done out of the teacher's supervision for which he may punish must be direct and immediate in their bearing upon the welfare of the school, or the authority of the master and the respect due to him. Cases may readily be supposed which lie very near the line, and it will often be difficult to distinguish between the acts which have such an immediate and those which have such a remote tendency. Hence each case must be determined by its peculiar circumstances.

* * * By common consent and by the universal custom in our New England schools, the master has always been deemed to have the right to punish such offenses. Such power is essential to the preservation of order, decency, decorum, and good government in schools. Upon this point the charge of the court was substantially correct.

II. The court charged the jury that although the punishment inflicted on the plaintiff was excessive in severity and disproportioned to the offense, still if the master in administering it acted with proper motives, in good faith, and, in his judgment, for the best interests of the school, he would not be liable; that the school-master acts in a judicial capacity, and that the infliction of excessive punishment, when prompted by good intentions and not by malice or wicked motives, or an evil mind, is merely an honest error of opinion, and does not make him liable to the pupil for damages. The plaintiff claims that this was erroneous.

* * *

We think the school-master does not belong to the class of public officers vested with such judicial and discretionary powers. He is included rather in the domestic relation of master and servant, and his powers and duties are usually treated of as belonging to that class.

* * *

It is also said that he stands *in loco parentis,* and is invested with all the authority and immunity of the parent. * * *

The parent, unquestionably, is answerable only for malice or wicked motives or an evil heart in punishing his child. This great, and to some extent irresponsible, power of control and correction is invested in the parent by nature and necessity. It springs from the natural relation of parent and child. It is felt rather as a duty than a power. * * * This parental power is little liable to abuse, for it is continually restrained by natural affection, the tenderness which the parent feels for his offspring, an affection ever on the alert, and acting rather by instinct than reasoning.

The school-master has no such natural restraint. Hence he may not safely be trusted with all a parent's authority, for he does not act from the instinct of parental affection. He should be guided and restrained by judgment and wise discretion, and hence is responsible for their reasonable exercise. The limit upon the parental authority transferred to the master is well expressed by Judge Blackstone. He says: "The master is *in loco parentis,* and has such a portion of the powers of the parent committed to his charge as may be necessary to answer the purposes for which he is employed." An English annotator, in a note to the passage, very properly adds: "This power must be temperately exercised, and no school-master should feel himself at liberty to administer chastisement co-extensive with the parent."

* * *

* * * The law, as we deem it to exist, is this: A school-master has the right to inflict reasonable corporal punishment. He must exercise reasonable judgment and discretion in determining when to punish, and to what extent. In determining upon what is a reasonable punishment, various considerations must be regarded, the nature of the offense, the apparent motive and disposition of the offender, the influence of his example and conduct upon others, and the sex, age, size, and strength of the pupil to be punished. Among reasonable persons, much difference prevails as to the circumstances which will justify the infliction of punishment, and the extent to which it may properly be administered. On account of this difference of opinion, and the difficulty which exists in determining what is a reasonable punishment, and the advantage which the master has

by being on the spot to know all the circumstances, the manner, look, tone, gestures, and language of the offender (which are not always easily described), and thus to form a correct opinion as to the necessity and extent of the punishment, considerable allowance should be made to the teacher by way of protecting him in the exercise of his discretion. Especially should he have this indulgence when he appears to have acted from good motives, and not from anger or malice. Hence the teacher is not to be held liable on the ground of excess of punishment, unless the punishment is clearly excessive, and would be held so in the general judgment of reasonable men. If the punishment be thus clearly excessive, then the master should be held liable for such excess, though he acted from good motives in inflicting the punishment; and in his own judgment considered it necessary, and not excessive. But if there is any reasonable doubt whether the punishment was excessive, the master should have the benefit of the doubt. * * *

     * * *

IV. Whether a rawhide was a proper instrument of punishment, was left to the jury with very suitable instructions.

The evidence to show that the rawhide was used in other schools in the vicinity was properly admitted to rebut the charge of malice, by showing that he did not resort to an unusual instrument of punishment.

The testimony to show the plaintiff did not claim an excess of punishment on the first trial was proper, as tending to prove that that claim on the then pending trial was not well founded.

Judgment reversed.

Teacher Has Authority to Punish Pupil for Offenses Committed After Returning Home from School

O'ROURKE v. WALKER

Supreme Court of Errors of Connecticut, 1925.
102 Conn. 130, 128 A. 25.

KEELER, J. (after stating the facts as above). It is conceded in the brief of the appealing plaintiff that the school board or other proper authority may make reasonable rules concerning the conduct of pupils, and inflict reasonable corporal punishment for the infraction of such rules, and that in the absence of rules so established, the teacher may make all necessary and proper rules for the regulation of the school. We so held in Sheehan v. Sturges, 53 Conn. 481, 2 A. 841. The plaintiff further concedes that—

> "The conduct of pupils outside of school hours and
> school property may be regulated by rules established by the

school authorities if such conduct directly relates to and affects the management of the school and its efficiency."

This we understand to be the rule abundantly established by authority. 5 C. J. 755. However, plaintiff proceeds to say that this conceded rule of law is qualified in this important particular:

"But no rule can be adopted which attempts to control the conduct of pupils outside of school hours after they have reached their homes."

Upon this last proposition plaintiff's appeal is entirely grounded. Counsel argue that the teacher stands in loco parentis while pupils are under his control and oversight in the school room; but when by a return to his home he has again come under parental control neither the teacher nor any other educational authority has any authority to follow him thither and to govern his conduct thereafter.

The authorities upon this point would not ordinarily be numerous, since it is a narrow one and restricted to transactions not usually forming the subject of litigation, and still less of consideration by appellate tribunals. In Lander v. Seaver, 32 Vt. 114, 76 Am.Dec. 156, a teacher whipped a pupil, who, after he had returned home from school, passed with other boys the home of the teacher, and made remarks insulting to the latter. The punishment was inflicted the next day in school. The court held that while ordinarily the control of pupils and the right of a teacher to use disciplinary measures with them ceased after they had reached home, yet where the acts done have a direct and immediate tendency to injure the welfare of the school and its usefulness, punishment may be inflicted upon a pupil for acts done after school hours and after his return home. In Hutton v. State, 23 Tex.App. 386, 5 S.W. 122, 59 Am.Rep. 776, defendant, a teacher, was convicted of assault and battery for whipping a pupil with a switch "about nine licks on the legs" for fighting after school hours in disobedience to a rule of the school. The court held that the fact that the fighting occurred after school hours did not deprive the teacher of his legal right to punish the pupil. In Burdick v. Babcock, 31 Iowa, 562, the court says:

"The view that acts, to be within the authority of the school board and teachers for discipline and correction, must be done within school hours, is narrow, and without regard to the spirit of the law and the best interest of our common schools. It is in conflict, too, with authority."

In this case the penalty inflicted was suspension by virtue of a rule to that effect.

We find no cases in point to the contrary of those cited above. There are many cases concerned with the power of school authorities to make and enforce rules forbidding activities and conduct outside of school hours and after the return of pupils to their homes, made punishable by expulsion or suspension, where the acts are likely to injuriously affect the proper operation and conduct of the school, and such rules have been upheld by the courts where adjudged to be reasonable. Citation is unnecessary; a full enumeration of the cases may be found in the note to Kinzer v. Directors, etc. (129 Iowa, 441, 105 N.W. 686, 3 L.R.A.[N.S.] 496), in 6 Ann.Cas. 998. The two cases cited by plaintiff, as particularly supporting his contention that the power of school authorities over the acts of pupils ends when they had passed within the curtilage of the parental abode, are concerned respectively with prohibitions of joining Greek letter secret societies, and refusing to wear a khaki uniform. In Mechem on Public Officers, § 730, the law is summarized in accordance with the decided weight of authority as follows:

> "The authority of the teacher is not confined to the school room or grounds, but he may prohibit and punish all acts of his pupils which are detrimental to the good order and best interests of the school, whether such acts are committed in school hours or while the pupil is on his way to or from school or after he has returned home."

Examination of the authorities clearly reveals the true test of the teacher's right and jurisdiction to punish for offenses not committed on the school property or going and returning therefrom, but after the return of the pupil to the parental abode, to be not the time or place of the offense, but its effect upon the morale and efficiency of the school, whether it in fact is detrimental to its good order, and to the welfare and advancement of the pupils therein. If the conduct punished is detrimental to the best interests of the school, it is punishable, and in the instant case, under the rules of the school board, by corporal infliction. The effect of the rule claimed by the plaintiff, if applied, would result in a serious loss of discipline in school, and possible harm to innocent pupils in attendance. Supposing that some strong-armed juvenile bully attending school lived upon the next block and sought for a brief moment the asylum of his home, and thence sallied forth and beat, abused, and terrorized his fellow pupils as they pass by returning home; then by the claim urged by plaintiff he would be immune from punishment by the school authorities, while if he began his assaults before he had passed within the bounds of his own front yard he would be liable to proper punishment for any harm done. Now the harm done to the morale of the school is the same. The injured and frightened pupils are dismayed and discouraged in going to and coming from the school, and demoralized while in attendance. It will not do to say, as plaintiff's counsel argue, that the proper resort to correct such an abuse is the parents of such offenders, or the public prosecutors. Some parents would dismiss the matter by saying that they could give no attention to children's quarrels; many would champion their children as being all right in their conduct. The public authorities would very properly say, unless the offense resulted in quite serious injury, that such affrays were too trifling to deserve their attention. Yet the harm to the school has been done, and its proper conduct and operation seriously harmed, by such acts. Correction will usually be sought in vain at the hands of parents; it can only be successfully applied by the teacher. It is not likely that any milder punishment than corporal infliction would act as a deterrent in cases like the present. The abuse of little girls by young bullies is a base and brutal offense.

In the instant case it will be observed that while the plaintiff had reached his home after school, his victims had not. This is an important fact, even if the rule claimed by plaintiff should be upheld as a general statement. The claim made in argument that the small girls who were abused were trespassers upon the property of plaintiff's mother is of no avail. There is nothing in the record to show that plaintiff was acting under direction of his mother, and even if he were, such conduct as the court has found to exist would not be lawful.

There is no error.

The other Judges concurred.

NOTES

1. In the case of Jones v. Cody, 132 Mich. 13, 92 N.W. 495, 62 L.R.A. 160 (1902), a principal enforced a requirement that pupils go directly home after school. A local storekeeper refused to allow the principal to enter her store to send some of the loitering pupils home. The principal then required strict adherence to his rule and the storekeeper sued the principal for loss of profits. The Court upheld the rule and indicated that it was not only the right, but the duty of the school to see that children went directly home from school. The Court reasoned that if the child did not reach home when scheduled, his parents would be put on notice and would go looking for him, thereby affording greater protection for the safety and well being of the child.

2. A Georgia court refused to enjoin enforcement of a rule prohibiting pupils from attending any movie, show, or social on any night except Friday or Saturday. See Mangum v. Keith, 147 Ga. 603, 95 S.E. 1 (1918).

3. Would a rule prohibiting pupils from attending movies or other social functions on school nights be upheld by courts today? In this regard, what limitations may be imposed on school officials today? Does such a rule grant too much authority to school officials?

4. *In loco parentis* was defined by a Nebraska court as follows: "general education and control of pupils who attend public schools are in the hands of school boards, superintendents, principals and teachers. This control extends to health, proper surroundings, necessary discipline, promotion of morality and other wholesome influences, while parental authority is temporarily superceded." Richardson v. Braham, 125 Neb. 142, 249 N.W. 557 (1933).

*Cruel and Unusual Punishment Clause of Eighth Amendment
Does Not Apply to Corporal Punishment in Schools*

INGRAHAM v. WRIGHT

Supreme Court of the United States, 1977.
430 U.S. 651, 97 S.Ct. 1401.

Mr. Justice POWELL delivered the opinion of the Court.

This case presents questions concerning the use of corporal punishment in public schools: first, whether the paddling of students as a means of maintaining school discipline constitutes cruel and unusual punishment in violation of the Eighth Amendment; and second, to the extent that paddling is constitutionally permissible, whether the Due Process Clause of the Fourteenth Amendment requires prior notice and an opportunity to be heard.

* * *

Petitioners' evidence may be summarized briefly. In the 1970–1971 school year many of the 237 schools in Dade County used corporal punishment as a means of maintaining discipline pursuant to Florida legislation and a local school board regulation. The statute then in effect authorized limited corporal punishment by negative inference, proscribing punishment which was "degrading or unduly severe" or which was inflicted without prior consultation with the principal or the teacher in charge of the school. The regulation, * * * contained explicit directions and limitations. * * *

Petitioners focused on Drew Junior High School, the school in which both Ingraham and Andrews were enrolled in the fall of 1970. In an apparent reference to Drew, the District Court found that "[t]he instances of punishment which could be characterized as severe, accepting the students' testimony as credible, took place in one junior high school." * * *

The District Court made no findings on the credibility of the students' testimony. Rather, assuming their testimony to be credible, the court found no constitutional basis for relief. * * *

A panel of the Court of Appeals voted to reverse. * * * Upon rehearing, the en banc court rejected these conclusions and affirmed the judgment of the District Court. * * *

* * *

II

In addressing the scope of the Eighth Amendment's prohibition on cruel and unusual punishment this Court has found it useful to refer to "[t]raditional common law concepts," * * * and to the "attitude[s] which our society has traditionally taken." * * * So too, in defining the requirements of procedural due process under the Fifth and Fourteenth Amendments, the Court has been attuned to what "has always been the law of the land," * * * and to "traditional ideas of fair procedure." * * * We therefore begin by examining the way in which our traditions and our laws have responded to the use of corporal punishment in public schools.

The use of corporal punishment in this country as a means of disciplining school children dates back to the colonial period. It has survived the transformation of primary and secondary education from the colonials' reliance on optional private arrangements to our present system of compulsory education and dependence on public schools. Despite the general abandonment of corporal punishment as a means of punishing criminal offenders, the practice continues to play a role in the public education of school children in most parts of the country. Professional and public opinion is sharply divided on the practice, and has been for more than a century. Yet we can discern no trend toward its elimination.

At common law a single principle has governed the use of corporal punishment since before the American Revolution: teachers may impose reasonable but not excessive force to discipline a child. * * * The basic doctrine has not changed. The prevalent rule in this country today privileges such force as a teacher or administrator "reasonably believes to be necessary for [the child's] proper control, training, or education." * * * To the extent that the force is excessive or unreasonable, the educator in virtually all States is subject to possible civil and criminal liability.

Although the early cases viewed the authority of the teacher as deriving from the parents, the concept of parental delegation has been replaced by the view—more consonant with compulsory education laws—that the State itself may impose such corporal punishment as is reasonably necessary "for the proper education of the child and for the maintenance of group discipline." * * * All of the circumstances are to be taken into account in determining whether the punishment is reasonable in a particular case. Among the most important considerations are the seriousness of the offense, the attitude and past behavior of the child, the nature and severity of the punishment, the age and strength of the child, and the availability of less severe but equally effective means of discipline. * * *

Of the 23 States that have addressed the problem through legislation, 21 have authorized the moderate use of corporal punishment in public schools. Of these States only a few have elaborated on the common law test of reasonableness, typically providing for approval or notification of the child's parents, or for infliction of punishment only by the principal or in the presence of an adult witness. Only two States, Massachusetts and New Jersey, have prohibited all corporal punishment in their public schools. Where the legislatures have not acted, the state courts have uniformly preserved the common law rule permitting teachers to use reasonable force in disciplining children in their charge.

Against this background of historical and contemporary approval of reasonable corporal punishment, we turn to the constitutional questions before us.

III

The Eighth Amendment provides, "Excessive bail shall not be required, nor excessive fines imposed, nor cruel and unusual punishments inflicted." Bail, fines and punishment traditionally have been associated with the criminal process, and by subjecting the three to parallel limitations the text of the Amendment suggests an intention to limit the power of those entrusted with the criminal law function of government. An examination of the history of the Amendment and the decisions of this Court construing the proscription against cruel and unusual punishment confirms that it was designed to protect those convicted of crimes. We adhere to this longstanding limitation and hold that the Eighth Amendment does not apply to the paddling of children as a means of maintaining discipline in public schools.

A

The history of the Eighth Amendment is well known. The text was taken, almost verbatim, from a provision of the Virginia Declaration of Rights of 1776, which in turn derived from the English Bill of Rights of 1689. The English version, adopted after the accession of William and Mary, was intended to curb the excesses of English judges under the reign of James II. * * *

      * * *

At the time of its ratification, the original Constitution was criticized in the Massachusetts and Virginia Conventions for its failure to provide any protection for persons convicted of crimes. This criticism provided the impetus for inclusion of the Eighth Amendment in the Bill of Rights. * * *

B

In light of this history, it is not surprising to find that every decision of this Court considering whether a punishment is "cruel and unusual" within the meaning of the Eighth and Fourteenth Amendments has dealt with a criminal punishment. * * *

      * * *

In the few cases where the Court has had occasion to confront claims that impositions outside the criminal process constituted cruel and unusual punishment, it has had no difficulty finding the Eighth Amendment inapplicable. * * *

C

Petitioners acknowledge that the original design of the Cruel and Unusual Punishments Clause was to limit criminal punishments, but urge nonetheless that the prohibition should be extended to ban the paddling of school children. Observing that the Framers of the Eighth Amendment could not have envisioned our present system of public and compulsory education, with its opportunities for noncriminal punishments, petitioners contend that extension of the prohibition against cruel punishments is necessary lest we afford greater protection to criminals than to school children. It would be anomalous, they say, if schoolchildren could be beaten without constitutional redress, while hardened criminals suffering the same beatings at the hands of their jailors might have a valid claim under the Eighth Amendment. * * * Whatever force this logic may have in other settings, we find it an inadequate basis for wrenching the Eighth Amendment from its historical context and extending it to traditional disciplinary practices in the public schools.

The prisoner and the schoolchild stand in wholly different circumstances, separated by the harsh facts of criminal conviction and incarceration. * * *

The schoolchild has little need for the protection of the Eighth Amendment. Though attendance may not always be voluntary, the public school remains an open institution. Except perhaps when very young, the child is not physically restrained from leaving school during school hours; and at the end of the school day, the child is invariably free to return home. Even while at school, the child brings with him the support of family and friends and is rarely apart from teachers and other pupils who may witness and protest any instances of mistreatment.

The openness of the public school and its supervision by the community afford significant safeguards against the kinds of abuses from which the Eighth Amendment protects the prisoner. In virtually every community where corporal punishment is permitted in the schools, these safeguards are reinforced by the legal constraints of the common law. Public school teachers and administrators are privileged at common law to inflict only such corporal punishment as is reasonably necessary for the proper education and discipline of the child; any punishment going beyond the privilege may result in both civil and criminal liability. * * * As long as the schools are open to public scrutiny, there is no reason to believe that the common law constraints will not effectively remedy and deter excesses such as those alleged in this case.

We conclude that when public school teachers or administrators impose disciplinary corporal punishment, the Eight Amendment is inapplicable. The pertinent constitutional question is whether the imposition is consonant with the requirements of due process.

IV

The Fourteenth Amendment prohibits any State deprivation of life, liberty or property without due process of law. Application of this prohibition requires the familiar two-stage analysis: we must first ask whether the asserted individual interests are encompassed within the Fourteenth Amendment's protection of "life, liberty or property"; if protected interests are implicated, we then must decide what procedures constitute "due process of law." * * * Following that analysis here, we find that corporal punishment in public school implicates a constitutionally protected liberty interest, but we hold that the traditional common law remedies are fully adequate to afford due process.

A

"[T]he range of interests protected by procedural due process is not infinite." * * *

* * * Among the historic liberties so protected was a right to be free from and to obtain judicial relief, for unjustified intrusions on personal security.

While the contours of this historic liberty interest in the context of our federal system of government have not been defined precisely, they always have been thought to encompass freedom from bodily restraint and punishment. * * * It is fundamental that the state cannot hold and physically punish an individual except in accordance with due process of law.

This constitutionally protected liberty interest is at stake in this case. There is, of course a *de minimis* level of imposition with which the Constitution is not concerned. But at least where school authorities, acting under color of state law, deliberately decide to punish a child for misconduct by restaining the child and inflicting appreciable physical pain, we hold that Fourteenth Amendment liberty interests are implicated.

B

"[T]he question remains what process is due." * * * Were it not for the common law privilege permitting teachers, to inflict reasonable corporal punishment on children in their care, and the availability of the traditional remedies for abuse, the case for requiring advance procedural safeguards would be strong indeed. But here we deal with a punishment—paddling—within that tradition, and the question is whether the common law remedies are adequate to afford due process. * * * Whether in this case the common law remedies for excessive corporal punishment constitute due process of law must turn on an analysis of the competing interests at stake, viewed against the background of "history, reason, [and] the past course of decisions." The analysis requires consideration of three distinct factors: "first, the private interest that will be affected * * * ; second, the risk of an erroneous deprivation of such interest * * * and the probable value, if any, of additional or substitute procedural safeguards; and, finally, the [state] interest, including the function involved and the fiscal and administrative burdens that the additional or substitute procedural requirement would entail." * * *

1

Because it is rooted in history, the child's liberty interest in avoiding corporal punishment while in the care of public school authorities is subject to historical limitations. * * *

The concept that reasonable corporal punishment in school is justifiable continues to be recognized in the laws of most States. * * * It represents "the balance struck by this country," * * * between the child's interest in personal security and the traditional view that some limited corporal punishment may be necessary in the course of a child's education. Under that longstanding accommodation of interests, there can be no deprivation of substantive rights as long as disciplinary corporal punishment is within the limits of the common law privilege.

This is not to say that the child's interest in procedural safeguards is insubstantial. The school disciplinary process is not "a totally accurate, unerring process, never mistaken and never unfair. * * *." * * * In any deliberate infliction of corporal punishment on a child who is restrained for that purpose, there is some risk that the intrusion on the child's liberty will be unjustified and therefore unlawful. In these circumstances the child has a strong interest in procedural safeguards that minimize the risk of wrongful punishment and provide for the resolution of disputed questions of justification.

We turn now to a consideration of the safeguards that are available under applicable Florida law.

2

Florida has continued to recognize, and indeed has strengthened by statute, the common law right of a child not to be subjected to excessive corporal punishment in school. Under Florida law the teacher and principal of the school decide in the first instance whether corporal punishment is reasonably necessary under the circumstances in order to discipline a child who has misbehaved. But they must exercise prudence and restraint. For Florida has preserved the traditional judicial proceedings for determining whether the punishment was justified. If the punishment inflicted is later found to have been excessive—not reasonably believed at the time to be necessary for the child's discipline or training—the school authorities inflicting it may be held liable in damages to the child and, if malice is shown, they may be subject to criminal penalties.

Although students have testified in this case to specific instances of abuse, there is every reason to believe that such mistreatment is an aberration. The uncontradicted evidence suggests that corporal punishment in the Dade County schools was, "[w]ith the exception of a few cases, * * * unremarkable in physical severity." Moreover, because paddlings are usually inflicted in response to conduct directly observed by teachers in their presence, the risk that a child will be paddled without cause is typically insignificant. In the ordinary case, a disciplinary paddling neither threatens seriously to violate any substantive rights nor condemns the child "to suffer grievous loss of any kind." * * *

In those cases where severe punishment is contemplated, the available civil and criminal sanctions for abuse—considered in light of the openness of the school environment—afford significant protection against unjustified corporal punishment. See, p. 1412, supra. Teachers and school authorities are unlikely to inflict corporal punishment unnecessarily or excessively when a possible consequence of doing so is the institution of civil or criminal proceedings against them.

* * *

3

But even if the need for advance procedural safeguards were clear, the question would remain whether the incremental benefit could justify the cost. Acceptance of petitioners' claims would work a transformation in the law governing corporal punishment in Florida and most other States. Given the impracticability of formulating a rule of procedural due process that varies with the severity of the particular imposition, the prior hearing petitioners seek would have to precede *any* paddling, however moderate or trivial.

Such a universal constitutional requirement would significantly burden the use of corporal punishment as a disciplinary measure. Hearings—even informal hearings—require time, personnel, and a diversion of attention from normal school pursuits. * * *

Elimination or curtailment of corporal punishment would be welcomed by many as a societal advance. But when such a policy choice may result from this Court's determination of an asserted right to due process, rather than from the normal processes of community debate and legislative action, the societal costs cannot be dismissed as insubstantial. * * * In view of the low incidence of abuse, the openness of our schools, and the common law safeguards that already exist, the risk of error that may result in violation of a schoolchild's substantive rights can only be regarded as minimal. Imposing additional administrative safeguards as a constitutional requirement might reduce that risk marginally, but would also entail a significant intrusion into an area of primary educational responsibility. <u>We conclude that the Due Process Clause does not require notice and a hearing prior to the imposition of corporal punishment in the public schools as that practice is authorized and limited by the common law.</u>

* * *

NOTES

1. In a Texas case a teacher whipped a pupil with a switch for fighting after school; the court held that the fact that the fighting occurred after school did not deprive the teacher of his legal right to punish the pupil. Hutton v. State, 23 Tex.App. 386, 5 S.W. 122 (1887).

The court stated:

The authority of the teacher is not confined to the school room or grounds, but he may prohibit and punish all acts of his pupils which are detrimental to the good order and best interests of the school, whether such acts are committed in school hours or while the pupil is on his way to or from school or after he has returned home.

2. In a New York case where a teacher was accused of being malicious in the punishment of a boy the teacher had been assigned to see that the pupils who were not taking part in class-day assembly should leave the school premises. One boy refused to leave; he had a record of bad behavior and he had been drinking. The boy used profane language when the teacher insisted that he leave. The teacher put his hands on the throat of the boy and either pushed or threw him over a hedge. The boy accused the teacher of assault and battery. The court ruled for the teacher and stated:

* * * people will differ as to what force is reasonable in manner and moderate in degree. Taking into consideration the prior conduct of the complainant, the lack of malice on the part of the defendant, the nature of the offense of the pupil, his motive, the effect of his conduct on other pupils, and his size and strength, I find and decide that the guilt of the defendant has not been proved beyond a reasonable doubt. People ex rel. Hogan v. Newton, 185 Misc. 405, 56 N.Y.S.2d 779 (1945).

3. <u>The past behavior of the pupil is an important factor in determining what is reasonable behavior</u>. In a New York case a pupil was punished by the school principal and the principal was indicted for criminal assault. The boy had dropped a book from a balcony to the seats of an auditorium. The lower court ruled for the pupil but the appellate court reversed the decision saying that <u>reports of the pupil's prior misbehavior should have been considered in deciding the reasonableness of the punishment</u>. People v. Mummert, 183 Misc. 243, 50 N.Y.S.2d 699 (1944).

4. Two cases that demonstrate excessive punishment were decided by courts of Arkansas and Connecticut. In the Arkansas case a teacher whipped a fifteen-year-old boy twice in the same day, with a paddle made of flooring, against the orders of the school board. The boy was whipped the first time for not repeating a riddle from a newspaper and the second time for throwing a paper wad. The punishment bruised the boy and the court

held the punishment was excessive. Berry v. Arnold School Dist., 199 Ark. 1118, 137 S.W.2d 256 (1940). In a Connecticut case a principal was accused of using unreasonable force on a small boy who struggled as the principal was dragging him to the school office. The principal threw the boy to the floor and sat on him. The court held that the principal had used unreasonable force and the boy had a right to resist such treatment in self-protection. Calway v. Williamson, 130 Conn. 575, 36 A.2d 377 (1944).

5. An example of excessive and unreasonable punishment by a teacher is also illustrated by an 1872 Kentucky case. In this case a teacher was taking part in a playground activity with the pupils and one pupil differed with the opinion of the teacher on a trivial matter. The teacher in turn beat the boy. The court said:

The authority of a teacher to hold his pupil to strict accountability in school for disorderly behavior did not justify him in assaulting and beating the pupil on the playground. Hardy v. James, 5 Ky. 36 (1872).

6. The courts have refused to uphold punishment of children for negligent or careless destroying of school property. The Supreme Court of Indiana has held that a "* * * teacher has the right to exact from pupils obedience to his lawful and reasonable demands and rules, and to punish for disobedience * * *," but the teacher may be found guilty of assault and battery when he attempts to enforce by chastisement a rule which requires pupils to "pay for wanton and careless destruction of school property." The court stated further: "Carelessness on the part of children is one of the most common, and yet one of the least blameworthy, of their faults. In simple carelessness there is no purpose to do wrong. To punish a child for carelessness, in any case, is to punish it when it has no purpose or intent to do wrong or violate rules. But beyond this no rule is reasonable which requires of the pupils what they cannot do. The vast majority of pupils, whether small or large, have no money at their command with which to pay for school property which they injure or destroy by carelessness or otherwise. If required to pay for such property, they would have to look to their parents or guardians for the money. If the parent or guardian should not have the money, or if they should refuse to give it to the child, the child would be left subject to punishment for not having done what it had no power to do." State v. Vanderbilt, 116 Ind. 11, 18 N.E. 266 (1888).

7. In an Indiana case involving corporal punishment, Judge Arterburn wrote a concurring opinion which suggests that a teacher has an inherent right to administer corporal punishment and cannot be deprived of this right by school board regulation. The judge said:

"A teacher, and a parent, have not only the right but the obligation to discipline a child, if necessary using corporal punishment, for the good of such child, as well as the protection of third parties offended or injured by the actions of such child. The failure to exercise such disciplinary action where the occasion requires it, is condemned by the law as much as an excessive and cruel punishment beyond requirements.

"In this case the teacher was confronted with an arrogant and impudent child interrupting classroom exercise by violent and abusive remarks towards the teacher. The medical testimony was un-

contradicted that this pupil had the mentality to know and understand her wrong-doing and to control it. The teacher had the duty
of protecting the interests of the remaining members of the class
from interruption and at the same time maintain order and respect
for authority among the children. A teacher has no choice in an
orderly society but to exercise physical force in stopping and removing the recalcitrant pupil and inflicting corporal punishment,
not only to the offending child for its benefit, but as an example to
the other pupils. Such matters may not be delayed until there is
time to talk and 'reason' with the pupil. Consideration has to be
given to the remaining pupils in the class where the incident occurred.

"I might further add that I have serious doubts that a teacher
confronted with such a situation and responsibility under the law
for maintaining order and a respect for authority before a classroom of pupils, can be deprived by a 'rule' of the right to use physical force to eliminate such a disturbance. As long as teachers or
parents are obligated under the law to educate, teach and train
children, they may not be denied the necessary means of carrying
out their responsibility as such teachers or parents." Indiana
State Personnel Board v. Jackson, 244 Ind. 321, 192 N.E.2d 740
(1963).

8. *Withholding Diploma.* It is within the sound judgment of school
authorities to determine if and when a pupil has completed the prescribed
courses entitling him to a diploma. However, there is no direct relationship
between participation in a graduation exercise and the issuance of a diploma. Once the pupil has completed successfully all of the required courses, the issuance of a diploma is a ministerial act which the school officials
must perform. Refusal of a pupil to perform some act which is not a part
of curriculum nor is required by school regulation prior to graduation will
not justify withholding of the diploma.

In a 1921 case where a student's refusal to wear a cap and gown to
graduation resulted in the board's withholding the pupils diploma, the court
mandated that the diploma be granted and stated:

A diploma, therefore, is *prima facie* evidence of educational worth,
and is the goal of the matriculate. * * * The issuance of a diploma by the school board to a pupil who satisfactorily completes
the prescribed course of study and who is otherwise qualified is
mandatory, and, although such duty is not expressly enjoined upon
the board by statute, it does arise by necessary and reasonable implication. * * * This Plaintiff, * * *, having complied
with all the rules and regulations precedent to graduation, may not
be denied her diploma by the arbitrary action of the school board
subsequent to her being made the recipient of the honors of graduation. Valentine v. Independent School Dist. of Casey, 191 Iowa
1100, 183 N.W. 434 (1921).

9. Ryan v. Board of Educ., 124 Kan. 89, 257 P. 945 (1927), concerned
a pupil who was accused of cheating on a final examination and thereby deprived of a diploma. Did the Court order the diploma issued when it decid-

ed that the evidence did not support the contention that the pupil had been guilty of cheating?

Constitutional Due Process

Each state has not only the duty, but also the responsibility to provide for the health, safety, and general welfare of its people. This we call the state's police power.

As pointed out elsewhere in this book, the Fourteenth Amendment to the Federal Constitution provides that no state shall deprive a person of his life, liberty or property without due process of law. Stated positively, a state may deprive a person of his life, liberty or property so long as the individual is given due process.

There are two types of due process. One is called procedural due process. This means that if an individual is to be deprived of his life, liberty, or property, a prescribed Constitutional procedure must be followed. The Supreme Court of the United States has said that in order to give an individual procedural due process as required by the Federal Constitution, three basic factors must be present. The individual must have proper notice that he is about to be deprived of his life, liberty, or property; he must be given an opportunity to be heard; and the hearing must be conducted fairly.

A second type of due process is called substantive due process. To satisfy this Constitutional requirement, if a state is going to deprive a person of his life, liberty, or property, the state must have a valid objective and the means used must be reasonably calculated to achieve the objective. Early interpretations by the U.S. Supreme Court recognized only the procedural aspects of due process of law.[7] It was not until 1923 that the Supreme Court defined due process of law as possessing "substantive" protections.[8]

Substantive Due Process

In that same year in Meyer v. Nebraska,[9] the Supreme Court related substantive protection of the due process clause of the Fourteenth Amendment to education when it held unconstitutional a Nebraska statute forbidding the teaching in public or private schools of foreign languages to pupils below the eighth grade. Since the U.S. Constitution provided no express relief for offending the statute, the Court, therefore, extended the due process clause to protect the teacher. The court related the teacher's right to teach to an expanded substantive interpretation of "liberty" and said:

> The problem for our determination is whether the statute as construed and applied unreasonably infringes the liberty

7. Hurtado v. California, 110 U.S. 516, 4 S.Ct. 111 (1884).

8. Adkins v. Children's Hospital, 261 U.S. 525, 43 S.Ct. 394 (1923).

9. 262 U.S. 390, 43 S.Ct. 625 (1923); See Pierce v. Society of Sisters, 268 U.S. 510, 45 S.Ct. 571 (1925).

guaranteed to the Plaintiff in error by the Fourteenth Amendment. 'No state shall * * * deprive any person of life, liberty, or property, without due process of law.'

While this court has not attempted to define with exactness the liberty thus guaranteed, the term has received much consideration and some of the included things have been definitely stated. Without doubt, it denotes not merely freedom from bodily restraint but also the right of the individual to contract, to engage in any of the common occupations of life, to acquire useful knowledge, to marry, establish a home and bring up children, to worship God according to the dictates of his own conscience, and generally to enjoy those privileges long recognized at common law as essential to the orderly pursuit of happiness by free men * * * The established doctrine is that this liberty may not be interfered with, under the guise of protecting the public interest, by legislative action which is arbitrary or without reasonable relation to some purpose within the competency of the State to effect.

* * * His [the teacher's] right thus to teach and the right of parents to engage him so to instruct their children, we think, are within the liberty of the Amendment.[10]

With this decision, the Supreme Court not only acknowledged the substantive protections of due process covering life, liberty and property but clearly extended them to protect a person's right of education,[11] travel,[12] and appearance.[13] Substantive due process rights generally encompass the First Amendment freedoms of religion, speech, press and assembly.

Procedural Due Process

Constitutional guarantees of procedural due process were originally assumed to be only applicable to proceedings of the judicial branch of government, i. e., a person's right to a trial by jury. However, in recent years the courts have made it abundantly clear that procedural due process is not confined to the courts but must also be afforded to individuals by administrative agencies, such as public schools, when the potential loss of a fundamental right is at stake. In other words, when a school district seeks to take action against a student which may permanently impair the student's education, then

10. Ibid.

11. Meyer v. Nebraska, supra; Pierce v. Society of Sisters, supra.

12. Ken v. Dulles, 357 U.S. 116, 78 S. Ct. 1113 (1958); United States v. Guest, 383 U.S. 745, 86 S.Ct. 1170

(1966); Shapiro v. Thompson, 394 U.S. 618, 89 S.Ct. 1322 (1969).

13. Richards v. Thurston, 424 F.2d 1281 (1st Cir. 1970); Breen v. Kahl, 296 F. Supp. 702 (D.C.Wis.1969), aff'd 419 F.2d 1034 (7th Cir. 1969), cert. denied 398 U.S. 937, 90 S.Ct. 1836.

certain due process procedures must be followed. In Soglin v. Kauffman,[14] the court said the point at which disciplinary actions should be subject to constitutional scrutiny is when the action involves suspension "for any period of time substantial enough to prevent one from obtaining credit for a particular term."

Care should be taken by the school administrator to provide the student with fair treatment under any circumstances. The circumstances and the interests of the parties involved are paramount in prescribing the standards of procedural due process.[15] The U.S. Supreme Court has said:

> Due process unlike some legal rules is not a technical conception with a fixed content, unrelated to time, place and circumstances * * * It is a delicate process of adjustment inescapably involving the exercise of judgment by those whom the Constitution entrusted the unfolding of its process.[16]

In providing procedural due process, the courts are not uniform in their requirements, but all insist that fundamental fairness must be afforded and "both sides must be given an opportunity to present their sides of the story in detail." [17]

In Due v. Florida A. & M. University,[18] the court outlined three minimal due process requirements.

> First, the student should be given adequate notice in writing of the specific ground or grounds and the nature of the evidence on which the disciplinary proceedings are based. Second, the student should be given an opportunity for a hearing in which the disciplinary authority provides a fair opportunity for hearing of the student's position, explanations and evidence. The third requirement is that no disciplinary action be taken on grounds which are not supported by any substantial evidence.

> Fundamental fairness prescribed in these early cases for long suspension or expulsion of students has been extended

---

14. 295 F.Supp. 978 (W.D.Wis.1968), aff'd 418 F.2d 163 (7th Cir. 1968).

15. Hobson v. Bailey, 309 F.Supp. 1393 (D.C.Tenn.1970); Zanders v. Louisiana State Bd. of Educ., 281 F.Supp. 747 (D.C.La.1968).

16. Joint Anti-Fascist Refugee Comm. v. McGrath, 341 U.S. 123, 71 S.Ct. 624 (1951) (concurring opinion of Justice Frankfurter).

17. Dixon v. Alabama State Bd. of Educ., 294 F.2d 150 (5th Cir. 1961),

cert. denied 368 U.S. 930, 82 S.Ct. 368. For an excellent discussion of procedural due process, see William G. Buss, "Procedural Due Process for School Discipline: Probing the Constitutional Outline," *University of Pennsylvania Law Review*, Vol. 119, pp. 545–641 (1971).

18. 233 F.Supp. 396 (D.C.Fla.1963).

to temporary, short-term suspensions by the U.S. Supreme Court.[19] The formality and intensity, though, of the procedural process is not fixed, the requirement being only that the process be commensurate with the length of suspension or the detriment which may be imposed on the student.

Procedural Due Process Required for Students

DIXON v. ALABAMA STATE BD. OF EDUC.

United States Court of Appeals, Fifth Circuit, 1961.
294 F.2d 150, cert. denied 368 U.S. 930, 82 S.Ct. 368.

RIVES, Circuit Judge. The question presented by the pleadings and evidence, and decisive of this appeal, is whether due process requires notice and some opportunity for hearing before students at a tax-supported college are expelled for misconduct. We answer that question in the affirmative.

The misconduct for which the students were expelled has never been definitely specified. Defendant Trenholm, the President of the College, testified that he did not know why the plaintiffs and three additional students were expelled and twenty other students were placed on probation. The notice of expulsion which Dr. Trenholm mailed to each of the plaintiffs assigned no specific ground for expulsion, but referred in general terms to "this problem of Alabama State College."

* * *

As shown by the findings of the district court * * * the only demonstration which the evidence showed that *all* of the expelled students took part in was that in the lunch grill located in the basement of the Montgomery County Courthouse. The other demonstrations were found to be attended "by several if not all of the plaintiffs." We have carefully read and studied the record, and agree with the district court that the evidence does not affirmatively show that *all* of the plaintiffs were present at any but the one demonstration.

* * * The most elaborate grounds for expulsion were assigned in the testimony of Governor Patterson:

"Q. There is an allegation in the complaint, Governor, that—I believe it is paragraph six, the defendants' action of expulsion was taken without regard to any valid rule or regulation concerning student conduct and merely retaliated against, punished, and sought to intimidate plaintiffs for having lawfully sought service in a publicly owned lunch room with service; is that statement true or false?

19. Goss v. Lopez, 419 U.S. 565, 95 S. Ct. 729 (1975).

"A. Well, that is not true; the action taken by the State Board of Education was—was taken to prevent—to prevent incidents happening by students at the College that would bring—bring discredit upon—upon the School and be prejudicial to the School, and the State—as I said before, the State Board of Education took—considered at the time it expelled these students several incidents, one at the Court House at the lunch room demonstration, the one the next day at the trial of this student, the marching on the steps of the State Capitol, and also this rally held at the church, where—where it was reported that—that statements were made against the administration of the School. In addition to that, the—the feeling going around in the community here due to—due to the reports of these incidents of the students, by the students, and due to reports of incidents occurring involving violence in other States, which happened prior to these things starting here in Alabama, all of these things were discussed by the State Board of Education prior to the taking of the action that they did on March 2 and as I was present and acting as Chairman, as a member of the Board, I voted to expel these students and to put these others on probation because I felt that that was what was in the best interest of the College. And the—I felt that the action should be—should be prompt and immediate, because if something—something had not been done, in my opinion, it would have resulted in violence and disorder, and that we wanted to prevent, and we felt that we had a duty to the—to the—to the parents of the students and to the State to require that the students behave themselves while they are attending a State College, and that is (sic) the reasons why we took the action that we did. That is all."

Superintendent of Education Stewart testified that he voted for expulsion because the students had broken rules and regulations pertaining to all of the State institutions * * *.

The evidence clearly shows that the question for decision does not concern the sufficiency of the notice or the adequacy of the hearing, but is whether the students had a right to any notice or hearing whatever before being expelled. * * * After careful study and consideration, we find ourselves unable to agree with the conclusion of the district court that no notice or opportunity for any kind of hearing was required before these students were expelled.

It is true, as the district court said, that " * * * there is no statute or rule that requires formal charges and/or a hearing * * * ," but the evidence is without dispute that the usual practice at Alabama State College had been to give a hearing and opportunity to offer defenses before expelling a student. * * *

Whenever a governmental body acts so as to injure an individual, the Constitution requires that the act be consonant with due process of law. The minimum procedural requirements necessary to satisfy due process depend upon the circumstances and the interests of the parties involved. * * *

The precise nature of the private interest involved in this case is the right to remain at a public institution of higher learning in which the plaintiffs were students in good standing. It requires no argument to demonstrate that education is vital and, indeed, basic to civilized society. Without sufficient education the plaintiffs would not be able to earn an adequate livelihood, to enjoy life to the fullest, or to fulfill as completely as possible the duties and responsibilities of good citizens.

There was no offer to prove that other colleges are open to the plaintiffs. If so, the plaintiffs would nonetheless be injured by the interruption of their course of studies in mid-term. It is most unlikely that a public college would accept a student expelled from another public college of the same state. Indeed, expulsion may well prejudice the student in completing his education at any other institution. Surely no one can question that the right to remain at the college in which the plaintiffs were students in good standing is an interest of extremely great value.

Turning then to the nature of the governmental power to expel the plaintiffs, it must be conceded, as was held by the district court, that that power is not unlimited and cannot be arbitrarily exercised. Admittedly, there must be some reasonable and constitutional ground for expulsion or the courts would have a duty to require reinstatement. The possibility of arbitrary action is not excluded by the existence of reasonable regulations. There may be arbitrary application of the rule to the facts of a particular case. Indeed, that result is well nigh inevitable when the Board hears only one side of the issue. In the disciplining of college students there are no considerations of immediate danger to the public, or of peril to the national security, which should prevent <u>the Board from exercising at least the fundamental principles of fairness by</u> giving the accused students notice of the charges and an opportunity to be heard in their own defense. Indeed, the example set by the Board in failing so to do, if not corrected by the courts, can well break the spirits of the expelled students and of others familiar with the injustice, and do inestimable harm to their education.

* * *

For the guidance of the parties in the event of further proceedings, we state our views on the nature of the notice and hearing required by due process prior to expulsion from a state college or university. They should, we think, comply with the following standards. The notice should contain a statement of the specific charges and grounds which, if proven, would justify expulsion under the regulations of the Board of Education. The nature of the hearing should vary depending upon the circumstances of the particular case. The case before us requires something more than an informal interview with an administrative authority of the college. By its nature, a charge of misconduct, as opposed to a failure to meet the scholastic standards of the college, depends upon a collection of the facts concerning the charged misconduct, easily colored by the point of view of the witnesses. In such circumstances, a hearing which gives the Board or the administrative authorities of the college an opportunity to hear both sides in considerable detail is best suited to protect the rights of all involved. This is not to imply that a full-dress judicial hearing, with the right to cross-examine witnesses, is required. Such a hearing, with the attending publicity and disturbance of college activities, might be detrimental to the college's educational atmosphere and impractical to carry out. Nevertheless, the rudiments of an adversary proceeding may be preserved without encroaching upon the interests of the college. In the instant case, the student should be given the names of the witnesses against him and an oral or written report on the facts to which each witness testifies. He should also be given the opportunity to present to the Board, or at least to an administrative official of the college, his own defense against the charges and to produce either oral testimony or written affidavits of witnesses in his behalf. If the hearing is not before the Board directly, the results and findings of the hearing should be presented in a report open to the student's inspection. If these rudimentary elements of fair play are followed in a case of misconduct of this particular type, we feel that the requirements of due process of law will have been fulfilled.

The judgment of the district court is reversed and the cause is remanded for further proceedings consistent with this opinion.

Reversed and remanded.

NOTES

1. *Standards for Procedural Due Process.* A joint committee comprised of representatives from the American Association of University Professors, U.S. National Student Association, Association of American Colleges, National Association of Student Personnel Administrators, and National Association of Women Deans and Counselors have drafted a Joint Statement on Rights and Freedoms of Students. This statement prescribes the following standards for providing students with procedural due process.

PROCEDURAL STANDARDS IN DISCIPLINARY PROCEEDINGS
* * *

The administration of discipline should guarantee procedural fairness to an accused student. Practices in disciplinary cases may vary in formality with the gravity of the offense and the sanctions which may be applied. They should also take into account the presence or absence of an honor code, and the degree to which the institutional officials have direct acquaintance with student life in general and with the involved student and the circumstances of the case in particular. The jurisdictions of faculty or student judicial bodies, the disciplinary responsibilities of institutional officials and the regular disciplinary procedures, including the student's right to appeal a decision, should be clearly formulated and communicated in advance. Minor penalties may be assessed informally under prescribed procedures.

In all situations, procedural fair play requires that the student be informed of the nature of the charges against him, that he be given a fair opportunity to refute them, that the institution not be arbitrary in its actions, and that there be provision for appeal of a decision. The following are recommended as proper safeguards in such proceedings when there are no honor codes offering comparable guarantees.

A. *Standards of Conduct Expected of Students*

The institution has an obligation to clarify those standards of behavior which it considers essential to its educational mission and its community life. These general behavioral expectations and the resultant specific regulations should represent a reasonable regulation of student conduct, but the student should be as free as possible from imposed limitations that have no direct relevance to his education. Offenses should be as clearly defined as possible and interpreted in a manner consistent with the aforementioned principles of relevancy and reasonableness. Disciplinary proceedings should be instituted only for violations of standards of conduct formulated with significant student participation and published in advance through such means as a student handbook or a generally available body of institutional regulations.

B. *Investigation of Student Conduct*

1. Except under extreme emergency circumstances, premises occupied by students and the personal possessions of students should not be searched unless appropriate authorization has been obtained. For premises such as residence halls controlled by the institution, an appropriate and responsible authority should be designated to whom application should be made before a search is conducted. The application should specify the reasons for the search and the objects or information sought. The student should be present, if possible, during the search. For premises not controlled by the institution, the ordinary requirements for lawful search should be followed.

2. Students detected or arrested in the course of serious violations of institutional regulations, or infractions of ordinary law, should be informed of their rights. No form of harassment should be used by institutional representatives to coerce admissions of guilt or information about conduct of other suspected persons.

C. *Status of Student Pending Final Action*

Pending action on the charges, the status of a student should not be altered, or his right to be present on the campus and to attend classes suspended, except for reasons relating to his physical or emotional safety and well-being, or for reasons relating to the safety and well-being of students, faculty, or university property.

D. *Hearing Committee Procedures*

When the misconduct may result in serious penalties and if the student questions the fairness of disciplinary action taken against him, he should be granted, on request, the privilege of a hearing before a regularly constituted hearing committee. The following suggested hearing committee procedures satisfy the requirements of procedural due process in situations requiring a high degree of formality.

1. The hearing committee should include faculty members or students, or, if regularly included or requested by the accused, both faculty and student members. No member of the hearing committee who is otherwise interested in the particular case should sit in judgment during the proceeding.

2. The student should be informed, in writing, of the reasons for the proposed disciplinary action with sufficient particularity, and in sufficient time, to insure opportunity to prepare for the hearing.

3. The student appearing before the hearing committee should have the right to be assisted in his defense by an adviser of his choice.

4. The burden of proof should rest upon the officials bringing the charge.

5. The student should be given an opportunity to testify and to present evidence and witnesses. He should have an opportunity to hear and question adverse witnesses. In no case should the committee consider statements against him unless he has been advised of their content and of the names of those who made them, and unless he has been given an opportunity to rebut unfavorable inferences which might otherwise be drawn.

6. All matters upon which the decision may be based must be introduced into evidence at the proceeding before the hearing committee. The decision should be based solely upon such matters. Improperly acquired evidence should not be admitted.

7. In the absence of a transcript, there should be both a digest and a verbatim record, such as a tape recording, of the hearing.

8. The decision of the hearing committee should be final, subject only to the student's right of appeal to the president or ultimately to the governing board of the institution.

Temporary Suspension Requires Procedural Due Process

GOSS v. LOPEZ

Supreme Court of the United States, 1975.
419 U.S. 565, 95 S.Ct. 729.

Mr. Justice WHITE delivered the opinion of the Court.

This appeal by various administrators of the Columbus, Ohio, Public School System (CPSS) challenges the judgment of a three-judge federal court, declaring that appellees—various high school students in the CPSS—were denied due process of law contrary to the command of the Fourteenth Amendment in that they were temporarily suspended from their high schools without a hearing either prior to suspension or within a reasonable time thereafter, and enjoining the administrators to remove all references to such suspensions from the students' records.

I

Ohio law, Rev.Code Ann. § 3313.64 (1972), provides for free education to all children between the ages of six and 21. Section 3313.66 of the Code empowers the principal of an Ohio public school to suspend a pupil for misconduct for up to 10 days or to expel him. In either case, he must notify the student's parents within 24 hours and state the reasons for his action. A pupil who is expelled, or his parents, may appeal the decision to the Board of Education and in connection therewith shall be permitted to be heard at the board meeting. The Board may reinstate the pupil following the hearing. No similar procedure is provided in § 3313.66 or any other provision of state law for a suspended student. Aside from a regulation tracking the statute, at the time of the imposition of the suspensions in this case the CPSS itself had not issued any written procedure applicable to suspensions. Nor, so far as the record reflects, had any of the individual high schools involved in this case. Each, however, had formally or informally described the conduct for which suspension could be imposed.

The nine named appellees, each of whom alleged that he or she had been suspended from public high school in Columbus for up to 10 days without a hearing pursuant to § 3313.66, filed an action under 42 U.S.C.A. § 1983 against the Columbus Board of Education and various administrators of the CPSS. The complaint sought a declaration that § 3313.66 was unconstitutional in that it permitted public school administrators to deprive plaintiffs of their rights to an education without a hearing of any kind, in violation of the procedural due process component of the Fourteenth Amendment. It also sought to enjoin the public school officials from issuing future suspensions pursuant to § 3313.66 and to require them to remove references to the past suspensions from the records of the students in question.

The proof below established that the suspensions arose out of a period of widespread student unrest in the CPSS during February and March 1971. Six of the named plaintiffs, Rudolph Sutton, Tyrone Washington, Susan Cooper, Deborah Fox, Clarence Byars, and Bruce Harris, were students at the Marion-Franklin High School and were each suspended for 10 days on account of disruptive or disobedient conduct committed in the presence of the school administrator who ordered the suspension. One of these, Tyrone Washington, was among a group of students demonstrating in the school auditorium while a class was being conducted there. He was ordered by the school principal to leave, refused to do so, and was suspended. Rudolph Sutton, in the presence of the principal, physically attacked a police officer who was attempting to remove Tyrone Washington from the auditorium. He was immediately suspended. The other four Marion-Franklin students were suspended for similar conduct. None was given a hearing to determine the operative facts underlying the suspension, but each, together with his or her parents, was offered the opportunity to attend a conference, subsequent to the effective date of the suspension, to discuss the student's future.

Two named plaintiffs, Dwight Lopez and Betty Crome, were students at the Central High School and McGuffey Junior High School, respectively. The former was suspended in connection with a disturbance in the lunchroom which involved some physical damage to school property. Lopez testified that at least 75 other students were suspended from his school on the same day. He also testified below that he was not a party to the destructive conduct but was instead an innocent bystander. Because no one from the school testified with regard to this incident, there is no evidence in the record indicating the official basis for concluding otherwise. Lopez never had a hearing.

Betty Crome was present at a demonstration at a high school other than the one she was attending. There she was arrested together with others, taken to the police station, and released without being formally charged. Before she went to school on the following day, she was notified that she had been suspended for a 10-day period. Because no one from the school testified with respect to this incident, the record does not disclose how the McGuffey Junior High School principal went about making the decision to suspend Crome, nor does it disclose on what information the decision was based. It is clear from the record that no hearing was ever held.

There was no testimony with respect to the suspension of the ninth named plaintiff, Carl Smith. The school files were also silent as to his suspension, although as to some, but not all, of the other named plaintiffs the files contained either direct references to their suspensions or copies of letters sent to their parents advising them of the suspension.

On the basis of this evidence, the three-judge court declared that plaintiffs were denied due process of law because they were "suspended without hearing prior to suspension or within a reasonable time thereafter," and that Ohio Rev.Code Ann. § 3313.66 (1972) and regulations issued pursuant thereto were unconstitutional in permitting such suspensions. It was ordered that all references to plaintiffs' suspensions be removed from school files.

Although not imposing upon the Ohio school administrators any particular disciplinary procedures and leaving them "free to adopt regulations providing for fair suspension procedures which are consonant with the educational goals of their schools and reflective of the characteristics of their school and locality," the District Court declared that there were "minimum requirements of notice and a hearing prior to suspension, except in emergency situations." In explication, the court stated that relevant case authority would: (1) permit "[i]mmediate removal of a student whose conduct disrupts the academic atmosphere of the school, endangers fellow students, teachers or school officials, or damages property"; (2) require notice of suspension proceedings to be sent to the students' parents within 24 hours of the decision to conduct them; and (3) require a hearing to be held, with the student present, within 72 hours of his removal. Finally, the court stated that, with respect to the nature of the hearing, the relevant cases required that statements in support of the charge be produced, that the student and others be permitted to make statements in defense or mitigation, and that the school need not permit attendance by counsel.

The defendant school administrators have appealed the three-judge court's decision. Because the order below granted plaintiffs' request for an injunction—ordering defendants to expunge their records—this Court has jurisdiction of the appeal pursuant to 28 U.S.C. A. § 1253. We affirm.

II

At the outset, appellants contend that because there is no constitutional right to an education at public expense, the Due Process Clause does not protect against expulsions from the public school system. This position misconceives the nature of the issue and is refuted by prior decisions. The Fourteenth Amendment forbids the State to deprive any person of life, liberty, or property without due process of law. Protected interests in property are normally "not created by the Constitution. Rather, they are created and their dimensions are defined" by an independent source such as state statutes or rules entitling the citizen to certain benefits. Board of Regents v. Roth, 408 U.S. 564, 577, 92 S.Ct. 2701, 2709, 33 L.Ed.2d 548 (1972).

* * *

The Due Process Clause also forbids arbitrary deprivations of liberty. "Where a person's good name, reputation, honor, or integrity is at stake because of what the government is doing to him," the minimal requirements of the Clause must be satisfied. Wisconsin v. Constantineau, 400 U.S. 433, 437, 91 S.Ct. 507, 510 (1971); Board of Regents v. Roth, supra, 408 U.S. at 573, 92 S.Ct. at 2707. School authorities here suspended appellees from school for periods of up to 10 days based on charges of misconduct. If sustained and recorded, those charges could seriously damage the students' standing with their fellow pupils and their teachers as well as interfere with later opportunities for higher education and employment. It is apparent that the claimed right of the State to determine unilaterally and without process whether that misconduct has occurred immediately collides with the requirements of the Constitution.

Appellants proceed to argue that even if there is a right to a public education protected by the Due Process Clause generally, the Clause comes into play only when the State subjects a student to a "severe detriment or grievous loss." The loss of 10 days, it is said, is neither severe nor grievous and the Due Process Clause is therefore of no relevance. Appellants' argument is again refuted by our prior decisions; for in determining "whether due process requirements apply in the first place, we must look not to the 'weight' but to the *nature* of the interest at stake." Board of Regents v. Roth, supra, at 570–571, 92 S.Ct. at 2705—2706. Appellees were excluded from school only temporarily, it is true, but the length and consequent severity of a deprivation, while another factor to weigh in determining the appropriate form of hearing, "is not decisive of the basic right" to a hearing of some kind. Fuentes v. Shevin, 407 U.S. 67, 86, 92 S.Ct. 1983, 1997 (1972). The Court's view has been that as long as a property deprivation is not *de minimis*, its gravity is irrelevant to the question whether account must be taken of the Due Process Clause. Sniadach v. Family Finance Corp., 395 U.S. 337, 342, 89 S.Ct. 1820, 1823 (1969) (Harlan, J., concurring); Boddie v. Connecticut, 401 U. S. 371, 378–379, 91 S.Ct. 780, 786 (1971); Board of Regents v. Roth, supra, 408 U.S., at 570 n. 8, 92 S.Ct., at 2705. A 10-day suspension from school is not *de minimis* in our view and may not be imposed in complete disregard of the Due Process Clause.

A short suspension is, of course, a far milder deprivation than expulsion. But, "education is perhaps the most important function of state and local governments," Brown v. Board of Education, 347 U.S. 483, 493, 74 S.Ct. 686, 691 (1954), and the total exclusion from the educational process for more than a trivial period, and certainly if the suspension is for 10 days, is a serious event in the life of the suspended child. Neither the property interest in educational benefits temporarily denied nor the liberty interest in reputation, which is also implicated, is so insubstantial that suspensions may constitutionally be imposed by any procedure the school chooses, no matter how arbitrary.

* * *

There are certain bench marks to guide us, however, Mullane v. Central Hanover Trust Co., 339 U.S. 306, 70 S.Ct. 652 (1950), a case often invoked by later opinions, said that "[m]any controversies have raged about the cryptic and abstract words of the Due Process Clause but there can be no doubt that at a minimum they require that deprivation of life, liberty or property by adjudication be preceded by notice and opportunity for hearing appropriate to the nature of the case." Id., at 313, 70 S.Ct. at 657. "The fundamental requisite of due process of law is the opportunity to be heard," Grannis v. Ordean, 234 U.S. 385, 394, 34 S.Ct. 779, 783 (1914), a right that "has little reality or worth unless one is informed that the matter is pending and can choose for himself whether to * * * contest." Mullane v. Central Hanover Trust Co., supra, 339 U.S. at 314, 70 S.Ct. at 657. At the very minimum, therefore, students facing suspension and the consequent interference with a protected property interest must be given *some* kind of notice and afforded *some* kind of hearing.

"Parties whose rights are to be affected are entitled to be heard; and in order that they may enjoy that right they must first be notified." Baldwin v. Hale, 1 Wall. 223, 233 (1864).

It also appears from our cases that the timing and content of the notice and the nature of the hearing will depend on appropriate accommodation of the competing interests involved. Cafeteria Workers v. McElroy, supra, 367 U.S. at 895, 81 S.Ct. at 1748; Morrissey v. Brewer, supra, 408 U.S. at 481, 92 S.Ct. at 2600. The student's interest is to avoid unfair or mistaken exclusion from the educational process, with all of its unfortunate consequences. The Due Process Clause will not shield him from suspensions properly imposed, but it disserves both his interest and the interest of the State if his suspension is in fact unwarranted. The concern would be mostly academic if the disciplinary process were a totally accurate, unerring process, never mistaken and never unfair. Unfortunately, that is not the case, and no one suggests that it is. Disciplinarians, although proceeding in utmost good faith, frequently act on the reports and advice of others; and the controlling facts and the nature of the conduct under challenge are often disputed. The risk of error is not at all trivial, and it should be guarded against if that may be done without prohibitive cost or interference with the educational process.

The difficulty is that our schools are vast and complex. Some modicum of discipline and order is essential if the educational function is to be performed. Events calling for discipline are frequent occurrences and sometimes require immediate, effective action. Suspension is considered not only to be a necessary tool to maintain order but a valuable educational device. The prospect of imposing elaborate hearing requirements in every suspension case is viewed with great concern, and many school authorities may well prefer the untrammeled power to act unilaterally, unhampered by rules about notice and hearing. But it would be a strange disciplinary system in an educational institution if no communication was sought by the disciplinarian with the student in an effort to inform him of his dereliction and to let him tell his side of the story in order to make sure that an injustice is not done. "[F]airness can rarely be obtained by secret, one-sided determination of facts decisive of rights. * * *" "Secrecy is not congenial to truth-seeking and self-righteousness gives too slender an assurance of rightness. No better instrument has been devised for arriving at truth than to give a person in jeopardy of serious loss notice of the case against him and opportunity to meet it." * * *

We do not believe that school authorities must be totally free from notice and hearing requirements if their schools are to operate with acceptable efficiency. Students facing temporary suspension have interests qualifying for protection of the Due Process Clause, and due process requires, in connection with a suspension of 10 days or less, that the student be given oral or written notice of the charges against him and, if he denies them, an explanation of the evidence the authorities have and an opportunity to present his side of the story. The Clause requires at least these rudimentary precautions against unfair or mistaken findings of misconduct and arbitrary exclusion from school.

There need be no delay between the time "notice" is given and the time of the hearing. In the great majority of cases the disciplinarian may informally discuss the alleged misconduct with the student minutes after it has occurred. We hold only that, in being given an opportunity to explain his version of the facts at this discussion, the student first be told what he is accused of doing and what the basis of the accusation is. Lower courts which have addressed the question of the *nature* of the procedures required in short suspension cases have reached the same conclusion. Tate v. Board of Education, 453 F.2d 975, 979 (CA8 1972); Vail v. Board of Education, 354 F. Supp. 592, 603 (NH 1973). Since the hearing may occur almost immediately following the misconduct, it follows that as a general rule notice and hearing should precede removal of the student from school. We agree with the District Court, however, that there are recurring situations in which prior notice and hearing cannot be insisted upon. Students whose presence poses a continuing danger to persons or property or an ongoing threat of disrupting the academic process may be immediately removed from school. In such cases, the necessary notice and rudimentary hearing should follow as soon as practicable, as the District Court indicated.

In holding as we do, we do not believe that we have imposed procedures on school disciplinarians which are inappropriate in a classroom setting. Instead we have imposed requirements which are, if anything, less than a fair-minded school principal would impose upon himself in order to avoid unfair suspensions. Indeed, according to the testimony of the principal of Marion-Franklin High School, that school had an informal procedure, remarkably similar to that which we now require, applicable to suspensions generally but which was not followed in this case. Similarly, according to the most recent memorandum applicable to the entire CPSS, see n. 1, supra, school principals in the CPSS are now required by local rule to provide at least as much as the constitutional minimum which we have described.

We stop short of construing the Due Process Clause to require, countrywide, that hearings in connection with short suspensions must afford the student the opportunity to secure counsel, to confront and cross-examine witnesses supporting the charge, or to call his own witnesses to verify his version of the incident. Brief disciplinary suspensions are almost countless. To impose in each such case even truncated trial-type procedures might well overwhelm administrative facilities in many places and, by diverting resources, cost more than it would save in educational effectiveness. Moreover, further formalizing the suspension process and escalating its formality and adversary nature may not only make it too costly as a regular disciplinary tool but also destroy its effectiveness as part of the teaching process.

On the other hand, requiring effective notice and informal hearing permitting the student to give his version of the events will provide a meaningful hedge against erroneous action. At least the disciplinarian will be alerted to the existence of disputes about facts and arguments about cause and effect. He may then determine himself to summon the accuser, permit cross-examination, and allow the student to present his own witnesses. In more difficult cases, he may permit counsel. In any event, his discretion will be more informed and we think the risk of error substantially reduced.

Requiring that there be at least an informal give-and-take between student and disciplinarian, preferably prior to the suspension, will add little to the factfinding function where the disciplinarian himself has witnessed the conduct forming the basis for the charge. But things are not always as they seem to be, and the student will at least have the opportunity to characterize his conduct and put it in what he deems the proper context.

We should also make it clear that we have addressed ourselves solely to the short suspension, not exceeding 10 days. Longer suspensions or expulsions for the remainder of the school term, or permanently, may require more formal procedures. Nor do we put aside the possibility that in unusual situations, although involving only a short suspension, something more than the rudimentary procedures will be required.

IV

The District Court found each of the suspensions involved here to have occurred without a hearing, either before or after the suspension, and that each suspension was therefore invalid and the statute unconstitutional insofar as it permits such suspensions without notice or hearing. Accordingly, the judgment is

Affirmed.

NOTES

1. The United States Court of Appeals for the Fifth Circuit held that due process does not preclude basing expulsions on hearsay testimony by the school principal which consisted mainly of reading or reciting statements made to him by teachers in response to his inquiries in the course of his investigation of charges against students. See Boykins v. Fairfield Board of Education, 492 F.2d 697 (5th Cir. 1974).

2. The United States Court of Appeals for the Eighth Circuit sustained the action of public school officials in the suspension of an Indian pupil. See Cameron v. Whirlwindhorse, 494 F.2d 110 (8th Cir. 1974).

3. The United States Court of Appeals for the Fifth Circuit held that a school board's action was constitutionally deficient where it simply confirmed the school principal's judgment in a dismissal proceeding without

independently evaluating and weighing the evidence on its own. Preconceived determination of guilt denies due process. See Lee v. Macon County Bd. of Educ., 490 F.2d 458 (5th Cir. 1974).

Procedural Due Process Is Required to Reassign Handicapped Children

MILLS v. BOARD OF EDUC. OF DIST. OF COLUMBIA

United States District Court, District of Columbia, 1972.
348 F.Supp. 866.

WADDY, District Judge. This is a civil action brought on behalf of seven children of school age by their next friends in which they seek a declaration of rights and to enjoin the defendants from excluding them from the District of Columbia Public Schools and/or denying them publicly supported education and to compel the defendants to provide them with immediate and adequate education and educational facilities in the public schools or alternative placement at public expense. They also seek additional and ancillary relief to effectuate the primary relief. They allege that although they can profit from an education either in regular classrooms with supportive services or in special classes adopted to their needs, they have been labelled as behavioral problems, mentally retarded, emotionally disturbed or hyperactive, and denied admission to the public schools or excluded therefrom after admission, with no provision for alternative educational placement or periodic review. * * *

THE PROBLEM

The genesis of this case is found (1) in the failure of the District of Columbia to provide publicly supported education and training to plaintiffs and other "exceptional" children, members of their class, and (2) the excluding, suspending, expelling, reassigning and transferring of "exceptional" children from regular public school classes without affording them due process of law.

The problem of providing special education for "exceptional" children (mentally retarded, emotionally disturbed, physically handicapped, hyperactive and other children with behavioral problems) is one of major proportions in the District of Columbia. The precise number of such children cannot be stated because the District has continuously failed to comply with Section 31–208 of the District of Columbia Code which requires a census of all children aged 3 to 18 in the District to be taken. Plaintiffs estimate that there are " * * * 22,000 retarded, emotionally disturbed, blind, deaf, and speech or learning disabled children, and perhaps as many as 18,000 of these children are not being furnished with programs of specialized education." According to data prepared by the Board of Education, Division of Planning, Research and Evaluation, the District of Columbia provides publicly supported special education programs of various descriptions to at least 3880 school age children. However, in a 1971 report to the Department of Health, Education and Welfare, the District of Columbia Public Schools admitted that an estimated 12,340 handicapped children were not to be served in the 1971–72 school year.

Each of the minor plaintiffs in this case qualifies as an "exceptional" child.

* * *

Although all of the named minor plaintiffs are identified as Negroes the class they represent is not limited by their race. They sue on behalf of and represent all other District of Columbia residents of school age who are eligible for a free public education and who have been, or may be, excluded from such education or otherwise deprived by defendants of access to publicly supported education.

* * *

PLAINTIFFS ARE ENTITLED TO RELIEF

Plaintiffs' entitlement to relief in this case is clear. The applicable statutes and regulations and the Constitution of the United States require it.

Statutes and Regulations

Section 31–201 of the District of Columbia Code requires that:

"Every parent, guardian, or other person residing [permanently or temporarily] in the District of Columbia who has custody or control of a child between the ages of seven and sixteen years shall cause said child to be regularly instructed in a public school or in a private or parochial school or instructed privately during the period of each year in which the public schools of the District of Columbia are in session.

* * * "

Under Section 31–203, a child may be "excused" from attendance only when

" * * * upon examination ordered by * * * [the Board of Education of the District of Columbia], [the child] is found to be unable mentally or physically to profit from attendance at school: Provided, however, That if such examination shows that such child may benefit from specialized instruction adapted to his needs, he shall attend upon such instruction."

Failure of a parent to comply with Section 31–201 constitutes a criminal offense. D.C.Code 31–207. The Court need not belabor the fact that requiring parents to see that their children attend school under pain of criminal penalties presupposes that an educational opportunity will be made available to the children. The Board of Education is required to make such opportunity available. * * *

The Constitution—Equal Protection and Due Process

* * *

In Hobson v. Hansen, 269 F.Supp. 401 (D.C.D.C.1967) Circuit Judge J. Skelly Wright considered the pronouncements of the Supreme Court in the intervening years and stated that "* * * the Court has found the due process clause of the Fourteenth Amendment elastic enough to embrace not only the First and Fourth Amendments, but the self-incrimination clause of the Fifth, the speedy trial, confrontation and assistance of counsel clauses of the Sixth, and the cruel and unusual clause of the Eighth." (269 F.Supp. 401 at 493, citations omitted). Judge Wright concluded "(F)rom these considerations the court draws the conclusion that the doctrine of equal educational opportunity—the equal protection clause in its application to public school education—is in its full sweep a component of due process binding on the District under the due process clause of the Fifth Amendment."

In Hobson v. Hansen, supra, Judge Wright found that denying poor public school children educational opportunities equal to that available to more affluent public school children was violative of the Due Process Clause of the Fifth Amendment. *A fortiori,* the defendants' conduct here, denying plaintiffs and their class not just an equal publicly supported education but all publicly supported education while providing such education to other children, is violative of the Due Process Clause.

Not only are plaintiffs and their class denied the publicly supported education to which they are entitled many are suspended or expelled from regular schooling or specialized instruction or reassigned without any prior hearing and are given no periodic review thereafter. Due process of law requires a hearing prior to exclusion, termination of classification into a special program. * * *

The Defense

The Answer of the defendants to the Complaint contains the following:

"These defendants say that it is impossible to afford plaintiffs the relief they request unless:

(a) The Congress of the United States appropriates millions of dollars to improve special education services in the District of Columbia; or

(b) These defendants divert millions of dollars from funds already specifically appropriated for other educational services in order to improve special educational services. These defendants suggest that to do so would violate an Act of Congress and would be inequitable to children outside the alleged plaintiff class."

This Court is not persuaded by that contention.

The defendants are required by the Constitution of the United States, the District of Columbia Code, and their own regulations to provide a publicly-supported education for these "exceptional" children. Their failure to fulfill this clear duty to include and retain these children in the public school system, or otherwise provide them with publicly-supported education, and their failure to afford them due process hearing and periodical review, cannot be excused by the claim that there are insufficient funds. In Goldberg v. Kelly, 397 U. S. 254, 90 S.Ct. 1011, 25 L.Ed.2d 287 (1969) the Supreme Court, in a case that involved the right of a welfare recipient to a hearing before termination of his benefits, held that Constitutional rights must be afforded citizens despite the greater expense involved. The Court stated at page 266, 90 S.Ct. at page 1019, that "the State's interest that his [welfare recipient] payments not be erroneously terminated, clearly outweighs the State's competing concern to prevent any increase in its fiscal and administrative burdens." Similarly the District of Columbia's interest in educating the excluded children clearly must outweigh its interest in preserving its financial resources. If sufficient funds are not available to finance all of the services and programs that are needed and desirable in the system then the available funds must be expended equitably in such a manner that no child is entirely excluded from a publicly supported education consistent with his needs and ability to benefit therefrom. The inadequacies of the District of Columbia Public School System whether occasioned by insufficient funding or administrative inefficiency, certainly cannot be permitted to bear more heavily on the "exceptional" or handicapped child than on the normal child.

IMPLEMENTATION OF JUDGMENT

* * *

Inasmuch as the Board of Education has presented for adoption by the Court a proposed "Order and Decree" embodying its present plans for the identification of "exceptional" children and providing for their publicly supported education, including a time table, and further requiring the Board to formulate and file with the Court a more comprehensive plan, the Court will not now appoint a special master as was requested by plaintiffs. * * *

JUDGMENT AND DECREE

* * * it is hereby ordered, adjudged and decreed that summary judgment in favor of plaintiffs and against defendants be, and hereby is, granted, and judgment is entered in this action as follows:

1. That no child eligible for a publicly supported education in the District of Columbia public schools shall be excluded from a regular public school assignment by a Rule, policy, or practice of the

Board of Education of the District of Columbia or its agents unless such child is provided (a) adequate alternative educational services suited to the child's needs, which may include special education or tuition grants, and (b) a constitutionally adequate prior hearing and periodic review of the child's status, progress, and the adequacy of any educational alternative.

2.   The defendants, their officers, agents, servants, employees, and attorneys and all those in active concert or participation with them are hereby enjoined from maintaining, enforcing or otherwise continuing in effect any and all rules, policies and practices which exclude plaintiffs and the members of the class they represent from a regular public school assignment without providing them at public expense (a) adequate and immediate alternative education or tuition grants, consistent with their needs, and (b) a constitutionally adequate prior hearing and periodic review of their status, progress and the adequacy of any educational alternatives; and it is further ORDERED that:

3.   The District of Columbia shall provide to each child of school age a free and suitable publicly-supported education regardless of the degree of the child's mental, physical or emotional disability or impairment.   Furthermore, defendants shall not exclude any child resident in the District of Columbia from such publicly-supported education on the basis of a claim of insufficient resources.

4.   Defendants shall not suspend a child from the public schools for disciplinary reasons for any period in excess of two days without affording him a hearing pursuant to the provisions of Paragraph 13.-f., below, and without providing for his education during the period of any such suspension.

5.   Defendants shall provide each identified member of plaintiff class with a publicly-supported education suited to his needs within thirty (30) days of the entry of this order. * * *

  * * *

9.   a.   Defendants shall utilize public or private agencies to evaluate the educational needs of all identified "exceptional" children and, within twenty (20) days of the entry of this order, shall file with the Clerk of this Court their proposal for each individual placement in a suitable educational program, including the provision of compensatory educational services where required.

  * * *

10.   a.   Within forty-five (45) days of the entry of this order, defendants shall file with the Clerk of the Court, with copy to plaintiffs' counsel, a comprehensive plan which provides for the identification, notification, assessment, and placement of class members.   Such plan shall state the nature and extent of efforts which defendants have undertaken or propose to undertake to

(1) describe the curriculum, educational objectives, teacher qualifications, and ancillary services for the publicly-supported educational programs to be provided to class members; and,

(2) formulate general plans of compensatory education suitable to class members in order to overcome the present effects of prior educational deprivations.

* * *

12. Within forty-five (45) days of the entry of this order, defendants shall file with this Court a report showing the expunction from or correction of all official records of any plaintiff with regard to past expulsions, suspensions, or exclusions effected in violation of the procedural rights * * *.

13. Hearing Procedures.

a. Each member of the plaintiff class is to be provided with a publicly-supported educational program suited to his needs, within the context of a presumption that among the alternative programs of education, placement in a regular public school class with appropriate ancillary services is preferable to placement in a special school class.

b. Before placing a member of the class in such a program, defendants shall notify his parent or guardian of the proposed educational placement, the reasons therefore, and the right to a hearing before a Hearing Officer if there is an objection to the placement proposed. * * *

* * *

e. Whenever defendants take action regarding a child's placement, denial of placement, or transfer * * * the following procedures shall be followed.

(1) Notice required hereinbefore shall be given in writing by registered mail to the parent or guardian of the child.

(2) Such notice shall:

(a) describe the proposed action in detail;

(b) clearly state the specific and complete reasons for the proposed action, including the specification of any tests or reports upon which such action is proposed;

(c) describe any alternative educational opportunities available on a permanent or temporary basis;

(d) inform the parent or guardian of the right to object to the proposed action at a hearing before the Hearing Officer;

(e) inform the parent or guardian that the child is eligible to receive, at no charge, the services of a federally or locally funded diagnostic center for an independent medical, psychological and educational evaluation and shall specify the name, address and telephone number of an appropriate local diagnostic center;

(f) inform the parent or guardian of the right to be represented at the hearing by legal counsel; to examine the child's school records before the hearing, including any tests or reports upon which the proposed action may be based, to present evidence, including expert medical, psychological and educational testimony; and, to confront and cross-examine any school official, employee, or agent of the school district or public department who may have evidence upon which the proposed action was based.

(3) The hearing shall be at a time and place reasonably convenient to such parent or guardian.

*   *   *

(5) The hearing shall be a closed hearing unless the parent or guardian requests an open hearing.

(6) The child shall have the right to a representative of his own choosing, including legal counsel. *   *   *

(7) The decision of the Hearing Officer shall be based solely upon the evidence presented at the hearing.

(8) Defendants shall bear the burden of proof as to all facts and as to the appropriateness of any placement, denial of placement or transfer.

(9) A tape recording or other record of the hearing shall be made and transcribed and, upon request, made available to the parent or guardian or his representative.

(10) At a reasonable time prior to the hearing, the parent or guardian, or his counsel, shall be given access to all public school system and other public office records pertaining the child, including any tests or reports upon which the proposed action may be based.

(11) The independent Hearing Officer shall be an employee of the District of Columbia, but shall not be an officer, employee or agent of the Public School System.

*   *   *

(13) The parent or guardian, or his representative, shall have the right to present evidence and testimony, including expert medical, psychological or educational testimony.

(14) Within thirty (30) days after the hearing, the Hearing Officer shall render a decision in writing. *   *   *

NOTES

1. A federal district court in Pennsylvania has held that: "Having undertaken to provide a free public education to all its children, including its exceptional children, the Commonwealth of Pennsylvania may not deny any mentally retarded child access to a free public program of education and training." Pursuant to this requirement a consent decree was issued

and affirmed by the court providing a "free, public program of education and training appropriate to the child's capacity, within the context of a presumption that, among the alternative programs of education and training required by statute to be available, placement in a regular public school class is preferable to placement in a special public school class [i. e., a class for "handicapped" children] and placement in a special public school class is preferable to placement in any other type of program of education and training　*　*　*" Pennsylvania Ass'n for Retarded Children v. Commonwealth, 334 F.Supp. 1257 (E.D.Pa.1971), 343 F.Supp. 279 (E.D.Pa.1972).

2. What if funds are insufficient to provide the special services needed for handicapped children? Does the court fully resolve this issue?

3. A statute which required parents to relinquish custody of their children to the welfare department in order for them to receive tuition assistance for an appropriate education in private programs was found to be unconstitutional. A Virginia statute provided for partial tuition reimbursement for handicapped children in private educational programs when no public programs were available. The court held that the requirement that parents relinquish custody of their children in order to obtain special education services violated the right to family integrity guaranteed by the Ninth and Fourteenth Amendment. Kruse v. Campbell, 431 F.Supp. 180 (E.D.Va. 1977).

Freedom of Speech and Expression

There are few areas of the law more misunderstood by laymen than those connected with First Amendment rights, especially as they relate to freedom of speech and expression. While it is true that the right to speak one's mind carries with it the moral obligation, at least, to mind one's speech, this rule of thumb is not the prevailing yardstick or standard used by the courts in resolving issues in this area.

The Supreme Court has relied primarily on two tests to determine whether the state can control freedom of speech or expression. These are: (1) clear and present danger and (2) material and substantial disruption. In 1919 the Court [20] said that "The rules require that before an utterance can be penalized by government it must, ordinarily, have occurred in such circumstances or have been of such a nature as to create a "clear and present danger" that would bring about "substantial evils" to the state. In subsequent decisions [21] the Court further defined the concept, Justice Brandeis said:

> "no danger flowing from speech can be deemed clear and present, unless the incidence of the evil apprehended is so imminent that it may befall before there is opportunity for full discussion. If there be time to expose through discussion the falsehood and fallacies, to avert the evil by the pro-

20. Schenck v. United States, 249 U.S. 47, 39 S.Ct. 247 (1919).

fornia, 314 U.S. 252, 62 S.Ct. 190 (1941).

21. Whitney v. California, 274 U.S. 357, 47 S.Ct. 641 (1927); Bridges v. Cali-

cesses of education, the remedy to be applied is more speech, not enforced silence." [22]

Government cannot limit speech where the dangers are merely perceived or are not "present" or "imminent." Justice Black observed that "What finally emerges from the 'clear and present danger' cases is a working principle that the substantive evil must be extremely serious and the degree of imminence extremely high before utterances can be punished." [23]

The second rationale "material and substantial disruption" is the standard applied to public education by the Supreme Court in the famous *Tinker* case. The Court in this case made it clear that school authorities would not be permitted to deny a student his fundamental right simply because of "a mere desire to avoid discomfort and unpleasantness that always accompany an unpopular viewpoint." [24]

The great weight of judicial authority supports the proposition that a board of education possesses the authority to regulate pupil dress and personal appearance if they become so extreme as to interrupt the school's decorum and favorable learning atmosphere. An illustration of this judicial position was provided several years ago when the Arkansas Appellate Court [25] upheld a school regulation which forbade the wearing of low necked dresses, any immodest dress, or the use of face paints or cosmetics. Of somewhat more recent vintage and application is the right of a school district to require pupils to participate in physical education programs and to wear clothing suitable for these occasions. The majority rule in these instances is that the pupil must participate in physical education programs, but they may not be required to wear "immodest" attire.[26]

Haircuts have been viewed as a form of expression and the advance sheets of many courts of record are literally filled with cases involving the prohibiting of male pupils from wearing long hair. Students and parents have relied on several legal issues in contesting student appearance regulations including freedom of speech of the First Amendment, the due process and equal protection clauses of the Fourteenth Amendment, the Ninth Amendment which provides for retention of rights by the people and even the Civil Rights Acts. The following cases convey the lack of agreement by the courts in the application of these rights to students in public schools. From the numerous cases which exist on this subject, it is quite difficult to identify a prevailing view of the courts. The courts, from the U.S. Courts

22. Whitney v. California, supra.

23. Bridges v. California, supra.

24. Tinker v. Des Moines Independent School Community Dist., 393 U.S. 503, 89 S.Ct. 733 (1969).

25. Pugsley v. Sellmeyer, 158 Ark. 247, 250 S.W. 538 (1923).

26. Mitchell v. McCall, 273 Ala. 604, 143 So.2d 629 (1962).

of Appeals down, appear to be about evenly split on the application of constitutional rights and haircuts. The courts are in general agreement in keeping with *Tinker,* that any hair style or dress that is disruptive of classroom decorum may be prevented, but it is quite difficult for many of the courts to see precisely how an untidy haircut can be so destructive to a favorable learning environment.

Denial of Freedom of Expression Must be Justified by a Reasonable Forecast of Substantial Disruption

TINKER v. DES MOINES INDEPENDENT COMMUNITY SCHOOL DIST.

Supreme Court of the United States, 1969.
393 U.S. 503, 89 S.Ct. 733.

Mr. Justice FORTAS delivered the opinion of the Court.

Petitioner John F. Tinker, 15 years old, and petitioner Christopher Eckhardt, 16 years old, attended high schools in Des Moines, Iowa. Petitioner Mary Beth Tinker, John's sister, was a 13-year-old student in junior high school.

In December 1965, a group of adults and students in Des Moines held a meeting at the Eckhardt home. The group determined to publicize their objections to the hostilities in Vietnam and their support for a truce by wearing black armbands during the holiday season and by fasting on December 16 and New Year's Eve. Petitioners and their parents had previously engaged in similar activities, and they decided to participate in the program.

The principals of the Des Moines schools became aware of the plan to wear armbands. On December 14, 1965, they met and adopted a policy that any student wearing an armband to school would be asked to remove it, and if he refused he would be suspended until he returned without the armband. Petitioners were aware of the regulation that the school authorities adopted.

On December 16, Mary Beth and Christopher wore black armbands to their schools. John Tinker wore his armband the next day. They were all sent home and suspended from school until they would come back without their armbands. They did not return to school until after the planned period for wearing armbands had expired— that is, until after New Year's Day.

This complaint was filed in the United States District Court by petitioners, through their fathers, under § 1983 of Title 42 of the United States Code. It prayed for an injunction restraining the respondent school officials and the respondent members of the board of directors of the school district from disciplining the petitioners, and it sought nominal damages. After an evidentiary hearing the District Court dismissed the complaint. It upheld the constitutionality of the school authorities' action on the ground that it was reasonable in order to prevent disturbance of school discipline. 258 F.Supp. 971 (1966). The court referred to but expressly declined to follow the Fifth Circuit's holding in a similar case that the wearing of symbols like the armbands cannot be prohibited unless it "materially and substantially interfere[s] with the requirements of appropriate discipline in the operation of the school." Burnside v. Byars, 363 F.2d 744, 749 (1966).

On appeal, the Court of Appeals for the Eighth Circuit considered the case *en banc.* The court was equally divided, and the District Court's decision was accordingly affirmed, without opinion. 383 F.2d 988 (1967). We granted certiorari. 390 U.S. 942, 88 S.Ct. 1050, 19 L.Ed.2d 1130 (1968).

I.

The District Court recognized that the wearing of an armband for the purpose of expressing certain views is the type of symbolic act that is within the Free Speech Clause of the First Amendment. * * * As we shall discuss, the wearing of armbands in the circumstances of this case was entirely divorced from actually or potentially disruptive conduct by those participating in it. It was closely akin to "pure speech" which, we have repeatedly held, is entitled to comprehensive protection under the First Amendment. * * *

First Amendment rights, applied in light of the special characteristics of the school environment, are available to teachers and students. It can hardly be argued that either students or teachers shed their constitutional rights to freedom of speech or expression at the schoolhouse gate. This has been the unmistakable holding of this Court for almost 50 years. * * *

* * *

The school officials banned and sought to punish petitioners for a silent, passive expression of opinion, unaccompanied by any disorder or disturbance on the part of petitioners. There is here no evidence whatever of petitioners' interference, actual or nascent, with the schools' work or of collision with the rights of other students to be secure and to be let alone. Accordingly, this case does not concern speech or action that intrudes upon the work of the schools or the rights of other students.

Only a few of the 18,000 students in the school system wore the black armbands. Only five students were suspended for wearing them. There is no indication that the work of the schools or any class was disrupted. Outside the classrooms, a few students made hostile remarks to the children wearing armbands, but there were no threats or acts of violence on school premises.

The District Court concluded that the action of the school authorities was reasonable because it was based upon their fear of a disturbance from the wearing of the armbands. But, in our system, undifferentiated fear or apprehension of disturbance is not enough to overcome the right to freedom of expression. Any departure from absolute regimentation may cause trouble. Any variation from the majority's opinion may inspire fear. Any word spoken, in class, in the lunchroom, or on the campus, that deviates from the views of another person may start an argument or cause a disturbance. But our Constitution says we must take this risk, Terminiello v. Chicago, 337 U.S. 1, 69 S.Ct. 894 (1949); and our history says that it is this sort of hazardous freedom—this kind of openness—that is the basis of our national strength and of the independence and vigor of Americans who grow up and live in this relatively permissive, often disputatious, society.

In order for the State in the person of school officials to justify prohibition of a particular expression of opinion, it must be able to show that its action was caused by something more than a mere desire to avoid the discomfort and unpleasantness that always accompany an unpopular viewpoint. Certainly where there is no finding and no showing that engaging in the forbidden conduct would "materially and substantially interfere with the requirements of appropriate discipline in the operation of the school," the prohibition cannot be sustained. Burnside v. Byars, supra, 363 F.2d at 749.

In the present case, the District Court made no such finding, and our independent examination of the record fails to yield evidence that the school authorities had reason to anticipate that the wearing of the armbands would substantially interfere with the work of the school or impinge upon the rights of other students. Even an official memorandum prepared after the suspension that listed the reasons for the ban on wearing the armbands made no reference to the anticipation of such disruption.

On the contrary, the action of the school authorities appears to have been based upon an urgent wish to avoid the controversy which might result from the expression, even by the silent symbol of armbands, of opposition to this Nation's part in the conflagration in Vietnam. It is revealing, in this respect, that the meeting at which the school principals decided to issue the contested regulation was called in response to a student's statement to the journalism teacher in one of the schools that he wanted to write an article on Vietnam and have it published in the school paper. (The student was dissuaded.)

It is also relevant that the school authorities did not purport to prohibit the wearing of all symbols of political or controversial significance. The record shows that students in some of the schools wore buttons relating to national political campaigns, and some even wore the Iron Cross, traditionally a symbol of Nazism. The order prohibiting the wearing of armbands did not extend to these. Instead, a particular symbol—black armbands worn to exhibit opposition to this Nation's involvement in Vietnam—was singled out for prohibition.

Clearly, <u>the prohibition of expression of one particular opinion</u>, at least without evidence that it is necessary to avoid material and substantial interference with schoolwork or discipline, <u>is not constitutionally permissible.</u>

In our system, state-operated schools may not be enclaves of totalitarianism. School officials do not possess absolute authority over their students. Students in school as well as out of school are "persons" under our Constitution. They are possessed of fundamental rights which the State must respect, just as they themselves must respect their obligations to the State. In our system, students may not be regarded as closed-circuit recipients of only that which the State chooses to communicate. They may not be confined to the expression of those sentiments that are officially approved. In the absence of a specific showing of constitutionally valid reasons to regulate their speech, students are entitled to freedom of expression of their views. As Judge Gewin, speaking for the Fifth Circuit, said, school officials cannot suppress "expressions of feelings with which they do not wish to contend." Burnside v. Byars, supra, 363 F.2d at 749.

* * *

If a regulation were adopted by school officials forbidding discussion of the Vietnam conflict, or the expression by any student of opposition to it anywhere on school property except as part of a prescribed classroom exercise, it would be obvious that the regulation would violate the constitutional rights of students, at least if it could not be justified by a showing that the students' activities would materially and substantially disrupt the work and discipline of the school. Cf. Hammond v. South Carolina State College, 272 F.Supp. 947 (D.C. S.C.1967) (orderly protest meeting on state college campus); Dickey v. Alabama State Board of Education, 273 F.Supp. 613 (D.C.M.D. Ala.1967) (expulsion of student editor of college newspaper). In the circumstances of the present case, the prohibition of the silent, passive "witness of the armbands," as one of the children called it, is no less offensive to the constitution's guarantees.

As we have discussed, the record does not demonstrate any facts which might reasonably have led school authorities to forecast substantial disruption of or material interference with school activities, and no disturbances or disorders on the school premises in fact occurred. These petitioners merely went about their ordained rounds in school. <u>Their deviation consisted only in wearing on their sleeve a band of black cloth, not more than two inches wide</u>. They wore it to exhibit their disapproval of the Vietnam hostilities and their advocacy of a truce, to make their views known, and, by their example, to influence others to adopt them. They neither interrupted school activities nor sought to intrude in the school affairs or the lives of others. They caused discussion outside of the classrooms, but no interference with work and no disorder. In the circumstances, our Constitution does not permit officials of the State to deny their form of expression.

We express no opinion as to the form of relief which should be granted, this being a matter for the lower courts to determine. We reverse and remand for further proceedings consistent with this opinion.

Reversed and remanded.

*Rule Banning Buttons Is Not Unconstitutional
If It Is Reasonably Related to Prevention
of Disruptive Conduct*

GUZICK v. DREBUS

United States Court of Appeals, Sixth Circuit, 1970.
431 F.2d 594.

MEMORANDUM OPINION AND ORDER

LAMBROS, District Judge. This is an action arising under the provisions of Title 42 U.S.C.A. § 1983. This section provides as follows:

"Every person who, under color of any statute, ordinance, regulation, custom, or usage, of any State or Territory, subjects, or causes to be subjected, any citizen of the United States or other person within the jurisdiction thereof to the deprivation of any rights, privileges, or immunities secured by the Constitution and laws, shall be liable to the party injured in an action at law, suit in equity, or other proper proceeding for redress."

The complaint, in summary, alleges the following: Thomas Guzick, Jr., is 17 years of age and is a student at Shaw High School in East Cleveland, Ohio. Defendant, Donald L. Drebus, is the principal of Shaw High School. The other defendants are: Nelson F. Leist, Superintendent of the East Cleveland School District; and Robert Henderson, Charles Hamilton, Leslie Reardon, Erwin Schrader, and George Beasley, who are members of the East Cleveland Board of Education. Plaintiff desires to wear a button on his lapel while attending school at Shaw High. The button reads:

"April 5 Chicago
G.I.Civilian
Anti-War
Demonstration
Student Mobilization Committee"

He wore this button to school on March 11, 1969. The school principal, Mr. Drebus, ordered the plaintiff to remove the button. Upon the plaintiff's refusal to remove the button, Mr. Drebus suspended him from Shaw High School until such time as he returned to school without the button. The complaint alleges that the acts of Mr. Drebus in suspending the plaintiff have been ratified, approved, or encouraged by the other defendants in their official capacities. Plaintiff alleges that his right to wear this button is protected by the First Amendment to the Constitution, and that his suspension deprives him of rights guaranteed by the Constitution; and, further, that his suspension was without just cause, without a hearing, and without due process of law. The complaint alleges that similar buttons are being worn in other high schools in the Cleveland area, and that the acts of the defendants denying the plaintiff his right to wear a similar button deprives him of the equal protection of the law as guaranteed by the Fourteenth Amendment. The complaint seeks a temporary restraining order enjoining the defendants from interfering with the plaintiff's right to wear the button while attending school and from refusing to reinstate the plaintiff. It also seeks a preliminary and permanent injunction directed toward securing the same relief. The complaint further seeks a declaratory judgment that any rule or regulation of the East Cleveland Board of Education proscribing the wearing of such buttons is unconstitutional, and the complaint further seeks damages in the amount of $1000.00 per day for every day the plaintiff is compelled to miss school and for costs and attorneys' fees.

*   *   *

In a case where there are substantial factual disputes raised by the testimony of the various witnesses, their demeanor on the stand and their relative degree of knowledge are particularly important. The Court has, therefore, reviewed the evidence and its impressions of the various witnesses and has reached its considered judgment as to the actual facts in this case.

The city of East Cleveland, Ohio, is a suburb located east of Cleveland. At one time, it was an almost exclusively white community. In the last few years, however, many negroes have moved into the community from Cleveland, which is immediately adjoining; and East Cleveland now is a racially mixed community.

*   *   *

Approximately 70% of the students at Shaw High School are black. Approximately 30% are white. There has been considerable friction between the students of the two races. There has also been friction among students of the same race. Nonetheless, Shaw High School has not, as yet, had a serious racial disturbance.

At the same time, many other high schools in the area have had such disturbances. At John Hay High, a predominately black school approximately one mile to the west, there have been repeated disturbances; and, in fact, John Hay High School was forced to close for a number of days as a result of these. East High School and Glenville High School have also had serious disturbances. East High was also required to close. Both of these high schools have a high percentage of black students.

Collinwood High School, which is racially mixed, has had serious disturbances. Indeed, these required the closing of the school at one time this year.

So far there have been no crippling disruptions at Shaw High. The situation, however, is not peaceful.

Although there have been no crippling disruptions of school activities, Shaw High has a significant, perhaps serious, discipline problem. Students have been threatened in both the men's rooms and locker rooms, among other places. These threats have often been accompanied by violence. Money has been extorted from students under these circumstances. The problem has been of such significance that the P.T.A. and other groups in the community have become concerned. There have been numerous fights at Shaw, both between blacks and whites and among students of the same race. These fights have occurred both during school hours and in the evening.

Tension at Shaw High is at an incendiary point. The school officials spend a great portion of their time disciplining students in an attempt to control this situation. In January of this year, black students attempted to organize a walkout. Such walkouts have occurred in a number of the other schools in the area. Shaw High officials were forced to call police to the school. The walkout was aborted, and only one student actually left the school.

These are but a few of the incidents described to the Court. It appears that the principal reason why more such incidents have not occurred is the extensive effort by school officials to avert such situations by maintaining discipline and discussing these problems with the students and their parents.

For many years Shaw High has had an informal rule with respect to the wearing of emblems and other insignia. The rule has never been published; nevertheless, it has been applied uniformly and consistently for at least forty years at both Shaw High School and Kirk Junior High. To summarize the rule, it provides that students will not be permitted to wear buttons, emblems, or other insignia on school property during school hours unless these emblems or insignia are related to a school activity.

This informal rule has been applied in a wide variety of situations. School officials have applied it against the high school fraternities and sororities which existed at Shaw in the 1940's. Emblems signifying or indicating membership in any of these fraternities were prohibited. Students wearing them were asked to remove them or leave school.

Subsequently, informal clubs replaced the outlawed high school fraternities. The rule was applied to these clubs. Pins, emblems, lavalieres, lettering on clothing, and other other insignia have not been permitted at Shaw High School.

* * *

The problem again exists as a result of the racial mixture at Shaw. Buttons, pins, and other emblems have been used as identifying "badges." They have portrayed and defined the divisions among students in the school. They have fostered an undesirable form of competition, division and dislike. <u>The presence of these emblems, badges</u> <u>and buttons are taken to represent, define and depict the actual divi-</u> <u>sion of the students in various groups</u>.

* * *

The rule has acquired a particular importance in recent years. Students have attempted to wear buttons and badges expressing inflammatory messages, which, if permitted, and as the evidence indicates, would lead to substantial racial disorders at Shaw. Students have attempted to wear buttons with the following messages inscribed thereon. "White is right"; "Say it loud, Black and Proud"; "Black Power." Other buttons have depicted a mailed black fist, commonly taken to be the symbol for black power.

There have been occasions when the wearing of such insignia has led to disruptions at Shaw and at Kirk Junior High. A fight resulted in the cafeteria when a white student wore a button which read "Happy Easter, Dr. King." (Dr. Martin Luther King was assassinated in the Easter season.) On another occasion, students at Kirk Junior High entered the corridors wearing a distinctive headdress. They proceeded down the corridors striking and attacking certain other students whom they had expected would join them in wearing the headdress, but who had not done so.

School authorities have attempted to eliminate the wearing of buttons, emblems, other insignia, and distinctive forms of dress characteristic of a particular club or group. The evidence discloses a number of instances in which various individuals and groups attempted to wear such insignia or clothing and in which the school officials prohibited it. * * *

On March 11, 1969, the plaintiff, Thomas Guzick, Jr., in the company of Hunter Havens, went to the office of the principal of Shaw High, Mr. Donald Drebus. Both the plaintiff and Mr. Havens wore a button on their clothing inscribed with the message:

"April 5 Chicago
G.I. Civilian
Anti-War
Demonstration
Student Mobilization Committee"

Alexander School Law MTB—14

Plaintiff also carried certain leaflets which he and Mr. Havens desired to distribute at Shaw High School.

The conversation had that morning between the two students and Mr. Drebus is in dispute. It appears, however, that the students requested permission to pass out the leaflets at the school. Mr. Drebus refused permission, stating that Shaw High had a policy against distribution of leaflets. Mr. Drebus demanded that the students remove the buttons which they were wearing. The students asserted that they had a constitutional right to wear such buttons. Hunter Havens removed his. The plaintiff, however, refused to remove his button, even after a warning by Mr. Drebus that he would suspend the plaintiff from school if he refused to remove it. Upon the plaintiff's further refusal to remove the button, he was suspended from school until such time as he returned without the button. Subsequently, the plaintiff filed suit with this Court seeking a legal determination whether he is entitled under the Constitution to wear this button at Shaw High School.

As outlined above, the Court has concluded that Shaw High School has had a long-standing and consistently-applied rule prohibiting the wearing of buttons and other insignia on school grounds during school hours, unless these are related to a school-sponsored activity. The Court finds that this rule has been a significant factor in preserving peace and good order at Shaw High School and in preventing provocations, distractions, and disruptive conduct. The Court finds that if this policy of excluding buttons and other insignia is not retained, some student will attempt to wear provocative or inciting buttons and other emblems. If these provocative buttons and insignia are permitted to be worn, they will further amplify an already serious discipline problem, they will exacerbate an already tense racial situation, and they will inevitably cause substantial disruptions in the educational process at Shaw High.

The Court further finds that if students are permitted to wear *some* buttons but not others, similar disruptions of the educational process will occur. Many students will not understand the justification for any rule that prohibits the wearing of certain buttons while permitting others. Many will not accept the distinction.

*   *   *

The Court finds that the prohibition of buttons and other insignia at Shaw High significantly contributes to the preservation of peace and order, and that the blanket prohibition of buttons and other insignia is reasonably related to the prevention of the distractions and disruptive and violent conduct at Shaw High. The Court finds that if all buttons are permitted or if any buttons are permitted, a serious discipline problem will result, racial tensions will be exacerbated, and the educational process will be significantly and substantially disrupted.

CONCLUSIONS OF LAW

On February 24, 1969, the United States Supreme Court decided Tinker v. Des Moines Independent Community School District, 393 U.S. 503, 89 S.Ct. 733. This is the landmark case in the area of the student's rights to free speech in the public schools, and it has formed the basis of this litigation.

* * *

The Court noted that the wearing of an expressive arm band is "closely akin" to "pure speech." It was, in substance, the silent expression of an idea.

* * *

The regulation in the *Tinker* case was not applied in an even-handed manner. Other buttons and symbols of political and controversial significance were permitted to be worn in the school. The Court concluded that the regulation was directed at the principle expressed in this particular demonstration—that is, opposition to the Vietman War. The school authorities, the Court concluded, wanted not to introduce the Vietnam controversy into the school.

Certain factors, present in the *Tinker* case, and upon which the Court rested its decision, are not present here. The rule prohibiting the wearing of emblems at Shaw High School is one of long standing. It has been applied evenhandedly both in politically controversial and noncontroversial areas. * * * They have applied this rule consistently; they have applied it equally. The rule is applied (and it is applied in this case) without regard to the content and the ideas sought to be expressed in the emblem. It is applied without regard to the status of the wearer or to the message, inflammatory or innocuous, sought to be expressed.

Furthermore, there is in the present case much more than an "undifferentiated fear or apprehension" of disturbances likely to result from the wearing of buttons at Shaw High School. The wearing of buttons and other emblems and insignia has occasioned substantial disruptive conduct in the past at Shaw High. It is likely to occasion such conduct if permitted henceforth. The wearing of buttons and other insignia will serve to exacerbate an already tense situation, to promote divisions and disputes, including physical violence among the students, and to disrupt and interfere with the normal operation of the school and with appropriate discipline by the school authorities.

* * *

The school authorities have adopted the policy of excluding all insignia and emblems, in view of the explosive situation and the likelihood of substantial disruption if provocative emblems are permitted. This Court is unprepared to say that the rule excluding all buttons is unreasonable, in view of the difficulty in applying a selective rule and in view of the real likelihood that such a rule would itself contribute to disruption. This Court is also unprepared to say that the school authorities were unreasonable in rejecting such a selective rule.

* * *

* * * This Court concludes that such a rule is reasonably related to the prevention of disruptive conduct at Shaw High School.

The wearing of buttons or, as in the *Tinker* case, wearing of arm bands is itself and without accompanying conduct "closely akin" to "pure speech." Nevertheless, wearing of such insignia has other characteristics different from pure speech. A button is not merely a statement; it is an identification tag. It identifies the wearer as an adherent or member of one group or class. It identifies him as not being a member of other groups or classes. This identification aspect exists independent of the nature of the message contained in the button. Thus, for example, a button on which appears a mailed black fist certainly identifies the wearer with a particular political persuasion. This is apart from any message sought to be conveyed by the button.

The button also demonstrates that the wearer has a particular and keen interest in the goals and outlook of the group with which the button identifies him. It marks the wearer as a proponent; it also may mark him as someone's opponent. In so doing, buttons have an inherent tendency to divide a body of individuals into separate subgroups, each identified by its own insignia, each declaring by a particular decoration its position in relation to other individuals. Such an effect may not be significant in the context of many high schools in this country. But because of the "peculiar situation" at Shaw High, this divisive influence is likely and, indeed, almost certain to lead to disruptive conduct. When there is added the fact that many of these expressive buttons are likely to convey that expression in a most inflammatory and, perhaps, insulting manner, it is apparent that a most dangerous situation will result.

Free speech is the single most important element upon which this nation has thrived. Wherever reasonably possible, it must be upheld, cherished, and nurtured. There are, however, situations in which free speech, or manifestations which are "closely akin" to free speech, must be exercised with care and restraint; and there are situations in which the manifestations of speech may even be prohibited altogether. It has been demonstrated that the identifying aspects of buttons and other insignia have led to considerable disruption at Shaw High in the past. It has also been demonstrated that such insignia would be likely and, indeed, more likely to lead to such disruptions if permitted now.

We bear in mind that the buttons and other insignia are not speech themselves. Rather, they are a pictorial manifestation of speech. As such, they acquire other characteristics which would not be possessed by the spoken word itself. Buttons and other insignia have an inherently identifying nature. They are in a sense "badges." It is this aspect of emblems and other insignia that has caused difficulty at Shaw High. It is this aspect, and not the actual speech of any of the students, which has been prohibited and which is at issue here.

* * *

* * * The prohibition of buttons and other insignia at Shaw High is the result of a history of problems which the Shaw High authorities have encountered as a result of this activity. The prohibition against buttons is reasonably related in preventing the occurrence of disruptive conduct. It is also reasonably related to what is administratively possible at Shaw High School. If any buttons are permitted to be worn at Shaw High, it is likely that students will require that all buttons be permitted. In any event, the wearing of any buttons will lead to disruptive, even violent, activities, will materially and substantially affect the normal educational processes at Shaw High, and will diminish significantly the ability of the school officials to maintain proper discipline.

In this case, it is relevant that the school authorities *did* prohibit the wearing of all symbols and applied the rule uniformly and consistently. This was not the case in *Tinker*.

It is also relevant that the wearing of a button by the plaintiff in this case was associated with a distribution of leaflets. This was not the case in *Tinker*.

An evidentiary pattern has developed in this case which specifically shows to this Court that the school authorities had a constitutionally valid reason to regulate student conduct regarding the wearing of buttons and other emblems and symbols. This was not the case in *Tinker*.

* * *

It is also relevant that leaflets of all kinds are being distributed and circulated throughout the public schools, and specifically at Shaw High School, and finding their way on the bulletin boards. Many of these are of a harmless nature, but many of these are downright immoral and sinister, such as, defendants' Exhibit B distributed by SDS, which was posted on the Shaw High School bulletin board. It encouraged a demonstration in Washington opposing our political leaders and, among other things, contained this phrase: "Don't let the bastards grind you down!"

It is also relevant in the instant case that one of the pamphlets which was circulated at Shaw High School by the Student Mobilization Committee advertised a city-wide meeting to consider a possible high school strike.

The regulation prohibiting the wearing of the button is an appropriate standard of behavioral conduct which is reasonably relevant to the mission and function of Shaw High School.

The regulation is not discriminatory nor unreasonable, arbitrary or capricious. The rule does not deny a federally protected constitutional right.

Upholding the Shaw High School rule prohibiting buttons or other symbols does not sound the death knell for student freedom of speech.

The evidence in this case has made it abundantly clear that the school authorities have a factual basis upon which to forecast substantial disruption of, or material interference with, school activities if student behavioral conduct regarding the wearing of buttons is not regulated.

Therefore, the Court finds the issues in this case in favor of the defendants; and the plaintiff's claim for injunctive relief and damages is denied.

It is, therefore, ordered that this cause be and is hereby dismissed and terminated.

NOTES

1. In a corollary case, a United States District Court in California upheld the suspension of high school pupils for ten days for use of profanity and/or vulgarity appearing in an off campus newspaper "Oink." The more damaging portions of the publication appeared to be a "* * * vulgar retouching of what appears to be a photograph of President Nixon * * *" Baker v. Downey City Bd. of Educ., 307 F.Supp. 517 (D.C.Cal.1969).

2. A clear case of disruptive school activities by non-students arose when twelve youths entered the office of the secretary of the school principal and told her "* * * they were going to interrupt us that day * * *.", locked the secretary out of her office, moved furniture about, scattered papers and dumped some books on the floor, all of which resulted in the dismissal of school. The conviction of the defendants was affirmed in State v. Midgett, 8 N.C.App. 230, 174 S.E.2d 124 (1970).

3. Suspension of black students for disrupting a student assembly because the tune "Dixie" was played was upheld by the United States Court of Appeals, Eighth Circuit. The Court said that "On the record we cannot say that the tune 'Dixie' constitutes a badge of slavery or that the playing of the tune under the facts as presented constituted officially sanctioned racial abuse. Such a ruling would lead to the prohibition of the playing of many of our most famous tunes." Tate v. Board of Educ. of Jonesboro, Arkansas, 453 F.2d 975 (8th Cir. 1972).

4. Students can be temporarily suspended from school for disrupting school by engaging in a sit-in and not attending classes. Gebert v. Hoffman, 336 F.Supp. 694 (E.D.Pa.1972).

5. Symbols and insignia such as Confederate flag, indicating desire to maintain segregated school must be removed. Smith v. St. Tammany Parish School Bd., 448 F.2d 414 (5th Cir. 1971).

6. In a state where no *de jure* segregation had existed, the federal court declined to change the school flag which resembled a Confederate flag. Banks v. Muncie Community Schools, 433 F.2d 292 (7th Cir. 1970).

Rule Prohibiting Heel Plates Is Reasonably Related
to Legitimate School Purpose

STROMBERG v. FRENCH

Supreme Court of North Dakota, 1931.
60 N.D. 750, 236 N.W. 477.

NUESSLE, J. This action was brought to restrain the defendants from enforcing the following rule adopted by the board of education of the city of Langdon, to wit: "Notice is hereby given that on and after September 29, 1930, any boy wearing metal heel plates on his shoes will be refused admittance to classes and will be suspended or expelled until the heel plates are removed."

* * * Murray Stromberg, at the direction of his father, G. E. Stromberg, wore metal heel plates. The plaintiff insisted that he had a right to do so and that the action of the board of education forbidding their use was unreasonable. The defendants threatened to enforce the rule. The plaintiff thereupon began the instant action to permanently enjoin them from doing so.

The case came to trial before the court without a jury. Evidence was offered in support of the contentions of the respective parties. The court held that the rule in question was a reasonable one and that the board of education had the right to make and enforce it, and accordingly ordered judgment in favor of the defendants. Plaintiff thereupon perfected the instant appeal.

The record discloses that at the beginning of the school year in September, 1930, some of the boys attending the Langdon High School were wearing shoes on the heels of which metal plates were affixed. The principal and superintendent, believing that the use of these plates resulted in undue noise when their wearers walked through the halls and in the classrooms of the school and caused unreasonable damage to the floors of the school, requested the boys wearing them to discontinue their use. The boys complied with this request. Murray Stromberg was one of the boys who used heel plates. His mother noticed that he had removed the plates and directed him to replace them. He complied with his mother's direction and the school authorities, objecting, sent him home until such time as he should remove the plates. Plaintiff was informed of this action of the principal and superintendent and at once interviewed them. He insisted that as a parent he had the right to determine what apparel his boy should wear at school, that therefore he had the right to direct Murray to wear heel plates, and that the action of the school authorities in forbidding their use was arbitrary and unreasonable, and he insisted that Murray be permitted to continue in school though he wore the forbidden heel plates. Thereupon, on September 25, 1930, the school board enacted the rule first above quoted.

It appears that heel plates are quite commonly worn on the heels of shoes. The plaintiff offered evidence tending to show that their use prolongs the life of the heel appreciably. On the other hand, defendants offered evidence tending to show that their use was a fad rather than a matter of practical advantage. The floors of the Langdon High School are of hardwood, varnished and polished. The testimony of the defendants further tended to show that the use of these heel plates by boys in the high school caused undue noise when they were passing through the halls, and that the floors were injured thereby more than they would be by ordinary leather or rubber heels. It further appears that a number of high school boys wore heel plates and that all were requested to discontinue their use for the above reasons. The trial court found, among other things:

"That such rule does not involve any element of oppression or humiliation to the pupils attending such High School, and that it imposes no affirmative duty upon such pupils, and that no more than a nominal consumption of time or expenditure of money is required to comply with it; and that in adopting said rule the members of said Board of Education acted wholly and entirely in good faith.

"That the floors of said High School building are made of hardwood, and that the wearing on their shoes of metal heel plates by the boys attending such High School was and is the direct cause of extraordinary and material damage to such floors, and was and is the direct cause of unusual and material expense to said Special School District.

"That the wearing on their shoes of such metal heel plates by the boys attending such High School also caused an excessive and great amount of unneccessary and unusual noise and confusion in and about the High School building and both directly and indirectly tended to prevent, hinder and interfere with the discipline, government and instruction of the pupils attending such High School."

And the court held that the rule in question was a reasonable one and that the defendants had the right to make and enforce it.

The plaintiff on this appeal challenges the findings of the trial court as being not supported by the evidence. He contends that, in any event, the rule of which he complains is unreasonable and arbitrary and that it infringes upon his parental right to determine what is reasonable and proper apparel for his son.

* * *

The Constitution of North Dakota, section 147 et seq., imposes upon the Legislature the duty of making provision for the establishment and maintenance of a system of public schools. While imposing this duty, the Constitution places no restrictions upon the Legislature as to its performance. "The Legislature, therefore, has the power to enact any legislation in regard to the conduct, control, and regulation of the public free schools, which does not deny to the citizen the constitutional right to enjoy life and liberty, to pursue happiness and to acquire property." Flory v. Smith, 145 Va. 164, 134 S.E. 360, 362, 48 A.L.R. 654. Pursuant to this constitutional mandate and authority, the Legislature made provision for the erection of special school districts and, among other provisions, enacted section 1251, C.L.1913, as follows:

"Each board of education shall have the power and it shall be its duty: * * *

"7. To have the custody of all school property of every kind and to see that the ordinances and by-laws of the city or village in relation thereto are observed. * * *

"11. To adopt, alter and repeal, whenever it may deem expedient, rules and regulations for the reception, organization, grading, government and instruction of pupils, their suspension, expulsion or transfer from one school to another. But no pupil shall be suspended or expelled except for insubordination, habitual indolence or disorderly conduct; such suspension shall not be for a longer period than ten days, nor such expulsion beyond the end of the current term of school. * * * *"

Thus the Legislature reposed a very broad discretion in boards of education with respect to the conduct and regulations of schools conducted by them.

The enactment of the defendant school board, of which the plaintiff complains, is clearly aimed at the conservation of school property and the maintenance of good order and discipline in the school. As a general rule the decision of a school board, "if exercised in good faith on matters affecting the good order and discipline of the school, is final so far as it relates to the rights of pupils to enjoy school privileges, and the courts will not interfere with the exercise of such authority unless it has been illegally or unreasonably exercised." 35 Cyc. 1135. See, also, 24 R.C.L. 574 et seq. "The power of the board of education to control and manage the schools and to adopt rules and regulations necessary for that purpose is ample and full. The rules * * * necessary to a proper conduct and management of the schools are, and must necessarily be, left to the discretion of the board, and its acts will not be interfered with nor set aside by the courts, unless there is a clear abuse of the power and discretion conferred." * * * Presumptively, rules and regulations established by a school board are reasonable and proper. * * * And whether or not such rules and regulations are reasonable is a question of law to be determined by the court. * * *

The plaintiff contends that the right of a parent to educate, discipline, and direct his children is paramount; that any rule or regulation which interferes with this right is unreasonable and must fall. So, in the instant case, he insists he has the right to determine the character and kind of apparel that his son shall wear and that the rule of which he complains denies this right. Of course, in most instances, the right of the parent is paramount, but sometimes the interests of the public generally require that the parent shall give way. We think this is so in the instant case. The trial court found, and we think rightly, that under the circumstances there was no abuse of authority and the rule was proper and reasonable. Certainly there was no hardship or indignity imposed upon the plaintiff or his son by it. It is aimed at the remedying of a condition which the school authorities consider detrimental to the best conduct of the school. Plaintiff argues that if such a rule may be enforced, then other rules may be enacted and enforced, and thus the school board enabled to prescribe absolutely the apparel that children must wear in order to enjoy the privileges of the school. But the plaintiff overlooks the safeguard of reasonableness which must always be considered.

Finally, plaintiff insists that the statute, section 1251 expressly limits the power of the school board to expel or suspend to those cases where the pupil is insubordinate, habitually indolent, or guilty or disorderly conduct. The record discloses that Murray Stromberg was an excellent student. No exception could be taken to his conduct. He violated no rule imposed by the school authorities excepting that with respect to the wearing of metal heel plates, and then only because of parental direction. Clearly he was not indolent or disorderly. The plaintiff contends that he was not insubordinate within the meaning of that term as used in the statute. Whatever he did was done without malice or willful disregard of rules and only because of parental command. It seems to us that even so his conduct amounted to insubordination. Any other construction put upon the term as used in the statute might result in an intolerable situation. No rule or regulation could be enforced, provided the parent directed the pupil not to observe it. So we hold that the action of Murray, though taken at the command of his parents, constituted insubordination within the meaning of that term as used in the statute.

It follows then that since the rule of which the plaintiff complains was enacted by the school board in the proper exercise of its authority and since, under the circumstances, this rule was reasonable, the plaintiff is not entitled to the relief which he seeks.

The judgment of the district court must be, and it is, affirmed.

NOTES

1. In the first quarter of the twentieth century a school board adopted a regulation which read: "The wearing of transparent hosiery, low necked dress or any other style of clothing tending toward immodesty of dress, or the use of face paints or cosmetics, is prohibited." Was this regulation upheld? Pugsley v. Sellmeyer, 158 Ark. 247, 250 S.W. 538 (1923). How would such a regulation fare in the courts today?

2. A Georgia pupil was refused permission to continue to attend classes while wearing slacks in the case of Matheson v. Brady, 202 Ga. 500, 43

S.E.2d 703 (1947). The case was decided on a technical basis. Hence, the primary issue was not resolved. Would such a rule or regulation be considered reasonable or unreasonable by contemporary standards?

Haircut Regulation Is Constitutionally Permissible

JACKSON v. DORRIER

United States Court of Appeals, Sixth Circuit, 1970.
424 F.2d 213.

PER CURIAM. This case involves the timely subject of long hair worn by teenage male high school students.

The Metropolitan Board of Education of Nashville and Davidson County, Tennessee, adopted the following regulation in 1961:

> "Pupils shall observe modesty, appropriateness, and neatness in clothing and personal appearance. A student is not appropriately dressed if he is a disturbing influence in class or school because of his mode of dress. The principal may suspend a student who does not meet this requirement."

Under this regulation the students at Donelson High School were told, as to hair on male students, that hair in the front may not come below the eyebrows, ears must show clear of hair and hair in the back is to be tapered and not be long enough to turn up.

Two male students, Michael Jackson and Barry Steven Barnes, who were members of a combo band known as "The Purple Haze," permitted their hair to grow longer than prescribed by school officials. After conferences with the students and their parents the students were suspended by the principal and sent home for violation of the regulation. After additional conferences a hearing was conducted before the Board of Education. The Board sustained the action of the principal.

* * *

The complaint charges that the student plaintiffs have been deprived of certain rights guaranteed by the Constitution of the United States; that the defendant school officials, having the authority and duty to promulgate plans, rules and regulations for the administration and operation of the public school system, wrongfully refused to enroll these two students at Donelson High School for the school year beginning September 1968 on the ground that their hair was too long, that they wore mustaches, and in the case of Barnes, a beard; and that the two students were informed that their appearance constituted "improper grooming" which amounted to "distracting attire." The complaint sought a declaration that the above quoted regulation is invalid. It prayed that defendants be compelled to readmit these two students to Donelson High School and that defendants be enjoined from conditioning attendance at school on the length of hair or the presence of a beard or mustache.

* * *

There is evidence to support the conclusion that the wearing of excessively long hair by male students at Donelson High School disrupted classroom atmosphere and decorum, caused disturbances and distractions among other students and interfered with the educational process. Members of faculty of Donelson High School testified that the wearing of long hair by Jackson and Barnes was an obstructing and distracting influence to a wholesome academic environment. A teacher of history and social studies stated that two boys with long hair were a distracting influence in her class; that they were "constantly combing, flipping, looking in mirrors and rearranging their hair," attracting the attention of other students and interfering with classroom teaching; and that the train of thought of both the students and teachers was interrupted. An English teacher testified that she often asked a boy to put away his comb and refrain from combing his hair in class. She described long hair on male students as a disturbing and distracting influence on educational processes in her classes and other school activities at Donelson High School. A teacher of industrial arts testified that girls with long hair were required to wear hair nets as a safety precaution and that long hair on boys was a safety hazard in shop work. One teacher said that other students pay more attention to a boy with long hair than to what the teacher is trying to teach. Another teacher testified that when her class was attended by the boys with long hair hardly a day would go by that she would not have to interrupt her teaching and say: "Put your combs away. This is not a beauty parlor. This is a school classroom."

* * *

The record establishes that the deliberate flouting by Jackson and Barnes of this well publicized school regulation created problems of school discipline.

It is contended that enforcement of the regulation deprived the two students of freedom of speech and expression in violation of the First Amendment. Neither of the students testified that his hair style was intended as an expression of any idea or point of view. We agree with the finding of the District Court that this record does not disclose that the conduct of Jackson and Barnes and the length of their hair were designed as an expression within the concept of free speech. Therefore Tinker v. Des Moines School Independent Community District, 393 U.S. 503, 89 S.Ct. 733, 21 L.Ed.2d 731 (1969), has no application. * * *

The record supports the finding of the District Judge that Jackson and Barnes pursued their course of personal grooming for the purpose of enhancing the popularity of the musical group in which they performed. We agree with Judge Gray that "the growing of hair for purely commercial purposes is not protected by the First Amendment's guarantee of freedom of speech."

It is further contended that the action of school officials violated the due process clause of the Fourteenth Amendment. <u>The evidence shows that the two students were afforded ample opportunity to be heard and that the procedural and substantive requirements of due process were met by conferences conducted by the school principal and by the hearing before the Board of Education</u>. * * *

> "To hold that the relationship between parents, pupils and school officials must be conducted in an adversary atmosphere and accordingly the procedural rules to which we are accustomed in a court of law would hardly best serve the interests of any of those involved."

We also agree with the District Court that the regulation enforced in this case is not void for vagueness and overbreadth, but to the contrary, as applied to these two students, was quite specific. The record shows that the principal of Donelson High School interpreted and administered the regulation in such a way as clearly to inform all students, including the two involved in this case, as to what was required of them with regard to personal grooming. <u>There can be no doubt that Jackson and Barnes had adequate notice of what was expected of them and deliberately chose not to comply with the regulation.</u>

Appellants further contend that they have been deprived of the equal protection of the law in violation of the Fourteenth Amendment. * * * As previously stated, substantial evidence supports the finding of the District Judge that the regulation has a real and reasonable connection with the successful operation of the educational system and with the maintenance of school discipline.

* * *

Having found no violation of constitutional rights, we are not prepared to hold that the regulation here in question and the interpretation and application placed upon it are beyond the power of school officials and the Board of Education, as applied to public elementary and high schools, provided there is adequate compliance with due process standards. The students here involved were accorded an adequate hearing before school authorities and the Board of Education and a thorough evidentiary hearing before the District Judge.

* * *

In the absence of infringement of constitutional rights, the responsibility for maintaining proper standards of decorum and discipline and a wholesome academic environment at Donelson High School is not vested in the federal courts, but in the principal and faculty of the school and the Metropolitan Board of Education of Nashville and Davidson County, Tennessee.

We follow Ferrell v. Dallas Independent School District, supra, in holding that the District Court committed no error in dismissing the present case.

Affirmed.

Hair Rule Violates Substantive Due Process

RICHARDS v. THURSTON

United States Court of Appeals, First Circuit, 1970.
424 F.2d 1281.

COFFIN, Circuit Judge. Plaintiff, a seventeen year old boy, was suspended from school at the beginning of his senior year because he refused to cut his hair, which a local newspaper story introduced into evidence described as "falling loosely about the shoulders". Defendant, the principal of the high school in Marlboro, Massachusetts, admits that there was no written school regulation governing hair length or style but contends that students and parents were aware that "unusually long hair" was not permitted.

On these sparse facts the parties submitted the case posed by plaintiff's request for injunctive relief against the deprivation of his rights under 42 U.S.C. § 1983. Each relied on the failure of the other to sustain his burden of proof, plaintiff claiming that he should prevail in the absence of evidence that his appearance had caused any disciplinary problems, and defendant maintaining that plaintiff had failed to carry his burden of showing either that a fundamental right had been infringed or that defendant had not been motivated by a legitimate school concern. The district court granted plaintiff's request for a permanent injunction and ordered plaintiff reinstated. Richards v. Thurston, 304 F.Supp. 449 (D.Mass.1969).

* * *

Plaintiff, too, advances a narrow argument for prevailing—the lack of any specific regulation authorizing suspension for unusual hair styles. We do not accept the opportunity. We take as given defendant's allegation in his answer that parents and students—including plaintiff—were aware that unusually long hair was not permitted. Moreover, we would not wish to see school officials unable to take appropriate action in facing a problem of discipline or distraction simply because there was no preexisting rule on the books.

Coming to the merits, we are aware of a thicket of recent cases concerning a student's wearing of long hair in a public high school. While several of the decisions holding against the student have relied on the prior occurrence of disruptions caused by unusual hair styles, we think it fair to say that many of those courts would hold against the student on a barren record such as ours, on the grounds that the student had not demonstrated the importance of the right he asserts. On the other hand, in few of the cases holding for the student was there any evidence of prior disruptions caused by hair styles. Despite the obvious disagreement over the proper analytical framework, each of the "pro-hair" courts held explicitly or implicitly that the school authorities failed to carry their burden of justifying the regulation against long hair.

What appears superficially as a dispute over which side has the burden of persuasion is, however, a very fundamental dispute over the extent to which the Constitution protects such uniquely personal aspects of one's life as the length of his hair, for the view one takes of the constitutional basis—if any—for the right asserted may foreshadow both the placement and weight of the evidentiary burden which he imposes on the parties before him. For this reason, we resist the understandable temptation, when one is not the final arbiter of so basic a constitutional issue, to proceed directly to an application of the constitutional doctrine without attempting to ascertain its source as precisely as possible.

It is perhaps an easier task to say what theories we think do *not* apply here. We recognize that there may be an element of expression and speech involved in one's choice of hair length and style, if only the expression of disdain for conventionality. However, we reject the notion that plaintiff's hair length is of a sufficiently communicative character to warrant the full protection of the First Amendment. * * * That protection extends to a broad panoply of methods of expression, but as the non-verbal message becomes less distinct, the justification for the substantial protections of the First Amendment becomes more remote. * * *

Our rejection of those constitutional protections in this case is not intended to denigrate the understandable desire of people to be let alone in the governance of those activities which may be deemed uniquely personal. As we discuss below, we believe that the Due Process Clause of the Fourteenth Amendment establishes a sphere of personal liberty for every individual, subject to reasonable intrusions by the state in furtherance of legitimate state interests.

The idea that there are substantive rights protected by the "liberty" assurance of the Due Process Clause is almost too well established to require discussion. Many of the cases have involved rights expressly guaranteed by one or more of the first eight Amendments. But it is clear that the enumeration of certain rights in the Bill of Rights has not been construed by the Court to preclude the existence of other substantive rights implicit in the "liberty" assurance of the Due Process Clause. * * *

We do not say that the governance of the length and style of one's hair is necessarily so fundamental as those substantive rights already found implicit in the "liberty" assurance of the Due Process Clause, requiring a "compelling" showing by the state before it may be impaired. Yet "liberty" seems to us an incomplete protection if it encompasses only the right to do momentous acts, leaving the state free to interfere with those personal aspects of our lives which have no direct bearing on the ability of others to enjoy their liberty. * * *

* * * The Founding Fathers wrote an amendment for speech and assembly; even they did not deem it necessary to write an amendment for personal appearance. We conclude that within the commodious concept of liberty, embracing freedoms great and small, is the right to wear one's hair as he wishes.

Determining that a personal liberty is involved answers only the first of two questions. The second is whether there is an outweighing state interest justifying the intrusion. The answer to this question must take into account the nature of the liberty asserted, the context in which it is asserted, and the extent to which the intrusion is confined to the legitimate public interest to be served. For example, the right to appear au naturel at home is relinquished when one sets foot on a public sidewalk. Equally obvious, the very nature of public school education requires limitations on one's personal liberty in order for the learning process to proceed. Finally, a school rule which forbids skirts shorter than a certain length while on school grounds would require less justification than one requiring hair to be cut, which affects the student twenty-four hours a day, seven days a week, nine months a year. * * *

Once the personal liberty is shown, the countervailing interest must either be self-evident or be affirmatively shown. We see no inherent reason why decency, decorum, or good conduct requires a boy to wear his hair short. Certainly eccentric hair styling is no longer a reliable signal of perverse behavior. We do not believe that mere unattractiveness in the eyes of some parents, teachers, or students, short of uncleanliness, can justify the proscription. Nor, finally, does such compelled conformity to conventional standards of appearance seem a justifiable part of the educational process.

In the absence of an inherent, self-evident justification on the face of the rule, we conclude that the burden was on the defendant. Since he offered no justification, the judgment of the district court must be affirmed.

Affirmed.

NOTES

1. The case of Ferrell v. Dallas Independent School District, 392 F.2d 697 (1968), involved a suit to enjoin school officials from refusing to enroll male pupils who had failed to comply with a school regulation banning long hair. The U. S. District Court for the Northern District of Texas denied

any injunctive relief and the pupils appealed. The Court of Appeals held that the regulation promulgated by the principal was valid.

2. In a 1968 California case, a 15-year-old minor was refused admission to high school because he had a beard. The beard was neat in appearance and was trimmed regularly. The pupil contended the board's "good grooming" policy as applied to him was unconstitutional because it violated his rights of freedom of speech and expression of his right of "liberty". Moreover, he claimed that because a beard cannot be put on and taken off like an article of clothing, the "good grooming" policy extended into his home life and violated his right of privacy.

The California Appellate Court said: "The decisive issue confronting us is simply whether the respondent school board's "good grooming" policy constitutes an unreasonable infringement of petitioners' constitutional rights." In order to determine this, the court declared that "* * * a governmental agency seeking to impose restrictions on the exercise of an individual's constitutional right must demonstrate that: (1) The government's restraint rationally relates to the enhancement of the public service; (2) The benefits that the public gains by the restraint outweigh the resulting impairment of the constitutional right; and (3) No alternatives less subversive of the constitutional right are available." Upon application of these three measures of constitutionality, the court held for the board of education and said concerning each of the tests: *First,* there had been ample testimony by experienced educators that the "good grooming" policy enhanced public education by precluding descriptions of the educational process and promoting a proper classroom atmosphere and decorum. Concerning the second test, the court said: "* * * the public derives benefit where public school students are academically trained in a classroom climate devoid of disruptive influences. Manifestly, the public assumes the cost of maintaining the public school system and is entitled to have its schools operated with a minimum of interruption. The parents of the majority of male students who are clean-shaven enjoy the right to have their youngsters educated in a classroom setting free of disturbances and distractions. Expert opinion established that it is injurious to the educational process when a deviation on the part of one student leads to the lack of acceptance on the part of many students. Good study habits and proper conduct on the part of youngsters constitute attributes which are beneficial to the general public and far outweigh the restraint on the peripheral right to grow a beard." The court concluded in applying the third test that no alternative less subversive of Kevin's right to grow a beard was available to defendant, board of education.

Finally, the court said that the claim that the school regulation was not an invasion of the pupil's right of privacy and quoted an earlier case saying "The domain of family privacy must give way insofar as a regulation reasonably calculated to maintain school discipline may affect it. The rights of the other students, and the interest of teachers, administrators and the community-at-large in a well run and efficient school system are paramount." Akin v. Board of Ed. of Riverside Unified School Dist., 262 Cal. App.2d 161, 187, 68 Cal.Rptr. 557 (1968).

3. The Fifth Circuit ruled against three male pupils who refused to shave in compliance with a good grooming rule of their school. The Fifth Circuit noted, with approval, the sentiment of the District Court that

"* * * the Court felt somewhat put upon by having to fit a controversy over shaving into an inordinately busy schedule. It was viewed as a problem for school administrators * * *. The entire problem seems miniscule in light of other matters involving the school system * * *." Stevenson v. Board of Education of Wheeler County, Georgia, 426 F.2d 1154 (5th Cir. 1970).

4. See Breen v. Kahl, 419 F.2d 1034 (1969), where 7th Circuit held hair regulation unconstitutional.

5. The United States Court of Appeals, Fourth Circuit in reviewing all the relevant appellate haircut decisions concluded that the state interest may overcome the student's constitutional interest if the evidence supports that the health and safety of the student or students are jeopardized, but the court found that proof that "jest, disgust, and amusement were evoked" by the long hair was insufficient to restrain the students constitutional interest. In so saying the court did hold that hair style is a constitutionally protected right, "to be secure in one's person" as guaranteed by substantive due process. Massie v. Henry, 455 F.2d 779 (4th Cir. 1972).

Student Publications

Freedom of the press is a cornerstone of the basic freedoms of the Constitution. In settling the Pentagon papers dispute between the New York Times and the United States Government, the Supreme Court said:

> "In the First Amendment the Founding Fathers gave the free press the protection it must have to fulfill its essential role in our democracy. The press was to serve the governed, not the governors. The Government's power to censor the press was abolished so that the press would remain forever free to censure the Government." [27]

While the Supreme Court has not ruled on the subject of restraint of student publications, the position taken by the court in Tinker v. Des Moines [28] suggests that the standard of "reasonable forecast of material and substantial interference" is a standard which may be applied to freedom of the press as well as freedom of speech and expression. In Dickey v. Alabama State Board of Education,[29] perhaps the leading case on student newspapers, a U.S. District Court in Alabama made it clear that First Amendment protections are extended to students and that the school or university can only restrict those rights through reasonable regulation.

According to the U.S. Court of Appeals, Sixth Circuit, however, the requirement of a showing of "reasonable forecast of material and substantial" disruption does not mandate that the school officials "delay action against the inciters until after the riot has started and the

27. New York Times Co. v. United States, 403 U.S. 713, 91 S.Ct. 2140 (1971).

29. 273 F.Supp. 613 (1967), vac'd 402 F. 2d 515.

28. 393 U.S. 503, 89 S.Ct. 733 (1969).

buildings have been taken over and damaged." [30] This court upheld the suspension of university students for distribution on campus of an underground newspaper which berated the student-body for apathy and urged them to "stand up and fight" the school administration by seizing campus buildings. The language, the court held, was "an open exhortation to the students to engage in disorderly and destructive activity." [31]

Freedom of speech protection does not apply equally to high school students and adults alike. In determining the extent of its application, the court may properly consider the age or maturity of those addressed. Therefore, publications may be protected when directed to adults but may not be appropriate for minors. A different set of judicial standards may validly apply to prior restraint when exercised at the high school level as opposed to the college level of education. First Amendment rights of children are not co-extensive with those of adults.[32]

Restraint of student publications in the absence of reasonable forecast of disruption, however, is not justified. The U.S. Court of Appeals, Seventh Circuit, has held that punishment of students was constitutionally unjustifiable where the board of education failed to produce evidence showing imminence of disruption.[33] The Court said:

> "We conclude that absent an evidentiary showing, and an appropriate balancing of the evidence by the district court to determine whether the Board was justified in a 'forecast' of the disruption and interference, as required under Tinker, plaintiffs are entitled to the declaratory judgment, injunctive and damage relief sought."

Public school officials may promulgate student newspaper reglations which prohibit distribution of material which will cause interference with school operation and discipline, but according to Eisner v. Stamford Board of Education, the school policy cannot be overbroad and unconstitutionally vague and where prior approval is required the policy must prescribe a definite brief period within which review of the submitted material is to be approved and by whom.[34]

30. Norton v. East Tennessee State University Disciplinary Committee, 419 F.2d 195 (6th Cir. 1969), certiorari denied 399 U.S. 906, 90 S.Ct. 2191.

31. Ibid.

32. Quarterman v. Byrd, 453 F.2d 54 (4th Cir. 1971).

33. Scoville v. Board of Education of Joliet Township High School District 204, 286 F.Supp. 988 (N.D.Ill.1968), affirmed 415 F.2d 860, reversed on rehearing 425 F.2d 10 (1970), certiorari denied 400 U.S. 826, 91 S.Ct. 51.

34. Eisner v. Stamford Board of Education, 440 F.2d 803 (2nd Cir. 1971).

Board Unable to Reasonably Forecast Disruption
from Student Publication

SCOVILLE v. BOARD OF EDUC. JOLIET TOWNSHIP HIGH SCHOOL DIST. 204

United States Court of Appeals, Seventh Circuit, 1970.
425 F.2d 10.

KILEY, Circuit Judge. The plaintiffs, minors, were expelled from high school after writing, off the school premises, a publication which was distributed in school and which contained, among other things, material critical of school policies and authorities. This civil rights action was brought for declaratory judgment, injunctive relief, and damages, alleging violation of First and Fourteenth Amendment rights, as well as an unconstitutional application of an Illinois statute. * * *

The plaintiffs are Raymond Scoville and Arthur Breen, students at Joliet Central High School, one of three high schools administered by the defendant Board of Education. Scoville was editor and publisher, and Breen senior editor, of the publication "Grass High." They wrote the pertinent material. "Grass High" is a publication of fourteen pages containing poetry, essays, movie and record reviews, and a critical editorial. Sixty copies were distributed to faculty and students at a price of fifteen cents per copy.

On January 18, 1968, three days after "Grass High" was sold in the school, the dean advised plaintiffs that they could not take their fall semester examinations. Four days thereafter plaintiffs were suspended for a period of five days. Nine days after that Scoville was removed as editor of the school paper, and both he and Breen were deprived of further participation in school debating activities.

* * * The Board expelled plaintiffs from the day classes for the second semester, by virtue of the Board's authority under Ill.Rev. Stat. Ch. 122, Sec. 10–22.6 (1967), upon a determination that they were guilty of "gross disobedience [and] misconduct." * * *

* * * At no time, either before the Board of Education or in the district court, was the expulsion of the plaintiffs justified on grounds other than the objectionable content of the publication. The Board has not objected to the place, time or manner of distribution. The court found and it is not disputed that plaintiffs' conduct did not cause any commotion or disruption of classes.

No charge was made that the publication was libelous, and the district court felt it unnecessary to consider whether the language in "Grass High" labeled as "inappropriate and indecent" by the Board could be suppressed as obscene. * * *

I

Plaintiffs contend that the expulsion order violated their First and Fourteenth Amendment freedoms. The same cases are cited by plaintiffs and defendants in support of their arguments on this contention. The authoritative decision, pertinent to the important issue before us, is Tinker v. Des Moines School District, 393 U.S. 503, 89 S.Ct. 733, 21 L.Ed.2d 731 (1969). *Tinker* is a high school "arm band" case, but its rule is admittedly dispositive of the case before us.

The *Tinker* rule narrows the question before us to whether the writing of "Grass High" and its sale in school to sixty students and faculty members could "reasonably have led [the Board] to *forecast* substantial disruption of or material interference with school activities * * * or intru[sion] into the school affairs or the lives of others" Tinker v. Des Moines School District, 393 U.S. at 514, 89 S. Ct. at 740. (Emphasis added.) We hold that the district court erred in deciding that the complaint "on its face" disclosed a clear and present danger justifying defendants' "forecast" of the harmful consequences referred to in the *Tinker* rule.

* * *

Plaintiffs' freedom of expression was infringed by the Board's action, and defendants had the burden of showing that the action was taken upon a reasonable forecast of a substantial disruption of school activity. No reasonable inference of such a showing can be drawn from the complaint which merely alleges the facts recited in the beginning of this opinion. The criticism of the defendants' disciplinary policies and the mere publication of that criticism to sixty students and faculty members leaves no room for reasonable inference justifying the Board's action. While recognizing the need of effective discipline in operating schools, the law requires that the school rules be related to the state interest in the production of well-trained intellects with constructive critical stances, lest students' imaginations, intellects and wills be unduly stifled or chilled. Schools are increasingly accepting student criticism as a worthwhile influence in school administration.

Absent an affirmative showing by the defendants, the district court, faced with the motion to dismiss, inferred from the admitted facts in plaintiffs' complaint and the presented exhibits that the Board action was justified. However, the district court had no factual basis for, and made no meaningful application of, the proper rule of balancing the private interests of plaintiffs' free expression against the state's interest in furthering the public school system. Burnside v. Byars, 363 F.2d at 748. No evidence was taken, for example, to show whether the classroom sales were approved by the teachers, as alleged; of the number of students in the school; of the ages of those to whom "Grass High" was sold; of what the impact was on those who bought "Grass High"; or of the range of modern reading material available to or required of the students in the school library. That plaintiffs may have intended their criticism to substantially disrupt or materially interfere with the enforcement of school policies is of no significance per se under the *Tinker* test.

The "Grass High" editorial imputing a "sick mind" to the dean reflects a disrespectful and tasteless attitude toward authority. Yet does that imputation to sixty students and faculty members, without more, justify a "forecast" of substantial disruption or material interference with the school policies or invade the rights of others? We think not. The reference undoubtedly offended and displeased the dean. But mere "expressions of [the students'] feelings with which [school officials] do not wish to contend" (Tinker v. Des Moines School District, 393 U.S. at 511, 89 S.Ct. at 739; Burnside v. Byars, 363 F.2d at 749) is not the showing required by the *Tinker* test to justify expulsion.

Finally, there is the "Grass High" random statement, "Oral sex may prevent tooth decay." This attempt to amuse comes as a shock to an older generation. But today's students in high school are not insulated from the shocking but legally accepted language used by demonstrators and protestors in streets and on campuses and by authors of best-selling modern literature. A hearing might even disclose that high school libraries contain literature which would lead students to believe the statement made in "Grass High" was unobjectionable.

We believe the discussion above makes it clear, on the basis of the admitted facts and exhibits, that the Board could not have reasonably forecast that the publication and distribution of this paper to the students would substantially disrupt or materially interfere with school procedures.

II

The sole authority for the Board's action is Ill.Rev.Stat. Ch. 122, Sec. 10–22.6 (1967), which gives the School Board the power "to expel pupils guilty of gross disobedience or misconduct." In view of our conclusion that the complaint "on its face" discloses an unjustified invasion of plaintiffs' First and Fourteenth Amendment rights, it follows that we agree with plaintiffs that the Board applied the Illinois statute in an unconstitutional manner.

We conclude that absent an evidentiary showing, and an appropriate balancing of the evidence by the district court to determine whether the Board was justified in a "forecast" of the disruption and interference, as required under *Tinker*, plaintiffs are entitled to the declaratory judgment, injunctive and damage relief sought.

The cause is remanded for further proceedings.

Reversed and remanded.

*Policy Requiring Prior Approval of Student Publication
Must be Sufficiently Specific to Prevent
Arbitrary Administration*

EISNER v. STAMFORD BD. OF EDUC.

United States Court of Appeals, Second Circuit, 1971.
440 F.2d 803.

IRVING R. KAUFMAN, Circuit Judge: The deceptively simple facts in this case generate legal problems which summon up many centuries of political and social thought and action concerning the relation between the rights and powers of men, women, and children, and their government. To resolve this problem we are required to consider principles and concepts which courts have fashioned over several decades of this century, giving concrete effect to the proscription of the first amendment against any law abridging freedom of expression, and apply them to the unique social structure prevailing in a public system of secondary schools.

The Board of Education of the City of Stamford, Connecticut, on November 18, 1969, adopted the following "policy":

"Distribution of Printed or Written Matter

"The Board of Education desires to encourage freedom of expression and creativity by its students subject to the following limitations:

> "No person shall distribute any printed or written matter on the grounds of any school or in any school building unless the distribution of such material shall have prior approval by the school administration.

"In granting or denying approval, the following guidelines shall apply.

> "No material shall be distributed which, either by its content or by the manner of distribution itself, will interfere with the proper and orderly operation and discipline of the school, will cause violence or disorder, or will constitute an invasion of the rights of others."

Plaintiffs are students at Rippowam High School in Stamford. They wish to distribute free of the restraint imposed by the quoted policy, or of any other similar restraint, a mimeographed newspaper of their own creation and other printed and written literature. The district court agreed with their contention that the Board's policy violates their right to freedom of expression. * * * The court therefore declared the policy unconstitutional and enjoined defendants from enforcing any requirement that students obtain prior approval before publishing or distributing literature within the Stamford public schools.

* * *

We affirm the decision below, 314 F.Supp. 832 (1970), insofar as it declares unconstitutional and enjoins the enforcement of the Board's policy of November 18, 1970, but we do so, as will shortly appear, with some reservations and for reasons significantly different from those advanced by the court below. * * * We do not agree with the district court, however, that reasonable and fair regulations which corrected those defects but nevertheless required prior submission of material for approval, would in all circumstances be an unconstitutional "prior restraint."

I.

* * *

The sensitive analysis of the constitutional validity of previous restraints of speech suggested by these cases requires that we address ourselves to the following questions. First, is the Board's policy justified as included within one or more of the categories of exceptional cases to which previous restraints are permissible? Second, is the policy as narrowly drawn as may reasonably be expected so as to advance the social interests that justify it or, to the contrary, does it unduly restrict protected speech, to an extent "greater than is essential to the furtherance of" those interests? * * *

II.

We agree with appellants that we need not and should not concern ourselves with the content or disruptive potential of the specific issue of the newspaper which plaintiffs sought unsuccessfully to distribute on school property. <u>The students are challenging the policy "on its face"</u> and not as applied to their particular publication.

* * *

Many cases, following in the choppy waters left by *Tinker*, have applied the quoted language either to validate or to restrain a school's attempt to prevent students from engaging in constitutionally protected activity. Nor need we search far for a theoretical underpinning for the authority of school officials to control disruptive speech, in view of the unassailable power of the state to suppress "words * * * which by their very utterance inflict injury or tend to incite an immediate breach of the peace." Chaplinsky v. New Hampshire, supra, or words which "have all the effect of force." Near v. Minnesota, 283 U.S. at 716, 51 S.Ct. at 631. These phrases have a venerable ancestry, descending from the principle at least as old and as formidable as Schenck v. United States, 249 U.S. 47, 52, 39 S.Ct. 247, 249, 63 L.Ed. 470 (1919), that "[t]he question in every case is whether the words are used in such circumstances and are of such a nature as to create a clear and present danger that they will bring about the substantive evils that Congress has a right to prevent."

The potential "evil," the School Board urges, is the disruption of the effort by the state of Connecticut through its system of public schooling, to give its children "opportunities for growth into free and independent well-developed men and citizens." Prince v. Massachusetts, 321 U.S. 158, 165, 64 S.Ct. 438, 442, 88 L.Ed. 645 (1944). As the *Tinker* court recognized, it has "repeatedly emphasized the need for affirming the comprehensive authority of the States and of school officials * * * to prescribe and control conduct in the schools." 393 U.S. at 507, 89 S.Ct. at 737. * * * Unless the policy, therefore, purports to delegate greater power to restrain the distribution of disruptive matter than *Tinker* allows, or unless it otherwise unreasonably burdens students' first amendment activity, it is valid.

III.

The policy criteria by which school authorities may prevent students from distributing literature on school property departs in no significant respect from the similarly very general and broad instruction of *Tinker* itself. Although the policy does not specify that the foreseeable disruption be either "material" or "substantial" as *Tinker* requires, we assume that the Board would never contemplate the futile as well as unconstitutional suppression of matter that would create only an *im*material disturbance. Thus, the regulation tracks the present state of the authoritative constitutional law, and while we realize this does not end the matter it does save the regulation from the charge that it is on its face fatally overbroad, since the policy statement does not purport to authorize suppression of a significant class of protected activity. * * *

Absence of overbreadth, of course, does not in itself absolve the policy statement of the plaintiffs' charge that it is also unduly vague. The phrase "invasion of the rights of others" is not a model of clarity or preciseness. But several factors present here lessen or remove the familiar dangers to first amendment freedoms often associated with vague statutes. Thus, the statement does not attempt to authorize *punishment* of students who publish literature that under the policy may be censored by school officials. If it did, students would be left to guess at their peril the thrust of the policy in a specific case and the resultant chill on first amendment activity might be intolerable. * * * Also, because any ban that school authorities may impose would apply only to students *on school property*, the policy statement does not threaten to foreclose, e. g., from the publisher of a newspaper, a significant market or block of potential buyers should the publisher guess wrongly as to the kind of literature that a school principal will tolerate under particular circumstances. Cf. Interstate Circuit, Inc. v. City of Dallas, 390 U.S. 676, 88 S.Ct. 1298, 20 L.Ed.2d 225

(1968). The policy does not in any way interfere with students' freedom to disseminate and to receive material outside of school property; nor does it threaten to interfere with the predominate responsibility of *parents* for their children's welfare. The statement is, therefore, in many ways narrowly drawn to achieve its permissible purposes, and indeed may fairly be characterized as a regulation of speech, rather than a blanket prior restraint.

In sum, we believe that the Board's policy statement is neither overbroad nor unconstitutionally vague, so far as it prescribes *criteria* by which school officials may prevent the distribution on secondary school property of written or printed matter. * * *

IV.

Since, however, the policy statement is in other ways constitutionally deficient, it would not be remiss for us to observe that greater specificity in the statement would be highly desirable. The Board would in no way shackle school administrators if it attempted to confront and resolve in some fashion, prior to court intervention, some of the difficult constitutional issues that will almost inevitably be raised when so broad a rule is applied to particular cases. For example, to what extent and under what circumstances does the Board intend to permit school authorities to suppress criticism of their own actions and policies? * * * Similarly, does the Board anticipate that school officials will take reasonable measures to minimize or forestall potential disorder and disruption that might otherwise be generated in reaction to the distribution of controversial or unpopular opinions, before they resort to banishing the ideas from school grounds? * * * The Board might also undertake to describe the kinds of disruptions and distractions, and their degree, that it contemplates would typically justify censorship, as well as other distractions or disorders that it would consider do not justify suppression of students' attempts to distribute literature. At the same time it would be wise for the Board to consider the areas of school property where it would be appropriate to distribute approved material.

Refinements of the sort we mention would lessen the possibility that the policy statement under attack here because of its tendency to over-generalization, will be administered arbitrarily, erratically, or unfairly, see Interstate Circuit, Inc. v. Dallas, 390 U.S. 676, 685, 88 S.Ct. 1298, 20 L.Ed.2d 225 (1968). * * *

Finally, greater specificity might reduce the likelihood of future litigation and thus forestall the possibility that federal courts will be called upon again to intervene in the operation of Stamford's public schools. It is to everyone's advantage that decisions with respect to the operation of local schools be made by local officials. The greater the generosity of the Board in fostering—not merely tolerating—students' free exercise of their constitutional rights, the less likely it will be that local officials will find their rulings subjected to unwieldy constitutional litigation.

V.

Although the Board's regulation passes muster as authorizing prior restraints, <u>we believe it is constitutionally defective in its lack of procedure for prior *submission* by students for school administration approval, of written material before "distribution."</u> * * *

* * *

* * * The policy as presently written is wholly deficient in this respect for it prescribes no period of time in which school officials must decide whether or not to permit distribution. <u>To be valid, the regulation must prescribe a definite brief period within which review of submitted material will be completed</u>.

<u>The policy is also deficient in failing to specify to whom and how material may be submitted for clearance</u>. Absent such specifications, students are unreasonably proscribed by the terms of the policy statement from distributing *any* written material on school property, since the statement leaves them ignorant of clearance procedures. Nor does it provide that the prohibition against distribution without prior approval is to be inoperative until each school has established a screening procedure.

Finally, we believe that the proscription against "distributing" written or printed material without prior consent is unconstitutionally vague. We assume that by "distributing" the Board intends something more than one student passing to a fellow student his copy of a general newspaper or magazine. Indeed, this assumption underpins most of our discussion concerning the constitutional validity of the policy statement, apart from the deficiencies we describe here. If students are to be required to secure prior approval before they may pass notes to each other in the hallways or exchange Time, Newsweek or other periodicals among themselves, then the resultant burden on speech might very likely outweigh the very remote possibility that such activities would ever cause disruption. We assume, therefore, that the Board contemplates that it will require prior submission only when there is to be a *substantial* distribution of written material, so that it can reasonably be anticipated that in a significant number of instances there would be a likelihood that the distribution would disrupt school operations. If the Board chooses to redraft its policy in light of what we have said in this opinion, it must make its intentions in this respect clear. Once it does, courts may better evaluate the potential "chill" of the policy on speech. The Board would be wise to be mindful of this danger zone.

<u>For the reasons stated above, we affirm the declaratory judgment by the district court that the Board's policy statement is unenforceable</u>. Because we disagree with the district court's conclusion that under all circumstances, any system for prior submission and re-

straint would be unconstitutional, <u>the district court must modify its grant of injunctive relief so as to restrain only the enforcement of this particular policy</u>. We therefore affirm and remand the case to the district court for entry of an appropriate judgment in accordance with this opinion.

NOTES

1. The U. S. Court of Appeals for the Fourth Circuit has provided propositions of law which must be followed in order for a school's prior restraint regulation to be constitutionally valid. These are:

(a) Secondary school children are within the protection of the first amendment, although their rights are not coextensive with those of adults.

(b) Secondary school authorities may exercise reasonable prior restraint upon the exercise of students' first amendment rights.

(c) Such prior restraints must contain precise criteria sufficiently spelling out what is forbidden so that a reasonably intelligent student will know what he may write and what he may not write.

(d) A prior restraint system, even though precisely defining what may not be written, is nevertheless invalid unless it provides for:

(1) A definition of "Distribution" and its application to different kinds of material;

(2) Prompt approval or disapproval of what is submitted;

(3) Specification of the effect of failure to act promptly; and

(4) An adequate and prompt appeals procedure.

Baughman v. Freienmuth, 478 F.2d 1345 (4th Cir. 1973).

2. A few "earthy words" relating to bodily functions and sexual intercourse are not obscene in the legal sense. Jacobs v. Board of School Commissioners, 490 F.2d 601 (1973), certiorari granted 417 U.S. 929, 94 S.Ct. 2638. The Supreme Court limited the scope of the obscenity exception of First Amendment protection to: "works which depict or describe sexual conduct" and which, taken as a whole, appeal to the prurient interest in sex, which portray sexual conduct in a patently offensive way, and which, taken as a whole, do not have serious literary, artistic, political, or scientific value. Miller v. California, 413 U.S. 15, 93 S.Ct. 2607 (1973).

3. First Amendment protection does not prohibit a school's regulation of student's off-campus sale of underground newspaper where prior submission rule was the product of an extensive and good faith effort to formulate a valid student conduct code. Sullivan v. Houston Ind. School District, 475 F.2d 1071 (5th Cir. 1973), rehearing denied 475 F.2d 1404, certiorari denied 414 U.S. 1032, 94 S.Ct. 461.

4. The United States Court of Appeals for the Seventh Circuit held that school board provisos between two distributions of literature were invalid and that occasional presence of "earthy" words in unofficial student newspaper did not render their newspaper obscene. See Jacobs v. Board of School Commissioners, 490 F.2d 601 (1973).

*Board Prohibition of Distribution of Sex Questionnaire
Is Not Violative of Constitution*

TRACHTMAN v. ANKER

United States Court of Appeals, Second Circuit, 1977.
563 F.2d 512, cert. denied 435 U.S. 925, 98 S.Ct. 1491 (1978).

LUMBARD, Circuit Judge: These are cross appeals from a judgment * * * which enjoined defendants from restraining plaintiffs' attempts to distribute a sex questionnaire to eleventh and twelfth-grade students at Stuyvesant High School in New York City and to publish the results in the student publication, "The Stuyvesant Voice." * * * We conclude that defendants' actions in prohibiting the proposed sexual survey did not violate any constitutional right of the plaintiffs. * * *

* * * Trachtman and Marks submitted for review a questionnaire consisting of twenty-five questions, which, they advised, was to be used as a means for obtaining information for an article on "Sexuality in Stuyvesant" to appear in the "Voice." The questions, which the district court described as "requiring rather personal and frank information about the student's sexual attitudes, preferences, knowledge and experience," covered such topics as pre-marital sex, contraception, homosexuality, masturbation and the extent of students' "sexual experience." The questionnaire included a proposed cover letter which described the nature and purpose of the survey; it stressed the importance of honest and open answers but advised the student that, "[y]ou are not required to answer any of the questions and if you feel particularly uncomfortable—don't push yourself."

The students sought permission to distribute the questionnaire on school grounds on a random basis. The answers were to be returned anonymously and were to be kept "confidential." The students were to tabulate the results and publish them in an article in the "Voice," which would also attempt to interpret the results.

* * * [Permission was denied]

* * *

On appeal both parties agree that the defendants' restraint of the students' efforts to collect and disseminate information and ideas involves rights protected by the First Amendment. See Tinker v. Des Moines Independent Community School District. Essentially, resolution of the issues here turns upon a narrow question: What was it necessary for the defendants to prove to justify the prohibition of the distribution of the questionnaire and did the defendants meet this burden of proof?

* * *

Essentially, the defendants' position is that the students here seek not only to communicate an idea but to utilize school facilities to solicit a response that will invade the rights of other students by subjecting them to psychological pressures which may engender significant emotional harm. Plaintiffs do not question defendants' authority to protect the physical and psychological well being of students while they are on school grounds, * * * rather, they contend that defendants have not made a sufficient showing to justify infringement of the students' rights to speech and expression.

In interpreting the standard laid down in *Tinker*, this court has held that in order to justify restraints on secondary school publications, which are to be distributed within the confines of school property, school officials must bear the burden of demonstrating "a reasonable basis for interference with student speech, and * * * courts will not rest content with officials bare allegation that such a basis existed." Eisner v. Stamford Board of Education. At the same time, it is clear that school authorities need not wait for a potential harm to occur before taking protective action. * * * Although this case involves a situation where the potential disruption is psychological rather than physical, *Tinker* and its progeny hold that the burden is on the school officials to demonstrate that there was reasonable cause to believe that distribution of the questionnaire would have caused significant psychological harm to some of the Stuyvesant students.

In support of their argument that students confronted with the questionnaire could suffer serious emotional harm, defendants submitted affidavits from four experts in the fields of psychology and psychiatry. Florence Halpern, professor of psychology at the New York University School of Medicine, stated that many adolescents are anxious about the "whole area of sex" and that attempts to answer the questionnaire by such students "would be very likely" to create anxiety and feelings of self-doubt; further, she stated that there were almost certainly some students with a "brittle" sexual adjustment and that for "such adolescents, the questionnaire might well be the force that pushes them into a panic state or even a psychosis." She concluded that distribution of the questionnaire was a "potentially dangerous" act that was "likely to result in serious injury to at least some of the students."

* * *

The record shows that the curriculum at Stuyvesant includes various courses on sex and sexuality and that professionally supervised peer-group discussions are sponsored by the school. The defendants have consistently treated the topic of sexuality as an important part of students' lives, which requires special treatment because of its sensitive nature. Thus, the school system has provided several courses on the physical and emotional aspects of sex; such courses are taught by teachers with special qualifications and administrative materials emphasize the sensitive nature of the topic. Further, the Board has consistently taken the postition that even professional researchers may not conduct "sexual surveys" of students without meeting certain specific requirements.

Plaintiffs offered statements from five experts, including Gilbert Trachtman, who is a professor of educational psychology at New York University. Plaintiffs' experts questioned the possibility that any emotional harm could be caused by students' attempts to answer the questionnaire, pointed out that the survey might be of substantial benefit to many students, and expressed the opinion that "squelching" the survey could have deleterious effects. They indicated that the topics covered in the questionnaire are of normal interest to adolescents and are common subjects of conversation; further some of these experts emphasized that students in Manhattan are bombarded with sexually explicit materials and that it was highly unlikely that any student could be harmed by answering the questionnaire. It is noteworthy, however, that at least two of plaintiffs' experts, one of whom was Gilbert Trachtman, recognized that there was some possibility that some students would suffer emotional damage as a result of answering the questionnaire.

* * *

In determining the constitutionality of restrictions on student expression such as are involved here, it is not the function of the courts to reevaluate the wisdom of the actions of state officials charged with protecting the health and welfare of public school students. The inquiry of the district court should have been limited to determining whether defendants had demonstrated a substantial basis for their conclusion that distribution of the questionnaire would result in significant harm to some Stuyvesant students. * * *

We believe that the school authorities did not act unreasonably in deciding that the proposed questionnaire should not be distributed because of the probability that it would result in psychological harm to some students. The district court found this to be so with respect to ninth and tenth-grade students. We see no reason why the conclusion of the defendants that this was also true of eleventh and twelfth-grade students was not within their competence. Although psychological diagnoses of the type involved here are by their nature difficult of precision, * * * we do not think defendants' inability to predict with certainty that a certain number of students in all grades would be harmed should mean that defendants are without power to protect students against a foreseen harm. We believe that the school authorities are sufficiently experienced and knowledgeable concerning these matters, which have been entrusted to them by the community; a federal court ought not impose its own views in such matters where there is a rational basis for the decisions and actions of the school authorities. * * * Their action here is not so much a curtailment of any First Amendment rights; it is principally a measure to protect the students committed to their care, who are compelled by law to attend the school, from peer contacts and pressures which may result in emotional disturbance to some of those students whose responses are sought. <u>The First Amendment right to express one's views does not include the right to importune others to respond to questions when there is reason to believe that such importuning may result in harmful consequences.</u> Consequently where school authorities have reason to believe that harmful consequences might result to students, while they are on the school premises, from solicitation of answers to questions, <u>then prohibition of such solicitation is not a violation of any constitutional rights of those who seek to solicit.</u>

In sum, we conclude that the record established a substantial basis for defendants' belief that distribution of the questionnaire would result in significant emotional harm to a number of students throughout the Stuyvesant population. * * *

* * *

Search and Seizure

The Fourth Amendment of the United States Constitution provides for "The right of people to be secure in their persons, houses, papers, and effects, against unreasonable searches and seizures shall not be violated, and no warrants shall issue, but upon probable cause * * *." <u>It is for the courts to ascertain what constitutes an unreasonable search or seizure</u>.

To search or not to search a pupil, his desk, or his locker or even his automobile is a question frequently confronting school administrators. Oftentimes, the issue must be decided forthwith because the gravity of the situation—bomb threats, dangerous weapons, illegal drugs—could result in serious injury to school pupils.

The issue of search and seizure in the public schools balances primarily on whether or not the court views the school teacher or administrator as a parent or a policeman. To assume that the school administrator or teacher represents the state and seeks to obtain seized goods for purposes of criminal prosecution would obviously require a warrant.

Whether the doctrine of *in loco parentis* gives school authorities unlimited control over students is therefore one fundamental question involved in search and seizure cases. A Texas court held that a principal was acting *in loco parentis,* not as an arm of the state [35] when he discovered marijuana upon requiring a student to empty the contents of his pockets on the principal's desk. By not being an arm of the state the principal's actions are not subject to restraint by the Fourth Amendment. <u>The Fourth Amendment was intended to protect indi-</u>

---

35. Mercer v. State, 450 S.W.2d 715 (Tex.Civ.App.1970).

viduals from unauthorized governmental searches and was not intended as a protection against searches by private persons. The Texas court did not view the Fourth Amendment as bestowing any search and seizure protections upon the student.

A New York court was more restrictive in its application of *in loco parentis* holding that the student had constitutional rights against illegal search and seizure and this right had to be weighed against the school authorities' power of *in loco parentis*.[36] Without unlimited right to search, the school authority can only search if he has "reasonable suspicion" that something of an illegal nature is in the possession of a student. The court commented:

"* * * a school teacher, to a limited extent at least, stands *in loco parentis* to pupils under his charge, * * *

The *in loco parentis* doctrine is so compelling in light of public necessity and as a social concept antedating the Fourth Amendment, that any action, including a search, taken thereunder upon *reasonable suspicion* should be accepted as necessary and reasonable." (emphasis added)

In reaching the same conclusion a Delaware court, held that a vice-principal's search of a student's jacket did not violate the constitution since the vice-principal stood *in loco parentis*.[37] But the court was careful to point out that the search was accompanied by a reasonable suspicion that contraband was secreted in the student's pockets. This court rejected the argument that a principal was a private individual, to whom search and seizure prohibitions do not apply, and concluded that his actions were those of a state official. For a state official to conduct a search without a warrant in the absence of the power of *in loco parentis* or other extenuating circumstances would, of course, offend the constitution.

Although the standard of "reasonable suspicion" is a lower standard than that of the "probable cause" required for police to obtain a warrant, it is not so unrestrictive as to place no restraint on school personnel.[38] A New York court held that school personnel concluding a strip search of fifth grade students after classroom thefts violated the children's Fourth Amendment rights because there were no acts which allowed the school officials to particularize which student might have actually taken the money. The court maintained that there must be some available facts which together provide reasonable grounds to search and the search must be conducted in order to further a legitimate school purpose, such as the maintenance and discipline in the school.

36. People v. Jackson, 65 Misc.2d 909, 319 N.Y.S.2d 731 (1971).

37. State v. Baccino, 282 A.2d 869 (Del.Super.1971).

38. Bellnier v. Lund, 438 F.Supp. 47 (N.D.N.Y.1977).

A student's freedom from unreasonable search and seizure must be balanced against the need for school officials to maintain order and discipline and to protect the health and welfare of all the students. Where an assistant principal threatened to call student's parents forcing the student to reluctantly, but voluntarily, empty his pockets producing a pipe and marijuana, the court held that such search was legitimate. Where the scope of intrusion is slight and there is no police involvement school officials are held only to a "reasonable cause to believe" standard.[39]

With regard to searching school lockers, the Supreme Court of Kansas [40] has held that the student does not have exclusive possession of the school locker against the school and its officials. The school locker does not possess the same attributes of sole possession that is found in one's dwelling, motor vehicle, or private locker.

The Kansas court was careful to indicate that the locker was opened on the principal's "own judgment" even though requested to do so by police. While not pursuing this point sufficiently, the court appeared to imply that the school principal must instigate the search of his own volition with reasonable suspicion on behalf of the school. But without the intervention of the principal, the police cannot search the locker for the primary purpose of obtaining evidence for criminal prosecution. With regard to school and police cooperation in the search of university dormitory rooms one court said:

> "True, the University retains broad supervisory powers which permit it to * * * [provide reasonable regulation] to further the University's function as an educational institution. The regulation cannot be construed or applied so as to give consent to a search for evidence for the primary purpose of a criminal prosecution. Otherwise, the regulation itself would constitute an unconstitutional attempt to require a student to waive his protection from unreasonable searches and seizures as a condition to his occupancy of a college dormitory room * * *. *Clearly the University had no authority to consent or join in a police search for evidence of crime.*[41] [emphasis added]

Although the courts have not decided the specific issue, it *may* be permissible for a school principal to search a student's car if he has reason to believe that something harmful to students or the school is hidden there.[42] Supporting such a conclusion is a federal district court's decision in Maine which held constitutional a search

39. M. v. Board of Educ. Ball—Chatham Community School Dist. No. 5, 429 F.Supp. 288 (S.D.Ill.1977).

40. State v. Stein, 203 Kan. 638, 456 P. 2d 1 (1969), certiorari denied 90 U.S. 966, 90 S.Ct. 966 (1970).

41. Piazzola v. Watkins, 442 F.2d 284 (C.A.Ala.1971).

42. People v. Jackson, supra. (*In loco parentis* does not end at the school door).

of a "corpsman" bag at a Job Corp Center, producing marijuana, which was conducted without a warrant and not incident to arrest. The search, according to the court, was a constitutional exercise of the administrator's authority "to maintain proper standards of conduct and discipline at the Center." "Quite plainly the investigation was conducted solely for the purpose of ensuring proper moral and disciplinary conditions of the Center, an obligation mandated by federal statute." [43]

A warrantless search of a student's automobile by police officers violates the Fourth Amendment if the police officers received information in sufficient time to obtain a warrant and there is no danger that the goods will be removed or transported away.[44]

Validity of Search Rests on Balance Between School's In Loco Parentis Authority and Student's Fourth Amendment Rights

STATE v. BACCINO

Superior Court of Delaware, New Castle, 1971.
282 A.2d 869.

BIFFERATO, Judge. The Court heard defendant's motion to suppress evidence in the above captioned case on April 6, 1971. The delay in deciding this case was due to the briefing. The Court finds the relevant facts to be as follows:

On October 20, 1970, at approximately 1:45 p.m. two students of Brandywine High School were brought to the Vice Principal's office after being found out of class illegally. The Vice Principal, Robert M. Barto, sent one of the boys to class and brought the second boy, Joseph A. Baccino, Jr., the defendant, to his assigned class. At that time the defendant was carrying a coat. The Vice Principal took the coat from the defendant to make sure that the defendant would go to class. Prior to the Vice Principal obtaining possession of the coat there was a tug-of-war over it, and, of course, the Vice Principal won. Because the defendant was out of class illegally and because the defendant was known to the Vice Principal to have experimented with drugs in the past, the Vice Principal made a search of the coat, finding ten packets of hashish. The State Police were called and the defendant was arrested for possession of a dangerous drug with intent to sell.

Defendant files this motion and claims that the Vice Principal, as an employee of the State Educational System, that he is bound to have probable cause before he makes a search and that the search

---

43. United States v. Coles, 302 F.Supp. 99 (D.C.Me.1969).

44. Caldwell v. Cannady, 340 F.Supp. 835 (D.C.Tex.1972).

made by the Vice Principal was without probable cause and, therefore, inadmissible.

The legal issue to be resolved is a narrow one. Is the principal of a high school a private individual to whom the prohibitions of the Fourth Amendment of the United States Constitution do not apply, * * * or government official or agent to whom the Fourth Amendment and the exclusionary rule applies. * * *

The rationale for the rule which allows unlawfully seized evidence by private individuals to be admitted, aside from the fact that it is not constitutional, is the notion that private individuals would not be deterred by an exclusionary rule. Ann. 36 A.L.R.2d 553, 559. While this may be true in the case of isolated private searches, it is inapposite to the situation of a school principal who has a duty to investigate unlawful activity.

* * *

Since 42 U.S.C.A. § 1983 requires the principals' actions to be "state action" in order for a Federal Court to recognize a cause of action, it is difficult to see how a principal could also be a private official for purposes of the Fourth Amendment at the same time. Therefore, I conclude that a principal is not a private individual for purposes of the Fourth Amendment but that his actions are those of a state official and are subject to the Fourth Amendment. This does not mean, however, that the entire law of search and seizure as it applies in the criminal law is automatically incorporated into the school system of this state. The Fourth Amendment is the line which protects the privacy of individuals including students but only after taking into account the interests of society.

In Delaware a principal stands in loco parentis to pupils under his charge for disciplinary action, at least for purposes which are consistent with the need to maintain an effective educational atmosphere. 14 Del.C. § 701 (1970).

Thus, the question becomes what is the relationship of the doctrine of loco parentis to the Fourth Amendment. There is a split of authority in the cases which have considered the issue. In Mercer v. State, Tex.Civ.App., 450 S.W.2d 715 (1970) the Court held that since the principal was acting in loco parentis, he was not an arm of the government. * * * However, in People v. Jackson, 65 Misc.2d 909, 319 N.Y.S.2d 731 (1971) the New York Supreme Court, Appellate Division, after classifying the Coordinator of Discipline as a government official, held that the doctrine of loco parentis was merely a compelling state interest to be balanced against the prohibitions of the Fourth Amendment. The result was the adoption of a standard of reasonable suspicion rather probable cause to justify a search in view of the "distinct relationship" between the high school official and the student.

New York has recognized that a student has a right to freedom from unreasonable searches and seizures. People v. Overton, 20 N. Y.2d 360, 283 N.Y.S.2d 22, 229 N.E.2d 596. Texas apparently does not. * * *

I believe the decisions of the United States Supreme Court, however, have made it clear that the Bill of Rights applies to juveniles. In re Gault, 387 U.S. 1, 87 S.Ct. 1428, 18 L.Ed.2d 527 (1967).

In Tinker v. Des Moines Independent Community School District, supra, the Supreme Court said that school officials do not possess absolute authority over their students and that students in state-operated schools are "persons" under the Federal Constitution, and are possessed of fundamental rights which the State must respect. Thus, in striking the balance we cannot ignore the students' constitutional rights. But various factual situations give rise to different standards and procedures in light of the Fourth Amendment. * * *

It is this court's duty to make sure schools do not become enclaves to totalitarianism, *Tinker*, supra, after taking into account the necessity to maintain discipline and an effective educational atmosphere.

Thus, I conclude that the doctrine of loco parentis 14 Del.C. § 701 must be balanced against the students' Fourth Amendment rights to determine whether or not those rights have been violated. The only question remaining is the standard to be used to strike the balance. I conclude, as did the majority in People v. Jackson, supra, that "[t]he in loco parentis doctrine is so compelling in light of public necessity and as social concept antedating the Fourth Amendment, that * * * a search, taken thereunder upon reasonable suspicion should be accepted as necessary and reasonable." 319 N.Y.S.2d 731, 736. This standard should adequately protect the student from arbitrary searches and seizures and give the school officials enough leeway to fulfill their duties.

Turning to the facts, the question is whether or not the principal had reasonable suspicion to believe that the defendant's jacket contained illegal drugs when he seized it. Or in the alternative, the question may be asked whether the principal was enforcing a reasonable school regulation when he seized the jacket and thereafter did he have reasonable suspicion that the jacket contained illegal drugs so that it became his duty to search it.

It is the Court's opinion that the Vice Principal had reasonable suspicion to believe that the defendant's jacket contained contraband. Defendant's motion to suppress the evidence is denied.

It is so ordered.

*School Authority with Reasonable Suspicion Can
Search Student Beyond School Grounds*

PEOPLE v. JACKSON

Supreme Court, Appellate Term, First Department, 1971.
65 Misc.2d 909, 319 N.Y.S.2d 731.

LUPIANO, Justice. On October 27, 1969 the Coordinator of Discipline at a city high school received information which caused him to proceed to a certain classroom. He sought out the defendant, a student, in the room and requested that he accompany him to his office. This the defendant did willingly. En route, the Coordinator observed a bulge in the defendant's left pants pocket and further observed him continually putting his hand in and taking it out of the pocket. As they neared his office, the defendant bolted for the door at the outside of the school. As he did this, the Coordinator noticed a policeman standing in front of his office and called out to him, "he's got junk and he's escaping". With that he pursued the defendant and caught up with him three blocks from the school. The Coordinator grabbed the defendant who still had his left hand in his left side pants pocket. Grabbing defendant's wrist, the latter's hand came out revealing the nipple of an eyedropper with other material clenched in his fist. The Coordinator held defendant's wrist and said, "give that to me"; thereupon the Coordinator opened his hand and found a set of "works", syringe, eyedropper, etc. This material, the subject matter of the motion to suppress, was then turned over to the police officer who also had pursued the boy and came upon the scene at that moment. The court below suppressed the evidence on the ground that the Coordinator, a governmental official, had searched the defendant without the prerequisite of probable cause, in violation of his constitutional rights.

Here, the Coordinator of Discipline of a city high school, acting with a high degree of suspicion, but short of probable cause, searched this student and found him in possession of a set of narcotics "works". While a student has the right to be free of unreasonable search and seizure, school authorities, in view of the "distinct relationship" between them and their students and the right of parents to expect that certain safeguards will be taken, have "the affirmative obligation of the school authorities to investigate any charge that a student is using or possessing narcotics", which "becomes a duty when suspicion arises" * * * A school official, standing *in loco parentis* to the children entrusted to his care, has, inter alia, the long honored obligation to protect them while in his charge, so far as possible, from harmful and dangerous influences, which certainly encompasses the bringing to school by one of them of narcotics and "works", whether for sale to other students or for administering such to himself or other students. I have read the citation of authorities given in the dissenting opinion relating to the "philosophy of loco parentis". Those cases are not affected by the doctrine and are inapposite.

What the Constitution (Fourth Amendment) forbids is not all searches and seizures, but unreasonable searches and seizures * * * Each search must be determined in its own setting. The Amendment, as it relates to seized property, after search, does not apply to private persons. Classifying the Coordinator as a governmental official, in his capacity and sphere of responsibility embracing the purpose and duties he is called upon to perform with respect to his charges, it would not be unreasonable or unwarranted that he be permitted to search the person of a student where the school official has reasonable suspicion that narcotics may be found on the person of his juvenile charge. Such action, of an investigatory nature, would and should be expected of him. Being justified, he would still be performing this important function, though three blocks from school, necessitated by the flight of this errant boy. As I view the incident, the Coordinator's function and responsibility went with him during the chase that took him and the boy away from the school. In loco parentis purpose did not end abruptly at the school door. The need to fulfill that purpose—including the making of a search—extended uninterruptedly beyond the school limits since the defendant chose to run away. This is a far cry from a situation not stemming from the school, without the nexus existing here. Absent that nexus, the search and seizure by the Coordinator would be unreasonable and unlawful for the obvious reason that his duties and responsibilities originate within the school.

To circumscribe the official's action, in these circumstances, within school limits would be akin to the incident where the cinematic county sheriff stops in hot pursuit of the wrongdoer at the county line, ruefully watching him cross over, powerless to do anything more.

The dissenting opinion emphasizes that the search and seizure happened away from the school and that the action of the policeman and the school official conjoined in making the search and seizure. This is misplaced emphasis, because proper place is not given to the official's right and duty to act as he did in the circumstances, originally and independently, in fulfillment of a quasi-parental obligation. Moreover, this right and duty did not make him a law enforcement officer as the dissent suggests. Rather as the doctrine suggests, and simply stated, he was acting in a limited manner, in place of the defendant's parents. In the landmark case, relating to the duty of teachers in the supervision of school children, the Court of Appeals in Hoose v. Drumm, 281 N.Y. 54, at page 57–58, 22 N.E.2d 233, at page 234 stated: "at recess periods, not less than in the class room, a teacher owes it to his charges to exercise such care of them as a par-

ent of ordinary prudence would observe in comparable circumstances." (Emphasis supplied)

Stated differently, a school teacher, to a limited extent at least, stands in loco parentis to pupils under his charge, and may exercise such powers of control, restraint and correction over them as may be reasonably necessary to enable him properly to perform his duties as a teacher and accomplish the purposes of education (C.J.S. Schools and School Districts § 493).

This doctrine is imbedded in the common law and has received implicit recognition by our State Legislature through the enactment of Sec. 35.10, Penal Law, McKinney's Consol.Laws, c. 40, which restates the former Penal Law, Sec. 246(4)(6). The section declares: "The use of physical force upon another person which would otherwise constitute an offense is justifiable and not criminal under any of the following circumstances:

1. A parent, guardian or other person entrusted with the care and supervision of a minor or an incompetent person, and a teacher or other person entrusted with the care and supervision of a minor for a special purpose, may use physical force, but not deadly physical force, upon such minor or incompetent person when and to the extent that he *reasonably believes it necessary to maintain discipline or to promote the welfare of such minor* or incompetent person." (Emphasis supplied)

Without proper recognition of the doctrine, the reasonableness of the official's conduct toward the defendant cannot be properly viewed and concluded. With full recognition, however, the action of the official toward the student, taken in school and away from school, partaking of their "distinct relationship", may be better understood and accepted as necessary and reasonable in light of loco parentis and in juxtaposition with the Fourth Amendment . * * *

* * *

The *in loco parentis* doctrine is so compelling in light of public necessity and as a social concept antedating the Fourth Amendment, that any action, including a search, taken thereunder upon reasonable suspicion should be accepted as necessary and reasonable. * * *

* * * While we are far advanced from the days of the Little Red Schoolhouse, such advancement has also brought great ills. Rampant crime and drug abuse threaten our schools and the youngsters exposed to such ills. Much could be written about the ponderous problems that beset parents and school authorities in their efforts to prevent and stave off the conditions all about us. We are well aware of the gravity of these conditions. There is no need for enlargement. In consequence, greater responsibility has fallen upon those charged with the well-being and discipline of these children. What they may do in that regard should be weighed, on balance, with

full appreciation of their duties and the nature of that greater responsibility. Only then can reasonableness be concluded in the context of the prevailing circumstances relating to the Fourth Amendment. Of course, absolute control should not be handed over in the everyday dealings with these children. Reasonable restraint is imposed, less what the school officials do shall take the form of authoritarian behavior, trammelling the rights of the students entrusted to them. Toward that end, a basis founded at least upon reasonable grounds for suspecting that something unlawful is being committed, or about to be committed, shall prevail before justifying a search of a student when the school official is acting *in loco parentis.*

I, therefore, conclude that within the framework of this happening, <u>no arbitrary invasion of the defendant's privacy resulted</u>. On the contrary, the search and seizure, based at least upon reasonable grounds for suspecting that something unlawful was being committed, or about to be committed, must be deemed a reasonable search and seizure within the intendment of the Fourth Amendment as applied to the "distinct relationship" of the high school official to his student.

Order referred on the law and the facts. Motion to suppress hypodermic needle and "works" denied and the case remitted to the court below for further appropriate proceedings.

School Officials May be Obligated to Inspect School Lockers

PEOPLE v. OVERTON

Court of Appeals of New York, 1967.
20 N.Y.2d 360, 283 N.Y.S.2d 22, 229 N.E.2d 596, affirmed on reargument
24 N.Y.2d 522, 301 N.Y.S.2d 479, 249 N.E.2d 366, 1969.

KEATING, Judge. Three detectives of the Mount Vernon Police Department having obtained a search warrant went to the Mount Vernon High School. The warrant directed a search of the persons of two students and, also, of their lockers.

The detectives presented the warrant to the vice-principal, Dr. Panitz, who sent for the two students, one of whom was the defendant, Carlos Overton. The detectives searched them and found nothing. A subsequent search of Overton's locker, however, revealed four marijuana cigarettes.

The defendant moved to invalidate that portion of the search warrant which directed a search of his locker, on the ground that the papers were defective upon which it was based. This motion was granted. The court denied the motion to suppress, however, on the grounds that the vice-principal had consented to the search and that he had a right to do so. The Appellate Term reversed and dismissed the information, holding that the consent of the vice-principal could not justify an otherwise illegal search. The People have appealed from this order of the Appellate Term.

It is axiomatic that the protection of the Fourth Amendment is not restricted to dwellings. A depository such as a locker or even a desk is safeguarded from unreasonable searches for evidence of a crime (United States v. Blok, 88 U.S.App.D.C. 326, 188 F.2d 1019).

There are situations, however, where someone other than the defendant in possession of a depository may consent to what otherwise would have been an illegal search. Such a case was United States v. Botsch, 364 F.2d 542 [2d Cir. 1966], cert. den. 386 U.S. 937, 87 S.Ct. 959, 17 L.Ed.2d 810. In that case, the defendant had rented a shed from one Stein. Stein retained a key to the shed and accepted deliveries on behalf of the defendant. When the police approached Stein and informed him of their suspicion that the defendant was receiving goods obtained through fraud, Stein consented to a search of the shed.

In upholding the search, the court noted two significant factors. First, Stein had a key to the shed and, second, more than a mere landlord-tenant relationship existed, since Stein was empowered to take deliveries on behalf of the defendant. The court also noted that Stein had a right to exculpate himself from implication in the defendant's scheme.

Considering all these factors cumulatively, the court concluded that, in this situation, Stein could give consent to the search. Thus, the search was not unreasonable in contravention of the Fourth Amendment.

Dr. Panitz, in this case, gave his consent to the search of Overton's locker. The dissenting opinion suggests, however, that Dr. Panitz' consent was not freely given, because he acted under compulsion of the invalid search warrant. If this were the case, his consent might be rendered somewhat questionable. However, Dr. Panitz testified that: "Being responsible for the order, assignment, and maintenance of the physical facilities, if *any* report were given to me by *anyone* of an article or item of the nature that does not belong there, or of an illegal nature, I would inspect the locker." (Italics supplied.)

This testimony demonstrates beyond doubt that Dr. Panitz would have consented as he did regardless of the presence of the invalid search warrant.

The power of Dr. Panitz to give his consent to this search arises out of the distinct relationship between school authorities and students.

The school authorities have an obligation to maintain discipline over the students. It is recognized that when large numbers of teenagers are gathered together in such an environment, their inexperience and lack of mature judgment can often create hazards to each other. Parents, who surrender their children to this type of environment, in order that they may continue developing both intellectually and socially, have a right to expect certain safeguards.

It is in the high school years particularly that parents are justifiably concerned that their children not become accustomed to antisocial behavior, such as the use of illegal drugs. The susceptibility to suggestion of students of high school age increases the danger. Thus, it is the affirmative obligation of the school authorities to investigate any charge that a student is using or possessing narcotics and to take appropriate steps, if the charge is substantiated.

When Overton was assigned his locker, he, like all the other students at Mount Vernon High School, gave the combination to his home room teacher who, in turn, returned it to an office where it was kept on file. The students at Mount Vernon are well aware that the school authorities possess the combinations of their lockers. It appears understood that the lock and the combination are provided in order that each student may have exclusive possession of the locker vis-à-vis other students, but the student does not have such exclusivity over the locker as against the school authorities. In fact, the school issues regulations regarding what may and may not be kept in the lockers and presumably can spot check to insure compliance. The vice-principal testified that he had, on occasion, inspected the lockers of students.

Indeed, it is doubtful if a school would be properly discharging its duty of supervision over the students, if it failed to retain control over the lockers. Not only have the school authorities a right to inspect but this right becomes a duty when suspicion arises that something of an illegal nature may be secreted there. When Dr. Panitz learned of the detectives' suspicion, he was obligated to inspect the locker. This interest, together with the nonexclusive nature of the locker, empowered him to consent to the search by the officers.

Accordingly, the order of the Appellate Term should be reversed and the matter remitted to that court for consideration of the other points raised by the defendant which were not decided on the prior appeal.

* * *

NOTES

1. Where the primary purpose of the school official's search was not to obtain convictions, but to secure evidence of student misconduct, the fact that evidence of crime is uncovered and prosecution results therefrom should not itself make the search and seizure illegal. In re Donaldson, 269 Cal.App.2d 509, 75 Cal.Rptr. 220 (1969).

2. A search of a student's automobile by officials of a nonpublic quasi-military academy has been upheld by federal district court in Maine. Plaintiff student was dismissed from the academy following a search of his car at the direction of the school disciplinary officer. The search produced a quantity of marijuana and a can of beer. Such a search, according to the

court, was a reasonable exercise of supervisory authority of the school. The court pointed out that the search was not conducted by a police officer. It should also be observed that this case has limited utility for public schools since the Fourth Amendment protects an individual from unwarranted search by government and does not protect against search by a private person or private school. Keene v. Rodgers, 316 F.Supp. 217 (D.C.Me. 1970).

3. Search of a student's locker and briefcase in a private university without a search warrant was upheld by the Supreme Court of California. Marijuana was found in the locker after other students reported an offensive odor coming from the locker. The court said:

> "Even if [the] University were a 'public' rather than a 'private' institution, the search here challenged would be reasonable within the meaning of the Fourth Amendment. It is true the search was conducted without a warrant, and the burden therefore rested upon the People to show justification. * * * But that burden was sustained in the case at bar by a compelling showing of facts bringing the search within the 'emergency' exception to the warrant requirement. In the case at bar * * * a 'compelling urgency' was clearly shown." * * * "* * * inasmuch as the students entitled to use the room had already been disturbed by this offensive odor throughout the preceding day, further delay in suppressing it would have been unjustifiable. Once the defendant's briefcase was discovered and opened, its contents were in plain sight. An observation from a lawful vantage point of contraband in plain sight is not, a 'search' in the constitutional sense." People v. Lanthier, 5 Cal.3d 751, 97 Cal.Rptr. 297, 488 P.2d 625 (1971).

Student Marriage and Pregnancy

Over the years educators have been concerned about the impact of teenage marriages on the educational process. This factor, coupled with the huge increase in enrollment in the public schools and the social and economic significance placed on the need for a high school diploma, has created problems heretofore unencountered by school personnel. School officials are placed in the precarious position of assisting the newlyweds to adjust to their new relationship and, at the same time, finding ways and means to discourage early marriages among their classmates.

Many procedures and policies have been adopted by school boards to cope with the problem of teenage marriages. These measures fall within three general categories: attempts to require married pupils to attend school; attempts to limit or prohibit participation of married pupils in school activities; and attempts to suspend or expel married pupils. These actions reflect an attitude of many school administrators that married pupils exert an undesirable influence on other pupils. Some of the reasons for this sentiment could be the general feeling that these pupils expect special considerations; they attend school irregularly; they discuss matters of a personal and intimate nature; and they show a marked decrease in scholarship.

While marriages, though, may be discouraged, the married student has a legal right to attend school. This particular issue was settled in 1929 when the Supreme Court of Mississippi invalidated a school board rule which prohibited married students from attending public schools because, the board argued, "marriage brings about views of life which should not be known to unmarried children." The Court in striking down this rule and ordering the student admitted observed that marriage is a domestic relation "highly favored by law" and is "refining and elevating, rather than demoralizing." [45]

The courts have given a mixed response to whether married students can participate in extracurricular activities of the school. The older view is that such restraints are valid because it is a legitimate school purpose to discourage early marriage and extracurricular activities tend to give married participants greater status and influence among their classmates.[46] The more recent view of the courts maintains that denial of participation in the full range of school activities constitutes an invasion of the students' protected right of marital privacy.[47] In this particular case the boy was an honor student and as a member of the baseball team had an opportunity to go on to play either college or professional baseball. The court observed that the boy had violated no law and the school rule had placed unendurable strain on his marriage. In another case, a federal district court in Tennessee held that a school board regulation against married student participation in extracurricular activities was not related to any reasonable educational purpose its sole purpose being to punish and discourage marriage. As such the rule impermissibly infringed on the student's rights as protected under both due process and equal protection clauses.[48] Most recently, the Colorado Court of Appeals reviewed this issue and found that the school board's rationale of forcing married students to concentrate on their basic studies was an insufficient justification to exclude them from extracurricular activities. Although this case became moot because the student graduated during the judicial process, the court's view, nevertheless, seems to represent the prevailing precedent today.[49]

There appears to be a custom existing in many school districts throughout the country to suspend or expel either married or unmarried pregnant students. Recent decisions by the federal courts have

45. McLeod v. State, 154 Miss. 468, 122 So. 737 (1929).

46. Kissick v. Garland Independent School Dist., 330 S.W.2d 708 (Tex.Civ. App. 1959).

47. Davis v. Meek, 344 F.Supp. 298 (D. C.Ohio 1972).

48. Holt v. Shelton Dist., 341 F.Supp. 821 (D.C.Tenn.1972). See also: Hollon v. Mathis Ind. School Dist., 358 F. Supp. 1269 (S.D.Tex.1973), vacated 491 F.2d 92; Romans v. Crenshaw, 354 F.Supp. 868 (S.D.Tex.1972).

49. Beeson v. Kiowa County School Dist., 567 P.2d 801 (Colo.1977).

been in opposition to these practices. School board justification for suspension of pregnant students has been traditionally justified on grounds that it protected the mental and physical health of the pregnant student or her child to be.

Board Regulation Mandating Withdrawal of Married Student from School Is Invalid

BOARD OF EDUC. OF HARRODSBURG v. BENTLEY

Court of Appeals of Kentucky, 1964.
383 S.W.2d 677.

DAVIS, Commissioner. This appeal tests the validity of a school board regulation requiring that any student who shall marry shall withdraw from the school, subject to being readmitted after one year. The trial court adjudged that the regulation is invalid and granted a permanent injunction against enforcement of the regulation as applied to appellee.

The Board of Education of Harrodsburg Independent School District (hereinafter designated as the Board) duly adopted the questioned resolution in 1957; the text of the resolution is:

"Any student, either boy or girl, who marries, automatically must withdraw immediately from school and cannot re-enter school for one full year, and then only as a special student with permission of the principal. A special student cannot attend home room or study halls or enter into any class activities, social events or athletics. If, upon re-entering school after the year has elapsed, the student becomes pregnant, she will automatically withdraw until after the birth of the child."

The record reflects that the Board's policy, as enunciated by the resolution, was widely publicized, and was known to the appellee prior to the time of her marriage. Although the text of the resolution remained unchanged, it is admitted that the Board had uniformly followed the policy of permitting a student to complete the six-week term in progress at the time of the marriage.

Appellee was a regularly enrolled student at Harrodsburg High School and a member of the junior class when she married April 10, 1964. The six-week term then current lacked one and a half weeks of completion. Appellee was permitted to remain as a student until the close of that six-week period; she was required to withdraw from school and dropped from its rolls April 24, 1964.

Appellee then enrolled in Mercer County High School, but remained there only a day and a half. Her mother withdrew her from that school, and sought to have her reinstated in Harrodsburg High School. The Board, at a specially called session, heard the request of appellee and her parents, but expressed the view that it could not make an exception as to appellee since it had uniformly invoked the rule theretofore. This suit resulted.

Certain fundamental precepts were recognized by the trial court, and are acknowledged by the litigants:

The Board is vested with the duty and power to control and manage the Harrodsburg High School. The Board is authorized to enforce reasonable regulations, including disciplinary rules. KRS 160.-160.

* * *

It is also recognized by all that KRS 158.100 mandatorily directs that each board of education shall provide public educational facilities for residents of its district who are under twenty-one years of age. There is no specific statutory provision dealing with the matter of married pupils under age twenty-one.

With these accepted principles in mind, we turn to the specific controversy at bar. The appellee was sixteen years old at the time of her marriage. The marriage ceremony was publicly performed in a Harrodsburg church. The marriage must have been approved by appellee's parents, pursuant to the provisions of KRS 402.210, although the record is silent as to that.

There is no suggestion that any sensationalism or scandal preceded or followed the wedding. It is admitted that appellee is now, and has been throughout her lifetime, a moral and respectable person. There has been no complaint of misbehavior or misconduct on her part. She has maintained a creditable, above average scholastic record.

For the Board, it was shown that the 1957 regulation had been adopted, upon public demand of parents and patrons, by reason of an "epidemic" of marriages of high school students. Moreover, the Board predicated its policy upon its belief, from experience and counsel of its superintendent, that such marriages during school term cause discussion and excitement, thereby disrupting school work and leading to dropping out of school. The Board expressed its view that student marriage is detrimental to the best interests and welfare of a good and successful school system.

It is recalled that the regulation in question provides for readmission of a married student after "one full year, and then only as a special student with permission of the principal." However, the record reflects that it has been the uniform policy in enforcment of the rule that the married student be permitted to complete the current six-week term. It was explained that the disruptive impact of student marriage is by reason of widespread student body discussion and excitement just prior to and just following the marriage. Apparently the regulation as originally promulgated sought to alleviate the disruption generally said to be attendant at the time just before and just following the marriage. As noted, however, quite the opposite practice has been consistently followed. The pupil (including the present appellee) is allowed to remain actively in full school routine during the immediate time following the marriage—but no longer than the end of the then current six-week term.

It is accepted, of course, that marriage is favored by public policy. 35 Am.Jur., Marriage, § 3. The General Assembly has imposed various requirements looking toward preservation of the institution of marriage. KRS Chapter 402. Specifically, Kentucky's legislature has placed its sanction upon marriage of a female who has attained age sixteen. KRS 402.020(5). The safeguard of written consent from one in *loco parentis* is demanded for marriage participants under age twenty-one. KRS 402.210.

On the other hand, no question arises as to the sincerity of purpose of the Board here. It has acted upon the counsel of its superintendent and its own experience in administration of the affairs of the school under its jurisdiction. We have neither the right nor the inclination to substitute our view for the Board's view as to the exercise of its sound discretion as it relates to matters within the province of the Board's responsibilities. It does become our function to examine the regulation and determine whether it is unreasonable or arbitrary, and therefore illegal. (There is no suggestion that the Board has acted maliciously.)

In 47 Am.Jur., Schools, § 155, it said:

"However, a pupil may not be excluded from school because married, where no immorality or misconduct of the pupil is shown, nor that the welfare and discipline of the pupils of the school is injuriously affected by the presence of the married pupil."

* * * It may be observed that the Tennessee decision just cited is the only one which may be said to lend support to the position of the Board here. In most of the cases just cited the courts upheld regulations prohibiting married students from certain cocurricular and extracurricular activities. In so doing, the courts adverted to the factor that the particular board was not making marriage, *ipso facto,* the basis for denial of the student's right to obtain an education.

For the appellee it is pointed out that all persons meeting the residence, moral and mental qualifications are entitled to an opportunity for publicly furnished education until attaining age twenty-one. In today's economy we judicially note the increasing demand for education as a prerequisite for employment. Certainly, there is no reason to suppose that the marriage of a student will diminish the need of that student for an education—indeed, just the contrary would appear the case.

It is our conclusion that the decision of the trial court is correct; the instant regulation is arbitrary and unreasonable, and therefore void. The fatal vice of the regulation lies in its sweeping, advance determination that every married student, regardless of the circumstances, must lose at least a year's schooling. Moreover, the manner of enforcement of the regulation accentuates the fact that the regulation is not realistically related to its purported purpose. It is asserted for the Board that the most intense disruptive impact of a student marriage occurs during the time just preceding and just following the marriage. Yet, under the uniformly followed pattern of administration of this regulation, the married student is permitted to remain in school during all of the time preceding the marriage, and may remain for a maximum of six weeks thereafter. Such procedure, even though premised on the Board's commendable desire to permit the student to complete the current term, effectively frustrates the prime purpose of the regulation. Additionally, after it may be reasoned that the disturbing influence of the event has subsided, the situation is returned to the "spotlight" of student attention by compelling withdrawal of the married student; after a year, assuming the principal is willing, the student is to be reinstated, thus injecting another occasion for student body agitation.

The regulation has a further inherent weakness in that it merely provides that a married student *may* be permitted to resume school if, but only if, the principal permits it. Of course, we will not assume that the principal would arbitrarily deny permission—but there is a complete absence of any standard or guideline for the principal; neither has the ousted student any gauge by which to estimate whether the principal's consent will be forthcoming after a year.

Implicit in this record is the desire of the Board to permit this appellee to "work something out" so that her education would not be interrupted. A review of the Board's minutes warrants the conclusion that the Board felt that its hands were tied—principally because it never had made any previous exception in such cases. The unreasonable and arbitrary effect of the regulation is thus demonstrated, since it imposes the identical result in every case, without regard to the circumstances of any case. The Board's discretion is foreclosed in advance, no matter what the facts. Such prejudgment is unreasonable and arbitrary.

We are not to be understood here as deciding that some reasonable and appropriate regulation in this area may not be adopted; we do hold the instant regulation invalid.

Without undertaking to restate the arguments which may be advanced in support of either side of the question, we state that we are persuaded that the view quoted (47 Am.Jur., Schools, Sec. 155) is sound. Consequently, it is our holding that the regulation here is an arbitrary and unreasonable one.

The judgment is affirmed.

NOTES

1. Would the court's decision have been otherwise if the Harrodsburg School Board had immediately expelled a pupil following his marriage rather than permitting him to complete the current six-weeks term?

2. Near the conclusion of the opinion of the Harrodsburg case, the Court states: "We are not to be understood here as deciding that some reasonable and appropriate regulation in this area may not be adopted. * * *" What would constitute the essential elements of a "reasonable and appropriate regulation in this area"?

3. Board of education has authority to adopt a regulation barring married high school students from participation in extra-curricular school activities. Estay v. LaFourche Parish School Board, 230 So.2d 443 (La. App.1969).

4. In the case of Cochrane v. Board of Education of Mesick Consolidated School District, 360 Mich. 390, 103 N.W.2d 569 (1960), the fathers of two sons enrolled in a secondary public school petitioned the Court to direct the school officials to reinstate the boys in cocurricular activities. The Court upheld the school policy forbidding the boys to play football because of their marital status.

5. The Michigan Attorney General intervened in the Cochrane case, supra, and contended that the school district policy was void. He said, " * * * The concern of the law is to protect, not to attack, the state of matrimony, and to exalt, not to undermine, the security of legal marriages * * * They are entitled, by law and public policy, to the respect and security of community acceptance in their married status, as well as to all the benefits of equal access to all public educational facilities, including their earned status in the cocurricular activities." How plausible is this position?

6. Two more cases involving pupil marriages and nonparticipation in cocurricular activities are State ex rel. Baker v. Stevenson, Ohio Com.Pl., 189 N.E.2d 181 (1962), and Starkey v. Board of Ed. of Davis County School Dist., 14 Utah 2d 227, 381 P.2d 718 (1963). Board policies were upheld in each of these cases.

In the Ohio case, a boy was married in February—wife was pregnant at the time. Board's policy against married pupil participation in extracurricular activities included leadership in school organizations, athletics, scholarship activities, band, glee club, social events, dramatic events, cheerleading, etc. Plaintiff challenged the rule as being arbitrary and unreasonable and that it penalized marriage and was therefore void. In upholding the board's actions the Court said it would not interfere with the board's ruling unless it was unreasonable. In this case the student was an outstanding basketball player given "hero" status. The court said further: "We have all witnessed the effect upon the entire student body caused when the 'star' football or basketball player decides to adopt a manner of speech, type of haircut, wear a particular kind of clothing, eat a particular kind of food, expresses a preference for a definite song, singer, playing record, actor or performer and ad infinitum."

It is a matter of common knowledge that a great segment of our adult population has likewise succumbed to the worship of the athlete. Many times the high school students have difficulty in securing seats at athletic contests because the adults have pre-empted their places."

"Untold thousands upon thousands of dollars have been reaped by manufacturers from the sale of razor blades, lotions, hair tonic, and creams, cigarettes and many, many other items made popular merely because used and consumed by Mickey Mantle, Frankie Robinson (we have yet to hear from Jerry Lucas), Oscar Robertson, et al."

"How much more susceptible, therefore, the high school student to the athletic 'star'". * * * "If any married students are in a position of idolization, the more desirous is the group to mimic."

"Any policy which is directed toward making juvenile marriages unpopular and to be avoided should have the general public's wholehearted approval and support."

Pregnant Unmarried Student Cannot be Excluded from School Attendance

ORDWAY v. HARGRAVES

United States District Court, District of Massachusetts, 1971.
323 F.Supp. 1155.

CAFFREY, District Judge. This is a civil action brought on behalf of an 18-year old pregnant, unmarried, senior at the North Middlesex Regional High School, Townsend, Massachusetts. The respondents are the Principal of the High School, Robert Hargraves, the seven individual members of the North Middlesex Regional High School Committee, and the School Committees of Pepperell and Townsend. The cause of action is alleged to arise under the Civil Rights Act, 42 U.S.C.A. § 1983, and jurisdiction of this court is invoked under 28 U.S.C.A. § 1343. The matter came before the court for hearing on plaintiff's application for preliminary injunctive relief in the nature of an order requiring respondents to re-admit her to the Regional High School on a full-time, regular-class-hour, basis.

At the hearing, eight witnesses testified. On the basis of the credible evidence adduced at the hearing, I find that the minor plaintiff, Fay Ordway, resides at East Pepperell, Massachusetts, and is presently enrolled as a senior in the North Middlesex Regional High School; and that plaintiff informed Mr. Hargraves, approximately January 28, 1971, that she was pregnant and expected to give birth to a baby in June 1971. There is outstanding a rule of the Regional school committee, numbered Rule 821, which provides: "Whenever an unmarried girl enrolled in North Middlesex Regional High School shall be known to be pregnant, her membership in the school shall be immediately terminated." Because of the imminence of certain examinations and the fact that school vacation was beginning on February 12, Mr. Hargraves informed plaintiff that she was to stop attending regular classes at the high school as of the close of school on February 12. This instruction was confirmed in writing by a letter from Mr. Hargraves to plaintiff's mother, Mrs. Iona Ordway, dated February 22, 1971, in which Mr. Hargraves stated that the following conditions would govern Fay Ordway's relations with the school for the remainder of the school year:

a) Fay will absent herself from school during regular school hours.

b) Fay will be allowed to make use of all school facilities such as library, guidance, administrative, teaching, etc., on any school day after the normal dismissal time of 2:16 P.M.

c) Fay will be allowed to attend all school functions such as games, dances, plays, etc.

d) Participation in senior activities such as class trip, reception, etc.

e) Seek extra help from her teachers during after school help sessions when needed.

f) Tutoring at no cost if necessary; such tutors to be approved by the administration.

g) Her name will remain on the school register for the remainder of the 1970–71 school year (to terminate on graduation day—tentatively scheduled for June 11, 1971).

h) Examinations will be taken periodically based upon mutual agreement between Fay and the respective teacher. * * *

At the hearing, Dr. F. Woodward Lewis testified that he is plaintiff's attending physician and that she is in excellent health to attend school. He expressed the opinion that the dangers in attending school are no worse for her than for a non-pregnant girl student, and that she can participate in all ordinary school activities with the exception of violent calisthenics. * * *

* * *

Dr. Mary Jane England, a medical-doctor and psychiatrist attached to the staff of St. Elizabeth's Hospital, expressed the opinion that young girls in plaintiff's position who are required to absent themselves from school become depressed, and that the depression of the mother has an adverse effect on the child, who frequently is born depressed and lethargic. She further testified that from a psychiatric point of view it is desirable to keep a person in the position of plaintiff in as much contact with her friends and peer group as possible, and that they should not be treated as having a malady or disease.

* * *

Plaintiff testified that her most recent grades were an A, a B-plus, and two C-pluses, and that she strongly desires to attend school with her class during regular school hours. She testified that she has not been subjected to any embarrassment by her classmates, nor has she been involved in any disruptive incidents of any kind. She further testified that she has not been aware of any resentment or any other change of attitude on the part of the other students in the school. * * *

　　　*　*　*

It is clear, from the hearing, that no attempt is being made to stigmatize or punish plaintiff by the school principal or, for that matter, by the school committees. It is equally clear that were plaintiff married, she would be allowed to remain in class during regular school hours despite her pregnancy. Mr. Hargraves made it clear that the decision to exclude plaintiff was not his personal decision, but was a decision he felt required to make in view of the policy of the school committee which he is required to enforce as part of his duties as principal. In response to questioning, Mr. Hargraves could not state any educational purpose to be served by excluding plaintiff from regular class hours, and he conceded that plaintiff's pregnant condition has not occasioned any disruptive incident nor has it otherwise interfered with school activities. Cf. Tinker v. Des Moines Independent Community School District, 393 U.S. 503, 514, 89 S.Ct. 733, 740, 21 L.Ed.2d 731 (1969), where the Supreme Court limited school officials' curtailment of claimed rights of students to situations involving "substantial disruption of or material interference with school activities."

Mr. Hargraves did imply, however, his opinion is that the policy of the school committee might well be keyed to a desire on the part of the school committee not to appear to condone conduct on the part of unmarried students of a nature to cause pregnancy. The thrust of his testimony seems to be: the regional school has both junior and senior high school students in its student population; he finds the twelve-to-fourteen age group to be still flexible in their attitudes; they might be led to believe that the school authorities are condoning premarital relations if they were to allow girl students in plaintiff's situation to remain in school.

It should be noted that if concerns of this nature were a valid ground for the school committee regulation, the contents of paragraph b), c) and d) of Mr. Hargraves' letter of February 22 to plaintiff's mother substantially undercut those considerations.

In summary, no danger to petitioner's physical or mental health resultant from her attending classes during regular school hours has been shown; no likelihood that her presence will cause any disruption of or interference with school activities or pose a threat of harm to others has been shown; and no valid educational or other reason to justify her segregation and to require her to receive a type of educational treatment which is not the equal of that given to all others in her class has been shown.

It would seem beyond argument that the right to receive a public school education is a basic personal right or liberty. <u>Consequently, the burden of justifying any school rule or regulation limiting or terminating that right is on the school authorities.</u> Cf. Richards v. Thurston, 424 F.2d 1281, at 1286 (1 Cir. 1970), where the court ruled:

> "In the absence of an inherent, self-evident justification on the face of the rule, we conclude that the burden was on the defendant."

On the record before me, respondents have failed to carry this burden. Accordingly, it is

Ordered:

1. <u>Respondents are to re-admit plaintiff to regular attendance at North Middlesex Regional High School until further order of this court.</u>

2. <u>This order will be effective as of the opening of school,</u> at 8:00 A.M., Monday, March 15, 1971.

NOTES

1. <u>A federal district court ruled that unwed mothers may not be expelled from school unless there is a showing that she is so lacking in moral character as to adversely affect the education of other pupils.</u> Judge Smith wrote, "* * * the fact that a girl has one child out of wedlock does not forever brand her as a scarlet woman undeserving of any chance for rehabilitation or the opportunity for future education." 300 F.Supp. 748 (D.C. Miss.1969).

2. <u>A student may not be excluded from school for the sole reason that she is an unwed mother.</u> Shull v. Columbus Municipal Separate School District, 338 F.Supp. 1376 (D.C.Miss.1972).

Sex Discrimination

<u>Prohibitions against discrimination on the basis of sex are found in the Equal Protection Clause of the Fourteenth Amendment, Title VI of the Civil Rights Act of 1964 and Title IX of the Education Amendments of 1972.</u> Each of these legal standards have had a great impact on the schools during the past few years affecting admission standards, quotas, facilities, and athletic programs.

The Fourteenth Amendment has been used to deal with all types of discrimination but only in the relative recent past has it been applied to sex discrimination. <u>Under the Supreme Court interpretations the Equal Protection Clause of the Fourteenth may be invoked using one of two standards, the rational relationship standard and the strict scrutiny standard.</u> The first approach, the rational relationship standard, has traditionally <u>given legislatures broad discretion in classifications of people for various reasons.</u> <u>Under this test the court presumes the legislature, or government agency, is acting ra-</u>

tionally, is not arbitrary, and the purpose of the legislations is reasonably related to a proper governmental objective. Under this standard the burden of proof is on the plaintiff to overcome this presumption. The second test, that of strict scrutiny, is invoked where the challenged legislation affects fundamental rights and bears on a suspect classification of people. This more active test shifts the burden to the government to show that it has a compelling interest in establishing such a classification. Race, color, and national origin are suspect classes which will invoke this standard. The Supreme Court has listed five ways by which a suspect class may be identified: (1) Does the class have an immutable characteristic, (2) is there a history of invidious discrimination against the class, (3) is the class a discrete and insular minority, (4) is the class politically powerless, and (5) does the classification stigmatize members of the class as inferior? [50] Regarding sex discrimination questions 3 and 5 are difficult to reconcile.

As a result, today, sex is not considered to be a suspect classification justifying the "strict scrutiny" standard, but recent cases suggest that the Supreme Court without actually applying the test does, in fact, give intensive analysis to the rationale for governmental action which may tend to discriminate. In Reed v. Reed[51] the Supreme Court rejected the strict scrutiny test, but nevertheless struck down an Idaho statute which discriminated against women.

In *Frontiero*,[52] four justices found that government regulations which discriminated against women in the armed forces should be strictly scrutinized, but four other justices held that the regulations should fall based on the *Reed* rational relationship test. Presently, the issue is in balance as to which test is to be utilized by the courts, but regardless of test the courts have systematically struck down a broad range of rules, regulations, and statutes as discriminatory.

In addition, however, vestiges of sex discrimination have been removed wholesale by application of a panoply of federal legislation.[53] Title VII of the Civil Rights Act of 1964 was amended by the Equal Employment Opportunity Act of 1972 prohibiting discrimination in employment on the basis of race, color, religion, national origin, or sex. Title VII (Section 799A) and Title VIII (Section 845) of the Public Health Service Act as amended by the Comprehensive Health Manpower Act and the Nurse Training Amendments Act of 1971 prohibits use of sex as a determination for admission. The Equal Pay Act of 1963 as amended by the Education Amendments of 1972

50. Frontiero v. Richardson, 411 U.S. 677, 93 S.Ct. 1764 (1973). See Mark A. Kadzielski, "Title IX of the Education Amendments of 1972: Change or Continuity," *Journal of Law and Education*, Vol. 6, No. 2, April, 1977, p. 185.

51. 404 U.S. 71, 92 S.Ct. 251 (1971).

52. 411 U.S. 677, 93 S.Ct. 1764 (1973).

53. See: Kadzielski, supra.

forbids discrimination in salaries based on sex. Title IX of the Education Amendments of 1972, patterned after Title VI of the Civil Rights Act of 1964, prohibits sex discrimination in educational institutions.[54]

All of these statutory efforts to end sex discrimination have had both direct and indirect impact on the operation of the public schools, but the one provision which has been most visible has been Title IX of the Education Amendments of 1972.

PUBLIC LAW 92–318

(Education Amendments of 1972).

TITLE IX—PROHIBITION OF SEX DISCRIMINATION

Sex Discrimination Prohibited

Sec. 901.   (a) No person in the United States shall, on the basis of sex, be excluded from participation in, be denied the benefits of, or be subjected to discrimination under any education program or activity receiving Federal financial assistance, except that:

(1) in regard to admissions to educational institutions, this section shall apply only to institutions of vocational education, professional education, and graduate higher education, and to public institutions of undergraduate higher education;

(2) in regard to admissions to educational institutions, this section shall not apply (A) for one year from the date of enactment of this Act, nor for six years after such date in the case of an educational institution which has begun the process of changing from being an institution which admits only students of one sex to being an institution which admits students of both sexes, but only if it is carrying out a plan for such a change which is approved by the Commissioner of Education or (B) for seven years from the date an educational institution begins the process of changing from being an institution which admits only students of only one sex to being an institution which admits students of both sexes, but only if it is carrying out a plan for such a change which is approved by the Commissioner of Education, whichever is the later;

(3) this section shall not apply to an educational institution which is controlled by a religious organization if the application of this subsection would not be consistent with the religious tenets of such organization;

54. Ibid. p. 186.

(4) this section shall not apply to an educational institution whose primary purpose is the training of individuals for the military services of the United States, or the merchant marine; and

(5) in regard to admissions this section shall not apply to any public institution of undergraduate higher education which is an institution that traditionally and continually from its establishment has had a policy of admitting only students of one sex.

(b) Nothing contained in subsection (a) of this section shall be interpreted to require any educational institution to grant preferential or disparate treatment to the members of one sex on account of an imbalance which may exist with respect to the total number or percentage of persons of that sex participating in or receiving the benefits of any federally supported program or activity, in comparison with the total number or percentage of persons of that sex in any community, State, section, or other area: *Provided*, That this subsection shall not be construed to prevent the consideration in any hearing or proceeding under this title of statistical evidence tending to show that such an imbalance exists with respect to the participation in, or receipt of the benefits of, any such program or activity by the members of one sex.

(c) For purposes of this title an educational institution means any public or private preschool, elementary, or secondary school, or any institution of vocational, professional, or higher education, except that in the case of an educational institution composed of more than one school, college, or department which are administratively separate units, such term means each such school, college or department.

Admission Standards and Quotas Favoring Male
Applicants Are Unconstitutional

BRAY v. LEE

United States District Court, District of Massachusetts, 1972.
337 F.Supp. 934.

CAFFREY, District Judge. This is a civil action brought pursuant to the Civil Rights Act, 42 U.S.C.A. § 1983 et seq. Jurisdiction of this court is invoked pursuant to 28 U.S.C.A. § 1343. Plaintiffs, who are female students in the Boston public school system, seeking permanent injunctive and declaratory relief against respondents, the members of the Boston School Committee, the Superintendent of Schools, the Headmaster of Boston Latin School, the Headmistress of Girls Latin School, and the Chief Examiner of the Boston Board of Examiners.

Briefly stated, the plaintiffs, who bring this action through their next friends, are a group of girl students, each of whom took the examination in March 1970 for admission as seventh grade students to the Girls Latin School for the academic year beginning in September 1970. Plaintiffs allege, and I find, that they are representatives of a class with an outside figure of 177 members, all of whom took the same examination for admission to Girls Latin School in September 1970, scored from 120 to 133, and, nevertheless, were not admitted in the fall of 1970. In their complaint plaintiffs allege that the various respondents illegally discriminated against them on the basis of their sex, for the reason that a boy who applied for admission to Latin School for the school year beginning September 1970 was admitted if he made a score on the examination of 120 or better out of a possible 200 points. Plaintiffs further allege that a girl who took the same examination was required to score 133 or better in order to gain admission at the same time to Girls Latin School. The accuracy of these factual representations is conceded by respondents.

* * *

To further understand the working and application of the admissions test, it should be noted that the Boys Latin building has a seating capacity for approximately 3,000 students and the Girls Latin building has a seating capacity for approximately 1,500 students. Because of the disparity in the seating capacity of the two buildings, the Boston School Department, in evaluating the results of examinations in the past, first made a determination of how many seats were available in the boys building. They then counted down from the top possible score of 200 until they had accepted a number of boys equal to the number of available seats for the following September. This established the cut-off mark for the admission of boys which, in 1970, turned out to be a mark of 120 out of a possible 200. Any boy who scored 120 or higher was then admitted to Boys Latin school for the school year beginning in September 1970.

Using the same technique with reference to the number of seats available in Girls Latin School, the School Department evaluated the result of the girls' examination by counting down from 200 until they reached a number equal to the number of seats available in September 1970 and thus determined that the cutoff mark for girls, because of the lesser number of seats available, was 133 out of a possible 200.

* * *

On the basis of the foregoing, I rule that the use of separate and different standards to evaluate the examination results to determine the admissibility of boys and girls to the Boston Latin schools constitutes a violation of the Equal Protection Clause of the Fourteenth Amendment, the plain effect of which is to prohibit prejudicial disparities before the law. This means prejudicial disparities between all citizens, including women or girls. I further find that on the basis of the record of this case female students seeking admission to Boston Latin School have been illegally discriminated against solely because of their sex, and that discrimination has denied them their constitutional right to an education equal to that offered to male students at the Latin school.

* * *

Accordingly, respondents are permanently enjoined from hereafter using a different standard to determine the admissibility of boys and girls, and are affirmatively ordered to use the same standard for admission of boys and girls to any school operated by the City of Boston, including the Boston Latin School.

* * *

An order will be entered in accordance with this opinion.

NOTES

1. In a 1979 decision the Supreme Court of the United States held that the Title IX statute created a private remedy under which an individual could challenge discriminatory acts. Prior to this decision the law had been interpreted as only establishing a procedure for the termination of federal financial support for institutions violating section 509 of the Title. The Supreme Court said:

> Title IX was patterned after Title VI of the Civil Rights Act of 1964. Except for the substitution of the word "sex" in Title IX to replace the words "race, color, or national origin" in Title VI, the two statutes use identical language to describe the benefited class. Both statutes provide the same administrative mechanism for terminating federal financial support for institutions engaged in prohibited discrimination. Neither statute expressly mentions a private remedy for the person excluded from participation in a federally funded program. The drafters of Title IX explicity assumed that it would be interpreted and applied as Title VI had been during the preceding eight years. Cannon v. University of Chicago, 47 U.S.L.W. 4549, May 14, 1979.

2. Higher admission standards for female than for male applicants for admission to a public college preparatory high school violates the Equal Protection Clause. Berkelman v. San Francisco Unified School District, 501 F.2d 1264 (9th Cir. 1974).

3. A state high school activities association which is a voluntary non-profit corporation created to regulate interscholastic activities acts under color of state law and is there subject to judicial scrutiny under the Civil Rights Act and the Fourteenth Amendment. An association rule that girls and boys shall not be members of the same athletic teams is unconstitutionally overbroad. Gilpin v. Kansas State High School Activities Assn., Inc., 377 F.Supp. 1233 (D.Kan.1973).

4. An Indiana court held that until girls' programs are comparable to those maintained for boys, the difference in athletic ability alone is not justification for a rule denying "mixed" participation in non-contact sports. Haas v. South Bend Community School Corp., 289 N.E.2d 495 (Ind.1972).

*League Rule Barring Girls Participation in Inter-
scholastic Athletics Is Unconstitutional*

BRENDEN v. INDEPENDENT SCHOOL DIST. 742

United States Court of Appeals, Eighth Circuit, 1973.
477 F.2d 1292.

HEANEY, Circuit Judge. This is a civil rights action brought under 42 U.S.C.A. § 1983 to enjoin enforcement of a rule promulgated by the Minnesota State High School League which bars females from participating with males in high school interscholastic athletics. The rule states:

> "Girls shall be prohibited from participation in the boys' interscholastic athletic program either as a member of the boys' team or a member of the girls' team playing the boys' team.

> "The girls' team shall not accept male members."

Minnesota State High School League Official Handbook, 1971–72.

Athletic Rules for Girls, Article III, Section 5.

The complaint charges that this rule discriminates against females in violation of the Equal Protection Clause of the Fourteenth Amendment to the United States Constitution.

The plaintiffs are Peggy Brenden and Antoinette St. Pierre, female high school students at Minnesota public high schools. Brenden attends the St. Cloud Technical High School in Independent School District 742 and St. Pierre attends Hopkins Eisenhower High School in Independent School District 274. Neither school district has appealed the judgment below. The defendant and sole appellant, the Minnesota State High School League, is a non-profit corporation which claims the membership of the state's 485 public high schools, including St. Cloud Technical High School and Hopkins Eisenhower High School.

The plaintiffs desired to participate in non-contact interscholastic sports: Brenden in tennis; St. Pierre in cross-country skiing and cross-country running. Neither of their schools provided teams for females in the respective sports. They did, however, provide such teams for males. Both plaintiffs would have liked to qualify for positions on the teams which have been established for males, but they were precluded from doing so on the basis of the above quoted rule. The trial court found that both were excellent athletes, and that neither would damaged by competition with males.

The court, after a trial on the merits, granted relief stating: * * * We affirm the decision of the trial court.

Having stated what this case is about, we would also like to emphasize what it is not about. First, because neither high school provided teams for females in the sports in which Brenden and St. Pierre desired to participate, we are not faced with the question of whether the schools can fulfill their responsibilities under the Equal Protection Clause by providing separate but equal facilities for females in interscholastic athletics. See generally, Note, Sex Discrimination in High School Athletics, 57 Minn.L.Rev. 339, 366–370 (1972). Second, because the sports in question are clearly non-contact sports, we need not determine if the High School League would be justified in precluding females from competing with males in contact sports such as football. See, Cynthia Morris et al., etc. v. Michigan State Board of Education et al., etc., 472 F.2d 1207 (6th Cir. 1973).

* * *

* * * In evaluating a claim that state action violates the Equal Protection Clause, the following three criteria must be considered:

" * * * [I] the character of the classification in question; [II] the individual interests affected by the classification; [III] and the governmental interests asserted in support of the classification. * * * "

Dunn v. Blumstein, 405 U.S. 330, 335, 92 S.Ct. 995, 999, 31 L.Ed.2d 274, 280 (1972).

I. *Sex-Based Classifications.*

* * *

* * * There is no longer any doubt that sex-based classifications are subject to scrutiny by the courts under the Equal Protection Clause and will be struck down when they provide dissimilar treatment for men and women who are similarly situated with respect to the object of the classification. * * * Furthermore, discrimination on the basis of sex can no longer be justified by reliance on "outdated images * * * of women as peculiarly delicate and impressionable creatures in need of protection from the rough and tumble of unvarnished humanity." Seidenberg v. McSorleys' Old Ale House, Inc., 317 F.Supp. 593, 606 (S.D.N.Y.1970).

* * * In this case, it is unnecessary for this Court to determine whether classifications based on sex are suspect and, thus, can be justified only by a compelling state interest because the High School League's rule cannot be justified even under the standard applied to test nonsuspect classifications. * * *

II. *The Plaintiffs' Interest in Interscholastic Athletics.*

The High School League contends that relief under the Civil Rights Act is inappropriate because participation in interscholastic sports is a privilege and not a right. We disagree. The Supreme Court has rejected "the concept that constitutional rights turn upon whether a governmental benefit is characterized as a 'right' or as a 'privilege.' * * * ". Graham v. Richardson, 403 U.S. 365, 374, 91

S.Ct. 1848, 1853, 29 L.Ed.2d 534 (1971). <u>The question in this case is not whether the plaintiffs have an absolute right to participate in interscholastic athletics, but whether the plaintiffs can be denied the benefits</u> of activities provided by the state for male students.

* * *

Discrimination in education has been recognized as a matter of the utmost importance. * * * In particular, "[d]iscrimination in education is one of the most damaging injustices women suffer. It denies them equal education and equal employment opportunity, contributing to a second class self image." * * *

<u>Discrimination in high school interscholastic athletics constitutes discrimination in education.</u> The Supreme Court of Minnesota has stated that:

> "* * * [I]nterscholastic activities * * * [are] today recognized * * * as an important and integral facet of the * * * education process. * * *

The importance of interscholastic athletics for females as part of the total educational process has been recently emphasized by the Minnesota State Board of Education. Its recent statement of policy and proposed action, Eliminating Sex Bias in Education (September 1972), states that:

> "* * * [O]ur educational system has helped perpetuate the division of the sexes into predetermined roles and has failed to provide freedom from discrimination because of sex * * *

> "The practice of stereotyping and socializing men and women into 'masculine' 'feminine' roles has resulted in prejudice, dominance, discrimination and segregation harmful to the human development of both sexes.

> *   *   *   *   *   *   *   *   *   *

> "The State Board of Education is concerned about four areas in particular: discrimination in hiring and promoting, *sex requirements for boys and girls to participate in sports and extra-curricular activities,* sex bias in curricular and teaching materials, and providing in-service training for administrators and teachers to overcome the habits and practices of teaching stereotyped social roles." (Emphasis added.)

In view of these circumstances, we must conclude that at the very least, the plaintiffs' interest in participating in interscholastic sports is a substantial and cognizable one. Thus, this case is properly before a federal court to determine if the High School League's actions are in conformity with the Equal Protection Clause. * * *

III. *The High School League's Interest.*

Because the defendant high schools have not provided teams for females in tennis and cross-country skiing and running, the effect of the High School League's rule is to completely bar Brenden and St. Pierre from competition in these non-contact interscholastic sports, despite their being fully qualified. The High School League argues, however, that its rule is justified in order to assure that persons with similar qualifications compete among themselves. They state that physiological differences between males and females make it impossible for the latter to equitably compete with males in athletic competition.

In evaluating the High School League's justification for their rule, we will, as we have indicated, apply the equal protection standard for evaluating non-suspect classifications. That standard is set forth in Reed v. Reed, supra, 404 U.S. at 76, 92 S.Ct. at 254.

> " * * * A classification 'must be reasonable, not arbitrary, and must rest upon some ground of difference having a *fair and substantial* relation to the object of the legislation, so that all persons in similar circumstances shall be treated alike.' * * * " (Citation omitted and emphasis added.)

It has been pointed out that in applying this standard, the Supreme Court's definition of what constitutes a rational relationship has become more rigorous, and that the Court has become "less willing to speculate as to what unexpressed legitimate state purposes may be rationally furthered by a challenged statutory classification." Green v. Waterford Board of Education, supra, 473 F.2d at 633.

We recognize that because sex-based classifications may be based on outdated stereotypes of the nature of males and females, courts must be particularly sensitive to the possibility of invidious discrimination in evaluating them, and must be particularly demanding in ascertaining whether the state has demonstrated a substantial rational basis for the classification. * * * This is especially true where the classification involves the interest of females in securing an education.

We believe that in view of the nature of the classification and the important interests of the plaintiffs involved, the High School League has failed to demonstrate that the sex-based classification fairly and substantially promotes the purposes of the League's rule.

(A)

First, we do not believe the High School League has demonstrated a sufficient rational basis for their conclusion that women are incapable of competing with men in non-contact sports. The trial court specifically found that the plaintiffs were capable of such competition and the evidence indicates that the class of women, like the class of men, includes individuals with widely different athletic abilities. * * *

Essentially, the testimony of those witnesses who concluded that females were wholly incapable of competing with men in interscholastic athletics was based on subjective conclusions drawn from the physiological difference between the sexes by individuals who were not themselves familiar with mixed competition. This subjective testimony is particularly susceptible to discrimination based on stereotyped notions about the nature of the sexes.

Furthermore, the High School League failed to show that it had established any objective nondiscriminatory minimum standards for evaluating qualifications for non-contact interscholastic athletics. The record indicates, in fact, that the schools had adopted no cut policies allowing male students, no matter *how untalented*, to participate in the non-contact interscholastic sports involved here.

* * *

(B)

Second, even if we assume, arguendo, that, on the whole, females are unlikely to be able to compete with males in non-contact interscholastic sports, this fact alone would not justify precluding qualified females like Brenden and St. Pierre from such competition. * * *

In *Reed,* the Court found unconstitutional a portion of the Idaho probate code which granted males a mandatory preference over females in competing for the right to administer an estate without regard for the individual qualifications of the female applicant. * * *

* * *

In our view, *Reed* precludes a state from using assumptions about the nature of females as a class, to deny to females an individualized determination of their qualifications for a benefit provided by the state.

In the present case, the underlying purpose of the High School League's rule is, as we have indicated, to insure that persons with similar qualifications will compete with each other. Yet, females, whatever their qualifications, have been barred from competition with males on the basis of an assumption about the qualifications of women as a class. The failure to provide the plaintiffs with an individualized determination of their own ability to qualify for positions on these teams is, under *Reed*, violative of the Equal Protection Clause. * * *

* * *

We are, of course, always reluctant to invalidate state and local action as unconstitutional. We have, however, no choice where a group of citizens has been deprived of the equal protection of the law. The likelihood of similar state action in this area being found unconstitutional in the future will be minimized if the League and the local school board affirmatively respond to the request of the Minnesota Department of Education to:

> " * * * Review all State Board rules and regulations and take steps to eliminate all sex-based requirements for courses and extra-curricular activities for students.

> "[And] * * * Provide equal access for all pupils to local school facilities, programs, equipment, staff services, and financial resources."

Affirmed.

Athletic Rules May be Reasonable if Justified by Distinct Differences Between the Sexes

CAPE v. TENNESSEE SECONDARY SCHOOL ATHLETIC ASS'N

United States Court of Appeals, District of Tennessee, 1977.
563 F.2d 793.

PER CURIAM. Tennessee Secondary School Athletic Association appeals from a judgment of the district court declaring that present TSSAA rules applicable to girls' basketball violate the Equal Protection Clause of the Fourteenth Amendment. The challenged rules call for six instead of five players on each team, impose half-court restrictions, and permit only forwards to shoot. A comparison of the TSSAA girls' rules and those published by the National Federation of State High School Associations (NFSHSA), as set forth in the trial judge's opinion, appears as an addendum hereto.

* * *

Plaintiff Victoria Ann Cape, a junior at the Oak Ridge High School in Oak Ridge, Tennessee, played as a guard on the Oak Ridge High School girls' basketball team during the 1975–1976 year. Plaintiff's complaint alleged that as a guard under the girls' rules, she was never able to "set up plays" and otherwise participate in the full playing and strategy of the game in such a manner as would be permitted under traditional basketball rules. She claimed that being deprived of the opportunity to play a full-court game and to shoot the ball (a function, which under the girls' rules, is confined to the forwards) makes it virtually impossible for her to obtain an athletic scholarship in basketball, as she lacks the necessary training in the shooting skills. Plaintiff points out that the State of Tennessee is only one of five states that continue to use separate rules for girls' basketball.

Following a trial on the merits, the district court specifically found no rational relationship between the different game rules and advancement of any of <u>five admittedly legitimate objectives which the defendants sought to achieve</u>:

1. To protect those student activities [sic] who are weaker and incapable of playing the full-court game from harming themselves.

2. To provide the opportunity for more student athletes to play in basketball games.

3. To provide the opportunity for awkward and clumsy student athletes to play defense only.

4. To provide a "more interesting" and "faster" game for the fans.

5. To ensure continued crowd support and attendance (game receipts) because these fans are accustomed to a split-court game.

Plaintiff did not sue as representative of a class and there is no indication that the other members of her sex who play girls' basketball under present rules share in any way plaintiff's views. Nevertheless, she has succeeded in procuring the order of a federal court which imposes her own personal notions as to how the game of basketball should be played upon not only the high school which plaintiff attends, but upon the approximately 526 junior and senior high schools, both public and private, in the State of Tennessee which are members of the Tennessee Secondary School Athletic Association.

<u>No challenge is made here to the most apparent sex-based classification in this case. Entirely separate basketball leagues for males and females are maintained on the basis of sex. It must therefore be assumed, for the purposes of this case, that this classification by gender is valid, as it serves important governmental objectives and is substantially related to the achievement of them.</u> * * *

When the classification, as here, relates to athletic activity, it must be apparent that its basis is the distinct differences in physical characteristics and capabilities between the sexes and that the differences are reflected in the sport of basketball by how the game itself is played. It takes little imagination to realize that were play and competition not separated by sex, the great bulk of the females would quickly be eliminated from participation and denied any meaningful opportunity for athletic involvement. Since there are such differences in physical characteristics and capabilities, we see no reason why the rules governing play cannot be tailored to accommodate them without running afoul of the Equal Protection Clause.

There is no evidence of any intent to discriminate between the sexes. There is no claim that defendants discriminated in furnishing services and facilities on the basis of sex. Plaintiff's remedy, if any, should more appropriately be directed to activity within the framework of the Association itself, a framework which is not shown to be inadequate to resolve issues of this sort.

Reversed and remanded for entry of judgment for the defendants. No costs, a public question being involved.

NOTES

1. For an athletic association to presume that girls as a group are athletically inferior to boys is to establish a permanent presumption that each and all girls are athletically inferior. Under the Due Process Clause of the Fourteenth such irrebuttable presumptions are unconstitutional. Yellow Springs Exempted Village School Dist. Bd. of Educ. v. Ohio High School Athletic Ass'n, 443 F.Supp. 753 (S.D.Ohio 1978).

2. Once state public schools decide to provide interscholastic competition it must be provided for all on equal terms. Separate comparable girls programs, coeducational teams or dropping all varsity sports are alternatives. Leffel v. Wisconsin Interscholastic Athletic Ass'n, 444 F.Supp. 1117 (D.C.Wis.1978).

Liability of School Districts and Officials for Violating Students' Civil Rights

A student's constitutional rights may be protected by the courts not only by injunctive relief but also through recent judicial application of the Civil Rights Act of 1871. Under this law denial of a student's constitutional rights can result in damages assessed by the court against the school board or an individual school board member, administrator or teacher. This act had been virtually dormant for almost 100 years when it was revived in the early 1960s in a famous Supreme Court case of Monroe v. Pape [55] at which time the Court opened the courts to actions against public officials. The law itself states:

> Every person who, under color of any statute, ordinance, regulation, custom, or usage, of any State or Territory, subjects, or causes to be subjected, any citizen of the United States or other person within the jurisdiction thereof to the deprivation of any rights, privileges or immunities secured by the Constitution and laws, shall be liable to the party injured in an action at law, suit in equity, or other proper proceeding for redress.[56]

This law was enacted by the Congress on April 20, 1871 after a month of debate during which time it became clear that there was great sentiment toward providing legal redress against those Southerners who repressed individual rights of Southern blacks. The press

---

55. 365 U.S. 167, 81 S.Ct. 473 (1961).   56. 42 U.S.C.A. § 1983 enacted 1871.

at that time called the legislation the Southern-outrage Repression bill.[57]

As written, the law provides for both injunctive and monetary relief to be awarded by the federal courts. Offenders against whom action may be instituted are statutory persons—"persons" as the law is written. The United States Supreme Court has had difficulty in deciding exactly who a "person" is, whether it is a public board or an individual official or employee. In *Monroe* the Court first held that Congress did not intend the word "person" to include municipalities or agencies of the government. Therefore, suits seeking relief under the Act were filed only against school officials and not school districts as entities. The result was that from 1961 to 1978 school districts insured the school officials against damages which may be incurred by lawsuit in such cases and the municipality was immune. On June 6, 1978 in Monell v. New York City,[58] this all changed when the Supreme Court voted 7 to 2 to overrule *Monroe* insofar as it provided immunity for municipalities. The Court, in so ruling, did not upset the interpretation of the *respondeat superior* doctrine, that a public school district is not responsible for the wrongdoing of its employees, but it did say that the school district could be held liable under Section 1983 if it adopts an unconstitutional policy or acquiesces in an unconstitutional custom. Justice Brennan stated in this regard:

> We conclude, therefore, that a local government may not be sued for an injury inflicted solely by its employees or agents. Instead, it is when execution of a government's policy or custom, whether made by its lawmakers or by those whose edicts or acts may fairly be said to represent official policy, inflicts the injury that the government as an entity is responsible under Section 1983.

Monell, therefore, taken in context with two other cases Wood v. Strickland [59] and Carey v. Piphus,[60] clearly permits courts to assess damages against either the governmental agency or an individual official of government if it or they suppress one's civil rights, whether it be a student, teacher, or some other party. *Wood* established the potential liability of school board members for denial of students due process rights, while *Carey* clarified the nature and extent of the damages which could be levied by the courts. In *Carey*, Justice Powell writing for the Court explained that there was a limitation to the damages which were possible under this kind of action. According to Powell, Section 1983 was not intended to provide purely punitive relief whereby the court would punish the wrongdoer for ill deeds, but

---

57. Ernest W. Williams, *Liability of Public Schools and Public School Officials for Damages Under 42 U.S.C. 1983*, unpublished thesis for Juris Doctor, Harvard Law School, 1975, p. 1.

58. 436 U.S. 658, 98 S.Ct. 2018 (1978).

59. 420 U.S. 308, 95 S.Ct. 992 (1975).

60. 435 U.S. 247, 98 S.Ct. 1042 (1978).

instead the Act was designed to compensate the victim for detriment and damage caused by the denial. In other words, damages could not flow from the unconstitutional behavior of the agency or official, but from the actual harm such as mental and emotional distress stemming from the constitutional deprivation. Compensatory damages of this nature are quite difficult to prove and the Supreme Court places this burden squarely on the shoulders of the plaintiff. In the absence of such proof the individual is entitled to collect only nominal damages which the Supreme Court set at one dollar. Therefore, although school districts and officials are liable for their acts, the chances of the aggrieved student demonstrating any substantial injury which is easily quantifiable in damages is slight, the net result being that Section 1983 actions may not be as beneficial to the plaintiff as once believed.

School Board Members May be Liable, as Individuals,
for Damages Under Section 1983 of the
Civil Rights Act of 1871

WOOD v. STRICKLAND

Supreme Court of the United States, 1975.
420 U.S. 308, 95 S.Ct. 992.

Mr. Justice WHITE delivered the opinion of the Court.

Respondents Peggy Strickland and Virginia Crain brought this lawsuit against petitioners, who were members of the school board at the time in question, two school administrators, and the Special School District of Mena, Ark., purporting to assert a cause of action under 42 U.S.C.A. § 1983, and claiming that their federal constitutional rights to due process were infringed under color of state law by their expulsion from the Mena Public High School on the grounds of their violation of a school regulation prohibiting the use or possession of intoxicating beverages at school or school activities. The complaint as amended prayed for compensatory and punitive damages against all petitioners, injunctive relief allowing respondents to resume attendance, preventing petitioners from imposing any sanctions as a result of the expulsion, and restraining enforcement of the challenged regulation, declaratory relief as to the constitutional invalidity of the regulation, and expunction of any record of their expulsion. * * *

I

The violation of the school regulation prohibiting the use or possession of intoxicating beverages at school or school activities with which respondents were charged concerned their "spiking" of the punch served at a meeting of an extracurricular school organization attended by parents and students. At the time in question, respondents were 16 years old and were in the 10th grade. The relevant facts begin with their discovery that the punch had not been prepared for the meeting as previously planned. The girls then agreed to "spike" it. Since the county in which the school is located is "dry," respondents and a third girl drove across the state border into Oklahoma and purchased two 12-ounce bottles of "Right Time," a malt liquor. They then bought six 10-ounce bottles of a soft drink, and, after having mixed the contents of the eight bottles in an empty milk carton, returned to school. Prior to the meeting, the girls experienced second thoughts about the wisdom of their prank, but by then they were caught up in the force of events and the intervention of other girls prevented them from disposing of the illicit punch. The punch was served at the meeting, without apparent effect.

* * *

* * * the board voted to expel the girls from school for the remainder of the semester, a period of approximately three months.

The board subsequently agreed to hold another meeting on the matter, and one was held approximately two weeks after the first meeting. The girls, their parents, and their counsel attended this session. The board began with a reading of a written statement of facts as it had found them. The girls admitted mixing the malt liquor into the punch with the intent of "spiking" it, but asked the board to forgo its rule punishing such violations by such substantial suspensions. * * * The board voted not to change its policy and, as before, to expel the girls for the remainder of the semester.

II

The District Court instructed the jury that a decision for respondents had to be premised upon a finding that petitioners acted with malice in expelling them and defined "malice" as meaning "ill will against a person—a wrongful act done intentionally without just cause or excuse." In ruling for petitioners after the jury had been unable to agree, the District Court found "as a matter of law" that there was no evidence from which malice could be inferred.

The Court of Appeals, however, viewed both the instruction and the decision of the District Court as being erroneous. Specific intent to harm wrongfully, it held, was not a requirement for the recovery of damages. Instead, "[i]t need only be established that the defendants did not, in the light of all the circumstances, act in good faith. The test is an objective, rather than a subjective one."

Petitioners as members of the school board assert here, as they did below, an absolute immunity from liability under § 1983 and at the very least seek to reinstate the judgment of the District Court. If they are correct and the District Court's dismissal should be sustained, we need go no further in this case. Moreover, the immunity question involves the construction of a federal statute, and our practice is to deal with possibly dispositive statutory issues before reach-

ing questions turning on the construction of the Constitution.
* * * We essentially sustain the position of the Court of Appeals
with respect to the immunity issue.

The nature of the immunity from awards of damages under §
1983 available to school administrators and school board members is
not a question which the lower federal courts have answered with a
single voice. There is general agreement on the existence of a "good
faith" immunity, but the courts have either emphasized different factors as elements of good faith or have not given specific content to
the good-faith standard.

* * *

Common-law tradition, recognized in our prior decisions, and
strong public-policy reasons also lead to a construction of § 1983 extending a qualified good-faith immunity to school board members
from liability for damages under that section. Although there have
been differing emphases and formulations of the common-law immunity of public school officials in cases of student expulsion or suspension, state courts have generally recognized that such officers should
be protected from tort liability under state law for all good-faith non-
malicious action taken to fulfill their official duties.

As the facts of this case reveal, school board members function
at different times in the nature of legislators and adjudicators in the
school disciplinary process. Each of these functions necessarily involves the exercise of discretion, the weighing of many factors, and
the formulation of long-term policy. "Like legislators and judges,
these officers are entitled to rely on traditional sources for the factual information on which they decide and act." * * * As with
executive officers faced with instances of civil disorder, school officials, confronted with student behavior causing or threatening disruption, also have an "obvious need for prompt action, and decisions
must be made in reliance on factual information supplied by others."

Liability for damages for every action which is found subsequently to have been violative of a student's constitutional rights and
to have caused compensable injury would unfairly impose upon the
school decisionmaker the burden of mistakes made in good faith in
the course of exercising his discretion within the scope of his official
duties. School board members, among other duties, must judge
whether there have been violations of school regulations and, if so,
the appropriate sanctions for the violations. Denying any measure of
immunity in these circumstances "would contribute not to principled
and fearless decision-making but to intimidation." * * * The imposition of monetary costs for mistakes which were not unreasonable
in the light of all the circumstances would undoubtedly deter even the
most conscientious school decisionmaker from exercising his judgment independently, forcefully, and in a manner best serving the
long-term interest of the school and the students. The most capable

candidates for school board positions might be deterred from seeking office if heavy burdens upon their private resources from monetary liability were a likely prospect during their tenure.

These considerations have undoubtedly played a prime role in the development by state courts of a qualified immunity protecting school officials from liability for damages in lawsuits claiming improper suspensions or expulsions. But at the same time, the judgment implicit in this common-law development is that absolute immunity would not be justified since it would not sufficiently increase the ability of school officials to exercise their discretion in a forthright manner to warrant the absence of a remedy for students subjected to intentional or otherwise inexcusable deprivations.

* * * We think there must be a degree of immunity if the work of the schools is to go forward; and, however worded, the immunity must be such that public school officials understand that action taken in the good-faith fulfillment of their responsibilities and within the bounds of reason under all the circumstances will not be punished and that they need not exercise their discretion with undue timidity. * * *

The disagreement between the Court of Appeals and the District Court over the immunity standard in this case has been put in terms of an "objective" versus a "subjective" test of good faith. As we see it, the appropriate standard necessarily contains elements of both. The official himself must be acting sincerely and with a belief that he is doing right, but an act violating a student's constitutional rights can be no more justified by ignorance or disregard of settled, indisputable law on the part of one entrusted with supervision of students' daily lives than by the presence of actual malice. To be entitled to a special exemption from the categorical remedial language of § 1983 in a case in which his action violated a student's constitutional rights, a school board member, who has voluntarily undertaken the task of supervising the operation of the school and the activities of the students, must be held to a standard of conduct based not only on permissible intentions, but also on knowledge of the basic, unquestioned constitutional rights of his charges. Such a standard imposes neither an unfair burden upon a person assuming a responsible public office requiring a high degree of intelligence and judgment for the proper fulfillment of its duties, nor an unwarranted burden in light of the value which civil rights have in our legal system. Any lesser standard would deny much of the promise of § 1983. Therefore, in the specific context of school discipline, we hold that a school board member is not immune from liability for damages under § 1983 if he knew or reasonably should have known that the action he took within his sphere of official responsibility would violate the constitutional rights of the student affected, or if he took the action with the malicious intention to cause a deprivation of constitutional rights or other injury to the student. That is not to say that school board members are "charged with predicting the future course of constitutional law." * * * A compensatory award will be appropriate only if the school board member has acted with such an impermissible motivation or with such disregard of the student's clearly established constitutional rights that his action cannot reasonably be characterized as being in good faith.

III

The Court of Appeals based upon its review of the facts but without the benefit of the transcript of the testimony given at the four-day trial to the jury in the District Court, found that the board had made its decision to expel the girls on the basis of *no* evidence that the school regulation had been violated:

> "To justify the suspension, it was necessary for the Board to establish that the students possessed or used an 'intoxicating' beverage at a school-sponsored activity. No evidence was presented at either meeting to establish the alcoholic content of the liquid brought to the campus. Moreover, the Board made no finding that the liquid was intoxicating. The only evidence as to the nature of the drink was that supplied by the girls, and it is clear that they did not know whether the beverage was intoxicating or not." 485 F.2d, at 190. * * *

* * * In its statement of facts issued prior to the onset of this litigation, the school board expressed its construction of the regulation by finding that the girls had brought an "alcoholic beverage" onto school premises. The girls themselves admitted knowing at the time of the incident that they were doing something wrong which might be punished. In light of this evidence, the Court of Appeals was ill advised to supplant the interpretation of the regulation of those officers who adopted it and are entrusted with its enforcement. * * *

When the regulation is construed to prohibit the use and possession of beverages containing alcohol, there was no absence of evidence before the school board to prove the charge against respondents. The girls had admitted that they intended to "spike" the punch and that they had mixed malt liquor into the punch that was served. * * *

Given the fact that there *was* evidence supporting the charge against respondents, the contrary judgment of the Court of Appeals is improvident. It is not the role of the federal courts to set aside decisions of school administrators which the court may view as lacking a basis in wisdom or compassion. Public high school students do have substantive and procedural rights while at school. * * * But § 1983 does not extend the right to relitigate in federal court evidentiary questions arising in school disciplinary proceedings or the proper construction of school regulations. The system of public education that has evolved in this Nation relies necessarily upon the discretion and judgment of school administrators and school board members and § 1983 was not intended to be a vehicle for federal-court correction of errors in the exercise of that discretion which do not rise to the level of violations of specific constitutional guarantees.

* * *

IV

* * *

Respondents have argued here that there was a procedural due process violation which also supports the result reached by the Court of Appeals. Brief for Respondents. But because the District Court did not discuss it, and the Court of Appeals did not decide it, it would be preferable to have the Court of Appeals consider the issue in the first instance.

The judgment of the Court of Appeals is vacated and the case remanded for further proceedings consistent with this opinion.

So ordered.

Students Are Entitled to Recover Only Nominal Damages Unless They Can Prove Actual Injury

CAREY v. PIPHUS

Supreme Court of the United States, 1978.
435 U.S. 247, 98 S.Ct. 1042.

Mr. Justice POWELL delivered the opinion of the Court.

In this case, brought under 42 U.S.C.A. § 1983, we consider the elements and prerequisites for recovery of damages by students who were suspended from public elementary and secondary schools without procedural due process. The Court of Appeals for the Seventh Circuit held that the students are entitled to recover substantial non-punitive damages even if their suspensions were justified, and even if they do not prove that any other actual injury was caused by the denial of procedural due process. We disagree, and hold that in the absence of proof of actual injury, the students are entitled to recover only nominal damages.

I

Respondent Jarius Piphus was a freshman at Chicago Vocational High School during the 1973–1974 school year. On January 23, 1974, during school hours, the school principal saw Piphus and another student standing outdoors on school property passing back and forth what the principal described as an irregularly shaped cigarette. The principal approached the students unnoticed and smelled what he believed was the strong odor of burning marihuana.   He also saw Piphus try to pass a packet of cigarette papers to the other student. When the students became aware of the principal's presence, they threw the cigarette into a nearby hedge.

The principal took the students to the school's disciplinary office and directed the assistant principal to impose the "usual" 20-day suspension for violation of the school rule against the use of drugs.   The students protested that they had not been smoking marihuana, but to no avail.   Piphus was allowed to remain at school, although not in class, for the remainder of the school day while the assistant principal tried, without success, to reach his mother.

A suspension notice was sent to Piphus' mother, and a few days later two meetings were arranged among Piphus, his mother, his sister, school officials, and representatives from a Legal Aid Clinic. The purpose of the meetings was not to determine whether Piphus had been smoking marihuana, but rather to explain the reasons for the suspension.   Following an unfruitful exchange of views, Piphus and his mother, as guardian *ad litem*, filed suit against petitioners in Federal District Court   *   *   *   charging that Piphus had been suspended without due process of law in violation of the Fourteenth Amendment.   The complaint sought declaratory and injunctive relief, together with actual and punitive damages in the amount of $3,000. Piphus was readmitted to school under a temporary restraining order after eight days of his suspension.

Respondent Silas Brisco was in the sixth grade at Clara Barton Elementary School in Chicago during the 1973–1974 school year.   On September 11, 1973, Brisco came to school wearing one small earring. The previous school year the school principal had issued a rule against the wearing of earrings by male students because he believed that this practice denoted membership in certain street gangs and increased the likelihood that gang members would terrorize other students.   Brisco was reminded of this rule, but he refused to remove the earring, asserting that it was a symbol of black pride, not of gang membership.

The assistant principal talked to Brisco's mother, advising her that her son would be suspended for 20 days if he did not remove the earring.   Brisco's mother supported her son's position, and a 20-day suspension was imposed.   Brisco and his mother, as guardian *ad litem,* filed suit in Federal District Court   *   *   *   charging that Brisco had been suspended without due process of law in violation of the Fourteenth Amendment.   The complaint sought declaratory and injunctive relief, together with actual and punitive damages in the amount of $5,000.   Brisco was readmitted to school during the pendency of proceedings for a preliminary injunction after 17 days of his suspension.

*   *   *

* * * We granted certiorari to consider whether, in an action under § 1983 for the deprivation of procedural due process, <u>a plaintiff must prove that he actually was injured by the deprivation before he may recover substantial "nonpunitive" damages.</u>

II

42 U.S.C.A. § 1983, enacted as § 1 of the Civil Rights Act of 1871, 17 Stat. 13, provides:

> "Every <u>person</u> who, under color of any statute, ordinance, regulation, custom, or usage, of any State or Territory, subjects, or causes to be subjected, any citizen of the United States or other person within the jurisdiction thereof to the deprivation of any rights, privileges, or immunities secured by the Constitution and laws, shall be liable to the party injured in an action at law, suit in equity, or other proper proceeding for redress."

The legislative history of § 1983, * * * demonstrates that it was intended to "create a species of tort liability" in favor of persons who are deprived of "rights, privileges, or immunities secured" to them by the Constitution.

* * *

A

Insofar as petitioners contend that the basic purpose of a § 1983 damages award should be to compensate persons for injuries caused by the deprivation of constitutional rights, they have the better of the argument. Rights, constitutional and otherwise, do not exist in a vacuum. Their purpose is to protect persons from injuries to particular interests, and their contours are shaped by the interests they protect.

Our legal system's concept of damages reflects this view of legal rights. "The cardinal principle of damages in Anglo-American law is that of *compensation* for the injury caused to plaintiff by defendant's breach of duty." * * * The Court implicitly has recognized the applicability of this principle to actions under § 1983 by stating that <u>damages are available under that section for actions "found</u> * * * <u>to have been violative of</u> * * * constitutional rights *and to have caused compensable injury* * * *." Wood v. Strickland, 420 U.S. 308, 319 (1975) (emphasis supplied). * * *

The Members of the Congress that enacted § 1983 did not address directly the question of damages, but the principle that damages are designed to compensate persons for injuries caused by the deprivation of rights hardly could have been foreign to the many lawyers in Congress in 1871. Two other sections of the Civil Rights Act of 1871 appear to incorporate this principle, and no reason suggests itself for reading § 1983 differently.　To the extent that Congress intended that awards under § 1983 should deter the deprivation of constitutional rights, there is no evidence that it meant to establish a deterrent more formidable than that inherent in the award of compensatory damages.　*　*　*

B

It is less difficult to conclude that damages awards under § 1983 should be governed by the principle of compensation than it is to apply this principle to concrete cases.　But over the centuries the common law of torts has developed a set of rules to implement the principle that a person should be compensated fairly for injuries caused by the violation of his legal rights.　These rules, defining the elements of damages and the prerequisites for their recovery, provide the appropriate starting point for the inquiry under § 1983 as well.

It is not clear, however, that common-law tort rules of damages will provide a complete solution to the damages issue in every § 1983 case.　In some cases, the interests protected by a particular branch of the common law of torts may parallel closely the interests protected by a particular constitutional right.　In such cases, it may be appropriate to apply the tort rules of damages directly to the § 1983 action.　*　*　*　In other cases, the interests protected by a particular constitutional right may not also be protected by an analogous branch of the common law of torts.　*　*　*　In those cases, the task will be the more difficult one of adapting common-law rules of damages to provide fair compensation for injuries caused by the deprivation of a constitutional right.

Although this task of adaptation will be one of some delicacy—as this case demonstrates—it must be undertaken.　The purpose of § 1983 would be defeated if injuries caused by the deprivation of constitutional rights went uncompensated simply because the common law does not recognize an analogous cause of action.　*　*　*　In order to further the purpose of § 1983, the rules governing compensation for injuries caused by the deprivation of constitutional rights should be tailored to the interests protected by the particular right in question—just as the common-law rules of damages themselves were defined by the interests protected in the various branches of tort law. We agree with Mr. Justice Harlan that "the experience of judges in dealing with private [tort] claims supports the conclusion that courts of law are capable of making the types of judgment concerning causation and magnitude of injury necessary to accord meaningful compensation for invasion of [constitutional] rights."　*　*　*　With these principles in mind, we now turn to the problem of compensation in the case at hand.

C

The Due Process Clause of the Fourteenth Amendment provides:

"nor shall any State deprive any person of life, liberty, or property, without due process of law; *   *   * ."

This Clause "raises no impenetrable barrier to the taking of a person's possessions," or liberty, or life.   *   *   *   Procedural due process rules are meant to protect persons not from the deprivation, but from the mistaken or unjustified deprivation of life, liberty, or property.   Thus, in deciding what process constitutionally is due in various contexts, the Court repeatedly has emphasized that "procedural due process rules are shaped by the risk of error inherent in the truth-finding process   *   *   * ."   *   *   *   Such rules "minimize substantively unfair or mistaken deprivations of" life, liberty, or property by enabling persons to contest the basis upon which the State proposes to deprive them of protected interests.

*   *   *

The parties   *   *   *   disagree as to the   *   *   *   holding of the Court of Appeals that respondents are entitled to recover substantial—although unspecified—damages to compensate them for "the injury which is 'inherent in the nature of the wrong,' " even if their suspensions were justified and even if they fail to prove that the denial of procedural due process actually caused them some real, if intangible, injury.   Respondents, elaborating on this theme, submit that the holding is correct because injury fairly may be "presumed" to flow from every denial of procedural due process.   Their argument is that in addition to protecting against unjustified deprivations, the Due Process Clause also guarantees the "feeling of just treatment" by the government.   *   *   *   They contend that the deprivation of protected interests without procedural due process, even where the premise for the deprivation is not erroneous, inevitably arouses strong feelings of mental and emotional distress in the individual who is denied this "feeling of just treatment."   They analogize their case to that of defamation *per se*, in which "the plaintiff is relieved from the necessity of producing any proof whatsoever that he has been injured" in order to recover substantial compensatory damages.

Petitioners do not deny that a purpose of procedural due process is to convey to the individual a feeling that the government has dealt with him fairly, as well as to minimize the risk of mistaken deprivations of protected interests.   They go so far as to concede that, in a proper case, persons in respondents' positions might well recover damages for mental and emotional distress caused by the denial of procedural due process.   Petitioners' argument is the more limited one that such injury cannot be presumed to occur, and that plaintiffs at least should be put to their proof on the issue, as plaintiffs are in most tort actions.

We agree with petitioners in this respect. As we have observed in another context, the doctrine of presumed damages in the common law of defamation *per se* "is an oddity of tort law, for it allows recovery of purportedly compensatory damages without evidence of actual loss." * * * The doctrine has been defended on the grounds that those forms of defamation that are actionable *per se* are virtually certain to cause serious injury to reputation, and that this kind of injury is extremely difficult to prove. Moreover, statements that are defamatory *per se* by their very nature are likely to cause mental and emotional distress, as well as injury to reputation, so there arguably is little reason to require proof of this kind of injury either. But these considerations do not support respondents' contention that damages should be presumed to flow from every deprivation of procedural due process.

First, it is not reasonable to assume that every departure from procedural due process, no matter what the circumstances or how minor, inherently is as likely to cause distress as the publication of defamation *per se* is to cause injury to reputation and distress. Where the deprivation of a protected interest is substantively justified but procedures are deficient in some respect, there may well be those who suffer no distress over the procedural irregularities. Indeed, in contrast to the immediately distressing effect of defamation *per se,* a person may not even know that procedures *were* deficient until he enlists the aid of counsel to challenge a perceived substantive deprivation.

Moreover, where a deprivation is justified but procedures are deficient, whatever distress a person feels may be attributable to the justified deprivation rather than to deficiencies in procedure. But as the Court of Appeals held, the injury caused by a justified deprivation, including distress, is not properly compensable under § 1983. This ambiguity in causation, which is absent in the case of defamation *per se,* provides additional need for requiring the plaintiff to convince the trier of fact that he actually suffered distress because of the denial of procedural due process itself.

Finally, we foresee no particular difficulty in producing evidence that mental and emotional distress actually was caused by the denial of procedural due process itself. Distress is a personal injury familiar to the law, customarily proved by showing the nature and circumstances of the wrong and its effect on the plaintiff. In sum, then, although mental and emotional distress caused by the denial of procedural due process itself is compensable under § 1983, we hold that neither the likelihood of such injury nor the difficulty of proving it is so great as to justify awarding compensatory damages without proof that such injury actually was caused.

* * *

III

Even if respondents' suspensions were justified, and even if they did not suffer any other actual injury, the fact remains that they were deprived of their right to procedural due process. "It is enough to invoke the procedural safeguards of the Fourteenth Amendment that a significant property interest is at stake, whatever the ultimate outcome of a hearing." * * *

Common-law courts traditionally have vindicated deprivations of certain "absolute" rights that are not shown to have caused actual injury through the award of a nominal sum of money. By making the deprivation of such rights actionable for nominal damages without proof of actual injury, the law recognizes the importance to organized society that those rights be scrupulously observed; but at the same time, it remains true to the principle that substantial damages should be awarded only to compensate actual injury or, in the case of exemplary or punitive damages, to deter or punish malicious deprivations of rights.

Because the right to procedural due process is "absolute" in the sense that it does not depend upon the merits of a claimant's substantive assertions, and because of the importance to organized society that procedural due process be observed, * * * we believe that the denial of procedural due process should be actionable for nominal damages without proof of actual injury. We therefore hold that if, upon remand, the District Court determines that respondents' suspensions were justified, respondents nevertheless will be entitled to recover nominal damages not to exceed one dollar from petitioners.

* * *

Chapter 9

DESEGREGATION

No one could have predicted that the pre-1850 education of a five-year-old child by the name of Sarah Roberts would have had such a profound effect on the historical development of the public schools. Sarah left home each day and walked through the streets of the City of Boston past five elementary schools for white children to reach the Smith Grammar School which had been established in 1820 for Negroes.

Not only was the school remote from the child's home, but an evaluation committee had reported that it was in poor condition— "the school rooms are too small, the paint is much defaced" and the equipment needed repair. Sarah's father tried repeatedly to place her in the better nearby schools for whites, but each time his efforts had failed. After persistent rebuffs, Mr. Roberts sought the most able lawyer, civil rights enthusiast, and later United States Senator, Charles Sumner, to represent his child and challenge the unequal treatment. From the ensuing legal conflict, the now famous and pernicious doctrine of separate-but-equal was born.

Citing passages from the Massachusetts Constitution, which would later be likened to the equal protection clause of the Fourteenth Amendment, Sumner maintained that compelling Negro children to attend separate schools was to effectively "brand a whole race with the stigma of inferiority and degradation." [1] Eloquently, Sumner pointed out that a segregated school could not be considered as equivalent to white schools because of the stigma of caste which mandatory attendance attached thereto. Sumner, effectively, expounded the same constitutional position which was to be the heart of the plaintiff's successful contention over 100 years later in Brown v. Board of Education, that separate schools "exclusively devoted to one class must differ essentially, in its spirit and character, from that public school known to the law, where all classes meet together in equality." [2]

Justice Shaw of the Massachusetts Court was, however, unconvinced and in his historical opinion set forth the "separate-but-equal" doctrine that was to prevail for so long. In theory he agreed with "the great principle" advanced by Sumner that all persons ought to stand equal before the law, but he went on to contrarily conclude that the standard of equality did not imply that all men and women were legally clothed with the same civil and political powers but that all were merely entitled to equal consideration and protection for their

---

1. Roberts v. City of Boston, 59 Mass.   **2.** Ibid.
   (5 Cush.) 198 (1850).

maintenance and security. What exactly the protected rights were was dependent on the laws adapted to their "respective relations and conditions." As one of these conditions, race was seen to be a legitimate rationale for classification. Judge Shaw failed to show, however, that there was any reasonable relationship between racial classification and a legitimate objective of the school system; he merely asserted that school segregation was for the good of both races. With this decision "separate-but-equal" had been born into education and it would not expire for over one hundred years. During the intervening years a Civil War would be fought, civil rights laws would be enacted by the U.S. Congress to little or no avail and the U.S. Supreme Court itself would transplant the unfortunate standard from the Massachusetts Constitution to the Constitution of the United States.

In 1868, the Fourteenth Amendment was ratified to assure the constitutionality of reconstruction statutes which had been enacted to proscribe racial discrimination. The third clause of the critical second sentence of the Amendment stated: "Nor shall any State * * * deny to any person within its jurisdiction the equal protection of the laws." In spite of the strength of the wording, the Amendment was to have little immediate effect as was evidenced by the Civil Rights Cases wherein the Supreme Court held that no application could be made to private discrimination such as occurred in inns, conveyances, restaurants and places of entertainment.[3]

The move from private discrimination to state sanctioned discrimination came about through interplay of an educationally irrelevant issue concerning interstate commerce by which a Mississippi statute requiring segregated train cars was upheld because it pertained solely to transportation within the state.[4] The Equal Protection Clause was thereby circumvented and state enforced classification of citizens by race was made possible. In the South state action began transforming the private custom of discrimination into state law. Jim Crow laws began in Florida in 1887 and soon engulfed the South.[5] Justice Powell, commenting much later, said "the Equal Protection Clause was virtually strangled in its infancy by post-Civil War judicial reactionism."[6]

3. See: Jethro K. Lieberman, *Milestones, 200 Years of American Law*, Oxford University Press and West Publishing Company, New York and St. Paul, Minnesota, 1976, pp. 256–257; Richard Kluger, *Simple Justice*, Vintage Books, New York, 1977, pp. 77–78.

4. Louisville, New Orleans and Texas R. Co. v. Mississippi, 133 U.S. 587, 10 S.Ct. 348 (1890).

5. Lieberman, *op. cit.* p. 260.

6. Regents of Univ. of Calif. v. Bakke, 438 U.S. 265, 98 S.Ct. 2733 (1978).

The capstone of segregation, though, came in 1896 with Plessy v. Ferguson [7] in which the separate-but-equal rationale of the Roberts Court was implanted as a national standard applying to the Fourteenth Amendment. In *Plessy* the Supreme Court maintained that an 1890 Louisiana law entitled "An Act to Promote the Comfort of Passengers" providing that "all railway companies carrying passengers in their coaches in this State, shall provide equal but separate accommodations for the white and colored races, by providing two or more passenger coaches for each passenger train, or by dividing the passenger coaches by a partition so as to secure separate accommodations" was not unconstitutional because state legislatures have wide discretion in promoting public peace and good order, and such actions will be upheld so long as they are reasonable. In a now infamous passage Justice Brown said: "In determining the question of reasonableness it (legislature) is at liberty to act with reference to the established usages, customs and traditions of the people, and with a view to the promotion of their comfort, and the preservation of the public peace and good order. Gauged by this standard, we cannot say that a law which authorizes or even requires the separation of the two races in public conveyances is unreasonable. * * * " [8] In essence, the Court made the Equal Protection Clause subject to custom and tradition in accordance with legislative interpretation, no matter how blatantly and objectionably the law affected a particular classification of people.

In a lonely dissent in *Plessy* Justice Harlan attacked the majority opinion and enunciated the law which would eventually become the prevailing view over one-half a century later. He maintained, "Our constitution is color-blind, and neither knows nor tolerates classes among its citizens. In respect to civil rights, all citizens are equal before the law." [9] He maintained that separation of the races was a "badge of servitude."

After *Plessy*, the precedent of separation of the races was quickly transferred to education and even extended. In Richmond County, Georgia, the school board discovering that it needed more facilities at the grade school level to accommodate Negro children discontinued the Negro high school and turned the building into a Negro elementary school. [10] The board advised the Negro high school students to seek their education in church-affiliated schools. Upon challenge, the U.S. Supreme Court held that in this matter the only interest of the Federal judiciary was to see that all citizens share equitably in the tax burden, but that the matter of education and how it was conducted, supported by that taxation, was solely a state concern.

7. Plessy v. Ferguson, 163 U.S. 537, 16 S.Ct. 1138 (1896).

8. Ibid.

9. Ibid.

10. Cumming v. Richmond County Bd. of Educ., 175 U.S. 528, 20 S.Ct. 197 (1899).

Further expansion of segregation in education was justified in 1908 in Berea College v. Kentucky [11] wherein the Supreme Court upheld a state law which forbade any institution as a corporation, to provide instruction to both races at the same time unless the classes were conducted at least twenty-five miles apart. The law, the "Day Law" as it was named after its author,[12] was enacted specifically to prohibit integration at Berea College, a small private college which had been founded in 1859 to provide nondiscriminatory education for needy students, both Negro and Caucasian. In upholding the law and sidestepping the direct issue of state enforced racial discrimination in the private sector, the Court simply asserted that the College as a corporation of Kentucky was subject to state regulation and was not entitled to all the immunities to which individuals were entitled. Since the College was the plaintiff and not Negro students, the Court was free to say that "a state may withhold from its corporations privileges and powers to which it cannot constitutionally deprive individuals." [13]

Plessy, Cumming and Berea College cases had not only fully established that the state could constitutionally maintain a separate system of education for blacks and whites, but that the arm of the state could reach into private education and require that it be segregated as well. Beyond this, Cumming laid the groundwork for almost unlimited state discretion in defining what constituted separate-but-equal. The federal courts would not intervene. Separation of the races in education was subsequently expanded to include not only black and white, but also yellow, brown and red as well. In Gong Lum v. Rice [14] in 1927 the Supreme Court held that states could segregate a Mongolian child from the Caucasian schools and compel her to attend a school for black children. Segregation of the Gong Lum type was formed in many states both North and South.

Erosion of Separate-but-Equal

As long as state legislatures had plenary power to define the limits of separate-but-equal the concept was accepted with little or no argument. By the 1930s, however, the National Association for Advancement of Colored People (NAACP) initiated a movement which was to pursue racial abuse and seek judicial clarification of the limits of separate-but-equal as a legal basis for segregation. At first, the intention was to attack segregation where equal facilities were obviously inadequate or nonexistent. As a result of these efforts in 1938, a landmark desegregation case Missouri ex rel. Gaines v. Canada was handed down by the Supreme Court. [15] By a vote of seven to

---

11. 211 U.S. 45, 29 S.Ct. 33 (1908).

12. See: Kern Alexander and Erwin Solomon, College and University Law, Michie Company, Charlottesville, Virginia, 1972, p. 518.

13. Berea College v. Commonwealth of Kentucky, op. cit.

14. 275 U.S. 78, 48 S.Ct. 91 (1927).

15. 305 U.S. 337, 59 S.Ct. 232 (1938).

one the Supreme Court held a Missouri law prohibiting Negroes from entering the University of Missouri Law School unconstitutional because there was no other public law schools in the state to which Negroes could go in the alternative. The ruling was singularly important because it not only placed some outward boundaries on implementation of separate-but-equal but more significantly it represented a reassertion of judicial authority in construing the Equal Protection Clause as a limitation on previously unfettered state action in education.

With the World War II years intervening little was accomplished during the next decade, but slowly a public attitude against separate-but-equal began to materialize which would set the stage for more direct judicial action. The foundation of separate-but-equal was shaken by the Supreme Court in 1950, another case involving a law school, this time the University of Texas.[16] Law schools were good targets for desegregation attorneys because judges and lawyers could more readily see the disparate condition in the legal field. In this case a black Houston mail carrier by the name of Sweatt sought admission to the University of Texas law school. Since the state had no law school for blacks, under the precedent of *Gaines* a lower Texas Court ordered that the state set up a law school for Negroes. The school that was established was woefully inadequate and Sweatt further challenged reasserting his claim to be admitted to the University of Texas Law School. Here the Supreme Court was presented with a rather different dilemma of comparing two schools and rendering a judgment as to their comparability. Thus, the high Court found itself in the uneasy role of a super accreditation agency. In ordering Sweatt admitted to the all-white law school Chief Justice Fred Vinson pointed out that the new law school "could never hope to be equal in reputation of the faculty, experience of the administration, position and influence of the alumni, standing in the community, tradition and prestige." [17]

Vinson virtually eliminated the use of separate law schools for blacks by further observing that "The law school to which Texas is willing to admit [Sweatt] excludes from its student body members of the racial groups which number 85 percent of the population of the State and include most of the lawyers, witnesses, jurors, judges, and other officials with whom [he] will inevitably be dealing when he becomes a member of the Texas Bar. With such a substantial and significant segment of society excluded, we cannot conclude that the education offered [Sweatt] is substantially equal to that which he would receive if admitted to the University of Texas Law School." [18]

The obvious educational infirmity of the separate-but-equal doctrine emerged with litigation in this case. Limitations on curricu-

16. Sweatt v. Painter, 339 U.S. 629, 70   17. Ibid.
    S.Ct. 848 (1950).   18. Ibid.

lum, faculty, educational atmosphere and professional development combined to draw into serious constitutional question the further maintenance of separate higher education facilities for both blacks and whites. On the same day that *Sweatt* was handed down, the Supreme Court ruled that if a state chose not to establish separate and substantially equal facilities for Negroes, it could not segregate them within the white school.[19] McLaurin, a black doctoral student in the College of Education at the University of Oklahoma, was allowed to enroll in the white school but was compelled to sit and study in designated sections for blacks while in the classrooms, library and dining hall. The Court held this treatment unconstitutional, as well.

Even though these cases served to expound the frailties of separate-but-equal they did little to help the black elementary and secondary school children who were denied equal opportunity with no relief in sight. With *Cumming* as the precedent, the Negro child attended school in ramshackled facilites, had poor and low instructors, and in most cases attended schools which were in session only for a minor portion of the year. This circumstance could not be corrected so long as the separate-but-equal doctrine stood.

Brown and the Demise of Segregated Schools

Several cases began making their way through the lower courts, each of which held potential for challenging the separate-but-equal doctrine head-on. Eventually five cases from Kansas, South Carolina, Virginia, Delaware, and Washington, D. C. reached the Supreme Court,[20] and were first argued in December, 1952.

Lower courts in each case, with the exception of the Delaware case, had denied relief to Negro children. In Delaware a decision by the Delaware Court of Chancery holding for the plaintiffs, requiring that Negro children be admitted to schools previously attended only by white children, was affirmed by the Supreme Court of Delaware. The defendants in this case applied for *certiorari* to the U. S. Supreme Court challenging the immediate admission of black children to the white schools. In Brown v. Board of Education the plaintiffs were Negro children of elementary age residing in Topeka. They brought action to enjoin a state statute which permitted, but did not require, cities in Kansas of more than 15,000 population to maintain separate facilities for Negro and white students. Under that authority the Topeka Board of Education chose to establish segregated elementary schools. The lower federal court held that segregation in public education had a detrimental effect on Negro children but denied plain-

19. McLaurin v. Oklahoma State Regents for Higher Educ., 339 U.S. 637, 70 S.Ct. 851 (1950).

20. Brown v. Board of Educ., 98 F. Supp. 797 (D.C.Kan.1951); Briggs v. Elliott, 98 F.Supp. 529 (D.C.S.C.1951); Davis v. County School Bd., 103 F. Supp. 337 (D.C.Va.1952); Belton v. Gebhart, 32 Del.Ch. 343, 87 A.2d 862 (1952); and Bolling v. Sharpe, cert. granted 344 U.S. 873, 73 S.Ct. 173 (1952).

tiffs relief because the facilities were substantially equal. In both the South Carolina and Virginia cases the lower courts had found the Negro schools to be inferior and had ordered improvements for equalization, but had not required admission of the Negro children to the schools for white children during the transition period. In the Washington, D.C. case, Negro children directly challenged school segregation in the nation's capital alleging that segregation deprived them of due process of law under the Fifth Amendment. It was necessary to couch this latter claim in the Fifth Amendment since the Fourteenth Amendment did not apply to Congress.

These cases combined then presented a range of situations by which the Supreme Court could comprehensively view the segregation issue. The Kansas case involved permissive segregation legislation in a northern state for elementary children; in the Virginia case a compulsory segregation law was used to segregate high school students in an upper southern state; and South Carolina represented the Deep South and Delaware a border state.[21] The District of Columbia case drew due process and congressional power into question. The differing circumstances and the wide geographical distribution gave the decision more importance and imbued it with a national flavor and aura.

The importance of the case was reflected in the Court's hesitancy to rush to judgment. Though the case was first argued on December 9, 1952, the Court reached no decision and on June 8, 1953, the court issued an order setting the case for reargument that Fall, for which date the court submitted a series of questions for litigants to address. The first question asked what evidence was there to indicate that congress and the states contemplated that the Fourteenth Amendment, when ratified, was intended to abolish school segregation. Second, the Court asked whether Congress had the power to abolish school segregation and what the limits of the Court's own powers were. Third, the Court sought opinions on the extent of its own powers to resolve the issue, should the answer to the first two questions be inconclusive. Fourth, the Court asked whether, in the event of a decision in favor of plaintiffs, desegregation should be immediate or gradual and whether the plaintiff children's grievance was personal and present. The fifth question concerned the procedural form the final decree should take.[22]

Within the parameters of these issues several alternatives were open to the Court. Ashmore[23] listed those which appeared to be within the realm of possibility.

---

21. Loren Miller, "The Petitioners," from Harold W. Horowitz and Kenneth L. Karst, *Law Lawyers and Social Change*, Bobbs-Merrill, Indianapolis, 1969, pp. 181–182.

22. Ibid.

23. Harry S. Ashmore, *The Negro and the Schools*, The University of North Carolina Press, Chapel Hill, 1954, pp. 42–43.

1. That there was <u>no need to rule on the constitutionality of segregation</u> *per se*, since each case might be disposed of on other grounds. (The Supreme Court had repeatedly declared that it would not rule on questions of a constitutional nature if a case could be decided by any other means.)

2. <u>That the "separate but equal" doctrine was still the law,</u> and <u>when the separate facilities were unequal the Court would allow a reasonable period for the facilities to be made equal in fact.</u>

3. That the "separate but equal" doctrine was still the law, but <u>when separate facilities were unequal the Court would require immediate admission of Negroes to the white schools pending the achievement of actual equality of facilities.</u>

4. That the "separate but equal" doctrine was still the law, but <u>the Court might require non-segregation in certain phases of public education which it deemed impossible of equality within the separate framework.</u> (In other words, the Court might conceivably hold that a particular course of activity could not be provided equally under segregation, as it had at least implied in the higher education cases.)

5. That <u>whether segregation in a given case was a denial of equal protection of the laws</u> was a question of fact, to be decided as are other questions of fact in the lower trial court.

6. <u>That segregation was unconstitutional</u>; the Court recognized the need for orderly progress of transition to non-segregation; but the Court would limit itself to minimum personal relief of the plaintiffs, leaving to Congress the job of legislating detailed rules for implementing desegregation in the schools generally. (This would be in keeping with the idea that the administration of local school systems involves a "political question.")

7. <u>That "separate but equal" was a clear denial of equal protection of the laws and thus unconstitutional;</u> but the <u>Court would permit a gradual change-over to a non-segregated system under the supervision of the District Courts, or under the direction of a master appointed by the Supreme Court itself.</u>

8. <u>That "separate but equal" was unconstitutional and must be ended immediately;</u> Negro plaintiffs in the case before the Court must be admitted at once to the white schools.

Realistically, the major point of the case could only have been decided one way, that separate-but-equal was unconstitutional. When asked how the court would decide, the Solicitor General of the United States responded that the court "properly could find only one answer." [24] The final judgment came in a unanimous decision written by Chief Justice Earl Warren. The Court ruled: "We conclude that in the field of public education the doctrine of separate but equal has no place. Separate educational facilities are inherently unequal." [25] For directness and finality the decision was a model. In overturning separate-but-equal, Warren did not dwell on other judicial precedents because the precise issue before the Court had not been presented before. The validity of separate-but-equal, since *Roberts*, had been assumed but had never been argued and validly established.

The case was not only a watershed in American education, but was one of the most important decisions ever rendered by the Supreme Court. For sheer impact on society it undoubtedly had the most far-reaching impact. Pollak commented: "Except for waging and winning the Civil War and World Wars I and II, the decision in the *School Segregation Cases* was probably the most important American governmental act of any kind since the Emancipation Proclamation." [26]

Separate-but-Equal Facilities Are
Inherently Unequal

BROWN v. BOARD OF EDUC. OF TOPEKA

Supreme Court of the United States, 1954.
347 U.S. 483, 74 S.Ct. 686.

Mr. Chief Justice WARREN delivered the opinion of the Court.

These cases come to us from the States of Kansas, South Carolina, Virginia, and Delaware. They are premised on different facts and different local conditions, but a common legal question justifies their consideration together in this consolidated opinion.

In each of the cases, minors of the Negro race, through their legal representatives, seek the aid of the courts in obtaining admission to the public schools of their community on a nonsegregated basis. In each instance, they have been denied admission to schools attended by white children under laws requiring or permitting segregation according to race. This segregation was alleged to deprive the plaintiffs of the equal protection of the laws under the Fourteenth Amendment. In each of the cases other than the Delaware case, a three-

24. Lieberman, *op. cit.* p. 276.

25. Brown v. Board of Educ., 347 U.S. 483, 74 S.Ct. 686 (1954).

26. Louis H. Pollak, *The Constitution and the Supreme Court, A Documentary History*, Vol. II, The World Publishing Company, 1966, p. 266.

judge federal district court denied relief to the plaintiffs on the so-called "separate but equal" doctrine announced by this Court in Plessy v. Ferguson, 163 U.S. 537, 16 S.Ct. 1138, 41 L.Ed. 256. Under that doctrine, equality of treatment is accorded when the races are provided substantially equal facilities, even though these facilities be separate. In the Delaware case, the Supreme Court of Delaware adhered to that doctrine, but ordered that the plaintiffs be admitted to the white schools because of their superiority to the Negro schools.

The plaintiffs contend that segregated public schools are not "equal" and cannot be made "equal," and that hence they are deprived of the equal protection of the laws. Because of the obvious importance of the question presented, the Court took jurisdiction. Argument was heard in the 1952 Term, and reargument was heard this Term on certain questions propounded by the Court.

* * *

In the first cases in this Court construing the Fourteenth Amendment, decided shortly after its adoption, the Court interpreted it as proscribing all state-imposed discriminations against the Negro race. The doctrine of "separate but equal" did not make its appearance in this Court until 1896 in the case of Plessy v. Ferguson, supra, involving not education but transportation. American courts have since labored with the doctrine for over half a century. In this Court, there have been six cases involving the "separate but equal" doctrine in the field of public education. In Cumming v. Board of Education of Richmond County, 175 U.S. 528, 20 S.Ct. 197, 44 L.Ed. 262, and Gong Lum v. Rice, 275 U.S. 78, 48 S.Ct. 91, 72 L.Ed. 172, the validity of the doctrine itself was not challenged. In more recent cases, all on the graduate school level, inequality was found in that specific benefits enjoyed by white students were denied to Negro students of the same educational qualifications. * * * In none of these cases was it necessary to re-examine the doctrine to grant relief to the Negro plaintiff. And in Sweatt v. Painter, supra, the Court expressly reserved decision on the question whether Plessy v. Ferguson should be held inapplicable to public education.

In the instant cases, that question is directly presented. Here, unlike Sweatt v. Painter, there are findings below that the Negro and white schools involved have been equalized, or are being equalized, with respect to buildings, curricula, qualifications and salaries of teachers, and other "tangible" factors. Our decision, therefore, cannot turn on merely a comparison of these tangible factors in the Negro and white schools involved in each of the cases. We must look instead to the effect of segregation itself on public education.

In approaching this problem, we cannot turn the clock back to 1868 when the Amendment was adopted, or even to 1896 when Plessy v. Ferguson was written. We must consider public education in the light of its full development and its present place in American life

<u>throughout the Nation</u>. Only in this way can it be determined if segregation in public schools deprives these plaintiffs of the equal protection of the laws.

Today, education is perhaps the most important function of state and local governments. Compulsory school attendance laws and the great expenditures for education both demonstrate our recognition of the importance of education to our democratic society. It is required in the performance of our most basic public responsibilities, even service in the armed forces. It is the very foundation of good citizenship. Today it is a principal instrument in awakening the child to cultural values, in preparing him for later professional training, and in helping him to adjust normally to his environment. <u>In these days, it is doubtful that any child may reasonably be expected to succeed in life if he is denied the opportunity of an education.</u> <u>Such an opportunity, where the state has undertaken to provide it, is a right which must be made available to all on equal terms.</u>

We come then to the question presented: <u>Does segregation of children in public schools solely on the basis of race, even though the physical facilities and other "tangible" factors may be equal, deprive the children of the minority group of equal educational opportunities?</u> We believe that it does.

In Sweatt v. Painter, supra, in finding that a segregated law school for Negroes could not provide them equal educational opportunities, this Court relied in large part on "those qualities which are incapable of objective measurement but which make for greatness in a law school." In McLaurin v. Oklahoma State Regents, supra, the Court, in requiring that a Negro admitted to a white graduate school be treated like all other students, again resorted to intangible considerations: "* * * his ability to study, to engage in discussions and exchange views with other students, and, in general, to learn his profession." Such considerations apply with added force to children in grade and high schools. To separate them from others of similar age and qualifications solely because of their race generates a feeling of inferiority as to their status in the community that may affect their hearts and minds in a way unlikely ever to be undone. The effect of this separation on their educational opportunities was well stated by a finding in the Kansas case by a court which nevertheless felt compelled to rule against the Negro plaintiffs:

> "Segregation of white and colored children in public schools has a detrimental effect upon the colored children. The impact is greater when it has the sanction of the law; for the <u>policy of separating the races is usually interpreted as denoting the inferiority of the negro group.</u> <u>A sense of inferiority affects the motivation of a child to learn.</u> Segregation with the sanction of law, therefore, has a tendency to [retard] the educational and mental development of Negro

children and to deprive them of some of the benefits they would receive in a racial[ly] integrated school system."

Whatever may have been the extent of psychological knowledge at the time of Plessy v. Ferguson, this finding is amply supported by modern authority. Any language in Plessy v. Ferguson contrary to this finding is rejected.

We conclude that in the field of public education the doctrine of "separate but equal" has no place. Separate educational facilities are inherently unequal. Therefore, we hold that the plaintiffs and others similarly situated for whom the actions have been brought are, by reason of the segregation complained of, deprived of the equal protection of the laws guaranteed by the Fourteenth Amendment. This disposition makes unnecessary any discussion whether such segregation also violates the Due Process Clause of the Fourteenth Amendment.

Because these are class actions, because of the wide applicability of this decision, and because of the great variety of local conditions, the formulation of decrees in these cases presents problems of considerable complexity. On reargument, the consideration of appropriate relief was necessarily subordinated to the primary question—the constitutionality of segregation in public education. We have now announced that such segregation is a denial of the equal protection of the laws. In order that we may have the full assistance of the parties in formulating decrees, the cases will be restored to the docket, and the parties are requested to present further argument on Questions 4 and 5 previously propounded by the Court for the reargument this Term. The Attorney General of the United States is again invited to participate. The Attorneys General of the states requiring or permitting segregation in public education will also be permitted to appear as *amici curiae* upon request to do so by September 15, 1954, and submission of briefs by October 1, 1954.

It is so ordered.

NOTES

1. On the same day as Brown, the Court also announced a decision stating that "racial segregation in the public schools of the District of Columbia is a denial of the due process of law guaranteed by the Fifth Amendment to the Constitution." The Fourteenth Amendment applies to the States, but not to the District of Columbia. It found racial segregation of the District schools a denial of due process under the Fifth Amendment. The Court stated: "Classifications based solely on race must be scrutinized with particular care, since they are contrary to our traditions and hence constitutionally suspect * * *" Bolling v. Sharpe, 347 U.S. 497, 74 S.Ct. 693 (1954).

2. One commentator has written as follows about the second Brown decision:

The admission of a few dozen children to a few dozen schools would have presented no very grave difficulties calling for a study of means of gradual adjustment. Seen in its totality, however, as involving some 5,000 school districts, nearly nine million white children and nearly three million colored, the situation exhibited great variety and complexity. To begin with, a vast number of statutes and regulations incorporating centrally or marginally the rule of segregation, would require change in order to conform to the new principle. Bickel, A., *The Least Dangerous Branch* (Bobbs-Merrill, New York, 1962), p. 248.

Interpreting Brown

Over a generation after *Brown* judicial decisions are still required to settle social and legal issues emanating from the circumstances surrounding desegregation. Full realization of the complexities brought on by the decision were probably, to a degree, foreseen by the Supreme Court when it first rendered its decision in 1954. Because of this awareness the Court delayed granting specific relief and invited the U. S. Attorney General and Attorneys General of all the States to submit their views regarding the ultimate order of the Court.

After due consideration of courses of action for implementation, the Court with Chief Justice Warren again delivering the opinion said that consideration should be given to "the public interest," as well as the "personal interest of the plaintiffs." In viewing this dichotomy the Court directed lower courts to fashion remedies which would permit desegregation "with all deliberate speed." [27] In retrospect the wisdom of the decision in *Brown II* has been called into question. Today, some maintain that the implementation decision, *Brown II*, allowed too much flexibility; others claimed not enough. But from the Supreme Court's perspective the wisest course was to allow the local federal district courts to settle the individual complaints on a case-by-case basis with due regard for equity for all concerned, and during the periods of transition the lower courts were to retain jurisdiction to see that desegregation was properly implemented. The Supreme Court sought to avoid unreasonable delays by requiring specifically that the lower courts "will require that the defendants make a prompt and reasonable start toward full compliance with our May 17, 1954 ruling." [28]

Considerable conflict followed the *Brown* decisions. Perhaps one of the most dramatic episodes occurred in Little Rock, Arkansas, where at first the National Guard was used to prevent Negro children from entering school and later Federal troops and the National Guard were used to protect the entrance of Negro children into the formerly white public schools.[29] Ultimately, the Supreme Court was called on to render a judgment in the Little Rock case. The question of nullification and interposition, the Civil War question, was again raised by

27. Brown v. Board of Educ. of Topeka, 349 U.S. 294, 75 S.Ct. 753 (1955).

28. Ibid.

29. Cooper v. Aaron, 358 U.S. 1, 78 S. Ct. 1401 (1958).

the Governor and the Legislature of Arkansas' asserting that they had no duty to obey federal court orders directed to them to effectuate desegregation.[30] The Court's response was direct and unambiguous, it said:

> In short, the constitutional rights of children not to be discriminated against in school admission on grounds of race or color declared by this Court in the Brown case can neither be nullified openly and directly by state legislators or state executive or judicial officers, nor nullified indirectly by them through evasive schemes for segregation whether attempted "ingeniously or ingenuously." [31]

During the years immediately after *Brown*, school districts experimented with various devices to avoid desegregation. Initially, some states sought to provide funding for private schools through tuition or voucher type arrangements. The most blatant example of this transpired in Virginia where, in Prince Edward County, the public schools were closed and private schools were operated with state and county assistance. In holding this scheme to be unconstitutional the Supreme Court said that, "* * * the record in the present case could not be clearer that Prince Edward's public schools were closed and private schools operated in their place * * *, for one reason, and one reason only: to ensure, * * *, that white and colored children in Prince Edward County would not, under any circumstances, go to the same school." [32]

Brown definitely proscribed government action which compelled or encouraged segregation, but did it require government intervention to integrate or mix the races in the schools?

When the *Briggs* case, a companion to *Brown*, was remanded to a federal district court in South Carolina, the lower court judge discussed desegregation versus integration and defined the situation thusly:

> [A]ll that is decided, is that a state may not deny to any person on account of race the right to attend any school that it maintains. * * * The Constitution, in other words, does not require integration. It merely forbids segregation.[33]

The difference between desegregation and integration was also emphasized later by northern courts which held that:

> * * * there is no constitutional duty on the part of the board to bus Negro or white children out of their neighbor-

---

30. Ibid.

31. Ibid.

32. Griffin v. County School Bd. of Prince Edward Cty., 377 U.S. 218, 84 S.Ct. 1226 (1964).

33. Briggs v. Elliott, 132 F.Supp. 776 (E.D.S.C.1955).

hoods or to transfer classes for the sole purpose of alleviating racial imbalance. * * *[34]

Contrarily, in another case in the South, the United States Court of Appeals for the Fifth Circuit held that there was indeed an affirmative duty on the part of government to integrate the schools where *de jure* segregation had existed prior to *Brown*.[35] This court distinguished *de facto* segregation, caused by housing patterns, from *de jure* segregation which governmentally promulgated and enforced such as existed in the South.

These cases taken together enunciated a rule of law which required affirmative action by school boards in the South, *de jure* states, but did not compel school boards in the North *de facto* states, to act affirmatively to move children about to assure that Negro children attended school with white children.

This issue was not treated by the U.S. Supreme Court until 1968 when it held that "freedom of choice" was an acceptable plan for desegregation only if it did in fact erase the vestiges of the past dual system of education. The Court said that: "The school officials have the continuing duty to take whatever action may be necessary to create an unitary, nonracial system."[36] The constitutionality of an "open door" or "freedom of choice" policy could be judged only in light of its utility in bringing about desegregation. Effectively the courts dismissed the distinction between integration and desegregation. The standard required that school districts be unitary and not dual. Where *de jure* segregation existed before, the state had an obligation to affirmatively assert itself to remove barriers to desegregation.

After waiting for fifteen years for the lower courts to effectuate the desegregation mandate of *Brown II,* the Supreme Court acted in 1969 to require that all school districts operating in states which had legal segregation in 1954 immediately become unitary.[37] It replaced "with all deliberate speed" with an "immediately" standard. Whether this was accomplished through rezoning, busing or other devices was not of concern to the Court, it simply required that all districts became unitary without further delay.

34. Bell v. School City, 324 F.2d 209 (7th Cir. 1964), cert. denied 377 U.S. 924, 84 S.Ct. 1223 (1964); Deal v. Cincinnati Bd. of Educ., 369 F.2d 55 (6th Cir. 1966), cert. denied 389 U.S. 847, 88 S.Ct. 39 (1967).

35. United States v. Jefferson County Bd. of Educ., 372 F.2d 836 (1966).

36. Green v. County School Bd. of New Kent County, Virginia, 391 U.S. 430, 88 S.Ct. 1689 (1968).

37. Alexander v. Holmes, 396 U.S. 19, 90 S.Ct. 29, reh. denied 396 U.S. 976, 90 S.Ct. 437 (1970).

State's Closing of Public Schools and Contributing
to the Support of Private Segregated Schools
Is Unconstitutional

GRIFFIN v. COUNTY SCHOOL BD. OF PRINCE EDWARD COUNTY

Supreme Court of the United States, 1964.
377 U.S. 218, 84 S.Ct. 1226.

Mr. Justice BLACK delivered the opinion of the Court.

This litigation began in 1951 when a group of Negro school children living in Prince Edward County, Virginia, filed a complaint in the United States District Court for the Eastern District of Virginia alleging that they had been denied admission to public schools attended by white children and charging that Virginia laws requiring such school segregation denied complainants the equal protection of the laws in violation of the Fourteenth Amendment. On May 17, 1954, ten years ago, we held that the Virginia segregation laws did deny equal protection. Brown v. Board of Education, 347 U.S. 483, 74 S. Ct. 686, 98 L.Ed. 873 (1954). On May 31, 1955, after reargument on the nature of relief, we remanded this case, along with others heard with it, to the District Courts to enter such orders as "necessary and proper to admit [complainants] to public schools on a racially nondiscriminatory basis with all deliberate speed * * * ." Brown v. Board of Education, 349 U.S. 294, 301, 75 S.Ct. 753, 757, 99 L.Ed. 1083 (1955).

Efforts to desegregate Prince Edward County's schools met with resistance. In 1956 Section 141 of the Virginia Constitution was amended to authorize the General Assembly and local governing bodies to appropriate funds to assist students to go to public or to nonsectarian private schools, in addition to those owned by the State or by the locality. The General Assembly met in special session and enacted legislation to close any public schools where white and colored children were enrolled together, to cut off state funds to such schools, to pay tuition grants to children in nonsectarian private schools, and to extend state retirement benefits to teachers in newly created private schools. The legislation closing mixed schools and cutting off state funds was later invalidated by the Supreme Court of Appeals of Virginia, which held that these laws violated the Virginia Constitution. Harrison v. Day, 200 Va. 439, 106 S.E.2d 636 (1959). In April 1959 the General Assembly abandoned "massive resistance" to desegregation and turned instead to what was called a "freedom of choice" program. The Assembly repealed the rest of the 1956 legislation, as well as a tuition grant law of January 1959, and enacted a new tuition grant program. At the same time the Assembly repealed Virginia's compulsory attendance laws and instead made school attendance a matter of local option.

In June 1959, the United States Court of Appeals for the Fourth Circuit directed the Federal District Court (1) to enjoin discriminatory practices in Prince Edward County schools, (2) to require the County School Board to take "immediate steps" toward admitting students without regard to race to the white high school "in the school term beginning September 1959," and (3) to require the Board to make plans for admissions to elementary schools without regard to race. Allen v. County School Board of Prince Edward County, 266 F.2d 507, 511 (C.A.4th Cir. 1959). Having as early as 1956 resolved that they would not operate public schools "wherein white and colored children are taught together," the Supervisors of Prince Edward County refused to levy any school taxes for the 1959–1960 school year, explaining that they were "confronted with a court decree which requires the admission of white and colored children to all the schools of the county without regard to race or color." As a result, the county's public schools did not reopen in the fall of 1959 and have remained closed ever since, although the public schools of every other county in Virginia have continued to operate under laws governing the State's public school system and to draw funds provided by the State for that purpose. A private group, the Prince Edward School Foundation, was formed to operate private schools for white children in Prince Edward County and, having built its own school plant, has been in operation ever since the closing of the public schools. An offer to set up private schools for colored children in the county was rejected, the Negroes of Prince Edward preferring to continue the legal battle for desegregated public schools, and colored children were without formal education from 1959 to 1963, when federal, state, and county authorities cooperated to have classes conducted for Negroes and whites in school buildings owned by the county. During the 1959–1960 school year the Foundation's schools for white children were supported entirely by private contributions, but in 1960 the General Assembly adopted a new tuition grant program making every child, regardless of race, eligible for tuition grants of $125, or $150 to attend a nonsectarian private school or a public school outside his locality, and also authorizing localities to provide their own grants. The Prince Edward Board of Supervisors then passed an ordinance providing tuition grants of $100, so that each child attending the Prince Edward School Foundation's schools received a total of $225 if in elementary school or $250 if in high school. In the 1960–1961 session the major source of financial support for the Foundation was in the indirect form of these state and county tuition grants, paid to children attending Foundation schools. At the same time, the County Board of Supervisors passed an ordinance allowing property tax credits up to 25% for contributions to any "nonprofit, nonsectarian private school" in the county.

In 1961 petitioners here filed a supplemental complaint, adding new parties and seeking to enjoin the respondents from refusing to operate an efficient system of public free schools in Prince Edward County and to enjoin payment of public funds to help support private schools which excluded students on account of race. The District Court, finding that "the end result of every action taken by that body [Board of Supervisors] was designed to preserve separation of the races in the schools of Prince Edward County," enjoined the county from paying tuition grants or giving tax credits so long as public schools remained closed. * * * At this time the District Court did not pass on whether the public schools of the county could be closed but abstained pending determination by the Virginia courts of whether the constitution and laws of Virginia required the public schools to be kept open. Later, however, without waiting for the Virginia courts to decide the question,[9] the District Court held that "the public schools of Prince Edward County may not be closed to avoid the effect of the law of the land as interpreted by the Supreme Court, while the Commonwealth of Virginia permits other public schools to remain open at the expense of the taxpayers." * * * Soon thereafter, a declaratory judgment suit was brought by the County Board of Supervisors and the County School Board in a Virginia Circuit Court. Having done this, these parties asked the Federal District Court to abstain from further proceedings until the suit in the state courts had run its course, but the District Court declined; it repeated its order that Prince Edward's public schools might not be closed to avoid desegregation while the other public schools in Virginia remained open. The Court of Appeals reversed, Judge Bell dissenting, holding that the District Court should have abstained to await state court determination of the validity of the tuition grants and the tax credits, as well as the validity of the closing of the public schools. Griffin v. Board of Supervisors of Prince Edward County, 322 F.2d 332 (C.A.4th Cir. 1963). We granted certiorari, stating:

> "In view of the long delay in the case since our decision in the Brown case and the importance of the questions presented, we grant certiorari and put the case down for argument March 30, 1964, on the merits, as we have done in other comparable situations without waiting for final action by the Court of Appeals." 375 U.S. 391.

For reasons to be stated, we agree with the District Court that, under the circumstances here, closing the Prince Edward County schools while public schools in all the other counties of Virginia were being maintained denied the petitioners and the class of Negro students

---

9. The Supreme Court of Appeals of Virginia had, in a mandamus proceeding instituted by petitioners, held that the State Constitution and statutes did not impose upon the County Board of Supervisors any mandatory duty to levy taxes and appropriate money to support free public schools. Griffin v. Board of Supervisors of Prince Edward County, 203 Va. 321, 124 S.E.2d 227 (1962).

they represent the equal protection of the laws guaranteed by the Fourteenth Amendment.

I.

* * *

* * * The case has been delayed since 1951 by resistance at the state and county level, by legislation, and by lawsuits. The original plaintiffs have doubtless all passed high school age. There has been entirely too much deliberation and not enough speed in enforcing the constitutional rights which we held in Brown v. Board of Education, supra, had been denied Prince Edward County Negro children. We accordingly reverse the Court of Appeals' judgment remanding the case to the District Court for abstention, and we proceed to the merits.

II.

In County School Board of Prince Edward County v. Griffin, 204 Va. 650, 133 S.E.2d 565 (1963), the Supreme Court of Appeals of Virginia upheld as valid under state law the closing of the Prince Edward County public schools, the state and county tuition grants for children who attend private schools, and the county's tax concessions for those who make contributions to private schools. The same opinion also held that each county had "an option to operate or not to operate public schools," 204 Va., at 671, 133 S.E.2d, at 580. We accept this case as a definitive and authoritative holding of Virginia law, binding on us, but we cannot accept the Virginia court's further holding, based largely on the Court of Appeals' opinion in this case, 322 F.2d 332, that closing the county's public schools under the circumstances of the case did not deny the colored school children of Prince Edward County equal protection of the laws guaranteed by the Federal Constitution.

Since 1959, all Virginia counties have had the benefits of public schools but one: Prince Edward. However, there is no rule that counties, as counties, must be treated alike; the Equal Protection Clause relates to equal protection of the laws "between persons as such rather than between areas." Salsburg v. Maryland, 346 U.S. 545, 551, 74 S.Ct. 280, 283, 98 L.Ed. 281 (1954). Indeed, showing that different persons are treated differently is not enough, without more, to show a denial of equal protection. * * *

Virginia law, as here applied, unquestionably treats the school children of Prince Edward differently from the way it treats the school children of all other Virginia counties. Prince Edward children must go to a private school or none at all; all other Virginia children can go to public schools. Closing Prince Edward's schools bears more heavily on Negro children in Prince Edward County since white children there have accredited private schools which they can attend, while colored children until very recently have had no available private schools, and even the school they now attend is a temporary expedient. Apart from this expedient, the result is that Prince Edward County school children, if they go to school in their own county, must go to racially segregated schools which, although designated as private, are beneficiaries of county and state support.

A State, of course, has a wide discretion in deciding whether laws shall operate statewide or shall operate only in certain counties, the legislature "having in mind the needs and desires of each." Salsburg v. Maryland, supra, 346 U.S., at 552, 74 S.Ct., at 284. A State may wish to suggest, as Maryland did in Salsburg, that there are reasons why one county ought not to be treated like another. But the record in the present case could not be clearer that Prince Edward's public schools were closed and private schools operated in their place with state and county assistance, for one reason, and one reason only: to ensure, through measures taken by the county and the State, that white and colored children in Prince Edward County would not, under any circumstances, go to the same school. Whatever nonracial grounds might support a State's allowing a county to abandon public schools, the object must be a constitutional one, and grounds of race and opposition to desegregation do not qualify as constitutional.

* * * Accordingly, we agree with the District Court that closing the Prince Edward schools and meanwhile contributing to the support of the private segregated white schools that took their place denied petitioners the equal protection of the laws.

III.

* * *

The District Court held that "the public schools of Prince Edward County may not be closed to avoid the effect of the law of the land as interpreted by the Supreme Court, while the Commonwealth of Virginia permits other public schools to remain open at the expense of the taxpayers." * * * At the same time the court gave notice that it would later consider an order to accomplish this purpose if the public schools were not reopened by September 7, 1962. That day has long passed, and the schools are still closed. On remand, therefore, the court may find it necessary to consider further such an order. An order of this kind is within the court's power if required to assure these petitioners that their constitutional rights will no longer be denied them. The time for mere "deliberate speed" has run out, and that phrase can no longer justify denying these Prince Edward County school children their constitutional rights to an education equal to that afforded by the public schools in the other parts of Virginia.

The judgment of the Court of Appeals is reversed, the judgment of the District Court is affirmed, and the cause is remanded to the District Court with directions to enter a decree which will guarantee that these petitioners will get the kind of education that is given in the State's public schools. And, if it becomes necessary to add new parties to accomplish this end, the District Court is free to do so. It is so ordered.

Judgment of Court of Appeals reversed, judgment of the District Court affirmed and cause remanded with directions.

Mr. Justice CLARK and Mr. Justice HARLAN, disagree with the holding that the federal courts are empowered to order the reopening of the public schools in Prince Edward County, but otherwise join in the Court's opinion.

*State Must Institute Affirmative Action Where
"Freedom of Choice" Fails to Create
Unitary System*

GREEN v. COUNTY SCHOOL BD. OF NEW KENT COUNTY, VIRGINIA

Supreme Court of the United States, 1968.
391 U.S. 430, 88 S.Ct. 1689.

Mr. Justice BRENNAN delivered the opinion of the Court.

The question for decision is whether, under all the circumstances here, respondent School Board's adoption of a "freedom-of-choice" plan which allows a pupil to choose his own public school constitutes adequate compliance with the Board's responsibility "to achieve a system of determining admission to the public schools on a non-racial basis * * *." Brown v. Board of Education of Topeka, Kan., 349 U.S. 294, 300–301, 75 S.Ct. 753, 756, 99 L.Ed. 1083 (*Brown II*).

Petitioners brought this action in March 1965 seeking injunctive relief against respondent's continued maintenance of an alleged racially segregated school system. * * *

* * *

The pattern of separate "white" and "Negro" schools in the New Kent County school system established under compulsion of state laws is precisely the pattern of segregation to which *Brown I* and *Brown II* were particularly addressed, and which *Brown I* declared unconstitutionally denied Negro school children equal protection of the laws. Racial identification of the system's schools was complete, extending not just to the composition of student bodies at the two schools but to every facet of school operations—faculty, staff, transportation, extracurricular activities and facilities. In short, the State, acting through the local school board and school officials, organized and operated a dual system, part "white" and part "Negro."

It was such dual systems that 14 years ago *Brown I* held unconstitutional and a year later *Brown II* held must be abolished; school boards operating such school systems were *required* by *Brown II* "to

effectuate a transition to a racially nondiscriminatory school system."
349 U.S., at 301, 75 S.Ct. at 756. It is of course true that for the
time immediately after *Brown II* the concern was with making an
initial break in a long-established pattern of excluding Negro children
from schools attended by white children. The principal focus was on
obtaining for those Negro children courageous enough to break with
tradition a place in the "white" schools. See, e. g., Cooper v. Aaron,
358 U.S. 1, 78 S.Ct. 1401, 3 L.Ed.2d 5. Under *Brown II* that immediate goal was only the first step, however. The transition to a unitary, nonracial system of public education was and is the ultimate
end to be brought about; it was because of the "complexities arising
from the transition to a system of public education freed of racial discrimination" that we provided for "all deliberate speed" in the implementation of the principles of *Brown I*. 349 U.S., at 299–301, 75 S.
Ct. at 755. Thus we recognized the task would necessarily involve solution of "varied local school problems." Id., at 299, 75 S.Ct. at 756.
* * *

It is against this background that 13 years after *Brown II* commanded the abolition of dual systems we must measure the effectiveness of respondent School Board's "freedom-of-choice" plan to
achieve that end. The School Board contends that it has fully discharged its obligation by adopting a plan by which every student, regardless of race, may "freely" choose the school he will attend. The
Board attempts to cast the issue in its broadest form by arguing that
its "freedom-of-choice" plan may be faulted only by reading the
Fourteenth Amendment as universally requiring "compulsory integration," a reading it insists the wording of the Amendment will not
support. But that argument ignores the thrust of *Brown II*. In the
light of the command of that case, what is involved here is the question whether the Board has achieved the "racially nondiscriminatory
school system" *Brown II* held must be effectuated in order to remedy
the established unconstitutional deficiencies of its segregated system.
In the context of the state-imposed segregated pattern of long standing, the fact that in 1965 the Board opened the doors of the former
"white" school to Negro children and of the "Negro" school to white
children merely begins, not ends, our inquiry whether the Board has
taken steps adequate to abolish its dual, segregated system. *Brown
II* was a call for the dismantling of well-entrenched dual systems tem-
pered by an awareness that complex and multifaceted problems would
arise which would require time and flexibility for a successful resolution. School boards such as the respondent then operating state-com-
pelled dual systems were nevertheless clearly charged with the affirmative duty to take whatever steps might be necessary to convert
to a unitary system in which racial discrimination would be eliminated root and branch. * * * The constitutional rights of Negro
school children articulated in *Brown I* permit no less than this; and
it was to this end that *Brown II* commanded school boards to bend
their efforts.

In determining whether respondent School Board met that command by adopting its "freedom-of-choice" plan, it is relevant that this first step did not come until some 11 years after *Brown I* was decided and 10 years after *Brown II* directed the making of a "prompt and reasonable start." This deliberate perpetuation of the unconstitutional dual system can only have compounded the harm of such a system. Such delays are no longer tolerable, for "the governing constitutional principles no longer bear the imprint of newly enunciated doctrine." * * * The burden on a school board today is to come forward with a plan that promises realistically to work, and promises realistically to work *now*.

The obligation of the district courts, as it always has been, is to assess the effectiveness of a proposed plan in achieving desegregation. There is no universal answer to complex problems of desegregation; there is obviously no one plan that will do the job in every case. The matter must be assessed in light of the circumstances present and the options available in each instance. It is incumbent upon the school board to establish that its proposed plan promises meaningful and immediate progress toward disestablishing state-imposed segregation. It is incumbent upon the district court to weigh that claim in light of the facts at hand and in light of any alternatives which may be shown as feasible and more promising in their effectiveness. Where the court finds the board to be acting in good faith and the proposed plan to have real prospects for dismantling the state-imposed dual system "at the earliest practicable date," then the plan may be said to provide effective relief. Of course, the availability to the board of other more promising courses of action may indicate a lack of good faith; and at the least it places a heavy burden upon the board to explain its preference for an apparently less effective method. Moreover, whatever plan is adopted will require evaluation in practice, and the court should retain jurisdiction until it is clear that state-imposed segregation has been completely removed. * * *

We do not hold that "freedom of choice" can have no place in such a plan. We do not hold that a "freedom-of-choice" plan might of itself be unconstitutional, although that argument has been urged upon us. Rather, all we decide today is that in desegregating a dual system a plan utilizing "freedom of choice" is not an end in itself. * * *

The New Kent School Board's "freedom-of-choice" plan cannot be accepted as a sufficient step to "effectuate a transition" to a unitary system. In three years of operation not a single white child has chosen to attend Watkins school and although 115 Negro children enrolled in New Kent school in 1967 (up from 35 in 1965 and 111 in 1966) 85% of the Negro children in the system still attend the all-Negro Watkins school. In other words, the school system remains a dual system. Rather than further the dismantling of the dual system, the plan has operated simply to burden children and their parents with a responsibility which *Brown II* placed squarely on the School Board. The Board must be required to formulate a new plan and, in light of other courses which appear open to the Board, such as zoning, fashion steps which promise realistically to convert promptly to a system without a "white" school and a "Negro" school, but just schools.

The judgment of the Court of Appeals is vacated insofar as it affirmed the District Court and the case is remanded to the District Court for further proceedings consistent with this opinion. It is so ordered.

Dual School Systems Are to be Terminated at Once and Unitary Systems Are to Begin Immediately

ALEXANDER v. HOLMES

Supreme Court of the United States, 1969.
396 U.S. 19, 90 S.Ct. 29, reh. denied 396 U.S. 976, 90 S.Ct. 437, 1970.

PER CURIAM. This case comes to the Court on a petition for certiorari to the Court of Appeals for the Fifth Circuit. The petition was granted on October 9, 1969, and the case set down for early argument. The question presented is one of paramount importance, involving as it does the denial of fundamental rights to many thousands of school children, who are presently attending Mississippi schools under segregated conditions contrary to the applicable decisions of this Court. Against this background the Court of Appeals should have denied all motions for additional time because continued operation of segregated schools under a standard of allowing "all deliberate speed" for desegregation is no longer constitutionally permissible. Under explicit· holdings of this Court the obligation of every school district is to terminate dual school systems at once and to operate now and hereafter only unitary schools. * * *

It is hereby adjudged, ordered, and decreed:

The Court of Appeals' order of August 28, 1969, is vacated, and the case is remanded to that court to issue its decree and order, effective immediately, declaring that each of the school districts here involved may no longer operate a dual school system based on race or color, and directing that they begin immediately to operate as unitary school systems within which no person is to be effectively excluded from any school because of race or color.

* * *

The Court of Appeals shall retain jurisdiction to insure prompt and faithful compliance with its order, and may modify or amend the same as may be deemed necessary or desirable for the operation of a unitary school system.

* * *

De Facto Segregation

De facto segregation is not unconstitutional whether it occurs in the South or the North. President Nixon summarized the law in this regard in 1969. He said: "There is a fundamental distinction between so-called 'de jure' and 'de facto' segregation: de jure segregation arises by law or by the deliberate act of school officials and is unconstitutional; de facto segregation results from residential housing patterns and does not violate the Constitution."

This legal position concerning *de facto* segregation has been reiterated several times by the courts in various decisions. A notable early example was the Bell decision in which the U.S. Court of Appeals for the Seventh Circuit said: " * * * there is no affirmative U.S. Constitutional duty to change innocently arrived at school attendance districts by the mere fact that shifts in population either increase or decrease the percentage of either Negro or white pupils." [38] Similarly, the Court of Appeals for the Fifth Circuit held that boards of education have no constitutional obligation to relieve racial imbalance which they do not cause or create. These are both decisions from northern states but fundamentally the law is the same whether the segregation occurs in the North or the South. If segregation is created by law of official act then an affirmative duty is required to integrate the schools. The Supreme Court summarized the Constitutional standard in a Denver, Colorado case. Thusly: "* * * we have held that where plaintiffs prove that a current condition of segregated schooling exists within a school district where a dual system was compelled or authorized by statute at the time of our decision in *Brown* * * *, the State automatically assumes an affirmative duty to 'effectuate a transition to a racially nondiscriminatory school system.'" [39] In this case the Supreme Court emphasized that the differentiating factor between *de jure* segregation and so-called *de facto* segregation is *purpose* or *intent*.

If school authorities practice purposeful segregation, then a *de jure* condition exists and the school district will be required to take affirmative measures to correct racial imbalance in the schools.

---

38. Bell v. School City of Gary, 324 F. 2d 209 (7th Cir. 1963).

39. Keyes v. School Dist. No. 1, Denver, 413 U.S. 189, 93 S.Ct. 2686 (1973).

School Board Actions May Have Effect of Creating
Unconstitutional De Jure Segregation

KEYES v. SCHOOL DIST. NO. 1, DENVER

Supreme Court of the United States, 1973.
413 U.S. 189, 93 S.Ct. 2686.

Mr. Justice BRENNAN delivered the opinion of the Court.

This school desegregation case concerns the Denver, Colorado, school system. That system has never been operated under a constitutional or statutory provision that mandated or permitted racial segregation in public education. Rather, the gravamen of this action, brought in June 1969 in the District Court for the District of Colorado by parents of Denver schoolchildren, is that respondent School Board alone, by use of various techniques such as the manipulation of student attendance zones, schoolsite selection and a neighborhood school policy, created or maintained racially or ethnically (or both racially and ethnically) segregated schools throughout the school district, entitling petitioners to a decree directing desegregation of the entire school district.

* * * The District Court found that by the construction of a new, relatively small elementary school, Barrett, in the middle of the Negro community west of Park Hill, by the gerrymandering of student attendance zones, by the use of so-called "optional zones," and by the excessive use of mobile classroom units, among other things, the respondent School Board had engaged over almost a decade after 1960 in an unconstitutional policy of deliberate racial segregation with respect to the Park Hill schools. The court therefore ordered the Board to desegregate those schools through the implementation of the three rescinded resolutions. D.C., 303 F.Supp. 279 and 289 (1969).

Segregation in Denver schools is not limited, however, to the schools in the Park Hill area, and not satisfied with their success in obtaining relief for Park Hill, petitioners pressed their prayer that the District Court order desegregation of all segregated schools in the city of Denver, particularly the heavily segregated schools in the core city area. But that court concluded that its finding of a purposeful and systematic program of racial segregation affecting thousands of students in the Park Hill area did not, in itself, impose on the School Board an affirmative duty to eliminate segregation throughout the school district. Instead, the court fractionated the district and held that petitioners had to make a fresh showing of *de jure* segregation in each area of the city for which they sought relief. Moreover, the District Court held that its finding of intentional segregation in Park Hill was not in any sense material to the question of segregative intent in other areas of the city. * * *

* * *

I

Before turning to the primary question we decide today, a word must be said about the District Court's method of defining a "segregated" school. Denver is a tri-ethnic, as distinguished from a bi-racial, community. The overall racial and ethnic composition of the Denver public schools is 66 Anglo, 14% Negro, and 20% Hispano. * * * What is or is not a segregated school will necessarily depend on the facts of each particular case. In addition to the racial and ethnic composition of a school's student body, other factors, such as the racial and ethnic composition of faculty and staff and the community and administration attitudes toward the school, must be taken into consideration. The District Court has recognized these specific factors as elements of the definition of a "segregated" school and we may therefore infer that the court will consider them again on remand.

We conclude, however, that the District Court erred in separating Negroes and Hispanos for purposes of defining a "segregated" school. We have held that Hispanos constitute an identifiable class for purposes of the Fourteenth Amendment. Hernandez v. Texas, 347 U.S. 475, 74 S.Ct. 667, 98 L.Ed. 866 (1954). * * * Indeed the District Court recognized this in classifying predominantly Hispano schools as "segregated" schools in their own right. But there is also much evidence that in the Southwest Hispanos and Negroes have a great many things in common. The United States Commission on Civil Rights has recently published two Reports on Hispano education in the Southwest. Focusing on students in the States of Arizona, California, Colorado, New Mexico, and Texas, the Commission concluded that Hispanos suffer from the same educational inequities as Negroes and American Indians. In fact, the District Court itself recognized that "[o]ne of the things which the Hispano has in common with the Negro is economic and cultural deprivation and discrimination." 313 F.Supp., at 69. This is agreement that, though of different origins Negroes and Hispanos in Denver suffer identical discrimination in treatment when compared with the treatment afforded Anglo students. In that circumstance, we think petitioners are entitled to have schools with a combined predominance of Negroes and Hispanos included in the category of "segregated" schools.

II

In our view, the only other question that requires our decision at this time is that subsumed in Question 2 of the questions presented by petitioners, namely whether the District Court and the Court of Appeals applied an incorrect legal standard in addressing petitioners' contention that respondent School Board engaged in an unconstitutional policy of deliberate segregation in the core city schools. Our conclusion is that those courts did not apply the correct standard in addressing that contention.

Petitioners apparently concede for the purposes of this case that in the case of a school system like Denver's, where no statutory dual system has ever existed, plaintiffs must prove not only that segregated schooling exists but also that it was brought about or maintained by intentional state action. Petitioners proved that for almost a decade after 1960 respondent School Board had engaged in an unconstitutional policy of deliberate racial segregation in the Park Hill schools. * * * This finding did not relate to an insubstantial or trivial fragment of the school system. On the contrary, respondent School Board was found guilty of following a deliberate segregation policy at schools attended, in 1969, by 37.69% of Denver's total Negro school population * * *. Respondent argues, however, that a finding of state-imposed segregation as to a substantial portion of the school system can be viewed in isolation from the rest of the district, and that even if state-imposed segregation does exist in a substantial part of the Denver school system, it does not follow that the District Court could predicate on that fact a finding that the entire school system is a dual system. We do not agree. We have never suggested that plaintiffs in school desegregation cases must bear the burden of proving the elements of *de jure* segregation as to each and every school or each and every student within the school system. Rather, we have held that where plaintiffs prove that a current condition of segregated schooling exists within a school district where a dual system was compelled or authorized by statute at the time of our decision in Brown v. Board of Education, 347 U.S. 483, 74 S.Ct. 686, 98 L.Ed. 873 (1954) (*Brown I*), the State automatically assumes an affirmative duty "to effectuate a transition to a racially nondiscriminatory school system," Brown v. Board of Education, 349 U.S. 294, 301, 75 S.Ct. 753, 756, 99 L.Ed. 1083 (1955) (*Brown II*), see also Green v. County School Board, 391 U.S. 430, 437–438, 88 S.Ct. 1689, 1693–1694, 20 L.Ed.2d 716 (1968), that is, to eliminate from the public schools within their school system all "vestiges of state-imposed segregation." Swann v. Charlotte-Mecklenburg Board of Education, 402 U.S. 1, 15, 91 S.Ct. 1267, 1275, 28 L.Ed.2d 554 (1971).

This is not a case, however, where a statutory dual system has ever existed. Nevertheless, where plaintiffs prove that the school authorities have carried out a systematic program of segregation affecting a substantial portion of the students, schools teachers, and facilities within the school system, it is only common sense to conclude that there exists a predicate for a finding of the existence of a dual school system. Several considerations support this conclusion. First, it is obvious that a practice of concentrating Negroes in certain schools by structuring attendance zones or designating "feeder" schools on the basis of race has the reciprocal effect of keeping other nearby schools predominantly white. Similarly, the practice of building a school—such as the Barrett Elementary School in this case—to a certain size and in a certain location, "with conscious knowledge that it would be a segregated school," 303 F.Supp., at 285, has a substantial reciprocal effect on the racial composition of other nearby schools. So also, the use of mobile classrooms, the drafting of student transfer policies, the transportation of students, and the assignment of faculty and staff, on racially identifiable bases, have the clear effect of earmarking schools according to their racial composition, and this, in turn, together with the elements of student assignment and school construction, may have a profound reciprocal effect on the racial composition of residential neighborhoods within a metropolitan area, thereby causing further racial concentration within the schools. We recognized this in *Swann* * * *.

In short, common sense dictates the conclusion that racially inspired school board actions have an impact beyond the particular schools that are the subjects of those actions. This is not to say, of course, that there can never be a case in which the geographical structure of, or the natural boundaries within, a school district may have the effect of dividing the district into separate, identifiable and unrelated units. Such a determination is essentially a question of fact to be resolved by the trial court in the first instance, but such cases must be rare. In the absence of such a determination, proof of state-imposed segregation in a substantial portion of the district will suffice to support a finding by the trial court of the existence of a dual system. Of course, where that finding is made, as in cases involving statutory dual systems, the school authorities have an affirmative duty "to effectuate a transition to a racially nondiscriminatory school system." *Brown II*, supra, 394 U.S., at 301, 75 S.Ct. at 756.

On remand, therefore, the District Court should decide in the first instance whether respondent School Board's deliberate racial segregation policy with respect to the Park Hill schools constitutes the entire Denver school system a dual school system. We observe that on the record now before us there is indication that Denver is not a school district which might be divided into separate, identifiable and unrelated units. * * *

* * * In any event, inquiry whether the District Court and the Court of Appeals applied the correct legal standards in addressing petitioners' contention of deliberate segregation in the core city schools is not at an end even if it be true that Park Hill may be separated from the rest of the Denver school district as a separate, identifiable, and unrelated unit.

III

The District Court proceeded on the premise that the finding as to the Park Hill schools was irrelevant to the consideration of the rest of the district, and began its examination of the core city schools by requiring that petitioners prove all of the essential elements of *de jure* segregation—that is, stated simply, a current condition of segregation resulting from intentional state action directed specifically to the core city schools. The segregated character of the core city schools could not be and is not denied. Petitioners' proof showed that at the time of trial 22 of the schools in the core city area were less than 30% in Anglo enrollment and 11 of the schools were less than 10% Anglo. Petitioners also introduced substantial evidence demonstrating the existence of a disproportionate racial and ethnic composition of faculty and staff at these schools.

On the question of segregative intent, petitioners presented evidence tending to show that the Board, through its actions over a period of years, intentionally created and maintained the segregated character of the core city schools. Respondents countered this evidence by arguing that the segregation in these schools is the result of a racially neutral "neighborhood school policy" and that the acts of which petitioners complain are explicable within the bounds of that policy. Accepting the School Board's explanation, the District Court and the Court of Appeals agree that a finding of *de jure* segregation as to the core city schools was not permissible since petitioners had failed to prove "(1) a racially discriminatory purpose and (2) a causal relationship between the acts complained of and the racial imbalance admittedly existing in those schools." 445 F.2d at 1006. This assessment of petitioners' proof was clearly incorrect.

Although petitioners had already proved the existence of intentional school segregation in the Park Hill schools, this crucial finding was totally ignored when attention turned to the core city schools. Plainly, a finding of intentional segregation as to a portion of a school system is not devoid of probative value in assessing the school authorities' intent with respect to other parts of the same school system. On the contrary where, as here, the case involves one school board, a finding of intentional segregation on its part in one portion of a school system is highly relevant to the issue of the board's intent with respect to the other segregated schools in the system. This is merely an application of the well-settled evidentiary principle that "the prior doing of other similar acts, whether clearly a part of a scheme or not, is useful as reducing the possibility that the act in question was done with innocent intent." 2 J. Wigmore, Evidence 200 (3d ed. 1940). * * *

Applying these principles in the special context of school desegregation cases, we hold that a finding of intentionally segregative school board actions in a meaningful portion of a school system, as in this case, creates a presumption that other segregated schooling within the system is not adventitious. It establishes, in other words, a prima facie case of unlawful segregative design on the part of school authorities, and shifts to those authorities the burden of proving that other segregated schools within the system are not also the result of intentionally segregative actions. This is true even if it is determined that different areas of the school district should be viewed independently of each other because, even in that situation, there is high probability that where school authorities have effectuated an intentionally segregative policy in a meaningful portion of the school system, similar impermissible considerations have motivated their actions in other areas of the system. We emphasize that the differentiating factor between *de jure* segregation and so-called *de facto* segregation to which we referred in *Swann* is *purpose* or *intent* to segregate. Where school authorities have been found to have practiced purposeful segregation in part of a school system, they may be expected to oppose system-wide desegregation, as did the respondents in this case, on the ground that their purposefully segregative actions were isolated and individual events, thus leaving plaintiffs with the burden of proving otherwise. But at that point where an intentionally segregative policy is practiced in a meaningful or significant segment of a school system, as in this case, the school authorities cannot be heard to argue that plaintiffs have proved only "isolated and individual" unlawfully segregative actions. In that circumstance, it is both fair and reasonable to require that the school authorities bear the burden of showing that their actions as to other segregated schools within the system were not also motivated by segregative intent.

＊　＊　＊

In discharging that burden, it is not enough, of course, that the school authorities rely upon some allegedly logical, racially neutral explanation for their actions. Their burden is to adduce proof sufficient to support a finding that segregative intent was not among the factors that motivated their actions. The courts below attributed much significance to the fact that many of the Board's actions in the core city area antedated our decision in *Brown*. We reject any suggestion that remoteness in time has any relevance to the issue of intent. If the actions of school authorities were to any degree motivated by segregative intent and the segregation resulting from those actions continues to exist, the fact of remoteness in time certainly does not make those actions any less "intentional."

＊　＊　＊

The respondent School Board invoked at trial its "neighborhood school policy" as explaining racial and ethnic concentrations within the core city schools, arguing that since the core city area population had long been Negro and Hispano, the concentrations were necessarily the result of residential patterns and not of purposefully segregative policies. We have no occasion to consider in this case whether a "neighborhood school policy" of itself will justify racial or ethnic concentrations in the absence of a finding that school authorities have committed acts constituting *de jure* segregation. It is enough that we hold that the mere assertion of such a policy is not dispositive where, as in this case, the school authorities have been found to have practiced *de jure* segregation in a meaningful portion of the school system by techniques that indicate that the "neighborhood school" concept has not been maintained free of manipulation.   *   *   *

*   *   *

IV

In summary, the District Court on remand, *first,* will afford respondent School Board the opportunity to prove its contention that the Park Hill area is a separate, identifiable and unrelated section of the school district that should be treated as isolated from the rest of the district. If respondent School Board fails to prove that contention, the District Court, *second,* will determine whether respondent School Board's conduct over almost a decade after 1960 in carrying out a policy of deliberate racial segregation in the Park Hill schools constitutes the entire school system a dual school system. If the District Court determines that the Denver school system is a dual school system, respondent School Board has the affirmative duty to desegregate the entire system "root and branch." Green v. County School Board, 391 U.S., at 438, 88 S.Ct. at 1694. If the District Court determines, however, that the Denver school system is not a dual school system by reason of the Board's actions in Park Hill, the court, *third,* will afford respondent School Board the opportunity to rebut petitioners' prima facie case of intentional segregation in the core city schools raised by the finding of intentional segregation in the Park Hill schools. There, the Board's burden is to show that its policies and practices with respect to schoolsite location, school size, school renovations and additions, student-attendance zones, student assignment and transfer options, mobile classroom units, transportation of students, assignment of faculty and staff, etc., considered together and premised on the Board's so-called "neighborhood school" concept, either were not taken in effectuation of a policy to create or maintain segregation in the core city schools, or, if unsuccessful in that effort, were not factors in causing the existing condition of segregation in these schools. Considerations of "fairness" and "policy" demand no less in light of the Board's intentionally segregative actions. If respondent Board fails to rebut petitioners' prima facie case, the District Court must, as in the case of Park Hill, decree all-out desegregation of the core city schools.

The judgment of the Court of Appeals is modified to vacate instead of reverse the parts of the Final Decree that concern the core city schools, and the case is remanded to the District Court for further proceedings consistent with this opinion.

*   *   *

It is so ordered.

NOTES

1. In taking the position that there is no affirmative duty to integrate where *de facto* segregation exists, one commentator had this to say. "Revolutionary as was the decision in *Brown* in its rendition and subsequent application, the Court has not sought to overturn the established principle of constitutional law that 'the unlawful administration by state officers of a state statute fair on its face, resulting in its unequal application to those who are entitled to be treated alike, is not a denial of equal protection unless there is shown to be present in it an element of intentional or purposeful discrimination.' Snowden v. Hughes, 321 U.S. 1, 64 S.Ct. 397 (1944). In one of its first cases, Virginia v. Rives, 100 U.S. 313 (1879), construing the equal protection clause of the Fourteenth Amendment, the Court held that a mere showing that Negroes were not included in a particular jury was not enough, there must be a showing of actual discrimination because of race. Virginia v. Rives, 100 U.S. 313 (1879). Down through the years, this has been the law of the land: "The purpose of the equal protection clause of the Fourteenth Amendment is to secure every person within the State's jurisdiction against intentional and arbitrary discrimination, whether occasioned by express terms of a statute or by its improper execution through duly constituted agents." Sunday Lake Iron Co. v. Township of Wakefield, 247 U.S. 350, 38 S.Ct. 495 (1918). No different purpose was attributed to the amendment by the Court either in *Brown* or any case since decided." Charles J. Bloch, "Does the Fourteenth Amendment Forbid De-Facto Segregation?," 16 Western Reserve L.Rev. 542 (1965). Permission to quote granted by: Wm. S. Hein and Company, Inc., Buffalo, New York.

2. A minority view regarding *de facto* segregation was expounded in a case in Washington, D.C. in 1967. The court, in this case, held that racially and socially homogeneous schools damage the mind and spirit of the child and whether segregation occurs by law or by fact, there is an affirmative duty to overcome the segregation. The court said further that aptitude and achievement tests used for "tracking," placing children in separate learning tracks, were middle class oriented and served to perpetuate segregation in the schools. Based on these conclusions, the court handed down a decree ordering the busing of volunteering children from predominantly Negro schools to predominantly white schools and also mandated the abolition of ability grouping of children by the "tracking" procedures which were being used at that time in Washington, D.C. Hobson v. Hansen, 269 F. Supp. 401 (1967). Affirmed on Appeal by United States Court of Appeals for District of Columbia.

3. The Court of Appeals for the Fifth Circuit said in United States v. Jefferson County Board of Education (372 F.2d 836) that:

The Constitution is both color blind and color conscious.

To avoid a conflict with the equal protection clause, a classification that denies a benefit, causes harm, or imposes a burden must not be based on race. But the Constitution is color conscious to prevent discrimination being perpetuated and to undo the effects of past discrimination. The criterion is the relevancy of color to a legitimate governmental purpose.

Quotas and Busing

If the vestiges of past state sanctioned segregation remain, then the courts may do whatever is reasonably necessary to desegregate the schools. What constitutes legitimate remedies to overcome past segregation to bring into effect a unitary school system has been the subject of controversy since the days of "freedom of choice." Beyond freedom of choice though the state is required to assert a positive policy of placement of either students or facilities to bring about integration.

The problem really has two aspects: the measurement of inequality and the physical process used by the courts to effectuate integration. In determining the degree of inequality the lower courts have tended to rely on quotas as a primary yardstick. In this regard, the Supreme Court has held that racial percentages of each school do not have to reflect the racial composition of the school system as a whole.[40] A fixed mathematical racial balance is not required and according to the Court should not be the sole criterion to determine appropriate movement toward a unitary state. The Supreme Court is consistent in this position in higher education as well as elementary and secondary. In the celebrated *Bakke* decision[41] the Supreme Court rejected the University of California's quota system for admission to medical school which specified a percentage of the student body be set aside for selected classifications of persons. The Court said:

> * * * it is evident that the Davis special admission program involves the use of an explicit racial classification never before countenanced by this court. It tells applicants who are not Negro, Asian, or "Chicano" that they are totally excluded from a specific percentage of the seats in an entering class * * * The fatal flaw in petitioner's preferential program is its disregard of individual rights as guaranteed by the Fourteenth Amendment.[42]

In both higher education and the public schools, the court has been consistent in allowing the use of quotas or percentage as one criterion or as a starting point, but has never required nor permitted it to be used as the sole determinant.

Several alternatives have been approved by the Supreme Court in overcoming *de jure* racial imbalances and transportation is one such acceptable remedy. Significantly, in Swann v. Charlotte-Mecklenburg, the court observed that, "Desegregation plans cannot be limited to walk-in schools."

40. Swann v. Charlotte-Mecklenburg Bd. of Educ., 402 U.S. 1, 91 S.Ct. 1267 (1971).

41. Regents of the Univ. of Calif. v. Bakke, 438 U.S. 265, 98 S.Ct. 2733 (1978).

42. Ibid.

*Busing to Overcome Racial Segregation Is a Judicially
Acceptable Alternative Where De Jure
Segregation Has Existed*

SWANN v. CHARLOTTE–MECKLENBURG BD. OF EDUC.

Supreme Court of the United States, 1971.
402 U.S. 1, 91 S.Ct. 1267.

Mr. Chief Justice BURGER delivered the opinion of the Court.

* * *

This case and those argued with it arose in States having a long history of maintaining two sets of schools in a single school system deliberately operated to carry out a governmental policy to separate pupils in schools solely on the basis of race. That was what Brown v. Board of Education was all about. * * *

The Charlotte-Mecklenburg school system, the 43d largest in the Nation, encompasses the city of Charlotte and surrounding Mecklenburg County, North Carolina. The area is large—550 square miles —spanning roughly 22 miles east-west and 36 miles north-south. During the 1968–1969 school year the system served more than 84,000 pupils in 107 schools. Approximately 71% of the pupils were found to be white and 29% Negro. As of June 1969 there were approximately 24,000 Negro students in the system, of whom 21,000 attended schools within the city of Charlotte. Two-thirds of those 21,-000—approximately 14,000 Negro students—attended 21 schools which were either totally Negro or more than 99% Negro.

* * *

In April 1969 the District Court ordered the school board to come forward with a plan for both faculty and student desegregation. Proposed plans were accepted by the court in June and August 1969 on an interim basis only, and the board was ordered to file a third plan by November 1969. In November the board moved for an extension of time until February 1970, but when that was denied the board submitted a partially completed plan. In December 1969 the District Court held that the board's submission was unacceptable and appointed an expert in education administration, Dr. John Finger, to prepare a desegregation plan. Thereafter in February 1970, the District Court was presented with two alternative pupil assignment plans— the finalized "board plan" and the "Finger plan."

The Board Plan. As finally submitted, the school board plan closed seven schools and reassigned their pupils. It restructured school attendance zones to achieve greater racial balance but maintained existing grade structures and rejected techniques such as pairing and clustering as part of a desegregation effort. The plan created a single athletic league, eliminated the previously racial basis of the school bus system, provided racially mixed faculties and administrative staffs, and modified its free-transfer plan into an optional majority-to-minority transfer system.

The board plan proposed substantial assignment of Negroes to nine of the system's 10 high schools, producing 17% to 36% Negro population in each. The projected Negro attendance at the 10th school, Independence, was 2%. The proposed attendance zones for the high schools were typically shaped like wedges of a pie, extending outward from the center of the city to the suburban and rural areas of the county in order to afford residents of the center city area access to outlying schools.

As for junior high schools, the board plan rezoned the 21 school areas so that in 20 the Negro attendance would range from 0% to 38%. The other school, located in the heart of the Negro residential area, was left with an enrollment of 90% Negro.

The board plan with respect to elementary schools relied entirely upon gerrymandering of geographic zones. More than half of the Negro elementary pupils were left in nine schools that were 86% to 100% Negro; approximately half of the white elementary pupils were assigned to schools 86% to 100% white.

The Finger Plan. The plan submitted by the court-appointed expert, Dr. Finger, adopted the school board zoning plan for senior high schools with one modification: it required that an additional 300 Negro students be transported from the Negro residential area of the city to the nearly all-white Independence High School.

The Finger plan for the junior high schools employed much of the rezoning plan of the board, combined with the creation of nine "satellite" zones. Under the satellite plan, inner-city Negro students were assigned by attendance zones to nine outlying predominately white junior high schools, thereby substantially desegregating every junior high school in the system.

The Finger plan departed from the board plan chiefly in its handling of the system's 76 elementary schools. Rather than relying solely upon geographic zoning, Dr. Finger proposed use of zoning, pairing, and grouping techniques, with the result that student bodies throughout the system would range from 9% to 38% Negro.

* * *

On February 5, 1970, the District Court adopted the board plan, as modified by Dr. Finger, for the junior and senior high schools. The court rejected the board elementary school plan and adopted the Finger plan as presented. Implementation was partially stayed by the Court of Appeals for the Fourth Circuit on March 5, and this Court declined to disturb the Fourth Circuit's order, 397 U.S. 978, 90 S.Ct. 1099, 25 L.Ed.2d 389 (1970).

On appeal the Court of Appeals affirmed the District Court's order as to faculty desegregation and the secondary school plans, but vacated the order respecting elementary schools. * * *

* * *

Nearly 17 years ago this Court held, in explicit terms, that state-imposed segregation by race in public schools denies equal protection of the laws. At no time has the Court deviated in the slightest degree from that holding or its constitutional underpinnings. None of the parties before us challenges the Court's decision of May 17, 1954, that

> "in the field of public education the doctrine of 'separate but equal' has no place. Separate educational facilities are inherently unequal. Therefore, we hold that the plaintiffs and others similarly situated * * * are, by reason of the segregation complained of, deprived of the equal protection of the laws guaranteed by the Fourteenth Amendment.
> * * *

* * *

The central issue in this case is that of student assignment, and there are essentially four problem areas:

(1) to what extent racial balance or racial quotas may be used as an implement in a remedial order to correct a previously segregated system;

(2) whether every all-Negro and all-white school must be eliminated as an indispensable part of a remedial process of desegration;

(3) what the limits are, if any, on the rearrangement of school districts and attendance zones, as a remedial measure; and

(4) what the limits are, if any, on the use of transportation facilities to correct state-enforced racial school segregation.

Racial Balances or Racial Quotas.

The constant theme and thrust of every holding from *Brown I* to date is that state-enforced separation of races in public schools is discrimination that violates the Equal Protection Clause. The remedy commanded was to dismantle dual school systems.

* * *

Our objective in dealing with the issues presented by these cases is to see that school authorities exclude no pupil of a racial minority from any school, directly or indirectly, on account of race; it does not and cannot embrace all the problems of racial prejudice, even when those problems contribute to disproportionate racial concentrations in some schools.

In this case it is urged that the District Court has imposed a racial balance requirement of 71%–29% on individual schools. The fact that no such objective was actually achieved—and would appear to be impossible—tends to blunt that claim, yet in the opinion and order of the District Court of December 1, 1969, we find that court directing "that efforts should be made to reach a 71–29 ratio in the various schools so that there will be no basis for contending that one school is racially different from the others * * *, [t]hat no school [should] be operated with an all-black or predominantly black student body, [and] [t]hat pupils of all grades [should] be assigned in such a way that as nearly as practicable the various schools at various grade levels have about the same proportion of black and white students."

The District Judge went on to acknowledge that variation "from that norm may be unavoidable." This contains intimations that the "norm" is a fixed mathematical racial balance reflecting the pupil constituency of the system. If we were to read the holding of the District Court to require, as a matter of substantive constitutional right, any particular degree of racial balance or mixing, that approach would be disapproved and we would be obliged to reverse. The constitutional command to desegregate schools does not mean that every school in every community must always reflect the racial composition of the school system as a whole.

As the voluminous record in this case shows, the predicate for the District Court's use of the 71%–29% ratio was twofold: first, its express finding, approved by the Court of Appeals and not challenged here, that a dual school system had been maintained by the school authorities at least until 1969; second, its finding, also approved by the Court of Appeals, that the school board had totally defaulted in its acknowledged duty to come forward with an acceptable plan of its own, notwithstanding the patient efforts of the District Judge who, on at least three occasions, urged the board to submit plans. * * *

We see therefore that the use made of mathematical ratios was no more than a starting point in the process of shaping a remedy, rather than an inflexible requirement. From that starting point the District Court proceeded to frame a decree that was within its discretionary powers, as an equitable remedy for the particular circumstances. As we said in *Green*, a school authority's remedial plan or a district court's remedial decree is to be judged by its effectiveness. Awareness of the racial composition of the whole school system is likely to be a useful starting point in shaping a remedy to correct past constitutional violations. In sum, the very limited use made of mathematical ratios was within the equitable remedial discretion of the District Court.

One-race Schools.

The record in this case reveals the familiar phenomenon that in metropolitan areas minority groups are often found concentrated in one part of the city. In some circumstances certain schools may remain all or largely of one race until new schools can be provided or neighborhood patterns change. Schools all or predominantly of one race in a district of mixed population will require close scrutiny to determine that school assignments are not part of state-enforced segregation.

In light of the above, it should be clear that the existence of some small number of one-race, or virtually one-race, schools within a district is not in and of itself the mark of a system that still practices segregation by law. The district judge or school authorities should make every effort to achieve the greatest possible degree of actual desegregation and will thus necessarily be concerned with the elimination of one-race schools. * * * Where the school authority's proposed plan for conversion from a dual to a unitary system contemplates the continued existence of some schools that are all or predominately of one race, they have the burden of showing that such school assignments are genuinely nondiscriminatory. The court should scrutinize such schools, and the burden upon the school authorities will be to satisfy the court that their racial composition is not the result of present or past discriminatory action on their part.

An optional majority-to-minority transfer provision has long been recognized as a useful part of every desegregation plan. Provision for optional transfer of those in the majority racial group of a particular school to other schools where they will be in the minority is an indispensable remedy for those students willing to transfer to other schools in order to lessen the impact on them of the state-imposed stigma of segregation. In order to be effective, such a transfer arrangement must grant the transferring student free transportation and space must be made available in the school to which he desires to move. * * * The court orders in this and the companion *Davis* case now provide such an option.

Remedial Altering of Attendance Zones.

The maps submitted in these cases graphically demonstrate that one of the principal tools employed by school planners and by courts to break up the dual school system has been a frank—and sometimes drastic—gerrymandering of school districts and attendance zones. An additional step was pairing, "clustering," or "grouping" of schools with attendance assignments made deliberately to accomplish the transfer of Negro students out of formerly segregated Negro schools and transfer of white students to formerly all-Negro schools. More often than not, these zones are neither compact nor contiguous; indeed they may be on opposite ends of the city. As an interim corrective measure, this cannot be said to be beyond the broad remedial powers of a court.

Absent a constitutional violation there would be no basis for judicially ordering assignment of students on a racial basis. All things being equal, with no history of discrimination, it might well be desirable to assign pupils to schools nearest their homes. But all things are not equal in a system that has been deliberately constructed and

maintained to enforce racial segregation. The remedy for such segregation may be administratively awkward, inconvenient, and even
bizarre in some situations and may impose burdens on some; but all
awkwardness and inconvenience cannot be avoided in the interim period when remedial adjustments are being made to eliminate the dual
school systems.

* * *

We hold that the pairing and grouping of noncontiguous school
zones is a permissible tool and such action is to be considered in light
of the objectives sought. * * * Maps do not tell the whole story
since noncontiguous school zones may be more accessible to each other in terms of the critical travel time, because of traffic patterns and
good highways, than schools geographically closer together. Conditions in different localities will vary so widely that no rigid rules can
be laid down to govern all situations.

Transportation of Students.

The scope of permissible transportation of students as an implement of a remedial decree has never been defined by this Court and
by the very nature of the problem it cannot be defined with precision.
No rigid guidelines as to student transportation can be given for application to the infinite variety of problems presented in thousands of
situations. Bus transportation has been an integral part of the public
education system for years, and was perhaps the single most important factor in the transition from the one-room schoolhouse to the
consolidated school. * * *

The importance of bus transportation as a normal and accepted
tool of educational policy is readily discernible in this and the companion case *Davis,* supra. The Charlotte school authorities did not
purport to assign students on the basis of geographically drawn zones
until 1965 and then they allowed almost unlimited transfer privileges.
* * *

Thus the remedial techniques used in the District Court's order
were within that court's power to provide equitable relief; implementation of the decree is well within the capacity of the school authority.

The decree provided that the buses used to implement the plan
would operate on direct routes. Students would be picked up at
schools near their homes and transported to the schools they were to
attend. The trips for elementary school pupils average about seven
miles and the District Court found that they would take "not over 35
minutes at the most." This system compares favorably with the
transportation plan previously operated in Charlotte under which
each day 23,600 students on all grade levels were transported an
average of 15 miles one way for an average trip requiring over an
hour. In these circumstances, we find no basis for holding that the
local school authorities may not be required to employ bus transporta-

tion as one tool of school desegregation. Desegregation plans cannot be limited to the walk-in school.

An objection to transportation of students may have validity when the time or distance of travel is so great as to either risk the health of the children or significantly impinge on the educational process. * * * It hardly needs stating that the limits on time of travel will vary with many factors, but probably with none more than the age of the students. The reconciliation of competing values in a desegregation case is, of course, a difficult task with many sensitive facets but fundamentally no more so than remedial measures courts of equity have traditionally employed.

The Court of Appeals, searching for a term to define the equitable remedial power of the district courts, used the term "reasonableness." In *Green,* supra, this Court used the term "feasible" and by implication, "workable," "effective," and "realistic" in the mandate to develop "a plan that promises realistically to work, and * * * to work *now."* On the facts of this case, we are unable to conclude that the order of the District Court is not reasonable, feasible and workable. However, in seeking to define the scope of remedial power or the limits on remedial power of courts in an area as sensitive as we deal with here, words are poor instruments to convey the sense of basic fairness inherent in equity. Substance, not semantics, must govern, and we have sought to suggest the nature of limitations without frustrating the appropriate scope of equity.

At some point, these school authorities and others like them should have achieved full compliance with this Court's decision in *Brown I.* The systems would then be "unitary" in the sense required by our decisions in *Green* and *Alexander.*

It does not follow that the communities served by such systems will remain demographically stable, for in a growing, mobile society, few will do so. Neither school authorities nor district courts are constitutionally required to make year-by-year adjustments of the racial composition of student bodies once the affirmative duty to desegregate has been accomplished and racial discrimination through official action is eliminated from the system. This does not mean that federal courts are without power to deal with future problems; but in the absence of a showing that either the school authorities or some other agency of the State has deliberately attempted to fix or alter demographic patterns to affect the racial composition of the schools, further intervention by a district court should not be necessary.

For the reasons herein set forth, the judgment of the Court of Appeals is affirmed as to those parts in which it affirmed the judgment of the District Court. The order of the District Court, dated August 7, 1970, is also affirmed. It is so ordered.

* * *

Interdistrict Desegregation

Since school districts in the South are generally quite large, geographically, most of the litigation has involved intradistrict desegregation. The courts found that much integration could be accomplished without going beyond the school district boundaries. Few instances are extant where it has been necessary to question the boundaries of the basic school district unit in order to effectuate a unitary educational system. Some cases have, however, been initiated in the South where it appeared that the school district boundaries were actually being used to thwart effective desegregation. In one such instance a town in Virginia exercised its discretion under Virginia municipal law and withdrew from the county, forming an independent municipality.[43] At the time of withdrawal of municipal functions the newly independent city decided to continue to operate the school system as a part of the overall county school system. Later, however, it was decided to also separate the independent city's school system from the countywide school district. This decision came about shortly after a federal district court had required a new desegregation plan for the entire county replacing the older freedom of choice plan. The new reorganization resulted in an increase in the proportion of blacks in the county schools and a decrease in the city schools although both systems would retain a majority of blacks. The U.S. Supreme Court enjoined the reorganization saying that the court must look to the effect of such action on the segregation of the schools. Where the effect is to exacerbate the problem of racial imbalance the court will frown on changing school district boundaries. The Supreme Court listed three factors supporting the conclusion under which such reorganizations may be judged constitutionally impermissible: first, the likelihood of increased segregation as white parents shifted their children to the new school district from private schools and the county system was apparent; second, the fact that the independent city schools in the state had traditionally been predominately white suggested that the same pattern might ensue here; and third, the timing of the city's decision was psychologically poor since it made it appear that the rationale for separating the school system was based on the lower court's prohibition of the use of a freedom of choice plan for the entire school system. Effectively, then the Supreme Court said that where segregation is perpetuated as a result of *de jure* governmental action, the Court will not be deterred from intervening even though the remedy goes beyond school district boundaries.[44]

43. Wright v. Council of the City of Emporia, 107 U.S. 451, 92 S.Ct. 2196 (1972).

44. See also: Lee v. Macon County Bd. of Education, 448 F.2d 746 (1971);

Stout v. Jefferson County Bd. of Education, 448 F.2d 403 (1971); Haney v. County Bd. of Education, 410 F.2d 920 (1969).

In another case rendered on the same day as the above decision, the Supreme Court refused to permit severance of Scotland Neck schools from those of surrounding Halifax County, North Carolina.[45] The Court reasoned that the motivation of Scotland Neck's departure from the county school system was prompted solely for purposes of segregation and the effect of the action would weld the two systems into a segregated pattern, the new city district being predominately white and the county schools would be basically black.

An entirely different situation was presented in the notable Richmond, Virginia case.[46] Here a federal district court required the merger of three large and separate school districts to bring about desegregation. Chesterfield and Henrico County school districts are the suburban school districts surrounding Richmond and, as in most large urban areas, the city school district had become progressively segregated over the years as white families moved beyond the city limits. Effectively, the federal district judge's decision would have made one large administrative unit of the three systems with a complex system of rezoning and busing among the school centers. On appeal, the United States Court of Appeals for the Fourth Circuit reversed the lower court decision holding that there was no evidence to indicate that there was ever any state action taken to keep blacks confined to a particular school district. The court said that:

> This court believes that the root causes of the concentration of blacks in inner cities of America are simply not known and that the district court could not realistically place on the counties the responsibility for the effect that inner city decay has had on the public schools of Richmond * * * The facts of this case do not show that state establishment and maintenance of school districts coterminous with the political subdivision of the city of Richmond and the counties of Chesterfield and Henrico have been intended to circumvent any federally protected right.[47]

In review of this decision by the U.S. Supreme Court, eight justices were unable to render a decision, deadlocking four to four. Justice Powell had removed himself from the case because he had formerly been a member of the Richmond school board. Thus, the decision by the Court of Appeals stood.

A similar but more complicated situation arose in Michigan where the school district pattern around Detroit was found by a lower federal district court to be so constituted as to create school segregation in the central city of Detroit.[48] Both the federal district court and the

45. United States v. Scotland Neck City Board of Education, 407 U.S. 484, 92 S.Ct. 2214 (1972).

46. Bradley v. Richmond School Board, 456 F.2d 6 (4th Cir. 1972); 416 U.S. 696, 94 S.Ct. 2006 (1974).

47. Ibid.

48. Milliken v. Bradley, 418 U.S. 717, 94 S.Ct. 3112 (1974).

federal Court of Appeals concluded that desegregation of Detroit schools was impossible, unless the racial composition of the entire metropolitan area was taken into account. Dismantling of segregation, therefore, according to these federal courts, required interdistrict busing between the Detroit core city and several suburban school districts. On appeal the U.S. Supreme Court in reversing the decision held that there was no evidence in the record to show that the original boundaries of the Detroit School District or any other school districts in Michigan were established for the purpose of segregation of the races.

Subsequent to the Supreme Court's decision in *Milliken,* the U.S. Court of Appeals for the Sixth Circuit upheld a federal district court decision which effectively merged the Louisville and Jefferson County, Kentucky school districts.[49] The court did not depart from the *Milliken* rationale but reached a different result because of the special circumstances which were attendant to the Louisville situation. The court found that there still remained vestiges of past *de jure* discrimination in the two large school districts which was not true in *Milliken.* The Court of Appeals found the crucial difference between the Louisville and Detroit cases to lie in the fact that in the past school district boundaries in Louisville had been ignored in order to segregate the schools. For example, it was shown that in pre-*Brown* days black high school students in the Jefferson County school district were sent to Central High School located in the Louisville school district. This was done because the Jefferson County system had no black high school. It was also shown that another city high school was actually located geographically in the county and students of both systems had attended school there. No such interplay was present or had ever transpired between the suburban school districts of Detroit and the central city. Further, school districts in Kentucky had been legally segregated in pre-*Brown* days and as such evinced a record of segregated past which was not present in Michigan.

The Detroit and Louisville cases, although reaching different results, continued a consistent legal rationale enunciating a rule of law which states essentially that school district integration will be required, by busing or other means, either within or among school districts, where it can be shown that segregation is the result of governmental action which tends to create, maintain or perpetuate segregation of the races. The rule applies to northern as well as to southern states. In the North, although schools were not segregated by statute before *Brown* in 1954, it is quite possible for subsequent government acts whether patent or latent to discriminate in such a way as to create patterns of racial imbalance in the schools. In such instances the segregation will not be viewed as *de facto* by the courts but as *de jure* and therefore unconstitutional.

49. Newburg Area Council, Inc. v. Gordon, 521 F.2d 578 (1975); Newburg Area Council, Inc. v. Board of Education, 510 F.2d 1358 (1974).

*Interdistrict Integration May Be an Improper Remedy
to Overcome Single-district Segregation*

MILLIKEN v. BRADLEY

Supreme Court of the United States, 1974.
418 U.S. 717, 94 S.Ct. 3112.

Mr. Chief Justice BURGER delivered the opinion of the Court.

We granted certiorari in these consolidated cases to determine whether a federal court may impose a multidistrict, areawide remedy to a single-district *de jure* segregation problem absent any finding that the other included school districts have failed to operate unitary school systems within their districts, absent any claim or finding that the boundary lines of any affected school district were established with the purpose of fostering racial segregation in public schools, absent any finding that the included districts committed acts which effected segregation within the other districts, and absent a meaningful opportunity for the included neighboring school districts to present evidence or be heard on the propriety of a multidistrict remedy or on the question of constitutional violations by those neighboring districts.

* * *

* * * In Brown v. Board of Education, 349 U.S. 294, 75 S.Ct. 753, 99 L.Ed. 1083 (1955) (*Brown II*), the Court's first encounter with the problem of remedies in school desegregation cases, the Court noted:

> "In fashioning and effectuating the decrees, the courts will be guided by equitable principles. Traditionally, equity has been characterized by a practical flexibility in shaping its remedies and by a facility for adjusting and reconciling public and private needs." Id., at 300, 75 S.Ct., at 756.

In further refining the remedial process, *Swann* held, the task is to correct, by a balancing of the individual and collective interests, "the condition that offends the Constitution." A federal remedial power may be exercised "only on the basis of a constitutional violation" and, "[a]s with any equity case, the nature of the violation determines the scope of the remedy." 402 U.S., at 16, 91 S.Ct., at 1276.

Proceeding from these basic principles, we first note that in the District Court the complainants sought a remedy aimed at the *condition* alleged to offend the Constitution—the segregation within the Detroit City School District. The court acted on this theory of the case and in its initial ruling on the "Desegregation Area" stated:

> "The task before this court, therefore, is now, and
> * * * has always been, how to desegregate the Detroit
> public schools." 345 F.Supp., at 921.

Thereafter, however, the District Court abruptly rejected the proposed Detroit-only plans on the ground that "while [they] would provide a racial mix more in keeping with the Black-White proportions of the student population [they] would accentuate the racial identifiability of the [Detroit] district as a Black school system, and would not accomplish desegregation." Pet.App., 56a. "[T]he racial composition of the student body is such," said the court, "that the plan's implementation would clearly make the entire Detroit public school system racially indentifiable" (Id., at 54a), "leav[ing] many of its schools 75 to 90 per cent Black." Id., at 55a. Consequently, the court reasoned, it was imperative to "look beyond the limits of the Detroit school district for a solution to the problem of segregation in the Detroit public schools * * * " since "[s]chool district lines are simply matters of political convenience and may not be used to deny constitutional rights." Id., at 57a. Accordingly, the District Court proceeded to redefine the relevant area to include areas of predominantly white pupil population in order to ensure that "upon implementation, no school, grade or classroom [would be] substantially disproportionate to the overall pupil racial composition" of the entire metropolitan area.

*   *   *

Viewing the record as a whole, it seems clear that the District Court and the Court of Appeals shifted the primary focus from a Detroit remedy to the metropolitan area only because of their conclusion that total desegregation of Detroit would not produce the racial balance which they perceived as desirable. Both courts proceeded on an assumption that the Detroit schools could not be truly desegregated—in their view of what constituted desegregation—unless the racial composition of the student body of each school substantially reflected the racial composition of the population of the metropolitan area as a whole. The metropolitan area was then defined as Detroit plus 53 of the outlying school districts. *   *   *

In *Swann*, which arose in the context of a single independent school district, the Court held:

> "If we were to read the holding of the District Court to require, as a matter of substantive constitutional right, any particular degree of racial balance or mixing, that approach would be disapproved and we would be obliged to reverse," 402 U.S., at 24, 91 S.Ct., at 1280.

The clear import of this language from *Swann* is that desegregation, in the sense of dismantling a dual school system, does not require any particular racial balance in each "school, grade or classroom." See Spencer v. Kugler, 404 U.S. 1027, 92 S.Ct. 707, 30 L.Ed.2d 723 (1972).

Here the District Court's approach to what constituted "actual desegregation" raises the fundamental question, not presented in *Swann*, as to the circumstances in which a federal court may order desegregation relief that embraces more than a single school district. The court's analytical starting point was its conclusion that school district lines are no more than arbitrary lines on a map drawn "for political convenience." Boundary lines may be bridged where there has been a constitutional violation calling for interdistrict relief but the notion that school district lines may be casually ignored or treated as a mere administrative convenience is contrary to the history of public education in our country. No single tradition in public education is more deeply rooted than local control over the operation of schools; local autonomy has long been thought essential both to the maintenance of community concern and support for public schools and to quality of the educational process. * * *

The Michigan educational structure involved in this case, in common with most States, provides for a large measure of local control, and a review of the scope and character of these local powers indicates the extent to which the interdistrict remedy approved by the two courts could disrupt and alter the structure of public education in Michigan. The metropolitan remedy would require, in effect, consolidation of 54 independent school districts historically administered as separate units into a vast new super school district. See n. 10, supra. Entirely apart from the logistical and other serious problems attending large-scale transportation of students, the consolidation would give rise to an array of other problems in financing and operating this new school system. Some of the more obvious questions would be: What would be the status and authority of the present popularly elected school boards? Would the children of Detroit be within the jurisdiction and operating control of a school board elected by the parents and residents of other districts? What board or boards would levy taxes for school operations in these 54 districts constituting the consolidated metropolitan area? What provisions could be made for assuring substantial equality in tax levies among the 54 districts, if this were deemed requisite? What provisions would be made for financing? Would the validity of long-term bonds be jeopardized unless approved by all of the component districts as well as the State? What body would determine that portion of the curricula now left to the discretion of local school boards? Who would establish attendance zones, purchase school equipment, locate and construct new schools, and indeed attend to all the myriad day-to-day decisions that are necessary to school operations affecting potentially more than three-quarters of a million pupils?

It may be suggested that all of these vital operational problems are yet to be resolved by the District Court, and that this is the purpose of the Court of Appeals' proposed remand. But it is obvious from the scope of the interdistrict remedy itself that absent a complete restructuring of the laws of Michigan relating to school districts the District Court will become first, a *de facto* "legislative authority" to resolve these complex questions, and then the "school superintendent" for the entire area. This is a task which few, if any, judges are qualified to perform and one which would deprive the people of control of schools through their elected representatives.

Of course, no state law is above the Constitution. School district lines and the present laws with respect to local control, are not sacrosanct and if they conflict with the Fourteenth Amendment federal courts have a duty to prescribe appropriate remedies. * * * But our prior holdings have been confined to violations and remedies within a single school district. We therefore turn to address, for the first time, the validity of a remedy mandating cross-district or interdistrict consolidation to remedy a condition of segregation found to exist in only one district.

The controlling principle consistently expounded in our holdings is that the scope of the remedy is determined by the nature and extent of the constitutional violation. *Swann,* 402 U.S., at 16, 91 S.Ct., at 1276. Before the boundaries of separate and autonomous school districts may be set aside by consolidating the separate units for remedial purposes or by imposing a cross-district remedy, it must first be shown that there has been a constitutional violation within one district that produces a significant segregative effect in another district. Specifically, it must be shown that racially discriminatory acts of the state or local school districts, or of a single school district have been a substantial cause of interdistrict segregation. Thus an interdistrict remedy might be in order where the racially discriminatory acts of one or more school districts caused racial segregation in an adjacent district, or where district lines have been deliberately drawn on the basis of race. In such circumstances an interdistrict remedy would be appropriate to eliminate the interdistrict segregation directly caused by the constitutional violation. Conversely, without an interdistrict violation and interdistrict effect, there is no constitutional wrong calling for an interdistrict remedy.

The record before us, voluminous as it is, contains evidence of *de jure* segregated conditions only in the Detroit schools; indeed, that was the theory on which the litigation was initially based and on which the District Court took evidence. With no showing of significant violation by the 53 outlying school districts and no evidence of any interdistrict violation or effect, the court went beyond the original theory of the case as framed by the pleadings and mandated a metropolitan area remedy. To approve the remedy ordered by the court would impose on the outlying districts, not shown to have committed any constitutional violation, a wholly impermissible remedy based on a standard not hinted at in *Brown I* and *II* or any holding of this Court.

In dissent, Mr. Justice WHITE and Mr. Justice MARSHALL undertake to demonstrate that agencies having statewide authority participated in maintaining the dual school system found to exist in Detroit. They are apparently of the view that once such participation

is shown, the District Court should have a relatively free hand to reconstruct school districts outside of Detroit in fashioning relief. Our
assumption, *arguendo,* that state agencies did participate in the maintenance of the Detroit system, should make it clear that it is not on
this point that we part company. The difference between us arises
instead from established doctrine laid down by our cases. *Brown,*
supra; *Green,* supra; *Swann,* supra; *Scotland Neck,* supra; and
Emporia, supra, each addressed the issue of constitutional wrong in
terms of an established geographic and administrative school system populated by both Negro and white children. In such a context, terms such as "unitary" and "dual" systems and "racially
identifiable schools," have meaning, and the necessary federal
authority to remedy the constitutional wrong is firmly established.
But the remedy is necessarily designed, as all remedies are, to restore
the victims of discriminatory conduct to the position they would have
occupied in the absence of such conduct. Disparate treatment of
white and Negro students occurred within the Detroit school system,
and not elsewhere, and on this record the remedy must be limited to
that system. *Swann,* supra, 402 U.S., at 16, 91 S.Ct., at 1276.

The constitutional right of the Negro respondents residing in Detroit is to attend a unitary school system in that district. Unless petitioners drew the district lines in a discriminatory fashion, or arranged for white students residing in the Detroit district to attend
schools in Oakland and Macomb Counties, they were under no constitutional duty to make provisions for Negro students to do so. The
view of the dissenters, that the existence of a dual system in *Detroit*
can be made the basis for a decree requiring cross-district transportation of pupils, cannot be supported on the grounds that it represents
merely the devising of a suitably flexible remedy for the violation of
rights already established by our prior decisions. It can be supported
only by drastic expansion of the constitutional right itself, an expansion without any support in either constitutional principle or
precedent.

III

* * * The Court of Appeals * * * held the State deriva-
tively responsible for the Detroit Board's violations on the theory that
actions of Detroit as a political subdivision of the State were attributable to the State. Accepting, *arguendo,* the correctness of this finding of state responsibility for the segregated conditions within the
city of Detroit, it does not follow that an interdistrict remedy is constitutionally justified or required. With a single exception, discussed
later, there has been no showing that either the State or any of the
85 outlying districts engaged in activity that had a cross-district effect.
The boundaries of the Detroit School District, which are coterminous
with the boundaries of the city of Detroit, were established over a
century ago by neutral legislation when the city was incorporated;

there is no evidence in the record, nor is there any suggestion by the respondents, that either the original boundaries of the Detroit School District, or any other school district in Michigan, were established for the purpose of creating, maintaining, or perpetuating segregation of races. There is no claim and there is no evidence hinting that petitioner outlying school districts and their predecessors, or the 30-odd other school districts in the tricounty area—but outside the District Court's "desegregation area"—have ever maintained or operated anything but unitary school systems. Unitary school systems have been required for more than a century by the Michigan Constitution as implemented by state law. Where the schools of only one district have been affected, there is no constitutional power in the courts to decree relief balancing the racial composition of that district's schools with those of the surrounding districts.

* * *

We conclude that the relief ordered by the District Court and affirmed by the Court of Appeals was based upon an erroneous standard and was unsupported by record evidence that acts of the outlying districts effected the discrimination found to exist in the schools of Detroit. Accordingly, the judgment of the Court of Appeals is reversed and the case is remanded for further proceedings consistent with this opinion leading to prompt formulation of a decree directed to eliminating the segregation found to exist in Detroit city schools, a remedy which has been delayed since 1970.

Reversed and remanded.

NOTES

1. In a suit seeking desegregation of the Indianapolis public schools, the litigation followed a course similar to that of *Milliken*. In its first opinion, the District Court held that the Indianapolis City public schools were de jure segregated; the Court of Appeals affirmed and the U.S. Supreme Court denied certiorari. 332 F.Supp. 655 (S.D.Ind.1971), affirmed 474 F.2d 81, certiorari denied 407 U.S. 920, 413 U.S. 920, 93 S.Ct. 3066. In subsequent proceedings to select a remedy, the District Court concluded that Indianapolis-only desegregation plans were inadequate and ordered the preparation of a metropolitan desegregation plan. 368 F.Supp. 1191 (S.D. Ind.1973). In 1969, after the filing of the suit, the Indiana Legislature had enacted a law consolidating the governments of Indianapolis and surrounding Marion County, but specifically excluding the area school districts from consolidation. The Court of Appeals for the Seventh Circuit vacated those portions of the District Court's opinion ordering a metropolitan remedy, citing *Milliken* 503 F.2d 68 (7th Cir. 1974).

2. Education, as pointed out elsewhere, is primarily a state function under our constitutional scheme. It is clear, however, that the federal government through the U.S. Constitution may limit state actions in the area of education. Also, the Congress of the United States may make the receipt of federal grants contingent upon prescribed conditions.

Almost a decade after Brown, Congress passed and the President signed into law the Civil Rights Act of 1964. Title VI of the Act provides the following:

> Section 601. No person in the United States shall, on the ground of race, color, or national origin, be excluded from participation in, be denied the benefits, or be subjected to discrimination under any program or activity receiving Federal financial assistance.

Section 602 of the Act authorized Federal departments and agencies to issue "rules, regulations, or orders of general applicability" to implement the purposes of the statute. These Sections, among others, eventually led to issuance by the U.S. Office of Education of a Statement of Policies for School Desegregation, better known as "guidelines."

The following year Congress passed the Elementary and Secondary Education Act of 1965, which provided federal aid to elementary and secondary education. The substantial funds made available by this and other federal education acts have made the policies and practices under regulations pursuant to the Civil Rights Act central questions for courts and school administrators.

In order to implement the mandate of Title IV of the Civil Rights Act of 1964, the Department of Health, Education and Welfare was charged with the responsibility of preparing "guidelines." They have two purposes: (1) to indicate to local and state authorities what is necessary for compliance with federal law; (2) to bind the agency in this one aspect of the determination of eligibility for federal funds.

The HEW guidelines have been given substantial weight by the courts in dealing with problems of desegregation. The application of the guidelines and their influence on the courts was discussed in United States v. Jefferson County Bd. of Educ. (372 F.2d 836, 1966) from which the following excerpt is taken:

"HEW Guidelines are based on decisions of this and other courts, are formulated to stay within the scope of the Civil Rights Act of 1964, are prepared in detail by experts in education and school administration, and are intended by Congress and the executive to be part of a coordinated national program. The Guidelines present the best system available for uniform application, and the best aid to the courts in evaluating the validity of a school desegregation plan and the progress made under that plan.

"HEW regulations provide that schools applying for financial assistance must comply with certain requirements. However, the requirements for elementary or secondary schools 'shall be deemed to be satisfied if such school or school system is subject to a final order of a court of the United States for the desegregation of such school or school system * * *.' 45 C.F.R. § 80.4(c) (1964). (The Guidelines are, of course, subject to this regulation). This regulation causes our decisions to have a twofold impact on school desegregation. Our decisions determine not only (1) the standards schools must comply with under Brown but also (2) the standards these schools must comply with to qualify for federal financial assistance. Schools automatically qualify for federal aid whenever a final court order desegregating the school has been entered in the litigation and the school authorities agree to comply with the order. Because of the second consequence of our decisions and because of our duty to cooperate with Congress and with the executive in enforcing Congressional objectives, strong policy considerations support our holding that the standards of court-supervised desegregation should not be lower than the standards of HEW-supervised desegregation.   The Guidelines, of course, cannot bind the courts; we are not abdicating any judicial responsibilities.   (In Singleton I, to avoid any such inference, we said: 'The judiciary has, of course, functions and duties distinct from those of the executive department * * *.   Absent legal questions, the United States Office of Education is better qualified * * *' 348 F.2d at 731.)   But we hold that HEW's standards are substantially the same as this Court's standards.   They are required by the Constitution and, as we construe them, are within the scope of the Civil Rights Act of 1964.   In evaluating desegregation plans, district courts should make few exceptions to the Guidelines and should carefully tailor those so as not to defeat the policies of HEW or the holding of this Court. * * *

"A.   Title IV authorizes HEW to give technical and financial assistance to local school systems in the process of desegregation. 78 Stat. 246–99, 42 U.S.C.A. § 2000c (1964).   Title VI requires all federal agencies administering any grant-in-aid program to see to it that there is no racial discrimination by any school or other recipient of federal financial aid.   School boards cannot, however, by giving up federal aid, avoid the policy that produced this limitation on federal aid to schools: Title IV authorizes the Attorney General to sue, in the name of the United States, to desegregate a public school or school system.   More clearly and effectively than either of the other two coordinate branches of Government, Congress speaks as the Voice of the Nation.   *The national policy is plain: formerly de jure segregated public school systems based on dual attendance zones must shift to unitary, nonracial systems—with or without federal funds.*

"To make Title VI effective, the Department of Health, Education, and Welfare (HEW) adopted the regulation, 'Nondiscrimination in Federally assisted Programs.'   45 C.F.R. Part 80, Dec. 4, 1964, 64 F.R. 12539.   This regulation directs the Commissioner of Education to approve applications for financial assistance to public schools only if the school or school system agrees to comply with a court order, if any, outstanding against it, or submits a desegregation plan satisfactory to the Commissioner.

"To make the regulation effective, by assisting the Office of Education in determining whether a school qualifies for federal financial aid and by informing school boards of HEW requirements, HEW formulated certain standards of guidelines.   In April 1965, nearly a year after the Act was signed, HEW published its first *Guidelines,* 'General Statement Policies under Title VI of the Civil Rights Act of 1964 Respecting Desegregation of Elementary and Secondary Schools.'   These *Guidelines* fixed the fall of 1967 as the target date for total desegregation of all grades.   In March 1966, HEW issued '*Revised Guidelines*' to correct most of the major flaws revealed in the first year of operation under Title VI.

"B.   The HEW Guidelines raised the question: To what extent should a court, in determining whether to approve a school desegregation plan, give weight to the HEW Guidelines? We adhere to the answer this Court gave in four earlier cases.   The HEW Guidelines are 'minimum standards', representing for the most part standards the Supreme Court and this court established *before the Guidelines were promulgated.* Again, we hold, 'we attach great weight' to the *Guidelines.* Singleton v. Jackson Municipal Separate School District, 5th Cir. 1965, 348 F.2d 729 (*Singleton I*).

"The congressional mandate, as embodied in the Act and as carried out in the HEW Guidelines, does not conflict with the proper exercise of the judicial function or with the doctrine of separation of powers. It does however profoundly affect constructive use of the judicial function within the lawful scope of sound judicial discretion. When Congress declares national policy, the duty the two other coordinate branches owe to the Nation requires that, within the law, the judiciary and the executive respect and carry out that policy. * * * The judicial branch too should cooperate with Congress and the executive in making administrative agencies effective instruments for supervising and enforcing desegregation of public schools. * * * "

3. The Equal Educational Opportunities Act, Elementary and Secondary Education Amendments of 1974, Title II, P.L. 93–380, 88 Stat. 514, 20 U.S.C.A. §§ 1701 et seq., 1951 et seq., Section 202 states:

   (a) The Congress declares it to be the policy of the United States that:

      (1) all children enrolled in public schools are entitled to equal educational opportunity without regard to race, color, sex or national origin; and

      (2) the neighborhood is the appropriate place for determining public school assignments.

   (b) In order to carry out this policy, it is the purpose of this part to specify appropriate remedies for the orderly removal of the vestiges of the dual school system.

Federal Officials Cannot Permit Funding Assistance to School Districts Not in Compliance with Civil Rights Act of 1964

ADAMS v. RICHARDSON

United States District Court, District of Columbia, 1972.
351 F.Supp. 636.

MEMORANDUM OPINION

JOHN H. PRATT, District Judge. This is a suit for declaratory and injunctive relief against the Secretary of Health, Education and Welfare and the Director of the Office for Civil Rights (OCR) of the Department of Health, Education and Welfare (HEW), complaining of alleged defaults on the part of defendants in the administration of their responsibilities under Title VI of the Civil Rights Act of 1964, as amended, 42 U.S.C.A. § 2000d et seq. (1970).

The responsibilities of the OCR include the administration and enforcement of HEW's regulation issued pursuant to Title VI and published at 45 C.F.R. Part 80. In addition, the OCR through agreement with other departments and agencies of the Executive

Branch, had been assigned responsibility for Title VI enforcement with respect to most federal financial assistance to elementary, secondary and higher education and for health and social welfare activities, including such assistance as is granted and administered by those departments and agencies.

* * *

FINDINGS OF FACT

A. *Higher Education*

* * *

B. *Elementary and Secondary School Districts—1970–71*

1. HEW has reported that as of the school year 1970–71, 113 school districts had reneged on prior approved plans and were out of compliance with Title VI. Some 74 of these districts are still out of compliance with Title VI.

2. Although HEW has known of the noncompliance of most of these districts since early in the 1970–71 school year, HEW has commenced administrative enforcement actions against only seven such districts, and of the eight cases referred to the Justice Department, only three have been sued.

3. HEW has attempted to excuse its administrative inaction on the grounds that it is still seeking voluntary compliance through negotiation and conciliation.

4. These non-complying districts have received and continue to receive substantial federal assistance from HEW.

C. *Compliance with Supreme Court Decisions*

1. In Alexander v. Holmes County Board of Education, 396 U.S. 19, 90 S.Ct. 29, 24 L.Ed.2d 19 (1969), the Supreme Court required desegregation "at once" of dual school systems in thirty Mississippi school districts. At the time of this decision (October 29, 1969), 87 school districts had HEW-approved desegregation plans which permitted segregation to be postponed until September, 1970. Despite the Supreme Court's directive, HEW took no steps to compel immediate desegregation in these 87 districts.

2. Following the decision of the Supreme Court in Swann v. Charlotte-Mecklenburg Board of Education, 402 U.S. 1, 91 S.Ct. 1267, 28 L.Ed.2d 554 (1971), which enunciated "a presumption against schools that are substantially disproportionate in their racial composition" HEW identified 300 non-court order school districts with one or more schools composed mostly of local minority students.

3. Initially, HEW eliminated 75 of the 300 districts from further consideration without any on-site investigation or communication with the districts because in HEW's judgment the racial disproportion of the schools in these districts was too small to constitute a violation

of *Swann*. HEW then eliminated 134 of the remaining 225 districts from further consideration still without any on-site investigation or communication with the districts. Although at least 85 of these districts have one or more schools substantially disproportionate in their racial composition, none was required to justify the substantial racial disproportion in its schools. HEW mailed letters to the remaining 91 districts in the summer of 1971, notifying them that additional desegregation steps may be required under the *Swann* decision. Of these 91 districts, HEW received desegregation plans acceptable to HEW from 37 districts, noticed three for administrative hearing, and found *Swann* "not applicable" to nine.

4. Thus, 42 districts which HEW deemed to be in presumptive violation of *Swann* remained so approximately a year later while HEW continues to review them.

5. These 42 school districts have been receiving federal funds from HEW throughout this period of over one year.

D. *Vocational and Other Schools*

* * *

E. *Districts Subject to Court Orders*

1. Some 640 school districts which receive HEW aid, including many of the largest school districts, are subject to school desegregation court orders in the 17 southern and border states.

2. Shortly after the passage of the statute in 1964, HEW issued a regulation which, in effect, deemed a district in compliance if it were subject to a final desegregation order and provided assurance that it will comply with said order including any subsequent modification thereof.

3. In 1968, Congress in amending § 2000d–5 of the statute, adopted the HEW regulation in part by providing that, for the purpose of determining whether an educational agency is in compliance with Title VI, compliance by such agency with a final court desegregation order shall be deemed to be compliance with said Title.

4. Once a school district has been placed under a court desegregation order and gives assurance "on paper" that it is in compliance with such order, it is the practice of HEW to regard such school district as in compliance with Title VI. HEW does not monitor said school districts to determine whether or not the court order is being obeyed.

5. HEW's justification for failure to monitor school districts under court order is allegedly based upon possible conflicts with the courts, possible conflicts with the Justice Department, and HEW's alleged lack of resources to provide systematic monitoring.

6. HEW has advanced and continues to advance substantial federal funds to school districts under court order.

F. *HEW's Record of Administrative Enforcement Proceedings*

1. Between the passage of the Civil Rights Act in 1964 and March 1970, HEW initiated approximately 600 administrative proceedings against noncomplying school districts. In 1968 alone, HEW initiated about 100 enforcement proceedings. In 1969 HEW initiated nearly the same number of proceedings.

2. From March 1970, the month in which defendant Pottinger assumed the position as director of HEW's OCR, until February 1971, no enforcement proceedings were initiated, and since February 1971, only a small, token number of such proceedings have been commenced.

3. As a result of such enforcement proceedings, 44 school districts were subject to fund terminations in 1968–69. Only two cutoffs occurred in 1969–70. No termination of funds have occurred since the summer of 1970.

4. Upon initiating an administrative enforcement proceeding, it is the practice of HEW to defer the school district's application for "new" programs funds only. HEW does not defer its advancement of funds under "continuing" and previously-approved programs.

5. HEW makes no attempt subsequently to recapture funds distributed to a district between the notice of hearing and the formal determination of its Title VI ineligibility.

6. Since administrative enforcement proceedings generally consume one or more years, HEW's limited deferral practice allows the continued flow of large federal aid to the respondent school districts.

7. Despite defendants' reluctance or failure to employ enforcement proceedings terminating funds, substantial progress toward compliance with Title VI has been made. Since 1968 the number of Negro pupils in 100% minority schools or mostly minority schools in eleven southern states has greatly declined, decreasing from 68% of the total Negro pupils in the region in 1968 to 9.2% in 1971–72. On the other hand, the number of said pupils in 51% or more majority white schools has substantially increased, rising from 18% in 1968 to 43% in 1971–72.

The basic issue presented for determination is whether defendants' exercise of discretion in relying largely on voluntary compliance to accomplish the progress achieved and to obtain compliance in the areas still unresolved meets their full responsibilities under the mandate of Title VI.

CONCLUSIONS OF LAW

* * *

3. In its enactment of Title VI of the Civil Rights Act of 1964, Congress clearly indicated its intent and purpose by providing in § 2000d that:

"No person in the United States shall, on the ground of race, color, or national origin, be excluded from participation in, be denied the benefits of, or be subjected to discrimination *under any program or activity receiving Federal financial assistance.*" (Emphasis supplied)

4. HEW and all other federal agencies empowered to grant federal assistance to any program or activity are directed by § 2000d–1 of Title VI to effectuate the provisions of § 2000d by the issuance of rules, regulations and orders of general applicability consistent with the objectives of the statute authorizing financial assistance. Agencies granting federal assistance are authorized to enforce compliance with such requirements (1) by termination of or by refusal to grant or continue such assistance after opportunity for hearing and an express finding on the record of a failure to comply with such requirement, or (2) by any other means authorized by law. Prior to such enforcement action, notice of failure to comply with the requirement must be given by the agency concerned and there must be a determination by the agency that compliance cannot by secured by voluntary means. After the enforcement action terminating or refusing to grant or continue assistance has been concluded, the agency is required to make a report to the appropriate committee of the House and Senate of the circumstances and grounds for such action, which shall not take effect until thirty days after the filing of such report.

5. The underlying thrust of the statute requires that the agency involved, i. e., in this case HEW, attempt at the outset to secure compliance by voluntary means, if such method is reasonably possible. This course involves negotiation, and negotiation takes time. To such extent, the defendants have discretion but such discretion is not unlimited.

6. Where a substantial period of time has elapsed, during which period attempts toward voluntary compliance have been either not attempted or have been unsuccessful or have been rejected, defendants' limited discretion is ended and they have the duty to effectuate the provisions of § 2000d by either administrative determination, after a hearing on the record, that there has been a failure to comply and that funds should be terminated, or by any other means authorized by law, such as reference to the Department of Justice. Under such circumstances, defendants cannot rely on their alleged complete discretion as justification for permitting the mandate of the statute to be unenforced.

7. Title VI of the Civil Rights Act of 1964 is not a new statutory provision. The record is replete with instances occurring over long periods of time since 1964, where defendants' efforts seeking voluntary compliance has either not been attempted or have been unsuccessful or have met with rejection. In these cases, defendants cannot in their discretion permit further advances of federal assistance in

violation of the statute, but have the duty of accomplishing the purposes of the statute through administrative enforcement proceedings or by other legal means.

8.   After the initiation and during the pendency of an administrative enforcement proceeding HEW can only defer a school district's application for new program funds.   After such initiation and during the pendency of administrative enforcement proceedings and until action by HEW terminating or refusing to grant or continue Federal assistance, defendants have no authority to withhold Federal payments to school systems or agencies under continuing and previously-approved programs.   Under the statute, said termination action is not to become effective (a) until the agency head makes a report to the appropriate Committees of Congress, and (b) thirty days have elapsed after the filing of said report.   Nor can HEW recapture funds distributed to a district between the notice of hearing and the final determination of Title VI ineligibility.

9.   Compliance by school districts and other educational agencies under final order of a federal court for the desegregation of the school or school system operated by such agency is, by virtue of § 2000d–5, to be deemed compliance with the provisions of Title VI. Until there has been a finding by the Court entering the order that its order has not been complied with, defendants are under no obligation to effectuate the provisions of Title VI through the means previously described.   To the extent that their resources permit, defendants have the duty to monitor school districts under court order and to bring their findings to the attention of the court concerned.   The responsibility for compliance by school districts and other educational agencies under court order rests upon the court issuing said order.

10.   In summary, the discretion implicitly vested in defendants by statute exists solely for the purpose of achieving voluntary compliance with the requirements of Title VI.   As the undisputed record demonstrates, defendants' efforts toward voluntary compliance have been unsuccessful in the case of many state and local educational agencies which continue to receive substantial federal funds in violation of the statute.   Defendants now have no discretion to negate the purpose and intent of the statute by a policy described in another context as one of "benign neglect" but, on the contrary, have the duty, on a case-by-case basis, to employ the means set forth in § 2000d–1 to achieve compliance.

*   *   *

Testing and Discrimination

In recent years a wave of official interest in testing of students, teachers, and other employees has swept the country. Several states have devised competency tests for students and various types of employment and evaluation tests for teachers, the results of which may racially discriminate or appear to discriminate. At this time the potential educational and social consequences of such tests are uncertain, but it is clear that unusually high percentages of blacks score relatively low even when the tests are corrected for so-called cultural bias.

Several years ago significant litigation took place in Washington, D.C. in Hobson v. Hansen [50] wherein a federal judge found the results of a school-wide testing program and tracking system to be unconstitutional. The court held that the testing and placement scheme was based on inaccurate test results which reflected "socio-economic or racial status, * * * environmental and psychological factors which have nothing to do with innate ability." [51] In another similar case, a federal district court in California enjoined the use of I.Q. tests to place elementary school pupils in classes for the educable mentally retarded.[52] The court found that two out of every three children placed in the EMR class were black, and as a result, the racial imbalance of the EMR classes made the testing program suspect. The school district was unable to sustain the burden of showing a relationship between the I.Q. tests results and the academic capabilities of black children. More recently, though, a federal district court in Florida held that a statewide literacy testing program was valid and did not contain cultural bias which would make it constitutionally objectionable.[53] In this case the court did, however, delay the implementation of the test three years until all potential high school graduates had the benefit of a full elementary and secondary education in a racially unitary school system.

The position of the U.S. Supreme Court on employee testing was enunciated in 1971 in Griggs v. Duke Power Co.[54] In this case the Court found that the Civil Rights Act of 1964, Title VII, prevented an employer from rejecting black job applicants on the basis of lack of completion of high school or on the results of a general intelligence test. Duke Power was unable to show that the general standards it had established were related to job performance. The Court said:

> The facts of this case demonstrate the inadequacy of broad and general testing devices as well as the infirmity of using diplomas or degrees as fixed measures of capability. * * * Nothing in the Act precludes the use of testing or measuring procedures; obviously they are useful. What Congress has forbidden is giving these devices and mechanisms controlling

50. 269 F.Supp. 401 (D.D.C.1967), aff'd sub nom., Smuck v. Hobson, 408 F.2d 175 (D.C.Cir.) (en banc).

51. Ibid.

52. P. v. Riles, 343 F.Supp. 1306 (N.D. Cal.1972) aff'd 502 F.2d 963 (9th Cir. 1974).

53. Debrah P. et al. v. Turlington, 474 F.Supp. 244 (1979). Case No. 78892 —Civ. T—C (1979).

54. 401 U.S. 424, 91 S.Ct. 849 (1971).

force unless they are demonstrably a reasonable measure of job performance.[55]

Lower courts have subsequently invalidated the use of the Graduate Record Examination and the National Teachers Examination as violative of due process and equal protection because the examinations were not job related. School districts in these instances were unable to shoulder the burden of showing job relatedness in the face of the high percentage of black teachers who were disqualified.[56]

Cognizant of the limitations of the above cases, school districts and governmental agencies have more recently been able to fashion tests which are more nearly related to job performance and, therefore, are constitutionally and statutorily valid. The Supreme Court in Washington v. Davis[57] upheld the validity of a written examination of verbal skills used to select recruits for the District of Columbia police department. The Court rejected the application of the "effect" standard of Title VII of the Civil Rights Act of 1964 and held that a mere showing that a higher percentage of blacks failed the tests was insufficient to establish a claim of racial discrimination. The Court, thereby, made it clear that plaintiffs must be able to show that a test has a racially discriminatory purpose, not simply show that the result or effect of a test was to produce a racially disparate impact on job applicants. For a plaintiff to show a discriminatory purpose is a relatively difficult standard to achieve, but the Supreme Court has suggested several evidentiary sources which can be helpful to the plaintiff: (1) historical background, (2) specific sequence of events leading to the passage or implementation of the testing program, (3) departure from accepted practices and normal procedures, (4) substantive departures, and (5) legislative and administrative history of the program.[58] In this case the court further commented that: "Determining whether invidious discriminatory purpose was a motivating factor demands a sensitive inquiry into such circumstances and direct evidence of intent as may be available. The impact of the official action * * * may provide an important starting point." [59]

The burden which the Supreme Court has placed on the plaintiffs in "test" cases, to show discriminatory purpose, was too much for plaintiffs to sustain in a recent challenge of the National Teacher Ex-

---

55. Ibid.

56. Armstead v. Starkville Municipal Separate School District, 325 F.Supp. 560 (N.D.Miss.1971), affirmed in part and reversed in part, 461 F.2d 276 (5th Cir. 1972); Chance v. Board of Examiners, 458 F.2d 1167 (2nd Cir. 1972); Baker v. Columbus Municipal Separate School District, 462 F.2d 1112 (5th Cir. 1972); United States v. Chesterfield County School District, 484 F.2d 70 (4th Cir. 1973); United States v. North Carolina, 400 F.Supp. 343 (E.D.N.C.1975) vacated, 425 F. Supp. 789 (E.D.N.C.1977).

57. 426 U.S. 229, 96 S.Ct. 2040 (1976).

58. Village of Arlington Heights v. Metropolitan Housing Development Corp., 429 U.S. 252, 97 S.Ct. 555 (1977).

59. Ibid.

amination used by the State of South Carolina for certifying public school teachers.[60] This judgment reversed the trend of lower court cases,[61] cited above, which had held that the National Teachers Examination was a constitutionally inappropriate measure of a school teacher's ability to teach. The federal district court refused to find a discriminatory purpose even though the state was aware that the NTE scores would disqualify a greater proportion of black teacher applicants and that it would place a higher percentage of black teachers in lower paying classifications. The court held for the state even in the face of the state's long history of resisting school desegregation.

The new trend is then for the courts to place a heavier burden on the plaintiffs to show that the state has a discriminatory purpose. Even though race is involved the courts are hesitant to invoke a strict scrutiny standard which would make it incumbent on the state to show that it not only had a legitimate legislative purpose in the testing program but that it had a compelling interest in evaluating teachers with the particular tests in use.[62] Judges realize that education is an important state governmental function and they generally recognize that the courts are not equipped to evaluate the instruments of academic evaluation for students and are unable to determine precisely what standards should be educational prerequisites for entering or evaluating employment in the teaching profession.

*Employment Standards and Tests which Are Not
Significantly Related to Job Performance Violate
the Civil Rights Act of 1964*

GRIGGS v. DUKE POWER CO.

Supreme Court of the United States, 1971.
401 U.S. 424, 91 S.Ct. 849.

Mr. Chief Justice BURGER delivered the opinion of the Court.

We granted the writ in this case to resolve the question whether an employer is prohibited by the Civil Rights Act of 1964, Title VII, from requiring a high school education or passing of a standardized general intelligence test as a condition of employment in or transfer to jobs when (a) neither standard is shown to be significantly related to successful job performance, (b) both requirements operate to disqualify Negroes at a substantially higher rate than white applicants, and (c) the jobs in question formerly had been filled only by white employees as part of a longstanding practice of giving preference to whites.

60. United States v. South Carolina, 445 F.Supp. 1094 (D.S.C.1977), aff'd mem., 434 U.S. 1026, 98 S.Ct. 756 (1978).

61. Supra, Note 56.

62. See: Donald Marion Lewis, "Certifying Functional Literacy: Competency Testing and Implications for Due Process and Equal Educational Opportunity", *Journal of Law and Education*, Vol. 8, No. 2, April 1979.

* * *

The objective of Congress in the enactment of Title VII is plain from the language of the statute. It was to achieve equality of employment opportunities and remove barriers that have operated in the past to favor an identifiable group of white employees over other employees. Under the Act, practices, procedures, or tests neutral on their face, and even neutral in terms of intent, cannot be maintained if they operate to "freeze" the status quo of prior discriminatory employment practices.

The Court of Appeals' opinion, and the partial dissent, agreed that, on the record in the present case, "whites register far better on the Company's alternative requirements" than Negroes. * * * Because they are Negroes, petitioners have long received inferior education in segregated schools and this Court expressly recognized these differences in Gaston County v. United States, 395 U.S. 285, 89 S.Ct. 1720 (1969). * * * Congress did not intend by Title VII, however, to guarantee a job to every person regardless of qualifications. In short, the Act does not command that any person be hired simply because he was formerly the subject of discrimination, or because he is a member of a minority group. Discriminatory preference for any group, minority or majority, is precisely and only what Congress has proscribed. What is required by Congress is the removal of artificial, arbitrary, and unnecessary barriers to employment when the barriers operate invidiously to discriminate on the basis of racial or other impermissible classification.

* * * The Act proscribes not only overt discrimination but also practices that are fair in form, but discriminatory in operation. The touchstone is business necessity. If an employment practice which operates to exclude Negroes cannot be shown to be related to job performance, the practice is prohibited.

On the record before us, neither the high school completion requirement nor the general intelligence test is shown to bear a demonstrable relationship to successful performance of the jobs for which it was used. Both were adopted, as the Court of Appeals noted, without meaningful study of their relationship to job-performance ability. * * *

The evidence, however, shows that employees who have not completed high school or taken the tests have continued to perform satisfactorily and make progress in departments for which the high school and test criteria are not used. The promotion record of present employees who would not be able to meet the new criteria thus suggests the possibility that the requirements may not be needed even for the limited purpose of preserving the avowed policy of advancement within the Company. * * *

The Court of Appeals held that the Company had adopted the diploma and test requirements without any "intention to discriminate against Negro employees." * * *

* * * But Congress directed the thrust of the Act to the consequences of employment practices, not simply the motivation. More than that, Congress has placed on the employer the burden of showing that any given requirement must have a manifest relationship to the employment in question.

The facts of this case demonstrate the inadequacy of broad and general testing devices as well as the infirmity of using diplomas or degrees as fixed measures of capability. * * *

* * *

Nothing in the Act precludes the use of testing or measuring procedures; obviously they are useful. What Congress has forbidden is giving these devices and mechanisms controlling force unless they are demonstrably a reasonable measure of job performance. Congress has not commanded that the less qualified be preferred over the better qualified simply because of minority origins. Far from disparaging job qualifications as such, Congress has made such qualifications the controlling factor, so that race, religion, nationality, and sex become irrelevant. What Congress has commanded is that any tests used must measure the person for the job and not the person in the abstract.

State Use of Test Scores for Both Certification Purposes and as a Salary Factor Does Not Violate Equal Protection Clause or Title VII of Civil Rights Act

UNITED STATES OF AMERICA v. STATE OF SOUTH CAROLINA

United States District Court, District of South Carolina, Columbia Div., 1977.
445 F.Supp. 1094, aff'd 434 U.S. 1026, 98 S.Ct. 756, 1978.

Before HAYNSWORTH and RUSSELL, Circuit Judges and SIMONS, District Judge.

ORDER

* * *

* * * The defendants are charged with violations of the Fourteenth Amendment to the Constitution of the United States and Title VII of the Civil Rights Act of 1964, as amended, 42 U.S.C. § 2000e, et seq., (1970), through the use of minimum score requirements on the National Teacher Examinations (hereinafter "NTE") to certify and determine the pay levels of teachers within the State.

* * *

For over thirty years the State of South Carolina and its agencies have used scores on the NTE to make decisions with respect to the certification of teachers and the amount of state aid payable to local school districts. Local school boards within the State use scores on the NTE for selection and compensation of teachers. From 1969 to 1976, a minimum score of 975 was required by the State for its certification and state aid decisions. In June, 1976, after an exhaustive validation study by Educational Testing Service (ETS), and after a critical review and evaluation of this study by the Board of Education's Committee on Teacher Recruitment, Training and Compensation and the Department Staff, the State established new certification requirements involving different minimum scores in various areas of teaching specialization that range from 940 to 1198.   *   *   *

Plaintiffs challenge each of the uses of the NTE. They contend that more blacks than whites historically have failed to achieve the required minimum score, and that this result creates a racial classification in violation of the constitutional and statutory provisions cited in their complaints.   *   *   *

I.   CONSTITUTIONAL ISSUES

We first consider whether the use by the State and its Board of Education of a minimum score requirement on the NTE violates the equal protection clause of the Fourteenth Amendment.

*   *   *

In disposing of the remaining constitutional claims, separate consideration must be given to the State's use of the test scores to certify teachers and to determine the amount of state aid for local school districts. Plaintiffs allege that the disparate racial impact of defendants' certification and compensation systems creates a racial classification in violation of the Fourteenth Amendment. In order to sustain that allegation, the Supreme Court's decision in Washington v. Davis, 426 U.S. 229, 96 S.Ct. 2040, 48 L.Ed.2d 597 (1976), requires plaintiffs to prove that the State intended to create and use a racial classification. If plaintiffs fail to prove intent (or defendants adequately rebut that proof), then we must evaluate this classification under the rational relationship standard required by the Fourteenth Amendment as to all such classifications.

A.   *Discriminatory Intent*

Because of its paramount importance under Washington v. Davis, we look first at whether the plaintiffs have proved that any of the challenged decisions of defendants were motivated by an intent to discriminate. The purpose or intent that we must assess is the purpose or intent that underlies the particular act or acts under review.
*   *   *

1. *Certification*

South Carolina requires persons who teach in the public schools to hold a certificate issued by the State Board of Education. S.C. Code § 21–354. From 1945 to the present the State has had four certification systems, each requiring prospective teachers to take the NTE. Candidates are able to take the NTE an unlimited number of times. (The tests are given by the State three or four times each year).

The record before us indicates that during this period, the racial composition of the South Carolina teacher force has closely paralleled the racial composition of the State's population. * * *

From 1945 through 1968, the State issued four grades of certificates: A, B, C and D. From 1945 through 1956, candidates were awarded certificates based on their relative standing with respect to test scores of all candidates in the State for the year: * * *

In 1957, a new system of absolute, rather than relative, requirements was instituted. Under this system, a score of 500 or more on the Common Examinations portion of the NTE was required for an *A* certificate; a score of 425 to 499 for a *B* certificate; a score of 375 to 424 for a *C* certificate; and a score of 332 to 374 for a *D* certificate. * * *

In 1969, the certification system was further revised by replacing the four-tiered system with two types of certificates: the professional certificate and the warrant. * * * Those who attained scores below 400 were not licensed. In the academic year 1969–70, the maximum score requirement of 400 on the Common Examinations eliminated approximately 41% of the graduates of predominantly black colleges and less than 1% of the graduates of predominantly white colleges. Similar results were obtained in succeeding years, despite the fact that a score of 400 is usually below the 11th percentile nationally, and almost 90% of the candidates who take these tests get a higher score.

In 1976, the certification system was again revised, the two-tiered system being replaced with a single certificate with separate minimum score requirements in each of the 18 fields of teaching specialty replacing the single minimum score requirement. These combined scores on both Common Examinations and Area Examinations ranged from 940 in Agriculture to 1178 in Library and Media Specialties; and are set forth in detail hereinafter. There are no statistics in the record indicating the impact of the new score requirements because they will be applied first to the class of 1977; however, plaintiffs predict that, under these requirements the disparate impact may be even greater.

* * *

With respect to the constitutional challenge to South Carolina's use of the NTE for certification purposes, we conclude that the plaintiffs have not demonstrated the required discriminatory intent with respect to any of the specific decisions setting certification standards based on NTE scores. This is especially true in connection with the State's 1976 change in requirements where there is no indication whatsoever that the State and its officers were motivated by anything more than a desire to use an accepted and racially neutral standardized test to evaluate the teacher applicants competing for relatively few jobs in South Carolina.

The NTE are developed and administered by ETS, an independent non-profit organization of recognized professional reputation. ETS recommends that minimum score requirements not be used as a sole determinant of certification decisions where other appropriate information or criteria are available.

In this case, the plaintiffs have come forth with no other reasonably appropriate criteria upon which certification may be properly based.

Neither have plaintiffs been able to establish any defect in the NTE indicating that the examinations themselves discriminate on the basis of race. The choices as to subject matter and question format are reasonable and well-documented on the record, and although other subject matters or other examination forms might be possible or even preferable, there is no proof of any inherent discrimination. The inference that plaintiffs would have us draw from the statistics which indicate that blacks as a group have lower average scores than whites is rebutted by the evidence with respect to the construction of the tests and their content validity. Since we find that the NTE create classifications only on permissible bases (presence or absence of knowledge or skill and ability in applying knowledge), and that they are not used pursuant to any intent to discriminate, their use in making certification decisions by the State is proper and legal.

2. Pay Scales

Plaintiffs raise a separate constitutional challenge to South Carolina's use of the NTE as a partial determinant of the salaries paid to public school teachers. The use of the NTE for salary purposes is distinct from, and, in significant ways, unrelated to the use of the NTE for certification purposes. Accordingly, we must again examine plaintiffs' proof with respect to intent.

* * *

We are unable to find a discriminatory intent from these facts, even though the historical background of a dual pay system and a delay in implementing a unitary system after the Fourth Circuit struck down a similar system in another state provide some support for such an inference. Such inference is adequately rebutted by the evidence with respect to what the Legislature actually did. The unitary pay system was based in part on the amount of educational training and years of teaching experience possessed by each teacher. Plaintiffs make no claim that the use of either of these factors was motivated by discriminatory intent, and it is evident that the monetary rewards available through these avenues alone, without regard to the grade of certificate, were significant. The link between the new unitary pay system and the new certification system is not without a reasoned basis. It was important to the State to use its limited resources to improve the quality of the teacher force and to put whatever monetary incentives were available in the salary schedule to that task. As before stated, we have found that no discriminatory intent has been established with respect to the decision in 1945 to adopt a certification system based in part on NTE scores; and, therefore, without independent proof, there is no associated discriminatory intent in linking the certification and salary systems.

* * *

Plaintiffs urge that the Legislature was motivated by an intent to discriminate because the state aid schedule provided fewer benefits and incentives for two classifications of teachers in which there were relatively more blacks than whites; the classifications continued to be based, if only in part, on examination scores; and the developer of the tests was later opposed to their use for this purpose. In the absence of any competent or persuasive direct evidence of intent, plaintiffs would have us draw an inference from the facts that are available. But such an inference can stand only if there is no equally persuasive explanation consistent with a legitimate intent. Here the reordering of priorities with respect to the limited resources available for teacher salaries appears entirely consistent with an intent to obtain the maximum incentive for improvement that could be accomplished with a fixed number of dollars. We are unable to find an intent to discriminate.

B. *Application of Rational Relationship Standard*

In the absence of discriminatory intent, the classifications of teachers for both certification and pay purposes may be assessed under the "rational relationship" standard required by the Fourteenth Amendment of all classifications.

The Supreme Court has defined this standard in the following terms:

> Although no precise formula has been developed, the Court has held that the Fourteenth Amendment permits the States a wide scope of discretion in enacting laws which affect some groups of citizens differently than others. The constitutional safeguard is offended only if the classification rests on grounds wholly irrelevant to the achievement of the State's objective. State legislatures are presumed to have

acted within their constitutional power despite the fact that, in practice, their laws result in some inequality. A statutory discrimination will not be set aside if any state of facts reasonably may be conceived to justify it.

McGowan v. Maryland, 366 U.S. 420, 425–26, 81 S.Ct. 1101, 1105, 6 L.Ed.2d 393 (1961).

We conclude that the State's use of the NTE for both certification and pay purposes meets the "rational relationship" standard of McGowan v. Maryland, supra, and consequently does not violate the equal protection clause of the Fourteenth Amendment. * * *

* * * we find that the defendants have offered a legitimate and important governmental objective for their use of the NTE. The State has the right to adopt academic requirements and to use written achievement tests designed and validated to disclose the minimum amount of knowledge necessary to effective teaching. * * * The evidence in the record supports a finding that South Carolina officials were concerned with improving the quality of public school teaching, certifying only those applicants possessed of the minimum knowledge necessary to teach effectively, utilizing an objective measure of applicants coming from widely disparate teacher training programs, and providing appropriate financial incentives for teachers to improve their acedemic qualifications and thereby their ability to teach. We conclude that these are entirely legitimate and clearly important governmental objectives.

In considering whether defendants' use of the NTE bears a fair and substantial relationship to these governmental objectives, we conclude that it does.

The record supports the conclusion that the NTE are professionally and carefully prepared to measure the critical mass of knowledge in academic subject matter. The NTE do not measure teaching skills, but do measure the content of the academic preparation of prospective teachers. * * * the NTE program "is neutral on its face and rationally may be said to serve a purpose the Government is constitutionally empowered to pursue." * * * Plaintiffs have not contended nor proved that the NTE are racially biased or otherwise deficient when measured against the applicable professional and legal standards.

Furthermore, there is ample evidence in the record of the content validity of the NTE. The NTE have been demonstrated to provide a useful measure of the extent to which prospective teachers have mastered the content of their teacher training programs. In a similar challenge to a bar examination the Fourth Circuit has held that proof of such content validity is persuasive evidence that the equal protection clause has not been violated. Richardson v. McFadden, 540 F.2d 744 (4th Cir. 1976). The Supreme Court has held that a substantial relationship between a test and a training program

—such as is found here—is sufficient to withstand challenge on constitutional grounds. Washington v. Davis, 426 U.S. at 248–52, 96 S. Ct. 2040. State officials surely have the right to require graduation from approved teacher training programs as a prerequisite to being certified to teach in South Carolina. Plaintiffs have acknowledged the substantial relationship between the academic training program and the job of teaching by advocating that a requirement of graduation from an approved program *alone* is sufficient to protect the public interest.

* * *

We also conclude that defendants' use of the NTE for salary purposes bears the necessary relationship to South Carolina's objectives with respect to its public school teaching force. Although the NTE were not designed to evaluate experienced teachers, the State could reasonably conclude that the NTE provided a reliable and economical means for measuring one element of effective teaching—the degree of knowledge possessed by the teacher. * * *

II. TITLE VII ISSUES

We turn now to the question whether defendants' uses of the NTE violate Title VII, 42 U.S.C.A. § 2000e, et seq. * * *

* * *

The remaining claims under Title VII must be tested under statutory standards. In Washington v. Davis, 426 U.S. 229, 96 S.Ct. 2040, 48 L.Ed.2d 597 (1976), the Supreme Court summarized the order of proof:

> Under Title VII, Congress provided that when hiring and promotion practices disqualifying substantially disproportionate numbers of blacks are challenged, discriminatory purpose need not be proved, and that it is an insufficient response to demonstrate some rational basis for the challenged practices. It is necessary, in addition, that they be "validated" in terms of job performance in any one of several ways, perhaps by ascertaining the minimum skill, ability or potential necessary for the position at issue and determining whether the qualifying tests are appropriate for the selection of qualified applicants for the job in question. (Id. at 246, 96 S.Ct. at 2051).

Thus, it was held not sufficient for the governmental entity to prove that the classification resulting from the test scores had a rational basis, that is, that it differentiated between persons who did and did not have some minimum verbal and communication skill. It was necessary, in addition, for the governmental entity to demonstrate that the minimum verbal and communication skill, in turn, had some rational relationship to the legitimate employment objectives of the employer. * * * that the employment practice must be a "business necessity." Id. at 431, 91 S.Ct. 849.

A. *Certification*

Plaintiffs have proved that the use of NTE scores by the State in its certification decisions disqualifies substantially disproportionate numbers of blacks. The burden of proof was thereby shifted to the defendants, and in an effort to meet this burden the State commissioned an extensive validity study by ETS. The design of this study is novel, but consistent with the basic requirements enunciated by the Supreme Court, and we accordingly hold such study sufficient to meet the burden placed on defendants under Title VII.

The study seeks to demonstrate content validity by measuring the degree to which the content of the tests matches the content of the teacher training programs in South Carolina. It also seeks to establish a minimum score requirement by estimating the amount of knowledge (measured by the ability to answer correctly test questions that have been content validated) that a minimally qualified teacher candidate in South Carolina would have.

* * *

We find that the results of the validity study are sufficiently trustworthy to sustain defendants' burden under Title VII. * * * Plaintiffs misconceive their burden once defendants have made a reasonable showing that the study was executed in a responsible, professional manner designed to produce trustworthy results. In order to rebut the presumption that trustworthy results were indeed produced, plaintiffs must not only show that the study was not executed as intended, but also that the results were adversely affected.

* * *

There remains, however, the question whether the State has satisfied the "business necessity" requirement set out in Griggs v. Duke Power Co., 401 U.S. 424, 91 S.Ct. 849, 28 L.Ed.2d 158 (1971). This "business necessity" doctrine appears neither in the explicit language nor the legislative history of Title VII. The Court in *Griggs* and subsequent Title VII cases did not establish judicial standards for determining whether a particular practice is a business necessity. The EEOC Guidelines are of little assistance because they were published before *Griggs* and have not been updated since that time.

We think that *Griggs* did not import into Title VII law the concept of "compelling interest" developed as a part of the "strict scrutiny" standard for assessing certain classifications under the Fourteenth Amendment. Under this concept, the Court would balance the disparate impact on blacks against the business purpose of the employer and uphold the business practice only if it were sufficiently "compelling" to overcome the disparate impact. It is our view that the Supreme Court intended an examination of the alternatives available with respect to the legitimate employment objective identified by the employer to determine whether there is available to the employer an alternative practice that would achieve his business purpose equally well but with a lesser disparate impact by race. In examining alternatives, the risk and cost to the employer are relevant.

Here, plaintiffs have suggested only one alternative to the use of the NTE for certification purposes. Plaintiffs contend that mere graduation from an approved program should be sufficient and would have a lesser disparate impact on blacks. We cannot find that this alternative will achieve the State's purpose in certifying minimally competent persons equally well as the use of a content-validated standardized test. The record amply demonstrates that there are variations in admissions requirements, academic standards and grading practices at the various teacher training institutions within the State. The approval that the State gives to the teacher training program is to general subject matter areas covered by the program, not to the actual course content of the program, and not to the means used within the program to measure whether individual students have actually mastered the course content to which they have been exposed. The standardized test scores do reflect individual achievement with respect to specific subject matter content, which is directly relevant to (although not sufficient in itself to assure) competence to teach, and thus the use of these scores for certification purposes survives the business necessity test under Title VII.

B. *Pay scales*

There remains, finally, the question whether the uses of the NTE for salary purposes are a violation of Title VII. * * *

We believe that a distinction for pay purposes between those who are qualified as well as between those who are not qualified survives the business necessity test. There appears to be no alternative available to the State, within reasonable limits of risk and cost, for providing the incentive necessary to motivate thousands of persons to acquire, generally on their own time and at their own expense, the necessary additional academic training so that they will be minimally competent teachers. Having made the investment of four years in an undergraduate education, it seems reasonable to try to upgrade the talent of unqualified teachers where possible, rather than rejecting them altogether.

In accordance with the foregoing findings and conclusions, we conclude that plaintiff and plaintiff-intervenors have failed to establish their right to any of the relief sought in their respective complaints. It is, therefore,

ORDERED that judgment be entered in favor of the defendants.

Percentage of Black Teachers in the School District Compared to Percentage of Blacks in the School Teacher Population in the Relevant Labor Market Is a Statistical Criterion of Discrimination

HAZELWOOD SCHOOL DIST. v. UNITED STATES

Supreme Court of the United States, 1977.
433 U.S. 299, 97 S.Ct. 2736.

Mr. Justice STEWART delivered the opinion of the Court.

The petitioner Hazelwood School District covers 78 square miles in the northern part of St. Louis County, Mo. In 1973 the Attorney General brought this lawsuit against Hazelwood and various of its officials, alleging that they were engaged in a "pattern or practice" of employment discrimination in violation of Title VII of the Civil Rights Act of 1964, as amended, 42 U.S.C.A. § 2000e et seq. The complaint asked for an injunction requiring Hazelwood to cease its discriminatory practices, to take affirmative steps to obtain qualified Negro faculty members, and to offer employment and give backpay to victims of past illegal discrimination.

Hazelwood was formed from 13 rural school districts between 1949 and 1951 by a process of annexation. By the 1967–1968 school year, 17,550 students were enrolled in the district, of whom only 59 were Negro; the number of Negro pupils increased to 576 of 25,166 in 1972–1973, a total of just over 2%.

From the beginning, Hazelwood followed relatively unstructured procedures in hiring its teachers. * * * Generally, those who had most recently submitted applications were most likely to be chosen for interviews.

Interviews were conducted by a department chairman, program coordinator, or the principal at the school where the teaching vacancy existed. Although those conducting the interviews did fill out forms rating the applicants in a number of respects, it is undisputed that each school principal possessed virtually unlimited discretion in hiring teachers for his school. The only general guidance given to the principals, was to hire the "most competent" person available, and such intangibles as "personality, disposition, appearance, poise, voice, articulation, and ability to deal with people" counted heavily. The principal's choice was routinely honored by Hazelwood's superintendent and Board of Education.

* * * As a buyer's market began to develop for public school teachers, Hazelwood curtailed its recruiting efforts. For the 1971–1972 school year, 3,127 persons applied for only 234 teaching vacancies; for the 1972–1973 school year, there were 2,373 applications for 282 vacancies. A number of the applicants who were not hired were Negroes.

Hazelwood hired its first Negro teacher in 1969. The number of Negro faculty members gradually increased in successive years: six of 957 in the 1970 school year; 16 of 1,107 by the end of the 1972 school year; 22 of 1,231 in the 1973 school year. By comparison, according to 1970 census figures, of more than 19,000 teachers employed in that year in the St. Louis area, 15.4% were Negro. That percentage figure included the St. Louis City School District, which in recent years has followed a policy of attempting to maintain a 50% Negro teaching staff. Apart from that school district, 5.7% of the teachers in the county were Negro in 1970.

Drawing upon these historic facts the Government mounted its "pattern or practice" attack in the District Court upon four different fronts. It adduced evidence of (1) a history of alleged racially discriminatory practices, (2) statistical disparities in hiring, (3) the standardless and largely subjective hiring procedures, and (4) specific instances of alleged discrimination against 55 unsuccessful Negro applicants for teaching jobs. Hazelwood offered virtually no additional evidence in response, relying instead on evidence introduced by the Government, perceived deficiencies in the Government's case, and its own officially promulgated policy "to hire all teachers on the basis of training, preparation and recommendations, regardless of race, color or creed."

The District Court ruled that the Government had failed to establish a pattern or practice of discrimination. The court was unpersuaded by the alleged history of discrimination, noting that no dual school system had ever existed in Hazelwood. * * *

The Court of Appeals for the Eighth Circuit reversed. After suggesting that the District Court had assigned inadequate weight to evidence of discriminatory conduct on the part of Hazelwood before the effective date of Title VII, the Court of Appeals rejected the trial court's analysis of the statistical data as resting on an irrelevant comparison of Negro teachers to Negro pupils in Hazelwood. The proper comparison, in the appellate court's view, was one between Negro teachers in Hazelwood and Negro teachers in the relevant labor market area. Selecting St. Louis County and St. Louis City as the relevant area the Court of Appeals compared the 1970 census figures, showing that 15.4% of teachers in that area were Negro, to the racial composition of Hazelwood's teaching staff. In the 1972-1973 and 1973-1974 school years, only 1.4% and 1.8%, respectively, of Hazelwood's teachers were Negroes. This statistical disparity, particularly when viewed against the background of the teacher hiring procedures that Hazelwood had followed, was held to constitute a prima facie case of a pattern or practice of racial discrimination.

* * * Applying that standard, the appellate court found 16 cases of individual discrimination, which "buttressed" the statistical proof. Because Hazelwood had not rebutted the Government's prima

facie case of a pattern or practice of racial discrimination, the Court of Appeals directed judgment for the Government and prescribed the remedial order to be entered. *   *   *

*   *   *

This Court's recent consideration in International Brotherhood of Teamsters v. United States, of the role of statistics in pattern or practice suits under Title VII provides substantial guidance in evaluating the arguments advanced by the petitioners. In that case we stated that it is the Government's burden to "establish by a preponderance of the evidence that racial discrimination was the [employer's] standard operating procedure—the regular rather than the unusual practice." We also noted that statistics can be an important source of proof in employment discrimination cases; *   *   *. Where gross statistical disparities can be shown, they alone may in a proper case constitute prima facie proof of a pattern or practice of discrimination.

There can be no doubt, in light of the *Teamsters* case, that the District Court's comparison of Hazelwood's teacher work force to its student population fundamentally misconceived the role of statistics in employment discrimination cases. The Court of Appeals was correct in the view that a proper comparison was between the racial composition of Hazelwood's teaching staff and the racial composition of the qualified public school teacher population in the relevant labor market. The percentage of Negroes on Hazelwood's teaching staff in 1972–1973 was 1.4% and in 1973–1974 it was 1.8%. By contrast, the percentage of qualified Negro teachers in the area was, according to the 1970 census, at least 5.7%. Although these differences were on their face substantial, the Court of Appeals erred in substituting its judgment for that of the District Court and holding that the Government had conclusively proved its "pattern or practice" lawsuit.

The Court of Appeals totally disregarded the possibility that this prima facie statistical proof in the record might at the trial court level be rebutted by statistics dealing with Hazelwood's hiring after it became subject to Title VII. Racial discrimination by public employers was not made illegal under Title VII until March 24, 1972. A public employer who from that date forward made all its employment decisions in a wholly nondiscriminatory way would not violate Title VII even if it had formerly maintained an all-white work force by purposefully excluding Negroes. For this reason, the Court cautioned in the *Teamsters* opinion that once a prima facie case has been established by statistical work force disparities, the employer must be given an opportunity to show "that the claimed discriminatory pattern is a product of pre-Act hiring rather than unlawful post-Act discrimination."

The record in this case showed that for the 1972–1973 school year, Hazelwood hired 282 new teachers, 10 of whom (3.5%) were

Negroes; for the following school year it hired 123 new teachers, five of whom (4.1%) were Negroes. Over the two-year period, Negroes constituted a total of 15 of the 405 new teachers hired (3.7%). Although the Court of Appeals briefly mentioned these data in reciting the facts, it wholly ignored them in discussing whether the Government had shown a pattern or practice of discrimination. And it gave no consideration at all to the possibility that post-Act data as to the number of Negroes hired compared to the total number of Negro applicants might tell a totally different story.

What the hiring figures prove obviously depends upon the figures to which they are compared. The Court of Appeals accepted the Government's argument that the relevant comparison was to the labor market area of St. Louis County and St. Louis City, in which, according to the 1970 census, 15.4% of all teachers were Negro. The propriety of that comparison was vigorously disputed by the petitioners, who urged that because the City of St. Louis has made special attempts to maintain a 50% Negro teaching staff, inclusion of that school district in the relevant market area distorts the comparison. Were that argument accepted, the percentage of Negro teachers in the relevant labor market area (St. Louis County alone) as shown in the 1970 census would be 5.7% rather than 15.4%.

The difference between these figures may well be important; the disparity between 3.7% (the percentage of Negro teachers hired by Hazelwood in 1972–1973 and 1973–1974) and 5.7% may be sufficiently small to weaken the Government's other proof, while the disparity between 3.7% and 15.4% may be sufficiently large to reinforce it. In determining which of the two figures—or very possibly, what intermediate figure—provides the most accurate basis for comparison to the hiring figures at Hazelwood, it will be necessary to evaluate such considerations as (i) whether the racially based hiring policies of the St. Louis City School District were in effect as far back as 1970, the year in which the census figures were taken; (ii) to what extent those policies have changed the racial composition of that district's teaching staff from what it would otherwise have been; (iii) to what extent St. Louis' recruitment policies have diverted to the city teachers who might otherwise have applied to Hazelwood; (iv) to what extent Negro teachers employed by the city would prefer employment in other districts such as Hazelwood; and (v) what the experience in other school districts in St. Louis County indicates about the validity of excluding the City School District from the relevant labor market.

It is thus clear that a determination of the appropriate comparative figures in this case will depend upon further evaluation by the trial court. As this Court admonished in *Teamsters*, "statistics * * * come in infinite variety * * *. [T]heir usefulness depends on all of the surrounding facts and circumstances." Only the trial court is in a position to make the appropriate determination after further findings. And only after such a determination is made can a foundation be established for deciding whether or not Hazelwood engaged in a pattern or practice of racial discrimination in its employment practices in violation of the law.

We hold, therefore, that the Court of Appeals erred in disregarding the post-Act hiring statistics in the record, and that it should have remanded the case to the District Court for further findings as to the relevant labor market area and for an ultimate determination of whether Hazelwood engaged in a pattern or practice of employment discrimination after March 24, 1972. Accordingly, the judgment is vacated, and the case is remanded to the District Court for further proceedings consistent with this opinion.

It is so ordered.

Chapter 10

TEACHERS AND THE LAW

The law relating to teacher personnel administration has many ramifications including issues pertaining to certification, contracts, and, in recent years, the many aspects of constitutional law as it affects teachers has come into play. The teacher—school board relationship may, therefore, manifest conditions of the employment contract but in addition the effects of state tenure and other statutes come to bear. Beyond statute, the state constitution and, particularly in recent years, the federal Constitution have had a profound impact on teacher employment practices. Federal civil rights legislation has further created new standards which has caused a substantial amount of litigation. This chapter attempts to summarize the prevailing view of the courts in each situation bearing on freedom of speech and expression, loyalty, self-incrimination, discrimination, and due process as well as the cases which are based on obligation of contracts and the strictures of tenure statutes.

Freedom of Speech and Expression

At an earlier point in our nation's constitutional development, public employment was viewed as a privilege and not a right.[1] This privilege-right dichotomy is no longer controlling; today public employees are not expected to shed their rights upon taking positions in public institutions.

In search of a new standard, the courts have developed a flexible rule which merely provides that the public's interests will be balanced against the private interest of the employee in each circumstance. This balancing, however, does not remove all vestiges of state restraint from teacher activities; on the contrary, the courts have reflected a strong belief that because of their sensitive position in the classroom, the teacher must be held accountable for certain activities both internal and external to the school.[2] The interest of the public is to a great extent dependent on the teachers' status, appearance, and stature in the community and in preserving the integrity of the learning processes of the school. Since a teacher enters the school setting with the constitutional presumption of freedom of speech and association, the school must have a compelling reason to overcome the teachers' interest. Valid rationale has been used by boards of education in dismissing teachers for activities ranging from in-school is-

1. Justice Holmes often quoted statement in McAuliffe v. New Bedford, 155 Mass. 216, 29 N.E. 517 (1892) is thought to be the first reference to this idea: "The petitioner may have a constitutional right to talk politics, but he has no constitutional right to be a policeman."

2. See: "Developments in the Law-Academic Freedom, "Harvard Law Review, Vol. 81, pp. 1045–1159 (1968).

sues such as insubordination and incompetency to out-of-school activities which tend to reflect on the welfare of the school such as alcoholism, sexual misconduct and gambling.

Political activity of teachers has been given a high degree of protection by the courts. In the leading case, Pickering v. Board of Education,[3] the U.S. Supreme Court found that even though free speech is not an "absolute right" it is nevertheless sufficiently strong to require a "compelling state interest" on the part of the state to overcome a teacher's right to speak out against a school board's handling of school fiscal matters. The Court equated the teacher's right of free speech with that of other members of the general public to criticize public policies and actions.

Extramural speech and association of the teacher may be questioned by the school board if they draw into question the teacher's competence to teach and convey to students any particular subject matter * and second, extramural activities may indicate the likelihood that a teacher will inculcate in students values which are inconsistent with those which are to be formally espoused by the public educational system as required by society. In either instance, both state legislatures and school boards have sought to rid the schools of those teachers who may seek to inculcate "subversive" doctrine through the mechanism of public education.

Oaths have been a favorite device of government to attempt to enforce allegiance of the citizenry and their popularity has apparently dwindled little. In one case,[4] under the Arizona law, one who subscribed to an oath and who is, or thereafter became a knowing member of an organization which had as "one of its purposes" the violent overthrow of the government was subject to discharge and criminal penalties. The U.S. Supreme Court held this particular oath unconstitutionally vague, violating the freedom of association protected by the First Amendment, because nothing in the oath purported to exclude association by one who does not subscribe to the organization's unlawful ends. The court explained that a person could be a knowing member of an organization but yet not subscribe to its goal of violent overthrow of government.[5]

The U.S. Supreme Court in viewing loyalty statutes has maintained: "we do not question the power of a State to take proper measures safeguarding the public service from disloyal conduct. But measures which purport to define disloyalty must allow public servants to know what is and is not disloyal." [6] An oath cannot be lacking in "terms susceptible of objective measurement." [7]

3.   391 U.S. 563, 88 S.Ct. 1731 (1968).

* Expounded on more fully in the chapter on Curriculum in this book.

4.   Elfbrandt v. Russell, 384 U.S. 11, 86 S.Ct. 1238 (1966).

5.   Ibid.

6.   Baggett v. Bullitt, 377 U.S. 360, 84 S.Ct. 1316 (1964).

7.   Cramp v. Board of Public Instruction, 368 U.S. 278, 82 S.Ct. 275 (1961).

The state does, of course, have justifiable reason in attempting to prevent the overt overthrow of the government but whether the loyalty oath route is desirable or even functional in preventing the belief in overthrow is another question. Mr. Justice Marshall in dissent in Connell v. Higginbotham [8] indicated that he believes the entire notion is obnoxious to the Constitution because the state uses the oath mechanism to punish one for his beliefs:

> "But in my view it simply does not matter what kind of evidence a State can muster to show that a job applicant 'believes in overthrow.' For state action injurious to an individual cannot be justified on account of the nature of the individual's beliefs, whether he 'believes in the overthrow' or has any other sort of belief. If there is any fixed star in our constitutional constellation, it is that no official, high or petty, can prescribe what shall be orthodox in politics, nationalism, religion, or other matters of opinion * * * ." [9]

The majority of the U.S. Supreme Court in *Connell* struck down the disclaimer portions of a Florida loyalty oath preserving only the portion of the oath which required a teacher to swear: "I will support the Constitution of the United States and of the State of Florida * * * ." [10]

The Court's decisions seem to clearly indicate that any oath disclaiming association will be viewed with strict scrutiny; vagueness and overbreadth in oath construction will render it unconstitutional. *Keyishian* makes clear that the state in administering its loyalty program must rely on overt acts or direct evidence of illegal intent and not merely on beliefs or knowing membership in a subversive organization." [11]

Teachers Have a Constitutional Right to Speak Out Freely on Matters of Public Concern

PICKERING v. BOARD OF EDUC.

Supreme Court of the United States, 1968.
391 U.S. 563, 88 S.Ct. 1731.

Mr. Justice MARSHALL delivered the opinion of the Court.

Appellant Marvin L. Pickering, a teacher in Township High School District 205, Will County, Illinois, was dismissed from his position by the appellee Board of Education for sending a letter to a local newspaper in connection with a recently proposed tax increase

8. 403 U.S. 207, 91 S.Ct. 1772 (1971).

9. Ibid.

10. Ibid. See also: Cole v. Richardson, 92 S.Ct. 1332 (1972).

11. Keyishian v. Board of Regents of University of State of New York, 385 U.S. 589, 87 S.Ct. 675 (1967).

that was critical of the way in which the Board and the district superintendent of schools had handled past proposals to raise new revenue for the schools. Appellant's dismissal resulted from a determination by the Board, after a full hearing, that the publication of the letter was "detrimental to the efficient operation and administration of the schools of the district" and hence, under the relevant Illinois statute, Ill.Rev.Stat., c. 122, § 10–22.4 (1963), that "interests of the schools require[d] [his dismissal]."

* * *

The letter constituted, basically, an attack on the School Board's handling of the 1961 bond issue proposals and its subsequent allocation of financial resources between the schools' educational and athletic programs. It also charged the superintendent of schools with attempting to prevent teachers in the district from opposing or criticizing the proposed bond issue.

The Board dismissed Pickering for writing and publishing the letter. Pursuant to Illinois law, the Board was then required to hold a hearing on the dismissal. At the hearing the Board charged that numerous statements in the letter were false and that the publication of the statements unjustifiably impugned the "motives, honesty, integrity, truthfulness, responsibility and competence" of both the Board and the school administration. The Board also charged that the false statements damaged the professional reputations of its members and of the school administrators, would be disruptive of faculty discipline, and would tend to foment "controversy, conflict and dissension" among teachers, administrators, the Board of Education, and the residents of the district. Testimony was introduced from a variety of witnesses on the truth or falsity of the particular statements in the letter with which the Board took issue. The Board found the statements to be false as charged. No evidence was introduced at any point in the proceedings as to the effect of the publication of the letter on the community as a whole or on the administration of the school system in particular, and no specific findings along these lines were made.

* * * It is not altogether clear whether the Illinois Supreme Court held that the First Amendment had no applicability to appellant's dismissal for writing the letter in question or whether it determined that the particular statements made in the letter were not entitled to First Amendment protection. In any event, it clearly rejected Pickering's claim that, on the facts of this case, he could not constitutionally be dismissed from his teaching position.

To the extent that the Illinois Supreme Court's opinion may be read to suggest that teachers may constitutionally be compelled to relinquish the First Amendment rights they would otherwise enjoy as citizens to comment on matters of public interest in connection with the operation of the public schools in which they work, it proceeds on a premise that has been unequivocally rejected in numerous prior decisions of this Court. * * * "[T]he theory that public employment which may be denied altogether may be subjected to any conditions, regardless of how unreasonable, has been uniformly rejected." Keyishian v. Board of Regents, supra, 385 U.S. at 605–606, 87 S.Ct. at 685. At the same time it cannot be gainsaid that the State has interests as an employer in regulating the speech of its employees that differ significantly from those it possesses in connection with regulation of the speech of the citizenry in general. The problem in any case is to arrive at a balance between the interests of the teacher, as a citizen, in commenting upon matters of public concern and the interest of the State, as an employer, in promoting the efficiency of the public services it performs through its employees.

The Board contends that "the teacher by virtue of his public employment has a duty of loyalty to support his superiors in attaining the generally accepted goals of education and that, if he must speak out publicly, he should do so factually and accurately, commensurate with his education and experience." Appellant, on the other hand, argues that the test applicable to defamatory statements directed against public officials by persons having no occupational relationship with them, namely, that statements to be legally actionable must be made "with knowledge that [they were] * * * false or with reckless disregard of whether [they were] * * * false or not," * * * should also be applied to public statements made by teachers. * * *

An examination of the statements in appellant's letter objected to by the Board reveals that they, like the letter as a whole, consist essentially of criticism of the Board's allocation of school funds between educational and athletic programs, and of both the Board's and the superintendent's methods of informing, or preventing the informing of, the district's taxpayers of the real reasons why additional tax revenues were being sought for the schools. The statements are in no way directed towards any person with whom appellant would normally be in contact in the course of his daily work as a teacher. Thus no question of maintaining either discipline by immediate superiors or harmony among coworkers is presented here. Appellant's employment relationships with the Board and, to a somewhat lesser extent, with the superintendent are not the kind of close working relationships for which it can persuasively be claimed that personal loyalty and confidence are necessary to their proper functioning. Accordingly, to the extent that the Board's position here can be taken to suggest that even comments on matters of public concern that are substantially correct * * * may furnish grounds for dismissal if they are sufficiently critical in tone, we unequivocally reject it.

We next consider the statements in appellant's letter which we agree to be false. The Board's original charges included allegations that the publication of the letter damaged the professional reputa-

tions of the Board and the superintendent and would <u>foment contro-</u>
<u>versy and conflict among the Board, teachers, administrators, and the</u>
<u>residents of the district.</u> <u>However, no evidence to support these alle-</u>
<u>gations was introduced at the hearing.</u> So far as the record reveals,
Pickering's letter was greeted by everyone but its main target, the
Board, with massive apathy and total disbelief. * * *

       * * *

In addition, the fact that particular illustrations of the Board's
claimed undesirable emphasis on athletic programs are false would
not normally have any necessary impact on the actual operation of
the schools, beyond its tendency to anger the Board. For example,
Pickering's letter was written after the defeat at the polls of the second proposed tax increase. <u>It could, therefore, have had no effect on</u>
<u>the ability of the school district to raise necessary revenue, since</u>
<u>there was no showing that there was any proposal to increase taxes</u>
<u>pending when the letter was written.</u>

More importantly, the question whether a school system requires
additional funds is a matter of legitimate public concern on which the
judgment of the school administration, including the School Board,
cannot, in a society that leaves such questions to popular vote, be
taken as conclusive. On such a question free and open debate is vital
to informed decision-making by the electorate. Teachers are, as a
class, the members of a community most likely to have informed and
definite opinions as to how funds allotted to the operation of the
schools should be spent. Accordingly, it is essential that they be able
to speak out freely on such questions without fear of retaliatory dismissal.

       * * *

What we do have before us is a case in which a teacher has
made erroneous public statements upon issues then currently the subject of public attention, which are critical of his ultimate employer
but which are neither shown nor can be presumed to have in any way
either impeded the teacher's proper performance of his daily duties in
the classroom or to have interfered with the regular operation of the
schools generally. In these circumstances we conclude that the interest of the school administration in limiting teachers' opportunities to
contribute to public debate is not significantly greater than its interest in limiting a similar contribution by any member of the general
public.

The public interest in having free and unhindered debate on matters of public importance—the core value of the Free Speech Clause of
the First Amendment—is so great that it has been held that a State
cannot authorize the recovery of damages by a public official for defamatory statements directed at him except when such statements
are shown to have been made either with knowledge of their falsity
or with reckless disregard for their truth or falsity. * * * It is

therefore perfectly clear that, were appellant a member of the general public, the State's power to afford the appellee Board of Education or its members any legal right to sue him for writing the letter at issue here would be limited by the requirement that the letter be judged by the standard laid down in New York Times.

This Court has also indicated, in more general terms, that statements by public officials on matters of public concern must be accorded First Amendment protection despite the fact that the statements are directed at their nominal superiors. * * *

While criminal sanctions and damage awards have a somewhat different impact on the exercise of the right to freedom of speech from dismissal from employment, it is apparent that the threat of dismissal from public employment is nonetheless a potent means of inhibiting speech. We have already noted our disinclination to make an across-the-board equation of dismissal from public employment for remarks critical of superiors with awarding damages in a libel suit by a public official for similar criticism. However, in a case such as the present one, in which the fact of employment is only tangentially and insubstantially involved in the subject matter of the public communication made by a teacher, we conclude that it is necessary to regard the teacher as the member of the general public he seeks to be.

In sum, we hold that, in a case such as this, absent proof of false statements knowingly or recklessly made by him, a teacher's exercise of his right to speak on issues of public importance may not furnish the basis for his dismissal from public employment. Since no such showing has been made in this case regarding appellant's letter, see Appendix, infra, his dismissal for writing it cannot be upheld and the judgment of the Illinois Supreme Court must, accordingly, be reversed and the case remanded for further proceedings not inconsistent with this opinion. It is so ordered.

Judgment reversed and case remanded with directions.

NOTES

1. Free speech protection does not entitle a teacher to be excessively critical and derisive of duly constituted school authority and to personally denounce and abuse other teachers. Amburgey v. Cassady, 370 F.Supp. 571 (E.D.Ky.1974).

2. Can a superintendent move a teacher to another school in the school system if the motivation for the transfer is based on the teacher's exercise of a constitutionally protected right? See: Adcock v. Board of Educ. of San Diego Unified School Dist., 10 Cal.3d 60, 109 Cal.Rptr. 676, 513 P.2d 900 (1973).

3. What political statements may a teacher make in the classroom?

4. A tenure teacher announced his candidacy for state representative. On the same day, the board of education adopted a rule requiring any candidate for public office to take a leave without pay beginning on the day the teacher becomes a candidate. Did the court uphold this regulation

which was made applicable to all teachers currently employed? See School City of East Chicago v. Sigler, 219 Ind. 9, 36 N.E.2d 760 and Adams v. State, 69 So.2d 309 (Fla.1954).

Evidence Must Show That Exercise of Constitutional Right Was the Motivating Factor Not to Rehire Before Remedial Judicial Action Is Justified

MT. HEALTHY CITY SCHOOL DIST. BD. OF EDUC. v. DOYLE

Supreme Court of the United States, 1977.
429 U.S. 274, 97 S.Ct. 568.

Mr. Justice REHNQUIST delivered the opinion of the Court.

Respondent Doyle sued petitioner Mt. Healthy Board of Education in the United States District Court for the Southern District of Ohio. Doyle claimed that the Board's refusal to renew his contract in 1971 violated his rights under the First and Fourteenth Amendments to the United States Constitution. After a bench trial the District Court held that Doyle was entitled to reinstatement with back pay. The Court of Appeals for the Sixth Circuit affirmed the judgment, * * *

* * *

Doyle was first employed by the Board in 1966. He worked under one-year contracts for the first three years, and under a two-year contract from 1969 to 1971. In 1969 he was elected president of the Teachers' Association, in which position he worked to expand the subjects of direct negotiation between the Association and the Board of Education. During Doyle's one-year term as president of the Association, and during the succeeding year when he served on its executive committee, there was apparently some tension in relations between the Board and the Association.

Beginning early in 1970, Doyle was involved in several incidents not directly connected with his role in the Teachers' Association. In one instance, he engaged in an argument with another teacher which culminated in the other teacher's slapping him. Doyle subsequently refused to accept an apology and insisted upon some punishment for the other teacher. His persistence in the matter resulted in the suspension of both teachers for one day, which was followed by a walkout by a number of other teachers, which in turn resulted in the lifting of the suspensions.

On other occasions, Doyle got into an argument with employees of the school cafeteria over the amount of spaghetti which had been served him; referred to students, in connection with a disciplinary complaint, as "sons of bitches"; and made an obscene gesture to two girls in connection with their failure to obey commands made in his capacity as cafeteria supervisor. Chronologically the last in the series of incidents which respondent was involved in during his employment by the Board was a telephone call by him to a local radio station. It was the Board's consideration of this incident which the court below found to be a violation of the First and Fourteenth Amendments.

In February of 1971, the principal circulated to various teachers a memorandum relating to teacher dress and appearance, which was apparently prompted by the view of some in the administration that there was a relationship between teacher appearance and public support for bond issues. Doyle's response to the receipt of the memorandum—on a subject which he apparently understood was to be settled by joint teacher-administration action—was to convey the substance of the memorandum to a disc jockey at WSAI, a Cincinnati radio station, who promptly announced the adoption of the dress code as a news item. Doyle subsequently apologized to the principal, conceding that he should have made some prior communication of his criticism to the school administration.

Approximately one month later the superintendent made his customary annual recommendations to the Board as to the rehiring of nontenured teachers. He recommended that Doyle not be rehired. The same recommendation was made with respect to nine other teachers in the district, and in all instances, including Doyle's, the recommendation was adopted by the Board. Shortly after being notified of this decision, respondent requested a statement of reasons for the Board's actions. He received a statement citing "a notable lack of tact in handling professional matters which leaves much doubt as to your sincerity in establishing good school relationships." That general statement was followed by references to the radio station incident and to the obscene gesture incident.

The District Court found that all of these incidents had in fact occurred. It concluded that respondent Doyle's telephone call to the radio station was "clearly protected by the First Amendment," and that because it had played a "substantial part" in the decision of the Board not to renew Doyle's employment, he was entitled to reinstatement with backpay. App. to pet., at 12a–13a. The District Court did not expressly state what test it was applying in determining that the incident in question involved conduct protected by the First Amendment, but simply held that the communication to the radio station was such conduct. The Court of Appeals affirmed in a brief *per curiam* opinion.

Doyle's claims under the First and Fourteenth Amendments are not defeated by the fact that he did not have tenure. Even though he could have been discharged for no reason whatever, and had no constitutional right to a hearing prior to the decision not to rehire him, Board of Regents v. Roth, 408 U.S. 564, 92 S.Ct. 2701, 33 L.Ed.2d 548 (1972), he may nonetheless establish a claim to reinstatement if the

decision not to rehire him was made by reason of his exercise of constitutionally protected First Amendment freedoms.   Perry v. Sindermann.

That question of whether speech of a government employee is
constitutionally protected expression necessarily entails striking "a
balance between the interests of the teacher, as a citizen, in commenting upon matters of public concern and the interest of the State
as an employer, in promoting the efficiency of the public services it
performs through its employees."   Pickering v. Board of Education.
There is no suggestion by the Board that Doyle violated any established policy, or that its reaction to his communication to the radio
station was anything more than an *ad hoc* response to Doyle's action
in making the memorandum public.   We therefore accept the District
Court's finding that the communication was protected by the First
and Fourteenth Amendments.   We are not, however, entirely in
agreement with that court's manner of reasoning from this finding to
the conclusion that Doyle is entitled to reinstatement with backpay.

The District Court made the following "conclusions" on this aspect of the case:

"(1) If a non-permissible reason, e. g., exercise of First
Amendment rights, played a substantial part in the decision
not to renew—even in the face of other permissible grounds
—the decision may not stand (citations omitted).

"(2) A non-permissible reason did play a substantial
part.   That is clear from the letter of the Superintendent
immediately following the Board's decision, which stated
two reasons—the one, the conversation with the radio station clearly protected by the First Amendment.   A court
may not engage in any limitation of First Amendment
rights based on 'tact'—that is not to say that 'tactfulness' is
irrelevant to other issues in this case."

At the same time, though, it stated that "in fact, as this
Court sees it and finds, both the Board and the Superintendent were faced with a situation in which there did exist in
fact reason * * * independent of any First Amendment
rights or exercise thereof, to not extend tenure."

Since respondent Doyle had no tenure, and there was therefore
not even a state law requirement of "cause" or "reason" before a decision could be made not to renew his employment, it is not clear
what the District Court meant by this latter statement.   Clearly the
Board legally *could* have dismissed respondent had the radio station
incident never come to its attention.   One plausible meaning of the
court's statement is that the Board and the Superintendent not only
could, but in fact *would* have reached that decision had not the constitutionally protected incident of the telephone call to the radio sta-

tion occurred. We are thus brought to the issue whether, even if that were the case, the fact that the protected conduct played a "substantial part" in the actual decision not to renew would necessarily amount to a constitutional violation justifying remedial action. We think that it would not.

A rule of causation which focuses solely on whether protected conduct played a part, "substantial" or otherwise, in a decision not to rehire, could place an employee in a better position as a result of the exercise of constitutionally protected conduct than he would have occupied had he done nothing. The difficulty with the rule enunciated by the District Court is that it would require reinstatement in cases where a dramatic and perhaps abrasive incident is inevitably on the minds of those responsible for the decision to rehire, and does indeed play a part in that decision—even if the same decision would have been reached had the incident not occurred. The constitutional principle at stake is sufficiently vindicated if such an employee is placed in no worse a position than if he had not engaged in the conduct. A borderline or marginal candidate should not have the employment question resolved against him because of constitutionally protected conduct. But that same candidate ought not to be able, by engaging in such conduct, to prevent his employer from assessing his performance record and reaching a decision not to rehire on the basis of that record, simply because the protected conduct makes the employer more certain of the correctness of its decision.

This is especially true where, as the District Court observed was the case here, the current decision to rehire will accord "tenure." The long term consequences of an award of tenure are of great moment both to the employee and to the employer. They are too significant for us to hold that the Board in this case would be precluded, because it considered constitutionally protected conduct in deciding not to rehire Doyle, from attempting to prove to a trier of fact that quite apart from such conduct Doyle's record was such that he would not have been rehired in any event.

* * *

Initially, in this case, the burden was properly placed upon respondent to show that his conduct was constitutionally protected, and that this conduct was a "substantial factor"—or to put it in other words, that it was a "motivating factor" in the Board's decision not to rehire him. Respondent having carried that burden, however, the District Court should have gone on to determine whether the Board had shown by a preponderance of the evidence that it would have reached the same decision as to respondent's reemployment even in the absence of the protected conduct.

We cannot tell from the District Court opinion and conclusions, nor from the opinion of the Court of Appeals affirming the judgment of the District Court, what conclusion those courts would have reached had they applied this test. The judgment of the Court of Appeals is therefore vacated, and the case remanded for further proceedings consistent with this opinion.

*Freedom of Speech Is Guaranteed to Teacher in
Private Communication with Employer*

GIVHAN v. WESTERN LINE CONSOLIDATED SCHOOL DIST.

Supreme Court of the United States, 1979.
439 U.S. 410, 99 S.Ct. 693, 58 L.Ed.2d 619.

Mr. Justice REHNQUIST delivered the opinion of the Court.

Petitioner Bessie Givhan was dismissed from her employment as a junior high English teacher at the end of the 1970–1971 school year.[1] At the time of petitioner's termination, respondent Western Line Consolidated School District was the subject of a desegregation order entered by the United States District Court for the Northern District of Mississippi. Petitioner filed a complaint * * * seeking reinstatement on the ground that nonrenewal of her contract * *. * infringed her right of free speech secured by the First and Fourteenth Amendments of the United States Constitution. In an effort to show that its decision was justified, respondent school district introduced evidence of, among other things, a series of private encounters between petitioner and the school principal in which petitioner allegedly made "petty and unreasonable demands" in a manner variously described by the principal as "insulting," "hostile," "loud," and "arrogant." After a two-day bench trial, the District Court held that petitioner's termination had violated the First Amendment. Finding that petitioner had made "demands" on but two occasions and that those demands "were neither 'petty' nor 'unreasonable,' insomuch as all of the complaints in question involved employment policies and practices at [the] school which [petitioner] conceived to be racially discriminatory in purpose or effect," the District Court concluded that "the primary reason for the school district's failure to renew [petitioner's] contract was her criticism of the policies and practices of the school district, especially the school to which she was assigned to teach." * * *

The Court of Appeals for the Fifth Circuit reversed. Although it found the District Court's findings not clearly erroneous, the Court

---

1. In a letter to petitioner dated July 23, 1971, District Superintendent C. L. Morris gave the following reasons for the decision not to renew her contract:

"(1)[A] flat refusal to administer standardized National tests to the pupils in your charge; (2) an announced intention not to cooperate with the administration of the Glen Allan Attendance Center; (3) and an antagonistic and hostile attitude to the administration of the Glen Allan Attendance Center demonstrated throughout the school year."

of Appeals concluded that because petitioner had privately expressed her complaints and opinions to the principal, her expression was not protected under the First Amendment.   *   *   *

This Court's decisions in *Pickering, Perry,* and *Mt. Healthy* do not support the conclusion that a public employee forfeits his protection against governmental abridgment of freedom of speech if he decides to express his views privately rather than publicly.   While those cases each arose in the context of a public employee's public expression, the rule to be derived from them is not dependent on that largely coincidental fact.

In *Pickering* a teacher was discharged for publicly criticizing, in a letter published in a local newspaper, the school board's handling of prior bond issue proposals and its subsequent allocation of financial resources between the schools' educational and athletic programs. Noting that the free speech rights of public employees are not absolute, the Court held that in determining whether a government employee's speech is constitutionally protected, "the interests of the [employee], as a citizen, in commenting upon matters of public concern" must be balanced against "the interest of the State, as an employer, in promoting the efficiency of the public services it performs through its employees."   *   *   *   The Court concluded that under the circumstances of that case "the interest of the school administration in limiting teachers' opportunities to contribute to public debate [was] not significantly greater than its interest in limiting a similar contribution by any member of the general public."   Here the opinion of the Court of Appeals may be read to turn in part on its view that the working relationship between principal and teacher is significantly different from the relationship between the parties in *Pickering,*   *   *   *   But we do not feel confident that the Court of Appeals' decision would have been placed on that ground notwithstanding its view that the First Amendment does not require the same sort of *Pickering* balancing for the private expression of a public employee as it does for public expression.

Perry and *Mt. Healthy* arose out of similar disputes between teachers and their public employers.   As we have noted, however, the fact that each of these cases involved public expression by the employee was not critical to the decision.   Nor is the Court of Appeals' view supported by the "captive audience" rationale.   Having opened his office door to petitioner, the principal was hardly in a position to argue that he was the "*unwilling* recipient" of her views.

The First Amendment forbids abridgment of the "freedom of speech."   Neither the Amendment itself nor our decisions indicate that this freedom is lost to the public employee who arranges to communicate privately with his employer rather than to spread his views before the public.   We decline to adopt such a view of the First Amendment.

While this case was pending on appeal to the Court of Appeals, Mt. Healthy City Board of Education v. Doyle, was decided. In that case this Court rejected the view that a public employee must be reinstated whenever constitutionally protected conduct plays a "substantial" part in the employer's decision to terminate. Such a rule would require reinstatement of employees that the public employer would have dismissed even if the constitutionally protected conduct had not occurred and, consequently, "could place an employee in a better position as a result of the exercise of constitutionally protected conduct than he would have occupied had he done nothing." Thus, the Court held that once the employee has shown that his constitutionally protected conduct played a "substantial" role in the employer's decision not to rehire him, the employer is entitled to show "by a preponderance of the evidence that it would have reached the same decision as to [the employee's] reemployment even in the absence of the protected conduct." Id., at 287, 97 S.Ct., at 576.

The Court of Appeals in the instant case rejected respondents' *Mt. Healthy* claim that the decision to terminate petitioner would have been made even if her encounters with the principal had never occurred:

> "The [trial] court did not make an express finding as to whether the same decision would have been made, but on this record the [respondents] do not, and seriously cannot, argue that the same decision would have been made without regard to the 'demands.' Appellants seem to argue that the preponderance of the evidence shows that the same decision would have been justified, but that is not the same as proving that the same decision would have been made. * * * Therefore [respondents] failed to make a successful 'same decision anyway' defense."

Since this case was tried before *Mt. Healthy* was decided, it is not surprising that respondents did not attempt to prove in the District Court that the decision not to rehire petitioner would have been made even absent consideration of her "demands." Thus, the case came to the Court of Appeals in very much the same posture as *Mt. Healthy* was presented in this Court. And while the District Court found that petitioner's "criticism" was the "primary" reason for the school district's failure to rehire her, it did not find that she would have been rehired *but for* her criticism. Respondents' *Mt. Healthy* claim called for a factual determination which could not, on this record, be resolved by the Court of Appeals.

Accordingly, the judgment of the Court of Appeals is vacated and the case remanded for further proceedings consistent with this opinion.

So ordered.

*Dress Constitutes Freedom of Expression which Cannot be
Restrained without Compelling Reason*

EAST HARTFORD EDUC. ASS'N v. BOARD OF EDUC.

United States Court of Appeals, Second Circuit, 1977.
562 F.2d 838.

OAKES, Circuit Judge: Appellants unsuccessfully sought below a declaratory judgment of the unconstitutionality of, and injunction against the enforcement of, the East Hartford public school teachers' dress code. Suit was brought under 42 U.S.C.A. §§ 1983 and 1988, and jurisdiction was invoked under 28 U.S.C.A. §§ 1331, 1343, 2201, and 2202. *　*　*

I. FACTS

Appellant Brimley teaches English and film-making in an East Hartford public high school. He objects to so much of the Board's dress code, *　*　*. In upholding a hair code for policemen, the Supreme Court emphasized the employment status of the police officer and the unquestioned "need for discipline, esprit de corps, and uniformity" in a police force. *　*　* We commence with the premise that quite different considerations apply here. Even though both teachers and policemen are employees of the state through local governmental units, terms like "discipline" and "esprit de corps," appropriate for members of a uniformed paramilitary force, are manifestly inappropriate for high school teachers. *　*　*

The right to control one's own body, recognized by Supreme Court decree as constitutionally derived, *　*　* extends in the minds and hearts of many individuals to the body's teguments, be they clothing or hair. People have been conscious of personal appearance and fashion from the time the first of our forebears crawled out of what Judge Learned Hand so onomatopoetically referred to as the "primordial ooze." *　*　*

Substantial creative efforts of mankind have been devoted to matters of dress, from the robes of the ancient Egyptians to King Henry VIII's armor, and dress has often conveyed a message, whether it be one of martyrdom in the sackcloth and ashes of the early Christians, respect for God in the skullcaps worn by many Jews, or achievement and calling in the regalia worn in academic processions. The mark of authority for priest and judge alike has been a robe, for monks baldness has been a sign of asceticism, and for English judges and our own founding fathers powdered wigs were a symbol of wisdom, authority, and sometimes affluence.

Conversely, recognizing the role clothing plays in giving individuals a sense of freedom and identity, the military, prisons, and other authoritarian institutions have long used strict uniformity of dress and hair style to effectuate conformity. Their purpose has been to deprive a person of his individuality in the interests of better discipline and related aims. * * *

History is replete with instances of oppression accomplished by body-tegument conformity. Following the Manchus' invasion of China in 1644, for example, the conquerors sought to consolidate their power by requiring the population to wear a prescribed hair style and prescribed clothing; thousands chose to die rather than accept these marks of servitude. * * * <u>Today, dictatorships of both the left and the right use hair and dress regulation as part of their programs of behavior regulation.</u> * * *

In view of these historical and contemporary factors, it would be difficult not to conclude that "a liberty interest within the Fourteenth Amendment," Kelley v. Johnson, supra, 425 U.S. at 249, 96 S. Ct. at 1447 (Powell, J., concurring), is involved in this case. * * * Along the "rational continuum which, broadly speaking, includes a freedom from all substantial arbitrary impositions and purposeless restraints," id. at 543, 81 S.Ct. at 1777, the liberty interest asserted by appellant here is a weighty one deserving our careful attention.

B.   Teaching and the First Amendment

In addition to the general liberty interest in one's appearance, in the teaching context there is a strong additional interest that must be weighed in the scales in determining the constitutionality of regulatory intrusions like the one at issue here. The claim appellant makes is not simply a symbolic speech claim. Rather, it is a claim that the inseparable complex of speech, conduct and character known as teaching is a First Amendment interest that in and of itself should be protected from needless regulation by the State.

The academic context has long been given special constitutional protection in our country, because the educational needs of a free people are of utmost importance. * * *

Freedom to teach in the manner of one's choice is a form of academic freedom that is universally recognized, if not invariably protected, at the college level, * * * and that has been accorded significant respect in cases involving public secondary school teachers, * * *.

In secondary schools, it is true, the idea of academic freedom may be balanced to a degree by the countervailing interest of states, acting through local school boards, to inculcate basic community values in students who may not be mature enough to deal with academic freedom as understood or practiced at higher educational levels. * * * This may mean that public secondary school boards have considerable discretion as to the substantive content of what is taught, but there is no reason to extend this wide discretion to the teaching process itself. There is, as we see it, a sharp distinction between content of curriculum and pedagogical methodology. * * * As long as the substantive values that the school board seeks to inculcate are not subverted by the way in which a teacher wishes to communicate with his students, * * * the teacher's freedom to choose teaching methods is entitled to be weighed in the constitutional scales.

This irreducible core of academic freedom extends, in our view, to the particular style of clothing that appellant wishes to wear here. As noted, he is subverting no community values; neatness, cleanliness and morality are not involved. Moreover, appellant is concededly sincere in his belief, which is certainly reasonable, that a slightly more informal mode of dress will make him a more effective teacher. It is a truism that, long after a student's substantive knowledge has been forgotten, it is the character of a good teacher—of which appearance and style are inevitably part—that is most remembered and that continues to inspire. * * * <u>Appellant's attempt to express himself on this level is, we hold, an interest entitled to First Amendment protection</u>.

III.   THE STATE'S COUNTERVAILING INTERESTS

The reasons advanced by appellees for their tie code are that it establishes "a professional image for teachers," that it promotes "good grooming among students," and that it aids maintenance of "respect" and "decorum" in the classroom. While other reasons for teacher dress codes might be generated by a fertile imagination, under recent Supreme Court authority we are required to limit our attention to legitimate, articulated, non-illusory state objectives. * * *

* * *

Moreover, even if the Board had authority to require teachers to maintain a "professional image," that phrase is almost meaningless as applied to neckties for men. Informality is making inroads even in the staid legal profession, *see In re DeCarlo*, 141 N.J.Super. 42, 357 A.2d 273 (App.Div.1976) (per curiam) (female attorney in slacks and sweater properly attired for court), and among other groups, male doctors, dentists, clergymen, engineers, and teacher—and particularly for the younger members of these groups—a tie is no longer mandatory and is far from typical. * * * Considering the wide variations in the attire worn by professionals today, the Board's statement that it wants its teachers to wear ties to enhance their "professional image" amounts to little more than a statement that it wants its teachers to wear ties because it wants them to wear ties. Such a purpose is plainly entitled to little or no weight.

As to the promotion of Good grooming among students, as an independent interest this also seems to be ultra vires the Board's statutory powers. <u>The student hair regulations of this very school board,</u>

moreover, have been held unconstitutional by a state court. * * * Finally, even were the Board's second purpose to be considered legitimate, the connection between teacher and student dress is so tenuous, as a glance at any public high school classroom will confirm, that the Board's means—requiring its male teachers to surround their necks with a tie—lack the requisite "significant relationship" to the Board's end. * * *

We turn, then, to the final asserted interest, the need for respect, discipline, and decorum in the classroom. This is certainly a valid concern of the school board, as Conn.Gen.Stat. § 10–221 makes clear. It is far from clear, however, that a tie code like that in issue here has any connection with respect or discipline. Indeed, appellant puts forward the seemingly more reasonably proposition, which we must accept at this stage, that being tieless helps him to maintain his students' respect. Teenagers, who are so often rebellious against authority, may find a tieless teacher to be a less remote, more contemporary individual with whom they can more easily interact, and hence to whom they are better prepared to listen with care and attention. It is highly questionable, and certainly not established on this motion for summary judgment, that the Board's valid end of promoting discipline is substantially, or even incrementally, furthered by its tie regulation.

IV. THE BALANCE

In view of our finding in the preceding section that the Board's articulated interests carry very little weight, we conclude that the decision below must be reversed. * * * Certainly a school board may make regulations that help to promote the effective and efficient education of children. It may not, however, make regulations that infringe on constitutional interests while not realistically and significantly furthering the board's proper purposes.

The regulation at issue here implicates both a Fourteenth Amendment liberty interest and a First Amendment interest. The intersection of these two interests calls for a higher degree of scrutiny of the government's countervailing interest than would the presence of either individual interest alone. * * * At this stage of the proceedings, the Board has plainly failed to carry this burden, and its asserted interests are far outweighed by the individual interests at stake.

We accordingly vacate the summary judgment and remand for a hearing on the merits.

Merely Knowing Membership without Specific Intent to Further Unlawful Aims of an Organization Is Not a Constitutionally Adequate Basis for Imposing Sanctions

KEYISHIAN v. BOARD OF REGENTS

Supreme Court of the United States, 1967.
385 U.S. 589, 87 S.Ct. 675.

Mr. Justice BRENNAN delivered the opinion of the Court.

Appellants were members of the faculty of the privately owned and operated University of Buffalo, and became state employees when the University was merged in 1962 into the State University of New York, an institution of higher education owned and operated by the State of New York. As faculty members of the State University their continued employment was conditioned upon their compliance with a New York plan, formulated partly in statutes and partly in administrative regulations, which the State utilizes to prevent the appointment or retention of "subversive" persons in state employment.

Appellants Hochfield and Maud were Assistant Professors of English, appellant Keyishian an instructor in English, and appellant Garver, a lecturer in philosophy. Each of them refused to sign, as regulations then in effect required, a certificate that he was not a Communist, and that if he had ever been a Communist, he had communicated that fact to the President of the State University of New York. Each was notified that his failure to sign the certificate would require his dismissal. Keyishian's one-year-term contract was not renewed because of his failure to sign the certificate. Hochfield and Garver, whose contracts still had time to run, continue to teach, but subject to proceedings for their dismissal if the constitutionality of the New York plan is sustained. Maud has voluntarily resigned and therefore no longer has standing in this suit.

Appellant Starbuck was a nonfaculty library employee and part-time lecturer in English. Personnel in that classification were not required to sign a certificate but were required to answer in writing under oath the question, "Have you ever advised or taught or were you ever a member of any society or group of persons which taught or advocated the doctrine that the Government of the United States or of any political subdivisions thereof should be overthrown or overturned by force, violence or any unlawful means?" Starbuck refused to answer the question and as a result was dismissed.

Appellants brought this action for declaratory and injunctive relief, alleging that the state program violated the Federal Constitution in various respects. A three-judge federal court held that the program was constitutional. 255 F.Supp. 981. We noted probable jurisdiction of appellants' appeal, 384 U.S. 998, 86 S.Ct. 1921, 16 L.Ed.2d 1012. We reverse.

We considered some aspects of the constitutionality of the New York plan 15 years ago in Adler v. Board of Education, 342 U.S. 485, 72 S.Ct. 380, 96 L.Ed. 517. That litigation arose after New York passed the Feinberg Law which added § 3022 to the Education Law, McKinney's Consol.Laws, c. 16. The Feinberg Law was enacted to implement and enforce two earlier statutes. The first was a 1917 law, now § 3021 of the Education Law, under which "the utterance of any treasonable or seditious word or words or the doing of any treasonable or seditious act" is a ground for dismissal from the public school system. The second was a 1939 law which was § 12–a of the Civil Service Law when *Adler* was decided and, as amended, is now § 105 of that law, McKinney's Consol.Laws, c. 7. This law disqualifies from the civil service and from employment in the educational system any person who advocates the overthrow of government by force, violence, or any unlawful means, or publishes material advocating such overthrow or organizes or joins any society or group of persons advocating such doctrine.

* * *

Adler was a declaratory judgment suit in which the Court held, in effect, that there was no constitutional infirmity in former § 12–a or in the Feinberg Law on their faces and that they were capable of constitutional application. But the contention urged in this case that both § 3021 and § 105 are unconstitutionally vague was not heard or decided. Section 3021 of the Education Law was challenged in *Adler* as unconstitutionally vague, but because the challenge had not been made in the pleadings or in the proceedings in the lower courts, this Court refused to consider it. 342 U.S., at 496, 72 S.Ct., at 386. Nor was any challenge on grounds of vagueness made in *Adler* as to subdivisions 1(a) and (b) of § 105 of the Civil Service Law.[4] Subdivision 3 of § 105 was not added until 1958. Appellants in this case timely asserted below the unconstitutionality of all these sections on grounds of vagueness and that question is now properly before us for decision. Moreover, to the extent that *Adler* sustained the provision of the Feinberg Law constituting membership in an organization advocating forceful overthrow of government a ground for disqualification, pertinent constitutional doctrines have since rejected the premises upon which that conclusion rested. *Adler* is therefore not dispositive of the constitutional issues we must decide in this case.

II.

A 1953 amendment extended the application of the Feinberg Law to personnel of any college or other institution of higher education owned and operated by the State or its subdivisions. In the same

4. The sole "vagueness" contention in *Adler* concerned the word "subversive," appearing in the preamble to and caption of § 3022, 342 U.S., at 496, 72 S.Ct., at 387.

year, the Board of Regents, after notice and hearing, listed the Communist Party of the United States and of the State of New York as "subversive organizations." In 1956 each applicant for an appointment or the renewal of an appointment was required to sign the so-called "Feinberg Certificate" declaring that he had read the Regents Rules and understood that the Rules and the statutes constituted terms of employment, and declaring further that he was not a member of the Communist Party, and that if he had ever been a member he had communicated that fact to the President of the State University. This was the certificate that appellants Hochfield, Maud, Keyishian, and Garver refused to sign.

* * *

Section 3021 requires removal for "treasonable or seditious" utterances or acts. The 1958 amendment to § 105 of the Civil Service Law, now subdivision 3 of that section, added such utterances or acts as a ground for removal under that law also. The same wording is used in both statutes—that "the utterance of any treasonable or seditious word or words or the doing of any treasonable or seditious act or acts" shall be ground for removal. But there is a vital difference between the two laws. Section 3021 does not define the terms "treasonable or seditious" as used in that section; in contrast, subdivision 3 of § 105 of the Civil Service Law provides that the terms "treasonable word or act" shall mean "treason" as defined in the Penal Law and the terms "seditious word or act" shall mean "criminal anarchy" as defined in the Penal Law.

Our experience under the Sedition Act of 1798, 1 Stat. 596, taught us that dangers fatal to First Amendment freedoms inhere in the word "seditious." See New York Times Co. v. Sullivan, 376 U.S. 254, 273–276, 84 S.Ct. 710, 722–724, 11 L.Ed.2d 686. And the word "treasonable," if left undefined, is no less dangerously uncertain. Thus it becomes important whether, despite the omission of a similar reference to the Penal Law in § 3021, the words as used in that section are to be read as meaning only what they mean in subdivision 3 of § 105. Or are they to be read more broadly and to constitute utterances or acts "seditious" and "treasonable" which would not be so regarded for the purposes of § 105?

Even assuming that "treasonable" and "seditious" in § 3021 and § 105, subd. 3 have the same meaning, the uncertainty is hardly removed. The definition of "treasonable" in the Penal Law presents no particular problem. The difficulty centers upon the meaning of "seditious." Subdivision 3 equates the term "seditious" with "criminal anarchy" as defined in the Penal Law. Is the reference only to Penal Law, McKinney's Consol.Laws c. 40, § 160, defining criminal anarchy as "the doctrine that organized government should be overthrown by force or violence, or by assassination of the executive head or of any of the executive officials of government, or by any unlawful means"?

But that section ends with the sentence "The advocacy of such doctrine either by word of mouth or writing is a felony." Does that sentence draw into § 105, Penal Law § 161, proscribing "advocacy of criminal anarchy"? If so, the possible scope of "seditious" utterances or acts has virtually no limit. For under Penal Law § 161, one commits the felony of advocating criminal anarchy if he "* * * publicly displays any book * * * containing or advocating, advising or teaching the doctrine that organized government should be overthrown by force, violence or any unlawful means." Does the teacher who carries a copy of the Communist Manifesto on a public street thereby advocate criminal anarchy? It is no answer to say that the statute would not be applied in such a case. We cannot gainsay the potential effect of this obscure wording on "those with a conscientious and scrupulous regard for such undertakings." Baggett v. Bullitt, 377 U.S. 360, 374, 84 S.Ct. 1316, 1323, 12 L.Ed.2d 377. Even were it certain that the definition referred to in § 105 was solely Penal Law § 160, the scope of § 105 still remains indefinite. The teacher cannot know the extent, if any, to which a "seditious" utterance must transcend mere statement about abstract doctrine, the extent to which it must be intended to and tend to indoctrinate or incite to action in furtherance of the defined doctrine. The crucial consideration is that no teacher can know just where the line is drawn between "seditious" and nonseditious utterances and acts.

Other provisions of § 105 also have the same defect of vagueness. Subdivision 1(a) of § 105 bars employment of any person who "by word of mouth or writing willfully and deliberately advocates, advises or teaches the doctrine" of forceful overthrow of government. This provision is plainly susceptible of sweeping and improper application. It may well prohibit the employment of one who merely advocates the doctrine in the abstract without any attempt to indoctrinate others, or incite others to action in furtherance of unlawful aims. * * * And in prohibiting "advising" the "doctrine" of unlawful overthrow does the statute prohibit mere "advising" of the existence of the doctrine, or advising another to support the doctrine? Since "advocacy" of the doctrine of forceful overthrow is separately prohibited, need the person "teaching" or "advising" this doctrine himself "advocate" it? Does the teacher who informs his class about the precepts of Marxism or the Declaration of Independence violate this prohibition?

Similar uncertainty arises as to the application of subdivision 1(b) of § 105. That subsection requires the disqualification of an employee involved with the distribution of written material "containing or advocating, advising or teaching the doctrine" of forceful overthrow, and who himself "advocates, advises, teaches, or embraces the duty, necessity or propriety of adopting the doctrine contained therein." Here again, mere advocacy of abstract doctrine is apparently included. And does the prohibition of distribution of matter "containing" the doctrine bar histories of the evolution of Marxist doctrine or tracing the background of the French, American, or Russian revolutions? The additional requirement, that the person participating in distribution of the material be one who "advocates, advises, teaches, or embraces the duty, necessity or propriety of adopting the doctrine" of forceful overthrow, does not alleviate the uncertainty in the scope of the section, but exacerbates it. Like the language of § 105, subd. 1(a), this language may reasonably be construed to cover mere expression of belief. For example, does the university librarian who recommends the reading of such materials thereby "advocate * * * the * * * propriety of adopting the doctrine contained therein"?

* * *

There can be no doubt of the legitimacy of New York's interest in protecting its education system from subversion. But "even though the governmental purpose be legitimate and substantial, that purpose cannot be pursued by means that broadly stifle fundamental personal liberties when the end can be more narrowly achieved." Shelton v. Tucker, 364 U.S. 479, 488, 81 S.Ct. 247, 252, 5 L.Ed.2d 231. The principle is not inapplicable because the legislation is aimed at keeping subversives out of the teaching ranks. In De Jonge v. State of Oregon, 299 U.S. 353, 365, 57 S.Ct. 255, 260, 81 L.Ed. 278, the Court said:

> "The greater the importance of safeguarding the community from incitements to the overthrow of our institutions by force and violence, the more imperative is the need to preserve inviolate the constitutional rights of free speech, free press and free assembly in order to maintain the opportunity for free political discussion, to the end that government may be responsive to the will of the people and that changes, if desired, may be obtained by peaceful means. Therein lies the security of the Republic, the very foundation of constitutional government."

Our Nation is deeply committed to safeguarding academic freedom, which is of transcendent value to all of us and not merely to the teachers concerned. That freedom is therefore a special concern of the First Amendment, which does not tolerate laws that cast a pall of orthodoxy over the classroom. "The vigilant protection of constitutional freedoms is nowhere more vital than in the community of American schools." Shelton v. Tucker, supra, 364 U.S., at 487, 81 S. Ct., at 251. The classroom is peculiarly the "marketplace of ideas." The Nation's future depends upon leaders trained through wide exposure to that robust exchange of ideas which discovers truth "out of a multitude of tongues, [rather] than through any kind of authoritative selection." United States v. Associated Press, D.C., 52 F.Supp.

362, 372. In Sweezy v. State of New Hampshire, 354 U.S. 234, 250, 77 S.Ct. 1203, 1211, 1 L.Ed.2d 1311, we said:

> "The essentiality of freedom in the community of American universities is almost self-evident. No one should underestimate the vital role in a democracy that is played by those who guide and train our youth. To impose any straitjacket upon the intellectual leaders in our colleges and universities would imperil the future of our Nation. No field of education is so thoroughly comprehended by man that new discoveries cannot yet be made. Particularly is that true in the social sciences, where few, if any, principles are accepted as absolutes. Scholarship cannot flourish in an atmosphere of suspicion and distrust. Teachers and students must always remain free to inquire, to study and to evaluate, to gain new maturity and understanding; otherwise our civilization will stagnate and die."

We emphasize once again that "[p]recision of regulation must be the touchstone in an area so closely touching our most precious freedoms," N. A. A. C. P. v. Button, 371 U.S. 415, 438, 83 S.Ct. 328, 340, 9 L.Ed.2d 405; "[f]or standards of permissible statutory vagueness are strict in the area of free expression. * * * Because First Amendment freedoms need breathing space to survive, government may regulate in the area only with narrow specificity." * * *

The regulatory maze created by New York is wholly lacking in "terms susceptible of objective measurement." Cramp v. Board of Public Instruction, supra, at 286, 82 S.Ct., at 280. It has the quality of "extraordinary ambiguity" found to be fatal to the oaths considered in *Cramp* and Baggett v. Bullitt. * * *

We therefore hold that § 3021 of the Education Law and subdivisions 1(a), 1(b) and 3 of § 105 of the Civil Service Law as implemented by the machinery created pursuant to § 3022 of the Education Law are unconstitutional.

IV.

Appellants have also challenged the constitutionality of the discrete provisions of subdivision 1(c) of § 105 and subdivision 2 of the Feinberg Law, which make Communist Party membership, as such, prima facie evidence of disqualification. The provision was added to subdivision 1(c) of § 105 in 1958 after the Board of Regents, following notice and hearing, listed the Communist Party of the United States and the Communist Party of the State of New York as "subversive" organizations. Subdivision 2 of the Feinberg Law was, however, before the Court in *Adler* and its constitutionality was sustained. But constitutional doctrine which has emerged since that decision has rejected its major premise. That premise was that public employment, including academic employment, may be conditioned upon the surrender of constitutional rights which could not be abridged by direct government action. Teachers, the Court said in *Adler*, "may work for the school system upon the reasonable terms laid down by the proper authorities of New York. If they do not choose to work on such terms, they are at liberty to retain their beliefs and associations and go elsewhere." 342 U.S., at 492, 72 S.Ct., at 385. The Court also stated that a teacher denied employment because of membership in a listed organization "is not thereby denied the right of free speech and assembly. His freedom of choice between membership in the organization and employment in the school system might be limited, but not his freedom of speech or assembly, except in the remote sense that limitation is inherent in every choice." Id., at 493, 72 S.Ct., at 385.

However, the Court of Appeals for the Second Circuit correctly said in an earlier stage of this case, "* * * the theory that public employment which may be denied altogether may be subjected to any conditions, regardless of how unreasonable, has been uniformly rejected." Keyishian v. Board of Regents, 345 F.2d 236, 239. Indeed, that theory was expressly rejected in a series of decisions following *Adler*. * * * In Sherbert v. Verner, 374 U.S. 398, 404, 83 S.Ct. 1790, 1794, 10 L.Ed.2d 965, we said: "It is too late in the day to doubt that the liberties of religion and expression may be infringed by the denial of or placing of conditions upon a benefit or privilege."

We proceed then to the question of the validity of the provisions of subdivision 1 of § 105 and subdivision 2 of § 3022, barring employment to members of listed organizations. Here again constitutional doctrine has developed since *Adler*. Mere knowing membership without a specific intent to further the unlawful aims of an organization is not a constitutionally adequate basis for exclusion from such positions as those held by appellants.

In Elfbrandt v. Russell, 384 U.S. 11, 86 S.Ct. 1238, 16 L.Ed.2d 321, we said, "Those who join an organization but do not share its unlawful purposes and who do not participate in its unlawful activities surely pose no threat, either as citizens or as public employees." Id., at 17, 86 S.Ct., at 1241. We there struck down a statutorily required oath binding the state employee not to become a member of the Communist Party with knowledge of its unlawful purpose, on threat of discharge and perjury prosecution if the oath were violated. We found that "[a]ny lingering doubt that proscription of mere knowing membership, without any showing of 'specific intent,' would run afoul of the Constitution was set at rest by our decision in Aptheker v. Secretary of State, 378 U.S. 500, 84 S.Ct. 1659, 12 L.Ed.2d 992." Elfbrandt v. Russell, supra, at 16, 86 S.Ct., at 1240. In *Aptheker* we held that Party membership, without knowledge of the Party's unlawful purposes *and* specific intent to further its unlawful aims, could not constitutionally warrant deprivation of the right to travel abroad. As we said in Schneiderman v. United States, 320 U.S. 118, 136, 63 S.Ct. 1333, 1342, 87 L.Ed. 1796, "[U]nder our traditions beliefs are personal and not a matter of mere association, and * * * men in adhering to a political party or other organization * * * do not subscribe unqualifiedly to all of its platforms or asserted principles." "A law which applies to membership without the 'specific intent' to further the illegal aims of the organization infringes unnecessarily on protected freedoms. It rests on the doctrine of 'guilt by association' which has no place here." *Elfbrandt*, supra, at 19, 86 S.Ct., at 1242. Thus mere Party membership, even with knowledge of the Party's unlawful goals, cannot suffice to justify criminal punishment, * * * nor may it warrant a finding of moral unfitness justifying disbarment. * * *

* * * <u>*Elfbrandt* and *Aptheker* state the governing standard: legislation which sanctions membership unaccompanied by specific intent to further the unlawful goals of the organization or which is not active membership violates constitutional limitations.</u>

Measured against this standard, both Civil Service Law § 105, subd. 1(c), and Education Law § 3022, subd. 2 sweep overbroadly into association which may not be proscribed. The presumption of disqualification arising from proof of mere membership may be rebutted, but only by (a) a denial of membership, (b) a denial that the organization advocates the overthrow of government by force, or (c) a denial that the teacher has knowledge of such advocacy. * * * Thus proof of nonactive membership or a showing of the absence of intent to further unlawful aims will not rebut the presumption and defeat dismissal. * * *

Thus § 105, subd. 1(c), and § 3022, subd. 2, suffer from impermissible "overbreadth." * * * They seek to bar employment both for association which legitimately may be proscribed and for association which may not be proscribed consistently with First Amendment rights. Where statutes have an overbroad sweep, just as where they are vague, "the hazard of loss or substantial impairment of those precious rights may be critical." * * *

<u>We therefore hold that Civil Service Law § 105, subd. 1(c), and Education Law § 3022, subd. 2, are invalid insofar as they proscribe mere knowing membership without any showing of specific intent to further the unlawful aims of the Communist Party of the United States or of the State of New York.</u>

The judgment of the District Court is reversed and the case is remanded for further proceedings consistent with this opinion.

Reversed and remanded.

Disclaimer Provisions of Loyalty Oath Are Unconstitutional

CONNELL v. HIGGINBOTHAM

Supreme Court of the United States, 1971.
403 U.S. 207, 91 S.Ct. 1772.

PER CURIAM. This is an appeal from an action commenced in the United States District Court for the Middle District of Florida challenging the constitutionality of §§ 876.05–876.10 of Fla.Stat. (1965), and the various loyalty oaths upon which appellant's employment as a school teacher was conditioned. The three-judge U.S. District Court declared three of the five clauses contained in the oaths to be unconstitutional,* and enjoined the State from conditioning employment on the taking of an oath including the language declared unconstitutional. The appeal is from that portion of the District Court decision, 305 F.Supp. 445, which upheld the remaining two clauses in the oath: I do hereby solemnly swear or affirm (1) "that I will support the Constitution of the United States and of the State of Florida"; and (2) "that I do not believe in the overthrow of the Government of the United States or of the State of Florida by force or violence."

On January 16, 1969, appellant made application for a teaching position with the Orange County school system. She was interviewed by the principal of Callahan Elementary School, and on January 27, 1969, appellant was employed as a substitute classroom teacher in the fourth grade of that school. Appellant was dismissed from her teaching position on March 18, 1969, for refusing to sign the loyalty oath required of all Florida public employees, Fla.Stat. § 876.05.

The first section of the oath upheld by the District Court, requiring all applicants to pledge to support the Constitution of the United States and of the State of Florida, demands no more of Florida public employees than is required of all state and federal officers. U.S. Const., Art. VI, cl. 3. The validity of this section of the oath would appear settled. * * *

The second portion of the oath, approved by the District Court, falls within the ambit of decisions of this Court proscribing summary dismissal from public employment without hearing or inquiry required by due process. * * * That portion of the oath, therefore, cannot stand.

Affirmed in part, and reversed in part.

---

* The clauses declared unconstitutional by the court below required the employee to swear: (a) "that I am not a member of the Communist Party"; (b) "that I have not and will not lend my aid, support, advice, counsel or influence to the Communist Party"; and (c) "that I am not a member of any organization or party which believes in or teaches, directly or indirectly, the overthrow of the Government of the United States or of Florida by force or violence."

NOTES

1. Appellee's employment at the Boston State Hospital was terminated when she refused to take the following oath required of all public employees in Massachusetts: "I do solemnly swear (or affirm) that I will uphold and defend the Constitution of the United States of America and the Constitution of the Commonwealth of Massachusetts and that I will oppose the overthrow of the government of the United States of America or of this Commonwealth by force, violence, or by any illegal or unconstitutional method." Appellee challenged the constitutionality of the oath statute. A three-judge District Court concluded that the attack on the "uphold and defend" clause was foreclosed by Knight v. Board of Regents, 390 U.S. 36, 88 S.Ct. 816, 19 L.Ed.2d 812, but found the "oppose the overthrow" clause "fatally vague and unspecific" and thus violative of the First Amendment. In response to a remand from this Court, the District Court concluded that the case was not moot, and reinstated its earlier judgment. _Held:_ The Massachusetts oath is constitutionally permissible.

(a) The oath provisions of the United States Constitution are not inconsistent with the First Amendment.

(b) The District Court properly held that the "uphold and defend" clause, a paraphrase of the constitutional oath, is permissible.

(c) The "oppose the overthrow" clause was not designed to require specific action to be taken in some hypothetical or actual situation but was to assure that those in positions of public trust were willing to commit themselves to live by the constitutional processes of our government.

(d) The oath is not void for vagueness. Perjury, the sole punishment, requires a knowing and willful falsehood, which removes the danger of punishment without fair notice; and there is no problem of punishment inflicted by mere prosecution, as there has been no prosecution under the statute since its enactment nor has any been planned.

(e) There is no constitutionally protected right to overthrow a government by force, violence, or illegal or unconstitutional means, and therefore there is no requirement that one who refuses to take Massachusetts' oath be granted a hearing for the determination of some other fact before being discharged.

Reversed and remanded.

Cole v. Richardson, 405 U.S. 676, 92 S.Ct. 1332 (1972).

2. Constitutional guarantees of free speech and free press do not permit a state to forbid or proscribe "advocacy" of overthrow of government in the abstract unless such advocacy is directed to inciting or producing imminent lawless action and is likely to incite or produce such action. Scales v. United States, 367 U.S. 203, 81 S.Ct. 1469 (1961), rehearing denied 366 U.S. 978, 81 S.Ct. 1912; Communist Party of Indiana v. Whitcomb, 414 U.S. 441, 94 S.Ct. 656 (1974).

Privilege Against Self-Incrimination

Teachers may as anyone else invoke the Fifth Amendment privilege against self-incrimination. To avail oneself of this Amendment refusing to provide information to the state because it may tend to incriminate cannot be interpreted as an admission of guilt. No presumption can be inferred from the act. In Slochower v. Board of Education,[12] the Supreme Court held that dismissal of a Brooklyn College professor for invoking the privilege before a congressional committee was unconstitutional. This principle cannot, however, be too broadly interpreted for only a short time later the Supreme Court held in Beilan v. Board of Education[13] that a teacher could be dismissed for refusing to answer questions posed by the school superintendent about allegedly past subversive activities. The Court found that the dismissal was not predicated on an impermissible inference of guilt drawn from refusal to answer, but instead on a finding of insubordination emanating from the fact that the teacher refused to answer.[14] *Slochower* was distinguished in that the refusal to answer in *Beilan* was directed toward questions posed by a superior in specific regard to fitness to teach and incompetency was specifically cited as the reason for dismissal.

The rationale of *Beilan*, though, comes under a shadow as the Court has ruled subsequently that disbarment of a lawyer for refusing to produce evidence in an ethical practices proceeding was unconstitutional.[15] Also, dismissal of a policeman for invoking the privilege in refusal to answer questions regarding his fitness and concerning conduct which could open him to criminal prosecution was held to be unconstitutional.[16] Although these cases can be distinguished in that the former involved disbarment and complete denial of future employment and the latter related to criminal evidence, the strength of the *Beilan* decision is somewhat diminished if the fitness of a teacher is viewed in the broader constitutional light of both *Pickering* and *Keyishian*.

Failure of Teacher to Answer Questions Posed by Superintendent Concerning Loyalty May be Incompetency

BEILAN v. BOARD OF PUBLIC EDUC. OF PHILADELPHIA

Supreme Court of the United States, 1958.
357 U.S. 399, 78 S.Ct. 1317.

Mr. Justice BURTON delivered the opinion of the Court.

The question before us is whether the Board of Public Education for the School District of Philadelphia, Pennsylvania, violated the Due Process Clause of the Fourteenth Amendment to the Constitution of the United States when the Board, purporting to act under the

12. 350 U.S. 551, 76 S.Ct. 637 (1956).

13. 357 U.S. 399, 78 S.Ct. 1317 (1958).

14. "Developments in the Law-Academice Freedom," *op. cit.* p. 1076.

15. Spevack v. Klein, 385 U.S. 511, 87 S.Ct. 625 (1967).

16. Garrity v. New Jersey, 385 U.S. 493, 87 S.Ct. 616 (1967).

Pennsylvania Public School Code, discharged a public school teacher on the ground of "incompetency," evidenced by the teacher's refusal of his Superintendent's request to confirm or refute information as to the teacher's loyalty and his activities in certain allegedly subversive organizations. For the reasons hereafter stated, we hold that it did not.

On June 25, 1952, Herman A. Beilan, the petitioner, who had been a teacher for about 22 years in the Philadelphia Public School System, presented himself at his Superintendent's office in response to the latter's request. The Superintendent said he had information which reflected adversely on petitioner's loyalty and he wanted to determine its truth or falsity. In response to petitioner's suggestion that the Superintendent do the questioning, the latter said he would ask one question and petitioner could then determine whether he would answer it and others of that type. The Superintendent, accordingly, asked petitioner whether or not he had been the Press Director of the Professional Section of the Communist Political Association in 1944. Petitioner asked permission to consult counsel before answering and the Superintendent granted his request.

On October 14, 1952, in response to a similar request, petitioner again presented himself at the Superintendent's office. Petitioner stated that he had consulted counsel and that he declined to answer the question as to his activities in 1944. He announced he would also decline to answer any other "questions similar to it," "questions of this type," or "questions about political and religious beliefs * * *." The Superintendent warned petitioner that this "was a very serious and a very important matter and that failure to answer the questions might lead to his dismissal." The Superintendent made it clear that he was investigating "a real question of fitness for [petitioner] to be a teacher or to continue in the teaching work." These interviews were given no publicity and were attended only by petitioner, his Superintendent and the Assistant Solicitor of the Board.

* * *

* * * The only question before us is whether the Federal Constitution prohibits petitioner's discharge for statutory "incompetency" based on his refusal to answer the Superintendent's questions.

By engaging in teaching in the public schools, petitioner did not give up his right to freedom of belief, speech or association. He did, however, undertake obligations of frankness, candor and cooperation in answering inquiries made of him by his employing Board examining into his fitness to serve it as a public school teacher.

"A teacher works in a sensitive area in a schoolroom. There he shapes the attitude of young minds towards the society in which they live. In this, the state has a vital concern. It must preserve the integrity of the schools. That the school authorities have the right and the duty to screen the officials, teachers, and employees as to their fitness to maintain the integrity of the schools as a part of ordered society, cannot be doubted." Adler v. Board of Education, 342 U.S. 485, 493, 72 S.Ct. 380, 385.

As this Court stated in Garner v. Board of Public Works, 341 U.S. 716, 720, 71 S.Ct. 909, 912. "We think that a municipal employer is not disabled because it is an agency of the State from inquiring of its employees as to matters that may prove relevant to their fitness and suitability for the public service."

The question asked of petitioner by his Superintendent was relevant to the issue of petitioner's fitness and suitability to serve as a teacher. Petitioner is not in a position to challenge his dismissal merely because of the remoteness in time of the 1944 activities. It was apparent from the circumstances of the two interviews that the Superintendent had other questions to ask. Petitioner's refusal to answer was not based on the remoteness of his 1944 activities. He made it clear that he would not answer any question of the same type as the one asked. Petitioner blocked from the beginning any inquiry into his Communist activities, however relevant to his present loyalty. The Board based its dismissal upon petitioner's refusal to answer any inquiry about his relevant activities—not upon those activities themselves. It took care to charge petitioner with incompetency, and not with disloyalty. It found him insubordinate and lacking in frankness and candor—it made no finding as to his loyalty.

We find no requirement in the Federal Constitution that a teacher's classroom conduct be the sole basis for determining his fitness. Fitness for teaching depends on a broad range of factors. The Pennsylvania tenure provision specifies several disqualifying grounds, including immorality, intemperance, cruelty, mental derangement and persistent and willful violation of the school laws, as well as "incompetency." However, the Pennsylvania statute, unlike those of many other States, contains no catch-all phrase, such as "conduct unbecoming a teacher," to cover disqualifying conduct not included within the more specific provisions. Consequently, the Pennsylvania courts have given "incompetency" a broad interpretation. * * *

"The term 'incompetency' has a 'common and approved usage'. The context does not limit the meaning of the word to lack of substantive knowledge of the subjects to be taught. Common and approved usage give a much wider meaning. For example, in 31 C.J., with reference to a number of supporting decisions, it is defined: 'A relative term without technical meaning. It may be employed as meaning disqualification; inability; incapacity; lack of ability, legal qualifications, or fitness to discharge the required duty' * * * * "

In the instant case, the Pennsylvania Supreme Court has held that "incompetency" includes petitioner's "deliberate and insubordinate refusal to answer the questions of his administrative superior in a vitally important matter pertaining to his fitness." 386 Pa. at page 91, 125 A.2d at page 331. This interpretation is not inconsistent with the Federal Constitution.

Petitioner complains that he was denied due process because he was not sufficiently warned of the consequences of his refusal to answer his Superintendent. The record, however, shows that the Superintendent, in his second interview, specifically warned petitioner that his refusal to answer "was a very serious and a very important matter and that failure to answer the questions might lead to his dismissal." That was sufficient warning to petitioner that his refusal to answer might jeopardize his employment. Furthermore, at petitioner's request, his Superintendent gave him ample opportunity to consult counsel. There was no element of surprise.

Our recent decisions in Slochower v. Board of Higher Education, 350 U.S. 551, 76 S.Ct. 637, 100 L.Ed. 692, and Konigsberg v. State Bar of California, 353 U.S. 252, 77 S.Ct. 722, 1 L.Ed.2d 810, are distinguishable. In each we envisioned and distinguished the situation now before us. In the Slochower case, 350 U.S. at page 558, 76 S.Ct. at page 641, the Court said:

> "It is one thing for the city authorities themselves to inquire into Slochower's fitness, but quite another for his discharge to be based entirely on events occurring before a federal committee whose inquiry was announced as not directed at 'the property, affairs, or government of the city, or * * * official conduct of city employees.' In this respect the present case differs materially from Garner [Garner v. Board of Public Works, 341 U.S. 716, 71 S.Ct. 909, 95 L.Ed. 1317], where the city was attempting to elicit information necessary to determine the qualifications of its employees. Here, the Board had possessed the pertinent information for 12 years, and the questions which Professor Slochower refused to answer were admittedly asked for a purpose wholly unrelated to his college functions. On such a record the Board cannot claim that its action was part of a bona fide attempt to gain needed and relevant information."

* * * In the instant case, no inferences at all were drawn from petitioner's refusal to answer. The Pennsylvania Supreme Court merely equated refusal to answer the employing Board's relevant questions with statutory "incompetency."

Inasmuch as petitioner's dismissal did not violate the Federal Constitution, the judgment of the Supreme Court of Pennsylvania is affirmed.

Plea of Constitutional Privilege against Self-incrimination
Bears No Presumption of Unfitness

BOARD OF PUBLIC EDUC. SCHOOL DIST. OF PHILADELPHIA v. INTILLE

Supreme Court of Pennsylvania, 1960,
401 Pa. 1, 163 A.2d 420.

CHARLES ALVIN JONES, Chief Justice.

The three appellants (Angelina Intille, Thomas Deacon and Sadie T. Atkinson) were teachers in the public schools of Philadelphia until the Spring of 1954 when they were dismissed by the Board of Public Education of the School District on a charge of "incompetency", preferred by Dr. Louis P. Hoyer, Superintendent of the Philadelphia public schools. In each case, the dismissal was based *solely* on the teacher's refusal to answer certain questions propounded by a Subcommittee (also known as the Velde Committee) of the Un-American Activities Committee of the House of Representatives concerning the witness' alleged membership in and association with the Communist Party. In refusing to testify in such regard, each of the appellants expressly relied upon the privilege against self-incrimination guaranteed by the Fifth Amendment of the Federal Constitution.

All of the proceedings below, which resulted in the final orders of dismissal, now before us, were conducted separately throughout but, since the basic legal questions raised (both Federal and State), are the same in all three appeals, they will be disposed of in this one opinion.

The appellants contend that their dismissals, as teachers, (1) violated the due process clause of the Fourteenth Amendment, and (2) abridged their privilege against self-incrimination under the Fifth Amendment in further violation of the Fourteenth Amendment and of Article VI of the Federal Constitution.

There is also an additional question raised by the Board's contention that the appellants' plea of privilege against self-incrimination under the Fifth Amendment constituted incompetency within the intent of Pennsylvania's Public School Code of 1949.

As teachers under contract prescribed by the Public School Code of 1949, the appellants were entitled to tenure as professional employees and, by virtue of the same statutory authority, were subject to dismissal from their teaching positions *only* for cause upon notice, hearing and right of appeal. One of the specified causes for removal, as prescribed by the School Code, is incompetency, which is the charge upon which Superintendent Hoyer suspended these teachers and recommended their dismissal to the Board of Education. The Superintendent based his finding of incompetency solely upon the fact that the appellants had refused to answer questions asked them by the Congressional Committee in reliance on their pleas of privilege under the Fifth Amendment against self-incrimination.

*   *   *

It follows from what we have said that the appellants' dismissals by the Board of Education, because they refused to answer certain questions of the Congressional Committee on a plea of the Fifth Amendment's protection against self-incrimination, deprived them of liberty and property without due process of law and, at the same time, worked abridgment by State action of the same constitutional privilege, all in violation of the Fourteenth Amendment.

*   *   *

For a public school teacher to plead a constitutional privilege, in appropriate circumstances, does not prove the teacher's incompetency within the intended scope of that term as used in our Public School Code; the plea is not even relevant as evidence of incompetency. Just as remaining mute, upon a plea of the Fifth Amendment, carries no implication of guilt of the matter inquired about in the unanswered questions   *   *   *   so also does the plea not carry an implication of the pleader's *incompetency*. Nor is it of any materiality to a question of the pleader's competency whether or not the propriety of the plea against self-incrimination is conceded or rejected by the inquiring body so long as the plea is made in good faith and is not plainly frivolous. There is no prerequisite to the exercise of the privilege against self-incrimination that the pleader must first establish affirmatively his good faith and lack of frivolity in entering the plea. The appellants' pleas of the Fifth Amendment did not prove their incompetency within the meaning of the Public School Code and, since their refusal to answer the Committee's questions, in reliance on the Fifth Amendment privilege, was all that was proven against them, the Board failed to make out a case for their dismissal.

But, the Board presently advances the idea that a teacher who refuses to answer a Congressional Committee's questions, implying possible subversive affiliations on the part of the witness, is incompetent within the meaning of the tenure provisions of our Public School Code. Such a contention transgresses what was thought to have been decided in Beilan, where we were assured that no question of loyalty was in any way involved. If the refusal to answer a particular question is to be made a basis for the discharge of a professional employee, the question should, obviously, have for its purpose the eliciting of information concerning some matter material to the fitness of the employee to continue at work. This is so whether the question propounded be by a Congressional Committee or by the Board of Education itself. And, if the only material matter to which the question relates is possible disloyalty or subversion on the part of the employee, then any proceeding looking to his dismissal for refusal to answer questions relating to his possible disloyal or subversive activities or affiliations must be brought under the Pennsylvania Loyalty Act of December 22, 1951, P.L. 1726, 65 P.S. § 211 et seq. In a proceeding under that statute a teacher may be discharged if it is determined "by a fair preponderance of the evidence" that he is a disloyal or subversive person; and "If the appointing authority shall be comprised of three or more members, a vote of two-thirds of the members shall be necessary in order to discharge a person." See Section 7 of the Act (65 P.S. § 217). What the Board of Education has attempted to do in these cases is to avoid the requirement of the Pennsylvania Loyalty Act that disloyalty or subversion, as a ground for the discharge of a public school teacher, must be proven "by a fair preponderance of the evidence." The Board's action evidences a belief that it has found a way to dismiss, without any evidence at all, teachers whom it suspects of disloyalty or subversion. Anything in the Beilan case to the contrary is herewith overruled for the future. In searching out and eliminating disloyalty or subversion among teachers in public schools the procedures of the applicable statute enacted for that purpose must be faithfully pursued, and violence must no longer be done the meaning of the word "incompetency" in order to circumvent the procedures of the Loyalty Act.

The orders of the courts below, now here on appeal at Numbers 331, 332 and 352, are severally reversed, and the records remanded for further proceedings not inconsistent with this opinion.

* * *

Certification

All state legislatures have enacted laws relating to the certification of teachers and when such are properly promulgated with no intent to discriminate, and are not arbitary, they will be upheld by the courts. These laws run the gamut from great particularity to gross generality. Hence, it is necessary to consider the specific laws of each state individually to determine its certification requirements.

The general rule is that if a teacher satisfies all the requirements set forth in the statutes and regulations relative to the issuance of a certificate, the certifying body may not arbitrarily refuse to issue the certificate. However, in most cases, the certificate issuing body is vested with discretionary authority. Also, the issuing agency may, in many instances, prescribe higher standards for certification than are contained in laws enacted by a state legislature.

Most states require than an applicant for a teacher's certificate be of good moral character. In order to remain eligible for either continued certification or renewal of an existing certificate, the teacher must continue to evidence a good moral character.

State Board of Education Will Not be Deprived of
Discretion in Granting Certificates

METCALF v. COOK

Court of Appeals of Maryland, 1935.
168 Md. 475, 178 A. 219.

BOND, Chief Judge. The question here is one of statutory construction, raised by a demand of the appellant for a writ of mandamus to compel the superintendent of schools to grant him a certificate authorizing him to teach in a high school of the state, notwithstanding a by-law of the state board of education limiting the issue of such certificates to those who have attained a higher rank in their own training. The appeal is from a denial of the writ upon an agreed statement of the facts supplemented by testimony.

The Code, art. 77, §§ 87 and 88, provides generally for the issue of teachers' certificates by the state superintendent, and section 83 limits employment as a teacher to a person holding a certificate. Section 85, subsec. 5, of the article provides that a high school teacher's certificate "may be granted to persons who are graduates of a standard college or university, or who have had the equivalent in scholastic preparation." Section 11 of the same article directs and empowers the state board of education to "determine the educational policies of the State," and "enact by-laws for the administration of the public school system, which when enacted and published shall have the force of law." And in pursuance of this authority the board, on September 19, 1930, enacted a by-law that "only such graduates as rank academically in the upper four fifths of the Class and who make a grade of 'C' or better in practical teaching, shall be issued Maryland Teachers' Certificates." The appellant ranked only in the lowest fifth of his class, and for that reason was denied the certificate which he now seeks through the courts. He contends that the passage of the by-law was not within the authority vested in the board by the statutes.

In 1927 he was awarded a scholarship to Western Maryland College, under the provision in article 77, section 243, which required that the winner of such a scholarship should give a bond to the state "that he will teach school within this State for not less than two years after leaving college." And having complied and attended the college, the appellant considers himself assured a teaching position by that provision of the statute. But we are unable to see in the requirement of a bond anything more than a measure to assure the state that it may derive so much benefit in return for its grant to the student. It secures the benefit in case the state should want it. No assurance is given the student, and no obligation assumed by the state toward him.

The provision in section 85, subsec. 5, that a high school teacher's certificate "may be granted," to persons of the specified experience, is construed by the appellant as the equivalent of "shall be granted," and therefore as prohibiting a choice among such persons by the board, limiting eligibility to those in the upper four-fifths of the classes. With this construction, too, the court is in disagreement. There seems to the court to be no intention manifested other than that of setting a minimum requirement for the board's selection of teachers. That seems to be a reasonable construction, in accord with the evident plan of the whole statute that the board shall be depended upon largely to make the educational system work properly. Discretion in selection from eligibles, whose fitness must differ greatly, would seem to be a very likely intention. And if the discretion is given, as we think it is, then when exercised it acquires by the express terms of the statute the force of law, not to be interfered with by the courts. * * *

    * * * the appellant argues that exercise of the authority retroactively could not be intended, so that after a student has started on his preparation a higher test than that with which he was faced at the start could be imposed. The by-law makes no change in courses of study and preparation; it concerns only the diligence and ability of the student in it, and the contention seems to be that the student had a right to take his work more easily. We see no vested rights in the standards of work which might restrict retroactive by-laws. Before the student is selected as a teacher he has no contract with the state, and no vested rights. He is only the recipient of the state's bounty, with the state left unrestrained in adopting requirements it might find desirable at any time.

    A further objection, that no notice was given the appellant of the adoption of this by-law, is subject to the same criticisms. There is no requirement of notice to individuals. Publication of the by-law is required by the statute, and it is not denied that there was publication; and in that the full measure of the statutory requirements was met. Upon publication, the by-law acquired the force of law.

    Order affirmed, with costs.

*Certificate May be Denied Where Board Has Evidence to
Question Good Moral Character of Applicant*

APPLICATION OF BAY

Supreme Court of Oregon, 1963.
233 Or. 601, 378 P.2d 558.

PERRY, Justice. Dean Norman Bay petitioned the circuit court of Union County for judicial review of the decision of appellant State Board of Education denying him issuance of a five-year elementary teacher's certificate. From the decree of the circuit court reversing the Board's decision for lack of competent evidence, appeal is made to this court.

In December of 1953 petitioner was tried and convicted in the state of Washington for his acts of breaking, entering, and grand larceny of several stores, the American Legion Club, and the local high school, committed while employed as a night policeman. At the time these acts were perpetrated, petitioner was 24 years old. After serving 18 months of a two-year sentence, he was paroled. He moved to La Grande, Oregon, where, in the fall of 1956 he enrolled at the Eastern Oregon College of Education. In 1958 the state of Washington restored to him his full civil rights.

In 1960 petitioner was granted a one-year elementary teacher's emergency certificate by the Superintendent of Public Instruction, and taught elementary school while completing his fourth year at the college. Following graduation he applied for a five-year elementary teacher's certificate, but his application was denied on June 14, 1961.

On September 13, 1961 a hearing was conducted before the Board, the primary purpose of which was to determine whether petitioner had furnished the evidence of good moral character which ORS 342.060(2) authorizes the superintendent to require of an applicant. Whereas numerous witnesses appeared at the hearing to testify of petitioner's good character and over-all reputation in the community, the sole evidence of bad character introduced was the record of the prior conviction. The Board concluded that petitioner had not met his burden of furnishing satisfactory evidence of good moral character and he thereupon petitioned the circuit court of Union County for review of the administrative order pursuant to ORS 183.-480. The court held that evidence as to a prior conviction was irrelevant and immaterial in determining present character where not accompanied by other evidence which related the prior act to the present, and therefore adjudged there was no competent evidence to support the Board's findings. The Board was ordered to issue petitioner the certificate, from which order this appeal is taken.

* * *

In order to properly discuss the issues presented it is first necessary to discuss the powers of the trial court in reviewing the Board's determination.

While the statute uses the language "as a suit in equity," it is quite clear that this language refers only to the fact that the review shall be made by the court, not a jury, and does not grant to a trial court the right on appeal to try the cause de novo. That is, the reviewing court is not granted the power to weigh the evidence and subsitute its judgment as to the preponderance thereof for that of the agency. The extent to which a reviewing court should review the action of an administrative agency has been expressed by this court, as follows:

"* * * Generally, they go no further than to determine whether the agency (1) acted impartially; (2) performed faithfully the duties delineated in the legislative acts which conferred jurisdiction upon it; (3) stayed within its jurisdiction; (4) committed no error of law; (5) exercised discretion judiciously and not capriciously; and (6) arrived at no conclusion which was clearly wrong." Richardson v. Neuner, 183 Or. 558, 564, 194 P.2d 989, 991.

The learned trial court recognized these guide posts and reached the conclusion that the finding of the Board as to lack of good moral character could not be sustained by the record. This conclusion of the court is based upon a finding that there was no evidence of bad moral character at the time of application and therefore the Board's conclusion was clearly wrong.

Whether or not the Board arrived at a conclusion which was clearly wrong depends upon whether a review of the entire record discloses any facts from which the conclusion drawn by the Board could be reached by reasonable minds. * * *

The Board made the following findings of fact which are pertinent to this appeal:

"1. That the applicant on December 9, 1953, was convicted of grand larceny of four counts in the Superior Court for Klickitat County, State of Washington and received a one to fifteen-year sentence by the said Court. That thereafter this sentence was fixed at a term of two years by the State Board of Terms and Parole of the State of Washington, and the applicant served an eighteen-month term at the Monroe Reformatory in the State of Washington.

"2. Thereafter upon his release he was placed on parole for approximately a year and moved to the City of La Grande, Oregon, and in the fall of 1956 entered the Eastern Oregon College of Education and enrolled in a teacher education course.

"3. That by act of the Governor of the State of Washington full civil rights were restored to him on July 3, 1958.

*   *   *   *   *   *   *   *

"8. The Board further finds the offenses committed by Mr. Bay consisted of breaking and entering various stores in Goldendale, Washington and grand larceny, and included safe burglaries at the American Legion Club, and Goldendale High School. That at the time, he committed the offenses for which he was imprisoned he had reached the age of 24 years; that his offenses numbered not one but several; that he was a man of superior intelligence as evidenced by his scores on intelligence tests in his subsequent college record.

"9. The Board further finds that at the time of the thefts he occupied a position of trust as a night policeman in the community and that while so engaged he committed the acts resulting in his conviction.

"10. That a teacher in a public school is the key factor in teaching by precept and example the subjects of honesty, morality, courtesy, obedience to law, and other lessons of a steadying influence which tend to promote and develop an upright and desirable citizenry, as required by ORS 336.240 and related statutes.

"11. That there has been no evidence submitted to the Board of any violations of law or deviations from normally considered moral conduct from the time of his release from the Monroe Reformatory to the present time."

The Board then made the following conclusions of law:

"1. That the applicant has not furnished evidence of good moral character deemed satisfactory and necessary by the Board to establish the applicant's fitness to serve as a teacher."

In resolving the question of moral character there must be kept in mind the distinction between character and reputation. "Character is what a man or woman is morally, while reputation is what he or she is reputed to be." Leverich v. Frank, 6 Or. 212; State v. Charlie Sing, 114 Or. 267, 229 P. 921.

"A person's 'character' is usually thought to embrace all his qualities and deficiencies regarding traits of personality, behavior, integrity, temperament, consideration, sportsmanship, altruism, etc. which distinguish him as a human being from his fellow men. His disposition toward criminal acts is only one of the qualities which constitute his character.
* * *

Since the crux of the question before the Board was good moral character, the fact that he had been guilty of burglarizing properties while he held a position of trust was most pertinent. These actions of petitioner clearly evidenced a lack of the moral fiber to resist temptation. The trial court therefore erred in holding there was no evidence of lack of good moral character.

The petitioner offered numerous witnesses from which a conclusion might properly be reached that this lack of moral fiber no longer exists. However, this condition, having been shown to have existed, it became a matter of judgment as to whether it had been overcome.

The power to decide such an issue was delegated by the legislature to the Board of Education, therefore, as previously pointed out, the courts are not permitted to substitute their judgment for that of the Board where there is substantial evidence to support the agency.

The judgment of the trial court is reversed with instructions to enter findings of fact and conclusions of law sustaining the action of the Board of Education.

NOTES

1. Under what circumstances and when would applicant Bay be eligible for a certificate?

2. One of the basic purposes of the certification laws is that a capable and competent instructor will be provided in every classroom. Consequently, a teacher's certificate is a prerequisite not only to employment and reemployment, but is necessary for schools to qualify for state aid. It is a common practice in several states to permit student teachers to assume complete control of a class in the absence of the regular teacher. This violates not only the spirit but also the letter of the law of many states because a student teacher is not a qualified teacher, but is seeking to become a qualified teacher. If a teacher teaches without a certificate, she is considered to be a volunteer and is entitled to no compensation for services rendered, See: Floyd County Bd. of Educ. v. Stone, 307 S.W.2d 912 (Ky.1957).

3. A teacher who has no certificate when entering into an employment contract with a school board could not recover salary for services rendered, even though he had obtained the license prior to actually beginning work. McCloskey v. School Dist., 134 Mich. 235, 96 N.W. 18 (1903); O'Conner v. Francis, 42 App.Div. 375, 59 N.Y.S. 28 (1899); Lee v. Mitchell, 108 Ark. 1, 156 S.W. 450 (1913).

4. A state board of education was held entitled to conclude that a teacher was unfit to teach and her teaching credentials could be revoked where the teacher had joined a "swingers" club, engaged in sexual acts with men other than her husband, and had appeared disguised on television to discuss nonconventional sexual behavior even though the teacher's school principal found her teaching satisfactory. Pettit v. State Bd. of Educ., 10 Cal.3d 29, 109 Cal.Rptr. 665, 513 P.2d 889 (1973).

5. The renewal of a teacher's certificate is as important as his initial right to the certificate. What happens if the superintendent refuses to recommend that a teacher's certificate be renewed? See Matteson v. State Bd. of Educ., 57 Cal.App.2d 991, 136 P.2d 120 (1943).

6. Assume that an individual completes all requirements for a teaching certificate in your state in August and immediately makes application to the proper officials for a teaching certificate. Due to a large number of similar requests, the certifying officials do not certify the individual herein until October 15. He has been teaching since the first day of September. Is the teacher entitled to compensation for services rendered from September 1 to October 15? No

Statute Forbidding Certification to Persons Who Are Not Citizens
and Have Manifested No Intent to Become Citizens
Is Not Violative of Equal Protection

AMBACH v. NORWICK

Supreme Court of the United States, 1979.
— U.S. —, 99 S.Ct. 1589.

Mr. Justice POWELL delivered the opinion of the Court.

This case presents the question whether a State, consistently with the Equal Protection Clause of the Fourteenth Amendment, may refuse to employ as elementary and secondary school teachers aliens who are eligible for United States citizenship but who refuse to seek naturalization.

I

New York Education Law § 3001(3) forbids certification as a public school teacher of any person who is not a citizen of the United States, unless that person has manifested an intention to apply for citizenship. The Commissioner of Education is authorized to create exemptions from this prohibition, and has done so with respect to aliens who are not yet eligible for citizenship. Unless a teacher obtains certification, he may not work in a public elementary or secondary school in New York.

Appellee Norwick was born in Scotland and is a subject of Great Britain. She has resided in this country since 1965 and is married to a United States citizen. Appellee Dachinger is a Finnish subject who came to this country in 1966 and also is married to a United States citizen. Both Norwick and Dachinger currently meet all of the educational requirements New York has set for certification as a public school teacher, but they consistently have refused to seek citizenship in spite of their eligibility to do so. Norwick applied in 1973 for a teaching certificate covering nursery school through sixth grade, and Dachinger sought a certificate covering the same grades in 1975. Both applications were denied because of appellees' failure to meet the requirements of § 3001(3). Norwick then filed this suit seeking to enjoin the enforcement of § 3001(3), and Dachinger obtained leave to intervene as a plaintiff.

* * *

II

* * *

Applying the rational basis standard, we held last Term that New York could exclude aliens from the ranks of its police force. Foley v. Connelie, 435 U.S. 291 (1978). Because the police function fulfilled "a most fundamental obligation of government to its constituency" and by necessity cloaked policemen with substantial discretionary powers, we viewed the police force as being one of those appropriately defined classes of positions for which a citizenship requirement could be imposed.   Accordingly, the State was required to justify its classification only "by a showing of some rational relationship between the interest sought to be protected and the limiting classification."

The rule for governmental functions, which is an exception to the general standard applicable to classifications based on alienage, rests on important principles inherent in the Constitution.   The distinction between citizens and aliens, though ordinarily irrelevant to private activity, is fundamental to the definition and government of a State.   The Constitution itself refers to the distinction no less than 11 times, see Sugarman v. Dougall, (Rehnquist, J., dissenting), indicating that the status of citizenship was meant to have significance in the structure of our government.   The assumption of that status, whether by birth or naturalization, denotes an association with the polity which, in a democratic republic, exercises the powers of governance.   The form of this association is important: an oath of allegiance or similar ceremony cannot substitute for the unequivocal legal bond citizenship represents.   It is because of this special significance of citizenship that governmental entities, when exercising the functions of government, have wider latitude in limiting the participation of noncitizens.

In determining whether, for purposes of equal protection analysis, teaching in public schools constitutes a governmental function, we look to the role of public education and to the degree of responsibility and discretion teachers possess in fulfilling that role.   Each of these considerations supports the conclusion that public school teachers may be regarded as performing a task "that go[es] to the heart of representative government."

Public education, like the police function, "fulfills a most fundamental obligation of government to its constituency."   The importance of public schools in the preparation of individuals for participation as citizens, and in the preservation of the values on which our society rests, long has been recognized by our decisions:

> "Today, education is perhaps the most important function of state and local governments.   Compulsory school attendance laws and the great expenditures for education both demonstrate our recognition of the importance of education to our democratic society.   It is required in the performance of our most basic public responsibilities, even service in the armed forces.   It is the very foundation of good citizenship.

Today it is a principal instrument in awakening the child to cultural values, in preparing him for later professional training, and in helping him to adjust normally to his environment." Brown v. Board of Education, 347 U.S. 483, 493 (1954).

* * * Other authorities have perceived public schools as an "assimilative force" by which diverse and conflicting elements in our society are brought together on a broad but common ground. * * * These perceptions of the public schools as inculcating fundamental values necessary to the maintenance of a democratic political system have been confirmed by the observations of social scientists. * * *

Within the public school system, teachers play a critical part in developing students' attitude toward government and understanding of the role of citizens in our society. Alone among employees of the system, teachers are in direct, day-to-day contact with students both in the classrooms and in the other varied activities of a modern school. In shaping the students' experience to achieve educational goals, teachers by necessity have wide discretion over the way the course material is communicated to students. They are responsible for presenting and explaining the subject matter in a way that is both comprehensible and inspiring. No amount of standardization of teaching materials or lesson plans can eliminate the personal qualities a teacher brings to bear in achieving these goals. Further, a teacher serves as a role model for his students, exerting a subtle but important influence over their perceptions and values. Thus, through both the presentation of course materials and the example he sets, a teacher has an opportunity to influence the attitudes of students toward government, the political process, and a citizen's social responsibilities. This influence is crucial to the continued good health of a democracy.

Furthermore, it is clear that all public school teachers, and not just those responsible for teaching the courses most directly related to government, history, and civic duties, should help fulfill the broader function of the public school system. Teachers, regardless of their specialty, may be called upon to teach other subjects, including those expressly dedicated to political and social subjects. More importantly, a State properly may regard all teachers as having an obligation to promote civic virtues and understanding in their classes, regardless of the subject taught. Certainly a State also may take account of a teacher's function as an example for students, which exists independently of particular classroom subjects. In light of the foregoing considerations, we think it clear that public school teachers come well within the "governmental function" principle recognized in *Sugarman* and *Foley*. Accordingly, the Constitution requires only that a citizenship requirement applicable to teaching in the public schools bears a rational relationship to a legitimate state interest. * * *

III

As the legitimacy of the State's interest in furthering the educational goals outlined above is undoubted, it remains only to consider whether § 3001(3) bears a rational relationship to this interest. The restriction is carefully framed to serve its purpose, as it bars from teaching only those aliens who have demonstrated their unwillingness to obtain United States citizenship. Appellees, and aliens similarly situated, in effect have chosen to classify themselves. They prefer to retain citizenship in a foreign country with the obligations it entails of primary duty and loyalty. They have rejected the open invitation extended to qualify for eligibility to teach by applying for citizenship in this country. The people of New York, acting through their elected representatives, have made a judgment that citizenship should be a qualification for teaching the young of the State in the public schools, and § 3001(3) furthers that judgment.

Reversed.

Contracts

The framers of the Constitution realized the importance of the sanctity of contracts. Provision for protecting the obligation of contracts was included in Article I, Section 10 of the U. S. Constitution.

The Supreme Court, in the famous Dartmouth College case,[17] interpreted Article I, Section 10 of the Constitution, declaring that states could not enact legislation which impairs the obligation of a contract. In this case, the English crown had granted a charter to Dartmouth College, which had been established in the Colony of New Hampshire as a private college. The college was governed by a self-perpetuating board of twelve members. A conflict developed between the college president and the board members which had political ramifications. Reacting to this controversy, the legislature of New Hampshire in 1816, enacted legislation which materially altered the charter making the college a state institution. The college trustees brought an action and claimed, in part, that the act of the legislature was unconstitutional and impaired the obligation of their contract, the original charter. The opinion of the Court delivered by Justice Marshall, stated:

> The points for consideration are: 1. Is this contract protected by the Constitution of the United States? 2. Is it impaired by the acts under which the defendant holds?
>
> 1. On the first point, it has been argued, that the word "contract" in its broadest sense, would comprehend the po-

17. Trustees of Dartmouth College v. Woodward, 17 U.S. (4 Wheat) 518 (1819).

litical relations between the government and its citizens, would extend to offices held within a state, for state purposes, and to many of those laws concerning civil institutions, which must change with circumstances, and be modified by ordinary legislation; which deeply concern the public, and which, to preserve good government, the public judgment must control * * *.

This (charter) is plainly a contract to which the donors, the trustees and the crown (to whose rights and obligation; New Hampshire succeeds) were the original parties. It is a contract made on a valuable consideration. It is a contract for the security and disposition of property. It is a contract, on the faith of which, real and personal estate has been conveyed to the corporation. It is, then, a contract within the letter of the constitution, and within its spirit also unless the fact that the property is invested by the donors in trustees, for the promotion of religion and education, for the benefit of persons who are perpetually changing, though the objects remain the same, shall create a particular exception, taking this case out of the prohibition contained in the constitution. * * *

The opinion of the court, after mature deliberation, is, that this is a contract, the obligation of which cannot be impaired, without violating the constitution of the United States. This opinion appears to us to be equally supported by reason, and by the former decisions of this court.

2. We next proceed to the inquiry, whether its obligation has been impaired by those acts of the legislature of New Hampshire, to which the special verdict refers?

From the review of this charter, which has been taken, it appears that the whole power of governing the college, of appointing and removing tutors, of fixing salaries, of directing the course of study to be pursued by the students, and of filling up vacancies created in their own body, was vested in the trustees. On the part of the crown it was expressly stipulated, that this corporation, thus constituted, should continue forever; and that the number of trustees should forever consist of twelve, and no more. By this contract the crown was bound, and could have made no violent alteration in its essential terms, without impairing its obligation.

By the Revolution the duties, as well as the powers, of government devolved on the people of New Hampshire. It is admitted, that among the latter was comprehended the transcendent power of parliament, as well as that of the executive department. It is too clear, to require the support of argument, that all contracts and rights respecting property, remained unchanged by the Revolution. The obligations, then, which were created by the charter to Dartmouth College, were the same in the new, that they had been in the old government * * * But the Constitution of the United States has imposed this additional limitation, that the legislature of a state shall pass no act "impairing the obligation of contracts." * * *

It results from this opinion, that the acts of the legislature of New Hampshire, which are stated in the special verdict found in this cause, are repugnant to the Constitution of the United States; and that the judgment on this special verdict ought to have been for the plaintiffs. The judgment of the state court must, therefore, be reversed.[18]

In an Indiana case, Article I, Section 10 of the Constitution of the United States is directly applied as a limitation on state legislative actions pertaining to public education. The Indiana legislature passed an act which repealed a 1927 law granting tenure to teachers. The teacher sought a writ of mandamus to compel her continued employment. She claimed the original act had granted her a continuing contract which could not be impaired nor breached by subsequent legislation. The original act provided:

It is further agreed by the contracting parties that all of the Teachers' Tenure Law, approved March 8, 1927, shall be in full force and effect in this contract.

The Supreme Court of Indiana ruled in favor of the defendant board of education and the teacher appealed. The Supreme Court of the United States reversed the Indiana Court.

Both of these decisions illustrate the constitutional requirements within which a state legislature must operate when dealing with contracts. Particular application may be noted where legislation such as tenure and retirement statutes may create a contract between the state and an individual.

There is a fine line between the constitutional rights of one individual and the rights of the people as exercised through the elected authority of the legislature to provide for the welfare of the state. This is demonstrated by the dissent of Justice Black in the Anderson v. Brand case where he said that the Supreme Court should not interfere with the determination of educational policy by the Indiana legislature because the legislature of a state cannot make and be held to a contract "with a few citizens, that would take from all the citizens, the continuing power to alter the educational policy for the best interests of Indiana school children * * *."

18. State ex rel. Anderson v. Brand,
303 U.S. 95, 58 S.Ct. 433 (1938).

A teacher's contract must satisfy the same requirements applicable to contracts in general. A school district is a legal entity, a corporate body with the power to sue and be sued; purchase, receive, hold and sell real and personal property, make contracts and be contracted with; and do all other things necessary to accomplish the purposes for which it is created.

Contracts of school districts must conform not only to the requirements of general contract law, but also must satisfy other statutory and case law demands as well. A contract may be defined as an agreement between two or more competent persons for a legal consideration on a legal subject matter in the form required by law. This definition includes the five basic elements inherent in every valid contract, to-wit:

1. Offer and acceptance
2. Competent persons
3. Consideration
4. Legal subject matter
5. Proper form

We shall discuss these elements in the order set out above.*

All contracts are agreements, but not all agreements are contracts. An agreement is an offer and an acceptance. Every valid contract contains an offer and acceptance. For example, a board of education offers a fifth grade teaching position in a particular school to an individual. There is no agreement unless and until the individual accepts the offer.

Several significant factors concerning agreements should be kept in mind. An offer can only be accepted by the individual or individuals to whom it is made. Unless otherwise stated, an offer must be accepted within a reasonable time after it made or it will be terminated automatically. Newspaper advertisements are usually considered to be invitations for offers and not offers. That is, the board of education is soliciting offers. Also, an offer cannot be accepted unless at the time the individual performed the act necessary to accept the offer he knew of the existence of the offer. By way of illustration, let us assume that vandals broke into a school building and the board of education offered a reward for information leading to the arrest and conviction of the vandals. The information was provided to the police by an individual who was unware of the reward offer. A majority of the States hold that the individual is not entitled to the reward because he could not have accepted the offer since he was unaware of its existence—there was no meeting of the minds.

* Appreciation is extended to Ray Corns for this discussion of contracts, see: Kern Alexander, Ray Corns, Walter McCann, Public School Law, West Publishing Company, St. Paul, 1969, pp. 390–392.

Each valid contract must be entered into between two or more competent persons—persons who have the legal capacity to contract. As already indicated, a board of education is considered a competent person under the law with full capacity to enter into contracts. However, there are certain classes of people who have limited capacity to contract. These include minors, married women, insane persons, drunken persons, and corporations.

A minor has the right to disaffirm his contract until a reasonable time after he reaches his majority, i.e., becomes an adult. If a board of education contracts with a minor, the minor has the prerogative of electing to avoid the contract within a reasonable time after he becomes an adult and no penalties for a contractual breach will be imposed against the minor. However, the board of education has no right or option to avoid its contract with the minor.

If an individual is so insane or drunk at the time he enters into a contract so that he does not know what he is doing, he may have the contract set aside because there was no meeting of the minds, which is always essential in every valid contractual situation.

At the common law, married women did not possess the legal capacity to contract. This was premised on the age old concept that when a man and woman married, the two became one and the man was that one. This contractual limitation has been removed by statutes in all states and women now possess the power to enter into contracts on the same basis as men.

Before entering into a contract with a corporation, a board of education should ascertain that the corporation has the power by statute or under its articles of incorporation to perform the services agreed upon.

Valid contracts must be supported by consideration—something of value. Consideration is divided into three types. These are good, valuable, and a promise for an act.

Good consideration is love and affection. For example, a mother may convey property to a child for good consideration. This notion is seldom invoked by courts today.

Valuable consideration is cash or its equivalent. Most deeds will recite that the property is being conveyed for good and valuable consideration.

The third type of consideration is that found in a unilateral contract—a promise for an act. For example, a board of education promises a reward of $500 for information leading to the arrest and conviction of vandals who damaged school property and an individual, knowing of the offer, provides the information that leads to the arrest and conviction of the vandals, is entitled to the reward. His consideration was the doing of the act requested.

All contracts to be valid must involve a legal subject matter. Most, if not all, states prohibit the holding of various types of assemblies, such as rooster fighting. If a board of education entered into a contract to lease school premises for the purposes of staging a rooster fighting conclave, such a contract would involve an illegal subject matter and would be declared void.

Contracts to be enforceable must be in the form required by law. For example, all agreements with respect to the sale or leasing of real estate must be in writing to be enforceable. An oral agreement to sell real property even if made in the town square before ten thousand people is unenforceable in the courts. This is but one example of the requirement that contracts must be in the proper form to be enforceable. Most states require that teacher's contracts be in writing.

Tenure Contracts Between the State and Teacher Cannot be Unilaterally Cancelled by the State

STATE OF INDIANA EX REL. ANDERSON v. BRAND

Supreme Court of the United States, 1938.
303 U.S. 95, 58 S.Ct. 443.

Mr. Justice ROBERTS delivered the opinion of the Court.

The petitioner sought a writ of mandate to compel the respondent to continue her in employment as a public school teacher. Her complaint alleged that as a duly licensed teacher she entered into a contract in September, 1924, to teach in the township schools and, pursuant to successive contracts, taught continuously to and including the school year 1932–1933; that her contracts for the school years 1931–1932 and 1932–1933 contained this clause: "It is further agreed by the contracting parties that all of the provisions of the Teachers' Tenure Law, approved March 8, 1927, shall be in full force and effect in this contract"; and that by force of that act she had a contract, indefinite in duration, which could be canceled by the respondent only in the manner and for the causes specified in the act. She charged that in July, 1933, the respondent notified her he proposed to cancel her contract for cause; that, after a hearing, he adhered to his decision and the county superintendent affirmed his action; that, despite what occurred in July, 1933, the petitioner was permitted to teach during the school year 1933–1934 and the respondent was presently threatening to terminate her employment at the end of that year. The complaint alleged the termination of her employment would be a breach of her contract with the school corporation. The respondent demurred on the grounds that (1) the complaint disclosed the matters pleaded had been submitted to the respondent and the county superintendent who were authorized to try the issues and had lawfully determined them in favor of the respondent; and (2) the Teachers' Tenure Law, Acts Ind.1927, c. 97, had been repealed in respect of teachers in township schools. The demurrer was sustained and the petitioner appealed to the state Supreme Court which affirmed the judgment. The court did not discuss the first ground of demurrer relating to the action taken in the school year 1932–1933, but rested its decision upon the second, that, by an act of 1933, Acts Ind.1933, c. 116, the Teachers' Tenure Law had been repealed as respects teachers in township schools; and held that the repeal did not deprive the petitioner of a vested property right and did not impair her contract within the meaning of the Constitution. * * *

* * *

As in most cases brought to this court under the contract clause of the Constitution, the question is as to the existence and nature of the contract and not as to the construction of the law which is suppose to impair it. The principal function of a legislative body is not to make contracts but to make laws which declare the policy of the state and are subject to repeal when a subsequent Legislature shall determine to alter that policy. Nevertheless, it is established that a legislative enactment may contain provisions which, when accepted as the basis of action by individuals, become contracts between them and the State or its subdivisions within the protection of article 1, § 10. If the people's representatives deem it in the public interest they may adopt a policy of contracting in respect of public business for a term longer than the life of the current session of the Legislature. This the petitioner claims has been done with respect to permanent teachers. * * *

* * *

The courts of Indiana have long recognized that the employment of school teachers was contractual and have afforded relief in actions upon teachers' contracts. An act adopted in 1899 required all contracts between teachers and school corporations to be in writing, signed by the parties to be charged, and to be made a matter of public record. A statute of 1921 enacted that every such contract should be in writing and should state the date of the beginning of the school term, the number of months therein, the amount of the salary for the term, and the number of payments to be made during the school year.

In 1927 the State adopted the <u>Teachers' Tenure Act</u> under which the present controversy arises. * * * By this act it was provided that a teacher who has served <u>under contract for 5 or more successive years, and thereafter enters into a contract for further service with the school corporation, shall become a permanent teacher and the contract, upon the expiration of its stated term, shall be deemed to continue in effect for an indefinite period, shall be known as an indefinite contract, and shall remain in force unless succeeded by a new contract or canceled as provided in the act.</u> The corporation may cancel the contract, after notice and hearing, for incompetency, insubordination, neglect of duty, immorality, justifiable decrease in the number of teaching positions, or other good or just cause, but not for political or personal reasons. The teacher may not cancel the contract during the school term nor for a period 30 days previous to the beginning of any term (unless by mutual agreement) and may cancel only upon 5 days' notice.

By an amendatory act of 1933 township school corporations were omitted from the provisions of the act of 1927. The court below construed this act as repealing the act of 1927 so far as township schools and teachers are concerned and as leaving the respondent free to terminate the petitioner's employment. But we are of opinion that the petitioner had a valid contract with the respondent, the obligation of which would be impaired by the termination of her employment.

Where the claim is that the state's policy embodied in a statute is to bind its instrumentalities by contract, the cardinal inquiry is as to the terms of the statute supposed to create such a contract. The State long prior to the adoption of the act of 1927 required the execution of written contracts between teachers and school corporations, specified certain subjects with which such contracts must deal, and required that they be made a matter of public record. These were annual contracts, covering a single school term. The act of 1927 announced a new policy that a teacher who had served for 5 years under successive contracts, upon the execution of another was to become a permanent teacher and the last contract was to be indefinite as to duration and terminable by either party only upon compliance with the conditions set out in the statute. The policy which induced the legislation evidently was that the teacher should have protection against the exercise of the right, which would otherwise inhere in the employer, of terminating the employment at the end of any school term without assigned reasons and solely at the employer's pleasure. The state courts in earlier cases so declared.

The title of the act is couched in terms of contract. It speaks of the making and canceling of indefinite contracts. In the body the word "contract" appears ten times in section 1, defining the relationship; eleven times in section 2, relating to the termination of the employment by the employer, and four times in section 4, stating the conditions of termination by the teacher.

The tenor of the act indicates that the word "contract" was not used inadvertently or in other than its usual legal meaning. By section 6 it is expressly provided that the act is a supplement to that of March 7, 1921, supra, requiring teachers' employment contracts to be in writing. By section 1 it is provided that the written contract of a permanent teacher "shall be deemed to continue in effect for an indefinite period and shall be known as an indefinite contract." Such an indefinite contract is to remain in force unless succeeded by a new contract signed by both parties or canceled as provided in section 2. No more apt language could be employed to define a contractual relationship. By section 2 it is enacted that such indefinite contracts may be canceled by the school corporation only in the manner specified.   The admissible grounds of cancellation, and the method by which the existence of such grounds shall be ascertained and made a matter of record, are carefully set out.   Section 4 permits cancellation by the teacher only at certain times consistent with the convenient administration of the school system and imposes a sanction for violation of its requirements.   Examination of the entire act convinces us that the teacher was by it assured of the possession of a binding and enforceable contract against school districts.

                    *   *   *

Our decisions recognize that every contract is made subject to the implied condition that its fulfillment may be frustrated by a proper exercise of the police power but we have repeatedly said that, in order to have this effect, the exercise of the power must be for an end which is in fact public and the means adopted must be reasonably adapted to that end, and the Supreme Court of Indiana has taken the same view in respect of legislation impairing the obligation of the contract of a state instrumentality.   The causes of cancellation provided in the act of 1927 and the retention of the system of indefinite contracts in all municipalities except townships by the act of 1933 are persuasive that the repeal of the earlier act by the later was not an exercise of the police power for the attainment of ends to which its exercise may properly be directed.

As the court below has not passed upon one of the grounds of demurrer which appears to involve no federal question, and may present a defense still open to the respondent, we reverse the judgment and remand the cause for further proceedings not inconsistent with this opinion.

So ordered.

A Contract Between a School Trustee and a Teacher to Pay "Good Wages" Is Too Indefinite to Enforce

FAIRPLAY SCHOOL TOWNSHIP v. O'NEAL

Supreme Court of Indiana, 1891.
127 Ind. 95, 26 N.E. 686.

ELLIOTT, J.   The complaint of the appellee alleges that she was duly licensed to teach school, and that her license was in force on the 31st day of March, 1888; that she entered into a verbal contract with the school trustee on that day, wherein she undertook to teach school for the term to be held in the school year 1888; that the school trustee promised in said oral contract to pay her "good wages;" that she has been ready and willing to teach, but the trustee refused to permit her to do so.   The question presented is whether there was such a contract as bound the school township, and made it liable for damages for a breach.   Our opinion is that there was no such contract.

The trustee is an officer clothed with statutory power, and all who deal with him are bound to take notice of the nature and extent of his authority. * * * The authority of the trustee respecting schools is vested in him for a public purpose, in which all the citizens of the township have an interest, and upon many phases of which they have a right to be heard by petition or remonstrance. This is especially so with regard to the employment of teachers. It is necessary, for the information of the citizens, that contracts made with teachers should be certain and definite in their terms; otherwise the citizens cannot guard their interests, nor observe the conduct of their officer. It is necessary that the contract should be definite and certain, in order that when the time comes for the teacher to enter upon duty there may be no misunderstanding as to what his rights are. Any other rule would put in peril the school interests. Suppose, for illustration, that a contract providing for "good wages," "reasonable wages," "fair wages," or the like, is made, and when the time comes for opening the schools there arises a dispute as to what the compensation shall be. How shall it be determined, and in what mode can the teacher be compelled to go on with the duty he has agreed to perform? Until there is a definite contract, it can hardly be said that a teacher has been employed, and the public interest demands that there should be a definite agreement before the time arrives for the schools to open; otherwise the school corporation may be at the mercy of the teacher, or else there be no school. We think that a teacher cannot recover from the school corporation for the breach of an executory agreement, unless it is so full and definite as to be capable of specific enforcement. * * * There is much reason for scrutinizing with care contracts made so far in advance of the opening of the school year as was that here sued on, and sound policy requires that the terms should be so definitely fixed and made known that all interested may have full and reliable information. It is, we may say in passing, not altogether clear that the statute does not require that all contracts shall be in writing and be recorded; but we do not deem it necessary to decide that question. Judgment reversed.

NOTES

1. Would the outcome of this case have been different if the contract had been written?

2. Teachers' general relationships with school boards are created by contract and governed by general principles of contract law. Kirk v. Miller, 83 Wash.2d 777, 522 P.2d 843 (1974).

3. Power to employ or discharge teachers is exclusively vested in the school board and cannot be delegated to any other body or official, such as a school superintendent. Snider v. Kit Carson School Dist. R–1, in Cheyenne County, 166 Colo. 180, 442 P.2d 429 (1968).

4. In order to have a valid teacher employment contract, as in other discretionary matters, the school board must act as a board and not as indi-

viduals. Landers v. Board of Educ. of Town of Hot Springs, 45 N.M. 446, 116 P.2d 690 (1941).

5. If a statute provides for nonrenewal of a teacher's contract for "cause" such cause cannot be found in constitutionally protected reasons; even nontenured teachers cannot be dismissed for exercising constitutional rights. Board of Trustees, Laramie County School Dist. No. 1 v. Spiegel, 549 P.2d 1161 (Wyo.1976).

6. Notice of nonrenewal of teacher's contract must contain a statement of probable cause which is sufficiently explicit for the individual teacher to reasonably determine what criteria and standards the board will be considering in making its final determination; anything less violates due process. Merely stating that nonrenewal is due to reduction in enrollment and financial reasons, without more specification, is not sufficient. Williams v. Board of Directors of Endicott School Dist. 308, 10 Wash.App. 579, 519 P.2d 15 (1974). Compare this case to Perry v. Sindermann, 408 U.S. 593, 92 S.Ct. 2694 (1972).

Scope of Teacher's Duties

There are many attendant duties outside the classroom which teachers are called upon to perform. These may include supervision of athletic events and field excursions, selling of tickets at student activities, loading of school buses and other related non-academic duties too numerous to mention.

The court cases to date on this subject indicate that a teacher may be required to perform tasks incidental to regular classroom work. Teachers may not be required to render such services as janitorial duties, traffic duty, school bus driving and similar activities not coming within the implied duties of a teacher's contract. All such common law legal principles may be altered, of course, by a collective bargaining contract.

*Assignment of Teacher to Supervise Athletic Events of
School Is Not Unreasonable and Is Within Scope
of Teaching Duties*

McGRATH v. BURKHARD

California District Court of Appeal, Third Dist. (1955).
131 Cal.App.2d 367, 280 P.2d 864.

SCHOTTKY, Justice. Plaintiff, a teacher in the Sacramento Senior High School, commenced an action for declaratory relief against defendant Superintendent of Sacramento City Unified School District, the Board of Education of said district and the individual members of said board, and the principal of the Sacramento Senior High School. Plaintiff sought declaratory relief on the ground that the non-classroom assignments, as hereinafter detailed, did not fall within the scope of his duties as a teacher under the terms of his contract of employment, and that such duties were unprofessional in nature. Plaintiff asked the court to declare the rights and duties under the contract of employment; that the non-classroom work was not within the scope of employment; that plaintiff should not be assigned duties on a teaching day which required more than eight hours per day to perform competently; that if more than eight hours may be assigned the court should declare the number of hours per day plaintiff is obligated to perform under the contract; that no duties be assigned on days for which he is not paid, i. e., Saturdays, holidays and most non-teaching days.

                    *   *   *

        *   *   * Before discussing the contentions made by plaintiff and appellant we shall summarize the factual situation which is not in substantial dispute.

        Appellant is a teacher in the Sacramento Senior High School. From 1942 to 1945 he was employed as a long term substitute teacher; from July, 1945, to July, 1948, he was employed as a probationary teacher and from July, 1948, to the date of this action he was employed as a permanent teacher. He achieved the status of tenure in 1948.

        At all times appellant has been employed under a written contract, which incorporates the rules of the respondent Board of Education.

        During his course of employment by respondents, appellant and other male teachers have been required to attend certain non-classroom activities and act in a supervisory capacity. The activities are school football and basketball games, which are under the auspices and control of the school authorities. These games may be held at places other than on the school grounds. Six of these athletic assignments are made to each male member of the faculty during each school year, three football games and three basketball games. At the beginning of the school year each male teacher selects the three football games at which he would prefer to supervise; at the end of such season he then selects the three basketball games at which he would prefer to attend in a supervisory capacity. To the extent possible the requests of the teachers are complied with in the scheduling of these assignments, but at times a teacher receives an assignment on a date other than the one he had selected. The teachers are selected impartially and without discrimination. For many years past this administrative practice of assigning the male teachers to supervise at the school athletic contests in football and basketball has been carried out to protect the welfare of the students. The teachers have no authority to act as police officers, but policemen are present at the games to handle any situation in which their authority is needed. Appellant testified that the teacher's duties at these games consisted of maintaining order in the student section of the stands, * * * controlling conduct of the students, preventing smoking in the gymnasium by students or adults and preventing spectators from entering the gymnasium with soft drinks, candy or other food. The female teachers of the school are given assignments to supervision of non-classroom activities, but of a different nature, as supervising in the cafeteria, variety shows and dances.

    *   *   *

Appellant first contends that he is under no contractual obligation in regard to the athletic assignments and that if so obligated, the required duties are unreasonable and not within the scope of teaching duties. He states that such obligation is nowhere set forth in the contract, the rules of the Board of Education, nor in the laws of the state of California. While it is true that this specific duty is not set forth, a study of the evidence and the provisions set forth in the Education Code and the Administrative Code reveals that the assignment complained of by appellant is and was within the contemplation of the parties when the contract of employment was entered into. Relevant portions of each are set out below:

> Education Code, section 2204. "The governing board of any school district shall: (a) Prescribe and enforce rules not inconsistent with law or with the rules prescribed by the State Board of Education, for its own government, and for the government of the schools under its jurisdiction."

> Education Code, section 13201. "The governing board of each school district shall fix and prescribe the duties to be performed by all persons in public school service in the school district."

These sections provide for the delegation of rule making authority, so that the correct body can prescribe exactly what the duties are. In connection with this, certain rules promulgated by the State Board of Education must be considered. The following excerpts are taken from the California Administrative Code, Title 5, Article 3, which is entitled "Duties of Principals and Teachers."

> "Section 16. Responsibility of Principal. The principal is responsible for the supervision and administration of his school."

> "Section 18. Playground supervision. Where playground supervision is not otherwise provided, the principal of each school shall provide for the supervision, by teachers, of the conduct and direction of the play of the pupils of the school or on the school grounds during recesses and other intermissions and before and after school. All athletic or social activities, wherever held, when conducted under the name or auspices of any public school, or any class or organization thereof, shall be under the direct supervision of the authorities of the district." * * *

* * * These provisions relate to all teachers in the public school system. Of course, the State Board of Education has expressed other duties which are required of teachers, as shown in the above excerpts from the Administrative Code. The local governing board has power delegated to it to make the necessary rules and regulations which its district requires. Ed.Code, secs. 2204, 13201. And finally, the principal has the necessary power which is inherent in his office to properly administer and supervise his school.

Appellant's contract expressly set forth that it was subject to the laws of California, the rules of the State Board of Education and of the local governing board. The trial court found that the rule of the Sacramento City Unified School District with reference to the athletic assignments was a part of appellant's contract. The code provisions relating to the duties of teachers do not set forth the particular duty which is the subject of this controversy. The rules promulgated by the State Board of Education do not set forth such specific duty. However, the rules in Article 3 of Title 5 of the Administrative Code do show that the principals and teachers are charged with certain duties * * *.

Appellant * * * asserts that the trial court should be reversed since the duties at the athletic contests were (1) in the nature of police work, (2) unprofessional, (3) foreign to the field of instruction, and (4) imposed unreasonable hours, and therefore were not within the scope of the teaching duties required by the contract. However, the record does not sustain appellant's contention in this regard. The teachers have no authority to act as police officers; in fact, they are expressly informed that their duties are supervisory only. At no time is a teacher to exert police powers. The teachers are to act in a supervisory capacity, much as they do at school assembly meetings, etc. They are acting to protect the welfare of the students. Appellant asserts that he has received no training for this type of work and that the evidence suggests, since women are not assigned this type of duty, that physical strength is a requisite and that the motivating reason for the assignments is to quell and put down disturbances, which is in the nature of police duty. The record refutes appellant's statement. From the deposition of Dr. Murphy, the principal at Sacramento Senior High School, it appears that he was asked questions directly on this point and he replied that the duties did not relate to physical strength or power and stated that he thought many of the female teachers could perform the duties at the games. He stated that he thought that a man's presence at the games was more effectual on the students than a woman's and that it just seemed to be more of a man's job. In explaining this he stated that the work in cafeteria supervision seemed to be more in line with a woman's presence than a man's. Appellant states that the duties were degrading, humiliating and unprofessional. Certain instances

are cited. Dr. Murphy admitted that the duty was disagreeable to
some, but he felt that it was the same with some women with the cafeteria assignments, or with anyone when they have to perform a task
which they do not like, and apparently this is especially so with some
teachers when they are faced with these types of supervisory duties.
All public school teachers have general duties as expressed by the Education Code, sections 13228, 13229 and 13230, supra, relating to the
control of the conduct of pupils, endorsement of rules and the training of them to be good American citizens. Coupled with these are
the rules of the State Board of Education in Article 3 of Title 5 of
the Administrative Code, which relate to certain duties, and section
24 in particular, quoted supra, which requires principals and teachers
to exercise careful supervision of moral conditions in the schools and
not to tolerate participation by students in gambling, profanity, the
use of intoxicating liquors, etc., on or off the schoolgrounds. Teachers are expected to perform these obligations. It is of great importance that the association of teacher and pupil should tend to inculcate in the latter principles of justice, fair-play, good sportsmanship,
good citizenship and respect for rules and authority. Viewing the duties at the games in light of the above, it is apparent that they are
not of an unprofessional nature. For as stated in the case of Parrish
v. Moss, supra, so strongly relied upon by appellant, "The day in
which the concept was held that teaching duty was limited to classroom instruction has long since passed."

Appellant's final contention is that the duties here involved impose unreasonable hours. The record shows that six of these assignments are made in a school year from September to the following
June. Generally, the hours are evening ones, from about six or seven
o'clock to ten o'clock. Some assignments fall on Saturday evenings
or on Thanksgiving Day. Appellant also claims that the Saturday or
legal holiday on which an assignment occasionally occurs is a day of
duty for which he is not paid. However, appellant is not paid on a
basis of so much per hour worked. Teachers are engaged in a professional employment. Their salaries and hours of employment are
fixed with due regard to their professional status and are not fixed
upon the same basis as those of day laborers. The worth of a teacher is not measured in terms of a specific sum of money per hour. A
teacher expects to and does perform a service. If that service from
time to time requires additional hours of work, a teacher expects to
and does perform it. If that service from time to time requires additional hours of work, a teacher expects to and does put in the extra
hours, without thought of measuring his or her compensation in
terms of a given sum of money per hour. A teacher's duties and obligations to students and the community are not satisfied by closing
the classroom door at the conclusion of a class. The direction and
supervision of extracurricular activities are an important part of his
duties. All of his duties are taken into consideration in his contract

for employment at the annual salary. All of this is, of course, subject to the test of reasonableness. It does not appear that six of these athletic assignments in an entire school year are unreasonable, nor that the hours of such assignments are unreasonable, under the circumstances. What is reasonable must necessarily depend upon the facts of the situation and the teachers are protected in that regard by the appropriate administrative and judicial procedure. Supervising the students and being present to protect their welfare at school athletic and social activities, conducted under the name and auspices of the school, is within the scope of the contract and such assignments are proper so long as they are distributed impartially, they are reasonable in number and hours of duty and each teacher has his share of such duty.

* * *

We believe that respondent school authorities had the right under the law and the contract with appellant to assign appellant to attend and assist in supervising these athletic contests. We believe that the presence of teachers at such contests should be helpful not only to the students but should be of benefit to the teachers themselves. We believe that the school authorities had the right to determine that such duties should be performed by the teachers assigned thereto. As stated by the learned trial judge in his memorandum opinion, "Have the parents not the right to expect, and, indeed, to demand, that all such school activities be under the supervision of the school authorities? If not, then who is to be in control? The answers to these questions seem obvious."

* * *

The judgment is affirmed.

NOTES

1. In the case of Parrish v. Moss, 200 Misc. 375, 160 N.Y.S.2d 577 (1951), New York teachers contested the right of a school board to assign incidental duties. The court held that teachers could be assigned only those duties related to their respective subject fields. English teachers could be required to coach plays and assist debate teams; band leaders would have to go with the band on field excursions; and physical education instructors could be required to coach intramural and inter school athletic teams.

2. Considering the decision in the California and New York cases, what criteria may be established to determine what outside assignments come within the "implied duties" portion of a teacher's contract.

Tenure

After meeting designated academic requirements and teaching within a school district for a prescribed number of years, if a teacher is recommended for re-employment, she acquires tenure in most states. This means usually that the teacher has a right of re-employment in the school district but no right to a particular school or position.

Once a teacher acquires tenure, she must be re-employed in that school district until she dies, resigns, or retires. The only way a tenure teacher contract can be terminated is for the board to prefer charges against the teacher and remove her for cause. The statutes usually specify what constitutes "cause"; or, as sometimes stated "good cause."

Many court cases have arisen concerning the transferring of a tenure teacher from one class or school to another class or school. Generally, a tenure teacher, like a teacher on a limited contract, may be assigned to any class or school in the district if she is qualified to teach in that position. The courts frown, however, upon any attempt of a school board or administrator to use "undesirable reassignment" as a means of getting at a teacher who has achieved continuing contract status. If a teacher has committed an act for which her contract may be terminated, the proper legal procedure should be followed to terminate her contract, rather than using "undesirable reassignment" as a substitute.

IN RE SANTEE APPEAL

Supreme Court of Pennsylvania, 1959.
397 Pa. 601, 156 A.2d 830.

PER CURIAM. The decree appealed from is affirmed on the following opinion of Judge Flannery for the court en banc.

"Miss Clara N. Santee has been a professional employee of the School District of the City of Hazleton where, since 1925, she has held the status of a teacher.

"For the school year 1956–1957 she was assigned to the D. A. Harman, Jr. High School teaching English and Mathematics in the 9th grade.

"On August 22, 1957, she was assigned to teach a 6th grade class in the Arthur Street School which assignment she regarded as a demotion and accepted under protest. Her salary was not affected by the transfer and is not here involved.

"Exercising her rights under the School Code she demanded restoration of her previous status and requested a hearing before the School Board. That was granted and her petition was denied. She appealed to the Superintendent of Public Instruction of the Commonwealth of Pennsylvania who, by decision dated June 11, 1958, dismissed her appeal. From that decision she appealed to this Court, and on October 3, 1958, we affirmed the decision and order of the Superintendent of Public Instruction.

* * *

"The question is narrow. Does an assignment from the 9th to the 6th grade constitute a demotion in type of position as contemplated by the Code? We believe it does not.

"The statute provides:

" ' * * * but there shall be no demotion of any professional employe either in salary or in type of position without the consent of the employe, or, if such consent is not received, then such demotion shall be subject to the right to a hearing before the board of school directors and an appeal in the same manner as hereinbefore provided in the case of the dismissal of a professional employe.'

* * *

"There was a salary distinction between 'elementary and secondary schools' under the Act of May 18, 1911, P.L. 309, as amended and revised. * * * But this distinction was swept away in the amendment of July 5, 1947, P.L. 1266, which provided for minimum salaries based on certification and academic qualifications and not on assignment and this system has been retained under the amendments to the Code. * * *

"Thus the Legislature has abolished the legal distinction between elementary and secondary schools and unless we can find in the law some differences between the two in importance, dignity, responsibility, authority and/or prestige—some distinguishing difference—the appellant cannot prevail.

"The definition of professional employee, as mandated in the Code, must be kept in mind. It provides:

" 'The term "professional employe" shall include teachers, supervisors, supervising principals, directors of vocational education, dental hygienists, visiting teachers, school secretaries the selection of whom is on the basis of merit as determined by eligibility lists, school nurses who are certified as teachers and any regular full-time employe of a school district who is duly certified as a teacher.'

* * *

"We construe these to be the 'type of position' referred to in Art. XI, Sec. 1151, which prohibits demotion of any professional employee either in salary or in type of position without the consent of the employee, as we have quoted above. Under this construction the appellant has not been demoted.

"There is no less importance, dignity, responsibility, authority, prestige or compensation in the elementary grades than in secondary. Here the young student still pliant, still susceptible, still in the formative stage, receives his earlier impressions, his inspiration, his direction. Here personality traits are brought out and developed, tastes are instilled, habit patterns are established, character is formed. This is perhaps the most important period of life; the most crucial. The period which may determine a child's ultimate moral, ethical and intellectual stature. To be charged with the responsibility for children in this critical time of their lives is no demotion."

Decree affirmed at appellant's costs.

NOTES

1. Tenure laws are enacted to provide job security to experienced teachers and to insure that they will not be discharged for insufficient and inadequate reasons. A system of tenure has as its objective the maintenance of an able teaching force who have undergone a period of probation with the concomitant result that because of such protections more talented personnel will be attracted to the teaching profession. State v. Redman, 491 P.2d 157 (1971), appeal after remand Redman v. Department of Educ., 519 P.2d 760 (Alaska 1974).

2. The broad purpose of teacher tenure is to protect worthy instructors from enforced yielding to political preferences and to guarantee employment regardless of the vicissitudes of politics. School District No. 8, Pinal County v. Superior Court of Pinal County, 102 Ariz. 478, 433 P.2d 28 (1967).

3. A continuing contract has as one of its central purposes the elimination of uncertainty in the employment plans of both teacher and school district. Peters v. South Kitsap School Dist., No. 402, 8 Wash.App. 809, 509 P.2d 67 (1973).

4. Tenure laws are not grants of power to school districts, but rather constitute a limitation on the power of the school district to freely contract with teachers. Carlson v. School District No. 6 of Maricopa County, 12 Ariz.App. 179, 468 P.2d 944 (1970).

5. Teaching of one-half days during school term does not prevent counting that term toward tenure. Independent School Dist. No. 10 of Seminole County v. Lollar, 547 P.2d 1324 (Okl.App.1976).

6. The Teacher Tenure Act of Colorado creates a contract by law between the school board and its teachers. Sedgewick County v. Ebke, 562 P. 2d 419 (Colo.1977).

7. A transfer involving a reduction in salary may be a violation of a teacher's tenure rights if such protection is expressly provided by statute. Such was the case in People ex rel. Callahan v. Board of Educ., 174 N.Y. 169, 66 N.E. 674 (1903).

8. Some courts construe the term "removal" as used in tenure laws to include a demotion in office by assigning the employee to a lower position with a reduction of compensation. See State v. Avoyelles, 199 La. 859, 7 So.2d 165 (1942).

9. Courts may hold that transfers which involve no salary reduction may violate tenure rights if the new position is of less dignity and prestige. See Smith v. School District No. 18, Pondera County, 115 Mont. 102, 139 P. 2d 518 (1943), and State v. Tangipahoa Parish School Bd., 12 So.2d 496 (La.App.1943).

10. The case of Board of School Trustees v. Moore, 218 Ind. 386, 33 N.E.2d 114 (1941), involved the legality of a salary schedule which provided a separate classification for inefficient, uncooperative, and uninterested teachers. In approving this schedule the Court said:

> In all walks of life it is expected that those who serve best will be appreciated most and will be best remunerated. There is no expression in the law which denies the school authorities the

right to weigh such considerations in classifying teachers and fixing their compensation. But, on the contrary, the vesting of discretion in school officers to maintain the school system for the good of the community would seem to command a consideration of such matters. Teachers' contracts may be canceled by the school authorities for incompetency, insubordination, or neglect of duty, but the statute does not command that contracts be canceled. There are no doubt degrees of incompetency, and insubordination and neglect of duty.

It is argued by the (district) that if teachers become lethargical in professional attitude, manifest defects in practical service, and fail to make progressive development in their qualification for work, and to manifest a seemly interest in the welfare of the schools, the board is confronted with a perplexing problem. It is said that teachers of this type are not essentially bad; that they may be potentially good; that the board may not desire to cancel their contracts, but may feel that something should be done to stimulate a desire upon the part of these teachers to improve their professional ability and service.

11.   In Rible v. Hughes, 24 Cal.2d 437, 150 P.2d 455 (1944), the Court upheld a salary schedule providing for increases for teachers who acquired additional college credits and reductions for those who did not. The Court said:

> The completion of a course of study one summer out of each four has a reasonable relation to a teacher's ability to discharge his professional duties. Although such training may not benefit all teachers equally, the basis of our educational system is that study enlarges one's capacity for accomplishment and leadership in any activity. Very certainly, a permanent teacher of long service, such as Miss Rible, who so far as the record shows, during more than 30 years of school work has not been in touch with any other phase of education than her own teaching, would benefit from college study not only with respect to the specific subjects from which she received credit but also from contact with modern educational processes. The Sacramento salary schedules are based upon this self-evident fact, and the determination of the board of education that compensation should be fixed each year in accordance with an estimation of ability is a reasonable one and, therefore, conclusive upon the courts.

Termination of Employment

Most states have enacted legislation specifying the grounds for and the manner in which a teacher's employment may be terminated. These laws may apply in instances of dismissal during the period of an annual contract or to termination of teachers who have either continuing contracts or tenure. The usual grounds for dismissal are incompetency and insubordination.

Incompetency has been construed by the courts to mean any physical or mental condition which tends to incapacitate a teacher to perform effectively. This rather broad definition has limitations, as noted in *Intille* above, but because of its breadth has been used by many boards as a catch-all for teacher dismissal. Insubordination, on the other hand, is narrower and imports a willful disregard for express or implied directions of the employer and repeated refusal to obey reasonable regulations.[19]

Other grounds for dismissal include immorality, misconduct, neglect of duty and other good or just cause. Every teacher is charged with the responsibility of setting a good example. Not only must a teacher be of good moral character, but her general reputation must attest to this fact. This is somewhat akin to the statement made so often in the trial of criminal cases that not only is a defendant entitled to a fair trial, but the trial should be conducted so fairly that he believes he had a fair trial. A teacher must not only be a moral person, but must conduct herself in such a manner that others will know of her virtue.

Although court's opinions are not uniform on the subject, it may generally be concluded that misconduct is a broader term than immorality and that different standards of proof are required for each.

*Incompetency and Immorality May be Interpreted by
the Courts to Broadly Mean a
General Lack of Fitness*

HOROSKO v. SCHOOL DIST. OF MOUNT PLEASANT

Supreme Court of Pennsylvania, 1939.
335 Pa. 369, 6 A.2d 866.

LINN, Justice. This appeal is from an order of the Superior Court reversing an order of the Common Pleas which had affirmed the action of a school board in discharging a teacher.

* * *

The difference of view between the two learned courts which have considered the case, arises from a different construction of the following provision in section 1205(a), 24 P.S. § 1126(a): "(a) The only valid causes for termination of a contract in accordance with the provisions of this section shall be—Immorality, incompetency, intemperance, cruelty, wilful and persistent negligence, mental derangement, persistent and wilful violation of the school laws of this Commonwealth on the part of the professional employe. * * * "

All the members of this court agree that the Superior Court's construction is much narrower than was apparently intended by the legislature; we also think the case calls for the application of the rule

19. School Dist. No. 8, Pinal County v. Superior Court of Pinal County, 102 Ariz. 478, 433 P.2d 28 (1967).

that findings of fact supported by competent evidence must be accepted on appeal. In the opinion of the Superior Court it is said—"It may be true, as counsel for appellee [the school board] argues, that appellant [teacher] now commands neither the respect nor the good will of the community, but these are not matters which the statute now recognizes as causes for dismissal." If the fact be that she "now commands neither the respect nor the good will of the community" and if the record shows that effect to be the result of her conduct within the clause quoted, it will be conclusive evidence of incompetency. It has always been the recognized duty of the teacher to conduct himself in such way as to command the respect and good will of the community, though one result of the choice of a teacher's vocation may be to deprive him of the same freedom of action enjoyed by persons in other vocations. Educators have always regarded the example set by the teacher as of great importance, particularly in the education of the children in the lower grades such as those attending the school in which this teacher had been employed; it was a country school with eighteen pupils classifying into eight grades.

Difficulties between this teacher and the board had been existing some time and grew out of her conduct with respect to a restaurant maintained by a man whom she married in August 1936, during the course of the period involved. In this restaurant beer was sold and a pin-ball and a slot machine were maintained and dice were played. The restaurant was across the road and about one hundred and twenty five feet from the school. In the opinion filed by the learned trial judge, he said:

"The evidence in the case is that: (1) While Miss Horosko used and was known by the name of Evelyn Horosko she was in fact married to one William Connors and lived with him as his wife; (2) That the said Connors was the proprietor of a lunch room and beer garden in which Evelyn Horosko acted as waitress and, on occasion, as bartender, such services being performed after school hours and during the summer vacation; (3) That in this beer garden and in the presence of several of her pupils whom she was tutoring, she (a) took an occasional drink of beer; (b) served beer to customers; (c) shook dice with customers for drinks; (d) played, and showed customers how to play a pin-ball machine on the premises. And further, that she was rated by A. H. Howell, County Superintendent of Schools, under the rating card provided by the Department of Education, as 43% competent, a rating of 50% being the 'passing' or average rating.

"Is such a course of conduct immoral or intemperate, and does it —in connection with her scholastic and efficiency rating—amount to incompetency? We hold it to be self evident that, under the intent and meaning of the act, immorality is not essentially confined to a deviation from sex morality; it may be such a course of conduct as offends the morals of the community and is a bad example to the youth whose ideals a teacher is supposed to foster and to elevate. Nor need intemperance be confined strictly to overindulgence in alcoholic liquors—temperance implies moderation, and a person may be intemperate in conduct without being an alcoholic addict. And so as to incompetency; as we take it, this means under the Act incompetency as a teacher—but does this mean that competency is merely the ability to teach the 'Three R's'?"

He concluded that it would be "just" (the word used in clause (j) of section 1205) to affirm the action of the school board in dismissing the teacher.

The opinion of the Superior Court is based, as we understand it, on a narrower construction of the word "incompetency" than that adopted by the trial court. The Statutory Construction Act of 1937, P.L. 1019, in section 33, 46 P.S. § 533, provides:

"Words and phrases shall be construed according to rules of grammar and according to their common and approved usage; but technical words and phrases and such others as have acquired a peculiar and appropriate meaning or are defined in this act, shall be construed according to such peculiar and appropriate meaning or definition.

"General words shall be construed to take their meanings and be restricted by preceding particular words."

The provisions of clause (a) which include the words "incompetency" and "immorality", are therefore to be construed "according to their common and approved usage", having regard, of course, to the context in which the legislature used them.

Among the definitions of "immorality" is "conduct inconsistent with moral rectitude." A large body of public opinion regards gambling as immoral. Gambling with a pin-ball or a slot machine, or with dice is prohibited by law. We are not prepared to say the learned judge erred in concluding that the teacher's shaking "dice with customers for drinks" and showing them how to play a pin-ball machine in the presence of school children, supported the finding of incompetency in the circumstances shown.

The term "incompetency" has a "common and approved usage". The context does not limit the meaning of the word to lack of substantive knowledge of the subjects to be taught. Common and approved usage give a much wider meaning. For example, in 31 C.J., with reference to a number of supporting decisions, it is defined: "A relative term without technical meaning. It may be employed as meaning disqualification; inability; incapacity; lack of ability, legal qualifications, or fitness to discharge the required duty." In Black's Law Dictionary, 3rd edition, page 945, and in 1 Bouv.Law Dict., Rawle's Third Revision, p. 1528, it is defined as "Lack of ability or fitness to discharge the required duty." Cases construing the word to the same effect are found in 4 Words and Phrases, First Series, page 3510, and

2 Words and Phrases, Second Series, page 1013. Webster's New International Dictionary defines it as "want of physical, intellectual, or moral ability; insufficiency; inadequacy; specif., want of legal qualifications or fitness.' Funk & Wagnalls Standard Dictionary defines it as "General lack of capacity of fitness, or lack of the special qualities required for a particular purpose."

In the circumstances, therefore, we must conclude that the order made in the Common Pleas was "just".

The order of the Superior Court is reversed and that of the Common Pleas is reinstated; each party to bear its own costs.

Word Misconduct Has Broad Scope and Is More Comprehensive Than Immoral Conduct or Immorality

GOVER v. STOVALL

Court of Appeals of Kentucky, 1931.
237 Ky. 172, 35 S.W.2d 24.

THOMAS, J. The appellant and plaintiff below, L. E. Gover, was employed by the Grayson graded common school board of education, of which appellees are members, as a teacher and as a football coach in the Prichard High School in Grayson, Ky., operated by the board. The employment was for the scholastic year of 1928–29, and, after he had served about one month under his employment, written charges were preferred against him and a trial of them was had before the board, resulting in his discharge. After the termination of the school year he filed this action against defendants in the Carter circuit court to recover judgment against them for $1,025.40, which was the difference between what he had earned and was able to earn during the time of the contract and what defendants agreed to pay him, which was, $1,600, he having earned, according to his petition, $574.60, which included his compensation up to the time he was discharged. The petition averred in general language that defendants discharged him over his protest, and "without sufficient cause and without any sufficient ground therefor." A demurrer filed to it by defendants was sustained, and plaintiff amended, and filed as an exhibit with his amendment what he said was an accurate copy of the testimony heard at his trial before the board, which was taken and transcribed by a stenographer agreed upon by the parties. In that pleading he averred that the only charge in the notice and to which any of the testimony was directed was that of "misconduct," and that the testimony was insufficient to establish it, and that his discharge was illegal and not for any of the grounds enumerated in the statute, which plaintiff alleged was section 4472 of the 1930 edition of Carroll's Statutes, and by reason of which it was unauthorized and wrongful, and that he was entitled to recover judgment for the amount prayed for in his petition. The demurrer was renewed to that amendment, and to the petition as amended, and the court sustained it and dismissed the action, upon plaintiff's refusal to further amend, and complaining of that judgment, he prosecutes this appeal.

The court filed a written opinion and based his judgment therein upon the ground that the action was a collateral attack of the board's dismissal order, which the court treated as a judgment of a duly created court, and, upon the theory that the board had jurisdiction of the subject-matter and of plaintiff's person, its order could not be attacked collaterally. But it is clear to our minds that the court was in error in so concluding. However, since for other reasons we have concluded the judgment was proper and the demurrer was properly sustained to the petition, we will consume neither time nor space in demonstrating the inaccuracy of the court's reason.

* * *

But, we also conclude that upon another ground the court's ruling was proper, even if it had been alleged in plaintiff's pleading that his contract was in writing. He averred, as we have hereinbefore stated, that the applicable statute to his case is section 4472 supra, of our present Statutes, and we think he is correct. It prescribes, inter alia, that an employed teacher may be dismissed by the board employing him "for immorality, misconduct, incompetency, insubordination or willful neglect of duty." The charge contained in the notice in this case, and the proof heard thereon and made a part of plaintiff's pleading, was: That, within a few weeks after plaintiff began his services as teacher under his employment, he and one Jack Jacobs, a young man residing in the town of Grayson where the school was situated, with three young ladies, who were Miss Marjorie Booth, a pupil in the school, and Misses Frances Jones and Irene Martin, went into the school building one night between 8 and 9 o'clock and remained in there from 45 minutes to an hour without turning on any lights, and that they kept such conduct a secret for a couple or more days, when those engaged in it were in some manner discovered. It had been known from the early morning after the escapade that someone had been in the school building the night before, and which was discovered by the janitor, who found bread crumbs, cigarette stubs, and other evidences of some one having been in the building after it was closed the evening before. Plaintiff, upon being asked on cross-examination why he kept the matter a secret, answered, in substance, that he did not want to expose the young ladies. He furthermore said that Jacobs, in the afternoon before the night visit to the schoolhouse was made, informed him of such contemplated party, and he requested Jacobs to "get him in on it," which was done.

Miss Booth, plaintiff's student, was asked:

"Q. If you thought it was not wrong, why did you close the doors? A. We didn't want anyone to watch us. * * *

"Q. Why were you so particular in keeping it away from the superintendent? A. Do you think we would want him to know it if we could get away with it?"

The testimony of the other witnesses was, in substance, to the same effect, but all participants testified that no immoral act was perpetrated or attempted during the stay of the party in the school building, nor did they have any such purpose in view, and the only reason given for not turning on the light (the building being equipped with electric lights) was to keep the matter a secret and that the moon gave sufficient light. The answers to the questions that we have inserted are sufficient to demonstrate a consciousness on the part of plaintiff and his witnesses that their conduct did not measure up to the correct standard, else there would have been no occasion for such cautiousness and secrecy.

Two of the definitions of the word "misconduct" given by Mr. Webster are: "To conduct amiss; bad behavior." The word has a broad scope, and is more comprehensive than "immoral conduct" or "immorality," since the acts composing them must necessarily be immoral in their nature. But, conduct might not be intrinsically immoral and yet be "misconduct" as growing out of the status and social relationship of the one engaged in it. According to the text in 40 C.J. 1220, it is defined as: "Bad behavior; improper conduct; mismanagement; or wrong conduct; in usual parlance, a transgression of some established and definite rule of action, where no discretion is left, except what necessity may demand."

Plaintiff in this case was a teacher in the public schools, and was so circumstanced as that both patrons and pupils regarded him in the light of an exemplar whose conduct might be followed by his pupils, and the law by necessary intendment demands and requires that he should not engage in any conduct inevitably calculated to invite criticism and of a nature and character justly productive of suspicions of immorality. That conduct like that proven against plaintiff was of the nature indicated there can be no doubt, and the testimony to which we have hereinbefore referred is conclusive proof that the participants so regarded it. The statute (section 4472) prescribing the grounds for dismissal employs, among others, the two terms "immorality" and "misconduct," showing that it was the intention and purpose of the Legislature to embrace more conduct than what is properly classified as "immorality" and to incorporate as additional grounds not embraced strictly within its scope, but to also include such other facts as lay within the adjacent zone of "misconduct," and vested the school authorities with a sound discretion to determine the intended application of that term; and, as indicated, we do not believe the board in this case disabused that discretion.

We do not mean by what we have said to prescribe a rule of conduct measuring up to the notions of the self-constituted moralist, nor to require the teacher to abstain from every act that is proscribed by blue law advocates, but we do say that, when he engages in conduct that in the minds of a prudent and cautious person would arouse suspicions of immorality, he is then guilty of such misconduct as is contemplated by the statute. We therefore conclude that the board did not err in finding that the proven and undenied conduct was sufficient ground to authorize plaintiff's dismissal, and the court properly dismissed the action.

Wherefore the judgment is affirmed.

Board's Inference That Teacher's Activities Constituted Social Misbehavior Was Arbitrary and Capricious

FISHER v. SNYDER

United States Court of Appeals, Eighth Circuit, 1973.
476 F.2d 375.

BRIGHT, Circuit Judge. Appellants, as members of the school board of a rural Nebraska county district, dismissed appellee, Frances Fisher, as a high school teacher at the close of the 1972 school year, giving as a reason her "unbecoming conduct" outside the classroom. Mrs. Fisher thereafter brought an action against the members of the board under 42 U.S.C.A. § 1983, alleging that constitutionally impermissible reasons underlay their dismissal action. The district court ordered her reinstatement, and the board members bring this appeal. We affirm the district court.

The relevant facts are not in dispute. Mrs. Fisher, a middle-aged [2] divorcee, was employed at the high school in Tryon, Nebraska, from 1970 to 1972. Her married son, then 26 years old, lived and taught in the neighboring town of Stapleton, Nebraska. Mrs. Fisher lived alone in a one-bedroom apartment. On several occasions, young ladies, married couples, and young men, who were friends of her son, visited Tryon. Because hotel and motel accommodations were generally sparse and unavailable in Tryon, Mrs. Fisher followed the advice of the secretary of the school board and allowed these guests to stay overnight at her apartment. Cliff Rowan, age 26, was a particularly frequent visitor. Rowan's parents lived in California. He, therefore, regularly visited Mrs. Fisher during his school vacations and at other times, and she referred to him as her second son. In the spring of 1972, Rowan spent about a week in Tryon visting school classes as a means of fulfilling certain of his college requirements. Mrs. Fisher made arrangements with school administrators for this visitation and it was reported in the local newspaper.

---

2. Mrs. Fisher's age is not disclosed by the record. The brief filed by amici curiae states that she is 55.

Following Rowan's visit, the school board notified Mrs. Fisher that her contract would not be renewed at the end of the 1972 school year. At her request, pursuant to provisions of Nebraska law, the board afforded Mrs. Fisher a hearing relating to the notice of dismissal. * * *

* * *

Nebraska by statute requires that notice and a hearing be given nontenured teachers who are to be terminated. Neb.Rev.Stat. § 79–1254. The appellees concede that the school board, in dismissing Fisher, complied with the statute, and its judgment, therefore, must be afforded judicial deference "so long as the board does not act unreasonbly, arbitrarily, capriciously, or unlawfully." Smith v. Board of Educ., 365 F.2d 770, 782 (8th Cir. 1966); * * *.

However, a high school teacher may successfully argue that his dismissal was arbitrary and capricious if he can prove:

> * * * that each of the stated reasons [underlying his dismissal] is trivial, or is unrelated to the educational process or to working relationships within the educational institution, or is wholly unsupported by a basis in fact. [McEnteggart v. Cataldo, 451 F.2d 1109, 1111 (1st Cir. 1971), cert. denied, 408 U.S. 943, 92 S.Ct. 2878, 33 L.Ed.2d 767 (1972).]

Thus, while a school board may legitimately inquire into the character and integrity of its teachers, * * * it must be certain that it does not arbitrarily or capriciously dismiss a teacher based on unsupported conclusions drawn from such inquiries.

In seeking to justify the dismissal in this case, the school board argues that the evidence developed at the board hearing supported its finding Mrs. Fisher guilty of conduct unbecoming a teacher. In the board's view, "the inferences from her social behavior are that there was a strong potential of sexual misconduct." The board does not actually accuse Mrs. Fisher of immoral conduct but "of social misbehavior that is not conducive to the maintenance of the integrity of the public school system." * * *

But here, there is no proof of improper conduct. The only whit of evidence offered as support for the board's conclusion that Mrs. Fisher was guilty of unbecoming conduct was the fact that she had overnight guests. But the presence of these guests in her home provides no inkling beyond subtle implication and innuendo which would impugn Mrs. Fishers' morality. Idle speculation certainly does not provide a basis in fact for the board's conclusory inference that "there was strong potential of sexual misconduct" and that, therefore, Mrs. Fisher's activity was "social misbehavior that is not conducive to the maintenance of the integrity of the public school system." We agree with the district court that "At most, the evidence may be said to raise a question of Mrs. Fisher's good judgment in her personal affairs, when measured against an undefined standard which someone could suppose exists in a small town in Nebraska." * * *

The record, furthermore, contains considerable evidence tending to negate any inference of improper or immoral conduct by Mrs. Fisher. She did not attempt to conceal the presence of her house guests but instead openly inquired of the school board's secretary about motel accommodations in Tryon for these guests. She was advised to keep them in her home because other accommodations were so limited. She formally introduced one of her guests at school so that he might observe classes to satisfy college requirements. The local Avon lady, wife of the pastor of a church in Tryon, called at Mrs. Fisher's residence on a Saturday morning during the 1970–1971 school year. Although Mrs. Fisher was apparently awakened by the visit, she invited the pastor's wife into her apartment. A young man who had been an overnight guest was also present in the apartment, and the three drank coffee together.

Two citizens of Tryon called as witnesses for the school board were subpoenaed. Their testimony cast no aspersions upon Mrs. Fisher's character or her fitness as a teacher. No evidence of a community reaction against Mrs. Fisher has been presented, * * * nor has she been shown incapable of maintaining discipline in her classes because of any inferences of impropriety drawn by her students or their parents.

This evidence, in the context of our review of the entire record, convinces us of the correctness of the district court's determination. The openness of the association, and the age differential between Mrs. Fisher and her guests, would seem to belie any inference of impropriety. The school board's inference of misconduct was arbitrary and capricious and therefore constituted an impermissible reason for terminating her employment, since the inference lacked any valid basis in fact.

Accordingly, we affirm the judgment of the district court.

NOTES

1. Where a tenured teacher made statements to an unauthorized assembly of students contradicting statements of the principal and superintendent and encouraging the students not to return to classes, the court held that the teacher's dismissal was valid as constituting insubordination and he was not effectively denied freedom of speech. Whitsell v. Southeast Local School District, 484 F.2d 1222 (6th Cir. 1973).

2. As grounds for dismissal, "immorality" must generally be shown to have an adverse effect upon fitness to teach. Where a teacher had sexual relations with a female minor student, the court held that such conduct was inherently detrimental to the teacher-student relation and was thus injurious to the welfare of the school. Denton v. South Kitsap School District, 10 Wash.App. 69, 516 P.2d 1080 (1973).

3. The conclusion of a board of education that a teacher is unable "to establish rapport with the students," without supporting evidence, is insufficient, standing alone, to establish "good or just cause" for dismissal. Powell v. Board of Trustees of Crook County School Dist. No. 1, 550 P.2d 1112 (Wyo.1976).

Homosexuality of Teacher Is Immorality Justifying Dismissal

GAYLORD v. TACOMA SCHOOL DIST. NO. 10

Supreme Court of Washington, 1977.
88 Wash.2d 286, 559 P.2d 1340.

HOROWITZ, Associate Justice. Plaintiff-appellant, James Gaylord, appeals a judgment of the trial court upholding Gaylord's discharge from employment as a high school teacher by defendant school district. * * *

Defendant school district discharged Gaylord—who held a teacher's certificate—from his teaching position at the Wilson High School in Tacoma on the ground of "immorality" because he was a known homosexual. * * *

We need consider only the assignments of error which raise two basic issues: (1) whether substantial evidence supports the trial court's conclusion plaintiff-appellant Gaylord was guilty of immorality; (2) whether substantial evidence supports the findings, that as a known homosexual, Gaylord's fitness as a teacher was impaired to the injury of the Wilson High School, justifying his discharge by the defendant school district's board of directors. The relevant findings of the trial court may be summarized as follows.

Gaylord knew of his homosexuality for 20 years prior to his trial, actively sought homosexual company for the past several years, and participated in homosexual acts. He knew his status as a homosexual, if known, would jeopardize his employment, damage his reputation and hurt his parents.

Gaylord's school superior first became aware of his sexual status on October 24, 1972, when a former Wilson High student told the school's vice-principal he thought Gaylord was a homosexual. The vice-principal confronted Gaylord at his home that same day with a written copy of the student's statement. Gaylord admitted he was a homosexual and attempted unsuccessfully to have the vice-principal drop the matter.

On November 21, 1972, Gaylord was notified the board of directors of the Tacoma School Board had found probable cause for his discharge due to his status as a publicly known homosexual. This status was contrary to school district policy No. 4119(5), which provides for discharge of school employees for "immorality." After hearing, the defendant board of directors discharged Gaylord effective December 21, 1972.

The court found an admission of homosexuality connotes illegal as well as immoral acts, because "sexual gratification with a member of one's own sex is implicit in the term 'homosexual.'" These acts were proscribed by RCW 9.79.120 (lewdness) and RCW 9.79.100 (sodomy).

After Gaylord's homosexual status became publicly known, it would and did impair his teaching efficiency. A teacher's efficiency is determined by his relationship with his students, their parents, the school administration and fellow teachers. If Gaylord had not been discharged after he became known as a homosexual, the result would be fear, confusion, suspicion, parental concern and pressure on the administration by students, parents and other teachers.

The court concluded "appellant was properly discharged by respondent upon a charge of immorality upon his admission and disclosure that he was a homosexual" and that relief sought should be denied.

Was Gaylord guilty of immorality?

Our concern here is with the meaning of immorality in the sense intended by school board policy No. 4119(5). School boards have broad management powers. RCW 28A.58. Under RCW 28A.58.-100(1) the school board may discharge teachers for "sufficient cause." Policy No. 4119(5) adopted by the school board and in effect during the term of Gaylord's teaching contract with defendant school district permits the Tacoma School Board of Directors to treat "immorality" as sufficient cause for discharge.

"Immorality" as used in policy No. 4119(5) does not stand alone. RCW 28A.67.110 makes it the duty of all teachers to "endeavor to impress on the minds of their pupils the principles of morality, truth, justice, temperance, humanity, and patriotism. * * *" RCW 28A.70.140 requires an applicant for a teacher's certificate be "a person of good moral character." RCW 28A.70.160 makes "immorality" a ground for revoking a teacher's certificate. Other grounds include the commission of "crimes against the laws of the state." The moral conduct of a teacher is relevant to a consideration of that person's fitness or ability to function adequately as a teacher of the students he is expected to teach—in this case high school students. * * *

"Immorality" as a ground of teacher discharge would be unconstitutionally vague if not coupled with resulting actual or prospective adverse performance as a teacher. * * * The basic statute permitting discharge for "sufficient cause" (RCW 28A.58.100(1)) has been construed to require the cause must adversely affect the teacher's performance before it can be invoked as a ground for discharge. * * *

The next question is whether the plaintiff's performance as a teacher was sufficiently impaired by his known homosexuality to be the basis for discharge. The court found that Gaylord, prior to his discharge on December 21, 1972, had been a teacher at the Wilson High School in the Tacoma School District No. 10 for over 12 years, and had received favorable evaluations of his teaching throughout this time. (Findings of fact Nos. 1 and 2). The court further found that "while plaintiff's status as a homosexual [was] unknown to others in the school," his teaching efficiency was not affected nor did his status injure the school. When, however, it became publicly known that Gaylord was a homosexual "the knowledge thereof would and did impair his efficiency as a teacher with resulting injury to the school had he not been discharged." (Finding of fact No. 9).

The court further found:

> A teacher's efficiency is determined by his relationship with students, their parents, fellow teachers and school administrators. In all of these areas the continued employment of appellant after he became known as a homosexual would result, had he not been discharged, in confusion, suspicion, fear, expressed parental concern and pressure upon the administration from students, parents and fellow teachers, all of which would impair appellant's efficiency as a teacher and injure the school.

(Finding of fact No. 10).

Gaylord assigns error to findings of fact numbers 9 and 10, contending there is no substantial evidence to support either. We do not agree.

First, he argues his homosexuality became known at the school only after the school made it known and that he should not be responsible therefor so as to justify his discharge as a homosexual. The difficulty with this argument is twofold. First, by seeking out homosexual company he took the risk his homosexuality would be discovered. It was he who granted an interview to the boy who talked to him about his homosexual problems. The boy had been referred to Gaylord for that purpose by the homosexual friend to whom Gaylord had responded favorably in answering his advertisement in the paper of the Dorian Society. As a result of that interview the boy came away with the impression plaintiff was a homosexual and later told the assistant high school principal about the matter. The latter in turn conferred with plaintiff for the purpose of verifying the charge that had been made. It was the vice-principal's duty to report the information to his superiors because it involved the performance capabilities of Gaylord. The school cannot be charged with making plaintiff's condition known so as to defeat the school board's duty to protect the school and the students against the impairment of the learning process in all aspects involved.

Second, there is evidence that at least one student expressly objected to Gaylord teaching at the high school because of his homosexuality.　Three fellow teachers testified against Gaylord remaining on the teaching staff, testifying it was objectionable to them both as teachers and parents.　The vice-principal and the principal, as well as the retired superintendent of instruction, testified his presence on the faculty would create problems.　There is conflicting evidence on the issue of impairment but the court had the power to accept the testimony it did on which to base complained of findings.　*　*　*　The testimony of the school teachers and administrative personnel constituted substantial evidence sufficient to support the findings as to the impairment of the teacher's efficiency.

It is important to remember that Gaylord's homosexual conduct must be considered in the context of his position of teaching high school students.　Such students could treat the retention of the high school teacher by the school board as indicating adult approval of his homosexuality.　It would be unreasonable to assume as a matter of law a teacher's ability to perform as a teacher required to teach principles of morality (RCW 28A.67.110) is not impaired and creates no danger of encouraging expression of approval and of imitation.　Likewise to say that school directors must wait for prior specific overt expression of homosexual conduct before they act to prevent harm from one who chooses to remain "erotically attracted to a notable degree towards persons of his own sex and is psychologically, if not actually disposed to engage in sexual activity prompted by this attraction" is to ask the school directors to take an unacceptable risk in discharging their fiduciary responsibility of managing the affairs of the school district.

We do not deal here with homosexuality which does not impair or cannot reasonably be said to impair his ability to perform the duties of an occupation in which the homosexual engages and which does not impair the effectiveness of the institution which employs him.　However, even the federal civil service regulations on which Gaylord relies to show a change in attitude towards homosexuals provides:

> [W]hile a person may not be found unsuitable based on unsubstantiated conclusions concerning possible embarrassment to the Federal service, a person may be dismissed or found unsuitable for Federal employment where the evidence establishes that such person's sexual conduct affects job fitness.

2 CCH Employment Practice's Guide ¶ 5339 (1975).　It must be shown that "the conduct of the individual may reasonably be expected to interfere with the ability of the person's fitness in the job or against the ability to discharge its responsibility."　2 CCH, supra.　These principles are similar to those applicable here.　The challenged findings and conclusions are supported by substantial evidence.

Affirmed.

NOTES

1.   Dismissal of a homosexual for immorality by a board of education must demonstrate a rational nexus between the conduct of the teacher and fitness to teach.   A showing of potential rather than actual harm to students will suffice.   Factors such as adverse effect on students or fellow teachers, adversity anticipated within school system, surrounding circumstances and possible chilling effects on discipline may be utilized to establish unfitness. Morrison v. State Board of Educ., 1 Cal.3d 214, 82 Cal.Rptr. 175, 461 P.2d 375 (1969).

2.   The dismissal of a teacher who underwent a change of sex has been held to constitute incapacity.   The tenured teacher changed his external anatomy to that of a female and was subsequently dismissed by the board which reasoned that the situation would cause emotional harm to students. The teacher's proficiency in the classroom was not in question.   According to the court, a teacher's fitness to teach is not based entirely upon academic proficiency but depends on a broad range of factors.   One of those factors, the court said, was the "teacher's impact and effect upon his or her students" and the impact in this case would be harmful to the children.   In re Grossman, 127 N.J. Super. 13, 316 A.2d 39 (1974).

3.   Arrest for homosexual act by a teacher was held to be sufficient grounds for board to dismiss him.   Although the teacher was later acquitted the court held that the difference in burden of proof in criminal and civil cases precludes application of the doctrine of res judicata.   The court said:

> * * * our legislature properly intended by the enactment of the pertinent sections of the Education Code to permit school boards to shield children of tender years from the possible detrimental influence of teachers who commit acts described therein even though they are not found guilty beyond a reasonable doubt * * * the criminal charge between defendant and the state was penal in nature while the case between defendant and the board is remedial, for the protection of young children.

Board of Educ. v. Calderon, 35 Cal.App.3d 490, 110 Cal.Rptr. 916 (1973); See also Pettit v. State Board of Educ., 10 Cal.3d 29, 109 Cal.Rptr. 665, 513 P.2d 889 (1973).

4.   Although illegally obtained evidence cannot be used against defendant teacher for alleged homosexual activity in a criminal proceeding, the same evidence is admissible in an administrative hearing by the school board to determine the teacher's fitness and moral character.   Governing Bd. v. Metcalf, 36 Cal.App.3d 546, 111 Cal.Rptr. 724 (1974).

5.   In a dismissal proceeding for immorality, the school board must relate the immoral conduct to the teacher's fitness.   In so doing the board may consider such matters as age and maturity of teacher's students, likelihood that the conduct will adversely affect students, the degree of adversity, proximity or remoteness of the conduct, the likelihood that the conduct would be repeated, and the underlying motives for the conduct.   Weissman v. Board of Educ. of Jefferson County School Dist. No. R-1, 547 P.2d 1267 (Colo.1976).

Procedural Due Process and the
Nontenured Teacher

Until recently it was generally presumed that teachers without tenure were not entitled to a hearing if they were not rehired at the end of their employment period. In several landmark cases, <u>teachers have maintained that they have a right of procedural due process whether they have statutory tenure or not</u>. In *Roth,* later reversed,[20] a federal district court in Wisconsin concluded that pretermination procedural due process required the following minimum rights:

(1) A statement of the reasons why the university intends not to retain him, to be furnished upon his request;

(2) Notice of a hearing at which he may respond to the stated reasons, to be provided upon his request: [21]

> "At such a hearing the professor must have a reasonable opportunity to submit evidence relevant to the stated reasons. The burden of going forward and the burden of proof rests with the professor. Only if he makes a reasonable showing that the stated reasons are wholly inappropriate as a basis for decision or that they are wholly without basis in fact would the university administration become obliged to show that the stated reasons are not inappropriate or that they have a basis in fact." [22]

The assumption on the part of this court was that a dependency or expectation of continued employment may be established between teacher and institution to such a degree that the termination may constitute a "grievous loss" within scope of the U.S. Supreme Court's rulings in welfare cases. In welfare cases the Supreme Court has held that <u>whether and to what extent procedural due process is afforded the individual is influenced by (a) the extent to which he may be "condemned to suffer grievous loss," and (b) whether the recipient's interest in avoiding that loss outweighs the governmental interest which involves a determination of the "precise nature of the governmental function involved as well as of the private interest that has been affected by government action."</u>[23]

In keeping with this standard the United States Court of Appeals, Fifth Circuit found that <u>a teacher's "expectancy of reemployment"</u>

---

20. Board of Regents of State Colleges v. Roth, 408 U.S. 564, 92 S.Ct. 2701 (1972).

21. William Van Alstyne, "The Constitutional Rights of Teachers and Professors," Duke Law Journal, Vol. 1970, No. 5, p. 851. Copyright © 1970 by Duke Law Journal. Reprinted with permission. Originally published at 1970 Duke L.J. 841.

22. Roth v. Board of Regents, supra.

23. Goldberg v. Kelly, 397 U.S. 254, 90 S.Ct. 1011 (1970).

could be of sufficient import to cause the court to invoke due process requirements.[24] The *Ferguson* court said:

> "* * * [A] college can create an obligation as between itself and an instructor where none might otherwise exist under the legal standards for the interpretation of contract relationships regularly applied to transactions in the market place if it adopts regulations and standards of practice governing nontenured employees which create an expectation of reemployment."[25]

These college cases are equally applicable to teachers in elementary and secondary schools, the test being a balancing of the nature of the government's function against the private interest that has been affected by governmental action.[26] The public schools' interest is the desirability of selecting and retaining an effective and competent teaching staff, while on the other side, the teacher's interest is his future employability, professional reputation and other career interests.[27] In Shrick v. Thomas, the court found that after weighing the teacher's interest against the school's, that due process required that she was entitled to not only a statement of reasons for dismissal, but also notice of a hearing at which she could respond to accusations. The court, however, would not go so far as to say that the teacher had to be furnished in advance with specifications of standards of teacher competence.

Coupled with the "expectancy of reemployment" doctrine, courts, of course, require procedural due process where a teacher can show that his dismissal emanates from an exercise of one of his fundamental freedoms such as free speech, expression and press. The state must show a compelling interest in order to suspend a fundamental right. "Simply because teachers are on the public payroll does not make them second-class citizens in regard to their constitutional rights."[28] Courts will invalidate denial of re-employment where the denial rests on an unconstitutional restriction of a fundamental liberty. In *Pred*, the court said the determination must rest on facts showing whether the denial of a continuing contract was "(a) a reprisal for these actions in expression of ideas, thoughts, or associations rather than permissable nondiscriminatory professional evaluations, and, if so, (b) whether under the circumstances in relation to the reasonable demands of a system of organized responsible learning these actions were protected."[29]

24. Ferguson v. Thomas, 430 F.2d 852 430 F.2d 945 (1st Cir. 1970).

25. Ibid.

26. Shrick v. Thomas, 447 F.2d 1025 (7th Cir. 1971). See also: Gouge v. Joint School District No. 1, 310 F. Supp. 984 (1970); Lucas v. Chapman, 430 F.2d 945 (1st Cir. 1970).

27. Shrick, supra.

28. Pred v. Board of Public Instruction of Dade County, 415 F.2d 851 (5th Cir. 1969).

29. Ibid.

In 1972, the Supreme Court of the United States clarified the rights of nontenure teachers in Board of Regents v. Roth holding that the terms of a nontenure teacher's employment affords no "property" interest in the teaching position. Therefore, to deny it did not require procedural due process. To simply hold a nontenure position does not give a teacher "expectancy of reemployment" requiring procedural due process in order to dismiss. This is true so long as no stigma is attached to his dismissal which would permanently impair his employment opportunities. "The nonretention of respondent, absent any charges against him or stigma or disability foreclosing other employment, are not tantamount to a deprivation of 'liberty' and the terms of respondent's employment accorded him no 'property' interest protected by procedural due process." [30]

The Supreme Court did say, however, in Perry v. Sindermann [31] that a lower federal district court erred in foreclosing determination of a teacher's claim where he alleged that nonrenewal of his contract violated his freedom of speech. In this case the court said that although subjective "expectancy" of tenure is not protected by the due process clause, that it is possible for a college [or school] to have a *de facto* tenure policy which entitled a teacher to a legitimate claim of job tenure which can only be terminated through a hearing process. Although upholding its denial of the validity of "expectancy of reemployment" in *Roth,* the Supreme Court here found an unusual situation where the college had implied a tenure arrangement. In fact, the faculty guide prepared by the college itself stated that "the College wishes the faculty member to feel that he has permanent tenure as long as his teaching services are satisfactory * * *." [32] The court concluded that "there may be an unwritten 'common law' in a particular university that certain employees shall have the equivalent of tenure." [33]

*Procedural Due Process Is Not Required Where Teacher Is
Not Deprived of Constitutional Right*

BOARD OF REGENTS OF STATE COLLEGES v. ROTH

Supreme Court of the United States, 1972.
408 U.S. 564, 92 S.Ct. 2701.

Mr. Justice STEWART delivered the opinion of the Court.

In 1968 the respondent, David Roth, was hired for his first teaching job as assistant professor of political science at Wisconsin State University-Oshkosh. He was hired for a fixed term of one academic year. The notice of his faculty appointment specified that his

30. Board of Regents v. Roth, 408 U.S.   32. Ibid.
   564, 92 S.Ct. 2701 (1972).

                                    33. Ibid.

31. 408 U.S. 593, 92 S.Ct. 2694 (1972).

employment would begin on September 1, 1968, and would end on June 30, 1969. The respondent completed that term. But he was informed that he would not be rehired for the next academic year.

The respondent had no tenure rights to continued employment. Under Wisconsin statutory law a state university teacher can acquire tenure as a "permanent" employee only after four years of year-to-year employment. Having acquired tenure, a teacher is entitled to continued employment "during efficiency and good behavior." A relatively new teacher without tenure, however, is under Wisconsin law entitled to nothing beyond his one-year appointment. There are no statutory or administrative standards defining eligibility for re-employment. State law thus clearly leaves the decision whether to rehire a nontenured teacher for another year to the unfettered discretion of university officials.

The procedural protection afforded a Wisconsin State University teacher before he is separated from the University corresponds to his job security. As a matter of statutory law, a tenured teacher cannot be "discharged except for cause upon written charges" and pursuant to certain procedures. A nontenured teacher, similarly, is protected to some extent *during* his one-year term. Rules promulgated by the Board of Regents provide that a nontenured teacher "dismissed" before the end of the year may have some opportunity for review of the "dismissal." But the Rules provide no real protection for a nontenured teacher who simply is not re-employed for the next year. He must be informed by February 1 "concerning retention or non-retention for the ensuing year." But "no reason for non-retention need be given. No review or appeal is provided in such case."

In conformance with these Rules, the President of Wisconsin State University-Oshkosh informed the respondent before February 1, 1969, that he would not be rehired for the 1969–1970 academic year. He gave the respondent no reason for the decision and no opportunity to challenge it at any sort of hearing.

The respondent then brought this action in Federal District Court alleging that the decision not to rehire him for the next year infringed his Fourteenth Amendment rights. (He attacked the decision both in substance and procedure. First, he alleged that the true reason for the decision was to punish him for certain statements critical of the University administration, and that it therefore violated his right to freedom of speech. Second, he alleged that the failure of University officials to give him notice of any reason for nonretention and an opportunity for a hearing violated his right to procedural due process of law.)

The District Court granted summary judgment for the respondent on the procedural issue, ordering the University officials to provide him with reasons and a hearing. 310 F.Supp. 972. The Court of Appeals, with one judge dissenting, affirmed this partial summary judgment.　446 F.2d 806.　We granted certiorari.　404 U.S. 909, 92 S.Ct. 227, 30 L.Ed.2d 181.　<u>The only question presented to us at this stage in the case is whether the respondent had a constitutional right to a statement of reasons and a hearing on the University's decision not to rehire him for another year.　We hold that he did not</u>.

I

The requirements of procedural due process apply only to the deprivation of interests encompassed by the Fourteenth Amendment's protection of liberty and property.　When protected interests are implicated, the right to some kind of prior hearing is paramount.　But the range of interests protected by procedural due process is not infinite.

The District Court decided that procedural due process guarantees apply in this case by assessing and balancing the weights of the particular interests involved.　It concluded that the respondent's interest in re-employment at Wisconsin State University-Oshkosh outweighed the University's interest in denying him re-employment summarily.　310 F.Supp., at 977–979.　Undeniably, the respondent's re-employment prospects were of major concern to him—concern that we surely cannot say was insignificant.　And a weighing process has long been a part of any determination of the *form* of hearing required in particular situations by procedural due process.　But, to determine whether due process requirements apply in the first place, we must look not to the "weight" but to the *nature* of the interest at stake.　* * *　We must look to see if the interest is within the Fourteenth Amendment's protection of liberty and property.

"Liberty" and "property" are broad and majestic terms.　They are among the "[g]reat [constitutional] concepts　* * *　purposely left to gather meaning from experience.　* * *　[T]hey relate to the whole domain of social and economic fact, and the statesmen who founded this Nation knew too well that only a stagnant society remains unchanged."　National Mutual Ins. Co. v. Tidewater Transfer Co., 337 U.S. 582, 646, 69 S.Ct. 1173, 1195, 93 L.Ed. 1556 (Frankfurter, J., dissenting).　For that reason, the Court has fully and finally rejected the wooden distinction between "rights" and "privileges" that once seemed to govern the applicability of procedural due process rights.　The Court has also made clear that the property interests protected by procedural due process extend well beyond actual ownership of real estate, chattels, or money.　By the same token, the Court has required due process protection for deprivations of liberty beyond the sort of formal constraints imposed by the criminal process.

Yet, while the Court has eschewed rigid or formalistic limitations on the protection of procedural due process, it has at the same time observed certain boundaries.　For the words "liberty" and "property" in the Due Process Clause of the Fourteenth Amendment must be given some meaning.

II

"While this court has not attempted to define with exactness the liberty * * * guaranteed [by the Fourteenth Amendment], the term has received much consideration and some of the included things have been definitely stated. Without doubt, it denotes not merely freedom from bodily restraint but also the right of the individual to contract, to engage in any of the common occupations of life, to acquire useful knowledge, to marry, establish a home and bring up children, to worship God according to the dictates of his own conscience, and generally to enjoy those privileges long recognized * * * as essential to the orderly pursuit of happiness by free men." Meyer v. Nebraska, 262 U.S. 390, 399, 43 S.Ct. 625, 626, 67 L. Ed. 1042. In a Constitution for a free people, there can be no doubt that the meaning of "liberty" must be broad indeed. See e. g., Bolling v. Sharpe, 347 U.S. 497, 499–500, 74 S.Ct. 693, 694, 98 L.Ed. 884; Stanley v. Illinois, 405 U.S. 645, 92 S.Ct. 1208, 31 L.Ed.2d 551.

There might be cases in which a State refused to re-employ a person under such circumstances that interests in liberty would be implicated. But this is not such a case.

The State, in declining to rehire the respondent, did not make any charge against him that might seriously damage his standing and associations in his community. It did not base the nonrenewal of his contract on a charge, for example, that he had been guilty of dishonesty, or immorality. Had it done so, this would be a different case. For "[w]here a person's good name, reputation, honor, or integrity is at stake because of what the government is doing to him, notice and an opportunity to be heard are essential." * * * In such a case, due process would accord an opportunity to refute the charge before University officials. In the present case, however, there is no suggestion whatever that the respondent's "good name, reputation, honor, or integrity" is at stake.

Similarly, there is no suggestion that the State, in declining to re-employ the respondent, imposed on him a stigma or other disability that foreclosed his freedom to take advantage of other employment opportunities. The State, for example, did not invoke any regulations to bar the respondent from all other public employment in state universities. Had it done so, this, again, would be a different case. For "[t]o be deprived not only of present government employment but of future opportunity for it certainly is no small injury * * *."

To be sure, the respondent has alleged that the nonrenewal of his contract was based on his exercise of his right to freedom of speech. But this allegation is not now before us. The District Court stayed proceedings on this issue, and the respondent has yet to prove that the decision not to rehire him was in fact based on his free speech activities.

Hence, on the record before us, all that clearly appears is that the respondent was not rehired for one year at one university. It stretches the concept too far to suggest that a person is deprived of "liberty" when he simply is not rehired in one job but remains as free as before to seek another.   *   *   *

III

The Fourteenth Amendment's procedural protection of property is a safeguard of the security of interests that a person has already acquired in specific benefits. These interests—property interests— may take many forms.

Thus, the Court has held that a person receiving welfare benefits under statutory and administrative standards defining eligibility for them has an interest in continued receipt of those benefits that is safeguarded by procedural due process. Goldberg v. Kelly, 397 U.S. 254, 90 S.Ct. 1011, 25 L.Ed.2d 287.   *   *   * Similarly, in the area of public employment, the Court has held that a public college professor dismissed from an office held under tenure provisions, Slochower v. Board of Education, 350 U.S. 551, 76 S.Ct. 637, 100 L.Ed. 692, and college professors and staff members dismissed during the terms of their contracts, Wieman v. Updegraff, 344 U.S. 183, 73 S.Ct. 215, 97 L.Ed. 216, have interests in continued employment that are safeguarded by due process. Only last year, the Court held that this principle "proscribing summary dismissal from public employment without hearing or inquiry required by due process" also applied to a teacher recently hired without tenure or a formal contract, but nonetheless with a clearly implied promise of continued employment. Connell v. Higginbotham, 403 U.S. 207, 208, 91 S.Ct. 1772, 1773, 29 L.Ed.2d 418.

Certain attributes of "property" interests protected by procedural due process emerge from these decisions. To have a property interest in a benefit, a person clearly must have more than an abstract need or desire for it. He must have more than a unilateral expectaiton of it. He must, instead, have a legitimate claim of entitlement to it. It is a purpose of the ancient institution of property to protect those claims upon which people rely in their daily lives, reliance that must not be arbitrarily undermined. It is a purpose of the constitutional right to a hearing to provide an opportunity for a person to vindicate those claims.

Property interests, of course, are not created by the Constitution. Rather they are created and their dimensions are defined by existing rules or understandings that stem from an independent source such as state law—rules or understandings that secure certain benefits and that support claims of entitlement to those benefits. Thus, the welfare recipients in Goldberg v. Kelly, supra, had a claim of entitlement to welfare payments that was grounded in the statute defining eligibility for them. The recipients had not yet shown that they were, in fact, within the statutory terms of eligibility. But we held that they had a right to a hearing at which they might attempt to do so.

Just as the welfare recipients' "property" interest in welfare payments was created and defined by statutory terms, so the respondent's "property" interest in employment at Wisconsin State University-Oshkosh was created and defined by the terms of his appointment. Those terms secured his interest in employment up to June 30, 1969. But the important fact in this case is that they specifically provided that the respondent's employment was to terminate on June 30. They did not provide for contract renewal absent "sufficient cause." Indeed, they made no provision for renewal whatsoever.

Thus, the terms of the respondent's appointment secured absolutely no interest in re-employment for the next year. They supported absolutely no possible claim of entitlement to re-employment. Nor, significantly, was there any state statute or University rule or policy that secured his interest in re-employment or that created any legitimate claim to it. In these circumstances, the respondent surely had an abstract concern in being rehired, but he did not have a *property* interest sufficient to require the University authorities to give him a hearing when they declined to renew his contract of employment.

IV

Our analysis of the respondent's constitutional rights in this case in no way indicates a view that an opportunity for a hearing or a statement of reasons for nonretention would, or would not, be appropriate or wise in public colleges and universities. For it is a written Constitution that we apply. Our role is confined to interpretation of that Constitution.

We must conclude that the summary judgment for the respondent should not have been granted, since the respondent has not shown that he was deprived of liberty or property protected by the Fourteenth Amendment. The judgment of the Court of Appeals, accordingly, is reversed and the case is remanded for further proceedings consistent with this opinion. It is so ordered.

Teacher with De Facto Tenure Is Entitled to a Hearing
Before Termination of Employment

PERRY v. SINDERMANN

Supreme Court of the United States, 1972.
408 U.S. 593, 92 S.Ct. 2694.

Mr. Justice STEWART delivered the opinion of the Court.

From 1959 to 1969 the respondent, Robert Sindermann, was a teacher in the state college system of the State of Texas. After teaching for two years at the University of Texas and for four years at San Antonio Junior College, he became a professor of Government and Social Science at Odessa Junior College in 1965. He was employed at the college for four successive years, under a series of one-year contracts. He was successful enough to be appointed, for a time, the cochairman of his department.

During the 1968–1969 academic year, however, controversy arose between the respondent and the college administration. The respondent was elected president of the Texas Junior College Teachers Association. In this capacity, he left his teaching duties on several occasions to testify before committees of the Texas Legislature, and he became involved in public disagreements with the policies of the college's Board of Regents. In particular, he aligned himself with a group advocating the elevation of the college to four-year status—a change opposed by the Regents. And, on one occasion, a newspaper advertisement appeared over his name that was highly critical of the Regents.

Finally, in May 1969, the respondent's one-year employment contract terminated and the Board of Regents voted not to offer him a new contract for the next academic year. The Regents issued a press release setting forth allegations of the respondent's insubordination. But they provided him no official statement of the reasons for the nonrenewal of his contract. And they allowed him no opportunity for a hearing to challenge the basis of the nonrenewal.

The respondent then brought this action in Federal District Court. He alleged primarily that the Regents' decision not to rehire him was based on his public criticism of the policies of the college administration and thus infringed his right to freedom of speech. He also alleged that their failure to provide him an opportunity for a hearing violated the Fourteenth Amendment's guarantee of procedural due process. The petitioners—members of the Board of Regents and the president of the college—denied that their decision was made in retaliation for the respondent's public criticism and argued that they had no obligation to provide a hearing. On the basis of these bare pleadings and three brief affidavits filed by the respondent, the District Court granted summary judgment for the petitioners. It concluded that the respondent had "no cause of action against the [petitioners] since his contract of employment terminated May 31, 1969, and Odessa Junior College has not adopted the tenure system".

The Court of Appeals reversed the judgment of the District Court. 430 F.2d 939. First, it held that, despite the respondent's lack of tenure, the nonrenewal of his contract would violate the Fourteenth Amendment if it in fact was based on his protected free speech. Since the actual reason for the Regents' decision was "in total dispute" in the pleadings, the court remanded the case for a full hearing on this contested issue of fact. Id. at 942–943. Second, the Court of Appeals held that, despite the respondent's lack of tenure, the failure to allow him an opportunity for a hearing would violate the constitutional guarantee of procedural due process if the respondent could show that he had an "expectancy" of re-employment. It, therefore, ordered that this issue of fact also be aired upon remand. Id. at 943–944. We granted a writ of certiorari, 403 U.S. 917, 91 S. Ct. 2226, 29 L.Ed.2d 694, and we have considered this case along with Board of Regents v. Roth, 408 U.S. 564, 92 S.Ct. 2701, 33 L.Ed.2d 548.

I

The first question presented is whether the respondent's lack of a contractual or tenure right to re-employment, taken alone, defeats his claim that the nonrenewal of his contract violated the First and Fourteenth Amendments. We hold that it does not.

For at least a quarter-century, this Court has made clear that even though a person has no "right" to a valuable governmental benefit and even though the government may deny him the benefit for any number of reasons, there are some reasons upon which the government may not rely. It may not deny a benefit to a person on a basis that infringes his constitutionally protected interests—especially, his interest in freedom of speech. For if the government could deny a benefit to a person because of his constitutionally protected speech or associations, his exercise of those freedoms would in effect be penalized and inhibited. This would allow the government to "produce a result which [it] could not command directly." Speiser v. Randall, 357 U.S. 513, 526, 78 S.Ct. 1332, 1342, 2 L.Ed.2d 1460. Such interference with constitutional rights is impermissible.

   *   *   *

Thus, the respondent's lack of a contractual or tenure "right" to re-employment for the 1969–1970 academic year is immaterial to his free speech claim. Indeed, twice before, this Court has specifically held that the nonrenewal of a nontenured public school teacher's one-year contract may not be predicated on his exercise of First and Fourteenth Amendment rights. * * * We reaffirm those holdings here.

In this case, of course, the respondent has yet to show that the decision not to renew his contract was, in fact, made in retaliation for his exercise of the constitutional right of free speech. The District Court foreclosed any opportunity to make this showing when it granted summary judgment. Hence, we cannot now hold that the Board of Regents' action was invalid.

But we agree with the Court of Appeals that there is a genuine dispute as to "whether the college refused to renew the teaching contract on an impermissible basis—as a reprisal for the exercise of constitutionally protected rights." 430 F.2d, at 943. The respondent has alleged that his nonretention was based on his testimony before legislative committees and his other public statements critical of the Regents' policies. And he has alleged that this public criticism was within the First and Fourteenth Amendments' protection of freedom of speech. Plainly, these allegations present a bona fide constitutional claim. For this Court has held that a teacher's public criticism of his superiors on matters of public concern may be constitutionally protected and may, therefore, be an impermissible basis for termination of his employment. Pickering v. Board of Education, supra.

For this reason we hold that the grant of summary judgment against the respondent, without full exploration of this issue, was improper.

II

The respondent's lack of formal contractual or tenure security in continued employment at Odessa Junior College, though irrelevant to his free speech claim, is highly relevant to his procedural due process claim. But it may not be entirely dispositive.

We have held today in Board of Regents v. Roth, 408 U.S. 564, 92 S.Ct. 2701, that the Constitution does not require opportunity for a hearing before the nonrenewal of a nontenured teacher's contract, unless he can show that the decision not to rehire him somehow deprived him of an interest in "liberty" or that he had a "property" interest in continued employment, despite the lack of tenure or a formal contract. In Roth the teacher had not made a showing on either point to justify summary judgment in his favor.

Similarly, the respondent here has yet to show that he has been deprived of an interest that could invoke procedural due process protection. As in Roth, the mere showing that he was not rehired in one particular job, without more, did not amount to a showing of a loss of liberty. Nor did it amount to a showing of a loss of property.

But the respondent's allegations—which we must construe most favorably to the respondent at this stage of the litigation—do raise a genuine issue as to his interest in continued employment at Odessa Junior College. He alleged that this interest, though not secured by a formal contractual tenure provision, was secured by a no less binding understanding fostered by the college administration. In particular, the respondent alleged that the college had a _de facto_ tenure program, and that he had tenure under that program. He claimed that he and others legitimately relied upon an unusual provision that had been in the college's official Faculty Guide for many years:

> "_Teacher Tenure_: Odessa College has no tenure system. The Administration of the College wishes the faculty member to feel that he has permanent tenure as long as his teaching services are satisfactory and as long as he displays a cooperative attitude toward his co-workers and his superiors, and as long as he is happy in his work."

Moreover, the respondent claimed legitimate reliance upon guidelines promulgated by the Coordinating Board of the Texas College and University System that provided that a person, like himself, who had been employed as a teacher in the state college and university system for seven years or more has some form of job tenure. Thus, the respondent offered to prove that a teacher with his long period of service at this particular State College had no less a "property" interest in continued employment than a formally tenured teacher at other colleges, and had no less a procedural due process right to a statement of reasons and a hearing before college officials upon their decision not to retain him.

We have made clear in _Roth_, * * * that "property" interests subject to procedural due process protection are not limited by a few rigid, technical forms. Rather, "property" denotes a broad range of interests that are secured by "existing rules or understandings." * * * A person's interest in a benefit is a "property" interest for due process purposes if there are such rules or mutually explicit understandings that support his claim of entitlement to the benefit and that he may invoke at a hearing. Ibid.

A written contract with an explicit tenure provision clearly is evidence of a formal understanding that supports a teacher's claim of entitlement to continued employment unless sufficient "cause" is shown. Yet absence of such an explicit contractual provision may not always foreclose the possibility that a teacher has a "property" interest in reemployment. For example, the law of contracts in most, if not all, jurisdictions long has employed a process by which agreements, though not formalized in writing, may be "implied." 3 A. Corbin on Contracts §§ 561–572A. Explicit contractual provisions may be supplemented by other agreements implied from "the promisor's words and conduct in the light of the surrounding circumstances." Id., at § 562. And, "[t]he meaning of [the promisor's] words and acts is found by relating them to the usage of the past." Ibid.

A teacher, like the respondent, who has held his position for a number of years, might be able to show from the circumstances of this service—and from other relevant facts—that he has a legitimate claim of entitlement to job tenure. Just as this Court has found there to be a "common law of a particular industry or of a particular plant" that may supplement a collective-bargaining agreement, United Steelworkers v. Warrior & Gulf Nav. Co., 363 U.S. 574, 579 * * * so, there may be an unwritten "common law" in a particular university that certain employees shall have the equivalent of tenure. This is particularly likely in a college or university, like Odessa Junior College, that has no explicit tenure system even for senior members of its faculty, but that nonetheless may have created such a system in practice. * * *

In this case, the respondent has alleged the existence of rules and understandings, promulgated and fostered by state officials, that may justify his legitimate claim of entitlement to continued employment absent "sufficient cause." We disagree with the Court of Appeals insofar as it held that a mere subjective "expectancy" is protected by procedural due process, but we agree that the respondent must be given an opportunity to prove the legitimacy of his claim of such entitlement in light of "the policies and practices of the institution." 430 F.2d, at 943. Proof of such a property interest would not, of course, entitle him to reinstatement. But such proof would obligate college officials to grant a hearing at his request, where he could be informed of the grounds for his nonretention and challenge their sufficiency.

Therefore, while we do not wholly agree with the opinion of the Court of Appeals, its judgment remanding this case to the District Court is affirmed.

Affirmed.

Mr. Justice POWELL took no part in the decision of this case.

NOTES

1. Procedural Due Process for Teachers

William Van Alstyne in the Duke Law Journal says that a rather "full panoply of particular procedural rights" for teachers might include all of the following.

"(1) Terminal action may not be taken other than pursuant to regularly established rules or standards which have been made available to the employee and which are reasonably precise and clear.

(2) Proceedings to terminate the employee must be preceded by specific notice of charges providing a statement of facts sufficient to warrant the action contemplated. Adequate time must be provided to enable the employee to prepare for the ensuing hearing, and a list of witnesses plus access to other evidence proposed for introduction at the hearing must be made available to him on request.

(3) The hearing must be held before an impartial trier of fact, the outcome of the hearing determined solely on the basis of material

placed in evidence in the course of the hearing, and a record must be made of the proceedings.

(4) The employee may be represented by counsel present during the proceedings; the employer must provide notice that counsel will be furnished upon request in the event the employee is unable to retain counsel.

(5) The employee is entitled to know the evidence offered against him, to confront adverse witnesses, to conduct cross-examination either personally or through counsel, to offer evidence and witnesses in his own behalf, and to testify in his own behalf or decline to do so within the privilege against self-incrimination.

(6) The teacher may appeal an adverse decision by briefs and oral argument, based on the record with the scope of review *de novo* on alleged errors of law (that is, an incorrect interpretation of the allegedly infringed rule) and limited on findings of fact to determine whether they are supported by substantial evidence in the record considered as a whole.

In fact, however, probably no instance of teacher termination would activate all of these possible procedural rights as a matter of constitutional law, and the particular combination of any two or more of them will vary in an extraordinary fashion depending upon a number of considerations."

William Van Alstyne, "The Constitutional Rights of Teachers and Professors," Duke Law Journal, Vol. 1970, No. 5, pp. 864–865.

2. The Supreme Court of Utah upheld the dismissal of a career (tenure) teacher for insubordination when he refused to accept a transfer to another school, which was recommended by the superintendent because of the friction which arose between the teacher and other certified personnel. Brough v. Board of Education of Millard County School District, 23 Utah 2d 174, 460 P.2d 336 (1970), rehearing denied 23 Utah 2d 253, 463 P.2d 567, certiorari denied 398 U.S. 928, 90 S.Ct. 1818.

3. Nonreemployment without a hearing of a nontenured teacher because of general ineffectiveness as a teacher does not violate the First and Fourteenth Amendments. Robinson v. Jefferson County Board of Education, 485 F.2d 1381 (5th Cir. 1973), rehearing denied 488 F.2d 1055.

4. Where a nontenured teacher had taught for ten years in a state with no tenure law and was not rehired, the court held that no substantive due process rights existed on behalf of the teacher which would invoke a cause of action under the Civil Rights Act § 1983, even though the only rationale used by the school board for dismissal was that the students of the teacher scored below expected levels on achievement tests. Scheelhaase v. Woodbury Central Community School District, 488 F.2d 237 (8th Cir. 1973).

5. Nontenured teacher's claim of entitlement to a position was, under the Illinois Tenure Act, insufficient to constitute a property interest within the Fourteenth Amendment. Appellant was unable to show that the tenure law limited in any way the authority of the school board to terminate employment prior to acquiring tenure status. Miller v. School District Number 167, Cook County, Illinois, 500 F.2d 711 (7th Cir. 1974).

6. Probationary teacher had no expectancy of reemployment vesting him with a property interest. McCullough v. Lohn, 483 F.2d 34 (5th Cir. 1973).

7. Where nontenured teacher was indicted for alleged sexual misconduct with students, the court held that, should he be convicted, the school board was not obligated to provide him with a hearing, however, in the event that he is exonerated by the court, the school board must provide a hearing in order for him to clear his name. The court found, in referring to Roth, though, that where a teacher is indicted it is not the obligation of the school board to hold a hearing prior to his trial in order to determine his guilt or innocence. To do so, according to the court, would have placed the board in the untenable position of dispensing findings which "in one direction would have injured the interests of the state, and in another direction would have damaged those of the teacher." Moore v. Knowles, 482 F. 2d 1069 (5th Cir. 1973).

8. A nontenured faculty member was held entitled to a hearing where the principal cause of his nonreappointment was the allegation that he was a racist. Wellner v. Minnesota State Junior College Board, 487 F.2d 153 (8th Cir. 1973).

9. Notice of nonrenewal of a nontenured teacher which is not posted nor published does not create a "stigma" upon the teacher's good name, reputation, honor or integrity sufficient to deprive her of "liberty" under the Fourteenth Amendment. Shirck v. Thomas, 486 F.2d 691 (7th Cir. 1973).

10. Where nontenured elementary teachers distributed a poem to students imploring them to throw off the dull discipline of the moral environment of their home life and enter into a new world of love and freedom—freedom to use acid and grass, freedom to engage in sexual activities, and freedom to use vulgarities, the court denied the teachers recovery under the Civil Rights Act. In so doing the court commented:

> "We do not believe that however much the reach of the First Amendment has been extended and however eager today's courts have been to protect the many varieties of claims to civil rights, the appellee school board had to put up with the described conduct of appellants."

Brubaker v. Board of Education, School District 149, Cook County, Illinois, 502 F.2d 973 (7th Cir. 1974).

11. A United States District Court in Minnesota listed five occasions where Roth and Sindermann dictated a hearing on nonrenewal:

a. Where the contract nonrenewal is related to the teacher's exercise of freedom of speech under the First Amendment.

b. Where the teacher is confronted with a charge that might seriously damage his or her standing and associations in the community.

c. Where the failure to reemploy the teacher imposes a stigma or other disability on him or her which forecloses future freedom to take advantage of other employment opportunities.

d. Where the teacher, by virtue of existing state policies, the contract terms, or similar understandings, has a reasonable expectancy of reemployment.

e. Where the adverse reports on which action is taken are prepared by the school's superiors or plaintiffs' compatriots and are fabricated, without any foundation or basis in fact whatsoever or are maliciously designed so as to use the freedom of the probationary period for reasons of personal calumny, hatred, vindication or dislike thus using the probationary period as a sword rather than a shield. Ferris v. Special School District No. 1, 367 F.Supp. 459 (D.Minn. 1973).

12. Where there was evidence that teachers' contracts had not been renewed in retaliation for their public comments regarding teacher's salaries and affiliation with a teacher's association, the court held that the nonrenewal of their contracts violated their First Amendment rights of freedom of speech and association. Greminger v. Seaborne, 584 F.2d 275 (8th Cir. 1978).

13. Allegation by teacher that nonrenewal of his contract was due to failure to shave his beard was held by the court to be unfounded and wholly insubstantial. Ball v. Board of Trustees of Kerrville, 584 F.2d 684 (5th Cir. 1978). See also: Carmichael v. Chambers County Bd. of Educ., 581 F. 2d 95 (5th Cir. 1978); Cain v. McQueen, 580 F.2d 1001 (9th Cir. 1978); Graves v. Duganne, 581 F.2d 222 (9th Cir. 1978).

Mandatory Leave for Pregnancy

Under the Due Process Clause an individual is protected from official acts which create "irrebuttable presumptions" thereby confining a person to a particular classification. This is a substantive aspect of due process which has been utilized by the court to proscribe arbitrary and overly broad generalizations which may or may not apply to each and every person. This principle can easily be seen when applied to the pregnancy of teachers in the public schools. While pregnancy may incapacitate some women after a given number of months, rendering them unable to effectively carry forth their duties, it is unreasonable to assume that all women are subject to the same limitations in the same manner and time frame. To assume so and to regulate the female teaching force accordingly, creates an unconstitutional presumption of their inability to teach.

Mandatory Leave Rules and Arbitrary Cut-off Dates
for Pregnant Teachers Violate Due Process

CLEVELAND BD. OF EDUC. v. LaFLEUR

Supreme Court of the United States, 1974.
414 U.S. 632, 94 S.Ct. 791.

Mr. Justice STEWART delivered the opinion of the Court.

The respondents in No. 72–777 and the petitioner in No. 72–1129 are female public school teachers. During the 1970–1971 school year, each informed her local school board that she was pregnant; each was compelled by a mandatory maternity leave rule to quit her job without pay several months before the expected birth of her child. These cases call upon us to decide the constitutionality of the school boards' rules.

I

Jo Carol LaFleur and Ann Elizabeth Nelson, the respondents in No. 72–777, are junior high school teachers employed by the Board of Education of Cleveland, Ohio. Pursuant to a rule first adopted in 1952, the school board requires every pregnant school teacher to take maternity leave without pay, beginning five months before the expected birth of her child. Application for such leave must be made no later than two weeks prior to the date of departure. A teacher on maternity leave is not allowed to return to work until the beginning of the next regular school semester which follows the date when her child attains the age of three months. A doctor's certificate attesting to the health of the teacher is a prerequisite to return; an additional physical examination may be required. The teacher on maternity leave is not promised re-employment after the birth of the child; she is merely given priority in reassignment to a position for which she is qualified. Failure to comply with the mandatory maternity leave provisions is ground for dismissal.

* * *

The petitioner in No. 72–1129, Susan Cohen, was employed by the School Board of Chesterfield County, Virginia. That school board's maternity leave regulation requires that a pregnant teacher leave work at least four months prior to the expected birth of her child. Notice in writing must be given to the school board at least six months prior to the expected birth date. A teacher on maternity leave is declared re-eligible for employment when she submits written notice from a physician that she is physically fit for re-employment, and when she can give assurance that care of the child will cause only minimal interference with her job responsibilities. * * *

* * *

II

This Court has long recognized that freedom of personal choice in matters of marriage and family life is one of the liberties protected by the Due Process Clause of the Fourteenth Amendment. * * * there is a right "to be free from unwarranted governmental intrusion into matters so fundamentally affecting a person as the decision whether to bear or beget a child."

By acting to penalize the pregnant teacher for deciding to bear a child, overly restrictive maternity leave regulations can constitute a heavy burden on the exercise of these protected freedoms. Because public school maternity leave rules directly affect "one of the basic civil rights of man," Skinner v. Oklahoma, supra, 316 U.S., at 541, 62

S.Ct., at 1113, the Due Process Clause of the Fourteenth Amendment requires that such rules must not needlessly, arbitrarily, or capriciously impinge upon this vital area of a teacher's constitutional liberty. The question before us in these cases is whether the interests advanced in support of the rules of the Cleveland and Chesterfield County School Boards can justify the particular procedures they have adopted.

The school boards in these cases have offered two essentially overlapping explanations for their mandatory maternity leave rules. First, they contend that the firm cutoff dates are necessary to maintain continuity of classroom instruction, since advance knowledge of when a pregnant teacher must leave facilitates the finding and hiring of a qualified substitute. Secondly, the school boards seek to justify their maternity rules by arguing that at least some teachers become physically incapable of adequately performing certain of their duties during the latter part of pregnancy. By keeping the pregnant teacher out of the classroom during these final months, the maternity leave rules are said to protect the health of the teacher and her unborn child, while at the same time assuring that students have a physically capable instructor in the classroom at all times.

It cannot be denied that continuity of instruction is a significant and legitimate educational goal. Regulations requiring pregnant teachers to provide early notice of their condition to school authorities undoubtedly facilitate administrative planning toward the important objective of continuity. But, as the Court of Appeals for the Second Circuit noted in Green v. Waterford Board of Education, 473 F.2d 629, 635:

> "Where a pregnant teacher provides the Board with a date certain for commencement of leave * * * that value [continuity] is preserved; an arbitrary leave date set at the end of the fifth month is no more calculated to facilitate a planned and orderly transition between the teacher and a substitute than is a date fixed closer to confinement. Indeed, the latter * * * would afford the Board more, not less, time to procure a satisfactory long-term substitute." (Footnote omitted.)

Thus, while the advance-notice provisions in the Cleveland and Chesterfield County rules are wholly rational and may well be necessary to serve the objective of continuity of instruction, the absolute requirements of termination at the end of the fourth or fifth month of pregnancy are not. Were continuity the only goal, cutoff dates much later during pregnancy would serve as well as or better than the challenged rules, providing that ample advance notice requirements were retained. Indeed, continuity would seem just as well attained if the teacher herself were allowed to choose the date upon which to commence her leave, at least so long as the decision were required to be made and notice given of it well in advance of the date selected.

In fact, since the fifth or sixth month of pregnancy will obviously begin at different times in the school year for different teachers, the present Cleveland and Chesterfield County rules may serve to hinder attainment of the very continuity objectives that they are purportedly designed to promote. For example, the beginning of the fifth month of pregnancy for both Mrs. LaFleur and Mrs. Nelson occurred during March of 1971. Both were thus required to leave work with only a few months left in the school year, even though both were fully willing to serve through the end of the term. Similarly, if continuity were the only goal, it seems ironic that the Chesterfield County rule forced Mrs. Cohen to leave work in mid-December 1970 rather than at the end of the semester in January as she requested.

We thus conclude that the arbitrary cutoff dates embodied in the mandatory leave rules before us have no rational relationship to the valid state interest of preserving continuity of instruction. As long as the teachers are required to give substantial advance notice of their condition, the choice of firm dates later in pregnancy would serve the boards' objectives just as well, while imposing a far lesser burden on the women's exercise of constitutionally protected freedom.

The question remains as to whether the cutoff dates at the beginning of the fifth and sixth months can be justified on the other ground advanced by the school boards—the necessity of keeping physically unfit teachers out of the classroom. There can be no doubt that such an objective is perfectly legitimate, both on educational and safety grounds. And, despite the plethora of conflicting medical testimony in these cases, we can assume, *arguendo*, that at least some teachers become physically disabled from effectively performing their duties during the latter stages of pregnancy.

The mandatory termination provisions of the Cleveland and Chesterfield County rules surely operate to insulate the classroom from the presence of potentially incapacitated pregnant teachers. But the question is whether the rules sweep too broadly. * * *

That question must be answered in the affirmative, for the provisions amount to a conclusive presumption that every pregnant teacher who reaches the fifth or sixth month of pregnancy is physically incapable of continuing. There is no individualized determination by the teacher's doctor—or the school board's—as to any particular teacher's ability to continue at her job. The rules contain an irrebuttable presumption of physical incompetency, and that presumption applies even when the medical evidence as to an individual woman's physical status might be wholly to the contrary.

* * *

* * * While the medical experts in these cases differed on many points, they unanimously agreed on one—the ability of any

particular pregnant woman to continue at work past any fixed time in her pregnancy is very much an individual matter. Even assuming, *arguendo*, that there are some women who would be physically unable to work past the particular cutoff dates embodied in the challenged rules, it is evident that there are large numbers of teachers who are fully capable of continuing work for longer than the Cleveland and Chesterfield County regulations will allow. Thus, the conclusive presumption embodied in these rules * * * is neither "necessarily [nor] universally true," and is violative of the Due Process Clause.

* * *

* * * While the regulations no doubt represent a good-faith attempt to achieve a laudable goal, they cannot pass muster under the Due Process Clause of the Fourteenth Amendment, because they employ irrebuttable presumptions that unduly penalize a female teacher for deciding to bear a child.

III

In addition to the mandatory termination provisions, both the Cleveland and Chesterfield County rules contain limitations upon a teacher's eligibility to return to work after giving birth. Again, the school boards offer two justifications for the return rules—continuity of instruction and the desire to be certain that the teacher is physically competent when she returns to work. As is the case with the leave provisions, the question is not whether the school board's goals are legitimate, but rather whether the particular means chosen to achieve those objectives unduly infringe upon the teacher's constitutional liberty.

Under the Cleveland rule, the teacher is not eligible to return to work until the beginning of the next regular school semester following the time when her child attains the age of three months. A doctor's certificate attesting to the teacher's health is required before return; an additional physical examination may be required at the option of the school board.

The respondents in No. 72–777 do not seriously challenge either the medical requirements of the Cleveland rule or the policy of limiting eligibility to return to the next semester following birth. The provisions concerning a medical certificate or supplemental physical examination are narrowly drawn methods of protecting the school board's interest in teacher fitness; these requirements allow an individualized decision as to the teacher's condition, and thus avoid the pitfalls of the presumptions inherent in the leave rules. Similarly, the provision limiting eligibility to return to the semester following delivery is a precisely drawn means of serving the school board's interest in avoiding unnecessary changes in classroom personnel during any one school term.

The Cleveland rule, however, does not simply contain these reasonable medical and next-semester eligibility provisions. In addition, the school board requires the mother to wait until her child reaches the age of three months before the return rules begin to operate. The school board has offered no reasonable justification for this supplemental limitation, and we can perceive none. To the extent that the three-month provision reflects the school board's thinking that no mother is fit to return until that point in time, it suffers from the same constitutional deficiencies that plague the irrebuttable presumption in the termination rules. The presumption, moreover, is patently unnecessary, since the requirement of a physician's certificate or a medical examination fully protects the school's interests in this regard. And finally, the three-month provision simply has nothing to do with continuity of instruction, since the precise point at which the child will reach the relevant age will obviously occur at a different point throughout the school year for each teacher.

Thus, we conclude that the Cleveland return rule, insofar as it embodies the three-month age provision, is wholly arbitrary and irrational, and hence violates the Due Process Clause of the Fourteenth Amendment. The age limitation serves no legitimate state interest, and unnecessarily penalizes the female teacher for asserting her right to bear children.

We perceive no such constitutional infirmities in the Chesterfield County rule. In that school system, the teacher becomes eligible for re-employment upon submission of a medical certificate from her physician; return to work is guaranteed no later than the beginning of the next school year following the eligibility determination. The medical certificate is both a reasonable and narrow method of protecting the school board's interest in teacher fitness, while the possible deferring of return until the next school year serves the goal of preserving continuity of instruction. In short, the Chesterfield County rule manages to serve the legitimate state interests here without employing unnecessary presumptions that broadly burden the exercise of protected constitutional liberty.

IV

For the reasons stated, we hold that the mandatory termination provisions of the Cleveland and Chesterfield County maternity regulations violate the Due Process Clause of the Fourteenth Amendment, because of their use of unwarranted conclusive presumptions that seriously burden the exercise of protected constitutional liberty. For similar reasons, we hold the three-month provision of the Cleveland return rule unconstitutional.

Liability of Administrators for Violating Teacher's Civil Rights

As discussed in the students rights chapter of this text, school officials may be held liable for violating the constitutional rights of either students or employees of the school system. Traditionally, teachers could recover damages or ask for judicial relief in specific performance in accordance with contract law, but more recently the Civil Rights Act of 1871 has come into play as an alternative action. As with students denial of a constitutional right, a teacher is protected by the Act and violation may result in damages. Monetary damage is not difficult to prove for the teacher who has been deprived of employment by denial of a right or interest. If, for example, the future employability of the teacher is harmed by action of a school board or official, the damages could be quite substantial.

Teacher Unconstitutionally Dismissed Can Claim Damages under Civil Rights Act of 1871

McLAUGHLIN v. TILENDIS

United States Court of Appeals, Seventh Circuit, 1968.
398 F.2d 287.

CUMMINGS, Circuit Judge.

This action was brought under Section 1 of the Civil Rights Act of 1871 (42 U.S.C. § 1983) [1] by John Steele and James McLaughlin who had been employed as probationary teachers by Cook County, Illinois, School District No. 149. Each sought damages of $100,000 from the Superintendent of School District No. 149 and the elected members of the Board of Education of that District.

Steele was not offered a second-year teaching contract and McLaughlin was dismissed before the end of his second year of teaching. Steele alleged that he was not rehired and McLaughlin alleged that he was dismissed because of their association with Local 1663 of the American Federation of Teachers, AFL–CIO. Neither teacher had yet achieved tenure.

*   *   *

The District Court granted the defendants' motion to dismiss the complaint, holding that plaintiffs had no First Amendment rights to join or form a labor union, so that there was no jurisdiction under the Civil Rights Act.[2] The District Court's memorandum opinion did not consider the alternative defense presented in the motion that defendants were immune from suit under the Illinois Tort Immunity Act (Ill.Rev.Stats.1967, Ch. 85, Sec. 2–201). Concluding that the First Amendment confers the right to form and join a labor union,

---

1. Section 1983 of Title 42 of the U.S. Code provides:

"Every person who, under color of any statute, ordinance, regulation, custom, or usage, of any State or Territory, subjects, or causes to be subjected, any citizen of the United States or other person within the ju-risdiction thereof to the deprivation of any rights, privileges, or immunities secured by the Constitution and laws, shall be liable to the party injured in an action at law, suit in equity, or other proper proceeding for redress."

we reverse on the ground that the complaint does state a claim under Section 1983.

It is settled that teachers have the right of free association, and unjustified interference with teachers' associational freedom violates the Due Process clause of the Fourteenth Amendment. * * * Public employment may not be subjected to unreasonable conditions, and the assertion of First Amendment rights by teachers will usually not warrant their dismissal. * * * Unless there is some illegal intent, an individual's right to form and join a union is protected by the First Amendment. * * *

Even though the individual plaintiffs did not yet have tenure, the Civil Rights Act of 1871 gives them a remedy if their contracts were not renewed because of their exercise of constitutional rights. * * *

* * * There is no showing on this record that plaintiffs' activities impeded "[the] proper performance of [their] daily duties in the classroom." * * * If teachers can engage in scathing and partially inaccurate public criticism of their school board, surely they can form and take part in associations to further what they consider to be their well-being.

* * *

Illinois has not prohibited membership in a teachers' union, and defendants do not claim that the individual plaintiffs engaged in any illegal strikes or picketing. Moreover, collective bargaining contracts between teachers' unions and school districts are not against the public policy of Illinois. * * * Illinois even permits the automatic deduction of union dues from the salaries of employees of local governmental agencies. Ill.Rev.Stats.1967, Ch. 85, Sec. 472. These very defendants have not adopted any rule, regulation or resolution forbidding union membership. Accordingly, no paramount public interest of Illinois warranted the limiting of Steele's and McLaughlin's right of association. Of course, at trial defendants may show that these individuals were engaging in unlawful activities or were dismissed for other proper reasons, but on this record we hold that the complaint sufficiently states a justifiable claim under Section 1983. There is nothing anomalous in protecting teachers' rights to join unions. Other employees have long been similarly protected by the National Labor Relations Act. * * *

The second ground of defendants' motion to dismiss was that they are protected against suit by the Illinois Tort Immunity Act (Ill.Rev.Stats.1967, Ch. 85, Sec. 2–201).[4] Under the Supremacy

---

4. Sec. 2–201 provides:

"Except as otherwise provided by Statute, a public employee serving in a position involving the determination of policy or the exercise of discretion is not liable for an injury resulting from his act or omission in determining policy when acting in the exercise of such discretion even though abused."

Clause, that statute cannot protect defendants against a cause of action grounded, as here, on a federal statute. Legislators and judges have broad immunity under Section 1983 because in enacting that statute Congress did not intend to overturn their pre-existing defense. * * * However, other officials, such as present defendants, retain only a qualified immunity, dependent on good faith action. * * * Even under the Illinois Act, immunity is conditioned upon a showing of good faith * * * and there has been no hearing on that question. In this Court and in their brief below the defendants also rely on common law immunity, but we rejected a similar contention in Progress Development Corp. v. Mitchell, 286 F.2d 222, 231 (7th Cir. 1961), where it was held that common law immunity did not extend to members of the Deerfield, Illinois, Park Board charged with discriminating against Negroes. Unless they can show good faith action, the reach of that decision extends to the present defendants who are alleged to have discriminatorily discharged Steele and McLaughlin for their union membership. To hold defendants absolutely immune from this type of suit would frustrate the very purpose of Section 1983. * * * At best, <u>defendants' qualified immunity in this case means that they can prevail only if they show that plaintiffs were discharged on justifiable grounds.</u> Thus here a successful defense on the merits merges with a successful defense under the qualified immunity doctrine.

* * *

The judgment of the District Court is reversed and the cause is remanded for trial.

School District, Trustees, and Superintendents Are "Persons" and Prayer for Back Pay Is Justified as Equitable Remedy

HARKLESS v. SWEENY INDEPENDENT SCHOOL DIST.

United States Court of Appeals, Fifth Circuit, 1970.
427 F.2d 319.

BELL, Circuit Judge: This appeal involves an action brought by ten Negro teachers alleging that the failure of the school district to renew their teaching contracts when the school system was desegregated denied them rights secured by the Fourteenth Amendment. They seek reinstatement and back pay. Jurisdiction is premised on 28 U.S.C.A. § 1343(3) and 42 U.S.C.A. § 1983.[1]

1. 28 U.S.C.A. § 1343(3), provides:
    "The district courts shall have original jurisdiction of any civil action authorized by law to be commenced by any person:
    * * * * * *
    "(3) To redress the deprivation, under color of any State law, statute, ordinance, regulation, custom or usage, of any right, privilege or immunity secured by the Constitution of the United States or by any Act of Congress providing for equal rights of citizens or of all persons within the jurisdiction of the United States;"

The complaint originally named each member of the board of trustees of the district and the superintendent in his individual as well as his representative capacity. * * * Because of the unwillingness expressed at the voir dire examination by two veniremen to assess monetary damages against the defendants as individuals, plaintiffs dismissed the complaint as to the defendants in their individual capacities. Thus the suit proceeded against the trustees and the superintendent as defendants only in their representative capacities. The suit also proceeded against the school district.

During the trial and after the defendants in their individual capacities had been dismissed, the applicability of Monroe v. Pape, supra, to the question whether a cause of action was stated was drawn into issue. Put differently, would a suit lie against defendants as being "persons" within the meaning of 42 U.S.C.A. § 1983? * * *

I.

The nub of this controversy is the breadth of the holding in Monroe v. Pape. We must follow that holding to its outer limits. The jurisdictional basis for this suit is 28 U.S.C.A. § 1343(3). It provides federal jurisdiction of civil actions authorized by law. As stated, the source of authorization claimed by appellants is 42 U.S.C.A. § 1983. The defendants contest this authorization on the basis of Monroe v. Pape.

* * *

Monroe v. Pape was an action to recover damages for the misconduct of police officers. The recovery was sought under § 1983 against the officers and also against their employer, the City of Chicago, under respondeat superior. The Supreme Court held that a cause of action could be maintained under § 1983 against the police officers but concluded that municipal corporations were not within the ambit of § 1983. Thus the *ratio decidendi* of the decision is that no cause of action lies against a municipality under § 1983 for damages under the doctrine of respondeat superior for the conduct of its police officers.

In footnote 50 to the opinion, the court stated with reference to its holding that a municipality was not included in § 1983: * * *

The district court read footnote 50 as meaning that municipalities were not "persons" within the meaning of § 1983 for any purpose —in law or in equity and based its decision on Monroe v. Pape in this

42 U.S.C.A. § 1983, provides:

"Every person who, under color of any statute, ordinance, regulation, custom, or usage, of any State or Territory, subjects, or causes to be subjected, any citizen of the United States or other person with the jurisdiction thereof to the deprivation of any rights, privileges, or immunities secured by the Constitution and laws, shall be liable to the party injured in an action at law, suit in equity, or other proper proceeding for redress."

posture. No suit would lie against a municipality under § 1983 under any circumstances.

The position of the district court was two-fold: Monroe v. Pape prohibited a suit against the school district under § 1983; perceiving no legal distinction between the school district and its trustees and superintendent acting in their representative capacities, it followed that no suit would lie against the trustees and superintendent. It is to be remembered that, at this point in the proceedings, plaintiffs had dismissed the trustees and the superintendent as individuals.

We do not read footnote 50 so broadly. We read it within the context of the holding of the court and the text to which it is appended. We think the court was saying in the footnote that the issue of damages against municipalities under respondeat superior was a question not raised in the equitable relief cases cited and that no inference may be drawn from those cases that a municipal corporation is a person within the meaning of § 1983 for the purposes of a damage claim against it under respondeat superior. * * *

* * *

While the question is not free from doubt, we are of the view that the school district here was included within the meaning of "person" in § 1983 for the equitable relief sought and that the district court erred in holding to the contrary.

II.

Turning then to the officials, the trustees and the superintendent, it seems well settled that § 1983 authorizes a suit against them. Federal judicial power has long been invoked to compel state officials to discharge their constitutional duties. * * *

In numerous cases since Monroe v. Pape, the Supreme Court has permitted relief under § 1983 against state officials sued as such, without mention of that case. * * *

We find no prohibition in Monroe v. Pape against the exercise of federal judicial power through § 1983 to redress constitutional wrongs through requiring appropriate official acts by officials sued in their representative capacities. We therefore conclude that § 1983 includes school district trustees and school superintendents, acting in their representative as well as their individual capacities, within the meaning of "person" as the term is used in § 1983 for the purposes of the equitable relief sought here. Thus, it follows that the district court erred in holding to the contrary.

III.

The last question to be reached is the propriety of the grant of a jury trial. The district court determined that the back pay and the factual issues involved in the prayer for injunctive relief presented jury issues and, therefore, granted defendants' demand for jury trial. The law seems otherwise.

Section 1983 was designed to provide a comprehensive remedy for the deprivation of federal constitutional and statutory rights. The prayer for back pay is not a claim for damages, but is an integral part of the equitable remedy of injunctive reinstatement. Reinstatement involves a return of the plaintiffs to the positions they held before the alleged unconstitutional failure to renew their contracts. An inextricable part of the restoration to prior status is the payment of back wages properly owing to the plaintiffs, diminished by their earnings, if any, in the interim. Back pay is merely an element of the equitable remedy of reinstatement. * * *

* * *

We conclude that these authorities teach that a claim for back pay presented in an equitable action for reinstatement authorized by § 1983 is not for jury consideration nor are the factual issues which form the basis of the claim for reinstatement. The Seventh Amendment does not so require. The plaintiffs' claim should have been determined by the court. The grant of jury trial was error.

Reversed and remanded for further proceedings not inconsistent herewith.

NOTES

A U.S. District Court in Pennsylvania has commented with regard to the Civil Rights Act of 1871:

We note that the United States District Courts are flooded with claims allegedly arising under the Civil Rights Act. Every act, every administrative decision of every state and local official is today threatened by federal litigation. This extends to every organization or institution that receives some financial support from state or local government sources. If state and local governments are to remain viable instruments of government and not become administrative agencies of the federal court system, there must remain some avenue by which local concerns are solved locally through the democratic process. Using the federal Civil Rights Act as a vehicle to threaten every exercise of discretion in matters legitimately within the area of a state's competence is not the purpose of this grant of jurisdiction to the federal courts. * * * The state has a right to make a legitimate inquiry into the competency of its teachers." King-Smith v. Aaron, 317 F. Supp. 164 (U.S. District Ct., W.D.Pa.1970).

Chapter 11

COLLECTIVE BARGAINING

Labor law in public education encompasses collective bargaining, strikes, wages, hours, and working conditions. With such broad import for the operation of the schools it is little wonder that the movement toward unionism has had such a profound effect on school administration. This has manifested itself at all levels from statutory provisions down to the day to day contract administration by the school building principal. The result has been that the administrative role has to a great extent shifted from discretionary activities to duties which are ministerial in nature. Public school labor relations is the story of this legal transition.

Developments of today in the public school labor relations closely track the precedents of the private sector of the 1930s. Differences do exist however between the public and private sectors which cannot be ignored thus preventing direct transference of private sector legal precedents into public practice. Both common law and statutory law today which govern public school labor relations are effectively a modification of the well established private sector view to realistic labor relations.

Historical Development

"Labor Relations in the Public Sector," Charles M. Rehmus, Paper
prepared for the 3rd World Congress, International Industrial
Relations Association, London, England (September 3–7, 1973)

Background of Public Employee Labor Relations

Workers in the industrial private sector in the United States were given the statutory right to organize and bargain collectively in the 1930's. By 1960, approximately 30 percent of all non-agricultural private sector employees were represented by unions. Yet by this same date there was practically no unionization in the public sector other than in the traditionally-organized postal service and in a few other isolated situations.

The reasons for the delay in union organization of employees in the public sector in the United States are complex. In part they stem from certain philosophical ideas long prevalent in the nation. Traditional concepts of sovereignty asserted that government is and should be supreme, hence immune from contravening forces and pressures such as that of collective bargaining. Related to this concept was that of the illegality of delegation of sovereign power. This assertion was that public decision-making could only be done by elected or appointed public officials, whose unilateral and complete discretion was therefore unchallengeable.

More practical considerations also delayed the advent of public employee unionism in the United States. The private sector unions and their international federations were fully occupied in trying to increase the extent of organization in the private sector. They had neither the money nor energy to turn to the public sector until the 1960's. Equally or more importantly, public employees were not generally dissatisfied with their terms and conditions of employment and therefore, except in isolated cases, did not press for collective bargaining rights. Though the wages and salaries of public employees in the United States had traditionally lagged slightly behind comparable private sector salaries, the greater fringe benefits and job security associated with public employment were traditionally thought to be adequate compensation.

By the late 1950's and early 1960's several of these practical considerations which had delayed public employee unionism had disappeared. Moreover, new factors came into play that are difficult to assess as to sequence or relative importance, but in total added to a new militancy. Change increasingly became endemic in American society as more and more groups, including public employees, found it commonplace to challenge the established order. Some public employees were made less secure by organizational and technological changes as government came under pressure to reduce tax increases and therefore turned to devices to increase efficiency and lower unit labor costs. Public employee wages and salaries began to lag further behind those in the unionized private sector as the post-war inflationary spiral continued. The private sector international unions saw the large and growing employment in the non-union public sector as a fertile alternative which might substitute for their failure after 1956 to increase membership steadily in the private sector. Finally, many observers of public employment both in and out of government began strongly and publicly to question the logic behind governmentally-protected collective bargaining in the private sector and government's complete failure to grant similar privileges and protections in the public sector.

By the 1960's these practical challenges to the traditional arguments of sovereignty and illegal delegation of powers came to be seen as overriding in a number of government jurisdictions. The City of New York, the school board of that same city, and the State of Wisconsin gave modification collective bargaining rights to their public employees. Most importantly, in 1962 President Kennedy by executive order gave federal employees a limited version of the rights that private employees had received 30 years before. These seminal breakthroughs in granting some form of bargaining right to public employees led increasingly to similar kinds of state legislation, particularly in the more industrialized states. Today over 30 American states have granted some form of collective bargaining rights to some or all of their public employees. President Nixon in two subsequent executive orders has expanded and clarified the bargaining rights of federal employees. *   *   *

Private versus Public Sector

Before 1932 labor relations in the United States was a product of common law. In our *laissez faire* economic system, the courts tended to favor industrial management since the damage done by work stoppages could be attributed to both social and economic disruption. In the period extending from about 1870 to 1930 business interests held hegemony in labor relations and the courts backed it up by liberal use of the injunction to suppress strikes, picketing and boycotts. Further, neither the courts nor the legislatures fashioned remedies for the employee to prevent employers from discriminating against union members. Consequently, by 1930 labor unions were quite weak and had relatively little influence on the American economic system.[1]

Aware of the onesidedness of the legal precedents and the suppressive nature of the injunction and its overuse by the courts, the Congress in 1932 enacted the Norris-LaGuardia Act which had as its primary purpose preventing federal courts from issuing injunctions against union activities occurring as a result of labor disputes. Several states followed suit and within a few years the scales were tipped in favor of unions making the use of the injunction almost impossible. Anti-injunction legislation was the seed which allowed labor to develop strength and to secure the favorable position it now holds in the country. Modern labor statutes have largely carried forth the anti-injunction theory allowing injunctions only if union activities violate the law or place the national health and safety in peril.[2]

Following the anti-injunction statute of 1932, the first broad labor relations act was the National Labor Relations Act of 1935 (The Wagner Act). Its purpose was to encourage collective bargaining as a means of promoting industrial peace. The Act established the National Labor Relations Board as a regulatory body to prosecute and remedy unfair labor practice. Additionally, the law created procedures for determining employee representation and placed a duty on both parties to bargain in good faith.

In 1947, the National Labor Relations Act was amended by the Labor Management Relations Act of 1947 more popularly known as the Taft-Hartley Act. With this law, more limitations were placed on union activities through more definitive regulation of unfair labor practices by the union. Later in 1959, the Taft-Hartley Act itself was amended by the Labor Management Reporting and Disclosure Act. This act was necessitated by widespread union mismanagement

1. *1975 Guidebook to Labor Relations,*   2. Ibid.
Commerce Clearing House, Inc., Chi-
cago, Illinois, 1975, pp. 8–9.

and corruption. A Senate investigating committee had found that unions in many cases had misused funds, had been infiltrated by gangsters, and had failed to conduct union business in a democratic manner. Designed to curb these abuses, the 1959 Act, specifically delineated employee rights as protection against union abuse, prescribed union election procedures, and established criminal penalties for misappropriation of union funds.[3]

The experience of private sector labor relations laid the groundwork for present statutory and judicial regulation of union activity. State statutes governing public employee collective bargaining reflect this in many ways; for example, scope of bargaining, representation procedures, impasse redress, etc. all have earmarks of the private experience.

Private and public sectors are, however, substantially different and the application of private labor relations to the public schools has proceeded slowly. Some contend, as did Franklin D. Roosevelt in 1937, that "The process of collective bargaining as usually understood cannot be transplanted into the public service."[4] This view maintains that decision-making in education is a sovereign prerogative which cannot be shared. Those who are elected and speak with the voice of the citizenry as a whole must exercise their discretion in such matters and this decision process which reflects the public will cannot be impaired nor delegated. Public employees reject this rationale arguing that the sovereign, legislature, or public agency is merely another employer with the power to delegate labor-management issues to the decision-making process of the bargaining table.

Most commentators admit, however, that the theoretical differences between the private and public sectors are probably of less practical importance than the more pragmatic distinctions relating to the strike, the process of governmental decision-making, existing civil service systems, and the different economic forces and motivations which bear on government as opposed to industry.[5]

At the heart of collective bargaining is the right to strike. From the viewpoint of the employee, if employees cannot strike, effective negotiations may be a hollow exercise. Labor's position is simply that "One cannot negotiate without ability to reject the proffered terms. The only way in which employees can reject an employer's offer is to stop work. Consequently, collective bargaining can hardly exist without preserving the right to strike."[6] With few exceptions, though, the people through their state legislature have re-

3. Ibid., p. 11.

4. See: Benjamin Werne, *Public Employment Labor Relations*, The Michie Company, 1974, p. 5.

5. Ibid., p. 6.

6. Speech by Jerry Wurf, International President of American Federation of State, County, and Municipal Employees, AFL–CIO, U.S. Conference of Mayors, Honolulu, Hawaii, 1967.

jected the right of public school teachers to strike. Where collective bargaining is permitted by statute legislation usually falls short of allowing strikes and in most instances provide express prohibition. No such restraint, of course, exists in the private sector.

Another essential difference is that in the public sector, especially where school teachers are concerned, statutory budget deadlines and taxing restrictions make the bargaining process dependent on direct legislative action. In states where local school district taxing leeway is limited much of the new money for education is derived each year from state tax revenues. In such a situation, the bargaining agreement for increased wages is usually subject to legislative appropriation regardless of the bargaining agreement. As state systems of school finance become more centralized this situation can only be expected to intensify.

A further very practical difference between the private and public sectors is that private employees have fewer inherent protections which public employees enjoy. In our system of government, as reviewed in other sections of this book, public school teachers have constitutional rights of equal protection and due process against arbitrary state action, a benefit not enjoyed by employees in the private sector. These constitutional protections coupled with statutory prohibitions of discrimination, state salary schedules, and fringe benefits of teacher retirement systems, sick leave, vacation leave, et cetera are examples of a public response to public employee needs which would probably not be found in the private sector in the absence of collective bargaining.

Finally, the normal market pressures of the private sector do not exist in the public schools. Public schools cannot lock out employees, go out of business or raise prices. Beyond this, when the legislature of a state becomes involved, laws can be enacted which quickly change the rules of the game, possibly, entirely redefining the criteria or certification for the teacher work force or unilaterally altering the nature of the public service in its entirety.

These distinctions, though, are held by many union leaders to be more apparent than real and it is certainly true that over the past decade a substantial erosion of the differences between private and public bargaining has transpired. To a large extent some of the traditional points of departure have become irrelevant, but throughout any discussion of this issue, one cannot help but observe that essential differences remain. The employee in the public sector as a citizen, taxpayer and human being has greater potential influence over his employment destiny than can be found in the private sector.

As Werne points out, "The employee in the private sector, except for the very devious method of shareholder voting, has no control over his management, unless by union contract. In the public sector, the employee can remove his employer from office and in not a few cases has effected such removal. In short, the strict dichotomy between employer and employee in the private sector has no exact counterpart in the public sector." [7]

Thus, the law pertaining to labor relations in the public schools may to a great extent be characterized as an adaptation of the private sector experience to the differing circumstances of the public schools.

The Right to Bargain Collectively

The rights of public employees to engage in collective bargaining entails important legal aspects. The employees right to organize, the authority of the school board to bargain, the right to strike, and the authority of the school board to submit to compulsory arbitration. Employees have a right to organize and join labor unions. A North Carolina law forbidding public employees from joining unions was held unconstitutional on its face as violative of the First and Fourteenth Amendments.[8] In AFSCME v. Woodward [9] the court held that employees not only have a right to join labor unions but may file suit for damages and injunctive relief under the Civil Rights Act of 1871 if this freedom is denied. In *Woodward* the court stated:

> The First Amendment protects the right of one citizen to associate with other citizens for any lawful purpose free from government interference. The guarantee of the "right of assembly" protects more than the "right to attend a meeting; it includes the right to express one's attitudes or philosophies by membership in a group or by affiliation with it or by other lawful means * * *" Griswold v. Connecticut, 381 U.S. 479, 85 S.Ct. 1678 (1965); N.A.A.C.P. v. Alabama, 357 U.S. 449, 78 S.Ct. 1163 (1958).[10]

In the absence of statute, authority to bargain may [11] be within the discretion of the local school board,[12] but there is no constitutional duty to bargain collectively with an exclusive bargaining agent.

> The refusal of [the School Board] to bargain in good faith does not equal a constitutional violation of plaintiffs-appellees' positive rights of association, free speech, petition, equal protection, or due process. Nor does the fact that the agree-

7. Werne, supra, p. 11; see also: *Collective Bargaining and Politics in Public Employment*, 19 U.C.L.A.L.Rev. 887 (1972).

8. Atkins v. City of Charlotte, 296 F. Supp. 1068 (D.N.C.1969).

9. 406 F.2d 137 (8th Cir. 1969).

10. Ibid.

11. This rule can vary among jurisdictions, for example, the Virginia Supreme Court has held that school boards do not have either statutory or constitutional authority to enter into collective bargaining agreements. Commonwealth v. Arlington County Bd., 217 Va. 558, 232 S.E.2d 30 (1977).

12. Chief of Police v. Town of Dracut, 357 Mass. 492, 258 N.E.2d 531 (1970).

ment to collectively bargain may be enforceable against a state elevate a contractual right to a constitutional right.[13]

Statutes prohibiting public employees right to strike do not violate the state or federal constitutional mandates of equal protection. This issue was settled in a New York case contesting the Taylor Law's prohibition against strikes. The New York Court of Appeals held:

> In view of the strong policy considerations which led to the enactment of the Taylor Law, it is our conclusion that the statutory prohibition against strikes by public employees is reasonably designed to effectuate a valid state policy in an area where it has authority to act. * * * [14]

Similarly, the Supreme Court has ruled that public school teachers have no inherent right to strike [15] and these judgments have been reinforced at the federal level where, following a strike by the United States postal workers in 1970, a three-judge panel held that government employees do not have a right to strike. The Court held that neither public nor private employees have an absolute right to strike without statutory authorization. The opinion stated:

> Given the fact that there is no constitutional right to strike, it is not irrational or arbitrary for the Government to condition employment on a promise to withhold labor collectively, and to prohibit strikes by those in public employment, whether because of the prerogative of the sovereign, some sense of higher obligation associated with public service, to assure the continuing functioning of the Government without interruption, to protect public health and safety or for other reasons.[16]

The public attitude against public employee strikes has become more moderate in recent years and even the courts, albeit usually in dissents, are tending to view the strike situation more liberally. In a dissent in an Indiana case involving teachers in the City of Anderson, Justice DeBruler summarized arguments in favor of public employee strikes.

1. State sovereignty is not necessarily infringed upon if collective bargaining and a limited right to strike are extended to public sector employees.

2. The difference between public and private sector employees is in many instances negligible.

3. The impact of a private sector strike might be more crippling than a strike by public employees.

13. 48 Am.Jur.2d, § 1027–1043.

14. City of New York v. DeLury, 23 N.Y.2d 175, 295 N.Y.S.2d 901, 243 N.E. 2d (1968).

15. Anderson Federation of Teachers v. School City of Anderson, 252 Ind. 558, 251 N.E.2d 15 (1969).

16. United Federation of Postal Clerks v. Blount, 325 F.Supp. 879, aff'd 404 U.S. 805, 92 S.Ct. 80 (1971).

4. Public employees are guaranteed the same irrevocable rights by the Constitution as employees working in the private sector.

5. Public employees must have some means to assert their rights, especially when such rights are not insured through legislation.

Compulsory interest arbitration has been utilized in the private sector as an alternative to the strike and may in the future become more common in public education. Impasse resolution in this manner provides that either party may request arbitration of the dispute and that the decision of the arbitrator is binding on both parties. Compulsory arbitration has been extended to fire fighters in Wyoming, Rhode Island, Massachusetts and New York. A statute in Oregon requires binding arbitration in the field of public education and Minnesota law provides for the Director of Mediation to resolve impasses by sending the dispute to arbitration.[17]

Without authorization from statute, however, school boards cannot generally, submit to binding arbitration. The Virginia Supreme Court has held that binding rights arbitration imposed by State Board Regulation constitutes an unlawful denial of local school board power and unwarranted delegation of authority and as such violates the Virginia Constitution which makes management of the teaching staff an essential function of the local school board.[18]

In Michigan, however, the courts have upheld a state statute which provided for compulsory arbitration. The city had maintained that the act violated the prerogative of city government as delineated in the Michigan constitution. The court held that validity of the statute should be upheld "unless the contrary clearly appears."[19] Although this case was later reversed on other grounds it clearly enunciated that state statute imposing arbitration on local government will be presumed to be valid unless in direct conflict with the state constitution. In the absence of such statute, however, local agencies are not required to delegate their authority to an arbitrator.

17. Hugh D. Jascourt, "Can Compulsory Arbitration Work in Education Collective Bargaining: An Introduction," *Journal of Law and Education*, Vol. 4, No. 4, October 1975.

18. School Bd. of the City of Richmond v. Parham, 218 Va. 950, 243 S.E.2d 468 (1978).

19. Dearborn Fire Fighters Union v. City of Dearborn, 42 Mich.App. 51, 201 N.W.2d 650 (1972).

The Rise and Fall of the Sovereignty Doctrine

K. Hanslowe, The Emerging Law of Labor Relations
in Public Employment 11–20 (1967)†

[V]arying policies have grown up at the state and federal levels with respect to the organizing and bargaining rights of public employees and * * * a discernible trend toward enhanced recognition and protection of these rights is now evident. At one time and place or another, however, virtually all aspects of collective bargaining have been deemed incompatible with government employment. Thus, courts have ruled that public employees can be prohibited from joining unions. To the assertion that this interferes with the constitutional right of freedom of association, government has responded that, there being no constitutional right to government employment, it may insist on non-membership as a condition of such employment because of the governmental right and need to maintain operations without interference and interruption. Consequently, it has been ruled that state governments may condition employment on relinquishment of the right to organize, and that no one has a constitutional right to work for the government on his own terms.

Even where public employees are allowed to join unions, this right has often been restricted to organizations not affiliated with the general labor movement. Where not so restricted, affiliation, in any event, must not be with an organization that asserts the right to strike against the government. The reason for the latter restriction is fairly obvious. Strikes of government employees are almost universally deemed to be unlawful. The reasons for the former restriction are thought to be as follows:

(1) Affiliation increases the possibility that conflicting loyalties will arise. For example, it is argued that policemen who are members of a labor federation such as AFL-CIO, or who are members of an international union also representing employees in private industry, cannot be expected to perform in disinterested fashion and with no reservations when called out to eliminate violence on a picket line maintained by their fellow union members.

(2) Affiliation increases the funds available to public employee organizations and thereby increases their capacity to strike.

(3) Affiliation increases the likelihood of sympathetic strikes by private or public employees to help their fellow union members.

(4) Affiliation with the general labor movement may result in placing too much power in the hands of organized labor. Employees in both sectors might use their respective political and economic pow-

† Reprinted by permission of the New York State School of Industrial and Labor Relations, Cornell University.

er each to enhance the position of the other group at the expense of the rest of society.

The government trend in recent years has been to relax previous restrictions on affiliation. Most jurisdictions which now allow their public employees to organize, also allow them to affiliate with the general labor movement, at least so long as the affiliations are not with organizations asserting the right to strike against the government. More stringent restrictions can still be found in some instances, however, especially with respect to bans on the affiliation of policemen's organizations with other unions.

Other facets of collective bargaining, familiar in the private sector, have been similarly deemed inappropriate in government employment. This is true not only of the strike, but of exclusive recognition of an organization representing a majority of the employees involved, the closed or union shop, the checkoff by the employer of union dues from the employees' wages, and the arbitration of disputes as well. Indeed, the very possibility of *bargaining* with the government has been questioned, and agreements reached between public officials and labor unions have been held invalid as constituting unauthorized abdications of governmental power with respect to conditions of public employment.

These views are reflected in legal opinion. For instance, the attorney general of Florida advised the city manager of Miami that:

> * * * no organization, regardless of who it is affiliated with, union or non-union, can tell a political sub-division possessing the attributes of sovereignty, who it can employ, how much it shall pay them, or any other matter or thing relating to its employees. To even countenance such a proposition would be to surrender a portion of the sovereignty that is possessed by every municipal corporation and such a municipality would cease to exist as an organization controlled by its citizens, for after all, government is no more than the individuals that go to make up the same and no one can tell the people how to say, through their duly constituted and elected officials, how the government should be run under such authority and powers as the people themselves give to a public corporation such as a city.[20]

A judicial decision, in 1946, asserted:

> There is an abundance of authority, too numerous for citation, which condemns labor union contracts in the public service. The theory of these decisions is that the giving of a preference [to unions and their members] is against public policy. It is declared that such preferences, in whatever

---

20. Florida Attorney General's Opinion, March 21, 1944, reproduced in Rhyne, *Labor Unions and Municipal Em-* *ployee Law* (Washington: National Institute of Municipal Law Offices, 1946), pp. 252–54.

form, involve an illegal delegation of disciplinary authority, or of legislative power, or of the discretion of public officers; that such a contract disables them from performing their duty; that it involves a divided allegiance; that it encourages monopoly; that it defeats competition; that it is detrimental to the public welfare; that it is subversive of the public service; and that it impairs the freedom of the individual to contract for his own services. *   *   *[21]

At the core of this position is the concept of sovereignty.

* * * In our polity, sovereignty, of course, ultimately reposes in the people but is, out of the practical necessities of circumstance, exercised for them by the constituted state governments and the federal government. It is these governments and their delegates (such as local governments, municipalities, and executive and administrative agencies) which exercise, within constitutional and statutory limitations, the sovereign power to make and enforce law. To the extent that collective bargaining entails joint determination of conditions of employment, such bargaining with the government is seen as unavoidably creating an interference in the sovereign's affairs. Unionization is similarly thought to involve intolerable splitting of the civil servant's loyalty between the government of which he is a part and his union. Furthermore, such practices as exclusive recognition, the closed or union shop, and the checkoff of union dues are thought not only to invite organized interference with the conduct of public business but to involve improper preference for one group at the expense of others in society. The use of arbitrators to resolve disputes is seen to entail an improper abandonment by the sovereign of a portion of his authority. And the strike, needless to say, involving, as it does, concerted coercion of the employer, falls little short of insurrection when the employer is the government.

What this position comes down to is that governmental power includes the power, through law, to fix the terms and conditions of government employment, that this power reposes in the sovereign's hand, that this is a unique power which cannot be given or taken away or shared, and that any organized effort to interfere with this power through a process such as collective bargaining is irreconcilable with the idea of sovereignty and is hence unlawful.

The [police] commission * * * not only had the power but it was the manifest duty to adopt and enforce the resolution [prohibiting policemen from joining a labor union]. * * * The failure to do so in effect would have amounted to a surrender of power, a dereliction of duty, and a relin-

21. Mugford v. Mayor and City Council of Baltimore, opinion Nov. 6, 1944, aff'd 185 Md. 266, 44 A.2d 745 (1946).

quishment of supervision and control over public servants it was their sworn duty to supervise and direct.[22]

This is the orthodox position. We shall see below that in practice it has been widely modified, although not wholly abandoned.

Still another line of analysis must be indicated. What has been said thus far flows from political or legal theory. It can also be argued that the theory is grounded in functional necessity. The sovereign, whether absolute or representative, acts for the entire political entity involved. The functions which the sovereign performs are governmental tasks which need to be discharged on behalf of the whole society. These tasks, whether they be national defense, local security, running an educational system, or whatever, are carried on to further the public weal. Any conduct which interferes with the performance of these tasks is inimical to that weal and is therefore intolerable. Strikes of civil servants clearly constitute such interference. So, likewise, to the extent that unionization and collective bargaining may have a tendency to lead to strikes, they can and, indeed, must be outlawed as running counter to the public interest. Thus the functional necessity of governmental tasks is asserted to combine with the theoretical nature of sovereign power to render collective bargaining on the part of public employees undesirable and unlawful.

Sovereignty Delimited

So goes the traditional argument. Its difficulty lies in the circumstance that life has a way of running ahead of logic and that history tends to be more complex than political theory. Implicit in the argument is the idea that the sovereign is absolute, all-powerful, and always right. The idea is open to question.

We derive our notions of sovereignty from the English common law which reposed sovereign authority in the king as the fountainhead of law, justice, and government. "The king can do no wrong," wrote Blackstone in his *Commentaries*. This maxim assumed concrete meaning in the context of law suits by citizens against the Crown. If the king can indeed do no wrong, the Crown is necessarily immune from suit. Applied to government employment, the Blackstone maxim means that, when the sovereign has fixed the terms of public employment, these are inescapably fair and just, and hence any employee effort to alter them is wrong and runs counter to law.

One difficulty with this is that, insofar as sovereign immunity from suit is concerned, the Blackstone maxim has been misunderstood, and the English kings did not enjoy the absolute immunity

---

22. Perez v. Board of Police Commissioners, 78 Cal.App.2d 638, 651, 178 P. 2d 537, 545 (1947).

commonly thought to be conveyed by the notion that they could "do no wrong." Professor Louis Jaffe writes:

> It is the prevailing view among students of this period that the requirement of consent [to be sued] was not based on a view that the King was above the law "[T]he king, as the fountain of justice and equity, could not refuse to redress wrongs when petitioned to do so by his subjects." Indeed, it is argued by scholars on what seems adequate evidence that the expression "the King can do no wrong" originally meant precisely the contrary to what it later came to mean. "[I]t meant that the king must not, was not allowed, not entitled to do wrong. * * *" It was on this basis that the King, though not suable in his court * * *, nevertheless endorsed on petitions "let justice be done," thus empowering his courts to proceed.[23]

The petitions referred to were "petitions of right." They were granted when other remedies against the government were unavailable. Thus legal procedure combined with political theory to delimit sovereign immunity even at its source—the kings of England. By what Professor Jaffe calls a "magnificent irony," these limitations upon sovereign immunity were substantially destroyed in North America when the Colonies, by revoking their allegiance to the Crown, eliminated the king who could "let justice be done."

So it seems that the king was not always absolutely right, and he has, of course, for a long time not been absolute. Absence of absolute power has, in any case, been a dominant characteristic of American government from the start. Yet the doctrine of sovereign immunity has had a sturdy history in American law which perhaps, helps to explain the reluctance with which American governments have moved in the direction of accepting collective bargaining with their employees.

     *   *   *

Mr. Justice Holmes spoke in favor of the immunity of the sovereign:

> A sovereign is exempt from suit, not because of any formal conception or obsolete theory, but on the logical and practical ground that there can be no legal right as against the authority that makes the law on which the right depends.[24]

Nevertheless, the doctrine of sovereignty, in areas other than the labor relations context, as well as in the labor relations field itself,

23. Louis Leventhal Jaffe, *Judicial Control of Administrative Action* (Boston: Little, Brown & Company, 1965), p. 199. Professor Jaffe's footnotes have been omitted.

24. Kawananakoa v. Polyblank, 205 U. S. 349, 353 (1907).

has come to be limited. Indeed, Professor Kenneth Culp Davis has recently written: "Sovereign immunity in state courts is on the run."

The traditional position, for one thing, has been substantially modified by legislative enactments, the effect of which is to "waive" sovereign immunity for certain purposes. A court of claims was established in 1855 to entertain citizens' claims that their private property has been unconstitutionally taken by the federal government for public use without just compensation. Tort claims against the federal government may be asserted under the Federal Tort Claims Act of 1946. Contract claims may be similarly asserted under the Tucker Act of 1948. Several states have legislated in similar vein.
* * *

More recently the courts, often without legislative aid, have, in Professor Davis' words, "abolish[ed] large chunks of immunity." According to Professor Davis, thirteen jurisdictions have so acted between 1957 and 1965. Some of the decisions collected by Professor Davis speak in such terms as:

> "[S]overeign immunity" may be a proper subject for discussion by students of mythology but finds no haven or refuge in this Court.[25]

With respect to municipal tort liability, the Supreme Court of Florida made this observation:

> The modern city is in substantial measure a large business institution. * * * To continue to endow this type of organization with sovereign divinity appears to us to predicate the law of the Twentieth Century upon an Eighteenth Century anachronism.[26]

> * * *

One may well ask, therefore, whether conceptions of sovereignty should remain as a barrier to collective bargaining in governmental labor relations. If the "sovereign" government is increasingly assuming ordinary legal responsibility in its relations with its citizens, why should not the same hold true for governmental relations with civil servants?

One point emerges. Whatever immunities the sovereign may possess, there is no barrier to such immunities being delimited. The sovereign power does, indeed, include the power within constitutional limitations to make policy. But does this not include the power to establish, as a matter of public personnel policy, a system of collective bargaining with respect to civil servants. This is, in fact, the position which seems to be emerging. One leading writer has concluded

25. Colorado Racing Commission v. Brush Racing Ass'n, 136 Colo. 279, 284 (1957).

26. Hargrove v. Town of Cocoa Beach, 96 So.2d 130, 133 (Fla.1957).

that, while *"the* [sovereignty] *doctrine is a clear and effective bar to any action on the part of government employees to compel the government to enter involuntarily into any type of collective bargaining relationship,* * * * *the doctrine does not preclude the enactment of legislation specifically authorizing the government to enter into collective bargaining relationships with its employees."* * * *[27]

Teachers May Organize and Bargain Collectively but Cannot Strike

NORWALK TEACHERS ASS'N v. BOARD OF EDUC. OF CITY OF NORWALK

Supreme Court of Errors of Connecticut, 1951.
138 Conn. 269, 83 A.2d 482.

JENNINGS, Justice. This is a suit between the Norwalk Teachers' Association as plaintiff and the Norwalk board of education as defendant for a declaratory judgment. * * *

* * * The plaintiff is a voluntary association and an independent labor union to which all but two of the teaching personnel of approximately 300 in the Norwalk school system belong. In April, 1946, there was a dispute between the parties over salary rates. The board of estimate and taxation was also involved. After long negotiations, 230 members of the association rejected the individual contracts of employment tendered them and refused to return to their teaching duties. * * * The contracts, subject to conditions precedent therein set forth, recognize the plaintiff as the bargaining agent for all of its members, defined working conditions and set up a grievance procedure and salary schedule. Similar contracts were entered into for the succeeding school years, including 1950–1951. From September, 1946, to the present and particularly with reference to the contract for 1950–1951, much doubt and uncertainty have arisen concerning the rights and duties of the respective parties, the interpretation of the contract and the construction of the state statutes relating to schools, education and boards of education. "In addition," the complaint states, "there has been the possibility of strikes, work stoppage or collective refusals to return to work by the teachers through their organization and the possibility of discharges or suspensions by the defendant by reason of difficult personnel relations, all of which tends to disharmony in the operation of the school system and to the ever present possibility that either, or both, the parties may be unwittingly violating statutes by reason of mistaken or erroneous interpretation thereon." The parties

---

27. Wilson R. Hart, *Collective Bargaining in the Federal Civil Service* (New York: Harper & Row, 1961), p. 44.

agreed that the contract for the school year 1949–1950 would govern their relations for the school year 1950–1951, that they would join in this action, and "that whatever contractual obligations exist will be forthwith modified so soon as they shall have received from the Court judgments and orders declaring their respective rights, privileges, duties and immunities." The specific points of dispute are stated in the questions reserved, printed in the footnote.[6]

* * *

Under our system, the government is established by and run for all of the people, not for the benefit of any person or group. The profit motive, inherent in the principle of free enterprise, is absent. It should be the aim of every employee of the government to do his or her part to make it function as efficiently and economically as possible. The drastic remedy of the organized strike to enforce the demands of unions of government employees is in direct contravention of this principle. It has been so regarded by the heads of the executive departments of the states and the nation. Most of the text writers refer to one or more of the following statements by three of our recent presidents. They are quoted, for example, in 1 Labor Law Journal 612 (May, 1950): "There is no right to strike against public safety by anybody anywhere at any time" (Calvin Coolidge on the Boston police strike). This same strike was characterized by President Wilson as "an intolerable crime against civilization." President Franklin D. Roosevelt said in a letter to the president of the National Federation of Federal Employees on August 16, 1937: "Particularly,

6. The plaintiff claimed a declaratory judgment answering and adjudicating the following questions:

"(a) Is it permitted to the plaintiff under our laws to organize itself as a labor union for the purpose of demanding and receiving recognition and collective bargaining?

"(b) Is it permitted to the plaintiff organized as a labor union to demand recognition as such and collective bargaining?

"(c) Is it permissible under Connecticut law for the defendant to recognize the plaintiff for the purpose of collective bargaining?

"(d) Is collective bargaining to establish salaries and working conditions permissible between the plaintiff and the defendant?

"(e) May the plaintiff engage in concerted action such as strike, work stoppage, or collective refusal to enter upon duties?

"(f) Is arbitration a permissible method under Connecticut law to settle or adjust disputes between the plaintiff and the defendant?

"(g) Is mediation a permissible method under Connecticut law to settle or adjust disputes between the plaintiff and the defendant?

"(h) If the answer to the previous questions is yes, are the State's established administrative facilities, such as the State Board of Mediation and Arbitration and the State Labor Relations Board, available, as they are available in industrial disputes, to the plaintiff and the defendant?

"(i) Does the continuing contract law, so-called, create a status of employment within which the plaintiff may claim employment subject to the right to bargain salaries and working conditions?

"(j) Has the plaintiff the right to establish rules, working conditions and grievance resolution procedures by collective bargaining?"

I want to emphasize my conviction that militant tactics have no place in the functions of any organization of Government employees. * * * [A] strike of public employees manifests nothing less than an intent on their part to prevent or obstruct the operations of Government until their demands are satisfied. Such action, looking toward the paralysis of Government by those who have sworn to support it, is unthinkable and intolerable. As the author of the article cited says, "The above statement by President Roosevelt, who certainly was no enemy of labor unions, epitomizes the answer to the problem. It seems to be axiomatic."

* * *

Few cases involving the right of unions of government employees to strike to enforce their demands have reached courts of last resort. That right has usually been tested by an application for an injunction forbidding the strike. The right of the governmental body to this relief has been uniformly upheld. It has been put on various grounds: public policy; interference with governmental function; illegal discrimination against the right of any citizen to apply for government employment (where the union sought a closed shop). * * *

The plaintiff, recognizing the unreasonableness of its claims in the case of such employees as the militia and the judiciary, seeks to place teachers in a class with employees employed by the municipality in its proprietary capacity. No authority is cited in support of this proposition. "A town board of education is an agency of the state in charge of education in the town * * *." * * * In fulfilling its duties as such an agency, it is acting in a governmental, not a proprietary, capacity. * * *

In the American system, sovereignty is inherent in the people. They can delegate it to a government which they create and operate by law. They can give to that government the power and authority to perform certain duties and furnish certain services. The government so created and empowered must employ people to carry on its task. Those people are agents of the government. They exercise some part of the sovereignty entrusted to it. They occupy a status entirely different from those who carry on a private enterprise. They serve the public welfare and not a private purpose. To say that they can strike is the equivalent of saying that they can deny the authority of government and contravene the public welfare. The answer to question (e) is "No."

Questions (a) and (b) relate to the right of the plaintiff to organize itself as a labor union and to demand recognition and collective bargaining. The right to organize is sometimes accorded by statute or ordinance. See, for example, the Bridgeport ordinance adopted June 17, 1946 (Bridgeport Munic.Reg. [1947] p. 15), discussed in National Institute of Municipal Law Officers Report No. 129, p. 51. The right to organize has also been forbidden by statute or regulation. Perez v. Board of Police Commissioners, 78 Cal.App. 2d 638, 178 P.2d 537. In Connecticut the statutes are silent on the subject. Union organization in industry is now the rule rather than the exception. In the absence of prohibitory statute or regulation, no good reason appears why public employees should not organize as a labor union. Springfield v. Clouse, 356 Mo. 1239, 1246, 206 S.W.2d 539. It is the second part of the question (a) that causes difficulty. The question reads: "Is it permitted to the plaintiff under our laws to organize itself as a labor union for the purpose of demanding and receiving recognition and collective bargaining?" The question is phrased in a very peremptory form. The common method of enforcing recognition and collective bargaining is the strike. It appears that this method has already been used by the plaintiff and that the threat of its use again is one of the reasons for the present suit. As has been said, the strike is not a permissible method of enforcing the plaintiff's demands. The answer to questions (a) and (b) is a qualified "Yes." There is no objection to the organization of the plaintiff as a labor union, but if its organization is for the purpose of "demanding" recognition and collective bargaining the demands must be kept within legal bounds. What we have said does not mean that the plaintiff has the right to organize for all of the purposes for which employees in private enterprise may unite, as those are defined in § 7391 of the General Statutes. Nor does it mean that, having organized, it is necessarily protected against unfair labor practices as specified in § 7392 or that it shall be the exclusive bargaining agent for all employees of the unit, as provided in § 7393. It means nothing more than that the plaintiff may organize and bargain collectively for the pay and working conditions which it may be in the power of the board of education to grant.

Questions (c) and (d) in effect ask whether collective bargaining between the plaintiff and the defendant is permissible. The statutes and private acts give broad powers to the defendant with reference to educational matters and school management in Norwalk. If it chooses to negotiate with the plaintiff with regard to the employment, salaries, grievance procedure and working conditions of its members, there is no statute, public or private, which forbids such negotiations. It is a matter of common knowledge that this is the method pursued in most school systems large enough to support a teachers' association in some form. It would seem to make no difference theoretically whether the negotiations are with a committee of the whole association or with individuals or small related groups, so long as any agreement made with the committee is confined to members of the association. If the strike threat is absent and the defendant prefers to handle the matter through negotiation with the plaintiff, no reason exists why it should not do so. The claim of the defendant that this would be an illegal delegation of authority is without merit. The authority is and remains in the board. This statement is not to be construed as approval of the existing contracts attached to the complaint. Their validity is not in issue.

As in the case of questions (a) and (b), (c) and (d) are in too general a form to permit a categorical answer. The qualified "Yes" which we give to them should not be construed as authority to negotiate a contract which involves the surrender of the board's legal discretion, is contrary to law or is otherwise ultra vires. For example, an agreement by the board to hire only union members would clearly be an illegal discrimination. Mugford v. Baltimore, 185 Md. 266, 270, 44 A.2d 745; Rhyne, Labor Unions & Municipal Employee Law, pp. 34, 137, 157. Any salary schedule must be subject to the powers of the board of estimate and taxation. "The salaries of all persons appointed by the board of education * * * shall be as fixed by said board, but the aggregate amount of such salaries * * * shall not exceed the amount determined by the board of estimate and taxation * * *." 21 Spec.Laws, p. 285, No. 315, § 3; Board of Education of Stamford v. Board of Finance, 127 Conn. 345, 349, 16 A.2d 601. One of the allegations of the complaint is that the solution of the parties' difficulties by the posing of specific issues is not satisfactory. Whether or not this is so, that course will be necessary if this discussion of general principles is an insufficient guide.

Question (f) reads, "Is arbitration a permissible method under Connecticut law to settle or adjust disputes between the plaintiff and the defendant?" The power of a town to enter into an agreement of arbitration was originally denied on the ground that it was an unlawful delegation of authority. Griswold v. North Stonington, 5 Conn. 367, 371. It was later held that not only the amount of damages but liability could be submitted to arbitration. Hine v. Stephens, 33 Conn. 497, 504; Mallory v. Huntington, 64 Conn. 88, 96, 29 A. 245. The principle applies to the parties to the case at bar. If it is borne in mind that arbitration is the result of mutual agreement, there is no reason to deny the power of the defendant to enter voluntarily into a contract to arbitrate a specific dispute. On a proposal for a submission, the defendant would have the opportunity of deciding whether it would arbitrate as to any question within its power. Its power to submit to arbitration would not extend to questions of policy but might extend to question of liability. Arbitration as a method of settling disputes is growing in importance and, in a proper case, "deserves the enthusiastic support of the courts." International Brotherhood of Teamsters v. Shapiro, 138 Conn. 57, 69, 82 A.2d 345. Agreements to submit all disputes to arbitration, commonly found in ordinary union contracts, are in a different category. If the defendant entered into a general agreement of that kind, it might find itself committed to surrender the broad discretion and responsibility reposed in it by law. For example, it could not commit to an arbitrator the decision of a proceeding to discharge a teacher for cause. So, the matter of certification of teachers is committed to the state board of education. General Statutes, §§ 1432, 1433, 1435. The best answer we can give to question (f) is, "Yes, arbitration may be a permissible method as to certain specific, arbitrable disputes."

From what has been said, it is obvious that, within the same limitations, mediation to settle or adjust disputes is not only permissible but desirable. The answer to question (g) is "Yes." The state board of mediation and arbitration and the state labor relations board, however, are set up to handle disputes in private industry and are not available to the plaintiff and defendant for reasons given in the opinion of the attorney general dated July 6, 1948. 25 Conn.Atty.Gen. Rep. 270. This was confirmed as to Norwalk teachers by an opinion dated June 12, 1950, not yet published. See also United States v. United Mine Workers, 330 U.S. 258, 269, 67 S.Ct. 677, 91 L.Ed. 884. The answer to question (h) is "No."

General Statutes, Sup.1949, § 160a, provides in part: "The contract of employment of a teacher shall be renewed for the following school year unless such teacher has been notified in writing prior to March first of that year that such contract will not be renewed." Question (i) asks whether this law creates "a status of employment within which the plaintiff may claim employment subject to the right to bargain salaries and working conditions?" The meaning of this is not clear and the briefs do not clarify it. It is the type of question that should be related to a specific state of facts. It cannot be answered in vacuo.

As to question (j), the plaintiff has no right to establish rules. As stated above, the right is and remains in the board.

Question (g) is answered, "Yes, but not under chapter 369 of the General Statutes as amended." Questions (e), (h) and (j) are answered "No." Question (i) is not answered. No purpose would be served by answering the other questions categorically. Questions (a) and (b) are answered, "Yes, with relation to the plaintiff's own members, provided its demands are kept within legal bounds." Questions (c) and (d) are answered, "Yes, with relation to the plaintiff's own members, provided that this answer shall not be construed as approval of any specific contract which has been or may be entered into between the parties." Question (f) is answered, "Yes, arbitration may be a permissible method as to certain specific, arbitrable disputes." In answering some of these questions we have gone beyond the requirements of the specific questions asked in order to render such assistance as we properly may in helping to solve the difficulties of the parties.

No costs will be taxed in this court to either party.

In this opinion the other judges concurred.

*Public Employees Must Have Express Legislative
Permission to Strike*

ANDERSON FEDERATION OF TEACHERS, LOCAL 519
v. SCHOOL CITY OF ANDERSON

Supreme Court of Indiana, 1969.
252 Ind. 558, 251 N.E.2d 15, reh. denied 254 N.E.2d 329, cert. denied
399 U.S. 928, 90 S.Ct. 2243.

GIVAN, Judge. On May 6, 1968, the Superior Court of Madison County found the appellant, Anderson Federation of Teachers, Local 519, in contempt of court for the violation of a restraining order which had been issued without notice on the 2nd day of May, 1968, directing the appellant, teachers' union, and its members to refrain from picketing and striking against the appellee school corporation. It is from this judgment of contempt that this appeal is taken.

The appellant is an organization of public school teachers employed by the appellee.

The appellee is a municipal corporation organized under the statutes of this state for the purpose of operating the public schools within the boundaries of the School City of Anderson, Indiana.

In the spring of 1968 the appellant and the appellees entered into negotiations concerning salary schedules for the following year. These negotiations apparently were not satisfactory to the appellant for on May 1, 1968, the appellant instituted a strike against the school corporation and established picket lines at the various schools operated by appellee. Evidence discloses that school children were unloaded in the public streets because of the presence of the picket lines. It was this action of picketing by the appellant which precipitated the temporary restraining order issued on May 2, 1968, and it was the continuation of this activity without regard for the restraining order upon which the trial court based its judgment after a hearing on May 6, 1968, that the appellant was in contempt of court for violating the restraining order.

The trial court was in all things correct in its finding and judgment of contempt of court.

It is the contention of the appellant that Indiana's "Little Norris-LaGuardia Act," also known as the anti-injunction statute, the same being Burns' Ind.Stat.Ann. § 40–501 et seq., is applicable in this case. This act prohibits the issuance of restraining orders and injunctions in matters involving labor disputes between unions and private employers. We do not agree with the appellant that this act is applicable to disputes concerning public employees. The overwhelming weight of authority in the United States is that government employees may not engage in a strike for any purpose.

The Supreme Court of the United States clearly enunciated the proposition that public employees did not have a right to strike and that the injunctive processes might properly be used to prevent or halt such strikes in the case of United States v. United Mine Workers (1947), 330 U.S. 258, 67 S.Ct. 677, 91 L.Ed. 884. This case has never been overruled or modified. * * *

* * *

This same proposition has been followed generally in most of the other state jurisdictions where it has been repeatedly held that strikes by public employees are or should be prohibited and that injunctions should be granted to halt or prevent them. * * *

We find only one case where an injunction to prevent a pending strike of public employees was denied. That case was Board of Education of City of Minneapolis v. Public School Employees Union (1951), 233 Minn. 141, 45 N.W.2d 797, 29 A.L.R.2d 424. That case, however was overruled in 1966 by the Supreme Court of Minnesota in Minneapolis Federation of Teachers Local 59, AFL-CIO v. Obermeyer, supra.

* * *

We thus see that both the federal and state jurisdictions and men both liberal and conservative in their political philosophies have uniformly recognized that to allow a strike by public employees is not merely a matter of choice of political philosophies, but is a thing which cannot and must not be permitted if the orderly function of our society is to be preserved. This is not a matter for debate in the political arena for it appears fundamental, as stated by Governor Dewey, public strikes would lead to anarchy, and, as stated by President Roosevelt, the public strike "is unthinkable and intolerable."

The Madison Superior Court, is, therefore, in all things affirmed.

Teachers' Sanctions Against Board Is Concerted
Action Toward Illegal End

BOARD OF EDUC. v. NEW JERSEY EDUC. ASS'N

Supreme Court of New Jersey, 1968.
53 N.J. 29, 247 A.2d 867.

WEINTRAUB, C. J. * * *

* * *

I.

In February 1967 a dispute arose between the secretary of the Board and defendant Haller, president of UBTA. Haller was a teacher in plaintiff's system but had not yet acquired tenure. On March 14, 1967 the Board met to consider teacher contracts for the following school year and decided not to offer one to Haller and two other nontenure teachers who were active in UBTA. Haller was so notified on March 29. UBTA held a special meeting of its membership on

March 31 at which a lengthy resolution was adopted listing 17 grievances.

*   *   *

Meanwhile, on April 12 UBTA resolved that "sanctions be imposed" against the Board and requested NJEA to follow suit. On April 21 the NJEA resolved to "impose sanctions" on the Board, and gave wide circulation to its resolution.

*   *   *

NJEA proclaimed through the local press that it would be "a violation of the professional code of ethics for any teacher to accept employment in Union Beach or for any administrator to offer employment in Union Beach as long as the sanctions which had been invoked were in effect."

II.

[1] It has long been the rule in our State that public employees may not strike. *   *   *

Defendants deny there was a "strike." They seek to distinguish the usual concerted refusal to work from what transpired here. As to the teachers employed by the Board, defendants say they merely resigned as of a future date, and with respect to the interference with the Board's recruitment of replacements, defendants, as we understand them, say a refusal to accept employment is inherently different from a quit. But the subject is the public service, and the distinctions defendants advance are irrelevant to it, however arguable they may be in the context of private employment. Unlike the private employer, a public agency may not retire. The public demand for services which makes illegal a strike against government inveighs against any other concerted action designed to deny government the necessary manpower, whether by terminating existing employments in any mode or by obstructing access to the labor market. Government may not be brought to a halt. So our criminal statute, N.J.S. 2A:98–1, N.J.S.A., provides in simple but pervasive terms that any two or more persons who conspire "to commit any act" for the "obstruction of *   *   * the due administration of the laws" are guilty of a misdemeanor.

Hence, although the right of an individual to resign or to refuse public employment is undeniable, yet two or more may not agree to follow a common course to the end that an agency of government shall be unable to function. Here there was such collective action by agreement both as to the quitting and as to new employment. As to the mass resignations, an agreement to that end must be inferred from the very adoption by the members through their teachers union of the program of sanctions which, despite some verbal obscurity in this regard, quite plainly imports an understanding to withdraw services when the union officialdom "imposes sanctions" upon a school district. The use of "unethical" in condemning new employment because of working conditions must mean it is also "unethical" to continue an existing employment under the same conditions. The full understanding must be that upon the imposition of sanctions, all services will be withdrawn. We have no doubt that the agreement to strike was not articulated because of the established illegality of that course. In any event, if it should be thought the plan did not include the obligation to quit in connection with the imposition of sanctions, we think it clear that the teachers entered into an agreement to quit when they voted in favor of mass resignations and then executed 36 of them. Although the Board accepted the resignations and hence does not ask that that work stoppage be ended, we are satisfied the stoppage was concerted action to an illegal end.

And with respect to blacklisting of the school district and the scheme of "sanctions" upon teachers who offer or take employment with a "sanctioned" school board, it can escape no one that the purpose is to back up a refusal of others to continue to work. At a minimum the object is to withhold additional services a school district may need to discharge its public duty, which, as we have said, is no less illegal. Such an illegal agreement may come into being at the time of the strike or may antedate it. If individuals enter into a union or association on terms that upon the occurrence of some stipulated event or signal they will impede government in its recruitment of services, that very arrangement constitutes an agreement the law denounces. An agreement not to seek, accept, or solicit employment in government whenever the upper echelon of the union makes a prescribed pronouncement is, no less than an accomplished shutdown, a thrust at the vitality of government, and comes within the same policy which denounces a concerted strike or quit or slowdown or other obstruction of the performance of official duties.

* * * That the conventional terminology of a "strike" nowhere appears is of no moment. The substance of a situation and not its shape must control. A doctrine designed to protect the public interest is equal to any demand upon it. It does not yield to guise or ingenuity.

* * *

* * * The trial court expressly added that "There is no intention, however, of restraining defendants from exercising the right of free speech concerning what they think the conditions are in the Union Beach school system."

What reappears in defendants' argument is a protest that "sanctions" are no more than an expression of disapproval of conditions in the school district and of the conduct of the Board. It is difficult, even in the abstract, to take that view of the terms used. Far from importing a mere denunciation of men and their work, the "imposition of sanctions" imports the imposition of a penalty. * * *

The imposition of "sanctions" was the stipulated signal for unlawful activity. The right to utter even a pleasantry may be lost if it is the agreed call for lawlessness. It need hardly be said that freedom of speech does not include the right to use speech as an instrument to an unlawful end. * * *

* * *

The judgment is affirmed. (for Board)

NOTES

Refusal to perform extracurricular duties constitutes a strike. "Extracurricular activities are a fundamental part of a child's education, making the supervision of such activities an integral part of a teacher's duty toward his or her students." Board of Educ. of City of Asbury Park v. Asbury Park Educ. Ass'n, 145 N.J. Super. 495, 368 A.2d 396 (1976).

Teachers Who Strike in Violation of Law May be
Disciplined Without a Prior Hearing

ROCKWELL v. THE BOARD OF EDUC. OF THE SCHOOL DIST. OF CRESTWOOD

Supreme Court of Michigan, 1975.
393 Mich. 616, 227 N.W.2d 736.

LEVIN, Justice. The issue is whether school teachers who strike may be discharged without a prior hearing.

Resolution requires construction of the Public Employment Relations Act (the PERA) in relation to the Teachers' Tenure Act and consideration of the teachers' claim that the PERA is violative of the Due Process Clause unless construed to require a prior hearing.

Section 6 of the PERA provides that public employees who, in concerted action with others, in support of efforts to obtain a change in compensation or other conditions of employment, fail to render services shall be deemed on strike. If the employee is disciplined by his employer for striking, he is entitled, on request, to a determination whether he violated the provisions of the act. The request is to be made "within 10 days *after* regular compensation of such employee has ceased or other discipline has been imposed." (Emphasis added.) If the employee is found to have violated the act, he may seek review by the circuit court.

In contrast, the Teachers' Tenure Act requires a hearing *before* discharge. That act provides that a teacher on continuing tenure may be discharged or demoted "only for reasonable and just cause, and only *after* such charges, notice, hearing and determination thereof." (Emphasis supplied.)

The circuit court found that the failure of the school board to proceed in accordance with the Teachers' Tenure Act required reinstatement of the teachers who were discharged. The Court of Appeals affirmed.

We conclude that a teacher, including a teacher on continuing tenure, who strikes in violation of the PERA may be disciplined without a prior hearing, and we reverse the circuit court and the Court of Appeals.

I

The Crestwood Education Association (the union) and the Board of Education of the School District of Crestwood (the school board) have been involved in a prolonged labor dispute. There has been no collective bargaining agreement since August, 1973.

When the school year commenced on September 3, 1974, the teachers, members of the union, did not report for work. This action was brought against the union and the school board on September 30, 1974, by the plaintiffs as homeowners, taxpayers and parents. By subsequent stipulation, the plaintiffs were dismissed and the litigation has continued on the cross-complaint of the school board.

Injunctive orders were issued in October and classes resumed. In December the teachers again did not report for work and classes were suspended. Contempt proceedings followed. Thereafter the school board adopted a resolution requiring the teachers either to report for work or to submit a letter of resignation by December 27, 1974, failing which their employment would be terminated. Thirty-eight teachers reported for work, one submitted a letter of resignation and the remaining 184 were, by school board resolution of December 30, 1974, deemed to have terminated their employment.

The school board hired substitute teachers and attempted to operate the schools.

The union had theretofore filed unfair labor practice charges with the Michigan Employment Relations Commission (MERC). The union then filed an amended charge complaining that the school board had not bargained in good faith and was attempting to destroy and interfere with the union. The teachers sought individual Section 6 hearings on January 6, 1975. On January 10th the circuit court set aside the school board's resolution of December 30, 1974 and directed reinstatement of the teachers and the resumption of classes. The Court of Appeals affirmed. The teachers returned to work.

II

The PERA defines "strike," prohibits strikes by public employees, and interdicts any public employer from authorizing a strike.

Section 6 of the PERA empowers the officer or body generally having disciplinary authority over an employee to terminate the employment of or impose other discipline on an employee who strikes in violation of the PERA. In providing that an employee's request for a hearing to determine whether he did violate the PERA be filed within 10 days *after* regular compensation has ceased or other discipline has been imposed, the Legislature manifested an intention that the officer or body may impose discipline without a prior hearing.

Section 6 begins with the words "[n]otwithstanding the provisions of any other law."

* * *

This Court has consistently construed the PERA as the dominant law regulating public employee labor relations. * * *

* * * The supremacy of the provisions of the PERA is predicated on the constitution (Const.1963, art. 4, § 48) and the apparent legislative intent that the PERA be the governing law for public employee labor relations.

The Teachers' Tenure Act was not intended, either in contemplation or design, to cover labor disputes between school boards and their employees. The 1937 Legislature in enacting the Teachers' Tenure Act could not have anticipated collective bargaining or meant to provide for the resolution of labor relations disputes in public employment. * * *

* * *

All teachers do not have rights of continuing tenure. Yet both tenured and non-tenured teachers are in a single public employee bargaining unit and have the same rights and obligations under Michigan's labor relations statutes.

A construction of the statutes providing uniform treatment of all public employee labor relations questions is more likely to effect a sound and expeditious resolution of labor disputes. Requiring hearings under both the Teachers' Tenure Act and the Michigan labor relations statutes, with review of the former by the circuit court and of the latter by the Court of Appeals, could result in competing claims and conflicting adjudications with untoward and costly delay.

Public employees may be disciplined under Section 6 of the PERA only for engaging in *concerted* strike action, while most disciplinary actions subject to the jurisdiction of the State Tenure Commission concern individual teachers. It should therefore be a rare case where the line separating disputes subject to the jurisdiction of the State Tenure Commission from those subject to the jurisdiction of the MERC will be unclear.

* * *

This construction of the two acts will not enable MERC to circumvent, at the request of school boards, the protection provided tenured teachers by the Teachers' Tenure Act. If the school board claims that a teacher was discharged for striking, the appeal is to the circuit court, not to MERC. If the school board claims that the teacher was discharged for a reason other than striking, MERC's jurisdiction is invoked only if the teacher claims he was discharged for activity protected under the PERA and the teacher himself files an unfair labor practice charge with the MERC; such a charge would not preclude the teacher from also defending against the discharge at a Teachers' Tenure Act hearing on the ground that it was not supported by reasonable and just cause.

III

Whether a teacher's employment can be terminated, consistent with the Due Process Clause, without a hearing need not be decided. The PERA provides for a hearing.

The claim that the Due Process Clause requires a *prior* hearing in every case of deprivation of a property right has been rejected by the United States Supreme Court.

* * *

In its most recent expression on the subject, the Supreme Court in Arnett v. Kennedy, supra, rejected a due process challenge to a statute allowing the discharge of a federal employee without a pre-disciplinary evidentiary hearing. A variety of rationales were espoused, but the uniform thrust of each opinion, including the dissents, is that the constitutional necessity of a pre-disciplinary hearing must be determined by balancing the competing interests of the government and employee.

* * *

When public employees strike, the public employer must, like a private employer, be able to hire substitute employees so that the public business is not interrupted. In order to hire competent replacements, it may be necessary for the public employer to offer permanent employment and thus displace strikers. Where essential services have been suspended, the hiring of replacements often cannot await time consuming adjudicatory processes.

The predominant interest secured by pre-disciplinary hearings, as advanced in *Arnett,* supra, is protection against removal of the wrong person and, assuming ultimate employee vindication, protection against interim financial deprivation.

The possibility of removal of a non-striker is minimized when, as here, the school board gives each striking teacher personal notice of the opportunity to return to the classroom before disciplinary action is taken. While on strike, a teacher receives no compensation; striking teachers do not suffer additional interim financial deprivation when disciplined.

IV

*   *   *

Although a strike begins as an economic strike, if it is determined that the employer engaged in an unfair labor practice, the strike may be held to be an unfair labor practice strike and the striking employees entitled to reinstatement.

Since an economic strike is protected concerted activity under the NLRA and the Michigan labor mediation act, it is an unfair labor practice for a private employer to discharge an employee for engaging in an economic strike before the employee has been replaced. The Crestwood school board discharged the school teachers before hiring replacements. However, in contrast with the NLRA and the Michigan labor mediation act, the PERA prohibits strikes in public employment; public employee strikes, therefore, are not protected "lawful concerted [activity] for the purpose of collective negotiation or bargaining or other mutual aid and protection" within the meaning of Section 9 of the PERA, modeled on Section 8 of the Michigan labor mediation act and Section 7 of the National Labor Relations Act.

The federal courts have held that a strike may be unlawful either because it has an unlawful purpose or unlawful means are used to accomplish a lawful purpose and strikers who engage in unlawful strike activity may be discharged.

The action of the Crestwood school board in discharging teachers for striking in violation of the provisions of the PERA prior to the hiring of replacements was not violative of that act. It does not necessarily follow, however, that these teachers may not be entitled to reinstatement should MERC determine that the school board engaged in an unfair labor practice.

V

*   *   *

If MERC should determine that the employing school district committed an unfair labor practice, MERC *may*, despite the illegality of the teachers' strike, order reinstatement.

*   *   *

Reversed. No costs, a public question.

When Clear and Present Danger Exists
Injunctive Relief is Justified

ARMSTRONG SCHOOL DIST. v. ARMSTRONG EDUC. ASS'N

Commonwealth Court of Pennsylvania, 1972.
5 Pa.Cmwlth. 378, 291 A.2d 120.

BLATT, Judge.   This is an appeal from an Order of the Court of Common Pleas of Armstrong County enjoining the appellant, the Armstrong Education Association ("Association"), from continuing to engage in a strike against the appellee, the Armstrong School District ("District").   The District has approximately 12,000 students, and it employs approximately 550 teachers, for whom the Association is the certified bargaining agent.   Since December, 1970, the District and the Association have been engaged in negotiations in an effort to arrive at a collective bargaining agreement for the 1971–1972 school year.

In their negotiations, the parties followed the procedures outlined in the Public Employe Relations Act, Act of July 23, 1970, * * * 43 P.S. § 1101.101, et seq. (hereinafter "Act No. 195"), but they reached an impasse.   In an effort to resolve this impasse, Association members began a strike against the District on April 27, 1971, and, in response to a complaint in equity filed on behalf of the District, the Court of Common Pleas of Armstrong County enjoined the strike on May 11, 1971, and ordered the teachers back to work. The teachers obeyed this Order and returned to work, finishing out the school year of 1970–1971.

Although negotiations continued, no agreement was reached and the teachers went out on strike again on August 30, 1971, just as the 1971–1972 school year was about to begin.   Another complaint in equity was filed on behalf of the District, contending that the strike created "a clear and present danger or threat to the health, safety or welfare of the public," thus bringing the matter within the provisions of Section 1003 of Act No. 195, 43 P.S. § 1101.1003, and making it ripe for injunctive relief.   Hearings were held by the Court of Common Pleas on September 1 and September 14, 1971, and the testimony at these hearings was substantially as follows:

The District Superintendent testified that the District was required to supply 180 instructional days prior to June 30, 1972 or be in danger of losing state subsidies, and that, with the school year scheduled to end on June 2, 1972, there might not be enough days remaining before June 30 to make up the time lost because of the strike.

* * *

Following the September 1 hearing, the Court denied the request for an injunction on the ground that it was premature, but, following the September 14 hearing, the Court issued the requested injunction, finding that a clear and present danger or threat to the health, safety or welfare of the public existed. Such a finding was based on the strained atmosphere in the community as evidenced by the harassment of School Board Directors and of the Judge, and on the fact that 12 days of school, which would have to be made up, had already been lost. The teachers were ordered back to work as of September 15, 1971. It is from this injunction that the Association has appealed.

* * *

It was long the law in almost all jurisdictions that strikes by public employees were illegal, and Pennsylvania was no exception to this rule. The last decade, however, has brought a tremendous increase in the unionization of public employees and a corresponding increase in illegal strikes by these employees, who claim to have found their remedies under the law inadequate. The leaders in this new militancy, perhaps with good reason, have often been school teachers.

In order to deal with the problem of public employee labor relations, the legislature in 1970 enacted Act No. 195. This Act explicitly recognized the right of public employees to organize and to bargain collectively, and it also established specific procedures for collective bargaining which were intended to lessen the possibility of the development of an impasse. The Act provided, however, that if all the procedures have been complied with, and yet an impasse has developed, the right of the employees to strike must be recognized. The public employer is then given the right to seek equitable relief, including injunctions, in the court of common pleas of the jurisdiction where the strike occurs. Section 1003 of Act No. 195 provides, however, that an injunction may not issue unless "* * * the court finds that the strike creates a clear and present danger or threat to the health, safety or welfare of the public."

* * * [T]he determination of whether or not a strike presents a clear and present danger to the health, safety or welfare of the public must, therefore, require the court to find that the danger or threat is real or actual and that a strong likelihood exists that it will occur. Additionally, it seems to us that the "danger" or "threat" concerned must not be one which is normally incident to a strike by public employees. By enacting Act No. 195 which authorizes such strikes, the legislature may be understood to have indicated its willingness to accept certain inconveniences, for such are inevitable, but it obviously intended to draw the line at those which pose a danger to the public health, safety or welfare.

The reasons indicated by the court for granting the injunction here fall generally into three categories: a) the disruption of routine procedures; b) the harassment of School Board Directors; and c) the danger of losing state subsidies because of the inability of the District to provide the full schedule of 180 instructional days.

The disruption and the harassment were certainly "clear and present" but they did not constitute a "danger" or "threat" as envisaged by Act No. 195. On the other hand, the loss of school subsidies was a "danger", but it was not, at least not yet, "clear and present".

The disruption of routine administrative procedures, the cancellation of extracurricular activities and sports and other such difficulties are most certainly inconvenient for the public, and especially for students and their parents. But these problems are inherent in the very nature of any strike by school teachers. If we were to say that such inconveniences, which necessarily accompany any strike by school teachers from its very inception, are proper grounds for enjoining such a strike, we would in fact be nullifying the right to strike granted to school teachers by the legislature in Act No. 195.

A more serious problem is raised by the community unrest and the harassment of public officials which have apparently occurred in reaction to the strike. The testimony gives no indication as to who has been involved in these incidents, although it was made clear as to some situations that the Association's members were *not* so involved. We deplore such activities and sympathize with the lower court's wish to bring them to an end. Enjoining the strike, however, was not a proper method of accomplishing this purpose. In this situation it does not seem to be the strike which was the "danger" to the public, but the reaction to it by persons unknown. We cannot find that Section 1003 of Act No. 195 was intended to permit striking employees to be penalized by having their strike enjoined because a number of citizens oppose their stand and choose to show this by disrupting the community. There are other laws available to deal with such disorders.

The danger that the District will lose state subsidies because of a strike would be proper grounds for enjoining the strike if such danger were "clear and present". And, although it is not certain that subsidies will in fact have to be withheld because of the strike, it is a possibility which cannot be ignored. If the strike lasted so long, therefore, that any continuation would make it unlikely that enough days would be available to make up the 180 required, the teachers could be properly enjoined from continuing it. At the time of the last hearing, however, the strike had lasted only 12 days, and the District had 20 days available in June plus 19 holiday dates which could be used to make up time lost. The possibility that the strike would extend longer than the make-up time available did not yet exist. If a strike is to be enjoined on the basis that insufficient make-up time actually will exist, the strike must at the very least have reached the point where its continuation would make it either clearly impossible or extremely difficult for the District to make up enough instructional days to meet the subsidy requirement within the time available. This strike was far from that point when the Court below enjoined it.

The fact that students and teachers might have to remain in school later in June than originally planned may be unfortunate, of course, but again it is merely an inconvenience inherent in the right of school teachers to strike, a right now guaranteed them by the law.

We must hold that at the time this injunction was issued, there were no reasonable grounds on which the lower court could find that the strike by the Association was a "clear and present danger or threat to the health, safety or welfare of the public". This is not to say, of course, that public employees may strike with impunity and ignore the public interest, nor that such inconveniences as those noted herein as incidental to a strike might not conceivably accumulate to such an extent, be continued so long or be aggravated by some unexpected development, so that the public health, safety and welfare would in fact then be endangered. We must hold, however, that the proper purpose of an injunction under Act No. 195 is to avert present danger, not to prevent danger which may never occur at all or which can only occur, if it does occur, at some future time before which the grievances concerned can reasonably be expected to be settled.

For the reasons stated, the order of the lower court is reversed and the injunction is hereby dissolved.

NOTES

1. An injunction against a teacher work stoppage was upheld where the teachers refused to work unless the school board reinstated certain provisions in a previously expired contract. The board refused to extend the terms of the old contract, and during the period when no contract was in existence, imposed interim operating regulations which eliminated protections of the old contract. The court said that the work stoppage was an illegal strike within the meaning of state statute prohibiting such stoppages for the purpose of inducing a "change in the conditions" of employment. Warren Educ. Ass'n v. Adams, 57 Mich.App. 496, 226 N.W.2d 536 (1975).

2. No civil action in tort can lie against teachers union for striking where employee relations act provides other remedies. The court reasoned that "public policy considerations interdict the creation of a new cause of action, which would unsettle an already precarious labor-management balance in the public labor relations sector." Lamphere Schools v. Lamphere Federation of Teachers, 400 Mich. 104, 252 N.W.2d 818 (1977).

Binding Arbitration Is an Unlawful Delegation
of Power Violating State Constitution

SCHOOL BD. OF THE CITY OF RICHMOND v. PARHAM

Supreme Court of Virginia, 1978.
218 Va. 950, 243 S.E.2d 468.

CARRICO, Justice. This is an appeal from the final order of the trial court awarding Margaret W. Parham (hereinafter, Parham), a Richmond public schoolteacher, a writ of mandamus against the

School Board of the City of Richmond (hereinafter, the School Board). The order compelled the School Board to submit to arbitration a grievance Parham had brought pursuant to the "Procedure for Adjusting Grievances," adopted by the State Board of Education (hereinafter, the State Board). The same order awarded the State Board, an intervenor in the proceeding, a declaratory judgment upholding the constitutionality of a provision of the Procedure which requires binding arbitration of certain disputes between local school boards and their non-supervisory employees. The sole question for decision is whether the provision for binding arbitration is constitutionally valid.

Adopted in 1973 and subsequently amended, the Procedure prescribes the method for settling employee grievances. * * *
* * *

In the present case, Parham unsuccessfully processed her grievance through the several administrative levels prescribed by the Procedure and ultimately presented the dispute to the School Board, where she received an adverse decision. When she called for arbitration, the School Board refused to arbitrate, stating that it questioned the constitutionality of the Procedure "insofar as it compels arbitration binding on school boards in Virginia." Parham then filed her petition for a writ of mandamus to compel the School Board to submit the matter to arbitration.

At the heart of the present controversy are the provisions of Article VIII of the Virginia Constitution, which article relates to education. In pertinent part, the article reads:

"* * *

"§ 2. *Standards of quality; State and local support of public schools.*—Standards of quality for the several school divisions shall be determined and prescribed from time to time by the Board of Education, subject to revision only by the General Assembly.

"* * *

"§ 4. *Board of Education.*—The general supervision of the public school system shall be vested in a Board of Education * * *.

"§ 5. *Powers and duties of the Board of Education.*—The powers and duties of the Board of Education shall be as follows:

"* * *

"(e) Subject to the ultimate authority of the General Assembly, the Board shall have primary responsibility and authority for effectuating the educational policy set forth in this Article, and it shall have such other powers and duties as may be prescribed by law.

"* * *

"§ 7. *School boards.*—The supervision of schools in each school division shall be vested in a school board * * * ."

The School Board recognizes that § 4 of Article VIII places "general supervision" of the public school system in the hands of the State Board. The School Board notes, however, that, under § 7 of Article VIII, the "supervision" of schools is vested in local school boards and that, implementing this constitutional mandate, the General Assembly has conferred upon such local boards extensive authority to execute their supervisory duties. * * *

The School Board argues, however, that "management of a school board's teaching staff and other employees is * * * an essential function of supervision" and that neither the General Assembly nor the State Board can divest local school boards of this function and place it "in an authority other than the local boards." Yet, the School Board asserts, the effect of the binding arbitration provision of the Procedure is to permit "an outside agency, in the form of an arbitration panel * * * to divest the local board of its essential function by the substitution of [the panel's] judgment for that of the board." As a result of the panel's action, the School Board maintains, a local school board's policies, rules, and regulations relating to the work activity of employees could be altered or rendered meaningless. This, the School Board concludes, is constitutionally impermissible under § 7 of Article VIII.

* * *

In analyzing the arguments of Parham and the State Board, it is interesting to note that neither of these parties specifically defends the binding arbitration provision of the Procedure; the arguments merely assert the validity of Procedure in general. The closest approach to a defense of the provision is a statement that "the arbitration panel has no authority whatsoever to make or enforce any decisions as to how the local school is to be operated." This merely evades, rather than answers, the School Board's contention that the arbitration provision permits "an outside agency, in the form of an arbitration panel * * * to divest the local board of its essential function [of managing its teaching staff] by the substitution of [the panel's] judgment for that of the board."

This contention of the School Board presents the real question in the case, *viz.,* whether the binding arbitration provision of the Procedure produces an unlawful delegation of power. * * *

There can be no doubt that a delegation of power is involved in the binding arbitration provision. Indeed, the very section of the Procedure which provides that an arbitration panel shall have authority to make a final and binding decision also states that the local school board "hereby delegates such authority to the Panel."

Whether, however, the arbitration provision results in an *unlawful* delegation of authority is a more difficult question. * * *

Although not involving binding arbitration provisions, Howard v. School Board of Alleghany County, 203 Va. 55, 122 S.E.2d 891 (1961), is pertinent to resolution of the present case. There, a state statute required the sale of school property if such disposition was favored by a majority of voters in a referendum. Ruling the statute invalid, we said that it was an "essential function" of a local school board's power of supervision, granted by what is now § 7 of Article VIII of the Constitution, "to determine whether a particular property is needed for school purposes and the manner in which it shall be used." The effect of the disputed statute, we stated, was "to divest the board of the exercise of that function and lodge it in the electorate," thus stripping the board "of any or all authority to exercise its judgment in the matter." 203 Va. at 58, 122 S.E.2d at 894. This is but another way of saying that the statute produced an unlawful delegation of power.

We believe the binding arbitration provision involved in the present case has the same effect as the offending statute in *Howard*, *viz.*, to remove from a local school board and transfer to others a function essential and indispensable to the exercise of the power of supervision vested by § 7 of Article VIII. * * *

Equally clear, the function of *applying* local policies, rules, and regulations, adopted for the management of a teaching staff, is a function essential and indispensable to exercise of the power of supervision vested by § 7 of Article VIII. This power of supervision would be an empty one, indeed, if a local school board, once having adopted a valid policy, rule, or regulation, found itself powerless to enforce what it had promulgated.

* * *

We conclude, therefore, that the binding arbitration provision of the Procedure produces an unlawful delegation of power, violative of § 7 of Article VIII of the Constitution. * * *

* * *

Reversed and final judgment.

Binding Arbitration Is Not an Illegal Delegation of School Board Power

CITY OF BIDDEFORD v. BIDDEFORD TEACHERS ASS'N

Supreme Judicial Court of Maine, 1973.
304 A.2d 387.

WEATHERBEE, Justice. These two complaints necessitate our first examination of the provisions of the Municipal Employees Labor Relations Law, 26 M.R.S.A. Chap. 9-A, which was enacted by the

Maine Legislature in 1969. The complaints direct our attention only to the application of the statute to teachers in the public schools.

In the fall of 1970 the Board of Education of the City of Biddeford and the representatives of the Biddeford Teachers Association entered into negotiations in an attempt to effect a contract for the professional services of teachers in the Biddeford public schools for the school year 1971–1972. When the Board and the Association were unable to reach an agreement, the fact-finding procedures provided in section 965(3) were called into play but they proved unsuccessful. Finally, in August of 1971 the parties resorted to the arbitration process found in section 965(4).

* * *

The purpose of the Municipal Public Employees Labor Relations Law is stated by 26 M.R.S.A. § 961 as follows:

> "It is declared to be the public policy of this State and it is the purpose of this chapter to promote the improvement of the relationship between public employers and their employees by providing a uniform basis for recognizing the right of public employees to join labor organizations of their own choosing and to be represented by such organizations in collective bargaining for terms and conditions of employment."

* * *

The Act makes it the obligation of the public employer and the bargaining agent to meet and bargain collectively and provides a four-step procedure consisting of negotiation, mediation (when jointly requested), fact finding and arbitration. The parties are first obligated to negotiate in good faith concerning "wages, hours, working conditions and contract grievance arbitration"—with the exception—

> "* * * [T]hat public employers of teachers shall meet and consult but not negotiate with respect to educational policies * * * ; "

Secondly, if the parties are unable to agree after negotiation they may jointly agree upon mediation procedures. Thirdly, if mediation procedures are omitted or are unsuccessful, either one or both may request fact-finding and the parties are then obligated to present their contending positions to the fact-finding board which will, after hearing, submit its findings to the parties. If a 30-day period of further effort to resolve the controversy is unsuccessful either party may make the findings public. Fifteen more days are then allowed to permit a further good faith effort to resolve the controversy. Fourth, and lastly, if, after another ten days they have not agreed as to an arbitration procedure, either party may request in writing that their differences shall be arbitrated in accordance with the procedure described in subsection 4.

In brief, this procedure requires each party to choose an arbitrator and the two so chosen shall name a "neutral" arbitrator. The three arbitrators shall then proceed to hear the matter. If the subject of the controversy has been salaries, pensions or insurance, the arbitrator shall *recommend* terms of settlement which are advisory only and may make findings of fact. As to other matters in dispute the arbitrators shall make determinations which are binding upon the parties and "the parties will enter into an agreement or take whatever other action that may be appropriate to carry out and effectuate such binding determinations". The determinations are subject to review in accordance with M.R.C.P., Rule 80B but, in the absence of fraud, the arbitrators' decisions upon questions of fact are final.

PART I

The Act obviously represents a fresh approach to municipal public employee labor relations problems and enters an area as yet unexplored here. In the field of education, particularly, it appears to clash with traditional concepts of school control and management. As a result, members of the Board here—as several school boards in other jurisdictions have done—protest that if the members entered into the proposed contract, as the arbitration award has ordered them to do—they would be surrendering their authority as public officers to persons who are in no way responsible to the electorate.

*   *   *

While the present actions present many issues concerning various areas of the arbitrators' award, we must first consider the constitutionality of the Act in so far as it requires local school boards, at the request of the teaching employees, to submit to binding arbitration disputes arising both out of the making of the labor contract and out of later employment under the contract. Can the superintending school committees constitutionally delegate this authority to arbitrators? In requiring them to do so, can the Legislature constitutionally take away the authority which local officials had traditionally exercised and repose it in persons who compose ad hoc boards of arbitration? If so, has there been such a valid delegation of authority here?

*   *   *

It appears that most of the cases holding that agreements to submit public employee labor disputes to binding arbitration are invalid attempts to delegate official responsibility come from states that had no legislation authorizing such agreements. On the other hand, serious concern over the problem is apparent in all the decisions and several of those often spoken of as favorable to the position urged here by the Association limit their holdings to grievance arbitration of contracts which municipalities have already entered into. It may be that the Rhode Island statute is the only one imposing upon the mu-

nicipalities binding arbitration in the areas of both interest and grievance, without specific constitutional authorization, which has been finally upheld. We consider that decisions involving arbitration in essential industries in the private sector such as hospitals and public
utilities give us little assistance as to this problem.

With scant solid precedent to guide us, we return to our own situation. We find that our Constitution gave the Legislature full responsibility over the subject matter of public schools and education
and empowered it to make all reasonable laws in reference to schools
and education for the "benefit of the people of this state". Opinions
of the Justices, 68 Me. 582 (1876). Except for the areas where the
Legislature has from time to time seen fit to impose its own requirements and except for the authority later given to the Commissioner
of Education, the responsibilities for operating the public schools
have remained in the local school boards.

The Legislature has now decided to take from the school boards
the ultimate authority they have exercised in certain areas of school
management—that is, as to "hours, and working conditions" and contract grievance arbitration—and to give it to ad hoc boards of arbitration.

It is settled beyond question that the Legislature may properly
conclude that the purposes of its legislation may best be carried out
through agents and that it may delegate to the agents a portion of its
power to facilitate the functioning of the legislative program.

There can be no doubt but that the Legislature, which is the
source of all municipal authority. Squires v. Inhabitants of City of
Augusta, 155 Me. 151, 153 A.2d 80 (1959), has also the power to take
back from municipal officers portions of the authority it has earlier
given them.

It is clear that the Legislature has recognized that the maintenance of a satisfactory quality of public education requires harmonious relations between school officials and the teaching staffs and that
disagreements inevitably arise during the carrying out of their respective responsibilities. The abrasive effect of the existence of unresolved grievances is one of the threats to harmonious relations which
the Legislature considers should be removed.

The lawmakers have recognized that policy making decisions
should remain in the local officials, responsible to the public, and that
while the citizens may properly be subjected to moral suasion as to
such matters as wages and pensions, the ultimate determination of
such matters with such heavy impact upon—and so limited by—municipal appropriations should be made by local officials.

The Legislature has apparently concluded, on the other hand,
that experience has taught that certain aspects of this dynamic and
complicated municipal employer-employee relationship no longer need
remain subject to arbitrary decision by the employer and that in the

area of working conditions and hours and of contract grievances the interests of the employees must in fairness be examined by impartial persons. The Legislature appears to believe that this much can be done without serious disruption of the balancing of operating costs against municipal appropriations.

We realize that in providing that the contract making process itself (as it affects working conditions and hours) is subject to binding arbitration, our Legislature has moved into an area forbidden by many courts. The Legislature must have concluded that the benefits which are sought by the statute can never be achieved if an impasse occurs at the very beginning of the relationship. This conclusion is not unreasonable.

True, the statute does not contemplate the delegation of authority to public administrative boards or agencies but instead gives it to ad hoc panels whose memberships are not to be controlled by governmental action. Here we are of the opinion that the Legislature, mindful of the denial to municipal employees of such economic weapons as strikes and work stoppages which are available to employees in private employment, has sought to avoid the disruptive feelings of resentment and bitterness which may result if the governmental employee may look only to the government for redress of his grievances.

Where the ultimate arbiter of the dispute is a representative of one side of the dispute, adverse decisions will be hard to accept and the tendency toward alienation will be strong.

We consider that there is a rational reason for the Legislature's decision that its purposes would be best effectuated if the parties are left to choose their own arbitrators in the limited non-policy areas which are subject to arbitration.

Agency Shop Does Not Violate First Amendment Rights

ABOOD v. DETROIT BD. OF EDUC.

Supreme Court of the United States, 1977.
431 U.S. 209, 97 S.Ct. 1782.

Mr. Justice STEWART delivered the opinion of the Court.

The State of Michigan has enacted legislation authorizing a system for union representation of local governmental employees. A union and a local government employer are specifically permitted to agree to an "agency shop" arrangement, whereby every employee represented by a union—even though not a union member—must pay to the union, as a condition of employment, a service fee equal in amount to union dues. The issue before us is whether this arrangement violates the constitutional rights of government employees who object to public sector unions as such or to various union activities financed by the compulsory service fees.

I

* * *

On November 7, 1969—more than two months before the agency-shop clause was to become effective—Christine Warczak and a number of other named teachers filed a class action in a state court, naming as defendants the Board, the Union, and several Union officials. Their complaint, as amended, alleged that they were unwilling or had refused to pay dues and that they opposed collective bargaining in the public sector. * * *

* * *

II

A

Consideration of the question whether an agency shop provision in a collective-bargaining agreement covering governmental employees is, as such, constitutionally valid must begin with two cases in this Court that on their face go far towards resolving the issue. The cases are Railway Employes' Department v. Hanson, * * * and International Association of Machinists v. Street, 367 U.S. 740, 81 S.Ct. 1784, 6 L.Ed.2d 1141.

In the *Hanson* case a group of railroad employees brought an action in a Nebraska court to enjoin enforcement of a union-shop agreement. The challenged clause was authorized, and indeed shielded from any attempt by a State to prohibit it, by the Railway Labor Act, 45 U.S.C.A. § 152, Eleventh. * * *

* * *

The record in *Hanson* contained no evidence that union dues were used to force ideological conformity or otherwise to impair the free expression of employees, and the Court noted that "[i]f 'assessments' are in fact imposed for purposes not germane to collective bargaining, a different problem would be presented." Id., at 235, 76 S. Ct., at 720. (footnote omitted). But the Court squarely held that "the requirement for financial support of the collective-bargaining agency by all who receive the benefits of its work * * * does not violate * * * the First Amendmen[t]." Id., at 238, 76 S.Ct., at 721.

The Court faced a similar question several years later in the *Street* case, which also involved a challenge to the constitutionality of a union shop authorized by the Railway Labor Act. In *Street,* however, the record contained findings that the union treasury to which all employees were required to contribute had been used "to finance the campaigns of candidates for federal and state offices whom [the plaintiffs] opposed, and to promote the propagation of political and economic doctrines, concepts and ideologies with which [they] disagreed." 367 U.S., at 744, 81 S.Ct., at 1787.

The Court recognized that these findings presented constitutional "questions of the utmost gravity" not decided in *Hanson,* id., at 749, 81 S.Ct., at 1789, and therefore considered whether the Act could fairly be construed to avoid these constitutional issues. Id., at 749–750, 81 S.Ct., at 1789–90. The Court concluded that the Act could be so construed, since only expenditures related to the union's functions in negotiating and administering the collective bargaining agreement and adjusting grievances and disputes fell within "the reasons * * * accepted by Congress why authority to make union-shop agreements was justified," id., at 768, 81 S.Ct. at 1800. The Court rule, therefore, that the use of compulsory union dues for political purposes violated the Act itself. Nonetheless, it found that an injunction against enforcement of the union-shop agreement as such was impermissible under *Hanson,* and remanded the case to the Supreme Court of Georgia so that a more limited remedy could be devised.

  * * *

  * * * A union-shop arrangement has been thought to distribute fairly the cost of these activities among those who benefit, and it counteracts the incentive that employees might otherwise have to become "free riders"—to refuse to contribute to the union while obtaining benefits of union representation that necessarily accrue to all employees. * * *

To compel employees financially to support their collective bargaining representative has an impact upon their First Amendment interests. An employee may very well have ideological objections to a wide variety of activities undertaken by the union in its role as exclusive representative. His moral or religious views about the desirability of abortion may not square with the union's policy in negotiating a medical benefits plan. One individual might disagree with a union policy of negotiating limits on the right to strike, believing that to be the road to serfdom for the working class, while another might have economic or political objections to unionism itself. An employee might object to the union's wage policy because it violates guidelines designed to limit inflation, or might object to the union's seeking a clause in the collective-bargaining agreement proscribing racial discrimination. The examples could be multiplied. To be required to help finance the union as a collective-bargaining agent might well be thought, therefore, to interfere in some way with an employee's freedom to associate for the advancement of ideas, or to refrain from doing so, as he sees fit. But the judgment clearly made in *Hanson* and *Street* is that such interference as exists is constitutionally justified by the legislative assessment of the important contribution of the union shop to the system of labor relations established by Congress. "The furtherance of the common cause leaves some leeway for the leadership of the group. As long as they act to promote the cause which justified bringing the group together, the individual cannot withdraw his financial support merely because he disagrees with the group's strategy. If that were allowed, we would be reversing the *Hanson* case, *sub silentio.*" * * *

B

* * *

The governmental interests advanced by the agency shop provision in the Michigan statute are much the same as those promoted by similar provisions in federal labor law. The confusion and conflict that could arise if rival teachers' unions, holding quite different views as to the proper class hours, class sizes, holidays, tenure provisions, and grievance procedures, each sought to obtain the employer's agreement are no different in kind from the evils that the exclusivity rule in the Railway Labor Act was designed to avoid. * * * The desirability of labor peace is no less important in the public sector, nor is the risk of "free riders" any smaller.

* * *

While recognizing the apparent precedential weight of the *Hanson* and *Street* cases, the appellants advance two reasons why those decisions should not control decision of the present case. First, the appellants note that it is *government* employment that is involved here, thus directly implicating constitutional guarantees, in contrast to the private employment that was the subject of the *Hanson* and *Street* decisions. Second, the appellants say that in the public sector collective bargaining itself is inherently "political," and that to require them to give financial support to it is to require the "ideological conformity" that the Court expressly found absent in the *Hanson* case. 351 U.S., at 238, 76 S.Ct., at 721. We find neither argument persuasive.

* * *

The distinctive nature of public-sector bargaining has led to widespread discussion about the extent to which the law governing labor relations in the private sector provides an appropriate model. To take but one example, there has been considerable debate about the desirability of prohibiting public employee unions from striking, a step that the State of Michigan itself has taken, Mich.Comp.Laws § 423.202. But although Michigan has not adopted the federal model of labor relations in every respect, it has determined that labor stability will be served by a system of exclusive representation and the permissive use of an agency shop in public employment. As already stated, there can be no principled basis for according that decision less weight in the constitutional balance than was given in *Hanson* to the congressional judgment reflected in the Railway Labor Act. The only remaining constitutional inquiry evoked by the appellants' argument, therefore, is whether a public employee has a weightier First Amendment interest than a private employee in not being compelled to contribute to the costs of exclusive union representation. We think he does not.

Public employees are not basically different from private employees; on the whole, they have the same sort of skills, the same needs, and seek the same advantages. "The uniqueness of public employment is *not in the employees* nor in the work performed; the uniqueness is in the special character of the employer." * * * The very real differences between exclusive agent collective bargaining in the public and private sectors are not such as to work any greater infringement upon the First Amendment interests of public employees. A public employee who believes that a union representing him is urging a course that is unwise as a matter of public policy is not barred from expressing his viewpoint. Besides voting in accordance with his convictions, every public employee is largely free to express his views, in public or private orally or in writing. With some exceptions not pertinent here, public employees are free to participate in the full range of political activities open to other citizens. Indeed, just this Term we have held that the First and Fourteenth Amendments protect the right of a public school teacher to oppose, at a public school board meeting, a position advanced by the teacher's union. * * * In so ruling we recognized that the principle of exclusivity cannot constitutionally be used to muzzle, a public employee who, like any other citizen, might wish to express his view about governmental decisions concerning labor relations, id., 97 S.Ct. at 426.

There can be no quarrel with the truism that because public employee unions attempt to influence governmental policy-making, their activities—and the views of members who disagree with them—may be properly termed political. But that characterization does not raise the ideas and beliefs of public employees onto a higher plane than the ideas and beliefs of private employees. It is no doubt true that a central purpose of the First Amendment "was to protect the free discussion of governmental affairs." * * * But our cases have never suggested that expression about philosophical social, artistic, economic, literary, or ethical matters—to take a nonexhaustive list of labels —is not entitled to full First Amendment protection. Union members in both the public and private sector may find that a variety of union activities conflict with their beliefs. * * * Nothing in the First Amendment or our cases discussing its meaning makes the question whether the adjective "political" can properly be attached to those beliefs the critical constitutional inquiry.

The differences between public and private sector collective bargaining simply do not translate into differences in First Amendment rights. Even those commentators most acutely aware of the distinctive nature of public-sector bargaining and most seriously concerned with its policy implications agree that "[t]he union security issue in the public sector * * * is fundamentally the same issue * * * as in the private sector. * * * No special dimension results from the fact that a union represents public rather than private employees." * * * We conclude that the Michigan Court of Appeals was correct in viewing this Court's decisions in *Hanson* and *Street* as controlling in the present case insofar as the service charges are applied to collective bargaining, contract administration, and grievance adjustment purposes.

C

* * *

Our decisions establish with unmistakable clarity that the freedom of an individual to associate for the purpose of advancing beliefs and ideas is protected by the First and Fourteenth Amendments. * * * Equally clear is the proposition that a government may not require an individual to relinquish rights guaranteed him by the First Amendment as a condition of public employment. * * * The appellants argue that they fall within the protection of these cases because they have been prohibited not from actively associating, but rather from refusing to associate. They specifically argue that they may constitutionally prevent the Union's spending a part of their required service fees to contribute to political candidates and to express political views unrelated to its duties as exclusive bargaining representative. We have concluded that this argument is a meritorious one.

One of the principles underlying the Court's decision in Buckley v. Valeo, 424 U.S. 1, 96 S.Ct. 612, 46 L.Ed.2d 659, was that contributing to an organization for the purpose of spreading a political message is protected by the First Amendment. Because "[m]aking a contribution * * * enables like-minded persons to pool their resources in furtherance of common political goals," id., at 22, 96 S.Ct. at 636, the Court reasoned that limitations upon the freedom to contribute "implicate fundamental First Amendment interests," id, at 23, 96 S.Ct. at 636.

The fact that the appellants are compelled to make, rather than prohibited from making, contributions for political purposes works no less an infringement of their constitutional rights. For at the heart of the First Amendment is the notion that an individual should be free to believe as he will, and that in a free society one's beliefs should be shaped by his mind and his conscience rather than coerced by the State. * * *

* * * They are no less applicable to the case at bar, and they thus prohibit the appellees from requiring any of the appellants to contribute to the support of an ideological cause he may oppose as a condition of holding a job as a public school teacher.

We do not hold that a union cannot constitutionally spend funds for the expression of political views, on behalf of political candidates, or towards the advancement of other ideological causes not germane to its duties as collective bargaining representative. Rarther, the Constitution requires only that such expenditures be financed from charges, dues, or assessments paid by employees who do not object to advancing those ideas and who are not coerced into doing so against their will by the threat of loss of governmental employment.

There will, of course, be difficult problems in drawing lines between collective bargaining activities, for which contributions may be compelled, and ideological activities unrelated to collective bargaining, for which such compulsion is prohibited. * * *

* * * All that we decide is that the general allegations in the complaint, if proven, establish a cause of action under the First and Fourteenth Amendments.

III

* * *

The judgment is vacated, and the case is remanded for further proceedings not inconsistent with this opinion.

It is so ordered.

NOTES

1. An agency shop fee or a "fair share fee" provided for in statute does not deny an individual teacher due process. In this case, decided by the Minnesota Supreme Court, the primary question was whether the fair share statute was constitutional since it did not provide for a hearing for individual nonunion teachers before imposition of the fair share fee. The court concluded that the governmental interest in securing the financial stability of the exclusive union representation was sufficiently strong to override the individual's interest in obtaining a prior determination of the fee's validity. Robbinsdale Educ. Ass'n v. Robbinsdale Federation of Teachers, 307 Minn. 96, 239 N.W.2d 437 (1976).

2. An agency shop provision in contract was held invalid in face of statute which granted public employees the right to voluntarily join, form, and participate in organizations of their own choosing. The court found that the statute assured the "right not to join" and the forced payment of dues or their equivalent "is tantamount to coercion or, at the very least, toward participation" in the labor organization as, expressly forbidden by statute. Churchill v. SAD No. 49 Teachers Ass'n, 380 A.2d 186 (Me.1977).

Scope of Negotiations Is Essentially a Question for
Legislative Guidance

KENAI PENINSULA BOROUGH SCHOOL DIST. v. KENAI PENINSULA EDUC. ASS'N

Supreme Court of State of Alaska, 1977.
572 P.2d 416.

CONNOR, Justice. These cases present important questions of labor law and constitutional law concerning the collective bargaining requirements for teachers in the public schools. * * *

I. *Introduction*

To facilitate the understanding of our more detailed legal discussion later in this opinion, we will summarize at the outset the contentions of the parties. The statutes at issue in this litigation are AS 14.20.550 and .610, which provide:

> "Sec. 14.20.550. *Negotiation with certificated employees.*
> Each city, borough and regional school board, shall negotiate with its certificated employees in good faith on matters pertaining to their employment and the fulfillment of their professional duties. (§ 1 ch 18 SLA 1970; am § 3 ch 71 SLA 1972; am § 21 ch 124 SLA 1975)."

> "Sec. 14.20.610. *Legal responsibilities of boards.* Nothing in §§ 550–600 of this chapter may be construed as an abrogation or delegation of the legal responsibilities, powers, and duties of the school board including its right to make final decisions on policies. (§ 1 ch 18 SLA 1970)."

> *   *   *

The school boards contend that the submission of educational policies to a good faith collective bargaining requirement would remove the final decisions on such matters from the boards, contrary to the intent of the legislature expressed in AS 14.20.610. The boards contend that to require bargaining on questions of educational policy would also contravene the Alaska Constitution, art. VII, § 1, which makes education the exclusive domain of the legislature. See Macauley v. Hildebrand, 491 P.2d 120 (Alaska 1971). Delegation of part of the decision-making power on educational policy to labor unions is unconstitutional, they urge, because the union is a private organization, unaccountable to the public. The union can use the power for its own ends, and is under no duty to foster educational policies which are in the general public interest.

The unions argue that such delegation is perfectly proper, and that there is no delegation of decision-making power inherent in a labor negotiations requirement. They further argue that they represent professional employees, and that their participation in good faith collective bargaining labor negotiations is an attempt by the legislature to provide professional advice to school boards on the management of the schools. *   *   *

*   *   *

II. *Scope of the Duty to Bargain*

If we were to look to the law concerning bargaining between labor unions and private employers, we would conclude that the scope of negotiable issues is broad. The law relating to the private sector has always contained, and still does contain, uncertainties. But the general trend has been to require that employers bargain in good faith on a wide range of items with respect to wages, hours, and other conditions of employment, without regard to whether the employers consider the items bargained for to be within the prerogatives of management. * * *

When we turn to employment in the public sector, and particularly in education, the question of what is properly bargainable is thrown into more doubt. If teachers' unions are permitted to bargain on matters of educational policy, it is conceivable that through successive contracts the autonomy of the school boards could be severely eroded, and the effective control of educational policy shifted from the school boards to the teachers' unions. Such a result could threaten the ability of elective government officials and appointive officers subject to their authority, in this case the school boards and administrators, to perform their functions in the broad public interest.

* * *

The school boards initially argue that to make matters of school operation and educational policy subject to collective bargaining amounts to an unconstitutional delegation of governmental power to the unions.

While courts in an earlier era often held laws unconstitutional on the ground that they delegated legislative power to private persons or groups. * * *

Furthermore, the statute merely requires the school board to negotiate with the union. It does not require the board to accept any particular proposal the union might offer. It does not require, and probably does not permit, the board to delegate to the union the sole power to make any decision. Therefore, cited cases invalidating outright grants of governmental power to private groups, * * * are not apposite.

The cases in other states rejecting the argument that collective bargaining with teachers' unions is an unconstitutional delegation of power, all involve statutes which fairly narrowly constrict either the scope of bargainable issues, or the school boards' duty to accede to union proposals, or both. * * * In this opinion, we similarly construe the Alaska statute. A statute defining the scope of collective bargaining as broadly as the union would have us do, might well present a more troubling constitutional question. But we find no constitutional infirmity in AS 14.20.550 and .610. The delegation of power problem still bears upon our task of statutory interpretation, however, for in interpreting the relevant statutes we will not readily assume that the legislature intended to divest the school boards of their power to determine matters of educational policy and school system management.

* * *

Put another way, a matter is more susceptible to bargaining the more it deals with the economic interests of employees and the less it concerns professional goals and methods. Bargaining over the latter topics presents particular problems because there is less likely to be any politically organized interest group other than the union concerned with these issues. The salaries of public employees have a direct financial effect on the taxpayers; on the other hand, a question such as teacher evaluation of administrators is unlikely to have any impact sufficiently direct to be discernible by laymen. Furthermore, it is such an abstract and abstruse subject that it is unlikely that any appreciable portion of the public will either understand it or care greatly about it. In such circumstances, the risk that effective power over the governmental decision will come to rest with the union is significantly greater. Moreover, it is more likely that there will be disagreements among union members on questions of this nature than on "bread and butter" issues; the risk that minority viewpoints within the union will not be meaningfully represented in the bargaining is a real one. *   *   *

III. *Specific Issues*

We will now consider the Alaska situation in more detail. At the outset it appears to us that questions concerning salaries, the number of hours to be worked, and amount of leave time are all so closely connected with the economic well-being of the individual teacher that they must be held negotiable under our statutes. The troubling question is what other items are bargainable.

The various trial courts in these cases considered such items as (1) relief from non-professional chores, (2) elementary planning time, (3) para-professional tutors, (4) teacher specialist, (5) teacher's aides, (6) class size, (7) pupil-teacher ratio, (8) a teacher ombudsman, (9) teacher evaluation of administrators, (10) school calendar, (11) selection of instructional materials, (12) the use of secondary department heads, (13) secondary teacher preparation and planning time, and (14) teacher representation on school board advisory committees.

The testimony adduced in the trial courts does not provide us with much enlightenment as to why any of these items should fall on one side of the line or another. Realistically the two areas, i. e., (1) educational policy, and (2) matters pertaining to employment and professional duties, merge into and blend with each other at many points. Logically and semantically it is nearly impossible to assign specific items to one category and not the other. *   *   *

*   *   *

*   *   * We are confronted, then, with a situation in which the legislature has not spoken with clarity and concerning which we possess no expertise. We can only conclude that salaries, fringe benefits,

the number of hours worked, and the amount of leave time are negotiable * * * we conclude that the other specific items * * * are, under the existing statutory language, non-negotiable.

It would be helpful if the legislature, through future enactments, provided more specific guidance on a number of the items which the unions seek to negotiate. Lacking that guidance, however, we cannot confidently say that the legislature intended any of these items to be bargainable. We cannot, therefore, read the statutes expansively as to the scope of what is negotiable.

As to matters which affect educational policy and are, therefore, not negotiable, we believe that there is nevertheless implicit in our statutes the intention that the school boards meet and confer with the unions. It is desirable that the boards consider teacher proposals on such questions. This will encourage teachers to give the boards the benefit of their expertise, and to make their positions known for the board's use in establishing educational policy.

　　*　*　*

Affirmed in Part, Reversed in Part.

NOTES

1. When teachers voluntarily surrender their individual academic freedom in exchange for protectionism of collective action and a group contract, they cannot later avoid their contractual commitments by recalling their constitutional freedoms. Where teachers maintained that school board policy unduly restricted use of certain books thus violating their First and Fourteenth Amendment rights, the court found that they had no redress since they had submitted themselves to an employer-employee contractual model which gave the school board the authority to control communication through the assignment of reading material. Cary v. Board of Educ. of Adams-Arapahoe School Dist., 427 F.Supp. 945 (D.Colo.1977).

2. Agreement by school board to confine itself in hiring to those applicants within the system is beyond the scope of bargaining and is therefore unenforceable. Board of Educ. of Township of North Bergen v. North Bergen Federation of Teachers, 141 N.J.Super. 97, 357 A.2d 302 (1976).

Freedom of Nonunion Teacher to Speak at Open Meeting Cannot be Curtailed

CITY OF MADISON v. WISCONSIN EMPLOYMENT RELATIONS COMM.

Supreme Court of the United States, 1976.
429 U.S. 167, 97 S.Ct. 421.

Mr. Chief Justice BURGER delivered the opinion of the Court.

The question presented on this appeal from the Supreme Court of Wisconsin is whether a State may constitutionally require that an elected Board of Education prohibit teachers, other than union representatives, to speak at open meetings, at which public participation is permitted, if such speech is addressed to the subject of pending collective-bargaining negotiations.

The Madison Board of Education and Madison Teachers, Inc. (MTI), a labor union, were parties to a collective-bargaining agreement during the calendar year of 1971. In January 1971 negotiations commenced for renewal of the agreement and MTI submitted a number of proposals. One among them called for the inclusion of a so-called "fair-share" clause, which would require all teachers, whether members of MTI or not, to pay union dues to defray the costs of collective bargaining. * * *

During the same month, two teachers, Holmquist and Reed, who were members of the bargaining unit, but not members of the union, mailed a letter to all teachers in the district expressing opposition to the "fair share" proposal. Two hundred teachers replied, most commenting favorably on Holmquist and Reed's position. Thereupon a petition was drafted calling for a one year delay in the implementation of "fair share" while the proposal was more closely analyzed by an impartial committee. The petition was circulated to all teachers in the district on December 6, 1971. Holmquist and Reed intended to present the results of their petition effort to the school board and to MTI at the school board's public meeting that same evening.

* * * During a portion of the meeting devoted to expression of opinion by the public, the president of MTI took the floor and spoke on the subject of the ongoing negotiations. He concluded his remarks by presenting to the board a petition signed by 1,300–1,400 teachers calling for the expeditious resolution of the negotiations. Holmquist was next given the floor, after John Matthews, the business representative of MTI, unsuccessfully attempted to dissuade him from speaking. Matthews had also spoken to a member of the school board before the meeting and requested that the board refuse to permit Holmquist to speak. Holmquist stated that he represented "an informal committee of 72 teachers in 49 schools" and that he desired to inform the Board of Education, as he had already informed the union, of the results of an informal survey concerning the "fair share" clause. He then read the petition which had been circulated to the teachers in the district that morning and stated that in the 31 schools from which reports had been received, 53% of the teachers had already signed the petition.

Holmquist stated that neither side had adequately addressed the issue of "fair share" and that teachers were confused about the meaning of the proposal. He concluded by saying: "Due to this confusion, we wish to take no stand on the proposal itself, but ask only that all alternatives be presented clearly to all teachers and more importantly to the general public to whom we are all responsible. We ask simply for communication, not confrontation." The sole response from the school board was a question by the president inquiring whether Holmquist intended to present the board with the petition. Holmquist answered that he would. Holmquist's presentation had lasted approximately two and one-half minutes.

Later that evening, the board met in executive session and voted a proposal acceding to all of the union's demands with the exception of "fair share." During a negotiating session the following morning, MTI accepted the proposal and a contract was signed on December 14, 1976.

(1)

In January 1972 MTI filed a complaint with the Wisconsin Employment Relations Commission (WERC) claiming that the Board had committed a prohibited labor practice by permitting Holmquist to speak at the December 6 meeting. * * *

* * *

(2)

The Wisconsin court perceived "clear and present danger" based upon its conclusion that Holmquist's speech before the school board constituted "negotiation" with the board. Permitting such "negotiation," the court reasoned, would undermine the bargaining exclusivity guaranteed the majority union under Wis.Stat. § 111.70(3)(a)4. From that premise it concluded that teachers' First Amendment rights could be limited. Assuming, *arguendo,* that such a "danger" might in some circumstances justify some limitation of First Amendment rights, we are unable to read this record as presenting such danger as would justify curtailing speech.

The Wisconsin Supreme Court's conclusion that Holmquist's terse statement during the public meeting constituted negotiation with the board was based upon its adoption of the lower court's determination that, "[e]ven though Holmquist's statement superficially appears to be merely a 'position statement,' the court deems from the total circumstances that it constituted 'negotiating.'" This cryptic conclusion seems to ignore the ancient wisdom that calling a thing by a name does not make it so. Holmquist did not seek to bargain or offer to enter into any bargain with the board, nor does it appear that he was authorized by any other teachers to enter into any agreement on their behalf. Although his views were not consistent with those of MTI, communicating such views to the employer could not change the fact that MTI alone was authorized to negotiate and to enter into a contract with the board.

Moreover, the school board meeting at which Holmquist was permitted to speak was open to the public. He addressed the school board not merely as one of its employees but also as a concerned citizen, seeking to express his views on an important decision of his government. We have held that teachers may not be "compelled to relinquish the First Amendment rights they would otherwise enjoy as citizens to comment on matters of public interest in connection with the operation of the public school in which they work." * * * Where the State has opened a forum for direct citizen involvement, it is difficult to find justification for excluding teachers who make up the overwhelming proportion of school employees and are most vitally concerned with the proceedings. It is conceded that any citizen could have presented precisely the same points and provided the board with the same information as did Holmquist.

* * *

(3)

The Employment Relations Commission's order was not limited to a determination that a prohibited labor practice had taken place in the past; it also restrains future conduct. By prohibiting the school board from "permitting employees to appear and speak at meetings of the Board of Education" the order constitutes an indirect, but effective, prohibition on persons such as Holmquist from communicating with their government. The order would have a substantial impact upon virtually all communication between teachers and the school board. The order prohibits speech by teachers "on matters subject to collective bargaining." As the dissenting opinion below noted, however, there is virtually no subject concerning the operation of the school system that could not also be characterized as a potential subject of collective bargaining. Teachers not only constitute the overwhelming bulk of employees of the school system, but they are the very core of that system; restraining teachers' expressions to the board on matters involving the operation of the schools would seriously impair the board's ability to govern the district. * * * The challenged portion of the order is designed to govern speech and conduct in the future, not to punish past conduct and as such it is the essence of prior restraint.

The judgment of the Wisconsin Supreme Court is reversed and the case is remanded to that court for further proceedings not inconsistent with this opinion.

Reversed and remanded.

Chapter 12

TORTS

The law grants to each individual certain personal rights with regard to conduct which others must respect. Some of these rights arise through the execution of a contract between individuals, for breach of which financial liability may result. The law also grants to each individual certain personal rights not of a contractual nature, such as freedom from personal injury and security of life, liberty, and property. The law imposes corresponding duties and responsibilities on each individual to respect the rights of others. If, by speech or other conduct, one fails to respect these rights, thereby damaging another, a tort has been committed and the offending party may be held liable.

A tort is a civil wrong independent of contract. It may be malicious and intentional or it may be the result of negligence and disregard for the rights of others. An action in tort compensates private individuals for harm caused to them by unreasonable conduct of others. Social norms have provided the basis for legal precedent in the determination of that which is considered unacceptable or unreasonable conduct.

The legally proper relationship between two persons may be breached by injury caused by either an act or an omission to act on the part of either party. The word tort is derived from the Latin word *"tortus"* or "twisted."[1] In personal relationships, the term "twisted" is applied to activity which in some way deviates from a normally acceptable pattern of behavior.

A tort is different from a crime and emanates from a separate and distinct body of law. A civil action for tort is initiated and maintained by the injured party for the purpose of obtaining compensation for the injury suffered, whereas in a criminal proceeding the action is brought by the state to protect the public from actions of a wrongdoer. In a criminal case the state prosecutes not to compensate the injured person, but rather to protect the public from further wrongful acts. Since criminal law does not, nor was ever intended to compensate an injured individual, social justice demanded the birth of the action in tort.

Grounds for actions in tort may be divided into three categories: (1) intentional interference, (2) strict liability, and (3) negligence.

1. William L. Prosser, *Law of Torts,* West Publishing Co., St. Paul, Minnesota, p. 1.

Intentional Interference

An intentional tort may result from an intended act whether accompanied by enmity, antagonism, maliciousness or by no more than a good-natured, practical joke.[2] With this type of tort it is not necessary for the wrongdoer to be hostile or desire to do harm to the injured party. Even where a person does not plan to injure another but proceeds intentionally to act in a way which invades the rights of another, he commits an intentional tort. In order for intent to exist the activity of an individual must, with substantial certainty, be the result of his act. If one does not know with substantial certainty the result of his act and injury results, then it is not an intentional tort but is negligence instead.

Assault. An intentional tort may be committed even if no physical "touching" takes place. To have assault there must be an "overt act or an attempt, or the unequivocal appearance of an attempt, to do some immediate physical injury to the person of another." The overt act must be a display of force or menace of violence of such a nature as to cause reasonable apprehension of immediate bodily harm.[3] It is assault where a person stands within striking distance of another and with sword drawn says, "I intend to run you through." Such words and acts may be sufficient to put the plaintiff in immediate apprehension of imminent harm and it is apparent that the offender has the present ability to effectuate the harm. Thus, an intentional tort may be consummated by an act which, while not involving physical contact, places a person in immediate fear that such action will transpire.

Battery. Technically, battery is an intentional tort which comes about through physical contact. Prosser points out that it is battery to injure a man in his sleep, even though he does not discover the injury until later, while it is an assault to shoot at him while he is awake, and frighten but miss him.[4] In both cases a person's interests are invaded. If a wrongdoer swings a bottle intending to strike the plaintiff, and the plaintiff sees the movement and is apprehensive for his own safety, there is assault and if the attack is consummated and the blow is actually landed, both assault and battery are present.

Teachers accused of assault and battery for administering corporal punishment are usually given considerable leeway as to the reasonableness of their action. In one case, the court explained the rule of law this way: "To be guilty of an assault and battery, the teacher must not only inflict on the child immoderate chastisement, but he

---

2. Reynolds v. Pierson, 29 Ind.App. 273, 64 N.E. 484 (1902); State v. Monroe, 121 N.C. 677, 28 S.E. 547 (1897).

3. State v. Ingram, 237 N.C. 197, 74 S. E.2d 532 (1953).

4. Prosser, *op. cit.* p. 37.

must do so with legal malice or wicked motives or he must inflict some permanent injury." [5]

Cases involving assault and battery by a teacher usually result from a teacher's attempt to discipline a child. The courts generally allow wide latitude for teachers in chastisement of pupils presuming that the teacher is innocent, has acted reasonably, and has done his duty until the contrary is proved.

The courts still uphold the ancient doctrine of *in loco parentis* which holds that the teacher stands in place of the parent and in such capacity has the right to chastise a pupil. The teacher's prerogatives are, of course, limited to the jurisdiction of the school and are not unlimited. Within these boundaries, the teacher may require pupils to abide by all reasonable commands and may inflict reasonable corporal punishment to enforce compliance. One court stated the situation in this manner:

> In the school, as in the family, there exists on the part of the pupils the obligations of obedience to lawful commands, subordination, civil deportment, respect for the right of other pupils, and fidelity to duty. Those obligations are inherent in any proper school system, and constitute, so to speak, the common law of the school.[6]

Courts do, however, make it quite clear that a teacher may be guilty of assault and battery if chastisement is cruel, brutal,[7] excessive,[8] or if administered in anger or insolence.[9] In one interesting old case, the court said that a teacher was not justified in beating a scholar so severely as to wear out two whips, striking two blows to the head with fists, and kicking the scholar in the face, because he misspelled a word and refused to try again.[10]

A case illustrating extreme conduct on the part of a teacher, resulting in a charge of assault and battery, took place in 1967 in Louisiana. The pupil sustained a broken arm when a physical education teacher tried to remove him from the basketball court. According to that teacher's testimony, the teacher twice ordered the boy off the basketball court and the boy returned a third time and was this time escorted from the court by the teacher. During this final episode the boy attempted to strike the teacher whereupon the teacher tried to restrain him with the resultant effect that the boy's arm was broken. This testimony was contradicted by the boy, who claimed he had not provoked the teacher other than by returning to the court and fur-

5. Suits v. Gover, 260 Ala. 449, 71 So. 2d 49 (1949).

6. State ex rel. Burpee v. Burton, 45 Wis. 150 (1878).

7. Gardner v. State, 4 Ind. 632 (1853).

8. Vanvactor v. State, 113 Ind. 276, 15 N.E. 341 (1888).

9. Cooper v. McJunkin, 4 Ind. 290 (1853).

10. Gardner v. State, 4 Ind. 632 (1853).

ther claimed that the teacher had menaced, chased, seized, lifted and shook him against the bleachers and suddenly let him fall on the floor fracturing his arm. The appellate court found that the teacher was five feet, eight inches tall and weighed 230 pounds, while the pupil was only five feet tall and weighed only 101 pounds. The court was unconvinced that the teacher actually believed that a blow from the pupil could harm him. The court in ruling for the pupil concluded that the lifting, shaking and dropping of the pupil was force in excess of that required to either protect himself or to discipline the pupil.[11]

Chastisement of a pupil may become assault and battery if the teacher does not administer the punishment reasonably. Criteria used by courts to identify excessive punishment include: (1) proper and suitable weapon, (2) part of person to which it is applied, (3) manner and extent of chastisement, (4) nature and gravity of offense, (5) age of pupil, (6) temper and deportment of the teacher,[12] and (7) history of pupil's previous conduct.

Both assault and battery may be criminal wrongs as well as tort where statutes so require. Criminal statutes usually define assault as attempted battery, requiring present ability. However, the reasoning pertaining to individual statutes may or may not have application to tort law.

Interference with Peace of Mind. In keeping with the theory that every man who is injured should have recompense, modern courts have had a tendency to recognize as a separate tort, interference with peace of mind, the infliction of mental or emotional anguish. In such cases it is necessary and quite difficult to prove mental suffering. The courts have not been able to precisely delineate between actual tortious actions and what may be considered everyday rough language or immoderate personal behavior which hurt one's feelings yet are so severe as to create an action in tort. One cannot recover simply because of hurt feelings.[13]

Courts have held that where an act is malicious, as distinguished from being merely negligent, there may be recovery for mental anguish, even though no physical injury results.[14] However, cases involving actions for mental anguish and suffering are easier to prove before a jury if the emotional distress has produced some visible or identifiable physical harm.

Another intentional tort is false imprisonment, sometimes called false arrest. Relatively few cases have occurred in this area, but the general rule is that an unauthorized person cannot detain or physical-

---

11. Frank v. Orleans Parish School Bd., 195 So.2d 451 (La.App.1967).

12. Cooper v. McJunkin, 4 Ind. 290 (1853), Danenhoffer v. State, 69 Ind. 295 (1879).

13. Wallace v. Shoreham Hotel Corp., 49 A.2d 81 (D.C.Mun.App. 1946).

14. Barnett v. Collection Service Co., 214 Iowa 1303, 242 N.W. 25 (1932).

ly restrain the movements of another. This type of tort is not applicable to the situation where a teacher confines a child in his classroom since a teacher is charged with the responsibility for overseeing pupil activities in the school setting and is authorized to confine a pupil, if necessary, in order to discipline him.

Strict Liability

Generally, liability for tort has been imposed with regard to "fault" on the part of the defendant. Both intentional interference and negligence are based on the supposition that someone was injured at the fault of another party. However, cases have arisen where a person has been injured through no actual, identifiable fault of anyone. Such cases have forced some courts to hand down damage awards based on strict liability of the defendant. In these instances a person may be liable even though he is not strictly at fault for the other party's injury. This rule was adopted in order to place the damages on the person best able to bear the burden. In these cases, the defendant's acts are not so important as the injury and suffering of the injured person. Underlying this type of decision is the older social justice reasoning that requires that "he who breaks must pay" regardless of whether the injury is knowingly or negligently caused.[15]

While fault is not a prerequisite to liability in these cases, the courts do generally require that the defendant has caused some unusual hazard to exist. The defendant's activity must be one which involves abnormal danger to others.

Today in the United States, strict liability will not be imposed unless the activity or thing is classified as hazardous or even "ultrahazardous."[16] While strict liability cases reported by appellate courts involving activities in the public schools are scarce, the possibility of such actions, nevertheless, exist. For example, the hazards in schools caused by laboratory experiments, shop activity, or field trips present possibilities of actions involving strict liability. However, this area makes up such a small element of the total tort liability picture in schools that it is more important at this point to move to a discussion of the much more prevalent tort of negligence.

Negligence *

Negligence differs from an intentional tort in that negligent acts are neither expected nor intended while an intentional tort may be both anticipated and intended. With negligence, a reasonable man in the position of the actor could have anticipated the harmful results. A teacher, for example, could not have reasonably foreseen that a

15. Prosser, *op. cit.* p. 315.

16. Restatement of Torts, pp. 519–520.

* See: Kern Alexander and Erwin Solomon, *College and University Law*, The Michie Co., Charlottesville, Virginia, 1972, pp. 590–602.

hidden can in an incinerator would explode and injure a child which the teacher had sent to empty the classroom wastebaskets.[17]

An accident which could not have been prevented by reasonable care does not constitute negligence. Many times what first appears to be an accident can be traced to someone's negligence; however, instances of pure accident do occur where someone is injured and no one is actually at fault. For example, where a child closed a music room door cutting off the tip of another student's finger the court found no negligence, merely an accident.[18]

A negligent act in one situation may not be negligence under a different set of circumstances. No definite rules as to what constitutes negligence apply. The standard of conduct of the actor is the key. The conditions embracing a negligent act have been described in this fashion:

> It is fundamental that the standard of conduct which is the basis of the law of negligence is determined by balancing the risk, in the light of the social value of the interest threatened, and the probability and extent of the harm, against the value of the interest which the actor is seeking to protect, and the expedience of the course pursued.[19]

In order for the court to strike a balance between the threatened harm and the actor's conduct [20], the court must establish a standard by which such activity can be measured. In attempting to set boundaries for negligent acts committed in different factual situations the courts have developed the reasonableness theory. For negligence to be present, someone must sustain an injury resulting from an "unreasonable risk" taken by another person. To determine unreasonableness the courts personify the test in the terms of the "reasonable man."

The Reasonable Man. The reasonable man has been described by different courts as a prudent man, a man of average prudence, a man of ordinary sense using ordinary care [21] and skill, and as a reasonably prudent man, he is an ideal, a model of conduct and a community standard. The model for the reasonable man, although a community ideal, varies in every case. His characteristics are: (1) the physical attributes of the defendant himself, (2) normal intelligence, (3) normal perception and memory with a minimum level of information and experience common to the community, and (4) such superior skill

---

17. Prier v. Horace Mann Ins. Co., 351 So.2d 265 (La.App.1977).

18. Lewis v. St. Bernard Parish School Bd., 350 So.2d 1256 (La.App.1977).

19. Terry, "Negligence," 29 Harv.L.Rev. 40 (1915); See also The Restatement of Torts, pp. 291–293.

20. William L. Prosser, *Law of Torts*, West Publishing Co., St. Paul, Minnesota, p. 123.

21. Ibid., p. 124.

and knowledge as the actor has or holds himself out as having.[22] While this standard of behavior provides a framework for the whole theory of negligence, the exact formula varies with attributes of the persons involved and with the circumstances.

The reasonable man then has the same physical characteristics as the actor himself and the acts in question are measured accordingly. Correspondingly, the man who is crippled is not held to the same standard as the man with no physical infirmities. The courts have also made allowances for the weaknesses or attributes connected with the sex [23] and age [24] of the individual. The courts have not, however, been so lenient with individuals who have mental deficiencies. The courts have traditionally held that a man with less mental ability than an average person must adjust and conform to the rules of society. He is not given an allowance by the courts for subnormal mentality, but, if a man is actually insane, a more convincing argument can be made for allowing for his particular incapacity.[25]

In this regard, courts have held that where a person is temporarily ill and loses control of his faculties, he may not be held strictly accountable for his actions. This is true only, however, where the illness is caused by circumstances beyond the control of the actor.

Elements of Negligence

To have a valid cause of action for negligence certain prerequisites must exist and are frequently summarized into four categories: (1) A *duty* on the part of the actor to protect others, (2) a *failure* on the part of the actor to exercise an appropriate standard of care, (3) the act must be the *proximate cause* or *legal cause* of the injury, and (4) an *injury*, causing damage or loss, must exist.

Duty

The routine of everyday life creates situations where persons constantly create risks and incur obligations for the safety of others. In negligence cases a person has a duty to abide by a standard of reasonable conduct in the face of apparent risks.[26]

The courts generally hold that no duty exists where the defendant could not have reasonably foreseen the danger of risk involved.

22. Lehmuth v. Long Beach Unified School Dist., 53 Cal.2d 544, 2 Cal.Rptr. 279, 348 P.2d 887 (1960).

23. Hassenyer v. Michigan Cent. R. Co., 48 Mich. 205, 12 N.W. 155 (1882).

24. Johnson v. St. Paul City Ry. Co., 67 Minn. 260, 69 N.W. 900 (1887); Kitsap County Transp. Co. v. Harvey, 15 F.2d 166 (9th Cir. 1927).

25. In criminal law the courts have applied the rule as established in

M'Naghten's Case, 10 Ct. & F. 200, 8 E.R. 718 (1843) which holds the defense of insanity can only be established by showing that the accused was "laboring under such a defect of reason, from disease of the mind, as not to know the nature and quality of the act he was doing; or, if he did know it, that he did not know he was doing what was wrong."

26. Morris v. Douglas County School Dist., 241 Or. 23, 403 P.2d 775 (1965).

A duty owed by one person to another may well intensify as the risk increases. In other words, the duty to protect another is proportional to the risk or hazard of a particular activity. In certain school functions where risks are greater to children, a teacher has an increased level of obligation or duty to the children. For example, whenever children perform a dangerous experiment, the teacher has a greater obligation for the children's safety than where he is merely supervising a study hall. One judge has explained the duty requirement in this way:

> Every person is negligent when, without intending any wrong, he does such an act or omits to take such a precaution that under the circumstances he, as an ordinary prudent person, ought reasonably to foresee that he will thereby expose the interest of another to an unreasonable risk of harm; a person is required to take into account such of the surrounding circumstances as would be taken into account by a reasonably prudent person and possess such knowledge as is possessed by an ordinary reasonable person and to use such judgment and discretion as is exercised by persons of reasonable intelligence under the same or similar circumstance.[27]

Therefore, the school district has no duty to protect a child who is injured when he leaves campus without permission. The district is not responsible for the student's welfare off school grounds unless the school assumes responsibility and has knowledge of the specific danger involved.[28]

Generally, the law holds that a person is not liable for an omission to act where there is not some definite relationship between the parties; no general duty exists to aid a person in danger. For example, even though a moral duty may be present, no legal duty mandates that a mere bystander aid a drowning person. If, however, a person acts affirmatively to assist a person in peril, he assumes a duty to the person and all his subsequent acts must be performed reasonably. Because of this requirement, passersby in many situations will not assist victims of auto wrecks or other mishaps. Some states, in order to encourage more humanitarian responses and to protect well meaning rescuers, have enacted laws which protect the "good Samaritan" from liability.

While a teacher has no more of a duty than anyone else to be a "good Samaritan" to the general public, he does have an obligation or duty to help a student under his jurisdiction when injured at school. Because of the teacher-student relationship, a teacher may be liable

---

27. Osborne v. Montgomery, 203 Wis. 223, 234 N.W. 372 (1931).

28. Hoyem v. Manhattan Beach City School Dist., 71 Cal.App.3d 866, 139 Cal.Rptr. 769 (1977).

for an omission to act as well as for an affirmative act. In such a case, though, the teacher is only required to provide such assistance as a person with the same training and experience in similar circumstances could reasonably provide.

Standard of Care

A legally recognized duty requires the actor to conform to a certain standard of conduct or care. As the risk involved in an act increases, the standard of care required of the actor likewise increases.[29] The standard of care of a woodshop teacher is, of course, greater than that of the school librarian because the risk of injury involved in handling power tools is much greater than the risk of being injured while reading a book. Similarly, chemistry classes require a high standard of care.[30]

The standard of care required by the courts is not uniform among all persons. Children and aged persons have generally been given substantially more leeway in their activities than is allowed a normal adult. While both children and aged persons are liable for their torts, they are not held to the same standard as others without impairments of age. Although it is difficult to pinpoint precise standards to determine the reasonableness of a child because of the great variations in age, maturity and capacity, the courts have nevertheless established as a subjective test that which is "reasonable to expect of children of like age, intelligence and experience." [31]

While most courts appear to follow the above criteria for determination of negligence of children, some courts have applied criminal law standards which prescribe the following criteria:

(a) Children between one and seven years cannot be liable for negligence. They theoretically have no capacity for negligence.[32]

(b) Children between the ages of seven and fourteen have a *prima facie* case for incapacity but it can be rebutted. In other words, children in this age group are presumed not to be capable of negligence until proved to the contrary.

Authorities generally agree that while arbitrary age limits for negligence have been established by some courts, it is not a generally acceptable rule of law. One court has said that the rule providing for a specific age limit

---

29. Cirillo v. Milwaukee, 34 Wis.2d 705, 150 N.W.2d 460 (1967).

30. Connett v. Freemont County School Dist. No. 6, 581 P.2d 1097 (Wyo.1978).

31. Prosser, *op. cit.* p. 127.

32. *The Restatement of Torts* § 464 states that: "Age is only one of the elements to be considered, along with experience and judgment, the latter involving discretion and power of self control, being predominant."

" * * * is arbitrary and open to the objection that one day's difference in age should not be the dividing line as to whether a child is capable of negligence or not. Under present-day circumstances, a child of six is permitted to assume many responsibilities. There is much opportunity for him to observe and thus become cognizant of the necessity for exercising some degree of care. Compulsory school attendance, the radio (television), the movies, and traffic conditions all tend to have this effect. Under the arbitrary cut-off rule, a child may be guilty of the most flagrant violation of duty and still be precluded from any presumption of negligence." *

With regard to teachers or others in the teaching profession, the generally accepted standard of care would be that of a reasonably prudent teacher, not that of a reasonably prudent layman. A New York court has put it this way:

> The standard of care required of an officer or employee of a public school is that which a person of ordinary prudence charged with his duties, would exercise under the same circumstances.[33]

A Vermont court has defined the "standard of care" owed to a pupil by a teacher in the following manner. A teacher's " * * * relationship to the pupils under his care and custody differs from that generally existing between a public employee and a member of the general public. In a limited sense the teacher stands in the parents' place in his relationship to a pupil * * * and has such a portion of the powers of the parent over the pupil as is necessary to carry out his employment. In such relationship, he owes his pupils the duty of supervision * * * " [34]

While the above is the prevailing view, some courts have held teachers to a lesser degree of care. These courts have said that a teacher may be charged only with reasonable care such as any person of ordinary prudence would exercise under comparable circumstances.

Proximate or Legal Cause

"Proximate cause" or "legal cause" is the connection between the act and the resultant injury. The question the court will ask is: "Was the injury a natural and probable consequence of the wrongful act, and ought it to have been foreseen in light of the attendant

33. Ohman v. Board of Educ. of City of New York, 300 N.Y. 306, 90 N.E.2d 474 (1949), rearg. denied 301 N.Y. 662, 93 N.E.2d 927.

34. Eastman v. Williams, 124 Vt. 445, 207 A.2d 146 (1965).

circumstances?" [35] The *Restatement of Torts* explains the necessity of adequate causal relation in this way:

> In order that a negligent actor shall be liable for another's harm, it is necessary not only that the actor's conduct be negligent toward the other, but also that the negligence of the actor be a legal cause of the other's harm.[36]

To establish proximate cause there must first be a duty or obligation on the part of the actor to maintain a reasonable standard of conduct. In most negligence cases, however, the courts will not refer to proximate cause but will rely solely on the duty or obligation of the defendant and the standard of conduct required to avoid liability. Proximate cause as a criterion of liability has been used most often where some doubt is present as to whether the injured person was within the zone of obvious danger.[37]

In these cases the courts require that the negligence of the defendant must be the "substantial" cause of the harm to the plaintiff. In other words, the cause must be substantial enough to lead reasonable men to conclude it is indeed the cause of injury. If the negligence is not a substantial factor in producing the harm then no liability will follow.

The actor's negligent act must be in continuous and active force up to the actual harm and the lapse of time must not be so great that contributing causes and intervening factors render the original negligent act to be an unsubstantial or insignificant force in the harm. Therefore, a teacher may be relieved of liability for negligent conduct if some intervening act is sufficient to break the causal connection between her act and a pupil's injury. For example, where a principal gave pupils permission to hold a race in a street and a "recklessly negligent" pupil ran into and injured a pedestrian, the court held that the causal relation was too remote to hold the principal liable.[38]

In order to break the chain of events causing injury, the intervening act must legally supersede the original negligent act. This rule is illustrated where a student was cleaning a power saw in shop class and another student turned on the switch starting the machine in violation of safety rules. The court in this instance held that the board's negligence in not having a guard over the beltdrive was not the proximate or legal cause of the injury.[39]

35. Scott v. Greenville Pharmacy, 212 S.C. 485, 48 S.E.2d 324 (1948).

36. Restatement, Second, Torts, § 430.

37. Prosser, *op. cit.* p. 252. See: Woodsmall v. Mt. Diablo Unified School Dist., 188 Cal.App.2d 262, 10 Cal.Rptr. 447 (1961); Munson v. Board of Educ., 17 A.D.2d 687, 230 N.Y.S.2d 919, aff'd 13 N.Y.2d 854, 242 N.Y.S.2d 492, 192 N.E.2d 272 (1962).

38. McDonell v. Brozo, 285 Mich. 38, 280 N.W. 100 (1938).

39. Meyer v. Board of Educ., 9 N.J. 46, 86 A.2d 761 (1952).

A different result might have been reached, however, if the intervening act had been foreseeable and could have been prevented by reasonable care on the part of the defendant. For example, were a teacher to send a child on an errand across a busy street and a motorist, while driving carelessly, injures the child, both the teacher and the motorist may be liable. Here the intervening negligent act is not substantial enough to entirely overcome the original act. In an actual case demonstrating this point, a school bus driver was negligent when a student was struck by an automobile after alighting from the bus. The driver of the automobile was also negligent; however, the court held that the negligent bus driver had a continuing obligation which was not ended by the negligence of the driver of the automobile. The automobile driver's negligence did not constitute a sufficient break in the causal connection to be a defense for the bus driver and was not a superseding or intervening cause.[40]

Injury or Actual Loss

A plaintiff, of course, cannot recover unless actual injury is suffered and is able to show actual loss or damages resulting from defendant's act. If the harm suffered is caused by more than one person, then damages may be apportioned among the tortfeasors. Sometimes both school district and teacher are joined together by a plaintiff student in a case wherein it is claimed that the injury was caused by acts by both parties.

Defenses for Negligence

In all cases involving negligence the defendant may attempt to show that he is not negligent because the injury was a mere accident, that his act was not the proximate or legal cause of injury or that some other act intervened and was responsible for the injury. However, aside from these essentials of a tort claim there are other rejoinders against negligence which may be classified as defenses. The more common of these are: (1) contributory negligence, (2) comparative negligence, (3) assumption of risk, and (4) immunity.

Of these defenses, contributory negligence and assumption of risk are most often used in school law cases. Immunity as a defense is where common or statutory law provides for sovereign immunity. Each of these concepts are briefly explained below:

Contributory Negligence. Contributory negligence involves some fault or breach of duty on the part of the injured person, or failure to exercise the required standard of care for his own safety. One court explained contributory negligence as conduct on the part of the injured party which caused or contributed to the injury and which would not have been done by a person exercising ordinary prudence

---

40. Mikes v. Baumgartner, 277 Minn.
423, 152 N.W.2d 732 (1967).

under the circumstances.[41] The *Restatement of Torts* defines contributory negligence in much the same manner as,

> * * * conduct on the part of the plaintiff which falls below the standard to which he should conform for his own protection, and which is legally contributing cause co-operating with the negligence of the defendant in bringing about the plaintiff's harm.[42]

As previously pointed out, a child is capable of negligence and his failure to conform to a required standard of conduct for a child of the same age, physical characteristics, sex and training will result in the court assigning fault to his actions. Thus, if an injured child is negligent and his negligence contributes to the harm, then a defendant, who is also negligent, may be completely absolved from liability. If the student has superior knowledge which would be protective then the courts will take it into consideration in adjudging fault. Where students knew that chemicals should not be held near a flame and the students intentionally set fire to the experiment and injury resulted, the court held the students were contributorily negligent because they should have known the consequences.[43]

However, since a child is not expected to act with the same standard of care as an adult, teachers have more difficulty in showing contributory negligence than if the plaintiff were an adult. A child is by nature careless and often negligent, and knowing this, a teacher should allow for an additional margin of safety. This is especially true with younger children. In fact, courts have said that where a child is concerned, the test to be employed is whether the child has committed a gross disregard of safety in the face of known, perceived and understood dangers.[44]

In a case where contributory negligence was found, a boy climbed on top of wire screening, fell through a hole and was injured, the jury found the boy to be contributorily at fault because he did not exercise a reasonable degree of care for his own protection.[45]

In other cases, courts have held that a pupil who was injured when he mixed chemicals in a school laboratory was guilty of contributory negligence because he knew the chemicals were dangerous; [46] and that a high school student who was injured while running in a school building after the lights were out was negligent.

41. Walsh v. West Coast Mines, 31 Wash.2d 396, 197 P. 2d 233 (1948).

42. Restatement, Second, Torts § 463.

43. Rixmann v. Somerset Public Schools, 83 Wis.2d 571, 266 N.W.2d 326 (1978).

44. Cormier v. Sinegal, 180 So.2d 567 (La.App.1965).

45. Basmajian v. Board of Educ., 211 App.Div. 347, 207 N.Y.S. 298 (1925).

46. Wilhelm v. Board of Educ. of City of New York, 16 A.D.2d 707, 227 N.Y. S.2d 791 (1962).

If a plaintiff's negligence or fault contributes to the injury, the court will bar recovery of any damages at all. Some courts have held that complete barring of any damages because of contributory fault is perhaps a litle drastic and have, therefore, endeavored to pro-rate damages based on degree of fault. This results in what is known as comparative negligence.

Comparative Negligence. Where contributory negligence on the part of the plaintiff is shown, the defendant is usually completely absolved from all liability. This, some courts and legislatures have felt, works a hardship on the negligent plaintiff who suffers injury but can recover nothing from the negligent defendant. This concern for the injured party has led legislatures in some states to enact statutes to determine degrees of negligence and allow recovery based on the relative degree of fault. While the specific provisions of "comparative negligence" statutes vary from state to state, the concept works this way: If the plaintiff's fault is found to be about equal to the defendant's, then the plaintiff will recover one-half the damages and must bear the remainder of the loss himself. If the plaintiff's negligence amounted to one-third the fault and the defendant's two-thirds, then the plaintiff could recover two-thirds of the damages.

Assumption of Risk. Assumption of risk is another defense against negligence. Herein, the plaintiff acts in a manner which effectively relieves the defendant of his duty or obligation of conduct. The plaintiff by expressed or implied agreement recognizes the danger and assumes the risk. Defendant is thereby under no legal duty to protect the plaintiff. With knowledge of the danger, the plaintiff voluntarily enters into a relationship with the defendant, and by so doing agrees to take his chances.[47]

Plaintiff's knowledge and awareness of the danger is an important factor in this defense. For example, a boy playing basketball was injured when his arm went through a glass pane in a door immediately behind the basketball backboard. The court later said that the boy had not assumed the risk of such an injury. The boy did not know the glass in the door was not shatterproof.[48] However, another court held that a boy had assumed the risk when he suffered an injury by colliding into a doorjamb in a brick wall while playing as a voluntary member of a team in a school gymnasium. The boy had played in the gym previously and knew the location of the basket, the door and the wall and, therefore, was aware of the danger involved in voluntarily playing in this particular gymnasium.[49] In a case where

47. Prosser, *op. cit.* p. 303. See: Passantino v. Board of Educ. of City of New York, 41 N.Y.2d 1022, 395 N.Y.S. 2d 628, 363 N.E.2d 1373 (1977).

48. Stevens v. Central School Dist. No. 1, 25 A.D.2d 871, 270 N.Y.S.2d 23 (1966).

49. Maltz v. Board of Educ. of New York City, 32 Misc.2d 492, 114 N.Y.S. 2d 856 (1952).

a batter in a softball game struck a classmate who was sitting on the third base line, the court said the child who was struck either assumed the risk or was contributorily negligent.[50]

Courts have generally established that the participant in athletic events, whether intramural or interscholastic, assumes the risk of the normal hazards of the game. This rule also applies to spectators attending sports or amusement activities. Spectators assume all the obvious or normal risks of being hurt by flying balls,[51] fireworks,[52] or the struggles of combatants.[53]

Everyone has seen spectators knocked down along the sidelines of football games by players careening off the field. A high school girl was injured precisely in this fashion as she was standing by the sidelines and was run over by football players. The court found against the plaintiff in following prevailing precedent and said that a spectator at a sporting event assumes risks incident to the game. This is especially true where the spectator chooses to stay at an unsafe place despite the availability of protected seating.[54]

Essential to the doctrine of assumption of risk is that the plaintiff have knowledge of the risks; if he is ignorant of the conditions and dangers, he does not assume the risk. If reasonable precautions are not taken to determine the hazards involved, then he has not assumed the risk but may have been contributorily negligent instead. However, neither a participant nor a spectator assumes the risk for negligence or willful or wanton conduct of others. For example, a spectator at an athletic contest does not assume the risk of the stands falling at a football game nor does he assume that by attending a baseball game, a player will intentionally throw a bat into the stands.

Immunity. Immunity from tort liability is generally conferred on (1) national and state governments unless abrogated by statute, (2) public officials performing quasi-judicial or discretionary functions, (3) charitable organizations granted immunity in some states, (4) infants under certain conditions, and (5) in some cases, insane persons.

Where public schools are concerned, the defense of immunity is usually employed to protect the public school district against liability.[55] This governmental or sovereign immunity is an historical

---

50. Benedetto v. Travelers Ins. Co., 172 So.2d 354 (La.App.1965).

51. Brisson v. Minneapolis Baseball and Athletic Ass'n, 185 Minn. 507, 240 N.W. 903 (1932); Kavafiam v. Seattle Baseball Club Ass'n, 105 Wash. 215, 177 P. 776 (1919).

52. Scanlon v. Wedger, 156 Mass. 462, 31 N.E. 642 (1891).

53. Dusckiewicz v. Carter, 115 Vt. 122, 52 A.2d 788 (1947).

54. Cadieux v. Board of Educ. of the City School Dist. for the City of Schenectady, 25 A.D.2d 579, 266 N.Y.S.2d 895 (1966).

55. Barr v. Bernhard, 562 S.W.2d 844 (Tex.1978).

and common law precedent which protects a state agency against liability for its torts. Because of the importance of this concept and its frequent applicability in public school tort cases, governmental or sovereign immunity is treated separately below.

Intervening Causative Factor May Absolve
School from Liability

ALBERS v. INDEPENDENT SCHOOL DISTRICT NO. 302 OF LEWIS CTY.

Supreme Court of Idaho, 1971.
94 Idaho 342, 487 P.2d 936.

McFADDEN, Justice.   This action was instituted by appellant Ray Albers, the father of Morris Albers, a minor, to recover damages from Independent School District No. 302 of Lewis County, respondent, for personal injuries suffered by his son Morris. A motion for summary judgment was made by the school district which the trial court granted. We affirm this judgment.

* * *

The record discloses that on December 23, 1967, during the Christmas holiday, Morris Albers, with five other boys, drove to the high school gymnasium of the district with the intention of playing an informal basketball game. Upon arrival they found the entrance locked; however, the custodian was working on the premises and was persuaded, perhaps reluctantly, to open the door and let the youths use the basketball court. The custodian went about his cleaning duties after admitting the boys.

Morris undertook to clean the playing surface of the gymnasium, by sweeping the court with a wide dust mop or broom for five or ten minutes, while his friends changed clothes. The boys then engaged in warming up activities, shooting baskets, using two worn leather basketballs which they found lying about, the equipment room of the gymnasium being locked.

At the time Morris was wearing standard basketball shoes and slacks. He was a member of the high school basketball team, an accomplished high school athlete, and participated in several other team sports. At least one of the other five boys was a teammate of his on the basketball team.

After warming up the boys split into two teams and played a "half-court" basketball game. Morris' deposition reflects that "it was a real clean game" from the standpoint of fouls and close calls. Sometime into their play a shot came off the backboard and "headed out towards [the] out of bounds line on the east side of the gym." Morris and an opposing player ran for the loose ball. As Morris reached to pick it up the two boys collided, Morris hitting his head against his opponent's hip. Morris fell to the floor on his back in a semi-conscious state. Morris suffered a fracture in the cervical area of his spine necessitating surgical correction and prolonged hospitalization.

*   *   *

Generally, schools owe a duty to supervise the activities of their students whether they be engaged in curricular activities or non-required but school sponsored extra-curricular activities. *   *   * Further, a school must exercise ordinary care to keep its premises and facilities in reasonably safe condition for the use of minors who foreseeably will make use of the premises and facilities. *   *   *

On the claim that the school district breached its duty to supervise the boys' game, the record lacks any evidence as to how the presence of a coach or teacher would have prevented the collision of the boys chasing the rebounding basketball. *   *   * Physical contact in such a situation in an athletic contest is foreseeable and expected. The general rule is that participants in an athletic contest accept the normal physical contact of the particular sport. *   *   * Nothing in the record would justify an exception to the rule here.

Regarding the allegation that the school district was negligent in allowing the youths to play on a dirty playing surface, the deposition of Morris Albers and his statements quoted above show there was no breach of any such duty. He had personally cleaned the floor and stated he saw no water spots or anything of that nature on the floor.

*   *   *

The summary judgment of the trial court is affirmed. Costs to respondent.

Reasonable Supervision Does Not Require
Constant Unremitting Scrutiny

FAGAN v. SUMMERS

Supreme Court of Wyoming, 1972.
498 P.2d 1227.

McINTYRE, Chief Justice. This case involves a suit for damages brought on behalf of seven-year-old George Fagan against a teacher's aid, Mrs. Lloyd Summers, and Park County School District No. 1.

During a noon recess a fellow student threw a small rock which hit a larger rock on the ground and then bounced up and struck George Fagan, causing him to lose the sight in his left eye. *   *   *

The trial court granted summary judgment for both Mrs. Summers and the school district. *   *   *

*   *   *

The Teacher

Regarding defendant Summers, she has stated by affidavit that she walked past the plaintiff and five or six other boys twice prior to the accident, while they were sitting on the ground near the school building. The boys were laughing and talking and she saw nothing out of the ordinary. After Mrs. Summers strolled by this group of youngsters, she had walked approximately 25 feet (taking about 30 seconds) when she heard an outcry from plaintiff. The accident happened in that interval.

There is no evidence or indication that Mrs. Summers' explanation is not true. Also, it is claimed on behalf of defendants that Mrs. Summers was reliable, conscientious and capable in her work and a good playground supervisor. This does not appear to be challenged in any of the evidence.

There is no requirement for a teacher to have under constant and unremitting scrutiny all precise spots where every phase of play activities is being pursued; and there is no compulsion that general supervision be continuous and direct at all times and all places. * * *

In Butler v. District of Columbia, 135 U.S.App.D.C. 203, 417 F.2d 1150, 1152, the court considered it common knowledge, susceptible of judicial notice, that small boys may indulge in horseplay when a teacher's back is turned. * * *

A teacher cannot anticipate the varied and unexpected acts which occur daily in and about the school premises. Where the time between an act of a student and injury to a fellow student is so short that the teacher has no opportunity to prevent injury, it cannot be said that negligence of the teacher is a proximate cause of the injury. * * *

As far as the instant case is concerned, counsel for appellant was asked during oral argument what should have been done by Mrs. Summers which was not done. His answer was to the effect that she could really not have done more than she did do and she could probably be dismissed from the suit. We consider counsel's answer frank and honest. In view of it and in view of what we have said about the absence of proximate cause on the part of Mrs. Summers, we hold summary judgment for her was proper.

The District

When counsel for appellant was asked during oral argument what the district should have done which was not done, his answer was that the district should have put the playground in better shape and should have provided more supervisors.

There is evidence that construction of a new school building was taking place. In connection with this construction, the blacktop of the playground had been torn up leaving clods of blacktop and a rough playground. It is also shown that this condition remained for approximately two years.

Although plaintiff alleged in his complaint that he had been hit with a piece of torn-up blacktop, counsel for appellant conceded in oral argument, as far as the record is concerned, plaintiff was hit with a rock. Counsel then advanced the theory that when the blacktop was torn up, it left rocks from beneath exposed.

There would be a possibility of this set of facts being proved if trial were had. Therefore, we will assume, for purposes of considering the propriety of summary judgment, that the playground was rough for a long period of time, with the blacktop torn up and rocks from beneath exposed. Although there appears to be no evidence as to where the rock which struck plaintiff came from, we will assume it was one which had been beneath the blacktop prior to ripping up of such blacktop.

We realize there are cases which hold a school district can be liable for injury resulting from a dangerous and defective condition of a playground. We have found no case, however, which holds rocks on the ground to be a dangerous and defective condition. Left on the ground, a rock will hurt no one.

Therefore, it we were to assume the school district was negligent for allowing rocks to be on the playground, we would have to hold the act of a third person who throws one of the rocks and injures the plaintiff an intervening cause of the accident.

* * *

In the case before us, plaintiff was not injured by negligence, if any, from rocks being on the playground. The injury was clearly caused by the intervening act of a third person—the boy who picked up and threw the rock. Appellant cites no authority for the proposition that such a result was reasonably foreseeable.

It is apparent from all we have said that the proximate cause of George Fagan's injury was the act of his fellow student in throwing a rock. It was not the failure of the Park County School District No. 1 to maintain the playground in a safe condition.

Appellant has made no effort to show that supervision of the playground was inadequate or that the accident would have been prevented if more supervisors had been present. We need not discuss counsel's casual suggestion that there may have been negligence in this regard.

Summary judgment for Mrs. Summers and for the school district was justified and proper.

Affirmed.

NOTES

1. *Liability of Teacher Aide for Pupil Injury.* When teacher aides are assigned tasks involving supervision, they are placed in position of potential liability for pupil injury. In such a situation, liability is likely to arise out of negligence on the part of the aide. Any person assigned such responsibilities is ignorant at his own peril. If he is not qualified to supervise playgrounds, then he should not attempt to perform the task.

In cases involving pupil injury, the courts have traditionally held the teacher to a higher "standard of care" than that owed to the general public. Likewise, a teacher aide, when placed in a supervisory capacity, owes the pupils a greater "standard of care" than is normally required in other personal relationships.

2. *Liability of Administrator or Supervisor for Negligent Acts of Teacher Aide.* Where the administrator or supervisor appoints a well qualified person to perform certain functions about the school and injury results, the administrator is not liable for negligence. The general rule of law is that in the public school situation the master is not liable for the commissions or omissions of his servant. In a Rhode Island case illustrating this principle, the court held that a school principal, who had authority over a school janitor, was not liable for injuries to a school teacher when he failed to warn her of a slippery floor in the school building. Gray v. Wood, 75 R. I. 123, 64 A.2d 191 (1949).

Therefore, a teacher or a principal is not liable for the negligent acts of a properly appointed and qualified teacher aide. On the other hand, if a teacher or a principal assigns duties for which the teacher aide is not qualified and the purposes of which do not fall within the scope of the aide's employment, the teacher or the principal may be liable for negligent acts by the aide.

3. An Illinois court in relating tort liability to the *in loco parentis* standard found that teachers are not subject to any greater liability than parents for injury to their children. Parents are liable only for willful and wanton misconduct, but not for mere negligence. Montague v. School Bd. of the Thorton Fractional Twp. North High School Dist. 215, 57 Ill.App.3d 828, 15 Ill.Dec. 373, 373 N.E.2d 719 (1978).

Reasonable Supervision Entails General Supervision Unless
Dangerous Situations Require Specific Supervision

MILLER v. YOSHIMOTO

Supreme Court of Hawaii, 1975.
56 Hawaii 333, 536 P.2d 1195.

KOBAYASHI, Justice.　*　*　*

The appellant instituted this negligence action for damages for the total loss of her left eye caused by the willful action of defendant Richard Yoshimoto, a minor (defendant). Appellant brought this action against both Yoshimoto and the appellee and alleged, *inter alia*, that appellee failed to provide proper supervision of students in or around the school area in which appellant was injured. The trial court gave judgment to the appellee. We affirm.

* * *

Aliamanu Intermediate School, hereinafter A.I.S., is a public school operated by the appellee. It is comprised of approximately 1600 students in the seventh and eighth grades.

Of the 1600 students approximately 80 percent use the buses to return home, while the other 20 percent walk home. Between 60 to 90 students walk home in the school campus area where the appellant was injured.

The principal of A.I.S., Mr. Harry Ono, had assigned various school personnel supervisory duties between 2:10 p. m. and 2:35 p. m.

On November 2, 1971, at about 2:10 p.m., Helen M. Miller, appellant, and her fellow students were dismissed from their classes at A. I.S. Accompanied by her friend, neighbor and classmate, Susan Colburn, appellant started walking home from her classroom in "B" Building at about 2:15 p.m. In order to reach home the girls had to walk between "F" Building and "B" Building and then across the school yard toward a flight of stairs which leads to Salt Lake Boulevard.

As appellant and Susan proceeded between "B" Building and "F" Building, Susan heard and appellant saw rocks being thrown from the end of "F" Building toward the area near "B" Building.

They recognized the two boys who were throwing the rocks as fellow students at A.I.S.

Appellant saw the boys throw three or four rocks; Susan saw the boys throw two or three rocks.

The girls then continued past the end of "F" Building and appellant asked the boys to stop throwing rocks as the rocks were going across the route where the girls would be walking. One of the boys then started to tease appellant.

As the girls continued walking the boys threw three or four rocks at the girls. Appellant again told the boys to stop throwing rocks, but the boys continued to throw rocks. These rocks came close enough to cause the girls to dodge them.

Appellant then told one of the boys that they "better not throw any more rocks" at her. Two more rocks were thrown at Susan and then appellant was struck in the eye by a rock.

Including the rock that injured appellant's eye, a total of between eight and twelve rocks were thrown by the boys at appellant and Susan.

The injury to appellant's eye required an enucleation of the left eye, an operation whereby the entire eye is removed from the socket. An artificial eye was later inserted.

* * *

It is widely recognized that the public school systems have a duty of reasonable supervision of the students entrusted to them. * * *

We agree with the above view and conclude that the appellee has a duty of reasonably supervising the public school students of Hawaii during their required attendance and presence at school and while the students are leaving school immediately after the school day is over. And, in our opinion, the duty of reasonable supervision entails general supervision of the students, unless specific needs, or a dangerous or a likely to be dangerous situation calls for specific supervision.

* * *

The critical question is whether the record herein shows that the appellee fulfilled its duty of reasonable supervision under the circumstances of this case.

* * *

Would the fact that there was no personnel assigned specifically to supervise the area in which appellant was injured be sufficient to show that appellee has breached its duty to provide reasonable supervision? We are of the opinion that, that in itself is not sufficient to show a breach by the appellee of its duty of reasonable supervision.

The duty of reasonable supervision does not require the appellee to provide personnel to supervise every portion of the school buildings and campus area. However, if certain specific areas are known to the appellee as dangerous, or the appellee should have known that a specific area is dangerous, or the appellee knew or should have known that certain students would or may conduct themselves in a manner dangerous to the welfare of others, duty of reasonable supervision would require specific supervision of those situations.

The appellant, however, failed to adduce any evidence showing that the area in which appellant was injured was dangerous in character or likely to be dangerous because of known deviant conduct of students or of others, requiring specific supervision by the appellee.

* * *

* * *[W]e are of the opinion that the evidence, in itself, is not sufficient to prove that the appellee failed to perform its duty herein.

* * *

* * * The record does not show that the findings of fact of the trial court are clearly erroneous.

The other issues urged upon this court by the appellant are without merit.

NOTES

The Supreme Court of Florida has attempted to set out an objective standard for review for damage awards. In the case of Bould v. Touchette, 349 So.2d 1181 (Fla.1977) the court stated:

Where recovery is sought for a personal tort, or where punitive damages are allowed, we cannot apply fixed rules to a given set of facts and say that a verdict is for more than would be allowable under a correct computation. In tort cases damages are to be measured by the jury's discretion. The court should never declare a verdict excessive merely because it is above the amount which the court itself considers the jury should have allowed. The verdict should not be disturbed unless it is so inordinately large as obviously to exceed the maximum limit of a reasonable range within which the jury may properly operate.

*Teacher's Leaving Schoolroom Not Proximate
Cause of Pupil's Injury*

SEGERMAN v. JONES

Court of Appeals of Maryland, 1969.
256 Md. 109, 259 A.2d 794.

SINGLEY, Judge. In 1968, Mary Latane Jones was a member of Mrs. Rita Segerman's fourth grade class at the Rollingwood Elementary School in Montgomery County. On 10 January of that year, Mrs. Segerman left the classroom for a few minutes on school business while the class was engaged in a program of calisthenics. During the teacher's absence and while the exercises were being performed, the back of Mary's head was struck by the feet of a fellow pupil, Robert Glaser (Bobby), and two of her front teeth were badly chipped. Mary's father, as Mary's next friend and in his individual capacity, brought suit against Mrs. Segerman and Bobby, alleging that Mary's injuries were the result of their negligence. Both defendants filed general issue pleas and the case went to trial before the Circuit Court for Montgomery County without a jury. At the end of the plaintiff's case, Bobby's motion for a directed verdict in his favor was granted, and judgment was entered in his favor for costs. From judgments against Mrs. Segerman entered on verdicts in amounts of $5,000.00 in Mary's favor and $1,131.00 in favor of Mary's father, Mrs. Segerman has appealed.

* * *

Mrs. Segerman testified that the physical education teacher came to Rollingwood on Fridays; that on other days, "It's up to the individual teacher to carry on her own phys. ed. program," and that since September, 1967, she had conducted exercise programs for Mary's class in the classroom. She also said that the members of her fourth grade class has been doing push-ups, sit-downs and jumping-jacks in the physical education class but that push-ups had never been previously done in her classroom, although jumping-jacks had.

According to Mrs. Segerman, the day when the accident occurred was in "a snowy week." She remembered "the entire week as being an indoor week", when "[t]he children could not go outdoors for phys. ed. during any part of that week at all."

Mrs. Segerman said that on 9 January, she asked the class if they were familiar with a record called "Chicken Fat" and when "so many of the children knew the record * * * asked them to bring it in." Margaret Wydro, a physical education teacher assigned to the Rollingwood area, described the record:

> "I think it was about five years ago. It was written specifically for the President's Council on Youth Fitness, to implement the program that President Kennedy had started. It was written by Meredith Willson, sung by Robert Preston; published by Capitol Records as a service to the Junior Chamber of Commerce, who was hopefully trying to distribute it at no cost to all schools throughout the country."

* * *

As Mrs. Segerman recounted it:

> "Q. Is that the record that you played that day? A. That is it.

> "Q. Mrs. Segerman, before playing this record that day that this girl in the class had brought in, did you go over it with the class? A. Yes.

> "Q. What did you do? How did you do it? A. First of all I asked, before I played the record, whether all the children knew it. And no one raised their hand to say that they did not know it. And I said we would listen to it first to make sure that we all knew how to do the exercises.

> "Q. Were they at the time sitting down; standing up? A. No. They were sitting down in their seats. I had not done anything. I just wanted them to listen to it first.

* * *

> "So we all were in our seats listening to the record. After the record played I asked the children then was there anyone who did not know how to do any of the exercises. And no one raised their hand. So to the best of my knowledge they all were aware of the exercises.

> "Q. Have they done all of these same exercises in gym class that you had see? A. Yes.

> "Q. All right. A. At that time, at that point I took the children and placed them around the room.

"Q. How did you place the children around the room? A. Generally as close to their desks as possible, or as close to this place they were supposed to be sitting; however, of course with the arrangement it would necessitate my moving certain children because the desks were close together, so that I utilized aisles and whatever space on the sides and front and back of the room that I had.

"Q. Do you know now just where you placed the children on that day? A. I could not place thirty of them if I had to.

"We could reconstruct it with the children, if we called the same children back again, I'm sure.

"Q. I mean do you know now? A. Not thirty of them, no.

"Q. Generally what would you do with respect to children that were on the same aisle, as these people would be sitting here, and these people would be there. That would give you six in an aisle. A. The normal procedure would be to place the children arms' distance apart, which is what I actually did.

"THE COURT: Place them what?

"A. Arms' distance apart.

"In other words, you have the child put their arm out, and the next child does that.

"After a while you get to judge the distance. You know approximately what is a safe distance between the children. And this is what I did with the group.

"Q. So you would take some people, instead of standing them by their seats, and move them in different places? A. Yes, definitely.

"Q. So you did this before you played the record the second time? A. Yes; oh, certainly.

"Q. Now, before you played the record the second time, did you say anything to the children there? A. Yes.

"Q. What did you tell them? A. First I made sure, as I said, that we all knew what was expected of them. I told them not to move from where I had placed them, that I was going into the office to attend to something and that I would be back in a few minutes and that they were to follow the instructions on the record.

"Q. Did you tell them not to move? A. Definitely.

* * *

"Q. Then what did you do when you put the record on? A. I waited to see how the procedure was going, and I

stayed for a few minutes to make sure that there was sufficient room and that things were going well.

"Q. The few minutes that you were there, did everything go all right?　A.　Yes."

Mrs. Segerman then left the classroom and walked across the
hall to the principal's office.　On cross examination, she said she assumed she was out of the classroom "four or five minutes."

What happened next is told by Mary:

"Mrs. Segerman put on a record, 'Chicken Fat'; and she
told us to follow the record.　And we'd started doing, working, and we went through the first side of the record.　And
then when we were starting the second side, Mrs. Segerman,
I think she told us that she's going out of the room, I'm almost positive she did, and she left.　And—and Bobby Glaser
was in the back of the room, and he moved up because he
couldn't hear the record player.　And he was doing his
push-ups, but he brought up his legs and was resting on his
knees.　And when he brought his feet down they went over
the back of my head and they came down on the floor.

"Q.　What came down on the floor?　A.　My head.

"Q.　Your head?　A.　And hit, my teeth hit the floor
and they came out.

"Q.　Your teeth came out?　A.　Yes."

*　*　*

It would appear that the court found that Mrs. Segerman was
negligent in leaving the classroom and that her failure to supervise
the exercises was the proximate cause of Mary's injury.　For reasons
which we shall develop, it is our view that Mrs. Segerman's motion
for a directed verdict should have been granted on the issue of proximate cause, which while ordinarily a question for the trier of facts,
was here a question of law, because the facts were undisputed and admitted of but one inference.　*　*　*

In structuring her appeal, Mrs. Segerman poses six questions:

"1.　Whether or not a teacher was negligent in leaving
her class room for four or five minutes on school business.

"2.　Whether the absence of the teacher from the class
room was the proximate cause of the plaintiff's injuries.

"3.　Whether or not a teacher is immune from suit
while acting within the scope of her employment.

"4.　Whether or not the Court committed error in failing to grant the defendant's motion for a directed verdict or
directed finding at the close of the plaintiff's case, and in
failing to grant the defendant's motion for a directed verdict

and to make a finding in behalf of defendant, at the close of all of the evidence.

"5. Whether or not the Court committed error in granting the defendant Robert Glaser's motion for a directed verdict or directed finding at the end of the plaintiff's case.

"6. Whether or not the Court committed error in finding against the defendant in favor of the plaintiff."

As we see the case, the significant issues are those presented by the second and fourth questions, because we believe that Mrs. Segerman's absence was not, as a matter of law, the proximate cause of Mary's injury. Even if we assume for the purposes of this opinion that Mrs. Segerman was negligent in leaving the room, it cannot be said that her absence or failure to supervise caused the injury, because Mrs. Segerman's presence could not have prevented it, and liability could be imposed only if the injury was reasonably foreseeable. "This is one of those events which could occur equally as well in the presence of the teacher as during her absence." Ohman v. Board of Education, etc., 300 N.Y. 306, 310, 90 N.E.2d 474, 475, aff'g 275 App.Div. 840, 88 N.Y.S.2d 273 (1949). As a consequence, we need not reach the other questions raised by the appeal.

In our view the proximate cause of Mary's injury was an intervening and wholly unforeseen force—the fact that Bobby Glaser left his assigned place and did not do his push-ups as he had been instructed to do them.

* * *

* * * In Holler v. Lowery, 175 Md. 149 at 161, 200 A. 353, 358 (1938) our predecessors said:

"There is no mystery in the doctrine of proximate cause. It rests upon common sense rather than legal formula. Expressed in the simplest terms it means that negligence is not actionable unless it, without the intervention of any independent factor causes the harm complained of. It involves of course the idea of continuity, that the negligent act continuously extends through every event, fact, act and occurrence related to the tortious conduct of the defendant and is itself the logical and natural cause of the injury complained of. In the statement of the doctrine an intervening cause means not a concurrent and contributing cause, but a superseding cause, which is itself the natural and logical cause of the harm."

* * *

If a rule can be developed from the teacher liability cases, it is this: a teacher's absence from the classroom, or failure properly to supervise students' activities, is not likely to give rise to a cause of action for injury to a student, unless under all the circumstances the possibility of injury is reasonably foreseeable. In Carroll v. Fitzsimmons, 153 Colo. 1, 3, 384 P.2d 81, 82 (1963), the Supreme Court of Colorado had before it the question whether an allegation "that the plaintiff was struck in the eye by a rock thrown by a fellow student" and "*   *   * that the defendant teacher permitted the rock to be thrown" stated a cause of action. In affirming the dismissal of the complaint, the court quoted from Nestor v. City of New York, supra, 28 Misc.2d 70 at 71, 211 N.Y.S.2d 975 at 977:

> "There is no requirement that the teacher have under constant and unremitting scrutiny the precise spots wherein every phase of play activity is being pursued; nor is there compulsion that the general supervision be continuous and direct."

The point is that a teacher could be liable to an injured student, whether or not the teacher could have prevented the injury, if the injury is a reasonably foreseeable consequence of absence of failure to supervise. Under such circumstances, the intervening force does not become a superseding cause which breaks the chain of causation, but becomes a part of the original tort. *   *   *

*   *   *

The test of foreseeability was well stated in McLeod v. Grant County School Dist. No. 128, 42 Wash.2d 316, 255 P.2d 360 (1953), a case which held the school district answerable in damages to a girl who was attacked in an unlighted room adjacent to the school gymnasium. There the Court said:

> "*   *   * Whether foreseeability is being considered from the standpoint of negligence or proximate cause, the pertinent inquiry in not whether the actual harm was of a particular kind which was expectable. Rather, the question is whether the actual harm fell within a general field of danger which should have been anticipated. [citing case]." 42 Wash.2d at 321, 255 P.2d at 363

having previously said:

> "The harm which came to appellant was not caused by the direct act or omission of the school district, but by the intervening act of third persons. The fact that the danger stems from such an intervening act, however, does not of itself exonerate a defendant from negligence. If, under the assumed facts, such intervening force is reasonably foreseeable, a finding of negligence may be predicated thereon. [citing case]." 42 Wash.2d at 320, 255 P.2d at 362.

*   *   *

If we apply this test to the facts of the case before us, it would be difficult to say that Mrs. Segerman could be held to have reasonably anticipated that any injury would result, whether the class performed the exercises while she was present in the room or after she had left it.

The testimony was uncontroverted that the members of the class had done push-ups before, possibly for as long as a year, in their physical education classes. She took the precaution of playing the record the first time with the children in their seats. She then spaced the children in the classroom and there is no testimony which would lead to the conclusion that this was done improperly. She then played one side of the record and observed the children doing the exercises before she left the room. <u>She had no reason to apprehend that any of the children would leave his assigned place or that any of the children would perform the exercises improperly, least of all Bobby Glaser, who, according to the testimony, was a good athlete.</u> The intervening force which became a superseding cause was the fact that Bobby chose to move from the place which had been assigned to him, and once there elected to do the push-ups by resting his knees on the floor rather than by supporting himself with the tips of his toes. If he had not changed his position or if he had changed his position and kept his toes on the floor, Mary would never have been hurt. <u>To say that Bobby's acts should have been foreseen by Mrs. Segerman would be sheer conjecture</u>.

Judgments reversed, costs to be paid by appellee.

NOTES

1. <u>The Supreme Court of California has held that the fact that another student's misconduct was the immediate precipitating cause of injury does not compel a conclusion that negligent supervision by the teacher was not the proximate cause of a student's death. The mere involvement of a third party nor the party's own wrongful conduct is sufficient in itself to absolve the defendants of liability, once a negligent failure to provide adequate supervision is shown.</u> Dailey v. Los Angeles Unified School Dist., 2 Cal.3d 741, 87 Cal.Rptr. 376, 470 P.2d 360 (1970).

2. Adequate supervision did not require a physical education teacher to provide a spotter for a student performing a forward roll when the student had been given proper instruction and had performed the routine on many occasions before without the assistance of a spotter. Lueck v. City of Janesville, 57 Wis.2d 254, 204 N.W.2d 6 (1973).

3. The intervening act of student throwing a bamboo high-jump cross bar, after school hours, and striking another student in the eye was the sole proximate cause of injury. High jumping equipment is not an "inherently dangerous" instrumentality which imposes a duty on teacher or school to provide supervision during nonschool hours. Bush v. Smith, 154 Ind.App. 382, 289 N.E.2d 800 (1973).

4. Requiring students to run to the dressing room, where time between classes is short, does not create an unreasonable risk. Driscol v. Delphi Community School Corp., 155 Ind.App. 56, 290 N.E.2d 769 (1973).

5. In preparation of a project for a science fair, a girl was burned when students attempted to light a defective burner which had gone out and alcohol exploded after the teacher had set the experiment up, checked that it worked correctly and returned to his regular class. The court, in holding the teacher liable for negligence, said: " * * * where one creates, deals in, handles or distributes an inherently dangerous object or substance, * * * an extraordinary degree of care is required of those responsible * * *. The duty is particularly heavy where children are exposed to a dangerous condition which they may not appreciate." The duty was to either positively warn the students not to try to light the burner or to personally supervise; the teacher did neither. Station v. Travelers Ins. Co., 292 So.2d 289 (La.App.1974).

Injured Student with Knowledge of Risk Involved Is Contributorily Negligent

HUTCHISON v. TOEWS

Court of Appeals of Oregon, Department 2, 1970.
4 Or.App. 19, 476 P.2d 811.

LANGTRY Judge. Plaintiff appeals from a judgment of involuntary nonsuit, entered on motion of both defendants at the conclusion of the plaintiff's case.

Plaintiff and his friend, Phillip Brown, both 15 years old, attempted to shoot a homemade pipe cannon which exploded, injuring plaintiff's hands. They had made the explosive charge by mixing potassium chlorate and powdered sugar.

Brown, as plaintiff's witness, testified that he and the plaintiff had "badgered" defendant Toews, the chemistry teacher at Phoenix High School, for potassium chlorate to use in fireworks experimentation. He said they had asked Mr. Toews for the material about a dozen times. The plaintiff said five or six times. Finally, Mr. Toews had given them some powered potassium chlorate, which they put in a baby food jar. A day or two later, when Mr. Toews left the separate chemical storage room unattended while he stepped into the adjoining chemistry classroom, Brown took, without Mr. Toews' knowledge or permission, some crystalline potassium chlorate also stored there. Brown positively identified this crystalline potassium chlorate as the substance used in the explosion. He was the one who mixed the ingredients. The plaintiff equivocated, first indicating that the powdered substance was what was used, but on cross-examination he said, "It looked like crystal." Brown waited approximately two years after the accident before he revealed to anyone that he had taken the crystalline substance and that it had caused the explosion. The plaintiff did not reveal that he knew the crystalline substance had been taken until after Brown's disclosure of the true facts. The injury occurred in November 1965. Plaintiff commenced this action for damages against defendant Toews only in June 1966, and filed in amended complaint in August 1967. In these complaints, plaintiff alleged that defendant Toews "supplied" the potassium chlorate to him.

* * *

Prosser says:

"* * * [T]he kind of contributory negligence which consists of voluntary exposure to a known danger, and so amounts to assumption of risk, is ordinarily a defense * * *." Prosser, Torts 539, § 78 (3rd ed. 1964).

We think the evidence construed in the light most favorable to plaintiff * * *, justifies the judgment of the court. The boys had purchased from a mail order firm in Michigan a pamphlet which gave 100 formulas for explosives. Together, they built the cannon and conducted their experiments. They admitted that they had looked at the warnings in the pamphlet. They had shown the pamphlet to defendant Toews, and he had cautioned them, and told them they should have supervision. He had declined their invitation to supervise them because of another commitment. Among other things, the pamphlet warned:

"* * * Some of the formulas listed in this booklet are very dangerous to make. Therefore, it is strongly suggested that the making of fireworks be left in the hands of the experienced.

* * *

They had previously experimented with homemade gunpowder in the cannon and in doing so had used up all of their fuses. When they mixed and placed the charge of potassium chlorate and powdered sugar in the cannon, they put the head of a paper match into the fuse hole and tried to light the paper end of the match in order to have time to take cover before the explosion. When Brown tried to light the paper match, wind impeded him. On Brown's request, plaintiff held his hands around the fuse hole to shield it from the wind. The charge exploded, and the closed pipe end "peeled like a banana." Plaintiff's hands were severly injured. The evidence is lengthy, but it is replete with statements from both of the boys that they knew the experiment conducted was dangerous. Plaintiff testified on cross-examination he knew "That you might get burned if you held onto it, or if you stood too close to it when it did shoot * * * that it might fly up or hit you in the face * * *."

* * * Plaintiff testified he knew that the pamphlet said the formula was very powerful.

* * *

There are many cases involving tort liability of suppliers of explosives to children. No purpose is served by a detailed discussion of them here. We note that they usually turn on whether the plaintiff had or should have had knowledge and understanding so that he could have avoided the explosion. * * *

In the case at bar, the only reasonable conclusion from the evidence was that plaintiff had knowledge of the risk involved, and that he was contributorily negligent as a matter of law.

Affirmed.

NOTES

1. Trade school welding student was not contributorily negligent when injured by exploding freon cylinder. Danos v. Foret, 354 So.2d 667 (La. App.1977).

2. Chemistry experiment in introductory high school course, requiring students to use materials which could explode, should be conducted under strictest supervision and personal attention of the teacher. (Mastrangelo v. West Side Union High School Dist. of Merced Cty., 2 Cal.2d 540, 42 P.2d 634 (1935).

Principal Liable Where He Assumed Additional Responsibility and Did Not Perform It Reasonably

TITUS v. LINDBERG

Supreme Court of New Jersey, 1967.
49 N.J. 66, 228 A.2d 65.

JACOBS, J. The Appellate Division affirmed a judgment for the plaintiffs against all three defendants, Lindberg, Smith and the Board of Education. We granted certification on the application of Smith and the Board of Education.

On October 25, 1963 the plaintiff Robert A. Titus, who was then nine years old and a student at the Fairview School in Middletown Township, rode off from home on his bicycle to school. He arrived at the school grounds at about 8:05 A.M., entered along the bus driveway, and headed for the bicycle rack on the west side of the school building. As he came around a corner of the building, he was struck by a paper clip which the defendant Richard Lindberg, then thirteen years old, had shot from an elastic band. Robert was seriously injured.

Lindberg was not then a student at Fairview but attended the Thompson School which was some distance away. Fairview had been designated by the school system's transportation coordinator as the pickup site for three schools including Thompson, and Lindberg was one of many students who customarily boarded school buses there. Up to two years earlier, Lindberg had attended Fairview and its records described him has a "very rough" and a "bully." On the morning of the incident he arrived early at Fairview, fooled around with an elastic band for a while, and struck a student in the back with a paper clip about 5 minutes before he shot the one which injured Robert.

Though the school doors at Fairview did not officially open until 8:15 A.M., it was customary for quite a few Fairview students to start arriving on the school grounds at about 8 A.M. Some would arrive on their bicycles, as did Robert, and others would arrive on foot. Oftentimes the students played the game of "keep away" before the school bell rang. An early arrival would obtain a ball from a classroom and a team of students would try to keep it away from a second team. The first bell rang at 8:15 A.M., the students were supposed to be in their seats by 8:30 A.M. when the late bell rang, and classes began at 8:35 A.M.

The defendant Smith had been principal of Fairview since 1960. He testified that he "did the supervising of the arrival of the children" and that, although he had known of prior pranks and deportment problems connected with Lindberg, he was not aware of any earlier incidents involving conduct such as his shooting of paper clips. Smith's practice was to arrive at the school grounds at 8 A.M. and he had instructed his teachers to arrive at that time and prepare for and be in their classes at 8:15 A.M. so that they could maintain order as the students filed in. On his arrival at 8 A.M. he would supervise deliveries by the milk truck and would watch out for the safety of children in the immediate area. He would then walk from the east side of the school to the west side where the buses began to arrive at 8:15 A.M. Sometimes he would walk through a corridor within the building and at other times he would walk along the outside of the building. At the time of the incident, he was walking inside the building. As he passed one of the windows of the building, he looked out and saw a group gathered around the stricken Robert. He went to the scene to administer assistance.

There were 560 students at Fairview and approximately 70 or 80 additional students arrived at the school grounds to board the buses. There were, in addition to administrative and part-time personnel, 19 full-time classroom teachers on the Fairview staff but none of them had been assigned any responsibilities in connection with the supervision of students before their entry into the classrooms. Smith testified that he made the rules governing the conduct of students on the school grounds and that he was charged with that responsibility. Although he stated that he told the students that school arrival time was from 8:15 A.M. to 8:30 A.M., he acknowledged his awareness that students began arriving at 8 A.M. and stated flatly that he maintained "supervision outside the building on the grounds between eight and 8:30."

The complaint, which was filed in the Law Division by Robert through his father Calvin as guardian *ad litem* and by his father individually, contained several counts. They charged the defendant Lindberg with having negligently shot the paper clip which injured Robert, the defendant Smith with having negligently failed to exercise supervision with the resulting injury, and the defendant Board of Education with having "actively and affirmatively failed to provide the necessary safeguards." After a full trial, the jury returned a verdict for the plaintiffs in the aggregate sum of $41,000 against all three defendants. A motion for new trial was denied by the trial court which also rejected a request that one-half the judgment be payable by Lindberg and the other half by Smith and the Board of Education. Its order directed that the judgment be borne proportionately by each of the three defendants. The defendant Lindberg sought no review but the defendants Smith and the Board of Education appealed to the Appellate Division which affirmed without opinion. We granted certification on application by Smith and the Board. 47 N.J. 571, 222 A.2d 23 (1966).

There is no dispute that Lindberg was soundly held liable for the injury caused by his conduct. And while there is dispute as to the liability of Smith, we are satisfied that the evidence fairly presented a jury question as to whether he had negligently failed to discharge his responsibilities with consequential injury to Robert. The duty of school personnel to exercise reasonable supervisory care for the safety of students entrusted to them, and their accountability for injuries resulting from failure to discharge that duty, are well-recognized in our State and elsewhere. * * *

In Cianci v. Board of Education, supra, a student was assaulted by another student in the school's play area and he brought an action for damages against the school principal and the board of education. New York's Appellate Division reversed the trial court's dismissal of the action against the principal, pointing out that "[q]uite apart from any liability imposed by statute, under the common law there was imposed upon her as the principal, both the duty to be reasonably vigilant in the supervision of the pupils and the liability for her negligent performance of such duty * * *. Similarly in Selleck v. Board of Education, 276 App.Div. 263, 94 N.Y.S.2d 318 (1949), motion for leave to appeal and rehearing denied 300 N.Y. 764, 90 N.E.2d 902 (1950), the court sustained a jury verdict for the plaintiff against both the supervising principal and the board of education where the evidence indicated that lack of proper supervision had resulted in a student's injury by another student who ran into him with his bicycle on the school grounds. 94 N.Y.S.2d at p. 321. See also the recent opinion in Eastman v. Williams, supra, where the Vermont Supreme Court made the following comments in the course of its holding that a jury question had been presented as to the liability of a teacher and a superintendent teacher for a student's injuries:

"In a limited sense the teacher stands in the parent's place
in his relationship to a pupil under his care and charge, and

has such a portion of the powers of the parent over the pupil as is necessary to carry out his employment. In such relationship, he owes his pupils the duty of supervision, and if a failure to use due care in such supervision results in injury to the pupil in his charge * * * [he is] * * * liable to such pupil. Common sense and fairness must call for the exercise of reasonable care in such duty of supervision, not only in the commission of acts that will not injure the pupil, but in a neglect or failure to act, when from such failure to act, injury results. See Doktor v. Greenberg, 58 N.J.Super. 155, 155 A.2d 793, 795; Guyten v. Rhodes, 65 Ohio App. 163, 29 N.E.2d 444, 445; 78 C.J.S. Schools and School Districts § 238, at 1197; 47 Am.Jur. Schools (1959 Supp.), § 60.1, p. 30. If the teacher is liable for misfeasance we find no sound reason why he should not also be held liable for nonfeasance, if his acts or neglect are the direct proximate cause of the injury to the pupil." 207 A.2d, at pp. 148–149.

Apparently Smith does not dispute the foregoing principles although he does seem to question that his responsibilities began before 8:15 A.M. We have no doubt on that score. In the first place he assumed the responsibility for supervising the school grounds beginning at 8 A.M. and was from that point on obligated to exercise due care * * *. In the second place, and wholly apart from the assumption it cannot in any fair sense be said that his legal responsibility began only upon the opening of the classrooms at 8:15 A.M. Obviously the students would be expected to and could properly come to the school grounds during some short period before the classrooms actually opened. They customarily began coming at 8 A.M. and that was reasonable. Smith undoubtedly knew of their coming and of their "keep away" games. When all this is coupled with the fact that Fairview was also a pickup site for the older students, the dangers and the need for reasonable supervision from 8 A.M. on were entirely apparent. See Conway, J. dissenting in Ohman v. Board of Education, 300 N.Y. 306, 90 N.E.2d 474, 478 (1949), motion for reargument denied 301 N.Y. 662, 93 N.E.2d 927 (1950):

"Children have a known proclivity to act impulsively without thought of the possibilities of danger. It is precisely this lack of mature judgment which makes supervision so vital. The mere presence of the hand of authority and discipline normally is effective to curb this youthful exuberance and to protect the children against their own folly."

Smith contends that he was entitled to a direction on the ground that there was insufficient evidence to enable a jury to find negligence on his part. The record discloses the contrary. He had not announced any rules with respect to the congregation of his students and their conduct prior to entry into the classrooms. He had assigned none of the teachers or other school personnel to assist him in supervising the students and he undertook the sole responsibility. He then failed to take any measures towards overseeing their presence and activities, except at the point of the milk delivery and by walking from east to west around or through the building. While he was walking through the building there was no semblance of supervision on the grounds outside and that was precisely when the injury to Robert occurred. Before then Lindberg had been fooling around and had struck another student while no supervisor was anywhere about. Bearing all of these circumstances in mind, it clearly cannot be said that the finding that Smith failed to take suitable supervisory precautions lacked reasonable support in the evidence. See Mayer v. Housing Auth. of Jersey City, 84 N.J.Super. 411, 423, 202 A.2d 439 (App. Div.1964), affirmed 44 N.J. 567, 210 A.2d 617 (1965).

Smith advances the further contention that, even if lack of due supervision be assumed, Lindberg's deliberate conduct rather than Smith's negligence was the "sole competent producing cause of the injury." The jury presumably found that conduct of the type engaged in by Lindberg was reasonably to be anticipated and guarded against and that Smith's failure to do so was a substantial factor in the occurrence. That being so, there was ample basis for finding proximate causation and holding Smith liable in addition to Lindberg.
* * *

Smith complains about the trial court's charge on the issue of proximate causation but we find it adequate. The jury was told, in line with one of the requests to charge submitted by the appellants, that the proximate cause was the efficient one which naturally and probably led to the result and without which the incident would not have occurred. It was also told that in order to hold Smith liable, it must find that there was a failure to exercise due supervisory care and that this failure was the cause of the injury within the court's definition of proximate cause. Reading the charge as a whole, we are satisfied that the jury could not have been misled and that no prejudice resulted from any lack of artistry or specificity in the language used by the trial court. See R.R. 1:5–3(a); Stackenwalt v. Washburn, 42 N.J. 15, 26–27, 198 A.2d 454 (1964).

We find no error in the verdict and judgment against Smith and come now to the liability of the Board of Education. * * * At the trial the appellants cited the statute which provides that no school district shall be liable for personal injury resulting "from the use of any public grounds, buildings or structures." L. 1933, c. 460 —now R.S. 18:5–30, N.J.S.A. The statute was ruled by the trial court to be inapplicable under the restrictive interpretation in Estelle v. Board of Education, 26 N.J.Super. 9, 19, 97 A.2d 1 (App.Div.1953), modified in other respects 14 N.J. 256, 102 A.2d 44 (1954). Cf. Thompson v. Board of Education, 11 N.J. 207, 209, 94 A.2d 206 (1953); Schwartz v. Borough of Stockton, 32 N.J. 141, 148, 160 A.2d

1 (1960). Apparently the appellants have accepted the trial court's ruling, for in their brief before us R.S. 18:5–30, N.J.S.A. is not at all relied upon or even cited; we consider it unnecessary to deal with it here.

The Board, placing some reliance on the vestiges of New Jersey's doctrine of "active wrongdoing", * * * complains that the trial court erred in its charge by referring in similar language to the Board's and Smith's duty of care. But that was the very approach taken in the requests to charge submitted by the appellants jointly. Thus in their fifth request they asked that the jury be charged that in order to find Smith and the Board responsible, it must find "negligence or failure to exercise reasonable care in the supervision of the children coming to school and prior to entering school on the morning in question." In their sixth request they asked for a finding in favor of Smith and the Board, if the act of Lindberg was found to be "an untoward event not reasonably to have been anticipated with an exercise of ordinary care on the part of the school principal and the Board of Education." And in their seventh and final request they asked for a finding in favor of Smith and the Board, if it was found that the exercise of "ordinary and reasonable care" in the supervision of the children prior to their entering school on the morning in question could not have prevented the shooting of the paper clip by Lindberg. In the light of the foregoing, the Board is in no position to press its present complaint about the trial court's charge. * * *

Though it was not cited to the trial court or the Appellate Division, Amelchenko v. Freehold Borough, 42 N.J. 541, 201 A.2d 726 (1964), is now cited by the Board in support of its contention that it was entitled to a directed verdict. See also Hoy v. Capelli, 48 N.J. 81, 222 A.2d 649 (1966); Visidor Corp. v. Borough of Cliffside Park, 48 N.J. 214, 225 A.2d 105 (1966). In _Amelchenko_ the plaintiff was injured when he fell in a municipal parking lot which had not been cleared after a heavy snowfall. The borough, with limited equipment and manpower, had planned its snow clearing program so as to give priority to the streets and had been unable to reach the parking lot despite work around the clock. We held that the borough's exercise of judgment would not be reviewed in the tort action and that the borough was entitled to a direction.

The situation in _Amelchenko_ may readily be differentiated from the case against the Board. The Fairview School had been designated as a pickup site by the school system's transportation coordinator and, as a result, many older students customarily congregated on the school grounds in addition to the arriving Fairview students. The dangers and the need for supervision were evident, yet the Board apparently made no supervisory plans and took no precautions. Under the evidence the jury could find that no rules or regulations had been promulgated, no supervisory personnel had been assigned to the area, no guidelines had been given to the coordinator or the principal, and no checkups had been made. Cf. Selleck v. Board of Education, supra, 94 N.Y.S.2d, at p. 321. On such finding, negligence on the Board's part could readily be determined without invading the holding or underlying policy of *Amelchenko*.

In any event, Smith having been found liable to the plaintiffs, the Board would be obliged under R.S. 18:5–50.4, N.J.S.A. to pay the judgment against him. That statute was originally enacted in 1938 (L. 1938, c. 311) and directed that each board of education shall save harmless and protect its individual teachers and members of supervisory and administrative staffs from financial loss arising out of claims and judgments "by reason of alleged negligence or other act resulting in accidental bodily injury to any person within or without the school building." A 1955 amendment carried the sympathetic legislative policy further by broadening the board's responsibility so as to include other board employees and claims and judgments for property damage as well as personal injury. L. 1955, c. 85. The proviso in the statute that the individual must be acting in the discharge of his duties within the scope of his employment or under direction of the board was clearly and fully satisfied here. Although it had been held that the statute did not create a new cause of action which could be maintained directly against the board (Hare v. Pennell, 37 N.J.Super. 558, 563, 117 A.2d 637 (App.Div.1955), the individual sued could readily join the board as a third party defendant (R.R. 4:14–1) and, viewed realistically, the board rather than the individual would be the truly interested party. See Cianci v. Board of Education, supra, 238 N.Y.S.2d, at p. 551; Shaw v. Village of Hempstead, 20 A.D.2d 663, 246 N.Y.S.2d 557, 558 (1964); cf. Sandak v. Tuxedo Union School District, 308 N.Y. 226, 124 N.E.2d 295 (1954), where the Court of Appeals, after referring to New York's various school enactments including its indemnity statute on which ours was modeled, noted "that for all practical purposes, even though the suit in name be against the teacher, it is the school district which is the real 'party against whom the claim is made.'" 124 N.E.2d, at p. 298. See Stearns v. Board of Education, 137 N.Y.S.2d 711, 713 (Sup.Ct.1955).

In view of the above, it can matter little to the Board that the judgment is against it as well as Smith except on the issue of proration. <u>On that issue, we agree with the Board that one-half of the judgment should be borne by Lindberg</u>. The New Jersey act (N.J.S. 2A:53A–1 et seq., N.J.S.A.) provides that there shall be contribution among joint tortfeasors but that "[a] master and servant or principal and agent shall be considered a single tortfeasor." N.J.S. 2A:53A–1, N.J.S.A. While there is little precedent on the subject (see Judson v. Peoples Bank and Trust Co., 25 N.J. 17, 37, 134 A.2d 761 (1957)), a fair construction of the act would lead to the conclusion that here the Board and its employee Smith should contribute no more than half of the judgment. The whole field of contribution is based on equitable considerations and the statutory provision expresses the widely held view that, by and large, it would be unfair to hold the master and servant or principal and agent for more than a single share. * * *

Lindberg's conduct was the most immediate and direct cause of the injury. The lack of due supervision was admittedly not as immediate and direct but was found on sufficient evidence to have been a proximate cause of the injury with resulting liability. These circumstances and the equitable considerations they delineate, clearly negate any suggestion that Lindberg should bear only one-third of the judgment with the remaining two-thirds to be borne by the Board in the light of R.S. 18:5–50.4, N.J.S.A. We are satisfied that the order below should be modified to the end that the Board and Smith be dealt with here as one tortfeasor within the contemplation of N.J.S., 2A:53A–1, N.J.S.A. and the judgment be borne one-half by Lindberg and one-half by the Board on behalf of itself and Smith. The plaintiffs are in any event to be paid the entire amount of the judgment. Subject to that modification, the judgment entered in the Law Division is:

Affirmed.

NOTES

1. A third grade pupil was directed by the teacher to water a plant located on the window ledge. The pupil used a chair to stand on while watering the plant with water poured from a glass milk bottle. The child fell off the chair, broke the bottle, and she sustained a severe wrist laceration. Was judgment rendered for or against the teacher? Why? See Gaincott v. Davis, 281 Mich. 515, 275 N.W. 229 (1937).

2. Suppose a teacher in inclement weather raised a window in the room in such a way as to cause a draft upon the pupils and the teacher did not permit the pupils to escape the effects of the draft and a child became ill as a direct result, would the teacher be liable for the consequential damages? See Guyten v. Rhodes, 65 Ohio App. 163, 18 O.O. 356, 29 N.E.2d 444 (1940).

3. May a teacher be held accountable for injuries sustained by a pupil who lost his sight in one eye because of a pencil thrown by another pupil during the teacher's absence from the room? See Ohman v. Board of Educ., 275 App.Div. 840, 88 N.Y.S.2d 273 (1949).

4. School bus driver was found not to be negligent for the death of a five-year-old child who had gotten off the school bus, crossed the street in front of the bus and then ran back under the rear wheels of the bus while chasing a blowing piece of paper. The bus driver was attentive, watched the child cross the street originally, but had not seen the child return. Johnson v. Svoboda, 260 N.W.2d 530 (Iowa 1978).

School District Negligent in Misclassification of Student

HOFFMAN v. BOARD OF EDUC. OF CITY OF NEW YORK

Supreme Court, Appellate Division, Second Department, 1978.
64 A.D.2d 369, 410 N.Y.S.2d 99.

SHAPIRO, Justice.   This is an appeal from a judgment of the Supreme Court, Queens County, which is in favor of the plaintiff, upon a jury verdict, in the principal amount of $750,000.   For the reasons hereafter stated, the judgment should be reversed and a new trial granted, unless plaintiff stipulates to accept to reduce the principal amount of the verdict to $500,000.

Shortly after starting kindergarten in September, 1956, plaintiff was placed in a class for Children with Retarded Mental Development (CRMD) based upon a determination by defendant's certified psychologist that the child had an intelligent quotient (I.Q.) of 74. *Seventy-five was the cut-off point fixed by the defendant, so that if plaintiff had been given a rating of 75 he would not have been found to be retarded and would not have been sent to a class for mentally retarded children.   He remained in classes for the retarded for 11 years,* until he was 17 years of age.   At that age he was transferred to the Occupational Training Center for the retarded.   He remained there for one year; at the start of the second year, in September, 1969, he was advised that he would not be continued there because an I.Q. test administered in May, 1969 showed that he was not retarded.

*   *   *

Plaintiff entered Kindergarten at his neighborhood school, P.S. 81, Queens, in September, 1956.   Four months later, on January 9, 1957, Monroe Gottsegen, a certified clinical psychologist who started his employment with defendant about a week earlier, administered the primarily verbal Stanford-Binet Intelligence Test.   At that time, Dr. Gottsegen had had his Master's degree for six years, during which period he had tested about 1,000 children.   His report, dated January 23, 1957, included the following:

"Mongolian tendencies, severe speech defects, slow in response. *   *   *

Eligible for placement in a CRMD class at P 77 Q in September 1957."

*   *   *

Finally, on May 12, 1969, *after he had been closeted with mentally retarded children for more than 12 years,* plaintiff was administered an I.Q. test by Dr. William F. Garber of the Bureau of Child Guidance.   At that time, plaintiff was one month past his 18th birthday and he was approaching the end of his first year at the Queens Occupational Training Center.   *   *   *

Plaintiff was administered a Wechsler Intelligence Scale for Adults (W.A.I.S.) test. He scored a verbal I.Q. of 85 and a performance I.Q. of 107 resulting in a full scale I.Q. of 94.

* * *

Neither plaintiff nor his mother was advised of the test results at that time. Plaintiff remained at the Occupational Training Center until the end of the spring semester. He returned to the OTC on September 8, 1969. * * *

In December, 1969, at the behest of plaintiff's counsel, plaintiff was examined by Dr. Lawrence I. Kaplan, a neurologist and psychiatrist. At that time plaintiff had been out of the school system for three months. Dr. Kaplan found that plaintiff had a marked stutter, that his articulation was not clear and that he had difficulty in making himself understood. On neurological testing he found him to be normal in all respects and he ruled out any brain damage. Dr. Kaplan elicited that plaintiff had been having symptoms of "being upset, shaking, unable to eat properly, crying, feeling depressed, not sleeping well, walking the floor, had no friends". His opinion was that plaintiff was not mentally retarded, but that he had a "defective self-image and feelings of inadequacy". This was because plaintiff had been placed in a class of mentally retarded children and "this result[ed] in an alteration in his concept of himself, particularly because he is intelligent enough to appreciate the position in which he is placed". * * *

* * * Dr. Abt concluded that plaintiff's learning potential had always been above average and that one of the reasons his intellectual development had been diminished was the assumption of the correctness of the school's diagnosis by his family and others, by reason of which they did not provide the stimulation that would otherwise have been given the child. The result was that, at the time Dr. Abt examined him, plaintiff felt that he was substantially without an education; that he did not know what he could do to earn a living; and that he did not know "where he fitted into the world, and even where he fitted into his family". All this was a competent producing cause of the condition of depression that he noted in plaintiff.

Plaintiff had no additional schooling up to the time of the trial. In August, 1970, when he was 19 years old, he was interviewed by the State Division of Vocational Rehabilitation. * * *

The Division of Vocational Rehabilitation provided a speech therapy program for him in the National Hospital for Speech Disorders. He was provided 40 weekly sessions of therapy and he showed slow improvement. In July, 1972, when he was 21 years old, he was referred by his rehabilitation counselor to Dr. Bernard Stillerman, who noted that plaintiff was "very dependent on his mother who not only made the appointment for him but is his verbal contact, for the most part, with the world * * *. * * * He is also moderately depressed because of the speech problem which precludes him from having friends. <u>In fact, he is preoccupied with the thought that he can make friends but cannot keep them because of his speech.</u>"

* * *

Plaintiff was trained by the Division of Vocational Rehabilitation to be a messenger and it obtained his first job for him.   Thereafter he had 11 different messenger jobs. * * *

At the age of 26 (as of the date of the trial) he had not made any advancement in his vocational life, nor any particular improvement in his social life. * * *

Defendant's principal argument for reversal is that Dr. Gottsegen's report of January 23, 1957 did *not* recommend that plaintiff be given another I.Q. test within two years * * *.   Dr. Gottsegen testified that "we wanted him *retested* within two years" and that it was his "feeling there was retardation" but that he "doubted some of the results and *therefore I suggested a retesting*" (emphasis supplied). * * *

It is defendant's position that the words "retest" and "re-evaluate" are words of art with different meanings.   "Retest", argues defendant, means to administer a further I.Q. test, while "re-evaluate" means observation of the child and noting his achievements as a basis for determining whether a new I.Q. test should be administered.

Defendant maintains that the continuous observation of plaintiff by his succeeding teachers, each of whom noted the scores on the semi-annual achievement tests, amounted to "a *constant* re-evaluation, with Dr. Gottsegen's report not overriding their own observations."   Defendant asserts that the record amply supported their judgments and, further, that if there was a difference of opinion as to this it was no more than an error of professional judgment not severe enough to constitute negligence.

Defendant's analysis flies in the face of the testimony of the expert witnesses on both sides to the effect that intelligence of children is determined in schools (and elsewhere) *only* by I.Q. testing, and that achievement tests and classroom evaluations do not determine the intelligence of a child.   Since Dr. Gottsegen's written recommendation was that plaintiff's "*intelligence* should be re-evaluated within a two year period", it could only mean that he was to be administered a new I.Q. test within that period.   If it did not have that meaning, it meant nothing, since a CRMD child is always being observed by his teacher for signs of improvement, and achievement tests were being given semi-annually to *all* CRMD children. * * *

If in fact Dr. Gottsegen's prescription was equivocal, or his recommendation that plaintiff's "intelligence should be re-evaluated" was puzzling or ambiguous, it was up to the school administration to find out what its own employee meant, for he was paid to give advice, not to intone as a Delphic oracle. In any event, an error due to his lack of clarity, if such there was, would be the responsibility of the Board of Education under the rule of *respondeat superior*. * * * Certainly the very least that can be said is that the jury could properly have concluded that if Dr. Gottsegen's 1957 report was ambiguous, each teacher, and therefore the defendant as their employer, was negligent in failing to inquire as to its true meaning. Thus, the failure to follow Dr. Gottsegen's recommendation for an intelligence retesting to determine so vital a matter as whether plaintiff should be continued in a class for retarded children was an egregious error committed on a wholesale basis.

* * *

Of course plaintiff's teachers could not have had the foresight to know that when plaintiff would reach the age of 18 his intelligence would be found to be well within the normal range. The indisputable fact remains (and defendant now concedes) that plaintiff's intelligence was *always* normal since one's intelligence does not leap from less than three-quarters of average (74) to average (100). * * *

* * *

Defendant's affirmative act in placing plaintiff in a CRMD class initially (when it should have known that a mistake could have devastating consequences) created a relationship between itself and plaintiff out of which arose a duty to take reasonable steps to ascertain whether (at least, in a borderline case) that placement was proper * * *. We need not here decide whether such duty would have required "intelligence" retesting (in view of plaintiff's poor showing on achievement tests) had not the direction for such retesting been placed in the very document which asserted that plaintiff was to be placed in a CRMD class. It ill-becomes the Board of Education to argue for the untouchability of its own policy and procedures when the gist of plaintiff's complaint is that the entity which did not follow them was the board itself.

New York State and its municipalities have long since surrendered immunity from suit. Just as well-established is the rule that damages for psychological and emotional injury are recoverable even absent physical injury or contact * * *. Had plaintiff been improperly diagnosed or treated by medical or psychological personnel in a municipal hospital, the municipality would be liable for the ensuing injuries. There is no reason for any different rule here because the personnel were employed by a government entity other than a hospital. Negligence is negligence, even if defendant and Mr. Justice DAMIANI prefer semantically to call it educational malpractice. Thus, defendant's rhetoric constructs a chamber of horrors by asserting that affirmance in this case would create a new theory of liability known as "educational malpractice" and that before doing so we must consider public policy   *   *   *   and the effects of opening a vast new field which will further impoverish financially hard pressed municipalities.   Defendant, in effect, suggests that to avoid such horrors, educational entities must be insulated from the legal responsibilities and obligations common to all other governmental entities no matter how seriously a particular student may have been injured and, ironically, even though such injuries were caused by their own affirmative acts in failing to follow their own rules.

I see no reason for such a trade-off, on alleged policy grounds, which would warrant a denial of fair dealing to one who is injured by exempting a governmental agency from its responsibility for its *affirmative* torts.   Such a determination would simply amount to the imposition of private value judgments over the legitimate interests and legal rights of those tortiously injured.   That does not mean that the parents of the Johnnies who cannot read may flock to the courts and automatically obtain redress.   Nor does it mean that the parents of all the Janies whose delicate egos were upset because they did not get the gold stars they deserved will obtain redress.   If the door to "educational torts" for nonfeasance is to be opened   *   *   *   it will not be by this case which involves *misfeasance* in failing to follow the individualized and specific prescription of defendant's own certified psychologist, whose very decision it was in the first place, to place plaintiff in a class for retarded children, or in the initial making by him of an ambiguous report, if that be the fact.

As Professor David A. Diamond noted (29 Syracuse L.Rev. 103, 150–151), when discussing this very case after the judgment at Trial Term,   *   *   *   "the thrust of the plaintiff's case is not so much a failure to take steps to detect and correct a weakness in a student, that is, a failure to provide a positive program for a student, but rather, affirmative acts of negligence which imposed additional and crippling burdens upon a student" and that "it does not seem unreasonable to hold a school board liable for the type of behavior exhibited in *Hoffman*."   I agree.

                    *   *   *

Therefore, not only reason and justice, but the law as well, cry out for an affirmance of plaintiff's right to a recovery.   Any other result would be a reproach to justice.   In the words of the ancient Romans: *"Fiat justitia, ruat coelum"* (Let justice be done, though the heavens fall).   However, the verdict should be reduced to $500,000.

Governmental Immunity

Governmental agencies have historically been immune from tort liability.   As a general rule, common law asserts that government is inherently immune unless the legislature specifically abrogates the privilege.   The immunity concept evolved to this country from England where the King could, theoretically, do no wrong. Various legal scholars maintain the concept was a product of the dark ages where custom established that the lord of the fief was also the law-maker and judge. As such the lord was singly responsible for all laws and justice and since he made and implemented the laws he could not be sued without his permission.[56] As the feudal system drew to a close and fiefdoms became consolidated into larger governmental units, immunity became immeshed with the "divine right of Kings" placing the King in a superior and preferred legal position.[57] Sovereign immunity became formalized in English law at least as early as the Thirteenth Century at which time the King could not be sued in his own courts.[58] Sovereign immunity apparently reached its zenith in Fifteenth Century England where it stabilized as a prerogative of the monarch. Judicial recognition of this power was taken when an English court held in 1607 that the King was not liable for damages to private property caused by the government's digging for saltpetre which was to be used in the manufacture of gunpowder.[59] In spite of his judicial sanction affirming sovereign immunity, the great jurist Coke held in the same year that the King could not sit as a judge in his own case.[60] Effectively this began a whittling away process of the sovereign immunity which was not to culminate until over 250 years later when the House of Lords held that a public entity was liable for the damages caused by acts of its employees.[61] Later, this rationale was applied to schools in England when a court held that if negligence occurred resulting in student injury either the teacher or the school could be liable.[62]

The sovereign immunity doctrine may have been transported across the Atlantic to the United States directly under the precedent of Russell v. The Men Dwelling in the County of Devon [63] as relied upon by a Massachusetts court in Mower v. The Inhabitants of Leicester in 1812.[64] It is unlikely, however, that the concept did traverse the Atlantic through a single precedent, especially since the court in *Russell* attributed its holding of nonliability to (1) the lack of a public treasury, (2) general judicial apprehension that imposing liability would encourage a flow of such actions, (3) the belief that

56. F. Pollock and F. W. Maitland, *The History of English Law Before the Time of Edward I*, Cambridge University Press, Boston. Little, Brown & Co., 1905.

57. Eugene T. Conners, "Governmental Immunity: Legal Basis and Implications for Public Education," Ph.D. dissertation, University of Florida, 1977.

58. Ibid.

59. *The Case of the King's Prerogative in Saltpetre*, 12 Co.Rep. 12 (1607).

60. *Prohibitions del Roy*, 12 Rep. 63, (1607).

61. Mersey Trustees v. Gibbs, L.R. 1 H.L. 93 (1866).

62. Crisp v. Thomas, 63 LINS 756 (1890).

63. 100 Eng.Rep. 359, 2 T.R. 667 (1788).

64. 9 Mass. 247 (1812).

public inconvenience should be avoided and (4) that no legislation existed imposing such liability. No direct judicial notice was taken of the doctrine of Crown Prerogative or the "King can do no wrong" doctrine. It seems more likely that sovereign immunity came to be commonly accepted in this country through the use by early lawyers and judges of English legal books and materials such as Blackstone's Commentaries which were used as standard references, and, of course, many of the notable jurists of early America received their legal training in the Inns of Court in London. Regardless of its origin, however, the U.S. Supreme Court and state courts adopted the principle that the sovereign could not be sued without its permission. The Supreme Court in 1869 commented that "It is a familiar doctrine of the common law, that the sovereign cannot be sued in his own courts without his consent * * *" [65] and in the same year in another case the court stated that "Every government has an inherent right to protect itself against suits * * *. The principle is fundamental [and] applies to every sovereign power." [66] The federal government abrogated immunity to a statutorily prescribed extent in the *Federal Tort Claims Act of 1946.*

Beginning from the point of nearly universal adherence to the immunity doctrine state courts have in recent years tended to move away from the doctrine in several notable examples. Most significant is the *Molitor* case which abolished immunity in Illinois and directly refuted the legal rationale which supported sovereign immunity.[67] In *Muskopf,* the California Supreme Court observed the trend away from immunity saying:

> Only the vestigial remains of such governmental immunity have survived; its requiem has long been foreshadowed. For years the process of erosion of governmental immunity has gone on unabated. The Legislature has contributed mightily to that erosion. The courts, by distinction and extension, have removed much of the force of the rule. Thus, in holding that the doctrine of governmental immunity for torts for which its agents are liable has no place in our law we make no startling break with the past but merely take the final step that carries to its conclusion an established legislative and judicial trend.[68]

Since *Molitor* the gradual trend away from immunity has carried to the point that today at least thirty states have case law precedents

---

65. The Siren, 74 U.S. (7 Wall.) 152 (1869).

66. Nichols v. United States, 74 U.S. (7 Wall.) 122 (1869).

67. Molitor v. Kaneland Community Unit Dist. No. 302, 18 Ill.2d 11, 163 N.E.2d 89 (1959).

68. Muskopf v. Corning Hospital Dist., 55 Cal.2d 211, 11 Cal.Rptr. 89, 359 P. 2d 457 (1961).

which place limits on sovereign immunity.[69]   Of these, eighteen of
the states have established by legislation types of tort claims acts.
Six states substantially abrogate immunity by statute while three
state legislatures specifically reinforce the immunity doctrine.[70]

Sovereign Immunity May be Abrogated by the Courts

MOLITOR v. KANELAND COMMUNITY UNIT DIST. NO. 302

Supreme Court of Illinois, 1959.
18 Ill.2d 11, 163 N.E.2d 89.

KLINGBIEL, Justice.   Plaintiff, Thomas Molitor, a minor, by
Peter his father and next friend, brought this action against Kaneland Community Unit School District for personal injuries sustained
by plaintiff when the school bus in which he was riding left the road,
allegedly as a result of the driver's negligence, hit a culvert, exploded
and burned.

The complaint alleged, in substance, the negligence of the School
District, through its agent and servant, the driver of the school bus;
that plaintiff was in the exercise of such ordinary care for his own
safety as could be reasonable expected of a boy of his age, intelligence, mental capacity and experience; that plaintiff sustained permanent and severe burns and injuries as a proximate result of defendant's negligence, and prayed for judgment in the amount of
$56,000.   Plaintiff further alleged that defendant is a voluntary unit
school district organized and existing under the provisions of sections
8–9 to 8–13 of the School Code and operates school buses within the
district pursuant to section 29–5.   Ill.Rev.Stat.1957, chap. 122, pars.
8–9 to 8–13 and par. 29–5.

The complaint contained no allegation of the existence of insurance or other nonpublic funds out of which a judgment against defendant could be satisfied.   Although plaintiff's abstract of the record
shows that defendant school district did carry public liability insurance with limits of $20,000 for each person injured and $100,000 for
each occurrence, plaintiff states that he purposely omitted such an allegation from his complaint.

Defendant's motion to dismiss the complaint on the ground that
a school district is immune from liability for tort was sustained by
the trial court, and a judgment was entered in favor of defendant.
Plaintiff elected to stand on his complaint and sought a direct appeal
to this court on the ground that the dismissal of his action would violate his constitutional rights.   At that time we held that no fairly de-
batable constitutional question was presented so as to give this court
jurisdiction on direct appeal, and accordingly the cause was trans-

---

69. Conners, *op. cit.* p. 72.   70. Ibid.

ferred to the Appellate Court for the Second District. The Appellate Court affirmed the decision of the trial court and the case is now before us again on a certificate of importance.

In his brief, plaintiff recognizes the rule, established by this court in 1898, that a school district is immune from tort liability, and frankly asks this court either to abolish the rule *in toto*, * * *.

* * *

Thus we are squarely faced with the highly important question —in the light of modern developments, should a school district be immune from liability for tortiously inflicted personal injury to a pupil thereof arising out of the operation of a school bus owned and operated by said district?

It appears that while adhering to the old immunity rule, this court has not reconsidered and re-evaluated the doctrine of immunity of school districts for over fifty years. During these years, however, this subject has received exhaustive consideration by legal writers and scholars in articles and texts, almost unanimously condemning the immunity doctrine. * * *

Historically we find that the doctrine of the sovereign immunity of the state, the theory that "the King can do no wrong," was first extended to a subdivision of the state in 1788 in Russell v. Men of Devon, 2 Term Rep. 671, 100 Eng.Rep. 359. As pointed out by Dean Prosser (Prosser on Torts, p. 1066), the idea of the municipal corporate entity was still in a nebulous state at that time. The action was brought against the entire population of the county and the decision that the county was immune was based chiefly on the fact that there were no corporate funds in Devonshire out of which satisfaction could be obtained, plus a fear of multiplicity of suits and resulting inconvenience to the public.

It should be noted that the Russell case was later overruled by the English courts, and that in 1890 it was definitely established that in England a school board or school district is subject to suit in tort for personal injuries on the same basis as a private individual or corporation. * * *

The immunity doctrine of Russell v. Men of Devon was adopted in Illinois with reference to towns and counties in 1870 in Town of Waltham v. Kemper, 55 Ill. 346. Then, in 1898, eight years after the English courts had refused to apply the Russell doctrine to schools, the Illinois court extended the immunity rule to school districts in the leading case of Kinnare v. City of Chicago, 171 Ill. 332, 49 N.E. 536, where it was held that the Chicago Board of Education was immune from liability for the death of a laborer resulting from a fall from the roof of a school building, allegedly due to the negligence of the Board in failing to provide scaffolding and safeguards. That opinion reasoned that since the State is not subject to suit nor liable for the torts or negligence of its agents, likewise a school district, as a governmental agency of the State, is also "exempted from the obligation to respond in damages, as master, for negligent acts of its servants to the same extent as is the State itself." Later decisions following the Kinnare doctrine have sought to advance additional explanations such as the protection of public funds and public property, and to prevent the diversion of tax moneys to the payment of damage claims. * * *

Surveying the whole picture of governmental tort law as it stands in Illinois today, the following broad outlines may be observed. The General Assembly has frequently indicated its dissatisfaction with the doctrine of sovereign immunity upon which the Kinnare case was based. Governmental units, including school districts, are now subject to liability under the Workmen's Compensation and Occupational Disease Acts. * * * The State itself is liable, under the 1945 Court of Claims Act, for damages in tort up to $7,500 for the negligence of its officers, agents or employees. (Ill.Rev.Stat. 1957, chap. 37, pars. 439.1–439.24.) Cities and villages have been made directly liable for injuries caused by the negligent operation of fire department vehicles, and for actionable wrong in the removal or destruction of unsafe or unsanitary buildings. (Ill.Rev.Stat.1957, chap. 24, pars. 1–13, 1–16.) Cities and villages, and the Chicago Park District, have also been made responsible, by way of indemnification, for the nonwilful misconduct of policemen. * * * In addition to the tort liability thus legislatively imposed upon governmental units, the courts have classified local units of government as "quasi-municipal corporations" and "municipal corporations." And the activities of the latter class have been categorized as "governmental" and "proprietary," with full liability in tort imposed if the function is classified as "proprietary." The incongruities that have resulted from attempts to fit particular conduct into one or the other of these categories have been the subject of frequent comment. * * *

Of all of the anomalies that have resulted from legislative and judicial efforts to alleviate the injustice of the results that have flowed from the doctrine of sovereign immunity, the one most immediately pertinent to this case is the following provision of the Illinois School Code: "Any school district, including any non-high school district, which provides transportation for pupils may insure against any loss or liability of such district, its agents or employees, resulting from or incident to the ownership, maintenance or use of any school bus. Such insurance shall be carried only in companies duly licensed and authorized to write such coverage in this state. Every policy for such insurance coverage issued to a school district shall provide, or be endorsed to provide, that the company issuing such policy waives any right to refuse payment or to deny liability thereunder within the limits of said policy, by reason of the non-liability of the insured school district for the wrongful or negligent acts of its agents and employees, and, its immunity from suit as an agency of the state performing governmental functions." Ill.Rev.Stat.1957, c. 122, § 29–11a.

Thus, under this statute, a person injured by an insured school district bus may recover to the extent of such insurance, whereas, under the Kinnare doctrine, a person injured by an uninsured school district bus can recover nothing at all.

Defendant contends that the quoted provision of the School Code constitutes a legislative determination that the public policy of this State requires that school districts be immune from tort liability. We can read no such legislative intent into the statute. Rather, we interpret that section as expressing dissatisfaction with the court-created doctrine of governmental immunity and an attempt to cut down that immunity where insurance is involved. The difficulty with this legislative effort to curtail the judicial doctrine is that it allows each school district to determine for itself whether, and to what extent, it will be financially responsible for the wrongs inflicted by it.

Coming down to the precise issue at hand, it is clear that if the above rules and precedents are strictly applied to the instant case, plaintiff's complaint, containing no allegation as to the existence of insurance, was properly dismissed. On the other hand, the complaint may be held to state a good cause of action on either one of two theories, (1) application of the doctrine of Moore v. Moyle, 405 Ill. 555, 92 N.E. 2d 81, or (2) abolition of the rule that a school district is immune from tort liability.

As to the doctrine of Moore v. Moyle, that case involved an action for personal injuries against Bradley University, a charitable education institution. Traditionally, charitable and educational institutions have enjoyed the same immunity from tort liability as have governmental agencies in Illinois. * * * The trial court dismissed the complaint on the ground that Bradley was immune to tort liability. The Supreme Court reversed, holding that the complaint should not have been dismissed since it alleged that Bradley was fully insured. Unfortunately, we must admit that the opinion in that case does not make the basis of the result entirely clear. However, the court there said, 405 Ill. at page 564, 92 N.E.2d at page 86: "* * * the question of insurance in no way affects the liability of the institution, but would only go to the question of the manner of collecting any judgment which might be obtained, without interfering with, or subjecting the trust funds or trust-held property to, the judgment. The question as to whether or not the institution is insured in no way affects its liability any more than whether a charitable institution holding private nontrust property or funds would affect its liability. These questions would only be of importance at the proper time, when the question arose as to the collection of any judgment out of nontrust property or assets. * * * Judgments may be obtained, but the question of collection of the judgment is a different matter." If we were to literally apply this reasoning to the present school district case, we would conclude that it was unnecessary that the complaint contain an allegation of the existence of insurance or other nonpublic funds. Plaintiff's complaint was sufficient as it stood without any reference to insurance, and plaintiff would be entitled to prosecute his action to judgment. Only at that time, in case of a judgment for plaintiff, would the question of insurance arise, the possession of nonpublic funds being an execution rather than a liability question. It cannot be overlooked, however, that some doubt is cast on this approach by the last paragraph of the Moore opinion, where the court said: "It appears that the trust funds of Bradley will not be impaired or depleted by the prosecution of the complaint, and therefore it was error to dismiss it." These words imply that if from the complaint it did not appear that the trust funds would not be impaired, the complaint should have been dismissed. If that is the true holding in the case, then liability itself, not merely the collectability of the judgment, depends on the presence of nontrust assets, as was pointed out by Justice Crampton in his dissenting opinion. The doctrine of Moore v. Moyle does not, in our opinion, offer a satisfactory solution. Like the provision of the School Code above quoted, it would allow the wrongdoer to determine its own liability.

It is a basic concept underlying the whole law of torts today that liability follows negligence, and that individuals and corporations are responsible for the negligence of their agents and employees acting in the course of their employment. The doctrine of governmental immunity runs directly counter to that basic concept. What reasons, then, are so impelling as to allow a school district, as a quasi-municipal corporation, to commit wrongdoing without any responsibility to its victims, while any individual or private corporation would be called to task in court for such tortious conduct?

The original basis of the immunity rule has been called a "survival of the medieval idea that the sovereign can do no wrong," or that "the King can do no wrong." (38 Am.Jur., Mun.Corps., sec. 573, p. 266.) In Kinnare v. City of Chicago, 171 Ill. 332, 49 N.E. 536, 537, the first Illinois case announcing the tort immunity of school districts, the court said: "The state acts in its sovereign capacity, and does not submit its action to the judgment of courts, and is not liable for the torts or negligence of its agents, and a corporation created by the state as a mere agency for the more efficient exercise of governmental functions is likewise exempted from the obligation to respond in damages, as master, for negligent acts of its servants to the same extent as is the state itself, unless such liability is expressly provided by the statute creating such agency." This was nothing more nor less than an extension of the theory of sovereign immunity. Professor Borchard has said that how immunity ever came to be applied in the United States of America is one of the mysteries of legal evolution. (Borchard, Governmental Liability in Tort, 34 Yale L.J. 1, 6.) And how it was then infiltrated into the law controlling the liability of local governmental units has been described as one of the amazing chapters of American common-law jurisprudence. * * *

We are of the opinion that school district immunity cannot be justified on this theory. As was stated by one court, "The whole doctrine of governmental immunity from liability for tort rests upon a rotten foundation. It is almost incredible that in this modern age of comparative sociological enlightenment, and in a republic, the medieval absolutism supposed to be implicit in the maxim, 'the King can do no wrong,' should exempt the various branches of the government from liability for their torts, and that the entire burden of damage resulting from the wrongful acts of the government should be imposed upon the single individual who suffers the injury, rather than distributed among the entire community constituting the government, where it could be borne without hardship upon any individual, and where it justly belongs." Barker v. City of Santa Fe, 47 N.M. 85, 136 P.2d 480, 482. Likewise, we agree with the Supreme Court of Florida that in preserving the sovereign immunity theory, courts have overlooked the fact that the Revolutionary War was fought to abolish that "divine right of kings" on which the theory is based.

The other chief reason advanced in support of the immunity rule in the more recent cases is the protection of public funds and public property. This corresponds to the "no fund" or "trust fund" theory upon which charitable immunity is based. This rationale was relied on in Thomas v. Broadlands Community Consolidated School Dist., 348 Ill.App. 567, 109 N.E.2d 636, 640, where the court stated that the reason for the immunity rule is "that it is the public policy to protect public funds and public property, to prevent the diversion of tax moneys, in this case school funds, to the payment of damage claims." This reasoning seems to follow the line that it is better for the individual to suffer than for the public to be inconvenienced. From it proceeds defendant's argument that school districts would be bankrupted and education impeded if said districts were called upon to compensate children tortiously injured by the negligence of those districts' agents and employees.

We do not believe that in this present day and age, when public education constitutes one of the biggest businesses in the country, that school immunity can be justified on the protection-of-public-funds theory.

In the first place, analysis of the theory shows that it is based on the idea that payment of damage claims is a diversion of educational funds to an improper purpose. As many writers have pointed out, the fallacy in this argument is that it assumes the very point which is sought to be proved, i. e., that payment of damage claims is not a proper purpose. "Logically, the 'No-fund' or 'trust fund' theory is without merit because it is of value only after a determination of what is a proper school expenditure. To predicate immunity upon the theory of a trust fund is merely to argue in a circle, since it assumes an answer to the very question at issue, to wit, what is an educational purpose? Many disagree with the 'no-fund' doctrine to the extent of ruling that the payment of funds for judgments resulting from accidents or injuries in schools is an educational purpose. Nor can it be properly argued that as a result of the abandonment of the common-law rule the district would be completely bankrupt. California, Tennessee, New York, Washington and other states have not been compelled to shut down their schools." (Rosenfield, Governmental Immunity from Liability for Tort in School Accidents, 5 Legal Notes on Local Government, 376–377.) Moreover, this argument is even more fallacious when viewed in the light of the Illinois School Code, which authorizes appropriations for "transportation purposes" * * * and authorizes expenditures of school tax funds for liability insurance covering school bus operations * * *. It seems to us that the payment of damage claims incurred as an adjunct to transportation is as much a "transportation purpose" and therefore a proper authorized purpose as are payments of other expenses involved in operating school buses. If tax funds can properly be spent to pay premiums on liability insurance, there seems to be no good reason why they cannot be spent to pay the liability itself in the absence of insurance.

Neither are we impressed with defendant's plea that the abolition of immunity would create grave and unpredictable problems of school finance and administration. We are in accord with Dean Green when he disposed of this problem as follows: "There is considerable talk in the opinions about the tremendous financial burdens tort liability would cast upon the taxpayer. In some opinions it is stated that this factor is sufficient to warrant the courts in protecting the taxpayer through the immunity which they have thrown around municipal corporations. While this factor may have had compulsion on some of the earlier courts, I seriously doubt that it has any great weight with the courts in recent years. In the first place, taxation is not the subject matter of judicial concern where justice to the individual citizen is involved. It is the business of other departments of government to provide the funds required to pay the damages assessed against them by the courts. Moreover, the same policy that would protect governmental corporations from the payment of damages for the injuries they bring upon others would be equally pertinent to a like immunity to protect private corporations, for conceivably many essential private concerns could also be put out of business by the damages they could incur under tort liability But as a matter of fact, this argument has no practical basis. Private concerns have rarely been greatly embarrassed, and in no instance, even where immunity is not recognized, has a municipality been seriously handicapped by tort liability. This argument is like so many of the horribles paraded in the early tort cases when courts were fashioning the boundaries of tort law. It has been thrown in simply because there was nothing better at hand. The public's willingness to stand up and pay the cost of its enterprises carried out through municipal corporations is no less than its insistence that individuals and groups pay the cost of their enterprises. Tort liability is in fact a very small item in the budget of any well organized enterprise." Green, Freedom of Litigation, 38 Ill.L.Rev. 355, 378.

We are of the opinion that none of the reasons advanced in support of school district immunity have any true validity today. Further we believe that abolition of such immunity may tend to decrease the frequency of school bus accidents by coupling the power to transport pupils with the responsibility of exercising care in the selection and supervision of the drivers. As Dean Harno said: "A municipal corporation today is an active and virile creature capable of inflicting much harm. Its civil responsibility should be co-extensive. The municipal corporation looms up definitely and emphatically in our law, and what is more, it can and does commit wrongs. This being so, it must assume the responsibilities of the position it occupies in society." (Harno, Tort Immunity of Municipal Corporations, 4 Ill.L.Q. 28, 42.) School districts will be encouraged to exercise greater care in the matter of transporting pupils and also to carry adequate insurance covering that transportation, thus spreading the risk of accident, just as the other costs of education are spread over the entire district. At least some school authorities themselves have recognized the need for the vital change which we are making. See Editorial, 100 American School Board Journal 55, Issue No. 6, June, 1940.

"The nation's largest business is operating on a blueprint prepared a hundred, if not a thousand years ago. The public school system in the United States, which constitutes the largest single business in the country, is still under the domination of a legal principle which in great measure continued unchanged since the Middle Ages, to the effect that a person has no financial recourse for injuries sustained as a result of the performance of the State's functions * * *. That such a gigantic system, involving so large an appropriation of public funds and so tremendous a proportion of the people of the United States, should operate under the principles of a rule of law so old and so outmoded would seem impossible were it not actually true." Rosenfield, Governmental Immunity from Liability for Tort in School Accidents, 9 Law and Contemporary Problems 358, 359.

We conclude that the rule of school district tort immunity is unjust, unsupported by any valid reason, and has no rightful place in modern day society.

Defendant strongly urges that if said immunity is to be abolished, it should be done by the legislature, not by this court. With this contention we must disagree. The doctrine of school district immunity was created by this court alone. Having found that doctrine to be unsound and unjust under present conditions, we consider that we have not only the power, but the duty, to abolish that immunity.

"We closed our courtroom doors without legislative help, and we can likewise open them." Pierce v. Yakima Valley Memorial Hospital Ass'n, 43 Wash.2d 162, 260 P.2d 765, 774.

NOTES

Sovereign immunity protected a school board in West Virginia from liability when a child fell through a footbridge and was injured. Boggs v. Board of Educ., 244 S.E.2d 799 (W.Va. 1978).

Proprietary Functions

Some courts, being reluctant to totally abrogate immunity, have sought ways to avoid direct confrontation with the issue. In order to sidestep the overall problem, courts have settled tort actions in several states on the basis of the activity or function which was being performed by the school district when the injury occurred. In this regard we should note that school districts operate in a dual capacity performing functions which are strictly governmental the majority of the time, but they also on some occasions perform proprietary functions or functions which may be performed by a private corporation.

Proprietary functions have been defined as things not normally required by law or things not governmental in nature. If a function is within the scope of the public school operation, as expressed or implied by statute, then the function is governmental and not proprietary. Courts have generally held that school athletic contests are governmental functions.[71] While the courts have rather consistently held that municipalities are liable for injuries arising out of functions where admission is charged or some financial gain is realized, they have been reluctant to generally apply this standard to school districts.

Thus, if a spectator or participant is injured at an athletic contest, the courts will not usually impose liability on the school district even when a fee is charged and the school has realized a profit. Of course, exceptions exist to all general rules, and in regard to this question one court held that where a school district leased its football stadium to another for a fee, the lessor was held to have been engaged in a proprietary activity and was liable for injury to a spectator who was injured when a railing broke.

In following the rule that school districts are immune from liability for incidents arising during functions which charge fees, a Tennessee court said:

The mere fact that an admission fee was charged by the high school does not make the transaction an enterprise for

71.　Sawaya v. Tucson High School Dist. No. 1, 78 Ariz. 389, 281 P.2d 105 (1955).

profit. * * * The duties of a County Board of Education are limited to the operation of the schools. This is a governmental function. Therefore, in legal contemplation, there is no such thing as such a Board acting in a proprietary capacity for private gain.[72]

Texas [73] and Kansas [74] courts have said, *in dicta*, that if a school district can and does perform proprietary activities, then it must answer in damages when guilty in tort for injuries resulting from such functions. The Supreme Court of Oregon has laid down a test for distinguishing proprietary from governmental functions. "The underlying test is whether the act is for the common good of all without the element of special corporate benefit or pecuniary profit." [75]

The rule, therefore, may probably be summarized; as long as the purpose of the activity is educational and for the common good and the profit accrued is only incidental, then the activity is governmental in nature.

Holder of a Free Pass to a Football Game Was an Invitee to Whom the School District Owed a Duty of Reasonable Care

TANARI v. SCHOOL DIRECTORS OF DIST. NO. 502

Supreme Court of Illinois, 1977.
69 Ill.2d 630, 14 Ill.Dec. 874,
373 N.E.2d 5.

UNDERWOOD, Justice: Plaintiff, Flora Tanari, brought an action * * * seeking damages for injuries she sustained when she allegedly was knocked to the ground by a group of children engaged in horseplay at a high school football game sponsored by defendant on its premises. The complaint alleged ordinary negligence on the part of defendant in failing to provide adequate supervision and control of children at the game. At the close of the evidence, the trial court granted the defendant's motion for a directed verdict on the ground that plaintiff was a licensee on defendant's premises; that defendant therefore only owed her the duty to refrain from wilful and wanton misconduct; and that breach of such duty had neither been alleged nor proved at trial. * * *

Plaintiff, age 64, was employed as a bus driver by an individual who had a contract with the defendant school district to transport students to and from school. She had been so employed for 27 years

72. Reed v. Rhea County, 189 Tenn. 247, 225 S.W.2d 49 (1949).

73. Braun v. Trustees of Victoria Ind. School Dist., 114 S.W.2d 947 (Tex.Civ. App.1938).

74. Koehn v. Board of Educ. of City of Newton, 193 Kan. 263, 392 P.2d 949 (1964).

75. Rankin v. School Dist. No. 9, 143 Or. 449, 23 P.2d 132 (1933).

and had attended all of the local high school football games for the last 25 years. On October 13, 1972, plaintiff attended the Hall Township High School homecoming football game with her daughter, son-in-law and grandchildren. The game was held on defendant's premises at a sports stadium under defendant's supervision and control. Plaintiff entered the stadium using a complimentary season pass issued by the defendant. As she was walking toward her seat, she noticed a crowd of boys and girls playing near the northwest end of the stadium, and the next thing she knew she had been knocked to the ground by a "big" boy who fell on top of her. The boy, who was never identified, got up, apologized and hurried away. * * *

* * *

The athletic director of Hall Township High School testified that he had hired off-duty policemen and teachers to keep order at all high school football games conducted by the defendant. * * * He responded in the affirmative when asked if he had seen boys and girls at almost every game "playing tag, or horseplaying and roughing it up" in the area in question. However, when he was later asked if there was "rowdiness and horseplaying by these kids in that area," he responded that he did not know whether it should be called rowdiness and horseplay but the children were definitely there. He further testified that on previous occasions he had tried to "correct" the children but that, as soon as he left, they were back at it again. He knew from his personal observation that a policeman was in the area of the accident on the night in question.

The trial court allowed the defendant's motion for a directed verdict on the sole ground that plaintiff was a licensee on the defendant's premises and that there was no proof whatsoever that defendant had breached its duty to refrain from wilful and wanton misconduct. * * * Considering the state of the record before us, we are unable to concur with the appellate court's conclusions regarding defendant's immunity under the above-referred-to statutes and are likewise unable to agree with the court's further determination that "irrespective of the standard of care which might have been required in this case, no verdict in favor of the plaintiff could stand as against the defendant school directors."

The Local Governmental and Governmental Employees Tort Immunity Act (hereafter referred to as the Tort Immunity Act) provides, *inter alia,* that "a public employee serving in a position involving the determination of policy or the exercise of discretion is not liable for an injury resulting from his act or omission in determining policy when acting in the exercise of such discretion even though abused." Section 2–109 of the Act also provides that "[a] local public entity is not liable for an injury resulting from an act or omission of its employee where the employee is not liable." * * *

At the time of plaintiff's injury section 24–24 of the School Code provided in pertinent part:

> "Teachers and other certificated educational employees shall maintain discipline in the schools. In all matters relating to the discipline in and conduct of the schools and the school children, they stand in the relation of parents and guardians to the pupils. This relationship shall extend to all activities connected with the school program and may be exercised at any time for the safety and supervision of the pupils in the absence of their parents or guardians."

Since the foregoing statute specifically confers upon educators the status of parent or guardian to the students, and since a parent is not liable for injuries to his child absent wilful and wanton misconduct * * * it therefore follows that the same standard applies as between educator and student. * * * We [have] held that section 24–24 of the School Code was intended to confer *in loco parentis* status in nondisciplinary as well as disciplinary matters. * * *

In our view, section 24–24 of the School Code is not applicable here in view of the absence of any *in loco parentis* relationship between the injured plaintiff and the certificated employees of the defendant school district who allegedly failed to exercise proper supervision. * * * [S]ection 24–24 reflects "a legislative determination that educators should stand in the place of a parent or guardian in matters relating to discipline, the conduct of the schools and the school children. It is this status as parent or guardian which requires a plaintiff to prove wilful and wanton misconduct in order to impose liability upon educators." That status is clearly lacking here, and it seems evident that the purpose of the immunity which arises from such status would not be served by extending it to immunize school districts from liability to third parties for ordinary negligence in situations such as that now before us. We accordingly hold that section 24–24 of the School Code does not provide any basis for affirmance of the trial court's decision in this case.

It is unnecessary to dwell at length on the common law distinctions between invitees and licensees which have evolved over the years. It suffices to observe that the general definition of an invitee is a visitor who comes upon premises at the invitation of the owner in connection with the owner's business or related activity. * * * Licensees are persons who have not been invited to enter upon the owner's premises and who come there for their own purposes and not those of the owner. * * * However, their presence is condoned by the owner, which distinguishes them from trespassers. The trial court concluded in the case at bar that since the plaintiff had not purchased a ticket but rather had attended the football game using a complimentary season pass, there was an absence of "commercial benefit" to the defendant school district, and she must therefore be considered a licensee. For the reasons hereafter stated, we must disagree with that conclusion.

In determining whether or not a person is an invitee or a licensee in a given situation, appellate courts in this State have often looked at the surrounding circumstances to determine whether, as between the visitor and the owner, there was a "mutuality of interest in the subject to which the visitor's business relates" * * * "a mutually beneficial interest" * * * a "mutuality of interest" * * * a "mutuality of benefit or a benefit to the owner" * * * or whether the visitor had come to "transact business in which he and the owner have a mutual interest or to promote some real or fancied material, financial, or economic interest of the owner" * * * Such inquiries into the purpose and nature of the visit were deemed relevant, particularly in cases involving implied invitations, to ascertain whether the visitor was upon the owner's premises within the scope and purpose of the invitation or for some other reason.

That type of analysis is not necessary here. In our opinion, the complimentary pass issued to plaintiff was tantamount to an express invitation to attend Hall Township High School football games, and there can be no question about the fact that at the time of her injury, plaintiff was acting within the scope of that invitation. Unlike a person who comes upon an owner's premises for his own purposes rather than those of the owner and whose presence is merely condoned by the owner, plaintiff in this case was expressly invited and encouraged to come to the defendant's football stadium to swell the crowd in support of its team. In this type of situation, it would be entirely illogical to conclude that a person attending the game using a complimentary pass provided by the school district should be owed a lesser duty of care than a person otherwise similarly situated who had purchased a ticket. In our view, both persons should be owed the same duty of reasonable care, and we so hold.

Upon application of a reasonable care standard to the case at bar, we cannot conclude that all of the evidence, when viewed in its aspect most favorable to the plaintiff, so overwhelmingly favors the defendant that no verdict for the plaintiff could ever stand. * * * The question of whether defendant failed to exercise reasonable care in supervising children attending the football game and whether such failure, if found to exist, was the proximate cause of plaintiff's injuries, should have been submitted to the jury.

* * *

Reversed and remanded.

School District Not Immune Regardless of Whether It Was
Performing a Governmental or Proprietary Function

BOARD OF SCHOOL COMMISSIONERS OF MOBILE
CTY. v. CAVER

Supreme Court of Alabama, 1978.
355 So.2d 712.

BLOODWORTH, Justice.   *   *   *

Plaintiff, Caver, a student who was allegedly injured by a Mobile County School Board bus while she was standing in the school yard, brought suit for negligence, and the Board moved to dismiss her complaint because of sovereign immunity.   *   *   *

Defendant, Board, contends that the issue of sovereign immunity was decided in its favor in Sims v. Etowah County Board of Education, 337 So.2d 1310 (Ala.1976), which held in a plurality decision, (based upon an interpretation of Tit. 52, § 99, Code of Alabama 1940) that a school board is immune from suit in tort.

Although at first blush, the Board's argument seems an appealing one, for *Sims* appears to foreclose further inquiry into this question, a close reading of *Sims* and an examination of Act No. 480, Acts of Alabama, Regular Session 1969, as well as § 270 of the Constitution of 1901, convinces us that the Mobile County School Board is amenable to suit in tort.

Mr. Justice Stakely, in Morgan v. Board of School Commissioners of Mobile County, 248 Ala. 22, 26 So.2d 108 (1946), gave the history of the Mobile County Board of School Commissioners. In that opinion, he pointed out that the Mobile County School Board has been exempted, in large part, from the general scheme of public school legislation ever since 1854 when the State of Alabama set up its first comprehensive school system.

That legislative policy, which is based upon the fact that Mobile County established its school system before the State did so, continues to this date, as evidenced by Section 270 of Article XIV of the Alabama Constitution.

*   *   *

This limitation on legislative power is restrictive in its scope and purpose and is to be strictly construed.   *   *   *

Act Number 480 (the latest amendatory act regulating the public schools in Mobile County) falls within neither one of these two exceptions. That act provides, *inter alia,* that, "The said Board shall be a body corporate; and may have a common seal; *may sue and be sued*   *   *   *." (Emphasis supplied.) Clearly, the authority to "sue and be sued" is not one of those educational areas in which the legislature may not act concerning the Mobile County School Board.

We stressed in Sims v. Etowah County Board of Education, supra, as well as in Enterprise City Board of Education v. Miller, 348 So.2d 782 (1977), that the sovereign immunity we held was due to be accorded those boards of education flowed directly from the statutes. In both cases, the pertinent statutes stated that the county and city boards of education, respectively, "may sue." There was no corresponding provision in those statutes that the respective boards could "be sued." For that reason, we said in each case, *inter alia,* that the respective boards of education were immune from suit in tort.

In the case at bar, by contrast, Act Number 480 clearly states that the Mobile County School Board "may sue and be sued." We hold, therefore, as we said in *Sims* and *Enterprise City Board,* that the statute must be given effect, and, therefore, the Mobile County School Board may be sued in tort.

Defendant Board argues, however, that the phrase "sue and be sued" is not an all encompassing term, and that if the county school board may be sued, it may only be sued for acts performed in its corporate or proprietary capacity as opposed to acts performed in its governmental capacity. In other words, defendant Board would have us resort to determining whether the act is governmental or corporate. As we held in Jackson v. City of Florence, 294 Ala. 592, 320 So.2d 68 (1975), * * * however, these distinctions are tenuous, at best, and our continued reliance upon them, in the context of sovereign immunity cases, would serve no useful purpose.

For the foregoing reasons, we hold that the trial judge's order is due to be affirmed.

Affirmed.

NOTES

Nuisance. Another device used by the courts to partially skirt the boundaries of immunity is the nuisance doctrine. A "nuisance" has been defined as "the existence or creation of a dangerous, unsafe, or offensive condition which is likely to cause injury, harm, or inconvenience to others." National Educational Association, op. cit. p. 21. A more complete definition has been given by a Connecticut Court.

> * * * to constitute a nuisance there must have arisen a condition, the natural tendency of which is to create danger or inflict injury upon person or property, * * * there must be more than an act or failure to act on the part of the defendant, * * * the danger created must have been a continuing one * * *. Bush v. City of Norwalk, 122 Conn. 426, 189 A. 608 (1937).

A leading case in which a school district was held to have created a nuisance was where snow had fallen from the roof of a school building onto adjacent property damaging the property and the owner was injured when he fell on the ice. The court held that in this case there was both nuisance and trespass. The court said:

The plaintiff had the right to the exclusive use and enjoyment of his property, and the defendant had no more right to erect a building in such a manner that the ice and snow would inevitably slide from the roof, and be precipitated upon the plaintiff's premises, than it would have to accumulate water upon its own premises, and then permit it to flow in a body upon his premises. Ferris v. Board of Educ. of Detroit, 122 Mich. 315, 81 N.W. 98 (1899).

In keeping with the legal definition a dangerous condition must be created by the school district for nuisance to exist. In Kansas, an action was brought to recover damages for injury sustained by a nine-year-old pupil who slipped and fell on a wet lavatory floor. Pupils had made the floor wet and slippery by throwing wet paper towels and splashing water. The plaintiff claimed the district was maintaining a nuisance and was therefore liable. In response, the court held that the school did not create the nuisance since pupils could be expected to splash water and throw wet towels on the floor while using the lavatory and that wash basins were a necessary part of the school building equipment. Jones v. Kansas City, 176 Kan. 406, 271 P.2d 803 (1954). The adequacy of supervision on the part of school personnel was another matter. Adequacy of supervision is not a question to be dealt with in a nuisance action, since to constitute nuisance there must be a continuing hazard and there must be more than a mere failure to act on the part of defendant. Rose v. Board of Educ., 184 Kan. 486, 337 P.2d 652 (1959). It seems safe to conclude that while the "nuisance" theory is a viable method of averting direct confrontation with the governmental immunity issue, the courts in other jurisdictions will not plunge headlong toward its use as piecemeal abrogation. Barnett v. City of Memphis, supra; Folk v. City of Milwaukee, supra; Anderson v. Board of Education, supra. This, of course, does not mean courts will never employ the device since it is an acceptable legal doctrine, but it does indicate a reluctance on the part of the courts to tamper with the doctrine of governmental immunity in this limited fashion.

Defamation

Defamation is constituted of the twin torts, libel and slander. On their face a distinction between libel as written and slander as oral communication are easily distinguishable, however, other forms of communication such as acts or gestures, motion pictures, radio or television complicate the dichotomy. Some courts simply maintain that defamation designed for visual perception is libel and all other forms of communication are slander.[76] General acceptance by the courts is found in the following definitions: libel is a malicious publication, expressed in either printing or writing, or by signs and pictures while slander is personal imputation effected by writings, pictures, or signs both of which tend to injure a party's situation in society.[77]

Teachers and school administrators are particularly susceptible to actions in defamation because of the sensitivity of personal infor-

---

76. 50 Am.Jur.2d 516.   77. Ibid.

mation with which they came into contact each day. Teachers as a matter of routine process and communicate information which relates to pupil performance the misuse of which could potentially harm the student's reputation and stigmatize his or her future. The problem of the administrator is even more complex in communication of information concerning teacher performance to other administrators or to school board members. Public interest in education, though, makes it absolutely essential that proper pupil and teacher evaluations are made and that public school officials and employees not be subjected to constant fear of personal liability. Because of this important public interest the courts have generally recognized that statements regarding school matters are qualifiedly privileged if made by persons having a common duty or interest in the information and acting in good faith.[78] "In the absence of malice, a school official is not liable to a teacher for performing the duties of his office." [79] A teacher likewise has a qualified or conditional privilege when acting in good faith in school matters but the qualified privilege is not unlimited and no privilege attaches to a teacher's entry in a school register to the effect that a certain pupil "was ruined by tobacco and whisky."[80] Absolute privileges are only afforded those individuals who perform vital governmental functions which the courts have defined as judicial proceedings, legislative proceedings, and certain executive proceedings. With the judiciary absolute privilege extends only to the particular statements which are relevant or pertinent to the case at bar.[81] In the legislature complete privilege extends to statements made in the course of debate, voting or reports on work performed in committees.[82] Public officers holding executive positions also have absolute immunity for communications made in connection with the performance of their official duties.

While courts generally hold that school superintendents have a conditional or qualified privilege, some courts have maintained that public policy requires that superintendents be given an absolute privilege in evaluating teacher activities before school board. Similarly, school board members have been held to have absolute privilege in imputing inefficiency and lack of qualification in evaluating a school superintendent's performance.[83]

The more common precedent to follow, though, is that officials, teachers and others dealing in public interest context have at least a qualified privilege. This conditional immunity can even extend to

78. *Restatement of Torts* § 596; 12 A. L.R. 147; 50 A.L.R. 339.

79. Barton v. Rogers, 21 Idaho 609, 123 P. 478 (1912).

80. Dawkins v. Billingsley, 69 Okl. 259, 172 P. 69 (1918).

81. Prosser, *op cit.* p. 609.

82. Coffin v. Coffin, 4 Mass. 1, 3 Am. Dec. 189 (1808).

83. Smith v. Helbraun, 21 A.D.2d 830, 251 N.Y.S.2d 533 (1964).

parents presenting a petition before a school board to the effect that a teacher was "incompetent." [84]

A qualified privilege requires that the statements be made in good faith and without malice. One court explained such privileges in this way:

> If a communication comes within the class denominated absolute privileged or qualifiedly privileged, no recovery can be had. Privileged communications are divided and defined as follows: (1) that the communication was made by the defendant in good faith, without malice, not voluntarily but in answer to an inquiry, and in the reasonable protection of his own interest or performance of a duty to society; (2) that the defendant must honestly believe the communication to be true; (3) there must have been reasonable or probable grounds known to him for the suspicion; (4) that the communication, if made in answer to an inquiry, must not go further than to truly state the facts upon which the suspicion was founded, and to satisfy the inquirer that these were reasons for the suspicion. [85]

Under this definition, it is clear that the communication must be made in good faith, without malice, upon reasonable grounds and in answer to inquiry and importantly it must be made with regard to assisting or protecting the interests of either of the parties involved or in performing a duty to society. The school official or employee's communication is qualifiedly privileged if it is prompted by a duty owed to either the public or a third party and is made in good faith and without malice.

In some states truth is a defense for a defamation action. In these jurisdictions it is not necessary to show that the statement is the literal truth, but it is adequate to show that the imputation is only substantially true. In a Texas case, the president of a commercial college was asked for information concerning a former student. He replied that the man had been a student at the institution but had not graduated. He related that, in fact, the student had been dismissed from school for stealing a typewriter and had been placed in jail. Consequently, the student sued for damages and was able to show that the statement was untrue. The president could not show that the statement was even substantially true; therefore, the case was decided in favor of the student. [86]

While some states still use truth as a defense, the more modern concept is that even if an utterance is the truth, it must be made

84.　Ottinger v. Ferrell, 171 Ark. 1085, 287 S.W. 391 (1926).

85.　Baskett v. Crossfield; 190 Ky. 751, 228 S.W. 673 (1921).

86.　Tyler Commercial College v. Lattimore, 24 S.W.2d 361 (Tex.1930).

with good intentions and for justifiable reasons. To volunteer damaging information where the interests of the school or children are not at stake may well be considered by the courts to constitute malice. Further, if an unintentionally erroneous report is made conveying information potentially harmful to a child's reputation, failure to correct the error may constitute malice sufficient to destroy a conditional privilege.[87]

Pupil Records and Information

Teachers, guidance counselors, and principals are generally involved in the release of pupil information and records to other teachers, professional personnel within the school, prospective employers outside the school or other educational institutions to which pupils may be applying for entrance. Considering these areas of pupil information flow, common law suggests the following rules be followed. First, information should not be related to other teachers or administrators unless the motive and purpose is to assist and enhance the educational opportunities of the pupil. Transmittal should be made in the proper channels and to persons assigned the responsibility for the relevant educational function. Gossip or careless talk among teachers, which is not calculated to help the student, is not protected by the cloak of qualified privilege. Second, pupil information should be transmitted to prospective employers only upon request. This protects the teacher from the presumption that the transmittal was made with malice.[88] A qualified privilege has been upheld where a communicator responded to a questionnaire and only gave answers to specific questions.[89] It is a good practice not to release information over a telephone unless the identity of the caller is absolutely certain. Third, records should be released to colleges and other institutions only if there is statutory or regulatory requirement for the transmittals or if the pupil himself requests the conveyance. Most states have laws or regulations which require the transfer of elementary and secondary school pupils' records when they change schools. This, of course, facilitates the transition for the pupil as well as the school and provides needed data for placement and is therefore proper.

Beyond the common law federal statute intervenes to further protect the student. The Family Educational Rights and Privacy Act was passed in August 1974 as an amendment to the Omnibus Education Bill.[90] The act establishes standards to which school districts

87. Vigil v. Rice, 74 N.M. 693, 397 P.2d 719 (1964).

88. Solow v. General Motors Truck Co., 64 F.2d 105 (2nd Cir. 1933).

89. Hoff v. Pure Oil, 147 Minn. 195, 179 N.W. 891 (1920).

90. Education Amendments of 1974, Public Law No. 93–380, 20 U.S.C.A. § 1232g. (Sometimes referred to as the Buckley Amendment).

must adhere in handling student records.   Failure to abide by the
law can result in the withdrawal of federal education funds.

Essentially, the amendment provides that parents and emancipated students shall have the right to review and inspect all official records, files, and data concerning the student.   Information routinely
gathered and shared by school personnel are included.   The data to
which access is given are not limited to completed grade reports,
achievement test scores, attendance data, health data, but also includes behavior reports and teacher and counselor ratings.   Personal
notes kept by teachers or counselors which are not communicated or
routinely shared are probably exempt.[91]

The school cannot release individual student information unless
written consent has been given by the student or his legal guardian
or the school is under court order or subpoena.   School officials, including all teachers with "legitimate educational interest" and school
officials of other schools and school systems to which the student is
transferred or intends to transfer have the right to see the student's
records.   In the event that records are transferred the parent or
emancipated student must be notified of the record transfer, receive a
copy if requested, and have the opportunity to have a hearing to
challenge the contents.

Negative Recommendation Is Protected by a Conditional Privilege

HETT v. PLOETZ

Supreme Court of Wisconsin, 1963.
20 Wis.2d 55, 121 N.W.2d 270.

Hett brought this action to recover damages for injury to his
professional reputation from an allegedly libelous publication by
Ploetz.   *   *   *

From 1956 to 1959 Hett had been employed as a speech therapist
in the school system of the city of Cudahy, Wisconsin.   His schedule
required that he travel to six different schools and teach those pupils
who were in need of his speciality.   *   *   *

*   *   *

Based upon their analysis of Hett's qualifications, the principals
of the six schools in which Hett taught reported to Ploetz that they
did not recommend renewal of Hett's contract for the 1959–1960
school year.

While the principals did not recommend Hett's retention for that
year, Ploetz decided that because he had been the superintendent for

---

91. David G. Carter, J. John Harris   ucational Researchers".   *Journal of*
    III, and Frank Brown, "Privacy in   *Law and Education*, Vol. 5, No. 4, Oc-
    Education: Legal Implications for Ed-   tober 1976, p. 470.

only six months it would be unfair to Hett to recommend his dismissal.

Ploetz informed Hett that his contract was not going to be renewed and told him that it would be in his best interest to resign so that a dismissal would not appear on his record. Hett resigned.
* * *

On November 9, 1959, Hett applied for a position as a speech therapist at the Southern Wisconsin Colony and Training School, Union Grove, Wisconsin. In his application he stated that the reason he left the Cudahy school system was that there was a lack of advancement opportunities. He listed Ploetz as a reference and gave permission to the Southern Colony officials to communicate with Ploetz.
* * *

* * *

GORDON, Justice. The plaintiff contends that he was libeled by the defendant's response to an inquiry from a prospective employer of the plaintiff. Hett had not only given Ploetz's name as a reference but had also given express permission to the prospective employer to communicate with Ploetz.

We must resolve two questions. The first is whether any privilege insulates the defendant's letter; the second is whether an issue of malice exists for trial.

Conditional Privilege

It is clear that Ploetz's allegedly defamatory letter was entitled to a conditional privilege. Ploetz was privileged to give a critical appraisal concerning his former employee so long as such appraisal was made for the valid purpose of enabling a prospective employer to evaluate the employee's qualifications. The privilege is said to be "conditional" because of the requirements that the declaration be reasonably calculated to accomplish the privileged purpose and that it be made without malice. * * *
* * *

Lord Blackburn has said:

> "Where a person is so situated that it becomes right in the interests of society that he should tell to a third person facts, then, if he *bona fide* and without malice does tell them, it is a privileged communication." See Rude v. Mass, supra, p. 329, 48 N.W. p. 557.

The public school official who expresses an opinion as to the qualifications of a person who has submitted an application for employment as a school teacher should enjoy the benefits of a conditional privilege.

The Absence of Malice

As previously noted, the employee had given Ploetz's name as a reference and had authorized that an inquiry be made of him. The letter contains certain factual matters as well as expressions of opinion. The factual portions are not contradicted by any pleading before this court. Thus, the following statement contained in the letter written by Ploetz stands unchallenged:

> "Last year, our six Principals and Elementary Coordinator unanimously recommended that he be no longer retained in our system as a speech correctionist. He, therefore, was not offered a contract to return this year."

The expression of opinion of which Hett complains is contained in the following portion of the defendant's letter:

> "We feel that Mr. Hett is not getting the results that we expected in this very important field. I, personally, feel that Mr. Hett does not belong in the teaching field. He has a rather odd personality, and it is rather difficult for him to gain the confidence of his fellow workers and the boys and girls with whom he works."

In our opinion, the record before us establishes that this expression of opinion is not founded in malice. The background of the relationship of Hett and Ploetz satisifactorily demonstrates that the latter's negative recommendation was grounded on the record and not upon malice. Ploetz was not an intermeddler; he had a proper interest in connection with the letter he wrote.

* * *

The plaintiff has failed to recite any evidentiary facts which are sufficient to raise questions for trial. His allegations that the letter contains defamatory material are mere conclusions. No presumption of malice has arisen; no showing of express malice has been presented.

In Otten v. Schutt (1962), 15 Wis.2d 497, 503, 113 N.W.2d 152, 155, this court stated:

> "The law relating to defamatory communications is based on public policy. The law will impute malice where a defamatory publication is made without sufficient cause or excuse, or where necessary to protect the interests of society and the security of character and reputation; but where the welfare of society is better promoted by a freedom of expression, malice will not be imputed. * * *

Public policy requires that malice not be imputed in cases such as this, for otherwise one who enjoys a conditional privilege might be reluctant to give a sincere, yet critical, response to a request for an appraisal of a prospective employee's qualifications.

* * * A thorough examination of the entire record compels our conclusion that the <u>respondent is entitled to the benefit of a con</u><u>ditional privilege</u>.

Judgment affirmed.

NOTES

1. If a statement is made by defendant in response to an inquiry by the plaintiff, then a conditional privilege may be elevated to the status of an absolute privilege. <u>An "absolute privilege is confined to relatively few</u> <u>situations. It is accorded judicial proceedings, legislative proceedings, pro</u><u>ceedings of executive officers charged with responsibility of importance,</u> <u>publications made</u> *with consent of the plaintiff* and communications be<u>tween husband and wife."</u> Prosser, *Law of Torts*, 2nd ed., West Publishing Company, Dec. 95, Walker v. D'Alesandro, 212 Md. 163, 129 A.2d 148 (1957).

The Supreme Court of Missouri has invoked this rule where a superintendent responded to a question by a teacher in a hearing before the school board.

"When plaintiff asked the defendant at the board meeting why she was not going to be re-employed the following school year the superintendent should be at liberty to say to her, 'Miss Williams, you have disobeyed school rules and regulations, you are insubordinate and are insufficient and inadequate with your students.' In that situation he (superintendent) is absolutely protected in his explanation to plaintiff."

Williams v. School Dist. of Springfield R–12, 447 S.W.2d 256 (Mo. 1969).

2. Would a school superintendent be protected by an absolute privilege in responding to a similar teacher inquiry at a teachers' meeting rather than at a school board meeting?

3. In the case of De Bolt v. McBrien, 96 Neb. 237, 147 N.W. 462 (1914), the Court applied the absolute privilege rule to a state superintendent of public instruction's statement to the county supervisor accusing the plaintiff of poker playing and being under the influence of liquor.

4. The Oklahoma Appellate Court found that defamatory statements about the school librarian made by the president and dean of the medical school at a session of the board of regents were absolutely privileged. See Hughes v. Bizzel, 189 Okl. 472, 117 P.2d 763 (1941).

5. In other related cases see Haskell v. Perkins, 165 Ill.App. 144 (1911); Forsythe v. Durham, 270 N.Y. 141, 200 N.E. 674 (1936); and Maurice v. Worden, 54 Md. 233 (1880).

6. Parents and patrons of the school have a qualified privilege in disclosing information at a school board meeting. Where school patrons presented the school trustees with a letter charging that the teacher failed to keep proper order and discipline and allowed older boys to take improper privileges with her and girl students, the court held that if the defendants believed that the school was conducted as stated then it was their right to complain to the trustees since they were the only ones authorized to remedy

it. According to the court the central issue was whether the letter was presented with malicious intent. In reversing a judgment in favor of the teacher, the court remanded the case for jury determination of whether malice existed. According to the court the jury should be instructed to find that malice was present if the publication by defendants was not made in good faith and had actually intended to injure the teacher not merely to correct the school situation. Malone v. Carrico, 16 Ky. Law Rev. 155 (1894).

7. Residents and patrons of a school district were held to be protected by a qualified privilege when they presented a petition to the school board stating that "we do not think she (plaintiff teacher) is a competent teacher and has but little control over the school." The court said that if the occasion, the motive, and the cause be proper, the publication or communication does not imply malice. To overcome a qualified privilege malice must be proved by the person claiming to have been defamed, and the mere falsity of the alleged defamatory matter is not sufficient. Hoover v. Jordan, 27 Colo.App. 515, 150 P. 333 (1915); see also, 40 A.L.R.3d 490.

8. Where tenured teacher and assistant principal were responsible for investigating suspected drug involvement of students and counseling with students and their parents, their communications to parent of high school student concerning sale of drugs in Plaintiffs' place of business were qualifiedly privileged. Comments were made in good faith and on an occasion which properly served their duty and under circumstances were fairly warranted by the occasion. Teacher and assistant principal were not liable to Plaintiffs for defamation in absence of showing of express malice. The Court defined *qualified privilege* as: "A communication, although it contains criminating matter, is privileged when made in good faith upon any subject in which the party communicating has an interest, or in reference to which he has a right or duty, if made to a person having a corresponding interest, right, or duty, and made upon an occasion to properly serve such right, interest, or duty, and in a manner and under circumstances fairly warranted by the occasion and the duty, right, or interest, and not so made as to unnecessarily or unduly injure another, or to show express malice." Chapman v. Furlough, 334 So.2d 293.

In defining *good faith* the court quoted an older Florida case saying: "Good faith, a right, duty, or interest in a proper subject, a proper occasion, and a proper communication to those having a like right, duty, or interest, are all essential to constitute words spoken, that are actionable per se, a privileged communication, so as to make the proof by the Plaintiff of express malice essential to liability. In determining whether or not a communication is privileged, the nature of the subject, the right, duty, or interest of the parties in such subject, the time, place and circumstances of the occasion, and the manner, character, and extent of the communication, should all be considered. When all these facts and circumstances are conceded, a court may decide whether a communication is a privileged one, so as to require the Plaintiff to prove express malice * * *." Abraham v. Baldwin, 52 Fla. 151, 42 So. 591 (1906).

FAMILY EDUCATIONAL AND PRIVACY RIGHTS ACT

20 U.S.C.A. § 1232g
(Education Amendments of 1974, Public Law 93–380)

Conditions for availability of funds to educational agencies or institutions; inspection and review of education records; specific information to be made available; procedure for access to education records; reasonableness of time for such access; hearings; written explanations by parents; definitions

(a) (1) (A) No funds shall be made available under any applicable program to any educational agency or institution which has a policy of denying, or which effectively prevents, the parents of students who are or have been in attendance at a school of such agency or at such institution, as the case may be, the right to inspect and review the education records of their children. * * * Each educational agency or institution shall establish appropriate procedures for the granting of a request by parents for access to the education records of their children within a reasonable period of time, but in no case more than forty-five days after the request has been made.

* * *
* * *

(2) No funds shall be made available under any applicable program to any educational agency or institution unless the parents of students who are or have been in attendance at a school of such agency or at such institution are provided an opportunity for a hearing by such agency or institution, in accordance with regulations of the Secretary, to challenge the content of such student's education records, in order to insure that the records are not inaccurate, misleading, or otherwise in violation of the privacy or other rights of students, and to provide an opportunity for the correction or deletion of any such inaccurate, misleading, or otherwise inappropriate data contained therein and to insert into such records a written explanation of the parents respecting the content of such records.

* * *

Release of education records; parental consent requirement; exceptions; compliance with judicial orders and subpoenas; audit and evaluation of Federally-supported education programs; record-keeping

(b) (1) No funds shall be made available under any applicable program to any educational agency or institution which has a policy or practice of permitting the release of education records (or personally identifiable information contained therein other than directory information, as defined in paragraph (5) of subsection (a) of this section) of students without the written consent of their parents to any individual, agency, or organization, other than to the following—

(A) other school officials, including teachers within the educational institution or local educational agency, who have been determined by such agency or institution to have legitimate educational interests;

(B) officials of other schools or school systems in which the student seeks or intends to enroll, upon condition that the student's parents be notified of the transfer, receive a copy of the record if desired, and have an opportunity for a hearing to challenge the content of the record;

(C) authorized representatives of (i) the Comptroller General of the United States, (ii) the Secretary, (iii) an administrative head of an education agency (as defined in section 1221e–3(c) of this title), or (iv) State educational authorities, under the conditions set forth in paragraph (3) of this subsection;

(D) in connection with a student's application for, or receipt of, financial aid;

(E) State and local officials or authorities to whom such information is specifically required to be reported or disclosed pursuant to State statute adopted prior to November 19, 1974;

(F) organizations conducting studies for, or on behalf of, educational agencies or institutions for the purpose of developing, validating, or administering predictive tests, administering student aid programs, and improving instruction, if such studies are conducted in such a manner as will not permit the personal identification of students and their parents by persons other than representatives of such organizations and such information will be destroyed when no longer needed for the purpose for which it is conducted;

(G) accrediting organizations in order to carry out their accrediting functions;

(H) parents of a dependent student of such parents, as defined in section 152 of Title 26; and

(I) subject to regulations of the Secretary, in connection with an emergency, appropriate persons if the knowledge of such information is necessary to protect the health or safety of the student or other persons. * * *

(2) No funds shall be made available under any applicable program to any educational agency or institution which has a policy or practice of releasing, or providing access to, any personally identifiable information in education records other than directory information, or as is permitted under paragraph (1) of this subsection unless—

(A) there is written consent from the student's parents specifying records to be released, the reasons for such release, and to whom, and with a copy of the records to be released to the student's parents and the student if desired by the parents, or

(B) such information is furnished in compliance with judicial order, or pursuant to any lawfully issued subpoena, upon condition that parents and the students are notified of all such orders or subpoenas in advance of the compliance therewith by the educational institution or agency.

* * *

Chapter 13

FINANCE

Fiscal affairs of school districts which broadly range from equity to taxpayers to equality of opportunity to students has, in recent years, become fertile ground for litigation. Because of the complexity of the matters involved and the tendency of issues of taxation and finance to go directly to the heart of the democratic processes, the courts have traditionally been hesitant to impose their power on legislative prerogative. Generally, the state legislature, in the absence of contrary constitutional restraints, has plenary power over state and local financing of schools. State constitutional provisions empowering the legislature to provide for a system of public schools expressly or impliedly confer on the legislature the authority to tax and distribute funds for public schools. Where litigation does arise it usually involves the methods used by the legislature to regulate and control revenues and expenditures in the exercise of this authority. A substantial amount of litigation is devoted to the legal requirements for taxation and taxpayers remedies for payment of illegal taxes as well as legal requirements for budgeting and accounting for school funds. Many cases question the legal authority of school districts to issue bonds, hold bond elections, and impose certain fees and charges on children and parents. Although the volume of cases is relatively small compared to other fiscal matters, the issue of constitutional rights of students and the resulting impact on state school finance has probably been the most widely publicized area of school finance litigation.

Recent court actions challenging the constitutionality of state school aid formulas under specific state constitutional provisions and the Equal Protection Clause of the Fourteenth Amendment represent an evolutionary step in judicial expansion of constitutional protections of individual rights. Constitutional rights of students have been extended, placing new limitations and restrictions on the police power of the state to regulate and control education. Courts once obliquely maintained that education was a privilege bestowed upon the individual by the good will of the state and that it could be altered or even taken away at state discretion. Today, however, this attitude has been changed and now the concept is that the student possesses a constitutional interest in an education. Under Due Process the litigation continues to test various provisions of state constitutions and their attendant ramifications. The theory that education is a protected interest has manifested itself in constitutional protections for students in both the substantive and procedural aspects of constitutional law.

The Equal Protection Clause of the Fourteenth Amendment has been a primary vehicle by which plaintiffs have sought to expand individual rights. With the desegregation cases as the basic source of precedent, some lower courts initially invoked equal protection rights as a means of forcing redistribution of state fund sources for education. In subsequent cases state constitutional provisions were utilized to contest the legitimacy of certain methods of school fund allocation. These cases harbored pervasive legal implications not the least of which was their impact on the traditional role of the legislature in setting governmental finance policy. Of all of the powers possessed by the legislative branch of government, the discretionary power to tax and distribute resources has been the most fundamental and jealously guarded. The courts, in treading on this hallowed ground, entered a "political thicket" as formidable as reapportionment and desegregation.

The school finance cases, therefore, represent an important step in legal precedents because they involve limitations not only on the police power of the state to regulate and control education but they also restrict a state's power to devise and implement its own system of taxation. Each of these issues has traditionally formed almost entirely separate precedents.

Taxation for Education

The power of taxation is an inherent power of the state, limited only by the 14th Amendment of the Federal Constitution and the constitution of the state. The states are not prevented by the equal protection clause from taxing according to reasonable classification. For example, a state may impose a heavier tax on nonresidents than on residents because of difficulties and expense of tax collection. However, a state may not impose taxes which impose an arbitrary or discriminatory burden upon a segment of the population.

The courts have held that school districts have no inherent power to levy taxes. This power must be expressly conferred upon the school district by the legislature. In the levy and collection of taxes, school districts must adhere strictly to the language of the statutory authority; the courts are hesitant to extend powers of taxation by statutory implication. The power of a local school district to tax for education funds is not implied by a statutory mandate to establish and operate a local school system. In the absence of contrary constitutional provisions, the legislature may choose to finance education entirely from a tax levied at the state level and redistributed to the school districts.

School districts must construe statutes strictly and expend the monies for the specific purposes as set out by the legislature. If a school tax levy is illegal because of failure to follow the prescribed procedure, the courts will make a determination depending on whether the statutory provision is mandatory or directory. If the provision is mandatory, the tax is invalid. However, the courts have established no clear guidelines for determining if a provision is mandatory or directory. In these situations courts are generally faced with the perplexing problem of finding a tax levy invalid and, thereby, harming the educational program. Because of this, the courts are usually very liberal in this regard and are hesitant to call a tax invalid. If a procedural error is relatively minor and does not deprive the taxpayers of a substantial or fundamental right, the courts will allow the tax to stand.

"THE DEVELOPMENT OF THE AMERICAN STATE AND LOCAL TAX SYSTEM" *

Colonial Taxation

The colonial governments in their early days subsisted on voluntary payments, subsidies and allowances abroad, quit-rents, and occasional fees and fines of early justice. When compulsory levies developed, the tax systems followed the pattern of the local economies. In the democratic New England communities almost every one owned land; and the distribution of property was fairly equal. Consequently, in New England, in addition to the poll tax, the colonies levied a tax on the gross produce of land, either actual or computed, according to the extent and quality of the land held. Gradually, this levy grew into a real property tax, which was soon expanded into a general property tax. The town artisans and other townsmen who subsisted on the fruit of their labor, instead of property, were not adequately taxed by the property levy. The "faculty tax" was added to reach these persons. The faculty tax was not an income tax, but instead a levy in a fixed amount, imposed rather arbitrarily, according to occupations and callings.[1]

An entirely different development took place in the Southern colonies, dominated by an aristocratic landed gentry with large holdings. There, the land tax played an insignificant role. After slavery was introduced, it became difficult to retain even the poll tax, which became in a sense a property tax on slaves. Consequently, the Southern colonies turned to excise taxes, particularly on imports and exports, which bore heavily on poorer consumers.

The middle colonies, particularly the New Netherlands, reflected the dominance of the moneyed interests and trading classes, who brought with them a Dutch tradition. Here, there was neither the more or less equal distribution of wealth charactistic of New England,

---

* With permission of Jerome R. Hellerstein, Third Ed., West Publishing Company, St. Paul, Minn. pp. 1–2 & pp. 70–72.

1. For the details of American faculty taxes, see Seligman, The Income Tax 367 (2d ed. 1914).

nor the preponderance of the landed interests typified by Virginia. Instead of a system of poll and property levies or of excises primarily on imports and exports, the fundamental characteristic of the tax structure was an excise system of taxation of trade, borrowed from Holland.

"Each section, therefore, had a fiscal system more or less in harmony with its economic conditions. It was not until these conditions changed during the eighteenth century that the fiscal systems began somewhat to approach each other; and it was not until much later that we find throughout the country a general property tax based not on the produce, but on the market value of property." [2]

The outstanding development in State and local taxation during the nineteenth century was the rise of the property tax. As stated by Professor Ely, during the period from 1796 to the Civil War "the distinguishing feature of the system of state and local taxation in America may be described in one sentence. It is the taxation of all property, movable or immovable, visible or invisible, or real or personal * * * at one uniform rate." [3]

Nevertheless, the divergence of economic systems was reflected in the development of the State fiscal systems. In the Southern States, with imports and exports as a source of revenue cut off by the Federal Constitution, land had to bear a large part of the tax burden. As increased revenues were needed, these States, dominated by landed proprietors at least until the Civil War, turned primarily to license and privilege taxes on peddlers, auctioneers, saloon keepers, traders in slaves and horses, keepers of ferries, toll bridges and turnpikes, and indeed virtually all occupations carried on outside the farms.

In the Northern States, where business interests were dominant, the license or privilege tax system did not take hold. To supplement property tax yields, banks, insurance companies, canals, railroads, and other businesses were taxed; and as corporations came to play a more important role in the economy, general corporate franchise taxes were enacted. These levies were the precursors of the present day corporate taxes on or measured by net income. The newer States adopted the current tax philosophy of the older States, making the property tax the cornerstone of their tax structures.

　　　*　*　*

Early Property Taxation. Although property taxes were regarded as an extraordinary source of revenue in early history, they, nevertheless, have ancient origins. In Athens, the land tax was originally levied on gross produce, but it gradually developed into a property tax imposed not only on land and houses but also on slaves, cattle, furniture and money. Rome taxed many forms of personalty as well as

2. See Seligman, Essay in Taxation 16–17 (10th ed. 1931), on which this section is based.

3. Taxation in American States and Cities 131 (1888).

realty. In Europe, the early property taxes were levied on land but were gradually extended to buildings and cattle, until they became general property taxes. As new types of movable and intangible property developed, evasion became prevalent and assessment difficult. The principle of the general property tax broke down and personal property taxes were gradually abandoned. By 1800, the base of European property taxes had largely dwindled down to land alone or land and buildings.

The Development of the General Property Tax in the United States. * * * the general property tax became formally established in this country for the States and localities during the nineteenth century.

At first the property tax was really a tax on land at a fixed sum per acre of different types of land—cleared and uncleared, cultivated and cleared, and so forth. It soon was expanded to include livestock, buildings, and personal property. Each item of taxable property was listed and taxed at a fixed sum for each cow, each barn, and so on. The increasing complexity of this taxable list led finally to (1) the general property tax—general taxation of all properties, instead of the growing lists of taxable specified properties; (2) appraisal of property—the tax rates were imposed as percentages of per millages of the property valuation, rather than as a fixed sum of money per unit of property; (3) the adoption of the principle of uniformity—whereas earlier laws provided for varying rates for different classes of property, the uniformity concept adopted by State constitutions required real and personal property to be taxed at a uniform proportion of value.

Authority to Levy Taxes Must be Found in Express Legislative Provision

MARION & McPHERSON RWY. CO. v. ALEXANDER

Supreme Court of Kansas, 1901.
63 Kan. 72, 64 P. 978.

CUNNINGHAM, J. The plaintiff in error in this action seeks to enjoin the collection of all taxes levied for school purposes in school district No. 79, Marion county, Kan., in excess of 2 per cent. on the taxable property owned by it in said district. A graded school district, No. 79, had been organized, identical in boundaries and inhabitants with school district No. 79; such organization being authorized by article 7, c. 92, of the General Statutes of 1889. That article generally provided for the organization of union or graded schools, its principal sections being as follows: Section 107 provides for the selection of a board of directors by the graded school district, and that such board shall consist of a director, clerk, and treasurer. Section

108 directs that such board of directors shall, in all matters relating to the graded schools, possess all the powers and discharge all the like duties of boards of directors in other districts. Section 109 provides that the union districts thus formed shall be entitled to an equitable share of the school funds, to be drawn from the treasurer of each district so uniting, in proportion to the number of children attending the said graded school for each district. Section 110: "The said union district may levy taxes for the purpose of purchasing a building or furnishing proper buildings for the accommodation of the school or for the purpose of defraying necessary expenses and paying teachers, but shall be governed in all respects by the law herein provided for levying and collecting district taxes." Section 111 provides certain duties for the clerk of the union district in relation to reports, and that the district treasurer shall apportion the amount of school moneys due the union district, and pay the same over to the treasurer of the union district on order of the clerk and director thereof. Section 112, that the clerk of the union district shall make report to the county superintendent, and discharge all the duties of clerk in like manner as the clerk of the district. Section 113, that the treasurer of the district shall perform all the duties of treasurer as prescribed in the act in like manner as the district treasurer. Section 115, that any single district shall possess power to establish graded schools in like manner and subject to the same provisions as two or more districts united. Section 28 of the same chapter (being the section which gives the general power for levying district taxes) provides: "The inhabitants qualified to vote at a school meeting, lawfully assembled, shall have power: * * * To vote a tax annually not exceeding two per cent. on the taxable property in the district, as the meeting shall deem sufficient for the various school purposes, and distribute the amount as the meeting shall deem proper in the payment of teachers' wages, and to purchase or lease a site."

These are all the sections which afford light for the solution of the question involved. From these, it is contended by plaintiff in error that while the inhabitants of one or more school districts may form a union or graded district, and create the machinery to run the same and to maintain any and all schools therein, the total levy "for the various school purposes" cannot exceed 2 per cent. on the taxable property in any one district annually. It is contended by the defendants in error that the various sections quoted, conferring as they do upon the various members of the graded school district board all the powers of like officers of ordinary district boards, and erecting a separate entity for the purpose of managing a separate school, and conferring upon that entity the power to levy taxes as found in section 110, give the power to such graded school district to make within its bounds an additional levy not to exceed 2 per cent.; that is, that it may levy as much as the original school district may, and this in addition to what the original district levies, and not that the total of both levies must be the limit fixed in section 28. The court below took this view of the question. In this we do not agree. We think that by section 28 the entire levy may not exceed 2 per cent.; and we are strengthened in this conclusion by the language of section 109, which says that a union district shall be entitled to "an equitable share of the school funds," and also by that in section 111,—"the district treasurer shall apportion the amount of school money due the union district and pay the same over to the union district." The law fixes the time for holding the annual meetings of the union or graded districts in June, while the annual meetings of school districts occur in July. All these provisions, taken together, indicate that it was the purpose of the legislature that, while the first meeting—that of the graded district—could suggest the levy desired for graded school purposes, the last one only possessed the power to vote the tax which for "the various school purposes" could not in any one year exceed 2 per cent. Or, at least, there must be such harmony in the action of both bodies that the aggregate levy may not exceed the limit found in section 28. We may say that the question is not one entirely free from doubt, but can hardly believe that the legislature would have left it in that condition, had its purpose been to confer the right to so largely increase the burden of taxation. The authority to levy taxes is an extraordinary one. It is never left to implication, unless it is a necessary implication. Its warrant must be clearly found in the act of the legislature. Any other rule might lead to great wrong and oppression, and when there is a reasonable doubt as to its existence the right must be denied. Therefore to say that the right is in doubt is to deny its existence. * * *

The levies sought to be enjoined are those for the years 1894 and 1895, and our conclusion is that the judgment of the district court must be reversed, and it be directed to make the injunction perpetual, enjoining all of the defendants from collecting all of said school taxes in excess of 2 per cent. All the justices concurring.

NOTES

1. "Neither municipalities nor school districts are sovereigns, and they have no original or fundamental power of legislation or taxation, but have only the right and power to enact those legislative and tax ordinances or resolutions which are authorized by act of the legislature." Appeal of School District of City of Allentown, 370 Pa. 161, 87 A.2d 480 (1952).

2. Taxes levied and collected for school purposes are state taxes whether they are collected by the school district or a municipality. In an Alabama case, the court said: "If the Constitution raises the fund and directs its use in furthering a state function, it continues to be such a state fund regardless of the sort of agency designated to administer it." City Board of Education of Athens v. Williams, 231 Ala. 137, 163 So. 802 (1935).

3. In relating legislative provisions for taxation to constitutional requirements the courts have held that revenue statutes must be given a rea-

sonable construction, and no statute can circumvent positively stated constitutional provisions. Mathews v. Board of Education of City of Chicago, 342 Ill. 120, 174 N.E. 35 (1930).

4. "The authority to levy taxes is an extraordinary one. It is never left to implication, unless it is a necessary implication. Its warrant must be clearly found in the act of the legislature. Any other rule might lead to great wrong and oppression, and when there is a reasonable doubt as to its existence the right must be denied   *   *   *." Marion and M. Ry. Co. v. Alexander, County Treasurer, 63 Kan. 72, 64 P. 978 (1901).

5. "The power of the board of education of a non-high school district to levy taxes is statutory. The language granting the power is to be strictly construed and will not be extended beyond the plain import of the words used." People ex rel. Smith, Co. Collector v. Wabash Railway Co. et al., 374 Ill. 165, 28 N.E.2d 119 (1940).

6. The intent of the legislature in enacting taxation statutes is many times difficult to interpret. A Pennsylvania court in determining that a statute prescribing taxation for "amusements" included admissions to "fair grounds" had this to say about statutory interpretation:

> The language of a statute must be read in a sense which harmonizes with the subject matter and its general purpose and object. The general design and purpose of the law is to be kept in view * * *.

School Dist. of Cambria Twp. v. Cambria Co. Legion Recreation Ass'n, 201 Pa.Super. 163, 192 A.2d 149 (1963).

7. Courts will not interfere with the exercise of sound business judgment on the part of taxing authorities, but will intervene only to prevent a clear abuse by such officers of their discretionary powers. People v. Baltimore & Ohio Southwestern Railway Co., 353 Ill. 492, 187 N.E. 463 (1933).

Taxpayer Cannot Recover Illegal Taxes which Were Paid Voluntarily and Without Protest

CORNELL v. HIGH SCHOOL DIST. NO. 99

Appellate Court of Illinois, Second Dist. 1936.
286 Ill.App. 398, 3 N.E.2d 717.

DOVE, Justice.   *   *   *

The complaint alleged that the plaintiffs were the owners of all beneficial interest and avails of sundry lots in Lyman Park subdivision in Downers Grove, Ill.; that in 1934 they first learned that none of this land lies within the territorial area of the defendant corporation, and therefore the defendant never had any authority or power to levy, extend, collect, or receive any taxes with reference to said real estate; that the defendant levied, assessed, extended, demanded, and collected taxes from the plaintiffs wrongfully and without any color or warrant of authority for the years 1925 to 1930, amounting to the aggregate sum of $1,000, which amount the plaintiffs paid through the regular DuPage county officers, and which amount the defendant now holds to the use and for the benefit of the plaintiffs. * * *

It is insisted by counsel for appellants that the lands of the plaintiffs, being outside of the appellee district, were not assessable for high school taxes, that they were wrongfully assessed and the taxes paid by mistake, and, as the district has obtained appellants' money without any color of authority, appellants are entitled to recover. * * *

        * * *

In Yates v. Royal Ins. Co., 200 Ill. 202, 65 N.E. 726, 727, which was an action by the insurance company against the state superintendent of insurance to recover taxes paid by it under an act of the Legislature thereafter held void, the court held there could be no recovery, and quoted the following from Colley on Taxation: "That a tax voluntarily paid cannot be recovered back, the authorities are generally agreed. And it is immaterial, in such a case, that the tax has been illegally laid, or even that the law under which it was laid was unconstitutional. The principle is an ancient one in the common law, and is of general application. Every man is supposed to know the law, and, if he voluntarily makes a payment which the law would not compel him to make, he cannot afterwards assign his ignorance of the law as the reason why the state should furnish him with legal remedies to recover it back." And in Swanston v. Ijams, 63 Ill. 165, which was an action brought against the county treasurer of McLean county to recover back taxes illegally assessed, the court held that there were two reasons why the plaintiff could not recover: First, he did not assert his rights when he might have done so; and, second, he voluntarily paid the tax, even though he did so in order to prevent a sale of his lands.

In our opinion, under the foregoing authorities, there can be no recovery under the allegations of the complaint, and the judgment of the trial court will therefore be affirmed.

Judgment affirmed.

NOTES

1. Where a wrongful tax is collected, the taxpayer may only recover on such remedies as are authorized by law, such as an appeal to set aside or cancel a tax deed and a tax protest. Wall v. M. & R. Sheep Co., 33 Cal.2d 768, 205 P.2d 14. An application for abatement is a proper remedy for a person who is not taxable by a school district. Orford School District No. 6 v. Orford, 63 N.H. 277 (1884).

2. A person who pays tax voluntarily and not under duress cannot recover the tax. Harding v. Wiley, 219 Ill.App. 1. A mere protest by a taxpayer is not sufficient to constitute payment under compulsion or duress.

3. A person may not question the legality of school funds unless he has a requisite interest in such funds. Chalupnik v. Savall, 219 Wis. 442, 263 N.W. 352 (1935).

4. Some states have statutory provisions for taxpayer protest in a court or board of tax review. The findings of fact or judgment by this court or board will not be disturbed unless clearly arbitrary or against the weight of evidence.

5. Taxpayers may not sit idly by and allow illegal systems of taxation to be installed without protesting and then take advantage of the illegality of the system by collaterally attacking the system when they are sued. In such a case the Court of Civil Appeals of Texas held that, although a scheme of taxation is illegal, the burden is on the taxpayers to show that they have suffered substantial financial loss as a result of the failure of the city and school district to assess property legally. City of Houston v. McCarthy, 371 S.W.2d 587 (1963).

State Has Sovereign Taxing Powers which Extend to Taxation of Instate Income Earned by Nonresidents

SHAFFER v. CARTER

Supreme Court of the United States, 1920.
252 U.S. 37, 40 S.Ct. 221.

Mr. Justice PITNEY delivered the opinion of the Court.

*   *   *

The Constitution of Oklahoma, besides providing for the annual taxation of all property in the state upon an ad valorem basis, authorizes (article 10, § 12) the employment of a variety of other means for raising revenue, among them income taxes.

The act in question is chapter 164 of the Laws of 1915. Its first section reads as follows:

"Each and every person in this state, shall be liable to an annual tax upon the entire net income of such person arising or accruing from all sources during the preceding calendar year, and a like tax shall be levied, assessed, collected and paid annually upon the entire net income from all property owned, and of every business, trade or profession carried on in this state by persons residing elsewhere."

*   *   *

Plaintiff, a nonresident of Oklahoma, being a citizen of Illinois and a resident of Chicago, in that state, was at the time of the commencement of the suit and for several years theretofore (including the years 1915 and 1916) engaged in the oil business in Oklahoma, having purchased, owned, developed and operated a number of oil and gas mining leases, and being the owner in fee of certain oil-producing land, in that state. From properties thus owned and operated during the year 1916 he received a net income exceeding $1,500,000, and of this he made, under protest, a return which showed that, at the rates fixed by the act, there was due to the state an income tax in excess of $76,000. The then state auditor overruled the protest and assessed a tax in accordance with the return; the present auditor has put it in due course of collection; and plaintiff resists its enforcement upon the ground that the act, in so far as it subjects the incomes of nonresidents to the payment of such a tax, takes their property without due process of law and denies to them the equal protection of the laws, in contravention of section 1 of the Fourteenth Amendment, burdens interstate commerce, in contravention of the commerce clause of section 8 of article 1 of the Constitution, and discriminates against nonresidents in favor of residents, and thus deprives plaintiff and other nonresidents of the privileges and immunities of citizens and residents of the state of Oklahoma, in violation of section 2 of article 4. He also insists that the lien attempted to be imposed upon his property pursuant to section 11 for taxes assessed upon income not arising out of the same property would deprive him of property without due process of law.

* * *

Under the "due process of law" provision appellant makes two contentions: First, that the state is without jurisdiction to levy a tax upon the income of nonresidents; and, secondly, that the lien is invalid because imposed upon all his property real and personal, without regard to its relation to the production of his income.

These are separate questions, and will be so treated. The tax might be valid, although the measures adopted for enforcing it were not. Governmental jurisdiction in matters of taxation, as in the exercise of the judicial function, depends upon the power to enforce the mandate of the state by action taken within its borders, either in personam or in rem according to the circumstances of the case, as by arrest of the person, seizure of goods or lands, garnishment of credits, sequestration of rents and profits, forfeiture of franchise, or the like; and the jurisdiction to act remains even though all permissible measures be not resorted to. * * *

It will be convenient to postpone the question of the lien until all questions as to the validity of the tax have been disposed of.

The contention that a state is without jurisdiction to impose a tax upon the income of nonresidents, while raised in the present case, was more emphasized in Travis, Comptroller v. Yale & Towne Mfg. Co., 252 U.S. 60, 40 Sup.Ct. 228, 64 L.Ed. 460, decided this day, involving the Income Tax Law of the state of New York (Laws 1919, c. 627). There it was contended, in substance, that while a state may tax the property of a nonresident situate within its borders, or may tax the incomes of its own citizens and residents because of the privileges they enjoy under its Constitution and laws and the protection they receive from the state, yet a nonresident although conducting a business or carrying on an occupation there cannot be required through income taxation to contribute to the governmental expenses of the state whence his income is derived; that an income tax, as against nonresidents, is not only not a property tax, but is not an excise or privilege tax, since no privilege is granted; the right of the noncitizen to carry on his business or occupation in the taxing state being derived, it is said, from the provisions of the federal Constitution.

This radical contention is easily answered by reference to fundamental principles. In our system of government the states have general dominion, and, saving as restricted by particular provisions of the federal Constitution, complete dominion over all persons, property, and business transaction within their borders; they assume and perform the duty of preserving and protecting all such persons, property, and business, and, in consequence, have the power normally pertaining to governments to resort to all reasonable forms of taxation in order to defray the governmental expenses. Certainly they are not restricted to property taxation nor to any particular form of excises. * * * That the state, from whose laws property and business and industry derive the protection and security without which production and gainful occupation would be impossible, is debarred from exacting a share of those gains in the form of income taxes for the support of the government, is a proposition so wholly inconsistent with fundamental principles as to be refuted by its mere statement. That it may tax the land but not the crop, the tree but not the fruit, the mine or well but not the product, the business but not the profit derived from it, is wholly inadmissible.

Income taxes are a recognized method of distributing the burdens of government, favored because requiring contributions from those who realize current pecuniary benefits under the protection of the government, and because the tax may be readily proportioned to their ability to pay. Taxes of this character were imposed by several of the states at or shortly after the adoption of the federal Constitution. * * *

The rights of the several states to exercise the widest liberty with respect to the imposition of internal taxes always has been recognized in the decisions of this court. * * *, while denying their power to impose a tax upon any of the operations of the federal government, Mr. Chief Justice Marshall, speaking for the court, conceded (4 Wheat. 428, 429, 4 L.Ed. 579) that the states have full power to tax their own people and their own property, and also that the power is not confined to the people and property of a state, but may be exercised upon every object brought within its jurisdiction, saying:

"It is obvious, that it is an incident of sovereignty, and is coextensive with that to which it is an incident. All subjects over which the sovereign power of a state extends, are objects of taxation," etc.

In Michigan Central Railroad v. Powers, 201 U.S. 245, 292, 293, 26 Sup.Ct. 459, 462 (50 L.Ed. 744), the court, by Mr. Justice Brewer, said:

> "We have had frequent occasion to consider questions of state taxation in the light of the federal Constitution, and the scope and limits of national interference are well settled. There is no general supervision on the part of the nation over state taxation, and in respect to the latter the state has, speaking generally, the freedom of a sovereign both as to objects and methods."
>
> *   *   *
>
And we deem it clear, upon principle as well as authority, that just as a state may impose general income taxes upon its own citizens and residents whose persons are subject to its control, it may, as a necessary consequence, levy a duty of like character, and not more onerous in its effect, upon incomes accruing to nonresidents from their property or business within the state, or their occupations carried on therein, enforcing payment, so far as it can, by the exercise of a just control over persons and property within its borders. This is consonant with numerous decisions of this court sustaining state taxation of credits due to nonresidents * * * and sustaining federal taxation of the income of an alien nonresident derived from securities held in this country. (De Ganay v. Lederer, 250 U.S. 376, 39 Sup.Ct. 524, 63 L.Ed. 1042).

That a state, consistently with the federal Constitution, may not prohibit the citizens of other states from carrying on legitimate business within its borders like its own citizens, of course is granted; but it does not follow that the business of nonresidents may not be required to make a ratable contribution in taxes for the support of the government. On the contrary, the very fact that a citizen of one state has the right to hold property or carry on an occupation or business, in another is a very reasonable ground for subjecting such nonresident, although not personally, yet to the extent of his property held, or his occupation or business carried on therein, to a duty to pay taxes not more onerous in effect than those imposed under like circumstances upon citizens of the latter state. * * *

* * * It clearly appears from the averments of the bill that the whole of plaintiff's property in the state of Oklahoma consists of oil-producing land, oil and gas mining leaseholds, and other property used in the production of oil and gas; and that, beginning at least as early as the year 1915, when the act was passed, and continuing without interruption until the time of the commencement of the suit (April 16, 1919), he was engaged in the business of developing and operating these properties for the production of oil, his entire busi-

ness in that and other states was managed as one business, and his entire net income in the state for the year 1916 was derived from that business. Laying aside the probability that from time to time there may have been changes arising from purchases, new leases, sales, and expirations (none of which, however, is set forth in the bill), it is evident that the lien will rest upon the same property interests which were the source of the income upon which the tax was imposed. The entire jurisdiction of the state over appellant's property and business and the income that he derived from them—the only jurisdiction that it has sought to assert—is a jurisdiction in rem; and we are clear that the state acted within its lawful power in treating his property interests and business as having both unity and continuity. Its purpose to impose income taxes was declared in its own Constitution, and the precise nature of the tax and the measures to be taken for enforcing it were plainly set forth in the act of 1915; and plaintiff having thereafter proceeded, with notice of this law, to manage the property and conduct the business out of which proceeded the income now taxed, the state did not exceed its power or authority in treating his property interests and his business as a single entity, and enforcing payment of the tax by the imposition of a lien, to be followed by execution or other appropriate process, upon all property employed in the business.

No. 531: Appeal dismissed.

No. 580: Decree affirmed.

NOTES

1. Tangible personal property which is located in a state other than in which the owner is domiciled may be taxed at the place of its location. Fennell v. Pauley, 83 N.W. 799 (1900). The "domicile" of a person is the place where he has his principle, true, fixed, permanent home, and to which he has, whenever he is absent, the intention of returning, and it also means the habitation, fixed in any place, from which a person does not have any present intention of removing. State v. Benny, 20 N.J. 238, 119 A.2d 155.

2. Intangible personal property is generally taxable at the domicile of the owner. Scripps v. Board of Review of Fulton Co., 55 N.E. 700 (1899). However, courts have upheld cases where the state legislature provides that intangible personal property shall be taxed where located other than where the owner is domiciled. In arriving at this conclusion a Minnesota court stated:

> For many purposes the domicile of the owner is deemed the situs of his personal property. This, however, is only a fiction, from motives of convenience, and is not of universal application, by yields to the actual situs of the property when justice requires that it should. It is not allowed to be controlling in matters of taxation. Thus, corporeal personal property is conceded to be taxable at the place where it is actually situated. A credit which cannot

be regarded as situated in a place merely because the debtor resides there, must usually be considered as having its situs where it is owned, at the domicile of the creditor. The creditor, however, may give it a business situs elsewhere; as where he places it in the hands of an agent for collection or renewal, with a view to reloaning the money and keeping it invested as a permanent business * * *.

The allegation to pay taxes on property for the support of the government arises from the fact that it is under the protection of the government. In re Washington County v. Estate of Jefferson, 35 Minn. 215, 28 N.W. 256 (1886).

3. In a case where property was assessed in the wrong district and the owner had means of knowing the mistake, he could not recover as having paid under a mistake of fact. A mistake of fact is one "not caused by the neglect of a legal duty on the part of the person making the mistake." Civ.Code, § 1577, San Diego Land & Town Co. v. La Presa School Dist., 122 Cal. 98, 54 P. 528 (1898).

Distribution of State School Funds *

Where constitutionality of a statute is questioned, all reasonable doubt will be resolved in favor of the questioned authority and the act will be declared constitutional unless it can be clearly demonstrated that the legislature did not have the power or authority exercised or that its authority was exercised arbitrarily and capriciously, for instance, as to classification or delegation of authority, to the prejudice of the rights of some of the citizens. Particularly, is this true where the act in question is * * * of great public concern involving the performance of an absolute duty imposed on the legislature by the basic law of the state.[4]

This statement describes the traditional position of the courts toward the judicial regulation of such important legislative functions as taxation for public education. Nonintervention has been the watchword for decades when courts have been asked to examine the constitutionality of legislatively prescribed methods of taxation for financing of education.

The courts have steadfastly adhered to the philosophy that an act of the legislature will not be rendered invalid unless the act obviously violates certain prescribed constitutional standards. With regard to the constitutionality of state school finance programs, the courts have traditionally only been asked to determine whether such

---

* This discussion is adapted from a chapter by Kern Alexander and K. Forbis Jordan in *Financing Education; Fiscal and Legal Alternatives*, edited by R. L. Johns, Kern Alexander and K. Forbis Jordan, Charles Merrill Company, 1972.

4. School District No. 25 of Woods County v. Hodge, 199 Okl. 81, 183 P.2d 575 (1947).

programs created unconstitutional classifications or violated equality and uniformity of taxation requirements. The Equal Protection Clause of the Fourteenth Amendment encompasses, but is not limited to, the same protections as the equality and uniformity of taxation provisions of most state constitutions. Even though the federal Equal Protection Clause encompasses much more than mere equality and uniformity of taxation, its broader aspects were not successfully invoked in challenging state school finance programs until recently.

The Equal Protection Clause was first described as a limitation on state revenue legislation by the Supreme Court of the United States in 1890. The "test" devised by the Supreme Court to determine constitutionality of state taxation has been restated by Justice Jackson:

> Equal protection does not require identity of treatment. It only requires that classification rest on real and not feigned differences, that the distinction have some relevance to the purpose for which the classification is made, and the different treatment be not so disparate, relative to the difference in classification, as to be wholly arbitrary.[5]

The equal protection clause establishes a minimum standard of uniformity to which state tax legislation must conform in addition to and over and beyond similar limitations imposed by state constitutional requirements.[6]

In practically all cases state constitutions have the equivalent of an "equal protection" provision—that is, some constitutional restriction against "unreasonable classifications." While the United States Supreme Court has the ultimate interpretative power regarding "reasonableness" under the federal Equal Protection Clause, state courts have the last word as to the meaning of reasonableness under their respective state constitutions.[7] The primary problem is, of course, the definition of reasonableness with regard to appropriate classification. There are apparently no universally applicable tests by which to determine the reasonableness or unreasonableness of a classification. The cases merely indicate a vague outline of reasonableness and in some instances a given basis may be valid with respect to one tax and invalid with another.[8] Justice Bradley, in *dictum* in the *Bell's Gap* case,[9] however, did give this explanation.

5. Bell's Gap Railroad Co. v. Commonwealth of Pennsylvania, 134 U.S. 232, 10 S.Ct. 533 (1890).

6. Wade J. Newhouse, *Constitutional Uniformity and Equality in State Taxation* (Ann Arbor: University of Michigan Law School, 1959, p. 602).

7. Ibid., p. 608.

8. Ibid., p. 603.

9. Bell's Gap Railroad Co. v. Pennsylvania, supra.

[The equal protection clause] was not intended to prevent a
state from adjusting its system of taxation in all proper and
reasonable ways. It may, if it chooses, exempt certain classes of property from any taxation at all, such as churches, libraries, and the property of charitable institutions. *   *   *
We think we are safe in saying, that the Fourteenth Amendment was not intended to compel the state to adopt an iron
rule of equal taxation. If that were its proper construction
it would not only supersede all those constitutional provisions and laws of some of the states, whose object is to secure equality of taxation, and which are usually accompanied with qualifications deemed material; but it would render nugatory those discriminations which the best interests
of society require. *   *   * [10]

The Equal Protection Clause of the Fourteenth Amendment is no
stranger to disputes over the distribution of school funds. As early
as 1912 the Supreme Court of Maine in Sawyer v. Gilmore handed
down an opinion which examined constitutional equality under both
the Maine and United States Constitutions as applied to both taxa-
tions and distribution of funds by the state.[11] The court in this case
maintained that the equality of taxation provision of the state constitution required only equality of assessment, not equality of distribution.

The logic in this case reflected a judicial philosophy which was
relied upon for over half a century. The courts steadfastly refused to
apply state constitutional uniformity and equality of taxing provisions to school fund distribution formulas. In fairness to the courts,
however, seldom, if ever, was a statute challenged where the legislature was not seeking to move toward greater equity in distribution of
resources among school districts. Plaintiffs were typically attempting to retard such process. Indeed, in most cases, state equality of
taxation and the federal Constitution were invoked in an attempt to
prevent the equalization of resources among school districts.

In Dean v. Coddington a South Dakota case, the constitutional
equality and uniformity arguments were raised in an attempt to prevent the initiation of a foundation or equalization program.[12] The
plaintiff, a taxpayer, asserted that the state foundation program act
was unconstitutional, violating both the equal and uniform provisions
of the South Dakota constitution and the equal protection clause of
the Fourteenth Amendment.

The plaintiff admitted that the taxes were probably uniformly
raised, but contended that uniformity requirement is not satisfied un-

10. Ibid.

11. Sawyer v. Gilmore, 109 Me. 169, 83,
     A. 673 (1912).

12. Dean v. Coddington, 81 S.D. 140,
     131 N.W.2d 700 (1964).

less the revenues derived from the taxes are uniformly distributed. The court, in upholding the constitutionality of the foundation program, commented on equality and uniformity of taxation of both the state and federal constitutions and then laid down guidelines to govern the legislature's apportionment of public funds. First, the court pointed out that the test of the uniformity of taxation provision under the South Dakota Constitution was substantially the same as that required by the Fourteenth Amendment to the United States Constitution. The rule was stated by the court as:

> It is generally held that the constitutional provisions requiring equality and uniformity relate to the levy of taxes and not to the distribution or application of the revenue derived therefrom; and hence statutes relative to the distribution or application of such money cannot be held invalid on this ground.[13]

In justifying state taxation programs the courts have not always adhered strictly to their philosophy of separation between taxation and distribution of revenues. Indeed, a court is forced into this very dilemma when it seeks to justify a legislative act on the basis of its rationality. In fact, the court in seeking to determine the reasonableness of a classification cannot avoid analyzing the impact of tax revenues on local school districts. Such an analysis forces a court to look at such things as fiscal ability, educational needs, high costs of programs, and other conditions peculiar to particular school districts.

As state legislatures have attempted to provide greater equalization of resources among school districts through various taxing and funding techniques, disputes have arisen over the constitutionality of these methods. Many states have constitutional provisions which require that state school funds be distributed in a particular manner, usually a flat amount per school census or population count.[14] Such constitutional provisions have been an impediment to legislatures seeking to equalize resources for poorer school districts. In the earlier cases these constitutional provisions were invoked by taxpayers from the wealthier school districts which sought to prevent state equalization of resources. A case in point is a 1924 Oklahoma case[15] where the legislature enacted a law providing additional money from the state general fund to support school districts which could raise enough resources from a 15 mill levy to operate an eight-month school term. The plaintiff maintained such legislation was unconstitutional because the state constitution mandated that monies from the state permanent school fund must be allocated on the basis of

---

13. Ibid.

14. See: Taylor v. School Dist. of City of Lincoln, 128 Neb. 437, 259 N.W. 168 (1935).

15. Miller v. Childers, 107 Okl. 57, 238 P. 204 (1924).

school population to all common school districts and also complained that state aid provided to only financially weak districts was special legislation constituting an unconstitutional classification. With regard to the first argument, the court held that the equalization monies were to be paid out of the state general fund and not out of the constitutionally restricted permanent school fund, thereby allowing the legislature flexibility in its method of allocation. The court dismissed the latter argument saying that the state aid to weak school districts applied to all districts alike, extending aid to those which were similarly situated in privation of resources.

This court also pointed out that the Oklahoma constitution placed the duty on the legislature to "establish and maintain a *system* [emphasis added] of free public schools wherein all children of the state may be educated.[16] Significantly, the court maintained that such wording meant that the legislature was to provide an "efficient and sufficient system, with competent teachers, necessary general facilities" and adequate length of school terms. The word "system," the court said, indicates a degree of uniformity and equality of opportunity, and by assuming the responsibility to provide for public education the state had the duty to provide "insofar as it is practical, equal rights and privileges to its youth, to obtain such mental and moral training as will make them useful citizens. * * * " This equality of treatment, the court said, was an "imperative governmental duty." [17]

Courts have been hesitant to invalidate legislative acts on the basis of unconstitutional classification because the source of taxation is often tightly interwoven with the government's plan for distribution of funds to local districts. The essence of an illegal constitutional classification is to arbitrarily classify local districts or persons with no regard for their actual conditions or needs. The United States Court of Appeals for the Ninth Circuit, speaks of this as fitting tax programs to needs:

> Traditionally classification has been a device for fitting tax programs to local needs and usages in order to achieve an equitable distribution of the tax burden. It has, because of this, been pointed out that in taxation, even more than in other fields, legislatures possess the greatest freedom in classification. Since the members of a legislature necessarily enjoy a familiarity with local conditions which this court cannot have, the presumption of constitutionality can be overcome only by the most explicit demonstration that a

16. Constitution of Oklahoma, Section 1, Art. 13. See also: Kennedy v. Miller, 97 Cal. 429, 32 P. 558 (1893); Piper v. Big Pine School Dist., 193 Cal. 664, 226 P. 926 (1924).

17. Miller v. Childers, 107 Okl. 57, 238 P. 204 (1924).

classification is a hostile and oppressive discrimination against particular persons and classes. The burden is on the one attacking the legislative arrangement to negate every conceivable basis which might support it.[18]

Even though the court denied that equality and uniformity of taxation requirements of both state and federal constitutions applied to the distribution of funds, it proceeded nevertheless to lay down "guiding principals" which govern the legislatures' distribution of tax funds. Quoting *Corpus Juris Secundum,* the court said:

> In the absence of constitutional regulation the method of apportioning and distributing a school fund, accruing from taxes or other revenue, rests in the wise discretion of the state legislature, which method, in the absence of abuse of discretion or violation of some constitutional provision, cannot be interfered with by the courts * * * the fact that the fund is distributed unequally among the different districts or political subdivisions does not render it invalid.[19]

In other words, the needs of the various types of school districts and the resulting impact of methods of taxation is a matter which is to be determined by the legislature.

In 1965, however, the theory was advanced that education was a constitutionally protected right and must be provided to all on equal terms, thus a state which gives fewer dollars for the child in a power school district may be held to deny equal protection rights.[20] It was argued that the state had no reasonable equal protection basis on which to justify making a child's education dependent on the wealth of the school district. The United States Supreme Court had laid the groundwork for this conclusion by previously holding that to classify persons on either the basis of poverty [21] or according to their location, homesite, or occupation was unreasonable.[22] Therefore, it was concluded, the quality of a child's education could not be contingent upon a state and local taxing and fund distribution system which is based on the property wealth of the local school district.

By 1968, several suits had been filed, each seeking to have state school finance programs rendered unconstitutional through the appli-

18. Hess v. Mullaney, 15 Alaska 40, 213 F.2d 635 (9th Cir. 1954), cert. denied Hess v. Dewey, 348 U.S. 836, 75 S.Ct. 50 (1954).

19. 79 C.J.S., Schools and School Districts, § 441.

20. "Is Denial of Equal Education Opportunity Constitutional?" *Administrator's Notebook,* No. 6. XIII (University of Chicago, Feb. 1965). See also: Arthur E. Wise, *Rich Schools Poor Schools* (Chicago: The University of Chicago Press, 1968).

21. Griffin v. Illinois, 351 U.S. 12, 76 S.Ct. 585 (1956).

22. Baker v. Carr, 369 U.S. 186, 82 S.Ct. 691 (1962); Gray v. Sanders, 372 U.S. 368, 83 S.Ct. 801 (1963).

cation of this logic. A three-judge federal district court in Florida [23] was apparently the first court to hold that a state school finance mechanism was unconstitutional as violative of the equal protection rights of a child. This court, relying largely on precedent by the United States Supreme Court in Reynolds v. Sims,[24] reasoned that the Equal Protection Clause requires "the uniform treatment of persons standing in the same relation to the governmental action." The court then departed from the traditional line of thought of the courts which had held that so long as the act in question applies uniformly there is no violation of equal protection, reasoning to the contrary that a uniform act of the legislature may indeed violate the equal protection clause if its effect is discriminatory. The court adopted the "rational basis" standard and concluded that a state must show a rational basis for its act or the act will be held unconstitutional. This decision was later vacated and remanded on other grounds by the U.S. Supreme Court.

Educators for some time have recognized that all children cannot be educated equally with equal resources. Some children with special learning deficiencies caused by cultural deprivation or mental or physical incapacities must be given special educational services. Today, some state aid programs partially take into account the differences in educational needs of children but most state finance programs do not adequately measure or compensate such educational needs by providing proportionately greater funds to school districts with high incidences of high cost children. Is a child denied a constitutional right of an equal education if he cannot hear the teacher, cannot enunciate clearly enough to progress normally in school, or has a cultural background placing him at such a learning deficit that he will be unable to ever catch up or compete? In such cases, equal expenditures or regular programs for all children may provide equal learning opportunity for normal, middle class children, but attendance in such regular middle class educational programs by the physically, mentally or culturally deprived provides for less than equal educational opportunity.

A fundamental legal question is whether a state's responsibility to provide a child with an opportunity for equal education is successfully discharged where no recognition was given to individual needs and deficiencies. It was this issue which was addressed in two 1968 cases which ultimately reached the Supreme Court.

In McInnis v. Shapiro,[25] the plaintiffs claimed that the Illinois finance system created large variations in expenditures per student from district to district, thereby providing some students with a good

23. Hargrave v. Kirk, 313 F.Supp. 944 (D.C.Fla.1970); vac'd and rem'd on other grounds sub. nom., Askew v. Hargrave, 401 U.S. 476, 91 S.Ct. 856 (1971).

24. 377 U.S. 533, 84 S.Ct. 1362 (1964).

25. 293 F.Supp. 327, aff'd 394 U.S. 322, 89 S.Ct. 1197 (1969).

education and depriving others who have equal or greater educational need. The court concluded that equal educational expenditures are not required by the Fourteenth Amendment and that variations created by taxation of property in the school districts do not discriminate. The court said:

> Unequal educational expenditures per student, based upon the variable property values and tax rates of local school districts, do not amount to an invidious discrimination. Moreover, the statutes which permit these unequal expenditures on a district to district basis are neither arbitrary nor unreasonable.[26]

The *McInnis* court declined to establish judicial standards for determining legislative allocations based on educational needs. Since *McInnis* was summarily affirmed by the Supreme Court of the United States [27], this statement represented precedent and had substantial impact on legal thought at that time.

The position in *McInnis* was summed by saying that there were no "discoverable and manageable standards by which a court can determine when the Constitution is satisfied and when it is violated." [28]

McInnis was closely followed by a second "educational need" case in Virginia.[29] In *Burruss*, plaintiffs relied more directly on the educational need argument than did the plaintiffs in *McInnis*. Specifically, plaintiffs claimed the state formula created and perpetuated substantial disparities in educational opportunities throughout the state of Virginia and failed to relate to any of the variety of educational needs present in the several counties and cities of Virginia.

To the former allegation, the court found that the system of finance was not discriminatory as it operated under a uniform and consistent state plan. With regard to educational needs, the court praised the equalization of educational opportunity as a worthy and commendable goal, but refused to interject the wisdom of the court in ascertaining what constituted educational need disparities. In following the hands-off course of *McInnis*, the court said:

> * * * the courts have neither the knowledge, nor the means, nor the power to tailor the public moneys to fit the varying needs of these students throughout the state. We can only see to it that the outlays on one group are not invidiously greater or less than that of another. No such arbitrariness is manifest here.[30]

Accordingly, *Burruss* denied relief to plaintiffs under either the "efficiency" provision of the Virginia Constitution or the equal protection

26. McInnis v. Shapiro, supra.

27. 394 U.S. 322, 89 S.Ct. 1197 (1969).

28. McInnis v. Shapiro, supra.

29. Burruss v. Wilkerson, 310 F.Supp. 572 (D.C.Va.1969) aff'd mem. 397 U.S. 44, 90 S.Ct. 812 (1970).

30. Burruss v. Wilkerson, supra.

clause of the Fourteenth Amendment. The United States Supreme Court summarily affirmed this decision.

Only a short time elapsed between *McInnis* and the now famous decision by the California Supreme Court in Serrano v. Priest.[31] In *Serrano*, the court handed down a well reasoned decision which strongly documents the establishment of a new equal protection application to school finance. The court here spoke of equalization only in terms of the relative wealth of the local school districts as measured in terms of property valuation. It did not attempt to define the equal protection argument in terms of educational needs of children or educational programs.

According to this court, in order to answer the primary constitutional question, does the California public school financing scheme violate the Equal Protection Clause, it was first necessary to determine whether (1) education is a fundamental interest protected by the constitution, (2) wealth is a "suspect classification," and (3) the state has a "compelling interest" in creating a system of school finance which makes a child's education dependent on the wealth of his local school district. In a short treatise on constitutional law, the court pointed out that the United States Supreme Court had employed two tests for determining the constitutionality of state legislation under the equal protection clause. In the first and more lenient test, the Supreme Court presumed that state legislation is constitutional and merely required the state to show that the distinctions drawn or classifications created by the challenged statute had some "rational relationship to a conceivable legitimate state purpose." On the other hand, if the state legislation touched on a "fundamental interest" of the individual or involved a "suspect classification," then the court would subject the challenged statute to "strict scrutiny" or active and critical analysis. If a fundamental interest or suspect classification is involved, the presumption of constitutionality is not with the state; on the contrary, the burden of establishing the necessity of the classification is with the state.

In critically analyzing the present California finance system the court pointed out that although the basic state aid program in California tends to equalize among school districts, the total system, including state and local funds combined, created great disparities in school revenues and the system as a whole generated school revenue proportional to the wealth of the individual school. After concluding that education was a "fundamental interest" and property wealth was a "suspect classification," the court then applied the "strict scrutiny" standard and found the system of finance unconstitutional.

Closely following *Serrano*, a United States District Court in Minnesota entertained a class action suit [32] wherein plaintiffs alleged de-

31. 96 Cal.Rptr. 601, 487 P.2d 1241 (1971).

32. Van Dusartz v. Hatfield, 334 F. Supp. 870 (D.C.Minn.1971).

nial of equal protection and violation of the Civil Rights Act.[33] Plaintiffs showed that rich districts in Minnesota enjoy both lower tax rates and higher spending. The court, in viewing the facts, arrived at the inescapable conclusion that, "the level of spending for publicly financed education in Minnesota is profoundly affected by the wealth of each school district." Education was considered to be a "fundamental interest" and wealth to be a "suspect classification" as held in *Serrano*. *Van Dusartz* though had limited utility as precedent because the court's comments were made merely in support of an order denying the defendant's motion to dismiss the action and the court deferred further action until after the 1972 Minnesota legislative session.

A significant decision by a federal three-judge court in Texas[34] followed both the California and Minnesota cases and reached the same conclusion. Here it was held that plaintiffs had been denied equal protection of the law by the Texas system of financing its public schools. Plaintiffs contended that the educational finance system of the state makes education a function of the local property tax base. The court observed that the school finance system of Texas erroneously assumes that the value of property in the various districts will be sufficiently equal to maintain comparable expenditures among districts. This inequality is not corrected to any substantial degree by state funds because when all state and local funds were combined to correct this unconstitutional inequality, *Rodriguez* established a standard of "fiscal neutrality." As was the case in both *Serrano* and *Van Dusartz*, the court maintained that fiscal neutrality did not require that all educational expenditures be equal for each child. The standard simply required that "the quality of public education may not be a function of wealth, other than the wealth of the state as a whole."

The rationale and precedents of the lower courts in *Serrano* and *Rodriguez*, that a child's education could not be contingent on the wealth of the local school district, were to come of no avail, however, for in 1973 the Supreme Court of the United States handed down a reversal of *Rodriguez*[35] effectively terminating such state school finance litigation under the Equal Protection Clause. On rehearing *Serrano* the California Supreme Court was forced to abandon the Fourteenth Amendment as the constitutional basis for overturning the state school aid formula and thereafter relied solely on an equal protection provision in the California constitution.

33. Also raised issue of discrimination under Civil Rights Act, 42 U.S.C.A. § 1983.

34. Rodriguez v. San Antonio Independent School Dist., 337 F.Supp. 280 (W.D.Texas 1971).

35. San Antonio Independent School Dist. v. Rodriguez, 411 U.S. 1, 93 S.Ct. 1278, reh. denied 411 U.S. 959, 93 S.Ct. 1919 (1973).

Justice Powell in upholding the constitutionality of the Texas method of financing its schools maintained that education was not a "fundamental" constitutional right under the Equal Protection Clause, as had been presumed from reading *Brown,* and as such education could not be viewed in special favor by the court so as to justify strict judicial scrutiny. In so holding the Court reverted to the traditional judicial position of leaving such matters to the wisdom of the legislature. In this regard Justice Powell concluded:

> Education, perhaps even more than welfare assistance, presents a myriad of "intractable economic, social, and even philosophical problems". The very complexity of the problems of financing and managing a statewide public school system suggests that "there will be more than one constitutionally permissible method of solving them," and that, within the limits of rationality, "the legislature's efforts to tackle the problems" should be entitled to respect.[36]

Immediately after this decision most if not all such litigation in the federal courts was abandoned. From the Supreme Court's position it was quite clear that any future actions, if they were to be successful in attacking methods of state school financing, would have to be pursued in reliance on state constitutional grounds rather than on the Fourteenth Amendment. Subsequent to and in accordance with the Supreme Court's decision in *Rodriguez* the Supreme Courts of Michigan[37] and Arizona[38] reversed previous precedent and upheld the constitutionality of their own state school finance programs. The Michigan Supreme Court had previously held that the Michigan school finance system violated the equal protection provision of the state constitution[39] but on rehearing found no violation of either the state or federal equal protection clauses. Similarly, the Supreme Court of Arizona in upholding that state's method of financing schools followed *Rodriguez* in finding that education was not a fundamental right deserving of strict judicial scrutiny.

Litigation in the realm of state school aid distribution has returned to state courts, and since *Rodriguez* the actions now test state formulas in light of only constitutional provisions. Bases for such litigation may be found in equal protection, uniformity, equality, thorough and efficient or other provisions of state constitutions. State equal protection was, as mentioned previously, the ultimate basis on which the California Supreme Court relied to hold the method of financing in that state unconstitutional after the U.S. Supreme Court

36. Ibid.

37. Milliken v. Green, 390 Mich. 389, 212 N.W.2d 711 (1973).

38. Shofstall v. Hollins, 110 Ariz. 88, 515 P.2d 590 (1973).

39. Governor v. State Treasurer, 389 Mich. 1, 203 N.W.2d 457 (1972).

in *Rodriguez* removed equal protection of the Fourteenth Amendment from contention.[40]

Rodriguez continues, though, to have substantial influence in shaping state courts view of their own constitutions. In a recent Louisiana case the court held that the method of school financing in that state did not differ significantly from that of Texas litigated in *Rodriguez* and that, as such, it was not unconstitutionally discriminatory against the poor people in poor school districts. The Supreme Court of Idaho held in a 3–2 decision that the education finance law of that state did not violate the "uniform system" requirement of that state's constitution.[41] In so doing, the court refused to recognize education as a "fundamental interest" under the Idaho Constitution and in the same vein turned back the plaintiffs equal protection claim. Decisions in Illinois,[42] Kansas,[43] Montana,[44] and Oregon [45] have likewise denied relief to plaintiffs where challenges to the school finance law were predicated on state constitutional provisions. In the Oregon case, the Oregon Supreme Court observed that it could interpret the equal protection clause of the Oregon Constitution more broadly than that placed on the federal constitution in *Rodriguez,* but it declined to do so. The Court refused to acknowledge that education was a fundamental right and the fact that education was mentioned in the Oregon Constitution was not sufficient to establish its fundamentality. Further, the Court found that the word "uniform" in constitution merely required that the legislature provide a minimum program of educational opportunity throughout the state. Complete uniformity, the court decided, would infringe on the state's reasonable objective to maintain local control of education.[46]

In an important case which departed from the influence of *Rodriguez,* the New Jersey Supreme Court relied on that state's "thorough and efficient" clause to invalidate the state school aid formula.[47] This court made it quite clear that the state had an obligation to correct the fiscal imbalances created by local school district organization and fiscal ability variations. It further found that the "thorough and efficient" requirement required equal educational opportunity and that if local government fails to so provide then the state must act to either compel local school districts to meet the constitutional man-

40. Serrano v. Priest, supra.

41. Thompson v. Engelring, 96 Idaho 793, 537 P. 2d 635 (1975).

42. Blase v. State of Illinois, 55 Ill.2d 94, 302 N.E.2d 46 (1973); People ex rel. Jones v. Adams, 40 Ill.App.3d 189, 350 N.E.2d 767 (1976).

43. Knowles v. State Board of Educ., 219 Kan. 271, 547 P.2d 699 (1976).

44. State ex rel. Woodahh v. Straub, 164 Mont. 141, 520 P.2d 776 (1974).

45. Olsen v. State ex rel. Johnson, 276 Or. 9, 554 P.2d 139 (1976).

46. Ibid.

47. Robinson v. Cahill, 62 N.J. 473, 303 A.2d 273 (1973).

date or the state must meet the obligation itself. In broadly defining the "thorough and efficient" standard, the court said:

> The Constitution's guarantee must be understood to embrace that educational opportunity which is needed in the contemporary setting to equip a child for his role as a citizen and as a competitor in the labor market.[48]

Unrestrained legislative authority in the allocation of state school funds was also brought into check in Connecticut where the court held that the state constitutional equal protection provision was violated by a state method school fund distribution which allocated money to local school districts on a flat grant basis ignoring the fiscal ability of local school districts.[49] The court reasoned that under the Connecticut Constitution education was a fundamental right because it was explicitly recognized in Article VIII, Section I, and the history and tradition of the state demonstrated a commitment to education of children. In holding the system unconstitutional and mandating that the legislative redress the faults, the court observed that absolute equality of resources was not required, and that cost differences due to variations in educational needs and economic conditions could be taken into account.

Positive lower court response to challenges to state school finance programs in New York,[50] and Ohio [51] portend a future of continuing litigation in this field. Although *Rodriguez* closed the door, successful federal equal protection challenges the entire controversy and has generated substantial legal momentum which will not quickly subside. The question of the fundamentality of education will continue to be a basic issue in these cases and state courts can be expected to disagree as to its relevance depending on the precise wording of each state's constitution.

48. Robinson v. Cahill, supra.

49. Horton v. Meskill, 172 Conn. 615, 376 A.2d 359 (1977), affirming 31 Conn.Sup. 377, 332 A.2d 113 (Hartford County Superior Court 1974).

50. Board of Educ., Levittown v. Hyquist No. 8208/74 (Nassau County Supreme Court).

51. Board of Educ. of the City School District of the City of Cincinnati v. Walter, No. A-7602725 (Hamilton County Court of Common Pleas 1978).

*Constitutional Provision Requiring That Taxes be Equal and
Uniform Is Not a Restraint on Legislative Authority
in Distribution of School Funds*

DEAN v. CODDINGTON

Supreme Court of South Dakota, 1964.
81 S.D. 140, 131 N.W.2d 700.

RENTTO, Judge. By the enactment of Ch. 67, Laws of 1959,
now SDC 1960 Supp. 15.2246, this state initiated a foundation program of state support to school districts. This act was in effect re-
enacted with amendments and additional provisions by Ch. 76, Laws
of 1961 and Ch. 77, Laws of 1963. * * *

In this proceeding plaintiff is asking that Ch. 77, Laws of 1963,
be declared invalid and that the defendants be enjoined from making
distribution of the 1963 appropriation. He asserts that said Ch. 77
violates that part of Sec. 17, Art. VI of our Constitution which provides that all taxation shall be equal and uniform. He makes the further claim that it denies him equal protection of the law in violation
of the 14th Article of Amendment to the Constitution of the United
States. The defendants' motion to dismiss the complaint for failure
to state a claim upon which relief could be granted was sustained.
This appeal is from the order of dismissal.

* * *

The act establishes a foundation program fund to include all funds
appropriated to, or designated to it by law, gift or grant including
any money appropriated by the Federal Congress for purposes of
equalizing school opportunity. It prescribes rules for determining the
eligibility of school districts to receive funds and sophisticated formulas concerning the amount thereof. The eligibility requirements and
payment formulas are designed to encourage improvement of education at the local level.

The stipulation by which the pertinent facts involved were
presented to the court reveals that plaintiff is a resident and taxpayer
of Lakeview Common School District No. 3 in Hutchinson County,
South Dakota. Such district did not maintain a secondary or an elementary school during the school year 1962–63, and did not plan to
maintain any during the 1963–64 school year. The students living in
the district attended school in the Independent School District of
Scotland Bon Homme County, South Dakota. * * *

The Lakeview district, under the Foundation Program, was not
eligible to receive any of the funds appropriated to the foundation by
Ch. 365, Laws of 1963 for the fiscal year ending June 30, 1964 because it had not operated a school during the previous school fiscal
year. Further, the Lakeview children attending the Scotland school
were by the formula counted in its enrollment thus enhancing the

payment from the foundation to the Scotland district. These results are complained of by the plaintiff and made the basis of his claim of unconstitutionality. He asserts that the effect of the law is to lower taxes in the Scotland district while leaving them constant in the Lakeview district.

Art. VI, § 17 of our Constitution, so far as here material provides: "all taxation shall be equal and uniform". The test of uniformity under this section is substantially the same as under the 14th Amendment to the United States Constitution. State ex rel. Botkin v. Welsh, 61 S.D. 593, 251 N.W. 189. * * *

The general rule applicable in this situation is stated in C.J.S. Taxation § 34 to be:

> "It is generally held that the constitutional provisions requiring equality and uniformity relate to the levy of taxes, and not to the distribution or application of the revenue derived therefrom; and hence statutes relative to the distribution or application of such money cannot be held invalid on this ground."

After observing that it was not unusual for states after collecting taxes on a statewide basis to make distribution of revenues to municipal corporations, particularly school districts, the court in Hess v. Mullancy, 213 F.2d 635, 15 Alaska 40, cert. denied Hess v. Dewey, 348 U.S. 836, 75 S.Ct. 50, 99 L.Ed. 659, goes on to say: "No requirements of uniformity or of equal protection of the law limit the power of a legislature in respect to allocation and distribution of public funds. Gen. American Tank Car Corp. v. Day, * * *

       *   *   *

In Acker v. Adamson, 67 S.D. 341, 293 N.W. 83, this court said "the legislative power of state legislatures is unlimited except as limited by the State or Federal Constitutions." In our view the money, the apportionment of which is here in question, is the property of the state and may be used for any public purpose the legislature deems wise.

We have consistently recognized that in determining what is a public purpose the legislature is vested with a large discretion which cannot be controlled by the courts unless its action is clearly evasive. Torigian v. Saunders, 77 S.D. 610, 97 N.W.2d 586. Expending state funds for the purpose of improving the educational opportunities afforded within the state has long been recognized as a public purpose. State ex rel. Clark v. Gordon, 261 Mo. 631, 170 S.W. 892. In Section 4 of the enabling act under which our state was admitted to the Union we assumed the responsibility for the establishment and maintenance of systems of public schools open to all the children of the state. This was declared our duty in Section 18 of Art. XXVI of our Constitution. We are satisfied that funds of the state expended to provide reasonable equality of education for all children in the state are spent for a public purpose. See 47 Am.Jur., Schools, § 89 and § 90. The distribution of funds as directed in Ch. 77, Laws of 1963, is upon a reasonable basis of classification within the taxing district involved.

The guiding principles which we think govern in this field are well stated in C.J.S. Schools and School Districts § 411, wherein it is written:

"In the absence of constitutional regulation the method of apportioning and distributing a school fund, accruing from taxes or other revenue, rests in the wise discretion of the state legislature, which method, in the absence of abuse of discretion or violation of some constitutional provision, cannot be interfered with by the courts. Apportionment statutes are designed to promote equality of facilities, and if the purpose of public welfare is kept in view in making the distribution, the fact that the fund is distributed unequally among the different districts or political subdivisions does not render it invalid."

Accordingly the trial court did not err in dismissing plaintiff's complaint.

* * *

Affirmed.

All the Judges concur.

NOTES

1. In a case questioning the authority of the legislature to establish a tax equalization board which would determine the market value of property and substitute such value for state school aid purposes, a Pennsylvania court held that the legislative prerogative to control the state's finances is subject only to constitutional limitations and that the appropriation and distribution of school subsidies is a peculiar prerogative of the legislature. School Dist. of Newport Tp. in Luzerne County v. State Tax Equalization Bd., 366 Pa. 603, 79 A.3d 641 (1951).

2. The legislative appropriation and distribution of school subsidies must be in accordance with terms of state constitutional requirements. Constitutional provisions mandating that the general assembly encourage, by all suitable means, the promotion of intellectual improvement infer that the legislature may provide support for the common schools. Kleen v. Porter, 237 Iowa 1160, 23 N.W.2d 904 (1946).

3. Most foundation aid programs have provisions requiring a specified local school district effort for participation. The courts have held that such a required local effort does not violate constitutional equality requirements, even when the power to raise money for school purposes is delegated to selectmen and not to a vote by the populace and the distribution formula results in some districts raising more money per pupil than others.

In a New Hampshire case, the court said:

> The fact that the receipt of this aid together with the computation
> of the operating costs of the district school according to a formula
> contained in the act authorizing the creation of such a district re-
> sults in one town in the district having to raise more dollars per
> pupil attending the cooperative school than another town in the
> same district does not place an unequal tax burden on any inhabi-
> tant of a particular taxing district which is the constitutional
> equality required * * *. The constitution does not guarantee
> that all taxing districts shall have an equal number of pupils to
> educate, or that the aggregate costs of education shall be identical.
> Town of Gilsum v. Monadnock Regional School Dist., 105 N.H. 361,
> 202 A.2d 790.

4. Constitutional requirements that taxes be uniform, apply to the levying and payment of taxes, and not to the distribution of the revenue arising therefrom. Mitchell v. Lowden, 288 Ill. 327, 123 N.E. 566. This position is substantiated by an Ohio case which held that so long as a tax is uniformly laid the legislature may appropriate the proceeds of that tax by a rule that is not uniform, so long as the appropriation of funds is reasonable and made in pursuance of a valid and legitimate state purpose.

In relating state financing of schools to a constitutional requirement to establish thorough and efficient system of schools throughout the state, the court had this to say:

> A thorough system could not mean one in which part or any num-
> ber of the school districts of the state were starved for funds. An
> efficient system could not mean one in which part or any number
> of the school districts of the state lacked teachers, buildings, or
> equipment. In the attainment of the purpose of establishing an
> efficient and thorough system of schools throughout the state it
> was easily conceivable that the greatest expense might arise in the
> poorest districts; that portions of great cities, teeming with life,
> would be able to contribute relatively little in taxes for the support
> of schools, which are the main hope for enlightening these dis-
> tricts, while districts underpopulated with children might repre-
> sent such taxation value that their school needs would be relatively
> over supplied.

Miller v. Korns, 107 Ohio St. 287, 140 N.E. 773 (1923).

5. In several states, constitutional provisions require the apportionment of school funds based on the average daily attendance or school populations. Such provisions are mandatory; and other measures which might cause allocation variations, such as equalization or effort calculations, cannot be used. State Board of Education v. Board of Education of Savannah and Chatham County, 186 Ga. 783, 199 S.E. 641.

6. A state constitutional provision requiring "equitable distribution" has been interpreted to mean that the state school funds should be distributed to school districts in proportion to the school children enumerated and living in the school district. The payment out of the school fund to any district for the tuition of children who do not belong in the district is not an

equitable distribution within the meaning of the Constitution. Taylor v. School Dist. of City of Lincoln, 128 Neb. 437, 259 N.W. 168 (1935).

7. Courts have attempted to set forth certain guides governing the assessment and equalization of property values within and among school districts. A Texas court set out the following guidelines:

It is now well settled that the assessment of property for tax purposes is a quasi-judicial function of boards of equalization and that no attack on valuations fixed by such boards can or will be sustained in the absence of proof of fraud, want of jurisdiction, illegality, or the adoption of an arbitrary and fundamentally erroneous plan or scheme of valuation. * * * Moreover, when their official action is attacked it will be presumed that such boards discharged their duties as public agencies according to law and acted in good faith. * * *

While it has been held that a grossly excessive valuation may, in law, be sufficient to establish such fraud or illegality as to render a valuation void, * * * it is held with equal emphasis that mere errors in judgment or the fact that a trial judge or jury differs with the valuation fixed will not suffice as a basis for avoiding the board's action. * * *

If a valuation fixed by a board of equalization is attacked on the ground of unlawful or arbitrary discrimination it is not sufficient to show, comparatively, that in other isolated instances, property of equal or greater value than that in suit, was valued at less. * * *

The Supreme Court, in State v. Houser, 138 Tex. 28, 156 S.W.2d 968, held that such valuations will not be set aside merely upon a showing that the same are in fact excessive. As we held in Hutchinson v. City of Dallas, Tex.Civ.App., 290 S.W.2d 253, the showing of mere excessiveness of value is not sufficient as a matter of law to raise a fact issue in a suit attacking the validity of an assessment on the ground of unlawful or arbitrary discrimination. It is necessary to go further and show that the valuation given the property was so grossly excessive as to constitute in law evidence of fraud, bad faith, or illegality on the part of the equalization board. * * * State v. Whittenburg, 153 Tex. 205, 265 S.W.2d 569.

Discrepancies in valuations are discussed further by another court:

A reasonable discrepancy between the true value of the property and the value at which it is assessed for taxes will be permitted to cover the difference in judgment as to the value of the property; but where the property is assessed at a value seven times as high as its true value, the discrepancy is too great. It does not evidence a mere difference in judgment as to the value of the property. (Citing authorities.)

On the other hand, one whose property has been assessed on substantially the same basis as the great bulk of the property on the same tax roll may not have his assessment cancelled merely because in isolated instances some of the other property on the tax roll has been assessed at less than its proportionate value. Mayne v. Duncanville Independent School Dist., Tex.Civ.App., 380 S.W.2d 682.

8. In a case where a taxpayer resisted the collection of school taxes assessed against his property, claiming the property valuations were not equal and uniform as compared to valuations placed upon other taxable property within the districts. The court pointed out that exact uniformity and equality of taxation is unattainable. A reasonable discrepancy between the true value of the property and the value at which it is assessed for taxes is permissible to cover the difference in judgment as to the value of the property. The court found that the valuations placed on this taxpayer's property did not exceed the reasonable discrepancy rule. Darby v. Borger Ind. School Dist., 386 S.W.2d 572 (Tex.Civ.App.1965).

State School Finance System which Results in Revenue Disparities Based on Fiscal Ability of School Districts Does Not Violate the Equal Protection Clause of the Fourteenth Amendment

SAN ANTONIO INDEPENDENT SCHOOL DIST. v. RODRIGUEZ

Supreme Court of the United States, 1973.
411 U.S. 1, 93 S.Ct. 1278, reh. denied 411 U.S. 959, 93 S.Ct. 1919.

Mr. Justice POWELL delivered the opinion of the Court.

This suit attacking the Texas system of financing public education was initiated by Mexican-American parents whose children attend the elementary and secondary schools in the Edgewood Independent School District, an urban school district in San Antonio, Texas. They brought a class action on behalf of schoolchildren throughout the State who are members of minority groups or who are poor and reside in school districts having a low property tax base. Named as defendants were the State Board of Education, the Commissioner of Education, the State Attorney General, and the Bexar County (San Antonio) Board of Trustees. The complaint was filed in the summer of 1968 and a three-judge court was impaneled in January 1969. In December 1971 the panel rendered its judgment in a *per curiam* opinion holding the Texas school finance system unconstitutional under the Equal Protection Clause of the Fourteenth Amendment. The State appealed, and we noted probable jurisdiction to consider the far-reaching constitutional questions presented. * * * For the reasons stated in this opinion, we reverse the decision of the District Court.

I

* * *

The school district in which appellees reside, the Edgewood Independent School District, has been compared throughout this litigation with the Alamo Heights Independent School District. This comparison between the least and most affluent districts in the San Antonio area serves to illustrate the manner in which the dual system of finance operates and to indicate the extent to which substantial disparities exist despite the State's impressive progress in recent years. Edgewood is one of seven public school districts in the metropolitan area. Approximately 22,000 students are enrolled in its 25 elementary and secondary schools. The district is situated in the core-city sector of San Antonio in a residential neighborhood that has little commercial or industrial property. The residents are predominantly of Mexican-American descent: approximately 90% of the student population is Mexican-American and over 6% is Negro. The average assessed property value per pupil is $5,960—the lowest in the metropolitan area—and the median family income ($4,686) is also the lowest. At an equalized tax rate of $1.05 per $100 of assessed property —the highest in the metropolitan area—the district contributed $26 to the education of each child for the 1967–1968 school year above its Local Fund Assignment for the Minimum Foundation Program. The Foundation Program contributed $222 per pupil for a state-local total of $248. Federal funds added another $108 for a total of $356 per pupil.

Alamo Heights is the most affluent school district in San Antonio. Its six schools, housing approximately 5,000 students, are situated in a residential community quite unlike the Edgewood District. The school population is predominantly "Anglo," having only 18% Mexican-Americans and less than 1% Negroes. The assessed property value per pupil exceeds $49,000, and the median family income is $8,001. In 1967–1968 the local tax rate of $.85 per $100 of valuation yielded $333 per pupil over and above its contribution to the Foundation Program. Coupled with the $225 provided from that Program, the district was able to supply $558 per student. Supplemented by a $36 per-pupil grant from federal sources, Alamo Heights spent $594 per pupil.

       *   *   *

Despite recent increases, substantial interdistrict disparities in school expenditures found by the District Court to prevail in San Antonio and in varying degrees throughout the State still exist. And it was these disparities, largely attributable to differences in the amounts of money collected through local property taxation, that led the District Court to conclude that Texas' dual system of public school financing violated the Equal Protection Clause. The District Court held that the Texas system discriminates on the basis of wealth in the manner in which education is provided for its people. 337 F. Supp., at 282. Finding that wealth is a "suspect" classification and that education is a "fundamental" interest, the District Court held that the Texas system could be sustained only if the State could show that it was premised upon some compelling state interest. Id., at 282–284. On this issue the court concluded that "[n]ot only are defendants unable to demonstrate compelling state interests *   *   *

they fail even to establish a reasonable basis for these classifications." Id., at 284.

Texas virtually concedes that its historically rooted dual system of financing education could not withstand the strict judicial scrutiny that this Court has found appropriate in reviewing legislative judgments that interfere with fundamental constitutional rights or that involve suspect classifications. If, as previous decisions have indicated, strict scrutiny means that the State's system is not entitled to the usual presumption of validity, that the State rather than the complainants must carry a "heavy burden of justification," that the State must demonstrate that its educational system has been structured with "precision," and is "tailored" narrowly to serve legitimate objectives and that it has selected the "less drastic means" for effectuating its objectives, the Texas financing system and its counterpart in virtually every other State will not pass muster. The State candidly admits that "[n]o one familiar with the Texas system would contend that it has yet achieved perfection." Apart from its concession that educational financing in Texas has "defects" and "imperfections," the State defends the system's rationality with vigor and disputes the District Court's finding that it lacks a "reasonable basis."

This, then, establishes the framework for our analysis. We must decide, first, whether the Texas system of financing public education operates to the disadvantage of some suspect class or impinges upon a fundamental right explicitly or implicitly protected by the Constitution, thereby requiring strict judicial scrutiny. If so, the judgment of the District Court should be affirmed. If not, the Texas scheme must still be examined to determine whether it rationally furthers some legitimate, articulated state purpose and therefore does not constitute an invidious discrimination in violation of the Equal Protection Clause of the Fourteenth Amendment.

II

The District Court's opinion does not reflect the novelty and complexity of the constitutional questions posed by appellees' challenge to Texas' system of school financing. In concluding that strict judicial scrutiny was required, that court relied on decisions dealing with the rights of indigents to equal treatment in the criminal trial and appellate processes, and on cases disapproving wealth restrictions on the right to vote. Those cases, the District Court concluded, established wealth as a suspect classification. Finding that the local property tax system discriminated on the basis of wealth, it regarded those precedents as controlling. It then reasoned, based on decisions of this Court affirming the undeniable importance of education, that there is a fundamental right to education and that, absent some compelling state justification, the Texas system could not stand.

We are unable to agree that this case, which in significant aspects is *sui generis*, may be so neatly fitted into the conventional mosaic of constitutional analysis under the Equal Protection Clause. Indeed, for the several reasons that follow, we find neither the suspect-classification nor the fundamental-interest analysis persuasive.

The wealth discrimination discovered by the District Court in this case, and by several other courts that have recently struck down school-financing laws in other States, is quite unlike any of the forms of wealth discrimination heretofore reviewed by this Court. * * *

The case comes to us with no definitive description of the classifying facts or delineation of the disfavored class. Examination of the District Court's opinion and of appellees' complaint, briefs, and contentions at oral argument suggests, however, at least three ways in which the discrimination claimed here might be described. The Texas system of school financing might be regarded as discriminating (1) against "poor" persons whose incomes fall below some identifiable level of poverty or who might be characterized as functionally "indigent," or (2) against those who are relatively poorer than others, or (3) against all those who, irrespective of their personal incomes, happen to reside in relatively poorer school districts. Our task must be to ascertain whether, in fact, the Texas system has been shown to discriminate on any of these possible bases and, if so, whether the resulting classification may be regarded as suspect.

The precedents of this Court provide the proper starting point. The individuals, or groups of individuals, who constituted the class discriminated against in our prior cases shared two distinguishing characteristics: because of their impecunity they were completely unable to pay for some desired benefit, and as a consequence, they sustained an absolute deprivation of a meaningful opportunity to enjoy that benefit. * * *

                            * * *

Only appellees' first possible basis for describing the class disadvantaged by the Texas school-financing system—discrimination against a class of definably "poor" persons—might arguably meet the criteria established in * * * prior cases. Even a cursory examination, however, demonstrates that neither of the two distinguishing characteristics of wealth classifications can be found here. First, in support of their charge that the system discriminates against the "poor," appellees have made no effort to demonstrate that it operates to the peculiar disadvantage of any class fairly definable as indigent, or as composed of persons whose incomes are beneath any designated poverty level. Indeed, there is reason to believe that the poorest families are not necessarily clustered in the poorest property districts. A recent and exhaustive study of school districts in Connecticut concluded that "[i]t is clearly incorrect * * * to contend that the 'poor' live in 'poor' districts * * *. Thus, the major factual assumption of *Serrano*—that the educational financing system discriminates against the 'poor'—is simply false in Connecticut." [53] Defining "poor" families as those below the Bureau of the Census "poverty level," the Connecticut study found, not surprisingly, that the poor were clustered around commercial and industrial areas— those same areas that provide the most attractive sources of property tax income for school districts. Whether a similar pattern would be discovered in Texas is not known, but there is no basis on the record in this case for assuming that the poorest people—defined by reference to any level of absolute impecunity—are concentrated in the poorest districts.

Second, neither appellees nor the District Court addressed the fact that, unlike each of the foregoing cases, lack of personal resources has not occasioned an absolute deprivation of the desired benefit. The argument here is not that the children in districts having relatively low assessable property values are receiving no public education; rather, it is that they are receiving a poorer quality education than that available to children in districts having more assessable wealth. Apart from the unsettled and disputed question whether the quality of education may be determined by the amount of money expended for it, a sufficient answer to appellees' argument is that, at least where wealth is involved, the Equal Protection Clause does not require absolute equality or precisely equal advantages. Nor indeed, in view of the infinite variables affecting the educational process, can any system assure equal quality of education except in the most relative sense. * * *

For these two reasons—the absence of any evidence that the financing system discriminates against any definable category of "poor" people or that it results in the absolute deprivation of education—the disadvantaged class is not susceptible of identification in traditional terms.

As suggested above, appellees and the District Court may have embraced a second or third approach, the second of which might be characterized as a theory of relative or comparative discrimination based on family income. Appellees sought to prove that a direct correlation exists between the wealth of families within each district and the expenditures therein for education. That is, along a continuum, the poorer the family the lower the dollar amount of education received by the family's children.

* * *

* * * These questions need not be addressed in this case, however, since appellees' proof fails to support their allegations or the District Court's conclusions.

* * *

53. Note, A Statistical Analysis of the School Finance Decisions: On Win- ning Battles and Losing Wars, 81 Yale L.J. 1303, 1328–1329 (1972).

This brings us, then, to the third way in which the classification scheme might be defined—*district* wealth discrimination. Since the only correlation indicated by the evidence is between district property wealth and expenditures, it may be argued that discrimination might be found without regard to the individual income characteristics of district residents. * * * Alternatively, as suggested in Mr. Justice MARSHALL's dissenting opinion, the class might be defined more restrictively to include children in districts with assessable property which falls below the statewide average, or median, or below some other artifically defined level.

However described, it is clear that appellees' suit asks this Court to extend its most exacting scrutiny to review a system that allegedly discriminates against a large, diverse, and amorphous class, unified only by the common factor of residence in districts that happen to have less taxable wealth than other districts. The system of alleged discrimination and the class it defines have none of the traditional indicia of suspectness: the class is not saddled with such disabilities, or subjected to such a history of purposeful unequal treatment, or relegated to such a position of political powerlessness as to command extraordinary protection from the majoritarian political process.

We thus conclude that the Texas system does not operate to the peculiar disadvantage of any suspect class. But in recognition of the fact that this Court has never heretofore held that wealth discrimination alone provides an adequate basis for invoking strict scrutiny, appellees have not relied solely on this contention. They also assert that the State's system impermissibly interferes with the exercise of a "fundamental" right and that accordingly the prior decisions of this Court require the application of the strict standard of judicial review. * * * It is this question—whether education is a fundamental right, in the sense that it is among the rights and liberties protected by the Constitution—which has so consumed the attention of courts and commentators in recent years.

       * * *

Nothing this Court holds today in any way detracts from our historic dedication to public education. We are in complete agreement with the conclusion of the three-judge panel below that "the grave significance of education both to the individual and to our society" cannot be doubted. But the importance of a service performed by the State does not determine whether it must be regarded as fundamental for purposes of examination under the Equal Protection Clause. * * *

* * * It is not the province of this Court to create substantive constitutional rights in the name of guaranteeing equal protection of the laws. Thus, the key to discovering whether education is "fundamental" is not to be found in comparisons of the relative societal significance of education as opposed to subsistence or housing.

Nor is it to be found by weighing whether education is as important as the right to travel. Rather, the answer lies in assessing whether there is a right to education explicitly or implicitly guaranteed by the Constitution. * * *

Education, of course, is not among the rights afforded explicit protection under our Federal Constitution. Nor do we find any basis for saying it is implicitly so protected. As we have said, the undisputed importance of education will not alone cause this Court to depart from the usual standard for reviewing a State's social and economic legislation. It is appellees' contention, however, that education is distinguishable from other services and benefits provided by the State because it bears a peculiarly close relationship to other rights and liberties accorded protection under the Constitution. Specifically, they insist that education is itself a fundamental personal right because it is essential to the effective exercise of First Amendment freedoms and to intelligent utilization of the right to vote. * * *

    * * * We need not dispute any of these propositions. The Court has long afforded zealous protection against unjustifiable governmental interference with the individual's rights to speak and to vote. Yet we have never presumed to possess either the ability or the authority to guarantee to the citizenry the most *effective* speech or the most *informed* electoral choice. That these may be desirable goals of a system of freedom of expression and of a representative form of government is not to be doubted. These are indeed goals to be pursued by a people whose thoughts and beliefs are freed from governmental interference. But they are not values to be implemented by judicial intrusion into otherwise legitimate state activities.

Even if it were conceded that some identifiable quantum of education is a constitutionally protected prerequisite to the meaningful exercise of either right, we have no indication that the present levels of educational expenditures in Texas provide an education that falls short. Whatever merit appellees' argument might have if a State's financing system occasioned an absolute denial of educational opportunities to any of its children, that argument provides no basis for finding an interference with fundamental rights where only relative differences in spending levels are involved and where—as is true in the present case—no charge fairly could be made that the system fails to provide each child with an opportunity to acquire the basic minimal skills necessary for the enjoyment of the rights of speech and of full participation in the political process.

    * * *

We have carefully considered each of the arguments supportive of the District Court's finding that education is a fundamental right or liberty and have found those arguments unpersuasive. In one further respect we find this a particularly inappropriate case in which to subject state action to strict judicial scrutiny. The present case, in another basic sense, is significantly different from any of the cases in which the Court has applied strict scrutiny to state or federal legislation touching upon constitutionally protected rights. <u>Each of our prior cases involved legislation which "deprived," "infringed," or "interfered" with the free exercise of some such fundamental personal right or liberty.</u> * * * <u>A critical distinction between those cases and the one now before us lies in what Texas is endeavoring to do with respect to education.</u> * * *

Every step leading to the establishment of the system Texas utilizes today—including the decisions permitting localities to tax and expend locally, and creating and continuously expanding the state aid—was implemented in an effort to *extend* public education and to improve its quality. Of course, every reform that benefits some more than others may be criticized for what it fails to accomplish. But we think it plain that, in substance, the thrust of the Texas system is affirmative and reformatory and, therefore, should be scrutinized under judicial principles sensitive to the nature of the State's efforts and to the rights reserved to the States under the Constitution.

It should be clear, for the reasons stated above and in accord with the prior decisions of this Court, that this is not a case in which the challenged state action must be subjected to the searching judicial scrutiny reserved for laws that create suspect classifications or impinge upon constitutionally protected rights.

We need not rest our decision, however, solely on the inappropriateness of the strict-scrutiny test. A century of Supreme Court adjudication under the Equal Protection Clause affirmatively supports the application of the traditional standard of review, which requires only that the State's system be shown to bear some rational relationship to legitimate state purposes. This case represents far more than a challenge to the manner in which Texas provides for the education of its children. <u>We have here nothing less than a direct attack on the way in which Texas has chosen to raise and disburse state and local tax revenues. We are asked to condemn the State's judgment in conferring on political subdivisions the power to tax local property to supply revenues for local interests. In so doing, appellees would have the Court intrude in an area in which it has traditionally deferred to state legislatures.</u> This Court has often admonished against such interferences with the State's fiscal policies under the Equal Protection Clause. * * *

Thus, we stand on familiar grounds when we continue to acknowledge that the Justices of this Court lack both the expertise and the familiarity with local problems so necessary to the making of wise decisions with respect to the raising and disposition of public revenues. Yet, we are urged to direct the States either to alter drastically the present system or to throw out the property tax altogether in favor of some other form of taxation. No scheme of taxation, whether the tax is imposed on property, income, or purchases of goods and services, has yet been devised which is free of all discriminatory impact. In such a complex arena in which no perfect alternatives exist, the Court does well not to impose too rigorous a standard of scrutiny lest all local fiscal schemes become subjects of criticism under the Equal Protection Clause.

In addition to matters of fiscal policy, this case also involves the most persistent and difficult questions of educational policy, another area in which this Court's lack of specialized knowledge and experience counsels against premature interference with the informed judgments made at the state and local levels. Education, perhaps even more than welfare assistance, presents a myriad of "intractable economic, social, and even philosophical problems." * * * The very complexity of the problems of financing and managing a statewide public school system suggests that "there will be more than one constitutionally permissible method of solving them," and that, within the limits of rationality, "the legislature's efforts to tackle the problems" should be entitled to respect. * * * On even the most basic questions in this area the scholars and educational experts are divided. Indeed, one of the major sources of controversy concerns the extent to which there is a demonstrable correlation between educational expenditures and the quality of education—and assumed correlation underlying virtually every legal conclusion drawn by the District Court in this case. Related to the questioned relationship between cost and quality is the equally unsettled controversy as to the proper goals of a system of public education. And the question regarding the most effective relationship between state boards of education and local school boards, in terms of their respective responsibilities and degrees of control, is now undergoing searching re-examination. The ultimate wisdom as to these and related problems of education is not likely to be divined for all time even by the scholars who now so earnestly debate the issues. In such circumstances, the judiciary is well advised to refrain from imposing on the States inflexible constitutional restraints that could circumscribe or handicap the continued research and experimentation so vital to finding even partial solutions to educational problems and to keeping abreast of ever-changing conditions.

It must be remembered, also, that every claim arising under the Equal Protection Clause has implications for the relationship between national and state power under our federal system. Questions of federalism are always inherent in the process of determining whether a State's laws are to be accorded the traditional presumption of constitutionality or are to be subjected instead to rigorous judicial scrutiny. While "[t]he maintenance of the principles of federalism is a foremost consideration in interpreting any of the pertinent constitutional provisions under which this Court examines state action," it would be difficult to imagine a case having a greater potential impact on our federal system than the one now before us, in which we are urged to abrogate systems of financing public education presently in existence in virtually every State.

The foregoing considerations buttress our conclusion that Texas' system of public school finance is an inappropriate candidate for strict judicial scrutiny. * * *

III

     * * *

Apart from federal assistance, each Texas school receives its funds from the State and from its local school district. On a state-wide average, a roughly comparable amount of funds is derived from each source. The State's contribution, under the Minimum Foundation Program, was designed to provide an adequate minimum educational offering in every school in the State. * * *

     * * *

By virtue of the obligation to fulfill its Local Fund Assignment, every district must impose an ad valorem tax on property located within its borders. The Fund Assignment was designed to remain sufficiently low to assure that each district would have some ability to provide a more enriched educational program. Every district supplements its Foundation grant in this manner. In some districts, the local property tax contribution is insubstantial, as in Edgewood where the supplement was only $26 per pupil in 1967. In other districts, the local share may far exceed even the total Foundation grant. In part, local differences are attributable to differences in the rates of taxation or in the degree to which the market value for any category of property varies from its assessed value. The greatest interdistrict disparities, however, are attributable to differences in the amount of assessable property available within any district. Those districts that have more property, or more valuable property, have a greater capability for supplementing state funds. * * *

     * * *

The "foundation grant" theory upon which Texas legislators and educators based the Gilmer-Aikin bills, was a product of the pioneering work of two New York educational reformers in the 1920's, George D. Strayer and Robert M. Haig. Their efforts were devoted to establishing a means of guaranteeing a minimum statewide educational program without sacrificing the vital element of local participation. The Strayer-Haig thesis represented an accommodation between these two competing forces. * * *

The Texas system of school finance is responsive to these two forces. While assuring a basic education for every child in the State, it permits and encourages a large measure of participation in and control of each district's schools at the local level. In an era that has witnessed a consistent trend toward centralization of the functions of government, local sharing of responsibility for public education has survived. * * *

The persistence of attachment to government at the lowest level where education is concerned reflects the depth of commitment of its supporters. In part, local control means, as Professor Coleman suggests, the freedom to devote more money to the education of one's children. Equally important, however, is the opportunity it offers for participation in the decisionmaking process that determines how those local tax dollars will be spent. Each locality is free to tailor local programs to local needs. * * * No area of social concern stands to profit more from a multiplicity of viewpoints and from a diversity of approaches than does public education.

* * * Appellees suggest that local control could be preserved and promoted under other financing systems that resulted in more equality in educational expenditures. While it is no doubt true that reliance on local property taxation for school revenues provides less freedom of choice with respect to expenditures for some districts than for others, the existence of "some inequality" in the manner in which the State's rationale is achieved is not alone a sufficient basis for striking down the entire system. * * * It may not be condemned simply because it imperfectly effectuates the State's goals. * * * Nor must the financing system fail because, as appellees suggest, other methods of satisfying the State's interest, which occasion "less drastic" disparities in expenditures, might be conceived. Only where state action impinges on the exercise of fundamental constitutional rights or liberties must it be found to have chosen the least restrictive alternative. * * * The people of Texas may be justified in believing that other systems of school financing, which place more of the financial responsibility in the hands of the State, will result in a comparable lessening of desired local autonomy. * * *

Appellees further urge that the Texas system is unconstitutionally arbitrary because it allows the availability of local taxable resources to turn on "happenstance." * * * But any scheme of local taxation—indeed the very existence of identifiable local governmental units—requires the establishment of jurisdictional boundaries that are inevitably arbitrary. It is equally inevitable that some localities are going to be blessed with more taxable assets than others. * * *

Moreover, if local taxation for local expenditures were an unconstitutional method of providing for education then it might be an equally impermissible means of providing other necessary services customarily financed largely from local property taxes, including local police and fire protection, public health and hospitals, and public utility facilities of various kinds. We perceive no justification for such a severe denigration of local property taxation and control as would follow from appellees' contentions. It has simply never been within the constitutional prerogative of this Court to nullify statewide measures for financing public services merely because the burdens or benefits thereof fall unevenly depending upon the relative wealth of the political subdivisions in which citizens live.

In sum, to the extent that the Texas system of school financing results in unequal expenditures between children who happen to reside in different districts, we cannot say that such disparities are the product of a system that is so irrational as to be invidiously discriminatory. * * * In its essential characteristics, the Texas plan for financing public education reflects what many educators for a half century have thought was an enlightened approach to a problem for which there is no perfect solution. We are unwilling to assume for ourselves a level of wisdom superior to that of legislators, scholars, and educational authorities in 50 States, especially where the alternatives proposed are only recently conceived and nowhere yet tested. The constitutional standard under the Equal Protection Clause is whether the challenged state action rationally furthers a legitimate state purpose or interest. * * * We hold that the Texas plan abundantly satisfies this standard.

      *   *   *

      *   *   * The consideration and initiation of fundamental reforms with respect to state taxation and education are matters reserved for the legislative processes of the various States, and we do no violence to the values of federalism and separation of powers by staying our hand. We hardly need add that this Court's action today is not to be viewed as placing its judicial imprimatur on the status quo. The need is apparent for reform in tax systems which may well have relied too long and too heavily on the local property tax. And certainly innovative thinking as to public education, its methods, and its funding is necessary to assure both a higher level of quality and greater uniformity of opportunity. These matters merit the continued attention of the scholars who already have contributed much by their challenges. But the ultimate solutions must come from the lawmakers and from the democratic pressures of those who elect them.

      Reversed.

Financing System Does Not Violate State Constitutional
Equal Protection Provision

MILLIKEN v. GREEN

Supreme Court of Michigan, 1973.
390 Mich. 389, 212 N.W.2d 711.

      *   *   * Two questions have been certified to this Court under the provisions of GCR 1963, 797. There is no need to restate or re-

iterate the text of these questions. In substance, they inquire whether the Michigan school financing system denies "substantially equal educational opportunity" under the Equal Protection Clauses of the Michigan Constitution (Const.1963, art. 1, § 2) or the Fourteenth Amendment to the United States Constitution.

Neither the evidence presented at the hearing nor the judge's findings support the legal arguments advanced against the present system of financing public education.

We are presented with generalized arguments concerning the nature of educational opportunity in this State. So that our opinion not be misconstrued, it is important to note that we are not presented with a concrete claim by either individual students or by school districts that they are suffering from particular specified educational inadequacies because of deficiencies in the school financing system. Such concrete claims, when and if raised, will stand or fall on their own merits and not on account of anything we say here. In short, we are not abandoning the school children of this State to legislative whim in derogation of any judicially enforceable right to an education they may have under our Constitution.

When this case was initially considered a majority of the Court found it unnecessary to reach the Federal constitutional claim, holding that, in any event, the school financing system violated the Michigan Constitution. Since our grant of a rehearing, the Federal constitutional question has been settled.

In San Antonio Independent School District v. Rodriguez, 411 U. S. 1, 93 S.Ct. 1278, 36 L.Ed.2d 16 (1973), the United States Supreme Court reversed a three-judge Federal District Court which had held the Texas system of financing its public schools violated the Equal Protection Clause.

* * *

Accordingly, the certified question raising plaintiffs' Federal Fourteenth Amendment claim must be answered negatively.

The decision of the United States Supreme Court in *Rodriguez* does not foreclose challenges to a school financing system premised on the provisions of a state's constitution. Indeed, after *Rodriguez,* the New Jersey Supreme Court struck down that state's education financing scheme on the basis of provisons in its constitution. * * * Significantly, the Court, having made that decision, withheld decreeing any relief, stayed the effectiveness of its own order and requested argument on the question of the form of the decree. As will appear, we prefer to know where the argued contentions are likely to take us and the people of Michigan before we announce new doctrine and, thereby, undertake to make it the governing law.

* * *

Opponents of the present school financing system base their challenge on the disparities among local school districts in the amount of taxable resources available for financing their schools. They do not directly challenge the right of the Legislature to create a system of local school districts with a high degree of local autonomy as to school operations and financing pursuant to Const.1963, art. 8, § 2. Nor do they directly challenge the choice of a locally imposed property tax as the primary method of financing education.

They ask us, rather, to focus on the variations among districts in the amount of revenue, per pupil, which will be collected under a uniform tax rate. It is argued that these variations in tax "burden" unconstitutionally deprive children in districts with relatively low taxable resources of educational opportunities equivalent to those available to children in districts with greater taxable resources. Presumably this is so because their parents and other taxpayers in the districts with fewer taxable resources will have to tax themselves at a higher rate (expend more "tax effort") in order to raise a given amount of revenue.

Opponents further argue that the disparities in local taxable resources for education are a deprivation of the equal protection of the laws. Then they, as many other lawyers and judges, seek to reduce all further argument to whether "fundamental interests" and "suspect classifications" are present.

All courts agree that the function of an equal protection clause is to protect against governmental discrimination. They also agree that governmental discrimination is not of itself unconstitutional. An equal protection clause forbids only unreasonable discrimination or, pejoratively, invidious discrimination.

There are a number of reasons why the Equal Protection Clause has not historically been thought to require that all legislation be applied equally to all citizens. First, government must be able to draw reasonable distinctions among its citizens in awarding benefits and imposing burdens. Second, there is the traditional deference of courts to the Legislature's expression of the will of the people. Third, any strictly egalitarian view of the Equal Protection Clause could not be justified historically in terms of the intention of those who drafted and ratified it. Fourth, "equality" is itself such an ephemeral concept that judicial review on an abstract "equality" standard is bound to be unmanageable.

* * *

Much of the argument in this case has been directed to the question of whether the disparities in local taxable resources signify concomitant disparities in "educational opportunity", a phrase which has not yet been defined in terms which are both sufficiently concrete to be used to compare school systems and, also, broad enough to encompass more than a tiny portion of the spectrum of opportunity exposures that some have in mind when they speak of equal educational opportunity.

There is a fundamental disagreement concerning a standard by which equal educational opportunity may be measured.

Defendant school districts have argued that educational opportunity should be evaluated in terms of "output", as measured by pupil accomplishment on certain achievement tests. The defendants have presented statistical evidence indicating that there is no significant correlation between the level of taxable resources in a given district (or the actual per pupil expenditures of the district) and the level of achievement of its students.

On the other hand, opponents of the present school financing system wish to define educational opportunity in terms of "input." Just as defendants have defined output narrowly in terms of achievement test scores, so, too, opponents have defined input narrowly in terms of the district's available taxable resources.

Without disagreeing with either theory of defining educational opportunity—inputs or outputs—we cannot accept without criticism either of the further-narrowed definitions offered by the parties. The reduction of the sum total output to the accomplishment of the pupils on a few achievement tests would be grossly unjust to both the educators and the pupils, for education must extend far beyond the limits of verbal facility or mathematical proficiency. With respect to the input received by a school, the level of taxable resources within a district is only one of the myriad inputs into an educational system.

The foregoing discussion serves to demonstrate the complexity of the concept of educational opportunity. We will not attempt a definition.

Yet it is important in terms of the constitutional analysis to clarify the point in contention. Although lawyers and judges in this and other cases have spoken in the grand term of educational opportunity, they have been in fact discussing what concededly is only a facet of that concept—the taxable resources available to finance each child's education.

Opponents of the present system do not press for a general requirement of equality of "educational opportunity" in all or even several of its dimensions. Instead, they are seeking equality as to one factor or input of the educational process—taxable resources.

We are not presented with particular students or particular school districts alleging that they are receiving an inadequate education in some particular regard as a result of the present financing system.

V

The wealth discrimination here significantly differs from those situations in which indigents are totally excluded from public benefits by their inability to pay. We repeat, opponents do not assert that they or any identifiable persons are educationally deprived, nor do they, in contrast with an indigent who seeks a decree alleviating his deprivation, present us with a workable and constitutional alternative to the present financing system which would improve the "educational opportunity" of students residing in low state equalized value (SEV) districts.

A rule requiring government in the distribution of benefits, such as education, to take into account and alleviate all differences in ability to pay would work a revolutionary change in the system of furnishing benefits.

* * *

We do not find appealing the suggestion that this Court honor the obvious fact that ad valorem taxation by school districts was contemplated by our State Constitution by directing now that the entire State be reorganized into one school district or a few very large districts.

The wide disparities of taxable resources among local school districts is not a new phenomenon. It was a prevalent phenomenon long before and at the time the people adopted the new Constitution.

* * *

The Constitution does not forbid disparities in wealth. It does not forbid persons residing in one taxing district from taxing themselves at a higher rate than persons residing in other districts are both willing and able to tax themselves. It does not forbid the expenditure of the relatively higher tax revenues produced for local governmental purposes, even purposes that the Legislature has an obligation to "maintain and support".

* * *

The State's obligation to provide each child with an education can be defined either in absolute terms—an education which leaves the child with certain minimally sufficient skills or an education which meets his educational needs or one which is sufficient to allow him to function usefully in society, etc.—or it can be defined relatively—an education (or an educational opportunity) equal to that received by his peers, at whatever level that may be.

However the state's obligation is defined, no evidence has been presented that specific, significant educational inequities exist as a result of the current school financing system, let alone evidence that such inequities would be alleviated by an opinion of this Court upholding the claims urged upon us.

Instead of substantiating with evidence their claims of educational inequities and demonstrating that a decree of this Court would overcome those inequities, all have concentrated exclusively on the disparities in taxable resources among local school districts. Such disparities are, no doubt, a cause of the disparities in per pupil expenditures that now exist among school districts. Disparities in expenditures may, indeed, contribute to disparities in educational programs offered students. Eliminating disparities in taxable resources would alleviate present disparities in expenditures. But it has not been shown that eliminating disparities in expenditures will significantly improve the quality or quantity of educational services or opportunity offered to Michigan school children.

There is simply no assurance that a declaration that the present school financing system is unconstitutional would result in an educationally significant increase in services or opportunity in a substantial number of school districts with relatively low taxable resources. For all that appears, even if larger sums were to reach these districts, the new found money might be used for other purposes, such as to make deferred expenditures without any discernable increase in educational services or opportunity.

Even if part of the larger sums were available to hire "better" teachers, there is no reason to believe that a significantly greater number of the better teachers would accept employment in districts with low SEVs or low socioeconomic status (SES) in preferences to high SEV/SES districts. Obviously, factors other than money play an important role in a teacher's choice of employment, especially if one is a "better" teacher and presumably, therefore, possessing greater mobility and choice. It is even arguable that if all districts had the same amount of money to spend, the "better" teachers would gravitate, more so than now, to the higher SEV/SES districts.

While it is true that districts which spend more for education can pay higher teachers' salaries and generally offer a greater variety of programs to their students, there is continuing debate regarding the point at which the marginal return on incremental expenditures becomes educationally significant. While a system which spends $1,000 per pupil should be able to offer significantly better educational programs than one which spends $100 per pupil, the same conclusion is not necessarily true when comparing expenditures of $730.87 per pupil and $537.75 per pupil.

We have not been provided with nor have we discovered any *evidence* which would help us establish the point at which the marginal return in incremental expenditures becomes educationally significant. The relationship of expenditures to educational opportunity is being sharply questioned and is the topic of much current debate among educators. We would be ill-advised, at this time, to intrude our personal suppositions into this debate in what could only be, in view of our limited judicial function, a heavy-handed manner.

Even if it were made to appear that more money would eliminate constitutionally significant disparities between districts in the quantity or quality of educational services or opportunity, the remedy need not be to discard altogether the present tax machinery. There might be a less radical alternative, such as simply requiring that funds be provided to eliminate such disparities.

We conclude that this Court could not responsibly declare the present system of financing schools unconstitutional to achieve a social goal which our decree might not achieve, and might, perhaps, even impede.

It must be apparent by now that we are of the opinion that the state's obligation to provide a system of public schools is not the same as the claimed obligation to provide equality of educational opportunity. Because of definitional difficulties and differences in educational philosophy and student ability, motivation, background, etc., no system of public schools can provide equality of educational opportunity in all its diverse dimensions. All that can properly be expected of the state is that it maintain and support a system of public schools that furnishes adequate educational services to all children.

* * *

Our response to the certified questions is:

1. On the authority of *Rodriguez*, we answer negatively the question raising a Federal Fourteenth Amendment claim.

2. It has not been shown that the Michigan financing system substantially denies students in school districts having relatively low state equalized value per pupil "equal educational opportunity." Thus, we find no discrimination violative of Michigan's Equal Protection Clause.

3. We further respond to the question posed in the originally filed opinion (which restated the question certified to us, addressed at the hearing and in the trial judge's findings made at our request and argued in the briefs filed with us) that the Michigan Constitution does not prohibit a school district from levying taxes to support a level of expenditure for the education of students in the district beyond the level of expenditure in other districts. Nor does the Michigan Constitution oblige the Legislature to supplement the revenues the other districts are able and willing to raise to bring the level of their expenditures up to the level of the district taxing and spending the most, or, failing that, to require the higher taxing and spending districts to reduce their tax levies and expenditures to a level the other districts, as supplemented by whatever appropriations the Legislature is willing to provide, can or are willing to maintain.

NOTES

The Supreme Court of Arizona held that the Arizona Constitution does establish education as a fundamental right, but went on to say that a school financing system which meets the mandates of that state's Constitution, that education be free, uniform, open a minimal number of months per year, and be open to all of the particular age group, needs to only be rational and reasonable and not discriminatory nor capricious. In so finding, the Court upheld the constitutionality of Arizona's school financing system. Shofstall v. Hollins, 110 Ariz. 88, 515 P.2d 590 (1973).

A School Finance Distribution Formula Without Significant Equalizing Effects Violates the State Constitution

HORTON v. MESKILL

Supreme Court of Connecticut, 1977.
172 Conn. 615, 376 A.2d 359.

HOUSE, Chief Justice. * * *

The cases were brought seeking (1) a declaratory judgment that the system of financing public elementary and secondary education in this state, at least as it affects the town of Canton, violates the Connecticut and the United States constitutions; * * *.

In essence, each action sought by declaratory judgment a judicial determination as to whether the Connecticut educational finance system, at least as it existed at the time of trial (1974), violates constitutional equal rights and equal protection guarantees and is constitutionally mandated "appropriate legislation"; Conn.Const. Art. VIII § 1; to provide free public elementary and secondary schools in the state. * * *

* * *

We turn now to the assignments of error addressed to the court's finding of facts. * * *

Without attempting to recite in detail the lengthy finding of facts, we note certain findings which are of special significance. The public schools in Canton, like those of all other towns in the state, are financed primarily by two means: funds raised by the town by assessment on property within the town and funds distributed by the state pursuant to legislation providing for a flat grant depending on the average number of pupils attending school daily. This grant is usually referred to as the ADM (average daily membership) grant. General Statutes § 10–262. The ADM grant paid during 1973–74 was $215 per pupil and has since been increased to $250 per pupil. It has been the principal source of the state's contribution to local public school education for about three decades though, by statute, the state provides for various other grant payments to each town or district for public and nonpublic school programs and activities. * * *

In Connecticut, the percentage contribution of the local, state, and federal governments has been approximately 70 percent local, 20 to 25 percent state, and 5 percent or less federal. * * *

* * *

Because local property taxes are the principal source of revenue for local public schools, a significant measure of the ability of the various towns to finance local education is the dollar amount of taxable property per pupil in each town which can be figured by dividing the grand list of a town by the number of pupils. For the 1972–73 school year, wide disparities existed in the effective yield per pupil ranging from approximately $20,000 per pupil to approximately $170,000 per pupil. During that year, the state average was $53,639. In Canton, it was $38,415.

* * *

The tax effort of a town to finance education may be measured by determining the net school mill rate which is that part of the net mill rate which a town spends on education. * * *

* * *

* * * [T]axpayers in property-poor towns such as Canton pay higher tax rates for education than taxpayers in property-rich towns. The higher tax rates generate tax revenues in comparatively small amounts and property-poor towns cannot afford to spend for the education of their pupils, on a per pupil basis, the same amounts that property-rich towns do. These facts were affirmed by a conclusion of the governor's commission on tax reform: "In short, many towns can tax far less and spend much more; and those less fortunate towns can never catch up in school expenditure because taxes are already as high as homeowners can tolerate. * * * This dual inequity—a family can pay more and get less for its children—is the fundamental issue of school finance." 2 Governor's Commission on Tax Reform, Local Government—Schools and Property, pp. 53–54.

The wide disparities that exist in the amount spent on education by the various towns result primarily from the wide disparities that exist in the taxable wealth of the various towns; the present system of financing education in Connecticut ensures that, regardless of the educational needs or wants of children, more educational dollars will be allotted to children who live in property-rich towns than to children who live in property-poor towns.

* * * Property-rich towns were and still are able, through higher per pupil expenditures, to provide a substantially wider range and higher quality of educational services than Canton in the areas of course offerings, special education, learning disability teachers and facilities, library resources, television teaching, and in numerous other areas, including higher ratios of classroom teachers to students, specialist teachers to students, guidance counselors to students, and other similar relationships. Because of the two-thirds reimbursement provision of the state aid statute for special education, towns that spend more on special education receive more state aid than towns that spend less. * * *

High education-spending towns, such as Darien, were and are able to obtain more special education funds from the state because they are better able to afford the one-third portion of the expense, better equipped to identify special education problems and better staffed to apply for funds.

*   *   *

The criteria for evaluating the "quality of education" in a town include the following: (a) size of classes; (b) training, experience and background of teaching staff; (c) materials, books and supplies; (d) school philosophy and objectives; (e) type of local control; (f) test scores as measured against ability; (g) degree of motivation and application of the students; (h) course offerings and extracurricular activities. In most cases, the optimal version of these criteria is achieved by higher per pupil operating expenditures, and because many of the elements of a quality education require higher per pupil operating expenditures, there is a direct relationship between per pupil school expenditures and the breadth and quality of educational programs.

*   *   *

It further found that substantial progress can be made toward equalizing the financial abilities of the local districts by redistributing the flat grant funds according to a different formula, which can be accomplished without the need for additional state taxes; that equalizing the ability of the various towns to finance education would not require that all towns spend the same amount for the education of each pupil since towns can be left free to choose the level of expenditures appropriate for their circumstances; and that there is no reason why local control needs to be diminished in any degree merely because some financing system other than the present one is adopted.

*   *   *

Since many of the conclusions of the court are interdependent, it is unnecessary to consider them seriatim. Obviously the most significant ones are those dealing with constitutional interpretation, and the tests applicable to that interpretation, generally, and to the equal rights and equal protection provisions, specifically.

This court has many times noted that the equal protection clauses of the state and federal constitutions have a like meaning and impose similar constitutional limitations. *   *   * Where the legislation impinges upon a fundamental right *   *   * it must be struck down unless justified by a compelling state interest. *   *   * Where the statute does not involve fundamental rights *   *   * the legislation will withstand constitutional attack if the distinction is founded on a rational basis." *   *   *

In the *Rodriguez* case, the United States Supreme Court adopted what appears to be a special test for determining whether education is a fundamental constitutional right: "[T]he key to discovering whether education is 'fundamental' is not to be found in comparisons of the relative societal significance of education as opposed to subsistence or housing. Nor is it to be found by weighing whether education is as important as the right to travel. Rather, the answer lies in assessing whether there is a right to education explicitly or implicitly guaranteed by the Constitution." San Antonio Independent School District v. Rodriguez, supra, 33, 93 S.Ct. 1297. The court concluded that no such right was guaranteed by the federal constitution and, accordingly, declined to apply a strict scrutiny test.

*   *   *

The *Rodriguez* case is very relevant to the appeal before us. The equal protection clauses of both the United States and Connecticut constitutions having a like meaning, the decisions of the United States Supreme Court defining federal constitutional rights are, at the least, persuasive authority, although we fully recognize the primary independent vitality of the provisions of our own constitution. *   *   *   In the area of fundamental civil liberties—which includes all protections of the declaration of rights contained in article first of the Connecticut constitution—we sit as a court of last resort, subject only to the qualification that our interpretations may not restrict the guarantees accorded the national citizenry under the federal charter. In such constitutional adjudication, our first referent is Connecticut law and the full panoply of rights Connecticut residents have come to expect as their due. Accordingly, decisions of the United States Supreme Court defining fundamental rights are persuasive authority to be afforded respectful consideration, but they are to be followed by Connecticut courts only when they provide no less individual protection than is guaranteed by Connecticut law.

In the *Rodriguez* case, the United States Supreme Court was called upon to review the financing system for education used in Texas, which system had been attacked as violating the equal protection clause of the federal constitution. Although there are significant differences between the Texas system and the Connecticut system, they are alike in that a substantial quantum of educational support is supplied by local districts with disparities in financial resources for the furnishing of such support. The trial court in the present cases observed: "[T]hose differences do not, in the opinion of this court, make inapplicable to the Connecticut system the reasons why the Texas system was held not to violate the United States Constitution." We agree with that conclusion.

*   *   *

In our consideration of the merits of the present appeals, we have not found material aid in the many decisions from the courts of other jurisdictions since most of them depend upon the controlling and differing provisions of the constitutions in the particular jurisdictions. Nor have we found the *Rodriguez* test for the fundamentality of the right to an education of particular help—although under that test it cannot be questioned but that in the light of the Connecticut constitutional recognition of the right to education (article eighth, § 1) it is, in Connecticut, a "fundamental" right.

As other courts have recognized, educational equalization cases are "in significant aspects sui generis" and not subject to analysis by accepted conventional tests or the application of mechanical standards. The wealth discrimination found among school districts differs materially from the usual equal protection case where a fairly defined indigent class suffers discrimination to its peculiar disadvantage. The discrimination is relative rather than absolute. Further, the children living in towns with relatively low assessable property values are afforded public education but, as the trial court found, the education they receive is to a substantial degree narrower and lower in quality than that which pupils receive in comparable towns with a larger tax base and greater ability to finance education. True, the state has mandated local provision for a basic educational program with local option for a program of higher quality but, as the trial court's finding indicates, that option to a town which lacks the resources to implement the higher quality educational program which it desires and which is available to property-richer towns is highly illusory. * * * With justification, the trial court found merit to the complaints of the plaintiffs about "the sheer irrationality" of the state's system of financing education in the state on the basis of property values, noting that their argument " 'would be similar and no less tenable should the state make educational expenditures dependent upon some other irrelevant factor, such as the number of telephone poles in the district.' * * *

We find our thinking to be sustantially in accord with the decisions of the New Jersey Supreme Court in Robinson v. Cahill, 62 N.J. 473, 303 A.2d 273, and the California Supreme Court in Serrano v. Priest, 18 Cal.3d 728, 135 Cal.Rptr. 345, 557 P.2d 929 (*Serrano II*), and whether we apply the "fundamentality" test adopted by *Rodriguez* or the pre-*Rodriguez* test under our state constitution (as the California Supreme Court did in *Serrano II*) or the "arbitrary" test applied by the New Jersey Supreme Court in Robinson v. Cahill, supra, 62 N.J. 492, 303 A.2d 273, we must conclude that in Connecticut the right to education is so basic and fundamental that any infringement of that right must be strictly scrutinized.

"Connecticut has for centuries recognized it as her right and duty to provide for the proper education of the young." * * * Education is so important that the state has made it compulsory through a requirement of attendance. General Statutes § 10–184. * * *

The present-day problem arises from the circumstance that over the years there has arisen a great disparity in the ability of local communities to finance local education, which has given rise to a consequent significant disparity in the quality of education available to the youth of the state. It was well stated in the memorandum of decision of the trial court, which noted that the "present method [of financing education in the state] is the result of legislation in which the state delegates to municipalities of disparate financial capability the state's duty of raising funds for operating public schools within that municipality. That legislation gives no consideration to the financial capability of the municipality to raise funds sufficient to discharge another duty delegated to the municipality by the state, that of educating the children within that municipality. The evidence in this case is that, as a result of this duty-delegating to Canton without regard to Canton's financial capabilities, pupils in Canton receive an education that is in a substantial degree lower in both breadth and quality than that received by pupils in municipalities with a greater financial capability, even though there is no difference between the constitutional duty of the state to the children in Canton and the constitutional duty of the state to the children in other towns."

We conclude that without doubt the trial court correctly held that, in Connecticut, elementary and secondary education is a fundamental right, that pupils in the public schools are entitled to the equal enjoyment of that right, and that the state system of financing public elementary and secondary education as it presently exists and operates cannot pass the test of "strict judicial scrutiny" as to its constitutionality. These were the basic legal conclusions reached by the court. * * * It suffices to note that the exhaustive finding of facts amply supports the conclusions of the court that the present legislation enacted by the General Assembly to discharge the state's constitutional duty to educate its children, depending, as it does, primarily on a local property tax base without regard to the disparity in the financial ability of the towns to finance an educational program and with no significant equalizing state support, is not "appropriate legislation" (article eighth, § 1) to implement the requirement that the state provide a substantially equal educational opportunity to its youth in its free public elementary and secondary schools.
     * * *

While the development of an appropriate legislative plan is not without its complexities, the problem is not insoluble. * * * Obviously, absolute equality or precisely equal advantages are not required and cannot be attained except in the most relative sense. Logically, the state may recognize differences in educational costs based on relevant economic and educational factors and on course offerings of special interest in diverse communities. None of the basic alternative plans to equalize the ability of various towns to finance education requires that all towns spend the same amount for the education of each pupil. The very uncertainty of the extent of the nexus between dollar input and quality of educational opportunity requires allowance for variances as do individual and group disadvantages and local conditions.
     * * *

There is no error; * * * the cases are remanded for further proceedings consistent with this opinion.

Budgeting and Accounting for School Funds

In order that the school district can effectively plan for educational activities and account for the expenditure of tax funds, provisions must be made for budgetary and accounting procedures. School boards are generally given wide latitude in the determination of how educational funds will be expended. The attitude of the courts has been that a school district, being charged with the responsibility for operating the schools, should have as much freedom as possible to determine how and where the funds will be spent.

The exception to this rule is where the legislature has prescribed that school boards be fiscally dependent on city government. In such cases, the board must submit its budget for review and approval by the city government. However, where a city council has the authority to fix the amount of the school budget, it may not direct the itemized expenditure of the gross amount authorized; the board may spend the money for any purpose permitted by law. In instances where the law requires only the submission of the budget and does not specify control or approval authority, the courts have held that the reviewing agency cannot reduce the budget.

A school district must expend monies for the purpose for which they are collected. If a statute requires fund accounting for special tax money, the school board must establish and deposit the money in such a fund. In such a case, a taxpayer may not require an accounting for the school funds beyond seeing that they are used for the purpose for which they were levied and collected.

Funds Collected and Allocated for a Particular Public Purpose Cannot be Lawfully Diverted to Another Purpose

SAN BENITO IND. SCHOOL DIST. v. FARMERS' STATE BANK

Court of Civil Appeals, Texas 1935.
78 S.W.2d 741.

SMITH, Justice. On May 16, 1932, Farmers' State Bank & Trust Company of San Benito was closed and its affairs were taken over by the state banking commissioner for administration, as provided by law. Up to that time San Benito Independent School District maintained four separate checking accounts in the bank, which was the district treasury, as follows:

First, an "interest and sinking fund account," from taxes assessed, collected, and deposited in said account for the purpose of paying interest and principal upon the district's bonded debt, in which account there was a balance, at the time the bank failed, of $12,942.68;

Second, a "local maintenance fund account," in which were deposited taxes assessed and collected for the specific purpose of local maintenance, exclusive of teachers' salaries, in which there was a balance of $318.25;

Third, an "interest and penalty refunding account," in which had been deposited interest and penalties unlawfully collected from the taxpayers, which under the law were required to be refunded to those paying them. In this account there was a balance, at the time the bank failed, of $124.16. The balances in the three foregoing accounts aggregated $13,385.09.

Fourth, a "state available warrant fund account," in which were deposited, as received, funds received from the state for the specific purpose of paying teachers' salaries. In this account, however, there was no balance on hand at the time the bank failed. Moreover, at that time the bank held unpaid district warrants drawn against that account in the aggregate amount of $3,409.18, which the bank carried, not as an overdraft, but as assets.

In this situation the district brought this action against the bank and banking commissioner to recover $13,385.09, being the amount of the balance of funds on deposit in the first three accounts mentioned, and prayed that the amount of the unpaid warrants held by the bank against the exhausted fourth, or "state available warrant fund account," be offset against the district's claim, leaving a balance of $9,975.91, for which net amount the district prayed judgment.

The bank and banking commissioner answered, setting up their claim of $3,409.18, represented by the unpaid district warrants held by them against the exhausted "state available warrant fund account," and, asserting that that claim against that fund could not lawfully be applied as an offset against the district's claim upon deposits in the other three specific fund accounts, prayed for direct judgment upon said warrants.

The trial court rendered judgment in favor of the district for the amount of its deposits in the bank, and in favor of the banking commissioner for the amount of the unpaid warrants held by him, but denied the district's prayer that the latter recovery be applied as an offset. The district has appealed.

* * *

It is too well settled to require citation, or any extended discussion, that a public fund collected and allocated for a particular public purpose cannot be lawfully diverted to the use of another particular public purpose. Under that wise rule, when applied here, when the taxpayer pays a certain tax for the specific purpose of liquidating a particular public bonded indebtedness of his school district, the funds derived therefrom cannot lawfully be used for the purpose of paying teachers' salaries, chargeable under the law to a different public fund; when lawful interest and penalties have been collected from the taxpayers and segregated into a particular fund, and is required by law to be refunded to the taxpayer, as is the case here, that fund may not lawfully be diverted to the payment of teachers' salaries chargeable to another specific fund, as is sought to be done by appellant; when a specific tax has been levied and assessed by a school district and paid by the taxpayers, for the particular purpose of "local maintenance" (exclusive of teachers' salaries), and the fund so collected has been segregated and allocated to that purpose, as was done here, the district may not divert that fund to another for the purpose of paying teachers' salaries, as is sought to be done by the district in this case.

So when the bank acquired the warrants against the district's "state available fund" account, which was exhausted, at least for the time being, it could not lawfully collect them by charging the amounts thereof to the accounts of the interest and sinking fund, or the local maintenance fund, or the interest and penalty refunding fund; it could only hold the warrants until the account against which they were drawn was replenished, and it was so holding them, as among its assets, when it ceased to do business.

The corporate school district, as are all municipal corporations, is but a trustee of guardian of the public funds coming into its possession under the law, and may disburse those funds only in the manner and for the purposes prescribed by law. As the funds in question were gathered in, the district, in obedience to law, allocated them to the several purposes for which they were paid in, and deposited them with the bank in appropriate separate accounts kept for each specific fund. When so segregated into separate accounts, the district had no power or authority to transfer any part of the funds from either account and apply it to the purposes of any other account, any more than a trustee of several persons or estates could divert the funds of one cestui que trust to the use of another. Nor could the bank, in this case, lawfully pay the warrants drawn on one particular account out of the funds of another particular account, any more than it could charge the draft of one individual depositor to the account of another. The rights, capacities and interests of the respective parties are thus fixed by settled principles of law, and there being no mutuality of rights, interests and capacities between the district as trustee of the "available state" fund and account, and the same entity as trustee of the other three specific funds and accounts, it could not appropriate the one to the uses of the others.

The inevitable conclusion is, then, that in balancing the accounts between the district and the bank, the claim of the latter against the "state available fund" of the former could not be applied as an offset against the obligations of the bank to the other three separate fund accounts. The bank could not enforce such offset in an action thereon, nor may the district enforce it in this action.

The judgment is affirmed.

NOTES

1. The extent of budget itemization necessary to meet statutory requirements has been described in an Arizona case. Arizona statute requiring budgetary information divided the school budget into major general categories and then subdivided these categories into subitems. The operating expense category was broken down into two broad sections, Administration and Instruction. Each of these sections were divided into 41 subitems. A controversy arose as to whether the 41 subitems were merely explanatory of the major categories or were the expenditures of the board of education restricted to the amounts in the subitems making transfer of funds among subitems illegal. The statute governing this question stated: " * * * No expenditure shall be made for a purpose not particularly itemized and included in such budget, and no expenditure shall be made, and no debt, obligation or liability shall be incurred or created in any year for any purpose itemized in such budget in excess of the amount specified for such item." The court in interpreting this statute defined the word "purpose" in light of judicial principle that where the language of a statute may be subject to more than one interpretation the court will adopt the one which is reasonable in view of the particular situation being litigated. The court said:

> Since the word 'purpose' as used in (the statute) is susceptible of more than one interpretation, we are bound to declare as the intention of the legislature the alternative which is reasonable and convenient. It appears to us that to bind either the school district or the superintendent to a forty-one line operating expense budget, as advocated by the (treasurer), would be impractical, unduly restrictive, and lead to absurd results.

Isley v. School District No. 2 of Maricopa County, 81 Ariz. 280, 305 P.2d 432 (1956).

2. An Oklahoma court upheld a state board of education directive requiring school districts to treat as a current expense certain items which taxpayers insisted should have been recorded as capital outlay expenditures. The state board of education had acted under a statute providing that the state board shall prescribe a list of appropriation accounts by which funds of school districts shall be budgeted. St. Louis-San Francisco Railway v. McCurtain Co., Okl., 352 P.2d 896 (1960).

3. Where a school tax levy raises revenues in excess of the requested budgetary amount, the school board is entitled to the surplus. In Montgomery County, Maryland, where the county levies the tax rate requested by the school district, the county tax collector on many occasions received more from the school tax levy than was requested by the school board. The surplus remained in the county treasury and amounted to over one million dollars. The school board brought suit against Montgomery County to obtain the funds. The court held that when the levy was actually and unconditionally made by the county, the statutes were explicit in declaring that no part of the sum levied for the use of the public schools be used for any other

purpose, and that the amount so levied each year be paid by the county treasurer to the school board. Board of Ed. of Montgomery County v. Montgomery County, 237 Md. 191, 205 A.2d 202 (1964).

4. In the case of a fiscally dependent school district, a Connecticut court has held that where a school budget is submitted to a municipal reviewing agency and the expenditures are for purposes described by statute to be within the board of education's authority to effectuate; the finance board has no power to refuse to include an appropriation for such expenditure in its budget. This statement is qualified by the fact that the reviewing agency may refuse appropriation if the financial condition of the town does not permit such expenditures. This is, of course, an extremely important limitation, since in that state it is within the review board's authority to pronounce that the town is not in a financial position to support such expenditures for education and thereby cut the school budget. Board of Ed. of Town of Stamford v. Board of Finance of Town of Stamford, 127 Conn. 345, 16 A.2d 601 (1940).

5. In another case involving the authority of the town board of finance to control educational expenditures in Connecticut school districts, the court held that placement of certain funds to be used for school purposes in the general government budget contravened a statute permitting the board of education to transfer unexpended or uncontracted-for portion of appropriations for school purposes to any other item and this constituted an illegal restriction on the appropriation. Board of Ed. of Town of Ellington v. Town of Ellington, 151 Conn. 1, 193 A.2d 466 (1963).

6. A school district may not, in the absence of statute expressly permitting it, accumulate surpluses beyond that required to operate for the ensuing year. The theory is that a school district levying taxes sufficient to maintain a large surplus should reduce its tax levy. One court held that a tax levy which created a surplus of over 50 per cent of the entire school district budget exceeded the amount reasonably contemplated for a contingency. The court went on to say that: "A tax levy is required to be a reasonable approximation of the amount required. It has not been the policy of the law to permit the creation of funds by taxation in large amounts for future use, except where statutory authorization exists as in the case of building funds, sinking funds, and the like." Kissinger v. School Dist. No. 49 of Clay County, 163 Neb. 33, 77 N.W.2d 767 (1956).

Money or Property Derived Under the Auspices of the Public School Are Accountable in Same Manner as Other Tax Funds

PETITION OF AUDITORS OF HATFIELD TP. SCHOOL DIST.

Superior Court of Pennsylvania, 1947.
161 Pa. 388, 54 A.2d 833.

ARNOLD, Judge. This appeal is from an order of the court below directing the officers, directors and supervising principal of the Hatfield Joint Consolidated School District to comply with a duces tecum subpoena issued by the official auditors calling for the production of various books, vouchers and papers.

The Hatfield Joint Consolidated School District was formed by the school districts of the borough of Hatfield and the township of Hatfield. Its bank account is carried by its treasurer in the Hatfield National Bank under the name, "Hatfield Joint Consolidated School District," hereafter called the "official account." The warrants or vouchers thereon are executed by the proper officers of the district.

In the same bank is an account called "Hatfield Joint School Accounts," and the sole right to withdraw funds therefrom is possessed by Elmer B. Laudenslager, the supervising principal. This we will refer to as the "activities account." The appellants challenge the right of the statutory auditors to examine this account.

    *   *   *

Appellants have asked us to determine whether the activities account is subject to official audit even though no tax monies were in it, and state: "This question is a matter of interest to every district in the Commonwealth. The decision in this case will affect every school district * * * [and] * * * will decide once and for all the status of such funds * * * even as the legislature established the status of the cafeteria funds. Section 8 of Act of 1931, P.L. 243, and Act of 1945, P.L. 688, 24 P.S. § 331." Indeed the evidence in this case disclosed four other nearby communities operating a similar system, and in fact the system is widespread. It is fraught with great danger. High school football and other athletics have achieved great popularity, and this means that almost any school district, depending in a degree upon the skill of the athletes, has athletic events the admission fees of which aggregate a large sum of money, probably in excess of $10,000. It would be a great blow to the public school system if by embezzlement or lack of care such funds should be lost. Not only has the school board a moral duty to perform but there is also a legislative imperative. The public school system of this commonwealth is entirely statutory. Within the constitutional limitations the legislature is supreme and there reposes in the courts no power to permit deviation from its commands; and neither the local school districts nor the State Department of Education may by-pass the duties enjoined.

In the so-called activity accounts various situations obtain. Of course if pupils of a class give money to a supervising principal to purchase for them class jewelry or similar things the school district has no official duty (although it may have a moral duty), for the supervising principal acts as agent of the pupils. This is the smaller end of the problem. At the other pole, a school district, acting under the express provisions of § 405 of the Code, 24 P.S. § 339, has athletic events. These activities produce large sums of money from paid admissions. Under the instant system these sums of money are not disbursed through the treasurer, nor through a resolution of the board, but are solely at the command of one individual, who has no statutory standing or duty. It is possible that some school district may neither

Alexander School Law MTB—28

directly nor *indirectly* furnish any money for the playing field or stadium; or for the coaching of the athletes, or for their uniforms or playing togs, or for the apparatus with which the sport is connected, or for the lighting of the field; although it is very doubtful whether such case exists. But it is certainly true that, if a school district operates and expends tax money for the acquisition, maintenance or lighting of the playing field, or for the payment of services of a coach, the admissions charged result from the use of public property and from the expenditure of tax monies and are the property of the school district, must go into the official account of the treasurer thereof, and are subject to audit.

The monies derived form the sale of admissions to witness the event in question come into being because of (1) the use and wear of the school building and grounds; (2) the use and wear of personal property owned by the district; (3) the payment to employes such as coaches for their services; (4) the payment by the district for light, heat and various maintenance charges, including janitor service. By reason of the use of these public funds the event takes place, and from it are reaped the admission fees paid to witness the performance. The pupils are not expected to and do not furnish any of the money. The admission fees could not belong to them, and indeed if taken they would be professionals instead of amateurs. The spectators are not to get their money back. No one has any investment except the school district. The money raised by admissions therefore belongs to the district, which by its property and funds made the admission fees possible.

Of lesser importance, but in the same category, are the admission fees charged for dramatic and musical enterprises held in the buildings of the district. These belong to the district for the same reasons and with the same results. For instance, the school districts usually and properly provide musical instruments, just as they provide equipment and uniforms for athletics. In the instant case admission fees were expended through the activities account for such instruments, but it was frankly admitted that when bought the instruments belonged to the district. So do the admission fees themselves.

We have not attempted to discuss each situation that may present itself, but where monies or property are derived directly or indirectly through the use of school buildings, or from the expenditure of public funds of the district, the monies thus derived are public property, must be handled exactly as tax monies and be paid to the district treasurer.

* * *

Order affirmed.

Public School Indebtedness

The authority of school districts to issue bonds must be clearly and expressly conferred by statute. The failure of a school board to comply with the statutory conditions for school bond issuance will render the bonds illegal.

Bonds issued for a specific purpose must be used for that purpose and no other. It has been held that bonds approved by the voters for "erecting and constructing a new roof" for a school building were illegal where the statute provided for bonds to be issued for the purpose of "erecting and equipping, or purchasing and equipping" school houses.[52] In another case a court held that a statute which authorized a bond election for the "erection and enlargement" of school buildings could not be construed to include the issuance of bonds for the purpose of equipping school buildings.[53]

While earlier cases generally held that statutory procedures for school bond elections were to be strictly followed and failure to do so would make the bonds illegal, more recent cases tend to allow some flexibility so long as irregularities do not affect the results of the election. It has been held that where the voters in a bond election authorize bonds for a greater amount than is consistent with the law, the voter authorization is not illegal, and the school board may issue bonds for the amount prescribed by law.

Generally the courts have held that a bondholder cannot recover on an illegal bond even if he is an innocent purchaser. This rule, however, has been modified in some states where it has been held that where illegal bonds have been sold and the funds applied to the improvement of the district, the bondholder may recover under the *quantum meruit*. Also, the courts will permit the holder of an illegal bond to recover if the money is identifiable and has not been commingled with other funds of the district. The courts, in some cases, have allowed the holder to recover property purchased with illegal bond proceeds if no other money of the district was used in payment for the property.

Constitutions of most states make provision for debt limitations the maximum percentage of which a local school district may not exceed. Courts have held that the percentage of indebtedness is to be computed using the amount of bonds which actually has been issued and not the amount which was projected at the time of a bond election. While a state legislature must conform to prescribed constitutional requirements regarding indebtedness, some state legislatures have sought to avoid stringent constitutional debt restrictions which severely limit educational facility construction. One such device re-

---

52. School Dist. No. 6, Chase County v. Robb, 150 Kan. 402, 93 P.2d 905 (1939).

53. Jewett v. School Dist. No. 25 in Freemount County, 49 Wyo. 277, 54 P.2d 546 (1936).

sorted to by a few states is the "holding company" or the "local school building authority." This method of financing school construction effectively increases the debt capacity of a local school district and has been upheld by the courts.[54]

Legislature Has Power to Direct Local Authorities to Create Debt for Public School Building

REVELL v. CITY OF ANNAPOLIS

Court of Appeals of Maryland, 1895.
81 Md. 1, 31 A. 695.

ROBINSON, C. J. The act of 1894, c. 620, provides for the erection of a public school building in the city of Annapolis, and, to pay for the same, it authorizes and directs the school commissioners of Anne Arundel county to borrow money, not exceeding the sum of $20,000, on bonds to be indorsed by the county commissioners; and for the same purpose it directs that the city of Annapolis shall issue bonds to the amount of $10,000, and that said bonds shall be issued without submitting the question of their issue to the voters of said city. The city of Annapolis has refused to issue the bonds as thus directed by the act, and the question is whether the legislature has the power to direct that the city authorities shall issue bonds to raise money to be applied to the erection of a public school building in said city. This power is denied, on the broad ground that it is not competent for the legislature to compel a municipal corporation to create a debt or levy a tax for a local purpose, in which the state has no concern, or to assume a debt not within the corporate powers of a municipal government. If the correctness of this general proposition be conceded for the purposes of this case, we do not see how it affects in any manner the validity of the act now in question. We cannot agree that the erection of buildings necessary for the public schools is a matter of merely local concern, in which the state has no interest. In this country the people are not only in theory, but in practice, the source of all governmental power, and the stability of free institutions mainly rests upon an enlightened public opinion. Fully recognizing this, the constitution declares that it shall be the duty of the legislature "to establish throughout the state a thorough and efficient system of free public schools, and to provide by taxation or otherwise" for their maintenance and support. * * * And the legislature has accordingly established a public school system, and has provided for its support by state and local taxation. It cannot be said, therefore, that the erection of buildings for public school purposes is a matter in which the state has no concern; nor can we agree that

54. Kees v. Smith, 235 Ind. 687, 137 N. E.2d 541 (1956); Waller v. George- town Bd. of Educ., 209 Ky. 726, 273 S.W. 498 (1925).

the creation of a debt for such purposes is not within the ordinary functions of municipal government. What is a municipal corporation? It is but a subordinate part of the state government, incorporated for public purposes, and clothed with special and limited powers of legislation in regard to its own local affairs. It has no inherent legislative power, and can exercise such powers only as have been expressly or by fair implication delegated to it by the legislature. The control of highways and bridges within the corporate limits; the power to provide for an efficient police force; to pass all necessary laws and ordinances for the preservation of the health, safety, and welfare of its people; and the power to provide for the support of its public schools by local taxation,—are all among the ordinary powers delegated to municipal corporations. And the public schools in Baltimore city are not only under the control and supervision of the city authorities, but are mainly supported by municipal taxation. It is no answer to say that the public schools in Annapolis are under the control of the school commissioners of Anne Arundel county, and that under its charter it has no power to create a debt or levy taxes for their support. The legislature may, at its pleasure, alter, amend, and enlarge its powers. It may authorize the city authorities to establish public schools within the corporate limits, and direct that bonds shall be issued to raise money for their support, payable at intervals during a series of years. There is no difference in principle between issuing bonds and the levying of a tax in one year sufficient to meet the necessary expenditure. * * *

If the legislature has the power to direct the city authorities to create a debt for a public school building, the exercise of this power in no manner depends upon their consent or upon the consent of the qualified voters of the city. We recognize the force of the argument that the question whether a municipal debt is to be created ought to be left to the discretion and judgment of the people who are to bear the burden. We recognize the fact that the exercise of this power by the legislature may be liable to abuse. But this abuse of a power is no argument against its exercise. The remedy, however, in such cases, is with the people to whom the members of the legislature are responsible for the discharge of the trust committed to them. It is a matter over which the courts have no control. If the debt to be created was for a private purpose, that would present quite a different question, for it is a fundamental principle, inherent in the nature of taxation itself, that all burdens and taxes shall be levied for public, and not for private, purposes. Be that as it may, it is well settled in this state that the legislature has the power to compel a municipal corporation to levy a tax or incur a debt for a public purpose, and one within the ordinary functions of a municipal government. * * *

In closing his argument, the counsel for the appellees suggested that the act was invalid because it was in conflict with the fourteenth amendment of the federal constitution which forbids the taking of "property without due process of law." * * * It is a sufficient answer to this objection to say that the act in question, which requires the city authorities to issue bonds to raise money to pay the cost of a public school building, is a lawful exercise of legislature power, and, this being so, taxes levied to pay such bonds are not open to the objection of taking property without due process of law. Nor can we agree that the act is in conflict with section 33, art. 3, of the constitution, which declares that the general assembly shall pass no special law for any case for which provision has been made by an existing general law. The general law provides, it is true, that the school commissioners of Anne Arundel county shall have the control and supervision of the public schools in said county, with power to build, repair, and furnish schoolhouses. But it does not authorize the commissioners to borrow money upon bonds to be indorsed by the county commissioners for such purposes, nor does it provide for the apportionment of the cost of a public school building to be erected in the city of Annapolis between the county and the city. This could only be done by special act, and, this being so, the special act is not in conflict with the constitution, which forbids the passing of a special act for any purpose for which provision has been made by an existing general law. It follows from what we have said that the judgment sustaining the demurrer in this case must be overruled. * * *

*Issuance of Municipal Bonds Without Statutory
Authorization Is Ultra Vires*

HEWITT v. BOARD OF EDUC.

Supreme Court of Illinois, 1880.
94 Ill. 528.

Mr. Chief Justice WALKER delivered the opinion of the Court:

This was an action of assumpsit, brought by Hewitt in the circuit court of McLean county, against the "Board of Education of Normal School District," on a bond for $500, and two coupons of $25 each. The bond was dated the 1st of September, 1873, payable five years after its date, with ten per cent interest, and it was payable to John Gregory or order. It was indorsed by him in blank, and he negotiated it to the Home Bank, of which appellant purchased, taking no further indorsement.

* * *

The evidence tended to show that the bond was not issued to pay for a school house site, or to erect a building thereon. It also tended to prove that Gregory was, at the time the bond was issued to him, a member of the board, and that appellant was aware of the fact when he purchased the bond. As these were controverted facts, and were found by the circuit court against appellant, and as the Appellate Court has affirmed the judgment of the circuit court, we must take the affirmance as a finding of the facts as they were found by the circuit court, and we are precluded from reviewing these controverted facts, but are bound by the finding of the Appellate Court.

The fact, then, that the bond was not issued for an authorized purpose, undeniably rendered it void. Municipal corporations are not usually endowed with power to enter into traffic or general business, and are only created as auxiliaries to the government in carrying into effect some special governmental policy, or to aid in preserving the order and in promoting the well-being of the locality over which their authority extends. Where a corporation is created for business purposes, all persons may presume such bodies, when issuing their paper, are acting within the scope of their power. Not so with municipalities. Being created for governmental purposes, the borrowing of money, the purchase of property on time, and the giving of commercial paper, are not inherent, or even powers usually conferred; and unless endowed with such power in their charters, they have no authority to make and place on the market such paper, and persons dealing in it must see that the power exists. This has long been the rule of this court. * * * We might refer to other cases where it has been held that bonds issued without authority are void, even in the hands of purchasers before maturity and without actual notice.

A person taking bonds of a municipal corporation has access to the records of the body, and it is his duty to see that such instruments are issued in pursuance of authority, and when without power, they must be held void in whosesoever hands they are found. If, therefore, this bond was not issued to purchase a school house site, or for erecting a school building, as the Appellate Court seem to have found, the bond is void, as it was issued without power, and this, too, in the hands of a person taking without actual notice.

Again, this bond was issued without authority, and was void * * *.

The judgment of the Appellate Court is affirmed.

*Exercise of Discretion by School Trustees in Issuance
of Bonds Is Not Defeated by Lapse of Time*

COVINGTON v. McINNIS

Supreme Court of South Carolina, 1928.
144 S.C. 391, 142 S.E. 650

WATTS, C. J. This is an application in the original jurisdiction of the court to permanently enjoin the issuance of bonds of Clio school district No. 9 of Marlboro county, in the state of South Carolina. The petitioner for himself and other taxpayers in the district seeks to have the proposed bonds declared illegal on two grounds specified in the agreed statement of facts, submitted as a controversy without action.

* * *

It is contended, first, by the petitioner that, as more than seven years has elapsed since the authority was given by the election to the trustees to issue the bonds and a part of said bonds having been issued and sold, after so long a lapse of time the trustees are now without authority to issue the remaining portion of said bonds or any part thereof.

This court has recognized the validity of bonds issued many years after the election. The voters in the election declared their willingness to have the school district issue $50,000 of bonds. At the time of the election on account of the 8 per cent. limitation of the Constitution the full amount of these bonds could not be issued, but this disability having been removed and in the opinion of the trustees it is necessary for the school district to come into funds to be used for the purposes for which the election was held, there can be no valid objection to the bonds being issued for that purpose. This court has recognized in the case of Robinson v. Askew et al., 129 S. C. 188, 123 S. E. 822, that bonds can be issued many years after the election authorizing it; in that case the issue being sold four years after the election. * * * The only limitation which should affect the right to issue bonds under these circumstances is where the purposes for which the bonds were originally voted have ceased to be necessary, or where the conditions have so changed that it would be inequitable to allow the bonds to be issued, and, unless one of these conditions clearly appears to the satisfaction of the court, the exercise of their discretion by the trustees should not be interfered with.

The second objection is that the constitutional amendment required a vote on bonds to be issued under its provisions and that an election held previous to the adoption of the amendment would not be a compliance therewith. This raises the question whether the provisions of the amendment were retroactive or prospective only. The decision of this question rests upon a matter of intention. If it was the intention of the Legislature that it should be retroactive, it will have that effect. The wording of the amendment throws no light on this question, and therefore the court can consider the conditions under which the amendment was passed. As shown in the agreed statement of facts, there had been voted by the school district an issue of $50,000 of bonds for a definite purpose as submitted to the voters. This purpose was unable to be carried out on account of the 8 per cent. constitutional limitation. To enable the purpose for which the original bonds were voted to be carried out, the amendment to the Constitution was adopted, and to carry out this purpose it was clearly the intention that, if an election had been previously held, it should be regarded as the election required by the amendment. In this view it was clearly the intention of the amendment that it should be retro-active, and we so hold.

.   *   *   *   In the view we have taken above it was clearly the in-tention, in order to meet the existing condition, that it should have a retroactive effect.

This disposes of all the objections of the petitioner to the issu-ance of these bonds. The petition is dismissed, and the injunction dissolved.

NOTES

1. The legislature through its plenary power over public schools may prescribe the conditions by which school bonds shall be issued. Failure to follow prescribed conditions will render the bonds illegal. Dupont v. Mills, 196 A. 168 (1937).

2. In an 1893 case the Federal Circuit Court for the District of Ne-braska held that a statute which provides that "any school district shall have power and authority to borrow money to pay for the sites of school-houses" does not confer authority on the school district to issue negotiable securities. Such securities issued by school districts are void even in the hands of an innocent purchaser. Ashuelot Bank v. School Dist. No. 7, 56 F. 197 (1893).

3. Statutes relating to school bond elections frequently state that the notice of election or resolution shall relate to a single purpose only. The notice or resolution must state specifically the issues in order that the voter can make a clear choice. Such a statutory provision in Ohio provides for the notice of a bond election for "one purpose" but defines one purpose quite broadly as being "in the case of a school district, any number of school buildings; and in any case, all expenditures, including the acquisi-tion of a site and purchase of equipment, for any one utility building, or other structure, or group of buildings or structures for the same general purpose *   *   *   included in the same resolution." Pursuant to this stat-ute an action was brought contesting a bond election for which the resolu-tion had provided for (1) the acquisition of real estate, construction of fire-proof school buildings and the provision of furniture and furnishing there-fore, and (2) improvement of non-fireproof school buildings and the provi-sion of furniture and furnishings therefore. The court held that this reso-lution violated the statutory mandate for "one purpose" and stated:

> The purpose of the statute is to prevent the union in one act of di-verse, incongruous and disconnected matters, having no relation to or connection with each other *   *   * ; to give electors a choice to secure what they desire without the necessity of accepting some-thing which they do not want *   *   * ; and to prevent double propositions being placed before a voter having but a single ex-pression to answer all propositions, thus making logrolling impos-sible *   *   * . In applying the rule, the courts invoke a test as to the existence of a natural relationship between the various structures or objects united in one proposition so that they form 'but one rounded whole'. *   *   *

State ex rel. Board of Education v. Thompson, 167 Ohio St. 23, 145 N.E.2d 668 (1957).

4. One court has held that a statute authorizing the school district to issue bonds "for the purpose of raising funds to pay the cost of the equipping, enlarging, remodeling, repairing, and improving" the schoolhouse and "the purchase, repairing and installation of equipment thereof" did not authorize rural high school district to issue bonds for the purpose of raising funds to pay the cost of removing a schoolhouse from one site to another. Byer v. Rural High School Dist. No. 4 of Brown Co., 169 Kan. 351, 219 P.2d 382 (1950).

Slight Clerical Defect in Notice of Election
Is Not Sufficient to Invalidate Bonds

STATE v. ALLEN

Court of Appeals of Ohio, 1955.
102 Ohio App. 315, 143 N.E.2d 159.

COLLIER, Judge.

*   *   *

The single question for determination is: Does this mistake of .7 mill in the county auditor's certificate to the board of education, stating the average annual tax levy, which incorrect figure was carried in the notice of election and on the face of the ballot render the bonds invalid?

Counsel have not cited any authority directly in point and we have been unable to find any decision in which this identical question has been determined. However, there are many reported cases in Ohio dealing with irregularities and omissions in similar proceedings. The earlier decisions held that the provisions of the Uniform Bond Law, Chapter 133, Revised Code, should be strictly construed. The more recent decisions hold that a substantial compliance with the statutory requirements is all that is necessary. In the case of State ex rel. Board of Education of Springfield Local School Dist., Summit County, v. Maxwell, 144 Ohio St. 565, 60 N.E.2d 183, 185, Judge Zimmerman states the rule as follows:

"It has been generally held that defects, variances and irregularities in the several steps relating to the issuance of bonds should be material, harmful or both before the proceeding may be successfully attacked. *   *   * It has also been held that unsubstantial irregularities in the resolution of a political subdivision inaugurating an election on a bond issue which do not prejudice anyone will be disregarded, especially where the proposed bond issue as submitted was approved by considerably more than the requisite number of electors."

The bond issue in the instant case carried by a majority of 75.8 per cent of the electors. Under the rule above quoted the test is whether the voters were misled by the mistake in the auditor's figures. To determine this question it is proper to consider the degree of the error, the nature of the calculation and the closeness of the vote. When we consider the length of the duration of the bonds and the fact that the amount of the tax list varies from year to year, the calculation of an additional tax levy could be only an estimate. This estimate could not be exact, owing to the further facts that interest requirements, where bonds are issued in a series, are based on a constantly decreasing principal; that the bonds may not be of exactly equal installments; that the decreasing scale may not decrease uniformly; and that the tax duplicate throughout the life of the issue is certain to change. These and other conditions would necessarily make the calculation of the county auditor merely an estimate. It is probable that the actual amount required to retire the bonds may vary from year to year to a greater degree than the error discovered in the auditor's calculation. A statute requiring a statement of costs in ballots used in an election with reference to a public improvement is to be given a practical construction. * * *

A vital consideration in the determination as to whether an election should be declared invalid is the reluctance to reach a decision which would result in the disfranchisement of the voters. In the instant case more than three-fourths of the voters were in favor of the bond issue.

In all the cases we have examined, where the courts of Ohio have held elections invalid, there was a complete omission of some vital and jurisdictional condition to be performed. In the instant case there was no departure from the regular procedure prescribed by statute and all the proceedings were in conformity with the statutes. The answer contains no averment that enough voters were misled to change the result of the election, and it has been held in the case of Anselmi v. City of Rock Springs, 53 Wyo. 223, 80 P.2d 419, 116 A.L. R. 1250, as stated in the A.L.R. headnotes, that:

"The burden is on one claiming that the affirmative result of a bond issue election was affected by a misleading statement in the notice of election amounting to no more than an irregularity, to establish that the result of the election was affected by such statement."

* * *

For the reasons above set forth, our conclusion is that the provisions of the statutes have been substantially complied with and the slight clerical defect in the notice of election and on the ballot is not sufficient to invalidate the bonds. Therefore the court finds, on the question of the invalidity of the bond proceeding, in favor of the relator. The demurrer to the answer is sustained, and, respondent not desiring to plead further, the writ is allowed.

Writ allowed.

NOTES

1. Courts have held that school district indebtedness, subject to legal limitations, extends only to voluntary indebtedness. A judgment against a school district for a sum of money is not considered the creation of a debt within the meaning of constitutional debt limitations. Such debt is not subject to collateral attack by a taxpayers' suit to avoid taxation. Edmundson v. Indiana School Dist., 98 Iowa 639, 67 N.W. 671.

2. It has generally been held that a school district whose boundaries overlap or are coterminous with a civil government has a separate computation in determining indebtedness. Vallelly v. Park Commissioners, 16 N.D. 25, 111 N.W. 615, 171 A.L.R. 732 (1907).

3. In determining whether an indebtedness limit has been exceeded, the amount of indebtedness is determined at the time the bonds are issued and not at the time the bonds are voted. Hebel v. School Dist. R–1, Jefferson County, 131 Colo. 105, 279 P.2d 673 (1955).

4. Refunding bonds do not increase the indebtedness of a school district. Prohm v. Non-High School Dist., 130 N.E.2d 917 (1955).

5. The constitutions in Indiana and Kentucky limit the indebtedness of school districts and other political subdivisions to a mere two per cent of the value of the taxable property in the district. These constitutional debt limitations are the lowest of any of the states in the nation. In order to by-pass or avoid these uncommonly strict limitations both states have enacted statutes which allow for the use of school building corporations in financing school construction. Such a procedure permits the formation of a holding company which is authorized to construct a school building and incur the indebtedness. The school building corporation contracts with the school district to lease the building to the district for a number of years and when the rental payments have paid off the bonded indebtedness the building becomes the property of the school district. This type of purchase on an installment arrangement does not increase the indebtedness of the school district. The Supreme Court of Indiana had this to say about the constitutionality of the procedure:

> The fact that the building company was willing to give the school building to the (school district) when the building company had been paid an amount equal to its investment * * * does not change the lease-contract into a contract to purchase. It is true that the (school district), through the device of a long term lease providing for annual rental payments, may become the owner of the school building which (under the constitutional limitation) it could not have acquired * * * by issuing bonds. But it does not follow that either the arrangement or the result constitutes an evasion of the limitations of the (Constitution). The lease-contract is not in contravention of (the Constitution) unless it necessarily created a legally enforceable debt obligation for an amount in excess of the amount permitted by (the Constitution).

Jefferson School Tp. v. Jefferson Tp., 212 Ind. 542, 10 N.E.2d 608 (1937); and Kees v. Smith, 235 Ind. 687, 137 N.E.2d 541 (1956).

Fees in Public Schools

Courts have generally held that tuition fees, "matriculation" or "registration" fees, and fees for particular materials, activities or privileges are invalid.[55] In most cases invalidating fees, the courts have reasoned that the fee was charged as a condition of attendance which violated the state's constitutional or statutory provisions establishing "free" public schools. Another reason often given by the courts for invalidating fees is the lack of statutory authority to exact the fee. Courts have usually held fees invalid where the fees have been charged for an essential element of a school's activity. Where fees have been upheld, the courts have found that there was statutory authorization for the fee, that the purpose for the fee was a reasonable one or that the term "free schools" did not include furnishing textbooks.[56]

Courts have on occasion distinguished tuition fees from incidental fees, and in at least one jurisdiction a court has upheld an incidental fee of twenty-five cents per pupil per month to be used for raising funds to pay for fuel to heat the schoolroom, for brooms to sweep the schoolroom, and for water buckets to contain water for drinking purposes was reasonable and proper.[57] Similarly, in the same jurisdiction an incidental fee for improvement of grounds, insurance, and other incidental expenses did not violate the state constitution.[58]

However, in other jurisdictions incidental fees have been held invalid. In Georgia,[59] a very early decision held that a state statute requiring each child upon entering municipal public schools to pay the board of education an "incidental fee" was "clearly unconstitutional."

More recently, in Illinois, a court ruled that the state constitutional provision requiring the establishment of a thorough and efficient system of free schools did not prevent the state legislature from authorizing school boards to purchase textbooks and rent them to pupils.[60]

In several cases, public school fees for activities, particular materials or privileges have been held invalid.[61] A $25 annual fee required by one school district as a condition to furnishing each high school student a transcript of courses studied and grades achieved was held to be unconstitutional in Idaho.[62] The fee consisted of $12.-

---

55.   41 A.L.R.3rd 755.

56.   Ibid.

57.   Kennedy v. County Bd. of Educ., 214 Ala. 349, 107 So. 907 (1926).

58.   Vincent v. County Board of Educ., 222 Ala. 216, 131 So. 898 (1931).

59.   Irvin v. Gregory, 86 Ga. 605, 13 S. E. 120 (1891).

60.   Hamer v. Board of Educ., 47 Ill.2d 480, 265 N.E.2d 616 (1970).

61.   Mathis v. Gordy, 119 Ga. 817, 47 S. E. 171 (1904).

62.   Paulson v. Minidoka County School Dist., 93 Idaho 469, 463 P.2d 935 (1970).

50 for school activity fees and $12.50 for textbook fees, and had to be paid before a student could receive his transcript. Responding to each of these separately, the court reasoned that the student activity fee was imposed on all students whether they participated in extra-curricular activities or not, therefore, the fee was on attendance not on activities and as such contravened the state constitutional mandate that public schools be free. The court did note that since social and extracurricular activities were not necessarily principal elements of a high school career, the state constitution did not prohibit the school district from setting activity fees for students who voluntarily participated. With regard to the textbook fee the court observed that since textbooks were necessary to the school, they were indistinguishable from other fixed educational expense items such as building maintenance and teachers' salaries, all for which fees could not be charged.[63]

The requirement that pupils purchase textbooks and school supplies has been held invalid in Michigan.[64] In this case the school district maintained the word "free" in the state constitution did not include textbooks and supplies. The Supreme Court of Michigan held that books and supplies were necessary elements of any school's activity and an integral and fundamental part of elementary and secondary education.

Textbook Fee in Elementary Grades Violates State Constitution

CARDIFF v. BISMARCK PUBLIC SCHOOL DIST.

Supreme Court of North Dakota, 1978.
263 N.W.2d 105.

SAND, Justice. * * *

Gary Cardiff and other parents of school children attending elementary schools in the Bismarck Public School District brought an action in Burleigh County district court challenging the authority of the school district to charge rental fees for the use of necessary school textbooks.

* * *

The basic issue for our resolution is whether or not § 148 of the North Dakota Constitution provides for free textbooks and prohibits the Legislature from authorizing school districts to charge for textbooks. The parents contend the constitutional provision prohibits charging for textbooks, and the school district contends it merely prohibits charging tuition.

* * *

---

63. Ibid.

64. Bond v. Public Schools of Ann Arbor School Dist., 383 Mich. 693, 178

N.W.2d 484 (1970). See also: Board of Educ. of Freeport v. Nyquist, 92 Misc.2d 43, 399 N.Y.S.2d 844 (1977).

To resolve the first issue we must examine and construe the provisions of § 148 of the North Dakota Constitution, which provides as follows:

> "The legislative assembly shall provide at their first session after the adoption of this constitution, for a uniform system of free public schools throughout the state, beginning with the primary and extending through all grades up to and including the normal and collegiate course."

In 1968 this section was amended, as follows:

> "The legislative assembly shall provide for a uniform system of free public schools throughout the state, beginning with the primary and extending through all grades up to and including schools of higher education, except that the legislative assembly may authorize tuition, fees and service charges to assist in the financing of public schools of higher education."

In construing a written constitution we must make every effort to determine the intent of the people adopting it.   *   *   *

We must examine the whole instrument in order to determine the true intention of every part so as to give effect to each section and clause. If different portions seem to be in conflict, we must make a true effort to harmonize them if practicable.

In interpreting clauses in a constitution we must presume that words have been employed in their natural and ordinary meaning. *   *   *

Both parties contended that contemporaneous construction, as an aid in construction and interpretation of the constitution, *   *   * favored its point of view on the construction of § 148 of the North Dakota Constitution.   *   *   *

           *   *   *

From this examination we are left with a firm conviction that the legislative acts referred to do not lend any significant comfort or aid to the resolution of the basic question under consideration, namely, what does the term "uniform system of free public schools" mean? Contemporaneous construction in this instance is not helpful to either party. The Journal entries of the constitutional convention are not very helpful in determining the meaning of the language, "free public schools."

The first item relating to public schools introduced at the North Dakota Constitutional Convention, as found in the Journal, was File No. 47, § 2, which provided, in part:

> "It shall be the duty of the Legislature to establish and maintain a system of free public schools, adequate for educa-

tion of all children in the state, between the ages of six and eighteen years, inclusive, in the common branches of knowledge, and in virtue and christian morality." * * *

From this brief review it is clear that the framers consistently had in mind a free public school.

A short survey of the constitutional provisions of other states and their case law will shed some light on our question.

ARIZONA:

"The Legislature shall provide for a system of common schools by which a free school shall be established * * *" Constitution, Article XI, § 6.

In Carpio v. Tucson High School District No. 1 of Pima County, 111 Ariz. 127, 524 P.2d 948 (1974), cert. denied 420 U.S. 982, 95 S.Ct. 1412, 43 L.Ed.2d 664, the court had under consideration Article XI, § 6, of the Arizona Constitution. The court held that textbooks were not required to be furnished to high school students. However, the court referred to an earlier decision, Shoftstall v. Hollins, 110 Ariz. 88, 515 P.2d 590 (1973), where the court held that these constitutional provisions had been satisfied when the legislature provided for the means of establishing required courses, qualifications of teachers, textbooks to be used in common schools, etc. Considering this statement and the statement in *Carpio* that "textbooks have not been provided free in high schools as they have been in the common schools" leaves the impression that under the constitutional provisions of Arizona textbooks in common schools were provided free of charge.

COLORADO:

"The general assembly shall * * * provide for the establishment and maintenance of a thorough and uniform system of free public schools * * *" Constitution, Art. IX, § 2.

In Marshall v. School District RE #3 Morgan County, 553 P.2d 784 (Colo.1976), the court held that the school district was not required to furnish books free of charge to all students.

INDIANA:

"* * * it shall be the duty of the General Assembly * * * to provide, by law, for a general and uniform system of Common Schools, wherein tuition shall be without charge, and equally open to all." Constitution, Article 8, Section 1.

In Chandler v. South Bend Community School Corporation, 160 Ind.App. 592, 312 N.E.2d 915 (1974), the court held that this constitutional provision did not require textbooks to be provided free, but merely to provide a system of common schools where tuition would be without charge.

ILLINOIS:

"Education in public schools through the secondary level shall be free." Constitution, Article X, section 1.

In Beck v. Board of Education of Harlem Consolidated School District No. 122, 63 Ill.2d 10, 344 N.E.2d 440 (1976), the court held that workbooks, and other educational material, were not textbooks so as to come within the statutory provision of free textbooks, and as such it did not preclude the school board from charging the parents a fee for supplying the students with such material.

Earlier, in Hamer v. Board of Education of School District No. 109, 47 Ill.2d 480, 265 N.E.2d 616 (1970), the court was specifically concerned with the constitutional provision and held that under its provisions the school board was not prohibited from purchasing textbooks and renting them to pupils. It further held that the legislature had the power to direct the district school boards to issue textbooks to students free of charge but the constitution did not require it. In a related case entitled Hamer v. Board of Education of School District No. 109, County of Lake, 9 Ill.App.3d 663, 292 N.E.2d 569 (1973), the court in effect re-affirmed its earlier decision in the *Hamer* case.

WISCONSIN:

"The legislature shall provide * * * for * * * district schools * * * and such schools shall be free and without charge for tuition * * *" Constitution, Article X, section 3.

The court in Board of Education v. Sinclair, 65 Wis.2d 179, 222 N.W.2d 143 (1974), held that the schools may charge a fee for the use of textbooks and items of similar nature authorized by statute and that such did not violate the constitutional provision commanding that schools shall be free without charge for tuition for all children. It basically held that the term "free" referred to school buildings and equipment and what is normally understood by the term "tuition."

IDAHO:

"* * * it shall be the duty of the legislature of Idaho, to establish and maintain a general, uniform and thorough system of public, free common schools." Constitution, Art. 9, sec. 1.

In Paulson v. Minidoka County School District No. 331, 93 Idaho 469, 463 P.2d 935 (1970), the court held that school districts could not charge students for textbooks under the state constitutional provision. It also held that public high schools in Idaho are "common schools."

MICHIGAN:

"The legislature shall maintain and support a system of free public elementary and secondary schools * * *" Constitution, Article 8, § 2.

In 1908 the Michigan Constitution, Article 11, § 9, in part provided:

"The legislature shall continue a system of primary schools, whereby every school district in the state shall provide for the education of its pupils without charge for tuition * * *"

The Michigan court in Bond v. Public Schools of Ann Arbor, School District, 383 Mich. 693, 178 N.W.2d 484 (1970), held that the 1963 constitutional provision meant that books and school supplies were an essential part of the system of free public elementary and secondary schools and that the schools should not charge for such items. We note that the 1908 Constitution provided "without charge for tuition," whereas the 1963 Constitution provides for a system of "free public elementary and secondary schools."

MONTANA:

"It shall be the duty of the legislative assembly of Montana to establish and maintain a general, uniform and thorough system of public, free, common schools." Constitution, Article XI, Section 1.

In Granger v. Cascade County School District No. 1, 159 Mont. 516, 499 P.2d 780 (1972), the school district, as the school district here, contended that the pertinent language simply meant "tuition-free" as far as required courses were concerned and did not prohibit fees and charges for optional extra-curricular or elective courses and activities. The Montana parents, however, contended that the schools could not impose fees or charges for anything, whether elective or required, that is encompassed in the constitutional requirement of a "thorough system of public, free, common schools." The fees involved more than just charges for workbooks and textbooks, as in this case. The Montana Supreme Court answered the question in the following manner:

"We believe that the controlling principle or test should be stated in this manner: Is a given course or activity reasonably related to a recognized academic and educational goal of a particular school system? If it is, it constitutes part of the free, public school system commanded by Art.

XI, Sec. 1 of the Montana Constitution and additional fees or charges cannot be levied, directly or indirectly, against the student or his parents. If it is not, reasonable fees or charges may be imposed."

The court, however, pointed out that its decision does not apply to supplementary instruction offered by the school district on a private basis during the summer recess or at special times. It should be observed that the school district in the *Granger* case, as well as in the instant case, argued that they had a system of waivers and charges for welfare recipients and other cases of economic hardship. The court rejected this argument.

NEW MEXICO:

"A uniform system of free public schools sufficient for the education of, and open to, all children of school age in the state shall be established and maintained." Constitution, Article XII, § 1.

The court, in Norton v. Board of Education of School District No. 16, 89 N.M. 470, 553 P.2d 1277 (1976), held that under this constitutional provision courses required of every student shall be without charge to the student. However, reasonable fees may be charged for elective courses. The court also recognized that the board of education shall define what are required or elective courses in the educational system of New Mexico.

SOUTH DAKOTA:

"* * * it shall be the duty of the legislature to establish and maintain a general and uniform system of public schools wherein tuition shall be without charge." Constitution adopted 1889, Article VIII, § 1.

We have found no South Dakota case law on the question of tuition or textbooks.

WEST VIRGINIA:

"The legislature shall provide by general law, for a thorough and efficient system of free schools." Constitution, Article XII, Section 1.

The court in Vandevender v. Cassell, 208 S.E.2d 436 (W.Va. 1974), held that furnishing textbooks free to needy students satisfied the constitutional requirement. But two of the five judges, in a concurring opinion, stated that they did not interpret "free" as pertaining only to indigent pupils. They further stated:

"It is clear to me [us], however, that where state constitutions contain language providing for free schools, such as Article XII, Section 1 of the West Virginia Constitution, that this means free schools for students of all economic classes."

MISSOURI:

"* * * schools and the means of education shall forever be encouraged in this state. [The legislature was required to establish schools] as soon as practicable and necessary, where the poor shall be taught gratis." Constitution of 1820, art. VI, § 1.

"A general diffusion of knowledge and intelligence being essential to the preservation of the rights and liberties of the people, the general assembly shall establish and maintain free public schools for the gratuitous instruction of all persons in this state within ages not in excess of twenty-one years as prescribed by law. * * *" Constitution, Art. IX, § 1(a), source Constitution of 1875, Art. XI, §§ 1 and 3.

The court held in Concerned Parents v. Caruthersville School District No. 18, 548 S.W.2d 554 (Mo.1977), that under this constitutional provision school districts were prohibited from charging registration fees or course fees in connection with courses for which academic credit was given.

WASHINGTON:

"The Legislature shall provide for a general and uniform system of public schools. The public school system shall include common schools, and such high schools, normal schools, and technical schools as may hereafter be established." Constitution, art. 9, sec. 2.

The Supreme Court of the State of Washington, in Litchman v. Shannon, 90 Wash. 186, 155 P. 783 (1916), said:

"Public schools are usually defined as schools established under the laws of the state, usually regulated in matters of detail by local authorities in the various districts, towns, or counties, and maintained at the public expense by taxation, and open without charge to the children of all the residents of the town or other district."

Earlier, the Supreme Court of Washington, in School District No. 20, Spokane County v. Bryan, 51 Wash. 498, 99 P. 28 (1909), defined "common school" as found in its constitution as "one that is common to all children of proper age and capacity, free and subject to, and under the control of, the qualified voters of the school district."

From this study we have concluded that the courts have consistently construed the language "without payment of tuition" or "wherein tuition shall be without charge" or such similar language to mean that a school is prohibited from charging a fee for a pupil attending school. This language has also been construed as not prohibiting the charging of fees for textbooks.

However, as to constitutions containing language such as "free public schools" or "free common schools" or similar language, the courts have generally held, with a few exceptions, that this language contemplates furnishing textbooks free of charge, at least to the elementary schools. The exceptions have generally relied upon extrinsic material such as contemporary construction, history, or practices, as well as the language itself. Although the cases involving language similar to that contained in the North Dakota Constitution are not in themselves conclusive, they nevertheless are helpful, if not persuasive.

A comparison of the key constitutional provisions and existing case law of states which entered the Union at the same time and under similar conditions as North Dakota will be very helpful and valuable in determining the intent of the people of North Dakota in adopting § 148 of the North Dakota Constitution.

At the time North Dakota formulated and adopted its Constitution, three other States—Montana, South Dakota, and Washington— were going through a similar process. All four States were included in the same Enabling Act, Chapter 180, 25 Statutes at Large, 676, and were required to meet the conditions in § 4, which provided:

> "That provision shall be made for the establishment and maintenance of systems of public schools, which shall be open to all the children of said states, and free from sectarian control."

The key language in the constitutional provisions of the four States are as follows:

> Montana: "* * * thorough system of public, free common schools."
>
> South Dakota: "* * * uniform system of public schools wherein tuition shall be without charge."
>
> North Dakota: "* * * uniform system of free public schools throughout the state * * *."
>
> Washington: "* * * uniform system of public schools * * *."

We are impressed with the different language employed in the constitutions of the four states, Montana, South Dakota, North Dakota, and Washington, which came into the Union at the same time and under the same Enabling Act. We must assume that each state had available the same information as the other states and was free to choose its constitutional provisions, provided they met the requirements of the Enabling Act. It is significant to note that Montana and North Dakota adopted the "free common schools" and the "free public schools" concept, whereas South Dakota adopted the "public schools wherein tuition shall be without charge concept, and Washington merely provided for a "uniform system of public schools."

We also note that the Washington Supreme Court in the *Bryan* case supra, under the Washington Constitution held that a common school district is free for all children of proper age even though its Constitution merely required a uniform system of public schools. Therefore, if the term "common schools" implies a school for which no tuition may be charged, then the expression "free public schools" should mean something more than merely not permitting the charging of tuition. This position becomes persuasive when we recognize that other states specifically provided that no charge for "tuition" would be allowed.

If the framers of the North Dakota Constitution and the people of North Dakota had in mind only to provide public schools without charging tuition they could have, and probably would have, used the language "without payment of tuition" or "wherein tuition shall be without charge," rather than the language "free public schools." We must assume that the framers of the constitution made a deliberate choice of words which reflected or expressed their thoughts. The term "free public schools" without any other modification must necessarily mean and include those items which are essential to education.

It is difficult to envision a meaningful educational system without textbooks. No education of any value is possible without school books. * * *

We cannot overlook the fact that attendance at school between certain ages was compulsory from the very beginning under penalty of law. This lends support to the contention that textbooks were to be included in the phrase "free public schools."

     * * *

The word "free" takes on its true and full meaning from the context in which it is used. There can be no doubt that the term means "without charge or cost." In the absence of any other showing we must conclude that the term was commonly understood by the people to mean "without charge or cost." Books and school supplies are a part of the education system. This is true whether we apply the necessary elements of the school's activities test or the integral part of the educational system test.

After a review of the case law and constitutional provisions of other states, and after a careful analysis of the key language of the four states which were admitted under the same Enabling Act, we have come to the conclusion that the term "free public schools" means and includes textbooks, and not merely "free from tuition."

However, our conclusion must necessarily apply only to the elementary schools, as they are the only ones covered in this action.

The action in district court was not a class action and factually involved only students enrolled in the elementary schools. * * * This opinion therefore is limited to textbooks used in elementary schools in the required subjects, as set out in [statute] * * *

    * * * to the extent that they apply to elementary textbooks are in conflict with § 148 of the North Dakota Constitution and are therefore invalid and unconstitutional as to elementary school textbooks.

    * * *

The judgment and order of the district court are both affirmed.

Chapter 14

PROPERTY

It goes without saying that the property is of prime importance in operating a public school system just as it is to all individuals and corporations alike. School property is state property held in trust for public school purposes.[1] By vesting a local school district with the power to acquire and hold property, the legislature does not relinquish its control. School property remains the property of the state and the power of the local district may be expanded or abolished at the will of the legislature. For example, it is conceivable that a state legislature may decide to vest the control of school property in another agency, other than a school district, at the local level. In such a case the school district would, abiding by the statute, relinquish control over the property in favor of the other agency.

The same reasoning prevails where the legislature decides to reorganize many small school districts into larger, more comprehensive district units. The property now owned by the smaller district becomes, by statute, the property of the new, larger, consolidated district. The state legislature in this case has merely changed the trustee in which control of school property is vested.

School Board Must Have Legislative Authority to Contract
an Indebtedness for Purchase of Land

ROBERTSON v. BOARD OF EDUC. OF YANCEY COUNTY

Supreme Court of North Carolina, 1926.
192 N.C. 765, 135 S.E. 863.

PER CURIAM. At the commencement of this action, defendant board of education of Yancey county was negotiating for the purchase of certain land in said county, to be used for school purposes. It proposed to incur an indebtedness of $30,000, for the purchase of said land, and to request the board of county commissioners to issue bonds of Yancey county, in said sum, to raise money to pay the purchase price for said land. It is conceded that there is no legislative authority for the board of education to purchase said land, or for the board of county commissioners to issue said bonds. It was therefore error to dissolve the temporary restraining order theretofore issued by Judge Stack. Tate v. Board of Education of McDowell County, 192 N.C. 516, 135 S.E. 336. Chapter 120, Public Laws 1924, Extra Session, does not apply to Yancey county. It is not contended, how-

---

1. Carson v. State, 27 Ind. 465 (1867).

ever, that the purchase of said land is required to enable the board of education of Yancey county to maintain public schools, as required by the Constitution, in said county.

Whether it is a wise policy for the board of education to purchase this land, for the reasons it assigns in its answer to the complaint, does not present a question of law for our decision. We decide only that neither the board of education nor the board of county commissioners has the power, without legislative authority, conferred by statute, either general or special, to contract an indebtedness for the purchase of land for school purposes.

The judgment must be reversed.

NOTES

1. "A community unit school district, like any other school district established under enabling legislation, is entirely subject to the will of the legislature thereafter. With or without the consent of the inhabitants of a school district, over their protests, even without notice or hearing, the state may take the school facilities in the district, without giving compensation therefore, and vest them in other districts or agencies. The state may hold or manage the facilities directly or indirectly. The area of the district may be contracted or expanded, it may be divided, united in whole or in part with another district, and the district may be abolished. The 'property of the school district' is a phrase which is misleading. The district owns no property, all school facilities, such as grounds, buildings, equipment, etc., being in fact and law the property of the state and subject to the legislative will." People v. Deatherage, 401 Ill. 25, 81 N.E.2d 581 (1948).

An Indiana court held that: "Under the constitution and laws of this state, school property is held in trust for school purposes by the persons or corporations authorized for the time being by statute to control the same. It is in the power of the legislature, at any time, to change the trustee." Carson v. State, 27 Ind. 465 (1867).

2. The courts have consistently held that school property may be taken from one school district and vested in other agencies. In a school district organization case which has implications for the school district's control over property an Illinois court held: "The state may, with or without the consent of the inhabitants or against their protest, and with or without notice or hearing, take their property [property of the district] without compensation and vest it in other agencies, or hold it itself, expand or contract the territorial area, divide it, unite our whole or part of it with another municipality, apportion the common property and the common burdens in accordance with the legislative will, and it may abolish the municipality [or school district] altogether." People ex rel. Taylor v. Camargo Community Consol. School Dist., 313 Ill. 321, 145 N.E. 154 (1924).

Legislative Authority to Acquire Schoolhouses Impliedly
Includes Land for the Schoolhouse

STATE ex rel. POST v. BOARD OF ED. OF CLARKSBURG

Supreme Court of Appeals of West Virginia, 1912.
71 W.Va. 52, 76 S.E. 127.

BRANNON, P. The school district of Clarksburg by vote authorized the incurrence of a debt and the issue of bonds for its payment
for the purpose of building one high school and two graded schools.
The bonds were sold, and their proceeds are in the treasury. The
board of education refused to build the high school and one graded
school out of such money, on the ground that to do so would call for
the purchase of ground for their erection, and the board doubted its
power to use any of the money coming from said bonds in acquiring
such ground. Howard Post asks of this court a mandamus to compel the board to build said high school and graded school, and to acquire sites for them, and use such bond money in doing so.

Act 1908, c. 27, § 13 (Code Supp.1909, c. 45, § 1571), says that
the board of education of every district shall provide by purchase or
condemnation "suitable schoolhouses and grounds." Act 1911, c. 70,
allows the board to "borrow money and issue bonds for the purpose
of building, completing, enlarging, repairing or furnishing schoolhouses." Does the word "schoolhouse," used in the statute, mean land, include necessary land? In Hawkins v. Wilson, 1 W.Va. 117, a sum-
mons in unlawful detainer demanded a house and appurtenances. On
authority there cited it was held that the word "house" imported
land. "A grant of a house includes land under it." Devlin on Deeds,
§ 863, citing 32 Am.D. 238, and 45 Id. 220. Devlin on Deeds, § 1200,
says: "Courts have frequently decided that a conveyance of a building or barn, used as a term of description, will convey the land on
which the building or structure is erected." Note 1 in 6 Cyc. 115 will
support this position; also Bouvier, Law Dict. 963. When the statute
says that the money may be used to build houses, it means that it
may be used to acquire land for schoolhouses. Necessarily so. It is
a necessary implication, if the words do not per se mean land, as here
used. Commanded to build schoolhouses, it is an incidental power because indispensable to attain the end. You cannot build a schoolhouse without land on which to build it.

In view of the law above stated, and in view of the purpose
which must have been in the minds of the legislators who enacted the
bond section, we hold that the word "schoolhouses" includes land for
schoolhouses. We hold that the section in giving the board of education power to apply the money arising from the bonds "for the purpose of building, completing, enlarging, repairing or furnishing
schoolhouses" meant to give the board power to acquire land on

which to build schoolhouses. We can see that the Legislature never designed to limit the use of the money to work and material of construction, and deny its use in acquiring the ground indispensable and preliminary to work of construction. This ground is the first thing requisite in carrying out the purpose of the statute—a sine qua non. Otherwise the statute might be abortive. Certainly it cannot be doubted that such bond money may be used "in completing, enlarging, or repairing" existing schoolhouses; and it would be unreasonable to say this could be done, but a site could not be acquired. * * *

It is suggested that as to ground for schoolhouses, section 13, serial section 1571, of Supplement Code of 1909, commands the board of education to purchase or condemn sites, but that this can be done only by current levy. The section does not so limit. I read the two sections together, both providing schoolhouses. Section 13 gives full power to acquire sites, and it is plausible to say that all means of providing money may be used where necessary, that, where the ordinary tax levy is not adequate, the people may vote for bonds to supply funds; the bond remedy being additional or cumulative remedy. The power to acquire land for the purpose is necessarily implied, because the board could not furnish schoolhouses without it. We have seen that the statute commands the board of education to provide by purchase or condemnation suitable schoolhouses and lands. The power to buy land is plainly implied. In the well-considered case of Supervisors v. Gorrell, 20 Grat. (Va.) 505, the court said: "No express power is given them to acquire land for any purpose. But power is expressly given them 'to build and keep in repair county buildings.' * * * How can they discharge these express powers and duties, without the power to acquire land? Suppose a county is without a courthouse, clerk's office or jail, and without land on which to build them; how are the board of supervisors to perform their express power and duty in such a case, 'to build and keep in repair county buildings,' without first acquiring the ground on which to erect these necessary buildings? The implied power to acquire the ground is as plainly given as the express power to erect the buildings. In the construction of the most naked powers, to which the strictest rules of construction are applied, there is no better settled rule than this, that every power necessary to the execution of an express power is plainly implied." All the authorities assert such necessary implied power. * * *

Being of the opinion that the board has ample power under these statutes to apply the money arising from said bonds for the acquisition of land, we award the mandamus.

*Absent Legislation to the Contrary, a School District, as
a State Agency, Is Not Subject to Local
Municipal Zoning Ordinance*

CITY OF BLOOMFIELD v. DAVIS CO. SCHOOL DIST.

Supreme Court of Iowa, 1963.
254 Iowa 900, 119 N.W.2d 909.

GARFIELD, Chief Justice. This is an action in equity by the City of Bloomfield to enjoin defendants, Davis County Community School District, and its contractor, Boatman, from installing in a restricted residence district in plaintiff city a bulk storage tank for gasoline and a pump to supply its school buses therewith. * * *

On September 19, 1933, the council of plaintiff city passed ordinance 84 designating and establishing a restricted residence district in the city. Section 2 of the ordinance provides: "That no buildings or other structures, except residences, school houses, churches, and other similar structures shall hereafter be erected, reconstructed, altered, repaired or occupied within said district without first securing from the city council permit therefor; * * *."

Section 3 of the ordinance provides: "Any building or structure erected, altered, repaired or used in violation of any of the provisions of this ordinance, is hereby declared to be a nuisance, * * *."

* * *

The only contention of defendants we find it necessary to consider is that ordinance 84 should not be held applicable to them to prevent installation on this school-owned site of this gasoline facility for servicing its school buses because the school district is an arm of the state and proposes to use its property for a governmental purpose.

* * *

The law seems quite well settled that a municipal zoning ordinance is not applicable to the state or any of its agencies in the use of its property for a governmental purpose unless the legislature has clearly manifested a contrary intent. * * *

* * *

C.J.S. Zoning, § 135 says, "Ordinarily, a governmental body is not subject to zoning restrictions in its use of property for governmental purposes."

The underlying logic of some of these authorities is, in substance, that the legislature could not have intended, in the absence of clear expression to the contrary, to give municipalities authority to thwart the state, or any of its agencies in performing a duty imposed upon it by statute.

There can be no doubt the school district is an arm or agency of the state and that the maintenance of public schools, including providing transportation to the pupils entitled to it as required by statute, is a governmental function. Certainly it is not a proprietary one. * * *

* * *

Code section 297.1, I.C.A. states, "The board of each school corporation may fix the site for each schoolhouse, * * *." Section 297.3 says, "Any school corporation * * * may take and hold an area equal to two blocks * * * for a schoolhouse site, and not exceeding thirty acres for school playground, stadium, or field house, *or other purposes for each such site*." (Emphasis added.)

Section 285.10, which requires local school boards to provide transportation for each pupil legally entitled thereto, states, in subsection 2, that local school boards "Establish, maintain and operate bus routes for the transportation of pupils so as to provide for the economical and efficient operation thereof * * *." Section 285.-10 also provides, in subsection 5, that local boards "Exercise any and all powers and duties relating to transportation of pupils enjoined upon them by law."

Section 285.11 provides that in the operation of bus routes and contracting for transportation, "The boards shall take advantage of all tax exemptions on fuel, equipment, *and of such other economies as are available*." (Emphasis added.)

We think furnishing economical transportation to pupils entitled to it is as much a school matter, over which the district has exclusive jurisdiction, as maintenance of the school buildings or location of the high school football field. (Plaintiff concedes a football stadium is generally held to come within the meaning of a schoolhouse. See also Livingston v. Davis, 243 Iowa 21, 27, 50 N.W.2d 592, 596, 27 A. L.R.2d 1237.)

* * *

No statute has come to our attention which indicates a clear legislative intent that the state or such of its agencies as defendant district, in the use of its property for a governmental purpose, must comply with a municipal zoning ordinance. Unless our decision is to be contrary to the uniform current of authority on the subject, we must hold defendant district, in the location of this tank and pump to supply fuel to its buses, is not subject to ordinance 84.

* * *

We think this opinion does not conflict with our decision in Cedar Rapids Community School Dist. v. City of Cedar Rapids, supra, 252 Iowa 205, 106 N.W.2d 655, that the school district was subject to certain building ordinances of the city in renovating and constructing school buildings. No zoning ordinance or question as to the district's right to make use of its property in performing a duty enjoined on it by law—such as transportation of pupils—was there involved. The two cases are further to be distinguished on the ground that here the state appears to have taken over the field of legislation pertaining to transportation of pupils and therefore municipalities may not interfere in that field. See C.J.S. Zoning § 10.

Defendants are entitled to an injunction to restrain plaintiff from interfering with their installation of the gasoline tank and pump on the ground owned by the school district north of the high school football field. For decree accordingly the cause is—reversed and remanded.

All Justices concur.

School District Is Obliged to Adhere to Minimum Building Code Standards

EDMONDS SCHOOL DIST. v. CITY OF MOUNTLAKE TERRACE

Supreme Court of Washington, 1970.
77 Wash.2d 609, 465 P.2d 177.

HALE, Judge. A kind of sibling rivalry in governmental affairs brings the Edmonds School District and the City of Mountlake Terrace here on a declaratory judgment suit. The school district's claim of sovereign immunity from the city's building code is met by the city's equally vehement claim of sovereign authority to enforce the code. Failing to obtain in the superior court a declaratory judgment that it need not comply with the building code, the district now appeals from a judgment favoring its intergovernmental rival.

*   *   *

The school district brings this suit for a declaratory judgment asking that ordinance No. 391, the building code of the City of Mountlake Terrace, be held inapplicable to and not binding upon the school district in the construction of its high school addition. From a summary judgment denying this relief and dismissing the complaint with prejudice, the district appeals.

Each party claims superior rights over the other deriving from their common source of governmental power, the sovereign state. They present two main questions: Has the state designated which of the two agencies should exercise its sovereign authority with respect to building permits and minimum setback requirements? Is there an irreconcilable dichotomy between the delegation to the school district of the sovereign's constitutional duty to educate the children of the state and the city's exercise of the police power in adopting and enforcing a building code?

Are the two sets of delegated powers in conflict? The school district says that the city, in forcing compliance with its building code, is transgressing and trespassing upon its powers and duties as an agency of the sovereign state, to build, operate and maintain public high schools. The district's function of providing the land, materials and designs for school buildings cannot, it contends, be lawfully preempted nor frustrated in any way by a municipality any more than a city could enforce its standards upon the sovereign state against its will.

Education is one of the paramount duties of the state. The duty and power to educate the people are not only inherent qualities of sovereignty but are expressly made an attribute of sovereignty in the State of Washington by the state constitution. Const. art. 9, §§ 1, 2. The state exercises its sovereign powers and fulfills its duties of providing education largely by means of a public school system under the direction and administration of the State Superintendent of Public Instruction, State Board of Education, school districts and county school boards.

School districts are, in law, municipal corporations with direct authority to establish, maintain and operate public schools and to erect and maintain buildings for that and allied purposes. RCW 28.-58. In essence, a school district is a corporate arm of the state established as a means of carrying out the state's constitutional duties (RCW 28.57.135) and exercising the sovereign's powers in providing education. The state has thus made the local school district its corporate agency for the administration of a constitutionally required system of free public education. * * * The state now requires school districts to have the plans and specifications, including those features pertaining to heating, lighting, ventilating and safety, approved by the county superintendent of schools before entering into any school building construction contracts. RCW 28.58.301.

But in other spheres of governmental activity, the state has allocated some of its sovereign powers and responsibilities to cities, too. Under Const. art. 11, § 11, a city may make and enforce all police and sanitary regulations within its limits which do not conflict with general laws. By statute, cities are charged with the sovereign exercise of the police power to maintain peace and good government and to provide for the general welfare of their inhabitants through law not inconsistent with the constitution and statutes of the state. RCW 35.24.290(18). A city and other kinds of municipal corporations, too, are agencies of the state to accomplish these ends. Columbia Irrigation Dist. v. Benton County, 149 Wash. 234, 270 P. 813 (1928). Among these police powers, of course, is the capability of adopting and enforcing building codes. Just as the state has vested in the state superintendent, state board, and the school districts many of its attributes of sovereignty pertaining to education, it has done the same to incorporated cities with respect to the general police powers, among which are zoning and building regulations.

The City of Mountlake Terrace cannot, under existing statutes, supersede, set aside, invalidate or impair the educational processes of or limit the standards prescribed by the state for the operation of the public schools (State ex rel. School Dist. No. 37 of Clark County v. Clark County, 177 Wash. 314, 31 P.2d 897 (1934)), for that would be an infringement upon state sovereignty. But the state, in delegating to school districts power to build, maintain and operate public schools, has not prescribed minimum standards for street offsets, nor directed that building permits be waived in the construction of public school buildings or additions. It has left its subordinate municipalities free to regulate each other in those activities which traditionally are thought to lie within their particular competence and are more proximate to their respective functions. Fixing minimum offsets for streets, alleys, front, side and back yards would, unless the state has said otherwise, fit more relevantly into a city building code than into the general rules for the operation and maintenance of a high school.

* * *

There is little doubt that the State of Washington, * * * has the constitutional power to prescribe standards for and regulate school construction, and may, as an attribute of its sovereignty, deprive municipalities of any voice in these matters. But the state has not thus far exercised this power nor prohibited cities from exacting a building permit fee, nor relieved school districts within the corporate limits of a city from paying such fee or complying with the setback provisions of the municipal building code. Unless the state has, so to speak, preempted the field of building standards or specifically ousted the municipality of jurisdiction over school construction, we think the school district is obliged to comply with the minimum standards set forth in the city's building code.

Arguments of the district and amicus curiae convey a concern that, if the court holds a school district amenable to a municipal building code, the ruling will ultimately operate to permit cities—and counties—to interfere with or impinge upon the operation, management and control of the public schools. These fears, we think, are illusory. In the matter of education, a school district is deemed to be an arm of the state for the administration of the school system. * * * It follows that the school district exercises the paramount power of the state in providing education and carries out the will of the sovereign state as to all matters involved in the educational processes and in the conduct, operation and management of the schools. We find nothing in the constitution or existing law which would enable a city legislative body to trespass or impinge upon or interfere with the conduct and operation of the public schools. We do not apprehend that requiring the Edmonds School District to pay for a building permit and set back its new addition from the street or property lines in accordance with the city building code empowers the city to assume any responsibilities or control over the way the educational process is conducted. Such matters as curriculum, textbooks, teaching methods, grading, school hours and holidays, extracurricular school activities or those concerning the selection, tenure and compensation of school personnel—indeed, the thousand and one activities and facilities by which the school districts of the State of Washington afford an education to the children of the state, and adults, too—remain outside of the authority and control of the cities.

Affirmed.

Courts May Step in Where School Directors Are Influenced by Considerations Other Than for the Public Interest

GEMMELL v. FOX

Supreme Court of Pennsylvania, 1913.
241 Pa. 146, 88 A. 426.

"The bill in this case was filed to restrain the defendants, as such school directors, from acquiring, by condemnation or otherwise, 12 certain lots or pieces of ground in the village of Janesville, in said township, for school purposes. The property proposed to be taken by the defendants is 700 or 800 feet distant from the present school property in Janesville, which consists of a plot of ground 120 feet in width and 200 feet deep, on which is erected a frame schoolhouse containing two rooms. The building is two stories in height and occupies but a small part of the lot. On either side of the present school ground there is land which can be had at reasonable rates for school purposes; and, in fact, a taxpayer in the township has offered to donate to the school district a lot 60 feet wide and 200 feet deep adjoining the said school property for school purposes. The property proposed to be taken by the defendants for school purposes is underlaid with coal, there being four or five different veins; and one of the veins, which is workable, lies within 30 feet of the surface.

   * * * There is the testimony of a large number of witnesses to the effect that there is no necessity whatsoever for the acquisition of this ground for school purposes, and that it would be a waste of school funds and a burden on the taxpayers without any corresponding benefits to be derived therefrom. There is nothing in the evidence to show that the present site is not sufficient in size for the erection of another room in connection with the present building. Neither has it been shown that the present location is unsuitable for school purposes. Nor does it appear that there is any proposition to abandon the present site, or that there are any considerations affecting the public health making it necessary to acquire the land proposed to be taken. Neither is there any evidence tending to show that the adoption of the new site would result in advantages bearing any reasonable proportion to the expenditure required.

"It is to be presumed, however, in the absence of anything to the contrary, that the school directors are acting within the limits of the discretion with which they are intrusted. The power of the courts to interfere with school directors in the performance of their duties is exceedingly limited; and they are permitted to interfere only where it is made apparent that it is not discretion that is being exercised but arbitrary will or caprice. Discretion involves the exercise of judgment incidental to the proper performance of the duty delegated. When the contention is that the proposed action is unwise, no matter by what consensus of opinion it is shown, the law will refer it to mistaken judgment over which it has no supervision. But if it cannot be so referred, if the facts admit of no other conclusion than that the determination of the board has been influenced by other considerations than the public interests, no matter what these may have been, the law will regard it as an abuse of power and disregard of duty, and it becomes the duty of the courts to interfere for the protection of the public. Lamb v. Redding, 234 Pa. 481, 83 Atl. 362. Inasmuch as under the evidence it is shown that one additional room will be sufficient to accommodate the pupils of Janesville for a period of years to come, we feel that the probable expenditure of the amount necessary to acquire the property in question, and in view of the further fact that under the uncontradicted evidence the property at present owned by the school district in Janesville, and in view of the further fact that the land adjoining the present school property may be had without cost to the district, we feel that the determination of the school board to acquire the property in question is influenced by other considerations than the public interest, and that it would be an abuse of discretion on the part of the defendants to acquire, under the circumstances, the property in question. It may be that upon final hearing, when we have the benefit of the testimony on the side of the defense, a different conclusion will be reached. But, as the case now stands, we are satisfied that the preliminary injunction should be continued until final hearing."

An order was entered in accordance with this opinion.

Purchase of Property for Special Purposes

Taxpayers have on many occasions questioned a board of education's use of tax money for the purchase of property which does not fall strictly within the generally accepted definitions of a school or classroom instructional purpose. The purchase of property for such things as athletic fields, playgrounds, recreational centers, and camps has been contested.

The weight of authority indicates that the courts tend to interpret the authority of a board of education in this area broadly, and especially in recent years have expanded their interpretation of the purposes and objectives of public education. However, there are boundaries beyond which it may be questionable for a board of education to tread. For example, a "liberal minded" Florida court held that it was permissible for a board of education to purchase property in another county for camp and recreational ground.[2] On the other hand, a more cautious Kentucky court has held that there was no authorization for a board of education to purchase a recreation center in another county.[3]

School Board Has the Implied Authority to Purchase Land Outside Geographical Boundaries of School District

IN RE BD. OF PUBLIC INST. OF ALACHUA CTY.

Supreme Court of Florida, 1948.
160 Fla. 490, 35 So.2d 579.

TERRELL, Justice. * * *

The question for determination is whether or not the Board of Public Instruction of Alachua County is authorized to purchase and take title to lands outside the geographical limits of the county for the purpose of administering its public school program.

Appellants contend that this question should be answered in the negative. To support this contention they rely on certain provisions of Chapter 230, Florida Statutes 1941, F.S.A., particularly, sections 230.22 and 230.23, defining the powers and duties of Boards of Public Instruction. * * * They contend that said statutes and decisions restrict the power of the Board of Public Instruction in the exercise of its school program to the county over which it exercises jurisdiction and that it is without authority to enter another county or to purchase lands beyond its borders for any purpose.

Prior to the enactment of Chapter 19,355, Acts of 1939, as amended by Chapter 23,726, Acts of 1947, F.S.A. § 227.01 et seq., hereafter referred to as the School Code, this contention might have been upheld, but as this Court pointed out in Taylor et al. v. Board of Public Instruction of Lafayette County, 157 Fla. 422, 26 So.2d 180, 181, the School Code "enlarged materially the scope of public school programs, public school plants, and public school activities." An adequate public school program is no longer limited to exploiting the three R's and acquiring such facilities as are necessary to do so. It contemplates the development of mental, manual and other skills that may not derive from academic training. It is predicated on the premise that a personality quotient is just as important as an intelligence quotient and that training the character and the emotions is just as

2. In re Bd. of Public Inst. of Alachua County, 160 Fla. 490, 35 So.2d 579 (1948).

3. Wilson v. Graves County Bd. of Ed., 307 Ky. 203, 210 S.W.2d 350 (1948).

important as training the mind if the product is to be a well balanced citizen.

* * * Section 230.23, among other things, authorizes the County Board of Public Instruction to assume such responsibilities as may be vested in it by law, or as may be required by the State Board of Education or as in the opinion of the County Board of Public Instruction are necessary to provide for the more efficient operation of the County school system in carrying out the purposes of the School Code. As to property ownership, the latter section provides that the County Board of Public Instruction shall retain possession of all property to which title is not held by the County Board and to attain possession of and accept and hold under proper title all property which may at any time be acquired by the County Board for educational purposes in the County.

* * * It is not at all clear that the legislature intended the words "in the county" to limit land purchase to lands in the county. It would be just as reasonable to conclude that the intent was to authorize the purchase of lands anywhere they might aid the county's school program.

The reason for purchasing the lands in question was to provide a camp and a recreational ground to aid the educational program of Alachua County. It was situated on a lake across the county line in Clay County but within easy reach of the schools of Alachua County. It is shown to be well adapted for that purpose and was being offered at a nominal price. Competitive sports are now a recognized part of the public school program. Eminent psychologists proclaim the doctrine that competitive sports contribute more to one's personality quotient and ability to work with people than any other school activity. Athletic coaches and physical directors tell us that the Olympic Games and other forms of physical competition have done more to put an end to class hatreds and promote international harmony than the United Nations Assembly. The reason being that they are conducted by a strict moral code that insures just treatment to all who participate in them.

This is a mere incident to the manner in which the public school program has been bounced out of its traditional groove and invaded by new experiments in education. An adequate school program is now as diversified as an experimental farm program and the very purpose of the School Code was to give sanction to such a program. The progenitors of the three R's would doubtless have "thrown a fit" if the school Board had talked about purchasing lands for a recreational center. The barn yard and the woodpile filled the need of a recreational center for them. It met the challenge of the time but its exponent, the three R's and the little red school house that symbolized it now repose in the museum of modern education. What we are concerned with is a system to cope with this machine age that we are in danger of becoming victims of if we do not become its masters.

We have learned that the public school program has a definite relation to the economy of our people, that the great majority of them must make their living with their hands and that those who do so must acquire different skills and trades from those who pursue the learned professions, various businesses and specialized activities. We have also learned that while skill in the three R's was adequate for a rural democracy when the nearest neighbor was three miles away and it was sometimes three hundred yards from the front door to the front gate, but that it is entirely inadequate for an urban democracy where you speak to your neighbor through the window and sometimes live with a flock of them under the same roof. A democracy in which we cultivate our farms with machines, travel by automobile, send our mail by airplane and flip a gadget to warm the house, start breakfast and relieve much of the day's drudgery. Such is the social era that the public school program must prepare the citizen for and the School Code was designed to provide the wherewith for such a program. County lines may be treated as a fiction rather than a barrier to such a program.

It follows that the question confronting us impels an affirmative answer. To construe the School Code otherwise would render it impossible to bring about a public school program adequate for the needs contemplated by the legislature. So the fact that the lands in question were without the geographical limits of Alachua County is not material if they are essential to carry out its public school program.

Affirmed.

NOTES

1. In a ruling similar to the Alachua County case the Kentucky Court of Appeals upheld a cooperative arrangement by which the Jefferson County Board of Education jointly with the Jefferson County Fiscal Court created a Jefferson County Board of Recreation. The activities of the recreation board were financed jointly by the cooperating agencies upon submission and approval of a budget to each agency. The primary legal question was, does a statute which provides that any school district may join with a city or county in "providing and conducting public playgrounds and recreational centers" extend sufficient authority for the school district to budget funds and purchase property for the establishment of playgrounds, parks and recreation centers. The court said it did and reasoned: "We think the statute is plain in extending the authority; it is subject to no other construction. It is true that there is no explicit provision for the expenditure by the board of such sum or sums as may appear to it in the exercise of reasonable discretion to further the intended purpose. The force of the argument is that while the school district may join in 'providing and conducting' the enterprise, the county must bear all incident expenses. The power and authority granted by a statute is not always limited to that which is specifically conferred, but includes that which is necessarily implied as incident to the accomplishment of those things which are expressly authorized."

Dodge v. Jefferson County Board of Education, 298 Ky. 1, 181 S.W.2d 406 (1944).

2. The authority of a school district to purchase or construct teachers' homes has been upheld by the courts. One court had this to say: "An adequate public school system program now contemplates the development of skills that flow from the head, the hand, the heart, * * * Expenditures for facilities that aid these purposes may be lawfully made from the public school funds." Taylor v. Board of Education of Lafayette County, Fla., 26 So.2d 181 (1946). Evidently, the reasoning of this court was that homes for teachers would enhance the educational process to a sufficient degree to pay dividends through increased educational attainment of the pupils.

Conversely, it has been held that public school funds may not be used to provide a house for the school superintendent. Fulk v. School Dist. No. 8 of Lancaster County, 155 Neb. 630, 53 N.W.2d 56 (1952). However, this view seems to be in the minority.

School Buildings

Since much of the educational dollar goes for capital outlay and by far the greatest portion of this money comes from local taxation, it is inevitable that people in the community will from time to time question the propriety of the expenditure of such money for certain capital construction purposes. In settling these disputes the courts have found it necessary to define just what the legislature meant when it provided for local school boards to construct "school buildings" and "schoolhouses." Such an interpretation naturally reverts to a discussion of the parameters of educational purpose and the means by which to accomplish such purposes.

For example, in discussing educational purpose the courts have held both for and against the construction of football stadiums; however, the precedent seems to support the conclusion that stadiums do serve a school purpose and thereby constitute a schoolhouse within the meaning of statute. The rule seems to be that a schoolhouse is a place where instruction and training is given in any branch or branches of the educational endeavor regardless of whether such exercises are mental or physical.

Term "Schoolhouse" Is Broad Enough to Imply Authority to Build a Stadium

ALEXANDER v. PHILLIPS

Supreme Court of Arizona, 1927.
31 Ariz. 503, 254 P. 1056.

LOCKWOOD, J. Plaintiff brought this action for the purpose of restraining the issue of some $80,000 in bonds of the Phoenix union high school district of Maricopa County, Ariz. * * *

* * * The second question is the vital point in the case. In substance it is: May a high school district in Arizona issue bonds to

build a "stadium"? The purpose for which school bonds may be issued is governed by the provisions of paragraph 2736, R.S.A.1913, Civil Code, as amended by chapter 24, Session Laws of 1925, which reads, so far as material to this feature of the case, as follows:

"2736. The board of trustees of any school district may, whenever in their judgment it is advisable, and must, upon petition of fifteen per cent. of the school electors, as shown by the poll list at the last preceding annual school election, residing in the district, call an election for the following purposes: * * *

"(3) To decide whether the bonds of the district shall be issued and sold for the purpose of raising money for purchasing or leasing school lots, *for building schoolhouses,* and supplying same with furniture and apparatus, and improving grounds, or for the purpose of liquidating any indebtedness already incurred for such purposes." (Italics ours.)

The matter then for our determination is whether a stadium is a "schoolhouse" within the provision of paragraph 2736. The word "stadium" comes from the Greek, and was originally a measure of distance. From this, by easy transition, the term was applied first to a foot race of that distance, and then to the place where the race was run, usually an open area some 600 feet long, and flanked by terraced elevations providing seats for the spectators of the race. The modern definition follows the old one, but is somewhat broader in its scope and is technically given as:

"A similar modern structure witn its enclosure used for athletic games," etc. Webster's New International Dictionary (1925 Ed.).

This is also the popular definition, and we may assume, therefore, that, when the question was submitted to the electors of the district, it was understood by them that the proceeds of the bonds would be used to erect a structure where various forms of athletic games could be given by the students of the high school and spectators could be properly accommodated while watching them.

Is such a structure a "schoolhouse"? The terms "schoolhouse" and "school" are properly defined as follows:

"Schoolhouse—a building which is appropriated for the use of a school or schools, or as a place in which to give instruction."

"School—a place for instruction in any branch or branches of knowledge." Webster's New International Dictionary (1925 Ed.).

Was the stadium for which the bonds of the district were to be issued a "building which is appropriated for the use of a school or schools"? * * * No one would maintain that it was within the unfettered discretion of the pupils, the teachers, or any independent set of men or women to determine what should be taught in our public schools. Only the people, speaking through the proper authorities, can determine this question, and the law therefore provides in what branches of human knowledge instruction may be given. We therefore hold that the proper definition of a "schoolhouse" within the meaning of paragraph 2736, supra, is: Any building which is appropriated for a use prescribed or permitted by the law to public schools.

* * * The founders of our first public schools believed all that was necessary, or at least then advisable, was the most elementary mental training, and therefore for many years public school education was confined principally to the teaching of the "three R's." But as the world progressed, it was recognized more and more fully that man, using the language of the motto of one of our great philanthropic institutions, is composed of "body, mind, and spirit," and that the complete citizen must be trained in all three fields. * * *

* * * For this reason the new generation of educators has added to the mental education, which was all that was given by the public schools of the past, the proper training of the body, and a gymnasium is now accepted to be as properly a schoolhouse as is the chemical laboratory or the study hall. Not only is this true, but the public is realizing that, even on the mental side, the field is broadening, and, whereas 50 years ago such a thing as an auditorium with a stage was practically unheard of in connection with the public school, now even the rural school of three or four rooms is not considered to be properly equipped without such a structure, either separate or in combination with the ordinary lecture room.

We thus see that the branches of human knowledge taught in the public schools have been vastly expanded in the last few generations. Has this expansion been sufficient to bring within its scope a structure of the class in question? It is a well-known fact, of which this court properly takes judicial notice, the large majority of the higher institutions of learning in the country are erecting stadiums differing from that proposed for the Phoenix union high school only in size, and it is commonly accepted that they are not only a proper but almost a necessary part of the modern college. This is true both of our privately endowed and our publicly maintained universities. That athletic games under proper supervision tend to the proper development of the body is a self-evident fact. It is not always realized, however, that they have a most powerful and beneficial effect upon the development of character and morale. To use the one game of football as an illustration, the boy who makes a successful football player must necessarily learn self-control under the most trying circumstances, courage, both physical and moral, in the face of strong opposition, sacrifice of individual ease for a community purpose, teamwork to the exclusion of individual glorification, and above all that "die in the last ditch" spirit which leads a man to do for a cause everything that is reasonably possible, and, when that is done, to achieve the impossible by sheer will power. The same is true to a greater or lesser degree of practically every athletic sport which is exhibited in a stadium.

It seems to us that, to hold things of this kind are less fitted for the ultimate purpose of our public schools, to wit, the making of good citizens, physically, mentally, and morally, than the study of algebra and Latin, is an absurdity. Competitive athletic games therefore, from every standpoint, may properly be included in a public school curriculum. The question then is, Does the law of Arizona so include them?

The Eighth Legislature has specifically directed that all public school pupils not physically disabled must take, as part of the regular school work, a course in physical education, which is declared to include "athletic games and contests." So far as the instant case is concerned, this of course is merely illustrative of the present trend of thought along the lines of physical education. At the time the election referred to was held, paragraph 2733, R.S.A.1913, Civil Code, provided, among other things, as follows:

"Under such conditions as are provided for by law, boards of trustees may employ such special teachers in drawing, music, domestic science, manual training, kindergarten, commercial work, agriculture and other special subjects as they shall deem advisable."

We think "other special subjects" reasonably includes physical education, and indeed, by virtue of this provision, not only practically all high schools in the state of Arizona, but many of the grammar schools, have for years employed physical and athletic directors, both men and women, and physical education for both boys and girls is a subject required in the courses of study adopted by a large majority of our high schools, and approved by the state board of education in pursuance of paragraph 2778, R.S.A.1913; the Phoenix union high school being among this number.

If physical education be one of the special subjects permitted by law, it is a matter for the reasonable discretion of our school authorities as to how such subject should be taught and no parent who has ever had a child participate in any form of the athletic games and contests recognized and given by the various schools of this state, and who has noted the increased interest shown and effort put forth by the participants when such games and sports are open to the view of their schoolmates, friends, and parents, both in intra and inter mural competition, but will realize the educational value both of the games and of a suitable place for giving them.

For the foregoing reasons, we are of the opinion (1) that physical education is one of the branches of knowledge legally imparted in the Phoenix union high school; (2) that competitive athletic games and sports in both intra and inter mural games are legal and laudable methods of imparting such knowledge; and (3) that a structure whose chief purpose is to provide for the better giving of such competitive athletic games and sports as aforesaid is reasonably a schoolhouse within the true spirit and meaning of paragraph 2736, supra.

In view of the foregoing conclusions, it is not necessary to consider the other legal questions raised by plaintiff.

The judgment of the superior court of Maricopa county is affirmed.

NOTES

1. The Kentucky Court of Appeals has held that an auditorium-gymnasium is a "school building" within the meaning of statutes. Ranier v. Board of Education of Prestonsburg, Ky., 273 S.W.2d 577 (1954). The court in this case distinguished its reasoning from an earlier case in which it held that a football stadium did not constitute a "school building." Board of Education of Louisville v. Williams, Ky., 256 S.W.2d 29 (1953). The court reasoned that in the Ranier case the use of the auditorium-gymnasium constituted a useful educational purpose where use of the stadium did not.

In the 1953 Louisville case, the court disagreed with the ruling in the case of Alexander v. Phillips, the principle case presented above, and said: "The case of Alexander v. Phillips [citation], apparently the leading case in point, differs in that the voters in that case specifically voted for construction of the stadium, where the Louisville voters only authorized an eight million dollar bond issue for school buildings." The Kentucky court further commented on the Arizona case saying: "The court apparently reasoned that, since a schoolhouse was a place for instruction, and since some athletic instruction took place in a stadium, a stadium was therefore a schoolhouse. This dubious logic was supported by a eulogy on the spiritual values of interscholastic athletic contests, of which the court took judicial notice. We think Alexander v. Phillips is not persuasive as to the intent of the Kentucky legislature in authorizing special taxes and special bond issues for "school buildings."

2. The Supreme Court of Oregon has ruled that a swimming pool falls within the statutory meaning of the term "school building." The court reasoned: "We believe that it was the legislative purpose to empower the issuance of bonds by school districts for the erection on school lands of any structure which the district was authorized to construct and which it deemed necessary or desirable in carrying out its educational program." In rejecting the criterion as to whether the pool was enclosed the court further stated: "The statute reflects the intent to make the function of the structure rather than its architectural design the criterion in determining whether the bonds may be issued." Petition of School Board, No. U2–20, Multnomah Co., 232 Or. 593, 377 P.2d 4 (1962).

3. Courts in other jurisdictions have upheld the authority of the school district to construct buildings for a gymnasium, Burlington ex rel. School Com'rs v. Burlington, 98 Vt. 388, 127 A. 892 (1925); building for dramatics and athletics, Woodson v. School Dist., 127 Kan. 651, 274 P. 728 (1929); recreation field, Wilkinsburg v. School Dist., 298 Pa. 193, 148 A. 77 (1929); building for gymnasium, home economics and vocational training, Young v. Linwood School Dist., 193 Ark. 82, 97 S.W.2d 627 (1936).

4. In a case questioning whether a constitutional provision for taxes for "school purposes" included school buildings the court held that:

> the unfettered term "school purpose" has an all-inclusive meaning including the erection of school buildings. In this case the court it seems used reverse implication in reasoning that: "If the General Assembly, [in redrafting the applicable constitutional amendment] had intended to limit the application of amendment to the usual and ordinary expenses of maintaining and operating schools or 'school district purposes excluding the erection of buildings,' it could have easily clarified the situation by the use of some such expression." Rathjen v. Reorganized School Dist. R–11 of Shelby County, 365 Mo. 518, 284 S.W.2d 516 (1955).

School Site Selection

A major responsibility of a school board is the location and selection of an appropriate property for the furtherance of the educational purposes of the school district. Many cases have arisen contesting the board's authority to select sites and the appropriateness of the selection. Usually such cases accrue from the efforts of a board to consolidate small schools into larger more centralized schools which provide not only more efficient operation but also greater educational opportunities for the children.

The courts have uniformly held that it is within the discretion of a board of education to determine what school site will best meet the educational needs of the children and the mere fact that others do not agree is not grounds for interfering with the board's decision.

Courts Will Not Intervene Unless Board's Decision Is Tainted with Fraud or Abuse of Discretion

MULLINS v. BOARD OF EDUC. OF ETOWAH CO.

Supreme Court of Alabama, 1947.
249 Ala. 44, 29 So.2d 339.

STAKELY, Justice. This is an appeal from a decree of the equity court sustaining the demurrer to the bill of complaint. * * * The purpose of the bill is to enjoin the respondents from constructing a proposed school building in a particular community in Etowah County or in the alternative to declare legal rights of the Board of Education and Superintendent of Education of Etowah County.

The allegations of the bill in substance show the following. The respondents have requested and received bids for the proposed construction of a school building to consist of 18 rooms or more, to be located in the Southside Community in Etowah County, Alabama. The building is to "consist of grammar school and high school grades, a vocational school and an agricultural school." * * *

* * *

The community now served by the John S. Jones Junior High School is more thickly populated and has more children of school age than the Southside Community. More students from the community served by the John S. Jones Junior High School would attend the proposed school than students of the Southside Community. The proposed plan would necessitate the transportation of a greater number of children for much greater distances and would remove the Junior High School grades from the John S. Jones Junior High School.

* * *

The plan, it put into effect, will result in the construction in the Southside Community of a school building larger than needed by that community to care for the school children residing therein and a portion of the building so constructed would remain empty and unused. The respondents further propose to remove from neighboring communities, including the John S. Jones community, sufficient students to fill the proposed building, which will leave portions of the school facilities now being used in the John S. Jones community empty and unused. In either event the result will be a waste of funds and facilities held by respondents to the detriment of the taxpayers in the county and will prevent construction of much needed school buildings in other communities in Etowah County. The construction of a smaller and less expensive building for Southside High School will be adequate and sufficient to serve the needs of school children living in Southside Community.

It is further alleged that "the proposed action of the defendants * * * is a gross abuse of the discretion vested in them by the laws of the State of Alabama."

This court is committed to the view that the courts of this state will not ordinarily seek to control the exercise of the broad discretion given by the statutes to the county board of education since the powers vested in it are quasi-judicial as well as administrative. This principle prevails even though in the exercise of discretion there may have been error or bad judgment. The courts will act, however, if the acts of county boards of education are tainted with fraud or bad faith or gross abuse of discretion. * * *

It is conceded by appellants that there is nothing to show either fraud or bad faith in the present bill.

It is insisted, however, that the allegations of the bill present a case showing gross abuse of discretion. So far as we are aware this court has not attempted to define precisely "gross abuse of discretion", perhaps for the reason that it is best to allow the facts and circumstances peculiar to each case to determine its presence or absence. In a general way, however, we say that it means such an arbitrary and unreasonable act or conclusion as to shock the sense of justice and indicate lack of fair and careful consideration. * * *

The broad powers conferred on the county board of education to which we have referred include the power to consolidate schools and to arrange for transportation of pupils to and from such consolidated school (§ 76, Title 52, Code of 1940), the power to determine the "kind, grade and location of schools" (§ 113, Title 52, Code of 1940) and the power to adopt "a building program adequate to the present and future needs of the schools in the county" (§ 116, Title 52, Code of 1940). Do the allegations of the bill remove the case from within the discretion of the board to an arbitrary, unreasonable and unjustifiable misuse of power? Do the allegations of the bill overcome the presumption which is in favor of the reasonableness and propriety of the action of the board? It does not appear so to us.

The proposed school is to replace a school destroyed by fire in a community now without a school. Construing the bill against the pleader, it does not appear with sufficient certainty how much money is to be used to consummate the plan or how much empty or waste space will be created in the new school or be left in the John S. Jones Junior High School. There is nothing to show the dimensions, area or topography of the proposed site. There is nothing to show to what extent the proposed site is or is not a suitable school center or in a central location from the standpoint of other communities, not just the community in which one school, the John S. Jones Junior High School, is located. There is nothing to show a bad location from the standpoint of roads or the condition thereof.

Beyond all this there is nothing to show that the plan is out of step with the future needs of the schools of the county so far as they may be reasonably foreseen. § 116, Title 52, Code of 1940, supra. In the absence of a contrary showing it must be assumed that the authorities gave careful and due consideration to the growing and expanding needs of education in the county. The statutes as well as the high purposes of education contemplate that a plan should be adopted that has vision and foresight. A sparsely settled community today may well be a populous community tomorrow. Matters which may create irritations today because of inconvenience etc., may be relatively unimportant in comparison with a long range plan.

The allegations of the bill will not be aided by the general allegation that "the proposed action of the defendants is a gross abuse of discretion" because this is "merely to apply an epithet without defining the act". * * * The court acted correctly in sustaining the demurrer to the bill.

Affirmed.

NOTES

1. In a later Alabama case contesting the school board's selection of a school site for a high school, it was alleged that (1) the population of proposed site area was not sufficient to support a high school, and (2) the geographical conditions were not suitable for a high school. The court cited

the principle case above, Mullins v. Board of Education of Etowah County, 249 Ala. 44, 29 So.2d 339 (1947) and said that it would not interfere unless the board's action constituted "gross abuse of discretion" and in this case the selection of this particular school site did not demonstrate such gross abuse. The court further said that the complainants must show a "gross abuse of discretion" and the board's action must be "such an arbitrary and unreasonable act or conclusion as to shock the sense of justice and indicate lack of fair and careful consideration," and they had failed to do this. Board of Ed. of Blount County v. Phillips, 264 Ala. 603, 89 So.2d 96 (1956).

2. In an Indiana case a taxpayer sought a writ of mandamus to compel the school trustee to build a school building at a specified site. The court denied the writ and held that mandamus does not lie to compel a school township trustee to provide for the construction of a school building —especially where it does not clearly appear that it is the trustee's duty to construct the building and that he has the means to do so. Good v. Howard, 174 Ind. 358, 92 N.E. 115 (1910). Of course, the authority of the old township trustee is of little relevance today except that the axiom holds true that a taxpayer cannot substitute his discretion for that of a school board or a trustee and compel the construction of a school building.

3. Where a board of education selected a site for a school building and a large group of taxpayers objected, signed a petition, and brought an action to prevent purchase of the site, the court found that the evidence concerning the adequacy of the site was conflicting and said: "We do not deem it necessary to go into a detailed analysis of the proof. It is not the court's duty to select a site; it is only to determine whether the board of education abused a sound discretion in performing that duty. The weight of proof is largely with the board of education; and, if we had any doubt upon the question, it must be resolved in favor of the board of education * * *. Not only does the good faith of the board of education stand unimpeached; but, under the rule by which we will not set aside a finding of fact by the [board of education] where the proof is contradictory we will not disturb [its] judgment in the case." Spaulding v. Campbell County Board of Education, 239 Ky. 277, 39 S.W.2d 490 (1931).

Eminent Domain

Eminent domain is the power of the government to take private property for public use. Through the right of eminent domain the state can reassert, for reason of public exigency and for the public good, its dominion over any portion of the property of a state. Therefore, when statute so provides, a public board of education can condemn and take for public use property needed for public school purposes, but without legislative authorization the right of eminent domain lies dormant and cannot be exercised.

Also, the power of eminent domain as exercised by local school boards must satisfy constitutional provisions of both the state and federal governments. Federal constitutional provisions which must be carefully observed are the Fifth Amendment which prohibits depriving any person of life, liberty, or property without due process of law and from taking private property for public use without just compensation; and the Fourteenth Amendment which prohibits any state from depriving any person of life, liberty, or property without due process of law and from denying any person within its jurisdiction the equal protection of the laws. Comparable clauses are included in state constitutions. Such constitutional provisions make it necessary that owners are justly compensated for their property. The question of what is just compensation has been the impetus for much litigation. Generally, however, the fair market value or the value of the property between a willing buyer and a willing seller is the measure of compensation to be awarded the owner.

In taking private property for public use the public agency must show a necessity for the land and, therefore, cannot condemn more property than public necessity dictates.

It is a general rule that a school board cannot take land which is already being used by another public agency; however, it has been held in some cases that where two public agencies need land the agency with the more necessary need will prevail.

School District Can Use Power of Eminent Domain to Condemn Only That Land Reasonably Necessary for Public Purposes

STATE EX REL. TACOMA SCHOOL DIST. v. STOJACK

Supreme Court of Washington, 1958.
53 Wash.2d 55, 330 P.2d 567.

WEAVER, Justice. By writ of certiorari, Tacoma School District No. 10 presents for review an order of the trial court refusing to enter a decree of public use and necessity that would have permitted the school district to condemn defendant's property. The order dismissed the school district's condemnation action.

Prior to the commencement of this action, the school district had acquired approximately 73 contiguous acres of land, by other means than condemnation, for the purpose of erecting a new high school in South Tacoma. The district desired to condemn approximately three acres of land, lying in the "extreme northeasterly portion of the proposed site for said new South Tacoma high school," owned by Frank Stojack.

The trial court concluded:

"II. That pursuant to the laws of the State of Washington and, in particular, Chapter 155 of the Session Laws of the State of Washington, Regular Session 1957 [quoted *infra*], it was the intent of the Legislature *to limit the size of sites for senior high school purposes to 40 acres.* (Italics ours.)

"III. That Tacoma School District No. 10, Pierce County, Washington, having already acquired approximately 73 acres of the proposed new South Tacoma senior high school site, is not entitled to condemn the property of the defendants, Stojack et ux., * * * ."

The statute (RCW (Sup.1957) 28.58.070), to which the trial court refers in the above-quoted conclusion of law, reads as follows:

"The board of directors of any school district of this state may proceed to condemn and appropriate not more than fifteen acres of land for any elementary school purpose, not more than twenty-five acres for any junior high school purpose and not more than forty acres for any senior high school purpose. Such condemnation proceedings shall be in accordance with the laws of this state providing for appropriating private property for public use." Laws of 1957, chapter 155, § 1, p. 573.

* * *

Nowhere in the history of the present statute (RCW 28.58.010) do we find an acreage limitation; upon the power of a school district to purchase land, except *school land* belonging to the state of Washington. * * *

A municipal corporation does not have an inherent power of eminent domain. It may exercise such power only when it is expressly authorized to do so by the state legislature. * * *

Of course, by statute, the state may delegate the power of eminent domain to one of its political subdivisions, but such statutes are strictly construed. * * *

* * *

Laws of 1903, chapter 111, § 1, p. 193, provided:

"Whenever any school district shall select any real estate as a site for a school house, or as additional grounds to an existing school house site, within the district, and the board of school directors of such district and the owner or owners of the site or any part thereof, or addition thereto so selected, shall be unable to agree upon the compensation to be paid by such school district to the owner or owners thereof, such school district shall have the right to take and acquire title to such real estate for use as a school house site or additional site, upon first paying to the owner or owners thereof therefor the value thereof, to be ascertained in the manner hereinafter provided."

This act, which provided the procedure to be followed, contained no limitation of acreage in an eminent domain proceeding by a school district, and none existed, except as there appeared to have been a condemnation acreage limitation on districts in incorporated cities, as pointed out heretofore.

In 1909, the legislature adopted a one hundred and forty-six page "School Code" (Laws of 1909, chapter 97, page 230 et seq.)

The quoted language of the 1903 act, supra, was re-enacted in 1909 (Laws of 1909, chapter 97, subchapter 20, § 1, p. 372) and now appears as RCW 8.16.010. However, the 1909 school code placed an acreage limitation on school *condemnation* proceedings. It provided

> "The board of directors of any school district of this state may proceed to condemn and appropriate sufficient land for a school house site not to exceed five acres in extent; * * * " Laws of 1909, chapter 97, § 13, p. 289.

In 1949, the condemnation acreage limitation was raised to fifteen acres. Laws of 1949, chapter 54, § 1, p. 133; Rem.Supp.1949, § 4788. In 1957, the acreage limitation in condemnation proceedings by school districts was raised to 40 acres for senior high schools; less for other schools. RCW (Sup.1957) 28.58.070; Laws of 1957, chapter 155, § 1, p. 573. The words "condemn and appropriate," as used in the existing statute, are peculiarly significant in an action of eminent domain. They have no application to the process of acquisition by purchase.

Two facts are apparent from this survey of the history of the present statutes: First, the power of school districts to acquire land by purchase, free of any acreage limitation, came into existence prior to the right of acquisition by eminent domain; and, second, the right of school districts to acquire property by eminent domain (which at first had no acreage limitation) was established as an independent, additional method of acquiring property. The power of condemnation was not an amendment to the statutory power of a district to purchase property, nor is it a limitation thereof, in the absence of an expressed intent of the legislature.

The trial court erred when it concluded that the school district was not entitled to condemn defendant's property because the district already owned 73 acres of land.

* * *

Public education is a public use for which private property may be appropriated under the power of eminent domain. If an attempt is made to take more property than is reasonably necessary to accomplish the purpose, then the taking of excess property is no longer a public use, and a certificate of public use and necessity must be denied.

In the selection of a site, the board of directors had the authority to determine the area of land reasonably necessary to accommodate suitable buildings, play grounds * * * student activity areas, and related facilities to establish an adequate senior high school in accordance with present day educational requirements. The board considered, as disclosed by the evidence, present, as well as possible and probable future needs; population increase and shift; school attendance areas; the increased cost of acquiring additional land, once a community has consolidated around a school house site; the present day concept of one-story school buildings to minimize cost and fire hazard; and the need and extent of student activity areas. The superintendent and the assistant superintendent of the Tacoma school district testified that, in their opinion, the entire tract, including defendant's land, was necessary to accomplish the purpose set forth in resolution No. 175 of the board, even though it be admitted that no buildings would be erected on defendant's land because of the nature of the terrain.

Generally, the action of a public agency or a municipal corporation having the right of eminent domain in selecting land for a public use will not be controlled by the courts, except for a manifest abuse of discretion, violation of law, fraud, improper motives, or collusion. This court has frequently held that, in eminent domain proceedings, selection of land to be condemned by the proper public agency is conclusive in the absence of bad faith, or arbitrary, capricious, or fraudulent action. * * *

Defendant introduced no evidence. There is nothing to indicate a manifest abuse of discretion by the school board, nor that its determination was arbitrary, capricious, fraudulent, or collusive. If the court's conclusion, quoted supra, is to be sustained, it must be on the theory that acquisition of defendant's property is in violation of law, a theory which we have demonstrated to be erroneous; hence, the court's conclusion cannot stand.

* * *

The order of December 9, 1957, denying order of public use and necessity is reversed. The case is remanded to the trial court, with instructions to enter an order of public use and necessity in accordance with the petition.

It is so ordered.

NOTES

1. A Florida statute illustrates a typical right of eminent domain conferred upon a school district. "There is conferred upon the county board in each of the several counties in the state the authority and right to take private property for any public school purpose or use when, in the opinion of the county board, such property is needed in the operation of any or all of the public schools within the county, including property needed for any school purpose or use in any school district or districts within the county. The absolute fee simple title to all property so taken and acquired shall vest in the county board of such county unless the county board seeks to appropriate a particular right or estate in such property." F.S.A. § 235.05.

2. Where a school district takes property by condemnation, and the statutes do not require title to be taken in fee simple, the courts have held that a school district obtains only an easement or a qualified fee. The court in a Pennsylvania case held that under a condemnation proceeding: "* * * whatever kind of right, estate, or easement, the school district acquired, terminated when it ceased to use it for the purpose for which the land was appropriated, and the title reverted to the original owner or those who hold under him." Lazarus v. Morris, 212 Pa. 128, 61 A. 815 (1905).

3. In order to condemn property boards of education must show that the property will be used for a public school use. An Alabama court has held that an administrative building for the school superintendent and his staff constitutes a public use and falls within statutory provisions which provide for condemnation for "other public school purposes." Smith v. City Board of Education of Birmingham, 272 Ala. 227, 130 So.2d 29 (1961).

Eminent Domain Can be Exercised to Condemn Property for "Public Use"

OXFORD CTY. AGRICULTURAL SOCIETY v. SCHOOL DIST. NO. 17

Supreme Judicial Court of Maine, 1965.
161 Me. 334, 211 A.2d 893.

WEBBER, Justice. On appeal. The defendant School Administrative District No. 17, a quasi-municipal corporation charged with the responsibility of providing public school education, seeks to take property of the plaintiff Oxford County Agricultural Society by eminent domain. The District requires the property for the location of a new high school. It has general statutory authority to take by eminent domain for its lawful purposes but it has never been given specific legislative authority to take the property of this plaintiff.

The * * * issue is whether or not the Society's property is devoted to public uses to such an extent and in such a manner as to provide it with an exemption from condemnation. The plaintiff conducts an annual fair on the property in question which has all the usual attributes of an agricultural fair with which Maine people have long been familiar. * * * The plaintiff is a private voluntary corporation chartered by the Legislature. It is not a political subdivision of the state nor is it invested with any political or governmental function. It was not created to assist in the conduct of government nor was it created by the sovereign will of the Legislature without the consent of the persons who constitute it. These persons may decline or refuse to execute powers granted by legislative charter. They may at any time dissolve and abandon it and are under no legal obligation to conduct an annual fair or to carry on or continue any of the activities which are said to benefit the public. The principles governing exemption from condemnation were well stated in Tuomey Hospital v. City of Sumter (1964) 134 S.E.2d (S.C.) 744, 747:

> "We recognize that it is difficult to give an accurate and comprehensive definition of the term 'public use.' The distinction between public and private use lies in the character of the use and must to a large extent depend upon the facts of each case. There are, however, certain essential characteristics which must be present if the use is to be deemed public and not private within the meaning of the law of eminent domain.
>
> * * *
>
> The general rule, to which we adhere, was thus stated in the case of the President and Fellows of Middlebury College v. Central Power Corporation of Vermont, 101 Vt. 325, 143 A. 384, 388: 'It is essential to a public use, as the term is used in proceedings involving the law of condemnation or eminent domain, that the public must, to some extent, be entitled to use or enjoy the property, not by favor, but as a matter of right. * * * The test whether a use is public or not is whether a public trust is imposed upon the property; whether the public has a legal right to the use, which cannot be gainsaid or denied, or withdrawn at the pleasure of the owner.' "

We are satisfied that the statement set forth in 18 Am.Jur. 720, Sec. 94, accurately summarizes the requirements for exemption:

> "To exempt property from condemnation under a general grant of the power of eminent domain, it is not enough that it has been voluntarily devoted by its owner to a public or semipublic use. If the use by the public is permissive and may be abandoned at any time, the property is not so held as to be exempt. The test of whether or not property has been devoted to public use is what the owner must do, not what he may choose to do. It is immaterial how the property was acquired; if its owner has devoted it to a public use which he is under a legal obligation to maintain, it comes within the protection of the rule exempting it from condemnation."

We conclude, as did the justice below, that the property of the Society is not immune from condemnation by the District.

* * *

Appeal denied.

NOTES

1. The prevailing view is that one public agency may condemn property belonging to another public agency if a "more necessary need" exists. In a case illustrating this view the Supreme Court of North Dakota held that the convenience to the public arising out of the use of certain property as a school site and grounds exceeded the convenience to the public arising from the use as a park." Board of Ed. of Minot v. Park Dist. of Minot, N.D., 70 N.W.2d 899 (1955). A Massachusetts court held that school property could be taken for use as a public road. The court weighed the need for the road against the harm incurred and ruled that the road was the "more necessary need." The court said in part "* * * there is much greater freedom of choice as to where a schoolhouse shall be put than where roads shall run * * *." Easthampton v. County Commissioners of Hampshire, 154 Mass. 424, 28 N.E. 298 (1891).

2. In a case illustrating the use of fair market value as the measure of damages, a school board in Louisiana contested a court's valuation of a condemned tract of land. The jury had assessed a value of $1,200 for a school site of 5.9 acres. On appeal the board showed that similar land in the neighborhood was selling for from $5.00 to $25.00 per acre. Based on this evidence the total award was reduced to $300.00. Ouachita Parish School Bd. v. Clark, 197 La. 131, 1 So.2d 54 (1941).

3. Under condemnation procedures the usual redress open to a landowner is an action to recover compensation and damages for the loss of property. The award to the owner is usually based on the appraised fair market value of property. However, some courts have used other measures such as the "substitute facility approach" in condemnation of special purpose property. For example, where a highway intersects a school campus, cutting growth potential or isolating a building, the courts may apply this alternative standard. Dept. of Highways v. City of Winchester, 431 S.W.2d 707 (Ky.1968). The U.S. Supreme Court has said: " * * * we are not to make a fetish of market value 'since it may not be the best measure of value in some cases'. Where the highest and best use of the property is for municipal or governmental purposes, as to which no market value properly exists, some other method of arriving at just compensation must be adopted, and the cost of providing property in substitution for the property taken may reasonably be the basis of the award." U. S. v. Cors, 337 U.S. 325, 69 S.Ct. 1086 (1949).

4. Should prior planning and potential land use be taken into account in condemnation of school property by another state agency?

Adverse Possession

Adverse possession is a means of acquiring property which is of occasional concern to school district authorities. All states have statutes which limit the times during which certain actions may be brought. These are called statutes of limitation and apply to not only matters concerning property but other areas of law such as actions for contracts under seal, actions for wrongful death and actions for liability for torts. Statutes of limitation for recovery of property have particular significance because the running of the statute has not only procedural but also proprietary significance. In other words, if the statute of limitation for recovery of possession of property is twenty years and the owner of land does not initiate an action within this time against someone in actual open possession of the property, then the owner loses his title to the land, his right of action is dead, and the person in possession of the property acquires title. However, in order to gain title to property by adverse possession the occupant must exercise dominion over the property in a manner which is actual, uninterrupted, open, notorious, hostile and exclusive, with a claim of ownership such as will notify parties seeking information that the property is not held in subordination to any claim by others, but is held against all titles and claims.[4]

Party Seeking to Acquire Property by Adverse Possession Must Establish an Open, Notorious and Hostile Claim

LOVEJOY v. SCHOOL DIST. NO. 46 OF SEDGWICK CTY.

Supreme Court of Colorado, 1954.
129 Colo. 306, 269 P.2d 1067.

HOLLAND, Justice. * * *

* * *

The sole question here involved is whether or not the district, by being in possession and holding school on the premises for a long period of time more than the statutory period of eighteen years, was entitled to possession and to have title quieted in it by adverse possession.

The fact that the district had established a school on the land involved about the year 1886, and that there had been continuously conducted a school thereon until the year 1947, is not disputed. The proof offered by the School District lacks any showing of a clear, positive and unequivocal act on the part of the district during any of the time involved that would disclose its claim or right to the land by adverse possession. Mere occupancy alone seems to be relied upon until after the spring of 1947, when a question arose between Phyllis Lovejoy, the fee owner of the quarter section, and District No. 68 as to the ownership of the building. Since the building was a permanent fixture, she authorized her attorney, on April 30, 1951, to write the president of School District No. 68, requesting the Board to remove the school building. This incident was notice to the District that she claimed ownership of the land, and there appears no denial of her claim at that time. If the District then claimed ownership of the land, there then was an open opportunity for it to assert such claim of ownership; however, it consulted an attorney and then decided to

4. Liles v. Smith, 206 Okl. 458, 244 P.
2d 582 (1952).

claim ownership by adverse possession. By such action, a strong presumption follows that the School District, in effect, admitted that its claim was not open, hostile and notorious, as is necessary in reliance upon adverse possession.

Numerous witnesses, of the community, were called by plaintiff, some of whom had resided there for many years, and one in particular who attended the second term of school in 1887. None of the witnesses could recall any incident whereby it was known that the District claimed ownership to the land, but all were of the same positive impression that the District owned the building. * * *

* * *

The very essence of adverse possession is that the possession must be hostile, not only against the true owner, but against the world as well. An adverse claim must be hostile at its inception, because, if the original entry is not openly hostile or adverse, it does not become so, and the statute does not begin to run as against a rightful owner until the adverse claimant disavows the idea of holding for, or in subservience to another, it actually sets up an exclusive right in himself by some clear, positive and unequivocal act. The character of the possession must become hostile in order that it may be deemed to be adverse. And this hostility must continue for the full statutory period. 1 Am.Jur., p. 871, § 137. The statute begins to run at the time the possession of the claimant becomes adverse to that of the owner, and this occurs when the claimant sets up title in himself, by some clear, positive and unequivocal act.

No one representing School District No. 68 ever asserted that the District owned the land until immediately before the commencement of this action. The District, without color of title to possession, had to be in possession under an open and notorious claim of ownership. Under the circumstances here, mere occupancy was not sufficient to put any of the true owners on notice that the District claimed the land, and the burden of proof, as to open, notorious and hostile claim, is upon the District when it claims title by adverse possession without color of title. Every reasonable presumption is made in favor of the true owner as against adverse possession. Evans v. Welch, 29 Colo. 355, 68 P. 776.

In support of the general trend of the testimony that it was never known that the District claimed the land, only the building, it is to be noted that the District first claimed that it had a full acre after that time a right of way ditch cut across the corner of the section, which left an area of more than two acres, and the school land up to the ditch as a playground, and the fences along the ditch were not shown to have been placed there by the School District. Had the District been making a claim to the ground, it follows that there would have been no uncertainty as to the extent and boundaries thereof. The school board knew almost two years before this suit was commenced that Phyllis Lovejoy claimed ownership of the land when she asked them to remove the building. If originally this was a case of permission to use the ground, it would be in subordination to the title and here the burden was upon the District to prove that such notice was given, which it failed to meet.

There is no reason to discuss the question of the judgment for damages, since our determination of the rights of the parties involved necessitates a reversal of the judgment, and that the complaint be dismissed.

The judgment is reversed and the cause remanded with direction to the trial court to dismiss the complaint.

NOTES

1. Adverse possession must be open, visible, continuous and exclusive, with a claim of ownership, such as will notify parties seeking information upon the subject that the premises are not held in subordination to any claim of others, but against all titles and claimants.

The placing of a permanent school building and other necessary appendages on the land of another, and conducting school * * * thereon is evidence of adverse and hostile possession under which title may be claimed after fifteen years. Liles v. Smith, 206 Okl. 458, 244 P.2d 582 (1952).

2. A court in Wyoming had this to say about adverse possession and its relationship to title by the true owner. "* * * the general rule in the United States is that possession will be presumed to be in subservience to the title of the true owner, and that the burden to prove adverse possession is upon the party who relies thereon. 2 C.J. 264. These rules, however, must be construed in the light of other rules, which have been adopted by our courts. Thus the intention to claim may be manifested either by words, or by acts, * * * Further, the term 'claim of right' has been treated as the equivalent of a hostile claim. (Citing authorities). The character of possession may give rise to a presumption, and it is generally held that the actual occupation, use, and improvement of the premises of the claimant as if he were in fact the owner thereof will, in the absence of explanatory circumstances showing the contrary, be sufficient to raise a presumption of his entry and holding as absolute owner, and, unless rebutted, will establish the fact of a claim of right. (Citing authorities). * * * Thus it is said in the last case cited:

'All reasonable presumptions are to be made in favor of the true owners, including the presumption that actual possession is subordinate to the right of the true owner, subject, however, to the limitation that actual, continuous, exclusive possession for the statutory period, unexplained, displaces a presumption in favor of the true owner and creates a presumption of fact that such possession, and the commencement of it, were characterized by all the requisites to title by adverse possession.' " (Emphasis added).

City of Rock Springs v. Sturm, 39 Wyo. 494, 273 P. 908 (1929).

Acceptance of Donations

It is well settled that it is within the power of the school district to accept and hold donations of property for school purposes. The courts liberally construe gifts for charitable and public uses in favor of the public.[5]

Such gifts will be voided by the courts in instances of bad faith on the part of the donor or there is a question of fraudulent activity on the part of school board members. "The courts are astute to impeach and invalidate any transaction where an official has any personal interest." [6] Such gifts must be free of undue influence on the statutory duties and actions of school board members which work a detriment on the citizens of a school district. In one case it was charged that a gift of land by a board member to the school district constituted an undue influence on other board members and increased the value of adjoining property owned by the donor. The court held that such a conveyance will not be avoided by reason of any interest the board member may have in adjoining premises, where no fraud or undue influence of such board member is shown or alleged, and where no claim is lodged that the site is not a proper and suitable one for the proposed school.[7]

Gifts for Charitable and Public Use Are Always
Construed Liberally in Favor of the Public

VESTAL v. PICKERING

Supreme Court of Oregon, 1928.
125 Or. 553, 267 P. 821.

COSHOW, J. It cannot be questioned that the state is competent to become the beneficiary of a last will and testament unless there is a statute prohibiting the state to exercise that power. There is no statute prohibiting this state from receiving property by will. It has been held that the United States government, which is a government of limited powers, is capable of receiving property by will unless prohibited by statute. * * *

There is much stronger reason for holding a state of the Union capable of receiving property by will in the absence of a statute forbidding it than for so holding in favor of the United States of America. The United States of America possesses only such powers as are granted to it by its Constitution. The several states of the Union

---

5. Vestal v. Pickering, 125 Or. 553, 267 P. 821 (1928).

6. Venable v. School Comm. of Pilot Mountain, 149 N.C. 221, 62 S.E. 902 (1908).

7. Territory ex rel. Maguire v. Board of Trustees for High School of Logan Cty., 13 Okl. 605, 76 P. 165 (1904).

possess all of the power of sovereignty not expressly taken from them by the Constitution of the United States or their own Constitutions. The right to pass the title to property by will is a statutory right. It comes from the state itself. It would be an anomalous condition of affairs if the state could not receive property from its own creature or exercise the power that it grants to its citizens individually where no prohibition is contained in its fundamental law or any of its statutes.

School districts of the state of Oregon are bodies corporate. Or. L. §§ 5145, 5152. Said districts are authorized to receive, to hold, buy and sell real property for school purposes. Such districts are authorized and competent to transact "all business coming under their jurisdiction." Or.L. § 5152.

Plaintiffs rely upon the well-established principle that a corporation possesses only such powers as are granted to it by its charter or general law, and that the power to receive property by will has never been granted to said school district No. 1. Plaintiffs also urge the well-established principle that a school district, including said school district No. 1, is not a corporation in the sense of a private business concern or of a privately owned and controlled corporation organized under the laws of a state for the conduct of a school. Plaintiffs urge in this connection that, said school district No. 1 being a body corporate, its functions are limited to the powers especially granted by the laws of the state and the power to accept and retain property devised by will has not been granted to said school district. They also urge that, notwithstanding said school district is a body corporate, it is only an agency or arm of the state organized as a body corporate for the express and sole purpose of conducting the schools for the education of its citizens. It must be conceded that under our form of government the conduct of the public schools is a governmental function.

We opine that school districts, including said school district No. 1, as a body corporate of the state, organized for the purpose of conducting the state's business of educating its citizens, would have the power to receive and retain property devised to it by will unless that power is prohibited because the school district is the state itself, exercising its sovereign function of educating future citizens.

We do not think the school districts would have authority to receive property for any other purpose than that of conducting the public school system. So long as the operations of the school district are limited to the purpose of maintaining and supporting the schools, it is not exceeding its powers by receiving a devise or legacy, though the capacity of receiving such a gift is not expressly mentioned in the statute.

       *   *   *

"The general rule today is that a city may receive a legacy or devise in trust for a proper purpose. The same has been said to hold true of a county, school, township. * * * " 28 R.C.L. 77, § 24.

"Each civil township and each incorporated town or city in this state is, by the statute, declared a distinct municipal corporation for school purposes, and is authorized to contract and be contracted with, to sue and be sued; and the primary purpose of the corporation is to receive and expend, in the support of our common schools, such funds as may lawfully come into its possession devoted to that purpose. It is therefore clearly consistent with the purposes for which the school corporation was instituted that it should become a trustee to receive funds bequeathed to it for the use of the public schools. Dascomb v. Marston [80] Me. [223] 13 A. 888." Skinner v. Harrison, 116 Ind. 139, 18 N.E. 529, 2 L.R.A. 137.

The law of Indiana is very similar to the law in Oregon. The Skinner Case is therefore directly in point. This state, in so far as it has considered this question, has held to the same effect. * * *

* * *

Undoubtedly school districts in this state are authorized to receive, hold, and sell property for the purpose of conducting the common schools of the state. That authority is expressly given by statute. It not being prohibited by law, that authority includes the power to receive property by will. 7 McQuillin, Mun.Corp. 6632, § 354. This power has been exercised by different school districts of the state and has been recognized as existing in the school districts by the Legislature of the state, Or.L. §§ 5393, and following, 5401, 5634.

* * *

Plaintiffs insist that the powers of corporations to receive property are strictly construed. This is not the law where the gift is for charitable and public uses. A gift to a school district for the benefit of the public at large is a gift for charitable uses, and such gifts are always liberally construed in favor of the public. * * *

The judgment and decree of the circuit court are affirmed.

Reversion of School Property

Conveyance of land may be made to school districts upon the same rules of future interests as a similar transaction between private persons. Under common law, the only way a fee simple estate could be created was by the use of the words, "and his heirs" or "and their heirs," however, under modern statutes these words of inheritance are not necessary to create a fee simple estate. The name of the grantee only is sufficient to take a fee simple estate unless a lesser estate is described.[8]

When a school district acquires property and the words used in the conveyance are, "to X school district" or to "X school district and his heirs," and the grantor does not indicate a lesser estate, the

8. Smith, Chester H., Survey of the Law of Real Property, (West Pub. Co., St. Paul, Minn.) 1956, p. 85.

school district obtains title in fee simple absolute. A fee simple absolute estate is the largest, exclusive, and most extensive interest that can be enjoyed in land. It is an estate where lands are given to a man or in our case, a school district, and to his heirs absolutely without limit or end.[9]

However, many times grantors who convey property to school districts for school purposes desire that the land will sooner or later revert to them when it is no longer used for school purposes. In such cases deeds making the conveyances of land must be unmistakably clear as to their intent and without sufficient clarity the courts will not permit a reversion. A New Jersey court had this to say about the interpretation of such deeds: "Conditions, when they tend to destroy estates, are stricti juris and to be construed strictly * * *. Conditions subsequent, especially when relied upon to work a forfeiture, must be created by express terms or clear implication, and are strictly construed * * *."[10]

The condition subsequent of which the court speaks is a determinable fee the limitations of which are usually identified by the words "so long as," "until," "while" or "during". An example of such a condition is: A, fee simple owner, conveys Blackacre to school district for so long as said property is used for school purposes. In this case the school district has a determinable fee simple and A has a possibility of reverter.

In a case where land was conveyed to a school district "for school purposes only," it was contended that the property should revert to the grantor when it was no longer used for school purposes. The court held that the words "for school purposes only" were neither preceded nor followed by words on condition such as those listed above. The court said: "The words upon which the appellant relies as debasing the fee are merely superfluous and not expressive of any intention of the parties to the conveyance as to the effect to be given to it.[11] In this case, the clause merely duplicated a limitation which was already imposed on school property anyway.

The following cases discuss the relationship between the grantor and the school district where conditions subsequent exist or are alleged to exist.

9. Black's Law Dictionary, Revised Fourth Edition, (West Pub. Co., St. Paul, Minn.) 1968, p. 742.

10. Board of Educ. of Borough of West Paterson v. Brophy, 90 N.J. 57, 106 A. 32 (1919).

11. Phillips Gas and Oil Co. v. Lingenfelter, 262 Pa. 500, 105 A. 888 (1919).

Reversionary Interest Does Not Come Into Play as Long
as Property Is Used for School Purposes

WILLIAMS v. McKENZIE

Court of Appeals of Kentucky, 1924.
203 Ky. 376, 262 S.W. 598.

TURNER, C. On the 29th of August, 1895, appellee, W. H. Mc-Kenzie, and one Melvin Fyffe conveyed to the trustees of common school district No. 8 of Johnson county a tract of land of less than one acre, about one-half of which was from the property of appellee, and the other half from that of Fyffe. The conveyance was made "in consideration of their respect for the system of common schools of Johnson county," and was absolute on its face except as hereinafter pointed out. The habendum clause is:

"To have and to hold the same, with all the appurtenances thereon, to the second party and their heirs and assigns forever, with covenants of general warranty."

However, after the description of the property there is appended the following:

"It is expressly understood that the aforesaid property is to belong to the aforesaid school district so long as it is used for common school purposes, but whenever the same is no longer so used it is to revert back to the parties of the first part, and the party of the second part is to have the right to remove the school building and fixtures on said premises."

As indicated in the face of the instrument, the property conveyed had been probably for some years before the conveyance used for school purposes; at any rate, a schoolhouse was erected on it, and it has been continuously used for school purposes at all times since that day, and is yet so used.

Thereafter by operation of law the title so held by the common school district became vested in the county board of education, and in November, 1920, the board of education, in consideration of $50 and the customary royalty, leased the same for oil and gas development to the appellant Junior Oil Company. Thereafter the latter under the lease drilled a well on that part of the school lot formerly belonging to appellee, McKenzie, and brought in thereon a producing oil well, whereupon, in December, 1921, McKenzie instituted this equitable action seeking to cancel the deed of August, 1895, and the lease so made by the board and to have it adjudged the title thereto was in him, and to enjoin the oil company from entering upon the same, or using or claiming the same, and asking for an accounting for the oil taken therefrom.

The original petition alleges, in substance, that the board of education had no right or authority to make the lease to the oil company for oil and gas development, and that the oil company had moved onto the property for the purpose of developing the same for such purposes, and asserting the right so to do, whereby a cloud was cast upon plaintiff's title. It is further alleged that the board of education had title to such lot only for the purpose of conducting thereon a common school for educational purposes, and that the conversion of same by it to commercial purposes was equivalent to an abandonment by it of the original purpose for which the grant was made, and by such acts it abandoned the property for the original purpose, whereby the title to same reverted to plaintiff.

* * *

It will be observed that by the deed of August, 1895, appellee parted with his whole interest in the property. He made no reservation or exception, nor was there a condition or restriction of any nature upon the present titled conveyed. He only provided that the title so conveyed should revert to him in the uncertain event that the property should ever cease to be used for common school purposes. He provided only for a mere possible reverter to himself if the property should ever cease to be used for such purposes. The questions, therefore, which it seems necessary to determine, are:

(1) What estate did the grantees take in the deed of 1895, and what are their rights in the property while the same is still being used for common school purposes?

(2) What estate, if any, remains in the grantor under that deed while the same continues to be used for common school purposes, and has he such a right or interest during that time as authorizes him to maintain an action for waste?

(3) Have school authorities owning property in use for school purposes the right or power to lease the same for mineral development purposes, the funds, if any, derived therefrom to be used for schools?

Questions 1 and 2 are in effect one and the same, for, if the grantees in the deed took such estate as entitles them to the unrestricted use of the property before the reversion provided for takes place, then it is clear there is no such right or estate left in the grantor as entitles him to maintain an action for waste.

The grantor clearly parted with his whole present interest, and after parting with it engrafts upon the estate conveyed a possible reversionary interest in himself if the property should ever cease to be used for common school purposes, which is manifestly a thing which may or may never happen. The thing which will operate as a reversion in the grantor is and can be only the action of the grantees themselves or their successors in title.

A qualified or determinable fee is defined in 10 R.C.L. 652, as follows:

"A qualified or determinable fee is an estate limited to a person and his heirs, with a qualification annexed to it by which it is provided that it must determine whenever that qualification is at an end. Because the estate may last forever it is a fee; and because it may end on the happening of the event it is called a determinable or qualified fee."

Such an estate is defined in 21 C.J. 922, in the following way:

"Although distinctions have been made or discussed by some authorities, the terms 'base fee,' 'qualified fee' and 'determinable fee' are generally used interchangeably to denote a fee which has a qualification subjoined thereto, and which must be determined whenever the qualification annexed to it is at an end. This estate is a fee, because by possibility it may endure forever in a man and his heirs; yet as that duration depends upon the concurrence of collateral circumstances which qualify and debase the purity of the donation it is therefore a qualified or base fee."

Manifestly the estate passing under the deed in question is embraced by these definitions. The grantor parted with all present interest in the property, and conveyed it to the grantees without limitation or restriction of title, with the lone qualification that, if it should ever cease to be used for common school purposes, the title should revert to him. In conveying such a title, with no other limitation or restriction, the grantor not only divests himself of all present title, but places the unlimited and unrestricted use and occupation of the property in his grantee until such time, if ever, the event happens which will determine the estate conveyed. Such an estate, being one which may last forever, is from necessity such as carries with it the unlimited right to use and control the property at all times before the happening of the event which will end the estate.

As said by Mr. Washburn (4th Ed. vol. 1, p. 89) in discussing the incidents of a determinable fee:

"So long as the estate in fee remains the owner in possession has all the rights in respect to it which he would have if tenant in fee simple, unless it be so limited that there is properly a reversionary right in another—something more than a possibility of reverter belonging to a third person, when, perhaps, chancery might interpose to prevent waste of the premises."

This quotation from Mr. Washburn was approved by this court in the case of Landers v. Landers, 151 Ky. 206, 151 S.W. 386. Ann. Cas.1915A, 223, and the court in that case held there was no equitable waste where one only used the property in such way a prudent man would have used his own.

In 21 C.J. 923, in discussing the incidents of such an estate, it is said:

"Until its determination such an estate has all the incidents of a fee simple; and, while this estate continues, and until the qualification upon which it is limited is at an end, the grantee or proprietor had the same rights and privileges over his estate as if it was a fee simple. He has an absolute right to the exclusive possession, use, and enjoyment of the land, and as complete dominion over it for all purposes as though he held it in fee simple."

* * *

Other authorities to the effect that the holder of a determinable fee before its determination has all the rights of a fee simple title holder, and that the holder of a mere possible estate in reversion has not sufficient right or interest in the property to authorize him to maintain an action for waste [citations].

The property in this case has been used for school purposes now for 30 years or more, and there is nothing in the pleadings or evidence to suggest any purpose upon the part of the school authorities to abandon its use for such purpose, and consequently there is nothing to indicate that the title conveyed to the school trustees will at any time in the near future be determined by the cessation of the use of the property for such purposes.

Appellee, however, relies upon a certain class of cases holding that, where property has been conveyed for school purposes and a reversionary clause is inserted, its use for other purposes works a forfeiture of the original grant, and the reversion takes place. But that class of cases has no application here whatsoever, for the very plain and sufficient reason that the property here is not being used for other than school purposes, or in any such way as to interfere with the efficient and orderly administration of the school. There is no allegation that the oil development has or will so interfere with the school; and, even if there was, appellee, who is not now a resident of the school district, is not in position to make that question.

But it is earnestly argued that, the county board of education being the creature of the statute for a specific purpose, its only duty and authority lies in the administration of educational affairs; that it is not authorized to go into the field of speculation and engage in hazardous industrial affairs, even though such activities might result profitably, and for that reason alone the oil lease given by the school board was invalid and properly cancelled. In the first place, the mere leasing of its property to others for development purposes is not engaging in a commercial venture, but is, properly speaking, only an effort to get from its property the real values therefrom, to the end that there may be a more efficient administration of school affairs.

In support of this argument reliance is had upon the case of Herald v. Board of Education, 65 W.Va. 765, 65 S.E. 102, 31 L.R.A.

(N.S.) 588. In that case it was held by a majority of the Supreme Court of West Virginia that a school board under the statutes of that state had no power to lease a schoolhouse lot for oil and gas purposes, even though the school authorities had the absolute fee simple title thereto.

Under the provisions of section 4437, Ky.Stats., 1915 Ed., which was in effect at the time the deed was made from appellee to the school board, such school trustees were authorized to "take, hold and dispose of real and personal estate for the maintenance, use and benefit of the common school of their district." * * *

Oil and gas are fugitive minerals; they are connected by underground streams or crevices by which they may be drained from one property onto another, and there brought to the surface. There can be no sound or practical reason given that will deprive school authorities who own property under which there are valuable minerals from entering into contracts for its development, and particularly would this seem to be true when the character of the mineral is such that adjoining landowners may profit at the expense of the school property by the failure of the school authorities to enter into such contracts. It is shown in this record that there are on adjoining lands other producing oil wells very near to the property lines of the school lot, and it is perfectly apparent that if the well on the school lot had not been drilled the oil on the school lot would soon have been drained from it by such wells, and the school authorities would have thereby been deprived of the chief wealth on the property to which they had title for the benefit of the school. There was, however, in the West Virginia case referred to, a strong dissenting opinion, in which we fully concur. That opinion, after discussing the West Virginia statute, said:

"I think the statute not only expressly but impliedly gives this board ample power to lease this property. This ought especially to be so where the product, as in this case, is oil and gas, fugitive in nature and which will be drained and carried away by operations on adjoining lands."

We are of the opinion, therefore, that under the statute in existence at the time the title was conveyed to the school authorities the board of education had the right to execute the lease in question, and, having the right to do so, it was its duty to do so to prevent the valuable mineral product on the school property from being appropriated by others.

The views which we have here expressed make it unnecessary to discuss the other questions presented.

The judgment is reversed, with directions to set aside the judgment entered, to dismiss the plaintiff's petition, and on the counterclaim and cross-petition to quiet the present title of the school board and to enjoin appellee from further claiming any present right or interest in the school lot.

Whole court sitting.

NOTES

1. Whether a board of education by conveyance obtains a fee simple title or some type of defeasible fee is explained by the Kentucky Court of Appeals.

"When a limitation merely states the purpose for which the land is conveyed, such limitation usually does not indicate an intent to create an estate in fee simple which is to expire automatically upon the cessation of use for the purpose named. Additional facts, however, can cause such an intent to be found. Among the facts sufficient to have this result are clauses in other parts of the same instrument, the relation between the consideration paid for the conveyance and the market value of the land in question, and the situation under which the conveyance was obtained." Scott Cty. Bd. of Educ. v. Pepper, 311 S.W.2d 189 (Ky.1958).

2. Property obtained by a school district with a fee simple determinable provision in the deed providing that if the land is abandoned and "not used for school purposes" then property reverts was held sufficient to take property from school district when property was no longer in use. School Dist. No. Six in Cty. of Weld v. Russell, 156 Colo. 75, 396 P.2d 929 (1964).

3. Can property with a reversionary interest be transferred from one school district to another in case of merger of two or more school districts? See: School District No. Six in Cty. of Weld v. Russell, supra.

4. Does B have an estate in fee simple absolute or in fee simple determinable in the following situation? A, owning Blackacre in fee simple absolute, transfers Blackacre to B and his heirs to and for the use of C school district and for no other purpose. Scott County Bd. of Educ. v. Pepper, 311 S.W.2d 189 (Ky.1958).

Construction Contracts

School districts generally have the power to contract for construction of school buildings. The power of the school district to enter into such contracts may be implicitly or expressly authorized by statute. However, it has been held and is a general rule of law that a school district cannot enter into a contract to construct a school building nor provide additions to school buildings where funds have not been appropriated for the purpose. A construction contract is invalid where the liability incurred from the construction will surpass the legal debt limitation of the school district.

In cases involving school building construction, the question often arises as to whether the contractor has constructed the building in conformance with the terms of the contract. Formerly, it was held in this country as well as England, that a contractor must fulfill the performance of the contract completely before he was entitled to recover; however, in more recent years the courts have been hesitant to deprive the contractor of his payment if he acted in good faith and "substantially performed" the contractual requirements. In instances where the contractor does not perform in complete accord with the terms of the contract but performs only "substantially" he is entitled to recover the contract price less deductions for the omissions in his performance.

Contractor May Recover in Quantum Meruit if Project Is
Incomplete but He Has Substantially Performed

DODGE v. KIMBALL

Supreme Judicial Court of Massachusetts, 1909.
203 Mass. 364, 89 N.E. 542.

KNOWLTON, C. J. The plaintiff, Dodge, made a contract in writing to erect a large building for the defendants in North Adams. He received many payments under the contract, and afterwards brought this suit to recover the balance of the contract price. Having become a bankrupt, his trustee was permitted to come into court and prosecute the suit. By agreement of parties the case was referred to a referee, whose determination of all matters of fact was to be final; his decision of questions of law being subject to review by the court. He reported that the plaintiff was not entitled to recover and judgment was ordered for the defendant on his report. The case comes before us on an appeal by the plaintiff, which presents for our consideration all questions of law that appear of record.

* * *

The price fixed by the contract was $96,500. It was admitted that the defendants were entitled to an allowance of $90 for a saving in the price of face brick, and that payments have been made amounting to $87,195. $9,215 is the balance claimed in this action.

There were many particulars in which the defendants contended that the plaintiff failed to perform his contract. In regard to some of these the findings of the referee were for the plaintiff. But besides the plastering, of which we shall speak hereafter, there were ten different particulars in which it was found that the contract was not performed, for each of which the defendants would be entitled to an allowance, if they were obliged to pay at all. The deductions that ought to be made on account of these departures from the contract were found by the referee to amount in the aggregate to $4,071. It is not contended that any error of law entered into these findings.

The specifications in regard to the plastering provided, among other things, that the first coat for the whole building should be "good lime and hair mortar and mixed when used with adamant plaster, two bags of adamant to one hod of lime mortar." It declared that "this mixture must be strictly adhered to without any deviation whatever." The findings on this point are as follows: "The adamant referred to in these specifications is a patented composition of the class commonly called hard plasters. It contains a considerable amount of plaster of paris. It sets more quickly than lime and mortar plastering and gives a harder surface, less liable to injury from blows of any kind, and is quite commonly used in modern office buildings. It is somewhat more expensive than lime and mortar plastering. I find that in plastering this building the plaintiff used less than half the adamant called for by the specifications. I find that this was an intentional departure from the contract in a substantial matter, which cannot be remedied afterwards without disproportionate expense. I further find that the composition of the plaster was not known to the architect until after the certificates given by him under the contract had all been issued. I further find that the plaintiff is not entitled to recover in this action. * * * I find that the cost of removing the plaster in the building and replastering with plastering mixed in accordance with the specifications, including the necessary retinting of walls, would be $7,000; but I further find that the owner would not be justified in incurring such expense, and that the difference between the value of the building as actually plastered and as it would have been if plastered in accordance with the specifications is $800."

The plaintiff contends that the conclusion of the referee in this particular is erroneous in law, and that the judgment should be reversed. This contention seems to be two-fold: First, that an intentional departure from the contract in a matter of this kind will not preclude the contractor from recovering on a quantum meruit; and, secondly, that, as matter of law, the referee could not find that there was not a substantial performance of the contract. It becomes necessary to consider the law of Massachusetts in these particulars.

     * * *

Formerly it was generally held in this country, as it is held in England, that a contractor could not recover under a building contract, unless there was a full and complete performance of it, or a waiver as to the parts not performed, and that he could not recover on a quantum meruit after a partial performance from which the owner had received benefit, unless there had been such subsequent dealings between the parties as would create an implied contract to pay for what had been done. * * * But in most of the American states a more liberal doctrine has been established in favor of contractors for the construction of buildings, and it is generally held that if a contractor has attempted in good faith to perform his contract and has substantially performed it—although by inadvertence he has failed to perform it literally according to its terms—he may recover under the contract, with a proper deduction to the owner for the imperfections or omissions in the performance. * * * It would seem that in cases of this kind, while the plaintiff recovers under the contract, not the contract price, but the contract price less the deduction, he ought to aver, not absolute performance, but only substantial performance of his contract and a right to recover only the balance after allowing the owner a proper sum for the failure to do the work exactly in the way required. * * * The rule very generally adopted is that, to entitle the plaintiff to recover, he needs to show only that he proceeded in good faith in an effort to perform the contract, and that the result was a substantial performance of it, although there may be various imperfections or omissions that call for a considerable diminution of the contract price. The reason for this construction of such contracts is in part the difficulty of attaining perfection in the quality of the materials and workmanship, and of entirely correcting the effect of a slight inadvertence, and the injustice of allowing the owner to retain without compensation the benefit of a costly building upon his real estate, that is substantially, but not exactly, such as he agreed to pay for. In none of the courts of this country, so far as we know, is the contractor left remediless under conditions like those above stated. The recovery permitted is generally upon the basis of the contract, with a deduction for the difference between the value of the substantial performance shown and the complete performance which would be paid for at the contract price.

In Massachusetts the hardship upon the contractor of leaving him without compensation, if, acting in good faith, he performs a contract substantially, but fails to perform it completely, was early recognized by the courts, and it was decided that under such circumstances he might recover upon a quantum meruit. In Massachusetts this method of obtaining relief has ever since been treated as the only one for such cases, and has often been referred to as the doctrine stated in Hayward v. Leonard, 7 Pick. 186, 19 Am.Dec. 268. Because of this rule it is held to this day that, if the declaration is upon the contract alone, there can be no recovery under a building contract unless there has been a complete performance of it. Allen v. Burns, 201 Mass. 74, 87 N.E. 194, and cases cited.

This anomalous form of proceeding in this commonwealth does not give the plaintiff any larger rights than those stated above under the rule which generally prevails in actions upon a building contract in other states. In the first place, it has always been held that he cannot recover upon a quantum meruit unless he has acted in good faith under the contract, in an endeavor to perform it. * * * If he abandons the contract without excuse when he has only half performed it, he has no remedy. Homer v. Shaw, 177 Mass. 1, 58 N.E. 160. In both these particulars the contractor is governed by the same rules as those which are adopted generally in other states. * * *

We think that the referee's finding of fact that the plaintiff was guilty of an intentional departure from the contract, in a substantial matter, is conclusive against his right to recover, as well under the rule in Massachusetts as it would be under that in other states. It shows a lack of good faith on the part of the plaintiff in his dealings with the defendants under the contract. We think the findings and decision of the referee, taken together, are a finding that there was not a substantial performance of the contract. On both grounds the report was rightly confirmed and judgment was rightly ordered for the defendants.

Judgment affirmed.

NOTES

In cases where a contract is "substantially complete" the contractor is entitled to recover for the work completed. A building is judged to be "substantially complete" when it has reached the stage of construction when it could be put into use for the purpose for which it was intended. This is true even though comparatively minor items remain to be furnished or performed in order to make it conform to the plans and specifications of a completed building. State v. Goodman, 351 S.W.2d 763 (Mo.1961).

Employment of Architects

The statutory power granted to a school district to construct school buildings is implied power for the school district to employ an architect. The services of an architect have generally been held to be a prerequisite in a building program which allows the district the opportunity to determine what kind of building is desired and the estimated costs of construction. Payment of an architect for drawing of plans for a building is appropriate even though the building may never be constructed. Since an architect's services for preliminary drawings are not a part of the actual building program, payment of the architects' fee may not be made from the building appropriation but must be made from the general fund.[12]

There seems to be a fine line drawn by the courts between payment of architects for preliminary drawings and payment for more detailed building plans and specifications. Several courts have held that a contract with an architect to furnish plans and specifications for a school building is unenforceable if the building costs exceed the school district's appropriations for the purpose.[13]

Statutory provisions which require bids to be taken for services performed do not apply to the employment of architects. The services rendered by an architect are considered to be of a professional nature and are, therefore, not subject to bid requirements. The theory seems to be that the services rendered by an architect are a combination of knowledge, ability and skills and such attributes cannot be properly measured and quantified for bid purposes.

12. Fiske v. School Dist. of the City of Lincoln, 59 Neb. 51, 80 N.W. 265 (1899).

13. Bair v. School Dist. No. 141, 94 Kan. 144, 146 P. 347 (1915); Pierce v. Board of Educ., 125 Misc. 589, 211 N. Y.S. 788 (1925).

*Architect May be Employed by School Board
Without Competitive Bidding*

COBB v. PASADENA CITY BD. OF EDUC.

District Court of Appeal, Second Dist., Div. 2, Cal.1955.
134 Cal.App.2d 93, 285 P.2d 41.

MOORE, Presiding Judge. The question here presented is whether a board of education is required to advertise for competitive bids before it may contract with an architect for his professional services to prepare plans for the city's school extension program.

* * *

Appellant urges upon this court that his cause is governed by sections 18051 and 18052 of the Education Code which require (1) respondent to advertise for bids from architects and (2) to award any contract to the lowest bidder. Because such procedure was not followed, appellant contends that the judgment should be reversed and that respondent should be enjoined from expending any public funds on a void contract.

The contention here made has long since been denied judicially and legislatively. It has been held that because an architect is an artist, that his work requires taste, skill and technical learning and ability of a rare kind, it would be bad judgment to advertise and get many bids when the lowest bidder might be also the least capable and most inexperienced and his bid absolutely unacceptable and therefore "the employment of a person who is highly and technically skilled in his science or profession is one which may properly be made without competitive bidding." City & County of San Francisco 1044; Miller v. Boyle, 43 Cal.App. 39, 44, 184 P. 421. Because all contracts for the construction of improvements must be subject to competitive bidding, and because such contracts must conform with the procedure prescribed in sections 18051 and 18052, supra, it does not follow that in the employment of an architect to prepare plans for a public building a board must comply with those sections. * * * Where competitive proposals do not produce an advantage, a statute requiring competitive bidding does not apply. Ibid.

But after the above-cited decisions, the Legislature in 1951 added section 53060 to the Government Code as follows:

"The legislative body of any public or municipal corporation or district may contract with and employ any persons for the furnishing to the corporation or district special services and advice in financial, economic, accounting, engineering, legal, or administrative matters if such persons are specially trained and experienced and competent to perform the special services required.

"The legislative body of the corporation or district may pay from any available funds such compensation to such persons as it deems proper for the services rendered."

That statute removes all question of the necessity of advertising for bids for "special services" by a person specially trained and experienced and competent to perform the special services required. Now, a board may pay from any available funds a fair compensation to capable and worthy persons for special services.

* * * Such employment, therefore, lies within the discretion of the board, with which courts will not interfere in the absence of fraud or abuse of discretion in the exercise of its legislative powers.

* * *

Affirmed.

NOTES

1. While competitive bids are not required to be taken for architects, statutes generally provide for bids to be taken from contractors for school building construction. In the absence of statutes requiring the letting of building contracts based on competitive bids, a board of education may use its discretion in deciding whether to take bids. An Illinois court had this to say concerning the board's discretion: "The legislature has provided for the creation of boards of education and has delegated to such boards, the power to build schoolhouses, upon receiving authority to do so from a majority of the electorate of the school district, * * *. The method to be employed in letting contracts for the construction of school buildings has been left to the discretion of the school boards of the respective school districts. * * * Where no limitation has been placed upon a school board by the vote of the people of the district, it has the right to use its discretion as to the character and cost of a school building which shall be adequate and proper for the use of the district * * *."

2. Where a statute requires a formal mode for the making of a contract this provision of the law is not merely directory, but is mandatory. An example of mode would be as follows: All contracts by a board of education involving an expenditure in excess of $1,000 must be made on a basis of competitive bidding and shall be in writing. In a case such as this any deviation in the formal mode of making the contract renders the contract unenforceable against the governmental agency involved. Luzerne Township v. County of Fayette, 330 Pa. 247, 199 A. 327 (1938).

3. Where statutes require that bids be let for school building construction to the "lowest responsible bidder," this does not mean merely to the lowest bidder, but the school board is allowed considerable latitude in the determination of what constitutes a "responsible" bid. "All that is required of officials is that they observe good faith and accord all bidders just consideration, thus avoiding favoritism and corruption. An honest exercise of discretion will generally not be disturbed." Rugo, Inc. v. Henson, 148 Conn. 430, 171 A.2d 409 (1961). The word "responsible" means "accountable" and "reliable" and should not only take into consideration cost, but also the experience, reputation and financial standing of the bidder. Meyer v. Board of Ed., Union Free School Dist. No. 7, 31 Misc.2d 407, 221 N.Y.S.2d 500 (1961). The burden of proof is on the bidder and there is no burden on the school board to go out and investigate blindly as to the responsibility of the bidder.

Performance of Building Contract

In contracting for construction of school buildings, boards of education generally wish to insure performance of the contract by the contractor or builder. The power of a board of education to require a bond for faithful performance of a building contract has been upheld by the courts even though such power is not specifically provided for by statute, but is merely implied by the statutory authority of the school district to construct school buildings. Where a bond is conditioned for the faithful performance of a contract, but not for the payment of claims for laborers and materialmen, such a bond does not inure to the benefit of the laborers or materialmen.[14] Where there is a bond for faithful performance of a contract and the contractor defaults, the liability of the surety is measured by the terms of the bond. Most courts have held that the failure of a school board to comply with specified statutory procedures does not relieve the surety of liability.

Some authorities have held that school board members failing to obtain bond will be personally liable for injury resulting from failure to perform the contract even in the absence of statute.[15] More generally, however, the courts have held that in the absence of statute requiring a bond board members are not liable.[16] In the case where statute requires a board to require a bond for payment of laborers and materialmen and the board fails to do so the school board or officers are liable for payment.

Power of School Board to Contract Implies Authority
to Demand a Performance Bond of the Contractor

BOARD OF PRESIDENT AND DIRECTORS OF THE ST. LOUIS PUBLIC SCHOOLS v. WOODS

Supreme Court of Missouri, 1883.
77 Mo. 197.

MARTIN, C. This action was commenced on the 12th of September 1877, upon a bond given by defendants to the plaintiff in November, 1872. On the 12th of November, 1872, Stephenson Woods and John W. Barnes, under the name and style of Woods & Barnes, entered into a contract with plaintiff to erect and finish a school house in the southeastern part of St. Louis, for the sum of $6,977. At the time of entering into this contract said Woods & Barnes, as principals, and Jephtha H. Simpson and Thomas R. Pullis, as securi-

14. Summerhill v. Weller, 110 Cal.App. 406, 294 P. 414 (1931).

15. Staffon v. Lyon, 110 Mich. 260, 68 N.W. 151 (1896).

16. Blanchard v. Burns, 110 Ark. 515, 162 S.W. 63 (1913).

ties, the defendants in this case, executed and delivered to the plaintiff their bond in the penal sum of $8,000. The conditions and covenants of the bond are set out in full in the petition, and are as follows:

"The condition of the foregoing obligation is such, that, whereas, Woods & Barnes have entered into the preceding building contract with the said Board of President and Directors of the St. Louis Public Schools. Now, if they, the said Woods & Barnes, shall well and faithfully perform and fulfill all and every one of the terms, conditions and covenants therein contained, and if they will well and truly pay or cause to be paid, all just claims of sub-contractors or others for work done or materials furnished on said building, whether such claims are made against the Board of President and Directors of the St. Louis Public Schools, or against said Woods & Barnes, then this obligation shall be void, otherwise to remain in full force.

* * * And it is covenanted and agreed by and between the parties hereto, that in case of the failure of the said Woods & Barnes to pay or satisfy any just claim against them, for or on account of work done on said building, the said Board of President and Directors of the St. Louis Public Schools, may, if it chooses to do so, either institute suits on this bond to the use of the claimants, or the said board may transfer or assign this bond to one or more of such claimants, each of whom may and shall by such assignment acquire a separate right of action against the said principals and securities for the recovery of such damages arising to them respectively from the nonpayment of their just claims, and such actions shall be maintainable until the just claims are paid, or until the penal sum herein provided has been exhausted by recoveries in such actions."

The petition then goes on to set out the breaches of the bond, and says that said Woods & Barnes have failed to perform and fulfill the terms, conditions and covenants of the building contract; that they failed and neglected to pay all just claims of all sub-contractors and others for work done and materials furnished on said building. The names of these sub-contractors and material men or laborers are specified in the petition along with the sums due to each, amounting in the aggregate to $2,304.97. It is alleged that all said sums are just claims in favor of the said several parties as sub-contractors for work done or materials furnished or both, on and for the building contracted for, and that they remain unpaid. It is also alleged that the plaintiff has not made any assignment of its right of action, but brings and prosecutes this suit for the benefit of all the claimants mentioned. The building contract referred to in the petition was filed as a part of it and is set out in the record.

The defendants demurred to the petition, and rest their argument in support of it upon the ground that the plaintiff has no power to sue upon such a bond, that no such power is given in the act which constituted the board a municipal corporation, and that the object and purpose of the bond are matters in which the board has no interest whatever. The circuit court sustained the demurrer, and judgment was rendered in favor of the defendants. On writ of error to the St. Louis court of appeals that judgment was reversed and the, cause remanded for further proceedings. The defendants have brought the case here on appeal, and ask that the judgment of the court of appeals be reversed and the judgment of the circuit court be affirmed.

I am unable to adopt the conclusion reached by the learned counsel for the appellant, to the effect that the bond now sued on was beyond the powers of the board to accept, or that it "is repugnant or inconsistent with the objects of its creation." By the act of incorporation, the board is vested with "the charge and control of the public schools and all the property appropriated to the use of public schools within said city." It is also empowered "to do all lawful acts which may be proper or convenient to carry into effect the object of the corporation." Laws Applicable to St. Louis County 1872, p. 521, §§ 1, 4.

The board of public schools certainly has the power to build school houses. It has the right to make contracts with contractors for the erection of school buildings. And as germane to these powers, I think it has the right like any other proprietor, to exact conditions from its contractors, which shall tend to secure and pay off the material men and laborers who unquestionably contribute most to the erection of such buildings. Viewed from the narrow standpoint of private economy, this must be the cheapest way to erect such costly and commodious structures. Otherwise as the statutes furnish no security to material men or laborers in the mechanics' lien law, as against the board, on account of its being a municipal corporation, they will be compelled to add something to the materials and labor going into the school buildings, on the well known principle which prevails throughout the business world, that high prices and high interest always attend bad security. In a wider sense, I think, the bond is germane to the corporate objects of the school board. I think the law is not inclined to deny the board, even if it is a municipal corporation, the satisfaction and ease of conscience which the private citizen is naturally supposed to experience, when he reflects that the structure he dwells in has been entirely paid for, from the mason who laid the foundation to the artist who frescoed the ceilings. By a little caution and prudence on the part of proprietors erecting buildings, this pleasing result can always be secured, and I think the school board has the same right to attain it in the conduct of its business that any one else has. I must decline to hold that the school board in the conduct of its business transactions ought to be controlled by such a phlegmatic sense of justice toward its builders, as the learned counsel for the appellants think so appropriate to it as a public corporation. The object and purpose of the bond being entirely within the powers of the board, and the board being constituted the trustee of an express trust in the bond, the right to sue on it ought not to be questioned.

The judgment of the court of appeals reversing the judgment of the circuit court and remanding the case for further proceedings, is affirmed. All concur.

NOTES

1. Where a school district is required by statute to procure bond to protect laborers and materialmen, and it does so, there is no further duty on the part of one board of education to see that the laborers or materialmen are paid. Sundheim v. School Dist. of Philadelphia, 311 Pa. 90, 166 A. 365 (1933).

2. A bond given by a contractor pursuant to a school building contract assumes the contractual provisions:

"Provision in contract with city for construction of school building required contractor to furnish satisfactory bond securing payment of all labor performed or furnished, and all materials used in the fulfillment of the contract, and for the faithful performance of its terms and conditions. Bond furnished was conditioned upon contractor faithfully performing contract and satisfying all claims and demands incurred for same, and fully indemnifying and saving city harmless from all costs and damages because of contractors default, and payment of all persons who had contracts directly with the contractor for labor and materials." Dolben v. Duncan Constr. Co., 276 Mass. 242, 177 N.E. 105 (1931).

INDEX

References are to Pages

DISCHARGE

Teachers, exclusive power of school board, 584

DISCIPLINE

Student rights, disciplinary proceedings, procedural standards, 349

Teachers, this index

DISCLAIMER

Teachers, provisions of loyalty oath, constitutionality, 557

DISCOVERY

Civil action, pretrial discovery, 15

DISCRETION

Abuse by school board,

Construction of school building, 865–867

Interference by court, 321–323

Book selection, discretion of school board, 309–312

Courts, substitution for authorized officers or boards, 101–106

Local school boards, 118

Nongraded school, board's discretion to establish and operate, 316–317

Redelegation by school board, restriction, 127–129

Rules governing exercise of discretionary authority, 101

School trustees to issue bonds, lapse of time, effect, 829–831

Selection of school site by school board, 865 et seq.

State board of education, granting teacher's certificates, 566, 567

Student rights, promulgation rules and regulations, 318

DISCRIMINATION

Desegregation, generally, this index

Percentage of black teachers in school district, statistical criterion, 526 et seq.

Separate-but-equal doctrine, 455 et seq.

Teachers, 531 et seq.

DISMISSAL

Teachers, this index

DISRUPTION

Students,

Disruptive conduct, rule banning buttons, constitutionality, 372 et seq.

Forecast of substantial disruption, denial of freedom of expression, 368 et seq.

DISTINCTION

Legislative and executive acts, 100

DISTRIBUTION

Sex questionnaire by students, board prohibiting constitutionality, 403 et seq.

State finance distribution formula, equalizing, violation of state constitution, 812 et seq.

State school funds, 776 et seq.

Equality and uniformity, constitutional requisite, effect, 789–791

DISTRICT COURTS

Federal court system, 18, 19

DISTRICTS

Schools and School Districts, generally, this index

DOCTRINES

Precedent, historical development of doctrine, 8–10

Separate-but-equal doctrine, 455 et seq.

Sovereignty, rise and fall of the sovereignty doctrine, 644 et seq.

Stare decisis historical development of doctrine, 8–10

DOMICILE OR RESIDENCE

Detrimental acts committed after return home by pupil, school master, authority to punish for, 325–329

Home instruction, 260 et seq.

Offenses by pupil committed after returning home from school, authority of teacher to punish for, 329–332

Return of pupil to home, detrimental acts to good order of school, power to punish for, 325–329

Taxation of nonresidents, in state income earned by, 771 et seq.

Teachers' homes, authority of school district to purchase or construct, 860

DONATIONS

School districts, authority to accept, 879–881

DRESS

Students and Student Rights, generally, this index

Teachers, freedom of expression, compelling reason to restrain, 545–548.

DUAL SCHOOL SYSTEM

Termination immediately, 478, 479

FLAG SALUTE
Generally, 248 et seq.

FOOTBALL
Participation, violation of rule, discretion of school board, 321–323
Stadiums, construction, 860
Torts, free pass holder to game, invitee, duty of care, 744–747

FORECAST
Disruption from student publication, school board unable to reasonably forecast, 394–396
Student rights, substantial disruption, denial of freedom of expression, 368 et seq.

FOREIGN COUNTRIES
Comparison of educational system, 1

FOREIGN LANGUAGES
Chinese speaking children, failure to provide English language instruction, civil rights violation, 313–315
Statute prohibiting teaching, validity, 298–300

FORMALITIES
Contracts, 578

FORMULA
State constitution, school finance distribution formula, violation, 812 et seq.

FOURTEENTH AMENDMENT
Desegregation, 455 et seq.
Distribution of state school funds, 776 et seq.
Expansion of individual rights, 763
School aid formulas, 762
Separate-but-equal doctrine, 455 et seq.
Sex discrimination, prohibition, 428–431

FOURTH AMENDMENT
Student rights, validity of search of student's clothing, 409–411

FRAUD
School board's decision to construct school building, 865–867
State board of education action, finality, 112 et seq.

FREE PRESS
Constitutional guarantee, abstract advocacy of overthrow of government, 558

FREEDOM
Academic freedom, extension to protect teacher using dirty word, 306–309
Choice, unitary school system, failure to create, affirmative action by state, necessity, 475–478
Constitutional rights of individuals, 49, 50

FREEDOM OF SPEECH
Constitutional guarantee, abstract proscribing advocacy of overthrow of government, 558
First Amendment rights, 366–368
Teachers, this index

FUNCTIONS
Courts, 4–7
Education, state function, 71 et seq.
Judicial functions, administrative agencies, 106 et seq.
State agencies, 85
State governmental function, commerce clause restricting intrusion by congress, 50 et seq.

FUNDS
Finance, generally, this index
Taxes and Taxation, generally, this index

GENERAL JURISDICTION
State courts, 17, 18

GENERAL WELFARE
Congressional powers expansive under, 50 et seq.
Education and general welfare, 44–47

GIFTS
Public use, liberal construction in favor of, 879–881
School districts, authority to accept, 879–881

GOOD ORDER
School master, power to punish pupil for detrimental acts to, 325–329

GOVERNMENT
Legislature, plenary power to govern educational system, 76–79
Local governance of schools, 118 et seq.

GOVERNMENTAL FUNCTION
School district, performance by, torts, immunity, 748, 749

GRADES
Textbook fee in elementary grades, constitutional violation, 836 et seq.

RECORDS

Appellate review, 17

School board meetings, 157

School records, open to the public, 154, 155

RECOVERY

Students, nominal damages, exception, 448 et seq.

RECREATION BOARD

Joint financing by cooperating agencies, 859

REFUNDING BONDS

Indebtedness, 834

REGULATIONS

Rules and Regulations, generally, this index

REHIRING

Teachers, failure to rehire, remedial judicial action, evidence, necessity, 538–541

REIMBURSEMENT

Parochial schools, tuition reimbursement, constitutionality, 214 et seq.

RELIGION

See, also, specific headings, this index

Generally, 35, 36

Act for establishing religious freedom, 171–173

Church and state, 166 et seq.

Exemption, compulsory attendance, 264 et seq.

Memorial and remonstrance against religious assessments, 173–176

Public school and religion, 176 et seq.

Release time for religious instruction, 232 et seq.

REMEDIES

Interdistrict integration, improper remedy to overcome single-district segregation, 499 et seq.

Teachers, judicial action, failure to rehire, evidence, 538–541

REMOVAL FROM OFFICE

Kickbacks from contractor by school board member, 133

Public officers, 133

Statutory procedure, 133

RENEWAL

Teacher's certificate, 571

REORGANIZATIONS

School districts, 162

REPAIRS

Parochial schools, grants, constitutionality, 204 et seq.

REPORTS

Horace Mann's 10th and 12th annual reports to Massachusetts board of education, 31 et seq.

RESERVATION

Education powers reserved by states, 43, 44

State powers over education, 43, 44

RESIGNATION

Public office, 133

RESTRAINT

Teachers, dress, compelling reason, necessity, 545–548

RESTRICTIONS

School board,

Discretionary power, redelegation, 127–129

Rule-making power, redelegation, 122 et seq.

REVENUES

Generally, 762 et seq.

Finance, generally, this index

Taxes and Taxation, generally, this index

REVERSIONARY INTEREST

Continued use of property for school purposes, limitation, 883 et seq.

School property, 881 et seq.

REVIEW

Appeal and Review, generally, this index

REVOCATION

Teaching credentials by state board of education, 571

RISK

Torts, injured student, knowledge of risk involved, contributory negligence, 718–720

ROLE

Federal government, 41 et seq.

RULES AND REGULATIONS

Athletic rules, reasonableness, justification by distinct differences between sexes, 439–443

VACCINATION

Compulsory attendance, exemption, 268 et seq.

VALIDITY AND VALIDATION

Board regulation mandating withdrawal of married students from school, 420–423

Fees, public schools, 835 et seq.

School bonds, clerical defect in notice of election, effect, 832, 833

Sex education course for all students, state requirement, validity, 304–305

Student rights, search of students clothing, 409–411

VENUE

Civil action, 13

VIOLATIONS

Due process, statute prohibiting teaching of foreign language, 298–300

English language instruction, failure to provide to Chinese speaking children, civil rights violation, 313–315

State constitution, restriction on expenditure of federal funds for, 65 et seq.

VIRGINIA

Jefferson's bill for more general diffusion of knowledge, 26–28

VOLUNTARY

Taxes, illegal, recovery by taxpayer, voluntary payment, 769, 770

VOTES AND VOTING

Local school district elections, equality of voting power, necessity, 143–145

One-man one-vote, constitutionality, appointive boards, 141, 142

School board meetings, 157

VULGARITY

Suspension of high school student, use in off campus newspaper, 380

WAGES

Compensation and Salary, generally, this index

WISDOM

Regulation of students, court, nonconcerned with wisdom but with reasonableness, 323–325

WITHDRAWAL

Married students from school, board regulation mandating, validity, 420–423

WORDS AND PHRASES

Adverse possession, 875
Civil law, 3
Common law, 3
Common school, 83, 84
Constitution, 2
Contracts, 578
Contributory negligence, 701
Eminent domain, 868
Nuisance, 749
Proprietary functions, 743
Public office, 132
Reasonable man, torts, 694
School law, 1
School reorganization, 162
Schoolhouse, 860
Statutes, 2, 3

WORKING CONDITIONS

Labor law in public education as encompassing, 636

WRONGFUL DEATH ACTION

Statutes of limitations, 875 et seq.

ZONING

School district, local municipal zoning ordinance, exception, 850–852

†